The Palgrave Handbook of Dark Tourism Studies

Philip R. Stone • Rudi Hartmann
Tony Seaton • Richard Sharpley
Leanne White
Editors

The Palgrave Handbook of Dark Tourism Studies

palgrave
macmillan

Editors
Philip R. Stone
University of Central Lancashire
Preston, UK

Rudi Hartmann
University of Colorado Denver
Denver, USA

Tony Seaton
University of Limerick
Limerick, Ireland

Richard Sharpley
University of Central Lancashire
Preston, UK

Leanne White
Victoria University
Melbourne, Australia

ISBN 978-1-137-47565-7   ISBN 978-1-137-47566-4 (eBook)
https://doi.org/10.1057/978-1-137-47566-4

Library of Congress Control Number: 2017964279

© The Editor(s) (if applicable) and The Author(s) 2018
The author(s) has/have asserted their right(s) to be identified as the author(s) of this work in accordance with the Copyright, Designs and Patents Act 1988.
This work is subject to copyright. All rights are solely and exclusively licensed by the Publisher, whether the whole or part of the material is concerned, specifically the rights of translation, reprinting, reuse of illustrations, recitation, broadcasting, reproduction on microfilms or in any other physical way, and transmission or information storage and retrieval, electronic adaptation, computer software, or by similar or dissimilar methodology now known or hereafter developed.
The use of general descriptive names, registered names, trademarks, service marks, etc. in this publication does not imply, even in the absence of a specific statement, that such names are exempt from the relevant protective laws and regulations and therefore free for general use.
The publisher, the authors and the editors are safe to assume that the advice and information in this book are believed to be true and accurate at the date of publication. Neither the publisher nor the authors or the editors give a warranty, express or implied, with respect to the material contained herein or for any errors or omissions that may have been made. The publisher remains neutral with regard to jurisdictional claims in published maps and institutional affiliations.

Cover illustration: Paul Hobart/Alamy Stock Photo

Printed on acid-free paper

This Palgrave Macmillan imprint is published by Springer Nature
The registered company is Macmillan Publishers Ltd.
The registered company address is: The Campus, 4 Crinan Street, London, N1 9XW, United Kingdom

"We've gone on holiday by mistake!" Richard E. Grant (Withnail and I, 1987)

This Handbook is dedicated to my daughter and son—Sara and Aaron—as they embark into adulthood and discover that life is not about finding yourself, life is about creating yourself.
Dr. Philip R. Stone (a.k.a. Dad)
Editor-in-Chief: The Palgrave Handbook of Dark Tourism Studies

Dark Tourism Themes, Issues and Consequences: A Preface

Man stands in his own shadow and wonders why it's dark. (Zen Proverb)

In 2015, a commissioning editor from the internationally renowned publishers Palgrave Macmillan approached me to suggest dark tourism warranted a subject 'Handbook'. Consequently, 'dark tourism' as a scholarly field of study had come of age and this Handbook was born. The aim of any academic Handbook is to offer a seminal 'must-go-to' reference text for a specific subject. The aim of the *Palgrave Handbook of Dark Tourism Studies* is no different. During the past 20 years or so, dark tourism research has permutated heritage tourism discourse, thanatology, and memory studies. As a result, the term 'dark tourism' has been branded into an internationally recognised taxonomy to denote travel to sites *of* or sites associated *with* death or 'difficult heritage' within global visitor economies.

Yet, dark tourism is a provocative and contested concept. It divides opinions and emotions both within academic practice and empirical circles. The concept is also often used by sensationalist media to hook readers or viewers with stories of apparent touristic malpractice or dubious ethical visitor behaviour. In essence, dark tourism attempts to capture contemporary (re)presentations of the Significant Other dead within economic paradigms of business supply and consumer demand, as well as highlighting issues of dissonance, politics and historicity, and furthering our sociological understandings of death, the dead and collective memory. Moreover, modern morality is encapsulated through the tourist gaze at mortality at 'dark sites'. Dark tourism also allows us to commercialise the dead and to retail tragic memories in safe and socially sanctioned tourist environments. Even so, the semi-compulsive nature of consuming dark tourism ensures we do not encounter the actual corpse, but instead mediate specific narratives of the known and unknown dead.

In turn, the dominion of dark tourism offers a selective voice and records tragedy across time, space and context and, subsequently, can provide reflectivity of both place and people. Different cultural, political and linguistic representations of dark tourism and varying interpretative experiences are complex and multifarious and cannot be taken at face value. Instead, dark tourism offers visual signifiers and multiplicity of meanings within touristic landscapes, as global visitor sites function as retrospective witnesses to acts of atrocity or tragedy. Contemporary memorialisation is played out at the interface of dark tourism, where consumer experiences can catalyse sympathy for the victims or revulsion at the context. Yet, despite the cultural complexity and managerial dilemmas of dark tourism, we disconnect the (tragic) past from the (fretful) present for our (hopeful) future. We gaze at dark tourism in the knowledge that the victims are already dead, though the precise context and history of the victims can never be truly or fully understood. Ultimately, dark tourism is about death and the dead, but through its current production and ephemeral consumption, it perhaps tells us more about life and the living.

It is upon these inherent complexities of dark tourism that I imagined this Handbook. Of course, I was never ever going to address every single issue of dark tourism in every single cultural context. For any oversights and omissions, then these are either purposeful or by mistake—and I take this opportunity to apologise for the latter. Rather, I wanted a reference tome that provided readers with a selective yet coherent framework of dark tourism studies. I wanted a Handbook that critically addressed the theoretical and practical complexities of dark tourism but also left readers with questions that can open up new avenues for future research. I also wanted a reference book that incorporated the views of internationally recognised authors along with new emerging scholars in the field. To that end, four Associate Editors from the UK, USA, Ireland and Australia joined me, along with 45 authors representing every continent who contributed 30 original chapters spread across six thematic sections. Undoubtedly, what has transpired is the first-ever comprehensive Handbook of Dark Tourism Studies that readers can explore contextualised issues, examine key theoretical topics, and evaluate practical consequences of difficult heritage from around the world. The Handbook chapters are introduced and summarised by the respective editor in the section introductions; but each chapter may be read as a stand-alone paper or in conjunction with other sign-posted chapters in the book. The six thematic sections are:

- *Section One—Dark Tourism History* (edited by Tony Seaton). The opening section offers thought-provoking and wide-ranging historical accounts of

dark tourism from touristic practices of yesteryear. In doing so, the first section underpins dark tourism not only as a contemporary phenomenon but also with foundations firmly rooted in historicity.
- *Section Two—Dark Tourism: Philosophy and Theory* (edited by Philip R. Stone). The second section outlines a number of different cultural frameworks and theoretical paradigms in which to conceptually locate dark tourism studies. As a result, the section provides a number of conceptual templates that offer future researchers a defined philosophical agenda to interrogate meta-narratives of dark tourism.
- *Section Three—Dark Tourism in Society and Culture* (edited by Richard Sharpley). The third section provides a number of themes that relate to dark tourism in practice. In doing so, the section offers the reader sociological and cultural issues that focus on dissonant heritage and interpretation, political and stakeholder approaches, notions of identity and nation building, tourism mobilities, as well as media representations of dark tourism.
- *Section Four—Dark Tourism and Heritage Landscapes* (edited by Rudi Hartmann). The fourth section focuses on geographical accounts of dark tourism and journeys through difficult heritage landscapes. As a result, the section provides a number of extensive and contextualised accounts of slavery tourism, battlefield tourism, and disaster tourism, as well as 'Holocaust tourism'.
- *Section Five—The 'Dark Tourist' Experience* (edited by Philip R. Stone). The penultimate section deliberates issues of tourist experiences and dark tourism consumption. The section provides critical insights into visualisation and interpretive experiences, the motivations of tourists at dark tourism sites, political and educational dimensions of visitation, as well as children's perspectives of visiting particular dark sites.
- *Section Six—The Business of Dark Tourism* (edited by Leanne White). The concluding section focuses on business aspects and commercialisation of dark tourism. In doing so, issues of marketing and retailing are examined, as are issues of exhibiting death, as well as the semiotics of tourist souvenirs, and online media and digital encounters of dark tourism.

On a final and personal note: editing, writing and leading this book project reminded me of what Anne Frank wrote in her diary—'The world will keep on turning without me; I can't do anything to change events anyway'. Of course, Anne Frank through her death at the hands of the Nazi regime during World War Two and subsequent memorialised reincarnation *did* change events. By the agency of her diary testaments she helped us to come out of the shadows of genocide; she helped us glimpse the fragility of life and precariousness of death and, as a result, return us to a world that did indeed keep on turning. This Handbook cannot change the tragic events that sadly inspire dark tourism, including that of Anne Frank. However, as an increasingly fragmented modern world appears to spin ever faster, the themes, issues and consequences discussed in this book can change our perceptions of how and why tragic events are interpreted, remembered and commemorated. It is for this reason that dark tourism and its scholarly endeavours must continue to shine a critical light on the darker recesses of humanity. Without it, we shall remain in the shadows.

Preston, UK   Philip R. Stone

Acknowledgements

While I thought that I was learning how to live, I have been learning how to die. (Leonardo Da Vinci)

I would like to thank Palgrave Macmillan for commissioning this *Handbook*. In particular, I am grateful to Andrew James as commissioning editor (Sociology & Education) for his professional intuition for a book of this nature.

I would also like to say a special thank you to all the authors in this volume for their patience during the compilation of this publication and for providing the Handbook with such rich material. The authors in this Handbook represent every continent, and I am very grateful for their critical insights and international perspectives of 'dark tourism' and 'difficult heritage'.

And finally, I would like to say a very special thank you to the Associate Editors of this volume—Rudi Hartmann, Tony Seaton, Richard Sharpley and Leanne White—for their scholarly passion and commitment, as well as their editorial expertise and professional diligence. *Gratia vobis ago!*

Dr. Philip R. Stone

Editor-in-Chief: *The Palgrave Handbook of Dark Tourism Studies*

Contents

Section 1   Dark Tourism History   1

1   Encountering Engineered and Orchestrated Remembrance:
    A Situational Model of Dark Tourism and Its History   9
    Tony Seaton

2   Crime, Punishment, and Dark Tourism: The Carnivalesque
    Spectacles of the English Judicial System   33
    Tony Seaton and Graham M. S. Dann

3   Death and the Tourist: Dark Encounters in Mid-Nineteenth-
    Century London via the Paris Morgue   77
    John Edmondson

4   The British Traveller and Dark Tourism in Eighteenth-
    and Nineteenth-Century Scandinavia and the Nordic Regions   103
    Kathryn Walchester

5   "The Smoke of an Eruption and the Dust of an Earthquake":
    Dark Tourism, the Sublime, and the Re-animation of the
    Disaster Location   125
    Jonathan Skinner

xiv   Contents

Section 2 Dark Tourism: Philosophy and Theory	151
6 Thanatourism: A Comparative Approach *Erik Cohen*	157
7 Dark Tourism in an Increasingly Violent World *Jeffrey S. Podoshen*	173
8 Dark Tourism in an Age of 'Spectacular Death' *Philip R. Stone*	189
9 Dionysus Versus Apollo: An Uncertain Search for Identity Through Dark Tourism—Palestine as a Case Study *Rami K. Isaac and Vincent Platenkamp*	211
10 Dark Tourism as Psychogeography: An Initial Exploration *Richard Morten, Philip R. Stone, and David Jarratt*	227

Section 3 Dark Tourism, Society, and Culture	257
11 Dark Tourism, Difficult Heritage, and Memorialisation: A Case of the Rwandan Genocide *Mona Friedrich, Philip R. Stone, and Paul Rukesha*	261
12 'Pablo Escobar Tourism'—Unwanted Tourism: Attitudes of Tourism Stakeholders in Medellín, Colombia *Anne Marie Van Broeck*	291
13 Tourism Mobilities, Spectralities, and the Hauntings of Chernobyl *Kevin Hannam and Ganna Yankovska*	319
14 Disasters and Disaster Tourism: The Role of the Media *Richard Sharpley and Daniel Wright*	335

15 Denial of the Darkness, Identity and Nation-Building
    in Small Islands: A Case Study from the Channel Islands   355
    Gilly Carr

Section 4 Dark Tourism and Heritage Landscapes   377

16 Sites of Suffering, Tourism, and the Heritage of Darkness:
    Illustrations from the United States   381
    Dallen J. Timothy

17 From Celebratory Landscapes to Dark Tourism Sites?
    Exploring the Design of Southern Plantation Museums   399
    *Stephen P. Hanna, Derek H. Alderman, and Candace Forbes
    Bright*

18 Dark Tourism to Seismic Memorial Sites   423
    Yong Tang

19 First World War Battlefield Tourism: Journeys Out
    of the Dark and into the Light   443
    Dominique Vanneste and Caroline Winter

20 Tourism to Memorial Sites of the Holocaust   469
    Rudi Hartmann

Section 5 The 'Dark Tourist' Experience   509

21 Unravelling Fear of Death Motives in Dark Tourism   515
    Avital Biran and Dorina Maria Buda

22 Politics of Dark Tourism: The Case of Cromañón and
    ESMA, Buenos Aires, Argentina   533
    Maximiliano E. Korstanje and David Baker

Contents

23 "I Know the Plane Crashed": Children's Perspectives in Dark Tourism — 553
Mary Margaret Kerr and Rebecca H. Price

24 Dark Tourism Visualisation: Some Reflections on the Role of Photography — 585
John J. Lennon

25 Educating the (Dark) Masses: Dark Tourism and Sensemaking — 603
Catherine Roberts

Section 6 The Business of Dark Tourism — 639

26 Marketing Dark Heritage: Building Brands, Myth-Making and Social Marketing — 645
Geoffrey Bird, Morgan Westcott, and Natalie Thiesen

27 'Death as a Commodity': The Retailing of Dark Tourism — 667
Brent McKenzie

28 Exhibiting Death and Disaster: Museological Perspectives — 693
Elspeth Frew

29 Souvenirs in Dark Tourism: Emotions and Symbols — 707
Jenny Cave and Dorina Buda

30 'Shining a Digital Light on the Dark': Harnessing Online Media to Improve the Dark Tourism Experience — 727
Peter Bolan and Maria Simone-Charteris

Index — 747

Notes on Contributors

Derek H. Alderman is the head of the Department of Geography at the University of Tennessee, USA, where he is also the Betty Lynn Hendrickson Professor of Social Science. His research interests include race, public memory, heritage tourism and the African-American experience in the south-eastern United States. Adopting a social and spatial justice approach, he examines the cultural and historical geography of transatlantic slavery, the Jim Crow and Civil Rights eras, and more contemporary black campaigns for equality and inclusion. He is the founder and co-coordinator of the Race, Ethnicity, and Social Equity in Tourism (RESET) Initiative and vice-president of the American Association of Geographers. He is the (co)author of over 110 journal articles, book chapters and other scholarly essays.

David Baker is an associate professor of hospitality management in the College of Business at Tennessee State University, USA. He also served as an advisor to the Tourism Division of the nation of St. Kitts/Nevis from 2007 to 2014. Baker also undertakes consulting work in the tourism field for the Islands of the Caribbean. Before assuming his current position, he worked as an associate professor and assistant professor of hospitality management at the University of Central Missouri, USA, an instructor at Eastern Illinois University, USA, and as a resort manager of the Frigate Bay Beach Hotel in the Caribbean Nation of St. Kitts/Nevis. David is also a visiting professor at Imus Institute, Manila, Philippines (2016).

Avital Biran is a senior lecturer at Bournemouth University, UK. Her research interests revolve around issues of consumer behaviour and experience in tourism and leisure, particularly within the context of heritage and dark tourism, where she has published extensively. Her work focuses on the conceptual and empirical understanding of these notions and their interrelationship, heritage interpretation and the role of dark sites in destination recovery. Avital is currently developing an interest in social responsibility in management, specifically in relation to conflict reconciliation through tourism, disability and accessibility, gender-related issues in tourism consumption, and supply and higher education. She has taught extensively on visitor attractions management, tourism marketing, heritage and dark tourism, social and cultural issues in leisure and tourism, and disciplinary perspectives in tourism studies.

Geoffrey Bird is an associate professor in the School of Tourism and Hospitality Management at Royal Roads University, Victoria, Canada. Geoffrey completed his PhD in 2011 at the University of Brighton, UK, focusing on the relationship between tourism, remembrance and landscapes of war. He recently co-edited *Managing and Interpreting D-Day's Sites of Memory: Guardians of Remembrance* (Routledge, 2016) and *Battlefield Events: Landscape, Commemoration and Heritage* (Routledge, 2016). His background includes 25 years in the field of education working in government, then as a project manager in the field of sustainable tourism and poverty alleviation in Malaysia and Vietnam. Geoffrey also served as an officer in the Royal Canadian Naval Reserve and as a heritage interpreter at the Canadian National War Memorial at Vimy Ridge, France. In 2016, he directed and produced the film documentary *War Memories Across Canada* (Canadian Heritage, Parks Canada and Royal Roads University).

Peter Bolan is a senior lecturer and director for International Travel and Tourism Management at the Ulster University Business School, UK. He holds a Bachelor Honours degree in geography, a master's degree in tourism management and eTourism, and a PhD focusing on authenticity and displacement in film-induced tourism. His core research interests and consultancy specialisms include film- and media-induced tourism, digital tourism, golf tourism and food tourism. Previous experience prior to academia includes management roles within the visitor attraction sector and hospitality industry. Peter also writes regularly for a number of Northern Ireland business and hospitality trade publications.

Candace Forbes Bright is an associate scientist in the Department of Political Science, International Development and International Affairs at The University of Southern Mississippi, USA. Her principal research interests focus on health disparities and disasters, racial geographies and social networks. As a member of the multi-institutional Race, Ethnicity, and Social Equity in Tourism (RESET) research team that received a National Science Foundation grant to study racialised heritage tourism landscapes, she has focused much of her research on the inclusion of slavery in the narratives of tourist plantations.

Dorina Buda is an assistant professor and a Rosalind Franklin Fellow at the University of Groningen in the Netherlands. She is the author of *Affective Tourism: Dark Routes in Conflict* (Routledge, 2015) and has published articles in *Annals of Tourism Research*, *Journal of Travel Research*, *Current Issues in Tourism*, and *International Journal of Culture, Tourism and Hospitality Research*, among others. Her work has been driven by a passion for tourism research, which revolves around interconnections between tourism, sociopolitical conflict, emotions and identity. Her current research focus is on travel to conflict areas, 'hot spots' and historical locations where 'dark' events took place. Dorina studies dark tourism with a specific focus on emotional dynamics between people and places, whereby these trips can act in an emotional or therapeutic way, or lead to more self-awareness. Dorina completed her doctoral research in the Geography and Tourism Programmes at the University of Waikato, Aotearoa, New Zealand, with a PhD thesis on 'Danger-zone tourism: Emotional performances in Jordan and Palestine'.

Gilly Carr is a senior lecturer and academic director at the University of Cambridge's Institute of Continuing Education, UK. She is also a Fellow and Director of Studies in Archaeology at St Catharine's College (University of Cambridge, UK). She has published widely in the fields of conflict archaeology and post-conflict heritage studies and is currently writing 'Victims of Nazism in the Channel Islands: A Legitimate Heritage?' (Bloomsbury Academic). Previous volumes include 'Legacies of Occupation: Heritage, memory and archaeology in the Channel Islands' (Springer, 2014) and 'Protest, Defiance and Resistance in the Channel Islands: German Occupation 1940–1945' (with Paul Sanders and Louise Willmot; Bloomsbury Academic, 2014). Her most recent co-edited volume was 'Heritage and memory of war: Responses from Small Islands' (with Keir Reeves; Routledge 2015).

Jenny Cave is a senior lecturer in events and tourism (management communication) at the University of Waikato, New Zealand. Her research focuses on the relationship between diaspora, material cultures, tourism and community development in islands, the Pacific region and China. This emerges from an academic background in anthropology, museology and tourism with 20 years' experience managing cultural industries in both Canada and New Zealand.

Erik Cohen is the George S. Wise Professor of Sociology (emeritus) at the Hebrew University of Jerusalem, Israel, where he taught between 1959 and 2000. He has conducted research in Israel, Peru, the Pacific Islands and, since 1977, in Thailand. He is the author of more than 200 publications and of several books, including *Contemporary Tourism: Diversity and Change* (Elsevier, 2004) and *Explorations in Thai Tourism* (Emerald, 2008). Erik is a founding member of the International Academy for the Study of Tourism. He was awarded the UN World Tourism Organization's Ulysses Prize for 2012. He presently lives and does research in Thailand.

Graham Dann has been researching tourist motivation and such allied topics as tourism promotion for the past four decades. He has been recognised for his contribution to their understanding by the award of a peer-reviewed higher doctorate. He is a founder member of the International Academy for the Study of Tourism and of the research committee on international tourism of the International Sociological Association where he correspondingly served a term as vice-president and president. His academic career (from the tropics to the tundra) began in 1975 with a 21-year attachment to the University of the West Indies in which he taught sociology and researched tourism. That was followed by an 11-year stint at the University of Luton (now University of Bedfordshire), UK. Followed by a period as professor of tourism at Finnmark University College, Alta, currently he is professor emeritus at the University of Tromsø, Arctic University of Norway, Alta campus. In relation to dark tourism, his contribution may be counted among some of the earlier theoretical attempts to elucidate the phenomenon. Beginning in 1998 when he had a working paper published on the 'Dark Side of Tourism', he has also written about such areas as *Slavery, Contested Heritage and Thanatourism* (with Tony Seaton) (2001), plantation tourism in Barbados (with Rob Potter) (2001) and *Children of the Dark* (2005). Additionally, from the foregoing experience gained, he was able to provide a review of Richard Sharpley and Philip Stone's *The Darker Side of Travel* book (2010).

John Edmondson is an independent scholar in the field of Victorian Studies, specialising in mid-nineteenth-century literature and society in England, cross-currents with Second Empire France, travel and tourism in literature, and urban space and place. He has published two books—*A Traveller's Literary Companion to France* (1997) and *Dickens on France* (2006)—and has contributed many articles and reviews to magazines and journals on literary, publishing and education topics. His most recent research interests have included the repeated journey as a means of textual interpretation and how perceptions of the city are mediated by proximity and distance—see, respectively, 'Making Sense of Place: A Short Walk in Paris with the Uncommercial Traveller' *Dickens Quarterly*, Vol. 31, No 2, 2014, 127–154, and 'From a Distance—the Remote Cityscape as Dream and Nightmare', *E-REA, Revue électronique d'études sur le monde anglophone*, Vol. 13, No. 2, 2016, https://erea.revues.org/4889 (open access). Among his other activities, John is editor of the bimonthly journal *Industry and Higher Education* and a publishing consultant. Until recently he was the co-owner and director of IP Publishing Ltd., a small independent publishing house founded in 1990 and specialising in academic journals—the company was sold to SAGE Publications in April 2016.

Elspeth Frew is an associate professor in tourism management in the Department of Management and Marketing at La Trobe University, Australia. Elspeth's research interests are within cultural tourism, with a particular focus on dark tourism, as well as festival and event management, and she has published numerous articles in these areas. She has also undertaken research into industrial tourism and the relationship between the media and tourism management. Elspeth's research is interdisciplinary since she considers aspects of tourism within particular frameworks of psychology, media studies, anthropology and sociology.

Mona Friedrich earned her PhD from the Institute for Dark Tourism Research (iDTR) at the University of Central Lancashire (UCLan), UK. Her doctoral thesis explored complexities of (genocide) memorialisation processes in Rwanda and consequences of tourism development in post-conflict spaces. She previously completed a bachelor's degree in development studies at the University of Sussex, UK. She later graduated with a MA in Tourism, Environment and Development from the

Geography Department at King's College London. Mona has published in numerous publications, including a contribution to the *Journal of Tourism and Cultural Change*, as well as presenting at international conferences, such as the 2013 Peace Conference in Wageningen, the Netherlands. Mona is currently engaged in a research role at the Max Planck Institute for the History of Science, Berlin.

Stephen P. Hanna is a professor of geography at the University of Mary Washington in Fredericksburg, Virginia, USA. His current research focuses on the ways commemorative landscapes and their meanings to societies today are created and reproduced through both practice and representation. As a member of the Race, Ethnicity, and Social Equity in Tourism (RESET) Initiative, he has applied these interests to the ways African-American memories are or are not made present at tourism plantations through the complex interactions among visitors, guides, management and landscapes.

Kevin Hannam is a professor of tourism mobilities in the Business School at Edinburgh Napier University, UK. He is a founding co-editor of the journals *Mobilities* and *Applied Mobilities* (Routledge) and a co-editor of the books *The Routledge Handbook of Mobilities Research*, *Tourism and Leisure Mobilities* and *Event Mobilities*. He has a PhD in geography from the University of Portsmouth, UK, and is a Fellow of the Royal Geographical Society (FRGS), vice-chair of the Association for Tourism and Leisure Education and Research (ATLAS) and a research affiliate at the University of Johannesburg, South Africa.

Rudi Hartmann is an associate professor (C/T) at the University of Colorado Denver, USA, where he has taught geography and tourism planning since 1992. He received his PhD in geography from the Technical University Munich, Germany, in 1983. Rudi has a long-time interest in the study of tourist experiences at heritage sites. He has closely examined heritage tourism at memorial sites of the Holocaust in Germany and in the Netherlands. He has also reviewed theoretical foundations and conceptual changes in the study of heritage sites, including places with a 'shadowed past'. During his long-time work in and commitment to the field of geography, Rudi has contributed to geographic education in various ways, among others with a volume jointly developed with Chinese geographers on a comparative analysis of China and of the USA. As a visiting scholar, he conducted research or taught at Clark University, Massachusetts; at Lund University, Sweden; at the University of California, Berkeley; and at Beijing Normal University, China. Rudi is also an Associate Editor of this volume—the *Palgrave Handbook of Dark Tourism Studies*.

Rami Isaac Born in Palestine, Rami Isaac did his undergraduate studies in the Netherlands and graduate studies in the UK and has earned his PhD (spatial sciences) from the University of Groningen, the Netherlands. He is currently a senior lecturer in tourism teaching at the undergraduate as well as postgraduate levels at the Academy for Tourism at the NHTV Breda University of Applied Sciences in the Netherlands. Additionally, he is an assistant professor at the Faculty of Tourism and Hotel

Management at Bethlehem University, Palestine. Currently he is the president of the Research Committee 50 on International Tourism, International Sociologist Association ISA (2014–2018). His research interests are in the area of tourism development and management, critical theory and political aspects of tourism. He published numerous articles and book chapters on tourism and political (in)stability, occupation, dark tourism, violence and transformational tourism.

David Jarratt is a senior lecturer in the School of Management at the University of Central Lancashire (UCLan), UK. His principal research interests focus on the tourist experience and fundamental interrelationships with sense of place. In particular, he has considered the traditional seaside resort, which is an enduring sociocultural construction and its contemporary meaning to tourists. David has published in the areas of coastal development and seaside heritage, as well as presenting at numerous international conferences on the subject of coastal town regeneration. David draws his scholarly inspiration from the subject fields of human geography and environmental psychology. His most recent research has centred on issues of nostalgia, spirituality and sense of place as experienced by visitors to traditional British seaside resorts.

Mary Margaret Kerr is a professor and chair of administrative and policy studies and a professor of psychology in education and psychiatry at the University of Pittsburgh, USA. Trained in children's mental health, she has responded to over 1000 child-related crises, including the TWA 800 and USAir 427 airline disasters. This work appears in her textbook, *School Crisis Intervention and Prevention*. Dr. Kerr's research team studies the experiences of children who visit the Flight 93 (9/11) National Memorial, the Pentagon Memorial, the Holocaust National Memorial Museum (USA) and other such dark heritage sites. Children now join her team as active researchers of their own tourism experiences.

Maximiliano E. Korstanje is the editor-in-chief of the *International Journal of Safety and Security in Tourism* (UP Argentina) and the *International Journal of Cyber Warfare and Terrorism* (IGI-GlobalUS). He is a senior researcher in the Department of Economics at the University of Palermo, Argentina. Maximiliano has been included in the biographical records for Marquis 'Who's Who in the World' since 2009. With more than 800 publications and 40 books, he has been nominated for five honorary doctorates for his contribution to the study of the effects of terrorism and tourism. In 2015, he was appointed as a visiting research fellow at the School of Sociology and Social Policy, University of Leeds, UK, and in 2016 as visiting professor at the University of La Habana, Cuba.

John J. Lennon is the assistant vice-principal at Glasgow Caledonian University, UK, responsible for business development and industry engagement. John is also the director of the Moffat Centre for Travel and Tourism Business Development. The Moffat Centre is responsible for the production of international consumer and market research in tourism, and it funds scholarships for students wishing to study travel and tourism (www.moffatcentre.com). Within the commercial sector of travel and tourism, John has undertaken over 550 tourism and travel projects in over 40 countries on behalf of private sector and public sector clients. He undertakes research and commercial work in the fields of tourism development, destination marketing and financial feasibility of tourism projects. John is the author of five books and over 80 articles and numerous reports on the global travel and tourism industry.

Brent McKenzie is an associate professor in the Department of Marketing and Consumer Studies, College of Business and Economics, University of Guelph, Canada. In addition to his current work in the field of dark tourism, Brent is a specialist on business and management issues within the Baltic states of Estonia, Latvia and Lithuania, as well as the former Soviet Union. He has engaged in extensive research fieldwork and conducted a number of academic and industry workshops, presentations and seminars in these countries. His research has been published in both academic and practitioner journals. He is an associate editor for the *Journal of Eastern European and Central Asian Research*, a regional editor for the *International Journal of Business and Emerging Markets* and a member of the Editorial Advisory Board of the *Baltic Journal of Management*.

Richard Morten is a PhD candidate of the Institute for Dark Tourism Research (iDTR) at the University of Central Lancashire (UCLan), UK. His work focuses specifically on the emergence of dark tourism in post-Soviet space, as well as looking at the processes of reconciliation by which difficult heritage becomes tourism commodity. Currently based in Bulgaria, his research into the dark tourism phenomenon has taken him around the world, from Cuba to Kazakhstan.

Vincent Platenkamp undertook his secondary education in Breda, Brussels and Rotterdam. He then studied philosophy and sociology at the University of Amsterdam, the Netherlands, and later earned his PhD from Wageningen University, the Netherlands. After his work in Amsterdam and The Hague, Vincent worked at the NHTV Breda University of Applied Sciences (the Netherlands) as a professor of cross-cultural understanding. He has participated in various educational projects in the Netherlands, Portugal, Indonesia, Thailand, Hungary, Poland, Cuba, Curacao and Bulgaria. He was also an editor of the Dutch Leisure Magazine from 1995 to 2001. His current research interests are within critical theory, power relations and cross-cultural understandings. Vincent has published numerous articles and books, and his most recent book is *Key Concepts in Tourism Research* (2013).

Jeffrey Podoshen is an associate professor in the Department of Business, Organizations and Society at Franklin and Marshall College in Lancaster, PA, USA. Jeff's primary area of research relates to death and violent consumption and dark tourism. Fully immersed in a liberal arts environment, he often blends and bridges theory from a variety of disciplines in order to explain phenomena and to build theory. His work has appeared in numerous journals including *Consumption,*

Markets & Culture, Marketing Theory, Tourism Management, Journal of Community & Applied Social Psychology and *International Journal of Consumer Studies*.

Rebecca H. Price has over a decade of experience teaching research skills in non-traditional education settings. Rebecca is currently a PhD candidate in social and comparative analysis at the University of Pittsburgh, USA. She also serves as an adjunct research and instruction librarian at Duquesne University, USA. In her current role in the Flight 93 (9/11) research team (University of Pittsburgh), Rebecca offers mentoring to undergraduates as they design and execute research studies related to children's experiences at dark heritage sites. Rebecca's research interests include engaging children and other novice researchers as they explore, shape and communicate their experiences on school trips, at museums and in other out-of-classroom settings.

Catherine Roberts principal research interests are focused on memory, identity and conflict. These reflect an industry background in heritage practice (including former roles at Imperial War Museums [UK]; project coordination of oral histories/exhibitions on FEPOW and LGBT conflict experiences; Cultural Olympiad programming around conflict resolution): and consultancy (researching/developing alternative tourist pathways in European cities for EC-funded *Discover Peace* project; MOOCs for Humanitarian and Conflict Response Institute, University of Manchester, UK). Catherine has contributed articles to *Museum Practice* and *Heritage 365* and co-authored (with Philip R. Stone) *Dark Tourism and Dark Heritage: Emergent Themes, Issues and Consequences* in *Displaced Heritage* (Boydell Press, 2014). She has previously taught undergraduate tourism and event management at the University of Central Lancashire (UCLan), UK. Catherine is an associate of the Institute for Dark Tourism Research (iDTR) at UCLan where her current PhD research appraises touristic encounters with Auschwitz-Birkenau through transactional analysis.

Paul Rukesha received a bachelor's degree in social sciences (sociology) at the National University of Rwanda (now University of Rwanda) in 2007. Paul is currently a digital content development team leader in the Education Department at the Kigali Genocide Memorial, Rwanda—a memorial run by the Aegis Trust. He is responsible for digital content development, content appraisal and validation, as well as daily coordinating digital content development staff. He has been employed by the Aegis Trust since July 2010, having previously worked for the National Service of Gacaca Courts, Rwanda—a governmental institution which coordinated the traditionally inspired Rwandan courts in charge of prosecuting Rwandan genocide cases.

Tony Seaton is a MacAnally Professor of Tourism Behaviour and Travel History at the University of Limerick, Ireland, and Emeritus Professor of Tourism Behaviour, University of Bedfordshire, UK. He has taught and published widely for more than 25 years on tourism behaviour and history, with special focus on thanatourism and literary travel and cultural tourism. He has consulted and researched for many international organisations including the UNWTO, EU, ETC, and six different governments and been advisor to academic and historical libraries in Ireland, America and the UK. His current research interests are in historical and social science aspects of thanatourism, Icelandic travel history, Midland (UK) industrial history and the iconography and representation of travel and tourism in graphic satire and literature. Tony is also an Associate Editor of this volume—the *Palgrave Handbook of Dark Tourism Studies*.

Richard Sharpley is a professor of tourism and development at the University of Central Lancashire (UCLan), UK. He is a co-editor of the journal *Tourism Planning & Development* and a resource editor for *Annals of Tourism Research*. His principal research interests are within the fields of tourism and development and the sociology of tourism, and his books include *Tourism and Development: Concepts and Issues, 2nd Edition* (2015, with David Telfer); *Tourism, Tourists and Society, 4th Edition* (2008); *The Darker Side of Travel: The Theory and Practice of Dark Tourism* (2009, with Philip R. Stone); and *Tourist Experience: Contemporary Perspectives* (2011) and *The Contemporary Tourist Experience: Concepts & Consequences* (2012), both co-edited with Philip R. Stone. Richard is also an Associate Editor of this volume—the *Palgrave Handbook of Dark Tourism Studies*.

Maria Simone-Charteris is a lecturer in travel and tourism management at Ulster University, UK, where she teaches at undergraduate as well as postgraduate levels. Her research interests focus on pilgrimage and religious tourism, dark and political tourism, peace and reconciliation through tourism, food and wine tours and festivals, and slow travel and tourism. Maria is currently completing a PhD on the potential interconnections between religious and political tourism in Northern Ireland and is a fellow of the Higher Education Academy.

Jonathan Skinner is a reader in anthropology in the Department of Life Sciences, University of Roehampton, UK. He is also a chair of TECHNE (AHRC Doctoral Training Programme) Training Group. He has a particular interest in interviewing skills and qualitative research methods. He has undertaken fieldwork in the Eastern Caribbean on the island of Montserrat (tourism and trauma, colonial relations and disaster recovery) and in the USA/UK (social dancing, arts health, contested heritage). He previously lectured at Queen's University Belfast and the University of Abertay Dundee, and held visiting fellowships at the University of Oxford, Keele University, University of Illinois and California State University, Sacramento. He has been Honorary Treasurer of the Association of Social Anthropologists, editor of the journal *Anthropology in Action* and publications officer for the European Association of Social Anthropologists. He is currently an adjunct fellow of the Centre for Cosmopolitan Studies, University of St Andrews, co-edits the book series *Movement and Performance Studies* for Berghahn Publishers with Professor Helena Wulff (University of Stockholm) and is advisor to the arts health charity Arts Care.

Philip R. Stone is the Executive Director of the Institute for Dark Tourism Research (iDTR) at the University of Central Lancashire (UCLan), UK. He is internationally recognised in the field of 'dark tourism' and 'difficult heritage' having presented numerous keynote conference addresses across the UK and continental Europe, North America, Asia and Australasia. Philip has been a consultant/interviewee to over 100 national and international print and broadcast media outlets, including BBC Television, BBC Radio, CNN, The New York Times, Huffington Post, The Guardian, The Economist, and The New Scientist. Philip, who has a PhD in thanatology, has published extensively in the area of dark tourism and difficult heritage, including being (co)author/(co)editor (with Richard Sharpley) of *The Darker Side of Travel: The Theory and Practice of Dark Tourism* (Channel View Publications, 2009), *Tourist Experience: Contemporary Perspectives* (Routledge, 2011) and *The Contemporary Tourist Experience: Concepts and Consequences* (Routledge, 2012). Philip is also the Editor-in-Chief of this volume—the *Palgrave Handbook of Dark Tourism Studies*.

Natalie Thiesen has over 10 years of experience in the tourism industry and is the market development manager for Tourism Winnipeg, Canada. She recently completed her Master of Arts degree in tourism management at Royal Roads University, Victoria, Canada. Her thesis examined marketing approaches for a war heritage site. She was also awarded the 2015 Juno Beach Centre Fellowship to conduct research into the marketing of Canadian war sites of memory in France. Previously, she worked as a heritage interpreter at the Canadian National War Memorial at Vimy Ridge, France. Natalie received her Bachelor of Commerce in Hospitality and Tourism Management from Ryerson University, Toronto, Canada. She has published in the *Journal of Hospitality and Tourism* and *Sustainability: Science, Practice and Policy*, as well as co-authored chapters in *Managing and Interpreting D-Day's Sites of Memory: Guardians of Remembrance* (Routledge, 2016).

Dallen J. Timothy is a professor of community resources and development at Arizona State University, USA, and senior sustainability scientist at the Global Institute of Sustainability. He holds visiting professorships in China, Italy, Spain and Indiana (USA). Timothy is the editor of the *Journal of Heritage Tourism*, serves on the editorial boards of 17 additional journals and is commissioning editor for four book series by Routledge and Channel View Publications. His current research interests include religious tourism; trails and routes; political boundaries; cultural heritage; heritage cuisines/food and identity; migration and diasporas; and the geopolitics of heritage. He has worked and travelled in more than 100 countries and currently has active research projects in Asia, North America, the Caribbean, Europe and the Middle East.

Anne Marie Van Broeck is a senior lecturer and researcher in the Department of Earth and Environmental Sciences, University of Leuven (KU Leuven), Belgium, and also at the Institución Universitaria Colegio Mayor de Antioquia, Medellín, Colombia. Her principal research interests are related to sociocultural dimensions of tourism, dark tourism and conflict-related issues (i.e. conflicts caused by tourism, tourism in a context of political tensions, contested heritage and 'gangster tourism').

She has a particular interest in Latin America, specifically in Colombia, where she has lived and worked for several years (1996–2000) and now visits annually. She is also a coordinator and researcher for the project 'Turismo Oscuro en México' (Dark Tourism in Mexico) at the Instituto de Geografía, Universidad Nacional Autónoma de México.

Dominique Vanneste is an associate professor in the Department of Earth and Environmental Sciences at the University of Leuven (KU Leuven), Belgium. She is involved in the research groups of Human Geography and Tourism and is the director of a research and development unit 'ASTOR' (Association for Tourism Research), as well as programme director for the KU Leuven part of an Erasmus Mundus Master in Sustainable Territorial Development. She represents KU Leuven with the UNITWIN-UNESCO network and with the UNWTO Knowledge Network. Her main research interests and lecturing topics are *economic geography* (regional development, networking and location factors), *historical geography* (relationship between landscape, heritage, identity and conservation) and *tourism* (sustainable tourism and governance, heritage tourism, geo-tourism, tourism as a regional development lever).

Kathryn Walchester teaches in the Department of English and Cultural History at Liverpool John Moores University, UK. Her research addresses European travel in the eighteenth and nineteenth centuries, particularly journeys alternative to the dominant modes of Home Tour and Grand Tour, including accounts by women and servants, and journeys to the North. Publications include *'Our Own Fair Italy': Nineteenth-Century Women's Travel Writing and Italy 1800–1844* (Peter Lang, 2007) and *Gamle Norge and Nineteenth-Century British Women Travellers in Norway* (Anthem, 2014). Kathryn is currently working on a monograph about working and travelling, *Servants and the British Travelogue 1750–1850*, and co-editing a glossary of travel writing terms, *Keywords for Travel Writing Studies* with Zoe Kinsley and Charles Forsdick. She is also a co-organiser of the annual Liverpool Travel Seminar and of Borders and Crossings/Seuils et Travers International Travel Writing Conference.

Morgan Westcott is a marketer with 13 years of experience and former director of Sales and Marketing for the Arts and Cultural Guide to British Columbia, Canada. For over a decade, she served as general manager of LinkBC, a provincial tourism organisation facilitating partnerships between post-secondary programmes and various tourism-related organisations. She co-edited the online textbook *Intro to Tourism and Hospitality in BC* (Capilano University, 2016), along with writing a number of other student and instructor resources. Morgan has been a content generator for the BC Lodgings and Campgrounds Association and has produced business-to-business guides for Destination British Columbia. She holds a BA in English from the University of British Columbia, Canada, a Diploma of Marketing Management from the British Columbia Institute of Technology, Canada, and a MA in Tourism Management from Royal Roads University, Victoria, Canada—where she is now an associate faculty member teaching marketing.

Notes on Contributors

Leanne White is a senior lecturer in the College of Business at Victoria University, Melbourne, Australia. Her doctoral thesis examined manifestations of official nationalism and commercial nationalism at the Sydney 2000 Olympic Games. Leanne's research interests include issues of national identity, commercial nationalism, popular culture, advertising, destination marketing and cultural tourism. She is the author of more than 50 book chapters and refereed academic journal articles. Leanne is the editor of *Commercial Nationalism and Tourism: Selling the National Story* (Channel View Publications, 2017) and co-editor of *Advertising and Public Memory: Social, Cultural and Historical Perspectives on Ghost Signs* (Routledge, 2017), *Wine and Identity: Branding, Heritage, Terroir* (Routledge, 2013), *Dark Tourism and Place Identity: Managing and Interpreting Dark Places* (Routledge, 2013) and *Tourism and National Identities: An International Perspective* (Routledge, 2011). Leanne is also a keynote speaker, reviewer of academic journal articles, doctoral thesis examiner and member of professional associations in tourism, marketing, leisure and sport. Leanne is also an Associate Editor of this volume—the *Palgrave Handbook of Dark Tourism Studies*.

Caroline Winter is a lecturer at the William Angliss Institute, Melbourne, Australia, where she teaches tourism and research methods. Her principal research interests focus on the First World War and the way in which social memory and remembrance are formed through tourist activities. Caroline has conducted a number of battlefield studies at museums, memorials and cemeteries; and memorial sites such as Pozières in France and Ieper/Ypres in Belgium are her preferred places to research. Caroline's early research focused on values (intrinsic and instrumental) for natural places, and she has recently extended this research interest to the ethical issues of thoroughbred horse racing.

Daniel Wright is a lecturer in tourism management in the Lancashire School of Business & Enterpriset, University of Central Lancashire (UCLan), UK. Daniel completed his PhD in disaster management where he specifically explored the role of the visitor economy in post-earthquake regeneration and development. Daniel is an associate of the Institute for Dark Tourism Research (iDTR) at UCLan and has published numerous journal articles and book chapters that focus on disaster tourism. Daniel has also presented his work internationally, most recently in Peru, where he examined post-disaster regeneration polices. Daniel's principal research interests revolve around dark tourism, tourism photography and tourism futurology.

Ganna Yankovska holds a master's degree in tourism from the University of Sunderland, UK. She has presented at numerous tourism management conferences, as well as taking part in political debates about the tourism industry in Ukraine.

Tang Yong is an associate professor of geography at the Chengdu University of Technology (CDUT), China. Tang's principal research interests are within tourism geography, landscape history and issues of public memory and commemoration, as well as heritage and cultural tourism. Tang has served as director of the Collaborative

Education Programme of Tourism Management between CDUT and Edge Hill University, UK, and has taught in the Department of Tourism Development and Management, CDUT. He was sponsored by the China Scholarship Council to visit the Geography Department at the University of Colorado at Boulder, USA, and the Geography Department at the University of Connecticut at Storrs, USA. Tang is currently researching (dark) tourism at earthquake disaster sites travel motivations, sought experiences and perceived benefits of tourists with their visits to memorial sites of earthquake.

List of Figures & Plates

Plate 2.1	The pillory	36
Plate 2.2	Drawn through the streets on a sledge	37
Plate 2.3	Peine forte et dure	39
Plate 2.4	Elizabethan executions: hanging, beheading, and dismembering	41
Plate 2.5	Body parts exhibited	42
Plate 2.6	The Gunpowder Plot	45
Plate 2.7	Execution of Charles I	46
Plate 2.8	The Restoration of Charles 11 in London 1666	47
Plate 2.9	Execution of the Earl of Kilmarnock, 1746	51
Plate 2.10	The new gallows, 1783	52
Plate 2.11	(Hogarth) Death of the idle apprentice	53
Plate 2.12	The burning of Phoebe Harris, 1786	55
Plate 2.13	A Red Barn broadside	57
Plate 2.14	The Manning murder	58
Plate 2.15	Ratcliff Highway I	65
Plate 2.16	Ratcliff Highway II	66
Plate 5.1	Santorini sunken caldera and burnt islands from Oia (Photo Source: Author 2016)	137
Plate 5.2	Historic Santorini eruption postcards (Photo Source: Author 2016)	138
Plate 5.3	Plymouth outskirts under the volcano (Photo Source: Author 2005)	142
Plate 5.4	Tour guide narrating from Jack Boy Hill (Photo Source: Author 2015)	142
Plate 10.1	'Psychogeographical Guide to Paris' by Guy Debord (Source: van Tijen 2017)	231

Fig. 10.1	A dark tourism cylinder: a conceptual model showing dark tourism experience within a heterotopian framework (Source: Stone 2013)	239
Fig. 10.2	Dark tourism within a psychogeographical framework	242
Fig. 11.1	Five emergent research themes in Rwanda's memorialscape	277
Plate 13.1	Abandoned house (Photo Source: Author)	328
Plate 13.2	Swimming pool (Photo Source: Author)	329
Plate 14.1	Commemoration at the student house (Photo Source: Author, D. Wright)	346
Fig. 14.1	Poem in memory of victims (Translated by: Author, D. Wright)	347
Plate 15.1	Decorations in St Peter Port in 2015 in readiness for Liberation Day (Photo Source: Author)	360
Plate 15.2	Inside the Command Bunker at Noirmont Point, Jersey (Photo Source: Author)	361
Plate 15.3	National symbols on display in Guernsey (Photo Source: Jonathan Bartlett)	362
Fig. 15.1	Relationship between a dark event, a dark legacy, dark heritage and dark tourism	364
Plate 15.4	The entrance posts of *SS Lager* Sylt, Alderney (Photo Source: Author)	368
Plate 15.5	The entrance posts of Lager Wick, Jersey (Photo Source: Author)	372
Plate 15.6	Information panel about Lager Wick, Jersey (Photo Source: Author)	373
Fig. 16.1	Heritage resource types and scales	392
Plate 17.1	Scenes from Middleton Place. South Flanker, reflecting pond, spring house, and chapel (Photo Source: Author—Hanna, S.P.)	401
Plate 17.2	Middleton Place site plan featuring the 'Beyond the Fields Tour' (Map by Author—Hanna, S.P.)	412
Plate 17.3	Oak Alley site plan featuring the "Slavery at Oak Alley Exhibit" (Map by Author—Hanna, S.P.)	414
Plate 17.4	Whitney Plantation site plan featuring route of main tour (Map by Author—Hanna, S.P.)	417
Fig. 19.1	Items from the interviews (nodes from the transcript analysis) (data from 2009, 2013 and 2014)	453
Plate 19.1	The international dimension of WWI commemoration events in Flanders (Photo Source [A]: Foto WO1.be, 11 Nov. 2011, Photo Source [B]: AP Photo Virginia May, 11 Nov. 2014)	455
Fig. 20.1	Four-quadrant model for a categorisation of 'victims/perpetrators' places	499
Fig. 20.2	Sites associated with the victims and perpetrators in Nazi Germany, 1933–1945	500

Plate 23.1	Toy plane left in 2002 at the crash site of Flight 93 (Photo Source: Mary Anne McMullen)	564
Plate 23.2	Children's items left in 2002 at the crash site of Flight 93 (Photo Source: Author)	564
Plate 23.3	A rejected comment card (Photo Source: Author)	566
Plate 23.4	An accepted comment card which reads (as original): "Dear Men i Miss You i Love You i know the plane crashed. Love g p 2004 APRiL" (Photo Source: Author)	566
Plate 23.5	Child's message left in 2011 at the Flight 93 National Memorial (Photo Source: Author)	568
Plate 23.6	Child's drawing depicting the World Trade Center crash in New York City (Of note: X-Ray technique, patriotic colors, and smiling victims) (Photo Source: Mary Anne McMullen)	569
Plate 23.7	Child's drawing depicting World Trade Center crash in New York City (Of note: X-ray technique and smiling victims) (Photo Source: Mary Anne McMullen)	570
Plate 23.8	Patriotic tile tied to the fence surrounding the Flight 93 crash site (Photo Source: Mary Anne McMullen)	571
Plate 23.9	Child's drawing depicting first responders (Photo Source: Mary Anne McMullen)	572
Plate 23.10	Flight 93 Memorial Junior Ranger booklet page (Photo Source: Mary Anne McMullen)	573
Plate 24.1	Visitor at Dachau Crematoria, Dachau Concentration Camp (Photo: D. Weber)	588
Plate 24.2	Retail offer at Auschwitz-Birkenau Museum and Memorial, Poland (Photo: A. Tézenas)	590
Plate 24.3	Former residential accommodation in Pripyat, near Chernobyl (Photo: A. Tézenas)	592
Plate 24.4	Prefectural Industrial Promotion Hall, Hiroshima, Japan (Photo: D. Mulhern)	594
Plate 24.5	Visitors at Auschwitz-Birkenau Museum and Memorial viewing historical photographic record (the past) at the current site (the present) (Photo: A. Tézenas)	595
Plate 24.6	Deserted fairground at Pripyat, near Chernobyl, Ukraine (Photo: A. Tézenas)	599
Fig. 1	At Gallipoli in Turkey, the tourist is reminded that the cemetery is a place to be respected and is not for games and picnics (Source: Author)	640
Fig. 2	This final section of the book explores the business of dark tourism focussing on the five topics of branding, retail, exhibitions, souvenirs, and online marketing	641
Fig. 26.1	Brand identity, positioning, and image and dark tourism-related issues and concepts (Adapted from Pike 2004; Morrison 2013)	652

List of Figures & Plates

Fig. 27.1	Word cloud for the Edinburgh Dungeon, UK	676
Fig. 27.2	Word cloud for the London Dungeon, UK	677
Fig. 27.3	Word cloud for the York Dungeon, UK	678
Fig. 27.4	Word cloud summarising the three (UK) Dungeon attractions	679
Fig. 27.5	Statue of Lenin holding a shopping bag (Photo Source: Author)	680
Fig. 27.6	A can of the 'last breath of communism' (Photo Source: Author)	681
Fig. 27.7	A Titanic-themed teddy bear available as a gift/souvenir (Photo Source: Author)	683

List of Tables

Table 2.1	Death sentences and executions: 1849–1848	59
Table 11.1	A taxonomy of Rwanda's genocide memorials (as of July 2014)	272
Table 16.1	Types of one-time, localized crises and catastrophes in the United States	391
Table 16.2	Nationwide and persistent problems in the United States	392
Table 18.1	Memorial sites and attractions associated with seismic disasters	427
Table 22.1	Commonalities and differences	548

Section 1

Dark Tourism History

Tony Seaton

Introduction

Until the late 1990s, tourism history was a Cinderella subject in tourism discourse. Though there had been intermittent works on the Grand Tour (Lambert, 1937; Trease 1967; Hibbert 1987), that institutional holiday for the sons of aristocrats and gentlefolk which was a precursor of modern tourism, there were few attempts to provide more systematic accounts of tourism development, nationally or internationally. A few illustrated texts designed for a general audience appeared at irregular intervals (Sigaux 1966; Loschburg 1979; Feifer 1985), and there were two pioneering accounts of British seaside holidays that still have authority (Pimlott 1947; Walton 1983). More sustained interest in tourism history only began to develop as tourism became a recognised subject in academic programmes during the 1990s, and as scholars in traditional curriculum subjects—particularly history, sociology, and literary studies—came to recognise that it offered a wide and socially important field of behaviour for applying their disciplinary skills. The result was a minor renaissance in tourism history that included scholarly studies of tourism development over specified time periods that began with Towner's (1996) history of European tourism, followed by other general histories (Withey 1997; Lofgren 1999). There were also more specialist histories, including studies of human involvement with the

---

T. Seaton (✉)
University of Limerick, Limerick, Ireland

Emeritus Professor, University of Bedfordshire, Bedfordshire, UK

sea (Corbin 1994), the beach (Lencek and Bosker 1998), Mediterranean (Mullen and Munson 2009) mountains (Macfarlane 2003), and, following Marples (1959) early study, the history and philosophy of walking (Jebb 1987; Solnit 2001). There were also new scholarly studies of the Grand Tour in which text dominated illustration (Black 1992, 2003; Sweet 2015).

But none of these initiatives extended to the history of thanatourism/dark tourism, which still lacks a book length history 20 years after it emerged, though there are articles that include historical content, scattered among tourism and non-tourism journals. Nor are there academics working exclusively in dark tourism history that come close to John Walton's commitment over more than 30 years to British tourism history, which eventually led to the formation of the *Journal of Tourism History* in 2009. The dearth of dark tourism scholars with a track record of historical research in the subjects included in this collection made it necessary to look outside tourism to writers from other subject areas to meet the brief. The intention was to commission writers who could provide an interesting and diverse range of historical, dark tourism cases on subjects which had not previously featured strongly in the literature. The subjects chosen were: the touristic history of public executions; 'dark' walking tourism in nineteenth century London and Paris; dark tourism history in Scandinavia; and the touristic history of natural disasters. The writers assembled include those with backgrounds in anthropology, sociology, history, literary studies and languages as well as tourism studies.

About This Section

Chapter 1 by Tony Seaton offers a broad orientation to dark tourism history which begins with a critical overview of dark tourism as practice and discourse. This highlights some of the problematics surrounding its meaning and effects, and the way they act as a barrier to constructing a coherent history. The chapter proposes a revised model of dark tourism—entitled the EOR model—that aims to avoid the difficulties within current definitions, by shifting the focus of thanatourism/dark tourism from that of tourism contact with *death*, to tourism encounters with *remembrance of fatality and mortality*. The implications of this category change are then specified in terms of the way they affect historical perspectives. The chapter concludes with a three-point, methodological approach to historical inquiry into the history of encounters with engineered remembrance that comprise attention to their: political origins and beginnings; aetiology; and phenomenological antecedents and effects. Tony Seaton has, with John Lennon, been involved with dark tourism—or 'thanatourism' as he prefers to call it—since its inception (Foley and Lennon 1996; Seaton 1996), and more recently with the historical representation of tourism in literature (Seaton 2015, 2016, 2017), and visual iconography in art and photography (Seaton 2013a, b, 2014, 2016).

Chapter 2 by Tony Seaton and Graham Dann examines the touristic history of public executions and corporal punishments, judicial practices that attracted large audiences in Britain for several centuries, before being outlawed in the mid-nineteenth century. Though covering a longer period, and differing in thematic emphases, it follows earlier work by Gattrel (1994) and Wilson (2008) on dark tourism and crime history. Graham Dann has been one of the best-known and prolific tourism academics for some 40 years who has written widely on tourism motivation, the sociology of tourism, and, since the mid-1990s, on dark tourism history and the semiotics of tourism representation (Dann 1996, 1998, 2005). These later works also included a co-edited volume with his colleague Tony Seaton (Dann and Seaton 2001). As a further collaboration, the present account describes how judicial punishments in public, particularly executions, were first engineered and orchestrated by royalty in the twelfth century, flourished under the Tudors, declined under the Stuarts, and were reconfigured in the eighteenth century when more than 200 crimes were punishable by death. Executions were constructed with considerable attention to semiotic effects, which were first designed to attract large audiences and deter would-be transgressors, but later became as much carnivalesque entertainment as cautionary warning. After the abolition of capital punishment in 1868 the relationship between criminal justice and public hedonism continued as the mass media profitably exploited the popular appeal of crime and punishment in news coverage and fictional presentations. The result was a hegemonic alliance between the state and the entertainment industry which continues to the present. Its effects were to create a market for the growth of crime-based museums, exhibitions, and displays, as well to mark out geographies of crime, some of which were packaged as itineraries for commercial crime tours.

Chapter 3 comprises John Edmondson's account of the dark attractions of death in popular culture in mid-nineteenth century Paris and London and complements the first and fifth chapters in exploring the variety of exhibitions, shows and sites that put mortality and fatality on display, including violent crime. Edmondson is an independent scholar who has specialised in the mid-nineteenth century history and literature of France and Britain and especially in the work of Charles Dickens (see for example Edmondson 2006, 2014). His chapter falls into two sections. The first focuses on contemporary accounts of English visitors to the morgue in Paris, which was opened in 1804 with the purpose of displaying unidentified corpses for the pragmatic purpose of getting them identified. However, the displays attracted large audiences, including substantial numbers of English tourists, and the morgue was gradually appropriated as a tourist attraction. It was described in popular tourist guide books, one of which featured a full-page, coloured illustration of corpses. Dickens, who visited it several times, was a fascinated but shocked observer and Edmondson (2006) summarises his speculations on what drew the crowds to the corpses:

> In Dickens's view, these onlookers are not contemplating their own inevitable future state; the corpse is no *memento mori* for them, but rather an object of curiosity with which they make no personal connection…

This view contrasts with recent studies that exposure to exhibitions of bodies induces in their audiences' reflections on their own death (Stone 2011). For Dickens the spectators were voyeurs indulging a sublime curiosity in staring at the dead, in the safety of knowing that the dead could not stare back. From Paris Edmondson moves his account to London and surveys the great diversity of transgressive attractions featuring criminality, deviance, and violence there, including: the Chamber of Horrors at Madame Tussaud's; prison visits and murder sites; the portrayals of violent fatality in peep shows and panoramas featuring battles and the Lisbon Earthquake; and the popularity of anatomical museums and mummy unrolling. The chapter affirms the critical role of the press, theatre and 'penny dreadful' pulp fictions in stimulating and supplying tastes in popular culture that widened dark tourism practices.

Chapter 4, by Kathryn Walchester, comprises an appraisal of dark tourism encounters by British travellers in Scandinavia in the eighteenth and nineteenth centuries and is the first specialist essay on the subject. She teaches in the Department of English and Cultural History at Liverpool John Moores University, UK, where she leads a course on the history of travel and travel writing. She has published on women travellers in Italy (Walchester 2007) and travel to the North (Walchester 2014). Her account straddles three main categories: visits to the death sites, tombs, and memorials associated with Scandinavian monarchs; general accounts of cemeteries and funereal practice; and accounts of ancient burial sites and places associated with the dark aspects of Viking sagas. She locates travel to Sweden, Denmark, and Iceland as part of the general 'discovery' of northern Europe by British travellers in the Romantic period, partly due to a belief that Nordic culture was part of Britain's literary and linguistic heritage, and also to the gothic connotations of their history, and the perceived Otherness of their physical features, particularly Iceland's, which became coded as 'sublime' sights. Among the most popular tourist destinations in Sweden were places associated with Charles XII of Sweden, who died in battle in 1718 in mysterious circumstances which centred around whether or not he was killed by enemies or his own men. It was not just his death that was the main fascination, but the competing versions of engineered remembrance attached to it. Walchester provides a suggestive survey of Iceland, 'land of ice and fire', which was virtually unknown to English travellers until the late eighteenth century, but thereafter flourished as a literary destination among a coterie of elite travellers who included: Lord Dufferin, Sabine Baring-Gould, Anthony Trollope, Richard Burton, William Morris, and W.H. Auden, as well as many lesser-known writers who all produced books describing its unique combination of volcanoes, glaciers, and saga myths.

Dr Jonathan Skinner is Reader in the Department of Life Sciences at the University of Roehampton University. He has written widely on substantive and methodological issues in the study of natural disasters and dark tourism (Skinner 2000, 2008, 2017 and Skinner and Theodossopoulos 2011). In Chapter 5 he surveys great natural disasters as objects of the tourism gaze in history, a topic that has received limited coverage in academic writing. Disasters have always been an infrequent, but catastrophic hazard for human life on the planet that has given them a place in the myths of world religions (the flood, fires from heaven, great plagues). Skinner is particularly well-placed to write about them since in 1995 he was researching on the island Montserrat when a volcanic eruption started, frequently billed as a modern-day Pompeii for its covering of the capital, Plymouth, in pyroclastic material. He has been able to follow its development as a geographical and social phenomenon. It contrasts as a tourist destination with the dark and disaster tourism to Santorini, the Bronze Age Pompeii. His historical account reveals how natural disasters first became prime objects of the tourist gaze in the eighteenth century with the excavations at Pompeii and later, Herculaneum, two Roman cities destroyed by volcanoes. Their discoveries created a sensation, a reanimation, that was fuelled by two, new European developments—the growth of news and tourism. In the centuries following the weight of interdiscursive remembrance they have received has made them global tourism attractions and world heritage sites. His account shows how Pompeii has for more than 200 years remained a kind of mythic benchmark against which later volcanic disasters were later represented. His chapter also includes an account of the travel effects of the other great natural disaster of mid-eighteenth century Europe, the earthquake that destroyed Lisbon in 1755. Great natural catastrophes achieve sublime status in the public imagination and dictate their own terms of remembrance by the number of fatalities they create.

Skinner shows how semiotic signification of disasters may change over time and be 'repurposed' according to the needs and interests of later generations. Devastation that may once have been seen as an Act of God may later be interpreted as a state's failure to prepare, or treated as show material with which to re-cast a modern-day spectacle. The chapter draws an interesting difference between volcanoes and earthquakes as objects of the tourist gaze in terms of the physical evidence they leave and engages with questions of what dark tourism is. At volcano sites, physical leftovers remain and increase with successive eruptions, while the chaos left behind by earthquakes is frequently lost to posterity as rebuilding takes place over ruins that disappear.

The five chapters were written independently of each other and there was no a priori, party line to which the writers were asked to conform, except for that of bringing into dark tourism discourse an interesting range of case studies which exemplified its diverse, historical manifestations. Nevertheless, all of them, in different ways, articulate how engineered and orchestrated remembrance are at the heart of dark tourism encounters, whether those commemorating the penal rigour of the law, the mystery of a monarch's death, the problematic identity of anonymous corpses exhibited in a French morgue, or geophysical catastrophes in Pompeii or Portugal.

References

Black, J. (1992). *The British abroad. The grand tour in the eighteenth century*. Stroud: Alan Sutton.

Black, J. (2003). *Italy and the grand tour*. New Haven/London: Yale University Press.

Corbin, A. (1994). *The lure of the sea. The discovery of the seaside in the Western world 1750–1840*. Cambridge: Polity Press.

Dann, G. M. S. (1996). *The language of tourism: A socio-linguistic perspective*. Wallingford/Oxford: CAB International.

Dann, G. M. S. (1998). The dark side of tourism. In L. Serie (Ed.), *Éudeset Rapports* (Vol. 14). Aix-en-Provence: Centre International de Recherches et d'ÉtudesTouristiques.

Dann, G. M. S. (2005). Children of the dark. In G. J. Ashworth & R. Hartmann (Eds.), *Human trauma and tragedy revisited: The Management of atrocity sites for tourism* (pp. 233–252). New York: Cognizant.

Dann, G. M. S., & Seaton, A. V. (Eds.). (2001). *Slavery, contested heritage and thanatourism*. New York: The Haworth Press.

Edmondson, J. (2006). *Dickens on France*. Oxford: Signal Books.

Edmondson, J. (2014). Making sense of place: A short walk in Paris with the uncommercial traveller. *Dickens Quarterly, 31*(2), 127–154.

Feifer, M. (1985). *Going places. The ways of the tourist from Imperial Rome to the present day.* London: Macmillan.
Foley, M., & Lennon, J. J. (1996). Editorial: Heart of darkness. *International Journal of Heritage Studies, 2*(4), 195–197.
Gattrel, V. (1994). *The hanging tree: Execution and the English people 1770–1868.* Oxford: Oxford University Press.
Hibbert, C. (1987). *The grand tour.* London: Thames Methuen.
Jebb, M. (1987). *Walkers.* London: Constable.
Lambert, R. S. (1937). *Grand tour. A journey in the tracks of the age of aristocracy.* New York: E.P. Dutton and Co., Inc.
Lencek, L., & Bosker, G. (1998). *The beach. The history of paradise on earth.* London: Secker and Warburg.
Lofgren, O. (1999). *On holiday. A history of vacationing.* Berkeley: University of California Press.
Loschburg, W. (1979). *A history of travel.* Leipzig: Edition Leipzig.
Macfarlane, R. (2003). *Mountains of the mind. A history of fascination.* London: Granta Books.
Marples, M. (1959). *Shanks's pony.* London: J.M. Dent.
Mullen, R., & Munson, J. (2009). *The smell of the continent. The British discover Europe 1814–1914.* London: Macmillan.
Seaton, A. V. (1996). Guided by the dark: From thanatopsis to thanatourism. *International Journal of Heritage Studies, 2*(4), 234–244.
Seaton, A. V. (2013a). The tourist experience in graphic satire, 1796–1914. In T. Rakic & J.-A. Lester (Eds.), *Travel tourism and art* (pp. 13–35). Farnham/Surrey: Ashgate.
Seaton, A. V. (2013b). Didron's women and the hand maidens of iconography in nineteenth century Britain. *IKON, Journal of Iconographic Studies, 7-2014*, 291–312. Faculty of Humanities and Social Sciences, University of Rijeka.
Seaton, A. V. (2014). The unknown mother: Metempsychotic remembrance and rituals after World War 1. In L. Sikorska (Ed.), *Of what is past, or passing, or to come. Travelling in time and space in literature in English.* Annual Work in Literature and Linguistics, Dept. of Literature and Linguistics, Adam Mickiewicz University, Peter Lang, Oxford and New York.
Seaton, A. V. (2015). Travel and touring in England by elite Quaker, industrial families in the long nineteenth century: The journeys of Mary-Anne Schimmelpenninck (nee Galton) of Birmingham (1776–1856). *Quaker Studies, 20*(1), 117–144.
Seaton, A. V. (2016). Getting socially on the road – The short, happy life of the anapaestic tourism narrative 1766–1830. In M. Henes & B. Murray (Eds.), *Modes of transport: Travel writing and form, 1760–1900* (pp. 115–138). Basingstoke: Palgrave Macmillan. Palgrave Studies in Nineteenth-Century Writing and Culture.
Seaton, T. (2017). Qualitative approaches to the phenomenology of VFR travel: The use of literary and cultural texts as resources. *International Journal of Tourism Research.* https://doi.org/10.1002/jtr.2100.

Sigaux, G. (1966). *History of tourism*. London: Leisure Arts.

Skinner, J. (2000). The eruption of chances peak, Montserrat, and the narrative containment of risk. In P. Caplan (Ed.), *Risk revisited* (pp. 156–183). London: Pluto Press.

Skinner, J. (2008). Ghosts in the head and ghost towns in the field: Ethnography and the experience of presence and absence. *Journeys: International Journal of Travel and Travel Writing, 9*(2), 10–31.

Skinner, J. (2017). 'Was here': Identity traces and digital footprints as survival writing. *Liminalities: A Journal of Performance Studies*. http://liminalities.net/. In press.

Skinner, J., & Theodossopoulos, D. (2011). Introduction: The play of expectation in tourism. In J. Skinner & D. Theodossopoulos (Eds.), *Great expectations: Imagination, anticipation, and enchantment in tourism* (pp. 1–26). Oxford: Berghahn Books.

Solnit, R. (2001). *Wanderlust a history of walking*. London/New York: Verso.

Stone, P. R. (2011). Dark tourism and the cadaveric carnival: Mediating life and death narratives at Gunter von Hagens' Body Worlds. *Current Issues in Tourism Research, 14*(7), 685–701.

Sweet, R. (2015). *Cities and the grand tour: The British in Italy*, c. 1690–1820, Cambridge: Cambridge Social and Cultural Histories.

Towner, J. (1996). *An historical geography of recreation and tourism in the Western world 1540–1940*. Chichester: Wiley.

Trease, G. (1967). *The grand tour: A history of the golden age of travel*. New York: Holt, Rinehart and Winston.

Pimlott, J. A. R. (1947). *The Englishman's holiday*. London: Faber and Faber.

Walchester, K. (2007). *'Our own fair Italy': Nineteenth-century Women's travel writing and Italy 1800–1844*. Oxford: Peter Lang.

Walchester, K. (2014). *GamleNorge and nineteenth-century British women travellers and Norway*. London: Anthem.

Walton, J. (1983). *The English seaside resort. A social history*. New York: Leicester University Press/St. Martin's Press.

Wilson, J. Z. (2008). *Prison, cultural memory and dark tourism*. Oxford: Peter Lang.

Withey, L. (1997). *Grand tours and Cook's tours. A history of leisure tourism 1750–1915*. London: Aurum Press.

1

Encountering Engineered and Orchestrated Remembrance: A Situational Model of Dark Tourism and Its History

Tony Seaton

Is a history of dark tourism possible? This may seem an odd question to pose in the historical section of a substantial handbook. However, over the 20 years during which dark tourism has been explored academically, a recurrent problematic has been debate about what it is; therefore, a discussion of its meaning is unavoidable because it affects where its history is deemed to start. This introductory chapter examines some of the issues about dark tourism's origins and beginnings—a distinction discussed later—as a preface to the conceptual position reflected in the content of the chapters on its history that follow.

The earliest approach to dark tourism[1] envisaged it as a motivational category made up of tourists engaging in "travel to a location wholly, or partly motivated by the desire for actual or symbolic encounters with death" (Seaton 1996: 240). It was seen as a consumption grouping in the same way that other interests and activities (golfing, skiing, diving, battlefield walking, art, and history) had attracted their own identifiable and identified tourist typologies. From this basic premise, researchers set about surveying visitors at sites presumed to be 'dark' in order to profile who and what their visitors were. Twenty years later, the answer to this question seems to be, 'Nobody' and 'Everybody'. Research has failed to locate dark tourists as a distinctive group who accept that encounters with death, actual or symbolic, are their prime motivation. Though they can be counted at sites associated with the dead, they do not see death as the motivation for being there but prioritise other factors—history,

---

T. Seaton (✉)
University of Limerick, Limerick, Ireland

University of Bedfordshire, Luton, UK

national pride, and pilgrimage—as in the case of Australian and New Zealand tourists at Gallipoli and the Dardanelles who see those places as sites where national identity was forged, rather than as death sites (Slade 2003; Cheal and Griffin 2013). In some instances, visitors have been initially unaware of the 'dark' features of sites they were visiting, as was the case with those staying in the eccentric writer William Beckford's hilltop folly in Bath who did not know of Beckford or that, on arrival, they would find that his home had a cemetery in the garden (Seaton 2009a, b).

The heterogeneity of dark tourism experiences and responses makes it difficult to distinguish a common motivation that fits all. Dark tourism was originally deemed to comprise five main consumer activity categories that included behaviour which ranged from witnessing public hangings, to visiting Madame Tussauds and attending "murder weekends" in hotels that allowed crime readers to play detective games (Seaton 1996: 240–242). Many other tastes and activities can be subsumed within the province of dark tourism: family outings to the London Dungeon; rides on ghost trains at funfairs; eating burghers in a *Dracula* restaurant in New York; visiting cemeteries, singing songs round the John Lennon memorial in Central Park; attending a tribute concert to Freddie Mercury or David Bowie. But is it possible to identify common motives in them that would be recognised by the people involved?

Attempts to identify motivations have been made, but most, if not all, of them have been based on specific kinds of dark event that could not be generalised to others. In a seminal article, John Lennon and Malcolm Foley suggested that dark tourists sought three kinds of experience as visitors to 'dark' sites—'remembrance, education and entertainment' (Lennon and Foley 1996: 195). In the book-length study that followed, the authors did not revisit these motives. Instead, they concentrated on *sites,* rather than motivations of *visitors* to them (Lennon and Foley 2000). The sites they analysed were commemorations of twentieth-century atrocities and tragedies—a choice that reflected two of their defining assumptions about dark tourism that have often been ignored in discussion since. The first assumption was that it was confined to events within the memory of those still alive to validate them. The second was the corollary of this—that events that lay outside living memory did not constitute dark tourism because, they argued, "they do not posit questions, or introduce anxiety and doubt about modernity and its consequences" (Lennon and Foley 2000: 12). Dark tourism was thus, in Lennon and Foley's view, a product of late modernity; therefore, its history is somewhat brief. It is a perspective that has governed Lennon's subsequent work, which has principally addressed the problematics of exhibiting major humanitarian disasters of the twentieth century for touristic consumption, particularly holocaust sites. It is also a perspective that governs Williams' account of memorial museums (Williams 2007).

Philip Stone offered a more individualistic, motivational explanation of dark tourism (Stone 2012; Stone and Sharpley 2008), drawing on previous work proposing analogies between thanatourism and thanatopsis (Seaton 1996: 235–240). Thanatopsis was a motivated practice, encouraged by the Catholic Church in the Middle Ages, which involved reflections on death, induced or aided by various forms of memento mori exhibit (human skulls, deaths head rings, treatises on dying, etc.). Stone (2011, 2012) proposed that dark tourism, as an encounter with the deaths of 'significant others', acted as a surrogate form of memento mori ritual, which allowed tourists to reflect on their own mortality in ways denied them in a modern society that keeps death and dying out of sight or 'sequestered'.

There have been other attempts to conceptualise dark tourism as a motivated consumption grouping, but none has overcome the two problems just described: the doubt about its existence *sui generis*, given its subjects' refusal to recognise themselves as part of a 'dark' grouping focused on death; and the difficulty in associating the wide variety of behaviours deemed "dark" under any common, motivational banner. Indeed, some studies suggest that even a single form of dark tourism behaviour may be driven by many, different motives—a finding particularly observable in surveys of cemetery and churchyard visitors (e.g., see Raine 2013; Seaton 2014).

The other way of exploring dark tourism has been through supply rather than demand—a more popular option if volume of research is anything to go by. Dann (1998) provided an early typology of dark tourism supply, partly linked to motivation, as five main categories of site and activities: 'Perilous Places', 'Houses of Horror', 'Fields of Fatality', 'Tours of Torment', and 'Themed Thanatos'. These were each divided into captioned, sub-categories: 'Towns of Terror', 'Dungeons of Death', 'Heinous Hotels', and so on (Dann 1998). Stone (2006) added to the supply perspective with a typology conceptualised as a spectrum that had first been suggested as a qualitative measure of thanatouristic *motivation* (Seaton 1996). Stone recast the spectrum as a colour-coded inventory of dark tourism *sites*, varying from 'lightest' to 'darkest'. Like Dann's typology, the spectrum comprised a variety of named categories: 'dark fun factories', 'dark resting places', 'dark camps of genocide', and so forth (Stone 2006). Sharpley (2005) added to this by linking sites to different types of visitor.

Both consumer-led and supply-side approaches failed to bring the heterogeneous variety of different behaviours and sites under a plausible, common banner. They tended to swell the literature of dark tourism as an endless list of events and activities with little conceptual unity, except some association with death (Seaton and Lennon 2004: 74–78). Moreover, they all had different histories. Touring the scenes of historic disaster, for example, began with the re-discovery of Pompeii in the 1740s (see Jonathan Skinner's chapter in this volume); the fashion for travel to graveyards of literary celebrities somewhat later (Westover 2012); battlefield tours began in 1815 after Waterloo, fanned increasingly by British, imperial ideology (Seaton 1999); Jewish holocaust tourism began after World War II and has grown exponentially since (Young 1994; Winstone 2010); and body parts exhibitions by Gunter Von Hagen began in the 1990s.

Ironically, despite the differences between supply and demand as investigative categories in dark tourism, they have had one thing in common. This is the refusal by many people categorised within them to accept that they belong there. Just as many dark tourists at different sites deny that death is the main motivator for being there, so many of those involved in 'dark tourism' organisations deny that their work should be seen as 'dark'. Toni and Valma Holt, for instance, pioneers of the oldest established battlefield tourism company in the UK, dismiss the word 'dark' as a description of their conducted tours to the battlefields of two world wars, seeing them instead as pilgrimages of homage to the fallen (Seaton and Stone 2012).[2] The Director of the Association of Significant Cemeteries in Europe refuses to accept that cemetery management is a 'dark' enterprise when it includes initiatives to extend the role of cemeteries in the community as a resource that can be used, among other things, to educate children in history and environmental awareness (Seaton 2010: 86–90). In a recent study of tourism developments in Rwanda that included public exhibition of human remains and relics of the civil war, tourism planners strongly rejected descriptions of their work as 'dark, seeing it as about reconciliation, through bringing post-bellum, warring factions face-to-face with the human havoc both sides had created (Friedrich 2016). If, therefore, both suppliers and tourists appear to reject 'dark tourism' as a pejorative and unwelcome label wished on them by academics, how is a credible history of dark tourism possible?

Before attempting to answer this question, it is worth observing that the problem of research *subjects* resisting labels imposed on them as *objects* by external researchers is not new. It represents a longstanding, epistemological problem in the social sciences about the methods and validity of labelling in exploring human behaviour. Are people best understood 'scientifically' through the observations, concepts, and reports of 'informed' outsiders (the sociologist, the anthropologist, and other 'authorised' observers) or through their own, self-defining accounts? There are two ways in which this epistemological impasse might be overcome in dark tourism discourse.

One way of relieving tensions between the labellers and the labelled might be to abandon the term 'dark tourism' as a concept and re-name it in a way that would detoxify its transgressive associations, which is one reason why 'thanatourism' was preferred by some writers. However, the difficulty in agreeing an acceptable way of thinking about what has been known as 'dark tourism' may be more than a matter of naming. The problem may lie in flaws of definition that have not been recognised and require examination.

The original definition of thanatourism/dark tourism was, as noted earlier, tourism, motivated by the desire for actual or symbolic encounters with death (Seaton 1996). This formulation is debatable on two counts. The first is the one that has already been aired—that death is rarely acknowledged as a primary motivation by tourists (Biran and Hyde 2013: 192). Secondly, and more fundamentally, dark tourism is not, and never can be, an encounter with 'actual' death for anything but the few who happen to be physically present when another dies. Even that contact lasts only until the removal and disposal of a body that imparts little information about itself, except for certain physiological indicators of absence of life. Death is unknown and permanently unknowable as no one returns to report back on the experience. Dark tourism encounters are, in reality, not encounters with death but *remembrance* of the death and the dead, induced by *symbolic representations*. This may seem like a pedantic distinction, but it has radical implications for dark tourism study and analysis. Once remembrance of the dead rather than death itself is the focus of investigation, a number of issues and questions, overlooked or impossible to ask under previous definitions, become evident.

First is the fact that exhibited remembrance of death is a *semiotic* construction—ordered and controlled not by the dead, but by the living. In private life, these semiotic dimensions are obvious. When an individual dies, family and friends make the funerary arrangements, which include deciding the means of disposal of the body (burial, cremation, etc.), the cultural aesthetics of the ceremony (religious, etc.), and forms of commemoration (obituary notices in a paper, a gravestone, memorial tablet, etc.). The development of material forms to expedite these choices may be described in abstract terms as the *engineering* and *orchestration* of remembrance, where engineering is the choice of form and medium (headstone, memorial tablet, epitaph, etc.), and orchestration is their content, layout, and style (gravestone design, memorial speech, mausoleum features, etc.). It is these commemorative forms that become central to much dark tourism.

The effects of engineered remembrance are time bound. Tributes paid to the dead at funerals and memorial services may be forgotten. Obituaries may be thrown away and unread after a few weeks. Gravestones may be neglected and grow over, the messages on them may fade or wear away. In the heavily urbanised areas of some countries, graves may be leased only for a period before being dug up and re-let. But some people are not so quickly consigned to oblivion. Their remembrance may be engineered and orchestrated with greater resources on a larger, more durable scale in time and place than that of many others. This can be seen in public memorials. The modern state is one of the most important institutional agents of engineered remembrance, particularly in memorials to political and cultural significant others and, especially, to soldiers who have fallen in different wars. In Britain, cemeteries and museums dedicated to the memory of soldiers of the different services of two world wars have been comprehensively inventoried and promoted by governments (Jones 2007; Kavanagh 1994; Saunders 1996).

All of this is to draw attention to the question of *human agency* in decisions about material forms and themes of memorials and remembrance which later become an object of the tourist gaze. Remembrance depends less on the living features of the dead, and more on third parties with the will and resources to commemorate them. The will to do so may not be just a function of what they achieved in life, but the manner of their death. This is made clear by distinguishing between death as *mortality* and death as *fatality*. *Mortality* is death from natural causes, a fate that awaits the majority, while *fatality* is death under extraordinary, often unexpected and violent conditions, affecting a much smaller number of people. Fatality is almost always more newsworthy, and remembrance of it is engineered and orchestrated more durably and widely (in the media, history books, on monuments, etc.), particularly if multiple deaths are involved. Fatality is also more striking to dark tourists than mortality, unless the deceased is some kind of celebrity. In cemeteries from Brookwood in England to Cuba's national cemetery in Havana, visitors pass by the remembrances of the mortality of thousands of private individuals, but stop to look at public memorials to air crash victims, firemen killed fighting famous fires, and soldiers killed in wars abroad and revolutionary struggles at home.

The reconfiguration of dark tourism as encounters with the remembrance of death, rather than death itself, can now be more formally stated:

> Dark tourism/thanatourism comprises encounters through travel with the engineered and orchestrated remembrance of mortality and fatality.

Engineered and orchestrated remembrance—*hereafter abbreviated as EOR*—is thus the true object of the tourist gaze. The definition works for *all* dark tourism's encounters, from trivial ones like eating in a *Dracula* restaurant or riding a ghost train, which are primed by tourists' semi-playful remembrance of death in gothic horror narratives, to visiting a national military shrine. Dark tourism is thus a site of *tryadic exchange* which brings together: the represented dead, whether victims of mortality or fatality; the engineers and orchestrators of representations about them; and visitors encountering both as the-represented-dead. Once this *transactional perspective* is made the unit of analysis in dark tourism, it makes possible historical study of individual dark tourism events that allows for recognition of their functional origins and the dynamics of their effects. In so doing, it sheds light on a number of issues not obvious in less precise definitions.

EOR as Interdiscourse

EOR of private individuals is, as we have seen, typically small-scale commemoration of a loved one at a single site—a gravestone or a memorial tablet—intended for a limited audience in time and space. The most influential forms of EOR are much more than this. They are *interdiscursive and intertextual*, which means that they occur not just as commemorative displays and memorials in one place. They appear across many multimedia and multi-institutional narratives and representations. Remembrance of J.F. Kennedy, the American President assassinated in 1963, has been engineered and orchestrated at many sites (Arlington Cemetery, the book depository in Dallas from which he was shot, his presidential library, etc.), and in prolific media and textual forms (film, TV, radio, published biographies, etc.). Similarly, the memory of Elvis Presley is not just commemorated for visitors to Graceland by the house itself; it exists from years of multimedia knowledge of his life and death through records, films, TV, and not least through the international ubiquity of Elvis impersonators. The reach and potency of EOR commemoration may thus be created and reinforced through time discursively and textually, off-site but on-message, in many different ways.

EOR as Text and Practice

Nor is EOR just exposure to—and encounters with—displayed signs and physical sites. It may also be taking part in commemorative *practices* near them or elsewhere. These may be large, officially engineered gatherings, such as ceremonies of remembrance at national memorials and periods of silence for the war dead. It may also be smaller, unofficial rituals like laying roadside memorials to friends killed in road accidents at the spot where they took place; or joining in the pub singalongs that take place annually in Henley-on-Thames, Oxford, as fans of the 1960s singer, Dusty Springfield, gather opposite the church in which she is buried, to celebrate her birthday. These travel encounters that are wholly motivated by a premeditated desire to visit sites of remembrance of the dead may be seen as the 'purest' examples of dark tourism rituals.

Do Dark Tourists Exist?

Perhaps, the most important effect of the EOR model of dark tourism is to scale down the need to identify motivated, dark tourists as a group *sui generis*. The relevant question may be less about who dark tourists are and why they seek dark encounters, than how they can avoid having them. Engineered remembrance is a ubiquitous part of the everyday, semiotic environment, and encounters with it are an almost unavoidable part of modern life at home or away. Remembrance is on public display in monuments, national memorials, churches, cathedrals, cemeteries, museums, and buildings with Blue Plaque signage. Many of these have been located in public spaces that are difficult to avoid—along main thoroughfares, in squares, in parks, on high ground. Dark tourism may be accidental encounters with remembrance, induced by the 'stopping power' of the engineering and orchestration that have gone into making them likely to happen. Thus, dark tourism behaviour may not be best understood by trying to distinguish between those who engage in it as a premeditated, motivated choice, and those who do not. Dark tourism encounters may be ones that *everybody* has *accidentally* or *incidentally*. They may even happen while people are engaging in a quite different activity. The most useful variables in exploring these possibilities may be differences between *premeditated voluntary, involuntary, accidental,* and *incidental* encounters. McKercher's (2002, 2003) work on different kinds of heritage tourists offers a suggestive start point for doing so. His five-point typology could be explored, in conjunction with a typology of what, in the absence of a better term we might call, the differential 'the stopping power' of the encountered memorial sites and activities. The aim would be to reveal the interactive effects between the nature of the encounter (Premeditated? Accidental?) and the scale and character of engineered and orchestrated remembrance that produced it (Interdiscursive publicity? On site promotion? Monumental size? etc.). The net result of the EOR model is thus to put greater emphasis on the ways in which remembrance is engineered and orchestrated to gain attention, and the different kinds of attention they achieve among the travelling population, rather than supposing some people engage in dark tourism and some people do not.

The previous argument does not, of course, mean ceasing to explore tourist motivation, but it may mean giving up on the expectation of finding common motivations applicable to all forms of dark tourism. Dark motivation may work at varying levels of intensity and awareness in different encounters. It may not exist before, but emerge *during* the encounter, or even in retrospective reflection after it has finished. Lennon and Foley may be right in suggesting that visiting atrocity sites is a uniquely different kind of tourism from anything that preceded it. Stone may be right to observe that body parts exhibitions may elicit thanatoptic reflections on one's own death (Stone 2011, 2012), but other kinds of dark tourism encounters never would. At Holocaust sites where mass victims of genocide are remembered, it is debatable whether thanatoptic reflections on one's mortality, rather than horror on behalf of others, is a prime visitor effect, except for Jewish contemporaries of the dead who may feel, like the novelist Primo Levi, guilt and anguish at being a concentration camp survivor when so many others were not.

The Dynamics of Remembrance: Beginnings and Origins

Half-hidden in the EOR model is a temporal dimension to dark tourism behaviour absent from earlier formulations. The implicit assumption has been that dark tourism was a straightforward supply and demand transaction involving *two parties*, a consumer and a supplier, both of whom could be identified and discussed unproblematically. The commodity linking them was death—a static and stable entity that could be brokered between consumer and supplier in the knowledge that it had an agreed value that remained identical and constant for both parties. Death wasn't going anywhere. It happened for keeps and stayed put.

The EOR model casts doubt on the stability of all of these assumptions. Once represented remembrance of the dead, rather than death, is recognised as the commodity on offer, it becomes clear that, unlike all physical products and most tourism ones, it may *change* in symbolic value for both its producers and consumers. Unexpected events or new information about the dead may change the nature of remembrance. Social and intellectual virtues they were once seen to represent may become devalued, pernicious, or unfashionable. Once this possibility is accepted, then conceptualising dark tourism as a supply and demand relationship involving two participants and a static commodity needs to be revised. In the EOR model, it emerges as a *site of exchange* which involves *three,* rather than two, protagonists: the engineers and orchestrators of remembrance; the people who encounter the representations they produce; and the *represented dead* who, unlike the actual dead, have a shifting afterlife they have no control over, but which has a potent influence on the living.

Two high-profile British case histories in the *dynamics* of engineered and orchestrated remembrance and the triadic relations involved illuminate these theoretical propositions. The first is the funeral and memorials for Jimmy Savile who died in 2015 after an astonishingly successful career as a disc jockey, charity worker, and fund raiser—and a favourite of Margaret Thatcher, a British Prime Minister, whose government recommended him to the Queen for knighthood. He was given a grand funeral in his native Yorkshire and an impressive, graveside memorial was erected, as well as lesser ones elsewhere. Within a few months, it became known that he had been a serial paedophile for more than 40 years. Almost overnight, remembrance of Savile changed from that of an altruistic member of the 'great and good' to vilification as a public enemy whose grave was targeted for vandalising by vengeful vigilantes. In response, his family removed the gravestone, and other memorial tablets at sites where he had worked were taken down. The second case is that of a statue of the imperial entrepreneur, Cecil Rhodes, at Oriel College, Oxford, which had been in place for over a century. In 2015, students called for its removal because of Rhodes's brutal exploitation of black populations in his mercenary, colonial ventures. After consultation with various groups including other students, past and present, the college decided to keep the statue but remove the memorial tablet (Guardian 2012). The two cases demonstrate that remembrance, like history which provides its materials, is never closed or completed.

A useful analytical distinction in exploring movements in functional remembrance over time is that between 'beginnings' and 'origins', deployed by Edward Said following Michel Foucault, to describe institutional change. 'Beginnings' they used to designate the start of formations deliberately brought into being with an internally, defined function and client base, both of which are maintained through time. In contrast, 'Origins' described formations that come into being from *external* influences rather than internal agendas, involving one kind of clientele, but which later change in their character and clients (Bilgrami 2005). The distinction was adapted in tourism discourse to explore how sites and localities, once serving a primary *original* function (e.g., as military bases, workhouses, or slave markets), might later metamorphose into tourism sites involving changes in infrastructure, staff, and clients (Seaton 2009b: 89–90). The case studies that follow include discussion of engineered remembrance that invites reflections on beginnings and origins.

The Commodification of Death?

Another issue the EOR perspective speaks to is the common criticism of dark tourism as the commodification of death as exploitation for financial gain. The EOR model suggests two qualifications to this view. One comes from recognition that, since death is not the true object of dark tourism but rather represented remembrance of the dead, it is representations that are traded, not death itself (e.g., in selling mementoes of dead celebrities at locations associated with their death; promoting tours and T-shirts at national disaster sites). But these forms of commercial remembrance are few, compared to the volume of other kinds of engineered remembrance comprised by multitudes of small, but costly, memorials in cemeteries, burial grounds, and churchyards to dead family members and friends, intended for a limited audience who pay no entry fees. Costs rather than profits are even greater for more ambitious and public kinds of remembrance, targeted at large domestic and international audiences. Public monuments, gardens of remembrance, memorial libraries, museums, and similar large-scale ventures demand special resources and heavy investments that are often intended to achieve political or cultural payoffs, rather than commercial ones. Once built, they involve continuing maintenance costs that do not come cheap (e.g., the upkeep of war graves, the renovation of monuments, and the restoration of old buildings). Commodification, therefore, accounts for a relatively small volume of engineered remembrance and, where it exists, is often focused on dead celebrity figures whose careers were extensively commodified while they lived.

EOR and Thanatology

In addition to its utility in tourism analysis, the EOR model allows dark tourism/thanatourism to be integrated into thanatology—a bigger discursive domain to which it inherently belongs as a subset, and which may itself be considered as a subset of even bigger ones, sociology and anthropology. A thanatological perspective informed early statements about dark tourism and the notion that it evolved from a nexus of historical practices, including thanatopsis and pilgrimage, by which Christian societies had confronted death since the Middle Ages, and which were later transformed into more secular forms (see Seaton 1996, passim, and 2009b: 534–535; also Stone and Sharpley 2008; Stone 2012). But there has been little discussion since of how dark tourism might be more conceptually integrated into thanatology and anthropology.

The EOR approach enables it to be specified in broad terms. The argument is as follows. All known societies have engineered remembrance of mortality and fatality in narratives that perpetuate the memory of significant figures in their culture. Some societies focus less on remembrance of individuals than collectivities—tribes, races, religious communities, or even smaller, more specific groups, such as the one on a memorial in Newfoundland commemorating those who died on the *Titanic*. Remembrance may be told in written, printed, or oral texts, but also through social networks. European cultures have typically used a combination of literary, monumental, and social methods to perpetuate the name of their significant others, often focused on particular places and sites. The Greeks and Romans produced epic poetry which featured 'praise' lists of heroes in remembrance of illustrious ancestors and their mythic dead. Christianity commemorated Christ, the prophets, and the saints in the Bible through a vast literature of amplification and commentary, produced by its different denominations. Both classical cultures and Christianity left memorials and inscriptions to the named dead. Christianity, Judaism, and Islam also paid great attention to the *social production* of remembrance by organising their members into churches which could be anything from lavishly appointed cathedrals, synagogues, and mosques, to small meeting houses where, as Christ said, it was only necessary to have 'two or three… gathered together'. Not all societies engineer remembrance geographically with named commemoration at specific locations. Muslims do not have elaborate epitaphs at gravesides. Nor in secular Europe today are named memorials always attached to specific internment locations. Something like 70 per cent of people, for example, in Britain are cremated, many of whose ashes are scattered, like those of David Bowie, anonymously in places distant from where they lived or died. In traditional cultures, oral history may be the main method of engineering remembrance, less for individuals, than for sanctifying ancestral grounds held sacred to a whole tribe or ethnic grouping, making them vulnerable to vandalism by imperial developers through ignorance or disregard. The highest form of commemoration may, paradoxically, be the rhetorical trope that none is necessary since the work the deceased did in life will survive as memorial. In his tribute to Shakespeare, John Milton (1608–1674) wrote:

> WHAT needs my Shakespeare for his honoured bones,
> The labour of an age of pilèd stones?
> Or that his hallowed relics should be hid
> Under a stary-pointing pyramid?

Answering his own question, Milton declared that Shakespeare's poetry would be his 'live-long monument', and its effect would be to make us, the reader, 'marble' with awe at his astonishing output. An even more famous instance of this elegiac trope is the memorial to Christopher Wren's in St Paul's Cathedral, the cathedral which he built. It reads, *Si monumentum requiris circumspice*—'If you want a memorial look around.' This suggests that public monuments are, perhaps, most necessary for those who have achieved fame or, more likely, fortune in their time, but leave little that is tangible to show for it. In the major cemeteries of the world from Woodlawn in New York to Melbourne in Australia, many obscure industrialists, politicians, military figures, and other successful careerists, lie under declamatory memorials designed to rescue them from anonymity for the brief moment a visitor stops by to wonder whose family could afford such a send-off.

All of this is to underline that the history of engineered and orchestrated remembrance is as long as the history of the world, but not all of it has been *place specific*—the necessary but not sufficient, condition for dark tourism encounters. Where commemoration has been engineered at a precise geographical location, some visitors have probably always had encounters with it. Some readers, for example, of the sepulchral epigrams that form part of 'The Greek Anthology' (Leslie 1929: 109–152)—a celebrated collection of epigraphs that circulated about famous Greeks (Plato, Homer, Democritus, Euripides, etc.)—may have been moved to find out where they were buried or commemorated. Similarly, the Romans made much of memorial inscriptions on tombs (see, e.g., Diehl 1912; Erasmo 2008). But there is little evidence to suggest that encounters with engineered remembrance in either society became a significant goal of travel for any but a small minority. Dark tourism/thanatourism involving a significant number of collective, travel encounters with engineered remembrance was a late development that evolved over several centuries, mainly in Western Europe. Three main periods have been identified as 'developmental' ones in Britain (see, Seaton 1996 passim, and 2009b: 526–534). They are sketched very briefly, as a contextual background to the historical case studies that follow.

The first identifiable phase of dark tourism in numbers was Christian Pilgrimage, which flourished between c. 500 AD and the mid-sixteenth century. This was focused predominantly on journeys to make contact with the engineered remembrance of Christ's death and the martyrdom of his disciples and saints. It was encouraged as an activity by the Catholic Church, which supplied pilgrims with relics of orchestrated remembrance that included body parts of saints and holy figures and artefacts associated with them. It also encouraged *ex voto* donations[3] and, on occasion, engineered 'miracles' (e.g., effigies or pictures of Madonnas that wept or martyrs who bled) that were put on display in cathedrals, churches, and monastic foundations along the routes to shrines at Canterbury, Rome, and other sacred sites. The second phase was from c. 1550 to the mid-eighteenth century when antiquarianism became a passion among an increasing number of educated males. This was a British quest—following precedents in Italy, France, and Germany[4]—for ancestral roots, by travelling to find records of the past at home and abroad. It provoked an intensive interest in exposure to, or the acquisition of, old manuscripts, early printed books, as well as a lot of transcribing of messages on tombs, memorials, and walls. It also stimulated the collecting of archaeological exhibits and relics—initially as historical evidence of the national past, but later as curiosities for their own sake. The third phase was the impact of Romanticism, a complex and hugely influential cultural movement that introduced key notions of the Picturesque, the Sublime, the Gothic, and 'Beautiful Death', all of which fed into dark tourism. It began in the mid-eighteenth century, raged through the nineteenth, and still structures a considerable amount of dark tourism as well as cultural and literary tourism.

Discussion

The EOR model elaborated in this chapter is an attempt to relocate the focus of dark tourism analysis from contact with death to *remembrance* of mortality and fatality, engineered and orchestrated through representations of the dead, by the living, for audiences in the present and future. Under this revised definition, the history of dark tourism is the longitudinal study of encounters at remembrance sites, including disturbances and changes over time in the triadic relations underlying them. The main ones are likely to be those caused by decline or improvement in the societal and social valuation of the represented dead; changes in the composition of the audiences encountering their remembrance; and changes in the composition and perspectives of those who have engineered and orchestrated the encounters.

This repositioning offers a more *theoretical* and *situational* account of what actually happens in thanatourism/dark tourism than earlier ones, which assumed that it was about unproblematic contact by the living with the dead. It thus addresses a common criticism of dark tourism discourse made in the past in the mantra that it has been 'theoretically fragile'. One can agree with that comment but wonder, 'Why the big surprise? What else would one expect at the birth pangs of a new domain of inquiry—in this case, tracing the unlikely connection between tourism and death? Few natural scientists would venture to theorise an unfamiliar domain before attaining the safe ground of at least some preliminary observations and, in many cases, only after several years of making them. It is only in certain kinds of prescriptive, social scientific thought that theory is expected to *precede* observation. Moreover, dark tourism may have been hard to theorise because the wrong object of study—death, rather than remembrance of fatality and mortality—was made its main focus.

One of the indications of theoretical advance in a study area is the new avenues of inquiry it calls forth that have been disregarded or less visible before. Conceptualising dark tourism as travel encounters with remembrance, rather than death, provokes many new questions which may be explored from three different directions, all designed to illuminate the nature of remembrance, the forms it may take, and the effects it may produce. These directions concern the politics, aetiology, and phenomenology of remembrance.

The Politics of Commemoration and Engineered Remembrance

The EOR model is a *sociological* one that makes issues of *power* and *representation* central to dark tourism. Engineered and orchestrated remembrance and the commemorative forms they take may look like the immemorial furniture of place and everyday life, but they are always the willed and developed outcomes of specific agents or agencies who have had their own reasons for establishing them. In both their genesis and effects, they reflect the interests of the living, as much as—maybe even, *more than*—the characteristics of the *dead*. These interests may, or may not, be apparent to visitors. The analysis of dark tourism encounters thus starts with assessing the shaping power(s) behind specific sites of remembrance, knowing how they were established, and with what intentions and effects. These issues may be explored through a number of questions. Who is being commemorated? Who has decided that they should be? Why did they choose to do so? Who engineers the setting up of the site as sponsor and financial backer? Why are specific locations chosen as memorial sites? Who decides on the timing, particularly the length of the gap between the death of the nominated person or event, and the inauguration of commemoration? What determines the number of memorial forms called into being for people and events receiving more than one form of commemoration? What should determine the distribution of engineered remembrance among majority and minority populations in multicultural societies? How many memorials are sufficient?—a question in the case of Holocaust memorials which, after roadside memorials to accident victims, constitute the most numerous and expanding categories of modern memorials in Europe? Less obviously, but crucially, when is the *absence* or *suppression* of commemoration a 'significant silence' worthy of discussion, a phenomenon found after military or ideological conflict, when the victor may deny the vanquished commemoration. At Waterloo, it took nearly two centuries before the French were able to commemorate their dead; at Isandwana in South Africa, it was over a century before Zulu memorials were allowed by the British. More recently, the efforts of the Taliban and Islamic State to destroy memorials of ancient religions represents an attempt to root out remembrance of other religions.

Questions about the politics of remembrance and dark tourism are similar to those raised in debates about heritage tourism, and the usage of the past by people in the present. All heritages comprise significant elements of engineered and orchestrated remembrance of mortality and fatality, but unlike thanatourism, it is not confined to those elements, as it includes other tangible and intangible components which are not specific to a specific location (e.g., cultural performances and traditional customs). David Lowenthal's work (1985, 1996) suggests the common problematics of dark tourism and heritage by tracing the many ways in which 'things past' can never be fully reclaimed, even when attempted by dedicated historians, French novelists, and ambitious heritage developers. Yet, however partially the past may be known, it provides the material for engineering and orchestration that may pass for potent truth, affecting the cultural identity and perspectives of those exposed to it (see particularly Lowenthal's account of knowing and changing the past 1985: 185–262; and his critique of heritage, 1996: 88–173).

In provoking discussion about power and commemoration, the EOR model introduces a critical edge into conceptual thinking about thanatourism/dark tourism that has existed for years in heritage discourse, not just in Lowenthal's work, but in that of others, including Ashworth and Tunbridge's (2005) concept of 'contested' heritage, and in Walton's edited collection of case studies in tourism history, exemplifying the relations between power and historical representation (Walton 2005). The EOR model is not, however, only a tool for critical analysis. In offering a clearer understanding of what thanatourism is about, it may be utilised by tourism practitioners in positioning their products. It may be particularly relevant for destination agencies seeking narratives through which to promote their regions. Identifying thanatourism opportunities in a place depends upon systematically inventorying historical resources that may lend themselves to engineering and orchestration as dark tourism narratives. A seven-point procedure for doing so has been reported in an illustrative study comparing the thanatouristic resources of Sicily and Ireland (Seaton 2017).

Aetiology: How Engineered and Orchestrated Remembrance Run Their Courses

Aetiology, in medical parlance, is the study of the causes and progress of disease. In the EOR model, it refers to the progressive orchestration of remembrance as physical representations (memorials, gravestones, commemorative artefacts), and the perceptual effects produced on those encountering them. Physical representation comprises *material* and *semiotic* choices which are commonly delegated to specialists (artists, sculptors, stone masons, architects, etc.), and constitute a field that has not often been taken into account in dark tourism analysis, though one that has been explored extensively in art history, architectural history, and literary history of funerary cultures. Material choices in commemoration may comprise the kinds of metals, wood, or gems used in memorial displays, calibrated according to the wealth and distinction of the deceased. National and regional factors may affect these choices including the supply of some memorial materials and the cost of importing others. Gravestone memorials in Cornwall and Wales have survived long and legibly because they were made from durable, local slate, whereas sandstone monuments and headstones in other counties have degraded.

Semiotic choices in the orchestration of remembrance are the symbolic choices made in design and imagery of commemorative forms and memorials. What factors account for their wide variations regionally and internationally? They are typically influenced by religious and cultural factors and stylistic fashions. Both the Escurial and the Taj Mahal are celebrated memorials to elite figures—one a Spanish monarch and the other an Indian princess—but they are very different architecturally and produce different kinds of encounter. Another area of symbolic difference may be in the semiotics of institutional memorials erected to elite, public figures, and those installed for private individuals. Orchestration also includes how the dead are addressed and remembered in the rubric of epitaphs, which often reflect contemporary, elegiac conventions in prose and poetry that may be part of their encountered meaning, but one which may change over time. Semiotic conventions that were understood in their day by contemporary audiences may lose their original effect, as is the case with the Latin texts attached to elite tombs before the eighteenth century, and also to funerary symbols such as the pineapple, the hourglass, and the death's head in old graveyards and cemeteries.

A critical variable in the aetiology of remembrance is the fluctuating status of the commemorated dead which may rise or fall, and with it their response from visitors. This may reflect the declining reputation of the individual (as in the Savile case), or the waning public importance of the occupational or professional category by which the dead were once remembered. High-ranking military personnel and church leaders are now less likely to have prominent memorials in Western Europe than they had in the past, while sports figures, TV stars, pop singers, and other cultural performers have risen in the hierarchies of engineered remembrance—a trend that is also inscribed in the changing composition of those commemorated in Madame Tussauds over the past century (Pilbeam 2003: 193–219).

Phenomenology of the Encounter

The phenomenology of dark tourism encounters has, in the past, been seen as a matter of understanding the visitor and the visitor experience, the underlying premise being that the dark tourist was a pre-motivated individual going to a precisely targeted, death site. The EOR model is a more situational orientation to encounters, conceptualising them as sites of exchanges between person and sites of remembrance, which may be affected by a varying combination of interacting factors before, during, and after the encounters take place. Politics and aetiology may play their part. This was the case with the launch of a political theme park outside Vilnius in 2008, made up of statues of former 'Iron Curtain' bigwigs, collected from all over Lithuania and elsewhere after the fall of the Berlin wall. It reconfigured their original political significance in ways that affected visitors differently. One kind of visitor saw the collective assembly as parodic entertainment depicting the officials as impotent shadows of their former selves. For older Lithuanians, the exhibition was a blasphemy in perpetuating the memory of those they remembered as icons of oppression and evil.

The situational orientation of the EOR model, which places less emphasis on prior motivation and more on the immediate circumstances of encounters with remembrance, means framing questions that allow the circumstances to be specified. A start will be determining the encounters that were *premeditated* since these constitute, as suggested earlier, the 'purest' form of dark tourism. Once they have been determined, the focus should move to visitors for whom the encounters were accidental. Further situational issues might then be explored by questions about the part the dark tourism encounter plays in overall trip patterning. Is it a discrete travel choice, or one taken as part of a longer trip pattern (e.g., an Auschwitz visit as part of a Polish package tour). To what extent is a trip affected by interdiscursive influences, derived from factual or fictional representations, near or away from the site, which may have prepared, shaped, and influenced the visitor's choice and response to the encounter? How does the relationship of the visitor to the represented dead, and the engineers of their remembrance, affect the choice and experience of the encounter? What variations in motive are discernible between visitors at remembrance sites? The extent to which the situational circumstances of thanatourism encounters can be reconstructed depends upon the insight and ingenuity of the investigator in framing questions that go beyond the typical multiple choice inventories commonly used in motivational studies.

The distinction between *fatality* and *mortality* is one that has not been systematically examined in dark tourism analysis. They have tacitly been treated as if they are interchangeable. Separating and distinguishing between them theoretically opens up to analysis the way in which their differences and similarities may, or may not, affect the engineering and orchestration of remembrance, and their impacts upon those who encounter them. A helpful way of thinking *into* their connotations is by reflection on the binary contrasts of their occurrence in everyday life. We all leave *mortal remains*, but not *fatal* ones. We have *fatal* accidents, but not *mortal* ones. We are more likely to die of a *fatal* illness rather than a *mortal* one. In sexual relationships, we are *fatally*, but not *mortally*, attracted to ill-judged partners. We make *fatal* mistakes, but not *mortal* ones. We are in *mortal* danger, but it is not *fatal*. What are the discriminations that are at work in these paired terms, and what nuances of denotation and connotation emerge in reflecting on their resonance in relation to commemoration? Fatality may perhaps be hypothesised, more sudden, more dramatic, more dynamic, more noteworthy, more public, more modern, more epic, and more singular; mortality, on the other hand, may be more prosaic, more passive, more old-fashioned, more stoic, more predictable, duller, and less remarkable. Whatever the contrasts between the two, the next step might be inspection of different commemorative sites of mortality and fatality to determine whether they are engineered and orchestrated differently in visual symbolism, scale, appearance, design, and so on. The third stage of investigation would then be to explore the differences, if any, in the way people encounter the two kinds of remembrance.

The most important phenomenological effect of the EOR model may be that it rescues thanatourists/dark tourists from allegations of transgressive indulgence in death, by re-focusing their encounters as ones with remembrance of the dead—activities that most humans engage in at some times during their lives. Remembrance takes many different forms and affects people differently at different times and in different contexts. It may evoke deeply private feelings, involving love for departed friends and relatives, or it may stimulate a more ritualised, public display of patriotism and national pride. Engineered remembrance may call forth emotions of nostalgia, remorse, pity, revenge, or desire for reconciliation (a growing impetus at international military memorials in Europe). Its uses may be to educate, to induce conformity, to instruct, to politicise, or to entertain. It is this recognition—that remembrance, rather than death, is the actual focus of dark tourism, and that it serves many legitimate purposes and public interests—that separates dark tourists from arms dealers, serial killers, and necrophiliacs whose relationship to death is incontrovertibly, more hands-on.

Conclusion

History plays a greater part in the practice and study of thanatourism than in any other kind of tourism except heritage, because remembrance always looks back to the past. EOR is a model that attempts to shift its focus from contact with death to encounters with remembrance. It proposes that these should be explored situationally, taking account of a number of variables that may interact in different dark tourism encounters. It directs attention to a number of conceptual separations, intended to facilitate exploration of the variables and their impact on thanatouristic encounters—that is, those between *engineering* and *orchestration* of remembrance; between remembrance of *fatality* and *mortality*; and between *politics, aetiology,* and *phenomenology* as dimensions of inquiry into encounters with remembrance.

In conclusion, the EOR model attempts to address some difficulties in approaching dark tourism and its history, in a way that allows issues relating to remembrance—the power to commemorate, the material and symbolic forms of commemoration, the changing valuation of the commemorated dead, and so on—to emerge as the prime objects of situationally based inquiry that has previously been focused on contact with death.

Notes

1. 'Thanatourism' was an alternative term coined at the same time as 'dark tourism'. Their referents are identical, but the connotations of the two terms are different and are briefly discussed later in this chapter.
2. They did so in conversations with the author and Dr Philip Stone at the launch of the Institute for Dark Tourism Research (iDTR) at the University of Central Lancashire, UK, in 2013.
3. *Ex votos* were offerings, left at shrines to saints and other divine figure in fulfilment of vows, or as reflections of homage and gratitude to them. Relics were objects associated with holy figures and events including body parts (bones, strands of

hair, etc.); pieces of clothing; fragments of the 'true cross' on which Christ was said to have died. Relics survive in modern museology as sacralised exhibits supporting biographical remembrance (e.g., the desks at which writers wrote, the first guitar rock artists owned). They may even be the basis for whole exhibitions (e.g., displays of Lady Diana's clothes, or the manuscripts of famous authors).
4. The most explicit articulation of antiquarianism as the pursuit of 'inheritance' (today's 'heritage') comes from John Weever's, never-completed, epic attempt to survey all the extant, ancient funeral monuments in Britain and Ireland, the aim of which was 'to continue the remembrance of the defunct to posteritie (1631)'. It describes how, 'with painfulle expences' he 'travailled over the most parts of England, and some part of Scotland' to 'collect such memorials of the deceased, as were remaining yet undefaced'. It began with a 'Discourse of Funerall Monuments' and was followed by a survey of Canterbury, London, and Norwich (Weever 1631, 'Author to reader' no page reference). Only the first volume was published.

References

Ashworth Tunbridge, J., & Ashworth, G. (2005). *Dissonant heritage: Managing the past as a resource in conflict*. Chichester: Wiley.

Bilgrami, A. (2005). Interpreting a distinction. In H. Baba & W. Mitchell (Eds.), *Edward Said: Continuing the conversation* (pp. 26–35). Chicago: University of Chicago Press.

Biran, A., & Hyde, K. F. (2013). New perspectives on dark tourism. *International Journal of Culture, Tourism and Hospitality Research, 7*, 191–198.

Cheal, F., & Griffin, T. (2013). Pilgrims and patriots: Australian tourist experiences at Gallipoli. *International Journal of Culture, Tourism and Hospitality Research, 7*, 227–241.

Dann, G. M. S. (1998). *The dark side of tourism, Studies and reports, Serie L. Sociologie/psychologies/philosophie/anthropology* (Vol. 14). Aix-en-Provence: Centre International de Recherches et d'Etudes Touristiques.

Diehl, E. (1912). *Inscriptiones Latinae*. Bonnae: A. Marcus et E. Weber.

Erasmo, M. (2008). *Reading death in ancient Rome*. Columbus: Ohio State University Press.

Friedrich, M. (2016). *Heritage interpretation of the dead as a tool for peace and reconciliation: The case of visitor development at Rwanda's post conflict memorialscape*. Unpublished PhD thesis, University of Central Lancashire, Preston, England.

Guardian. (2012). *Jimmy Saville's £4000 headstone removed to be used as landfill*. https://www.theguardian.com/media/2012/oct/10/jimmy-savile-headstone-removed. Accessed 14 Sept 2016.

Jones, T. (2007). *On Fames's eternal camping ground. A study of First World War epitaphs in British cemeteries of the Western Front*. Pinner: T.G. Jones.

Kavanagh, M. (1994). *Museums and the First World War. A social history*. Leicester: Leicester University Press.

Lennon, J. J., & Foley, M. (1996). Editorial: Heart of darkness. *International Journal of Heritage Studies, 2*(4), 195–197.

Lennon, J. J., & Foley, M. (2000). *Dark tourism. The attraction of death and disaster*. London/New York: Continuum.

Leslie, S. (1929). *The Greek anthology*. London: Ernest Benn.

Lowenthal, D. (1985). *The past is another country*. Cambridge: Cambridge University Press.

Lowenthal, D. (1996). *The heritage crusade and the spoils of history*. London: Viking.

McKercher, B. (2002). Towards a classification of cultural tourists. *International Journal of Tourism Research, 5*(1), 29–38.

McKercher, B. (2003). Testing a cultural tourism typology. *International Journal of Tourism Research, 5*(1), 45–58.

Pilbeam, P. M. (2003). *Madame Tussaud and the history of waxworks*. London: Hambledon, Continuum.

Raine, R. (2013). A dark tourism spectrum. *International Journal of Culture, Tourism and Hospitality Research, 7*(3), 242–225.

Saunders, D. (1996). *Britain's maritime memorials and mementoes*. Yeovil: Patrick Stephens.

Seaton, A. V. (1996). Guided by the dark: From thanatopsis to thanatourism. *International Journal of Heritage Studies, 2*(4), 234–244.

Seaton, A. V. (1999). War and thanatourism: Waterloo 1815–1914. *Annals of Tourism, 26*(1), 130–158. *Research*.

Seaton, A. V. (2009a). Beckford and the tourists: Gothic performances at Lansdown Tower, Bath. *The Beckford Journal, 15*, 61–82. The Beckford Society, Spring.

Seaton, A. V. (2009b). Thanatourism and its discontents: An appraisal of a decade's work with some future directions. In T. Jamal & M. Robinson (Eds.), *The Sage handbook of tourism studies* (pp. 521–542). London: Sage.

Seaton, A. V. (2010). Purposeful otherness: Approaches to the management of thanatourism. In R. Sharpley & P. R. Stone (Eds.), *The darker side of travel. The theory and practice of dark tourism* (pp. 75–108). Bristol: Channel View Publications.

Seaton, A. V. (2017). Patrimony, engineered remembrance and ancestral vampires: Appraising thanatouristic resources in Ireland and Italy. In G. Hooper & J. J. Lennon (Eds.), *Dark tourism practice and interpretation* (pp. 55–68). Abingdon: Routledge.

Seaton, A. V., & Lennon, J. J. (2004). Moral panics, ulterior motives and alterior desires: thanatourism in the early 21st century. In T. V. Singh (Ed.), *New horizons in tourism: Strange experiences and stranger practices* (pp. 63–83). Wallingford: CAB International.

Seaton, A. V., & Stone, P. R. (2012). *In conversation with the Holts at the launch of the Institute for Dark Tourism Research (iDTR)*. Preston: University of Central Lancashire.

Sharpley, R. (2005). Travels to the edge of darkness. Towards a typology of dark tourism. In C. Ryan, S. Page, & M. Aicken (Eds.), *Taking tourism to the limit: Issues, concepts, and managerial perspectives* (pp. 215–226). London: Elsevier.

Slade, P. (2003). Gallipoli Tourism. *Annals of Tourism Research, 3*(4), 779–794.

Stone, P. R. (2006). A dark tourism spectrum: Towards a typology of death and macabre related tourist sites, attractions and exhibitions. *Tourism: An Interdisciplinary Journal, 54*(2), 145–160.

Stone, P. R., & Sharpley, R. (2008). Consuming dark tourism: A thanatological perspective. *Annals of Tourism Research, 35*, 574–595.

Stone, P. R. (2011). Dark tourism experiences: Mediating between life and death. In R. Sharpley & P. R. Stone (Eds.), *Tourist experience: Contemporary perspectives* (pp. 21–27). Abingdon/Oxford: Routledge.

Stone, P. R. (2012). Dark tourism and significant other death: Towards a model of mortality mediation. *Annals of Tourism Research, 39*(3), 1565–1587.

Walton, J. (2005). *Histories of tourism. Representation, identity and conflict*. Bristol: Channel View.

Westover, P. (2012). *Necroromanticism travelling to meet the dead, 1750–1860*. London: Palgrave Macmillan.

Williams, P. (2007). *Memorial museums. The global rush to commemorate atrocities*. Oxford/New York: Berg.

Winstone, M. (2010). *The holocaust sites of Europe. A historical guide*. London: I.B. Tauris.

Young, J. E. (1994). *The art of memory. Holocaust memorials in history*. Munich/New York: Prestel.

2

Crime, Punishment, and Dark Tourism: The Carnivalesque Spectacles of the English Judicial System

Tony Seaton and Graham M. S. Dann

Introduction

Trial and punishment may seem far removed from the hedonism of travel and tourism, but they have been associated throughout history. The Romans, who ruled Europe for 1000 years, crucified political prisoners, criminals, and escaping slaves along the Via Appia—the main highway that led travellers in and out of Rome. The Crucifixion of Christ was staged by the Romans in Jerusalem, as a recreational spectacle on the feast of the Passover—a Jewish public holiday. And, Rome's most famous ruin, the Colosseum, was once the leading tourist attraction for thousands of Romans, who came to watch the

---

We limit our analysis mainly to the United Kingdom, not simply because dark tourism is not to be found elsewhere, but rather due to the realisation that the accompanying language of connotation is culturally homogenised and temporarily predicated, thus allowing the similar cases that it describes to be compared. By contrast, examples from such Anglophone countries as the United States (e.g. Alcatraz tours) and Australia (Ned Kelly and Old Melbourne City Jail) set up a different system of signs and signifiers. As for the non-English speaking world, the full interpretive sense and capturing of such idiosyncratic meanings may well be "lost in translation" on account of associated linguistic variation. In this connection, we can think of such sites as Lima's Museo de la Inquisición or the Père Lachaise cemetery in Paris.

T. Seaton (✉)
University of Limerick, Limerick, Ireland

University of Bedfordshire, Luton, UK

G. M. S. Dann
University of Tromsø – Arctic University of Norway, Tromsø, Norway

© The Author(s) 2018
P. R. Stone et al. (eds.), *The Palgrave Handbook of Dark Tourism Studies*, https://doi.org/10.1057/978-1-137-47566-4_2

execution of Christians and other enemies of the state, who had been sentenced to death in gladiatorial contests with wild beasts.

This chapter sketches out the historical relationship between judicial systems and the tourist gaze in Britain. It explores how the trial and punishment of wrongdoers were for centuries transformed into ritualised, public spectacles designed to draw spectators, and how in mediated form, they remain so today. The conceptual analysis draws on the works of four twentieth-century cultural theorists—Gramsci, Goffman, Debord, and Bakhtin—which together offer insights into the historical relationship between state power, semiotic display, and the legal and ideological direction of public behaviour (also see Chap. 10).

Judicial Spectacle: Crime and Punishment on Display

All political regimes, ranging from the most benign to the most tyrannical, establish judicial systems which, to be effective, have to be known and obeyed. Every citizen must be made aware of what is legally permissible and the penalties incurred for related transgression. The phrase, "justice must be seen to be done", is not just a figure of speech, but alludes to the practical necessity of translating the convolutes of legal language into do's and don'ts that can be easily grasped by all citizens. In the past, before the rise of the mass media, which began with the spread of printing and reached its modern apogee with broadcasting and digital technology, judicial systems were made known to the public by displaying the machinery of trial, sentence, and punishment as "live" shows. By so doing, they aimed to impress those present as spectators with the legitimacy, omnipresence, and ineluctable reach of the laws that bound them. Furthermore, after these live performances of the law had been carried out, records of them were compiled and stored as the engineered and orchestrated remembrance of the law in action.

Ritualised, public spectacle evolved as an element of statecraft in controlling populations. The Romans engaged in crowd-pulling displays that made visible their power at home and abroad. Edward Gibbon described how they translated imperial conquests abroad into theatrical spectaculars at home by triumphal parades of captives drawn in chains through the streets, along with wagons laden with the spoils of war. Theatrical performance and ritual display have not disappeared from public life in modern times. The sociologist, Erving Goffman, devoted his career to analysing modern society as theatre.[1] He viewed many social interactions as *performances* in which people acted out formal and informal roles, and responded to those enacted by others. These roles, he believed, were performed through a mixture of verbal and non-verbal semiotic codes. He saw the judicial system as a particularly ritualised theatre of performance, in which the physical construction of courtrooms (their furnishings, spatial allocations, seating positions, etc.) and the norms of verbal and non-verbal behaviour imposed upon the "actors" (their dress, bodily positioning, and freedom to speak or stay silent) were symbolically ordered to control interactions, demarcating positions of dominance and submission (see, e.g. Goffman 1959, 1971 *passim*). In Goffman's eyes, all trials were, in one sense, "show trials"[2] because they involved theatrical staging and semiotic management.

Following Goffman, this chapter offers a view of the evolution of English criminal justice as a theatre of scripted roles and performances. It will suggest how trial and punishment evolved as *engineered and orchestrated spectacles* in which people acted out the roles allocated to them semiotically. Attendance by audiences exposed them to the deterrent might of the law, and engaged them in a public complicity that signified a tacit approval of its legitimacy. This historical evolution will be traced down to modern times when spectacles of public trial and punishment largely disappeared, giving way to less brutal, but more pervasive and diverse, displays vested in popular culture, which mediated, engineered, and orchestrated the criminal justice system to the general public. One of them was dark tourism and the ideological practices and perceptions produced within it, which may be seen as encounters with engineered and orchestrated remembrance (see Chap. 1).

For much of its pre-modern history, criminal justice in England was personal, physical, and public. Before a national, policed system of law enforcement existed, medieval criminals were mainly apprehended, tried, and punished by and before local communities. Detection of crime was made by an accuser's deposition naming a suspect individual. Guilt or innocence was then adjudicated through processes within the community. Following the Norman Conquest in 1066, William the Conqueror in that same year introduced two highly public methods of criminal trial—combat and ordeal. In combat, the accused, or a nominated substitute, fought his accuser and if he won was declared innocent. Ordeal came in two forms: by submersion in water (if the accused floated s/he was guilty, if not, s/he sank); or by fire which involved the accused holding, or walking over, heated metal, having the resultant wound dressed, and then, if it healed cleanly within a given time span, the accused was deemed innocent. For women, ordeal might involve ducking stools. Punishment was also a public performance, but did not include capital punishment. Under William, preferred punishments were variations of bodily mutilation—blinding, castration, and the removal of hands—which acted as durable forms of visible indictment. For murder, he introduced a cash payment—the "murdrum" charge (Bartlett 2000: 184). Less violent public punishments in the Middle Ages included the naming and shaming in the pillory or the stocks, in which wrongdoers were exhibited with their head and hands or feet, in wooden frames in public spaces, where passers-by could see, mock, and sometimes abuse them verbally or physically (a common practice was throwing rubbish at them) (Plate 2.1).

After William's death in 1087, his son, Henry I, introduced capital punishment in public for serious crimes like murder, coining, and forgery. In 1124, a record number of thieves and other malefactors were hanged at Huncote in Leicester (Poole 1987: 404), with six blinded and castrated (Bartlett 2000: 184). In 1225, criminals who had tampered with the royal coinage were rounded up and deprived of their testicles and right hands. By the reign of Henry II, crimes punishable by execution or mutilation included treason, homicide, arson, robbery, and rape (Bartlett 2000: 184). In 1166, the sheriffs of London and Middlesex presided over 34 trials by ordeals, 14 male mutilations, 14 men hanged, and 5 duels (Poole 1987: 404).

Plate 2.1 The pillory

Tyburn, located near what is now Marble Arch, began to develop around 1187 as the theatre of London executions, and with it the ritual processions to the gallows by the condemned in carts, or for the less fortunate, drawn along the ground to the gibbet, or on a sledge tied behind a horse—the fate of William de Morisco, executed in 1135 for murdering a king's messenger (Plate 2.2).

A semiotic practice at Tyburn, designed to increase the number of spectators and intensify the spectacle, was hanging criminals from very high gallows. This was the fate of the Scottish rebel, William Wallace in 1305, who was then cut down, drawn, and quartered and his body was hung alongside some of his Scottish supporters for 20 days on a gibbet. At the end of this period, his head was placed on London Bridge, where it was an unavoidable sight for travellers crossing the Thames to go into or out of the capital (Marks n.d.: 99).

Punishment in public as judicial practice reached a peak under the Tudors who came to power after Henry VII triumphed over Richard III at the Battle of Bosworth in 1485. The dynasty lasted from 1485 until 1603, a period during which public torture and execution of dissidents became routine judicial practice. Henry's victory had ended a century of conflict between warring, feudal barons, but both he and his successors always feared rebellions to their rule. The earliest of these, by Perkin Warbeck, came in the first decade of Henry's reign. After it was crushed, 169 ringleaders were rounded up in the Tower of London, "railed in robes like horses in a cart", and 150 of them were shuttled out of town and, "hanged about the seacoasts in Kent, Essex, Sussex and Norffolke" (Marks n.d.: 120–121). The coastal dispersion might sound like the seaside stopovers of a touring theatre company. It was intended as a

Plate 2.2 Drawn through the streets on a sledge

cautionary display aimed to reach areas of potential, Catholic resistance most vulnerable to foreign invasion. It made local populations aware of the perils of plotting sedition, or supporting uninvited Spanish or French visitors landing on their shores.

Henry VIII, son of Henry VII, used terror as a weapon of statecraft the longer he reigned. Brutal tortures and public executions were meted out to political opponents and to churchmen who refused to convert from Catholicism to Protestantism and accept Henry's takeover of the English Church from the Pope. Prominent figures, including Cardinal Wolsey, Thomas More, and Thomas Cromwell, who had once been his ministers and allies, fell from grace and were beheaded, as were three of the king's wives. His victims were also lesser known churchmen, among them the heroic, Carthusian monks of London who were hanged, drawn, and quartered for refusing to renounce their faith, or accept his claims to be the head of the Catholic Church in England. Another cleric, Richard Byfield, was carried to Smithfield to be burned, passing his wife and ten children along the way (Hooper 1935: 85). These grandstanding political and religious executions were only the tip of a much larger iceberg beneath which were mass executions of common felons. One estimate suggests that 72,000 were executed during Henry VIII's 38-year reign (Cawthorne 2006: 141), and there was not one year when 300–400 were not regularly brought to justice in "one place and another" (Whibley 1916, quoting Cardan and Harrison 1916: 495).

Henry was succeeded by his daughter, Mary, a Catholic, whose aim was to turn the clock back and restore the Pope as head of the Catholic Church in Britain. She used torture and public burnings for heresy as a means of eliminating Anglican churchmen and other dissenters. In a six-year reign that began in 1556, she presided over 279 public executions in fires at Smithfield, which included those of 5 bishops and 16 priests (Dickens 1989: 293–295; Duffy 2009). Executions were staged in areas of greatest anti-Catholic sympathisers—London, Essex, and Kent (Dickens 1989: 297), and drew large crowds. Three of the most infamous victims of Mary's Catholic fanaticism were Latimer, Ridley, and Hooper—the latter being burned at the stake in front of 7000 spectators (Cawthorne 2006: 143). The memorial in Oxford to all three is still a prominent tourist landmark in St Giles near the City's centre (Dickens 1989: 297).

Elizabeth, who became queen after Mary's death, was more "moderate" than her predecessors. Yet, in the 45 years of her reign, she presided over as many executions as Mary had done in her 6 years. From the beginning of her reign until the end of the seventeenth century (1558–1603), high treason and all felonies, except petty larceny, were punishable by death. For anyone refusing to plead, there was the torture called "peine forte et dure", a gradual pressing—till death, if necessary—under increasing weights(Underhill 1950: 400), a practice that formed part of a museum display in Victorian England (see Ichenhauser n.d.) (Plate 2.3).

THE PEINE FORTE ET DURE, 1721.

Plate 2.3 Peine forte et dure

The Tudors regarded treason and heresy as "personal" crimes, which is why they were met with such carefully orchestrated public savagery to inspire terror in onlookers, and engineer their remembrance for the future (Babington 1968; Underhill 1950). The executions of non-royal malefactors began, as they had in medieval times, with an escorted procession through the streets from gaol to place of execution. The sites of executions—Tyburn or Newgate—were prominent public spaces in London. Royal executions took place on the elevated site of Tower Hill. Protestant subjects were burned by Mary at Smithfield Market where there was space for large crowds and bonfires could be burnt freely. The central, theatrical feature of public executions was the scaffold itself, which was mounted on a raised platform that resembled a mini outdoor stage set with the audience, as in the performance of Shakespeare's plays, standing around below, or looking down from windows of houses they had hired for the performance. Scaffolds varied in design. They could be rectangular with cross struts allowing many people to be hanged like washing on a line, side by side. Another design was a triangular oddity for executions in threes.

Execution was preceded by speeches from the platform that might include prayers and attempts at comfort by clerics, invitations to the victim to confess, or to address the crowd with some final words of penitence or remorse. Audience participation supported the theatricality with responses that could be cries of approval, dissent, or shocked silence. The climax was the physical act of despatch by an executioner dressed for the occasion. In executions by hanging, an official hangman, practised in knot tying and rope positioning, would place the fatal noose round the neck of a blindfolded or hooded victim and then choose the moment to release the trap door for the terminal drop. In beheadings, an axman appeared in hood and tunic and then went to the business of decapitation (Plate 2.4).

If drawing and quartering were involved, the cruellest form of despatch, the victim was first hanged and then cut down from the scaffold while still alive, and then dismembered with his body parts removed in front of his eyes. Burning demanded different, technical preliminaries involving attention to the logistics of positioning the victim on the bonfire for briefest, or longest, torment in the encroaching flames. These decisions depended on judging where to apply the flaming brands to ignite the bonfire quickly or slowly, depending on weather conditions prevailing before or during the execution. The wetter the bonfire, the slower the death, and the longer the suffering of the condemned.

The lessons of the scaffold did not end with the execution. The aim was often to engineer remembrance among a much larger audience than the one that had been "on the spot" witnesses. This was commonly achieved by taking

EXECUTIONS AT TYBURN, *temp.* ELIZABETH.

Plate 2.4 Elizabethan executions: hanging, beheading, and dismembering

the bodies, or body parts, of the executed on tour to selected locations. There they were left on gibbets or in cages—the practice called "hanging in chains"—at crossroads, on bridges, and near other public highways (Plate 2.5).

A more durable way of commemorating crime and punishment that later made the exhibition of body parts redundant was a new technological inven-

> [Roxb. Coll. I. 490, 491.]
>
> **The godly end and wofull lamenta-**
> tion of one John Stevens, a youth that was
> hang'd, drawne, and quartered, for High-treason,
> at Salisbury, in Wiltshire, upon Thursday, being
> the seventh day of March last, 1632, with the
> setting up of his quarters on the City gates.
>
> TO THE TUNE OF *Fortune, my foe, etc.*
>
> Now, like the swan, before my death I sing,
> And, like the raven, heavy newes I bring:
> Oh dismall fate and cruell destiny,
> Which brought me here in this same sort to die!

Plate 2.5 Body parts exhibited

tion. This was the printing press, developed in Europe in the second half of the fifteenth century. The Protestant Tudors were the first English dynasty to use printing for disseminating official, judicial information across the land. Two key printed works gave them ideological coverage of the whole British population for many years before there were national newspapers. The first was the English Prayer book which, from its beginnings in 1562, spelled out Anglican orthodoxy, hailing the crown as the head of the church.

The other great, anti-Catholic propaganda volume was Foxe's *Book of Martyrs*,[3] first published in English in 1563, which remained in print for over 300 years (Cross and Livingstone 2005). It detailed Catholic persecutions of Protestants across Europe, supplying gory details on how and where they met their deaths, with an abundance of illustrations, featuring scenes of torture and execution in named locations. The book was placed in parish churches, as well as being widely available for private purchase. In 1720, religious propaganda appeared in a different, national geographic text, *Magna Britannia*, an eight-volume county gazetteer of Britain. Part of the entry for each county was a section headed, "Martyrs of this County", describing Catholic oppression of Protestants. This represented an early attempt to orchestrate and commemorate certain locations as transgressive settings that was to be repeated on a much greater scale a century later (Anon 1720, *passim*).

Catholics engaged in their own printed propaganda to combat what they regarded as the heresy in Britain—a Protestant country that had replaced the Pope with an excommunicated monarch. They were only able to do so safely during the brief reign of Queen Mary because of the draconian laws and punishments for spreading Catholicism. Many Catholics fled abroad and only dared to publish from the safety of mainland Europe. Anglicanism, therefore, won the religious propaganda war because the Tudor monarchs—Henry VIII, Edward VI, and Elizabeth—and later the Stuarts, had monopolistic control of the judicial system, and the printed press for most of the sixteenth and seventeenth centuries. They were thus able to transmit "official" Anglican doctrine without much opposition.

The reigns of the Tudors and Stuarts represented a high point in the despotic use of torture and public execution for political and religious dissent. Total executions peaked at around 700 a year under Henry VIII over the period 1536–1547, when the Reformation in England and his confrontation with the Pope were raging. The numbers fell to around 400 per year in Elizabeth's reign, which lasted 44 years. The scale and frequency of public executions offended even the lawyer Edmund Coke who commented, "What a lamentable case to see so many Christian men and women strangled on that cursed tree of the gallows" (Marks n.d.: 77; Underhill 1950: 398). The number of political and religious executions declined under the early Stuarts—James I and Charles I. However, they included two of the most sensational in British history: those of the Gun Powder plotters, a group of Catholic sympathisers who planned to blow up Parliament; and that of King Charles I himself who, on 30 January 1649, was beheaded. For more than a decade afterwards, Britain was a republic ruled by Oliver Cromwell until the monarchy was restored in 1660. The century that followed was one of intensive propaganda by the state and the Anglican church during which the *Book of Common Prayer* was changed to include three special days, not unlike saints' days, which had prayers commemorating and celebrating the triumph of the monarchy over threats to the crown. One of these was 5 November, popularly known as "Bonfire Night" , celebrating Britain's deliverance from the Gun Powder plot which still survives as a patriotic, public event to this day. Another special day was 29 January, when prayers were said in memory of the execution of King Charles I in 1649, who was virtually canonised in another widely reprinted book—*Ikon Basiliske*—which presented him as a martyr. The third day of celebratory prayer was 30 May, the date on which Charles II was restored to the throne (Plates 2.6, 2.7, and 2.8).

Once safely installed, the new king wreaked brutal, public revenge on the regicides who had killed his father, having 29 of them hanged, drawn, and quartered between 13 and 18 October 1660 (Marks n.d.). Nor did he spare those who were no longer alive to be tried and judged. In January 1661, three of the regicide ringleaders—Oliver Cromwell, Ireton, and Bradshaw—were disinterred, transported to a triangular gallows at Tyburn, and publicly "hanged at the several angles of the Triple-Tree" (Marks n.d.: 71). It was the last major occasion of collective, judicial punishment in public for political beliefs by an English king. It was not, however, the end of executions of common criminals in front of large crowds. Diarist Samuel Pepys described the public execution of one Colonel Turner for robbery:

> And there I got for a shilling to stand upon the wheel of a cart in great pain, above an hour before the execution was done; he delaying the time by long discourses and prayers, one after another in the hopes of a reprieve; but none came, and at last he was flung off the ladder in his cloak. A comely looking man he was and kept his countenance to the end. I was sorry to see him. It was believed that there were at least 12,000 to 14,000 people in the street, (i.e., Leadenhall Street, London). (Farrington 1996: 167)

Nevertheless, political and religious executions declined as an era of greater religious tolerance replaced the violence of the previous centuries. Catholics were no longer tortured and hanged for their beliefs but marginalised by exclusion from public life. During the 1700s, they produced their own annals of the persecutions they had suffered between 1577 and 1684, compiled by Richard Challoner (Challoner 1741–1742). This was still being printed with wood-engraved illustrations of tortures and executions nearly a century later (Anon 1836). In the early twentieth century, lavish travel guidebooks to the places where Catholics had suffered or lived were published, serving to encourage pilgrimages by the faithful to the "homes and haunts" of their martyrs,

Plate 2.6 The Gunpowder Plot

Plate 2.7 Execution of Charles I

Crime, Punishment, and Dark Tourism: The Carnivalesque... 47

Plate 2.8 The Restoration of Charles 11 in London 1666

whose lives and biographies had been silenced for so long (Camm 1910 [1936]; Hamilton 1904, 1906; Newton 1950).

Crime and Punishment in the Long Eighteenth Century (1690–1837)

In the eighteenth century, the nature of crime and criminality changed. Capital and corporal punishment were used less for political and religious challenges to the Crown or established Church than for a range of new crimes against property, land, and person, committed by artisans and labourers. This situation came about because a growing capitalist and mercantile class, with an appetite for property and land, dominated the English Parliament and were able to get laws of enclosure and trespass passed or amended, that allowed them to acquire land and spaces traditionally enjoyed as customary rights by the people. New laws criminalising trespass, hunting, poaching, and collecting wood were passed that could be enforced by brutal corporal and capital punishments (see Gattrel 1994 for a detailed account of public hanging in the mid-eighteenth and nineteenth centuries). The effect was to reduce the means by which many of the poor obtained food, fuel, and employment (Thompson 1991; Linebaugh 2002, *passim*). Between 1690 and 1800, 128 new crimes were added to the law books. In 1723, the Waltham Black Act specified approximately 220 hanging offences in Britain. The peccadilloes counted as crimes included: appearing with a sooty face on the highway, cutting down an ornamental shrub, burning a hayrick, writing on Westminster Bridge, theft of goods to the value of 12 (old) pence, or being in the company of gypsies for one month (Farrington 1996: 151). Though some were repealed in 1819, Britain still led the world in capital punishment, with 180 offences punishable by death (Babington 1968: 38–47). The result was the prosecution and public punishment of the poor, often for petty crime, in the interests of landed elites. The effect was to initially increase the visibility of public executions. On 19 December 1713, a newspaper making its annual report on the Sessions at the Old Bailey concluded that "it had not been known for many Years, that so many Persons received Sentence of Death at any one time". The condemned totalled 23, of whom 6 were women and 17 men; 7 were condemned for burglary, 5 for shoplifting, and 4 for entering houses and stealing goods above the value of 40 shillings.

In London, executions were staged as spectacles that drew large crowds and were conducted in carnivalesque conditions. The carnivalesque is a concept formulated by Bakhtin to describe special occasions, such as religious festivals and customary holidays, when the normal hierarchical distance between classes was suspended and a promiscuous mixing between them took place, in raucous circumstances. The carnivalesque was thus a temporary period of disorder for letting off steam, licensed by those in authority, provided that order was restored after the event (Hirschkop and Shepherd 2001: 85–91). Public executions often took place on market days or declared public holidays, thereby augmenting the crowd, the majority of which was typically composed of women (Seal 2015: 67) and, in some cases, children, particularly young girls.

Hangings were heavily ritualised and semiotically coded (Babington 1968: 53–60). In London on the Sunday morning preceding one or more executions, a service was held in Newgate prison where a hellfire sermon was preached to the condemned, but also targeted at the assembled congregation. On the day of the execution, the event was announced by the great bell of St Sepulchre's Church tolling a ritualistic dozen times within earshot of the condemned in nearby Newgate jail awaiting their fate. Shortly after, the prisoners had their fetters removed by the Yeoman of the Halter and their hands were then tied in front of them, symbolising that they needed to pray when they reached Tyburn, while a halter or rope was placed around their necks. From as early as 7 am, the anticipatory funeral procession of the guilty began to wind its way to Tyburn. The pub of wholesome Beer Street, and the contrasting gin palace of Gin Lane were favourite *en route* ports of call. There the condemned would indulge in typical male drinking behaviour even on the day of their execution. The stoppages had the effect of extending the march by up to three hours, thereby keeping an often unruly and alcoholically restive crowd waiting until 10 am. There was a brief halt at the halfway Hospital of St Giles in the Fields for prisoners to partake of the "cup of charity", a practice instigated by Matilda, wife of King Henry I (Collie 2002; Farrington 1996; Thornbury 1878), whereby the condemned were offered a "parting cup" comprising a whole "bowl" of ale, to add to the vast quantities of cheap gin and brandy already consumed.

At Tyburn itself, the drunken mob would respectively cheer or jeer at the guilty as folk heroes or villains, often pelting the latter with garbage and dead animals, and all the while scuffling and fighting among themselves (Farrington 1996). At the first sound of nearby church bells, the cry "Hats off" was heard, a message addressed to those blocking the tourist gaze in order to make room for those with otherwise restricted vision, while comic songs such as, "Oh my, think I've got to die" drowned out the hymn, sermon, and last words of the condemned. The din was enhanced by the shouts of street vendors hawking quantities of food and more drink to the spectators, and lewd jokes were exchanged within the mob. In the confusion, pickpockets flourished, some of whom may have made more money from their thefts than the small sums for which the criminal arraigned for robbery might have been condemned to death.

Superstitions developed around public hangings and, in particular, the health benefits that they could bestow (Farrington 1996). Touching any part of a felon's already dead body was said to reduce external lumps or skin complaints, while brushing up against a hanged man's hand was believed to cure everything from goitre, tumours, and ulcers, to cancers. Alternatively, if a nurse brought children to stroke the hand of the recently deceased, then that act would result in the general good health of the child, while barren women were able to conceive just by touching the dead man's hand. Placing a withered limb against the neck of a recently executed criminal was reckoned as being sufficient to completely restore that limb to its natural state, while spreading the death sweat of the convicted was apparently able to eliminate tuberculosis. All these cures were available without the necessity of expensive surgery, hospitalisation, or medicines. In 1818, an enterprising hangman was charging spectators half a crown to touch a corpse. In addition to getting tips, a free house, and a pension, hangmen raised extra funds in a black economy that allowed them to sell off the clothes and personal effects of the condemned, and later the rope that hanged him/her as dark tourism souvenirs (Farrington 1996: 158). Touching the rope was thought to eliminate headaches and epileptic fits, to bring luck and fortune to gamblers, and even to insure against one's own hanging. The gallows itself was believed to promote health benefits. In an unconscious parody of the medical cures once attributed to monastic relics of the True Cross in the Middle Ages, the splinters of the gallows were thought to cure toothache, while a bagful of chippings was said to eliminate fever. These mementoes in the nineteenth century came to be offered to Madame Tussaud's waxwork exhibition. Her display of homicidal artefacts for tourists led *Punch* magazine to name it the "Chamber of Horrors", a title that still survives (Chapman 1984, *passim*).

More affluent members of the public paid to attend the executions of particularly notorious criminals, buying their place for ringside seats where the pew admission was by ticket only. Most people attending executions came on foot, but some came from greater distances. The size of the audiences was seen as astonishing in its time, amounting to a Dark Tourism epidemic that lasted for a century. In February 1696, a plot to assassinate William III in Richmond Park was discovered and led to executions of the perpetrators: one of them, a man ironically called Friend, attracted greater crowds, "exceeding all precedent" (Marks n.d.: 215–216). In the 1740s, the novelist Samuel Richardson found the pressure of the mob at executions in London almost incredible, given their monthly regularity and marvelled at the carnivalesque atmosphere which literally stopped the traffic on a day when five executions took place:

> All the way up Holborn the Croud was so great, as every twenty or thirty yards to obstruct the Passage. The behaviour of my Countrymen is past accounting for; every Street and Lane I passed through, bearing rather the Face of a Holiday, than that of sorrow which I expected to see. (Ibid: 236–238)

A particularly large crowd witnessed the execution of the Earl of Kilmarnock for his part in the Jacobite uprising that concluded with the Battle of Culloden in 1746 (Plate 2.9).

In 1776, the execution of the twin brothers, Robert and Daniel Perreau, for forging a bank bond was witnessed by 30,000. A year later, a fashionable preacher, named Dodd, who got into debt and had according to report, "fallen so low as to become the editor of newspaper", was condemned to death for forging Lord Chesterfield's signature on a bond for £4200. On 27 June, he was hanged in front of "the greatest concourse of people ever drawn together by a like spectacle" (Ibid: 261–262). A year later, one of the most celebrated public executions was that of "John the Painter" who was hanged from a high gallows for a crime that changed the law. He had set fire to the rope house in Portsmouth dock yard, the result of which was to add a new capital crime to the 200 already on the statute book, "setting fire to private dockyards" (Ibid: 257). In 1783, executions were transferred from Tyburn to the outside of

Plate 2.9 Execution of the Earl of Kilmarnock, 1746

Newgate Prison, ending the procession through the streets which was thought to attract large crowds. Dr Johnson, the well-known dictionary writer, regarded this as a retrograde step as, in his opinion, it reduced the deterrent effect of public shaming. "Sir", he declared, "executions are intended to draw spectators" (Marks n.d.: 267) (Plate 2.10).

It was not just public hanging but lesser forms of corporal punishment that could be viewed by visiting spectators. Bridlewell and other houses of correction attracted a higher class of clientele than hangings. Some, like John Howard the prison reformer, visited prisons for humanitarian reasons. For others, witnessing floggings in Bridlewell was a dark pleasure, "a diversion for the curious and those whose appetites ran to watching the flogging of half-naked women" (Byrne 1989: 67).One effect of this unparalleled era of live "crime and capital punishment" spectacles was the appearance of new kinds of printed "true crime" texts. In addition to the proclamatory notices posted on the outside of prison gates by the authorities, commercial printers published single-sheet broadsides that were hawked around the assembled crowds like football programmes today, providing details of the offences committed and biographies of those tried and punished for them (Farrington 1996: 167). They were often illustrated with cheap, woodcut engravings of the event along with the supposed last words of the felon and, even, the odd poem or ballad. The Rev. Paul Lorraine, the ordinary of Newgate between 1698 and 1719,

Plate 2.10 The new gallows, 1783

issued 50 broadsheets describing the execution and last speeches of those condemned to his keeping (Marks n.d.: 228).

The great artist, William Hogarth, left a graphic record of mass behaviour at public executions in his famous series of engravings, "Industry and Idleness" which contrasts the life and fate of a hardworking apprentice with that of an idle one who ends up on the scaffold at Tyburn. Plate 2.11 shows him seated in a tumbrel next to his coffin, while the pike-bearing soldiers follow on horseback in a group behind (Trusler 1827; Paulson 1965). There is a preacher nearby bearing a volume entitled Wesley (a reference to the morality of Wesley's Methodist comfort book and anticipating the hellfire sermon preached to the condemned man at the place of execution), while the Ordinary from Newgate is the official presiding clergyman to witness the hanging. The assembled crowd is enjoying its cheap brandy while the hangman nonchalantly smokes his pipe. The fate of Tom is contrasted with that of the industrious prentice, Francis Goodchild. He is depicted as a hard worker carrying out his weaver apprenticeship in order to earn the favour of his master, marry his daughter, and become Lord Mayor of London. Tom, by contrast, is shown as a drunkard, a cheat, a gambler in the churchyard during the divine service, and frequenter of prostitutes.

There were more durable texts for richer folk with libraries. They included multivolume, trial reports (e.g. Anon 1742) from the Old Bailey Sessions, and other courts in the vicinity of London which remain one of the best sources for the legal history of the period (Langford 1989). There were also more

Plate 2.11 (Hogarth) Death of the idle apprentice

populist "chronicles" of criminal case histories with illustrations, including the *Tyburn Chronicle* which dealt with, "the lives, adventures, tryals, executions and last dying speeches of the most notorious malefactors whose crimes included: bigamy, forgery, highway-robberies, housebreaking, piracy, sodomy, with details of their executions and punishments" (Anon 1768). The most successful of these was the *Newgate Calendar*, printed and reprinted in four or five volumes from the 1780s to the 1830s (Anon 1770s/1780s; Knapp and Baldwin 1824). These helped to make Newgate and Tyburn infamous names in popular culture as places synonymous with criminality and retribution, promoting a topography of transgression for "dark excursions" that was to increase over the next two centuries (Langford 1989).

The carnivalesque spectacles of eighteenth-century punishments were less well publicised in the provinces than for London, but still drew crowds. When a new gallows was set up in front of Aylesbury gaol on 28 March 1812, a father named White turned up to see his son, Joseph, executed for horse theft. He watched the execution, "with the utmost composure", an attitude that disgusted even the large crowd (Gibbs 1872: 46). Women were not spared public executions, but, mystifyingly, it was regarded as kinder to burn them. In 1782, a woman named Rebecca Downing was burned at the stake in Heavitree near Exeter for poisoning her bullying employer with arsenic. In 1786, the burning of Phoebe Harris for counterfeiting, while her male accomplices hanged, attracted an outcry that helped to lead to the abolition of burning in the following year (Plate 2.12).

As the eighteenth century progressed, fewer and fewer people who had received death sentences were actually executed. Though much can be made of the trivial offences theoretically punishable by death among the 200 on the statute book, in reality, most executions were for serious ones that included: the monetary crimes of forgery, coining, clipping, and counterfeiting, which threatened the economy and hit the rich most of all; serious kinds of burglary and theft, particularly highway robbery; and violent crimes of rape and murder (Marks n.d: 221–268). For lesser crimes, as one legal historian has observed, "capital punishment operated to deter the prosecutor, magistrate, jury and judge", except in exceptional circumstances (Tobias 1967: 235). In the 20 years before 1772, Howard, the penal reformer, reckoned that only half of those sentenced to death in London went to the gallows, while in the Norfolk circuit it was less than a third, and in the Midlands less than a quarter (Hammond and Hammond 1933 [1952]: 321). By the end of the eighteenth century, no more than one in three sentences of death were carried out in London and Middlesex. In 1783, Tyburn spectacles were abolished and thereafter hangings took place outside the jail.

OLD BAILEY INTELLIGENCE.—Execution of Six Unfortunate Malefactors, and the Barbarious Execution and Burning of Phœbe Harris, for Coining Silver, on the 21st of June, 1786.

The following male convicts, viz., Edward Griffiths, George Woodward, William Watts, Daniel Keefe, Jonathan Harwood, and William Smith, were executed pursuant to their sentence, on the scaffold usually erected opposite Newgate. They were brought out at half-past seven in the morning, and the platform dropped about eight o'clock. Woodward was so exceedingly weak, that he was obliged to sit down till the executioneer had tied up the rest, and was then supported by two men.

The Barbarious Execution and Burning of Phœbe Harris.

Soon after the above execution, Phœbe Harris, convicted the session before last of coining silver, was brought out at the debtor's door, from whence she walked to a stake fixed in the ground, about half way between the scaffold and Newgate street. She was immediately tied by the neck to an iron bolt fixed near the top of the stake, and after praying very fervently for a few minutes, the steps on which she stood were drawn away, and she immediately became suspended. The executioner, with some assistants, put a chain round her body, which was fastened by strong nails to the stake. Two cart-loads of faggots were then piled round her, and after she had hung about half an hour, the fire was kindled. The flames presently burning the halter, the convict fell a few inches, and was then suspended by the iron chain passed over her chest and affixed to the stakes. Some scattered remains of the body were perceptible in the fire at half-past ten o'clock. The fire had not quite burnt out even at twelve. The unhappy woman was so exceedingly affected on Monday night, that it was generally supposed (and indeed wished) that she could not have survived.

Phœbe Harris was a well made little woman, something more than thirty years of age, of a pale complexion, and not of disagreeable features. When she came out of prison she appeared languid and terrified, and trembled greatly as she advanced to the stake, where the apparatus for the punishment she was about to experience seemed to strike her mind with horror and consternation, to the exclusion of all power of recollectedness in preparation for the approaching awful moment. A great concourse of people attended on the melancholy occasion.

Plate 2.12 The burning of Phoebe Harris, 1786

The decline in death sentences and the increase in reprieves for anything but serious crimes continued into the nineteenth century (Radzinowicz 1948). In the years from 1815 to 1829, the annual rate of executions fluctuated between 35 and 97 a year. Between 1828 and 1834, of 8483 capital convictions in England and Wales, only 355, less than 5 per cent, were carried out (Tobias 1967). Failures to convict and execute were increasingly affected by broad changes in moral attitudes. The public exhibition of corporal and capital punishments, particularly for women and children, was becoming morally unacceptable to a growing number of evangelical Christians of all denominations. There was a recurring fear among the middle and upper classes, especially in London, of the threat to civil and social order posed by the carnivalesque assembly of crowds. A particular nightmare was that the anarchy of French Revolutionary mobs in Paris, who had howled and cheered the guillotining of aristocrats and gentry during the Reign of Terror, might be copied by radicalised mobs in Britain. Large crowds also posed a considerable health and safety risk that was demonstrated outside the Old Bailey in London in 1807 when 27 people were trampled to death in the rush to see Holloway and Haggerty hanged for a murder on Hounslow Heath (Gibbs n.d. c.1880: 28). However, public executions were not abolished immediately. Hangings for murder continued to attract record crowds across England. For the Red Barn murder of Maria Marten, William Corder was hanged outside Bury St Edmond's Gaol in August 1828 (Worsley 2016) an event which sold one million broadsheet accounts (Collison 1972) (Plate 2.13).

Another notorious case that drew large audiences was the execution of Maria (née de Roux) and Frederick Manning (Allcock 2008 based on James Rymer's account in *Lloyds Weekly Newspaper*) that attracted, on 13 November 1849, an audience of between 30,000 and 50,000, until then the largest assembled crowd ever to witness a public hanging (Worsley 2016), most of whom had assembled the night before; 2,500,000 broadsides were run off for the easy-viewing rooftop spectators, drawn from all classes. At one extreme of the social spectrum were well-dressed, genteel ladies seated for a then considerable fee of two guineas in nearby houses, roofs, and gardens with opera glasses to their eyes, who gazed admiringly upon the black satin gown (later to be sold on to Tussaud's) of the Swiss woman of noble and brave demeanour. There was a larger segment of proletarian bystanders who drank in local gin shops and night houses filled to overflowing, or danced quadrilles, polkas, and jigs outside in the foggy streets. Additionally, there were card parties, drinking, and smoking, while vendors passed by with festive brandy balls, hot potatoes and pies, and Maria Manning's peppermints as souvenirs. All this gustatory and haptic sustenance took place to the sounds, sights, and smells of squibs, crackers and other fireworks (Alcock 2008). This street entertainment was thus a multisensory prototype of dark tourism at it most carnivalesque (Plate 2.14).

In other provincial towns and cities, public executions attracted large crowds in the early nineteenth centuries. In York on 5 April 1830, many thousands witnessed the execution of a seducer who had killed the woman he

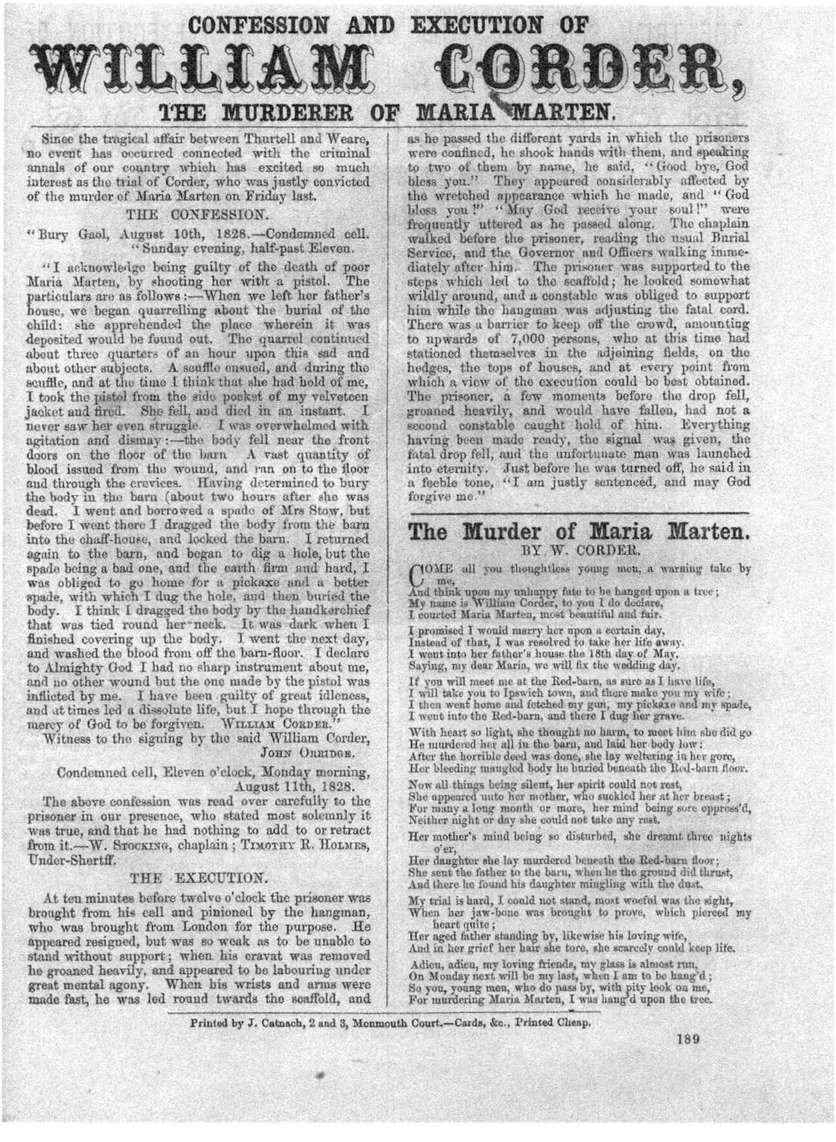

Plate 2.13 A Red Barn broadside

seduced (Collison 1972). Thousands walked all night from the country to Exeter to see Mrs Winsor hanged for child murder (Ibid: 41). At Moretonhampstead on Friday, 12 August 1836, a crowd estimated at 20,000 saw Thomas Oliver hanged for murdering a farmer (Ibid: 43). In 1839, the second year of Queen Victoria's reign, a railway company ran an excursion

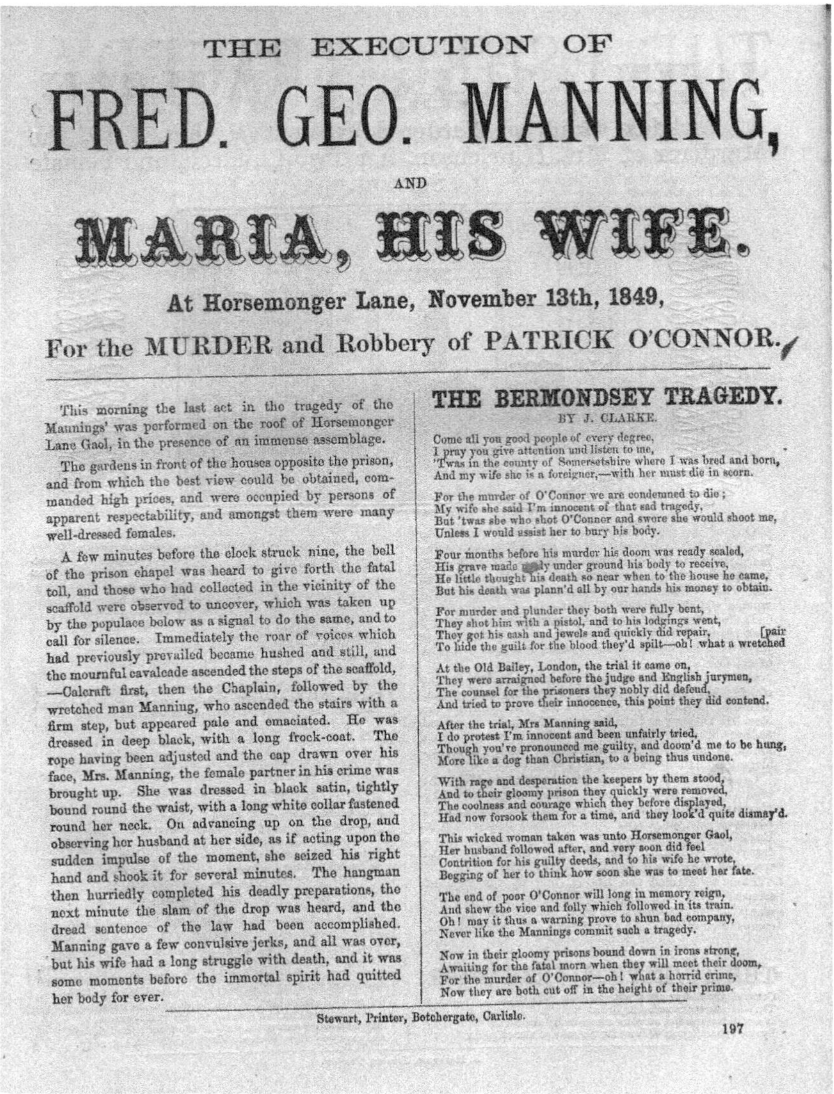

THE EXECUTION OF

FRED. GEO. MANNING,

AND

MARIA, HIS WIFE.

At Horsemonger Lane, November 13th, 1849,

For the MURDER and Robbery of PATRICK O'CONNOR.

This morning the last act in the tragedy of the Maunings' was performed on the roof of Horsemonger Lane Gaol, in the presence of an immense assemblage.

The gardens in front of the houses opposite the prison, and from which the best view could be obtained, commanded high prices, and were occupied by persons of apparent respectability, and amongst them were many well-dressed females.

A few minutes before the clock struck nine, the bell of the prison chapel was heard to give forth the fatal toll, and those who had collected in the vicinity of the scaffold were observed to uncover, which was taken up by the populace below as a signal to do the same, and to call for silence. Immediately the roar of voices which had previously prevailed became hushed and still, and the mournful cavalcade ascended the steps of the scaffold, —Calcraft first, then the Chaplain, followed by the wretched man Manniug, who ascended the stairs with a firm step, but appeared pale and emaciated. He was dressed in deep black, with a long frock-coat. The rope having been adjusted and the cap drawn over his face, Mrs. Manning, the female partner in his crime was brought up. She was dressed in black satin, tightly bound round the waist, with a long white collar fastened round her neck. On advancing up on the drop, and observing her husband at her side, as if acting upon the sudden impulse of the moment, she seized his right hand and shook it for several minutes. The hangman then hurriedly completed his deadly preparations, the next minute the slam of the drop was heard, and the dread sentence of the law had been accomplished. Manning gave a few convulsive jerks, and all was over, but his wife had a long struggle with death, and it was some moments before the immortal spirit had quitted her body for ever.

THE BERMONDSEY TRAGEDY.

BY J. CLARKE.

Come all you good people of every degree,
I pray you give attention und listen to me,
'Twas in the county of Somersetshire where I was bred and born,
And my wife she is a foreigner,—with her must die in scorn.

For the murder of O'Connor we are condemned to die;
My wife she said I'm innocent of that sad tragedy,
But 'twas she who shot O'Conner and swore she would shoot me,
Unless I would assist her to bury his body.

Four months before his murder his doom was ready sealed,
His grave made ready under ground his body to receive,
He little thought his death so near when to the house he came,
But his death was plann'd all by our hands his money to obtain.

For murder and plunder they both were fully bent,
They shot him with a pistol, and to his lodgings went,
They got his cash and jewels and quickly did repair,
To hide the guilt for the blood they'd spilt—oh! what a wretched [pair

At the Old Bailey, London, the trial it came on,
They were arraigned before the judge and English jurymen,
The counsel for the prisoners they nobly did defeud,
And tried to prove their innocence, this point they did contend.

After the trial, Mrs Manning said,
I do protest I'm innocent and been unfairly tried,
Though you've pronounced me guilty, and doom'd me to be hung,
More like a dog than Christian, to a being thus undone.

With rage and desperation the keepers by them stood,
And to their gloomy prison they quickly were removed,
The coolness and courage which they before displayed,
Had now forsook them for a time, and they look'd quite dismay'd.

This wicked woman taken was unto Horsemonger Gaol,
Her husband followed after, and very soon did feel
Contrition for his guilty deeds, and to his wife he wrote,
Begging of her to think how soon she was to meet her fate.

The end of poor O'Connor will long in memory reign,
And shew the vice and folly which followed in its train.
Oh! may it thus a warning prove to shun bad company,
Never like the Mannings commit such a tragedy.

Now in their gloomy prisons bound down in irons strong,
Awaiting for the fatal morn when they will meet their doom,
For the murder of O'Connor—oh! what a horrid crime,
Now they are both cut off in the height of their prime.

Stewart, Printer, Botchergate, Carlisle.

197

Plate 2.14 The Manning murder

train package, taking a tour party from Wadebridge to the nearby town of Bodmin to witness the hanging of two murderers. "Since the Bodmin gallows were in clear sight of the uncovered station, excursionists enjoyed the view without leaving the open railway carriages" (Boorstin 1987: 87). This was an early example of the "staycations" that were to become a familiar feature of Thomas Cook tours.

Table 2.1 Death sentences and executions: 1849–1848

	1840	1843	1846	1848
Death sentences	77	97	56	60
Executions	9	13	12	12

Source: Parliamentary *Accounts and Papers* 1838–1849, *Crime convictions, gaols, police* Vols. 8 (1838), 8 (1845), 15 (1849)

However, in the early years of Queen Victoria's reign, official statistics showed that executions were running at under a dozen a year, a fraction of the death sentences passed (see Table 2.1).

Offences carrying the death penalty were gradually struck from the statute book. Between 1841 and 1843, those removed included: rape, felonious riot, returning from transportation, malicious cutting and wounding, and simple burglary and robbery. The growth of crime coverage meant it was no longer important for punishments and executions to be seen to be believed. The workings of the criminal justice system were reaching far bigger audiences across Britain via the press than "live" performances. Improving literacy and cheap printing were creating a mass market of readers which was so obvious that, by the 1830s, the phenomenon was satirised as "The March of Intellect". Only one thing initially slowed down this trend, the price of newspapers which was kept artificially high by duties payable on paper and newsprint, known popularly as "taxes on knowledge". In 1855, the last of these taxes was abolished. The effect was a fall in the price of newspapers and the launch of new cheap ones, resulting in an expansion of newspaper readership that continued throughout the century. Crime and punishment became favoured reading for millions across Britain, in homes, offices, workplaces, clubs and pubs (where news was often read aloud to the less literate), and on train journeys. The press was becoming the main mediator of the criminal justice system to the general public.

In 1868, 13 years after the last "tax on knowledge" was removed, public hanging was abolished. Two of the last executions were for sensational murders that became national news. The first took place in November 1864 when a German named Franz Mueller became the first person to be convicted for murder on a train; 50,000 people gathered to see him hanged (British Broadcasting Corporation 2015). The final public execution was of Michael Barrett, convicted for his part in an Irish Fenian explosion in Clerkenwell that killed more than a score of people, who was hanged in front of Newgate jail (Farrington 1996). Thereafter, hardly anyone was allowed to witness capital punishment in England. Hanging was carried out behind the high walls of prisons until capital punishment was abolished in Britain in 1965. Only one occupational group was not excluded from attending live executions—newspaper reporters—an exception that implicitly recognised the importance of media coverage as a way of engineering and orchestrating awareness and respect for the criminal justice system.

Crime and Punishment in Fact and Fiction in Modern Society

The abolition of crime and punishment as "live" spectator sports did not end dark tourism's relationship with criminal justice as engineered and orchestrated public performance. From the second half of the 1800s, crime was reconfigured, in fact and fiction, across a wide range of popular culture with results that were to generate new forms of crime-related tourism far more pervasive than occasional, day outings at the scaffold. One consequence was to create audiences for exhibitions and museum displays of true crime. Pre-eminent among these was the showbiz empire of Madame Tussaud who had started her career in France making death masks of guillotined victims of the French Revolution. She came to Britain in the early nineteenth century and took her waxwork show on the road, before settling in permanent premises in London. There her exhibition became a household name and a must-see attraction for all visiting the capital. The most popular exhibits were those collectively named in *Punch* magazine, the "Chamber of Horrors", a display of the perpetrators, victims, and settings of notorious murders (see Chap. 3). A century later, the Tussaud's concept—that crime and horror pay as public entertainment—was copied with the launch of the London Dungeon, a branded attraction since expanded to other UK cities in Edinburgh, Blackpool, York, and Warwick Castle—as well as to Berlin, Hamburg, Amsterdam, and San Francisco. These Dungeon attractions now form part of the American mega-corporation, Merlin, which also owns Legoland, Sea Life, and Madame Tussaud's worldwide.

There were smaller, temporary exhibitions. A Bond Street gallery in the 1880s mounted a display of "'Instruments of torture from the Royal Castle of Nurenberg", a collection that was lent out for the occasion by its owner, the Earl of Shrewsbury and Talbot (Ichenhauser, c. 1880). It included devices used in Tudor and Stuart times to extort confessions from those accused of major crimes, including the "Iron Maiden" (*Eiserne Jungfrau*)—a name later adopted by a heavy metal band. A less accessible exhibition was the so-called, "Black Museum"—a collection of artefacts connected with major crimes which was established in the early twentieth century by the police. It has only been open to special guests, among them: W.S. Gilbert and Arthur Sullivan, King George V, and Edward, Prince of Wales (Honeycombe 1970).

In recent times, one of the most imaginative and novel exhibitions of the judicial system on display to tourists was that mounted in Reading Gaol in September and October 2016. Appropriately called "Inside", it was the brainchild of Artangel, an organisation whose remit is the exhibition of art in nonconventional settings. It was themed around the last years of Oscar Wilde, some of it in the cell in which he served a two-year sentence for gross indecency. It featured the work of artist, Nan Goldin, with that of other artists and writers, and included readings from Wilde's gaol writings, especially *De Profundis*. Gaol visits are not new in dark tourism[4] but the nexus of elements in the Artangel exhibition was unique. They constituted a historical interrogation of the tourism interface between art, literature, gay sexuality, and the criminal judicial system. It is one worthy of discussion and reflection among all with an interest in the uses and purposes of thanatourism, cultural tourism, literary tourism, and heritage. It demonstrated how engineered and orchestrated remembrance can simultaneously commemorate several things: the appalling conditions in which all Reading prisoners were once kept; the vicious laws in place against homosexuality at the time and the struggle for gay emancipation; and the hounding of Oscar Wilde through the humiliation he suffered to an early death at the age of 44 in exile 2 years after his release.

All of these exhibitions and performances were made possible because of news coverage. From the late nineteenth century, crime became a staple feature of mass-circulation newspapers. It also produced a wider literature of police memoirs, accounts of criminal investigations, and trial transcripts (e.g. Griffiths 1902). *Famous Trials*, a series launched in the 1920s, ran to 20 volumes and included the Oscar Wilde case. In the twentieth century, the film, radio, TV, and digital stations greatly increased levels of true crime coverage in news and feature journalism. BBC Radio pioneered the first UK, true crime series in the late 1940s, presented by Edgar Lustgarten and, a decade later, "Fabian of Scotland Yard" became the first TV series, based on the real-life cases of a London detective. In the 1980s, true crime on TV morphed into the ultimate kind of virtual travel in the badlands of law and order with "Crimewatch". This was, and remains, partly a live action, bulletin board of unfinished police business, providing details of unsolved crimes and also, extending an invitation to viewers to come forward as witnesses, providers of evidence, and participants in virtual identity parades, requiring them to recognise suspects from video footage and photographic "mugshots". The complicity between the police, the media, and their audiences is now so great that few object when news channels take advantage of pre-arranged filming opportunities to show violent police raids by officers in militarised, combat gear, breaking down the doors of suspects' homes in spectral imitation of the action in "rogue cop" films, starring Clint Eastwood or Bruce Willis.

If true crime has radically affected media news content, untrue crime has radically affected the fictions of imaginative literature and performance, particularly in the theatre, the novel, the radio play, the TV series, and film. Late Regency and early Victorian theatre impresarios were the first to recognise the potential of violent crime to fill theatre seats. An early example of theatrical exploitation of murder was the staging of the previously mentioned "Maria Marten, the Murder in the Red Barn" (see also Worsley 2016; Wikipedia 2015b). This was a theatrical melodrama built around the case of the shooting of a 24-year-old woman, Maria Marten, by her younger male lover, William Corder. The besotted couple had arranged to meet on 18 May 1827 at what became called "The Red Barn" in the village of Pollstead in Suffolk prior to their intended elopement to Ipswich. She was never seen again, but her body was discovered and dug up after her stepmother dreamt where she was buried. Eventually, in the absence of a convincing alibi, Corder was tried and executed in Bury St Edmunds for her murder, before a crowd variously estimated at between 7000 and 20,000. At times, this and other melodramas assumed the exaggerated qualities of pantomime, so much so that Worsley (2016) collectively referred to such ribaldry as "the murder entertainment industry", a direct analogue, perhaps, of the dark tourism industry. The Red Barn Murder still resonates today as sensational melodrama (Carr 2016).

Theatre presentations were not just confined to real-life cases. They also included the "blood and thunder" fictions of what came to be known as, "grand guignol" theatre. This was a generic, horror genre that had developed first in France, and in England featured characters like Sweeney Todd, the demon barber of Fleet Street, and other homicidal grotesques. Melodramas went down particularly well in "penny gaffs" and music halls attended by the urban poor (Disher 1949; Sheridan 1981, *passim*), and were even included in Victorian, toy theatres for children (Speaight 1946).

Crime and punishment also became holiday entertainment at seaside resorts. Pier head amusements included slot machines featuring peep shows lasting a few minutes. For a penny, the viewer watched a murder or execution scene come to life. Laurie Lee, the author of the classic, rural memoir, "Cider with Rosie", remembered a day-out excursion by charabanc to Weston-Super-Mare in the 1930s from his home in Gloucestershire, and the guilty excitement he and his friends felt as they sought out the melodramatic thrills of the pier:

> One glided secretly to one's favourite machine, the hot coin burning one's hand to command a murder, a drunk's delirium, a haunted grave or Newgate hanging. This last of course was my favourite; what dread power one's penny pur-

chased- the painted gallows, the nodding priest, the felon with the face of doom. At a touch they jerked through their ghastly dance, the priest, the hangman and the convict, joined together by rods and each one condemned to perpetual torment. (Lee 1959: 236–237)

Crime drama did not just feature in slot machines on piers. From the late 1940 to the 1980s, repertory companies and theatres would include detective plays in their summer programmes at seaside resorts. Meanwhile in London, Agatha Christie's play the "Mousetrap", which opened in 1952, still remains the longest running stage thriller, and a major tourist attraction in its own right.

One literary development, more than any other, exploited the public's fascination with criminal justice so successfully that it became a new literary genre. This was the detective story. It first appeared in a tale by the American writer, Edgar Alan Poe, called "Murders in the Rue Morgue" (1841). It was followed by the works of Emile Gaboriau (1866–1868) in France and by Wilkie Collins' novel "The Moonstone" (1868) in England. All were bestsellers, but it was not until the first appearance of Sherlock Holmes in a Christmas supplement to a monthly magazine, written by Arthur Conan Doyle—later, the first thriller writer to be knighted—that the genre took off. It spawned a succession of fictitious detectives, all with their branded idiosyncrasies, but usually united by one feature, that they were mostly smarter than the police in solving crimes (Cuddon 1982; Scott 1953; Steel 1955). With the coming of the broadcast media detective fictions were adapted to radio, film, and TV as popular forms and eventually, through the work of directors like Alfred Hitchcock and the *film noir* exponents in France,[5] achieved status as bone fide works of art with "highbrow" critics.

Topography and Transgression

One of the most unexpected impacts of the media's assiduous focus on crime and punishment was on place imagery. This was because of the way in which crimes were reported. Like football teams and cheeses, they were primarily identified by where they came from. For particularly sensational crimes, the effect was to fast-track certain locations into public awareness, as people clamoured for information on the whereabouts of crimes, their victims, the criminals, and the institutions where they were tried and punished. The outcome was the proliferation of sites that rose and fell as names in national and regional topographies of transgression.

This was not entirely new. In Shakespeare's time, some parts of London were represented as dens of iniquity by hack pamphleteers in guides intended, partly for "strangers" (aka tourists) as places to avoid in visiting the capital; and, partly, as useful information for those already living there (Seaton 2012). What was a relatively minor, "underground" subcultural phenomenon in Elizabethan England became more visible in the eighteenth century, as the myths of deviant and criminal communities in parts of London, and the courts and prisons for dealing with them, received wider publicity in print culture. This was why Tyburn, Newgate Prison, the Fleet Prison, and the Old Bailey became well-known London landmarks. In the Regency and Victorian periods, the gazetteer of transgression spread beyond London to the provinces on occasions when sensational crimes were widely reported by the media. The Red Barn murder in 1811, described earlier, turned Pollstead in Suffolk into a (dark) tourist attraction, attracting many visitors who stripped the partially red tiled, partially thatched roof of the barn for souvenirs. Worsley refers to them as "murder tourists" who might with hindsight be seen as the historical vanguard of committed "dark tourists" (Worsley 2016). The crime and location still attract attention today (see Spaul and Wilbert 2017).

Another atrocity in the provinces that became nationally infamous was that of Dr William Palmer in Staffordshire, convicted of poisoning his friend and possibly several others, including three of his infant children. His crimes became so well known throughout the county that the trial had to be moved to the Old Bailey (Wikipedia 2016). A crowd variously estimated at 20,000–50,000 came to see him hanged at Stafford Gaol. After his death, he secured a prominent biographical entry in *Bibliotheca Staffordiensis*, a monumental work on the literature and history of Staffordshire, which recorded that his life, crimes and trial had been reported in, "nearly every newspaper of the day", and were the subject of 16 different books or tracts, one of them by Charles Dickens (Simms 1894: 345–346).

London, however, remained the gold standard of transgressive topography because of its size, the supply of murders, and the number of reporters to cover them. During the century, the named locations of sensational crimes in the capital diversified, taking in districts, neighbourhoods, roads, and even specific houses. One sensational case in 1811 set an early precedent on the indelible effect a major crime could have in branding a previously obscure location. This was Ratcliff Highway, a main thoroughfare from the East End to London where, at number 29, a serial killer named John Williams slaughtered the Marr household—a husband, wife, baby, and servant, and later three others. He committed suicide before he could be tried, and was buried at the

Cannon Street crossroads with a stake through his heart. The murder was a national cause célèbre, inspiring illustrated broadsides, and becoming a prime subject in Madame Tussaud's Chamber of Horrors; 125 years after it happened, it was twice featured in a series of illustrated articles on the East End published in a monthly magazine by the Commercial Gas Company, a big employer based in the area. Its workers read how the murders inspired such terror in their day that the Prince Regent ordered a double guard to be put on duty at the Royal Palace, and Lord Macaulay recalled a shopkeeper who sold 300 alarm rattles in 10 hours to terrified locals (Anon 1931, Vol 2: 281–287; Anon 1935, Vol 5: 186–187). The name of Ratcliff Highway became so toxic that it was changed to George Street to purge its evil associations (Plates 2.15 and 2.16).

As the nineteenth century progressed, the public's fascination with low-life London was exploited in books with titles that emphasised its otherness, written by journalists cultivating the role of explorers reporting from a hidden, no-man's land of transgression. The titles included "Outcast London", "The Lights and Shadow of London Life", "The Night Side of London", and "Low Life Depths", and, in the early twentieth century, the American writer, Jack London, added his contribution "Children of the Abyss". The effect was to promote a form of metropolitan "orientalism" in which Manichean

Plate 2.15 Ratcliff Highway I

Plate 2.16 Ratcliff Highway II

comparisons between richer, civilised neighbourhoods and the "otherness" of those of the poor were constructed as polarities, similar to those Edward Said asserted imperialists had drawn between the West and the East on an international scale (Said 1987). Defined through this "otherness", the East End attracted social workers and religious groups to investigate and mitigate (e.g. Booth 1902), as well as less committed sightseers who were early representatives of both slum tourism and dark tourism. Charles Dickens was both a consumer and producer of this otherness. John Edmondson (see Chap. 3) describes his trips around the darker neighbourhoods of London and his novel, *Oliver Twist*, contributed to the mythology of the transgressive "rookeries" around Oxford Street where Fagin's criminal associates lived. Even more influential than Dickens' works were the penny dreadfuls by G.W.M. Reynolds, the bestselling, pulp fiction writer of the century, whose serial publications, "Mysteries of London" and "Mysteries of the Court of London", provided weekly or monthly accounts of illustrated melodrama that sold in hundreds of thousands during the 1840s and 1850s.

In the 1880s, London's place as the epicentre of transgression was consolidated with the serial killings of prostitutes in and around Whitechapel by an unknown murderer who became immortalised as "Jack the Ripper". They gave the East End mythic status as a transgressive locality which, though qualified in more pluralistic accounts since (Rose 1951; Fishman 1988; Ramsey 1997), attracted many visitors at the time, and still does so. Ripper trippers began visiting from the time of the murders and, by 1905, there were organised tours, one of which was led by a police surgeon. There were eventually several tours that occasionally crossed each other's paths. Arthur Conan Doyle and literary members of the "Crime Club" were among Whitechapel excursionists (Worsley 2016).

In the twentieth century, low-life London continued to exert its fascination, providing writers with further opportunities for passing as expert guides to places most people did not know. Thomas Burke was one who made a literary career as a seasoned traveller to obscure corners of a London which began with the bestseller, *Lime House Nights*, a book about drugs and Chinamen living near the Thames waterfront. A sceptical commentator mocked the kind of tourists he thought Burke's book would attract. They would, he suggested, be those who:

> having read of sensational accounts of opium dens and of vicious life in "Chinatown"… from a distance (would come) to see Limehouse in the expectation of being thrilled, and who, being unable to discover the things they thought to, find something in the stillness of the night, and (be) awed by shadows. (Anon 1935: 179–180)

If real-life crime created transgressive locations, fictional crime has played a lesser, but still significant, part in promoting place. The success of Arthur Conan Doyle's detective, Sherlock Holmes, was partly established by his iconic address at 14b Baker Street—a real street but a non-existent house number. It was only one of many named places in London that gave Doyle's stories verisimilitude. His work featured 19 named railway stations, including Blackfriars, Imperial Wharf, London Bridge, and Whitechapel, and many real neighbourhoods and streets, including the exotic Upper Swandham Lane, "a foul alley, lurking behind the high wharves which line the north side of the river to the east of London Bridge, between a slop shop and a gin shop". It is there that Dr Watson met up with Sherlock Holmes, disguised as a "filthy opium-smoking wreck" in the story "The man with the twisted lip" (Hamilton 1968: 56–57).

In modern times, place has been a key element in crime writing. Three of the most successful detectives in book and TV have been: Ian Rankin's Inspector Rebus; Ellis Peters' monastic sleuth, Cadfael; and Colin Dexter's, Inspector Morse. All of them carried out their investigations in real-life places that were later promoted in tour guides. The 20 Rebus novels were set in

Edinburgh and supported with website itineraries, a guidebook by Bruce-Gardyne and Skinner; another by Rankin himself (Rankin 2005), and a joint effort with other Edinburgh writers (Attwood, Rankin and Welsh (2010). Cadfael's investigations took place in medieval Shropshire and the Welsh Borders for which a lavishly illustrated tour guide was published (Talbot and Whiteman 1990). Inspector Morse's Oxford was the subject of several guidebooks (Goodwin 2002; Leonard 2004 and Leonard 2008). In Jericho, the area of Oxford where Morse operated, which was once an artisan district of terraced houses, house prices have risen astonishingly over the decades of his popularity and now (2016) cost in excess of half a million pounds. In 1988, two enterprising Americans, recognising the topographical appeals of detective fiction, produced an all-England guide to crime fiction (Dale and Hendershott 1988).

Exploitation of the synergy of crime and topography has been taken to new levels in the last 30 years because of two developments that have elevated them as raw materials for tourism trails. The first is the rise and rise of city marketing and regional development programmes, mounted in the face of the decline in Britain's manufacturing and industrial output since the 1980s. The second is the extraordinary advance in communication technologies that have increased the number of TV stations, generating round-the-clock programming, and creating social networking which is significantly primed by shared tourism experiences with photographs.

For broadcasters, the trends have created needs for frequent, low-budget, programme series to fill the schedules on mainstream and cable TV, and they have found that crime news and police documentaries with a national or regional connection are cheap to make and popular with audiences. Similarly, the exploits of fictional detectives and crime busters hailing from identifiable areas of Britain, provide long-running and repeatable series that can also have, as we have seen with Morse and Co., modest tourism impacts. The result is that British TV programming today abounds in crime programmes with distinctive, geographic settings that are regularly repeated to appeal to the armchair detective, the murder connoisseur, and the tourist sleuth. Alongside these broadcast developments has come a publishing expansion in national and regional guides to crime and punishment in many parts of Britain. History has been ransacked for crime narratives that have provided the content for a national, region-by-region murder guide (Tibbals 1993); murder guides to London (Butler 1973; Fido 1986; Le Vay 2007 and Edinburgh (Knight 2002)); crime itineraries around provincial towns and cities including Wolverhampton, Walsall, Wednesbury and West Bromwich (Robinson 2013),

Birmingham (Eddleston 1997), and Manchester (Hayhurst 2009); murder guides to provincial regions and individual counties including the Midlands (Posner 1973), the Wirral (Longman 2006), Berkshire (Long 1990), and Lancaster (Sailor 1994); and guides to "Prisons and Punishments" (Byrne 1989). One spatial study of transgression has offered a micro-analysis of murder settings by street types, buildings (houses, banks), types of room, and transport forms (e.g. taxis, railways) (Gaute and Odell 1986).

Conclusion

Judicial punishment was, for centuries, staged as a public spectacle, engineered and orchestrated to teach cautionary lessons about obedience to the law, and the punishments for transgression to subjects, brought face-to-face with the remorseless power of the state. In the late Middle Ages, this was mainly concentrated in the hand of semi-despots anxious to deter religious and political opponents, as well as keeping order among their subjects. In the eighteenth century, the state came to reflect broader, less aristocratic interests as new, gentrified, and mercantile classes gained influence in parliament and used it to secure and protect their economic interests. To do so, they reinvigorated or passed new laws of property and land entitlement, criminalising activities previously enjoyed as common law rights by the poor, and enforcing them with physical and capital punishments. Many of the laws were withdrawn as magistrates refused to convict for crimes that carried the death penalty, and criticism mounted among liberal and religious opinion.

Public hanging was abolished in 1868 and with it the carnivalesque enjoyments of public executions as "live shows". But it did not end the public's appetite for vicarious contact with crime and punishment that flourished in the media and popular culture in the consumption of crime reports, detective stories, police documentaries, and "crime watch" bulletins, which established transgressive locations that attracted tourism practices that sometimes evolved spontaneously, or were promoted. The public's fascination with criminality, criminals, and crime detection procedures is one of the unanticipated consequences of history. Judicial authorities certainly never predicted it when the police were first set up in England in the 1840s and were suspected and feared by some sectors of the population as enforcers of a legal system invented by the dominant classes to oppress them. Yet, the longstanding impact of representations of the judicial system at work in the media and popular culture has been to familiarise and normalise, not subvert, criminal justice. They thus act as powerful ideological endorsements of the forces of law and order and constitute instruments of state hegemony, in the sense theorised by the Italian sociologist Gramsci (Santucci 2010), serving to maintain its legitimacy. This conservative effect was recognised many years ago, as a particular feature of the detective story by a former Lord Chief Justice Lord Hewart:

> The detective story as distinct from the crime story flourishes only in a settled community where the reader's sympathies are on the side of the law and order and not on the side of the criminal who is trying to escape from justice. (Scott 1953: 15)

All of which makes the days of printed proclamations, broadsides, dying speeches, and patriotic prayers for deliverance from rebellion and sedition look primitive. Similarly, the staging of beheadings, hangings, correction house floggings, and the exhibition of body parts on bridges would now seem crude, transient, and offensive mechanisms of engineered and orchestrated awareness of judicial legitimacy. The modern citizen is now *a permanent virtual tourist* of the judicial system through the global and spectacular reach of printed news, film, TV, and digital media. Moreover, virtual tourism becomes *actual* when audiences are attracted to attend museums, wax works, and galleries: to take crime walks; and to tour gaols, dungeons, and other obsolete judicial settings.

The media and popular culture are expert orchestrators of the spectacular. Guy Debord, drew attention to media spectacle, as a central element in late industrial society (Debord 1967), suggesting that it was orchestrated distraction by forces of a status quo that masked unpalatable social realities, and were intended to narcoticise populations into a state of permanent passive consumption (also see Chap. 10). The account of judicial spectacle in history offered here is that spectacle is not necessarily a distraction, but is the promotion and imposition of reality, which has always been necessary in communicating judicial processes to populations. The major changes in judicial spectacle over the centuries have been the way in which it has been mounted, and the changing emphasis from punishment, to detection, and apprehension. The mediated spectacles of both true crime and crime fiction now place less emphasis on draconian punishment and more on the inevitability of being found out. The spectacles have moved from the live performance of punishment on the streets, to the mediated reach and pervasiveness of the global media, which is where most judicial systems hope it will stay.

Notes

1. Shakespeare had, of course, done so in *Twelfth Night* in the famous "All the world's a stage…" speech, but his account was quite different from Goffman's. Shakespeare saw the theatre of human life consisting of seven finite stages which followed each other from birth to death. Goffman imagined the theatre of life as a much more complex, stage on which we all daily play several parts and roles which change according to our roles in different social contexts or as he called, our "definition of the situation".
2. This phrase was derogatively applied during the 1930s and 1940s, to staged trials in Russia and Germany where "enemies of the state" were put on trial and filmed. Western critics argued that the trials, though public, were a sham as guilt had previously been assumed and was always confirmed by the verdict, despite the appearance of due legal process.
3. This was its popular title. Its actual title was *Acts and Monuments,* which it claimed, "set forth at large…the bloody times, horrible troubles, and great persecutions against the true martyrs of Christ, fought and wrought as well by heathen Emperors, as now lately practised by Romish prelates, especially in the realm of England and Scotland" (*Acts and Monuments*, 8th edition, 1641).
4. See among several studies: J. Lennon 2010, Strange, C and M. Kempa (2003) Shades of Dark Tourism: Alcatraz and Robben Island. *Annals of Tourism Research, 30 (2): 386–403*; J.Z. Wilson (2008) Prison: Cultural Memory and Dark Tourism. Peter Lang, Oxford; Hodgkinson and Urquhart (2017) Prison tourism. Exploring the spectacle of punishment in the UK, In Glenn Hooper and John J.J. Lennon (eds), *Dark Tourism. Practice and Interpretation*: 40–54, Routledge, Abingdon.
5. Film noir referred to a genre of film that appeared in France in the 1940s. The films were typically "pulp fiction" thrillers that derived an aesthetic distinction in the eyes of intellectuals from their sharp, laconic dialogue, and black and white photography that used lighting and camera angles to create a shadowed, claustrophobic atmosphere, lending them an introspective alterity, different from the typical fast-moving, all-action thrillers of Hollywood. Alfred Hitchcock was the great mascot of film noir directors.

References

Allcock, J. (2008). *Rymer's account for Lloyds Weekly Newspaper.* www.John Allcock. blogspot.co.uk/2008/09/execution-of-mannings.html. Accessed 17 Feb 2015.

Anon. (1720). *Magna Britannia et Hibernia Antiqua et Nova, or a new survey of Great Britain* (Vol. 8). Savoy: Liz Nutt.

Anon. (1742). *Select trials at the sessions house in the Old Bailey* (Vol. 4). Dublin: Smith, Faulkner and Wilson.

Anon. (1768). *The Tyburn chronicle: Or villainy display'd in all its branches, containing an authentic account of the lives, adventures, Tryals, executions, and last dying speeches of the most notorious malefactors* (Vol. 4). London: J. Cooke.

Anon. (1836). *The complete modern British martyrology: Commencing with 'the reformation', A.D. 1535, 26th Henry VIII to A.D. 1684, 24th Charles II*. London: T. Jones.

Anon. (1935). *The co-partnership herald* (Vol. 5, pp. 179–180).

Anon. (n.d. 1770s/1780s). *The Newgate calendar; or malefactors bloody register* (Vol. 5). London: J. Cooke.

Attwood, M., Rankin, I., & Welsh, I. (2010). *Crimestopping: an Edinburgh crime collection*.

Babington, A. (1968). *The power to silence. A history of punishment in Britain*. London: Robert Maxwell.

Bartlett, R. (2000). *England under the Norman and Angevin kings 1075–1225*. Oxford: Clarendon Press.

Boorstin, D. (1987). *The image: A guide to pseudo-events in America* (25th anniversary ed.). New York: Atheneum.

Booth, C. (1903). *Life and labour of the people in London*. London: Macmillan.

British Broadcasting Corporation. (2015). Murder on the Victorian Railway. *BBC2*, 21 March 20.15–21.15.

Bruce-Gardyne, T., & Skinner, J. (2007). *Rebus's favourites. The Deuchar guide to Edinburgh pubs, with a forward by Ian Rankin*. Orion Book Company.

Butler, I. (1973). *Murderers' London*. London: Robert Hale.

Byrne, R. (1989). *Prisons and punishment of London*. London: Harrap.

Camm, D. B. (1910 [1936]). *Forgotten shrines. An account of some old Catholic halls and families in England and of relics and memorials of the English martyrs*. London: Macdonald and Evans.

Carr, G. (2016). Guilty landscapes and the selective construction of the past: Dedham vale and the murder of the red barn. In G. Hooper & J. Lennon (Eds.), *Dark tourism: Principles and practice* (pp. 83–95). Abingdon: Routledge.

Cawthorne, N. (2006). *Public executions. From ancient Rome to the present day*. London: Capella/Arcturus.

Challoner, R. (1741-1742). *Memoirs of priests… That have suffered death in England 1577–1684*. London: Thomas Richardson & Son.

Chapman, P. (1984). *Madame Tussaud's chamber of horrors. Two hundred years of crime*. London: Constable.

Collison, R. (1972). *The story of street literature. Forerunner of the popular press*. London: J.M. Dent.

Collie, J. (2002). *Hidden London*. www.Britannia.com/hiddenlondon/stgilesfields.html. Accessed 17 Apr 2015.

Cross, F. L., & Livingstone, E. A. (2005). *The Oxford Dictionary of the Christian church* (3rd ed., revised). Oxford: Oxford University Press.

Cuddon, J. A. (1982). *A dictionary of literary terms*. London: Penguin Books.

Dale, A. S., & Sloan Hendershott, B. (1988). *Mystery reader's walking guide: London.* Lincolnwood: Passport Books.
Debord, G. (1967 [Trans. 2010]). *The society of the spectacle.* Detroit: Black and Red.
Dickens, A. G. (1989). *The English reformation* (2nd ed.). London: B.T. Batsford.
Disher, M. W. (1949). *Blood and thunder. Mid-Victorian melodrama and its origins.* London: Frederick Muller.
Duffy, E. (2009). *Fires of faith. Catholic England under Mary Tudor.* Newhaven/London: Yale University Press.
Eddleston, J. J. (1997). *Murderous Birmingham. The executed of the twentieth century.* Derby: Breedon Bocks.
Farrington, K. (1996). *Dark justice: A history of punishment and torture.* New York: Smithmark Publishers.
Fido, M. (1986). *Murder guide to London.* London: Weidenfeld and Nicholson.
Fishman, W. J. (1988). *East end 1888.* London: Duckworth.
Gattrel, V. (1994). *The hanging tree: Execution and the English people 1770–1868.* Oxford: Oxford University Press.
Gaute, J. H. H., & Odell, R. (1986). *Murder whereabouts.* London: Harrap.
Gibbs, R. (n.d. c.1880). *Buckinghamshire. A record of local occurrences and general events chronologically arranged* (Vol 3, A.D. 1801 to 1840). Aylesbury: Robert Gibbs.
Gibbs, R. (1880). *Buckinghamshire. A record of local occurrences and general events chronologically arranged* (Vol. 3, p. 46). Aylesbury: Robert Gibbs.
Goffman, E. (1959). *The presentation of self in everyday life.* New York: Doubleday.
Goffman, E. (1971). *Relations in public.* New York: Anchor Books.
Goodwin, C. (2002). *Inspector Morse country: An illustrated guide to the world of Oxford's famous detective.* London: Headline Books Company.
Griffiths, A. (1898). *Mysteries of crime and the police.* London: Virtue.
Haigh, C. (1993). *English reformations. Religion, politics and society under the Tudors.* Oxford: Clarendon Press.
Hamilton, D. A. (1904). *The chronicle of the English Augustinian Canonesses, regular of the Lateran, at St. Monica's in Louvain (now at St Augustine's priory, Newton Abbot, Devon) 1548–1625.* Edinburgh/London: Sands and Co.
Hamilton, D. A. (1906). *The chronicle of the English Augustinian Canonesses, regular of the Lateran, at St. Monca's in Louvain (now at St Augustine's priory, Newton Abbot, Devon) 1625–1644.* Edinburgh/London: Sands and Co.
Hamilton, J. R. (1968). *My life with Sherlock Holmes. Conversations in baker St. by John H. Watson, M.D.* London: John Murray.
Hammond, J. L., & Hammond, B. (1933 [1952]). Crime, poverty, philanthropy. In A. S. Turbeville (Ed.). *Johnson's England. An account of the life and manners of his age* (pp. 300–335). Oxford: Clarendon Press.
Hayhurst, A. (2009). *Greater Manchester murders.* New York: The History Press.
Henderson, W. (1937). *Victorian street ballads.* London: Country Life.
Hirschkop, D., & Shepherd, D. (2001). *Bakhtin and cultural theory.* Manchester/New York: Manchester University Press.

Hodgkinson, S., & Urquhart, D. (2017). Prison tourism. Exploring the spectacle of punishment in the UK. In G. Hooper & J. J. Lennon (Eds.), *Dark tourism. Practice and interpretation* (pp. 40–54). Abingdon: Routledge.

Honeycombe, G. (1970). *The murders of the Black Museum 1870–1970*. London: Hutchinson.

Hooper, E. (1935). *History of Newgate and the Old Bailey and a survey of the fleet and other old London gaols*. London: Underwood Press.

Ichenhauser, J. (n.d. c1880). *Illustrated catalogue of the original collection of instruments of torture from the Royal Castle of Nuremberg…lent for exhibition by the Right Honourable Earl of Shrewsbury and Talbot*. London. Art expert exhibited in New Bond Street. Correspondence to be addressed to S. Lee Bafferty F.R.G.S.

Knapp, A., & Baldwin, W. (1824). *The Newgate calendar: Interesting memoirs of the most notorious characters who have been convicted of outrages on the laws of England* (Vol. 4). London: J. Robins.

Knight, A. (2002). *Close and deadly: Chilling murders in the heat of Edinburgh*. Edinburgh: Black and White Publishing.

Langford, P. (1989). *A polite and commercial people: England 1727–1783*. Oxford: Oxford University Press.

Le Vay, B. (2007). *Eccentric London*. Chalfont St. Peter: Bradt Travel Guides.

Lee, L. (1959). *Cider with Rosie*. London: Hogarth Press.

Lennon, J. J. (2010). Dark tourism and sites of crime. In D. Botterill & T. Jones (Eds.), *Tourism and crime* (pp. 167–179). Oxford: Goodfellow.

Leonard, K. W. (2004) *The Oxford of Inspector Morse*. Location Guides, no place of publication.

Leonard, B. (2008). *The Oxford of Inspector Morse and Lewis*. Stroud: The History Press.

Linebaugh, P. (2002). *The London hanged. Crime and civil society in the eighteenth century*. London/New York: Verso.

Long, R. (1990). *Murder in Old Berkshire*. Buckingham: Barracuda Books.

Longman, D. K. (2006). *Criminal Wirral*. Stroud: Sutton.

Marks, A. (n.d. c1910). *Tyburn tree. Its history and annals*. London: Brown, Langham and Co.

Newton, D. (1950). *Catholic London*. London: Robert Hale.

O'Hagan, P. (2016, September 6). In jail with Oscar Wilde. *The Guardian Newspaper*, G2: 16–17.

Poole, A. L. (1987). *Domesday book to Magna Carta 1087–1216* (2nd ed.). Oxford: Clarendon Press.

Posner, M. (1973). *Midland murders*. Wolverhampton: STAR Publishers.

Radzinowicz, L. (1948–1956). *History of the English Criminal Law* (Vol 1), *passim*.

Ramsey, W. G. (1997). *The east end then and now*. London: Battle of Britain Prints International Ltd.

Rankin, I. (2005). *Rebus's Scotland*. Edinburgh: Orion Books.

Robinson, P. (2013). *Tales from four towns – death, destruction and notable news from the nineteenth century*. Wolverhampton/Walsall/Wednesbury: West Bromwich/Lulu.Com.

Rose, M. (1951). *The east end of London*. London: Cresset Press.

Said, E. (1978). *Orientalism*. London: Routledge and Kegan Paul.

Sailor, D. (1994). *The county hanging town: Trials, executions and imprisonment at Lancaster*. Lancaster: Challenge.

Santucci, A. (2010). *Antonio Gramsci*. New York: Monthly Review Press.

Scott, S. (1953). *Blood in their ink. The march of the modern mystery novel*. London: Stanley Paul.

Seal, L. (2015). *Capital punishment in twentieth century Britain: Audience, justice, memory*. UK: Taylor and Francis.

Seaton, A. V. (2012). Wanting to live with common people? The literary evolution of slumming. In F. Frenzel, K. Ko, & M. Steinbrink (Eds.), *Slum tourism. Poverty, power and ethics* (pp. 21–48). Abingdon: Routledge.

Sheridan, P. (1981). *Penny theatres of Victorian London*. London: Dennis Dobson.

Simms, R. (1894). *Bibliotheca Staffordiensis, or a bibliographical account of books and other printed matter relating to… The county of Stafford… Giving biographical notices of authors and printers*. Lichfield: A.C. Lomax.

Spaul, M., & Wilbert, C. (2017). Guilty landscapes and the selective reconstruction of the past: Dedham Vale and the murder in the Red Barn. In G. Hooper & J. J. Lennon (Eds.), *Dark tourism. Practice and interpretation* (pp. 83–95). London: Routledge.

Speaight, G. (1946). *Juvenile drama. The history of the toy theatre*. London: Macdonald and Co. Green's Juvenile Drama, "Jack Shepherd" as Home Entertainment.

Steel, K. (1955). Detective story. In J. T. Shipley (Ed.), *Dictionary of world literary terms* (pp. 94–95). London: George Allen and Unwin.

Strange, C., & Kempa, M. (2003). Shades of dark tourism: Alcatraz and Robber Island. *Annals of Tourism Research, 30*(2), 386–403.

Talbot, R., & Whiteman, R. (1990). *Cadfael country: Shropshire and the welsh border*. London: Macdonald.

Thornbury, W. (1878). *Old and New London* (Vol. 3, pp. 197–218). London: Cassell, Petter and Galpin.

Thompson, E. P. (1991). *Customs in common*. London: Merlin Press.

Tibbals, G. (1993). *The murder guide to Great Britain*. London: Boxtree.

Tobias, J. J. (1967 [1972]). *Crime and industrial society in the nineteenth century*. London: Pelican.

Underhill, A. (1950). The law. In Anon (Ed.), *Shakespeare's England. An account of the life and manners of his age* (Vol. 1, pp. 381–412). Oxford: Clarendon Press.

Whibley, C. (1916 [1950]). Rogues and Vagabonds. In Anon (Ed.), *Shakespeare's England. An account of the life and manners of his age* (Vol 11, pp. 484–510). Oxford: Clarendon Press.

Whiteman, R., & Talbot, R. (1991). *Cadfael country: Shropshire and the Welsh borders*. London: Macdonald.

Wikipedia. (2015). www.en.wikipedia.org/wiki/Red_Barn_Murder. Accessed 21 Apr 2016.

Wilson, J. Z. (2008). *Prison, cultural memory and dark tourism*. Oxford: Peter Lang.

Worsley, L. (2016). *A very British murder*. A three part series first shown in 2013 and repeated in 2016. BBC 4.

Worsley, L. (2016, February 21). Detection most ingenious. Episode 2 of *A Very British Murder*, BBC4, 9pm–10pm.

3

Death and the Tourist: Dark Encounters in Mid-Nineteenth-Century London via the Paris Morgue

John Edmondson

The prospect of looking at a corpse is not among the most obvious of enticements to visit a tourist attraction. Yet, it was precisely this prospect that drew crowds of visitors throughout the nineteenth century to the Morgue in Paris, with its macabre and apparently compelling display of the city's recent, unidentified dead. It is because it provides such an extreme example of dark tourism, and because of the direct encounter it enabled between the living and the dead, that I begin this chapter with a trip to the Paris Morgue and a discussion, with the help of eyewitness reports, of what led to its appropriation as a tourist site. The nature of the attraction and its visitors, and the confrontation of the living with the dead, make it an essential point of reference for the history and development of death-related tourism[1] and a backdrop for the exploration that follows of dark sites in Victorian London.

The Morgue opened in 1804 in a small building on the Quai du Marché-Neuf on Île de la Cité, close to Notre-Dame. Reconstructed and extended in 1830, it stayed there until 1864, when the building was demolished in the process of *Haussmannisation* and the Morgue was moved to a new, much larger home behind the Cathedral. It remained open to the public until the early twentieth century. The first Morgue—and the one that became internationally famous, or infamous—was a "small, low, substantial Doric building, constructed of massive, roughly-hewn stones" (Head, 1852, 43), next to a

J. Edmondson (✉)
Independent Scholar, London, UK

lively fruit and vegetable market ("indeed, the nice, fresh, green vegetables in the last of the booths ranged along the wall of the Quai actually touched it"— Head, 1852, 43). According to Charles Dickens:

> Those who have never seen the Morgue, may see it perfectly, by presenting to themselves an indifferently paved coach-house accessible from the street by a pair of folding-gates; on the left of the coach-house, occupying its width, any large London tailor's or linendraper's plate-glass window reaching to the ground; within the window, on two rows of inclined planes, what the coach-house has to show; hanging above, like irregular stalactites from the roof of a cave, a quantity of clothes… (Dickens, 1863, 221[2])

What "the coach-house has to show" is described graphically in Murray's 1864 *Handbook for Visitors to Paris*:

> […] a glazed partition will be seen, behind which are exposed the bodies of men and women found dead or drowned, and unowned. They are naked with the exception of a piece of leather over the loins, and stretched upon black marble slabs; the clothes hang on pegs above them, and a stream of water is trickling over the bodies. (Anon, 1864, 191–192)[3]

The purpose of the Morgue was to facilitate the identification of people found dead in the streets of the city or in the Seine. The idea was that friends, relatives or family members of missing people would visit to see whether they could identify one of the corpses on display. It served, in other words, the same purpose, but in a strikingly more uncompromising way, as the "Found Drowned" or "Body Found" handbills that would have been a familiar sight to Victorian Londoners.[4] It seems to have had reasonable success in fulfilling that aim of identification: around two-thirds of the bodies displayed in the 1840s and 1850s were recognized.[5] On average, 350–370 bodies were exhibited each year.[6] Many were suicides or assumed suicides; others were victims of accidents, sudden death and, to a much lesser extent, murder.[7]

From its early days, the Morgue attracted many more people than those in search of the missing. When the English novelist and travel writer Frances Trollope visited it in 1835, "about a dozen persons" entered at the same time (Trollope, 1836, 362). Trollope also mentions "the thousands who flocked to the Morgue" to see the severely mutilated body of the victim of a brutal murder (358). Subsequent writers emphasized the scale and variety of the crowd. Dickens, in his 1856 *Household Words* article "Railway Dreaming," noted:

> It is wonderful to see the people at this place. Cheery married women, basket in hand, strolling in, on their way to or from the buying of the day's dinner;

children in arms with little pointing fingers; young girls; prowling boys; comrades in working, soldiering, or what not. (Dickens, 1856, 375)[8]

Zola identifies a similar variety of visitors in his 1867 novel *Thérèse Raquin*:

> Des ouvriers entraient, en allant à leur ouvrage, avec un pain et des outils sous le bras [...] Puis venaient des petits rentiers, des vieillards maigres et sec, des flâneurs qui entraient par désœuvrement [...] Les femmes étaient en grand nombre; il y avait de jeunes ouvrières toutes roses, le linge blanc, les jupes propres, qui allaient d'un bout à l'autre du vitrage, lestement, en ouvrant de grands yeux attentifs, comme devant l'étalage d'un magasin de nouveautés; il y avait encore des femmes du peuple, hébétées, prenant des airs lamentables, et des dames bien mises, traînant nonchalamment leur robe de soie [...] Par moments, arrivaient des bandes de gamins, des enfants de douze à quinze ans, qui couraient le long du vitrage, ne s'arrêtant que devant les cadavres de femmes. (Zola, 1867, 101–102; ch. 13)[9]

And F.B. Head, in his 1852 travelogue *A Faggot of French Sticks*, tries to note down descriptions of the various people he sees coming into the Morgue: "the tide, however, in and out was so great, the stream of coming-in faces and departing backs was so continuous and conflicting, that I found it to be utterly impossible" (Head, 1852, 46). Murray's 1864 *Handbook for Visitors to Paris* refers to the popularity of the place in similar language, describing a "perpetual stream of men, women, and children" flowing in and out (Anon, 1864, 192).

These crowds of visitors were by no means limited to Parisians, or domestic French tourists. By mid-century, the Morgue's reputation was international. As Dickens writes in "Railway Dreaming," "All the world knows this custom…" (Dickens, 1856, 137). British visitors were much in evidence—according to Maillard (1860, 92), "les étrangers la visitent, principalement les Anglais" ("foreigners visit it, predominantly the English"). It was included in the major guidebooks—Galignani's *New Paris Guide* of 1852, for example, includes a dispassionate description and gives the location (Anon., 1852, 84). Murray's 1864 *Handbook*, on the other hand, devotes a substantial entry to it (191–192), describing it in detail and at the same time expressing profound disapproval:

> [...] it is not easy to understand how so disgusting and revolting an exhibition can be tolerated in a civilized country [...] (Anon., 1864, 192)

The graphic description that precedes the moral outrage could, of course, have done little other than whet the curiosity of many of Murray's readers.

Can we, then, glean anything from the contemporary reports and narratives that give us clues as to why so many tourists chose to step inside the

Morgue to contemplate its especially gloomy exhibition? Does this extreme example of dark tourism tell us anything about the phenomenon as a whole?

The first aspect to note is that the Morgue, as its notoriety spread, became one of the sights to see for visitors to Paris—at least for those who had the stomach for it. Its macabre curiosity value rose as reports and descriptions of it increased. And, as Vita points out, "its proximity to the cathedral [Notre-Dame] made it readily accessible to tourists" (Vita, 2003, 241). Indeed, the author of the *Household Words* article "Dead Reckoning at the Morgue" explains that he went in "on my way, by the route which most people take, to Nôtre Dame" (Anon., 1853a, 113). Veyriras notes too that most tourist visitors would have looked in as part of a general tour of the city, following the entries in their guidebook—"puis ils vont en d'autres lieux, de plaisir, de culture" ("then they go on to other places for pleasure, for culture") (Veyriras, 1982, 58). This certainly accords with the account of the not so talented poet (Anon., 1857) who narrates his 1856 visit to Paris in verse:

And then our march we took arm-in-arm
To St.-Germain, St. Roch, and the great Notre-Dame;
Inspecting La Morgue in the course of our roam,
And Napoleon's Column in the Place Vendôme[10]

For this tourist, as perhaps for many others, a visit to the Morgue was just one of the things to do in Paris, along with visits to Notre-Dame, the rue de Rivoli, and so on, and if you were on your way to or from Notre-Dame, it was conveniently at hand.

A gentle satire on British Continental tourists published in *The Times* in August 1858 implicitly confirms that the Morgue was both very widely known and on a well-trodden tourist itinerary:

In the hottest weather it is necessary to start immediately after breakfast to see half-a-dozen churches, as many public buildings, several picture galleries, a library, a palace, to ascend the highest spot near the town, and always to see something horrible in the shape of a Morgue, a Capuchin burial ground, an elaborate Calvary, a St. Anthony, or some other mortifying spectacle. (Anon., 1858, 6)

The Morgue is not even specified as the *Paris* Morgue—the writer assumes that the newspaper's readers will know what it is and that it is on the tourist circuit. And this jibe from the *Times* journalist raises another motivation for visiting it—the pull of the macabre, the desire to "see something horrible." In *Paris and the Parisians*, Frances Trollope admits to precisely this attraction:

> I have, in common with most people, I believe, a very strong propensity within me for seeing everything connected directly or indirectly with any subject or event which has strongly roused my curiosity, or interested my feelings; but, strange to say, I never feel its influence so irresistible as when something of shuddering horror is mixed with the spectacle. (Trollope, 1836, 361)

This may explain part of the attraction the Morgue held for Dickens, who visited it on several occasions. In "Travelling Abroad" he confesses:

> Whenever I am at Paris, I am dragged by invisible force into the Morgue. I never want to go there, but am always pulled there. (Dickens, 1860, 88)[11]

Dickens's "invisible force" and Trollope's "irresistible influence" articulate the attraction–repulsion interplay that is discernible in various accounts of visits to the Morgue and, more generally, in our responses to the Gothic, the bloody and the macabre.

Both writers, however, also find less immediately apparent explanations for the curious popularity of the corpses at the Paris Morgue. In his paper "Some Recollections of Mortality," Dickens focuses on the confrontation of the living with the dead. He studies the crowd's expressions as they contemplate a newly delivered corpse:

> And there was a much more general, purposeless vacant staring at it – like looking at a waxwork, without a catalogue, and not knowing what to make of it. But all these expressions concurred in possessing the one underlying expression of *looking at something that could not return a look*. (Dickens, 1863, 223) (Emphasis in original)

In addition to the privilege of staring without having the stare returned, there is a lack of recognition by the onlookers that the object of their attention was, until very recently, like themselves, a human being. On the contrary, their response suggests a confrontation with an Other—an alien somebody or something that has no direct relationship to their own lives or their sense of self. In Dickens's view, these onlookers are not contemplating their own inevitable future state; the corpse is no memento mori for them, but rather an object of curiosity with which they make no personal connection—hence the image of the waxwork exhibition.[12]

For Trollope the impact of the spectacle at the Morgue is heightened by the contrast of the bustling life and the energy of the city: "this citadel of death; – this low and solitary roof in the very centre of moving, living, laughing Paris" (Trollope, 1836, 361). Dickens too writes of the bustling life immediately outside, with street performers, the neighbouring market and people on their way to Notre-Dame (Dickens, 1860, 88), "and once the performing dog who had a wait in his part, came and peeped in, with a red jacket on, while I was alone in the contemplation of five bodies, one with a bullet through the temple" (Dickens, 1856, 375). So, the dark sights that the Morgue had to offer gained greater potency and fascination through their stark contrast with the energy, noise and colour of the city just outside its doors.[13]

This darkest of dark sites in nineteenth-century Paris thus furnishes us, through contemporary accounts and subsequent analyses, with several key motivations that help to explain, in combination or in isolation, its long and widespread notoriety and popularity—motivations that derive, respectively, from its appropriation as an accepted, if controversial stop on the tourist trail; its relationship to the tourist's thrill seeking and desire to "see something horrible" and so add variety to the business of sightseeing; the opportunity it afforded to gaze at the dead without reserve (and often with an apparent lack of engagement) in the safety of an official, controlled environment; and the dramatic contrast between the vibrant life of the city of light just outside and the stillness and otherness of the silent exhibition behind the glass divide.

Although Victorian London did not number an open-to-all-comers Morgue among its dark attractions, the Victorian visitors to the little building on the Île de la Cité would have been no strangers to graphic accounts and representations of violence and death, and, not least, of their perpetrators. The rapid rise of the popular press in the middle of the century (see, for example, Crone, 2012, ch. 6; Brake and Demoor, 2009, 152–153 and 501) both fed and increased the appetite for gory details. Dickens satirizes this appetite in *Great Expectations*. Parish clerk and aspiring thespian Mr Wopsle reads the newspaper aloud to a group of friends sitting round the fire at a country inn:

> A highly popular murder had been committed, and Mr. Wopsle was imbrued in blood to the eyebrows. He gloated over every abhorrent adjective in the description, and identified himself with every witness at the Inquest. (Dickens, 1860–61, 133)

The reports, like the one Wopsle appears to be reading, were very detailed, often verbatim or purportedly verbatim, reports of inquests and trials—today's tabloid editors would consider many of the descriptions their Victorian counterparts chose to publish too intimate and upsetting for their readers. London's popular press abounded with headlines on the latest murder, and were anything but shy of the sensational when the opportunity offered: "Atrocious case of theft, forgery and murder" (*Lloyd's Weekly Newspaper*, 13 January 1850); "Inhuman murder and mutilation" (*Lloyd's Weekly Newspaper*, 3 February 1850); "Horrible murder in Essex" (*Reynolds's Newspaper*, 13 February 1853); "Frightful murder in the Haymarket" (*The Morning Chronicle*, 26 February 1858); and so on.

The more famous of the murder cases, popularized through the popular press and street literature (e.g. the broadsheet), provided, as Crone puts it, "ideal material for melodramas as playwrights liberally manipulated the specifics of the story to fit within inherited plot structures" (Crone, 2012, 141)—the reality of the crime, in other words, adding spice to tried and tested genre pieces. The 1820s murder of Maria Marten by William Corder in what came to be known as the Red Barn, for example, became an enduringly popular subject for melodrama long into the century.[14]

Some of these stories penetrated so deeply into the popular culture that they even provided a merchandising opportunity. Crone (2012, 93–94) and Flanders (2011, facing 172) include in their accounts photographs of some of the china figurines of famous murderers and models of the locations of famous murders that must, bizarrely enough, have graced more than a few Victorian mantelpieces.

It is not too surprising, then, that models of murderers on a much larger scale, and in wax, became a key attraction at one of London's best-known tourist venues, Madame Tussaud's. Tussaud's, originally a touring exhibition, had become established in Baker Street in the 1830s (it moved to the Marylebone Road, where it still is, in the 1880s).[15] By the mid-century, when Madame Tussaud died, it was among the most famous of London's tourist destinations, readily listed alongside other tourist landmarks: "So you have been up, I suppose, to have a day's holiday in London – to see Saint Paul's, the British Museum, and Madame Tussaud's waxworks?" asks the narrator of "The Buckinghamshire Man" (Anon., 1859, 504), published in *All the Year Round*. The author of another article in *All the Year Round* confirms the extent of the exhibition's fame and popularity:

> Visitors from the country go to see these waxworks if they go nowhere else; tradesmen living in the neighbourhood put "Near Madame Tussaud's" on their cards; the omnibuses which run down Baker-street announce that they pass that deceased lady's door, as a means of getting customers; and there is scarcely a cab-horse in London but would make an instinctive "offer" to stop as he went by the well-known entrance […] (Anon., 1860b, 250)[16]

The same author, wondering whether the huge popularity of the exhibition is more attributable to the general display of famous historical characters or to "the profound and awful misery of the place which provides the Englishman with an entertainment that does not make him happy," decides that "the last-named of these two attractive elements has the most to do with the inconceivably great success of Madame Tussaud's." He is referring, of course, to the room that came to be known as the Chamber of Horrors. John Timbs provides a list of its contents in his *Curiosities of London*:

> The Chamber of Horrors contains portrait figures of the murderers Rush and the Mannings, Good and Greenacre, Courvoisier and Gould, Burke and Hare; Dumollard and his wife, believed to have murdered seventeen or eighteen persons; Nana Sahib; George Townley. Pierri, Pianori, and Orsini, who attempted to assassinate the Emperor of the French. William Palmer and Catherine Wilson, the poisoners. Oxford and Francis, who shot at Queen Victoria. Franz Müller, murderer; Fieschi and the infernal-machine; Marat, taken immediately after his assassination; heads of French Revolutionists; the knife and lunette used in decapitating 22,000 persons in the first French Revolution, purchased from M. Sanson, the grandson of the original executioner, now residing in Paris. Also a model of the guillotine, &c.; this being a class of models in which Madame Tussaud excelled in her youth. (Timbs, 1867, 820)

This is a relatively selective list. In its Catalogue entries of 1876 for the Chamber of Horrors, Tussaud's describes no fewer than 45 wax models of notorious murderers, 6 "Models and Relics" and 5 "Heads" (including that of Robespierre "taken immediately after his execution"). The short narratives, bearing stylistic similarities to the contemporary "sensation" fiction, crystallize the appeal—Tussaud's knew its audience. For example:

> WILLIAM PALMER. The annals of crime have not produced a more cold-blooded murderer. Under the guise of love and friendship, he sacrificed his victims to gratify his lust for gold; and, callous to the voice of nature, he coolly smiled at the torture he inflicted, calculating the effect of each dose of poison, and the time that it would take effect. Palmer was educated as a surgeon. He was executed at Stafford, for the murder of J. P. Cook, June 14, 1856. (Madame Tussaud & Sons, 1876, 43)

These novelistic potted histories are preceded by a defence and a justification for both Tussaud's staging of the exhibition and the visitor's compulsion to visit it:

> "He is a shallow critic," pithily remarks the "Daily Telegraph" in its leading article (March 20, 1868), on the Todmorden murder, "who wonders at the public interest in great crimes, and finds fault with it."

> In consequence of the peculiarity of the appearance of the following highly interesting Figures and Objects, they are placed in a separate room. The sensation created by the crimes of Rush, Mannings, &c, was so great that thousands

were unable to satisfy their curiosity. It therefore induced Madame Tussaud & Sons to expend a large sum in building a suitable room for the purpose; and they need scarcely assure the public that so far from the exhibition of the likenesses of criminals creating a desire to Imitate them, Experience teaches them that it has a direct tendency to the contrary. (Madame Tussaud & Sons, 1876, 41)

Thus, tourists who might otherwise worry about the propriety of their compulsion to visit the Chamber of Horrors could be comforted by the knowledge that the compulsion was both normal and respectable. Their desire to engage with the deviant was to some extent sanctioned by Tussaud's own defence of its exhibition and, perhaps most importantly, by the very popularity of the Chamber—if the desire is common, it is not deviant.

Unlike visitors to the Paris Morgue, Tussaud's customers had a catalogue but, like the Morgue's visitors, they had the irresistible opportunity to stare in safety at an Other. Like corpses, waxworks cannot "return the look." Like waxworks, corpses are in a state—inevitably beyond the empathetic comprehension of the living—of not-being. The onlooker may shudder but the threat is in the imagination, safely contained and in secure, officially approved surroundings. Some accounts of visits to the Chamber of Horrors, for which, incidentally, Tussaud's charged extra,[17] are redolent of Frances Trollope's notion that a sense of "shuddering horror" was a key element in the attraction of the Paris Morgue. One-time visitor to London, the Italian writer Edmondo De Amicis, "hurried through the room dedicated to England's most notorious criminals" (De Amicis, 1873, 51), although he had presumably paid the extra fee to visit it. His description reveals something of the atmosphere of the Chamber:

> [...] those savage and cretinous faces and furtive expressions, those clothes stained with blood – all in semi-darkness, which makes them seem almost real – horrified me. If someone behind a curtain had let out a scream I would easily have believed one of those murderers had plunged a knife into their heart. (De Amicis, 1873, 51–52).

All the Year Round's "Eye-witness" also recommends entering the Chamber "at a swift pace and without pausing for an instant" (Anon., 1860b, 252), although, on his visit, he seems to have missed very little:

> There is Horror in the dull cold light descending from above upon those figures in the Old Bailey dock, all with the same expression on their faces, upturned, inquisitive, bewildered. There is Horror in the unpicturesqueness of this aspect of crime – crime in coats and trousers being more horrible (because nearer to us) than crime in doublets and truck-hose. There is Horror in the inflated smiling heads, cast after death by hanging. There is Horror in the basket by the side of

the guillotine – a basket just the length of a body without the head, and filled with blood-drinking sawdust [...] There is Horror in the smell of the wax figures, in the folds of the empty clothes, in the clicking of machinery behind the scenes, and in the faces of most of the visitors to the place. (Anon., 1860b, 252)

Others, however, were less affected. "Eye-witness" reports "a young man from the provinces" eating a pork pie while contemplating Marat assassinated in his bath (Anon., 1860b, 253). In a letter to *The Times* of 5 February 1849, "S.G.O.," while acknowledging the attraction of the Chamber of Horrors, notes that "there is always a something in the waxen features which shows the hoax of the whole thing." S.G.O., perhaps not atypical of the average visitor, takes his encounters with Tussaud's display of murderers and murderers' accessories in his touristic stride. His indifference recalls that of visitors to the Paris Morgue:

[...] we applaud the ingenuity of the attempt; but we neither turn sick ourselves at the exhibition, nor do our children eat one bun less at the pastry-cook's at the corner of the next street. (S.G.O., 1849, 5)

Other responses to the Chamber of Horrors again echo those to the Morgue. "Eye-witness" finds that its effect is heightened by the contrast with its immediate surroundings:

An inexpressible dreariness is added to the other horrors of this Chamber of Despair by the sounds of distant music which reach it from without, at gusty intervals. The band which plays in the principal and less horrible room outside, is audible in this ghastly apartment in some of the stormier and more untidy passages of the overture to the Bronze Horse, as well as in the last tune but one of the Maritana Quadrilles. (Anon., 1860b, 252–253)

As we have seen, Dickens, Head and Trollope were all struck by the contrast of the inside of the Morgue with the energy and life all around it. Here, the music intrudes into the Chamber of Horrors just as Dickens's performing dog intrudes into the Morgue, reminding the visitor of the vibrant life and colour just beyond its walls, and so increasing and intensifying its effect.

Negative press coverage expressed similar moralistic disgust to that we find in Murray and elsewhere in relation to the Morgue. Again, no doubt, the coverage served mainly to entice readers to satisfy their curiosity with a visit. An article in *The Times* of 27 December 1856 complained,

The only objectionable part of the exhibition is that known as the Chamber of Horrors, directly calculated as it is to minister to a morbid curiosity in great criminals and to invest them with a mischievous interest. Of this abundant proof was furnished yesterday in the large number of people, mostly young people of the humbler class of both sexes, who crowded the apartment throughout the day [...] (Anon., 1856, 8)

The constant flow of visitors too recalls the crowds at the Morgue, as witnessed by Dickens, Head, Trollope, and Zola. Despite the contention of the *Times* journalist, there is evidence to suggest that visitors were by no means limited to the "humbler" classes. The *Guide Chaix* (Anon., 1851a, 184) describes the exhibition as "fort en vogue" (much in fashion) and the *Guide Joanne* of 1874 (Rousselet, 1874, 126) refers to the Chamber's "visiteurs fashionables."

Fashionable visitors were also much in evidence among the spectators at murder trials (see, for example, Crone, 2012, 83–85). A journalist in the *Illustrated London News* of 8 March 1845, bemoaning the fascination among people of all classes, especially those "who would think themselves injured if the appellation of respectable were denied to them," describes by way of illustration the scene at a murder trial in a provincial town:

[...] that court was crowded with the "rank and fashion" of the locality! The judicial bench itself was occupied by ladies, dressed as gaily, and with as much care, as if the occasion had been one of festivity, and for the whole of a long day they sat gazing on the criminals, over whom the shadow of death was closing darker and more dark with every lapsing minute [...] (Anon., 1845, 150)

The crowd watches the trial as it might watch a play, exhibiting a similar lack of connection with the accused to that exhibited by the visitors to the Paris Morgue who gazed at the corpses as they would at waxworks. In London, the most famous such "theatre" was the Old Bailey, where many of the most notorious murderers were tried. The price of admission depended on the "popularity" of the trial in process:

The stranger is admitted on payment of at least 1*s*. to the officer whose perquisite it is, but this perquisite is regulated by the officer himself, according to the importance of the trials that are on. (Anon., 1851b, 137)

One such officer tells a *Household Words* journalist, "We charge according to the cases tried; sometimes it's one thing, sometimes another. Why, sir, sometimes you can't come in under a pound" (Anon., 1853b, 495).[18] And in Dickens's *Great Expectations*, Pip, newly arrived in London and wandering past Newgate, encounters one lowly entrepreneur on the lookout for tourists in search of ghoulish entertainment:

> While I looked about me here, an exceedingly dirty and partially drunk minister of justice asked me if I would like to step in and hear a trial or so: informing me that he could give me a front place for half-a-crown, whence I could command a full view of the Lord Chief Justice in his wig and robes – mentioning that awful person like waxwork, and presently offering him at the reduced price of eighteenpence. As I declined the proposal on the plea of an appointment, he was so good as to take me into a yard and show me where the gallows was kept, and also where people were publicly whipped, and then he showed me the Debtor's Door, out of which culprits came to be hanged: heightening the interest of that dreadful portal by giving me to understand that "four on 'em" would come out that door the day after tomorrow at eight in the morning, to be killed in a row. (Dickens, 1860–61, 165–166)[19]

Prisons too might well have been on the Victorian dark tourist's agenda. Many contemporary guidebooks provide details of how visitors could gain admission. The *Guide Chaix,* for instance, includes a description for French tourists of all the main London prisons and mentions how to obtain permission to visit (Anon., 1851a, 249–252). Murray's *Handbook* of the same year includes the complete postal address for application to visit Millbank Penitentiary, then the largest of the London prisons. M.L. Moreau-Christophe, Inspecteur Général des Prisons de France, deplored the ease with which outsiders could obtain permission to visit Millbank. His account of what he saw on his visit interestingly echoes the distaste which Murray's *Handbook for Visitors to Paris* displayed for the open-access policy of the French Morgue:

> Le jour de ma visite à Milbank [*sic*], il y avait plusieurs *gentlemen* et une jeune *lady* qui avaient été admis à regarder les détenus à travers les grilles, comme on regarde les animaux au jardin des Plantes. (Moreau-Christophe 1839, 50)[20]

Once again the sense in the onlooker of separation from the subject of his or her contemplation is clearly perceptible in the commentary. And, again, the dark adventure with its attendant thrills can be experienced in the safety of a controlled, official environment that, through its sanction, renders the activity unexceptionable and, in the case of prison visits, supposedly in the social interest.

The Victorian dark tourist's fascination with murder was not limited to the perpetrators: the sites of the crimes were also core attractions. "The landlord upon whose premises a murder has been committed is now-a-days a made man," wrote the journalist Albany Fonblanque in 1837[21]:

The place becomes a show—the neighbourhood as the scene of a fair. The barn in which Maria Martin [*sic*] was murdered by Corder, was sold in toothpicks: the hedge through which the body of Mr Weare was dragged, was purchased by the inch. Bishop's house bids fair to go off in tobacco-stoppers and snuff-boxes; and the well will be drained—if one lady has not already finished it at a draught—at the rate of a guinea a quart. Really, if people indulge in this vile and horrid taste, they will tempt landlords to get murders committed in their houses, for the great profit accruing from the morbid curiosity! (Fonblanque, 1837, 194)[22]

According to an article in the *Illustrated London News* of 1 September 1849,[23] "for the first day or two after the murder," the house in Bermondsey where Maria and Frederick Manning killed Patrick O'Connor and buried him under the kitchen floor, "was surrounded by crowds of people." But, on that occasion, the commercial potential of the site was not realized:

[…] but the attraction soon ceased. The back-kitchen, where the victim was buried, and the house have been well cleaned. The landlord (Mr. Coleman) determined not to satisfy the morbid curiosity of the thousands who wished to look over the house, and it has therefore, very properly, been kept closed. It will not be let again for the present. (Anon., 1849, 3)

Later in the century, the horrific Whitechapel Murders and their unidentified perpetrator "Jack the Ripper" not only provided material for plays, novels, peep shows, ballads, and so on (see, for example, Flanders, 2011, 452–466 and White, 2007, 346), but also furnished tour organizers with a lucrative and long-term business prospect—guided walks around the East End to visit the sites of the various murders continue to thrive in twenty-first-century London.

Victorian street and fair entertainers reflected the commercial potential of murder and violence in their choice of subject. In his *London Labour and the London Poor*, Henry Mayhew interviews a peep show exhibitor.[24] The man, who presents a small peep show on the London streets, explains that the "caravan" shows, which are "much larger than the others, and are drawn by a horse or a donkey" specialize in "recent battles and murders" (Mayhew, 1861, 96). They tour the country, he says, in the spring and summer months and then often return to London in the winter.

People is werry fond of the battles in the country, but a murder wot is well known is worth more than all the fights. There was more took with Rush's murder than there has been even with the battle of Waterloo itself. (Mayhew, 1861, 97)[25]

Upmarket from the street entertainers, the panoramas (a major popular art form throughout the first half of the century), while often focusing on travel and topography, also drew heavily on famous battles for their spectacles. Natural disasters too provided subjects for extremely successful productions, especially the *Cyclorama of Lisbon Before and After the Earthquake in 1755*, presented in the purpose-built "Cyclorama" at the Colosseum in Regent's Park, with its spectacular lighting and sound effects adding to the violent "realism" of the experience.[26]

The touristic fascination with death and the associated spectacle of the corpse may at least partially explain the proliferation of another type of popular exhibition, which concentrated exclusively on the construction and deconstruction of the body. The anatomical museum, which had its origins in the eighteenth century, saw a popular revival in the middle of the nineteenth. At the high end of the market was the museum of the Royal College of Surgeons, with its Hunterian collection purchased from the estate of John Hunter in the 1790s. Many of the other anatomical exhibitions, however, had a more ambiguous appeal. Like Tussaud's Chamber of Horrors, they claimed the respectability of educational purpose, and the claim may well have been valid, but they also appealed in their many advertisements to that other desire, articulated by Frances Trollope after her visit to the Paris Morgue, for the excitement of "shuddering horror," and they again offered an opportunity to contemplate what was normally forbidden. Typically, the displays were of wax models of corpses and body parts, sometimes with the addition of preserved specimens. According to an advertisement in the *Illustrated London News* of 28 March 1846, the Museum of Pathological Anatomy on Regent Street boasted "upwards of one thousand models, cast from and coloured after nature; comprising every part of the human frame in every state of disease."

One type of waxwork model that attracted much attention was the "anatomical Venus" or "Florentine Venus." These Venuses were models of the naked corpse of a beautiful young woman that could be taken apart to show all the internal organs. Dr Kahn's Museum, the best known and the most frequently advertised of the mid-century anatomical exhibitions, boasted a Venus with 85 pieces (see Bates, 2006, 319 and Altick, 1978, 340). There were various similar models on display at other museums, including the very popular "Titian Venus" at Savile House in Leicester Square, as advertised in *The Times*:

> THE TITIAN VENUS: ANATOMICAL MODEL. – The Great Point of Attraction – the numerous visitors to this new and exquisite work of art express themselves in the highest degree pleased and instructed with the exhibition. The demonstrations, made by a medical gentleman, include a popular account of the various organs,

their uses and functions, and are equally interesting to the profession and the public. Admission 1s. Ladies admitted on Fridays. (7 June 1845)

The restriction of visits by women, so that the more indelicate aspects of the exhibition could be removed for them, also, of course, left men free to contemplate the Venus and all her secrets without female company. As the advert implies with its description of the model as a "work of art," and as Bates suggests, "anatomical Samsons and Venuses were … intentionally reminiscent of classical sculptures, a familiar and inoffensive representation of the human form" (Bates, 2006, 619). The true attraction of these beautiful "corpses" remains ambiguous, but it is hard not to think back to the Paris Morgue with the opportunity it afforded for a safe, normally forbidden encounter with the Other, and the various reactions the unresponsive bodies there provoked—among them fear, horror, sexual curiosity and the privilege of gazing at something "that could not return a look."

The popular anatomical museums, in one sense, represented a commercialization and commodification of the body/corpse, bringing it to centre stage in their shows. This could equally be applied to the fascination with the unrolling of mummies, which was at its height in the 1830s and 1840s (Daly, 1999, 86).[27] Here, the corpse is the Other not just because of its state of not-being, but also because it embodies, literally, the alien culture of the inscrutable Orient. The commercial opportunity was not neglected. An advertisement for the unrolling of the "Memphis Mummy" by Thomas Pettigrew, the surgeon and antiquary and prominent expert on Egyptian mummies, to take place at Exeter Hall in the Strand included the following booking information:

> A limited number of seats will be reserved, immediately around the tables on which the Mummy will be placed, at Six Shillings. Seats in the Balconies and Platform, Four Shillings. Gallery, Two Shillings and Sixpence. (*The Standard*, 17 March 1837)

The unrolling was thus envisaged as a theatrical-style performance, with those in the most expensive seats close enough to touch the bandages as they were removed. And the star of the show was the corpse.

It would be wrong, however, to end this essay without acknowledging that not all death-related tourism in the middle of the nineteenth century involved the body/corpse as spectacle. Visiting the burial places of famous people was a common tourist activity then as it is now. *Murray's Handbook for Modern London* of 1851, for example, includes a four-page list of "Eminent persons buried in London and its immediate vicinity," specifying the location of the grave in each case, as well as a section on "Cemeteries," with detailed descriptions of Kensal Green Cemetery and Bunhill Fields Burial Ground, among others. And the type of death-related tourism that these guidebook pages both reflect and encourage appears to be attributable to motivations that are largely distinct from those that have been discussed so far.

In a previous paper (Edmondson, 2014), I have applied Seaton's theory of metempsychosis, in combination with ideas from Walter Benjamin and Marcel Proust, to explore the relationship between a physical site or location and the individual onlooker, focusing on how places and spaces contain meaning and can become enriched with deeper meaning. In his essay "The Unknown Mother: Thanatourism and Metempsychotic Remembrance after World War I," which tracks the photographically recorded journey of a bereft mother to her son's grave in northern France, Seaton provides an intricate interlacing of his theory of metempsychosis with the process of grieving,[28] highlighting how landscape and buildings associated in some way with her son acquire new meaning for the mother and, consequently, as we examine the journey, for us.

The notion that specific physical space, place and things contain memory or, in some sense, absorb the consciousness of a person or event is frequently encountered in literature. In his novel *Les Misérables*, published in 1862, Victor Hugo crystallizes the process in his description of the site of the battle of Waterloo at night, when the landscape of the past becomes superimposed on that of the present:

> [...] une espèce de brume visionnaire s'en dégage, et si quelque voyageur s'y promène, s'il regarde, s'il écoute, s'il rêve comme Virgile devant les funestes plaines de Phillipes, l'hallucination de la catastrophe le saisit. L'effrayant 18 Juin revit; la fausse colline-monument s'efface [...] le champ de bataille reprend sa réalité; des lignes d'infanterie ondulent dans la plaine, des galops furieux traversent l'horizon ! le songeur effaré voit l'éclair des sabres, l'étincelle des bayonettes, le flamboiement des bombes, l'entre-croisement monstrueux des tonnerres; il entend, comme une râle au fond d'une tombe, la clameur vague de la bataille fantôme; ces ombres, ce sont les grenadiers; ces lueurs, ce sont les cuirassiers; ce squelette, c'est Napoléon; ce squelette, c'est Wellington; tout cela n'est pas plus et se heurte et combat encore [...] (Hugo, 1862, Vol 2 bk. 1 ch. xvi 420–421)[29]

The present incarnation of the place retains and contains past incarnations and acquires meaning from its history. In Chapter 35 of Thackeray's novel *Vanity Fair,* published in 1847–48, Mr Osborne, whose son George has been killed at Waterloo, makes "a journey which thousands of his country-men were then taking" a few months after the battle. Like Seaton's "Unknown

Mother," Osborne follows in the footsteps of his son and encounters the places associated with the closing days of George's life:

> He saw the point of the road where the regiment marched into action on the sixteenth, and the slope down which they drove the French cavalry who were pressing on the retreating Belgians. There was the spot where the noble Captain cut down the French officer who was grappling with the young Ensign for the colours [...] and here was the bank at which the regiment bivouacked under the rain of the night of the seventeenth. (Thackeray, 1847–48, 167)[30]

Similarly, in Dickens's *Bleak House*, Lady Dedlock asks Jo the crossing sweeper to guide her to the various locations associated with her former lover, a poor law-writer:

> Can you shew me all those places that were spoken of in the account I read? The place he wrote for, the place he died at, the place where you were taken to and the place where he was buried? (Dickens, 1852–53, 261)

The significance of place and thing[31] in personal grieving, and the meaning they contain for the griever, tell us something about the more general attraction of grave visiting in death-related tourism. The grave, or the headstone, becomes a point of contact, and contains meaning through its association with the work and/or life of the person it now represents. In that way, it connects us to the person—just as two very ordinary items in Flaubert's pavilion at Croisset, which have become extraordinary through association, connect the narrator of Barnes's *Flaubert's Parrot* to their illustrious owner:

> Two exhibits in a side cabinet are easy to miss: a small tumbler from which Flaubert took his last drink of water a few moments before he died; and a crumpled pad of white handkerchief with which he mopped his brow in perhaps the last gesture of his life. Such ordinary props, which seemed to forbid wailing and melodrama, made me feel I had been present at the death of a friend. (Barnes, 1984, 21)

The importance of a sense of "personal" connection in grave visiting appears to have intensified in the nineteenth century and to have played a role in the development of this important sector of death-related tourism. In her chapter "An Anthology of Corpses" in *The Literary Tourist* (23–55), Nicola Watson provides convincing argument for and evidence of a shift in the nineteenth century away from what she characterizes as "a public act of grateful homage" (Watson, 2008, 28) by eighteenth-century visitors to Westminster Abbey's Poets' Corner to the desire for "a personal, sentimental relation between the physical remains of the poet and the literary pilgrim" (29)—a shift which made the memorials, as opposed to the graves, in the Abbey less meaningful to the dark literary tourist.[32] In his 1847 work *Literary and Historical Memorials of London*, the historian J. Heneage Jesse reflects this perception:

> If there are poets buried in Poets' Corner to whom there are no monuments, so also are there monuments to poets whose burial-places are far away. [...] That Poets' Corner should have been selected to hold the monuments of these celebrated men, is in a great degree to be regretted, inasmuch as we are apt to misplace our sentiment by imagining that we are standing on the dust of departed genius, whereas we are only gazing on their cenotaphs. (Jesse, 1847, 421–422)[33]

That sought-for sense of personal connection is thus dependent on a tangible association of the place visited or the object contemplated with the dead—the skeleton beneath the tombstone, the house they lived in, the street they walked down, the glass that was by their bedside, the desk they wrote on, and so on. These associations appear to make the connection in some way "authentic" and weave the emotional thread.

If this form of death-related tourism seems essentially to derive from a desire, whether sharply or obscurely perceived, to achieve a personal emotional connection with the dead, it differs in that important respect from the other forms we have sampled in this chapter, which predominantly situate the corpse, and people and things associated with it, as spectacle. But all these varying performances—from the self-directed lone visit to a poet's grave through the macabre exhibits in Tussaud's Chamber of Horrors and the reality drama of murder trials to the carefully curated display of corpses at the Paris Morgue—reflect fundamental aspects of the relationship between the living and dead. In mid-nineteenth-century London, a burgeoning press, scientific progress, the development of mass tourism and the centrality of the theatre in popular entertainment combined to provide fertile ground for multiple explorations and exploitations of that relationship, and so furnished the dark tourist with an Aladdin's Cave of new and exciting encounters with death.

Notes

1. I use the phrase "death-related tourism" in preference to "necrotourism" as it seems to me more neutral and less suggestive of prior assumptions.
2. "Some Recollections of Mortality" was published in Dickens's journal *All the Year Round* on 16 May 1863. It is reprinted in *Dickens' Journalism*. I discuss

this paper in detail in the context of Seaton's theory of metempsychosis in Edmondson, 2014.
3. For detailed descriptions of the Morgue see, for example, "Dead Reckoning at the Morgue" (Anon., 1853a); "Railway Dreaming" (Dickens, 1856) and "Some Recollections of Mortality" (Dickens, 1863) among other papers by Dickens; *A Faggot of French Sticks* (Head, 1852, 42–51); and *Paris and the Parisians* (Trollope, 1836, 358–363).
4. Such handbills, for example, paper the walls of Gaffer Hexam's room in Dickens's *Our Mutual Friend* (Dickens, 1864–65, 31–32).
5. See, for example, Maillard's statistics (Maillard, 1860, 80–81) for each year from 1837 to 1859. On the basis of these figures, roughly 60% of the corpses were identified in a typical year. According to an 1853 article in *Household Words*, "Dead Reckoning at the Morgue," the "proportion of bodies recognized" was then "nine-tenths of the whole number exposed" (Anon., 1853a, 113), but that information was given to the journalist by the clerk of the Morgue, who very possibly exaggerated its efficacy. The article, published anonymously but identified by Lohrli (1973, 115) as the work of Dudley Costello, includes an eyewitness account of a mother discovering that one of the bodies on display is that of her son.
6. See Maillard (1860, 80–81) for precise statistics for the years 1837–59. According to Dudley Costello's *Household Words* article (Anon., 1853a, 114), the average per year was 364. F.B. Head (1852, 51) puts the figure at 300, but Maillard's statistics, taken directly from the registers at the Morgue, suggest Head's number is somewhat understated.
7. Maillard's figures (1860, 73) suggest that, for the period 1836–46, around 63% were suicides, 22% victims of accidents, 12% victims of sudden death and 3% murder victims. Some 65% of the bodies exhibited during that period were those of people who had drowned.
8. The article appeared in *Household Words* on 10 May 1856 and is reprinted in *Dickens' Journalism*.
9. "Workmen came in on their way to work, with their bread and tools under their arms […] Then there were shabby genteel types, wasted and dry old people and *flâneurs* who wandered in for want of something better to do and who looked at the corpses with the foolish, weak eyes of mild and sensitive men. Women were there in great numbers; there were young, rosy-cheeked working women in white linen and clean skirts, who walked nimbly from one end of the window to the other, their sharp eyes wide open as if they were walking past the window display of a fashionable clothes shop; then again there were poor women, looking stupefied and pathetic, and elegant ladies whose silk dresses trailed casually along the ground […] Every now and then gangs of young boys would turn up, kids of twelve to fifteen, and they would run the length of the window, pausing only in front of the corpses of women" (Author's translation).

10. This extract is from the anonymously and apparently self-published *My Rambles in Paris, Versailles, St. Cloud, &c., &c., 1856*, p 6. I am grateful to Veyriras (1982, 58–59) for bringing this useful item to my attention, but Veyriras mistakenly writes that the narrator visits the Morgue with his wife and children. In fact, he travels to Paris with a friend (see his Preface and the opening lines of the verse narrative).
11. Published in *All the Year Round* on 7 April 1860 and reprinted in *Dickens' Journalism*. Dickens describes an especially disturbing visit to the Morgue in this paper.
12. Dickens returns to this image later in "Some Recollections..." (1863, 224) and, interestingly, in another paper in which he describes the "keeper of the Morgue going about with a fading lantern, busy in the arrangement of his terrible waxwork for another sunny day" ("A Monument of French Folly," published in *Household Words*, 8 March 1851; see Dickens, 1851, 333).
13. Veyriras (1982, 59) and Edmondson (2006, 127), among others, identify this contrast as one of the factors that gave the Morgue its enduring fascination. As Veyriras puts it, "La mort paraît plus horrible – et plus fascinante – du fait de la proximité de ces plaisirs, du fait aussi que la Morgue, sise en plein Paris, offre d'étonnants contrastes entre la mort et la vie..." ("Death seems more horrible – and more fascinating – because of the proximity of these pleasures, and also because the Morgue, situated in the midst of Paris, offers astonishing contrasts between death and life...").
14. Crone (2012, ch. 4) provides a useful account of the treatment of murder in the popular melodramas, including the Maria Marten case. See also Flanders, 2011, 45 ff.
15. See the books by Berridge (2006), Leslie and Chapman (1978), and Pilbeam (2003) for detailed and illuminating accounts of the history of Tussaud's and its exhibits, and of the life and career of Marie Tussaud.
16. Berridge also draws on this article in her biography of Madame Tussaud, but wrongly attributes it to Dickens (Berridge, 2006, 269). The piece was published anonymously in *All the Year Round*, and may well have been edited by Dickens, but it was written by Charles Allston Collins, who contributed all the "Eye-Witness" articles and later collected them in volume form as *The Eye-Witness: Evidence About Many Wonderful Things*, published in 1860 (see Collins, 1860, 176–189 for the article on Tussaud's). See also Drew (2003, 214, note 20) and Dickens's letter to Collins of 19 November 1859 (Storey, 1997, 165): "Don't let the Eye-Witness drop [...] it is your own idea and one that you may stand by for years."
17. "Madame Tussaud's Wax Works, Baker-street, Portman-square ... Admission, 1*s*. Chamber of Horrors 6*d. extra*" (Anon., 1860a, xlii).
18. This article, published anonymously, is now known to have been written by Henry Morley (Lohrli, 1973, 112).

19. I do not cover public executions in this chapter as they form the subject of another chapter in this volume.
20. "The day of my visit to Millbank, there were several gentlemen and a young lady there who had been admitted to look at the prisoners behind bars, just as we look at the animals in the Jardin des Plantes."
21. Fonblanque was the editor of *The Examiner* from 1830 to 1847.
22. Fonblanque mentions three notorious murders in this passage. They took place in the 1820s and 1830s and remained in the popular consciousness for many years afterwards. Maria Marten (which Fonblanque spells "Martin") was murdered in 1827 by her lover William Corder in what came to be known as the Red Barn. William Weare, a gambler, was murdered in 1823 by John Thurtell in the (mistaken) belief that he was carrying a large amount of money. The attempts of Thurtell and his partner in crime to hide the body received extensive coverage in the press. In 1831, John Bishop, in partnership with Thomas Williams, murdered a poor Italian boy by drowning him in a garden well and then attempted to sell his body for dissection.
23. I am grateful to Jerry White's *London in the Nineteenth Century* (346) for drawing this article to my attention.
24. For a concise and well-illustrated history of the peep show, see Balzer (1998).
25. James Blomfield Rush, a tenant farmer, murdered his landlord Isaac Jermy and Jermy's son in November 1848. He was executed in 1849. Crone (2012, 46) and Altick (1978, 174) provide further evidence of the popularity of notorious murders as subjects for peep shows and related entertainments.
26. See, for example, Altick, 1978, 158–159. For a history of the panoramas and reprints of some of the narrative programmes that accompanied them, see the five volumes of *Panoramas, 1787–1900 Texts and Contexts*, under the General Editorship of Laurie Garrison (Garrison, 2013).
27. In his *Modernism, Romance and the Fin de Siècle*, Daly provides a fascinating analysis of this craze for mummy unrolling, both discussing it in the context of the commodification of the body and relating the process of unrolling to a symbolic if partial unveiling, in the Western imagination, of the mysterious Orient (Daly, 1999, 84–89). I am very grateful to Dr Rachel Harrison for bringing this work to my attention.
28. For Seaton on metempsychosis, see in particular his papers "Cultivated Pursuits: Cultural Tourism as Metempsychosis and Metensomatosis" (Seaton, 2013); "In the Footsteps of Acerbi: Metempsychosis and the Repeated Journey" (Seaton, 2001) and "Tourism as Metempsychosis and Metensomatosis: the Personae of Eternal Recurrence" (Seaton, 2002).
29. "[…] a kind of visionary mist emerges from it, and if some traveller wanders there, if he looks, if he listens, if he dreams like Virgil in the doom-laden plains of Philippi, the hallucination of the disaster takes hold of him. The terrible 18 June comes to life again; the artificial hill topped by the monument fades away […] the battlefield regains its reality; lines of infantry undulate over the plain, there is furious galloping across the horizon! The dismayed

dreamer sees the flash of sabres, the sparkle of the bayonets, the flare of the bombs, the frightful interchange of thunder; he hears, like a death-rattle in the depths of a tomb, the distant clamour of the phantom battle; these shadows, they are the grenadiers; these glimmers, they are the cuirassiers; this skeleton, it's Napoleon; this skeleton, it's Wellington; all these are no more and still they clash and struggle [...]" (Author's translation.)

30. In addition to being a destination for the grieving, Waterloo was also a popular site for a less sensitive form of dark tourism. In the same passage, Thackeray describes "peasants and relic-hunters" who were "offering for sale all sorts of mementoes of the fight, crosses, and epaulets, and shattered cuirasses, and eagles" (Thackeray, 1847–48, 165).
31. I use the word "thing" here because it best describes my meaning: I do not intend any echo of or reference to Thing Theory.
32. Westover also refers to the perceived importance of the physical remains, suggesting that "the draw of the grave was that literal, material proximity and limit, that sense that the author *was*, not just had been, there" (Westover, 2012, 12, emphasis in original).
33. I am grateful to Nicola Watson's excellent book *The Literary Tourist* (Watson, 2008, 29) for drawing this comment to my attention and referring me to Jesse's work.

References

Altick, R. D. (1978). *The shows of London*. Cambridge, MA: Belknap Press of Harvard University Press.
Anon. (1845). Another instance has just occurred which shows that the degrading appetite for horrors has an undiminished hold upon the public. *Illustrated London News,* 8 March 1845, 150.
Anon. (1849). The Bermondsey murder. *Illustrated London News,* 1 September 1849, 3.
Anon. (1851a). *Guide Chaix: Nouveau guide à Londres pour l'Exposition de 1851*. Paris: Librarie Centrale des Chemins de Fer de Napoléon Chaix et Cie.
Anon. (1851b). *Murray's handbook for modern London; or, London as it is*. London: John Murray.
Anon. (1852). *Galignani's new Paris guide*. Paris: A. and W. Galignani & Co.
Anon. (1853a). Dead reckoning at the morgue. *Household Words,* 1 October 1853, 112–116. [Published anonymously, author subsequently identified as Dudley Costello.]
Anon. (1853b). In the presence of the sword. *Household Words,* 23 July 1853, 492–498. [Published anonymously, author subsequently identified as Henry Morley.]
Anon. (1856). Madame Tussaud's. *The Times,* 27 December 1856, 8. *The Times Digital Archive*. Web. 26 September 2015.

Anon. (1857). *My Rambles in Paris, Versailles, St. Cloud, &c., &c., 1856.* Greenwich.
Anon. (1858). Goldsmith tells people to console themselves. *The Times*, 24 August 1858, 6. *The Times Digital Archive.* Web. 1 August 2015.
Anon. (1859). The Buckinghamshire man. *All the Year Round*, 17 September 1859, 500–504.
Anon. (1860a). *Murray's modern London 1860: A visitor's guide.* Moretonhampstead: Old House Books, 2003 (facsimile edition).
Anon. (1860b). Our eye-witness in great company. *All the Year Round,* 7 January 1860, 249–253. [Published anonymously, author subsequently identified as Charles Allston Collins.]
Anon. (1864). *A handbook for visitors to Paris.* London: John Murray.
Balzer, R. (1998). *Peepshows: A visual history.* New York: Henry N. Abrams.
Barnes, J. (1984). *Flaubert's parrot.* London: Picador, 1985.
Bates, A. W. (2006). Dr Kahn's museum: Obscene anatomy in Victorian London. *Journal of the Royal Society of Medicine, 99*, 618–624.
Berridge, K. (2006). *Waxing mythical: The life and legend of Madame Tussaud.* London: John Murray.
Brake, L., & Demoor, M. (Eds.). (2009). *DNCJ: Dictionary of nineteenth-century journalism.* Gent/London: Academia Press and the British Library.
Collins, C. A. (1860). *The eye-witness: Evidence about many wonderful things.* London: Sampson Low, Son, and Co.
Crone, R. (2012). *Violent Victorians: Popular entertainment in nineteenth century London.* Manchester: Manchester University Press.
Daly, N. (1999). *Modernism, romance and the Fin de Siècle: Popular fiction and British culture, 1880–1914.* Cambridge: Cambridge University Press.
De Amicis, E. (1873). *Memories of London.* (trans. Stephen Parkin). Richmond: Alma Classics, 2014.
Dickens, C. (1851). A monument of French folly. In Michael Slater (Ed.), *The amusements of the people and other papers,* The Dent Uniform Edition of Dickens' Journalism, Vol 2, 329–338. London: J.M. Dent, 1996.
Dickens, C. (1852–53). *Bleak House.* London: Penguin, 1996.
Dickens, C. (1856). Railway dreaming. In Michael Slater (Ed.), *'Gone astray' and other papers from Household Words.* The Dent Uniform Edition of Dickens' Journalism,Vol 3, 369–376. London: J.M. Dent, 1998.
Dickens, C. (1860). Travelling abroad. In Michael Slater and John Drew (Ed.), *'The Uncommercial Traveller' and other papers, 1859–70.* The Dent Uniform Edition of Dickens' Journalism, Vol. 4, 83–96. London: J.M. Dent, 2000.
Dickens, C. (1860–61). *Great expectations.* London: Penguin, 1996.
Dickens, C. (1863). Some recollections of mortality. In Michael Slater and John Drew (Ed.), *'The Uncommercial Traveller' and other papers, 1859–70.* The Dent Uniform Edition of Dickens' Journalism,Vol. 4, 218–228. London: J.M. Dent, 2000.
Dickens, C. (1864–65). *Our mutual friend.* London: Penguin, 1997.

Drew, J. (2003). *Dickens the journalist*. Basingstoke: Palgrave Macmillan.
Edmondson, J. (2006). *Dickens on France*. Oxford: Signal Books.
Edmondson, J. (2014). Making sense of place: A short walk in Paris with the Uncommercial Traveller. *Dickens Quarterly, 31*(2), 127–154.
Flanders, J. (2011). *The invention of murder: How the Victorians revelled in death and detection and created modern crime*. London: Harper Press.
Fonblanque, A. (1837). *England under seven administrations* (Vol. II). London: Richard Bentley.
Garrison, L. (Ed.). (2013). *Panoramas, 1787–1900: Texts and contexts* (Vol. 1–5). London: Pickering & Chatto.
Head, F. B. (1852). *A faggot of French sticks* (Vol. 2). London: John Murray.
Hugo, V. (1862). *Les Misérables*. Paris: Éditions Garnier Frères, 1963.
Jesse, J. H. (1847). *Literary and historical memorials of London* (Vol. 1). London: Richard Bentley.
Leslie, A., & Chapman, P. (1978). *Madame Tussaud: Waxworker extraordinary*. London: Hutchinson.
Lohrli, A. (1973). *Household Words: A weekly journal 1850–1859 conducted by Charles Dickens. Table of contents, list of contributors and their contributions based on the Household Words office book*. Toronto/Buffalo: University of Toronto Press.
Madame Tussaud & Sons. (1876). *Exhibition catalogue*. London: Madame Tussaud & Sons.
Maillard, F. (1860). *Recherches historiques et critiques sur la Morgue*. Paris: Adolphe Delahays.
Mayhew, H. (1861). *London labour and the London poor* (Vol. III). London: Charles Griffin and Company.
Moreau-Christophe, M. L. (1839). *Rapport sur les prisons de l'Angleterre, de l'Écosse, de la Hollande, de la Belgique et de la Suisse*. Paris: Imprimerie Royale.
Pilbeam, P. (2003). *Madame Tussaud and the history of waxworks*. London/New York: Hambledon and London.
Rousselet, L. (1874). *Londres et ses environs*. Paris: Collection des Guides Joanne, Librarie Hachette et Cie.
S.G.O. (1849). A new exhibition. Letter to the Editor. *The Times*, 5 February 1849, 5. *The Times Digital Archive*. Web. 26 September 2015.
Seaton, A. V. (2001). In the footsteps of Acerbi: Metempsychosis and the repeated journey. In E. Jarva, M. Mäkivuoti, & T. Sironen (Eds.), *Tutkimusmatkalla Pohjoisseen, Acta Universitatis Ouliensis. B40*, 121–138. Oulu: Oulu University Press.
Seaton, A. V. (2002). Tourism as metempsychosis and metensomatosis: The personae of eternal recurrence. In G. M. S. Dann (Ed.), *The tourist as a metaphor of the social world*, 135–168. Wallingford: CABI.
Seaton, A. V. (2013). Cultivated pursuits: Cultural tourism as metempsychosis and metensomatosis. In M. Smith & G. Richards (Eds.), *The Routledge handbook of cultural tourism*, 19–27. London: Routledge.

Seaton, A. V. (2014). The unknown mother: Thanatourism and metempsychotic remembrance after World War I. In L. Sikorska (Ed.), *Of what is past, or passing, or to come: Travelling in time and space in literature in English*, Studies in Literature in English, Vol. 5. Frankfurt am Main: Peter Lang.

Storey, G. (Ed.). (1997). *The Letters of Charles Dickens, Volume Nine, 1859–1861*. The British Academy Pilgrim Edition. Oxford: Clarendon Press.

Thackeray, W. M. (1847–48). *Vanity fair*. London: Smith, Elder, & Co., 1890.

Timbs, J. (1867). *Curiosities of London*. London: John Camden Hotten.

Trollope, F. (1836). *Paris and the Parisians in 1835* (Vol. I). London: Richard Bentley.

Veyriras, P. (1982). Visiteurs Brittaniques à la Morgue de Paris au dix-neuvième siècle. *Cahiers Victoriens & Edouardiens*, No. 15 (Avril 1982), 51–61.

Vita, P. (2003). Returning the look: Victorian writers and the Paris Morgue. *Nineteenth-Century Contexts*, 25(3), 241–256.

Watson, N. J. (2008). *The literary tourist*. Basingstoke: Palgrave Macmillan.

Westover, P. (2012). *Necromanticism: Traveling to meet the dead, 1750–1860*. Basingstoke: Palgrave Macmillan.

White, J. (2007). *London in the nineteenth century*. London: Jonathan Cape.

Zola, É. (1867). *Thérèse Raquin*. Paris: Fasquelle, 1984.

4

The British Traveller and Dark Tourism in Eighteenth- and Nineteenth-Century Scandinavia and the Nordic Regions

Kathryn Walchester

Introduction

The north has, since Classical times, been regarded as a place of darkness, horror, and even hell. "The journey northward is imagined as a journey into unimaginable barbarism", notes Peter Davidson in his account of the Roman geographer Strabo (2005: 22: Fjågesund 2014). The connection between evil and the north pertained into the eighteenth century when travellers, such as Charles Boileau Elliott, were inspired to note the "death-like" aspect of Scandinavia and its northern extremes which experienced perpetual day light and darkness (1832: 66). Eighteenth- and nineteenth-century tourism to the north featured much of the same thanatopic impulses as that of other European destinations, including an interest in graveyards and funereal rituals as part of a more general account of cultural practice. Discourses around thanatouristic sites in Scandinavia and the Nordic regions also reflect popular contemporary modes such as the Gothic and accounts of national histories. However, the geography of the region had an impact on the chronology and the focus of some aspects of thanatouristic practice. The main challenge to travel to Scandinavia, Finland, and Iceland before the mid-nineteenth century was the fact that sea travel was unreliable and dangerous before steamship lines were established. Travel across the interior of many Scandinavian and northern countries was arduous because of the lack of infrastructure and difficult terrain.

K. Walchester (✉)
Liverpool John Moores University, Liverpool, UK

© The Author(s) 2018
P. R. Stone et al. (eds.), *The Palgrave Handbook of Dark Tourism Studies*,
https://doi.org/10.1057/978-1-137-47566-4_4

Thus, as a whole, tourism to the north was slower to develop than that of southern Europe. The other factor, partially connected to the first, was that a widespread interest by the British in the history, culture, and literature of the north did not become fully established until the latter part of the nineteenth century, compared to the culture of Italy and Greece, where an interest in the classics had been evident from the beginning of the eighteenth century. In the middle of the nineteenth century prompted by newly established steamship routes to transport emigrating Scandinavians to America, there was a considerable increase in the numbers of British travellers visiting the region. Many more middle-class travellers made the journey, and among them were significant numbers of women. Following the region's success in attracting travellers for sport tourism, to hunt and to fish in the first part of the century, a number of large hotels had been built on the Scandinavian Peninsula to accommodate travellers, and an infrastructure of steamships across its fjords and railways was established. Later in the period, travellers began to focus in greater numbers on the region's culture and history in their writing, inspired by the translation of sagas in Britain and extensive archaeological work, such as that conducted by Hjalmar Stolpe on the Viking centre of Birka near to Stockholm. The geographical focus of this chapter extends beyond the Scandinavian Peninsula, referring out to travel literature which addresses Iceland, Denmark, and Finland (see Hall et al. 2009: 3–4). Travel to Iceland saw a similar, if slightly delayed, pattern of that to Scandinavia, with a concentration of travelogues produced in the 1860s and 1870s, which focused on the effects of volcanic eruptions and the sites of Viking sagas (Burton 1875; Hare 1885; Morris 1911).

Thanatouristic accounts of Scandinavia and Nordic regions by British travellers therefore trace a modified trajectory to those identified in other parts of Europe in which this "minor tourist form" developed in parallel and overlapping course with Romanticism (Seaton 1996: 243; Sharpley and Stone 2009). From the mid-eighteenth until the end of the nineteenth century, travellers' accounts of Scandinavia largely featured accounts of its natural beauty and positive effects on health and well-being (Barton 1998; Fjågesund and Symes 2003; Walchester 2014). However, alongside this dominant discourse, there ran a dark contraposition. Prompted by a Romantic predisposition to the sublime and the Gothic, eighteenth-century travellers to Scandinavia visited sites of famous battles and burial, often to engage in secular pilgrimage (Seaton 1996; Ryan 2007; Butler and Suntikul 2012). Particularly popular was Fredrikshald which saw the fall in 1718 of Charles XII of Sweden and allowed travellers to speculate on the mysterious circumstances of his death in battle. This chapter considers the writing by British travellers about the Scandinavian Peninsula and Iceland in terms of three main areas: visits to the death sites, tombs, and memorials associated with Scandinavian monarchs, most particularly Charles XII; general accounts of cemeteries and funereal practice; and accounts of ancient burial sites and places associated with the dark aspects of Viking sagas.

The Mystery of Charles XII's Death: Scandinavian Memorials and History

In early accounts, thanatouristic practices centre on Scandinavian history and provide prompts for their authors' discussions of kings and leaders of the region. As Stephen Bann has argued, the Romantic period saw new understandings of the history, and a "widespread and popular cult of the past" emerged (Bann 1995: 107). Thus, the extensive accounts and genealogical tables in travelogues such as those by William Coxe and Edward Daniel Clarke may be understood in terms of their contribution to a wider movement, which was attempting to configure a version of the foundations of modern Britain. The dominant mode of discussion of Scandinavian thanatouristic sites from the late eighteenth century is exemplified by William Coxe's description of Halden, the site of the murder of Charles XII of Sweden in 1718. Coxe (1747–1828), the son of the physician to the Royal Household, travelled extensively in northern Europe in 1784 (Fjågesund and Symes 2003: 22). His influential account informed the style of several subsequent accounts and is referenced in the travelogues of Wollstonecraft (1796) and Clarke (1823). Taking Voltaire's appellation of Charles as "the northern lion, as he is sometimes titled", Coxe's meticulous account of his visit to Halden is centred on his search for "complete information concerning the probable cause of the king's death", in particular, whether he was shot by his enemy or, as some contemporary commentators such as Mottraye and Voltaire speculated, by one of his own troops (Voltaire 1731: 190; Coxe 1792: 25, 27). The travelogue includes a script of his interview with 96-year-old Benk Enkelson, who had been a gunner in the Danish garrison, which leads Coxe to conclude accounts of Charles's assassination by his own troops to be "merely vague anecdotes and uncertain conjectures" and that he was killed by a small shot from the enemy positions (29). Coxe's motivation in visiting the exact spot of Charles's death therefore is that it allows him a privileged epistemological position, evaluating and confirming recent Swedish history. His writing does not feature reflections on mortality or expressions of emotive engagement with Charles's story or the way in which the site informs his own response; his primary focus is establishing an authoritative perspective. Although expressing less laudatory views of the monarch and not concerned with the details of his death, Mary Wollstonecraft also writes of her brief visit to Halden and its association for her with Charles. She notes:

> Arriving at Halden, at the siege of which Charles XII lost his life, we had only time to take a transient view of it, whilst they were preparing us some refreshment. Poor Charles! I thought of him with respect. (Wollstonecraft 1796: 95)

Wollstonecraft had certainly read Coxe's account, citing his account of the snow on the mountains around Christiania in Letter 13 (Wollstonecraft 1796: 195). However, she does not concur with Coxe's opinions of the monarch; despite her expressions of sadness about his death, she notes the effect of heavy taxation to fund his military campaigns on the people of Sweden in Letter 3 and does not enter into discussion about the circumstances of his death.

In the early nineteenth century, Halden became a "sacralised sight", according to the term outlined by Seaton, as so many visitors such as Edward Daniel Clarke and Henry Inglis, perhaps prompted by Coxe's investigations, also concerned themselves with the mystery and were driven to visit the site and some to write poetry, such as Bishop Esaias Tegnér's 1818 poem "Charles XII on the Centenary of his Death" (Seaton in Atkinson: 1999: 140). In 1829, Inglis, under the pseudonym Derwent Conway, discusses the uncertainty around the events of the king's death. Inglis notes that "it is a matter of dispute to this day, whether Charles XII was killed by a shot from one of the enemy's batteries, or from some outwork of which his own troops had possession; the latter opinion I found to be the more common tradition here". After his own examination of the site, Inglis concludes that "the tradition may be true" (1829: 276). As late as 1862, Horace Marryat alluded to the continued uncertainty around the king's death. His account of Halden included a long section describing the latest exhumation of Charles XII's body, giving typically gory descriptions of that alongside the previous examinations of the body, before concluding:

> That suspicions were aroused in the mind of Charles's surgeon is evident. The arguments of the learned men who examined the king's body may be unanswerable; but why, if proof is so positive, must the site of the murder be changed only a few weeks previous to the installation of a monument erected by the Swedish army to his memory? (1862: 193)

Marryat's apparent irritation with the continuation of speculation about Charles's death is a rhetorical strategy which permits him further discussion of the thanatopic details. Although many subsequent travellers visited the site of Charles's death, fewer travel writers expressed interested in solving the mystery of his death, in spite of the intrigue never having been completely resolved (Nordling 1998).

Accounts of the sites associated with the death of Charles XII during the early part of the nineteenth century indicate a move from such intellectual or reasoned accounts of his death with an attempt to establish verifiable details, as in Coxe's travel writing, to more physical accounts of the death site. Edward Daniel Clarke's travelogue, first published in 1810, and describing his travels with Thomas Malthus, William Otter, and a young pupil, John Martens Cripps, in 1799, indicates a transition between these two modes (Fjågesund and Symes 2003: 235). Clarke's travelogue describes the continued speculation around Charles XII's death as well as a very detailed account of the circumstances of the assassination of King Gustav III in 1792 but includes much more physical and sensorial detail of the experience of visiting the sites associated with death than earlier texts had done. In a similar way to William Coxe's discussion and interest in the death of Charles XII, Clarke engages with several aspects and sites associated with Gustav III's death in Stockholm. Gustav III had died in March 1792 after being shot by political opponents; he had begun a campaign to unite European monarchs against the Revolution in France.

Clarke writes of going to see the site in the Swedish capital where the king was shot outside the opera house, visiting a wax image of him, in addition to seeing a display of the clothes in which he died in Stockholm's Royal Armoury, where they are still exhibited (1823: 158). He details the shirt "covered with blood" and the "holes made in the sash and jacket". He notes that "even the napkin and rags which were hastily collected at the time of his assassination [...] were carefully preserved" and that "the nails, the knife, and other articles taken from the king's body" were "exhibited to us" (158). The proximity of Gustav's death is also highlighted by the fact that, like Coxe, Clarke is able to make "some inquiry of persons who had been eye-witnesses of all that passed upon the occasion, as to the behaviour of the king, when he found that the wound he had received was mortal" (159). Gustav's assassination was only eight years before Clarke's visit and its rawness resonates in his text through the details of artefacts preserved from the king and the reverence with which they are regarded. Clarke's travelogue, as well as containing a sketch of the accused assassin, Ankarström, chained to a post, includes considerable detail of his public flogging, display, and execution. Writing of the support shown by some for Gustav's murderer, Clarke concludes by making reference to the Revolution in France:

> That such an act of cruelty and cowardice should have met with its admirers would have been indeed incredible, had not the after-events, in the years

subsequent to this transaction, proved that there are no deeds of bloodshed and horror which mankind will not tolerate, when instigated by revolutionary persons. (158)

Clarke's visit to the sites and artefacts of Gustav III's death resonate within his travelogue because of both the proximity of the incident and ensuing events in Revolutionary France. Mark Davies suggests that for nineteenth-century travellers to Sweden, the artefacts presented for visitors a way of thinking about the current state of the nation in addition to its history. He asserts that it "offered history-evoking tombs and trophies; a suitable setting for discourse on royal reputations, and Sweden's *present* condition" (2000: 87). Clarke's visit to these thanatouristic displays allows him to consider not only the state of society in Sweden, and furthermore the horrific events further afield in Europe. His investigation about the circumstances of King Gustav's assassination indicates a similarity to Coxe's approach but also illustrates a move towards a more physical and emotional engagement with the sites of thanatouristic interest.

Clarke's engagement with the physical reminders of Charles XII's death also occurs at Riddarholm Church in Stockholm, at Charles's grave rather than at the site of his death. Clarke describes how the coffin has been recently opened, "by order of the young King [Gustav IV]" who, Clarke speculates, wanted to examine the injuries to the skull, which might offer clues to the nature, size, and direction of the fatal shot (1823: 227). In the absence of eye-witness accounts, Clarke's testimony foregrounds his proximity to the coffin:

> The coffin, meanwhile, was exposed to view; it was covered with crimson velvet, and adorned with gold fringe. We observed that it was still in as perfect preservation as when the burial took place; the fringe being so strong, that we had difficulty in pulling off a few threads to bear away as a memorial. Some of the party present complained of an unpleasant odour coming from this coffin; but we considered it as imaginary, the sepulchre having been some time open, and the coffin carefully closed immediately after the King's visit. (1823: 227)

Clarke prioritises the sensorial details and the presence of the coffin over the intellectual debate about the circumstances of the king's death. He and his party are prompted to gather a souvenir of their encounter, despite having to deface the cloth which covered the coffin. The emphasis on the physical, in this case of having actually seen Charles's coffin and retained a piece of cloth which had touched it, is an important element of the thanatouristic experience in Scandinavia during the Romantic period.

Travellers continued to be fascinated by the physical reminders of Charles's death into the nineteenth century, particularly by his grave in Stockholm and the marker of his death at Halden. For Charles Boileau Elliott, travelling in 1830, the marble stone, against which Charles was leaning when he was shot, becomes the conduit between the past and present. He writes:

> This block, rudely chiselled, now forms his monumental stone. Conscience has since smitten me for bringing away a piece of it; for if every traveller did the same, Charles would be left without a local memorial. (Elliott 1832: 89)

Elliott's succinct description of Charles's death does not allude to its surrounding intrigue as Coxe had done, noting simply, "he was leaning on a block of marble when a shot struck his head" (Elliott 1832: 89). Elliott's response to the site of death, motivated to take some part as memento, recalls Clarke's removal of the fringing from the cover of Charles's coffin. Elliott worries about the effects—that there would no longer be a monument if all travellers did the same—but cannot resist. Seeing the clothes worn by Charles at the time of his death, Elliott discusses the significance to him of such material reminders of the past:

> The clothes are exhibited in which the first of these great kings and warriors was shot at Frederickstein. From that place I carried away a portion of rock on which he leaned at the moment, and which now forms his monumental stone. Historical associations of this kind are peculiarly dear to me. They are fraught with classical interest, without carrying the mind back to periods where she is lost in the wide expanse of the past. (224–5)

Elliott's appreciation recalls the Romantic fascination with objects of art, which, as Kenneth S. Calhoon notes, are "ultimately the most poignant reminder of human mortality", but his interest is those reminders of the near past, which the mind can grasp, and not in any terrifying spans into antiquity (Calhoon 1987: 5).

Accounts such as Clarke's discussion of visiting and taking artefacts associated with Charles XII's death indicate a growing tourist interest in the material memorials of death by visitors during the period. Although, as Seaton has argued, thanatouristic practice has a long history, and visitors have always been motivated to take objects from sacralised sites, eighteenth- and nineteenth-century accounts of visits to Scandinavia indicate a shift from largely intellectual engagements with thanatouristic sites to a greater focus on the material and physical environment (Seaton 1999: 131). In the case of the sites of the assassinations of Charles XII and Gustav III in 1718 and 1792, respectively, the interest in objects signifying or associated with their deaths grew as time passed. This increased significance of the material object in the imaginings and constructions of the past which developed during the Romantic period has been noted by Stephen Bann and Stuart Semmel (Bann 1995; Semmel 2000). Semmel, in his account of nineteenth-century tourism to the site of the Battle of Waterloo, notes how "the tangible has often been enlisted as a window onto the all too intangible past" (Semmel 2000: 29). In his account of war and tourism in the nineteenth century, John K. Walton identifies "souvenir-hunters" as one of the types of visitors who came to Waterloo to see where "history had been made" (Walton in Butler and Suntikul 2012: 70; Singh 1998).

Romantic literary language and imagery of the Gothic informs the accounts of many visitors to the memorials of the Swedish kings, Charles XII, Gustav III, and Eric XIV. In their accounts of the memorials to Charles XII, John Barrow describes the "elegant sarcophagus of black marble, at the foot of which is suspended the sword which he was in the habit of wearing in battle" at the Riddarholm Church in his travel account from 1834 (154), and Isabella Blundell in her 1862 travelogue, *Gamle Norge*, describes how "a few stones piled together, serve to commemorate" the fall of the "Swedish hero" (1862: 242). The rustic memorial incited the imaginative response of a number of travellers such as Henry Inglis, who notes:

> Whatever may have been the merits of Charles XII., as a captain, or however much "the Swede" deserves to be coupled with "Macedonia's madman", there is something so romantic in the character and career of Charles, that we are more apt to regard him in the light of a hero of romance than as a mere warrior. (1829: 276)

Inglis indicates that he has been caught in what he calls the "romance", noting that "it was nearly dark before I left the fortress in search of the inn". He continues:

> When I stood within the shade of the cypress trees, that wave over the simple record of his fall, I could not help catching a portion of that enthusiasm that was once so kindled within him, and which is irresistibly associated with the spot where it was quenched forever. (1829: 276)

Charles Boileau Elliott's Romantic account of Fredrikshald likewise focuses on the natural elements of the site, which inspire an emotional reaction. The account of the site is introduced in terms of its picturesque landscape:

On the left, in the foreground, the Glomen rushes violently down a precipice in three successive cataracts; being hidden from the view, before the waves have regained a tranquil state, by a forest rising on the projecting angle of a chain of hills; in the distance, through a defile of woody mountains, we overlooked a fiord, at the extremity of which the tower of Frederickshall is seen in miniature, with a background of dark green forests on the heights above. (Elliott 1832: 88)

Elliott's account evokes the accounts of landscapes from the Gothic novels by writers such as Ann Radcliffe in the 1790s, which anticipated scenes of kidnap and imprisonment and murder. Instead, Elliott's description of Halden precedes his account of the death of Charles XII, "the fall of Sweden's glory" (1832: 88).

Cemetery Visits and Funereal Practices

Alongside the visits to sites of thanatouristic interest specific to Scandinavia, travellers to the northern regions, like eighteenth- and nineteenth-century travellers to other parts, often included accounts of their local funereal practices as part of more general quasi-anthropological descriptions. In his analysis of thanatouristic practices on the Tiwi Islands in Northern Australia, anthropologist Eric Venbrux proposes that "Cemeteries and mortuary rites of indigenous people have become tourist attractions" and suggests the similarities between anthropologists and tourists, "anthropologists may be regarded as cultural tourists *par excellence*, seeking to gain insight into what makes other people tick" (2010: 42). Even before the eighteenth century, visits to cemeteries by travellers had, as Seaton has shown, been established for several centuries—its roots being in the mediaeval pilgrimage (Seaton 2002: 73; Lennon and Foley 2000: 3; Lickorish and Jenkins 1997). Travellers to Scandinavia in the late eighteenth and early nineteenth centuries were no less fascinated by local cemeteries as indicators of cultural practices and beliefs. As Huntington suggests, "the issue of death throws into relief the most important cultural values by which people live their lives and evaluate their experiences" (1991: 25).

In their visits to Scandinavian graveyards, British travellers frequently noted differences from funereal practices at home, such as the tradition of leaving a likeness of the deceased above their grave. Edward Daniel Clarke and his party's visit to the tombs in the cathedral at Uppsala at the turn of the nineteenth century is an early example of this. He writes how "A custom is observed, which we also noticed in some of the churches in Denmark, of placing a deceased person's portrait over his tomb" (1823: 145). As in other observations of cultural practice, travellers were often quick to extrapolate and generalise about death rituals; Charles Henry Scott, in his account of a mid-nineteenth-century trip to Denmark, noted:

> We wandered through the cemetery outside the town; it was in good order, but we were astonished to see in the adjoining grave to an open one, coffin after coffin piled up within a foot of the surface [...] supposing this to be the usual arrangement – there must exist a great mass of coffins having scarcely any earth between or above them. (1856: 7)

Later in the century, Robert Anderton Naylor gives an extensive account of his party's tour of the sites in Kalmar in Sweden, including their explorations of the cemetery. His observations contradicted those of Scott in Denmark as he notes that "the inhabitants have patches of ground, say fifteen feet square, with well-kept fences round. The reason assigned for having so much space is that the authorities will only permit one person to be interred in the same grave" (1884: 28). He describes the custom of "placing on the tombs of friends bows of ribbon, with some choice sentiment printed thereon" as well as noting that "on the inscriptions you don't notice the words born or died, as in England, but a star and a cross to denote the birth and decease" (1884: 28). In the following chapter, Naylor reflects further on the impressions of the graveyard at Kalmar; the memories of the walk evidently linger in Naylor's mind more prominently than those of its other sites. He describes how "We might have some lingering thoughts of our ramble among the tombs of the departed, as they remind us, amid the pleasures of the present, of our own mortality" (1884: 34). His conclusions are positive though, remembering the flowers, ribbons, and well-kept graves as "all proofs that though dead yet not forgotten", and he cites Thomas Campbell's famous poem from 1825, "Hallowed Ground", "For to live in hearts we leave behind is not to die" (1839: 38).

Travelling to the Scandinavian Peninsula in the middle of the century, Charles Henry Scott's visit to a burial site also prompts repeated contemplations of mortality. However, rather than being explored through a discourse of cultural comparison, Scott's emphasis indicates a profound engagement with the conventions of the Gothic during his visit to the cathedral of Odense in Denmark in order to visit the grave of Canute or Knud IV. The view of the bodies through the glass lids incites reflections on mortality which is both personal and then directed more generally by the narrator:

> In a small chapel in the cathedral, side by side, are two coffins with glass lids, through which we looked upon the mouldering bones of Canute and Benedict [his brother]. "To this complexion we must come at last", we mentally ejaculated, and turned to examine some other interesting monuments. (1856: 53)

On his visit to Stockholm, it is the armour belonging to the former Swedish monarch which excites a rush of morbid thoughts. When the traveller sees the altar, he is aware of:

> …moving within the precincts of a huge sepulchre. Then one remarks the rigid stillness of the chevaliers, and finds each a suit of armour that once encased the body of a King, now serving only to cover a figure made of rubbish; that each helmet, now concealing but a block of wood, once held a royal brain, whence emanated thoughts and plans that stirred up passions, to quench the fire of which required the blood of victim thousands. Where are now those fiery brains, those stalwart bodies? Ah, poor mortality! They rot and moulder in the crypts beneath our feet, as worthless as the very blocks and rubbish that here constitute their effigies. (1856: 301–2)

Scott's response indicates a rather belated use of the language and style of the Gothic novel from over half a century. However, Scott's effusive emphasis on symbols and images of death is seen in a number of travel texts from the mid-century. Horace Marryat's 1862 *One Year in Sweden; including a visit to the Isle of Götland* is a particularly extreme example of extensive recourse to Gothic imagery and conventions. In addition to his account of the exhumation of Charles XII, mentioned earlier, his text abounds with gruesome artefacts and stories regarding his sojourn in Sweden and later trip to Norway, including an account of the exhumation of two women at Malmö, who were discovered to have three large toads sat on each of their corpses, to signal protest that the terms of the women's will had been ignored, a description of a mummified hand, a Viking burial site, and the viewing of Descartes's skull at Lund (1862: 7, 11, 54, 157). The Gothic highlight of his trip, however, is the death of the Catholic Dowager Queen of Sweden, Desideria, in December 1860:

> We saw Queen Desideria lie in state, her body exposed upon a "castrum doloris". The vast hall was hung with black cloth powdered in gold crowns, and many thousand lights burning; around her state ladies and others high in office, clad in deep mourning robes, with long black veils. (1862: 452)

Marryat's description of the unusual circumstances of the eccentric queen's death—she had arrived in the royal box at the opera just as the performance had ended before returning home to die—comes in the final section of the text. Ultimately however Marryat's is not a reverent appreciation of the thanatouristic elements of Sweden. In his concluding comments, Marryat accounts for the contents of his travelogue. He begins by ventriloquising a fictional version of one of his critics:

> A very trifling foolish book – all about necks, hobgoblins, bad kings" cries good Mrs. Squaretoes, wife of the—reviewer, who reads for her husband—"with not one word of politics, statistics, hospitals (foundling, no doubt). Then, too, the morals of the people—when we k-n-o-w how the men drink and the women—h-o-r-r-i-d!
> Books of travels are not literature, but "ephemerides" – things of the day to read and throw by. (1862: 460)

According to Marryat, superstition, stories, and the supernatural, although not conventionally considered a valid part of travel writing, should be included in it, albeit to be discarded before long.

Viking Sagas and Sites

The main thanatopic focus in the north for British travellers from the mid-nineteenth century was those sites associated with chivalry, warfare, and most particular Viking sagas (Holman 2007; Richards 2005; Smith 1998). In the preface to *The Danes and the Swedes* from 1856, Scott draws attention to what was to become the dominant view of Scandinavia:

> There is a wild romance about the history of these Northern regions that rivals even those thrilling annals of the East to which so many readers fly for excitement or amusement. Indeed no countries are richer in stirring legends, in heroic actions, in tragic deeds, than Denmark and Sweden. (Scott 1856: vi)

As Burchardt, among others, has argued, interest in Norse subjects and history in Britain was "intimately bound up with the Romantic movement, and though it was an outcome and not the origin of that movement, it had a considerable power in inspiring and accelerating its development" (1974:80; Fjågesund and Symes 2003: 42; Barton 2007: 28). The second half of the nineteenth century saw an increased intellectual and cultural interest in Icelandic and Scandinavian history prompted by the excavation of Viking sites on the shores of the Christiania Fjord and the burial mounds at Uppsala in Sweden and the translation of sagas, such as George Stephen's 1839 translation of Bishop Esaias Tegnér's *Frithiof's Saga: A Legend of Ancient Norway*, Samuel Laing's 1844 *The Heimskringla; or, Chronicle of the Kings of Norway*, and George Dasent's 1861 translation of *Njál's Saga*.

Sites of ancient burial in Scandinavia had not always inspired enthusiastic responses. Although aware of the potential thanatopic significance of the mounds at Uppsala, noting that "tradition has assigned to the bodies of *Odin, Frigga*, and *Thor*", Edward Daniel Clarke and his party do not stop to visit them (Clarke 1823: 214). Clarke's emphasis is on the uncertainty around the tumuli and Scandinavian history more generally, as if to exonerate his own ignorance of the importance of these landmarks:

> A little time spent upon the spot may hereafter enable some curious travellers to ascertain the real nature of these *tumuli*. If they should be proved to be places of burial, there is little probability of their having been constructed by the ancestors of the present race of Swedes, who in the period when such mounds were raised over the dead in the north of Europe were not inhabitants of *Sweden*. (1823: 215)

Bror Emil Hildebrand began the excavations of the mounds at Uppsala in 1846, but even after the discoveries, all travellers did not regard them with interest. In her 1853 account *Life in Sweden*, Irish traveller Selina Bunbury is unenthusiastic about her visit to the recently excavated mound:

> It is now a poor village, lying among great green mounds, which are supposed to be each an ättenhög or tomb of the old pagan kings and deities. One of them has been excavated. I penetrated into it, and the professor who brought me there told me I saw an urn within the railing, which is put up to defend the tomb, supposed to be, I think, that by Odin; but I found the sunshine on top of it pleasanter. (1853: 308)

Bunbury is, like a number of travellers in the early part of the period, attracted by the customs and landscape of the northern regions rather than by its ancient history. She has been brought by the professor, rather than by her own interest and makes no reflections on its significance.

More generally however, in the second half of the nineteenth century, ancient thanatouristic sites inspired British travellers to visit Scandinavia and Iceland. The sites became concomitant in Britain's construction of its past, that is, through a re-narrativising of British history in which Britain was seen to have been developed from Viking heritage. The former Viking inhabitants of Norway, Iceland, and Finland were often regarded as "forefathers" to the

British, particularly inspiring and underpinning their own imperial efforts (Fjågesund and Symes 2003: 137). In this case, accounts of thanatourism indicate contemporary cultural and national concerns, in addition to foregrounding particular authoritative historical narratives and personalised reflections on mortality as earlier encounters had done.

Writing about her 1881 trip to Norway accompanied by her husband John, Olivia Stone makes much of her visit to the "lately excavated" Viking longboat in Christiania at the university. The ships buried at Tune and Gokstad in Norway were extensive sites of human burial—the ship at Gokstad, for example, being 24 metres long and 5 metres wide (Fjågesund and Symes 2003: 139). In her seminal text on death rituals in the Viking culture, Hilda Roderick Ellis speculates that the Gokstad ship might have been the grave of Olaf of Geirstaðr who died in his 50s in about AD 840 (Ellis 1943: 19). Stone expresses disappointment with the condition of the first ship she sees, but then, realising that this had been the ship excavated at Tune in 1867, describes in much more detail the Gokstad ship, which she asserts is "in an almost perfect state of preservation" (4):

> What a curious thrill passes through one when standing face to face with armour or weapons that have been used by our species in the past ages! Notably does this feeling overwhelm one in the Tower of London. We wish this or that helmet would speak, and we fancy if only a visor were raised we should see a countenance beneath. We touch shrinkingly the sword-hilt which a hand, now mouldered into dust, once grasped firmly. With a similar feeling – but ten times intensified – we stood beside the Viking ship. Not only were we awe-struck by its form and workmanship, but the past warriors filled it from beam to beam; the forms of our – in part, at least – progenitors flitted ghost-like over the planks; hardy sailors manned the oars. What were they like, who were they, these bold Creek-men, our piratical ancestors? Long, long before the relics of the Tower, they lived and moved, fought and died. (4)

Stone's viewing of the ship encourages her to reflect not only on her own mortality and the passing of time, it also prompts her comparison between ways of living in the times of the Vikings and those of her own experience. She compares the standard of boat-building, concluding that "there are several points in the build of this galley which would indicate that retrogression rather than progression may have actually taken place" (4). Stone's concerns about regression, in the standards of boat-building at least, hint at other wider, fin-de-siècle fears of the cultural and physical degeneration of the British population. These concerns were played out in some fiction of the period, which featured inter-national marriages between British and Norwegians, such as

Marie Corelli's *Thelma* (1887) and *A Hardy Norseman* by Edna Lyall (1889). Having considered both the contents and the workmanship of the longboat, Stone turns to its Viking travellers and concludes, "England would not now be at the head of the nations had not her sons inherited the blood of these Vikings" (5).

Icelandic sites also featured in Victorian travelogues anxieties about degeneration in Britain. Andrew Wawn in *The Vikings and the Victorians* notes that "While several Victorian travellers worry about the faded glory of Iceland, one or two of them even dare to reflect on the possibility of future decline in Britain" (2000: 299). In his account of the travel writing of Sabine Baring-Gould, Wawn notes that "Baring-Gould believes that engagement with the old north, whether in travel book, novel or saga translation, can arrest the onset of such degeneracy" (2000: 299). Emblematic in his fascination with the region of a number of British intellectuals such as Charles Stuart Forbes, Lord Dufferin, Frederick Metcalfe, and S.E. Waller, Reverend Sabine Baring-Gould travelled to Iceland in the early 1860s, and with interest in travel, he was an avid collector of folktales and traditional stories (Dufferin 1857; Forbes 1860; Metcalfe 1856; 1858; 1861; Baring-Gould 1863; Colloms 2004). The following decade was to bring more attention to the region as William Morris, Anthony Trollope, and Richard Burton visited the country, and a subsequent wealth of saga recounts, poetry, and observations on the history and nature were published (Seaton in Atkinson 1989: xxvii; Chapman 1897; Burton 1875; Hare 1885; Morris 1911). Where accounts from the turn of the century, such as those by George Atkinson and Andrew Swinton, had focused on the geography, geology, and social customs of the region, travelogues featuring Iceland from the latter part of the nineteenth century highlighted the influence and settings of the sagas, a large number of which had thanatopic elements (for example Everest 1829). For example, Charles Forbes's text features considerable emphasis on extracts from Walter Scott's *Abstract of the Eyrbiggia Saga*, which had been reprinted as part of Mallet's *Northern Antiquities* in 1847, and S.E. Waller's 1874 *Six Weeks in the Saddle* exclaimed that he was "wild to visit the scene of such a tremendous tragedy" after being inspired by *Njál's Saga* (Forbes 1860; Waller 1874: 1).

Sabine Baring-Gould's appreciation of the thanatopic aspect of Viking stories is manifest in his 1863 account, *Iceland: Its Scenes and Sagas*. His travelogue features *The Story of Burnt Njal*, which had been translated in 1861 to critical acclaim, and Grettir's saga, the retelling of which forms the structure of his travelogue (Dasent 1861). Although the text is built around a series of stories from the saga featuring deaths and battles, Baring-Gould's most vivid engagement with thanatopsis is when the party is travelling towards Vatnsdalr and encounters the grave of Glámr the vampire, who was slain by Grettir.

Baring-Gould was to republish this story in *A Book of Ghosts* in 1904. The Icelandic landscape introduces the thanatopic elements of the site:

> As I stand by the cairn, the wind soughs up from the north, lashing the viscous pool into ripples, rustling among the reeds, humming with a strange mournful note through the crevices of the dead man's home, then rolls onward, to furrow the snows on Eiriks jökull. (1863: 116)

When asked to retell the story of the vampire's death by one of his party members, Baring-Gould replies melodramatically, "You shall hear, but if you get the blue-devils by listening to my story, blame your own inquisitiveness" (116). Thus, employing a common feature of the Gothic novel, the reader of the travelogue becomes voyeur to Baring-Gould's story-telling. Although, as Ellis notes, the figure of the draugr or vampire is "impressively drawn" in Grettir's saga, it is a recurring feature in the Icelandic sagas (Ellis 1943: 93). Mrs. Mary Disney Leith's numerous trips to Iceland at the end of the century were similarly informed by the sagas. In "Farewell", a poem written after her first trip to Iceland in the early 1890s, she appeals to the country, "Wilt teach me thy praises to utter, /With heart by thy sagas beguiled" (Leith 1895: 49). Her subsequent travel text featured visits to the dark sites of the sagas, such as Vatnsdalr, and its appendix included a poem "Gunnar's Holm" by Jonas Hallgrimsson from *Njáls Saga* (Leith 1897).

There were challenges particular to the exploration of thanatouristic sites in Iceland, however. The most evidence of these was the island's volcanic landscape. Baring-Gould notes the difficulty of the terrain for themselves and their ponies, describing how:

> Lava is always rock in ruin, never picturesque, always horrible: for during its flow gases generated in its fiery womb have exploded, shivering its whole mass, tilting the sides of these domes into the air with their jagged edges exposed, and blowing snags and splinters into cairn-like heaps all around. (1863: 103)

Earlier in the century, George Clayton Atkinson's account of 1833 had also described the arduous travelling for the ponies (Atkinson 1989: 107). Likewise, Charles Forbes notes Iceland's inhospitable landscape, both for residents and visitors. He describes, "Two tracks across this desert serve for communication between north and south; but not a blade of grass or shrub exists in that death-like solitude – lava, lava, lava, is the eternal vista" (1860: 24–5). Travellers were often frustrated in their attempts to visit relics of saga sites because of the results of Iceland's destructive landscape. As Wawn asserts,

"There is often the sense with Baring-Gould that the real Viking- and saga-age relics were forever just evading his grasp, as they decay, collapse, or are buried under lava shortly before his arrival" (299).

Whilst descriptions by travellers to Iceland could not often feature tangible reminders of its Viking past, their accounts instead offer extended accounts of dark Norse mythology set in the barren, lava-ruined vistas as well as detailed accounts of the fatalities caused by the volcanoes. Charles Forbes writes in detail of the eruptions of several volcanoes, but in most detail, that of Skaptar Jokull in 1783. In apocalyptic terms, Forbes describes how:

> Vast columns of smoke arose in the vicinity of the yökul, ashes and pumice were borne down in showers on the strong north gale, and immense quantities of ice were melted, causing rivers to overflow their banks. Two days afterwards the eruption burst forth with an infernal fury which seemed to threaten the end of all things. (1860: 287)

Forbes's account continues detailing the terrifying ordeal of the Icelanders, who were "enveloped in almost total darkness by the clouds of smoke and ashes, and half-suffocated by the noxious gases emitted" until the volcano erupted in earnest and they were "actually unearthed by fiery or boiling floods" (1860: 287). "Escape was almost impossible", he adds.

The landscape around Skaptar Jokull also impelled Lord Dufferin to break with the largely flippant tone of his 1857 travelogue, *Letters from High Latitudes*. His description of the impact of the Skaptar Jokull volcano eruption highlights its devastating effects at length, using statistics from Magnus Stephensen to underline its human and animal cost. Stephensen's account had been published as an appendix to William Jackson Hooker's travelogue about his tour of Iceland in 1809. Dufferin notes that:

> For a whole year a canopy of cinder-laden cloud hung over the island [...] Mephitic vapours tainted the atmosphere of the entire island; – even the grass, which no cinder rain had stifled completely withered up; – the fish perished in the poisoned sea. A murrain broke out among the cattle, and a disease resembling scurvy attacked the inhabitants themselves. Stephenson [sic] has calculated that 9,000 men, 28,000 horses, 11,000 cattle, 190,000 sheep died from the effects of this one eruption. (1857: 66)

Dufferin's listing of the effects and his central use of Stephensen's account, in contrast to its earlier peripheral inclusion, draws attention to an increased interest in the details of the human tragedy rather than merely the geological. Mrs. Alec Tweedie, in *A Girl's Ride in Iceland* from 1889, notes that the eruption of Skaptar Jokull "is chronicled in all works on Iceland" (1889: 151).

In addition to the volcanoes, the frozen landscape of the far north allowed for other striking encounters with death for travellers. Arriving on Spitzbergen on their return journey, the dread expressed by Dufferin's melancholy manservant, Wilson, who was "ever prepared for the worst", is evidently justified (1857: 166). Pulling in at English Bay, Dufferin observes an open coffin containing a skeleton:

> Half-imbedded in the black moss at his feet, there lay a grey deal coffin falling almost to pieces with age; the lid was gone – blown off probably by the wind – and within were stretched the bleaching bones of a human skeleton. A rude cross at the head of the grave still stood partially upright, and a half obliterated Dutch inscription preserved a record of the dead man's name and age [...] It was evidently some poor whaler of the last century to whom his companions had given the only burial possible in this frost-hardened earth, which even the summer sun has no strength to penetrate beyond a couple of inches, and which will not afford to man the shallowest grave. (1857: 174–5)

Despite the bleakness of this scene, Dufferin is not prompted to consider his own mortality. Rather, having offered the prosaic explanation for the presence of the cadaver on the beach, he cites Norse mythology, recounting the words of the Vala to Odin in Niflheim. Furthermore, Dufferin goes on to highlight the difference between himself and the skeleton asserting:

> It was no brother mortal that lay at our feet, softly folded in the embraces of 'Mother Earth', but a poor scarecrow, gibbeted for ages on this bare rock, like a dead Prometheus; the vulture, frost, gnawing forever on his bleaching relics, and yet eternally preserving them! (1857: 175)

Once more Dufferin presents his vision of death in mythological terms, and using the florid literary language of his account, he distances himself from the dead man. Dufferin notes that Magdalena Bay contains the bodies of men who died "upwards of 250 years ago, in such complete preservation that, when you pour hot water on the icy coating which encases them, you can actually see the unchanged features of the dead" (1857: 175). The frozen north of Spitzbergen then provides a freakish display of death for Dufferin and his party, but not one to which he can relate or which inspires reflection, rather one which becomes a Gothic spectacle.

From the beginning of the century, the most popular site on Iceland for tourists to visit was that of the Icelandic assembly at Thingvellir. A place of law-making and trials, it was adopted as thanatopic element of many tours. On his tour with Sir Henry Holland, George Mackenzie visited Thingvellir, and in his account of the assembly, he dwells on the darker aspects of the site, describing the punishments meted on those found guilty, including "those culprits who were condemned to die, were beheaded on a small island in the river Oxeraa", and notes that "the females were drowned in a deep pool below the lava" (1811: 208). Later in the century, other accounts embellished the details, such as Dufferin's account of the Norwegian Christians who invaded Iceland in the tenth century and a description of the Althing and the "Pool of Execution" under the waterfall of Almanna Gja. Dufferin sees Iceland's past as a dark reflection of its lack of Christian belief. In typically humorous style, he notes how:

> At the foot of the fall the waters linger for a moment in the dark, deep, brimming pool, hemmed in by a circle of ruined rocks; to this pool, in ancient times all women convicted of capital crimes were immediately taken, and drowned. Witchcraft seems to have been the principal weakness of ladies in those days, throughout the Scandinavian countries. (1857: 59)

By the end of the nineteenth century, many more travellers made the journey by steamship, the number of trips rising threefold from around 10 trips per year in the 1870s to "30–35 trips per year" in 1898–1903, and the ancient sites such as Thingvellir remained an important feature in Iceland's tourist itinerary (Sæþórsdóttir et al. 2011: 263). Many more women formed a part of the tourist groups. Identifying the dark aspects of Thingvellir, Mrs Alec Tweedie, for example, having crossed Iceland with her party in 1886, observes that "our notice was likewise directed to the 'blood stone'", on which, she describes, "the criminals were condemned to have their backs broken, after which barbarous punishment they were hurled backwards and fell into the chasm below" (Tweedie 1889: 108).

Conclusion

Two main strands dominate the thanatouristic practices in Scandinavia and the Nordic regions in the eighteenth and nineteenth centuries: an early preoccupation with the construction of recent history through individual visits to the death sites of, or memorials to, Scandinavian monarchs and, secondly, later in the period, a much more widespread interest in ancient deaths, recounted in sagas and indicated by Viking burial mounds. These propensities were limited in part by the geography and geology of the regions; the Scandinavian Peninsula was mountainous with remote habitation and there was lava-strewn, rugged terrain in Iceland. Despite the particularity of thanatouristic sites and practices in the north, the travel literature which describes them is informed by and in turn contributes to other Romantic and Victorian literature, especially an interest in wild nature, the Gothic, and later the Viking sagas.

References

Atkinson, G. C. (1989) *Journal of an expedition to the Feroe and Westman Islands and Iceland 1833*. Edited and Introduced by A. V. Seaton. Newcastle upon Tyne: Bewick-Beaufort Press.
Bann, S. (1995). *Romanticism and the rise of history*. New York: Twayne.
Baring-Gould, S. (1863). *Iceland: Its scenes and sagas*. London: Smieth, Elder & Co.
Barton, H. A. (1998). *Northern Arcadia: Foreign travelers in Scandinavia 1765–1815*. Carbondale: Southern Illinois University Press.
Barton, H. A. (2007). The discovery of Norway abroad, 1760–1905. *Scandinavian Studies, 79*(1), 25–40.
Burchardt, C. B. (1974 [1920]). *Norwegian life and literature: English accounts and views, especially in the nineteenth century*. Westport: Greenwood Press.
Burton, R. (1875). *Ultima Thule; or, a summer in Iceland*. London: Nimmo.
Butler, R., & Suntikul, W. (2012). *Tourism and war*. London: Routledge.
Campbell, T. (1839). *The poetical works of Thomas Campbell*. London: Edward Moxon.
Chapman, A. (1897). *Wild Norway: With chapters on Spitsbergen, Denmark etc.* London: Edward Arnold.
Clarke, E. D. (1823). *Travels in various countries of Europe, Asia and Africa. Part the third: Scandinavia* (Vol. 6). London: T. Cadell.
Colloms, B. (2004). 'Gould, Sabine Baring – (1834–1924)', *Oxford Dictionary of National Biography*. Oxford: Oxford University Press.
Coxe, W. (1792). *Travels into Poland, Russia, Sweden and Denmark*. 5 Vols. (Vol. V, 4th ed.). London: T. Cadell.
Dasent, G. W. (1861). *Njál's Saga: The story of Burnt Njal or life in Iceland at the end of the tenth century*. Edinburgh: Edmonston and Douglas.
Davidson, P. (2005). *The idea of north*. London: Reaktion.
Dufferin, L. (1857). *Letters from high latitudes*. London: John Murray.

Elliott, C. B. (1832). *Letters from the north of Europe, or a journal of travels in Holland, Denmark, Norway, Sweden, Finland, Russia, Prussia, and Saxony*. London: Henry Colburn and Richard Bentley.

Ellis, H. R. (1943). *The road to Hel; A study of the conception of the dead in Old Norse literature*. Cambridge: Cambridge University Press.

Everest, R. (1829). *A journey through Norway, Lapland, and Sweden: With some remarks on the geology of the country; its climate and scenery; the ascent of some of its principal mountains – The present political relations of the two countries – Statistical tables, meteorological observations*. London: Thomas and George Underwood.

Fjågesund, P. (2014). *The dream of the north: A cultural history to 1920*. Amsterdam: Rodopi.

Fjågesund, P., & Symes, R. (2003). *The Northern Utopia: British perceptions of Norway in the nineteenth century*. Amsterdam: Rodopi.

Forbes, C. S. (1860). *Iceland: Its volcanoes, geysers and glaciers*. London: John Murray.

Hall, C. M., Müller, D. K., & Saarinen, J. (2009). *Nordic tourism: Issues and cases*. Bristol: Channel View.

Hare, A. J. C. (1885). *Sketches in Holland and Scandinavia*. London: Smith, Elder and Co.

Holman, K. (2007). *The northern conquest: Vikings in Britain and Ireland*. Oxford: Signal.

Inglis, H. D. [pseud. Derwent Conway]. (1829). *A Personal Narrative of a journey through Norway, Parts of Sweden and the Islands and States of Denmark*. London: Hurst, Chance and Co.

Leith, M. D. (1895). *Verses and translation*. London: J. Masters.

Leith, M. D. (1897). *Three visits to Iceland*. London: J. Masters and Co.

Lennon, J., & Foley, M. (2000). *Dark tourism: The attraction of death and disaster*. London: Continuum.

Mallet, H. P. (1847). *Northern antiquities*. London: G. Bohn.

Metcalf, P., & Huntington, R. (1991). *Celebrations of death: The anthropology of mortuary ritual*. Cambridge: Cambridge University Press.

Metcalfe, F. (1856). *The Oxonian in Norway; or notes of excursions in that country* (2nd ed., revised ed.). London: Hurst and Blackett.

Metcalfe, F. (1858). *The Oxonian in Thelemarken; or notes of travel in South-Western Norway in the summers of 1856 and 1857. With glances at the legendary lore of that district* (2 Vols.) London: Hurst and Blackett.

Morris, W. (1911). *Collected works Vol. VIII, Journal of Travels in Iceland 1871, 1873*. London: Longman, Green and Co.

Nordling, C. (1998). The death of King Charles XII – The forensic verdict. *Forensic Science International, 96*(2), 75–89.

Richards, J. D. (2005). *The Vikings: A very short introduction*. Oxford: Oxford University Press.

Ryan, C. (2007). *Battlefield tourism: History, place and interpretation*. Amsterdam/London: Elsevier.

Sæþórsdóttir, A. D. C., Hall, M., & Saarinen, J. (2011). Making wilderness: Tourism and the history of the wilderness idea in Iceland. *Polar Geography, 34*(4), 249–273.

Scott, C. H. (1856). *The Danes and the Swedes*. London: Longman, Brown, Green and Longmans.

Seaton, A. V. (1996). Guided by the dark: From thanatopsis to thanatourism. *International Journal of Heritage Studies, 2*(4), 234–244.

Seaton, A. V. (1999). War and thanatourism: Waterloo 1815–1914. *Annals of Tourism Research, 26*, 130–158.

Seaton, A. V. (2002). Thanatourism's final frontiers? Visits to cemeteries, churchyards and funerary sites as sacred and secular pilgrimage. *Tourism Recreation Research, 27*(2), 73–82.

Semmel, S. (2000). Reading the tangible past: British tourism, collecting and memory after Waterloo. *Representations, 69*, 9–37.

Sharpley, R., & Stone, P. (Eds.). (2009). *The darker side of travel: The theory and practice of dark tourism*. Bristol: Channel View.

Singh, T. V. (Ed.). (2004). *New horizons in tourism: Strange experiences and stranger practices*. Wallingford: CABI Publishing.

Smith, V. (1998). War and tourism: An American ethnography. *Annals of Tourism Research, 25*, 202–227.

Stone, O. (1889). *Norway in June*. London: Marcus Ward.

Stone, P. R. (2012). Dark tourism and significant other death: Towards a model of mortality and mediation. *Annals of Tourism Research, 39*(3), 1565–2597.

Tweedie, Mrs. A. (1889). *A girl's ride in Iceland*. London: Griffith, Farran, Okeden and Welsh.

Waller, S. E. (1874). *Six weeks in the saddle; A painter's journal in Iceland*. London: Macmillan and Co..

Walton, J. K. (2012). War and tourism. The nineteenth and twentieth centuries. In R. Butler & W. Suntikul (Eds.), *Tourism and war* (pp. 64–74). London: Routledge.

Wawn, A. (2000). *The Vikings and the Victorians: Inventing the old north in nineteenth-century Britain*. Cambridge: D. S. Brewer.

5

"The Smoke of an Eruption and the Dust of an Earthquake": Dark Tourism, the Sublime, and the Re-animation of the Disaster Location

Jonathan Skinner

> The lightnings around Vesuvius increase in their vivid and scorching glare [....] now of a lurid and intolerable crimson, gushing forth through the columns of smoke, far and wide, and lighting up the whole city from arch to arch—then suddenly dying into a sickly paleness, like the ghost of their own life! (*The Last Days of Pompeii*, Edward George Bulwer-Lytton 1834)

> The most curious thing I've seen on my voyage is Pompeii. (*Rome, Naples et Florence*, Stendhal 1826)

> Earthquakes and volcanoes are at last claiming, by their very intrusive activity, the attention of observers, who are able to look through the smoke of an eruption, and the dust of an earthquake, at the real geological importance of the terrible demonstration. (*The American Naturalist*, WT. Brigham 1868)

Introducing a Dark and Stormy Tourism

The first quotation above from *The Last Days of Pompeii* (1834) describes the start of the eruption of Mount Vesuvius on 24 August 79 AD. It is written imaginatively by the popular Victorian writer Edward George Bulwer-Lytton, the gothic novelist who coined the expression "It was a dark and stormy night". The book uses characters to describe religious and classical

---

J. Skinner (✉)
University of Roehampton, London, UK

© The Author(s) 2018
P. R. Stone et al. (eds.), *The Palgrave Handbook of Dark Tourism Studies*,
https://doi.org/10.1057/978-1-137-47566-4_5

tensions between the Ancients—Glaucus, an Athenian in a Roman seaside resort town, falling in love with Nydia, the sister of a priest worshipping the Egyptian Goddess Isis—all set in a racy context of feasts and seduction in the shadow of Mount Vesuvius. The book was an instant bestseller, partly due to its launch just after the eruption of Vesuvius again on 23 August 1834 and partly because it dealt with issues to do with civilisation, colonialism and catastrophe—developing preoccupations of modern urban Victorian Britain. It became a "school of catastrophe" text (Dahl 1953) associated also with the adventure and dystopia writing of the age, but also evolution, extinction and early ecology writing (Scott 2014). This is an extension of what McCormick (1998: 5) describes as the "black visions" of Tennyson and other Victorian writers extending Blake's lament for a lost rural idyll before the rise of the "dark satanic mills". It is explained by Ferguson (2013: 2) as a consequence of living through the "radically altered spatial and temporal environment" of the mid- to late nineteenth century and became a reference text for the Grand Tour travellers and visitors who gazed upon Antiquity and pilfered, researched, wrote, painted, and gazed upon the site first explored in the mid-eighteenth century. Readers appreciated the fetishisation of simple landscape. Mary Shelley (1844: 279) found that he had "peopled its silence …. peopled its desert streets" when she revisited Pompeii in 1843. Londoners empathised with the bustling cosmopolitan "untechnological" Pompeii re-animated by Bulwer-Lytton Pompeii in 1843 after having read the historical novel. Bulwer's narrative overwrote other versions of visits to "the City of the Dead" as Sir Walter Scott had described it (Lockhart 1838). As such, the site and its stories were reworked and restaged from on-site picnics (Chard 2007) to Pompeiian plays in London's West End and mass-scale transatlantic "pyrodrama" spectaculars with up to 10,000 spectators (St Clair and Bautz 2012: 376), films—over nine films with the title between 1900 and 1950 (Daly 2011: 276)—television comedies ("Up Pompeii"), and even science fiction travels such as Dr Who's "The Fires of Pompeii" (Hobden 2009). Most recently we have the 2014 film of Robert Harris's 2003 bestseller *Pompeii* and Mary Beard's (2008) *Pompeii: The Life of a Roman Town* and related BBC show "Pompeii: New Secrets Revealed with Mary Beard". If one cannot visit the site as a traveller, then there are opportunities as a reader and a viewer to reimagine and reconstruct the past (cf. Harper 1993). Failing that one can flirt with danger from a distance with the "faux disaster" ruins one can float past on the "Escape from Pompeii" amusement park ride at Busch Gardens in Williamsburg, Virginia.

Pompeii is writ large in the contemporary imagination and has held this dramatic status from the French Revolution to post-9/11 Apocalyptic riskscape. It will continue to attract attention and tourist visits to the foothills of the volcano as well as to the ever-expanding number of related destinations. "Magnificence, mysterious grandeur, divine wrath, and terrific catastrophe, all portrayed on a huge scale, still can be forceful and exciting" suggests Curtis Dahl (1956: 147). The disaster narrative is fetching, compelling, enticing. More recently, Mary Manjikian (2012) refers to this attraction as the "romance of the world's end". It has led to the continual repurposing and "remediation" (Ekström 2016) of a Janus-facing Pompeii that gives us insight simultaneously into Antiquity and Apocalypse. There is a seduction to this calamitous aesthetic for the tourist gaze, not dissimilar to the "subtle, corrupting fascination" for Auschwitz identified by Steiner (1971: 30) or for the Ground Zeros that pockmark the globe, each an instantiation of new time, space and body configurations (cf. Feldman 2002). Tourists have an appetite for disaster, horror, and death. The question in this chapter is: in the context of natural disasters, is this a new phenomenon?[1]

Visiting Knebworth House, Bulwer-Lytton's gothic stately home—as well as film set, educational centre, and rock concert venue in Hertfordshire—one finds an exhibition dedicated to the writer and his *The Last Days of Pompeii*. There are memorabilia from his writings and visits to Pompeii, lodestones to the past, gifts and souvenirs from his visits—in particular two skulls of Pompeii's victims he kept on his writing desk and on display as muses and memento mori (Lazer 2009: 104), a perverse display of real skulls to realise fictional characters (Goldhill 2012). Predating Bulwer-Lytton, dilettante and gothic revivalist Horace Walpole visited Herculaneum in 1740, during what Moorman (2015) refers to as the treasure-hunt phase from 1710 to 1755 before archaeological digs were instituted and extended by 1805. While Bulwer-Lytton was attracted to the historical imagination of the place, and aroused by the curving bosom and nape of the cast of a young woman—an archaeological trace, an erotic imprint re-animating warm flesh from cold ash (Goldhill 2014)—Walpole took away what was unique for him, exotic souvenirs that appealed to his sensibilities. One of his many letters (Walpole 1890[1740]) to his friend Richard West describes his visit to "this reservoir of antiquities":

Naples, 14 June, 1740
 Dear West, — One hates writing descriptions that are to be found in every book of travels; but we have seen something to-day that I am sure you never read of, and perhaps never heard of. Have you ever heard of a subterraneous town? A whole Roman town, with all its edifices, remaining underground?

> Don't fancy the inhabitants buried it there to save it from the Goths: they were buried with it themselves; which is a caution we are not told that they ever took. [...] This underground city is perhaps one of the noblest curiosities that ever has been discovered.

Walpole brought home petrified dates that he housed in a small casket in his Tribune room, a shrine-like treasure store for storylines to visitors. His sole comment about them was that "they are burnt to a coal, but the shapes and rivelled skins are entire" (Walpole 1774: 97). They were guarded by a small bronze bust of Caligula with silver eyes. Walpole cooed over it and relished his role as custodian, describing the piece in a guidebook he constructed for visitors to his Strawberry Hill House:

> A small bust in bronze of Caligula, with silver eyes. This exquisite piece is one of the finest things in the collection, and shows the great art of the ancients. It is evidently a portrait, carefully done, and seems to represent that Emperor at the beginning of his madness. (Walpole 1774: 87)

Bulwer-Lytton modelled partly himself upon this dilettante writer. This curiosity-collecting habit is also found in Sir Walter Scott, Bulwer's contemporary, who mixed his curiosities, taking flags, body armour, and buttons as souvenirs from the site of the battle of Waterloo in 1815 (a month after Wellington's great victory) and exhibiting them back home alongside Napoleon's blotting paper and pen tray, a lock of Nelson's hair, Rob Roy's purse, and two model cast skulls of Robert the Bruce and a Guardsman from Waterloo. Goldhill suggests that writers such as these have a competitive and perverse relationship with the past that lies somewhere between archaeological record and the historical fictions of their novels, "the materiality of the real against the nonreferentiality of fiction" (Goldhill 2012: 112). Bulwer-Lytton was given his skulls by scientist, Vesuvius scholar, traveller, and guide John Auldjo that they might become a part of Knebworth's shrine to posterity:

> I know they will be taken and probably remain undisturbed for ages at Knebworth, where, perhaps, they may be found by Macaulay's New Zealander, when Knebworth House will be visited as one of the shrines of England. (Cited in Goldhill 2012: 97)

All three writers' houses have become popular contemporary tourist attractions. On a recent tour of Knebworth, given by current heir Henry Lytton-Cobbold, the skulls are still on display, labelled and named. Scott's "conundrum castle" can be visited as a site of national interest in Scotland. And Walpole's Strawberry Hill

House, though now empty of possessions after a bankruptcy sale in 1842, is a popular tourist attraction for the gothic imagining tourist. I volunteer as a room steward in the now empty Tribune room, watching tourists reconstruct the room in their imagination: where Caligula's silver eyes gazed and how the Walpole cabinet, now sitting in room 118a, case six of the Victoria and Albert Museum, might have looked in the centre wall of the room near the Japanese box of Roman dates. Tourists piece together a version of the past, curious about the curiosities formerly exhibited. Walpole, Scott, and Bulwer-Lytton, each in their own right romantic chroniclers, fêted the theatrical and atmospheric and have maintained the interests of readers and visitors across the centuries.

The medium for viewing Pompeii has changed from historical novel to Hollywood blockbuster, from newspaper report to science fiction episode or documentary. Equally, the demography of those visiting and the mode of transport that conveys them have changed from encounters by horse-drawn carriages to "flying visit" in a coach tour party. Nevertheless, the nature of the attractions to Pompeii remains the same. The motivations to tour, to visit, to be educated and experienced, and to understand the catastrophe and the past lives of its victims have changed little. The reconstructions at work in the visitors' imaginations endure, prompted by the marketing that stimulates and frames their expectations (Skinner and Theodossopoulos 2011), which has been called by Leite the commodification of collective "tourism imaginaries …. those shared, composite images of place and people" (2014: 264). There is also, perhaps, an unchanged relief in the safe, return home with a touch of schadenfreude, which has recently been linked to a Freudian death drive (*thanatos*) by Buda (2015). *Plus, ça change, plus c'est la même chose.* Some things are timeless, especially the personal experienr that travel affords articulated in the eighteenth-century quip made by William Bennet, Cambridge Don and Bishop of Cloyne: "Travellers always buy experience which no books can give" (Black 1999: 301).

Natural Catastrophe and the Sublime

Tourists have long been attracted to grand telluric forces and their impact from the eruptions of Vesuvius and its creation of Pompeii, to the religious fires and tsunami floods following the great earthquake of Lisbon on All Saint's Day, 1755. This "catastrophism" was international, killing upwards of 10,000 local citizens by fire, flood, and quake (Aguirre 2012). Humans repurpose events, establish meaning over them, and draw equations between them. Here is Clarence King (1877: 460), the first director of the US Geological Survey:

> If poor, puny little Vesuvius could immortalize itself by burying the towns at its feet, if the feeble energy of a Lisbon earthquake could record itself on the gravestones of thousands of men, then the volcanic period in Western America was truly catastrophic. Modern vulcanism, is but the faint, flickering survival of what was once a world-wide and immense exhibition of telluric energy, one whose distortions and dislocations of the crust, whose deluges of molten stone, emissions of mineral dust, heated waters, and noxious gases could not have failed to exert destructive effect on the life of considerable portions of the globe.

An anonymous article in US art magazine *The Aldine*, "Loitering around Lisbon" (Anon. 1872), addresses Grand Tour tourism to Lisbon in the same period as seen through the eyes of William Beckford (1760–1844), a wealthy inheritor, letter writer, and gothic revivalist aping Horace Walpole; he once described Walpole's residence as a "a gothic mousetrap" (Melville 1910: 299). The article is built around Beckford's (1835) two-volume Grand Tour, *Italy; with Sketches Of Spain and Portugal*, a travel memoir written as a diary of his movements (see also Seaton's introduction to this section). The letter from 30 June 1787 details part of his tour of Lisbon during the glowing, last phases of The Inquisition:

> We sallied out after dinner to pay visits. Never did I behold such cursed ups-and-downs, such shelving descents and sudden rises, as occur at every step one takes in going about Lisbon. I thought myself fifty times on the point of being overturned into the Tagus, or tumbled into sandy ditches, among rotten shoes, dead cats, and negro beldames, [...] I saw one dragging into light as I passed by the ruins of a palace thrown down by the earthquake. [...] We traversed the city this evening in all its extent in our way to the Duke d'Alafoens's villa [...] We walked part of the way home by the serene light of the full moon rising from behind the mountains on the opposite shore of the Tagus, at this extremity of the metropolis above nine miles broad. Lisbon, which appeared to me so uninteresting a few hours ago, assumed a very different aspect by these soft gleams. The flights of steps, terraces, chapels, and porticos of several convents and palaces on the brink of the river, shone forth like edifices of white marble, whilst the rough cliffs and miserable sheds rising above them were lost in dark shadows. (Beckford 1835, Letter XVI)

Beckford and other tourists sought out the contrasts between the old Lisbon and the new Lisbon, between the ruined, lost, and dark to the east of the city and the modern, rejuvenated, and "curious medley" of the "distasteful" (Anon. 1872: 44) alongside the river Tagus. These Grand Tourists enjoyed the contrasts of Lisbon, and the drama of the All Saints' Day narrative nearly 30 years earlier, an event that caught the imagination of European scholars with debates on humanity and omnipotence, god in nature, and the sublime—all cast through this first global catastrophe of the Enlightenment; Rousseau blamed the victims whereas Voltaire "heard them cry", to paraphrase moral philosopher Susan Neiman (2004: 138); Kant explained events with recourse to the descriptive sciences (cf. Brightman 1919), and Edmund Burke (1767[1756]: 152) added a "suddenness" to his aesthetics of the sublime. They also sought out the English gentry named in the local graveyards (Paice 2008). Prime Minister Sebastião José de Carvalho e Melo, first Marquis of Pombal, rebuilt the city along secular lines with city squares excluding the church's pre-quake presence (Walker 2015): a "violent subterranean transformation, both physical and philosophical" in the City of Death (Hamblyn 2008: 109, 113), still the epicentre for The Inquisition with its buried dungeons. Hamblyn (2008: 114) continues: "[i]t was as though Lisbon had been built and rebuilt over a pit of horrors, to which the earthquake had given concrete geophysical expression." Science trumped theodicy in Lisbon, and the visitors were drawn to the city they had read about and seen inked as disaster images in their newspapers—a print capitalism aesthetics of distant disaster spectators that precipitates not just tourism but also a cosmopolitan sense of commonality that lies at the heart of universal human rights according to Sharon Sliwinski (2011). Taking a leaf from Adorno, Neiman (2004: xvi) suggests that the Lisbon earthquake—Goethe's (1848: 19) "demon of terror"—became the equivalent for us "moderns" of Auschwitz, a *Zeitgeist* shock, the sublime as collective trauma, that taken together bookend the beginning and the end of the modern period. These moral aftershocks are with us today with the meaning of the Lisbon earthquake heralding a sublime environment that is neither God's nor God's gift. They have influenced the disaster tourists of yore and continue to influence them today on spectacular volcanic disaster islands such as Montserrat and Santorini.

Enlightenment figures—enthralled by a mix of fear and fascination—described the Lisbon earthquake as "sublime", an emotional response to the immensity of forces at play around them. Like Pompeii, the natural disaster has a dramatic human dimension to it. And, like Pompeii, the "natural" disaster was restaged for the curious Victorian public. The Colosseum Theatre in London's Regent's Park ran a successful—if controversial—show production, *Cyclorama of Lisbon Before and After the Earthquake in 1755* (see Chap. 4) that "dazzled" and "frightened the senses" of even William Thackeray (1899: 177) with the crashing of buildings, shrieks of the dying, flashes, and thunder assaulting his senses. Kant was influenced by the quake in his third critique that sought to develop an analytical understanding of human response to the magnitude and might of nature, to that which is "absolutely great" (2000[1790]: 131), surpassing measure of the senses and hence becoming something that we fear. It haunts the text as a "negative presentation" (Ray 2004: 10), dark and unfathomable, present by not being mentioned. To generalise, the Kantian sublime is thus uncontainable, dynamic, exciting, violent—as in the examples in this chapter—and scary. Read through a Marxist lens, this "negative pleasure" (Kant 2000: 129; cf. Burke's "negative pain"), the sublime is, as Gene Ray (2004: 6) appositely phrases it, "a 'manly' solution" to the problem of the beautiful with its feminine associations. With the sublime, the romantic—and bourgeois—traveller could, and still can, contemplate the awesomeness of nature, its thrills, and spills but without feeling effeminate.

Ray comments further on the implications for the scientific and literary naming—this new-found appreciation in spectators near and far. To describe, to visit, to tour is to represent, to commodify, to take control. Disaster tourism domesticates. For Ray, again, the sublime is central to this transition: "through the power of reason and its moral law, the great evil of natural catastrophe is elevated, transfigured and 'sublimed' into a foil for human dignity" (Ray 2004: 11). Contra Ray, Heringman suggests that the natural disaster is beyond domestication, just as it is beyond comprehension for it to be sublime. Volcano and earthquake are alien processes to us. They are, in fact, Other—wild nature to be mediated through metaphor or aesthetic medium such as poetry or art; the spewing volcano suffers us with its painful birth pang. The earthquake catastrophe is understood through the lens of the religious as a curse, the secular as sublime, the new discipline of the geological scientist as seismic. And so we colonise the formerly uncertain and incomprehensible through hyperbole. The sublime is just one of these tropes to mediate our experiences. Literary critic Noah Heringman (2003: 97) articulates this through natural philosopher Humphrey Day's declaration that the volcanoes are "the most sublime of the phenomena belonging to our globe" before going on to note that the earthquake also represents topical issues of the day to people (2003: 98). Earthquake and volcano narratives have an evanescence about them; the earth convulses with us as human witnesses before we die and/or are buried.

How, then, do the large-scale disasters and catastrophes such as the eruptions of Italy's Vesuvius, Greece's Santorini, and Montserrat's Soufriere Hills—not to mention Japan's Mount Aso, the USA's Mount St Helens, Iceland's Eyjafjallajökull, Hawaii's Kilauea, and many others—square with a niche form of tourism located on the cusp of modernity/post-modernity? These complex events are repurposed for the tourist and by the tourist. But, if dark tourism is "an intimation of post-modernity", as John Lennon and Malcolm

Foley (2000: 11) declare, then can it be accurately applied to physical events that are outwith living memory and our everyday experience of time? (See Chap. 1.)

From Santorini to Montserrat: Pompeii as a Disaster Tourism Trope

To assess this proposition, I wish to examine two examples where "Pompeii" features as the disaster tourism trope in use. They comprise Santorini, a Greek island and archipelago in the southern Aegean Sea in the Mediterranean, an inhabited remnant of a volcanic caldera; and Montserrat, a British Overseas Territory in the Eastern Caribbean, the site of an on-going eruption in the Soufriere Hills. The issue is as to whether or not these are contemporary dark tourism destinations? Patricia Erfurt-Cooper notes that contemporary tourists are certainly attracted to volcanoes. These volcano tourists are intrigued by temperamental nature around them, often heedless of the risk of explosion, gas poisoning, and burning. She defines the practice as follows:

> Volcano tourism involves the exploration and study of active volcanic and geothermal landforms. Volcano tourism also includes visits to dormant and extinct volcanic regions where remnants of activity attract visitors with an interest in geological heritage. (2010a: 3)

It is a niche form of eco- or nature tourism. Visitors are in awe of these exciting but deadly nature shows writ large across the landscape from Hawaii to Iceland. Often the visits are associated with spa trips to thermal springs and mud baths. Some are educational visits to admire and make sense of the geology in progress. Others are historical with a walk-through/sail-around the site of the 1883 eruption of Krakatoa. Writing in their extensive *Volcano and Geothermal Tourism* volume, Erfurt-Cooper (2010b: 148) features the fascinating volcano attractions on the Japanese island of Kyushu where concrete bunkers line the tourist routes as potential shelters should an eruption take place. One of the attractions is a "Buried Village" where 43 died under pyroclastic flows from Mt. Unzen. Locals renarrate their experiences as "a close call" with nature. A memorial hall records the event, quite literally using the reel from a camera found in the debris that contained footage of the pyroclastic flow as it approached the unfortunate spectators. Their last view of the spectacle is replayed to the tourists in a theatre that uses a vibrating floor and hot winds to simulate the pyroclastic flows on 3D large screens in front of them. Artefacts line a 39-metre glass-enclosed floor with light running through it at 100 km/second speed billed as "the phenomenon itself" (Anon. 2016b). This automated modern show trades off proximity to the site, the authenticity of materials on display (e.g., the camera), the advances in simulated experience for the visitor. The result is what Bell and Lyall (2002) refer to as an "accelerated sublime", an enhanced kinaesthetic experience of the landscape. This postmodern technology works as an innovative revamping of the historical cyclorama to "(re)activate the sublime" (cf. Bell and Lyall 2002: xii). Theirs is not a passive viewing of geo-nature. It is immersive and disturbing though the plight of the 43 is downplayed in favour of a sensorial engagement with the disaster. You sit watching their fate unfold in front of you just as they did. The disaster is re-animated for you the dark tourist. But you escape when they did not.

Santorini: Bronze Age Pompeii

There are no memorials on Santorini or Montserrat for the deceased. On these islands, the tourists' motivations are very different. The locations also differ considerably: classical caldera landscape to classic phreatic volcano peak, one a marine site breathtaking in its massive vertiginous heights, the other a contrast between "the green and the gritty" (Skinner 2015)—between the north and the south of the island. One has beauty in its absence, in a crater filled with Mediterranean waters pockmarked by remnants of volcanic activity, with human civilisation clinging to the walls of the caldera and bobbing gently in nature's new harbour for the cruise ship visitor. The other is an "island-of-extremes" (CTONews 2015) visited by plane that flies over an empty, grey, ashy moonscape till you come to land in the tropical green north, landing near to settlements full of life and contrasting with the dead, part-covered former capital. Both are seen as Pompeiis: Walter Friedrich (2009) describes Santorini as "a bronze age Pompeii" in his book about the island. Writing for a Fox News piece, Blane Bachelor (2014) headlined Montserrat as "a modern-day Pompeii in the Caribbean". Peter Hohenhaus (2016a), who runs the Dark-Tourism.com website, notes how this location has become a metonym for volcano disasters in general, standing for the entire cluster of eruptions involving the unfortunate loss of life and destruction to property that can be viewed by the visitor:

> The word "Pompeii" is often taken as almost a generic term, or as a metonym standing for all kinds of volcanic disasters, esp. of course if they involve some place getting covered in ash or lava. Thus you find expressions such as "a modern-day Pompeii" – as a descriptive term for the former capital of the Caribbean

island Montserrat, Plymouth, which was destroyed in a Soufriere Hills volcano eruption and buried by a pyroclastic flow. Similarly, on Heimaey, Iceland, an excavation project in which houses covered by lava in 1973 are currently being dug up calls itself "Pompei[i] of the North" (which also demonstrates what a marketing asset an association with Pompeii can be…).

Hohenhaus appreciates the temporal dimension in dark tourism, linking the activity with twentieth-century commodification but also recognising that Pompeii has contemporary caché because the Vesuvius volcano is still considered to be dangerous and is by no means extinct. Souvenir hunters continue to seek out their piece of Vesuvius rock from the crater (Karkut 2010: 239). It serves as a lodestone to the past and anchors the tourist to the explosion millennia ago that caused such loss of life. This is what rained down on the poor citizens, a curio for the mantelpiece as a poor match for the aristocrats' souvenirs from the ruins.

Santorini, a corruption on Saint Irene, is a Greek island 200 km from the mainland, 90 km square in size, and with a population of approximately 15,000. It is also the name for an island archipelago formed from a collapsed volcano caldera measuring 12 km by 7 km. The caldera is water filled, creating a sublime volcano lagoon surrounded by a 1000-foot-high cliff face. The water is 400 m deep, broken by the tops of two volcanoes that formed the small islands Palia and Nea Kameni (Old and New Burnt Island) from past and present eruptions (1600 BC to 1950 with other particular eruptions in 47 AD, 726 AD and 1707). Over half a million tourists visit the islands every year. Tourists visiting by cruise ship enter via the Old Port and take a cable car up the cliffs to the capital Fira. The views and sunsets from there and Oia are considered some of the most spectacular in the world. Volcano tourists can visit the islands and bathe in heated waters. Shops on the main island sell volcano soaps, pumice, ashtrays shaped like a volcanic caldera for cigarette ash to fall in the centre, and postcards of previous eruptions (photographs from 1950, newspaper prints from 1707 and 1866). The tourists have been seduced by the 360-degree visuals online that advertise the islands and the hotels (Anon. 2016b). They are attracted to the site of what is considered to have been the largest volcanic eruption in the world: to the remains of a colossal Minoan eruption approximately 1600 BC that could be heard across three continents, cast a shadow over the Mediterranean and caused global cooling as far as China. Few tourists feel unsafe or consider the volcano site a danger to visit. The fear lies in the altitude of the island towns where tourists perch for photographs, take the cable car journey up the steep slopes, and endure scary car and coach journeys winding around roads cut into the mountain sides.

Walter Friedrich's (2009: 125) *Santorini* text covers the volcano, natural history and mythology associated with the island. He refers to Santorini as "the bronze age Pompeii", the reason being that it is the epicentre of an eruption 3600 years ago that is thought to have destroyed the Minoan civilisation on the island and nearby Crete by not only ash but also a tsunami of classical and Biblical proportion—quite literally potentially linking Santorini to the fabled island of Atlantis described by Plato and instigating the 10 plagues of Egypt mentioned in Exodus. French volcanologist Ferdinand Fouqué uncovered ruins when visiting a quarry in the south of the island in 1867, painted rooms with ceramics in, paved streets and three-storey houses, the jaw bone and pelvis of a man. Buried in pumice, but missing the human element as though an evacuation had taken place, Akrotiri is a town buried in pumice that visitors can once again walk through, peeping into houses along the way. The burial of the city and its remarkable state of preservation have led to the association with Italy's Pompeii. Under the headline and byline "Akrotiri—Santorini's own Pompeii—Akrotiri untouched for more than 3000 years" (Anon. 2016c), holiday promoters draw explicit parallels with the more recent Pompeii:

> Just like Pompeii, this Minoan city was buried with little warning beneath tons of volcanic ash with its building, city squares, shops and houses preserved in pumice for later generations. Today, holiday visitors to Santorini can walk its streets and peep into homes that have remained little disturbed since 1500 BC.

Besides the artefacts "unpumiced" throughout the site, archaeologists were able to use recovery techniques from Pompeii to reconstruct the shape of wooden beds and furniture that had rotted away by using the pumice as a mould. Unlike Pompeii, however, there were no imprints of bodies in contorted horror. Santorini's volcanic devastation lay across the waters where people had evacuated themselves to. The site and its associations with Pompeii do not translate into an immediate form of dark tourism, but neither is it an example of dark tourism at a distance. There is no evidence of death on Santorini but this is where the ripples of death and destruction emanated from. Volcano Discovery is a tourist company organising bespoke package holidays to volcano sites all around the world to provide tourists with "unforgettable memories" (Volcano Discovery 2016). Organised by volcanologists, Santorini is their "fascination volcano" full of picturesque contemporary towns, prehistoric ruins and awesome landscapes. It is the geology more than the human-interest story that is the focus of these volcano tourists (Plates 5.1 and 5.2).

Plate 5.1 Santorini sunken caldera and burnt islands from Oia (Photo Source: Author 2016)

Dark Montserrat?

Tourists visiting the island of Montserrat come by ferry or plane from neighbouring Antigua. The island is mountainous, tropical and the shape of a teardrop. It measures 16 km in length and 11 km in width, 100 km square, and has a current population of just over 5100 predominantly British Overseas Territory Citizens. The highest point on the island is Chances Peak on the Soufriere Hills in the centre of the south of the island, 915 m above sea level. The Peak is currently the summit of a dynamic volcano that has been active since 1995 with various periods of dramatic and catastrophic eruption with pyroclastic mudflow. The south of the island is currently divided into five zones with access depending upon a separate five-point hazard level scale that ranges from "Unrestricted" to "Daytime Transit" to "Controlled Access" and "Essential Access" only, depending upon the current hazard status. The north of the island, 40 per cent of the island, is relatively unaffected by the volcano and eruptions apart from ash fall. Tropical, lush, and frequently described as "verdant" to invoke a connection with Ireland (cf. Skinner 2003), Montserratians now in the north of the island have endured evacuation, resettlement and problematic aid and development difficulties ever since the volcano began erupting in 1995. In her study of environmental change on the island and its social implications for disaster recovery and sustainable development, Anja Possekel (1999) suggests that they have come to terms with the loss of their capital, Plymouth, and the devastation of much of their island,

Plate 5.2 Historic Santorini eruption postcards (Photo Source: Author 2016)

developing a resilience to "living with the unexpected". Whereas Possekel stresses the need for vision and planning, here I attend to the role of tourism in the regeneration of not just the economy on the island but also to the re-animation of the buried city of Plymouth that was "overrun" in 1997.

A visit to Montserrat is a visit of extreme contrasts. Friendly liveliness in the north and a barren empty wasteland in the south interrupted by lorries transporting volcanic sand and the occasional volcano tour taxi or minibus. The volcano has stabilised in recent years, if that is a word that can describe a slow erupting volcano, and people have started returning to the island or migrating to it from other Caribbean islands. The population remains at half the approximate 10,000 inhabitants from pre-1995 levels. Further, tourism levels are a quarter of what they used to be at 9000 tourist visits in 2015 (DiscoverMNITeam 2016). In 2015, small cruise ships have started to call at the island, changing their itinerary from sailing past lava flows when it was erupting to stopping at Plymouth jetty for tourists to be driven past the capital to the safe zone for their visit to begin. "People are coming back – Montserrat is back alive", declared Hans Birkholz, CEO of Windstar Cruises (Sloan 2015). In the past, tourists would visit the north of the island and watch the volcano from the safe distance of the Montserrat Volcano Observatory. This bird's eye view of the volcano also used to include a tour of the seismographs by the station scientists for what one guesthouse manager refers to as her "lava-loving travelers 'volcanophiles'" (Bachelor 2014). It has been replaced by a video explaining the history of the volcano and a collection of souvenirs from the volcano such as a melted coca cola bottle in what one US tourist described as "a cabinet of curiosities" (bcdonthego 2016), not too far removed from Walpole's cabinet in his Tribune room. The authenticity of an active, real live site has been maintained. The MVO helicopter outside on a helipad that flies daily measurement and observation missions adds to the frisson of a real-life disaster taking place outside of the window, on the other side of the valley, "over there". Then, the tourists can continue the tour of the island by visiting Plymouth—"the lost city" (Bergeron 2016), "the buried city" (VisitMontserrat 2016), "a modern day Pompeii" (Bachelor 2014 for FOX News). Tourists can visit the periphery of Plymouth, viewing the city from Richmond Hill, having driven past "Danger" signs, through deserted cleared streets approaching the city.

With permits, the tourists can visit the city and walk on the pyroclastic material that is the depth of half a storey, peer through windows and figure out the use of twisted, rusted shapes. Tim Edensor (2005) writes of walks through industrial ruins, the hybrid nature of the tourist consumption, personal and different. One has to pick one's own path through these ruins.

The tourist's path has been deconstructed with weird mixtures of objects and nature fused and confused, reframed and mutated in front of them, to the side, over and under. The ruin, for Edensor (2005: 141), is "an allegory of memory", temporal rather than timeless, spectral and shocking in its fatality and physicality. It can be described as the end of the life of structures and objects. It is sobering for the walker or tourist, especially so with an ominous volcanic peak puffing away above. "Now she puffs but will she blow? Trust the Lord and pray it's no!" is a popular Montserrat souvenir slogan T-shirt. One can imagine the pyroclastic cast of a burnt body in one of these lifeless rooms, but it is a violation of personal space when tourists flout and flaunt their visits such as the crew of the Sy Skye who posed in people's houses for social media, drinking from leftover bars but also dressing up in clothes from people's closets. This was considered too close to home for comfort for many Montserratians, actions mocking the islanders, and behaviour devoid of "empathy" for their suffering (Pierre 2016).

Plymouth is a grey, ghostly city. In a world of colour it has turned monochrome. Ash covers everything, balanced and perched on items, crusted along surfaces. Human contact marks and imprints on it. "Take only photographs, leave only footprints" was a slogan meant for tidal sand. Here, even the ash on windows remains, and tourists write graffiti with their fingertips cleaning the glass: "I woz here" as though survival letters to the future visitor (Skinner 2017). The ghosts of inhabitants now populate the city. But is this a dark tourism experience? Dark Montserrat? There are certainly "ghosts in my head" (Skinner 2008) as I lived ten months in Plymouth before and during the start of the volcano crisis in 1995. The voices, characters, activities continue for me the ethnographer. But it is not a death site or a place of atrocity except by association for Hohenhaus (2016b). It is promoted as "mysterious" with the "volcano-buried city" (Rogers 2016), "Apocalyptic" (Bachelor 2014), "Another Paradise lost" (Newsweek Staff 1997) even. Further, it is no island of Dr Moreau, and the connection is with Columbus and not Jules Verne—who visited Santorini during the 1866–1870 eruptions before writing about Captain Nemo and his crew visiting an erupting island. No deaths occurred in Plymouth, but there was an ill-fated eruption on 25/26 June 1997 down the north-east side of the volcano, 400-degree-centigrade pyroclastic material flowing at 126 kph, destroying the island airport and catching 19 Montserratians working and visiting villages on the slopes. Further eruptions in August and in subsequent years including one on 28 July 2008 have encroached on and devastated the capital. Writing in the same Erfurt-Cooper and Cooper (2010a) volume, Nick Petford, John Fletcher, and Yegani Morakabati (2010) link volcano tourism with dark tourism, suggesting that it becomes lighter over time. For them (Petford et al. 2010: 85), volcano tourism is "a mix of danger and thrill seeking, combined with scientific or educational curiosity". Ironically, tourists are more attracted to the recently erupted destinations, but those are the least acceptable in terms of visiting places of disaster. Pompeii, for them, is the most authentic site of death and suffering, and hence one of the darkest (Petford et al. 2010: 90). Plymouth, Montserrat, had similar levels of destruction but no loss of life within it, and hence is not a site of death and suffering. In their words, it is "in effect a modern-day Pompeii minus human casualties" (Petford et al. 2010: 91). One can walk the streets of Plymouth on the western side of the island without feeling "ghoulish". But, perhaps, viewing the volcano from observation posts on the other side of the mountain, from Jack Boy Hill, one can see where pyroclastic flows swallowed up W.H. Bramble Airport and created a fan of new-island growth in the waters. There is a picnic site and an observation deck with fixed binoculars from where you can see the flanks of the volcano, flames, sulphur dioxide plumes, and one can trace the flow over the villages and farm land on the eastern side of the island where 19 Montserratians were killed. It is advertised as the most user-friendly site for viewing the volcano but is only accessible along decaying old roads and best approached in a four-wheel drive vehicle. It is a calm viewing spot, enlightening for the tourist. There is no mention of the fatalities at the location or in the TripAdvisor reviews. It is too close temporally to the loss of life for it to be commercially exploited as a dark tourism destination and is, thus, only a dark tourism spot from a guest demand, rather than supply, perspective.

Writing about "Reconceptualising Dark Tourism", Biran and Poria (2012) point out that the "dark" adjective need not necessarily directly equate with death. Dark tourism can be an umbrella term. It can link to the viewing of suffering, to dark play, to schadenfreude, and to meditations upon mortality—often through the sublime. As such, the volcano observatory on the east side of Montserrat brings more than "devastation" and "disaster" to the tourist experience found on the western side of the island. Informally, tour guides often take tourists to the viewing deck and talk about the accidents that occurred at the airport during its existence; they narrate the rescue operations that took place in 1997 when pyroclastic flows threatened and ultimately claimed the site and 19 lives. This can take place before tourists fly off the island from the new runway built in the centre of the island that can only accommodate small planes. It becomes a nerve-wracking, personalised experience, more than a "surreal" and "a humbling reminder of nature's awesome power" as tourism to Montserrat is positioned by VisitMontserrat (2016) (Plates 5.3 and 5.4).

Plate 5.3 Plymouth outskirts under the volcano (Photo Source: Author 2005)

Plate 5.4 Tour guide narrating from Jack Boy Hill (Photo Source: Author 2015)

Dark Tourism: New for Old

The twentieth century is the century when access to leisure expanded from the leisure class to the wider society (Seabrook 1995). It is also the time period when anthropology as a discipline as well as other social sciences developed. Late twentieth century is when we see the convergence of tourism and anthropology in the preceding sections o f this chapter as well as a developing engagement with the subject of dark tourism as an offshoot of thanatourism. This, then, would appear to be the era of escape, according to sociologist Chris Rojek (1993: 136) who ties in "fatal attractions" to our new postmodern landscape. It is jaded by "black spots": "commercial developments of grave sites and sites in which celebrities or large numbers of people have met with sudden and violent death" (Rojek 1993: 136). According to Rojek, these locations—from Auschwitz to Graceland and the Killing Fields of Cambodia—are predicated on a new mass production of commodities and a desire for the spectacular rather than the meaningful. They encourage a projection into the personalities and ways of life portrayed (Rojek 1993: 144). This is described as a "nostalgia in modernity" (Rojek1993: 145), a reaction to our contemporary living. "Under postmodernity, it might be said, everyone is a permanent *émigré* from the present", Rojek (1993: 168) professes. Yet even Rojek accepts that fin de siècle America filled Luna Park in Coney Island with simulations of the Fall of Pompeii and the eruption of Vesuvius, as well as the Pennsylvania Johnstown flood of 1889 and the 1902 eruption of Mount Pelée in Martinique that killed over 30,000 residents—the worst volcanic disaster of the twentieth century. In another part of the United States, Arlington Park, Denver's third amusement park, opened in 1892. A purpose-built leisure centre for amusement and escapism, it featured tennis courts, baseball field and theatre. It was built by dredging a creek and creating a lake with island. The main attraction at the park was "The Last days of Pompeii" show set up across the lakeside writ across a 52-foot canvas. Lights simulated the eruption of Mount Vesuvius. Park historian David Forsyth (2016: 17) explains how this attraction worked:

> Openings in the stage allowed smoke and flames to shoot up through the set, each series of events controlled electronically. To create the illusion of lava flowing down the sides of Vesuvius, a red light was set up behind the canvas; holes cut through the material allowed it to shine through, while a man moved the light around behind the screen to control the lava flow.

It did not last long, however. The park was remodelled five years later with the Pompeii key attraction giving way to a diving elk show and a scenic railway ride around the park. In 1901, tramps or arsonists burnt the park down permanently (Forsyth 2016: 18). Whereas traces of such Pompeiis are less visible in contemporary leisure sites, the Lisbon earthquake and tsunami might be imaginatively reflected in the contemporary Valley of the Waves theme park in South Africa's Sun City where waves crash through the swimming pool and earthquakes perform to an hourly timescale for the intrepid explorer tourist.

Pompeii figures in the imagination of the leisure tourist and amusement park visitor, perhaps the latter as a pre-tourist. Rojek is wrong to associate the fatal attractions with late-modernity/postmodernity. As shown above, fatal attractions have captured the imagination of the public whether or not they were in a position to realise their interests. Since the Roman Empire, leisure and hedonism were associated with military triumph and gladiator fights were organised following a military tragedy or natural disaster (Korstanje 2008: 17). In a similar argument to Rojek, but about a very different historical period, French studies academic Goran Blix (2013) suggests that changes to the *Ancien Régime*, the consequences of the French Revolution and the industrialisation of society resulted in a gap between the past and the present/future. People harped back for the golden age when there was less social and economic turbulence. This nostalgia manifested in an anxiety and nostalgia chronicled by Blix (2013) in his study *From Paris to Pompeii: French Romanticism and the Cultural Politics of Archaeology*. For Blix (2013: 1), "[t]he mortality of cultures was a key experience of modernity". These were Apocalyptic, indeterminate times. Writing about them "embalmed" the ephemeral for Balzac, whilst Schopin and Bruillov painted out their fears and fascinations with their own respective *Last Days of Pompeii*—the latter of which was viewed by Bulwer-Lytton before he wrote his own catastrophic version. In so doing, the Romantics projected themselves and their present-day fears into a past they visited literally and existentially.

The discovery of Pompeii exemplified for them the most radical alterity, a Lost City allowing access to a Lost World of Antiquity. Blix (2013: 160) explains: "Egypt and Pompeii were less models or lessons, less sites of mourning or ornament, than nostalgic surrogate homes, imaginary homelands that poets exiled in modernity yearned to visit". Blix interprets the Romantic fascination with Pompeii, the idle tourism there, the pilgrimages, the souvenirs, the artworks—to which we can add the subsequent, postmodern, multimedia representations—as a playful identification with the Other. There is pain in this. Not just because of the emptiness of time and the disconnect with one's place, but also the loss of lives, the geological extinction of civilisation that can still only be glimpsed askance. This is one revolution after another, the social after the sublime to juxtapose the geological tremors and eruptions with the upheavals in the social and feudal hierarchy. These are transitions and accelerations that have been with us across the *longue durée*. They are not just fin de -20th-siècle.

Emma Willis (2014) alludes to the issue of tourism and alterity in her recent work on dark tourism and theatricality. The dead are the Other by their haunting absence. We memorialise them and try to develop or maintain a relationship to close the void. This takes place in a theatrical "aesthetically mediated aftermath" (Willis 2014: 36) to the initial event. Whether crawling through the Cu Chi tunnels dressed up as Viet Cong soldiers, boating past a Pompeii son et lumière, or signing graffiti at the "Pompeii of the West" (Anon. 2016d) on the island of Montserrat, we engage with re-animations of the past, often "playing" the boundaries of presence and absence, the real and the reproduced. We are both spectators and witnesses. And, as such, we are complicit, implicated in the victimisation reproduced. For Willis, there is no neutrality in viewing. There are no spectatorial sidelines or theatrical wings in genocide memorial, catastrophe curiosity visiting, disaster gawping. There is, though, a sense of co-presence—of being with the Other of the past—and there is a co-subject construction as this visiting impacts upon the identity of the viewer and leads to an identification with the viewed. This is implication, interpellation and witnessing with Pompeii—whether ruin or excavation, literary re-animation, sublime geological education or spectacular leisure entertainment.

Notes

1. Tourism equates to one of Giddens's (1991: 112) "fateful moments" and in the context of this chapter approximates Rojek's "fatal attractions" (1993: 136). These visitor experiences are built around contrast. In terms of emotions and arousal, Gillen points out that "tourism can and does provide the opportunity to experience a contrasting emotional landscape, where the familiar self can be felt in an unfamiliar way" (2001, author's emphasis). For him, these emotions can be bought and sold as commodities open for circulation. In terms of the dark tourism literature, the discussion in this section of the volume is whether or not this commoditisation is a new phenomenon and whether the label dark tourism is sanguine and appropriate to describe what is taking place. Space does not allow engagement with distinctions between "natural" as opposed to the man-made "cultural" disasters (cf. Lowenthal 2005) or the thesis of the disaster as "man-made" constructions arising from 'modernising pressures' (cf. Torry 1979: 518; Skinner 2000).

References

Aguirre, B. (2012). Better disaster statistics: The Lisbon earthquake. *Journal of Interdisciplinary History, 43*(1), 27–42.

Anon. (1872). Loiterings around Lisbon. *The Aldine, 5*(2), 44–47.

Anon. (2016a). *Mt. Unzen Disaster Memoriael Hall Gamadasu Hall*. http://planetyze.com/en/japan/nagasaki/mt-unzen-disaster-memorial-hall-gamadasu-hall. Accessed 2 July 2016.

Anon. (2016b). *Landmarks*. Santorini360Hotels. http://www.santorini360hotels.com/landmarks/nea-kameni/nea-kameni-volcano. Accessed 5 Aug 2016.

Anon. (2016c). *Akrotiri – Santorini's own Pompeii*. Greek Island Holidays. http://www.greek-island-holidays.co.uk/guides/akrotiri-santorini.html. Accessed 15 Aug 2016.

Anon. (2016d, May 2). *ISU geosciences group recounts trip to the volcanic Caribbean Island Montserrat, featuring the "Pompeii of the West"*. http://www.isu.edu/headlines/title-8757-en.html. Accessed 3 May 2016.

Bachelor, B. (2014, February 20). Montserrat: A modern-day Pompeii in the Caribbean. *Fox News*. http://www.foxnews.com/travel/2014/02/20/montserrat-modern-day-pompeii-in-caribbean.html. Accessed 1 Sept 2016.

bcdonthego. (2016, July 13). Worth the drive, but don't expect too much. *Tripadvisor Montserrat Volcano Observatory Review*. https://www.tripadvisor.co.uk/ShowUserReviews-g147333-d316387-r392324792-Montserrat_Volcano_Observatory-Montserrat.html#REVIEWS. Accessed 20 Aug 2016.

Beard, M. (2008). *Pompeii: The life of a Roman town*. London: Profile Books.

Beckford, W. (1835). *Italy; with sketches of Spain and Portugal* (Vol. I). London: Richard Bentley. http://www.gutenberg.org/files/41150/41150-h/41150-h.htm. Accessed 21 Aug 2016.

Bell, C., & Lyall, J. (2002). *The accelerated sublime: Landscape, tourism, and identity*. London: Praeger.

Bergeron, E. (2016, June 9). Lost city of Plymouth - Montserrat - Volcano exclusion zone - UAV Drone Caribbean - WeBeYachting.com. https://www.youtube.com/watch?v=t9F-ws8T0Jw. Accessed 28 Aug 2016.

Black, J. (1999). *The grand tour in the eighteenth century*. London: Sandpiper Books Ltd.

Blix, G. (2013). *From Paris to Pompeii: French romanticism and the cultural politics of archaeology*. Philadelphia: University of Pennsylvania Press.

Brigham, W. T. (1868). Earthquakes. *The American Naturalist, 2*(10), 539–547.

Brightman, E. (1919). The Lisbon earthquake: A study in religious valuation. *The American Journal of Theology, 23*(4), 500–518.

Buda, D. (2015). The death drive in tourism studies. *Annals of Tourism Research, 50*(1), 39–51.

Bulwer-Lytton, E. G. (1834). *The last days of Pompeii*. Paris: Baudry.

Burke, E. (1767[1756]). *A philosophical enquiry into the origin of our ideas of the sublime and beautiful.* London: J. Dodsley. https://books.google.co.uk/books?id=CUgJAAAAQAAJ&printsec=frontcover#v=onepage&q&f=false. Accessed 15 Sept 2016.

Chard, C. (2007). Picnic at Pompeii: Hyperbole and digression in the warm south. In V. Coates & J. Seydl (Eds.), *Antiquity recovered: The legacy of Pompeii and Herculaneum* (pp. 115–132). Los Angeles: J. Paul Getty Museum.

CTONews. (2015). *The island of Montserrat is on the rebound,* Caribbean Tourism Organisation. http://www.onecaribbean.org/the-island-of-montserrat-is-on-the-rebound/. Accessed 5 Sept 2016.

Dahl, C. (1953). Bulwer-Lytton and the school of catastrophe. *Philological Quarterly, 32,* 428–442.

Dahl, C. (1956). Recreators of Pompeii. *Archaeology, 9*(3), 182–191.

Daly, N. (2011). The volcanic disaster narrative: From pleasure garden to canvas, page, and stage. *Victorian Studies, 53*(2), 255–285.

DiscoverMNITeam. (2016, February 12). *2015 tourism figures released.* http://www.discovermni.com/2016/02/2015-tourism-figures-released/. Accessed 1 Sept 2016.

Edensor, T. (2005). *Industrial ruins: Space, aesthetics and materiality.* Oxford: Berg.

Ekström, A. (2016). Remediation, time and disaster. *Theory, Culture & Society.* Prepublished January 2016. https://doi.org/10.1177/0263276415625336.

Erfurt-Cooper, P. (2010a). Introduction. In P. Erfurt-Cooper & M. Cooper (Eds.), *Volcano and geothermal tourism: Sustainable geo-resources for leisure and recreation* (pp. 3–31). London: Earthscan Ltd.

Erfurt-Cooper, P. (2010b). Volcano and geothermal tourism in Kyushu, Japan. In P. Erfurt-Cooper & M. Cooper (Eds.), *Volcano and geothermal tourism: Sustainable geo-resources for leisure and recreation* (pp. 142–154). London: Earthscan Ltd.

Feldman, A. (2002). Ground zero point one: On the cinematics of history. *Social Analysis: The International Journal of Social and Cultural Practice, 46*(1), 110–117.

Ferguson, T. (2013). Introduction. In T. Ferguson (Ed.), *Victorian time: Technologies, standardizations, catastrophes* (p. 1–15). London: Palgrave Macmillan.

Forsyth, D. (2016). *Denver's Lakeside Amusement Park: From the White City beautiful to a century of fun.* Boulder: University of Colorado Press.

Friedrich, W. (2009). *Santorini: Volcano, natural history, mythology.* Aarhus: Aarhus University Press.

Giddens, A. (1991). *Modernity and self-identity: Self and society in the late modern age.* Cambridge: Cambridge University Press.

Gillen, S. (2001). *A moving experience? Investigating the social significance of emotion in tourism.* Unpublished MA thesis, University of Lancaster. http://www.arasite.org/sgma1.htm. Accessed 6 June 2005.

Goldhill, S. (2012). A writer's things: Edward Bulwer Lytton and the archaeological gaze; or, what's in a skull? *Representations, 119*(1), 92–118.

Goldhill, S. (2014). *The buried life of things: How objects made history in nineteenth-century Britain.* Cambridge: Cambridge University Press.

Hamblyn, R. (2008). Notes from underground: Lisbon after the Earthquake. *Romanticism, 14*(2), 108–118.

Harper, M. (1993). Narratives for a liminal age: Ballanche, Custine, Nerval. In S. Nash (Ed.), *Home and its dislocations in nineteenth-century France* (pp. 65–84). Albany: State University of New York Press.

Harris, R. (2003). *Pompeii*. London: Hutchinson.

Heringman, N. (2003). The style of natural catastrophes. *Huntington Library Quarterly, 66*(1/2), 97–113.

Hobden, F. (2009). History meets fiction in "doctor who", the fires of Pompeii': A BBC reception of ancient Rome on screen and online. *Greece & Rome. Second Series, 56*(2), 147–163.

Hohenhaus, P. (2016a). Pompeii. Dark-Tourism.com, http://www.dark-tourism.com/index.php/italy/15-countries/individual-chapters/492-pompeii. Accessed 22 Aug 2016.

Hohenhaus, P. (2016b). Montserrat. Dark-Tourism.com, http://www.dark-tourism.com/index.php/montserrat-west-indies. Accessed 22 Aug 2016.

Kant, I. (2000). *Critique of the power of judgment*. Cambridge: Cambridge University Press.

Karkut, J. (2010). Under the volcano – Can sustainable tourism development be balanced with risk management? In P. Erfurt-Cooper & M. Cooper (Eds.), *Volcano and geothermal tourism: Sustainable geo-resources for leisure and recreation* (pp. 233–246). London: Earthscan Ltd.

King, C. (1877). Catastrophism and evolution. *The American Naturalist, 11*(8), 449–470.

Korstanje, M. (2008). The leisure in Ancient Rome: Chronicles of an empire rise. *Revista de Turism, 8*(8), 14–21.

Lazer, E. (2009). *Resurrecting Pompeii*. Abingdon: Routledge.

Leite, N. (2014). Afterword. Locating imaginaries in the anthropology of tourism. In N. Salazar & N. Graburn (Eds.), *Tourism imaginaries: Anthropological approaches* (pp. 260–278). Oxford: Berghahn Books.

Lennon, J., & Foley, M. (2000). *Dark tourism: The attraction of death and disaster*. Padstow: Continuum.

Lockhart, J. (1838). *Life of sir Walter Scott*. London: Murray.

Lowenthal, D. (2005). Natural and cultural heritage. *International Journal of Heritage Studies, 11*(1), 81–92.

Manjikian, M. (2012). *Apocalypse and post-politics: The romance of the end*. Plymouth: Lexington Books.

McCormick, J. (1998). *Catastrophe and imagination: English and American writings from 1870 to 1950*. New York: Transaction Publishers.

Melville, L. (1910). *The life and letters of William Beckford of Fonthill*. London: William Heinemann.

Moorman, E. (2015). *Pompeii's ashes: The reception of the cities buried by Vesuvius in literature, music, and Drama*. Berlin: Walter de Gruyter.

Neiman, S. (2004). *Evil in modern thought: An alternative history of philosophy*. Princeton: Princeton University Press.
Newsweek Staff. (1997, August 18). Another paradise lost. *Newsweek*. http://europe.newsweek.com/another-paradise-lost-172414?rm=eu. Accessed 3 July 2016.
Paice, E. (2008). *Wrath of god: The great Lisbon earthquake of 1755*. London: Quercus/Penguin Group.
Petford, N., Fletcher, J., & Morakabati, Y. (2010). On the economics and social typology of volcano tourism with special reference to Montserrat, West Indies. In P. Erfurt-Cooper & M. Cooper (Eds.), *Volcano and geothermal tourism: Sustainable geo-resources for leisure and recreation* (pp. 85–93). London: Earthscan Ltd.
Pierre, C. (2016, May 13). Sailors violate exclusion zone. Montserrat reporter online. https://www.themontserratreporter.com/sailors-violate-exclusion-zone/. Accessed 14 Sept 2016.
Possekel, A. (1999). *Living with the unexpected: Linking disaster recovery to sustainable development in Montserrat*. Berlin: Springer.
Ray, G. (2004). Reading the Lisbon earthquake: Adorno, Lyotard, and the contemporary sublime. *The Yale Journal of Criticism, 17*(1), 1–18.
Rogers, M. (2016, July 5). Mysterious Montserrat: Volcano-buried city, Beatles legacy. *USA Today*. http://www.usatoday.com/story/travel/experience/caribbean/2016/06/28/montserrat/86437812/. Accessed 1 Sept 2016.
Rojek, C. (1993). *Ways of escape: Modern transformations in leisure and travel*. London: The Macmillan Press Ltd.
Scott, H. (2014). *Chaos and cosmos: Literary roots of modern ecology in the British nineteenth century*. Pennsylvania: The Pennsylvania State University Press.
Seabrook, J. (1995). From leisure class to leisure society. In C. Critcher, P. Bramham, & A. Tomlinson (Eds.), *The sociology of leisure: A reader* (pp. 97–104). London: Chapman and Hall.
Shelley, M. (1844). *Rambles in Germany and Italy in 1840, 1842, and 1843* (Vol. 2). London: Edward Moxon.
Skinner, J. (2000). The eruption of chances peak, Montserrat, and the narrative containment of risk. In P. Caplan (Ed.), *Risk revisited* (pp. 156–183). London: Pluto Press.
Skinner, J. (2008). Ghosts in the head and ghost towns in the field: Ethnography and the experience of presence and absence. *Journeys: International Journal of Travel and Travel Writing, 9*(2), 10–31.
Skinner, J. (2015, May 21). Let's get gritty on the black and green. *MNIalive.com – Global Caribbean Media*. http://www.mnialive.com/articles/let-s-get-gritty-on-the-black-and-green. Accessed 21 May 2015.
Skinner, J. (2017). "Was here": Identity traces and digital footprints as survival writing. *Liminalities: A Journal of Performance Studies*. http://liminalities.net/12-5/washere.pdf. Accessed 20 Sept 2017.
Skinner, J., & Theodossopoulos, D. (2011). Introduction: The play of expectation in tourism. In J. Skinner & D. Theodossopoulos (Eds.), *Great expectations:*

Imagination, anticipation, and enchantment in tourism (pp. 1–26). Oxford: Berghahn Books.
Sliwinski, S. (2011). *Human rights in camera*. Chicago: University of Chicago Press.
Sloan, G. (2015). Back on the map for cruisers: Montserrat. *USA Today*. http://www.usatoday.com/story/cruiselog/2015/03/19/windstar-cruises-montserrat/24983199/. Accessed 5 Aug 2016.
St Clair, W., & Bautz, A. (2012). Imperial decadence: The making of the myths in Edward Bulwer-Lytton's: The last days of Pompeii. *Victorian Literature and Culture, 40*, 359–396.
Steiner, G. (1971). *Bluebeard's castle: Some notes towards the redefinition of culture*. New Haven: Yale University Press.
Stendhal. (1987[1826]). *Rome, Naples et Florence*. Paris: Gallimard.
Thackeray, W. (1899). *The works of William Makepeace Thackeray: Contributions to "Punch," etc*. London: Harper & Brothers.
Torry, W. (1979). Anthropological studies in hazardous environments: Past trends and new horizons. *Current Anthropology, 20*(3), 517–540.
VisitMontserrat. (2016). *Explore*. http://www.visitmontserrat.com/buried-city/. Accessed 8 Sept 2016.
Volcano Discovery. (2016). *Fascination volcano*. https://www.volcano-adventures.com/italy/volcanoes_italy_tour.html. Accessed 15 Aug 2016.
von Goethe, J. W. (1848). *The auto-biography of Goethe: Truth and poetry: From my own life*. London: H.G. Bohn.
Walker, T. (2015). Enlightened absolutism and the Lisbon earthquake: Asserting state dominance over religious sites and the church in eighteen-century Portugal. *Eighteenth-Century Studies, 48*(3), 307–328.
Walpole, H. (1774). *A description of the villa of Horace Walpole, youngest son of Sir Robert Walpole Earl of Orford, at Strawberry-Hill, near Twickenham. With an inventory of the furniture, pictures, curiosities, &c. Strawberry-Hill*. London: Thomas Kirkgate.
Walpole, H. (1890). In C. Yonge (Ed.), *Letters of Horace Walpole: Volume 1 (1736–1764)*. London: T. Fisher Unwin. http://www.fullbooks.com/Letters-of-Horace-Walpole1.html. Accessed 25 May 2016.
Willis, E. (2014). *Theatricality, dark tourism and ethical spectatorship: Absent others*. New York: Palgrave Macmillan.

Section 2

Dark Tourism: Philosophy and Theory

Philip R. Stone

Introduction

Memorials are dead. Memorialisation has failed. Or at least there is a contention that some war memorials in particular are not fit for purpose and have neglected to adequately recall horrific memories of the hostile past (Jones 2016). Of course, memorials not only pay reverence to the deceased, but also act as symbolic markers of our own mistakes, fights and follies. Past (and present) struggles have witnessed totalitarian regimes across the world thrive on a mantra of intolerance whereby swathes of populations have been tyrannised, persecuted, or murdered. Now, an apparent rise of the anti-liberal right in the West and rejection of globalisation under the political parlance of *populism* means that seeds are once again being sown for democracy's 'other' to return. Prejudice is a stain on society and the chaos of hatred, bigotry, and unreason cannot be easily conveyed through bleak memorials for the (conflict) dead which, subsequently, are strategically placed in the (dark) tourism landscape for contemporary consumption. Arguably, artistic abstract memorials that act as sombre tourist attractions and civic symbols have failed to remind the masses of fascism and xenophobia of yesteryear wars (Gold 2017; Jones 2016). However, the issue is not with memorialisation itself but with memory—or at least shared narratives of collective memory. The Holocaust, for instance, was not only the bureaucratic calculus of death by a Nazi German State but also

P. R. Stone (✉)
University of Central Lancashire, Preston, UK

involved demonic passions of the populace. Holocaust memorials rarely convey this message; and as tourists consume places of pain and shame, 'we would be utter fools to think it can't happen again, or that the world will never have any more reason to build memorials' (Jones 2016: 1).

Therefore, the ability to locate ourselves in a 'dark tourism world' where memorials are insufficiently narrating hurtful memories calls out for philosophical responses. At a rudimentary level, philosophising is the ability to extract ourselves from a busy, engaged world of making and doing things, and to disengage and pause for reflection and thought especially about meaning and purpose (Tribe 2009). The ability to offer philosophical approaches to dark tourism that are grounded in conceptual frameworks and meta-narratives is crucial to our understanding of signifying death within the visitor economy. Indeed, deaths of significant Others and destruction of physical places is often transformed into memory and historicity through a fluctuating process of socio-cultural and political production and construction, as well as performance and consumption of commemorative visitor sites. 'Heritage that hurts' (Uzzell and Ballantyne 1998) and sites of dark tourism are not automatically sanctified or deemed of historical note simply because an act of atrocity or disaster has occurred. Rather, spaces of dark tourism are continuously (re)negotiated and (re)constructed into places of meaning and meaning-making through human interaction and semiotics. Cultural expressions of tragic memory are both generated and informed by colloquial or official pasts and displayed within auratic memorial landscapes, as well as being consumed by polysemic tourist experiences (see also Section 5). It is within public places of tourism that memory mediates between dominant and usually authorised narratives and individual consumption. Tourism sites of tragic history are places where public and vernacular histories and memories intersect and act in dialogue (Sather-Wagstaff 2011). Yet, the question remains as to the relevance and application of this dialogue, and whether dark tourism and inherent memorial messages are getting through.

About This Section

This section outlines a number of different but complementary philosophical viewpoints of dark tourism, its challenges and components, as well as offering conceptual frameworks for locating future dark tourism studies. In the first chapter (Chap. 6), Erik Cohen addresses dominant Western-centric perspectives within dark tourism research and, subsequently, offers a comparative conceptual framework in which to locate dark tourism (or thanatourism as Cohen refers). Drawing upon the paradigmatic approach offered by Stone

(2012) in which Western dark tourism could be seen as a functional secular substitute for religious institutions in the face of mortality; Cohen examines dark tourism within non-Western emergent world regions. In so doing, Cohen offers a much-needed examination of dark tourism from an Asian context and, in particular, outlines a conceptual framework of dark tourism based on different ontological assumptions of death. Using a range of empirical illustrations including from Thailand, Cambodia, Malaysia, Vietnam, Laos, Japan, and China, Cohen argues that Asian dark tourism sites might differ from Western counterparts because of a fundamental difference in the theology of death and soteriology of the main Asian religious traditions.

In the second chapter (Chap. 7), Jeffrey Podoshen locates dark tourism within a dystopian world with ever-increasing violent narratives that embrace moral decay and atrocity images. Podoshen provides a deliberately provocative account of dark tourism at the intersection of death, its contemporary consumption, and consumer culture theoretics. He proposes that dark tourism denotes a *form of signalling* as well as a *form of preparation* and, consequently, the study suggests dark tourism is an extension of conspicuous consumer behaviour in a modern world where death can be immersed as a consumer activity.

The third chapter (Chap. 8) by Philip Stone draws upon the work of Jacobsen (2016) and, as a result, completes his trilogy of thanatological-themed papers within dark tourism (the first one being Stone and Sharpley 2008 and, the second, Stone 2012). In particular, Stone extends his earlier conceptual works which located dark tourism within a secular response to mortality mediation and an historical mentality of the 'forbidden' (or absence) death. Specifically, he contends that contemporary dark tourism is now a distinct component of what has been termed 'spectacular death'. Where death, dying, and mourning have, arguably, become increasing spectacles in Western societies, Stone suggests dark tourism offers a re-reversal of so-called 'forbidden' death. Ultimately, Stone argues that dark tourism as a mediating institution of mortality has the paradoxical tendency of making death linger uneasily between (market) liberation and denial as well as (heritage) autonomy and control.

In the fourth chapter (Chap. 9) by Rami Isaac and Vincent Platenkamp, a Nietzscheism approach is adopted to the study of dark tourism. Specfically, with Western morality ending in a form of relativism that rejects any substantial value in the norms of the modern world, a resultant crisis of identity emerges. In what Nietzsche compared to as a state of 'passive nihilism' in which no criterion can deliver the foundations of any identity; Nietzsche views an alternative to nihilism in the form of human (Greek) tragedy and the relationship between Apollo and Dionysus. It is here where Isaac and Platenkamp take their philosophical cue and, subsequently, examine the Apollonian (dreams and harmony) and the Dionysian (intoxication and chaos) as guiding principles within identity construction through dark tourism. Using the Palestinian/Israeli conflict as a contextual case study, Isaac and Platenkamp offer a thought-provoking account of confrontation, interpretation, authentication, and national identity through binary Apollonian/Dionysian perspectives of dark tourism.

The final chapter (Chap. 10) in this section by Richard Morten, Philip Stone, and David Jarratt examines dark tourism as an intrinsically emotional, subjective, and phenomenological place-based pursuit. In particular, they address spatial subjectivity within dark tourism environments and, as a result, the specific effects of geographical environments on the emotions and behaviours of individuals. The study suggests a transactional nature to the production and consumption of dark tourism; a process entirely influenced by a very personal framework of knowledge, memory, and associations. Adopting a psychogeographical approach, and drawing upon the work of Foucault and Debord, the study considers dark tourism not as a passive mode of tourism, but rather as a dynamic and individualistic way of interacting with space and place. Ultimately, Morten, Stone, and Jarratt argue that dark tourism exists by way of deeply personalised responses to geographic places and, consequently, the chapter is the first ever to comprehensively locate dark tourism as a specific form of psychogeography.

As a final note, this section offers a thematic approach that is selective and not exhaustive. That said, given the dynamic and complex nature of dark tourism across the globe and the ever-increasing significance accorded to the subject as a focus of contemporary consumption, dark tourism as a concept requires further theoretical underpinnings. Indeed, philosophical approaches to dark tourism as the production and consumption of 'difficult heritage' provide meta-narratives in which to conceptually frame future empirical research. It is hoped, therefore, that the chapters in this section will not only contribute to knowledge and understanding of a phenomenon that continues to grow in social and cultural significance, but will also act as a catalyst for future scholarship within dark tourism and heritage and memory studies.

References

Gold, T. (2017, March 13). Smile for the Auschwitz selfie: Why Holocaust memorials have failed. *The New Statesmen*. Available at: http://www.newstatesman.com/culture/2017/03/smile-auschwitz-selfie-why-holocaust-memorials-have-failed. Accessed 21 Mar 17.

Jacobsen, M. H. (2016). 'Spectacular death' – Proposing a new fifth phase to Philippe Ariè's admirable history of death. *Humanities, 5*(19). https://doi.org/10.3390/h5020019.

Jones, J. (2016, December 9). War memorials have failed – We have forgotten the chaos of fascism. *The Guardian*. Available at: https://www.theguardian.com/artanddesign/jonathanjonesblog/2016/dec/09/war-memorials-have-failed-peter-eisenman-holocaust. Accessed 21 Mar 17.

Sather-Wagstaff, J. (2011). *Heritage that hurts: Tourists in the Memoryscapes of September 11*. Walnut Creek: Left Coast Press.

Stone, P. R. (2012). Dark tourism and significant other death: Towards a model of mortality mediation. *Annals of Tourism Research, 39*(3), 1565–1587.

Stone, P. R., & Sharpley, R. (2008). Consuming dark tourism: A thanatological perspective. *Annals of Tourism Research, 35*(2), 574–595.

Tribe, J. (Ed.). (2009). *Philosophical issues in tourism*. Bristol: Channel View Publications.

Uzzell, D. L., & Ballantyne, R. (1998). Heritage that hurts: Interpretation in a postmodern world. In D. L. Uzzell & R. Ballantyne (Eds.), *Contemporary issues in heritage and environmental interpretation: Problems and prospects* (pp. 152–171). London: The Stationery Office.

6

Thanatourism: A Comparative Approach

Erik Cohen

Introduction

Philip Stone (2012) has proposed a paradigmatic approach to thana (death) tourism in contemporary secular Western, "death-denying" societies, departing from Giddens' (1991) argument on the weakening of "ontological security" in the contemporary world (also see Chap. 8). Stone proposed that sites of dark tourism constitute what could be seen as a functional substitute for religious institutions which in the past enabled individuals to come to terms with their mortality (Stone 2012; Stone and Sharpley 2008). Dark tourism is thus conceived as a non-religious mediating institution between the living and the dead, offering an opportunity of thanatopic contemplation in face of inevitable (and meaningless) death. Stone quotes Lennon and Foley's (2000) assertion that dark tourism is "primarily a Western phenomenon" (Stone 2006: 149). This resounds with my own conviction in the past that "tourism" is primarily a Western phenomenon. However, such Eurocentric attitudes have been recently dispelled by a revised conceptual approach, which argues that tourism is a global phenomenon, though manifested in diverse ways in various parts of the world (Cohen and Cohen 2015a). We should ask, therefore, do dark tourism phenomena exist in non-Western emergent world regions, though based on different ontological assumptions about death, than those of the secular West? Stone's paradigmatic approach could thus be broadened into

E. Cohen (✉)
Hebrew University of Jerusalem, Jerusalem, Israel

© The Author(s) 2018
P. R. Stone et al. (eds.), *The Palgrave Handbook of Dark Tourism Studies*,
https://doi.org/10.1057/978-1-137-47566-4_6

a comparative conceptual framework, in which Western thanatourism would be just one particular case. This procedure resembles one I have recently applied to the comparative study of roadside memorials, a phenomenon first studied in the contemporary West, but found in different disguises in many societies outside the West (Cohen 2012).

In this chapter, therefore, I seek merely to outline an approach to the comparative study of thanatourism and support it by examples taken from particular Asian countries. I have neither the resources nor the space for a systematic comparison of thanatourism in the emergent world regions.

Theoretical Approach

The crucial point of Stone's paradigmatic approach is the modern secular "theology" of life and death. For present purposes this can be concisely presented in a few basic premises:

1. Human life is a once-only event;
2. Death is an inevitable terminal point of individual life, the point of the ontological cessation of individual existence;
3. There is no afterlife, either as eternal life or as rebirth;
4. Hence, death is meaningless; there is no hope.

Under these premises, thanatouristic sites offer a potential opportunity for thanatopsis. That is, the contemplation of one's own death, and its stoical acceptance, without striving to overcome it by some act of faith or belief. However, students of thanatourism have recently stressed that not all thanatourist sites are equally dark; rather, there are various "shades of darkness," which implies that dark tourism combines degrees of both "darkness" and "lightness" (Heuermann and Chhabra 2014; Stone 2006; Sharpley 2005). Several typologies of Western thanatourism have been proposed to scale those phenomena along a dark-to-light axis (Stone 2006). Thanatourists will assumedly differ in their motivations and experiences along this axis, with the strongest thanatopic experiences at the darkest sites. Empirical studies, however, have shown that there is a wide diversity of motivations and experiences even among visitors to the same dark site (Biran et al. 2011). The darkness of sites and the depth of thanatopic experiences of visitors are possibly related, but not overlapping; these variables have therefore to be separately investigated. This is particularly important in the case of dark tourist sites in the emergent regions, which are visited by both a foreign and a domestic public.

My proposal for a comparative framework of thanasites in the West and in the emergent regions is based on four major dimensions: the kind of thanatourist sites, the respective theologies of death and soteriological teachings, the relations to and with the dead, and the motivations and experiences of domestic visitors to those sites.

Recent literature offers increasing evidence of the existence of thanatourist sites and of thanatourism in the emergent regions, for example, in Africa (Mudzanani 2014; Strange and Kempa 2003; Werdler 2012), in South America (Wyndham and Read 2012), and particularly in Asian countries, such as India (Verma and Jain 2013), China (Biran et al. 2014; Tang 2014), Singapore (Muzaini et al. 2007), Cambodia (Sofield 2009), Thailand (Rittichainuwat 2008), Vietnam (Hayward and Tran 2014), and Japan (Cooper 2006; Yoneyama 1999; Yoshida 2004). However, the motivations and experiences of thanatourists in those regions have been less studied. Researchers sought primarily to demonstrate that the phenomenon exists outside the West (Hayward and Tran 2014), but have not dealt systematically with the differences between Western thanatourism and that in other world regions. While such an enterprise is beyond the limits of this chapter, I seek to offer an approach to the comparative study of thanatourism by presenting and analyzing some selected thanatourism examples from Asian countries.

Ancestor Worship as Background to Asian Thanatourism

I distinguish two main varieties of thanatourist phenomena in contemporary Asia, both drawing on long-established religious traditions, particularly ancestor worship. The first expands the customs of ancestor worship unto sites of deceased non-kin persons, especially celebrities, attracting mainly domestic visitors. The other applies those traditions more loosely and selectively to the commemoration and worship on recent historical sites of massive death, such as battlefields and places where atrocities were committed or disasters occurred. These are often visited by both domestic and international visitors. All major Asian religions, Hinduism, Buddhism, Chinese folk religion, or Shinto, believe in the survival of the soul/spirit after death, but differ in their soteriological teachings. I shall focus here mainly on the Hindu-Buddhist traditions, and the ancestor worship rituals based on them.

Matthew Sayers (2013) states in his study of ancient Indian ancestor worship an opening question: "What is the ultimate goal of the individual in Hinduism? Liberation from rebirth? An eternal place in heaven? The tension between the ascetically oriented soteriology of liberation and that of the ritualistic tradition that aims at heaven is at the core of Hindu practices relevant to the ultimate end of the religious life"(ibid: 1). The Brahmins advocate the "renunciation of rituals and worldly life for the attainment of salvation. The ritualists endorse ritual activity as the way to the ultimate goal, an eternal stay in heaven"; the latter have created a "long tradition of ancestor worship" (ibid: 1). Sayers points out that "the centrality of reincarnation to the contemporary conception of Hinduism…belies a long and rich history of ancestor worship in South Asia. The funerary offerings made to one's dead parents in contemporary India are the survival of a tradition that stretches back to the Vedas… [which] revolves around the translation of the deceased to the next world" where "the ancestors live on the food offered to them in ritual" (ibid: 1). This ritual has "persisted for more than two thousand years after the development of the concept of transmigration" (ibid: 1).

Buddhism has similarly condoned ancestor worship, even though it denied permanence to the self: the Buddhist doctrine of conditioned origination "describes a world in which nothing is permanent, including the self" (Sayers 2013: 10). But, while Buddha had taught that the ultimate goal is nirvana, the extinction of the self, "the Buddhist authors did not reject the ubiquitous ritual practices of the householder (hospitality, divine rites and ancestral rites); they have merely reinterpreted them in various ways, for example, reconceptualizing their underpinning assumptions or offering a moral interpretation" (ibid: 11).

Extension of Ancestor Rituals to Popular Non-kin Deceased Persons

Ancestor worship, involving the practice of feeding the ancestors or even transferring objects to them, is found in all major Asian religions, notwithstanding theological or soteriological differences. In contemporary folk Buddhism, for example, the Buddhist monks may be taken recourse to as mediators with the spirits of the dead and serve to transfer objects from laymen to the ancestors. Ladwig (2011: 19) reports that in Laos, "the ritual transfer of objects to the spirits of the deceased… plays a crucial role in large rituals that are part of the Lao ritual cycle." Ladwig (2011: 19) points out that "the transfer of objects to non-human beings plays a crucial role in establishing a link between humans and the spirits of the dead." However, some critics see this belief as [erroneous] "folk Buddhism" and claim that only merit (*boun*) is transferred to the deceased, while the objects stay with the monks (ibid: 19).

I shall restrict the discussion of the extension of ancestor rituals to non-kin deceased to Thailand, since it renders the best examples of this process which I am familiar with. Ancestor worship is a principal form of the ritual system of spirit veneration, a major component of Thai folk religion. Adjoining most spirit houses for the Earth spirit (*phra phum*) at Thai dwellings, there is a lower shrine for the spirits of the ancestors (*taa-yaay*). Shrines are also put up for the spirits of mountains or semi-mythical heroes, local potentates, or notables, referred to, in terms of an adapted kinship terminology, by the honorifics *chao pho* (Lord Father) or *chao mae* (Lady Mother). Such shrines are locally venerated and mostly do not have a wider audience or appeal to domestic or foreign tourists.

However, a recent, though still rare, phenomenon is the erection of memorial shrines for notables or celebrities who have died in road accidents (a variety of Western "roadside memorials" [Cohen 2012]), or in mishaps, or who suffered a premature death from other causes. In contrast to the standardized *taa-yaay*, and even *chao pho-chao mae* shrines, such sites are devoted to widely known personalities and potentially appeal to a wider audience; they are thus potential thanatouristic attractions. I shall offer three examples of sites devoted to deceased celebrities in Thailand:

> The shrine of Hanni [Honey] Sri Isan, a *mo-lam* (a form of folk song [Champadeang 2010]) songstress from the northeastern (Isan) region of Thailand, who was killed at an early age in a road accident. A shrine in the form of an enlarged spirit house was established at the site, with a large photograph of the deceased on a billboard in front of it and one of her costumes displayed inside. People pray at the shrine and leave votive objects, particularly figurines of children (Hanni died childless) and ask the spirit of the songstress for good luck. (Cohen 2012: 353–357)

Another notable example is the shrine of Mitr Chaibancha, a popular Thai actor of the 1960s (Jaiser 2012: 37), who died in 1970 after a helicopter accident in Chonburi Province. A shrine in his memory was established in Thailand's leading seaside resort city, Pattaya, located in the same province. From humble beginnings, the shrine has been upgraded and embellished several times, most recently in 2012. It displays a life-size metal sculpture of the actor holding a pistol, photographs from his motion pictures, and other memorabilia (*Wikipedia* n.d.). The shrine acts as a memorial, but it also serves as a place of worship of the spirit of the actor, resembling the worship of a *chao pho* (Lord Father) (Cohen 2012: 349). These two sites, though commemorating deceased celebrities, have not (yet) achieved the level of popularity to be called a thanatourist attraction. However, though the dividing line is fuzzy, the third site commemorating the songstress Pumpuang Duangjan (1961–1992), who had enjoyed nation-wide popularity, appears to qualify as a thanatourist attraction (Cohen 2012: 347–349).

Pumpuang Duangjan was the most popular Thai *Luk Thung* (a popular vocal music style [Jaiser 2012: 43–51]) songstress and actress of her generation. Born to very poor villagers in the central province of Suphanburi, she was an illiterate prodigy, who started performing at the age of 15 and was soon propelled to stardom with her innovative style and daring appearance (Siriyuvasak 1998: 192–194). However, exploited by her managers and exhausted from being overworked, Pumpuang died from a blood illness at the age of 31. Her funeral rites took place in Wat (temple) Thap Kradan in Song Phi Nong district in her native Suphanburi, and her ashes were deposited in an urn at the temple. Soon after her death, the temple turned the main hall on its ground floor into a commemorative site for the deceased songstress. Her life-size likenesses, dressed in her outfits and holding a microphone, were placed at several locations within the temple, accompanied by continuous broadcasts of her songs. In the temple hall, her personal belongings, dresses, shoes, and even some intimate articles were displayed in glass cases, resembling the display of personal belongings of a deceased abbot in some other temples.

Wat Thap Kradan has attracted vast numbers of visitors who worshipped the spirit of the songstress and presented her with objects to use in her afterlife, just as such objects are "transferred" to deceased ancestors. These included not only dresses and other personal objects but also a large number of toilet chests, which had filled the space around the display of her personal belongings (author's observations). The donations by devotees made the temple prosperous. In the early 2000s, for instance, it was able to initiate a major renovation and expansion, whereby in addition to a display of the songstress' likenesses and photos in the main hall, several small shrines devoted to her were constructed within the temple's premises—one containing her gilded funerary urn and the others her likenesses. Additionally, an open shrine, with the image of the songstress dressed in white, was placed under an old banyan tree. Like the shrines to the spirits of prominent local women, marked by the honorific *chao mae* (Lady mother), an altar in front of the image was loaded with votive objects, its access flanked by a pair of animal figures. Moreover, hundreds of dresses donated to the dead songstress were hung on the branches of the banyan tree (author's observations).

Wat Thap Kradan is often visited by excursionists as a specific attraction, within a broader weekend trip to the area; the visitors often venerate and make presentations to the deceased songstress. However, closer observation reveals a personal motive behind this veneration: people beseech the spirit of the songstress to bestow them with luck—particularly, to reveal winning numbers in a forthcoming lottery draw. This, rather than commemoration, seems to be often the worshippers' principal motivation to visit Wat Thap Kradan (Cohen 2012: 347–349).

The only other Asian example I was able to find resembling such a site comes from Malaysia, the Bai Guang Memorial. A musical tomb in the shape of a piano for the remembrance of the late legendary Bai Guang songstress is the first musical tomb in Malaysia. The musical tomb plays one of her famous songs "If Without You" when one approaches the piano. Today, the Bai Guang Memorial tomb is well known and has become a key visitor attraction within the Nirvana Memorial Park [a private cemetery with branches in several Asian countries] (*Celebrity memorial* http://www.nirvana-asia-ltd.com/malaysia/bramches/nirvana-memorial-park-semenyih/celebrity-memorial/). But, in contrast to Pumpuang's memorial site, this songstress' spirit does not inhabit the tomb nor are supplications to it made by visitors.

An intensive search of the literature and the Internet failed to locate much information on other Asian examples of memorial sites for celebrities, but this might be due to the fact that this is as yet an emergent phenomenon. Thus, in the communist states of Asia, China, Vietnam, and Laos, public commemoration has in the past been restricted to monuments and other edifices devoted to revolutionary heroes, so memory sites for celebrities and other private persons could not be erected. However, things seem to be changing, with one study pointing out that in post-communist China, "state-led projects of patriotic education… ensured coexistence in commercial pop-culture of revolutionary idols and contemporary celebrities, via memory sites associated with… historical locations, museums and monuments of 'red tourism'" (Jeffreys 2012). However, I was unable to find any studies of memory sites associated with contemporary Chinese celebrities. I suggest that if such sites emerge, in China or elsewhere in Asia, they will be built upon, and expand, existing traditions rather than contrast with them, as Elvis Presley's Graceland in Memphis, Kentucky, contrasts, as a new kind of sacred place, with modern Western secularism (Rigby 2001).

Memorials of War, Atrocities, and Disasters

Many thanatourist sites have been established in Asia for the commemoration of the fallen in the Second World War as well as the Vietnam War, for the victims of atrocities in Cambodia, and for the casualties of major disasters, such as the 2004 tsunami in the Indian Ocean. Some of these have been created by the Western powers for their war dead and are outside the scope of this chapter. Other sites have been established by the initiative of the authorities of Asian countries and attract both a foreign and a local public. However, the literature on these sites remains scarce and uneven, dealing primarily with their history and structure and much less with the customs and conduct associated with them. I shall in this section discuss three examples of Asian thanatourist sites found in the literature. Firstly, a Buddhist temple devoted to the commemoration of the victims of the Khmer Rouge regime in Cambodia. Secondly, a notorious prison in Vietnam, and lastly, the Hiroshima Peace Memorial Park in Japan. I shall dwell upon the extent to which the customs associated with those sites deploy elements of prevailing religious traditions, especially ancestor worship, on sites of death on a massive scale.

Trevor Sofield (2009: 176) offers a detailed description of the Khmer New Year commemoration of relatives killed by the Pol Pot regime, conducted at a Buddhist temple on the holy Sampau mountain, close to the city of Battambang in Cambodia. The temple was destroyed by the Khmer Rouge, and its site has been deliberately desecrated. Indeed, its sacred cave was used as a torture prison and the ravines of the mountain for mass killings by hurling "enemies of the state" to their death. After the fall of the regime, the temple was rebuilt. At the temple:

> …a small group of nuns and monks [are] praying 24 hours a day in perpetuity trying to rescue the souls of those killed who, in Buddhist theology, are 'lost and hungry ghosts' because they were denied a proper burial… These dark places today experience a Cambodian form of thanatourism at the Khmer New Year when more than 30,000 pilgrims each day of the New Year holiday provide offerings for the monks and nuns to recite continuous prayers for their 'lost' relatives. Many pilgrims detour from the temple to the killing sites and caves to burn incense and recite prayers. Temporarily, however, not enough time has elapsed since the horrors of the democide to fade for most Cambodians; and the 'Cambodian thana- tourism' to the so-called Killing Fields of Pol Pot that may be found in many parts of Cambodia is not a form of visitation for most Cambodians. Such sites are shunned by most Cambodians. (Sofield 2009: 176)

Sofield goes on to report:

> In 2007, for example, 140,978 international visitors toured the Choeung Ek Killing Fields…where…mass graves containing the remains of 27,000 victims have been exhumed: but only 8569 Cambodians…entered the site. (ibid: 176)

The Cambodians do not neglect those sites; rather, it seems that they are unable to bear the intensity of the thanatopic experience at those sites of recent large-scale atrocities.

A similar thanatourist site has been described by Hayward and Tran (2014) in their study of tourism to Vietnam's Con Dao archipelago. The authors found that visits to the sites and memorials of the prisons on Con Son Island, in which dissidents have been incarcerated during successive French, South Vietnamese, and US administrations, constituted "the cornerstone of tourism in the archipelago since 1975 and the fundamental to the area's contemporary brand identity" (ibid: 117). According to the authors, domestic tourists began to visit the prisons in the late 1970s, initially in the form of self-organized visits to sites of imprisonment and/or demise of relatives, friends, and inspirational figures in Vietnam's extended struggle for self-determination. The physical remnants of the prisons and their associated grave sites became a key attraction for tourists, and the displays subsequently installed within them provided a chilling and vivid representation of the barbaric conditions in which dissidents were held and in which many perished (Hayward and Tran 2014).

Hayward and Tran (2014: 117) quote from Bodnar's (2001: x) foreword to Ho Tai's edited volume the observation that "successful memorialisation of War dead in Vietnam has to combine 'predictable tropes of patriotism' with the acknowledgment that there is a deep social attachment to 'rituals that signified that the dead would be reborn in an 'otherworld' where they would join a community of ancestors,' with the latter aspect providing as powerful a point of connection to the past and inspiration for the future as the former." The authors argue that "Con Son's only Buddhist pagoda… combines [these] two aspects in its daily chants" (ibid: 117). As an example, they quote a line from a chant, sung during a requiem mass by the pagoda's senior monk: "we believe that the fallen will watch over and provide guidance toward peace and happiness of present people and future generations" (ibid: 117).

The presentation of the prison sites consisted initially of "a simple opening-up of the former closed prison facilities to public visitation… revealing the horrors of incarceration" under previous regimes. However, with growing numbers of visitors and a rise in awareness of the prisons' significance, steps were taken toward "the maintenance and organization of prison sites for visitors and the provision of signage and documentation to enhance visitor experience." The latter involved "the installation of sculptures of shackled and emaciated prisoners in old prison buildings," providing, in the authors' view, "one of the 'darkest' imaginable thanatouristic experiences" (Hayward and Tran 2014; 118). At a large cemetery on the island, "20,000 deceased prisoners have been buried, 712 of whom have been identified and are commemorated with individually named headstones" (Hayward and Tran 2014: 118). The authors point out that individual graves of particularly revered patriots are also major centers of attraction and visitation.

Among the most visited graves is that of "Vietnam's most celebrated female revolutionary patriot, Vo Thi Sau [who] was executed by firing squad on Con Son in 1952 after two years of imprisonment during which she actively defied prison rules. Her revolutionary zeal and early death, aged 19, have contributed to a cult-status for her – akin to that of [a] secular revolutionary 'saint.' There are two distinct pilgrimage sites associated with her. While visitors to patriots' graves routinely bring bouquets of flowers, offerings of rice, meals, fruit or wine, Sau's memorials are also subject to gifts of materials that reflect her youth and femininity (such as lipstick, mirrors, combs etc.). The visitors' gifts are both marks of respect and also offerings that are made in anticipation of inspiration, guidance and/or good fortune deriving from the secular pilgrimage" (Hayward and Tran 2014: 118). The spirit of the communist heroine Vo Thi Sau in Vietnam is thus venerated and supplicated in a similar manner as the celebrity songstress Pumpuang in Thailand.

Of all Asian countries, Japan has by far the greatest number of memorial sites devoted to those killed in the Second World War. According to Yoshida (2004), the country features at least 85 memorial museums and memorials. I shall here limit myself to the most prominent and best known memorial site, the Hiroshima Peace Memorial Park.

I have argued above that the customs of the veneration of the dead on thanatourist sites in Asian Buddhist countries constitute an extension and adaptation of the prevailing traditional ancestor worship. In Japan, however, ancestor worship came to be merged with state Shinto rituals. According to Smith (1974: 2), "following the Meiji Restoration in 1868… official efforts to link Shinto emperor worship with 'Buddhist'… ancestor worship… proved dazzlingly successful." Consequently, "up to 1945 ancestor worship was tied… to the politics and objectives of the State." However, though the link has been formally broken after Japan's defeat in the Second World War, it has left its traces in the establishment and structure of the Peace Memorial Park, as Yoneyama's (1999) detailed study clearly demonstrates:

> In tracing the development of Japan's architectural modernism from the 1920s to the 1940s, the historian Inoue Shôichi offers an interesting account of the possible aesthetic origins of the Hiroshima Peace Memorial Park. Situated at the heart of the city, close to the site of the atomic bomb's detonation, the park was built on a vast open field of ashes created by the explosion. The park's location

was once the city's downtown commercial and residential district, crowded with shops, residences, inns and theaters. Today, the commemorative space accommodates a number of memorials and monuments, museums and lecture halls, and draws over a million visitors annually. It also provides the ritual space for the annual 6 August Peace Memorial ceremony, which is sponsored by the city of Hiroshima. The design for the Peace Memorial Park was selected following a public competition that took place in 1949, while Japan was still under Allied Occupation. According to Inoue, the park's stylistic origin can be traced back to a nearly identical ground plan that has been adopted three years before Japan's surrender as part of a grand imperial vision, the Commemorative Building Project for the Construction of Greater East Asia.

Both designs were the creation of the world-renowned architect Tange Kenzô. For the 1942 competition Tange proposed a grandiose Shintoist memorial zone to be built on an open plain at the foot of Mount Fuji. With the collapse of Japan's empire that followed defeat by the Allied Forces and, more important, by anti-imperialist resistance against Japan in Asia and the Pacific, Tange's 1942 plan was forever aborted. Yet the majestic space that he envisioned as monumentalizing the concept of the Greater East Asia Co-Prosperity [Sphere] appears to have been revived in his 1949 postwar design; it was subsequently realized in 1954, albeit at [a] much reduced scale, with the completion of Hiroshima's Peace Memorial Park.

Nothing epitomizes the Heideggerian irony of Japan's imperial modernity more solemnly than the incorporation of the monumentalized ruins of what is called the Atom Bomb Dome into the park. As in Tange's earlier plan, the central worshipping axis extends from the entrance, through the central cenotaph, to the ruins. This commemorative site is the artificially preserved remains of what used to be the Industry Promotion Hall, a quintessential sign of Japan's early-twentieth-century imperial modernity. Designed by an architect from Czechoslovakia, this continental Secession-style building, crowned with a distinctive dome-shaped roof, was completed in 1915. [In 1945] the atomic blast caused extensive damage to the building, leaving only some brick walls and the exposed iron frame of the dome-shaped canopy: hence the name of the ruin the Atom Bomb Dome.

In the postwar plan, the earlier concept of a sixty-meter Shintoist-style commemorative structure was scaled down and transfigured into the more human-sized, arch-shaped design of the central cenotaph that is now officially named the Hiroshima Peace City Commemorative Monument. In this newly recrafted public space, people congregate – not to celebrate the modernity, enlightenment, civilization, and dreams promised by the pan-Asian co-prosperity sphere, but rather to remember the inaugural moment of the nuclear age and to imagine possible self-annihilation of civilization.

The structural continuity between the two ritual spaces and, more crucially, the widespread failure to recognize their analogies alert us to the conventional status of Hiroshima memories, both nationally and in global contexts. The unproblematized transition of Hiroshima's central commemorative space from celebrating imperial Japan to honoring the postwar peaceful nation, suggests the persistence of pre-war social and cultural elements, even at the iconic site that supposedly symbolizes the nation's rebirth and departure from the past. (Yoneyama 1999: 1–3)

The Hiroshima Monument is ostensibly at one with other thanatourist sites, serving as monuments to mass death and destruction, such as Ground Zero in New York or Auschwitz-Birkenau in Poland, which seem to respond to "a deep human need to understand human tragedy and violence" (Neuberger 2014: 67). Beneath the surface, however, lurks a Shintoist memorial to the dead that is devoted to the victims of the atomic bomb on Hiroshima rather than the celebration of Japan's imperialist dreams (as intended in the original 1942 project, of which the Monument is a postwar permutation).

Conclusion

I have argued in this chapter that, in contrast to some claims, thanatourism, conceived as visits to places of death and suffering, is not an exclusively Western phenomenon. Indeed, thanatourist sites and visitations are found in non-Western regions of the globe and attract significant numbers of visitors. However, as my discussion of several examples from Asia indicates, they do not necessarily elicit the same thanatopic motivations and experiences of contemplation of death that are deemed iconic in Western thanatourism. Rather, on the basis of these examples, I argue that non-Western thanatourism differs from its Western counterpart with regard to most of the dimensions listed in the introduction.

I have distinguished between two major kinds of thanatourist sites in Asia. Firstly, memorial sites to popular non-kin deceased persons and, secondly, memorials of war, atrocities, and disasters. The former is devoted to famous individuals who suffered an early or unnatural death and is comparable to such celebrity memorial sites in the West as Graceland—the former home and resting place of Elvis Presley. The latter are sites of massive death of mostly anonymous individuals, which resemble Western war memorials.

However, despite these similarities, the conduct, motivations, and experiences of visitors to these sites might differ considerably, mainly owing to a fundamental difference in the theology of death and soteriology of the main Asian religious traditions. Asian countries have not been secularized, contrary to the Western secular "theology" of death as a terminal point of life in which the individual ceases to exist. The theologies of Asian religions teach survival after death and diverse ways of salvation. This softens the "darkness" of death as an ontological cessation of existence and opens the way for potential interaction with the dead at thanatouristic sites.

The case examples from several Asian countries indicate that visitors' interaction with the dead at thanatourist sites is generally patterned on traditional customs of ancestor worship, more closely at memorial sites of popular individuals and less so at sites of mass death. Visitors seek to access the spirits of the dead in various ways: by praying to or for them, rendering them assistance by feeding them, or transferring objects to them, but also by beseeching them for assistance and good luck. The latter is particularly common in Thailand but was also found at a memorial for a communist heroine in Vietnam.

Consequently, this leads to three principal conclusions:

1. Thanatourist sites in Asia emerged as an extension from prevailing traditions, particularly ancestor worship, and are not a novel phenomenon. Moreover, the spirits of the individual dead tend to be gradually incorporated into the pantheon of divinities and other mythical beings of the respective Asian religions.
2. Visitors to thanatourist sites in Asia may mourn for the dead, pay homage to them, desire to assist them, and make merit for themselves by worshipping at the sites, or even supplicate the deceased for personal benefits. But I have not found any evidence of the thanatopic motivation or experience presumed by theoreticians to be the crucial mark of (Western) thanatourism: the contemplation of their own mortality. This may well be the basic difference between Western and Asian thanatourism, derived from differences between the secular Western "theology" of death and its Asian religious counterparts.
3. It therefore follows from the above, that the concept of "mediation" of thanatourist sites, helping individuals to come to terms with inevitable and meaningless death, which is deemed central to the approach to (Western) thanatourism, should be broadened to include different kinds of mediation. In turn, this may release the study of thanatourism from its current Eurocentric bias. While thanatourist sites certainly play a mediating role in Asian thanatourism, the nature of that role varies between cultures and religions. In order to be globally applicable, the study of thanatourism needs to undergo a similar transformation as the Eurocentric paradigmatic approaches to tourism in general are presently undergoing (Cohen and Cohen 2015b).

References

Biran, A., Poria, Y., & Oren, G. (2011). Sought experiences at (dark) heritage sites. *Annals of Tourism Research, 38*(3), 820–841.

Biran, A., Liu, W., Li, G., & Eichhorn, V. (2014). Consuming post-disaster destinations: The case of Sichuan, China. *Annals of Tourism Research, 47*(1), 1–17.

Bodnar, J. (2001). Foreword. In H.-T. HoTai (Ed.), *The country of memory: Remaking the past in late socialist Vietnam*. Berkeley: University of California Press.

Celebrity memorial. http://www.nirvana-asia-ltd.com/malaysia/bramches/nirvana-memorial-park-semenyih/celebrity-memorial/

Champadeang, S. (2010). The role of molam in solving social problems. *Journal of Social Science, 6*(3), 365–368.

Cohen, E. (2012). Roadside memorials in northeastern Thailand. *OMEGA; Journal of Death and Dying, 66*(4), 343–363.

Cohen, E., & Cohen, S. (2015a). A mobilities approach to tourism from emerging world regions. *Current Issues in Tourism, 18*(1), 11–43.

Cohen, E., & Cohen, S. (2015b). Beyond eurocentrism in tourism: A paradigm shift to mobilities. *Tourism Recreation Research, 40*(2), 157–168.

Cooper, M. (2006). The Pacific War battlefields: Tourist attractions or war memorials? *International Journal of Tourism Research, 8*(3), 213–222.

Giddens, A. (1991). *Modernity and self-identity*. Cambridge: Polity.

Hayward, P., & Tran, G. T. H. (2014). At the edge: Heritage tourism development in Vietnam's Con Dao archipelago. *Journal of Marine and Island Cultures, 3*(2), 113–124.

Heuermann, K., & Chhabra, D. (2014). The darker side of dark tourism: An authenticity perspective. *Tourism Analysis, 19*(2), 213–225.

Jaiser, G. (2012). *Thai popular music*. Bangkok: White Lotus.

Jeffreys, E. M. (2012). Modern China's idols: Heroes, role models, stars and celebrities. *Portal: Journal of Multidisciplinary International Studies, 9*(1).

Ladwig, P. (2011). Can things reach the dead? The ontological status of objects and the study of Lao Buddhist rituals for the spirits of the deceased. In K. Lauser & A. Lauser (Eds.), *Engaging the spirit world in modern Southeast Asia* (pp. 19–41). Oxford: Berghahn.

Lennon, J. J., & Foley, M. (2000). *Dark tourism: The attraction of death and disaster*. London: Continuum.

Mudzanani, T. (2014). Why is death so attractive? An analysis of tourist motives for visiting the Hector Peterson Memorial and Museum in South Africa. *Mediterranean Journal of Social Sciences, 5*(15). Retrieved March 15, 2015, from http://mcser-org.ervinhatibi.com/journal/index.php/mjss/article/view/3265

Muzaini, H., Teo, P., & Yeoh, B. S. A. (2007). Intimations of postmodernity in dark tourism: The fate of history at Fort Siloso, Singapore. *Journal of Tourism and Cultural Change, 5*(1), 28–45.

Neuberger, J. (2014). Memorial and the macabre: Conflict resolution in memorial space. *Journal of Peace and Conflict Studies, 1*(1), 60–69.

Rigby, M. (2001). Graceland: A sacred place in a secular world? In C. M. Cusack & P. Oldmeadow (Eds.), *The end of religion? Religion in an age of globalization*. Sydney: Department of Studies in Religion, University of Sydney.

Rittichainuwat, B. N. (2008). Responding to disaster: Thai and Scandinavian tourists' motivations to visit Phuket, Thailand. *Journal of Travel Research, 46*(4), 422–432.

Sayers, M. R. (2013). *Feeding the dead: Ancestor worship in ancient India*. Oxford: Oxford University Press.

Sharpley, R. (2005). Travels to the edge of darkness: Towards a typology of dark tourism. In C. Ryan, S. Page, & M. Aitken (Eds.), *Taking tourism to the limits; issues, concepts and managerial perspectives* (pp. 217–228). Oxford: Elsevier.

Siriyuvasak, U. (1998). Thai pop music and cultural negotiation in everyday politics. In K.-H. Chen (Ed.), *Trajectories: Inter-Asian cultural studies* (pp. 184–204). London: Routledge.

Smith, R. J. (1974). *Ancestor worship in contemporary Japan*. Stanford: Stanford University Press.

Sofield, T. H. B. (2009). Year zero! From annihilation to renaissance: Domestic tourism in Cambodia. In S. H. Singh (Ed.), *Domestic tourism in Asia* (pp. 151–180). London: Earthscan.

Stone, P. R. (2006). A dark tourism spectrum: Towards a typology of death and macabre related tourist sites, attractions and exhibitions. *Tourism, 54*(2), 145–160.

Stone, P. R. (2012). Dark tourism and significant other death. *Annals of Tourism Research, 39*(3), 1565–1587.

Stone, P. R., & Sharpley, R. (2008). Consuming dark tourism: A thanatological perspective. *Annals of Tourism Research, 35*(2), 574–595.

Strange, C., & Kempa, M. (2003). Shades of dark tourism: Alcatraz and Robben Island. *Annals of Tourism Research, 30*(2), 386–405.

Tang, Y. (2014). Dark tourist perception: Motivations, experiences and benefits interpreted from the visits to seismic memorial sites in Sichuan province. *Journal of Mountain Science, 11*(5), 1326–1341.

Verma, S., & Jain, R. (2013). Exploring tragedy for tourism. *Research on Humanities and Social Sciences, 3*(8), 9–23.

Werdler, K. (2012). An introduction to dark tourism in Africa: Contested heritage or opportunity for a new proposition? *Mawazo; the Journal of the College of Humanities and Social Sciences, Makerere University, 11*(2), 103–113.

Wikipedia. (n.d.). Mitr Chaibancha.

Wyndham, M., & Read, P. (2012). Filling the void of trapped memories: The liberation of a Pinochet Centre of Torture. *Journal of Iberian and Latin American Research, 18*(1), 41–54.

Yoneyama, L. (1999). *Hiroshima traces: Time, space, and dialectics of memory*. Berkeley: University of California Press.

Yoshida, T. (2004). Whom should we remember? Japanese museums of war and peace. *Journal of Museum Education, 29*(2/3), 16–20.

7

Dark Tourism in an Increasingly Violent World

Jeffrey S. Podoshen

Introducing Dark Tourism and Death Consumption

This chapter theoretically examines dark tourism in an increasingly violent world. While early conceptualizations of dark tourism guide us in examining the phenomena of exposure to death-related tourism, a more violent age in a post-9/11, post-Charlie Hebdo world forces us to come to terms with a more violent existence. Violent death and orchestrated mass murder, once largely sequestered for many in the West, are now ever more evident in our own personal spaces and communities. Indeed, ISIS and violent extremism, not necessarily a stranger to those in the perpetually war-torn Middle East, is now in the forefront of the minds of those in the UK, Continental Europe and North America. Moreover, entertainment and the media incorporate increasingly violent narratives, including an emphasis on gruesome experiences in dystopian worlds whereby there is an embracing focus on moral decay, personal responsibility, and atrocity images (Podoshen et al. 2014). Resultantly, the study of death and its intersection with consumption has gained significant momentum in the literature (Dobscha et al. 2012; Dobscha 2016; Levy 2015; Podoshen 2016; Stone and Sharpley 2013; Venkatesh et al. 2014).

J. S. Podoshen (✉)
Franklin and Marshall College, Lancaster, PA, USA

Consequently, Podoshen et al. (2015a, b) note that a seemingly more violent world and a stronger closeness to death in contemporary society require new conceptualizations. As scholars, this requires a more forceful and direct approach to theory building in the realm of dark tourism. There are relationships and phenomena that cannot be explained by positivism alone or by existing conceptualizations. While positivism can assist us in strengthening existing frameworks and help in examining relationships between variables involved in dark tourism, both the discipline and the (visitor) experience require fresh theoretical inquiry. In this chapter, therefore, I present two particular conceptualizations of dark tourism consumption. These conceptualizations blend and bridge theory from tourism as well as consumption and consumer culture theory (CCT) (Ozcaglar-Toulouse and Cova 2010). Firstly, I discuss the relationship between conspicuous consumption and dark tourism, arguing that engaging in dark tourism in the age of the 'selfie' denotes *a form of signaling behavior* (Iqani and Schroeder 2016; also see Chap. 24). Secondly, I present the concept of dark tourism as *a form of preparation*. In this instance, engaging in dark tourism activities allows individuals to aptly prepare for a more violent existence. Thus in this chapter, I respond to Askegaard and Linnet's call for the strengthening of more macro-social frameworks of an exploratory nature in consumption-related research adjacent to the phenomenology of actual experiences (Askegaard and Linnet 2011). As a special note, I offer ideas that may be considered controversial by some. I do so wholeheartedly and in defense of non-positivism in dark tourism theory building. Ultimately, I argue that the positivist-dominated world of tourism studies can only take us so far in terms of explanation and breaking new ground in understanding the 'why' of tourist experiences.

Dark Tourism as Signaling

Conspicuous consumption is a practice whereby one displays wealth through a high degree of luxury expenditure on consumption and services (Trigg 2001). It can also involve competitive or extravagant consumption practices as well as those that are niche or non-mainstream (Patsiaouras and Fitchett 2012; Schaefers 2014). This consumption is often separated from general consumption in the sense that the primary need satisfied is prestige (Belk 1988), and that satisfaction is often tied very strongly from the admiration of others (Podoshen and Andrzejewski 2012; Wong 1997). As Segal and Podoshen (2013) explain, the concept and target of conspicuous consumption altered in the 1980s whereby luxury goods became accessible to many, not just to the higher socio-classes. As such, those looking to display increased levels of conspicuousness moved from tangible items, which became obtainable by many, to more 'cutting edge' purchases such as liposuction and plastic surgery. Closely related to materialism conspicuous consumption, by its very definition, cannot be conspicuous if the consumption is not noticeable by others (Podoshen and Andrzejewski 2012). In other words, consumption needs to be hierarchal in order to maintain the social order. If everyone is able to display and consume the conspicuous item, the item is no longer conspicuous and merely becomes a commodity. For example, it is not enough to possess a Hermes handbag, but rather the exclusive and extremely limited Birkin bag (at US$16,000). Of course, the ante rises as the prized consumption item becomes increasingly commoditized and thus available. Subsequently, the notion of 'luxury' is now accessible to the mass markets (Atwal and Williams 2009), and even very prestigious brands have created entry-level commodities. Therefore, it is unsurprising perhaps that current research in consumption alludes to a relationship between high uniqueness and high evaluation (Childs and Jin 2016). As what was once unique becomes more attainable, individuals will seek things that are even more unique. Arguably, at the same time, the role of materiality and conspicuous goods and services help maintain the social order, either for better or for worse, and as part of an externally based reference system (Heisley and Cours 2007; Chatterjee et al. 2000). As such, we can turn to tourism as an activity that allows for conspicuous consumption, and, as with tangible goods, finds itself moving in new directions to newer levels of conspicuousness.

Crouch (2013) considers tourism as a form of socially driven behavior and elucidates on how some individuals choose conspicuous destinations or experiences. Destinations can be perceived by others to be conspicuous or inconspicuous (Phillips and Back 2011), and travel choices can be influenced by the desire to enhance social identities (Sirgy and Su 2000). Carr (2005) suggests that some tourists are even willing to take on debt to go on holidays and that these holidays, when shared with peers, constitute a form of conspicuous consumption. This conspicuousness derives from a destination's image (Correia et al. 2014). Importantly, while sharing photos and stories about exotic and expensive destinations is nothing new, either inside or outside of social media, destinations or at least destination image and their perceptions are changing. For instance, recent news media have alluded to a growth in dark tourism especially that related to death and crime (Coldwell 2013; Podoshen 2013; Woollaston 2015) and have even raised issues of the 'selfie' spectacle at solemn destinations such as Auschwitz or at Ground Zero. As Murray (2015) notes, the selfie phenomenon is something many might associate with narcissism and shallow personal representation, which, of course, mirrors that of thoughts associated with overtly conspicuous consumers. Arguably, therefore, social media-driven selfies at remote, shocking, or abject-oriented places put the tourist in a situation whereby s/he is attempting to display a more exclusive form of tourism—that is, moving ahead of and away from the pack. Thus, it is one thing to display oneself at a Four Seasons resort or similar exclusive tourist destination; it is another (even more exclusive) notion to share images and experiences at places many do not dare even attempt to visit. As Iqani and Schroeder (2016) argue, nouveau selfie styles are featuring people in front of open caskets and funerals. The selfie, as Gram (2013) also argues, can be a way for people to turn themselves into objects. Hence, if this idea is taken further, a selfie in a 'rare' or unique instance can allow an individual to turn *him/herself* into a *rare object*. The repulsiveness of the abject and fear of death, for many, then creates a unique landscape for the unique object creation and the ability to create a distinct narrative of the self.

Buda and Shim (2015a) present the idea of 'a desire for novelty' in their explanation for increases in North Korean tourism. They dovetail this with 'danger-zone tourism' in their introspection on dark tourism motivation in the greater public consumerscape (Buda et al. 2014). The capstone of this quest for the novel and dangerous is what they term 'desire as recognition.' In their sense, recognition by others which is valued by the tourist. In essence, this is a conspicuousness in consumption and clearly a form of signaling behavior. It is not a very far stretch to see the operationalization of their novel theory by examining the wealth of attention of the few who are able to tour North Korea. Undoubtedly, the communist implemented dystopia of North Korea allows the tourist to engage in tourism that may center on the secretive and the highly dangerous (Buda and Shim 2015b). Those who are able to successfully venture to North Korea are able to garner a great deal of press and maybe even an appearance or two on cable television programming (Vice 2015).

Disaster and atrocity tourism in today's environment of selfie sticks and competitive conspicuousness requires a revised look at theory related to atrocity and disaster attractiveness. Ashworth and Hartmann (2005) provide a solid foundation in theorizing atrocity attraction and provide three main arguments for this type of tourism motivation. These are curiosity, empathy, and horror. Ashworth and Hartmann's *curiosity* argument likens atrocity tourism to the quest for unique satisfaction of human curiosity—similar to the desire to visit Stonehenge or Niagara Falls. Meanwhile, *empathy* as a motivator relies on the ability and need to identify with the victims in the atrocity being toured. This offers some synergy with the educational value and feelings of hope tourists can feel in disaster or grief tourism (Biran and Poria 2012; Seaton 2009; Sharpley 2009). Lastly, Ashworth and Hartmann posit *horror* as a motivation which goes back to our very nature and drive as humans to seek out fear and heightened emotional states—a morbid fascination with death (Seaton 1996; Seaton and Lennon 2004). Other scholars have put forth the notion that this type of tourism activity assists in the contemplation of one's own mortality (Stone and Sharpley 2008; Stone 2012). Therefore, contemplating one's own mortality at particular dark tourism sites provides an emotional state to share with others that is clearly unique and novel.

Biran et al. (2014) offer an interesting framework for understanding motivations to sites of disaster and carnage (also see Chap. 21). In particular, their examination of post-earthquake tourism determined that some tourists are actually motivated to tour disaster sites for leisure pursuits—including that of prestige. This is a significant finding in the sense that disaster tourism motivations are not just relegated to issues of understanding, empathy, or affect-oriented desires—they are also driven by status. However, while there has not been much exploration of this type of tourist motivation, it does appear that feelings of terror can have a positive effect on materialistic disposition (Rindfleisch and Burroughs 2004). These types of findings, which may be shocking to many, should not really surprise us in today's age as we witness individuals taking smiling selfies at Auschwitz or at Ground Zero for consumption on social media (Daily Mail 2014). It is not enough to tour a dark site, but you have to show that you have been there.

This then brings us back to the examination of the presentation of the self and the quest for uniqueness in a marketplace filled with ubiquity. Specifically, over a decade after Ashworth and Hartmann's (2005) work, I present here an additional motivation to consider—one based on conspicuousness and a desire to show others specific tourism activity as a form of signaling. Drawing upon Murray (2015), we integrate narcissism and the tendencies to promote one's selective and exclusive activities as a motivator. Indeed, both Carr (2015) and Acocella (2014) theorize that selfies are a product of a culture fixated on media and combined with high levels of self-absorption—an insatiable need to consume and display. One taking a selfie at a disaster site might not be as concerned with empathy or even helping victims, but rather in how others perceive the activity. By way of illustration, this may be similar to the American high school student who is only really concerned with playing video games and watching sport but spends some time cleaning up a local park (with photos to match) so that his/her resume is padded for a better shot at getting into the university of his/her choosing. Therefore, the selfie in essence becomes a condensed and widely disseminated promotional message (Podoshen 2014). Tourists can post selfies at disaster sites, even in the act of 'helping the recovery,' and can immediately share their act of (conspicuous) aiding with potentially thousands of onlookers. The destination image, therefore, is one that embodies not just a mere signal of something in the vein of wealth or status but one that signals a heightened level of empathy—whether that empathy actually exists in the mind of the tourist or not. Arguably, empathetic and educational aspects of the destination matter far less than desire to promote one's own image. Promoting one's image and fishing for 'likes' is, of course, a key driver of social media in today's self-obsessed age. Potentially then we are left with outcomes of a destination image being altered through the meaning and exposure of dark tourism as individuals tour dark sites with a new feeling of vapidity.

In terms of altering or evolving meanings along the lines of dark tourism for conspicuous purposes, we have to re-examine the 'sequestration of death' thesis and the 'absent-present death' paradox Stone (2009) presents in explanation of dark tourism consumption. While Stone's theory clearly still holds strong in a wealth of dark tourism situations, for some 'dark tourists' there may be an evolution from the conceptualization of motivation based on reducing individual levels of anxiety related to death to that of confronting death with a conspicuous and daring zeal (also see Chap. 8). Potentially then, as death consumption becomes less sequestered in contemporary societies, there is the compounding goal of death-related tourism that is more and more dangerous and extreme. The more extreme, unique, and abject, the more attention the tourist might receive. Ultimately, this brings death fervently from private space into public consumption.

The modern ubiquity of social media spurs the commoditization of 'common' tourism destinations as does the newly wealthy tourists from Asia or Russia who previously did not exist in great numbers during the last major global consumption booms. With increased 'competition' emulating from social media sharing, the world becomes a more challenging place for one to stand out in the clutter. Images of abjection, death, or extreme behavior and images at dark sites, for now at least, still stand out and are going to draw attention. In this respect, the morality of dark tourism is likely to be questioned as tourists flock to places associated with death not necessarily for reflection and commemoration, but as a personal platform to engage in and display conspicuous behavior.

Dark Tourism as Preparation

As noted earlier, an increasingly violent post-9/11 world means it is time to update conceptualizations and theory about dark tourism and 'absent death.' While the past 20 years has given us some interesting, if not contested, insights into the realm of death-related consumption and tourism, specifically related to dark heritage sites, the contemporary manifestation of real death, dying, and the abject (Kristeva 1982) has put death into more places to consume than ever before. Additionally, as our politically fractious world finds itself in seemingly never-ending conflict, the opportunities for death-related tourism are apparently increasing. Indeed, it is difficult to not consume death and abjection in today's world, no matter how hard one tries to avoid it (Drummond and Krszjzaniek 2016). In the past, news media often sanitized images for public consumption; however, today through internet distributed ISIS propaganda videos, for example, individuals can view horrific, unsanitized, and unedited videos within seconds of the actual death event. Media and shared media sites such as Reddit allow us to witness real death/murder often very quickly after or during the event. For instance, in 2015 we witnessed a news reporter and cameraman murdered on live US television—and the question remains, is this an anomaly or merely a preview? However, in terms of dark tourism theory, novel insights must be synthesized and created to ensure fresh theory building in light of recent happenings in the media, politics, and a globalized world. With this in mind, it is important to contrast the study of death and tourism in the pre-9/11 and post-9/11 worlds.

Mellor (1993), Mellor and Shilling (1993), and Willmott (2000) all pointed to a sequestration of death in the pre-9/11 world whereby dying was conceptualized as a largely private affair. Hence, much of dark tourism scholarship that occurred during this time focused on heritage-based, (secular) pilgrimage or commemorative experiences that took tourists to physical locations of dark events but also allowed them to commemorate on their own and distance from actual killing (Ashworth 1996; Foley and Lennon 1996; Seaton 1996, 2002). However, after the Islamist terrorism attack in New York on 9/11, these conceptualizations of death (and dark tourism) started to evolve (also see Chap. 8). Indeed, Stone (2009) in his seminal essay—'Making Absent Death Present: Consuming Dark Tourism in Contemporary Society'—critically examines the tourist gaze upon death and dying at Ground Zero whereby tourists are directly confronted with a sense of mortality. Stone (2009) notes the discourse of 'actual' death in the public sphere and its conceptualization as 'taboo.' Similarly, Sharpley (2012) suggests tourists can come face to face with the remnants of genocidal actions and discusses the question of how 'genocidal tourism' can be a reality (also Beech 2009; Schaller 2007). As previously mentioned, this discourse and activity brings death—once absent in the contemporary gaze—to have a presence even though the inevitability of death continues to be disavowed. With the bloody rise of ISIS and increasing global violence and strife interspersed with economic upheaval, the presence of death and 'life-endings' becomes even more pervasive. This makes attempting to understand the escape of death even more compelling.

Adding to his earlier theory building, Stone (2012) introduces the philosophy of *bracketing* in his conceptualization of dark tourism consumption. Bracketing is a process whereby the tourist may feel or create a perceived immunity from death by engaging in dark tourist activity. This then allows the tourist to confront death with a neutralizing effect and a sanitization of the subject matter. It is important to note that Stone (2012) places bracketing within the confines of exposure to the relics of death and not the actual reality of death. In other words, tourists are consuming what once 'was' and not what 'now is.' We can integrate bracketing with Podoshen et al.'s (2015b), take on exposure to violent consumption, and deduce that there may be theoretical differences in why one exposes him/herself to death given the moderating factor of the closeness to the actuality of death in situ. In this respect, tourists in today's world searching and touring death as it happens may not be engaging in bracketing to sanitize the subject matter of death but rather to get closer to it in a rather non-sanitized form. For example, during the Gaza/Israel war of 2014, a number of tourists watched bombs and rockets in real-time, live as it happened (Mackey 2014). While some were disgusted by these events, it is plausible that the characterization of the tourists was not one of bloodlust or perverse pleasure but rather a closeness to the act of war itself—to see what might come next as enemy fire appeared to inch closer and closer. While Israeli citizens were, for years, largely isolated from Gaza-based rocket fire, the range of Hamas-fired weapons increased and this put Israeli citizens in a direct path of harm that previously was not there.

With this theoretical framework in mind, we are challenged to rethink (or even extend) the notion of morality in consuming dark tourism. Engaging in this type of activity is, for many, not voyeurism as Lennon and Foley (2000) generalized as the key motivating factor for dark tourism. Arguably, it is much more profound than that. Indeed, cheering or applauding in times of war is nothing new, but understanding the dispositions, thoughts, and emotions behind the cheers is paramount to assessing the entire picture. Of course, there are reasons for cheering that are firmly based in the emotional contagion, which is going to be at the cusp of this type of activity. However, there are also the factors of motivation and contemplation that occur before and after the activity. Questions that may arise include: What motivated tourists to watch war unfold? Was it to cheer or was it something else? How do the tourists feel after engaging in cheering after close-up pictures of bodies are viewed, and those involved can witness the aftermath of destroyed homes and schools requires massive economic redevelopment at monstrous cost? To deride real-time dark tourism as merely emotionally based activity purveyed by bloodthirsty tourists, therefore, is shortsighted and problematic without understanding the antecedents and outcomes.

In the present climate, however, with lingering and violent realities ever close by we find ourselves in a world that has apparently gone backwards in race relations, has witnessed rapidly developing economic strife and collapse of markets, and a wealth of ambiguity about the future of humanity. There has been an increase of random acts of violence across the globe—even in places once thought to be 'immune' to it—for instance, recent terrorist attacks in Norway. Of course, this leads to an increasing number of sites and locations related to and immersed in death and disaster. At the same time, consumers have been flocking to more experiential consumption as traditional shopping experiences become more mundane and/or move to the online realm (Schmitt 1999; Williams 2006). Consumers searching for affect, once found in shopping malls and physical stores, find themselves looking for new venues that make the experience of consuming more than simply the act of purchasing required items. Cookie cutter shopping malls and the allure of leisurely mall experiences such as *Fast Times at Ridgemont High* are largely over. Arguably, therefore, dark tourism consumption for some people for some of the time fills that experiential void, and there has been some early work that has examined the burgeoning experientially minded immersion tourism experiences (Dalton 2014; Knudsen 2011a, b; Robb 2009).

Understanding Dark Tourism: Emergent Perspectives

Heritage tourism allows a connection with the past and an ability to educate oneself about past events, culture, and history. Meanwhile dark tourism today can allow a connection with the future. Wars such as World War I have been labeled 'the war to end all wars' along with other shortsighted slogans, only to remind us that war is really never ending. Additionally, tourism to dark places not only allow us to connect or reconnect with events of the past and generate memories, but rather give us a unique perspective into what may happen to us in the future.

In recent years, dark tourism scholarship has permeated top journals in the field of tourism studies, and that's certainly a positive development. However, as discussed in this chapter, much about dark tourism has still yet to be discovered, and changing environments calls for casting a wider net in epistemology and ontology. With this, it is paramount that dark tourism inquiry be expanded in ways that the dominant positivist orientation cannot fully explain. Consumer culture theory (CCT) as a tradition (Arnould and Thompson 2005) can assist tourism scholars in the quest to build theoretical insights and address questions we ordinarily would not be able to answer or to reduce to simple positivist and normative inquiry. The nature of dark tourism today is multifaceted and multidimensional and that requires a blending and bridging of theory from multiple subject fields. In order to open up this path, dark tourism scholars should immerse themselves in the field and rely more strongly on interpretative methods that give rise to introspection based on lived experiences and the socializing function (Dunkley 2015; Tunbridge and Ashworth 1996) that may exist in the activity (Dunkley 2015). While some have embraced this method of inquiry wholeheartedly (Buda et al. 2014; Healy et al. 2016; Miles 2014; Reijnders 2011), there is still a great deal that remains unexplored or unexplored in significant detail at the field level. Prasad and Prasad (2002) and Sandberg (2005) demonstrate the value of interpretative methods in explaining the lived experiences of human behavior—yielding new forms of knowledge. Deep, immersive inquiry allows for more intensive and sharper identity work that can assist in understanding more nuanced subcultures of consumption which can elucidate the microcultures, consumer tribes (Cova et al. 2007), and consumption communities that underlie identity work (Arnould and Thompson 2015). Thus, while some may be turned off by tourism and related commerce that is intertwined with death, the reality is that we have just scratched the surface in understanding dark tourism phenomena. Areas of exploration in dark tourism are wide open.

As noted in Podoshen (2015), death consumption was once viewed as largely commemorative, religious, or historical. Later, some likened it to morbid fascination or mere curiosity. Today, however, individuals across the globe are more prone in their search for answers in their ever increasingly violent world with death right on their doorstep, in their markets, their concert halls or public squares. Death consumption can no longer be derided as a mere transgressive activity or something people might engage in for 'fun' but rather as part of quest for deeper immersion in the world we actually exist in.

References

Acocella, J. (2014, May 12). Selfie: How big a problem is Narcissism. *The New Yorker*. http://www.newyorker.com/magazine/2014/05/12/selfie

Arnould, E., & Thompson, C. (2005). Consumer culture theory (CCT): Twenty years of research. *Journal of Consumer Research, 31*(4), 868–882.

Arnould, E., & Thompson, C. (2015). Consumer culture theory: Ten years gone (and beyond). In A. Thyroff et al. (Eds.), *Research in consumer behavior vol. 17: Consumer culture theory* (pp. 1–24). Bingley: Emerald Group.

Ashworth, G. (1996). Holocaust tourism and Jewish culture: The lessons of Krakow Kazimierz. In M. Robinson et al. (Eds.), *Tourism and cultural change* (pp. 1–12). Sunderland: Business Education Publishers.

Ashworth, G., & Hartmann, R. (2005). *Horror and human tragedy revisited: The management of sites of atrocities for tourism*. NY: Cognizant Communication Corporation.

Askegaard, S., & Linnet, J. T. (2011). Towards an epistemology of consumer culture theory: Phenomenology and the context of context. *Marketing Theory, 11*(4), 381–404.

Atwal, G., & Williams, A. (2009). Luxury brand marketing – the experience is everything! *Journal of Brand Management, 16*(5), 338–346.

Beech, J. (2009). Genocide tourism. In R. Sharpley et al. (Eds.), *The darker side of travel: The theory and practice of dark tourism* (pp. 207–223). Clevedon: Channel View.

Belk, R. W. (1988). Third world consumer culture marketing and development: Toward broader dimensions. *Research in Marketing, Supplement, 4*, 103–127. Greenwich: JAI Press.

Biran, A., & Poria, Y. (2012). Re-conceptualizing dark tourism. In R. Sharpley et al. (Eds.), *Contemporary tourist experience: Concepts and consequences* (pp. 57–70). London: Routledge.

Biran, A., Liu, W., Li, G., & Eichhorn, V. (2014). Consuming post-disaster destinations: The case of Sichuan, China. *Annals of Tourism Research, 47*, 1–17.

Buda, D. M., d'Hauteserre, A. M., & Johnston, L. (2014). Feeling and tourism studies. *Annals of Tourism Research, 46*, 102–114.

Carr, N. (2005). Poverty, debt, and conspicuous consumption: University students' tourism experiences. *Tourism Management, 26*(5), 797–806.

Carr, D. (2015). Selfies on a stick, and the social-content challenge for the media. *New York Times*, 4 January 2016. Available at: http://www.nytimes.com/2015/01/05/business/media/selfieson-a-stick-and-the-social-content-challenge-for-the-media.html?_r=0

Chatterjee, A., Hunt, J. M., & Kernan, J. B. (2000). Social character of materialism. *Psychological Reports, 86*, 1147–1148.

Childs, M., & Jin, B. (2016, in press). Do status symbols in marketing increase product evaluations? An experimental analysis of group differences on product evaluations for scarce and brand-presence products. *Journal of International Consumer Marketing, 28(3)*, 154–168.

Coldwell, W. (2013, October 31). Dark tourism: Why murder sites and disaster zones are proving popular. *The Guardian*. Available at: http://www.theguardian.com/travel/2013/oct/31/dark-tourism-murder-sites-disaster-zones. Accessed 12 Jul 2015.

Correia, A., Kozak, M., & Reis, H. (2014). Conspicuous consumption of the elite social and self-congruity in tourism choices. *Journal of Travel Research* 55(6), 738–750.

Cova, B., Kozinets, R., & Shankar, A. (2007). Tribes, Inc.: The new world of tribalism. In B. Cova et al. (Eds.), *Consumer tribes* (pp. 1–7). Oxford: Butterworth-Heinemann.

Crouch, G. I. (2013). Homo sapiens on vacation: What can we learn from Darwin? *Journal of Travel Research, 52(5)*, 575–590.

Daily Mail. (2014). I wouldn't do anything differently, *Daily Mail online*. Available at: http://www.dailymail.co.uk/news/article-2702161/I-wouldnt-differently-Teenager-took-selfie-Auschwitz-unrepentant-trend-posing-memorials-including-Ground-Zero-grows.html. Accessed 27 Aug 2015.

Dalton, D. (2014). *Dark tourism and crime*. Oxford: Routledge.

Dobscha, S. (2016). *Death in a consumer culture*. Oxford: Routledge.

Dobscha, S., Drenten, J., Drummond, K., Gabel, T., Hackley, C., Levy, S., Podoshen, J., Rook, D., Sredl, K., Tiwaskul, R. A., & Veer, E. (2012). Death and all his friends: The role of identity, ritual, and disposition in the consumption of death. In Z. Gurhan-Canli et al. (Eds.), *Advances in consumer research volume 40* (pp. 1098–1099). Duluth: Association for Consumer Research.

Drummond, K., & Krszjzaniek, E. (2016). Theatre of the abject: Body worlds and the transformation of the cadaver. In S. Dobscha (Ed.), *Death in a consumer culture* (pp. 242–254). Oxford: Routledge.

Dunkley, R. A. (2015). Beyond temporal reflections in thanatourism research. *Annals of Tourism Research, 52*, 177–179.

Foley, M., & Lennon, J. J. (1996). JFK and dark tourism: A fascination with assassination. *International Journal of Heritage Studies, 2(4)*, 198–211.

Gram, S. (2013). The young-girl and the selfie. Textual relations. http://text-relations.blogspot.it/

Healy, N., van Riper, C. J., & Boyd, S. W. (2016). Low versus high intensity approaches to interpretive tourism planning: The case of the Cliffs of Moher, Ireland. *Tourism Management, 52*, 574–583.

Heisley, D., & Cours, D. (2007). Connectedness and worthiness for the embedded self: A material culture perspective. *Consumption, Markets and Culture, 10(4)*, 425–450.

References

Iqani, M., & Schroeder, J. (2016, in press). #selfie: Digital self-portraits as commodity form and consumption practice. *Consumption, Markets and Culture, 19*(5), 405–415.

Knudsen, B. T. (2011a). Thanatourism: Witnessing difficult pasts. *Tourist Studies, 11*(1), 55–72.

Knudsen, B. T. (2011b). Deportation day: Live history lesson. *Museum International, 63*(1–2), 109–118.

Kristeva, J. (1982). *The powers of horror: An essay on abjection*. New York: Columbia University Press.

Lennon, J. J., & Foley, M. (2000). *Dark tourism*. Andover: Cengage Learning EMEA.

Levy, S. (2015). Olio and integraphy as method and the consumption of death. *Consumption, Markets & Culture, 18*(2), 133–154.

Mackey, R. (2014, July 14). Israelis watch bombs drop on Gaza from front row seats, *New York Times*. Available at: http://www.nytimes.com/2014/07/15/world/middleeast/israelis-watch-bombs-drop-on-gaza-from-front-row-seats.html?_r=0. Accessed: 6 Jul 2015.

Mellor, P. (1993). Death in high modernity: The contemporary presence and absence of death. In D. Clarke (Ed.), *The sociology of death* (pp. 11–30). Oxford: Blackwell.

Mellor, P., & Shilling, C. (1993). Modernity, self-identity and the sequestration of death. *Sociology, 27*, 411–431.

Miles, S. (2014). Battlefield sites as dark tourism attractions: An analysis of experience. *Journal of Heritage Tourism, 9*(2), 134–147.

Murray, D. (2015, in press). Notes to the self: The visual culture of selfies in the age of social media. *Consumption, Markets and Culture, 18*(6), 490–516.

Ozcaglar-Toulouse, N., & Cova, B. (2010). A history of French CCT: Pathways and key concepts. *Recherche et Applications en Marketing, 25*(2).

Patsiaouras, G., & Fitchett, J. A. (2012). The evolution of conspicuous consumption. *Journal of Historical Research in Marketing, 4*(1), 154–176.

Phillips, W. J., & Back, K. J. (2011). Conspicuous consumption applied to tourism destination. *Journal of Travel & Tourism Marketing, 28*(6), 583–597.

Podoshen, J. S. (2013). Dark tourism motivations: Simulation, emotional contagion and topographic comparison. *Tourism Management, 35*(1), 263–271.

Podoshen, J. S. (2014). Reactionary modernism: An essay on the post-postmodern condition. *Journal of Research for Consumers, 25*, 1.

Podoshen, J. S. (2015). Examining death and learning about life. In S. Dobscha (Ed.), *Death in a consumer culture*. Oxford: Routledge.

Podoshen, J. S., & Andrzejewski, S. A. (2012). An examination of the relationships between materialism, conspicuous consumption, impulse buying, and brand loyalty. *Journal of Marketing Theory and Practice, 20*(3), 319–334.

Podoshen, J. S., Andrzejewski, S. A., & Hunt, J. M. (2014a). Materialism, conspicuous consumption, and American hip-hop subculture. *Journal of International Consumer Marketing, 26*(4), 271–283.

Podoshen, J. S., Venkatesh, V., & Jin, Z. (2014b). Theoretical reflections on dystopian consumer culture: Black metal. *Marketing Theory, 14*(2), 207–227.

Podoshen, J. S., Venkatesh, V., Wallin, J., Andrzejewski, S., & Jin, Z. (2015a). Dystopian dark tourism: An exploratory examination. *Tourism Management, 51*(December), 316–328.

Podoshen, J. S., Andrzejewski, S., Venkatesh, V., & Wallin, J. (2015b). New approaches to dark tourism inquiry: A response to Isaac. *Tourism Management, 51*(December), 331–334.

Prasad, A., & Prasad, P. (2002). The coming age of interpretative organizational research. *Organizational Research Methods, 5*(1), 4–11.

Reijnders, S. (2011). Stalking the count: Dracula, fandom and tourism. *Annals of Tourism Research, 38*(1), 231–248.

Rindfleisch, A., & Burroughs, J. (2004). Terrifying thoughts, terrible materialism? Contemplations on a terror management account of materialism and consumer behavior. *Journal of Consumer Psychology, 14*(3), 219–224.

Robb, E. M. (2009). Violence and recreation: Vacationing in the realm of dark tourism. *Anthropology and Humanism, 34*(1), 51–60.

Sandberg, J. (2005). How do we justify knowledge produced within interpretative approaches? *Organizational Research Methods, 8*(1), 41–68.

Schaefers, T. (2014). Standing out from the crowd: Niche product choice as a form of conspicuous consumption. *European Journal of Marketing, 48*(9/10), 1805–1827.

Schaller, D. J. (2007). Genocide tourism – Educational value or voyeurism? *Journal of Genocide Research, 9*(4), 513–515.

Schmitt, B. (1999). Experiential marketing. *Journal of Marketing Management, 15*(1–3), 53–67.

Seaton, A. V. (1996). From thanatopsis to thanatourism: Guided by the dark. *Journal of International Heritage Studies, 2*(4), 234–244.

Seaton, A. (2002). Thanatourism's final frontiers? Visits to cemeteries, churchyards and funerary sites as sacred and secular pilgrimage. *Tourism Recreation Research, 27*(2), 73–82.

Seaton, A. V. (2009). Thanatourism and its discontents: An appraisal of decade's work with some future issues and directions. In T. Jamal et al. (Eds.), *The Sage handbook of tourism studies* (pp. 521–542). London: Sage.

Seaton, A. V., & Lennon, J. J. (2004). Thanatourism in the early 21st century: Moral panics, ulterior motives and ulterior desires. In T. Singh (Ed.), *New horizons in tourism: Strange experiences and stranger practices* (pp. 63–82). Cambridge, MA: CABI Publishing.

Segal, B., & Podoshen, J. S. (2013). An examination of materialism, conspicuous consumption and gender differences. *International Journal of Consumer Studies, 37*(2), 189–198.

Sharpley, R. (2009). Shedding light on dark tourism: An introduction. In R. Sharpley et al. (Eds.), *The darker side of travel: The theory and practice of dark tourism* (pp. 3–22). Bristol: Channel View Publications.

Sharpley, R. (2012). Towards an understanding 'genocide tourism': An analysis of visitors' accounts of their experience of recent genocide sites. In R. Sharpley et al. (Eds.), *Contemporary tourist experience: Concepts and consequences* (pp. 95–109). Oxford: Routledge.

Sirgy, M. J., & Su, C. (2000). Destination image, self-congruity, and travel behavior: Toward an integrative model. *Journal of Travel Research, 38*(4), 340–352.

Stone, P. R. (2009). Making absent death present. In R. Sharpley et al. (Eds.), *The darker side of travel: The theory and practice of dark tourism* (pp. 23–38). Tonawanda: Channel View.

Stone, P. R. (2012). Dark tourism and significant other death: Towards a model of mortality mediation. *Annals of Tourism Research, 39*(3), 1565–1587.

Stone, P. R., & Sharpley, R. (2008). Consuming dark tourism: A thanatological perspective. *Annals of Tourism Research, 35*(2), 574–595.

Stone, P., & Sharpley, R. (2013). Deviance, dark tourism and 'dark leisure': Towards a (re)configuration of morality and the taboo in secular society. In S. Elkington et al. (Eds.), *Contemporary perspectives in leisure: Meanings, motives and lifelong learning.* Abington: Routledge.

Trigg, A. (2001). Veblen, Bourdieu, and conspicuous consumption. *Journal of Economic Issues, 35*(1), 99–115.

Tunbridge, J., & Ashworth, G. (1996). *Dissonant heritage: The management of the past as a resource in conflict.* Chichester: John Wiley & Sons.

Venkatesh, V., Podoshen, J., Urbaniak, K., & Wallin, J. (2014). Eschewing community: Black metal. *Journal of Community and Applied Social Psychology, 26*(1), 66–81. https://doi.org/10.1002/casp.2197.

Vice Television. (2015). The vice guide to North Korea. Available at: http://www.vice.com/video/vice-guide-to-north-korea-1-of-3

Williams, A. (2006). Tourism and hospitality marketing: Fantasy, feeling and fun. *International Journal of Contemporary Hospitality Management, 18*(6), 482–495.

Willmott, H. (2000). Death. So what? Sociology, sequestration and emancipation. *The Sociological Review, 4,* 649–665.

Wong, N. (1997). Supposed you own the world and no one knows? Conspicuous consumption, materialism and self. In M. Brucks et al. (Eds.), *Advances in consumer research 24* (pp. 197–203). Ann Arbor: Association for Consumer Research.

Woollaston, V. (2015, June 10). Why are we so fascinated by Auschwitz? 'Dark tourism' to 'death sites' helps us deal with our mortality, study reveals. *Daily Mail.* Available at: http://www.dailymail.co.uk/sciencetech/article-3118013/Why-fascinated-Auschwitz-Dark-tourism-death-sites-helps-deal-mortality-study-reveals.html. Accessed 12 Jul 2015.

8

Dark Tourism in an Age of 'Spectacular Death'

Philip R. Stone

Introduction

We live in a dominion of the dead. We have always done so. Throughout history the pact between the living and the dead has been one of mutual obligation. We ritualise the dead with a memorialised afterlife, where the deceased depend on the living to maintain their memory. In return, the dead counsel us to know ourselves, provide procedure to our lives, systematise our social relations, and help restrain our ravaging impetuous exploits. In essence, the dead maintain our social and cultural order and, consequently, act as our immortal custodians. We offer the dead a commemorative future so that they may bequeath us an honoured past: we help them live on in memory so that they may help us go forward (Harrison 2003). Yet, while death is universal across time and cultures, dying is not. In other words, death is a finite ending to a biological life while dying embraces varying socio-cultural processes that are inherently influenced by life-worlds.

It is these individual and collective life-worlds that provide us with *deathscapes* (e.g., cemeteries, memorials, exhibitions, former battlefields, shrines,

---

Death is the problem of the living. Dead people have no problems.
Norbert Elias (2001: 3)

P. R. Stone (✉)
University of Central Lancashire, Preston, UK

© The Author(s) 2018
P. R. Stone et al. (eds.), *The Palgrave Handbook of Dark Tourism Studies*,
https://doi.org/10.1057/978-1-137-47566-4_8

etc.) that have changed throughout history and culture (Maddrell and Sidaway 2010). Yet, death—the crux of dark tourism representations—or more specifically the knowledge of mortality is an incessant task for the living as we deal with life. Indeed, society and culture, including religions, are a kind of contrivance to make life with death bearable (Bauman 2006). Death in itself is simply the cessation of life and a natural fact, but the deathscape in which it occurs is fluid and transforms over time. Therefore, death becomes a 'social construct' which continuously changes within a myriad of life conditions (Howarth 2007). Changes in our comprehension and attitudes towards death are brought to bear through transformations in society, culture, politics, religion, and technology, as well as through a sense of historicity (Jacobsen 2017). In other words, we need to comprehend and locate death within broader socio-cultural and historical circumstances in order to better understand contemporary Western (secular) deathscapes (also see Chap. 6). One of these contemporary deathscapes is 'dark tourism', in which significant death of Others is commodified as a spectacle within visitor economies and, subsequently, consumed as tourist experiences. Arguably, therefore, a component of the (post)modern deathscape has become spectacular in the late twentieth and early twenty-first centuries (Debord 1977; Connolly 2011; Jacobsen 2016). As part of this spectacularisation of death in contemporary society, dark tourism mediates Other death as a visual signifier of our own mortality. It is here where relationships between death and binary public/private space are becoming increasingly blurred (Young and Light 2016), and where consuming dark tourism deathscapes helps revive, rediscover, recycle, and reinvent the social construction of death.

Thus, drawing upon Michael Jacobsen (2016) and his outstanding review of Philippe Ariès' seminal history of death mentalities (Ariès 1974, 1981, 1985), my chapter suggests rather than asserts that dark tourism offers a display of the dead which can be spectacular. Consequently, dark tourism helps usher in a contemporary mentality of death in secular society where it is now produced as extravagant and consumed as mediated tourist experiences. Moreover, my chapter completes a trilogy of thanatological essays within dark tourism (the first one being Stone and Sharpley 2008; and the second, Stone 2012a). In particular, I extend my earlier conceptual works which located dark tourism within a secular response to mortality mediation and a historical mentality of the 'invisible/forbidden' or sequestered death. Specifically, I contend in this chapter that contemporary dark tourism is now a distinct element of what has been termed the new age of 'spectacular death' (after Jacobsen 2016). Particularly, where death, dying, and mourning have, arguably, become increasing spectacles in Western societies, I suggest dark tourism offers a potential revival of the so-called forbidden death. Ultimately, I argue that dark tourism as a mediating institution of mortality has the paradoxical tendency of making death linger uneasily between (market) liberation and (heritage) autonomy and control. Therefore, before appraising a new age of spectacular death as a historical extension of death mentalities, and the subsequent role of dark tourism, I first review how dark tourism as a concept can enlighten death in practice within contemporary visitor economies.

Enlightening Dark Tourism

Despite the title of this handbook, there is no such thing as 'dark tourism'—or at least there is no universally accepted definition of what dark tourism actually is or entails (Stone 2016a). Indeed, tourism may be defined simply as the movement of people, while 'dark' has so many subjective and contrasting connotations and linguistic complexities that it is almost futile to define 'darkness' in dark tourism. That said, however, and notwithstanding inherent cultural and semantic intricacies of the terminology, dark tourism is now an international scholarly brand that represents a taxonomy of heritage sites, exhibitions, and visitor attractions that all have commonality—that is, an interpretation of death for the modern visitor economy (Lennon 2017; Baillargeon 2016). Heritage tourism sites that interpret death, whether untimely or in violent or calamitous circumstances, often exist across the world for (secular) pilgrimages, memorialisation, or educative purposes (Lennon and Teare 2017; Oddens 2016; Collins-Kreiner 2015; Roberts and Stone 2014). However, these sites are also part of a broader service sector whereby tourism and the commodification of culture and heritage have been mainstay for many years. Of course, issues and impacts of commodifying cultural heritage are well rehearsed and are not repeated here; yet, the problems of 'packaging up' diverse global *sites of death* or heritage sites *associated with dying* remain (Light 2017; Lennon et al. 2017).

Moreover, whether we can accurately classify 'dark visitor sites' and identify which tourism destinations are indeed 'dark' remains an academic conundrum (Hooper and Lennon 2016). To some extent it matters little if agreement cannot be reached amongst the intelligentsia of what is or what is not 'dark' in dark tourism. Arguably, what matters more is scholarly recognition of heritage sites that seek to interpret death-events which have perturbed the collective consciousness. More importantly, academic interrogation is required to ascertain visitor behavioural reactions to such sites as well as identifying fundamental interrelationships with the cultural condition of society. That said, however, there has been a concerted academic effort to offer typological frameworks of death-related tourism over the past 20 years or so (Seaton 1996; Dann 1998; Lennon and Foley 2000; Miles 2002; Stone 2006; Dunkley et al. 2007; Jamal and Lelo 2011; Biran and Poria 2012). Much of this effort has focussed on the conceptual shading of dark tourism and whether some sites are 'darker' than others (Strange and Kempa 2003). An obvious point of course is that the notion of a death-event being more despairing and distressing than another is open to a multitude of personal meanings and selective heritage interpretations. What is less obvious is how particular sites can be affixed by various conceptual parameters that can lead to a fluid, if not subjective, continuum of intensity—both for producing such heritage sites and for divergent visitor experiences: for instance, visitor sites with explicit political or commemorative interpretation, sites that are anchored in edification, memorialisation, or *edutainment*, sites that possess locational authenticity or have chronological distance to the actual death-event, as well as the extent of sites adopting neo-liberal business marketing to drive tourist footfall (also see Chap. 26). While this list is not exhaustive and open to evident critique, particularly how to determine such intrinsic features (Seaton 2009a), conceptually positioning visitor sites that portray death-events allow enlightenment of the politics, history, management, and socio-cultural consequences of difficult heritage (Stone 2006).

Dark tourism and its difficult heritage are concerned with encountering spaces of death or calamity that have political or historical significance, and that continues to impact upon the living (Tarlow 2005). Moreover, dark tourism has, to some extent, domesticated death and exposes a cultural institution that mediates between the ordinary Self and the significant Other dead (Stone 2012a). Yet, the production of these deathscapes within the visitor economy and, consequently, the consumption of recent or distant trauma within a collectively endorsed tourism environment raise important questions of the associations between morality, mortality, and contemporary approaches to death and representation of the dead (Stone and Sharpley 2014). As I will discuss later, in a Western secular society where ordinary death is often sequestered behind medical and professional façades, yet extraordinary death is remembered for popular consumption, dark tourism mediates a potential, if not complex, relative social filter between life and death. Furthermore, ethical ambiguities inherent within dark tourism are systematic of broader secular moral dilemmas in conveying narratives of death. Moral boundaries and ethical relativity are often questioned and (re)negotiated in places of dark tourism (Stone 2009a). In turn, the secular institution of dark tourism signifies a communicative channel of morality warning against our excesses, whereby dark tourism may not only act as a guardian of tragic history, but also plays a moral guardian of a modern society which forever pushes the ethical envelope.

While dark tourism as an academic field of study has brought the interest of visiting deathscapes into the contemporary imagination, numerous conceptual challenges are evident. These multidisciplinary challenges remain outside of the scope of my chapter, yet dark tourism in its broadest sense can be considered dialogic and mediatory. Dark tourism exposes particularities of people, place, and culture, where visiting sites of mortality can reveal ontological anxieties about the past as well as the future. Dark tourism also symbolises sites of dissonant heritage, sites of selective silences, sites rendered political and ideological, sites powerfully intertwined with interpretation and meaning, and sites of the imaginary and the imagined. Therefore, analysing distinctions of dark tourism as a concept and researching its mediating interrelationships with the cultural condition of society is important in contributing to our understanding of the complex associations between (dark) heritages and the tourist experience. It is these associations that provide the rationale to study dark tourism where scholarly investigations can enlighten critical approaches to a contemporary social reality of death.

One of these approaches is locating dark tourism within the milieu of Other death. Arguably, therefore, dark tourism sites are unique auratic spaces whose evolutionary diversity and polysemic nature demand managerial strategies that differ from other visitor sites (Seaton 2009b). This notion of 'aura' from a tourist experience perspective calls for an affective design and interpretation on the part of heritage memory managers. Difficult heritage and its representation should allow visitors to feel alive in their reconnection with the past and to feel empathy with victims. Indeed, within the context of business practice and consumer research, dark tourism experiences will always evoke emotional tensions, albeit to varying degrees, between diverse stakeholders. Even so, dark tourism in practice should extend unbiased, if not balanced, interpretation that offers an opportunity for catharsis and acceptance, as well as grieving for a sense of loss of both people and place (also see Chap. 25). However, while dark tourism as a term may exist within academic imaginations and signifies a broach church of death-related heritage attractions, there are no corresponding 'dark tourists'. Dark tourists by implication of so-called dark tourism do not exist—only people interested in the social reality of their own life-worlds. Nonetheless, dark tourism in practice is identifiable where social scientists may scrutinise multidisciplinary quandaries that impact on death and the dead as contemporary commodities (Stone 2011a; Ashworth and Isaac 2015; Grebenar 2017). As a result, dark tourism exposes a cultural practice that blurs the line between commemoration of the dead and commodification of death. Therefore, it is how death has become 'packaged up and touristified' in contemporary Western society that my chapter now turns. In particular, I outline successive death mentalities as conceptual underpinning and as an established historic frame of reference. Thereafter, I argue for the emergence of a new pluralistic death mentality in a cosmopolitan age, whereby the re-ritualisation of death through dark tourism is becoming increasingly mediated, commodified, and, thus, spectacular.

Death Mentalities: A Historical Overview

French historian Philippe Ariès in his three major works on the social history of death (Ariès 1974, 1981, 1985) describes how the mentality of death has transformed over the last millennium in Western Europe (and to some extent North America). Despite the many years since publication, the works of Ariès (who passed away in 1984) remain seminal points of reference in the social scientific study of death. Indeed, his much-cited and often criticised work (see, e.g., Bauman 1992; Walter 1994; Elias 2001) offers a rather simplified, if not detailed, linear approach to the history of death. As such, Ariès proposed four key developmental stages of death from the Middle Ages to the late twentieth century. Arguably, Ariès' division of the past millennium into four distinct death phases—'tamed death [up until the 15th century]; one's own death/death of the Self [17th century]; thy death/death of the Other [18th/19th century]; and forbidden/invisible death [20th century]'—offers an almost unavoidable determinist and reductionist approach in their sequential ordering. Yet, by the same token, the amount of connected and partially connected social history into a decipherable and analytical schema makes the framework germane. Ariès (1981) goes on to add a fifth stage—the sixteenth century *remote and imminent death*—which appeared between death of the Self and death of the Other. Notwithstanding this addition, I will concentrate on the original four-stage version in this chapter as a conceptual foundation to contemporary deathscapes. Of course, transformations in the collective cultural psychology of any historic epoch mean that a history of death cannot have a starting point or, for that matter, an end point. Instead, I take the work of Ariès to suggest an interpretive framework to access contemporary social practices and attitudes of death, rather than testing it for historical accuracy. In turn, I offer an indicative discussion rather than conclusive discourse, which is much more polemical than historically precise. Ultimately, by outlining the work of Ariès and even going beyond Ariès (Jacobsen 2016), our cultural organisation of deathscapes such as dark tourism can be scrutinised.

The Tamed Death

Despite the social history of dying having a much longer chronicle (Davies 2005; Kellehear 2007; Kerrigan 2007), the analytical commencement point for Ariès was the *tamed death* of the medieval period. It is here that for Ariès the tame[d] death was so different from contemporary death in almost every respect. In an age where most people led a relatively short and often unpleasant existence, death became a relief from the vagrancies of feudal life. As the English political philosopher Thomas Hobbes once remarked of pre-modern society—it was 'solitary, poor, nasty, brutish and short' (Hobbes cited in Warbuton 2012)—thus, arguably, the medieval death tamed life. Indeed, during this period, Ariès argues that there was a societal fluency with death where the living and the dead co-existed in a physical and spiritual proximity. For instance, evident in the *Danse Macabre* (Dance of Death)—an artistic genre of late-medieval allegory on the universality of death—medieval populaces 'were as familiar with the dead as they were familiar with the idea of their own death' (Ariès 1974: 25). The shadow of the Grim Reaper—and remains of the decomposing deceased—was never far away as medieval inhabitants lived and died in propinquity. The final farewell at the medieval deathbed, in the presence of angels and demons in religious imagery and iconography, would witness communities gathering to communicate with dying. This communitas death collided with religious sentiments and proscribed (mainly Catholic) rituals that, in turn, ensured death was pacified in public. As Jacobsen (2016: 4) notes, 'death was a prepared, accepted and solemn event without theatrics in which the dying presided'. In short, without any genuine medicinal aid, death may have been ghastly and dying intrinsic with pain, yet the tamed deathbed was a fundamental feature of medieval society in which death was seen as a seemingly welcome end to a short hard-lived lifespan and the beginning of a long afterlife.

Death of the Self

As the tamed death gave way to a period of *one's own death/death of the Self*, the emphasis morphed from the communitas of death to a more individualised encounter. Indeed, death of the Self 'marked a shift in death mentality that instead of focusing on death as such was more concerned with the individual and the time of death as a moment of *maximum awareness*' (Jacobsen 2016: 4, original emphasis). As a result, the deathbed became 'reserved for the dying man alone and one which he contemplates with a bit of anxiety and a great deal of indifference' (Ariès 1974: 34). The beginning of this individualised deathbed meant that death became more personal, and matters conducted in life would influence any quest for celestial perpetuity. Thus, death of the Self was concerned with how the individual, within religiosity and its control, could prepare for, confront, and reconcile with the mortal coil.

Death of the Other

The increased alienation and distance of death of the Self, where attention was on the dying making amends before meeting his or her maker, was supplanted by a death mentality that witnessed a collision with the Romantic period in European art and literature. In the subsequent period of *thy death/death of the Other*, the emphasis shifted away from the dying to the bereaved, and to what has sometimes been referred to as the *beautiful, Romantic*, or *good death* (Walter 2003). Indeed, mortality was a major subject of Romantic art, literature, and travel which 'turned death into sensibility – not so much a religious and moral mediation in the medieval, *memento mori* tradition, [but] as an imaginative dwelling on fatality for aesthetic gratification' (Seaton 2009a: 531).

As a mourning culture took hold and 'a new intolerance of separation' (Ariès 1974: 59) of losing a loved one became the norm, funerary rituals became more melancholic and ostentatious, and the discernible despair of grieving and loss were hallmarks of death of the Other. Jacobsen (2016: 5) goes on to note, 'pietistic and spiritualistic *cults of the dead* testified to just how much death was now seen as a rupture… therefore making mourners desperately seeking contact with the deceased' [original emphasis]. Gothic style theatrics and familial bonds saw the Victorian death of the Other evolve through a waning of eternal damnation messages prescribed by ecclesiastics, with advancements in medicines prescribed by doctors. Moreover, with the emergence of the urbanised family with its new structures of feeling (Porter 1999a), attention became fixed not on the decedent but on those who continued to live. Influenced through Romanticism, including the quixotic depiction of death in art, literature, and poetry, the rituals of death became much more sentimental, if not morbid, and mourning became a family concern that perpetuated the memory of the deceased (Westover 2012). Indeed, the death of the Other became a death-with-dignity, a kind of good death where calmness prevailed in readiness for a dignified departure from the mortal world. The death of the Other was an illustration of how we paid respectful deference to the laws of nature, and how the time of passing became an opportunity to put 'things in order'. Moreover, the death of the Other was signified by the writing of wills with final bequests bestowed, sanctimonious instructions given to survivors, forgiveness sought both from companions and from God, promises of reunions made, and final words spoken. As Tercier (2005: 12) suggests, 'the business of the [Romantic] deathbed became just that: the tidying and tying up of unfinished business'. Thus, the Romantic reconstruction of thy death was nothing more distressing than a final peaceful sleep. With a darkened room, family and loved ones at the bedside, affairs in order, peace made with both survivors and God, and with a few gentle and quiet farewells, the decedent would dignifiedly drift off into an eternal slumber. Of course, this romanticised death of the Other was an ideal in the mindscape of a Victorian society who came to think of death as simply way of 'expiring consumption' (Jalland 1996). In its ultimate form, the death of the Other appeared to be a perfect coincidence of both social dying and biological death, which did not rely (solely) upon ontological continuity. However, while spiritual aspects were still important to thy death and religious forms still embraced the hope of an eternal existence, deathbeds that were increasingly secular found solace in medicinal relief from pain and discomfort. In short, the romantic Other death (re)created death and the dead for (re)evaluation and contemplation for the living (Stone 2014). Importantly, however, throughout the protracted history of the three aforementioned discrete death mentalities within Western culture, a number of dynamisms are evident:

> [processes of] individualisation, secularisation, urbanisation, the rise of humanism and the advancement of natural science were some of the main driving forces behind the gradual shift from one phase to the other and in many of the changes taking place in the planning, use and appearance of cemeteries, burial and disposal practices, relations between the living and the dead, eschatological beliefs, the time and place of dying and everything else associated with what is referred to as the *domain of the dead*. [Ariès 1981: 595] Jacobsen 2016: 5)

The Invisible/Forbidden Death

Following the death of the Other, the domain of the dead underwent a metamorphosis during the twentieth century, which according to Ariès saw the emergence of the *invisible* or *forbidden death*. It is within this phase that Ariès reveals his revulsion for modern developments and suggests modernity is marked by a waning of faith, especially for an (eternal) afterlife. Kellehear (2007) later characterised the invisible death as the *shameful death* for the lack of overt social exchanges between dying individuals and those who institutionally care for them. Hence, with the full onset of secularisation, the invisible death was signified by sequestration (Mellor and Shilling 1993) and the role of institutions, especially the medical establishment where increasing bureaucratisation and hospitalisation, as Ariès (1981: 559) alleges, 'robbed the dead and dying of all dignity'. Therefore, the invisible or forbidden death, where deaths were sequestered and 'disappeared' from the community gaze, is largely due to the process of medicalisation and professionalisation of the modern deathbed. Certainly, the position of the physician at the nineteenth century (Romantic) deathbed became entrenched and consolidated through advancements in therapeutic techniques and pathophysiology, as well as an expanding pharmacopoeia (Porter 1999b). Augmenting the position of the physician as an authority over death were technical advances and acceleration of the bureaucratic super-structure that became the foundation of the modern State. With increasing hospitals (and later hospices) and dispensaries, combined with professionalisation of disposal through regularisation of death certificates, post-mortems, advances in funerary technology, and the storage of cadavers, the invisible death became almost just that: concealed and obscured behind the façade and machinery of a (new) death, dying, and disposal industry.

Consequently, with increasingly industrialisation being applied to the deathbed, in terms of both processes and procedures, Porter (1999a: 84) notes, 'rather as the philosophes rationalised death, modern man has in effect denied his own mortality, and death has become taboo'. As the twentieth century progressed, the physicians' control over the process of dying increased, and death moved out of the familiar environs of the family and community to become institutionalised under a medical gaze. Thus, the transfer of power and emphasis from priest to doctor is now almost complete, and the care of the soul and body has shifted realms from post-mortem religious ritual to ante-mortem medical protocol. Finally, deritualisation and the lack of communal mourning of the invisible death meant that time-saving and minimalistic practices became associated with death and dying. Consequently, the individual, when confronted with mortality, is left to find his or her own peace and purpose. The gradual demise of collective meaning-making and communal support meant, according to Ariès at least, that death rituals in the past had provided people with a good death. In its place was a medicalised, institutionalised, and professionalised deathbed that offered some relief from the pain of dying yet, paradoxically, provided for a bad death. As Tercier (2005: 13) states:

> In the ideal modern death, biological, social and ontological death not only coincide but are meant to occur in such an instant that, perhaps, the whole business [of mortality] can be ignored, allowed to slip past unnoticed. Hence the invisibility of death.

The De-sequestration of Death: Towards the Spectacular Death

Undoubtedly, Phillippe Ariès left a legacy of stimulating if not contentious accounts of the social history of Western deathbeds. Yet, since his passing in 1984, society has changed remarkably and the death mentality and private/public deathscape bonding has also changed (Jacobsen 2016; Jonsson and Walter 2017). Moreover, sociologists have attempted to capture epochal transformations and the new collective conscience during the late twentieth and early twenty-first centuries with a plethora of polemic labels. These include terms, including but not limited to, postmodernity, reflexive modernity, late modernity, radicalised modernity, supermodernity, second modernity, or liquid modernity (see, for instance, Giddens 1990, 1991; Fornäs 1995; Ray 1999; Bauman 2000; González-Ruibal 2008; Beck and Grande 2010). While a discussion of the main processes embodying and driving these societal and cultural developments is beyond the scope of my chapter, they do point to how our contemporary world differs in many respects from that of the first two-thirds of the twentieth century. This includes death and how 'death in advanced modernity is qualitatively different from modern death' (McManus 2013). Therefore, Jacobsen (2016) argues that Ariès' final appellation of the 'invisible/forbidden' death is too parochial to properly designate contemporary death today. That said, Jacobsen acknowledges certain insights from Ariès' social history of death still persist, such as death remaining an integral element of a controlling, medicalising, and sequestering mentality. However, the invisible/forbidden death as a historical classification is now too limited to wholly describe contemporary death, because 'it is challenged by a death that is gradually coming out of the closet, as it were, and now confronts us in ways unimaginable to our grandparents' generation' (Jacobsen 2016: 10).

A key feature of Ariès' invisible/forbidden death thesis advocated it was concealed, denied, and tabooed. Yet, as Walter (1991) notes over a quarter a century ago, death is hidden rather than forbidden and it is the modern individual, not modern society, that denies death. Similarly, Mellor (1992) argued that while death remains hidden in the sense that it is generally sequestered from public space, as noted earlier, there is a contemporary presence of death, not least in popular culture, cyberspace, cultural heritage exhibitions, and the mass media (Walter et al. 1995; Sion 2014; Sayer and Walter 2016). Consequently, 'a sociological consideration of death must reflect upon, and attempt to explain, the apparent contradiction between the absence and presence of death in contemporary society' (Mellor 1992: 11; also see Stone and Sharpley 2008; Stone 2012a). By the same token, Walter (1994) argued that dying and mourning beliefs and customs are continually evolving and, as a result, death was being revived from its repression. In an update to his 'revival of death' proposition, Walter (1994, 2014) suggested that while conversational norms still govern public discourse on death, death is in fact no longer taboo. To illustrate further colloquial death conversations with another analogous societal taboo—that is, sex—Walter (2014: online) playfully notes that 'I don't talk to my students about what I did in bed last night, but that doesn't mean sex is a taboo topic in our society'. Moreover, Geoffrey Gorer's (1955) prophetic claim of a 'pornography of death' in society meant that the prudency of sequestered natural death re-emerges as reprehensibly graphic representations of violent death within the public media realm (also Tercier 2013). Importantly, therefore, Jacobsen (2016: 10) captures the rupture of the absent/present death paradox and suggests a new death mentality has now emerged and that 'death shall have a new dominion'. As a result, Jacobsen applies the epithet of *spectacular death* to denote present-day death as it is experienced, constructed, and performed in what Kellehear (2007) called our 'cosmopolitan age'. In other words, spectacular death exists where many of our traditions, practices, and beliefs are reinterpreted to fit new socio-cultural circumstances.

While not the first to use the term 'spectacular death' (Connolly 2011; Pavićević 2015), Jacobsen (2016) draws his main inspiration of his new mentality of death from the French situationist theorist Guy Debord (1977; also see Chap. 10). Debord proposed the idea of 'a society of the spectacle' in which the semiotics of contemporary society are consumed in a kind of hyper-realism. To that end, Jacobsen (2016: 10, original emphasis) argues that '*spectacular death* is a death that has for all practical intents and purposes been transformed into a *spectacle*'. Indeed, as Debord first envisaged, our contemporary society is saturated with signs and symbols whereby primary direct experiences are replaced by mere representations. Therefore, for Jacobsen, the spectacular death in our cosmopolitan age is an extension of the death mentalities proposed by Ariès, whereby contemporary death is now de-sequestered and returned to the public domain through display and symbolic representations. As Jacobsen (2016: 10) notes:

> Spectacular death thus inaugurates an obsessive interest in appearance that simultaneously draws death near and keeps it at arm's length – it is something that we witness at a safe distance with equal amounts of fascination and abhorrence, we wallow in it and want to know more about it without getting too close to it.

While I have examined elsewhere the symbolic display and de-sequestration of death within a dark tourism framework, particularly within a structural analysis of death and a Western secular response to mortality mediation (Stone and Sharpley 2008; Stone 2009b, 2012a), the notion of how such de-sequestration occurs has been overlooked until now. If Jacobsen's idea of a new death mentality in the form of 'spectacular death' is to have traction, then some of the dimensions of the spectacular death mentality require elucidation. Of course, as Jacobsen points out, there are many thanatological dimensions of and socio-cultural facets to spectacular death—too many and irrelevant to discuss here. Therefore, for the remainder of my chapter, I will concentrate on three key aspects of how the spectacle of dark tourism cements a new era of the de-sequestered and spectacular death and, thus, helps revive death in the public domain. These key aspects, as denoted by Jacobsen (2016), are, firstly, *the new mediated/mediatised visibility of death*; secondly, *the commercialisation of death*; and, finally, *the re-ritualisation of death*.

Dark Tourism as Spectacular Death

If death was hidden or forbidden as claimed by Ariès, then we would neither see it nor encounter it. Indeed, as suggested earlier, the taboo of death in a death-denying Western secularised society has lost its grip and, consequently, death is becoming increasingly anchored in new structures that expose us to mortality. One of those new structures is a *new mediated/mediatised visibility of death* in which extraordinary death of often ordinary people is presented to us in visual and mediated forms (Jacobsen 2016). Of course, this is nothing like the tamed death of the medieval period where 'real-life death' surrounded the masses. Instead, the new mediated forms of significant Other deaths, either as a result of recent or historic trauma, are safely displayed to us as spectacle for contemporary consumption—firstly in the mass media, then later within the realms of dark tourism (also see Chap. 14). Thus, dark tourism, like the media, is one of numerous institutions of mortality in contemporary society that mediates and visualises a particular kind of death for some people for some of the time (Walter 2009; Stone 2011b). However, despite being exposed to an incongruent assortment of 'mortality moments' within dark tourism (Stone 2009b), we remain divorced from the social reality of death and, in comparison to bygone death mentalities, we rarely experience directly real-death events. Instead, we 'encounter corpses' in dark tourism that have been selected, politicised, commemorated, or celebrated through the heritage touristification process (Convery et al. 2014). That said, however, we do not encounter the actual corpse but a visualised chronicle of the often tragic or horrid circumstances in which the death occurred (Stone 2016b). As a result, the contemporary memento mori that dark touristic deaths mediate can seem empty without accompanying meaningful narratives which, consequently, can make death more of a spectacle than an existential topic.

The new visibility of mediatised death within dark tourism is there is to provoke, impact, educate, or to entertain. Notwithstanding inherent and well-rehearsed complexities in difficult heritage processes or memorialisation practices, dark tourism as spectacular death brings back the forbidden or invisible dead. Ghosts are returning to the feast and are resurfacing and multiplying in a multitude of dark tourism sites across the world. In this way, death—or at least as a mediated and mediatised phenomenon—is much more pervasive in touristic landscapes than even a few decades ago. Therefore, 'death is very much present whilst being bizarrely absent' (Jacobsen 2016: 11) and, thus, 'death is everywhere yet nowhere in Western culture' (Horne 2013: 231). Death in contemporary society is spectacularly present through dark tourism despite its apparent absence. As Bauman (1992: 7, original emphasis) contends, 'the impact of death is at its most powerful and creative when death *does not appear under its own name*; [and] in areas and times which are not explicitly dedicated to it'. Moreover, if Geoffrey Gorer's aforementioned 'pornography of death' acted as a kind of transferral for the repression of Ariès' forbidden death, and as an outlet for such cultural fears, then the visibility of mediatised death through dark tourism helps fuel a new cultural fascination with death.

A second and closely related dimension of 'spectacular death', according to Jacobsen (2016), is the *commercialisation of death* (also see Chap. 27). Death sells and probably always will either through macabre intrigue, genuine interest, or puerile titillation. While Jacobsen focussed his commercialisation of death dialogue on the increasingly mercantile nature of funerary practice, as well as the use of death as entertainment in popular culture, I suggest a euphoric consumerism of death exists in dark tourism. Therefore, death is not only turned into a spectacle through mediated visual representations in dark tourism but is also part of a broader entrepreneurial exercise. Indeed, the business of death within dark tourism has evolved from Gothic aesthetic interests, including Romantic-era death-related tourism where travel to meet dead authors' homes or deceased artists' final resting places became journeys of 'necromanticism' (Westover 2012). Tourism as the movement of people, of course, is dictated to by supply-and-demand vagaries of market forces as well as complex push-and-pull factors inherent within commerce and industry; and dark tourism and its difficult heritage are no different. Neo-liberal market processes and practices are bought to bear on packaging up, marketing, and retailing the dead for contemporary consumption. Whether under the guise of public memorialisation or private money-making, the significant Other dead in dark tourism are kept alive and promoted as spectacles for the living. Memory managers of difficult heritage are striving to commemorate and document tragedy and death, yet also strive to shape the sacred design and choreography of visitor experiences in dark tourism places. In (re)framing acts of atrocity and disaster, dark tourism often commercialises sites of secular pilgrimage, which in turn can lead to rites of political and socio-cultural passage (Hansen-Glucklich 2014). Therefore, the commercialisation of death inherent in dark tourism, and as a dimension of the new spectacular death mentality, means our concern and exposure to death has not decreased. Conversely, we are witnessing an increase in supply of and demand for 'death-related visitor attractions' (Lennon and Foley 2000), which in many respects is fuelled by commercialised and consumerised dark tourism.

Equally as an expression and consequence of this contemporary exposure to death and its commercialisation through dark tourism is a third dimensioning of spectacular death—that is, *the re-ritualisation of death* (Jacobsen 2016). The invisible/forbidden death mentality of Ariès' modern society suggested death was being reversed through its minimalistic and less elaborate rituals. At the same time, the meaning-making importance—both personal and religious—of such death rituals diminished and, consequently, individuals were left increasingly isolated in the face of mortality. However, as Jacobsen (2016: 12) argues, 'as a new counterculture to this disappearance or denigration of many death rituals so characteristic just a century and a half ago, we [are] now gradually see[ing] the rise of new rituals and the reappearance and reinvention of old ones'. The complexities of these new rituals have been explored in dark tourism and the collective heritage of remembrance and forgetting (Benton 2010), including in places of pain and shame and how difficult heritage re-enacts them (Logan and Reeves 2008). Moreover, as they have been an apparent 'global rush to commemorate atrocities', memorial museums and accompanying dark tourism have witnessed 'an extraordinary boom in a new kind of cultural complex' (Williams 2007). Consequently, this 'memorial mania' according to Doss (2010) invokes the re-ritualisation of death as a spectacle in public spaces, akin to the Victorian 'death of the Other' where there was also a desire to publicly mark and celebrate the remembrance of the deceased. Notwithstanding other obvious contemporary re-rituals of death, including in funerary and burial practice or digital legacies, dark tourism offers a re-ritualising of death through its evanescent visitor experience and ephemeral consumption. As such, dark tourism can offer a potential 'mortality capital' to some individuals whereby absent death is made present within the public domain, and ritually revived through a substitute of recreated tragic situations and commemoration (Stone 2012b).

The spectacular death, and dark tourism being just one element of its defining features, is of course a challenge to and an extension of Ariès' forbidden, hidden, denied, silenced, repressed, and tabooed death thesis. As Jacobsen (2016: 14) rhetorically suggests, 'it seems that while we successfully kicked death out of the front door of modernity, it appears to have sneaked its way in through the back door or has squeezed through the cat flap in contemporary society'. In many ways, therefore, the spectacular death thesis as proposed by Jacobsen and augmented in my chapter is testament to the aforementioned revival of death thesis by Walter (1994, 2014). Indeed, I have argued elsewhere (Stone 2012a) that dark tourism joins the family of mediating institutions in which a neo-modern death mentality ushers in open-mindedness and individualistic encounters with mortality. As such, Jacobsen (2016: 15) suggests:

> [that] we are reviving, retrieving, rediscovering and reinventing death in a process in which the old and almost forgotten practices and ideals are mixed with the new social conditions characteristic of contemporary equally individualised, globalized, mediate/mediatised and technologically advanced late-modern, post-modern or liquid-modern society.

To that end, dark tourism may indeed be 'an imitation of post-modernity' as first claimed by Lennon and Foley (2000); yet, when examined under a structural analysis of historic death mentalities, dark tourism represents a spectacular 'new (old) death' (Schillace 2015).

Importantly, however, while the de-sequestration of death and a subsequent revival of death thesis may have valuable conceptual clout, Jacobsen reminds us that the seemingly liberation and revival of death in the public domain involves new forms of administration, limitations, and subjectification in the way we comprehend and construct spectacular death. In what Jacobsen (2016: 15) terms a 'partial re-reversal' of death—in recognition of the remaining attributes of Ariès' invisible/forbidden modern deathbed—he goes on to suggest that we are witnessing something new and heretofore unseen in death landscapes. I contend here that dark tourism is part of this new spectacular death landscape. In turn, dark tourism means that we do not face the Grim Reaper directly but, instead, consume the mortality spectacle of significant Others. Dark tourism in an age of the spectacular death ensures that mediatised/mediated death lingers uneasily between the liberation of market and commercial forces, yet is subject to cultural heritage selection and control. Dark tourism presents, in many respects, paradoxical deaths in that we collectively remember (or forget) tragic death in the hope that we have an authentic and autonomous death after a long and fulfilled life. Consequently, heritage processes selectively seek to manage, contain, control, dilute, or politicise dark tourism deaths; yet, the spectacular death mentality of dark tourism brings us into a new dominion of the dead. As such, dark tourism in a new age of spectacular death means that death of the Other is served to us as a contemporary spectacle, yet death of the Self continues to haunt the consciousness of the living and is hitherto to be tamed.

Conclusion

Death is universal to all societies which must simultaneously deny its existence yet accept its inevitability. The age of any spectacular death will have to conform to that eternal rule. Through an analysis of seminal historic mentalities of death as proposed by Philippe Ariès, and augmenting the 'revival of death' and 'spectacular death' theses suggested by Tony Walter and Michael Jacobsen respectfully, my chapter has outlined how successive deathbed histories reveal a contemporary age of the spectacular death. Moreover, I have argued how dark tourism is manifested as a defining institution of spectacular death through its key features of mediated/mediatised visibility of death, commercialisation of death, and the re-ritualisation of death. Spectacular death in dark tourism exposes mortality that is regulated and structured by heritage production, yet at the same time commodifies death as a form of visitor economy consumption. Thus, consuming the spectacle of death in dark tourism might mean a de-sequestration and de-taboo of death in public, but it may also perhaps reinforce the sting of death in private. Whether the age of the spectacular death and concomitant dark tourism experiences usher in a new death mentality, or intensify certain characteristics of the forbidden death, death is undoubtedly being revived, rediscovered, recycled, and reinvented. Of course, it remains to be seen what role dark tourism as a contemporary behavioural phenomenon plays in the (re)construction of death, and future research will enlighten this new dominion of the dead. Ultimately, however, despite everything, death remains a problem for the living because dead people do not care.

References

Ariès, P. (1974). *Western attitudes towards death from the middle ages to the present.* Baltimore: John Hopkins University Press.

Ariès, P. (1981). *The hour of our death* (trans: Weaver, H.). Oxford: Oxford University Press.

Ariès, P. (1985). *Images of man and death*. Cambridge: Harvard University Press.

Ashworth, G. J., & Isaac, R. K. (2015). Have we illuminated the dark? Shifting perspectives on 'dark' tourism. *Tourism Recreation Research, 40*(3), 316–325.

Baillargeon, T. (2016). Behind the scenes of science: Interview with Dr Philip Stone, Executive Director of the Institute for Dark Tourism Research. *Téoros, 35*(1). Available at https://teoros.revues.org/2906. Accessed 2 May 2017.

Bauman, Z. (1992). *Mortality, immortality and other life strategies*. Cambridge: Polity Press.

Bauman, Z. (2000). *Liquid modernity*. Cambridge: Polity Press.

Bauman, Z. (2006). *Liquid fear*. Cambridge: Polity Press.

Beck, U., & Grande, E. (2010). Varieties of second modernity: The cosmopolitan turn in social and political theory and research. *The British Journal of Sociology, 61*(3), 409–443.

Benton, T. (2010). *Understanding heritage and memory*. Manchester: Manchester University Press.

Biran, A., & Poria, Y. (2012). Reconceptualising dark tourism. In R. Sharpley & P. R. Stone (Eds.), *Contemporary tourist experience: Concepts and consequences* (pp. 59–70). Abington/Oxon: Routledge.

Collins-Kreiner, N. (2015). Dark tourism as/is pilgrimage. *Current Issues in Tourism, 19*(12), 1185–1189.

Connolly, T. (Ed.). (2011). *Spectacular death – Interdisciplinary perspectives on mortality and (un)representability*. Chicago: The University of Chicago Press.

Convery, I., Corsane, G., & Davis, P. (Eds.). (2014). *Displaced heritage: Responses to disaster, trauma, and loss*. Woodbridge: Boydell and Brewer.

Dann, G. M. S. (1998). The dark side of tourism. In *Etudes et Rapports, Serie L* (Vol. 14, pp. 1–31). Aix-en-Provence: Centre International de Recherches et d'Etudes Touristiques.

Davies, D. (2005). *A brief history of death*. Oxford: Blackwell.

Debord, G. (1977). *Society of the spectacle*. Detroit: Black and Red.

Doss, E. (2010). *Memorial mania: Public feeling in America*. Chicago: Chicago University Press.

Dunkley, R. A., Morgan, N., & Westwood, S. (2007). A shot in the dark? Developing a new conceptual framework for thanatourism. *Asian Journal of Tourism and Hospitality, 1*(1), 54–63.

Elias, N. (2001). *The loneliness of the dying*. London: Continuum.

Fornäs, J. (1995). *Cultural theory and late modernity*. London: Sage Publications.

Giddens, A. (1990). *The consequences of modernity*. Cambridge: Polity Press.

Giddens, A. (1991). *Modernity and self-identity: Self and society in the late modern age*. Stanford: Stanford University Press.

González-Ruibal, A. (2008). Time to destroy: An archaeology of supermodernity. *Current Anthropology, 49*(2), 247–279.

Gorer, G. (1955). The pornography of death. *Encounter, 5*(4), 49–52.

Grebenar, A. (2017). *The commodification of dark tourism: Conceptualising the visitor experience.* Unpublished PhD, University of Central Lancashire (UCLan), Institute for Dark Tourism Research, Preston.

Hansen-Glucklich, J. (2014). *Holocaust memory reframed: Museums and the challenges of representation.* New Brunswick: Rutgers University Press.

Harrison, R. P. (2003). *The dominion of the dead.* Chicago: The University of Chicago Press.

Hooper, G., & Lennon, J. J. (Eds.). (2016). *Dark tourism: Practice and interpretation.* London: Routledge.

Horne, J. (2013). Unsettling structures of otherness: Visualising the dying individual and end of life care reform. In M. Aaron (Ed.), *Envisaging death: Visual culture and dying* (pp. 224–242). Newcastle-upon-Tyne: Cambridge Scholars Publishing.

Howarth, G. (2007). *Death and dying: A sociological introduction.* Cambridge: Polity Press.

Jacobsen, M. H. (2016). 'Spectacular death' – Proposing a new fifth phase to Philippe Ariès's admirable history of death. *Humanities, 5*(19). https://doi.org/10.3390/h5020019.

Jacobsen, M. H. (Ed.). (2017). *Postmortal society: Towards a sociology of immortality.* Abington/Oxon: Routledge.

Jalland, P. (1996). *Death in the Victorian family.* Oxford: Oxford University Press.

Jamal, T., & Lelo, L. (2011). Exploring the conceptual and analytical framing of dark tourism: From darkness to intentionality. In R. Sharpley & P. R. Stone (Eds.), *Tourist experience: Contemporary perspectives* (pp. 29–42). Abington/Oxon: Routledge.

Jonsson, A., & Walter T. (2017). Continuing bonds and place. *Death Studies.* Available at http://dx.doi.org/10.1080/07481187.2017.1286412. Accessed 1 June 2017.

Kellehear, A. (2007). *A social history of dying.* Cambridge: Cambridge University Press.

Kerrigan, M. (2007). *The history of death: Burial customs and funeral rites from the ancient world to modern times.* Guilford: The Lyons Press.

Lennon, J. J. (2017). Conclusion: Dark tourism in a digital post-truth society. *Worldwide Hospitality and Tourism Themes, 9*(2), 240–244.

Lennon, J. J., & Foley, M. (2000). *Dark tourism: The attraction of death and disaster.* London: Continuum.

Lennon, J. J., & Teare, R. (2017). Dark tourism – Visitation, understanding and education: A reconciliation of theory and practice? *Worldwide Hospitality and Tourism Themes, 9*(2), 245–248.

Lennon, J. J., Seaton, A. V., & Wight, C. (2017). Directions, disconnect and critique: Round table discussion. *Worldwide Hospitality and Tourism Themes, 9*(2), 228–239.

Light, D. (2017). Progress in dark tourism and thanatourism research: An uneasy relationship with heritage tourism. *Tourism Management, 61*, 275–301.

Logan, W., & Reeves, K. (Eds.). (2008). *Places of pain and shame: Dealing with 'difficult heritage'*. London: Routledge.

Maddrell, A., & Sidaway, J. D. (Eds.). (2010). *Deathscapes: Spaces for death, dying, mourning and remembrance*. Aldershot: Ashgate.

McManus, R. (2013). *Death in a global age*. London: Palgrave Macmillan.

Mellor, P. A. (1992). Death in high modernity: The contemporary presence and absence of death. *The Sociological Review, 40*, 11–30.

Mellor, P. A., & Shilling, C. (1993). Modernity, self-identity and the sequestration of death. *Sociology, 27*(3), 411–431.

Miles, W. (2002). Auschwitz: Museum interpretation and darker tourism. *Annals of Tourism Research, 29*(4), 1175–1178.

Oddens, P. J. (2016, December 18). From dark ages to dark tourism: Death, spirituality and the modern tourist. *MMNieuws*. Available at http://www.mmnieuws.nl/article/from-dark-ages-to-dark-tourism-death-spirituality-and-the-modern-tourist/. Accessed 31 May 2017.

Pavićević, A. (2015). *From mystery to spectacle – Essays on death in Serbia from the 19th to the 21st century*. Belgrade: Etnografski Institut SANU.

Porter, R. (1999a). Classics revisited: The hour of Philippe Aries. *Mortality, 4*(1), 83–90.

Porter, R. (1999b). *The greatest benefit to mankind. A medical history of humanity from antiquity to the present*. London: Fontana.

Ray, C. (1999). Endogenous development in the era of reflexive modernity. *Journal of Rural Studies, 15*(3), 257–267.

Roberts, C., & Stone, P. R. (2014). Dark tourism and dark heritage: Emergent themes, issues and consequences. In I. Convery, G. Corsane, & P. Davis (Eds.), *Displaced heritage: Responses to disaster, trauma, and loss* (pp. 9–18). Woodbridge: Boydell and Brewer.

Sayer, D., & Walter, J. (2016). Digging the dead in a digital media age. In H. Williams & M. Giles (Eds.), *Archaeologists and the dead* (Vol. 9780198753537, pp. 367–395). Oxford: Oxford University Press.

Schillace, B. (2015). *Death's summer coat: What the history of death and dying can tell us about life and living*. London: Elliott & Thompson.

Seaton, A. V. (1996). Guided by the dark: From thanatopsis to thanatourism. *International Journal of Heritage Studies, 2*(4), 234–244.

Seaton, A. V. (2009a). Thanatourism and its discontents: An appraisal of a decade's work with some future issues and directions. In T. Jamal & M. Robinson (Eds.), *The sage handbook of tourism studies* (pp. 521–542). London: Sage.

Seaton, A. V. (2009b). Purposeful otherness: Approaches to the management of thanatourism. In R. Sharpley & P. R. Stone (Eds.), *The darker side of travel: The theory and practice of dark tourism* (pp. 75–108). Bristol: Channel View.

Sion, B. (Ed.). (2014). *Death tourism: Disaster sites as recreational landscape.* New York: Seagull Books.

Stone, P. R. (2006). A dark tourism spectrum: Towards a typology of death and macabre related tourist sites, attractions and exhibitions. *Tourism: An Interdisciplinary International Journal, 54*(2), 145–160.

Stone, P. R. (2009a). Dark tourism: Morality and new moral spaces. In R. Sharpley & P. R. Stone (Eds.), *The darker side of travel: The theory and practice of dark tourism* (pp. 56–72). Bristol: Channel View.

Stone, P. R. (2009b). Making absent death present: Consuming dark tourism in contemporary society. In R. Sharpley & P. R. Stone (Eds.), *The darker side of travel: The theory and practice of dark tourism* (pp. 23–38). Bristol: Channel View.

Stone, P. R. (2011a). Dark tourism: Towards a new post-disciplinary research agenda. *International Journal of Tourism Anthropology, 1*(3/4), 318–332.

Stone, P. R. (2011b). Dark tourism experiences: Mediating between life and death. In R. Sharpley & P. R. Stone (Eds.), *Tourist experience: Contemporary perspectives* (pp. 21–27). London: Routledge.

Stone, P. R. (2012a). Dark tourism and significant other death: Towards a model of mortality mediation. *Annals of Tourism Research, 39*(3), 1565–1587.

Stone, P. R. (2012b). Dark tourism as 'mortality capital': The case of ground zero and the significant other dead. In R. Sharpley & P. R. Stone (Eds.), *Contemporary tourist experience: Concepts and consequences* (pp. 71–94). London: Routledge.

Stone, P. R. (2014). Review: Necromanticism: Traveling to meet the dead, 1750–1860. *Journal of Heritage Tourism, 9*(1), 84–86.

Stone, P. R. (2016a). Enlightening the 'dark' in dark tourism. *Interpretation Journal.* Association of Heritage Interpretation (AHI), *21*(2): 22–24. Available at: http://works.bepress.com/philip_stone/47/. Accessed 21 May 2017.

Stone, P. R. (2016b) *'A commodification of death' – Dark tourism and difficult Heritage.* 'Packaging up death and the dead' for the contemporary visitor economy: A dark tourism and heritage perspective, ESRC 'Encountering Corpses' Seminar Series 2014–2017. Lancaster Castle, Lancaster, 19 October.

Stone, P. R., & Sharpley, R. (2008). Consuming dark tourism: A thanatological perspective. *Annals of Tourism Research, 35*(2), 574–595.

Stone, P. R., & Sharpley, R. (2014). Deviance, dark tourism and 'dark leisure': Towards a (re)configuration of morality and the taboo in secular society. In S. Elkington & S. Gammon (Eds.), *Contemporary perspectives in leisure: Meanings, motives and lifelong learning* (pp. 54–64). London: Routledge.

Strange, C., & Kempa, M. (2003). Shades of dark tourism: Alcatraz and Robben Island. *Annals of Tourism Research, 30*(2), 386–405.

Tarlow, P. E. (2005). Dark tourism: The 'appealing 'dark' side of tourism and more. In M. Novelli (Ed.), *Niche tourism: Contemporary issues, trends and cases* (pp. 47–58). Amsterdam: Elsevier.

Tercier, J. (2005). *The contemporary deathbed: The ultimate rush.* Basingstoke: Palgrave Macmillan.

Tercier, J. (2013). The pornography of death. In H. Maes (Ed.), *Pornographic art and the aesthetics of pornography* (pp. 221–235). London: Palgrave Macmillan.

Walter, T. (1991). Modern death: Taboo or not taboo? *Sociology, 25*(2), 293–310.

Walter, T. (1994). *The revival of death*. London: Routledge.

Walter, T. (2003). Historical and cultural variants on the good death. *British Medical Journal, 327*(7408), 218–220.

Walter, T. (2009). Dark tourism: Mediating between the dead and the living. In R. Sharpley & P. R. Stone (Eds.), *The darker side of travel: The theory and practice of dark tourism* (pp. 39–55). Bristol: Channel View.

Walter, T. (2014, October 17). *The revival of death: Two decades on*. End of life studies, University of Glasgow. Available at http://endoflifestudies.academicblogs.co.uk/the-revival-of-death-two-decades-on-by-tony-walter/#comments. Accessed 1 June 2017.

Walter, T., Littlewood, J., & Pickering, M. (1995). Death in the news: Public invigilation of private emotion. *Sociology, 29*(4), 579–596.

Warburton, N. (2012). *A little history of philosophy*. London: Yale University Press London.

Westover, P. (2012). *Necromanticism: Traveling to meet the dead, 1750–1860*. London: Palgrave Macmillan.

Williams, P. (2007). *Memorial museums: The global rush to commemorate atrocities*. Oxford: Berg.

Young, C., & Light, D. (2016). Interrogating spaces of and for the dead as 'alternative space': Cemeteries, corpses and sites of dark tourism. *International Review of Social Research, 6*(2), 61–72.

9

Dionysus Versus Apollo: An Uncertain Search for Identity Through Dark Tourism—Palestine as a Case Study

Rami K. Isaac and Vincent Platenkamp

Introduction

According to Nietzsche, European civilization has entered a phase of nihilism. The catastrophes of the twentieth century confirm this image. Adorno's moral dictum that art and thinking become impossible after the Holocaust refers to this image (Isaac and Platenkamp 2015; Tiedemann 2003). Western morality has ended in a form of relativism that rejects any substantial value in the everyday life of the Western world (Mann 1948a). This pessimistic line of thought leads to a devastating and completely relativized concept of identity. Identities are floating around without any point of anchorage. Nietzsche compares this situation to a state of passive nihilism in which no criterion can deliver the foundation of any identity. As an alternative to this nihilism, Nietzsche also talks about human tragedy. Nietzsche sees the origin of ancient Greek tragedy in the relation between Dionysus and Apollo—the birth of the tragedy in the first book by Nietzsche published in 1872. Nietzsche was at that time classics professor at Basle. He presents himself immediately as the great philosopher who is not confined to specialist considerations, but is searching for the bigger picture. *The Birth of Tragedy* is an early work, all the themes Nietzsche would elaborate upon in later works, including the will to power, moral criticism, the *amor fati*, and the eternal return.

One theme stands out in *The Birth of Tragedy*, however, essential: the Greek culture. Nietzsche shows how it has evolved from the dynamics of two

R. K. Isaac (✉) • V. Platenkamp
Academy for Tourism, NHTV Breda University of Applied Sciences, Breda, The Netherlands

principles: the Apollonian and the Dionysian. The Apollonian represents the world of dreams and harmony, the Dionysian intoxication and chaos. Nietzsche shows how these instincts have not only left their mark on Greek culture, but also by influencing the entire development of European culture. Within the first pages of *The Birth of Tragedy* (pp. 21 and 24), Nietzsche brings the Apollonian and the Dionysian in conjunction with the dream, respectively, intoxication. He sees Apollo and Dionysus as art gods (p. 21); the Apollonian and Dionysian forces therefore as art or art impulses which come from nature itself and dress in the visual world of dreams, respectively, in the ecstatic world of intoxication. Nietzsche sees the dream as a mere visual power, as health-giving appearance, as fantasy, delusion, and illusion. The dream is described as something pleasant: we have *Lust am Schein* (pleasure in appearance) and will therefore continue to dream the dream. Our everyday life seems to pass by in an ordinary and structured manner but then Dionysus enters the stage and destroys this seemingly ordered world. In moments of ecstasy, Man is confronted with the gruesome and dark side of life. And then Man awakens from these moments of ecstasy and Apollo enters the stage by trying to find a symbolical form for these ecstatic experiences he had just been gone through. Symbolically, therefore, modern Man needs to confront these tragedies of life, because this confrontation can contribute a refreshed zest for life that enables us to forget the desperate empty everyday world we live in. This awareness is essential to understanding the tragedy of life Nietzsche talks about. The modern human tragedy demands a new "human being" that looks catastrophes of the world in the eye and tries to understand the eternal suffering of the humankind as its own suffering. In this context, dark tourism becomes a potential way to make contact with particular human tragedy and is, arguably, crucial for modern Man (also see Chap. 25). Indeed, modern Man is uncertain about his own identities and is being confronted at the same time with human tragedies of the twentieth century through dark tourism.

By way of illustration, this chapter will examine Palestine as a case study. In particular, this study aims to explore the floating and relativized identities of modern Man within the context of dark tourism. Specifically, this chapter addresses how to revitalize these weakened and silenced identities within the Palestinian context. Moreover, authentication is "a process by which something – a role, product, site, object or event – is confirmed as 'original', 'genuine', 'real' or 'trustworthy'" (Cohen and Cohen 2012, p. 1296). Authentication can take place in two ways, namely hot or cool. The concept of hot authentication will be used as a contribution to this revitalization. Cool authentication corresponds with accepted common sense and dictionary definition of the term. The authority of the claim is based on scientific proof delivered by authorized persons or institutions according to formal criteria and accepted procedures. It is declarative and can be best compared to a claim of objective authenticity. The authority of hot authentication is based on belief, commitment, or devotion. There is no single identifiable authorized agent or institution, and there are no formal criteria. It includes rituals, offering, communal support, and resistance and can be best compared to a claim of existential authenticity (Cohen and Cohen 2012). This hot authentication could stimulate the subjective feelings of Palestinian identity in the context of domination and oppression.

Dionysus Versus Apollo: The Tragedy of Modern Life

Nietzsche's thinking is impregnated with a radical pessimism that implies a disbelief in any metaphysical world which denies any meaning of life outside life itself. In his *Die Geburt der Tragödie* (*The Birth of Tragedy*), this pessimism is inextricably connected with the core of his thoughts. For example, the imprisoned satyr Silenus is crying out laughing about the destiny of human mankind:

> … dasbeste ist für dich gänzlich unerreichbar: nicht geboren zu sein, nicht zu sein, nichts zu sein. Das Zweitbeste ist für dich bald zu sterben. (Nietzsche 1980, p. 30)
>
> […..To make the best is utterly beyond your reach: not to be born, not to be, to be nothing. The second best for is to die soon].

There is only one way out of this pessimism and that comes from art. In Nietzsche's vision on art there is a Dionysian ground on which an Apollonian order will be installed. Indeed, the Apollonian stands for a beautiful appearance of the world and the eternal presence as a dream product, while the Dionysian stands for original unity that destroys the appearance of the world but then repairs it again. Apollo explains the world and rescues us in its appearances, but then again Dionysus destroys this too beautiful appearance and opens the way to the core of things in all its ruthless ecstasy. And then, out of this tension between Dionysus and Apollo, Nietzsche situates the birth of ancient Greek tragedy. In a (Apollonian) dream world, once again, humans experience whole life:

> ...die ganze 'göttliche Komödie' des Lebens, mit dem Inferno, zieht an ihm vorbei, nicht nur wie ein Schattenspiel – denn er lebt und leidet mit in diesen Szenen – und auch nicht ohne jene flüchtige Empfindung des Scheins. (Nietzsche 1980, p. 22)

> [.... All the ' Divine Comedy' of life, with the Inferno, passes behind him, not only as a shadow play – because he lives and suffers within these scenes –. And not without that fleeting sensation of illusion.]

Humans will come to rest in this quiet trust in the appearances that Apollo is able to offer them, but then of course, they will shudder again because the Dionysian lusts emerge in an ecstasy to the surface. The "subject" forgets itself completely, the artist sinks away in Dionysian drunkenness, and in an Apollonian dream (work of art) the unity with the ground of the world will be revealed to him. Philosophically therefore, human beings are being protected against the complete knowledge of this gruesome life while at the same time their lust to live is being refreshed through these dark Dionysian sources that make him forget the desolate everyday life. Thus, tragedy for Nietzsche means an image of Dionysian wisdom through an Apollonian means of art. Tragic Man is a Dionysian man and a tragic culture has as its ultimate aim not science, but wisdom that looks to the world with an untouched gaze and tries to understand the eternal suffering of human mankind as its own suffering through this gaze.

What we need, therefore, is a strong human being that dares to give meaning, which is eager to search for new values and identities in this tragic life. Thomas Mann (1948, p. 124), a German writer, formulated this need in his careful way by saying:

> ... Und so ist der Mensch die geheime Hoffnung der Welt und aller Kreatur, zu welchem gleichsam alle Wesen sich vertrauensvoll hindrängen, und auf den sie auf ihren möglichen Erlöser und Heiland erblicken.

> [... And man is the secret hope of the world and to every creatures, to which all beings move at the same time, full of trust, and to which they see on their potential redeemer and savior.]

Despite his tragic destiny and in spite of all the calamities that came upon him, especially during the twentieth century, Man remains the secret hope of this world. This conclusion suddenly contains a very stimulating and hopeful element that could be very well expressed within dark tourism. The Palestinian identities that were sad to float in a nihilist, completely relativized context could get a revitalized content through this principle of hope.

Dark Tourism: The Return of Dionysus Through the Dream World of Apollo

Dark tourism was first introduced almost 20 years ago into the then growing field of tourism studies (Ashworth and Isaac 2015). One of the most interesting trends has been a focus on heritage sites with a controversial history, including locations of war, occupation (Isaac 2013), atrocity, and horror (Ashworth and Hartmann 2005), which are expressions of the Dionysus power of human nature. These studies have nurtured a critical debate about the nature of tourism at controversial locations (Hartmann 2013). Novelli (2005) states that increasing attention paid to the phenomenon of dark tourism in recent years may arguably be symptomatic of the trend within academic circles to identify and label specific forms of tourism, or to subdivide tourism into niche products and markets. On the other hand, however, dark tourism may also be an example of media hype responding to a presumed fascination in death and dying (Sharpley 2009). Stone (2006) further argues that for as long as people have been able to travel, they have been drawn, purposefully or otherwise, towards sites, attractions, places, or events that are linked in one way or another with death, tragedies, and disaster.

Through these sites, places, or events, an Apollonian dream world has been created in which the dark tragedies of life are given expressions. Nevertheless, in spite of the long history and increasing contemporary evidence of travel to sites and attractions associated with death and suffering, it is only relatively recently that academic attention has been focused upon what has collectively been referred to as "dark tourism". Foley and Lennon (1996) first introduced the term "dark tourism" in the mid-1990s to describe death-related tourism. In recent years, dark tourism has attracted increasing academic and media interest and has become a popular area of research. However, despite the recent attention paid to dark tourism, it is not a new phenomenon. Travelling to and experiencing spaces associated with death is an act that has been undertaken by tourists since the eleventh century (Dale and Robinson 2011), and arguably before. Stone (2006), for example, states that the Coliseum may be considered one of the first dark tourism attractions. More specifically, the publication of Lennon and Foley's (2000) *Dark Tourism: The Attraction of Death and Disaster* introduced the term to a wider audience, stimulating a significant degree of academic interest and debate. Furthermore, the launch of a UK university research centre by Philip Stone in 2012 which is dedicated to dark tourism scholarship attracted significant global attention (see www.darktourism.org.uk).

Dark tourism research has been focusing on three main perspectives: the demand-side, the supply-side of dark tourism, or adopting a more holistic view, studying both demand and supply. Thus, dark tourism research has contained largely descriptive accounts of a supply-side perspective of visitor sites of death and tragedy (Sharpley 2009). Indeed, recent studies have stressed the diversity and variety of dark sites, focusing on defining and classifying dark tourism manifestations based on specific attributes of sites (Kang et al. 2012). Consequently, Miles (2002) distinguishes between dark, darker, and darkest sites, and Stone's (2006) "Dark Tourism Spectrum" typological model offers a conceptual framing of visitor sites ranging from "lightest" to "darkest" sites. Until now, this approach has been criticized as leading to an increasing weakening and fuzziness of the notion of dark tourism as it arbitrarily combines evidently diverse visitor experiences (Sharpley 2009). As such, a supply-side perspective raises questions as to whether it is justifiable or appropriate to collectively classify as "dark tourism" tourists' experiences at themed attractions, such as the London Dungeon, alongside experiences of visitors to genocide camps, and whether the concept of dark tourism is indeed helpful at all for broader tourism research (Biran and Hyde 2013).

Stone and Sharpley (2008) suggest that potential motives for visiting death-related sites have not yet been fully or systematically examined, thus allowing only weak conceptualizations of dark tourism. A visit to a site associated with death and suffering is generally considered as dark tourism (Dunkley et al. 2007). However, the use of the term "dark tourism" is not without criticism. In particular, authors have addressed specific shortcomings of dark tourism and its theoretical justification as well as its loose conceptualization (Biran and Poria 2012; Jamal and Lelo 2011; Stone and Sharpley 2008). Moreover, Biran and Poria (2012) state problems of the use of the term "dark tourism". For instance, the meaning of "dark" in Western cultures has particular negative connotations, while visits to dark places are certainly not merely for negative reasons, nor do such visits produce purely negative responses. Biran and Poria (2012) also argue that conceptual notions of "darkness" are socially constructed. Therefore, they suggest using the term "dark tourism" only for deviant tourist behaviour. Similarly, Jamal and Lelo (2011) object to the overuse of the term "dark tourism". In addition, Bowman and Pezzullo (2009, p. 199) have gone so far as to suggest that it may be "time to even abandon the term 'dark tourism' insofar as it may present an impediment to detailed and circumstantial analyses of tourist sites and performances in all their mundane or spectacular particularity and ambiguity".

Recently, empirical research by Isaac and Cakmak (2014) at the former Nazi transit camp Westerbork in The Netherlands confirmed some of the theorizations and practical observations previously mentioned. Meanwhile, Isaac and Cakmak (2014) argued that the term dark tourism should be replaced by a "site associated with death and suffering". They also argue that dark tourism does not exist but the experience does. In this context, therefore, Dionysus gives the experience an overwhelming significance that needs to be understood in an Apollonian dream world. This experience refers to the process of authentication that uses subjective feelings, emotions, and values in order to revitalize Palestinian identities. Therefore, we need to look on a more tangible level how this process has been taken care of in the Palestinian case.

The Palestinian Case

The 1948 war that led to the creation of the State of Israel resulted in the devastation of Palestinian society. At least 80 per cent of Palestinians lived in the major part of Palestine which became Israel and more than 77 per cent of Palestinians became refugees living in the West Bank, Gaza Strip, Jordan, Syria, and Lebanon (Isaac 2010a). The minority of Palestinians, from between 60,000 and 156,000 people—depending on the sources—who remained behind, became nominal citizens of the newly established Jewish state, subject to a separate system of military administration by a government that also confiscated the bulk of Palestinian resources and their lands (Abu-Lughod and Sa'di 2007). For Palestinians, the 1948 war as well as the 1967 war are known as *"Al-Nakba"*—The "Catastrophe". The forced expulsion of 800,000 Palestinians from 1948 to 49 was part of a long-standing Zionist plan to manufacture an ethnically pure Jewish state (Pappé 2006). The second catastrophe was during the 1967 war, when 350,000 Palestinians were forced out of the West Bank and Gaza Strip. The slow transfer policy of the State of Israel added another 500,000 Palestinians to the list of homeless Palestinians (Andoni 1993). A society disintegrated, a people dispersed, and a complex and historically changing but taken-for-granted communal life was violently ended. The *Al-Nakba* has thus become, both in Palestinian memory and history. After 1948, the lives of the Palestinians at individual, community, and national levels were dramatically and irreversibly changed.

The destruction of Palestinian society was dominated by the heavy presence of what was represented and understood internationally as a birth or rebirth. In other words, the death-rebirth tension is a philosophical notion with enormous purchase in both religious and Western secular thought, and has been applied to the Jewish people (Abu-Lughod and Sa'di 2007). The 1948 war that led to the creation of the State of Israel was made to symbolize their rebirth within a decade after their persecution in Europe and subjection to the Nazi Genocide. This horrible Jewish Dionysian experience has been given expression in many Apollonian dream worlds at many places. Heritage sites such as Auschwitz (Biran et al. 2011) in Poland or Buchenwald in Germany are the testimony of these dark Apollonian dream worlds. Many Jewish generations visit these heritage sites in order to never forget this historical past, and during this process of authentication, their sense of identity becomes revitalized (Thurnel-Read 2009). Meanwhile, Palestinians were excluded from the unfolding of this history. Their "Dionysian catastrophe" was either disregarded or reduced to a question of ill-fated refugees, similar to the many millions around the world, and those who wandered in Europe following the end of the World War II, or those displaced or forced to flee the conflict that accompanied the partition of India in 1947. Excluded from history as the trace of a nation whose right to independence, statehood, and even existence was denied, Palestinian refugees were seen as a humanitarian case, and what often has been experienced as the demeaning support of United Nations agencies (Peteet 2005).

Consequently, Elias Sanbar (2001), a Palestinian historian and writer, articulates in his essay *"Out of Place, Out of Time"* the strange exclusion of Palestinians from the unfolding of Palestinian history, particularly in the Western world and thought:

> The contemporary history of the Palestinians turns on a key date: 1948. That year, a country and its people disappeared from maps and dictionaries ... The Palestinian people does not exist, said the new masters, and henceforth the Palestinians would be referred to by general, conveniently vague terms, as either "refugees" or in the case of a small minority that had managed to escape the generalised expulsion, "Israeli Arabs". A long absence was beginning. (p. 87)

Arguably, therefore, for Palestinians, the need for dark tourism places as the Apollonian expression of their Dionysian experiences became urgent, because of this historical exclusion. Dark tourism and its Apollonian dream world could give expression to the secret hope and search for identity that humankind should cherish and that Tomas Mann was talking about.

Initiatives for the Search of Palestinian Identity Through Dark Tourism

There are a growing number of establishments and civil society organizations in Palestine and Israel which are working to counter the mainstream discourse with regard to Palestine. These include official tour operators in the region who attempt to provide a counter narrative. Indeed, the mainstream discourse with regard to Palestine in Israeli society requires some clarification. For instance, a key myth for Westerners about this conflict is that they perceive Arabs and Jews have been fighting for thousands of years and that they will continue to fight.

However, Jews flourished in the Arab world at the time when they were being persecuted all over Europe. European Jews then started to argue that they needed a Jewish state in the land of Palestine. The mainstream Israeli-Jewish society believe through a process of education and myth-making that Palestine was somehow empty and, indeed, had been empty when the Jewish settler came to settle there. The question is, of course, who paid the price when they settled there? Of course Palestine at that time was not empty. It was populated by Palestinian Arabs, who had a long history and a high level of culture and education, with farms, markets, and towns and villages, roads and commerce, and lots of interaction with the rest of the world. As for a counter narrative, the following contextual examples attempt to readdress the mainstream discourse.

The Alternative Tourism Group (ATG) is a Palestinian NGO specializing in tourism and presents a critical first-hand experience, and examines the culture, history, and politics of Palestine, as well as its complex relationship with Israel. ATG was established in 1995 and operates according to the tenets of "justice tourism" and "solidarity tourism"—that is, tourism that holds as its central goals the creation of economic opportunities for the local community, positive cultural exchange between guest and host through one-on-one interaction, protection of the environment, and political/historical education (Isaac 2010a; Isaac and Hodge 2011). Kassis (cited in Isaac 2010a, pp. 30–31) adds that "at the global level 'justice tourism' is a social and cultural response to the policy of cultural domination as reflected in the case of tourism in Palestine – a good example of a policy capable of changing the history of Palestine, subverting of its identity, and causing restrictions, closures and difficulties for tourists to enter Palestinian cities". Currently, ATG offers tours for all types of tourists from university students to diplomats, or groups looking for alternatives, to more traditional mass pilgrimage in both Palestine and

Israel. ATG also runs several thematic tours, which include one-day political tours and solidarity tours, where tourists are introduced to the refugee camps in Palestine. During the tour experience tourists can listen to stories of the Palestinian expulsion and force displacement from their homelands during the wars of 1948 and 1967, as well as the recent displacements of many Palestinian families from their homes as a result of the construction of the Segregation Wall (Isaac 2009, 2010a, b). Hence, tourists may learn about the complexity of life of Palestinians, and the restriction of movements for Palestinians when travelling within the West Bank, including the checkpoints and road blocks, which are all examples of oppression and occupation in a country controlled by the state of Israel.

In December 2009, Palestinian Christian leaders launched the Kairos document that shared their daily realities of life under occupation. The Kairos calls on Christian sisters and brother and Churches worldwide to be witnesses to these realities, to be in solidarity, and to take action. The following is an excerpt:

> Today we have reached a dead end in the tragedy of the Palestinian people. The decision makers content themselves with managing the crisis rather than committing themselves to the serious task of finding a way to resolve it…It is a policy in which human beings and identities are destroyed, and this must be of concern to the Church…These days, everyone is speaking about peace in the Middle East and the peace process. So far, however, these are simply words; the reality is one of Israeli occupation of Palestinian territories, deprivation of our freedom and all that results from this situation…. (Kairos 2010, p. 3)

Kairos is an ancient Greek word meaning the right or opportune moment. The Kairos message is a clear one. Therefore, "justice tourism" to Palestine has its ultimate goal: "promoting peace with justice for the people in the Holy Land". Engaging churches, social movements, and faith-based organizations to promote Pilgrimages for Transformation, it is hoped that pilgrims will be inspired by and will work for justice-based peace and reconciliation for both Palestinians and Israelis. Transformational pilgrims to Palestine are also justice tourists, seeking to understand and make a positive difference in the lives of people whose lands they visit. Meeting Palestinians who are living under occupation is an act of solidarity that brings hope to the people and contributes to their economic development.

Zochrot (Remembering) is an organization founded by Eitan Bronstein based in Tel Aviv. Established in 2002 as an Israeli NGO, Zochrot helps raise awareness of the *Al-Nakba*, the Palestinian catastrophe of 1948. The *Al-Nakba* is an unspoken taboo in Israeli discourse, its memory erased from the official history of the country and from its physical landscape. Yet, the *Al-Nakba* is also the central trauma of the Israeli-Palestinian conflict, and its legacy continues to unfold today—in the institutionalization of inequality and violence, in the erasure of the past, and in the identity and a deteriorating plight of the Palestinian refugees. Therefore, the aim of Zochrot is to inform individuals that the organization "will act to challenge the Israeli Jewish public's preconceptions and promote awareness, political and cultural change within it to create the conditions for the Return of Palestinian Refugees and a shared life in this country" (Selwyn 2014, p. 117). Zochrot also runs several tours for Israelis and other tourists to both Israel and Palestine, and to various Palestinian villages destroyed during 1948, while working with former residents to recall and describe the buildings, such as mosques, churches, schools, and the social and cultural life of the villages. The tours present the 1948 *Al-Nakba* as "the destruction, expulsion, looting, massacres and incidents of rape of the Palestinian inhabitants of this country. Keeping the refugees out by force at the end of the war, in order to establish the Jewish state" (Selwyn 2014, p. 117).

This Dionysian outburst of violence needs an Apollonian dream world again. The Palestinian narrative of exclusion, displacement, and destruction needs to be revitalized by dark tourism sites that appeal to a growing Palestinian identity. Zochrot offers this Apollonian "dream world by exhibiting photographs, testimonies, maps of destroyed Palestinian villages, as well as conducting political educational programmes and other visual research" (Zochrot 2015) (http://www.zochrot.org). All these activities are done to seek recognition for the injustice done by the state of Israel. For instance, the charge of anti-Semitism has become a psychological weapon in the hands of Zionists, who use it to traumatize Israel's opponents and suppress its critics. Consequently, Said in his 2003 book *Culture and Resistance* points out that "there is a great difference between acknowledging Jewish oppression and using that as a cover for the oppression of another people" (p. 178). Land and people are separated into a web of bypass roads and military zones that link Israeli illegal settlements and integrate them into Israel proper (Nahleh 2006). Indeed, there are approximately 200 built colonies of Israel in Palestine that are connected by a network of roads, which separates each Palestinian city, town, and village from each other which, in turn, limits Palestinian communities' ability to expand. These settlements serve to separate the 700 Palestinian towns and villages from each other and to curb any contiguous rural and urban development between them. Recently, and particularly after the second *Intifada* uprising in October 2000, erected roadblocks, settlements, and outposts became Israel's new military borders, "not only formalizing the split-up between the Gaza Strip from the West Bank and East Jerusalem, but also progressively isolating each Palestinian area from its neighbor" (Usher 2003, p. 22). According to the Israeli journalist Amira Hass "the level of connection between West Bank cities and villages is fast approaching that of 150 years ago" (Hass 2003, p. 185). The erection of the Wall (Isaac 2009), which includes trenches, sniper, patrol roads, and barbed wire, has "resulted in the confiscation of even more agricultural land, destroying even more houses, and further tightening the noose on the already besieged Palestinian towns and villages" (Abu Nahleh 2006, p. 107). In the process, it is indeed breaking the social fabric and identity of Palestinian society and separating communities and families from each other, from their homes and land, their social activities, and from their daily services.

Therefore, this kind of prospective education and learning through (dark) tourism and specific organized tours can open up potential new ways of (re)constituting Jewish and Palestinian identities, as well as rebuilding relations between Israelis and Palestinians so that they can be founded on respect, recognition, and responsibility. Subsequently, approximately every two months Zochrot hosts free public tours to sites of destroyed Palestinian localities. With a diverse range of tour participants, including Arabs and Jews from various backgrounds, the tours cater to students, activists, artists, journalists, refugees, and residents amongst others. Indeed, a recent Zochrot tour catered for approximately 120 people to the destroyed Palestinian village of Al-Manshiyya, near Akka (Acre). Almost half of the participants were foreign students and activists, and the others Jewish Israelis and Palestinians with Israeli citizenship (Zochrot 2015).

Conclusion: The Return of Dionysus in Dark Tourism and an Uncertain Search for Identity

In this chaotic situation identity is not a self-evident concept. As far as identity is characterized by an unchanging sameness of a group of people (Palestinians) this becomes complex in situations where groups are displaced and exiled within a country but are still connected in various ways. Several identities are being constructed simultaneously and Palestinian identities need to be understood in the everyday interaction of this situation. Thus, this search for identity in the context of dark tourism in this region is heavily related to the historical and violent interaction between Israelis and Palestinians. This whole violent situation calls for an Apollonian dream world, in which these interactions and concomitant identification of all people involved can be presented. In this dream world, human beings are being protected against the complete knowledge of this gruesome reality, while at the same time creates a refreshed vision of Palestinian identity in these dark periods of violence.

Dark tourism, therefore, offers an inimitable opportunity to develop a forum in which Palestinians can not only seek identity but ascertain uniqueness in an uncertain and turbulent environment. Through these contextual initiatives presented in this chapter, Palestinians may again develop a sense of belonging, cohesion, legitimization, socialization, and confirmation. Ultimately, dark tourism as a phenomenon becomes more relevant for Palestinians, for the re-birth of their identities in this Dionysian context. This process of searching for identity is well associated with hot authentication (Cohen and Cohen 2012). Hot authentication fits best into the idea of the Apollonian dream world that was introduced in this chapter. In an Apollonian dream world, belief and commitment emerge and a strong subjective experience refers to the communal support and resistance that belong to the Palestinian heritage. During this communal support, many identification arise in this process of authentication. It provides abundant opportunities for all people involved to revitalize their identities in relation to the disturbing events that took place in Palestine. As Isaac (2014, p. 139) states, "an important difference with the discussion about dark tourism sites, like Auschwitz and the former sites of the slave trade on the Ghanaian coast (Finley 2004) is the situation. In Ghana and Auschwitz, these sites and places are constructed because they are related to heritage and memory. While in Palestine, the situation is 'real' and genuine". Similar dark tourism sites about the Palestinian heritage could be constructed as places of identification within a real but catastrophic context.

References

Abu Nahleh, L. (2006). Six families: Survival and mobility in times of crises. In L. Taraki (Ed.), *Living Palestine: Family survival, resistance, and mobility under occupation*. New York: Syracuse University Press.

Abu-Lughod, L., & Sa'di, A. (2007). Introduction. In A. H. Sa'di & L. Abu-Lughod (Eds.), *Nakba: Palestine, 1948 and the claims of memory*. New York: Colombia University Press.

Andoni, G. (1993). *Non-violence tax resistance in Beitsahour*. Beitsahour: Palestinian Centre for Rapprochement between People.

Ashworth, G. J., & Hartmann, R. (2005). *Horror and human tragedy revisited: The management of sites of atrocities for tourism.* New York: Cognizant.

Biran, A., & Hyde, K. (2013). Guest editorial. New perspectives on dark tourism. *International Journal of Culture, Tourism and Hospitality Research, 7*(3), 191–198.

Biran, A., & Poria, Y. (2012). Reconceptualising dark tourism. In R. Sharpley & P. R. Stone (Eds.), *Contemporary tourist experience: Concepts and consequences* (pp. 59–70). Abingdon: Routledge.

Biran, A., Poria, Y., & Oren, G. (2011). Sought experiences at (dark) heritage sites. *Annals of Tourism Research, 38*(3), 820–841.

Bowman, M. S., & Pezzullo, P. C. (2009). What's so dark about 'dark tourism'? Death, tours and performances. *Tourist Studies, 9*(3), 187–202.

Cohen, E., & Cohen, S. (2012). Authentication: Hot and cool. *Annals of Tourism Research, 39*(3), 1295–1314.

Dale, C., & Robinson, N. (2011). Dark tourism. In P. Robinson, S. Heitemann, & P. Dieke (Eds.), *Research themes for tourism* (pp. 205–218). Wallingford: CABI.

Dunkley, R. A., Morgan, N., & Westwood, S. (2007). A shot in the dark? Developing a new conceptual framework for thanatourism. *Asian Journal of Tourism and Hospitality, 1*(1), 54–63.

Finley, C. (2004). Authenticating dungeons, whitewashing castles: The former sites of the slave trade on the Ghanaian coast. In D. M. Lasansky & B. McLaren (Eds.), *Architecture and tourism*. Oxford: Berg.

Foley, M., & Lennon, J. (1996). JFK and dark tourism: A fascination with assassination. *International Journal of Heritage Studies, 4*, 198–211.

Hartmann, R. (2013). Dark tourism, thanatourism, and dissonance in heritage tourism management: New directions in contemporary tourism research. *Journal of Heritage Tourism*. https://doi.org/10.1080/1743873X.2013.807266.

Hass, A. (2003). *Reporting Ramallah*. Cambridge, MA: MIT Press.

Isaac, R. K. (2009). Can the segregation wall in Bethlehem be a tourist attraction? *Tourism and Hospitality: Planning & Development, 6*(3), 247–254.

Isaac, R. K. (2010a). Alternative tourism: New forms of tourism in Bethlehem for the Palestinian tourism industry. *Current Issues in Tourism, 13*(1), 21–36.

Isaac, R. K. (2010b). Moving from pilgrimage to responsible tourism: The case of Palestine. *Current Issues in Tourism, 13*(6), 579–590.

Isaac, R. K. (2013). Palestine: Tourism under occupation. In D. Butler & S. Wantanee (Eds.), *Tourism and war* (pp. 143–158). London: Routledge.

Isaac, R. K. (2014). A wail of horror: An empathic 'atrocity' tourism in Palestine. In H. Andrews (Ed.), *Tourism and violence* (pp. 125–144). London: Sage.

Isaac, R. K., & Cakmak, E. (2014). Understanding visitor's motivations at sites of death an disaster. The case of former transit camp Westerbork, The Netherlands. *Current Issues in Tourism, 17*(2), 164–179.

Isaac, R. K., & Hodge, D. (2011). An exploratory study: Justice tourism in controversial areas. The case of Palestine. *Tourism Planning & Development, 8*(1), 101–108.

Isaac, R. K., & Platenkamp, V. (2015). Concrete U(dys)topia in Bethlehem: A city of two tales. *Journal of Tourism and Cultural Change*. https://doi.org/10.1080/14766 825.2015.1040413.

Jamal, T., & Lelo, L. (2011). Exploring the conceptual and analytical framing of dark tourism: From darkness to intentionality. In R. Sharpley & P. R. Stone (Eds.), *Tourist experience: Contemporary perspectives* (pp. 29–42). Abingdon: Routledge.

Kairos. (2010). *Come and see: A call from the Palestinian Christians*. Beitsahour: Kairos.

Kang, E., Scott, N., Lee, T. J., & Ballantyne, R. (2012). Benefits of visiting a 'dark tourism' site: The case of the Jeju April 3rd Peace Park, Korea. *Tourism Management, 33*(2), 257–265.

Lennon, J. J., & Foley, M. (2000). *Dark tourism*. London: Continuum.

Mann, T. (1948a). *Nietzsches Philosophie in Lichte Unserer Erfahrung*. Berlin: Schwabe Verlag Basel.

Mann, T. (1948b). *Nietzsches Philosophie in Lichte unserer Erfahrung*. Berlin: Suhrkamp vorm S. Fischer.

Miles, W. (2002). Auschwitz: Museum interpretation and darker tourism. *Annals of Tourism Research, 29*, 1175–1178.

Nietzsche, F. (1980). *Die Geburt der Tragödie :Uit Werke I*. Frankfurt: J.B. Metzler.

Pappé, I. (2006). *The ethnic cleansing of Palestine*. Oxford: Oneworld.

Peteet, J. (2005). *Landscape of hope and despair: Palestinian refugee camps*. Philadelphia: University of Pennsylvania Press.

Said, E. (2003). *Culture and resistance*. Cambridge, MA: South End Press.

Sanbar, E. (2001). Out of place, out of time. *Mediterranean Historical Review, 16*(1), 87–94.

Selwyn, T. (2014). Tourism, sight prevention and cultural shutdown: Symbolic violence in fragmented landscapes. In H. Andrews (Ed.), *Tourism and violence*. Surrey: Ashgate.

Sharpley, R. (2009). Shedding light on dark tourism: An introduction. In R. Sharpley & P. R. Stone (Eds.), *Tourist experience* (pp. 3–22). London: Routledge.

Stone, P. R. (2006). A dark tourism spectrum: Towards a typology of death and macabre related tourist sites, attractions and exhibitions. *An Interdisciplinary International Journal, 54*(2), 145–160.

Stone, P. R., & Sharpley, R. (2008). Consuming dark tourism: A thanatological perspective. *Annals of Tourism Research, 35*(2), 574–595.

Thurnel-Read, T. (2009). Engaging Auschwitz: An analysis of young travelers' experience of Holocaust tourism. *Journal of Tourism Consumption and Practice, 1*(1), 26–52.

Tiedemann, R. (Ed.). (2003). Theodor W. Adorno. *Can one live after Auschwitz*. Stanford: Stanford University Press.

Usher, G. (2003). Facing defeat: The Intifada two years on. *Journal of Palestine Studies, 32*(2), 21–40.

Zochrot. (2015). Zochrot tours report. http://www.zochrot.org/en/tour/53548. Accessed 3 Mar 2015.

10

Dark Tourism as Psychogeography: An Initial Exploration

Richard Morten, Philip R. Stone, and David Jarratt

Introduction

The study of 'dark tourism' may be a relatively recent phenomenon, but the practice itself—including commemorative, educational or even leisure visits to places associated with death and/or suffering—is by no means a new social behaviour (Stone 2007). Scholarly examination of dark tourism has raised fundamental lines of multidisciplinary interrogation, not least issues that focus on notions of deviance and moral concerns of consuming or producing 'death sites' within the global visitor economy (Stone and Sharpley 2013). Discourse often revolves around visitor motives and tourist engagement (Yuill 2003), as well as issues of how 'dark heritage' should be managed (Hartmann 2014). While motivation is of a personal and subjective nature, managing or producing dark tourism sites is fraught with political difficulties and moral quandaries (also see Chap. 22). Importantly however, the (dark) tourist experience at sites of difficult heritage is a process of 'co-creation' between visitor site interpretation and individual meaning-making.

Thus, dark tourism is an intrinsically emotional, subjective and phenomenological place-based pursuit. Moreover, due to the highly subjective nature

---

Richard Morten is the founder of The Bohemian Blog (http://www.thebohemianblog.com/) and also writes under the pseudonym *Darmon Richter*.

R. Morten (✉) • P. R. Stone • D. Jarratt
University of Central Lancashire, Preston, UK

of the touristic experience, some visitors at some sites for some of the time may be engaging in so-called 'dark' tourism while others are not. As Stone (2007: 1) notes, 'if you have ever visited a Holocaust museum, taken a tour around former battlefields, or had an excursion to Ground Zero, then you've participated – perhaps unwittingly – in dark tourism.' Elsewhere, Stone (2005: 1) defines dark tourism as 'the act of travel, whether intentional or otherwise, to sites of death, destruction or the seemingly macabre.' Notions of the 'unwitting' or 'unintentionality' within dark tourism suggest that places may exist where tragic history—or its *darkness*—is not commonly perceived. For example, historic UK battlefields of state-sanctioned killing are often marked for touristic encounters within a broader rural idyll, where wildlife lovers mingle with battle enthusiasts in traumascapes of yesteryear (Conduit 2005; Stone 2012). However, while other commodified tourist places and 'attractions' may be considered intrinsically 'dark' in nature—due to the nature of atrocity or associated depravity or level of horror—the broader practice of dark tourism is a deeply personal transaction rooted in memory and perception.

The purpose of this chapter, therefore, is to address spatial subjectivity within dark tourism environments. Specifically, the chapter asks, through a broad-ranging conceptual and contextualised discussion, a number of interrelated questions: Who makes the association of 'darkness' to a place? Is the label 'dark tourism' applied by those offering (and commoditising) the visitor experience? Alternatively, is any 'dark' significance to be evaluated and decided upon by the tourists themselves? If the latter is the case, is it possible that one visitor to a (dark) site might be participating in dark tourism while another is not? Hence, the chapter suggests a transactional nature to the production and consumption of the dark tourism experience—a process entirely influenced by a very personal framework of knowledge, memory and associations. To that end, the research adopts a *psychogeography* approach—that is, the specific effects of the geographical environment on the emotions and behaviours of individuals. Ultimately, the chapter considers dark tourism not as a passive mode of tourism, but rather as a dynamic and individualistic way of interacting with space and place. In other words, dark tourism exists by way of deeply personalised responses to geographic places and, subsequently, the study seeks to present dark tourism as a very specific form of 'psychogeography.' The chapter aims to be a foundational text in which to conceptually locate dark tourism and its fundamental interrelationships with psychogeographical elements and, in so doing, offer a transdisciplinary challenge to human geography gatekeepers.

Exploring Psychogeography

The conceptual assembly of both geography and psychology may be enough to satisfy some of the broader definitions that have been offered for psychogeography (Hay 2012). However, it speaks very little to the *flâneur* philosophy (the idea of a connoisseur explorer) and the spirit of *dérive* (an unplanned journey or drifting through a place) which was integral to the original meaning of psychogeography (Debord 1958). Indeed, Western philosophers have long been interested in the various ways that different people view and interpret our shared world. For instance, the German existentialist Martin Heidegger used the term *Dasein* to denote the transactional process of 'being in the world.' In other words, we are not being in the world simply by the act of existing within space, but rather as a performance of sorts, in which every aspect of our knowledge and character plays a role in dictating our subjective interactions with our surroundings (Heidegger et al. 1962). This interest in spatiality and its subjectivity provided the bedrock for the post-war psychogeography movement. Specifically, in Paris, in the wake of World War II, a group of avant-garde philosophers who called themselves 'the Situationist International' began chronicling their interactions with space. They sought to explore ways in which people created their own meaningful (inter)relationships with their surroundings. As a result, Guy Debord—one of the Situationists' founding members—proposed psychogeography as 'the study of the precise laws and specific effects of the geographical environment, whether consciously organized or not, on the emotions and behaviour of individuals' (Debord 1955: website; also see Chap. 1). Therefore, psychogeography offered a potential new way of 'being in the world.' The psychogeographical pilgrim/traveller (or 'drifter')—the *flâneur*—would eschew the objectivity of maps in favour of 'letting the city speak for itself.' They would *drift* according to whim, following emotions rather than street signs as they traced the 'psychogeographical contours... constant currents, fixed points and vortexes' of their (usually urban) surroundings (Debord 1956: website). This mode of exploration was known as the *dérive* (from the French word for 'drifting') and constituted 'playful-constructive behaviour and awareness of psychogeographical effects' which immediately distinguished it 'from the classic notions of journey or stroll' (Debord 1956: website). The rules of the dérive, according to the Situationists, were simply that 'one or more persons during a certain period drop their relations, their work and leisure activities, and all their other usual motives for movement and action, and let themselves be drawn by the attractions of the terrain and the encounters they find there' (Debord 1956: website).

The Situationists' response was to create new designs of urbanised space, while promising enhanced opportunities for experimenting through mundane expression. Arguably, Guy Debord's intention was to unify two different factors of so-called 'soft and hard ambiances' that, taking a Debordian perspective, determined the values of urban landscape. In short, Debord's vision was a combination of two realms of opposing ambiance—the *soft ambiance* (light, sound, time and the association of ideas) and the *hard ambiance* (or the actual physical constructions of place). Hence, the Situationist philosophers drifted about Paris (often frequenting bars) and drew their own maps to describe the urban landscape before them. However, these maps did not conform to objective and conventional cartography, but rather the Situationists experimented with their own new forms to create maps that might act as a narrative rather than as a tool of 'universal knowledge' (McDonough 1994). These maps were created by slicing up conventional street plans and rearranging the component parts joined by arrows that indicated the subjective currents experienced by a *flâneur* exploring the city. These were maps of emotion and experience and, subsequently, replaced traditional and literal representations of streets and city blocks. For example, Plate 10.1 illustrates a 'Psychogeographical Guide to Paris' as conceived by Guy Debord. It exemplifies the city, as he perceived it, not as a comprehensive street plan but rather as a collection of nodal points of interest that possesses emotive value and joined by passages of potential movement—as indicated by the arrows. A caption on the map explains these arrows and nodes as 'psychogeographical slopes of drift and the location of ambiance units.'

Unsurprisingly, perhaps, this casual and rather bohemian approach to spatial geography has attracted some criticism. Even a member of the Situationist International, the artist Ralph Rumney, offered a playful critique of the psychogeographical practice:

> …as Debord defined *dérive* it was going from one bar to another, in a haphazard manner, because the essential thing was to set out with very little purpose and to see where your feet led you, or your inclinations… You go where whim leads you, and you discover parts of cities, or come to appreciate them, feel they're better than others, whether it's because you're better received in the bar or because you just suddenly feel better. (Rumney cited in Ward 2000: 169)

Meanwhile, Debord's biographer Vincent Kaufman states that the 'apparently serious term "psychogeography" comprises an art of conversation and drunkenness, and everything leads us to believe that Debord excelled at both' (Kaufman 2006: 114)—a sardonic reference, perhaps, to the frequentation of

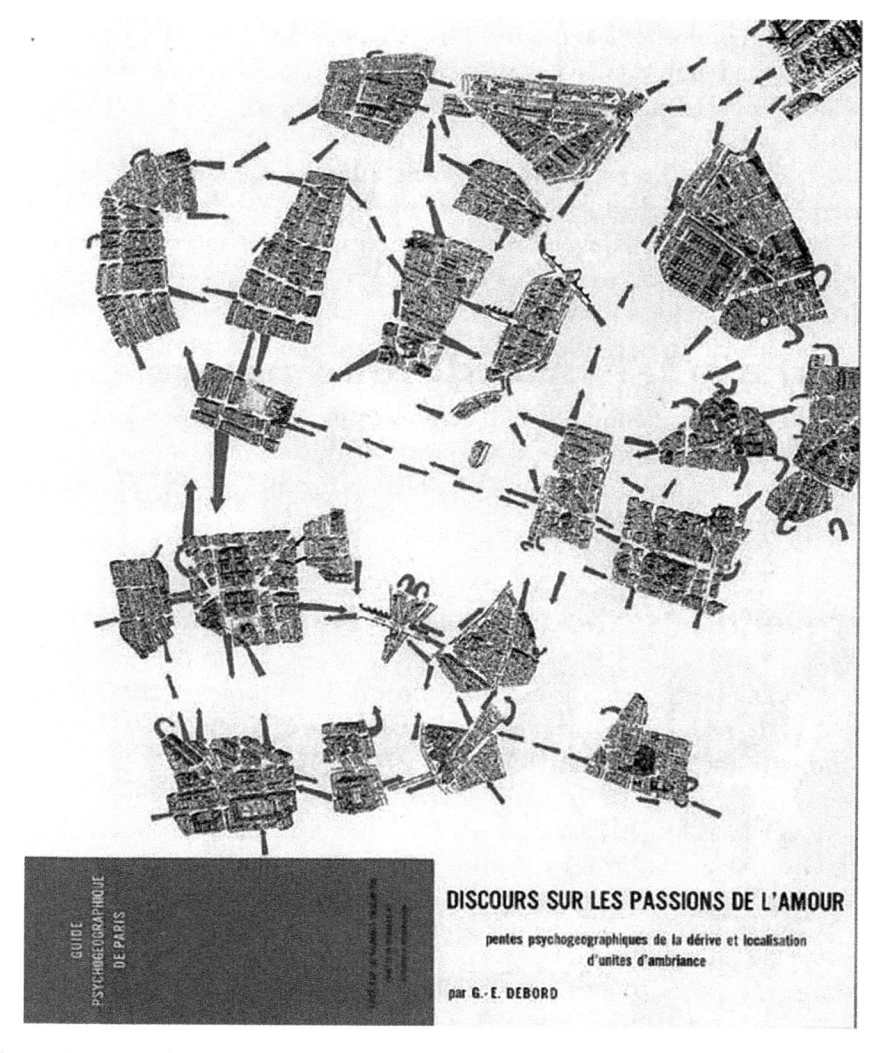

Plate 10.1 'Psychogeographical Guide to Paris' by Guy Debord (Source: van Tijen 2017)

Parisian bars noted earlier. Even Debord himself remarked the fate of 'urban relativity' and psychogeography and goes on to admit:

> ...the sectors of a city... are decipherable, but the personal meaning they have for us is incommunicable, as is the secrecy of private life in general... None of this is very clear. It is a completely typical drunken monologue... with its vain phrases that do not await response and its overbearing explanations. And its silences. (Debord 1961: website)

Arguably, the philosophical origins of psychogeography lie within inebriated yet enlightened 'pub-crawls' of post-war Paris. Yet, despite some obvious critique of the conceptual and empirical foundations of psychogeography, it has nevertheless established itself as an enduring mode of spatial geography—and a subject field that has attracted increasing attention over the past few years (Coverley 2006; Richardson 2015). Consequently, psychogeography may offer an alternative to conventional narratives on social spaces. Indeed, psychogeography seems set to become ever more popular in a contemporary society hallmarked by increasing privatisation of public spaces (Kayden 2000), as well as an alienation of traditional human interactions in favour of ever more superficial entertainment—or what Debord (1967) referred to as the 'Society of the Spectacle.' Of course, a full analysis of psychogeography and its contemporary application is beyond the scope of this chapter, though a critical overview is now offered to provide a backdrop for subsequent discussions of dark tourism.

Discovering Psychogeography (Within Tourism)

Psychogeographical definitions range from the simple—a practice that 'explains the relationship between psychology and geography' (Hay 2012: website)—to the more esoteric:

> …we, as human beings, embed aspects of our psyche… memories, associations, myth and folklore… in the landscape that surrounds us. On a deeper level, given that we do not have direct awareness of an objective reality but, rather, only have awareness of our own perceptions, it would seem to me that psychogeography is possibly the only kind of geography that we can actually inhabit. (Moore 2013: website)

In recent decades, a 'new school' of psychogeography has emerged, largely because of the work of London-based journalists and scholars such as Iain Sinclair (1997), Stewart Home (2004) and Will Self (2007). However, Sinclair (1997: 4) appears to emulate Debord in his description of interacting with the city:

> Walking is the best way to explore and exploit the city… the changes, shifts, breaks in the cloud helmet, movement of light on water. Drifting purposefully is the recommended mode, tramping asphalted earth in alert reverie, allowing the fiction of an underlying pattern to reveal itself.

Placing these textural similarities to one side, there are notable differences between the original Parisian psychogeographers of the post-war period and the more recent emergence of the London school of thought. Particularly, contemporary psychogeography appears to adopt a primarily literary form, albeit one that perhaps encourages action on the part of the reader. For instance, Williams (2008: website), in his review of Will Self's (2007) *Psychogeography*, describes it as 'a Romantic text whose associations of writing and walking have less to do with Guy Debord's influence on London-based writers and more to do with Wordsworth and Coleridge.' In contrast, psychogeography for the Situationist International was a purely tactile and phenomenological pursuit with Debord cautious of the idea of 'psychogeographical texts'—going on to lament that 'written descriptions can be no more than passwords to this great game' (Debord 1956: website). Similarly, Sinclair (2006: website) is also critical of Will Self's journalism and treatment of psychogeography and suggests that it has 'absolutely no connection whatsoever to whatever psychogeography was originally, or in its second incarnation.' Sinclair goes on to argue that psychogeography has 'become the name of a [newspaper] column by Will Self, in which he seems to walk the South Downs with a pipe, which has got absolutely nothing to do with psychogeography. There's this awful sense that you've created a monster' (Sinclair cited in Jeffries 2004: website).

Another difference between the Parisian and London-based approaches is evident in the focus. The Situationists were concerned with the future and the 'soulless' restrictive nature of post-war construction projects. In turn, they had sought to provide a critique of mid-twentieth-century advanced capitalism (Plant 1992). However, contemporary psychogeographers appear to be more interested in the history informing the fabric of their urban surroundings. As Duncan Hay, author of the *Walled City* blog, puts it, 'where Parisian psychogeography orients its critique of the city around a utopian projection towards a newly revivified post-revolutionary city, London psychogeography finds the strength of its critique in the past' (Hay 2012: 1). Yet, despite the inherent and obvious complexities of psychogeography—both as a concept of spatial geography and an application of psychosocial connections—it can serve as a 'brand name for more or less anything that's vaguely to do with walking or vaguely to do with the city... a new form of tourism' (Sinclair 2006: website).

Consequently, tourism studies have long examined subjective and phenomenological aspects of the tourist experience (Cohen 1979), as well as the role personal (secular) pilgrimages (or tourist journeys) play in our (post) modern society (Urry 1990; Urry and Larsen 2011). Arguably, therefore, tourism simply defined as the 'movement of people' is allied to the central psychogeographical premise of exploring relationships between psychology and geography (Hay 2012). Moreover, tourism is concerned with inherent personal emotions and behaviours of the 'journey' to and within any given place. Importantly, tourism is a deeply personal process of meaning-making. In other words, tourism can be an often-directionless and sometimes unplanned pursuit of leisurely interaction with space and, as such, can be entirely removed from our usual mode of being in the world. This may constitute a very specific, if not unintentional, form of psychogeography. Importantly, similar arguments may be made for dark tourism. In other words, dark tourism is *dark* precisely because of a perceived 'darkness' assigned to certain locations and geographic areas; even allowing for the application of shades or 'degrees of darkness' as a measure of that emotional depth (Sharpley 2009). The very nature of dark tourism relates to emotional attachment within place, where the tourist can play the role of a phenomenological pilgrim. However, in order to delineate particular places of darkness—for example, cemeteries, specific museum exhibitions, memorial sites and so forth—and in terms of bridging Debord's notion of *geographical ambiance*, it is worth considering the work of another French spatial philosopher, Michel Foucault. Indeed, Foucault examined spaces of unusual ambiance and places of extra-normative social significance within his conceptual work of the heterotopia, to which this chapter now turns.

Bridging Psychogeography: Heterotopia and Other (Tourism) Places

'Heterotopia' is a concept within spatial geography that denotes a place outside of the typical liminal systems of topography. First introduced by Michel Foucault, the idea of heterotopia holds that some social spaces function in a different way to the regular terrain of our day-to-day lives. The term 'heterotopia' is derived from 'Other places' and builds upon subtle yet significant distinctions between *place* and *space*. On the one hand, 'space' is defined as 'a continuous area or expanse which is free, available, or unoccupied,' while, on the other hand, 'place' is defined as 'a particular position, point, or area in space – a location designated or available for or being used by someone.' There is a great deal of subtlety that connects—but also differentiates—the two concepts of space and place. Indeed, the concepts are layered with meaning derived from a myriad of social, political, historical, geographical and anthropological structures. If *place* is to be understood as a location with particular meaning or significance attached, then that meaning, ultimately, renders the distinction highly subjective. As Agnew (1987) notes, place is more than just a location, but a composite of 'location,' 'locale' and a 'sense of place.' Furthermore, Cresswell (2004: 6) argues that 'place, then, is both simple (and that is part of its appeal) and complicated.' This complexity is also recognised by Harvey (1993: 5) who points out:

> The first step down the road is to insist that place, in whatever guise, is, like space and time, a social construct. The only interesting question that can be asked is, by what social process(es) is place constructed?

The social processes by which 'place' might be constructed can be viewed through the prism of definition. Cresswell (2015), for example, suggests that place can be defined as different from space by the process of naming it. Lippard (1997) notes that place may be defined by its nostalgic value, by its familiarity, and as *local* places (Lippard 1997; also Jarratt and Gammon 2016). Meanwhile, both Relph (1976) and Tuan (1977) advocate that place can be defined by the subjective experience of 'people in a world of places.' It is here that place possesses 'the notion of a meaningful segment of geographical space' (Cresswell 2008: 134), while Tuan (1977) argues 'what begins as undifferentiated space becomes place as we get to know it better and endow it with value… the ideas 'space' and 'place' require each other for definition.'

Subsequently, the issue of space/place has now moved towards less reductive models, emphasising instead the way in which 'places' are constructed by the people moving through them. In other words, there has been a subjective and transitory definition of the concept that has been described as a 'global' or 'progressive' approach to knowing *place* (Massey 1993, 2004). The study of embodiment, for instance, has presented new perspectives on what it means to be in place (Csordas 1994); while other researchers have broadened the focus to consider how place is experienced through the senses (such as 'smellscapes'—see Dann and Jacobsen 2003). Arguably, however, psychogeography might be seen as a conceptual and relational, if not contested, process that bridges the two ideas of space and place. In short, psychogeography reveals the subjective pilgrimage that looks for meaning in typically overlooked spaces, thus forming areas of new or unexpected significance and emotion and, thus, rendering these spaces into *places*—or *Other places* as Foucault would have it. Indeed, Cresswell (2015) describes the 'sense of place' in language that resonates with original writings of the Situationist International and their efforts to resist the homogenisation of post-war Paris. He goes on to note that 'it is commonplace in Western societies in the twenty-first century to bemoan a loss of a sense of place as the forces of globalization have eroded local cultures and produced homogenized global spaces' (Cresswell 2015: 14).

Of course, it is beyond the remit of this study to consider all of these approaches to place. Instead, the chapter defines *place* simply as the product of building subjective relations to *space*. In turn, this emphasises a process that was the very essence of early psychogeography and, subsequently, allows for the identification of the principles for Foucault's heterotopia and 'Other places.'

Principles of Heterotopia

Foucault introduced the perplexing and contested term 'heterotopia' to describe an assortment of places and institutions that interrupt the apparent continuity and normality of ordinary everyday space (Foucault 1967a [1984]). More of a philosophical ramble than a codified concept, Foucault suggested *heterotopias*—as opposed to *utopias* as invented places—are real spaces where the boundaries of normalcy within society are transgressed. Foucault argued that heterotopias inject a sense of alterity into the sameness, where change enters the familiar and difference is inserted into the commonplace. Indeed, heterotopias are spaces of contradiction and duality, as well as places of physical representation and imagined meaning. In short, heterotopias may be broadly seen as real places, but which are perceived to stand outside of known space and, thus, create a sense of the alternative (Topinka 2010). Stripped of its philosophical verbiage, the idea of heterotopias as alternative social spaces existing within and connected to conventional places offers a thought-provoking concept that can stimulate investigation into fundamental interrelationships between space, experience and culture. Ultimately, heterotopias can be physical or mental spaces that act as 'Other places' alongside existing spaces. As revealed shortly, heterotopias conform to a number of principles and include places where norms of conduct are suspended either through a sense of crisis or through deviation of behaviour. Heterotopias also have a precise and determined function and are reflective of the society in which they exist. They also have the power to juxtapose several real spaces simultaneously as well as being linked to the accumulative or transitory nature of time. Heterotopias are also places that are not freely accessible as well as being spaces of illusion and compensation. In short, Foucault argued that we are now in an era of simultaneity, juxtaposition, of proximity and distance, of side-by-side, and of the dispersed. The principles of Foucault's heterotopias are summarised here:

Principle #1: Foucault claimed that heterotopias were universal and would appear across all cultures. He went on to highlight two specific types—the heterotopia of *crisis* and the heterotopia of *deviation*. Here, Foucault argued that these were 'forbidden' places (such as care homes) and were places for people in a state of crisis in relation to their place in society or culture. Meanwhile, Foucault's deviation heterotopias were places reserved for those whose behaviour is deemed deviant to social norms (for example, prisons).

Principle #2: The heterotopia can be acted upon by society in order to serve different *roles and functions* over time. Foucault offers the example of a cemetery; an internment site where the appearance, function and traditional location within a settlement has changed over the centuries in relation to changing cultural attitudes to death and disposal of the dead.

Principle #3: The heterotopia has the power to *juxtapose*, in a single real space, several spaces that are in themselves incompatible. In other words, they can become spaces for the representation of ideas, and places bigger than themselves. Foucault offers the example of the theatre and the cinema, but also the garden as a kind of heterotopia symbolic of the larger outside world.

Principle #4: Foucault's fourth principle stated that heterotopias were heterochronous—that is, linked to specific slices of time. On the one hand, Foucault suggested the museum or library as examples of places of 'perpetual and indefinite accumulation of time.' Conversely, on the other hand, Foucault also argued heterotopias as places of fleeting time linked to a specific moment or moments. Here, Foucault gave the example of travelling fairgrounds that are dismantled after the fair has ended.

Principle #5: A fifth principle suggests heterotopias possess a system of *(de) valorisation* that allows places to be both isolated but also penetrable. In other words, places are, in some way, both opened and closed and can only be accessed from the surrounding world by way of barriers or cultural rituals. Foucault gave examples of religious institutions or military barracks—each protected by 'barriers' that can only be breached by stating correct words or undertaking social gestures, or by submitting to a specific process of initiation.

Principle #6: Finally, Foucault states that heterotopias maintain a function relative to all the space that remains. In turn, the final trait of heterotopias is that they create *illusions* and *compensations* that expose all real spaces and, as a result, create a place that is *Other*. Foucault offers examples of the colony and the brothel as way of illustration, where the outside world is made to seem more accessible by way of illusion, or perhaps in some cases perfected, reordered or compensated in the way of a model town.

With its all-encompassing and vaguely defined parameters, Foucault's idea of heterotopia has been a source of both inspiration as well as confusion in the application of conceptual frameworks that shape public space (Dehaene and De Cauter 2008). Furthermore, Heynen (2008) argues that heterotopia, while being a 'slippery' term to employ, offers potentially rich and productive readings of different spatial and cultural constellations and, accordingly, justifies the continuing use of the concept. While a full critique of 'heterotopology' is beyond the scope of this chapter, the paradox of heterotopia is that they are spaces both *separate from* yet *connected to* all other places. Therefore, in our contemporary world heterotopias are everywhere and, consequently, highlight the public-private binary opposition (Dehaene and De Cauter 2008). Indeed, heterotopian places are collective or shared in nature, and often perceived as marginal, interstitial and subliminal spaces. It is in this conceptual framework that heterotopias open up different, if not complex, layers of psychogeographical relationships between space and its consumption.

By way of contextualising notions of heterotopias and broader psychogeography, particularly within dark tourism, Stone (2013) offered a conceptual analysis of Chernobyl—the site of the world's worst nuclear accident. That analysis is summarised here in the following case example (Case Study 1). Specifically, Stone (2013: 90) asks whether Chernobyl as a heterotopia could 'provide a blueprint of how other 'dark tourism' sites might be constructed as marginal spaces.' Therefore, this study contextualises another dark tourism site as a potential heterotopian place—Auschwitz-Birkenau Memorial and Museum—a site synonymous with the Holocaust and the scale of atrocities that still haunts contemporary imagination (Case Study 2).

Case Study 1: The Chernobyl Exclusion Zone as a Heterotopia
The 'Exclusion Zone' or 'Zone of Alienation' marks an arbitrary 30 km radius around the nuclear reactor at Chernobyl (including the nearby abandoned town of Pripyat), Ukraine, which in 1986 went into meltdown, resulting in the worst radioactive accident in history. Recently, however, the site has begun a new life as a tourism destination—and with its obvious themes of death and suffering, it has become a notable destination for dark tourism (Dobraszczyk 2010; Stone 2011, 2013). Particularly, Stone (2013) seeks to evaluate this dark site against the (six) heterotopian principles suggested by Foucault (also Fig. 10.1):

1. The Chernobyl site, so intrinsically connected to Cold War binaries, offers an example of Foucault's heterotopia of crisis. Chernobyl and its dead zone is a place of sociocultural and political crises, a remnant 'forbidden' place

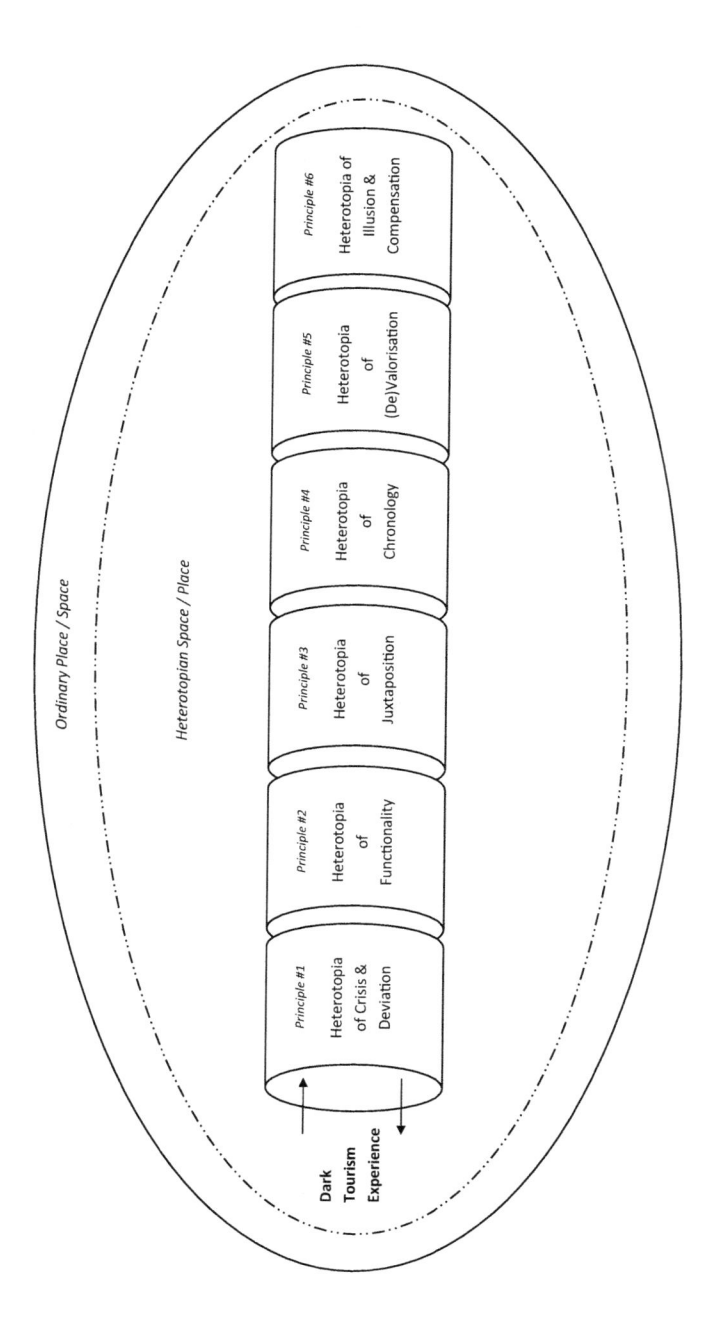

Fig. 10.1 A dark tourism cylinder: a conceptual model showing dark tourism experience within a heterotopian framework (Source: Stone 2013)

that highlights the upheavals and divisions of the Cold War and its sustained state of political and military tension. Today, Chernobyl as a heterotopia of crisis is where tourists can not only separate crises of the past, but also (re)connect to current global predicaments and contemplate future quandaries. Subsequently, however, post-Cold War tourism to the site perhaps reflects a more deviant approach to leisure and tourism (Stone and Sharpley 2013) in that it strays from accepted norms. In essence, Chernobyl (and its tourism) emerges from a landscape of historical and political crisis as an apparent 'deviant heterotopia.'

2. Stone (2013) suggests the Chernobyl site satisfies the idea of a 'heterotopia of functionality,' in that it possesses duality of function and it serves changing roles in relation to contemporary society. On the one hand, the site functions as a symbol of 'a failed political dogma as well as being symbolic of distant utopian ideals and Soviet power' (Stone 2013: 86). On the other hand, 'the site is also consumed by tourists as a pyramid of our technical age, a tomb of technological tragedy, and a symbol of our ruin to generations to come and, so, connects us to the fragility of our progress outside the Zone' (Stone 2013: 86).

3. In the abandoned nearby town of Pripyat—a 'modern Pompeii' (Todkill 2001)—multiple realities appear juxtaposed. Tourists can now experience tragedy and loss, the memorialised remnants of a nuclear accident, but set against the ruins of a past (would-be) utopia. This place of juxtaposition is what Stone (2013) refers to as an empty meeting ground of both the familiar and the uncanny. In turn, 'juxtapositions of the real… with the surreal… allow tourists to consume not only a sense of ruinous beauty and bewilderment, but also a sense of anxiety and incomprehension in a petrified place that mirrors our own world' (Stone 2013: 87).

4. Chernobyl offers a tourist experience where a sense of both the accumulation and transition of time occurs. As such, the site can be considered heterochronous. Similar to Foucault's museum, Stone (2013: 87) points to the way in which Chernobyl seems to exist outside of regularly functioning time: 'it accumulates time and collects evidence of an age in a perpetual and indefinite manner.' Thus, tourists not only consume the nuclear accident at Chernobyl, but also the historical era in which the disaster occurred. It is this museumification of Chernobyl that allows for a heterotopia of chronology in that time is seen in its most futile, most transitory and most precarious state (Foucault 1967b).

5. The fifth principle concerns access rituals and social constructs that serve to form a barrier separating the heterotopia from the world around it. Termed by Stone (2013) as heterotopias of (de)valorisation, heterotopian

places must have a system of 'purifications' (Foucault 1967b), where spaces are valorised (opened up) and then de-valorised (closed down) to visitors. In the case of Chernobyl, this can be seen in the militarised checkpoints that surround the Zone of Exclusion. Here, physical barriers are enforced and made all the more meaningful by the social ritual of tourists having to apply for formal access to the site, paying access fees and signing personal medical disclaimers to alleviate the State of any potential wrongdoing.

6. Finally, in the sense that heterotopias maintain a function relative to the space that remains, Stone (2013) argues that Chernobyl might serve as a 'heterotopia of illusion and compensation.' Chernobyl brings the binaries between the real and the surreal into focus, and serves to be compensate us for a ruined past while providing an illusion of a life-enhancing response. In turn, Chernobyl provides 'a (relatively) safe and socially sanctioned environment in which feelings of helplessness of preventing the accident stimulates an enhanced awareness of the fragility of our modern world' (Stone 2013: 89). Ultimately, as Dobraszczyk (2010: 387) states, 'if the voices of Chernobyl and Pripyat are to speak to us clearly, they must do so through the ruin that bears witness to them... in this sense, ruins become the foundation on which to build the future.'

Case Study 2: Auschwitz-Birkenau Memorial and Museum as a Heterotopia

Auschwitz-Birkenau Memorial and Museum is a former German Nazi concentration and extermination camp located on the outskirts of Oświęcim in Poland. KZ Auschwitz has become a symbol of state-sanctioned terror, genocide and the Holocaust. With over one million people systematically murdered at the site, mostly Jews, Auschwitz as a museum and memorial was created in 1947. Today, with over a million annual visitors to the site (Auschwitz.org. 2016a), the post-camp relics and structures are preserved to serve as a 'warning from history.' In terms of Foucault's heterotopian principles (Fig. 10.2):

1. Auschwitz-Birkenau is a place of crisis. It was a place of incarceration and mass execution for those considered socially 'deviant' by the German Nazi regime. Detention to this forbidden place was dictated by spurious criteria, including religion, culture, ethnicity, ableness or sexuality. This contrasts to its current role as a visitor site of powerful emotional and educational value, where modern-day tourists often report the kind of extraordinary, transformative or even 'life-changing' experiences that Foucault alluded to when detailing his heterotopias of crisis and deviation (e.g. see Woods 2016).

```
                    Psychogeography

    Heterotopias  ←——  Dark Tourism  ——→  Homotopias

    ┌──────────┐   ┌──────────┐   ┌──────────┐
    │          │   │          │   │          │
    │Foucauldian│   │          │   │ Debordian│
    │   dark   │   │Experience│   │   dark   │
    │  tourism │   │          │   │  tourism │
    │          │   │          │   │          │
    └──────────┘   └──────────┘   └──────────┘

    ←————————  Meaning Making  ————————→
                    Sense of Place
```

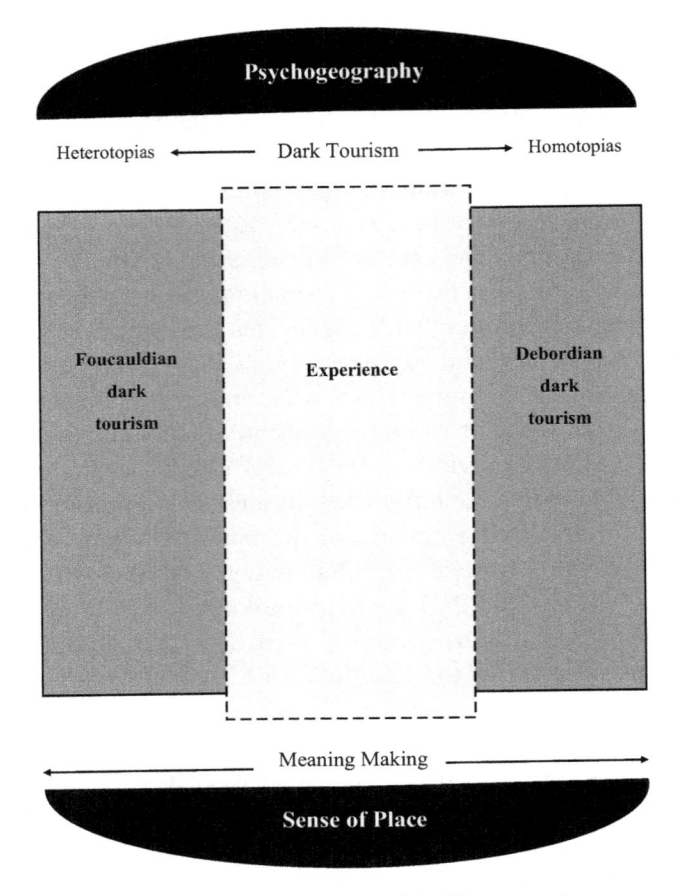

Fig. 10.2 Dark tourism within a psychogeographical framework

2. In terms of functionality, Auschwitz-Birkenau as a site has served multiple changing roles in relation to demands of society and various political ideologies. Auschwitz I was formerly an Austrian and, later, Polish army barracks, before the German Nazis commandeered it as a prison and concentration camp (Dwork and van Pelt 2002). Since 1947, operating as a museum, the place of Auschwitz-Birkenau has served multiple functions (and political ideologies) during Poland's membership of the Warsaw Pact and EU. The site now functions as a (mass tourism) memorial to Holocaust victims, as well as being a place of religious, political and cultural significance, a symbol of nation building and victimhood, and offering immense educational and historical value.

3. A touristic visit to Auschwitz-Birkenau is awash with juxtapositions. The place combines horror and tragedy in a setting that many tourists have

described as naturally beautiful—'the grounds at Auschwitz-Birkenau were really pretty, primarily because everything was so clean and the spring grass was full,' reads one of the many online articles written by visitors to the site (Mullins 2001). It is here where conventional landscapes and buildings are juxtaposed with the calamity of what occurred within the deathscapes of Auschwitz-Birkenau. As tourists now wander through the 'mansions of the dead' (Keil 2005), the return of normality (through tourism) is played out at the intersection of being in, what is arguably, one of the world's largest cemeteries.

4. Auschwitz-Birkenau Memorial and Museum is a heterotopia of chronology, being a place, as Foucault (1967b) puts it, of the 'perpetual and indefinite accumulation of time.' However, unlike a typical museum or library, which will often reflect all of time in a timeless setting, Auschwitz-Birkenau is focussed on a very specific slice of time (Dwork and van Pelt 2002). Specifically, the site interprets time of the Holocaust up until the camp's liberation in 1945. As such, the site arrests time at liberation and modern-day tourists now consume perpetual and unrelenting narratives of fear, murder and terror. Subsequent museumification of Auschwitz-Birkenau ensures the ever-recurring and habitual nature of tourism, where the site is revealed within heterochronism and where time is fleeting and (tourist) journeys transient. Indeed, tourists visiting the site are regulated to spend relatively short periods consuming memories of the Holocaust dead. It is here that heterotopias of chronology come together, both by witnessing the accumulation of time at Auschwitz-Birkenau and by the temporary touristic consumption of its deathscapes.

5. The obvious symbols of accessing the original Auschwitz-Birkenau site, namely, the watchtowers, electric fences or the guard points, are preserved for locational authenticity and perpetuity. However, other valorisation processes and commercial rituals exist for modern-day tourists that both open up and close down the site. While sight of the camps' fortifications reinforces a sense of entering into an 'Other' space, the systematic procedures of processing over a million visitors ensures Auschwitz-Birkenau is a heterotopia of de(valorisation). As Foucault (1967b cited in Dehaene and De Cauter 2008: 21) notes, 'one can only enter [and leave] with a certain permission and after having performed a certain number of gestures.' For example, various levels of visitor 'Entry Passes' available to individuals or tour groups to gain physical access to the site, the obligatory use of headphones and tour guides (or site 'Educators') for group visits, the period of year and times when only accompanied tour groups are permitted on site, and a host of other visitor rules, regulations and prohibitions (Auschwitz.org. 2016b).

6. The delusion of Auschwitz-Birkenau as a site of 'Arbeit Macht Frei' (Work Sets You Free) is, perhaps, the ultimate illusion of this place. Indeed, the reality of Auschwitz-Birkenau is now consumed as a surreal tourist attraction under curatorial remits and museum codes. However, as tourists consume genocide memories and attempt to capture the horror of the Holocaust, the Otherness of the place begins to elude the senses and a feeling of the sublime can give way of a pervasive anxiety inherent in contemporary society. Yet, despite the illusion of 'Never Again' (genocides have occurred and, sadly, continue to occur since the Holocaust), Auschwitz-Birkenau represents a microcosm of an apocalyptic world; the ordinary world outside the camp's perimeters is brought to the fore and exposed for all its geopolitical disorder and fragile societal frameworks in which we are all located. Yet, the tourist experience in the Other place at Auschwitz-Birkenau can produce a heterotopia of compensation. Indeed, the place of Auschwitz-Birkenau offers an educative counterbalance space that links us to present-day dangers of fascism, isolationism and the rise of Far Right political ideologies.

Evolving Heterotopia

Arguably, while Foucault's original definition of a heterotopia is a good fit for the kinds of commoditised *Other* places portrayed as 'dark tourism'—at least evidenced by the two case examples above—it is worth noting that the idea of the heterotopia itself has evolved since its conception. More contemporary interpretations have suggested heterotopias to better describe modern urban landscapes (Dehaene and De Cauter 2008), while new technologies and cybernetic realities allow for new ways of experiencing and examining heterotopias—not to mention the idea of 'virtual heterotopias' (Rousseaux and Thouvenin 2009). However, some heterotopias appear to manifest in different heterotopic forms over time. For example, and taking the case examples of both Chernobyl and Auschwitz-Birkenau in this study, both have been shown to function as heterotopias in their current touristic states; but while their dark tourism appeal may be new, their status as heterotopia is not. In other words, the nuclear power station (Chernobyl) and the Nazi prison/concentration camp (Auschwitz-Birkenau), during their functional pasts, arguably met the heterotopic principles originally suggested by Foucault. Yet, presently, the Nazi prison/concentration camp has become a museum, while the power plant (perhaps comparable to Foucault's factory) and its surrounding area have been preserved as an exclusion zone.

It seems, therefore, that Foucault has accounted for this heterotopia evolution when he described such places as progressive and functioning relatively to outside society (Foucault 1967b), while Topinka (2010: 56) suggests that heterotopias are universal, 'although the forms they take are heterogeneous' from one culture to the next. The changing functions of these heterotopias might reflect a deeper truth of Foucault's Sixth Principle; that is to say, heterotopias, while being in many ways isolated from the outside world, continue to function in a relative manner. Of course, while Chernobyl and Auschwitz-Birkenau are incomparable in terms of purpose, they have nevertheless both changed, in time, from original spaces of 'function' towards a new existence as (visitor) places of commodified experience. Consequently, this transition from intended function to contemporary touristic phenomenology relates to earlier discussions of space and place; to the relationship between geography and psychology; and thereby to the psychogeographers who sought to explore the latent emotional value contained within the urban environment. Therefore, for the remainder of this chapter, the study offers the idea of both *psychogeography as dark tourism*, and *dark tourism as psychogeography* and, by way of summary, outlines the notion of *Foucauldian Dark Tourism* and *Debordian Dark Tourism*.

Psychogeography as Dark Tourism

As noted earlier, Iain Sinclair is widely regarded as one of the most prolific psychogeographers of the London tradition, and his work has always tended towards the macabre. In a review of Sinclair's work, Jeffries (2004: 1) notes 'devoid of bucolic heritage idylls… (t)he poet's journey will take him past plague pits, over sewers and burial mounds … across the occult vortices of Hawksmoor churches, Ripper landmarks and gangland haunts.' In 1975, Sinclair published one of his most iconic works: the part-fiction/part-poetic collection of occult-heavy London psychogeography, *Lud Heat* (Sinclair 1975). Here, Sinclair is concerned with highlighting the esoteric symbolism of the British capital, drawing parallels and links between the legacies of historical characters such as William Blake, Nicholas Hawksmoor and Jack the Ripper. Much of Sinclair's narrative takes the form of a 'stream of consciousness,' or dense, epic poetry—but there are sections too that describe Sinclair's own experiences as he heads out on foot to trace symbolic shapes across a map of London.

Lud Heat is not, strictly, psychogeography—at least not as Guy Debord would have judged it. As discussed earlier, the Parisian *dérive* was a process of tracing the underlying current—those 'psychogeographical slopes'—by feeling alone, the process of discovering place within space. Sinclair, conversely, sets out with a pre-conceived mythology of London landmarks although his writing does nevertheless adhere to the principle of playful-constructive behaviour and awareness of psychogeographical effects (Debord 1958). As a result, the author begins his journey from *place*, rather than *space*. Sinclair appears to acknowledge this when he admits:

> For me, [psychogeography is] a way of psychoanalysing the psychosis of the place in which I happen to live. I'm just exploiting it because I think it's a canny way to write…. (Sinclair cited in Jeffries 2004: website)

However, psychogeographical traditionalism aside, the book is recognised as a significant work in the London psychogeography canon, and it's interesting to note that many passages of *Lud Heat* also adhere clearly to the academic definition of 'dark tourism.' Throughout the book, Sinclair demonstrates a seeming preoccupation with sites of death and suffering which are manifested from ancient history. For example, 'it is all here in the coastal ridges of Dorset: burial chamber stones heaped over with earth' (Sinclair 1975: 81), to more casual dark tourism—'take my lunch to Tower Hamlets Cemetery' (Sinclair 1975: 41). Sinclair also investigates sites of ritual murders, while his fascination with occult lore and morbid detail serves to turn even a commonplace stroll through London into an apparent dark tourism experience:

> They have circumnavigated the Roman Wall, they have followed the Hawksmoor trail east, from Blake's grave and the glimpse of St Luke's, Old Street, …to the place of the lichen-pattern on the grave, to the crossroads, the staked vampire pit, St-George's-in-the-East. (Sinclair 1975: 129)

That same vein of 'witting' premeditation which differentiates Sinclair's contemporary psychogeography from that of the early 1950s psychogeographical *dérive*, also serves to qualify his work as dark tourism; he walks the streets of London, encountering dark heritage at every turn, amongst the crowds of pedestrians and conventional tourists who do not experience the city as he sees it. Sinclair does not visit packaged-up commoditised sites of dark tourism, but rather through application of his own form of psychogeography he becomes a so-called 'dark tourist.'

Dark Tourism as Psychogeography

While psychogeography in certain contexts might be perceived as a kind of contemporary dark tourism, dark tourism might also be viewed as contemporary psychogeography. By way of illustration, the study highlights the travel narrative of a self-confessed 'dark tourist.' Namely, the collection of travel stories in *The Dark Tourist: Sightseeing in the world's most unlikely holiday destinations* by Dom Joly (2010a, also see Joly 2010b) is based on Joly's visits to numerous dark tourism destinations around the world. In turn, Joly's travelogue is briefly assessed for its psychogeographical content (Hay 2012), as well as the more precise rules of the *dérive*, as outlined by Debord (1955, 1956) and as noted earlier in this chapter.

Joly paints with a broad brush in his application of the term 'dark tourism.' His travelogue highlights six visitor destinations across the world, each with varying degrees of 'darkness.' Specifically, he outlines a visit to Iran, a trip across the USA (focussing on locations such as Ground Zero, and famous assassination sites at Dallas, Memphis and New York), the Killing Fields of Cambodia, the Chernobyl Exclusion Zone in Ukraine, a package tour of North Korea and, finally, a trip to conflict-scarred Beirut in Lebanon. While some of these destinations may stand out as notably 'dark destinations' (such as Chernobyl, the Killing Fields or Ground Zero), others are perhaps more debatable. As Hohenhaus (2010) comments in a review of Joly's work, 'his choice of Iran and North Korea had less to do with the "dark" in the sense of death and disaster, but rather with experiences of what's it like to live under *dark regimes.*' Of course, not everything a tourist may encounter in either Iran or North Korea is 'dark' and so to label generically tourism to these countries as 'dark tourism' reveals a very personal system of meaning-making. Indeed, commonplace activities at these destinations—Joly goes skiing in Iran, and walks through the streets of Pyongyang, North Korea—are affected by his own preconceptions of 'darkness' or 'dark regimes.' Arguably, therefore, this synthesis of geography and psychology would seem to position *The Dark Tourist* as a work of psychogeography—at least according to some of the definitions of psychogeography as noted earlier in this chapter.

Taking Joly's account of his Iranian visit as way of contextualisation, he appears to satisfy a more conservative *Debordian* definition of the term 'psychogeography.' Joly details his journey to Tehran, his emotions on arrival and the people he meets there, some experiences of touring the city streets and, finally, a skiing trip in the mountains above the city. His justification for calling this 'dark tourism' comes early in the chapter:

> As a founding member of George W. Bush's 'Axis of Evil' club – infamous for religious extremism, anti-Western rhetoric and being not impartial to the occasional hostage taking – it's most people's idea of a holiday in hell. For a Dark Tourist like me, however, it's a dream destination. (Joly 2010a: 5)

Once again, the author details a perceived darkness associated with the place, in lieu of visiting specific locations of death or suffering. Joly explicitly describes the way in which he drops his usual motives for movement and action (Debord 1980) when he explains his motivation for visiting Iran—'I just needed an angle – something to actually go and do there'—before finding unexpected inspiration in the form of photographs from an Iranian ski resort (Joly 2010a: 5). This would seem to satisfy Debord's *flâneur* principle of letting oneself be drawn by the attractions of the terrain and the encounters one finds there (Debord 1980).

Throughout the travelogue, Joly (2010a: 9) reiterates the draw of the terrain—'I was longing to see Tehran and wondered what touristic delights awaited me.' Moreover, his descriptions of human interactions provide the essence of his travel encounters: from suspicious border guards, to his friendly-yet-cautious driver, to meeting the denizens of Tehran's central bazaar—'we wandered up and down through the crowds in the covered alleys. I was the only Westerner in the whole place but I was met with nothing but smiles and friendship' (Joly 2010a: 11). *The Dark Tourist* also offers a great deal of reflection of the author's own emotions and behaviour, as an effect of the environment. Upon arrival to Iran, Joly (2010a: 8) comments, 'as I stepped off our plane it was bitingly cold and incredibly bleak outside. I felt depressed.' A little later, passing through airport security, he notes, 'they still didn't have a clue as to why I was coming into their country but the atmosphere had definitely lifted' (Joly 2010a: 9). In accordance with Tehran's psychogeographical contours, constant currents and fixed points and vortexes (Debord 1958), Joly is clearly guided by a subjective experience (rather than an objective itinerary) of the city. He fails to mention any of the Iranian capital's most celebrated landmarks, commenting only that 'the drive into Tehran was ugly, very ugly… the centre of Tehran was equally ugly,' before finding himself captivated instead by pieces of political street art and graffiti (Joly 2010a: 9).

Finally, Debord's psychogeography calls for a certain degree of playful-constructive behaviour and awareness of psychogeographical effects, which Joly demonstrates at times when he allows the terrain around him to drive passages of reflection and abstract connection building. Throughout the travelogue, Joly comments on the psychology of his surrounding geography—for instance, 'The further we drove into the mountains, the less I felt the grip of the Islamic State' (Joly 2010a: 13). On other occasions, he follows these trains of thought into playfully constructive streams of consciousness. For example, upon leaving the capital city behind, he notices fewer men with beards, and begins to ponder: 'what the relationship between facial hair and revolution was all about' (Joly 2010a: 13). This kind of playful reflection inspired by observation of often-overlooked details of the geographical environment seems to resonate with the very core principles of Debordian psychogeography.

Arguably, though Joly appears to be unaware of the psychogeography concept in his work, *The Dark Tourist* does appear to satisfy key criteria of psychogeographical writing. Consequently, the broad church of psychogeography offers an insight into potential new research avenues of 'Foucauldian Dark Tourism' and 'Debordian Dark Tourism.'

Towards New Conceptual Frameworks: Foucauldian Dark Tourism and Debordian Dark Tourism

In summary, psychogeography is a practice concerned with making meaning—with finding place in space—and seems to be at its most authentic in locations where the desired tourism experience is not already provided. Though contemporary psychogeographical definitions have broadened to encompass all manner of emotionally reflective tourism pursuits, the Debordian *flâneur* requires only a blank canvas (the landscape) with which to begin. Arguably, therefore, dark tourism appears to exist between two opposing poles. Firstly, there are those well-defined packaged-up sites of dark tourism (e.g. massacre sites, morbid museums or memorials to tragedy) at which it is almost impossible for a visitor not *to be doing* dark tourism. Secondly, there is a kind of free-range dark tourism, where the *darkness* is less explicit and those passing through the space may be so-called dark tourists or not, according to a very personal system of pre-conditioning, knowledge and perceptions. To refer to the spatial philosophy of Michel Foucault, as discussed earlier, organised sites of commoditised dark tourism might sometimes be considered heterotopias or 'Other places.' Consequently, this study set out to evaluate dark tourism as a form of psychogeography and, arguably, dark tourism is at its most psychogeographical when conducted at places other than Foucault's Other places—at *homotopias*, as termed here. It is within the *homotopias* where the (dark) tourist is required to interpret 'darkness' for themselves, rather than reading about it in museum panels, captions or in tourist guidebooks. In short, the chapter offers two distinct and separate modes of dark tourism as schematically illustrated in Fig. 10.2.

On the one hand, there is *Foucauldian dark tourism*. This is defined here as being conducted in heterotopia space(s)—at distinct and distinctly dark locations where a sense of darkness may be universally perceived. *Foucauldian dark tourism* occurs at locations filled with juxtaposition, with chronological significance, in some way representative of the space outside and contained within a clearly recognised system of barriers that are physical, psychical or social. Ultimately, *Foucauldian dark tourism* is packaged dark tourism.

On the other hand, *Debordian dark tourism* is an intrinsically personal process of meaning-making conducted in regular, non-heterotopic space, where dark associations emerge from a private system of knowledge, memory, experience, culture and preconceptions. *Debordian dark tourism* allows dark tourism experiences that are not packaged (up), commoditised or endorsed, but rather are constructed as a product of geography and psychology. They may be similar spaces, or places with similarities, but the process of individualised meaning-making ensures a homotopia. Ultimately, *Debordian dark tourism* pays attention to psychogeographical slopes and fixed units of ambiance, and develops through interactions with people encountered in the terrain. *Debordian dark tourism* provides for a phenomenological journey that might not be shared by other tourists inhabiting the same space.

Conclusion

This chapter set out to evaluate dark tourism within a conceptual psychogeographical framework. The study introduced the subject of psychogeography—a process of finding place within space—as well as identifying theoretical notions of heterotopias and their application to psychogeography. The study also demonstrated, rather than empirically tested, two case examples of how dark tourism locations may adhere to heterotopia principles. The chapter also discussed how accounts of dark tourism at non-heterotopic locations followed behavioural patterns more indicative of psychogeography. As a result, the research has revealed two conceptual frameworks in which to locate contemporary dark tourism. Indeed, the chapter highlights how two schools of geographical thought (psychogeography and heterotopia) correspond to very different (yet equally valid) forms of dark tourism. As a result, the authors suggest an original framework for this duality in the form of 'Foucauldian dark tourism' and 'Debordian dark tourism.'

Of course, the conceptual study presented in this chapter is far from conclusive, and features only a limited discussion on locales and application. Nonetheless, the intention of this study was to frame a potential new paradigm within which to consider the practice of dark tourism. In so doing, a plethora of fresh and exciting future research avenues into the production and consumption of dark tourism has emerged. That said, however, it should be noted that the idea of 'Foucauldian' or 'Debordian' dark tourism should not be taken as a mutually exclusive binary. In other words, many examples of dark tourism across the world and within different cultures may satisfy elements of both philosophies—for instance, whether it be 'dark tourists' explaining the relationship between psychology and geography as they visit heterotopic sites of commoditised dark tourism or students of Foucault tracing theoretical heterotopias around the slopes and vortices of a *dark dérive*.

Therefore, rather than promoting such a reductive model, it is hoped that the conceptual frameworks presented in this chapter will provide a useful way to consider the degree of investment, of interaction, inherent in the process of dark tourism consumption. Thus, a psychogeographical perspective reminds us that *darkness* is not always universally perceived, but rather is a personal response found often at the synthesis of geography and psychology. To return to the example of Auschwitz-Birkenau one last time, consider the mindscape of a Jewish visitor touring the site as compared to that of a visitor from some other ethnic background who is not implicitly connected to the history of the place. As Alfred Korzybski suggested 'the map is not the territory,' and in the case of Auschwitz, even the most rigidly planned and carefully curated visitor experience is not necessarily predictive of the psychological journey experienced from one individual to the next (Korzybski 1933).

Finally, understanding dark tourism as a broader system of processes—in terms of transactional, created or perceived darkness, rather than simply by the act of visiting a known dark tourism location—might lead to a more holistic understanding of the motivations and experiences inherent in dark tourism consumption. The commodification of dark tourism destinations may encourage a more predictable, controlled experience, but the psychological effect of the geography itself—its slopes, its drift, its vortices and ambiance—ought not to be overlooked.

References

Agnew, J. (1987). *Place and politics: The geographical mediation of state and society.* Boston: Allen and Unwin.

Auschwitz.org. (2016a). *Visitors to the Auschwitz site.* Available at http://70.auschwitz.org/index.php?option=com_content&view=article&id=82&Itemid=173&lang=en. Accessed 6 Nov 2016.

Auschwitz.org. (2016b). *Visitors regulations of the Auschwitz-Birkenau State Museum.* Available at http://visit.auschwitz.org/regulamin-zwiedzania-panstwowego-muzeum-auschwitz-birkenau.html?lang=en. Accessed 6 Nov 2016.

Cohen, E. (1979). A phenomenology of tourist experiences. *Sociology, 13*(2), 179–201.
Conduit, B. (2005). *Battlefield walks: Northumbria & the Scottish borders*. Wilmslow: Sigma Press.
Coverley, M. (2006). *Psychogeography*. Harpenden, Hertfordshire: Pocket Essentials.
Cresswell, T. (2004). *Place: A short introduction*. Malden: Blackwell Pub.
Cresswell, T. (2008). Place: Encountering geography as philosophy. *Geography, 93* (Part 3, Autumn), 132–139.
Cresswell, T. (2015). *Place: An introduction*. Chichester: Wiley Blackwell.
Csordas, T. J. (1994). *Embodiment and experience: The existential ground of culture and self*. Cambridge: Cambridge University Press.
Dann, G., & Jacobsen, J. K. S. (2003). Tourism smellscapes. *Tourism Geographies: An International Journal of Tourism Space, Place and Environment, 5*(1), 3–25.
Debord, G. (1955, September). Introduction to a critique of urban geography. *Les Lèvres Nues*, (6). Republished at *Situationist International Online* [website], translated by Knabb, K. Available at: http://www.cddc.vt.edu/sionline/presitu/geography.html. Accessed 1 Dec 2016.
Debord, G. (1956). Theory of the Dérive. *Les Lèvres Nues*, (9). Republished at *Situationist International Online* [website]. Trans. K. Knabb. Available at: http://www.cddc.vt.edu/sionline/si/theory.html. Accessed 1 Dec 2016.
Debord, G. (1961). Critique of separation. *Dansk-Fransk Experimentalfilmskompagni*. Republished at *Situationist International Online* [website]. Trans. K. Knabb. Available at: http://www.cddc.vt.edu/sionline/si/separation.html. Accessed 1 Dec 2016.
Debord, G. (1967). *The society of the spectacle*. Trans. D. Nicholson-Smith. New York: Zone Books.
Dehaene, M., & De Cauter, L. (2008). Heterotopia in a postcivil society. In M. Dehaene & L. De Cauter (Eds.), *Heterotopia and the city: Public space in a postcivil society* (pp. 3–9). Abingdon: Routledge.
Dobraszczyk, P. (2010). Petrified ruin: Chernobyl, Pripyat and the death of the city. *City: Analysis of Urban Trends, Culture, Theory, Policy, Action, 14*, 37–41.
Dwork, D., & van Pelt, R. J. (2002). *Auschwitz*. New York: Norton.
Foucault, M. (1967a [1984], October). Des espaces autres. Une conférence inédite de Michel Foucault. Architecture, Mouvement, *Continuité 5*, 46–49.
Foucault, M. (1967b). *Of other spaces*. Trans L. De Cauter & M. Dehaene. In M., Dehaene & L. De Cauter (Eds.) (2008) *Heterotopia and the City: Public space in a postcivil society* (pp. 13–29). Abingdon: Routledge.
Hartmann, R. (2014). Dark tourism, thanatourism, and dissonance in heritage tourism management: New directions in contemporary tourism research. *Journal of Heritage Tourism, 9*(2), 166–182.
Harvey, D. (1993). From space to place and back again. In J. Bird, B. Curtis, T. Putnam, G. Robertson, & L. Tickner (Eds.), *Mapping the futures* (pp. 3–29). London: Routledge.

Hay, D. (2012). Transforming psychogeography: From Paris to London [Blog]. *Walled City*. Available at: http://walled-city.net/transforming-psychogeography-from-paris-to-london. Accessed 18 Feb 2016.

Heidegger, M., Macquarrie, J., & Robinson, E. (1962). *Being and time*. Malden: Blackwell.

Heynen, H. (2008). Heterotopia unfolded? In M. Dehaene & L. De Cauter (Eds.), *Heterotopia and the city: Public space in a postcivil society* (pp. 311–323). Abingdon: Routledge.

Hohenhaus, P. (2010). Review: The dark tourist by Dom Joly. *Dark Tourism* [website]. Available at: http://www.dark-tourism.com/index.php/18-main-menus/mainmenussubpages/779-review-the-dark-tourist-vy-dom-joly. Accessed 24 Sept 2016.

Home, S. (2004). *Down and out in Shoreditch and Hoxton*. London: The Do-Not Press.

Jarratt, D., & Gammon, S. (2016). We had the most wonderful times': Seaside nostalgia at a British resort. *Tourism Recreation Research, 41*(2), 123–133.

Jeffries, S. (2004, April 24). On the road. On *Guardian.com* [website]. Available at: https://www.theguardian.com/books/2004/apr/24/featuresreviews.guardianreview14. Accessed 23 Sept 2016.

Joly, D. (2010a). *The dark tourist: Sightseeing in the world's most unlikely holiday destinations*. London: Simon & Schuster.

Joly, D (2010b, September 11). My travels: Dom Joly in North Korea. *The Guardian* [website]. Available at: https://www.theguardian.com/travel/2010/sep/11/dom-jolly-north-korea-pyongyang. Accessed 24 Sept 2016.

Kaufman, V. (2006). *Guy Debord: Revolution in the service of poetry*. Minneapolis: University of Minnesota Press.

Kayden, J. S. (2000). *Privately owned public space: The New York City experience*. New York: Wiley.

Keil, C. (2005). Sightseeing in the mansions of the dead. *Social & Cultural Geography, 6*(4), 479–494.

Korzybski, A. (1933). A non-Aristotelian system and its necessity for rigour in mathematics and physics. *Science and Sanity, 1933*, 747–761.

Lippard, L. R. (1997). *The lure of the local: Senses of place in a multicentered society*. New York: New Press.

Massey, D. (1993). Power-geometry and a progressive sense of place. In J. Bird, B. Curtis, T. Putnam, G. Robertson, & L. Tickner (Eds.), *Mapping the futures* (pp. 59–69). London: Routledge.

Massey, D. (2004). The responsibilities of place. *Local Economy, 19*(2), 91–101.

McDonough, T. F. (1994, Winter). Situationist space. In *October* (Vol. 67, pp. 58–77). Cambridge: The MIT Press.

Moore, A. (2013, May 7). Alan Moore interview. *Reasons I do not dance* [website]. Available at: http://neverdances.blogspot.co.uk/2013/05/alan-moore.html. Accessed 18 Feb 2016.

Mullins, W. (2001). Auschwitz-Birkenau Barracks. *Remembrance and hope* [website]. Available at: http://remembranceandhope.freeservers.com/photo5.html. Accessed 1 Dec 2016.

Plant, S. (1992). *The most radical gesture*. New York: Routledge.

Relph, E. (1976). *Place and placelessness*. London: Pion.

Richardson, T. (Ed.). (2015) *Walking inside out: Contemporary British psychogeography*. London: Rowman & Littlefield.

Rousseaux, F., & Thouvenin, I. (2009). Exploring informed virtual sites through Michel Foucault's heterotopias. *International Journal of Humanities and Arts Computing, 3*(1–2), 175–191.

Self, W. (2007). *Psychogeography*. London: Bloomsbury.

Sharpley, R. (2009). Shedding light on dark tourism: An introduction. In R. Sharpley & P. Stone (Eds.), *The darker side of travel: The theory and practice of dark tourism* (pp. 3–22). Bristol: Channel View Publications.

Sinclair, I. (1975). *Lud heat and suicide bridge*. London: Albion Village Press.

Sinclair, I. (1997). *Lights out for the territory*. London: Granta.

Sinclair, I. (2006, August 29). 'When in doubt, quote Ballard': An interview with Iain Sinclair. *Ballardian* [website]. Available at: http://www.ballardian.com/iain-sinclair-when-in-doubt-quote-ballard. Accessed 3 Mar 2016.

Stone, P. R. (2005). Dark tourism consumption – A call for research. *e-Review of Tourism Research (eRTR), 3*(5). Available at http://agrilife.org/ertr/files/2012/09/224_a-3-5-2.pdf. Accessed 13 Nov 2017.

Stone, P. R. (2007). Dark tourism: The ethics of exploiting tragedy. *Travel Weekly*. Available at: http://works.bepress.com/philip_stone/21. Accessed 23 Sept 2016.

Stone, P. R. (2011). Dark tourism: Towards a new post-disciplinary research agenda. *International Journal of Tourism Anthropology, 1*(3/4), 318–332.

Stone, P. R. (2012). 'Licenced death': Consuming landscapes of war through thanatourism. iDTR Working Paper/Presentation Series 2012/2013. Available at https://works.bepress.com/philip_stone/42/. Accessed 23 Nov 2016.

Stone, P. R. (2013). Dark tourism, heterotopias and post-apocalyptic places: The case of Chernobyl. In L. White & E. Frew (Eds.), *Dark tourism and place identity*. Melbourne: Routledge.

Stone, P. R., & Sharpley, R. (2013). Deviance, dark tourism and 'dark leisure': Towards a (re)configuration of morality and the taboo in secular society. In S. Elkington & S. Gammon (Eds.), *Contemporary perspectives in leisure: Meanings, motives and lifelong learning*. Abington: Routledge.

Todkill, A. (2001). Overexposure: The Chernobyl photographs of David McMillian. *CMAJ, 164*(11), 1604–1605.

Topinka, R. J. (2010, September). Foucault, Borges, heterotopia: Producing knowledge in other spaces. *Foucault Studies*, (9), 54–70.

Tuan, Y. (1977). *Space and place: The perspective of experience*. Minneapolis: University of Minnesota Press.

Urry, J. (1990). *The tourist gaze: Leisure and travel in contemporary societies*. London: Sage.

Urry, J., & Larsen, J. (2011). *The tourist gaze 3.0*. London: Sage.

van Tijen, T. (2017). *Literary psychogeography. Imaginary museum projects*. Available at http://imaginarymuseum.org/LPG/Mapsitu1.htm. Accessed 13 Nov 2017.

Ward, A. (2000). *The map is not the territory*. Manchester: Manchester University Press.

Williams, M. P. (2008). Review: Will self, psychogeography. *Literary London: Interdisciplinary Studies in the Representation of London, 6*(2). Available at: http://www.literarylondon.org/london-journal/september2008/williams.html. Accessed 18 Feb 2016.

Woods, J. (2016, January). *Visiting Auschwitz: How it changed my teaching*. University of Southern California Shoah Foundation [website]. Available at: http://sfi.usc.edu/blog/jeannie-woods/visiting-auschwitz-how-it-changed-my-teaching. Accessed 21 Sep 2016.

Yuill, S. M. (2003). *Dark tourism: understanding visitor motivation at sites of death and disaster*. Unpublished MA Thesis, Texas A&M University, Texas.

Section 3

Dark Tourism, Society, and Culture

Richard Sharpley

Introduction

An intimate relationship exists between tourism and society. In other words, the manner in which tourist sites, attractions, and events are understood and experienced is socially determined or, as Urry (1990: 23) puts it, "explaining the consumption of tourist services cannot be separated off from the social relations in which they are embedded." Tourists, for example, almost inevitably travel within a cultural 'bubble' (cf. Cohen 1974) and, hence, their experiences of places and people are to a lesser or greater extent influenced by their socio-cultural background. Equally, the significance of tourist sites and events to local communities is also culturally determined; how local communities understand and respond to particular sites and events and, indeed, to the tourists visiting them, will reflect the cultural meaning of those sites and events and the cultural influences that shape their interpretation. In short, tourism in general cannot be fully understood without a consideration of the cultural condition of the societies within which it occurs (Sharpley 2008).

Such a consideration is, arguably, of heightened importance in the context of dark tourism, particularly in the case of sites or attractions that, according to Stone's (2006) typology, may be located towards the 'darker end of the spectrum'. That is, whilst more frivolous or entertaining forms of dark tourism, such as Houses of Horror or ghost tours, are of possibly limited cultural

R. Sharpley (✉)
University of Central Lancashire, Preston, UK

significance (though the desire on the part of tourists to be frightened—to challenge the ontological security of modern society—may be culturally determined), sites which commemorate/interpret meaningful dark events, or those that have impacted upon, transformed, or shaped contemporary society in one way or another, are likely to be of immense cultural significance and susceptible to cultural influences. For example, battlefield sites 'are the constructions of reactions to individual stories, wider social constructs and ideologies that informed our past and inform our present and future' (Ryan 2007: 4). Hence, the interpretation and experience of battlefields may convey powerful, culturally saturated messages relevant to the cultural condition of contemporary societies: for instance, Gallipoli as the 'psychological birthplace' of Australia and New Zealand as nations (Slade 2003: 780), or Bannockburn in Scotland as a symbol of Scottish independence and identity (McCrone et al. 1995). Similarly, destinations may be culturally defined by dark events they have experienced, whether natural disasters (e.g., Hurricane Katrina in New Orleans in 2005, or the 2011 earthquake in Christchurch, New Zealand), terrorist attacks (New York and '9/11'; Bali and the bombing of the Sari Nightclub in 2002), or genocide (Auschwitz-Birkenau; Cambodia's 'Killing Fields'; or the Srebrenica Massacre in 1995 during the Bosnian War). Whatever the dark event being represented or commemorated (or not, as the case may be), a complete understanding of the presentation, interpretation, and experience of such sites is dependent on an exploration of their relationship with the cultural context within which they are located.

About This Section

The chapters in this third section of the Handbook address this relationship from a variety of perspectives. In the first (Chap. 11), Mona Friedrich, Philip Stone, and Paul Rukesha examine the memorialisation of one of the most momentous dark events of recent times, namely, the Rwandan genocide of 1994. Although it occurred more than 20 years ago, the genocide remains fundamental to contemporary Rwanda; it lives in the cultural memory of those who survived (and participated) in it, and it very much defines Rwanda today. Drawing on research amongst policymakers, staff, and both international and domestic visitors at genocide memorial sites, the chapter explores how the genocide is in general presented and interpreted as a form of 'cultural politics'. More specifically, it considers the extent to which the memorials are (in)effective in presenting a narrative that is free of dissonance and that contributes to peace and reconciliation within Rwanda, and to a deeper understanding of the genocide and its aftermath amongst international visitors.

In contrast, in Chap. 12, Anne Marie Van Broeck considers the dilemma facing a city with a dark history that it wishes to forget but which nevertheless is an attraction to tourists. The city is Medellin in Colombia, and its dark, unwanted past relates to its notoriety during the 1980s as a centre of drug trafficking and, in particular, the violence related to the power struggles of the Medellin Drugs Cartel and its infamous leader, Pablo Emilio Escobar Gaviri. Although one of many involved in the drugs trade, Escobar became the 'face' of drugs-related violence in Medellin and, following his death in 1993, his memory is not only a powerful element of Medellin's recent cultural history but has also become a commercially valuable asset. Not only does the production of numerous books, plays, movies, and T-shirts with his image (including one designed by his son) reveal the continued interest in Escobar, but he has become a tourist attraction, with Pablo Escobar tours being offered in Medellin. Hence, as the chapter discusses, the city must find a way of balancing its desire to put its notorious past behind it whilst accommodating the needs of tourists attracted by that past.

For many, contemporary society is defined, or can be explained by, the concept of mobilities. That is, the modern world is a world that is mobile: people, goods, money, technology, and information are all constantly mobile, to the extent that contemporary society is fundamentally mobile (and tourism is, therefore, symbolic of that mobility). In Chap. 13, the third in this section, Kevin Hannam and Ganna Yankovska apply the concept of mobilities to memory and memory-making at Chernobyl, the site of the world's worst nuclear accident in 1986. It is now possible to visit Chernobyl and the nearby ghost town of Pripyat, and increasing numbers of people do so, including both international visitors and former residents of the area who wish to see where they used to live. Reporting on research undertaken amongst the latter group, the chapter explores how the concept of mobilities can contextualise the shifting or mobile memories of former residents, in contrast to the 'fixed' or official memories presented in the commemorative space of Chernobyl.

Often overlooked in the analysis of dark tourism in general, and disaster tourism in particular, is the role of the media in framing, creating, and directing the nature of the tourist experience. In other words, through the manner in which they report disasters, newspapers and other forms of media act as cultural mediators, often depicting a disaster through particular tragedies or particular acts of heroism. In so doing, the media may play a powerful role in directing the focus of 'disaster tourists' whilst influencing understanding of a disaster more generally. In Chap. 14, Richard Sharpley and Daniel Wright address this gap in the dark/disaster tourism literature through an examination of the media reporting of the earthquake in L'Aquila, Italy, in 2009. They reveal that the media acted predictably—specifically, highlighting a particular tragedy that might be considered most 'newsworthy'—and that, as a consequence, tourists initially sought out specific sites within the ruined city. Hence, it is argued that media influence on dark/disaster should be anticipated and better managed.

In the final chapter in this section (Chap. 15), Gilly Carr argues that nations (or national identity) reside in the imagination; they are cultural artefacts that reflect the heritage that nations symbolise, imagine, construct (or deny), or build upon to define themselves. In some instances, that heritage may be difficult or dark, whilst a heritage that might be denied may be overlooked in the construction of a contemporary national identity. Drawing on research undertaken in The Channel Islands, the chapter discusses how heritage relating to the German occupation of the Islands during the Second World War has been, if not denied, manipulated in order to remove the 'darkness' from the (visitor) experience. In other words, both local people and tourists consume a 'whitewashed' version of the German occupation, a culturally constructed heritage based more on myth than history; in the search for a modern national identity the darkness has been banished and is, perhaps, only detectable by outsiders. Hence, this chapter neatly concludes this section by epitomising how dark tourism, in both its production and consumption, is culturally laden.

References

Cohen, E. (1974). Who is a tourist? A conceptual clarification. *The Sociological Review, 22*(4), 527–555.

McCrone, D., Morris, A., & Kiely, R. (1995). *Scotland: The brand. The making of Scottish heritage.* Edinburgh: Edinburgh University Press.

Ryan, C. (2007). Introduction. In C. Ryan (Ed.), *Battlefield tourism: History, place and interpretation* (pp. 1–10). Oxford: Elsevier.

Sharpley, R. (2008). *Tourism, tourists and society* (4th ed.). Huntingdon: Elm Publications.

Slade, P. (2003). Gallipoli thanatourism. *Annals of Tourism Research, 3*(4), 779–794.

Stone, P. R. (2006). A dark tourism spectrum: Towards a typology of death and macabre related tourist sites, attractions and exhibitions. *Tourism: An Interdisciplinary International Journal, 54*(2), 145–160.

Urry, J. (1990). The consumption of tourism. *Sociology, 24*(1), 23–35.

11

Dark Tourism, Difficult Heritage, and Memorialisation: A Case of the Rwandan Genocide

Mona Friedrich, Philip R. Stone, and Paul Rukesha

Introduction

The International Handbook on Tourism and Peace offers an optimistic foreword in which the global tourism industry is described as:

> [a] worldwide social and cultural phenomenon that engages people of all nations as both hosts and guests, [generating] … connections, [which] spur dialogue and exchange, break down cultural barriers and promote values of tolerance, mutual understanding and respect. In a world constantly struggling for harmonious coexistence, these values espoused by tourism could be integral to building a more peaceful future. (Rifai (2014: 11)

Despite this sanguine if not somewhat naïve claim, tourism as a viable memorial mechanism for peace building in destinations that have witnessed war, conflict, or atrocity is fraught with complexities and contradictions. Moreover, the 'difficult heritage' (Logan and Reeves 2009) that is often a legacy in post-conflict destinations is now regularly consumed as tourist experiences at

---

M. Friedrich
Max Planck Institute for the History of Science, Berlin, Germany

P. R. Stone (✉)
University of Central Lancashire, Preston, UK

P. Rukesha
Aegis Trust, Kigali Genocide Memorial, Kigali, Rwanda

© The Author(s) 2018
P. R. Stone et al. (eds.), *The Palgrave Handbook of Dark Tourism Studies*,
https://doi.org/10.1057/978-1-137-47566-4_11

various conflict-related visitor sites, attractions, or exhibitions. This is particularly evident in post-conflict regions in the Global South, where guided tours, museums, and memorials within the broader visitor economy have encouraged the growth of a practice frequently referred to as 'dark tourism' (Foley and Lennon 1996), 'thanatourism' (Seaton 1996), 'atrocity heritage' (Ashworth 2002), or 'grief tourism' (Blom 2000).

Dark tourism in post-conflict destinations is a potentially influential yet ethically laden phenomenon. As a result, dark tourism may symbolise visitor sites of discordant heritage, sites of selective silences, sites rendered political and ideological, and sites powerfully intertwined with interpretation and meaning (Stone 2013). Even so, the development of dark tourism and the difficult heritage it seeks to portray, as well as the potential memorialisation it can offer, has significant implications for societies recovering from conflict. This touristic development might include visitors' relations with the sites in question, as well as impacts, experiences, personal reflections, and contemplations pre-, during, and post-visit. Equally imperative are critical assessments of the *memorialscape* itself that embrace location, design, and the construction of post-conflict narratives at these often sanctified and sacred spaces (Foote 2003; Seaton 2009; Carr 2012).

Visitor encounters with sites of conflict or atrocity may generate new incentives and dialogues in which moral boundaries and ethical principles are questioned or renegotiated (Stone and Sharpley 2013). The production of post-conflict visitor sites also has the potential to suffer from a selective amnesia of memories. In other words, sites of difficult heritage are often 'subjectively presented to enhance cultural and political cohesion' since the formation of any heritage product is a direct consequence of selectivity (Logan and Reeves 2009: 2). Therefore, difficult heritage may disinherit certain non-participating social, ethnic, or regional groups, as their distinctive historical experiences of particular conflicts may be discounted, marginalised, distorted, or even ignored. As Tunbridge and Ashworth (1996: 30) succinctly note, 'history is to a greater or lesser extent hijacked by one group or another for one purpose or another.' This complexity of presenting difficult national heritage within the broader visitor economy as well as in a politically charged post-conflict environment is extremely problematic. This is no more so than in Rwanda, a country in central Africa that witnessed a series of political upheavals and which culminated in the cataclysm of genocide in 1994. Now evident within Rwanda's *genocidal memorialscape* is a variety of opposing priorities and political tensions, including between victims and perpetrators, national and international visitors, as well as between legislative authorities, private enterprise, and international development organisations (McKinney 2014; Sharpley and Friedrich 2017).

The purpose of this chapter, therefore, is to examine memorialisation and cultural processes and practices within the broader context of dark tourism and difficult heritage in Rwanda. In so doing, it offers an exploratory empirical insight into cultural memory at dark tourism sites of the Rwandan genocide. While such sites may create an intimate environment that provide a sense of comfort to survivors, they can also foster critical reflection on collective societal processes, including human rights reform, nation-building and identity, as well as violence prevention or transitional justice (Hamber et al. 2010). Examining Rwandan memorial visitor sites as places that encourage individual, national, or international reflection and action within broader peace building and heritage discourse, the chapter also serves as an incentive for future critical dialogues between stakeholders involved in the production and consumption of memory in post-conflict spaces (Friedrich and Johnston 2013; Friedrich 2016; also see Chap. 25). Ultimately, this chapter presents preliminary research into national and international visitor experiences of the Rwandan memorialscape and, in particular, ascertains whether dark tourism can contribute to social reconciliation, national restoration and individual recovery. Firstly, however, dark tourism and difficult heritage offers a conceptual framework in which to locate Rwandan memorialscapes and it is this that the chapter now turns.

Difficult Heritage(s): The Stuff of 'Dark Tourism'

Inherent complexities within memorialisation and the diverse impacts upon visitor experiences signify that dark tourism must adopt a multidisciplinary approach; encompassing a broad range of social, cultural, geographical, anthropological, political, managerial, and historical concerns (Stone 2013). Indeed, the overall nature of the (dark) visitor experience depends on both the characteristics and presentation of the site, attraction, or exhibition, and the manner in which this affects the needs, expectations, and perceptions of the individual (Sharpley and Stone 2009). Of course, sites dealing with the extreme trauma and pain of genocide should represent a dignified public space of mourning and remembrance for survivors and victims. As Buckley-Zistel and Schaefer (2014) note, these sites should be places that put past wrongs right and hold perpetrators accountable, as well as to contributing to potential peace-building initiatives through education and edification. However, actualisation of such features, as well as their positioning within the broader visitor economy, poses numerous ethical dilemmas in practice. Indeed, with regard to conceptualising the contemporary phenomenon of visiting such sites, the term 'dark' as in dark tourism may hint at a voyeuristic or even morbid interest in the macabre. Moreover, 'dark tourism' may attach a potentially manipulative label to the supply and production of such sites, exhibitions, or experiences (Sharply and Stone 2009). In short, dark tourism might advocate a latent exploitation of death and tragedy by marketing and commercialising the pain and suffering of others. Additionally, tourism to such 'dark sites' may exacerbate social and cultural tensions as opposed to alleviating them. As a case in point, the Korean Demilitarized Zone (DMZ) special exhibition at the Korean War Memorial in Seoul underscores the political schism between North and South Korea rather than attempting to repair social relations which, in turn, results in a staged 'cartography of paradox' (Kim 2011). Another example of this inherent narrative tension may be found in Northern Ireland and its former sites of The Troubles, where some tour guides are seemingly keen to promote victimhood by utilising 'Them and Us' descriptions. Consequently, remembering and forgetting the dead of The Troubles are shaped by a 'conflictual consensus' (Graham and Whelan 2007). As Graham and Whelan (2007) further note, this contested heritage and a hierarchical victimhood undermines any attempt to suppress burdens of the past in such an 'unagreed society'.

Hence, visitor experiences within the diverse and contested phenomenon of dark tourism do not express the multifaceted nature of visiting spaces *of* or places associated *with* death. Accordingly, Stone (2006) proposes seven different types of dark tourism sites with consequent visitor experiences on a theoretical 'dark-light' typology and, as such, offers various conceptual parameters to anchor this 'dark tourism spectrum'. These parameters include political, geographical, presentational, as well as chronological issues. As Stone's taxonomical model suggests, Rwanda's genocide memorials are at the darkest end of the dark tourism spectrum and, therefore, possess a higher political influence than other 'lighter' and less politically charged sites. Moreover, memorial visitor sites in Rwanda are historic-centric (i.e. a focus upon conservation and/or commemoration) and are mostly oriented towards education and genocide prevention. Furthermore, many of these memorial spaces are located off the beaten track and need to be deliberately sought by visitors (Friedrich 2016). Arguably, therefore, Rwandan memorial sites are less likely to be encountered serendipitously and are often created within a less-developed tourism infrastructure. This is reinforced by the relatively short time scale to the actual genocide event (just over two decades ago) and the geographical authenticity of locations where the majority of memorials are positioned at the actual murder sites.

Nonetheless, there have been some tendencies towards an expansion of the dark tourism typological base, with new locations and visitor experiences being brought into the body of research (Roberts and Stone 2014). Therefore, the oft-cited dark tourism spectrum taxonomy requires refining and, specifically, will need to address inherent challenges within the formation of collective memories in traumatised communities. Indeed, many of these challenges revolve around dissonance and disharmony at sites of former violence. This discordance often adopts binary, if not complex, relationships between those involved in the consumption process (e.g. victims, perpetrators [including children of perpetrators/second generation], national and international tourists, and so forth) and amongst those producing the memory (for instance, government ministries, memorial managers, or external agencies such as international NGOs). However, in societies where various groups are considered social equals, the affirmation of heritage identity by one group does not necessarily affect any other. This should not innately cause dissonance in other groups by depriving a particular heritage (Tunbridge and Ashworth 1996). Indeed, such an ideal society would be able to embrace multiple heritages without this leading to conflict or contestations. However, where social, political, religious, or economic relations between groups are experienced or perceived as unequal and where competing social, cultural, political, or ethnic divergence exists, disinheritance can lead to conflicting corollaries (Tunbridge and Ashworth 1996). In such cases, both the interpretation and identification of heritage in favour of a dominant group may entail the disinheritance of those who 'physically created it at the behest of their masters, or were dispossessed from it by their advent in the first place' (Tunbridge and Ashworth 1996: 31). Additionally, the empowerment of a former subservient or subaltern social group may lead to the destruction, decay, or marginalisation of the heritage from which they were previously excluded which, in turn, could eventually impede the formation of social cohesion and unity (Tunbridge and Ashworth 1996). Moreover, much of this dissonance is often exposed when difficult pasts are played out at museological interfaces, whereby museum exhibitions 'package up' death and suffering for the visitor economy.

Dissonant Heritage: Constructing (Hi)stories

Museums are an increasing component of a 'global institutional development' (Williams 2007: 7). In other words, contemporary museology constitutes a set of conventions and funding conditions to determine which objects and images may be displayed and how. Museums as tourist attractions are also firmly embedded within the broader visitor economy and, as such, can specify the manner and role of dark tourism within international development frameworks. As part of this developmental process, specialists and experts from subject fields including memorialisation studies, violence prevention, and transitional justice are increasingly cooperating (Friedrich 2016). This professional cooperation is perpetuating an inevitable fusion of local requirements and national imaginaries with international, if not already well-established Western norms and interpretation practices (Ibreck 2013). While it is apparent that professional outsiders can indeed plan and implement memorial projects, especially if they have a qualified skill set not readily available in survivor communities, it should always be ascertained whether they assist in bringing disparate groups together without creating unrealistic expectations or generating additional hostility (Barsalou 2014). In any case, it is necessary that museum practitioners include all stakeholders from affected communities to gain management insights for future practices, as well as establishing what role they play in public memory realms (Logan and Reeves 2009). However, such critical stakeholder dialogues will almost certainly demonstrate conflicting expectations, priorities, memories, and realities. As noted earlier, this dissonance in (re)presenting painful pasts is what Ashworth and Hartmann (2005: 253) define as dissonant heritage: a 'lack of congruence at a particular time or place between people and the heritage with which they identify.' Therefore, it is crucial for heritage specialists to identify, determine, and attempt to alleviate narrative tensions within the interpretation of dark tourism sites.

In the case of Rwanda, as discussed later, the display of human remains and genocide artefacts offer a critical and often contested insight into such divergent understandings, not only amongst the local and national populace but also amongst international visitors. A well-rehearsed argument for preserving artefacts and actual sites of past violence is that they add to the construction of a precise record of what has occurred (Tunbridge and Ashworth 1996). Moreover, an appeal is often made to notions of authenticity as a justification and criteria for the selection and interpretation of particular objects and locations. However, it should be noted that heritage is not 'the totality of the history of a place or even facets of that totality' (Tunbridge and Ashworth 1996: 10). Rather, heritage is a co-created process that is continuously recreated according to ever-changing sociocultural attitudes and political demands. Arguably, therefore, heritage sites and exhibitions are perhaps more telling about the present cultural condition of society rather than the actual past being presented (Tunbridge and Ashworth 1996). To that end, authenticity may derive its legitimacy from visitor experiences and the extent to which those experiences satisfy personal conditions of a particular history—however gruesome that history may be. Consequently, Viebach (2014) suggests that preservation of the past through the caretaking of shared artefacts and human remains offers a sense of denotation, by way of telling the outside world a story of extreme and ruthless violence. Thus, not only do artefacts and mass human remains serve as proof to counter genocide denial (as there was limited immediate media coverage of the Rwandan genocide (Williams 2007)), but further 'transform into a collective artefact as pain and suffering become shareable in our midst' (Viebach 2014: 92). Nonetheless, Guyer (2009: 163) expresses concern that the open display of cadavers (as is the case for some Rwandan genocide memorials) is profane and there is little value in 'remember[ing] the dead through the sheer anonymity of these bones [which] means that no one is or can be remembered [individually]… a pile of unrelated bones or a shelf with rows of carefully arranged skulls does not commemorate a person.' Arguably, therefore, this anonymity of bones offers little more than an undignified resting place for victims of slaughter and political mayhem.

Despite this, dissonance is not an unanticipated or unfortunate by-product of the heritage formation process that can be simply removed by improving the creation process itself. Rather, dissonance is inevitable, because during the construction of heritage, certain national or universal evidence must be purposefully selected. In turn, this implies a conscious deselection of alternative narratives or (hi)stories. Indeed, the implication of 'inheritance' entails the existence of 'disinheritance' and, consequently, any formation of inherited heritage from the past may disinherit someone completely, partially, actively, or potentially (Tunbridge and Ashworth 1996). Of course, developing a blueprint formula for designing (genocide) memorials is beyond the scope of this chapter, if indeed a universal memorial design formula could ever exist. Even so, it is important to evaluate potential consequences of such disinheritance within memorialisation in order to ascertain appropriate ways to tackle conceivable effects. Certainly, whole sites (and stories) and their difficult history might be absent from the public consciousness because memory managers perceive them as politically irrelevant or because they perpetuate recalls of pain, shame, or controversy. In turn, sites of atrocity and associated memories might be considered politically detrimental to complex peace-building processes and thus viewed as best forgotten. Kenneth Foote (2003) highlights this particular issue when examining 'shadowed landscapes' in the United States that played a significant role in the evolution of American society, but which are no longer marked in the public sphere. Foote (2003) classifies sites of memory into four different categories; firstly, *sanctification* (events/memories that certain people wish to commemorate); secondly, *obliteration* (shameful/

controversial events that people wish to forget, the evidence of which is destroyed); thirdly, *designation* (the simple marking of a site to remember); and finally, *rectification* (removing signs of violence and returning a site to use, suggesting no lasting positive or negative meaning).

Despite the constructive framing offered by Foote, memorialisation remains an underdeveloped and multifarious field of study. This is because memorials are often regarded as being located outside any political process—'relegated to the "soft" cultural sphere as art objects, to the private sphere of personal mourning, or to the margins of power and politics' (Meierhenrich 2011: 285). Even so, this chapter argues that Rwanda's memorialscape needs to be reviewed in light of new events, new information, and new population developments, just as any dynamic place of memory requires continuous reassessment in accordance with growth (also Friedrich 2016). In any case, it is acknowledged that memorial design and subsequent narratives cannot guarantee the continuity and supremacy of one particular account, nor can they prevent the event from being subjected to individual reinterpretations (Buckley-Zistel and Schaefer 2014). Since remembrance and commemoration is a discrete and often private affair, it is inadequate to base arguments on broad stereotypical assumptions or to simply analyse them through general societal developments (Viebach 2014). Indeed, attempts should focus on distinct contemplations of sensitive sites of memory as well as memorials not only 'being susceptive to change, but as being an agent of change in and of itself' (Buckley-Zistel and Schaefer 2014: 7). Therefore, the remainder of this chapter empirically addresses these issues in the case of Rwanda, but firstly a background and methodology to the Rwandan genocide case study.

Rwanda: The Genocide

Over the past 20 years or so, scholarly and political discourse have critically examined events and issues leading up to, during, and after the 1994 genocide in Rwanda. While a comprehensive historical discussion of the Rwandan genocide is beyond the capacity of this chapter, commonly cited and broad-ranging accounts of Rwanda's history include, but are not limited to Prunier (1995/1997), Gourevitch (1998), Des Forges (1999, 2011), Melvern (2009), Mamdani (2002), and Dallaire (2004).

When Europeans first arrived in Rwanda in 1916, most notably Belgian colonists, they found a society divided into three social groups: Hutu, Tutsi, and Twa, which were linguistically and culturally more or less homogeneous (Prunier 1997). Prior to colonisation, Rwanda was a functioning kingdom with flexible social organisation that allowed the three ethnic groups to achieve a degree of social mobility, even if under a controlling and hegemonic kingship (Prunier 1997). While brutal conflict that has come to characterise the two main ethnic groups—Hutu and Tutsi—had not been recorded before the arrival of the Europeans, extreme violence did occur, mostly amongst the descendants of the ruling class over their heritage and the throne (Des Forges 2011). It was during this turbulent period that the Belgians arrived in Rwanda, bringing with them a racial theory that allocated supremacy to the Tutsi ethnic minority—an ideology that resulted in years of violent outbreaks (Prunier 1997). Indeed, the Belgian colonists upon their arrival segregated the populace and produced identity cards classifying people according to their ethnicity. Tutsi are often taller and thinner than their Hutus counterparts, with apparent Ethiopian ancestry (BBC 2011). Subsequently, during the genocide, 'the bodies of Tutsis were thrown into rivers, with their killers saying they were being sent back to Ethiopia' (BBC 2011).

During this colonial period and up to independence from Belgium in July 1962, the Belgians considered the Tutsi to be superior to the Hutu and, as a result, the Tutsis enjoyed better jobs and educational opportunities than their neighbours. As resentment amongst the Hutus grew, a series of riots in 1959 culminated in over 20,000 Tutsis being killed, while many more fled into exile to neighbouring countries of Burundi, Tanzania, and Uganda. After gaining independence in 1962, the presidency of Gregoire Kayibanda replaced a centuries-old kingship of Rwanda. With majority Hutus now in power, the Tutsis were then portrayed as scapegoats for every political and economic crisis during subsequent decades (BBC 2011). This was also the case in the immediate years before the genocide. Post-independence witnessed some Tutsi refugees in neighbouring countries organising themselves into a force in order to destabilise Rwanda and regain power from the 'Hutu republic'. Their aim was to overthrow the Hutu regime and secure their right to return to their homeland. Attacks by Tutsi exiles not only failed, but also resulted in retaliations against the internal Tutsi population in Rwanda (Prunier 1997). In 1973, Juvénal Habyarimana gained power through a military coup and founded the second republic that sought the reunion of the state. However, this coup failed to resolve the refugee crisis. Consequently, Rwandan refugees which were mostly Tutsi, formed a political party called the Rwandese Alliance for National Unity (RANU) that later became the Rwandan Patriotic Front (RPF). The RPF comprised an armed militia that launched war into Rwanda from Uganda in 1990 (Prunier 1997). The ensuing civil war and the initiation of multi-party politics, as well as the construction of ethnicity by 'colonial outsiders,' inherent class struggles, Rwanda's north-south divide, and a series of unprecedented economic shocks—some resulting directly from strict stipulations imposed by the IMF and the World Bank—exacerbated existing tensions which set the conditions for genocide (Pottier 2002).

In August 1993, after numerous attacks and months of political negotiations, a tentative peace accord was signed between President Habyarimana and the RPF. However, the peace accord did little to halt the continuing unrest and when Habyarimana's aeroplane was shot down in April 1994, resulting in his death, the Rwandan genocide commenced. While those responsible for murdering President Habyarimana (along with the President of Burundi and many chief members of staff who were also travelling on the aircraft) has never been fully established, the effect of the killing was both instantaneous and catastrophic. In Kigali, the capital of Rwanda, the presidential guard directly initiated a campaign of ferocious retribution. Leaders of the political opposition were murdered and almost immediately the systematic killing of Tutus (and moderate Hutus) began (BBC 2011). In only 100 days, from 6 April to 4 July 1994, between 800,000 and one million Tutsi and moderate Hutu men, women, and children were murdered throughout all parts of Rwanda. The sadistic slaughter was mercilessly carried out mostly at close quarters with rudimentary farming tools, such as hoes and axes as well as wooden clubs and machetes. The early organisers of the genocide included military officials, politicians, and businessmen. However, many others soon joined in the mayhem and government soldiers as well as organised gangs of militias hacked and butchered their way through the Tutsi population. Indeed, sanctioned by the presidential guard and encouraged by radio propaganda, a militia group called the Interahamwe ('attack together') was mobilised and had 30,000 members at its peak of operation. Soldiers and police officers often encouraged ordinary citizens to participate in the atrocities and, in some cases, Hutus were forced by the military to murder their Tutsi neighbours. Perpetrators were also often provided with incentives to kill, notably in the form of food or money, and some were even told they could appropriate the land or property of those they executed (BBC 2011).

Numerous massacres took place, including in and around churches where people had sought sanctuary against extremist militia groups and radical army units (Des Forges 1999). In a misconstrued belief that the sacredness and inviolability of churches would protect victims as they had in previous violent outbreaks, and that churches would shelter people from death, whole communities perished inside ecclesiastical refuges, leaving a path of utter destruction and despair (Viebach 2014). The slaughter was characterised by an intensity of violence that not only turned friends and neighbours into enemies, but also broke years of family ties. The genocide was largely ignored by Western powers and the broader international community after ten UN soldiers were killed. As a result, the slaughter went unabated until finally, the RPF military captured Kigali in July 1994 and the genocide ceased. As soon it became apparent that the RPF was victorious, an estimated two million Hutus fled to Zaire (now the Democratic Republic of Congo), where many of the Hutu refugees have since been implicated in the genocide (BBC 2011).

The genocide ensured a collapsed economy, a completely demoralised population and a country left haunted by the vehement butchery (Melvern 2009). In the immediate aftermath, the genocide left streets, churches, and schools filled with corpses and personal belongings. Many of the unidentified victims were left unburied as cadaver memorials and as an appalling reminder that the atrocity was indeed *genocide*—a determined and methodical attempt to eradicate an entire ethnic group (Viebach 2014). A multi-ethnic government was set up after the genocide with Pasteur Bizimungu (a Hutu) as President, while Mr. Kagame (a Tutsi) became his deputy. However, Bizimungu was later jailed on charges of inciting ethnic violence and Kagame became the Rwandan President. Though the genocidal killing in Rwanda has stopped, the presence of Hutu militias in DR Congo has ensured years of conflict there, causing up to five million deaths (BBC 2011). Moreover, the Tutsi-led Rwandan government has twice invaded DR Congo under the pretext of wishing to wipe out Hutu forces. Additionally, a Congolese Tutsi rebel group remains active today and refuses to lay down its arms, citing that Tutsis remain at the risk of genocide. The United Nations currently has the world's largest peacekeeping force in the region—yet has been unable to end the fighting.

In the aftermath of genocide, and the need for remembrance, Rwanda's memorialscape presently comprises more than 400 memorial sites, of which seven are being restored for educational as well as commemorative purposes. The memorials attract both national and international visitors throughout the year (Friedrich 2016). The sites are maintained by the National Commission for the Fight against Genocide (CNLG), a government body responsible for commemoration and remembrance. Each of the memorials, apart from the Kigali Genocide Memorial (KGM), represents a site of significant massacre and extreme violence (Table 11.1). Particularly, the genocide site at Murambi—a former technical college—houses over 850 corpses conserved in powdered lime and has become a place which 'perhaps epitomises the horror of the genocide in terms of both atrocities that occurred there and in the manner in which they are presented' (Sharpley 2012: 103; also Table 11.1 [M2]).

Table 11.1 A taxonomy of Rwanda's genocide memorials (as of July 2014)

Memorial	Location	Biography and site design	Particularity	Site creation	Condition of site	Visitation	Site instigator
Kigali genocide memorial (KGM) (M1)	Central, in Gisozi District in Kigali	Museum including mass graves holding 250,000 victims, memorial gardens, three permanent exhibitions (new panels currently being installed), a children's memorial room, an illustration on the history of genocides around the world, museum café and gift shop. Survivors of the genocide are trained as guides at the centre and provide educational facilities	Largest memorial out of the seven national sites. Not an actual preserved killing site, but created for those victims killed in and around Kigali	1999—mass graves 2004—opening of the completed memorial centre	Good condition, modern museum, including text and photo panels, documents, artefacts, multi-media installations	Highest visitor numbers out of all sites, about 4000 per month in 2013 (international & local). Local numbers peak during commemoration. Over 9000 Rwandans visited the site in April 2014 (KGM visitor statistics)	Aegis trust, Kigali City council, Rwandan government
Murambi (M2)	Marginal, in the south of Rwanda, close to the town of Gikongoro	Former technical college where about 50,000 people were killed in a very short period of time. The site was situated in the controversial zone turquoise, occupied by the French military and displays around 850 bodies preserved in powdered lime, as well as artefacts. Holds an exhibition and a guide are usually present	Extremely shocking site. Only one of the 7 national sites, where complete bodies are on display, with clear mutilations visible	1995 Exhibition was established in 2011	The human remains and artefacts are exposed to the visitors/weather without sufficient protection, multi-media installations are not working (2014)	High visitor numbers during commemoration (mainly Rwandans). International tourists, usually visit on their way to Nyungwe Forest. Around 400 visitors per month	District, CNLG, Aegis trust (exhibition)

(continued)

Table 11.1 (continued)

Memorial	Location	Biography and site design	Particularity	Site creation	Condition of site	Visitation	Site instigator
Nyamata (M3)	Relatively central, 35 km south east of Kigali, Bugesera region, located close to the Ntarama Church Memorial. Visitors usually visit both sites	10,000 victims from the surrounding area took refuge in this Catholic church. On 10th April nearly all of them were slaughtered by the Interahamwe and army. Pews filled with blood-stained clothes/personal belongings of victims/blood stains on the walls. Human remains displayed within an inside crypt and in grave chambers outside of the church, which hold over 41,000 remains of victims. CNLG guides present	Single casket in the crypt holds the remains of a woman who was raped and tortured by the militia. The coffin symbolises the horrific violence committed against women during the genocide	Used as a place to remember since 1994	Artefacts, human remains exposed and not protected and are degrading. Although mass graves have been implemented in the church's garden	Higher visitor numbers (since located less than an hour away from Kigali), particularly during commemoration. Recommended in travel guides	District, local community (now CNLG)
Ntarama (M4)	Relatively central, 30 km south east of Kigali, Bugesera region (remote from the main road)	Catholic church, where 5000 people were killed. Ceiling covered with clothes, shelves stacked with coffins and human remains. Grenade holes in the walls used as entry points by killers. Separate room dedicated to children who suffered atrocious deaths, as revealed by blood stains on the wall. No mass graves present. CNLG guide present	The region is known for its violence against the Tutsi, since resettlements took place in 1963. The Nyabarongo river was flooded with dead bodies in 1994 and its large swamp area offered an unbearable hiding place for those persecuted	Used as a place to remember since 1994	Artefacts, human remains exposed not protected and are degrading.	Higher visitor numbers (since located less than an hour away from Kigali), particularly during commemoration. Recommended in travel guides	District, local community (now CNLG)

(continued)

Table 11.1 (continued)

Memorial	Location	Biography and site design	Particularity	Site creation	Condition of site	Visitation	Site instigator
Nyarubuye (M5)	Marginal, located in the Eastern Province	Former convent. Main building includes tables stacked with human remains, clothes and killing utensils. The gardens offer a dignified resting place for the 60,000 victims who lost their lives in this area. No guide/exhibition present	Known for stories of cannibalism, which state that perpetrators smashed the heads of victims, shredded their brains and drank their blood out of traditional wooden bowls	Used as a place to remember since 1994	Artefacts, human remains are openly exposed and not protected, but the site has recently been undergoing renovations and glass cabinets are being installed (2014)	Fewer visitors, since inaccessible with no public transport connection	District, local community (now CNLG)
Bisesero (M6)	Marginal, located in the Northern Province	Tutsi from nine different communities resisted the genocide with stones and spears in this area for weeks until they were slaughtered. Nine houses holding human remains now symbolically represent the struggle. Mass graves at the site house the remains of approximately 60,000 people of this region. CNLG guide present, no exhibition	Known for strong resistance. The area is also named the 'hill of resistance'	Used as a place to remember since 1998.	Less-developed site, however, refurbishments are taking place (2014). No glass cabinets to protect human remains	Fewer visitors; very isolated. Own private transport is needed and the roads are in poor condition	District, local community (now CNLG)

(continued)

Table 11.1 (continued)

Memorial	Location	Biography and site design	Particularity	Site creation	Condition of site	Visitation	Site instigator
Rebero (M7)	Central, Kigali City	Cemetery (14,000 victims), including graves of 12 politicians who were killed at the beginning of the genocide. No guide or exhibition	Known for politicians who resisted the extremist government (including Hutu)		Good condition, mainly a cemetery, no exhibition, guides or artefacts	Few visitors, mainly during commemoration.	Rwandan government (now CNLG)
Nyanza (M8)	Kicukiro, a suburb southeast of Kigali City	6,000 victims buried in concrete mass graves, surrounded by walls with lists of victim names. IBUKA (survivor's organisation) headquarters are located on the site. IBUKA staff provides site information, otherwise no exhibition or artefacts on display. Victims took refuge in the École Technique Officielle (ETO) which fell under the protection of Belgian troops from the United Nations assistance mission for Rwanda (UNAMIR). Following their withdrawal after the assassination of 10 Belgian soldiers, the Tutsis were left unprotected and ultimately taken to the less noticeable site at Nyanza and massacred	Many come to know about this site because of the American film *Shooting Dogs* which was located here and portrays the true story of the former British headmaster of the ETO who was killed in the genocide	Used as a place to remember since 1994	Mass graves and list of names, though fading due to the elements (2014)	Average visitor numbers. Rwandans come mainly during commemoration, but tourists visit due to its significant history and movie attachments	District, Rwandan government (now CNLG) IBUKA

Adapted from Friedrich (2016)

Rwanda's Memorialscape: An Empirical Analysis

The research for this chapter was implemented in a progressive and sequential manner and formed part of broader study into genocide memorialisation in Rwanda (Friedrich 2016). A comprehensive period of data collection was conducted between May and August 2014— during and after Kwibuka20— Rwanda's 20th annual commemoration of the genocide. This tribute anniversary offered the study an ideal context to both observe and interact with various participants involved in the consumption and production of official commemorative events. The interview sampling frame included a purposeful sample of selected groups which, in turn, represented an expansive range of people involved in memorialisation (e.g. politicians, heritage managers, NGO staff), as well as those experiencing Rwanda's genocide memorialscapes (including international tourists, local visitors, and members of the diaspora community). In total, 100 semi-structured interviews were conducted, of which this chapter selects and reports on a sub-sample of 22 interviews (see Friedrich 2016 for a full methodology).

A concerted political endeavour to create social cohesion in a post-genocide Rwanda means that ethnic distinctions and the labelling of ethnicity is discouraged in the country today. Indeed, political principles revolve around creating an all-embracing 'Rwandanness' and subsequent national identity. As a *special note* for this chapter, however, where research respondents occasionally made ethnic references during interviews, any ethnic references are reported verbatim. Key themes emerged from the empirical study and focussed on five main areas as highlighted in Fig. 11.1.

Authenticity and Educational Value

Education was a key emergent theme from this study and frequently mentioned in relation to the KGM, which provides for specific educational initiatives within its museum experience. This includes a mobile exhibition that travels around the country, and attempts to break down stereotypes and to educate communities on active bystandership, as well as demonstrating various peace initiatives. The aim of this exhibition, in contrast to the permanent one at the KGM, is to focus on the future, rather than on the horrific genocidal past. Indeed, some see the KGM as "an educative and venerable space" (Rwandan Interviewee 6), exemplifying how political and tribal ideologies have developed:

> ...*a very professional place for a museum in this region, very educational and informative.* (German Interviewee 16)

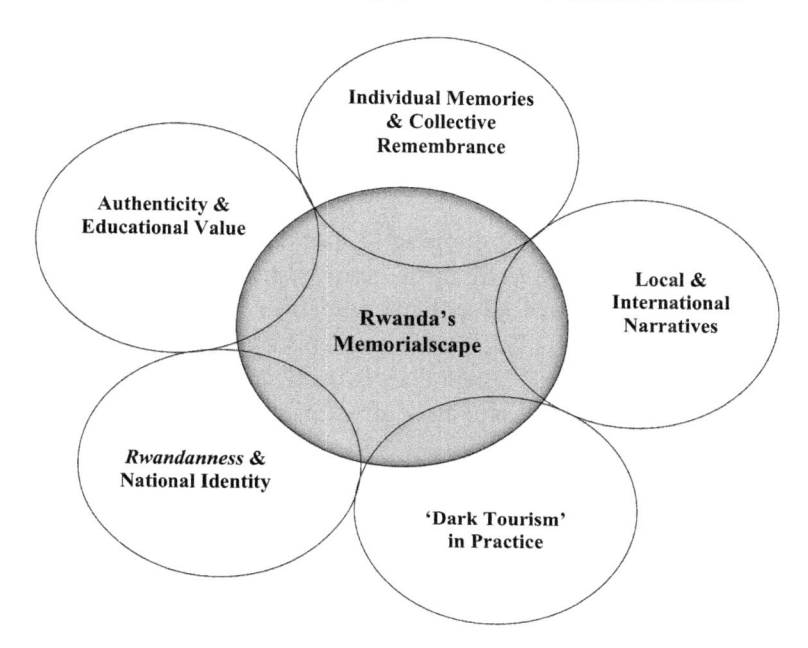

Fig. 11.1 Five emergent research themes in Rwanda's memorialscape

> *[a]… dignified place to pay respect in the gardens or at the graves.* (German Interviewee 13)

Others, however, describe the KGM as a rather 'sanitised version of what went on' (Canadian Interviewee 1), thereby encouraging visits to more provocative sites including the unburied cadavers at other massacre locations, including at Murambi and other churches (Table 11.1, [M2, M3 & M4]). Indeed, many respondents recount experiences at these sites as both shocking and confusing:

> *I remember feeling so shocked, I did not know what to feel. I almost froze. An open display of hundreds of skulls on tables, with no introduction whatsoever. I had an image in my head but nothing prepares you for it. It is enormous and grotesque, with no sense of escape, no breathing space to process what you are seeing. It is very confronting.* (Australian Interviewee 10)

Respondents also suggested that such site experiences have the potential to re-traumatise individuals, as well as placing further guilt on certain groups (Rwandan Interviewee 11). As a Canadian visitor noted in relation to a guided experience at Nyamata Church (Table 11.1 [M3]):

> ...for us seeing these images, it makes it real. The bones, the skulls, I understand why they are doing it, but I can't comment on whether this is right or wrong. I just remember a lady at Nyamata pointing to a skull in the tombs and saying this is her son, but that we should look at all of them, because they are equally important. (Canadian Interviewee 7)

Interestingly, a number of international respondents regarded these sites as being potentially manipulated by those involved in the production of memory. This suggestion of professional manipulation included the purposeful display of unburied corpses being used to silence questions or as 'something orchestrated for shock value' (Australian Interviewee 10). However, as often highlighted by respondents, the necessity for proof of atrocities remains apparent that, in turn, would make genocide denial impossible (Cook 2006). Yet, how this evidence is effectively displayed and incorporated into memorial designs requires further development and negotiation. While some respondents suggest authenticity of the object requires no or little context, most memorial museums should, arguably, provide minimum authentication through exhibit labelling, guidebook marking, or physical guides. In turn the visitor is instructed as to the context and background of the object under the gaze. Evidently, this is not sufficiently provided at various memorial sites throughout Rwanda. As a result, profound issues of memorial spaces as educative and reflective places of individual memories and collective remembrance remain.

Individual Memories and Collective Remembrance

The correlation between individual memories and collective remembrance is complex and fraught with difficulties. Indeed, as a Rwandan respondent suggested, 'it will take more than twenty years in Rwanda to end a conflict that is so deeply rooted in centuries of violence and suppression from all sides' (Rwandan Interviewee 16). Attempts to reformulate and instil a set of collegial social norms in Rwanda will undoubtedly mean that tragic memories will require remembering but that the 'origins of collective violence… lie in repressing memory and misconstruing the past' (Bartov 2007: 201). Yet, the clamour to remember past tragedy is not universal as a Rwandan respondent stated:

> ...one day all memories will be talked about in the public, but it is good that it is not done now. If you start pushing divisive discussions when everything is still raw, you will destroy all you have built on. (Rwandan Interviewee 8)

Similarly, another Rwandan respondent argued:

> ...*everything takes its own time and cannot be solved at once; the country is struggling with many things. Building something from scratch is not easy and then there are those in exile trying to deny that genocide ever happened. Maybe it is time to remember [some] people now. There will be another time for others.* (Rwandan Interviewee 9)

Meanwhile, another respondent emphasised issues of societal unity and bonding in that 'the memorialization of Tutsi does not help social cohesion, because grandchildren might start to hate the new generation of Hutus through these sites and through the memorials. It is a very one sided view' (Rwandan Interviewee 4). Issues of remembering Hutu offenders was also noted by another Rwandan respondent who states that 'perpetrators will of course not feel comfortable, as they feel ashamed' (Rwandan Interviewee 3); a view emphasised by a Tutsi who declared that memorials exert a general blame on the Hutu population and are therefore unapproachable (Rwandan Interviewee 15).

Despite issues of when and what to remember, a key concern amongst a number of respondents was that comparing the crime of genocide to other acts of violence in Rwanda, either before, during or after 1994 would, in effect, devaluate the horrific extent of the situation. In turn, this could be potentially regarded by some as a form of collective repudiation and genocide denial. Arguably, therefore, connecting or as some might say, blurring the lines of crimes committed in various political contexts at that time would not serve the purpose of a genocide memorial nor to its many victims. Generally, however, this research suggests that diverging individual memories should be stimulated so that the act of collective remembrance from different histories can play a more active role in national memorialisation. Certainly, inclusion of different voices and individual memories was highlighted by a research respondent who identified himself of Twa (Batwa) origin and states:

> [memorials]... *don't help the peace process, because they show that we are different. I know we are all Rwandans, but when we go to memorial sites, we notice the difference. All three groups lost families. But in that period* [official commemoration] *we only talk about one.* (Rwandan Interviewee 5)

In short, the respondent here is referring to the issue that the Batwa ethnic group have been excluded from public discourse and while they remain a largely subordinate ethnic minority in Rwanda, they have been equally affected by the genocide (Beswick 2011). Indeed, during the genocide, the Batwa, who compose 0.4% of Rwanda's population of eight million, lost an estimated 30% of their populace (Lewis, cited in Beswick 2011; also Matthews 2006). Ultimately, and perhaps unsurprisingly, individual memories from all ethnic groups require a definitive voice within collective remembrance, and no more so when local and international narratives of genocide perpetration, victims, and survivors are considered.

Local and International Narratives

While Rwanda's memorialscapes and consequent 'dark tourism' signify genocidal memory for Rwandans, the visitor sites are also becoming increasingly imperative for external audiences. Designed and preserved to serve both home and foreign visitor markets, Rwanda's national memorial sites largely diverge from hundreds of local memorials which, as an Australian visitor put it:

> [are] *low key and rarely visible in an obvious open space. They are often located in people's backyards or in market places and might consist of a small group of stones, a carving into a tree or photographs.* (Australian Interviewee 10)

As Steele (2006) argues, national memorials surpass the relevance of victims and society by focusing on humanity and legal principles. It is here that potential dissonance emerges and, specifically, between local memorial sites constructed for friends and family members—which are used for private remembrance—and interpretation of the genocide for international visitors within the context of national memory (Tadjo 2010; Ibreck 2013). Distinctions between local and national memorials are further made when visitor patterns are taken into account. As Friedrich (2016) points out, most local visitations to Rwanda's national memorials occur during official commemoration periods or as part of family commemoration ceremonies that honour death anniversaries of relatives and friends, or as part of work, community or district initiatives. While the KGM and Murambi sites offer broad educational accounts of genocide prevention, other sites (Table 11.1: M3, M4, M5, & M6) directly confront visitors with explicit remnants of the dead and offer scant narratives delivered by sporadically available tour guides.

Even so, for some people memorialscapes play an important role in the local community at large. They offer a reflexive space where sharing and communicating collective pain can be made. As a number of Rwandan visitors noted:

> *The genocide is part of my life, and visiting the ones we have lost makes me appreciate my life and the chance I was given.* (Rwandan Interviewee 2)

> *…commemoration and remembrance is not a sad period for me. At these* [memorial] *places I can meditate and think about where I came from and where I want to go.* (Rwandan Interviewee 18)

For others however, visits can be challenging reminders of the past. Consequently, as these Rwandan visitors suggest, a visit to a particular memorial may not offer any sense of educational value or reflexive mediation and, as a result, simply become sites of 'dark tourism':

> *I lived through it* [the genocide] *and it was horrific; I am not strong enough and do not want to put myself back into that position.* (Rwandan Interviewee 19)

> *These* [memorial] *sites started affecting me psychologically. Why do I have to look at the bodies of kids when I think that I know the history?* (Rwandan Interviewee 9)

'Dark Tourism' in Practice

As part of a developing visitor economy in Rwanda, tourism plays an important role in mediating the country's tragic past for present-day visitors. As a key component of this mediation, a KGM tour guide suggested the memorial site offered positive reflections on the future (Rwandan Interviewee 21), a sentiment shared by a Canadian visitor who described the KGM memorial as a place of 'sombreness but also lightness. It left me with a sense of beauty, it told a story, but it did not feel like all was lost' (Canadian Interviewee 22). Despite an ostensible sanguineness of some, the optimistic outlook of the majority of international visitor appears to be less clear. Indeed, many international visitors often described their tourist experiences to Rwandan's memorialscapes as shocking and traumatising which, subsequently, left them in a state of despair and with a sense of hopelessness.

That said, however, the political/professional shift now within Rwandan's memorialscape is to modify focus towards the present and future as well as Rwanda's achievements over the past 20 years or so. As a Rwandan research participant pointed out:

> *We are trying to be dynamic, just as the country has been dynamic. We want to show the end of the ICTR, the end of Gacaca and show how improvements were made. We need to highlight the developments for all Rwandans and the process of social cohesion, unity and peace.* (Rwandan Interviewee 6)

Arguably, therefore, the touristic development of Rwandan's memorialscapes may contribute to a mutual understanding that specific memorials 'are not fabricating guilt and victimisation and might be utilised as tools of reconciliation' (Rwandan Interviewee 11) and 'they might even serve as mediators' (Rwandan Interviewee 20). Generally, however, the inherent voyeuristic perception of (dark) tourism in practice—or, at least the term 'dark tourism' in theory—may be considered problematic for Rwanda's difficult heritage and its memorialscapes. Indeed, visits to such places can be associated with danger, fear or deviance (Buda and McIntosh 2013), as well as a certain curiosity to 'learn about our horrible side of humanity' (British Interviewee 12). Nonetheless, 'dark tourism' in practice needs to embrace polysemic visitor interpretations and to manage diverse auratic site qualities that are evident within memorialscapes in present-day Rwanda. This is particularly important as national identity and a sense of 'Rwandanness' is projected through its visitor economy.

'Rwandanness' and National Identity

Inherent complexities at places of memory in Rwanda are clear with visitor sites facing ethical as well as social and political dilemmas within an ever-developing tourism industry. This is particularly evident when the prescribed universal national identity suggests that 'we are all Rwandan now, not Hutu or Tutsi or Twa' (Rwandan Interviewee 17). The issue of national identity is further complicated with ingrained ethnicity at memorial sites, and to the wider discourse surrounding memorialisation processes in general (Hohenhaus 2013). While the Tutsi were predominantly targeted by Hutu perpetrators, this should not preclude the danger of fostering a continuing collective guilt within one section of the population, as well as creating a subsequent victimisation of another. Indeed, as a Rwanda research participant stated:

> ...those memorials remind me of who died and who killed them. Tutsi died by extremist Hutu, Hutu killed in the name of Hutu. Even though I might not have a relationship or family ties to this group, the fact that I belong in this category, makes me bear the shame of the crimes. I feel involved, worried that people who see me, may be linking me to the Genocide. (Rwandan Interviewee 11)

While not all aspects of Rwanda's past are portrayed at national memorial sites, it was evident that alternative histories will always exist within private spheres (McLean Hilker 2011), and will be susceptible to reinterpretations and contentious negotiations (Buckley-Zistel and Schaefer 2014). By way of illustration, a Rwandan research participant noted that:

> [Rwandans are]... *an introvert people. Nonetheless, they do talk about controversial issues, but only if you are in their community, within their private circle and at their home place.* (Rwandan Interviewee 8)

Nonetheless, McLean Hilker (2011) argues that covert discussions about the genocide may bear the risk of leaving alternative Hutu and Tutsi versions of the past unchallenged that, in turn, can reinforce a dangerous ethnic logic. However, given Rwanda's diverse society and its difficult heritage, just as other global sites of pain and shame tend to support the prevailing national narrative (Graham et al. 2000), there has been a dominated international approach towards memorialisation in Rwanda. That said, this study has illustrated that local practices of remembrance do take place in less obvious (private) spaces, in the form of more sequestered rituals, which are less traumatising for survivors than being exposed to explicit massacre sites.

Moreover, this chapter highlights the necessity of evidence, as a measure of preventing genocide denial in and outside of the country; though the effectiveness remains to be questioned, given the anonymity of the bones and cadavers and the individual's experiences/roles during the genocide. Additionally, this study suggests that those memorials displaying exclusively authentic graphic images (of the dead) do not help an understanding of the genocide and the ideology leading up to it. Therefore, without accompanying personal testimonies and facts epitomised by these (graphic) artefacts, any understanding of what happened, why and how it can be prevented, remains elusive (Brandstetter 2010). Furthermore, these spaces are predominantly created for an outside audience, since Rwandans who experienced the events of 1994 appear uncomfortable with frequent trips to these sites and, consequently, mainly visit them as part of larger and organised commemorative events or burial ceremonies. As such, national memorial spaces in Rwanda are mainly utilised by international tourists, whose experiences can be upsetting when accustomed to a general 'sequestration of the dead' within (Western) societies (Hohenhaus 2013: 154). As a British research respondent pointed out:

> *I was shocked, but not overly emotional at the church, because I could not grasp what I was seeing. It was a totally different experience than the one at the Memorial Centre, where I was deeply touched by the individual testimonies.* (British Interviewee 12)

Arguably, therefore, memorial policymakers in Rwanda need to agree on the purposes that memorial sites should fulfil and whom they should address. Indeed, heritage is created through deliberate action of certain stakeholders, which needs to be identified and managed with regard to overall aims and objectives of such sites (Ashworth and Hartmann 2005). Target groups are required to be identified in order to implement strategies which will cater to the needs of a diverging visitor base. For instance, a particular negotiation could be to expose a few of the cadaver artefacts at the sites, protecting them from decay, as well as placing them into context through accompanying genocide narratives. It is clear that Rwanda is still in the midst of reconstructive and transformative developments that foster conflicting priorities. Nevertheless, it should be stressed that if no investment (e.g. stakeholder analysis, research, preservation, conservation, or exhibition implementations) into certain sites takes place, then the valuable legacy as well as the potential to contribute to broader societal processes will be undermined. In terms of protecting authenticity within the confines of difficult heritage, a Rwandan research participant aptly notes:

> …we just cannot walk on their clothes, or personal belongings and leave them in the dust, we will destroy them. I understand the purpose of keeping it as raw as possible, because that is what moves us the most. But if we don't protect them now, everything will be gone. (Rwandan Interviewee 14)

This chapter demonstrates that the KGM and to a lesser extent Murambi, are largely perceived as memorial sites offering (some) educational value, in addition to their commemorative purpose. However, their actual contribution to the formation of social cohesion, national identity, and peace remains in question. While the majority of research participants in this study suggest that the potential is there, certain changes would need to be implemented. These include focusing on positive examples of reconciliation at community level as well as offering training on active bystandership for dedicated individuals. Arguably, therefore, current exhibitions should be evaluated on the basis of:

- …whether discussions of multiple perspectives of memory as a tool for dismantling myths and exploring the diversities of ethnic and political identities are encouraged throughout the site visit;
- …whether visitors change their opinions after visits, as well as forming or enhancing an emotional understanding of the human consequences of such a tragedy and whether a collective conscience is formed;

- ...whether critical thinking is motivated and engaged;
- ...and, whether new understandings of civic agency and personal responsibility are formed. (Adapted from Hamber et al. 2010: 405)

Conclusion

Memorials are expressions of broader processes of memorialisation which are constantly changing in accordance with a country's post-conflict development. Shifts in the memory landscape are produced by interactions between particular contestations and negotiations at the local level, developments at the national level and, in some cases, through external influences. This can be an extensive process in which new relations between stakeholders are forged while existing spaces might fade into oblivion or increase in force (Klep 2014). While some memorials in Rwanda have been quite static over the past 20 years, overall their preservation and construction is a result of local, national, and international efforts to come to terms with the realities of extreme violence, as well as of international political guilt about non-intervention. However, focus should now be on creating catalysts which can communicate significant change upon the world. This can only be realised if the memorials change the way they interact with Rwanda itself and local and international visitors. Exhibitions and designs should not only recount the (tragic) history but incorporate sequences of mobilisation and hope, which then translate into opportunities for immediate action within local Rwandan populations, but also for foreign visitors. Those involved in the production of such sites need to support the understanding, reconciliation, and healing of genocide for the local population and, therefore, should implement concrete changes at particularly graphic sites of memory in order to reduce the level of distress and trauma experienced by visitors. Stakeholder analysis should therefore include the impact indicators examined in this chapter to gain a better insight into Rwanda's complex visitor base, to see how such experiences can be utilised to create sites of humanitarian stimulation, rather than places of abject shock and horror. While interaction with the community is non-negotiable, so should be the recognition that the context in which 'memorial experts' operate in is always political. Memorialisation is therefore a 'form of cultural politics, which links ideology, public policy, national and community identity formation' to remembrance (Logan and Reeves 2009: 13); just as much as it is concerned with technical issues, such as the preservation of artefacts and conservation of former sites of conflict and violence.

Specifically, foreign memorial managers and consultant experts should adopt a cooperative cross-cultural approach in all stages of the Rwandan commemoration process, including an adequate study of local needs, priorities, and interests (Ibreck 2013; Barsalou 2014). Of course, it would be impossible to include *all* narratives and selected memories into national sites of remembrance that, in turn, might provide an equal voice to all members of society. Thus, the aim should be to create a safe socially sanctioned space that will foster critical reflection and serious dialogue for all those visiting. While some research respondents in this study highlighted a need for increased discourse of the more sensitive issues of the past, others stressed the differences in historical experiences to avoid confusion or denial. The dissonance here is evident and its management needs to be prioritised and incorporated into policymaking processes as well as into future preservation and exhibition initiatives.

Ultimately, this chapter has addressed memorialisation and visitor economy themes from broad disciplinary perspectives, demonstrating that 'dark tourism' can be located within the field of peace and conflict studies. Therefore, rather than excluding dark tourism as a morbid marketing niche within the wider tourism industry, it may well be the case that touristic visits to former sites of violence and death carry the potential to contribute to peace-building efforts in post-conflict communities.

References

Ashworth, G. (2002). Holocaust tourism: The experience of Krakow-Kazimierz. *International Research in Geographical and Environmental Education, 11*, 363–367.

Ashworth, G., & Hartmann, R. (2005). *Horror and human tragedy revisited – The management of sites of atrocities for tourism.* New York: Cognizant Communication Corporation.

Barsalou, J. (2014). Reflecting the fractured past: Memorialisation, transitional justice and the role of outsiders. In S. Buckley-Zistel & S. Schaefer (Eds.), *Memorials in times of transition* (pp. 47–67). Cambridge: Intersentia.

Bartov, O. (2007). *Erased: Vanishing traces of Jewish Galicia in present-day Ukraine.* Princeton: Princeton University Press.

BBC. (2011). Rwanda: How the genocide happened. [Online] Available from http://www.bbc.co.uk/news/world-africa-13431486. Accessed 2 Jul 16.

Beswick, D. (2011). Democracy, identity and the politics of exclusion in post genocide Rwanda: The case of the Batwa. *Democratization, 18*(2), 490–511.

Blom, T. (2000). Morbid tourism – A postmodern market niche with an example from Althorp. *Norsk Geografisk Tidsskrift – Norwegian Journal of Geography, 54*, 29–36.

Brandstetter, A. (2010). *Contested pasts: The politics of remembrance in post-genocide Rwanda* (pp. 6–22). Amsterdam: Netherlands Institute for Advanced Study in the Humanities and Social Sciences. 6th Ortelius Lecture, Antwerp 1 April 2010. Wassenaar: NIAS.

Buckley-Zistel, S., & Schaefer, S. (2014). *Memorials in times of transition*. Cambridge: Intersentia.

Buda, M. D., & McIntosh, J. A. (2013). Dark tourism and voyeurism: Tourist arrested for "spying" in Iran. *Culture, Tourism and Hospitality Research, 7*(3), 214–226.

Carr, G. (2012). Examining the memorialscape of occupation and liberation: A case study from the Channel Islands. *International Journal of Heritage Studies, 18*(2), 174–193.

Cook, S. E. (2006). *Genocide in Cambodia and Rwanda*. New Brunswick: Transaction Publishers.

Dallaire, R. (2004). *Shake hands with the devil: The failure of humanity in Rwanda*. London: Arrow.

Des Forges, A. (1999). *Leave none to tell the story. Genocide in Rwanda*. New York: Human Rights Watch.

Des Forges, A. (2011). *Defeat is the only bad news: Rwanda under Musinga, 1896–1931*. Madison: University of Wisconsin Press.

Foley, M., & Lennon, J. (1996). JFK and dark tourism: A fascination with assassination. *International Journal of Heritage Studies, 2*(4), 198–211.

Foote, K. (2003). *Shadowed ground: America's landscapes of violence and tragedy* (Revised Ed.). Texas: Texas University Press.

Friedrich, M. (2016). *Heritage interpretation of the dead as a tool for peace and reconciliation: The case of visitor development at Rwanda's post-conflict memorialscape*. Unpublished PhD, University of Central Lancashire, Preston.

Friedrich, M., & Johnston, T. (2013). Beauty versus tragedy: Thanatourism and the memorialisation of the 1994 Rwandan genocide. *Journal of Tourism and Cultural Change, 11*(4), 302–320.

Gourevitch, P. (1998). *We wish to inform you that tomorrow we will be killed with our families*. New York: Picador.

Graham, B., & Whelan, Y. (2007). The legacies of the dead: Commemorating the troubles in Northern Ireland. *Environment and Planning D: Society and Space, 25*, 476–495.

Graham, B., Ashworth, G. J., & Tunbridge, J. E. (2000). *A geography of heritage*. New York: Oxford University Press.

Guyer, S. (2009). Rwanda's bones. *Boundary 2 – An International Journal of Literature and Culture, 36*(2), 155–175.

Hamber, B., Ševčenko, L., & Naidu, E. (2010). Utopian dreams or practical possibilities? The challenges of evaluating the impact of memorialisation in societies in transition. *The International Journal of Transitional Justice, 4*(3), 397–420.

Hohenhaus, P. (2013). Commemorating and commodifying at the Rwanda genocide memorial sites in a politically difficult context. In L. White & E. Frew (Eds.),

Dark tourism and place identity: Managing and interpreting dark places (pp. 142–155). Abington/Oxon: Routledge.

Ibreck, R. (2013). International constructions of national memories: The aims and effects of foreign donors' support for genocide remembrance in Rwanda. *Journal of Intervention and State building, 7*(2), 149–169.

Kim, S. Y. (2011). Staging the 'cartography of paradox': The DMZ special exhibition at the Korean War Memorial, Seoul. *Theatre Journal, 63*(3), 381–402.

Klep, K. (2014). Memorialisation and social action in Santiago de Chile. In S. Buckley-Zistel & S. Schaefer (Eds.), *Memorials in times of transition* (pp. 199–219). Cambridge: Intersentia.

Logan, W., & Reeves, K. (2009). *Places of pain and shame. Dealing with 'difficult heritage'*. Abingdon: Routledge.

Mamdani, M. (2002). *When victims become killers: Colonialism, nativism, and the genocide in Rwanda*. Princeton: Princeton University Press.

Matthews, L. (2006). The people who don't exist. [Online] *Cultural Survival-Indigeneity in Africa, 30*(2). Available from: http://www.culturalsurvival.org/publications/cultural-survival-quarterly/rwanda/people-who-dont-exist. Accessed 1 Jun 2015.

McKinney, S. (2014). Between violence and romance: Gorillas, genocide and Rwandan tourism. In B. Sion (Ed.), *Death tourism: Disaster sites as recreational landscapes* (pp. 289–309). New York: Seagull Books.

McLean Hilker, L. (2011). Young Rwandans' narratives of the past [and present]. In S. Straus & L. Waldorf (Eds.), *Remaking Rwanda: State building and human rights after mass violence* (pp. 316–330). Madison: University of Wisconsin Press.

Meierhenrich, J. (2011). Topographies of remembering and forgetting – The transformation of Lieux de memoire in Rwanda. In S. Straus & L. Waldorf (Eds.), *Remaking Rwanda: State building and human rights after mass violence* (pp. 283–296). Madison, Wisconsin: University of Wisconsin Press.

Melvern, L. (2009). *A people betrayed-the role of the west in Rwanda's genocide*. London: Zed Books Ltd.

Pottier, J. (2002). *Re-imagining Rwanda, conflict, survival and disinformation in the late twentieth century*. Cambridge: Cambridge University Press.

Prunier, G. (1995/1997). *The Rwanda crisis: History of a genocide*. London: Hurst & Company.

Rifai, T. (2014). Foreword. In C. Wohlmuther & W. Wintersteiner (Eds.), *International handbook on tourism and peace* (p. 11). Klagenfurt/Celovec: Drava Verlag.

Roberts, C., & Stone, P. R. (2014). Dark tourism and dark heritage: Emergent themes, issues and consequences. In I. Convey, G. Corsane, & P. Davis (Eds.), *Displaced heritage: Dealing with disaster and suffering* (p. 2014). Woodbridge: Boydell & Brewer.

Seaton, A. V. (1996). Guided by the dark: From thanatopsis to thanatourism. *International Journal of Heritage Studies, 2*(4), 234–244.

Seaton, T. (2009). Purposeful otherness: Approaches to the management of thanatourism. In R. Sharpley & P. R. Stone (Eds.), *The darker side of travel. The theory and practice of dark tourism* (pp. 75–108). Bristol: Channel View Publications.

Sharpley, R. (2012). Towards an understanding of 'genocide tourism': An analysis of visitors' accounts of their experience of recent genocide sites. In R. Sharpley & P. R. Stone (Eds.), *Contemporary tourist experience: Concepts and consequences* (pp. 95–109). Abington: Routledge.

Sharpley, R., & Friedrich, M. (2017). Genocide tourism in Rwanda: Contesting the concept of the 'dark tourist'. In G. Hooper & J. J. Lennon (Eds.), *Dark tourism: Practice and interpretation* (pp. 134–146). Abington/Oxon: Routledge.

Sharpley, R., & Stone, P. R. (2009). Life, death and dark tourism: Future research directions and concluding comments. In R. Sharpley & P. R. Stone (Eds.), *The darker side of travel. The theory and practice of dark tourism* (pp. 247–251). Bristol: Channel View Publications.

Steele, S. L. (2006). Memorialisation and the land of the eternal spring: Performance practices of memory on the Rwandan genocide [Online] Available from: http://www.lawapps.law.unimelb.edu.au/cmcl/seminars/Passages_paper_S_Steele_final.pdf. Accessed 22 May 2012.

Stone, P. R. (2006). A dark tourism spectrum: Towards a typology of death and macabre related tourist sites, attractions and exhibitions. *Tourism: An Interdisciplinary International Journal, 54*(2): 145–160. Available from http://www.iztzg.hr/en/publications/tourism/latest_issue/?clanakId=100&brojId=6

Stone, P. R. (2013). Dark tourism scholarship: A critical review. *Culture, Tourism and Hospitality Research, 7*(3), 307–318.

Stone, P. R., & Sharpley, R. (2013). Deviance, dark tourism and 'dark leisure': Towards a (re)configuration of morality and the taboo in secular society. In S. Elkington & S. Gammon (Eds.), *Contemporary perspectives in leisure: Meanings, motives and lifelong learning*. Abington/Oxon: Routledge.

Tadjo, V. (2010). Genocide: The changing landscape of memory in Kigali. *African Identities, 8*(4), 379–388.

Tunbridge, J. E., & Ashworth, G. J. (1996). *Dissonant heritage – The management of the past as a resource in conflict*. Chichester: John Wiley & Sons Ltd.

Viebach, J. (2014). Alétheia and the making of the world: Inner and outer dimensions of memorials in Rwanda. In S. Buckley-Zistel & S. Schaefer (Eds.), *Memorials in times of transition* (pp. 69–94). Cambridge: Intersentia.

Williams, P. (2007). *Memorial museums – The global rush to commemorate atrocities*. New York: Berg.

12

'Pablo Escobar Tourism'—Unwanted Tourism: Attitudes of Tourism Stakeholders in Medellín, Colombia

Anne Marie Van Broeck

Introduction

Various cities and countries have a dark past which the local population and policy makers want to put behind them, to forget. Such a past may relate to particular political periods, wars, atrocities, or even specific people associated with a place. Often, however, there may not be consensus about whether a dark past should be denied or forgotten, and the debate may be further complicated by the opportunities offered by the apparent desire of tourists who want to know that past. In other words, although a place may wish to move on from a dark past, that past may represent a significant attraction to tourists (also see Chap. 22).

This chapter reflects on such a dilemma faced by Medellín (Colombia), a city often linked to drugs and the related violence, and specifically to the Medellín Cartel and Pablo Escobar, the infamous mafia leader, in the 1980s. Since then, the city has transformed and, in particular, has been striving to project a different image. With less drugs-related violence,[1] tourism has returned to the city, yet some tourists are now looking to find out more about this past. Thus, my main focus in this chapter is to explore the attitudes of key tourism stakeholders (policy makers, official entities, and tourism agencies) regarding the demand and supply of (dark) tourism related to Pablo Escobar and this era. As will be seen, the results demonstrate that there is a strong

A. M. Van Broeck (✉)
University of Leuven, Leuven, Belgium

preference to obliterate the past and to replace it by referring to Medellín's transformation through the contemporary architectural and social processes in the city. This 'transformation' and 'social urbanism' are central concepts in the political discourse of the city. Nevertheless, there is evidence of a move toward accepting the city's recent dark past, and even presenting it to tourists, but there is a long way to go.

'Unwanted (Moments in the) Past'[2]

As noted above, a number of cities and countries have experienced events or periods in their past which most of the local population and policy makers wish to put behind them to move forward. Indeed, their history might comprise episodes that they may even wish to obliterate from memory and/or dissociate themselves from, such as wars and atrocities as in the case of the Second World War and the Holocaust, the Rwanda Genocide, the Atlantic Slave Trade, or the imposition of South Africa's Apartheid (also see Chaps. 11, 16, and 20). Other countries have suffered political regimes they want to distance themselves from: the socialist regimes in Eastern Europe, fascist regimes in Spain and Italy, the Nazis in Germany, or the dictatorial regimes in several Latin American countries. Equally, other 'unwanted' pasts are provoked by crimes and criminal organizations (Al Capone in Chicago, the mafia in Sicily, Dutroux in Belgium, Fred and Rosemary West in UK) or one-off events with long-lasting impacts such as the terrorist attacks of 9/11.

These 'unwanted' pasts have left material legacy (heritage) and, as such, Knudsen (2011, p. 57) uses the concepts of not only 'difficult past' but also 'difficult heritage', defining the latter by referring to Macdonald (2006, p. 9) as 'a heritage that the majority of the population would prefer not to have'. Macdonald (2006) nevertheless uses the concept 'undesirable heritage', an unwished for legacy, and considers it a subcategory of what Tunbridge and Ashworth (1996) term 'dissonant heritage'. The 'unwanted' past and its related heritage are clearly not cherished and celebrated. Instead of commemorating and remembering—or as Foote (1997) calls it, 'sanctification' and 'designation'—them, societies and their members are more inclined toward denying, forgetting (oblivion) and erasing these past events (even engaging in historical revisionism), and altering or destroying the undesirable physical space and heritage (or in Foote's terms, 'rectification' and 'obliteration').

Poria (2007) also observes that no interest exists in conserving heritage related to 'bad active sections' of history, referring to those negative actions in the past undertaken by someone from one's social group. This history provokes embarrassment, discomfort, and feelings of shame, which leads often to collective forgetting or disagreement within the social group. In other words, heritage related to the commemoration of the victims (from within their own society) provokes feelings as sadness and revenge but, conversely, generally tension arises when dealing with heritage and places related to the victimizer (e.g. in Germany, Hitler's Eagle's Nest; in Spain, Franco's Valle de los Caídos; in Italy, Predappio, birthplace of Mussolini).

Young and Kaczmarek (2008) identify three strategies for dealing with an undesired past. These strategies, although employed in the specific context of post-communist places, are equally applicable to other circumstances. The first involves erasing the past from (urban) space by, for instance, removal of cultural landscapes related to this past. The second strategy is to return to the preceding period, a more glorious past. And the third is to connect the country/city to others through globalization, Westernization, or Europeanization, that is, looking for connections with the external world with more desirable characteristics.

While places have to deal internally with their past, the situation is further complicated by tourism. As Wielde Heidelberg (2015, p. 74) states: 'Fame from notorious events often transfers to the city where it happened, (…) whether the community likes it or not. This fame transfer creates a shared city "ghost" lingering in its shadows, but draws curiosity seekers from around the globe.' Frequently tourists are very keen to learn more about the 'ghost' of a place, the past, the 'bad history', and the 'dark' history, and want to visit related places, an interest which may be far from welcomed by local authorities and inhabitants. These stakeholders, however, often have little influence over the ways in which their 'dark' past is promoted; such dark tourism is rarely initiated by them, but mainly by external influences (Light 2000a). Many of the key sights are constructed as 'attractions' for the gaze of tourists and, consequently, leads Light (2000a, p. 158) to state that this is 'a heritage which is defined by its consumers'.[3]

Several studies have been published in the last decade focusing on tourism and controversial heritage,[4] raising the question of how to show it to the tourists. Yet, as Wielde Heidelberg (2015, p. 74) states: 'The local government component [of dark tourism] has been overlooked in this field of study'. The cases of Berlin, Budapest, and Bucharest illustrate the strategies these cities 'have adopted to negotiate and accommodate such [communist heritage] tourism without compromising post-communist identities' (Light 2000a, p. 157). A memory of the past was created; the heritage was stripped of the original meaning and symbolic references by 'decontextualization' either in space by the removal of objects, monuments, statues, or other architectural elements from their original place, such as moving them from the central civic square where they had a meaning to a park in the outskirts of the city, to 'spatial isolation' (Otto 2008), or in meaning by making them clearly a monument or a memorial or museumifying them with interpretative panels, thus transforming them into a tourist attraction and, as such, an element of the past: 'spatial reframing' (Otto 2008). For example, since the original Checkpoint Charlie guard house in Berlin was actually removed and placed in a museum, what tourists nowadays experience at the famous location is completely 'constructed, organized for tourism consumption, [a] deliberately contrived heritage space' (Light 2000a). In contrast in Bucharest, tourism drew another card and a completely new story is told to the tourists in the former House of People, completely silencing the Ceausescu era, the original purpose of the building or, in short, denying the socialist past—what Otto (2008) refers to as 'narrative reframing'.

Dann and Seaton (2001, p. 27) ask the question: 'How far back in the past must they [the committed atrocities and acts of repression] have occurred in order to be memorialized or discarded in heritage terms?' We could add, 'or be shown to an outsider's public, among others to tourists'. For instance, in 1996 the Hungarian National Museum opened a gallery interpreting the post-war period—'The rise and fall of communism (1945–1990)'—and, as such, presents the communist period as just another era in Hungary's history. Light (2000a, p. 168) interprets this as a sign that there is a clear break with the past; communism is considered history, and 'the country is sufficiently relaxed about its experience of communism to have few reservations about remembering it'. Probably no exact timing can be given, but without doubt, it is related to the moment when locals have been able to give it a place as part of their history.

One of the several moral issues raised is the possibility or objective of obtaining economic benefits from tourists, exploiting the 'unwanted past' and, therefore, directly or indirectly exploiting the victims. Is it acceptable to profit or engage in commerce stemming from tragedy, and should such (dark) tourism be used as a tool for economic development? Cities don't want to be known 'as "the dead city" that exploits their dead for benefit' (Wielde Heidelberg 2015, p. 75). Therefore:

> Cities may want to disassociate themselves with dark tourism to protect professional integrity. For a city admitting that there might be an economic benefit in being involved in interpretative programming for dark tourism might make the city look opportunistic and exploitative. (Wielde Heidelberg 2015, pp. 84–85)

Conversely, individuals might more swiftly spot the opportunities offered by visitors and respond by arranging different guided tours of sites associated with the unwanted era (Light 2000b). Additionally, in the case of tourism, even more opposition and controversy among the local authorities and within the local community may be observed when the focus of the (tourist) gaze is on the victimizer and their legacy. For instance, in Chicago, the city leaders have lent little support to tourism related to its 'gangster' past: no plaques are placed at important sites; buildings with connection to Al Capone have been razed; and brochures for related tours are forbidden in tourist-centric locations. Moreover, according to Reaves (2010), opposition from the large Italian-American community further influenced the city's reticence to profit from Al Capone. Yet Al Capone's legacy endures and the rather public negative attitude has been a boon to the private businesses running Al Capone tours. According to them, the sense that it is an 'underground' thing, though sanctioned by the city, often works their favor, since it entices tourists even more to their tours (Reaves 2010).

Similarly, controversy has been observed in Germany and beyond, when Hitler or the Nazi period was/is proposed as a focus for tourism. In 2011, a British tour company was strongly criticized (according to some, even sanctioned—Nayer 2011) for offering a 'Hitler tour' around Germany, titled 'Face of Evil: The Rise and Fall of the Third Reich', with visits to sites such as the lakeside villa where the Holocaust was planned, Berghof, and the spot where Hitler committed suicide (Nayer 2011). David Cesarani, a well-known and respected British expert on Nazi Germany, stated, 'German historians have confronted the Nazi past with seriousness. But there is a danger of sensationalism when it is incorporated in what I'd call a holiday tour. If you focus on the sites most pertinent to Hitler, you are concentrating on the cult of that personality. The trip in effect becomes a perverse pilgrimage' (Mudie 2011).[5] Much controversy was also provoked by the Hitler exhibition held in Berlin the same year (Connolly 2010; Crossland 2010; Paterson 2010; Rinne 2010 a.o.).

Generally, there is no clear answer as to how involved citizens and city officials should be in 'accommodating public interest in the ghost that made them famous' (Wielde Heidelberg 2015, p. 75), yet Wielde Heidelberg goes on to argue that suppressing the ghost is a mistake, stating that:

> Cities have a chance to provide a voice in the ghost enterprise, provide context, and ensure that the story is based on current research, regardless of how the event is presented by other sectors. (2015, p. 75)

Medellín's Unwanted Past: Drugs, Violence in the 1980s, and ... Pablo Escobar

Medellín, Colombia's second largest city, is without doubt associated with drugs and the related violence reflecting the power struggles of the Medellín Drugs Cartel and Pablo Emilio Escobar Gaviria (1949–1993), its globally notorious leader, during the 1980s. In 1989, *Forbes* magazine estimated Escobar to be the seventh richest man and one of 227 billionaires in the world, while his Medellín Cartel controlled 80% of the global cocaine market.

The power Pablo Escobar managed to acquire throughout his years in the drug trafficking business has been widely documented.[6] To a large extent, his power rested on a well-tailored way of doing business, which included both legal and illegal activities, the use of violence, and corruption at all levels with political, social, and religious support. Visibility through 'investments' in basic community needs gave him an aura of a 'good man' among the inhabitants of poorer barrios, who saw him as a Robin Hood character. In return, they gave him their support, which helped him build his power structure. Escobar's power cannot be assessed without a closer look at the politics, economics, and culture of the Department of Antioquia of which Medellín is the capital. He was a product of the Antioquia's idiosyncrasy where entrepreneurship and money-driven ethics exceed the rest of Colombia.[7]

The Medellín Cartel was quick to attract many enemies, including their primary rival and former associate, the Cali Cartel, the right-wing paramilitaries who were equally once associates of Escobar, as well as the vigilante group known as 'People Persecuted by Pablo Escobar' and, of course, the Colombian Government. Conflicts between these groups resulted in a circle of violence (assassinations, drive-by shootings by hitmen, car bombs), leading to the deaths of hundreds of individuals including civilians, politicians, journalists, policemen, government officials, and judges. Indeed, during the 1980s and early 1990s, Medellín became the world's murder capital with 25,100 violent deaths in 1991 and 27,100 in 1992 (Inter-American Commission on Human Rights 1993).

When the United States increased pressure on Colombia to extradite Pablo Escobar, the drug lord negotiated with the government and, in exchange for a reduced sentence in Colombia, he surrendered in 1991. He was held prisoner in 'La Catedral', his own luxurious private prison where he enjoyed preferential treatment, and from which he escaped after just one-year incarceration. In 1993, after several months on the run, he died during a confrontation with a special police unit.[8] His death, and the dismantling of the different cartels in the following years, brought back some superficial respite to the city.

Nevertheless, nowadays, other power structures have overtaken crime and drugs business and violence has not been completely erased from the city.

Pablo Escobar and the Medellín Cartel was just one of the many causes of the violence in the city, yet as if he was the only protagonist, it is primarily Escobar who is associated with the past violence in the city and who, according to some of our informants, has been accorded undue importance. Many citizens want to forget him and 'his' era but, at the same time, his memory sells. In Colombia, innumerable television series—so-called *narconovelas*—are made and broadcasted on drugs-related topics, or on Pablo Escobar and other important drug lords, one of the most popular being the 'Escobar: El Patron del Mal' in 2012. Books by national and international authors aimed at both adults and children, including a sticker book sold with pictures of 'Escobar: El Patron del Mal', movies and theater plays, and T-shirts (including a 'designer' shirt produced by his son) all illustrate the interest in him and the commercial value of his memory. And now there are also tourism and Pablo Escobar tours. In short, the world's once most notorious criminal has become one of the city's tourist attractions.

Medellín's Pride and Present: Transformation

In 2004, under the leadership of the then-mayor Sergio Fajardo, Medellín started a transformation process rooted in the policy of 'social urbanism'. The city decided to invest significant resources in the vulnerable areas of the city, the poorest and more violent parts of town which had previously often been neglected by city policies. New schools; prestigious architecture in public spaces, such as public libraries; new spaces for recreation and sports; connecting transportation systems (metro, metro cable, and electric stairways); new housing projects; and mobility, security, and green zones were created.

These physical-spatial changes, together with social interventions, were considered an effective means of social and cultural transformation, and they appear to have been successful according to quality-of-life indicators and decreased levels of violence. While Medellín was once characterized by drug trafficking, violence, poverty, and social inequality, the city is now defined by transformation, optimism, modernization, co-existence, education, culture, and innovation.[9] Over the last decade, the City of Eternal Spring[10] has received more and more positive attention. Indeed, in 2013 Medellín was the winner of the 'City of the Year' competition organized by *The Wall Street Journal*, Citi, and the Urban Land Institute, beating the other finalists, Tel Aviv and New York City, as the most innovative city in the world.

Tourism in Medellín

In its attempt to develop its tourism industry, Colombia has long suffered from a negative image owing to his history of violence.[11] Yet, some changes are appearing at the horizon and, little by little, the country is overcoming this problem. Tourism to Colombia has grown strongly in recent years and, since 2006, the number of international visitors has almost doubled (author's calculations based on tourism statistics between 2006 and 2015; see Mincomercio Industria y Turismo 2007–2015). The average annual growth of global international arrivals between 2000 and 2010 was around 3.2%; average annual growth in international arrivals to Colombia in the same period was 10.6%, a significant indicator of development of tourism in Colombia in those years (Alcaldía Medellín 2012, p. 28). Within Colombia, Medellín is the third most visited destination by foreign tourists after Bogotá and Cartagena, receiving approximately 10% of all international visitors (ibid.).

In newspaper articles and travel blogs related to Medellín, the 'unwanted past' (e.g. 'murder capital'; 'home of Pablo Escobar') is still often referred to, though typically in the past tense. Nevertheless, although Medellín is nowadays a different city, the 'ghost' of Pablo is still present. Moreover, he has suddenly become something new: a tourist attraction and a favorite especially among many of the young backpackers who have discovered this attractive city while traveling in Colombia. Indeed, many tourists know little or nothing of Medellín before they arrive other than its association with the violent era and Escobar's Medellín Cartel,[12] and many want to know more about this once they arrive.

Undoubtedly, Pablo Escobar 'sells', leading to a boom in Pablo Escobar tours. The first Pablo Escobar tours date from about 2007 when just one or two small agencies offered them. They were rather discrete and were mostly offered through the Internet. Subsequently, however, Pablo Escobar tours became promoted more widely in travelers' hostels and worldwide media reported on this phenomenon. Newspapers such as *The Guardian* (Baker 2011), *New York Times* (Alford 2013), *Der Spiegel* (Käufer 2013), and even *Aljazeera* (Arsenault 2014) have run articles on the tours, making them more well-known.

During the time frame of the research discussed here, various operators were offering tours. A detailed analysis of these tours, the providers, and the discourse are beyond the scope of this chapter (see Giraldo et al. 2014) although generally, these are half-day tours involving visits to the house where Pablo Escobar was killed, his grave, and some properties where he lived and from where he operated, such as the Monaco and Dallas buildings. There are no markers on these places and they are as such not outstanding in any sense when viewed from the street. However, for the purpose of this chapter, it is important to mention that apart from the longest running tour (offered by Paisa Road[13]), the most popular tours are those organized by or with the help of Roberto Escobar, the brother of the drug lord, who was also the cartel's book-keeper and who was released from prison in 2003 after serving a sentence for drugs-related crimes. After visiting some related places, the tour comes to the home of Roberto, once a hideout of Pablo and now something of a museum,[14] where he welcomes the tourists. Needless to say, the story is told from his and his family's viewpoint.

Methodology

This chapter presents partial results from ongoing research on Pablo Escobar tourism in Medellín which commenced in 2010. In a one-year project co-financed by the Instituto Universitario Colegio Mayor de Antioquia, the attitudes of official tourism-related entities (policy makers and tourism agencies) on Pablo Escobar-related tourism were explored. Therefore, several important official tourism stakeholders were interviewed in March and April 2012, these being the representatives of Subsecretaria de Turismo–Alcaldía de Medellín; Oficina de Dirección de Fomento Turístico la Gobernación de Antioquia; Medellín Convention & Visitors Bureau (responsible for the promotion of the city); Proexport, actually ProColombia (the entity that promotes, among other things, international tourism); ANATO (Colombian Association of Travel & Tourism Agencies); and ASOGUIAN (the departmental association of tour guides).[15] The interviews were recorded and transcribed. In this chapter, the citations are translated from Spanish to English and slightly modified for fluent reading and are anonymized. The information presented is extended and contextualized by the author's empirical research during several years living and working in Colombia.

A Past Medellín Wants to Forget (and Definitely Not to Show)

'Medellín's Pablo Escobar tours cause discomfort with authorities' was a headline of an online article in 2011 (Wells 2011). And indeed, during our interviews, our informants were often hesitant or reluctant to consider tourism with an interest in Pablo Escobar or a tourism product related to this particular moment in the past. The representative of the tour guides association, for example, declared that (notwithstanding individual guides) they would not even mention Pablo Escobar to the tourists unless asked explicitly about him. Their mission is, he said, to show the good side of the city. Also, the Association of Travel Agencies declared that their members who deal with incoming tourism would not sell Pablo Escobar-related tours. Nevertheless, having contacted a sample of them, some do offer such tours when explicitly requested (Giraldo et al. 2014).

Although all our informants had heard about Pablo Escobar tours, and disapproved of them, they admitted to not knowing what was really told or shown, and (as it was an official interview) claimed that they had neither participated in a tour nor contacted any relevant tour operator. The general tone of responses was, nevertheless, prejudiced about these tours, and sometimes even slightly tended to resemble a kind of witch-hunt. Governmental tourism agencies in general will not provide any support, assistance, or encouragement for Pablo Escobar tours.[16]

When asked what they feared most about offering tours about Pablo Escobar, or what made them most uncomfortable, most commonly mentioned were concerns about the image of the city, the fear of wrong or incomplete information, perpetuating the problems of the past, and attracting unwelcome visitors. These concerns are obviously very much intertwined.

The (Bad) Image of Medellín: Connecting Medellín with Tragedy and Violence

Many of the tourism administrators remain concerned that Medellín (as well as Colombia) will—through such tours—continue to be associated with and, therefore, stigmatized as a city (and country) of violence and drugs. This is very much related with Wielde Heidelberg's concern about 'connecting the home territory with tragedy' (2014, pp. 5–6) or 'unwanted association with the event' (2014, p. 9), which causes resistance to mentioning the past.

> What perception do they have about us out there? A negative one! Travel warnings! So we must all the time be telling what our good points are, 'this is good, that is good, look at the numbers, the homicides are low…'. It's like always being contradicting the image that they usually have in Europe. Many of them still see us as a dangerous country. (Respondent 1)

The fear exists that tourists will come to Medellín only to learn about the history of Pablo Escobar and what happened in the 1980s and that by engaging in tourism related to these topics, visitors will once again take only this image home with them.

Nevertheless, the fact that Medellín's image is still related to this past is rather slowly but steadily diminishing. As a study of foreign tourists in Medellín indicates, in 2010 only 25% of the interviewed tourists could recall the 1980s in Medellín as an era of narcotics trafficking (Giraldo and Muñoz 2010). Also, in the interviews some informants mentioned that they believed this image to be fading.

> Why would I have to mention that everything is safe now, if he [my Russian interlocutor] did not even know?! Why not raise it positively and not continue to see it negatively. (Respondent 1)

The negative image of Medellín is not only perpetuated abroad, and not only by tourism and these tours. Colombians themselves often judge their own society very harshly and many who lived this era perpetuate a negative image. Although some people might be prudently optimistic because of the transformation of the city, owing to experience they remain fearful that it may not last. It is difficult to change such a perception although some respondents noted that for the younger generations the reality might be different and, therefore, the negative image might be weakening.

> This [image of the 80s] has certainly been changing and will change each time when generations pass by. My generation, I was born in the late 60s, we lived in that era of very complex violence; and let's say for the generations which are a little older, living outside Colombia, the perception of this city is still associated with the 80s, early 90s, when there was Pablo Escobar, the Medellín cartel. And when we travel internationally we still find a lot that perception. This begins to change because the new generations are living this transformation process and today Medellín begins for some of these generations to be a model of transformation. And this is something this city is doing and certainly, as it happens for example with my daughters who are 20 years, the subject of Pablo Escobar and the theme of the Medellín cartel becomes a thing of which they say that it befell to their mom. But I grew up in a different atmosphere. So when those generations of 20 will be 40 years, possibly the image of Medellín will be different, but we still have a long road ahead for our communication strategy to be different. (Respondent 2)

Drug Culture, Drug Use: 'Vulnerable Communities' (6)

Talking about the drug lord could, in the perception of the authorities, attract unwanted visitors. On the one hand, there might be those interested in a gangster; on the other hand, they might be interested in drugs. Some informants feared that these tours would or do stimulate drug use by the tourists, directly (for instance, during the tours) or indirectly. Since drugs are still available in society, there exists the fear that 'to show it is to (indirectly) promote it':

> The theme of drug trafficking has not yet gone away and if you for some reason show it, you seem to promote it; so, the great difficulty is that it is a fact that has not been overcome and since it has not been overcome, you seem to promote it, which is different from what happens in other countries where these issues are at stake, for instance the Italian or Californian mafia. (Respondent 4)

There is no doubt that narcotourism exists in Colombia, defined by the United Nations Office on Drugs and Crime (UNODC) as a 'kind of tourism in which domestic and foreign people visit one or more specific areas of a country, with the intention to acquire, consume and transport drugs, mainly marijuana, cocaine and heroin, and even to visit plantations and clandestine laboratories to get to know the elaboration process' (UNODC 2013, p. 4; translated by author). As a study by UNODC observes, such tourists might come to Colombia in search of drugs, motivated by the image created by the history of the cartels in the 1980s and 1990s and by Pablo Escobar as an icon of that era. Nevertheless, research is needed to conclude definitively that a Pablo Escobar tour would contribute to narcotourism or to establish a clear link between narcotourism and such tours. Indeed, although some participants of these tours might have consumed drugs, others might genuinely be interested in the past of Medellín in particular and of Colombia more generally.

Related to this, there also exists the fear among respondents that drugs will again permeate Colombian society, thereby reactivating local trafficking, together with other social problems such as the sexual exploitation of children and adolescents and prostitution.[17] One of our informants referred to the 'vulnerable communities' in society (Respondent 6). And besides this societal component, the institutions interviewed did not want to be seen to be promoting this kind of tourism and, by implication, this broader business.

Unwelcome Sensationalism: And Glorification of a Perpetrator?

The interview respondents feared that during the tours, incomplete or incorrect information is or will be given. For instance, they feared that the narrative of the tours obliterates the bad that Pablo Escobar did to the city and society and that therefore he will be glorified as a kind of Robin Hood character.

> They distort reality; that is, they give information that is not complete, they inform in such a way that he's an idol but come on, let's talk reality, the damage he did to this city. (Respondent 2)

> The tours have a version of the reality, where they are the heroes, they saved people, but they do not tell about all the negative impact it had. (Respondent 5)

Another fear, related to this point is that, if neither the historical context nor the transformed present are mentioned, as the respondents believe occurs during Pablo Escobar tours, the tourists will leave the city with only this image of this one man, without seeing the broader perspective, without seeing the new city.

While the tours which include visit to Pablo Escobar's brother, Roberto, as discussed above, are of course less objective and twist reality more than once, this is not necessarily the case for all tours offered. Equally, it should be recognized that the problem does not only lie with tourism. More specifically, Pablo is not only promoted in tours to tourists, but he also appears frequently in the media, particularly in the aforementioned *narconovelas*, arousing among some youngsters of vulnerable communities the images and dreams of making quick money, as *el patron*. There still remains some admiration for and fascination in the drug lords.

It Is (Not) 'Behind Us': Open Wounds

There is a very strong contradiction when one analyzes the discourse of the respondents. On the one hand, they mentioned that the era of violence of the 1980s is behind them; it is past, manifested not least in the transformation processes that the city has gone through. Thus, the tours remind them of the past one wants to forget.

> I think that the fact of making the tour is reminding people of something we were and that we are not anymore, that one doesn't even remember that it had existed. (Respondent 3)

On the other hand, our respondents referred to the fact that although Medellín has made a lot of process, the city still faces violence and a drug trade; these are still a part of the reality they live in. Moreover, many of those (or their relatives) who suffered in the past are still alive; hence, the tours are seen as putting salt on open wounds (Respondent 4). People have not yet overcome the past and its pain; even more, it isn't over yet!

The wounds are open, so when you have not yet healed, when one speaks about a subject that is painful, it creates repulsion. (…) When you still see that it is an issue that did so much damage to this city, and that we are still living many very complex things that originated from that, it's when you ask 'this is the time to do it'!? How are you selling it when we know that young people are killing themselves?! It is obvious that the wounds are open and that's has not allowed us [to create a tour]. (..) The wound is open and you cannot do something when the wound is bleeding because it generates pain and rejection. (Respondent 2)

It is a denial of reality, when we think it is better not to speak of it to avoid we go back to an image they had of us; I think that's it, an image that remained in the minds of everyone, even now, many years later, after we have recovered; and I think even people from outside don't remember, that is, they remember as history, but they do not think that here still passes somethings similar; I don't think that. Anyway, here unconsciously it is a grief that has not yet passed as it should be, I think. (Respondent 3)

Our informants also mentioned what Wielde Heidelberg describes as 'the concern for integrity':

Cities may want to disassociate themselves with dark tourism to protect professional integrity. For a city, admitting that there might be an economic benefit in being involved in interpretative programming for dark tourism might make the city look opportunistic and exploitative. (Wielde Heidelberg 2015, p. 84)

They stated it as follows:

Today the issue is still an open wound for us, and as I said, it would a bit hard for us to make the administration or the ordinary people understand that we organize a tour of Pablo Escobar. (Respondent 2)

We are in the time period that there are still people affected by bombs, that is, my reading about why today the institutions do not address this is because that it is not yet past, better said it is not history, it is not history, it is still real in this country and in this city, and so the wound still hurts. (Respondent 4)

The Official Story Told: Medellín's Transformation

In 'Plan de Desarrollo Turístico, Medellín 2011–2016' (Alcaldia Medellín 2012), four strategic axes are defined for tourism development in the city: business tourism (MICE), health tourism, nature tourism, and cultural tourism. When inquiring with our informants about the attractions for cultural tourism, a variety of elements were mentioned: cultural traditions, such as fairs and festivals (La Feria de las Flores, El Festival del Tango, and the 'alumbrados', when Christmas lights decorate the whole city and, in particular, the river from bank to bank). Also, with reference to religious tourism, churches, processions in Semana Santa, and Christmas stables in December were all mentioned. Only very rarely were museums or art (or even Botero's sculptures) brought up in the interviews, while the history of Medellín and the city's historical monuments and buildings did not seem to be considered part of touristic attractions. Most frequently, respondents mentioned the traditions and the idiosyncrasy of the city and region as attractions: the way of living, talking, the expressions, proverbs, the ballads, the aguardiente, and the traditional gastronomy.

This is very much in line with the attractions generally found, but there was clearly a new buzzword. More than anything else, the word that was frequently mentioned in the interviews was 'transformation'. Talking about Medellín is definitely not to talk about the (dark) past but about the new present, the transformed Medellín with 'buildings that make one think one is not in Colombia, but outside of Colombia' (Respondent 2). This is the success story the public administration wants the world to hear.[18] Indeed, it is noteworthy that in all the interviews, our informants almost immediately put the emphasis on this new city and this process of transformation:

> Rather than selling the Museum of Antioquia, or the Museum of Modern Art, or Pedro Nel, or the Castillo, more than selling the Explore Park or the Botanical Garden as elements of our culture, what we are selling is: the city of today is another one, the city of today went through a process of transformation, where you will find sites that you did not expect to find. (Respondent 2)

> The central axis in our discourse is the transformation of the city. What is really attractive, that is, why would you come today to Medellín? Because today it is a city that has been transformed and has many things to show in this transformation process. (Respondent 2)

Also in the 'Plan de Desarrollo Turístico – 2011–2016', we can find (although less prominent) references to the transformation:

> To position the brand Medellín as a tourist destination, the construction of a strategy for international promotion is based on different elements that make the city a major tourist center: its culture and transformation, its historic sites, recreational areas, convention and conference centers. One can add to this the

changes in urbanistic infrastructure, modernity, public transport and fairs and festival with an international character, (...). In this context, an important aspect that should be developed is the process of social transformation that Medellín underwent: the problems that showed an unattractive image in the international context and isolated the city from the investment opportunities for a long time, and didn't allow to present it as a tourist destination of relevance, today, they have been the way to make it a city with opportunities; this thanks to the transformation projects of the Municipal Administration, which allow to visualize the city as an important to invest, visit and do business destination. One should capitalize on the image of the city, positioned in relation to changes and its transformation, because it is an important resource for tourism promotion. (Alcaldia de Medellín 2012, p. 79)

Yet, when talking about the progress the city has made, our informants barely mentioned what the situation had been previously. More significantly, the progress mentioned mainly refers to social and urbanistic development, and little mention is made with respect to violence. Indeed, our informants became tangled up in their answers when asked if and when one should mention Pablo Escobar or in broader terms the violence of the 1980s, in this transformation discourse. Most indicated that they prefer not to mention him. Or, in any case, they would mention him only as an antecedent, as if it's a minor detail. Pablo Escobar is generally swept under the carpet or brushed out, as soon as possible.

> We are promoting a city that was transformed from a reality where not only Pablo Escobar was present, but many other things that made our town live a dark and violent era. So yes, we talk with clarity about a transformation process – but we are not getting out there to promote Medellín today as the place where you go to make the tour of Pablo Escobar, but as the place where you will discover a city that is transformed, which had a complex past and which through some interventions that have been done in recent years, today knows a different reality. Its structure, its culture, through this transformation process, can be very appealing for you to come to visit the city a weekend or to go to the flower fair. (Respondent 2)

It is the present that matters, the focus is the transformation.

> Tours of the transformation tell you this historic information, but they go to the core, as I told you, they do not stay in the historic data, idealizing and mythologizing and dignifying, no, they tell it but they advance. OK, this was in the past; this was the reality, the scourge that underwent the community. And where are we now, the transformation. (Respondent 6)

Toward a New Vision and Role for the Policy Makers

During the interviews, the respondents often went back and forth when wondering what to do with the past, although a strong tendency (or habit) to conceal the past was present, such as:

> Again, and I repeat, it is a fear, a terror, a morbid curiosity or a suspicion to a theme we say it's better to keep it covered with a blanket, that's what I sense. (Respondent 1)

Nevertheless, some of the informants seemed to become more and more aware that something should be done, primarily since there is definitely a demand from the tourists and nothing is officially provided.

> It seems to me that not mentioning the topic of Pablo Escobar in the tours in Medellín, is like trying to cover the sun with a finger. It's like not talking about something that everybody knows. Maybe we do not see it and maybe we believe it is not so important, but outside Medellín it is something that everyone knows about Medellín. I guess that those who will come to visit Medellín, have read something about it, and expect that when he comes here, someone will tell him about this topic, or that he will find something. But, as there is almost nothing out there, nothing is signalized, … 'this was the house where he died', a plate, marker, anything that the tourist can see when he passes by or is taken on a tour … But there doesn't exist any historical description done professionally so to speak. (Respondent 3)

> When the tourist comes to town, he should know that there is a tour, that he will find a (hi)story that is very clear and that everyone in the world knows. That we have to have because if not the tourist is disappointed. As I was telling you right now, we asked some foreigners who did a [official city] tour and they told me that they felt as if they were not told half of the story. So, we should take care, the product must exist with a very clear script. (Respondent 5)

Some informants pointed out that not having a tour is counterproductive. Indeed, when nothing is offered officially, alternative tours will have the only say about this part of the history.[19]

> [We need] something institutional, because if a tourist comes and wants to know the history of Medellín the only option left are these [unofficial tours] and what they are showing them, and how they are showing it; but if the institutions show it, they can do it with a focus they want. (Respondent 4)

And, as mentioned above in the case of Chicago, it is always more exciting to bite the forbidden apple.

> Tourists are not going to wait and so it is becoming an illegal operation, even more, it becomes a journey of discovery and that seems to them even more exciting because as it is clandestine; it looks even more exciting and it seems closer to the reality. (Respondent 4)

> One has to tell the story, the story cannot be omitted; yes, I think it's more counterproductive to hide it because accepting it is to assume that this process has passed and that the city is now in another story, but to hide it or do things below is like feeding it. (Respondent 5)

Also, one of the informants dared to formulate the economic interest in having these tours:

> One misses the opportunity – that these foreigners come, extend their stay in the city – which is what concerns us all, that they spend and consume in the city and that they find what they have to find, yes, a tour of Paul Escobar, let's call him by name, I do not know how you should call it… Maybe that's the name people use to refer to it. Now one has to analyze whether one wants to sell this tour, but this product has to exist. But one should not promote the city itself as such. (Respondent 5)

One of our collocutors proposed a clear and defined place for the drug lord in the story to be told 'before the transformation'.

> But what do I think? That this has to change and we'll reach the point, as does Chicago with Al Capone for example, to have a tour that talks about our past, but included the transformation and that is the success of the thematic. If we speak of a past which we cannot hide and also without which we would not have the present as we have today, then we should not hide it or cover it or delete it. And that's how we will structure this past, which harmed us very much but which also gave us so much strength to build present we are building. This is how to organize the tour of Pablo Escobar in function of today, not staying in yesterday, not showing him as an idol, not showing him around drugs but, OK, we have a tour of Pablo Escobar, how is the 'Cathedral' [name of the prison he was incarcerated], what happened here, we'll tell stories about the 'Cathedral', where he escaped, and about the house in Laureles where he was killed, what happened here. And construct in that house the museum, showing here pictures of him and explaining what he did. We show the poorer neighborhoods where we talk a little bit about the pain but also about the transformation which took

> place in these neighborhoods. About what is happening about now, in terms of a hopeful and a constructive present. I am convinced that we have to get to this. (Respondent 2)

Yet, this requires a new vision and a new role for policy makers. For now, all informants concurred that there is no official position by the Mayor's Office/City Hall on what to do.

> Imagine, since it is a fact – it is a real tourist fact, there is a demand, that is undeniable – the problem is how the government deals with it and has not agreed on how to approach it. (Respondent 4)

> It is very clear that there should be a very clear position of mayor's office (city hall) because it is a city issue. (Respondent 5)

One factor which might make talking about the violent past easier is the societal changes underpinned by the *Ley de Víctimas* (law of the victims; Ley 1448, 2011, and a state council statement in 2014[20]) and, for Medellín in particular, the construction and working of the museum, Museo Casa de la Memoria.[21] New winds are blowing, since violence and victims are now discussed openly. For one of our informants, this could represent some new opportunities.

> The other thing is to exalt the aggressor; showing him is putting the image of the one who assaulted at the foreground. Now, Colombia has taken the first step to recognize victims, so it could for example take the issue of Pablo Escobar from the standpoint of the victims of the trafficking, not from the perpetrator, what still hurts us, but from the victims linked to the new law that we have which is very important, it gives us a future, a hope for peace. They don't have in New York at Ground Zero a museum dedicated to Bin Laden, no, you have there the recognition of the victims; and in this Colombia is barely starting to work, in recognition of the victims. In the United States you will see the theme of the Twin Towers from the victim's standpoint, not from the perpetrator's. In this case it is about the victimizer! Colombia just formulated a law on victims last year with this government, because so far we didn't even recognize the victims. But the victims do remember and it hurts them. So notice the change Colombia is passing through, when it says that there are victims of violence, of all violence, state, non-state, the other, OK. Already saying this is a giant step, that is new. But at least there should be an institutional option to have the subject told otherwise… So that's why in the United States are memorials, because they have valued the victims, something Colombia has not done, we are just releasing the concept of victim, are debuting and the Museum of Memory has barely two years, it is under construction, we we're entering levels of thinking of another power, today we are not in it. (Respondent 4)

Conclusions: In Search of a Balance

Without any doubt, Medellín is on a threshold. On one hand, the 1980s are temporally long gone; Pablo Escobar died in 1993 and much has since changed. Yet, on the other hand, the violence isn't completely gone. Medellín society is still looking for a balance—one foot in, one foot out this violence era—in a still very shaky reality. Also, the wounds have not yet healed, and society has still to come to terms with the past and its pain.

Yet, there is another challenge the city is facing. While several years ago Medellín (and Colombia) was considered too dangerous for tourists to visit, now that they have finally been able to travel there more safely, some of the tourists want to know more about what happened, to understand the past and the present. It is indeed hard to understand Medellín today without the knowledge of its past, of which the 1980s are a key element. Yet, the inhabitants (and tourism stakeholders) want to look to the future! The city desires to deny or at least forget Escobar and the 1980s, while, at least from the perspective of many tourists, they are part of the city's culture and heritage.

In this chapter we have presented the views of several key tourism stakeholders with regard to tourism related to this 'unwanted past', in general, and Pablo Escobar, in particular, and their search for what to do with it. The results of the research suggest that they indeed would prefer to wipe out this 'ghost' for both themselves and also for tourists. With reference to Young and Kaczmarek (2008), their strategy therefore seems related to the eradication of the past and the connecting of the city with globalization and modernization, manifested in 'the transformed city'. It reminds us of Otto's 'narrative decontextualization', where a new story (the transformation) is told and some other story (Pablo Escobar and the 1980s) is wiped out.

When analyzing the fears and objections revealed by our informants about the existing Pablo Escobar-related tours, many of them were phrased in relation to the tourists (they would leave with a bad image of Colombia; they would not receive the correct information; they would use drugs; they would think Pablo is a hero, …). Since society has not yet completely overcome the past nor become stable, our informants feared these tours might counteract the new developments and progress. Although this might be a risk, from closer analysis, it would appear rather that fears related to ongoing internal processes are projected on to the tourists. In other words, the fears and objections about the tours reflect similar ongoing internal societal processes, such as glorification of the past, the drug trade and lords, and so on, which are internal restraints on social progress that must be resolved from within.

Tourists are and will be interested in Medellín's past, and the city will have to find a way how to deal with this 'unwanted' demand. Suppressing the 'ghost' is a mistake, as is not telling the story, since this just triggers the attention and makes it possibly more tempting for tourists to search for it. In the absence of an official story, tourists are directing themselves to the offered alternatives. Thereby, this gives way to all kinds of versions of the history. And, although several operative tours actually are striving to tell the story in an (more or less) objective, informative way, is leaving way to tours visiting Pablo's brother who's giving his side of the story such a good idea?

It is clear that it is a long process, and the steps are taken little by little. One needs time to be able to consider it 'history' (past).

> Why is the tour of Al Capone in Chicago today successful? Because it happened many years ago, many years and today this is part of the history, but if that had been mounted 10 years after it had occurred, probably it would not have been successful as it is today, because today the city looks back at it like it is passed. We are in the process but we know it is going to take a long time. (Respondent 2)

The city has to become ready to be able to talk about what happened.

> What happens is that this is a process, a process where we have to go healing wounds and where we have to organize ourselves internally so that we all speak the same language. (Respondent 2)

Developments, such as the Museum Casa de la Memoria, show that there is a way and that Medellín is on the way. Recognizing the victims and talking about them and the damage done to the society—instead of focusing (solely) on the perpetrator(s)—might offer an alternative to talk not only internally, but also to the visitors, about the violence Colombia lived with, also in the era of the 1980s.

Coming to terms with the past, accepting it has passed, maybe even seeing it as part of their cultural heritage, and also of interest to tourists, will take some courage and time, but the process is on its way. There were also several voices, suggesting to accept the past as theirs, and recognizing it as an attractive for tourists, such as other places have added a dark spot on their list. The discussion is growing: Medellín and its stakeholders are already on its way, to look for a balance and find their 'middle ground'.

> So what do we have to do? It is not shutting off, but it is living a gradual process, where we will arrive, in some near future, to have with all clarity Pablo Escobar

tours, and we will have many serious companies offering distinctive variations of that tour; rather than stigmatizing this, we should ask: are we ready as a city? (Respondent 2)

I do not know how much we are prepared for that but it has to be an alternative, sooner rather than later. (Respondent 4)

Only the future will tell whether Medellín continues to try to hide Pablo Escobar or, maybe at best, accept tours that talk about him. Or, whether the city will find a way to deal with the past and be able to offer the tourists a tour 'from the 1980s to 2010s', in which they also include the other half of the (hi)story, acknowledging and enclosing this as part of who they were, are, and will be.

Epilogue While completing this chapter, a polemic started following an article published in August 2015 by Semana on the commercialization of Pablo Escobar tours (on the website of Despegar.com),[22] which implied formalizing/institutionalizing them as a tourist product. In a discussion on Facebook about this topic,[23] outrage about such tours was found, with similar arguments and fears expressed by informants a few years earlier. Conversely, several contributors did not understand/accept this indignation against tourists and tour operators, pointing clearly out that, while criticizing tourists for having an interest, most locals watch greedily the *narconovelas* on television. Similarly, while criticizing the tourism industry for profiting from this era, Colombian television channels are producing them also for profit, and the city itself gives support to international filmmakers, including for movies on their local anti-heroes.[24]

Notes

1. The worst period of violence of the narco-era is over; homicide rate has fallen, yet there is still violence experienced in the 'comunas'. As Polit Dueñas describes it, 'Although violence in Colombia is anything but over, Medellín is no longer experiencing the extreme situation it did 20 years ago, when Pablo Escobar was alive and urban violence was fundamentally caused by emerging narcos. The endemic forms of violence experienced in Medellín in the 1980s have diminished, but the comunas still are very violent places.' See Polit Dueñas, G. *Narrating Narcos*. Culiacán and Medellín, University of Pittsburgh Press, 2013, p. 176.

2. The concept of 'unwanted past' was coined by Light (2000b). Since then, it has been cited in various publications, such as Young and Kaczmarek (2008) and Balockaite (2012).
3. This is of course different when public policy choses to remember and memorize aspects of their past, in which case tourism can be promoted to participate in this.
4. Such as Light (2000a, b, 2001 on Bucharest, Berlin, and Budapest), Ivanov (2009 on Bulgaria), Balockaite (2012 on Lithuania and Poland), Bagnaresi et al. (2013 on Forli and Predappio), Van Daele (2012 on Obersalzberg, Germany), Vloeberghs (2013 on Sicily); several contributions on places in Latin American in Bilbija, K. and Payne, L.A. (eds; 2011).
5. Notwithstanding the wave of criticisms when the tour was launched, it is still offered by 'Historical Trips' (2015).
6. For more information on Pablo Escobar's life and power, see Salazar (2001) and Cañon (1994). There are also the books written by his right hand, the paid assassin, alias Popeye (Velásquez 2012), by his mistress (Vallejo 2007), and by several of his relatives, such as his brother (and brother-in-crime, Roberto Escobar 2000).
7. Even today entrepreneurship is highly validated in Medellín. In 'Plan de Mercadeo de Medellín, 2006–2016' (Alcaldía de Medellín 2006), we could find a new strategic concept for positioning the city: 'Medellín, the city where creativity flourishes', described as 'Medellín has always been the cradle of recursive people, who driven by their interests in growth, progress and entrepreneurship, found solutions and proposals, which make the city a place where ideas flourish and are projected with great force' (slide 24). Ironically Escobar was very much one of those recursive people.
8. There exist various versions of how he died, whether he was shot by a member of the special police unit or whether he committed suicide in view of his capture.
9. Since this paper is not about this transformation process and its alleged results, we only refer to the way the process has been officially presented, generally in very positive terms.
10. *La Ciudad de Eterna Primavera* is one of Medellín's epithets.
11. Besides the narcotrafficking-related violence, Colombia has known several decades-long armed conflicts.
12. Nevertheless, this is for most tourists not the reason to come to Medellín. The modern transformed city, its people, and climate are among the reasons. For backpackers, the fame as a city to party is also important.
13. http://www.paisaroad.com/tour-pablo-escobar
14. There have circulated other ideas about museums of Pablo Escobar, yet so far none has been realized. In the National Museum of Police History in Bogota, some of his belongings can be found, as well as information about the manhunt for drug criminals such as Pablo Escobar.

15. Public stakeholders: Subsecretaria de Turismo—Alcaldía de Medellín; Oficina de Dirección de Fomento Turístico la Gobernación de Antioquia; Proexport—actually ProColombia.

    Private stakeholders: Medellín Convention & Visitors Bureau; ANATO (Colombian Association of Travel & Tourism Agencies); ASOGUIAN (Association of Guides in Antioquia).
16. An individual guide told us how in one occasion she was prevented to talk about Pablo Escobar, and even denied access at a city event, when she didn't comply. It also appeared in our interviews that some people offering tours related to Pablo Escobar, looking for some institutional help, had not obtained the attention of those institutions. And, among the recommendations of the report realized by UNOCD on narcotourism, we can find:

    > Likewise, it is recommended that all travel agencies are associated with ANATO in order to accredit them and generate a control over those who are responsible to sell the city as a space of sex and drugs, or as the temple of the leader of the Medellín Cartel, Pablo Escobar. (2013, pp. 45–46)

17. The study of UNODC (2013) confirmed the links between drug use and prostitution.
18. Medellín hosted in 2014 UN Habitat's World Urban Forum on the future of cities. During the forum, several organized tours (Medellín Lab Tours) were offered with visits to schools, libraries, parks, transportation infrastructure, and other signs of the transformation (Brodzinsky 2014; Medellín.travel 2014, and personal observations).
19. Some guidelines for Pablo Escobar tours might be desirable.
20. Although at first victims of narcotrafficking were not included—the law only considered and benefited victims of armed conflict, not of organized nor common crime, after 1985, since 2014, through a state council statement, victims of narcotrafficking are considered victims of the armed conflict.
21. The first idea to construct a center of documentation for the memory of the armed conflict dated from 2004. During the consecutive years, a lot of research was realized, and preparations started. Finally the building was inaugurated in December 2012 and in the following year started operating as museum (Museo Casa de la Memoria and INER 2014, pp. 10–11). In July 2015, together with other institutions, Museo Casa de la Memoria initiated the research project 'Medellín, ¡Basta Ya!' in which they want, through the narratives of the victims and citizens, reconstruct the violent past in the city (1980–2013).
22. A platform similar to Booking.com and Expedia.com, yet with a strong presence in Latin America. Semana, 'Polémica por el "Pablo Escobar Tour"', Despegar.com, August 18, 2015, http://www.semana.com/nacion/articulo/polemica-por-el-pablo-escobar-tour-de-despegarcom/439110-3

23. https://www.facebook.com/elespectadorcom/posts/10153590796559066?comment_id=10153591011309066&notif_t=comment_mention
24. http://latino.foxnews.com/latino/entertainment/2015/08/24/tom-cruise-in-colombia-for-cartel-related-movie-meets-with-medellín-mayor/. Referencing to the making of *Mena*, a film with Tom Cruise.

References

Alcaldía de Medellín. (2012). *Plan de Desarrollo Turístico Medellín 2011–2016*. Medellín: Litografía Dinámica.

Bagnaresi, D., Battilani, P., & Bernini, C. (2013, October 9–11). A controversial heritage as cultural tourism product: The resident's perception of the fascist Regime's architecture in Forlì and Predappio, unpublished paper presented at "Post-Conflict, Cultural Heritage and Regional Development: an International Conference", Wageningen.

Balockaite, R. (2012). Coping with the unwanted past in planned socialist towns: Visaginas, Tychy and Nowa Huta. *Slovo, 24*(1), 41–57.

Bilbija, K., & Payne, L. A. (Eds.). (2011). *Accounting for violence. Marketing memory in Latin America*. Durham: Duke University Press.

Cañon, L. (1994). *El Patrón: Vida y Muerte de Pablo Escobar*. Bogota: Planeta.

Dann, G., & Seaton, A. V. (2001). Slavery, contested heritage and thanatourism. *International Journal of Hospitality & Tourism Administration, 2*(3/4), 1–29.

Escobar Gaviria, R. (2000). *Mi hermano Pablo*. Bogota: Quintero Editores.

Foote, K. (1997). *Shadowed ground. America's landscapes of violence and tragedy*. Austin: University of Texas Press.

Giraldo, C., & Muñoz, T. (2010). El perfil del turista extranjero que visitó Medellín en el año 2010. Unpublished document, Colegio Mayor de Antioquia, Medellín.

Ivanov, S. (2009). Opportunities for developing communist heritage tourism in Bulgaria. *Tourism, 2*, 177–192.

Knudsen, B. (2011). Thanatourism: Witnessing difficult pasts. *Tourist Studies, 11*(1), 55–72.

Light, D. (2000a). Gazing on communism: Heritage tourism and post-communist identities in Germany, Hungary and Romania. *Tourism Geographies, 2*(2), 157–176.

Light, D. (2000b). An unwanted past: Contemporary tourism and the heritage of communism in Romania. *International Journal of Heritage Studies, 6*(2), 145–160.

Light, D. (2001). 'Facing the future': Tourism and identity – Building in post-socialist Romania. *Political Geography, 20*(8), 1053–1074.

Macdonald, S. (2006). Undesirable heritage: Fascist material culture and historical consciousness in Nuremberg. *Journal of Heritage Studies, 12*(1), 9–28.

Museo Casa de la Memoria and INER. (2014). *Aunque no estés conmigo*. Medellín: Museo Casa de la Memoria and INER.

Otto, J. E. (2008). Representing communism: Discourses of heritage tourism and economic regeneration in Nowa Huta, Poland. Retrieved from the University of Minnesota Digital Conservancy. http://purl.umn.edu/56305

Poria, Y. (2007). Establishing cooperation between Israel and Poland to save Auschwitz concentration camp: Globalizing the responsibility for the massacre. *International Journal Tourism Policy, 1*(1), 45–57.

Salazar, A. (2001). *La parabola de Pablo. Auge y Caída de un gran capo del narcotráfico*. Bogota: Planeta.

Tunbridge, J. E., & Ashworth, G. J. (1996). *Dissonant heritage: The management of the past as a resource in conflict*. Chichester: J. Wiley.

UNODC. (2013). Estudio Exploratorio Descriptivo de la dinámica delictiva del tráfico de estupefacientes, la trata de personas y la explotación sexual comercial asociada a viajes y turismo en el municipio de Medellín, Colombia, Alcaldía de Medellín y Oficina de las Naciones Unidas contra la Droga y el Delito.

Vallejo, V. (2007). *Amando a Pablo, odiando a Escobar*. Mexico: Random House Mondadori.

Van Daele, C. (2012). Toerisme op een voormalige nazi-locatie: de controverses rond de Obersalzberg (Tourism on a former Nazi location: The controversies surrounding the Obersalzberg). Unpublished Master thesis to obtain the title of Master in Tourism. KULeuven, Belgium.

Velásquez, J. (2012). *Sobreviviendo a Pablo Escobar: "Popeye" el sicario, 23 años y 3 meses de cárcel*. Bogota: Ediciones DIPON.

Vloeberghs, S. (2013). Anti-maffiatours van Addiopizzo Travel in Sicilië: 'Dark Tourism' en de herinneringsmarkt (Anti-mafia tours of Addiopizzo Travel in Sicily: Dark tourism and the memory market), unpublished master thesis to obtain the title of Master in Tourism, Belgium.

Wielde Heidelberg, B. A. (2015). Managing ghosts: Exploring local government involvement in dark tourism. *Journal of Heritage Tourism, 10*(1), 74–90.

Young, C., & Kaczmarek, S. (2008). The socialist past and Postsocialist urban identity in central and Eastern Europe: The case of Lódz, Poland. *European Urban and Regional Studies, 15*(1), 53–70.

Websites

Alcaldía de Medellín. (2006). Plan de Mercadeo de Medellín 2006–2016. Resumen ejecutivo (202 slides). http://www.powershow.com/view1/283d31-ZDc1Z/Presentacin_Licitacin_Plan_de_Mercadeo_de_Medelln_powerpoint_ppt_presentation

Alford, H. (2013). I just got back from Medellín!. http://www.nytimes.com/2013/01/20/travel/i-just-got-back-from-medellín.html?_r=1. Published in *New York Times*, January 18, 2013.

Arsenault, C. (2014). Pablo Escobar tours entice Colombia visitors. http://www.aljazeera.com/indepth/features/2014/06/pablo-escobar-tours-entice-colombia-visitors-201463104320799241.html. Published in *Aljazeera*, June 7, 2014.

Baker, V. (2011). In Pablo Escobar's footsteps. http://www.theguardian.com/travel/2011/sep/13/pablo-escobar-tour-medellín-colombia. Published in *The Guardian*, September 13, 2011.

Brodzinsky, S. (2014). From murder capital to model city: Is Medellín's miracle show or substance? http://www.theguardian.com/cities/2014/apr/17/medellín-murder-capital-to-model-city-miracle-un-world-urban-forum. Published in *The Guardian*, April 17, 2014.

Connolly, K. (2010). Germany's first Hitler exhibition opens in nervous Berlin museum. http://www.theguardian.com/world/2010/oct/14/germany-first-hitler-exhibition-opens. Published in *The Guardian*, October 14, 2010.

Crossland, D. (2010). An opportunity missed: The failure of Berlin's Hitler exhibition to break new ground. http://www.spiegel.de/international/germany/an-opportunity-missed-the-failure-of-berlin-s-hitler-exhibition-to-break-new-ground-a-723784.html. Published in *Spiegel*, October 18, 2010.

Historical Trips. (2015). The face of evil: The rise and fall of the Third Reich. http://www.historicaltrips.com/tour/17/Germany/The-Face-of-Evil.html

Inter-American Commission on Human Rights. (1993). Second Report on the Situation of Human Rights in Colombia. Chapter II The violence Phenomenon. http://www.cidh.org/countryrep/colombia93eng/chap.2.htm. Organization of American States – OEA/Ser.L/V/II.84 -Doc. 39 rev. Published October 14, 1993 Original: Spanish.

Käufer, T. (2013). Pablo-Escobar-tour in Medellín: Souvenir mit Drogenbaron. http://www.spiegel.de/reise/staedte/pablo-escobar-tour-in-medellín-souvenir-mit-drogenbaron-a-936814.html#spRedirectedFrom=www&referrrer=%20 http://m.spiegel.de/reise/staedte/a-936814.html. Published in *Spiegel*, December 3, 2013.

Medellín.travel. (2014). Tourists Plans WUF7 2014 http://www.otroviaje.com/?index.php&vp=1&ver=1&id=4325&micro2=otroviaje&ingles=true

Mincomercio Industria y Turismo. (2007–2015). Estadísticas de turismo. http://www.mincit.gov.co/publicaciones.php?id=16590

Mudie, K. (2011). Having a Nazi time, wish you were here – Tourists to visit Hitler's haunts. http://www.dailystar.co.uk/posts/view/171171. Published in *Daily Star*, January 10, 2011.

Nayer, M. (2011). British tour company criticized for offering 'Hitler Tour' around Germany. http://gadling.com/2011/01/10/hilter-tour-around-germany/3/. Published in *Gadling*, January 10, 2011.

Paterson, T. (2010). Hitler exhibition breaks Germany's last taboo. http://www.independent.co.uk/arts-entertainment/art/news/hitler-exhibition-breaks-germanys-last-taboo-2106121.html. Published in *The Independent*, October 14, 2010.

Reaves, J. (2010). Capone's legacy endures, to Chicago dismay. http://www.nytimes.com/2010/04/23/us/23cnccapone.html. Published in *The New York Times*, April 22, 2010.

Rinne, J. D. (2010). Controversy: Hitler exhibit now open in Berlin. http://www.budgettravel.com/blog/controversy-hitler-exhibit-now-open-in-berlin,11533/. Published in *Budget Travel*, November 10, 2010.

Wells, M. (2011). Medellín's Pablo Escobar tours cause discomfort with authorities. http://colombiareports.com/medellíns-pablo-escobar-tours-cause-discomfort-with-authorities/. Published in *Colombia Reports*, December 21, 2011.

13

Tourism Mobilities, Spectralities, and the Hauntings of Chernobyl

Kevin Hannam and Ganna Yankovska

> *Interviewer: Why do you think so many tourists are visiting Chernobyl Zone? Respondent: I don't know; maybe to see our city, see how it was before, understand or explore the difference. It was so beautiful and now it's just a ghost-city. Interview: November, 2015.*

Introduction

The literature on dark tourism has sought to understand tourist's engagement with a range of sites that are associated with various traumatic events. Indeed, in an earlier chapter we interpreted the Chernobyl site from the perspective of dark and toxic tourism (Yankovska and Hannam 2014). A key problem with much of the literature on dark and toxic tourism is that it has a tendency to conceptualise such sites as being fixed or static when they are open to multiple interpretations—interpretations which are often highly fluid and mobile. This certainly becomes the case when we consider people's memories of such sites. Indeed, the dynamic role of memory can be traced back to the earlier

K. Hannam (✉)
Edinburgh Napier University, Edinburgh, UK

G. Yankovska
Independent Researcher, Sunderland, UK

work of Bartlett (1932: 213) who argued that memories are influenced by the presence of others and by the social and cultural worlds we inhabit:

> [r]emembering is not the re-excitation of innumerable fixed, lifeless and fragmentary traces. It is an imaginative reconstruction, or construction, built out of the relation of our attitude towards a whole active mass of organized past reactions or experience.

In this chapter, we wish to more explicitly examine how a mobilities perspective could better help us to understand the attraction of dark tourism sites through a focus on memories of landscapes and the ways in which these may lead to a degree of "hauntedness" or spectrality—indeed in the opening quotation above Chernobyl is referred to as a *ghost-city* by a former resident (also see Chap. 24). Mobilities research draws upon and develops post-humanistic theory in an attempt to create innovative ways of understanding the ways in which human subjects are decentred by the blurring of the boundaries between the human and non-human. This chapter thus reconceptualises the human-non-human divide in terms of dark tourism landscapes. We begin by outlining some of the key aspects of what has become known as tourism mobilities (Sheller and Urry 2004; Rickly et al. 2016). We then go on to consider work which has emphasised the "spectral" nature of landscapes which have been understood in terms of the ways in which these can be "haunted" by past and present memories of former residents and tourists (also see Chap. 19). Finally, we examine the example of Chernobyl to flesh out our theoretical arguments.

Tourism Mobilities

A mobilities approach to tourism and leisure encourages us to think beyond the mobilities of tourists to ways in which tourism and leisure experiences bring other mobilities into sync, or disorder, and as a result reconceptualises social theory. In so doing, mobilities studies advances an agenda that thinks relationally about the politics that hinder, encourage, regulate, and inform mobilities at various scales, from the microbiological to the bodily to the national, as well as the mobility of information and non-human objects. Researching leisure and tourism mobilities involves an understanding of complex combinations of movement and stillness, realities and fantasies, play, and work (Sheller and Urry 2004; Hannam et al. 2014). In short, proponents of the mobilities paradigm argue that the concept of mobilities is concerned with mapping and understanding both the large-scale movements of people, objects, capital, and information across the world, connected with more local processes of daily transportation, movement through public space, and the travel of material things within everyday life simultaneously (Hannam et al. 2006). Studies of leisure and tourism mobilities have examined the experience of the different modes of travel that tourists undertake, seeing these modes in part as forms of material and sociable dwelling-in-motion, dwelling-in-tourism (Obrador 2003), places of and for various activities. These "activities" can include specific forms of leisure, work, or simply information-gathering, but almost always involve being connected, maintaining a moving presence with others that holds the potential for many different convergences or divergences of global and local physical presence (Hannam et al. 2006, 2014).

Non-representational theory, Thrift (1997: 126–127) argues, is about "practices, mundane everyday practices, that shape the conduct of human beings toward others and themselves at particular sites." Such a theoretical position sought to address the ways in which ordinary people incorporate "the skills and knowledges they get from being embodied beings" (Thrift 1997: 127). Drawing upon this insight, in tourism studies it has thus been frequently argued that we need to move beyond simply analysing the social construction of practices to develop a more informed theoretical analysis of the everyday embodiment and performances of tourism (Coleman and Crang 2002). Much of this work has been centred on notions of tourists' agency and has in turn developed ideas concerned with the body in tourism (Jokinen and Veijola 1994; Obrador 2003). This has subsequently led to a more in depth discussion of the various sensuous and morally loaded encounters of hosts and guests sharing food, dancing and other forms of hospitality as well as forming new relationships (Mostafanezhad and Hannam 2014).

Non-representational theory has, however, been criticised for its overemphasis on the embodied nature of tourism encounters. Hence, "more than representational theory" has been put forward, as a way of analysing the coupling of representations to the non-representational embodied practices discussed above through the notion of "performativity" (Adey 2010). The concept of performativity is an attempt to "find a more embodied way of rethinking the relationships between determining social structures and personal agency" (Nash 2000: 654). Nash (2000: 655) further argued that the notion of performativity, "is concerned with practices through which we become 'subjects' decentered, affective, but embodied, relational, expressive and involved with others and objects in a world continually in process. The emphasis is on practices that cannot adequately be spoken of, that words can-not capture, that texts can-not convey – on forms of experience and movement that are not only or never cognitive." This is a particularly important point that Nash (2000) raises for work in the dark tourism research area, as many of the emotions felt by tourists at such sites often "cannot adequately be spoken of." There is, we argue, a fundamental problem in representing in academic language the frequently highly emotive experiences of tourists at dark tourism sites.

The notion of performativity is thus concerned with the ways in which people know the world without knowing it, the multisensual practices and experiences of everyday life and is central to mobilities research (Hannam 2006). As Adey (2010: 149) notes: "[t]his is an approach which is not limited to representational thinking and feeling, but a different sort of thinking-feeling altogether. It is a recognition that mobilities … involve various combinations of thought, action, feeling and articulation." Adey (2010: 149) draws upon the work of Tim Ingold (2004) who proposes a rethinking of practices of walking as a combination of both "thought and unthought." Macpherson (2010: 1) further emphasises the links between human bodies and the landscapes that they inhabit as being "in a constant process of 'becoming.'" A post-humanistic mobilities approach thus aims to explore new modes of being and becoming in the contemporary world. In light of this, post-humanistic geographers have challenged the singular model of the human subject and have attempted to reconceptualise the blurring boundaries between humans and non-human things that may not necessarily be known cognitively but may be *affective* nonetheless (Castree and Nash 2006; Lorimer 2009; Danby and Hannam 2016). We can develop this further by examining traumatic memories and the development of what have been terms "spectro-geographies."

Traumatic Memories and Spectrality

Dark tourism research has focused on the active contestation of performances of collective memories implicitly and/or explicitly (see, e.g. Mowatt and Chancellor 2011; Stone 2012; Podoshen 2013; Kidron 2013). Trauma as a cultural process is also closely connected with the formation of collective memories. Cultural trauma may affect a whole social group and does not need to be experienced by every group member. Events may not be traumatic by themselves but they are attributed a traumatic meaning collectively (Alexander 2004; Eyerman 2004; Ashworth 2008). Ferron and Massa (2014: 23) have argued that "studying how collective memories are formed, particularly in the case of trauma, is important because they persist for entire generations and they play a crucial social role, in that the interaction of the cultural elements involved can influence attitudes not only toward the past but also toward the present of current societies." Traumatic events, nevertheless, can be conceptualised as a fundamental "disruption" of social life in some form (Birtchnell and Büscher 2011). Philosophically, traumatic events can also be considered as the "intrusion of something new which remains unacceptable for the predominant view" (Zizek 2014: 77).

In terms of understanding the collective memories of traumatic events, empirical research has focused on how such events can produce widespread collective mourning, commemorative ceremonies as well as the construction of physical monuments as sites of remembrance (Johnson 1995; Knox 2006). Whilst monuments are usually symbols of only one person or one ideal, war memorials and other landscapes such as cemeteries, commemorate many people or whole communities (Heffernan 1995). War memorials can be seen as ways in which to commemorate those men and women who gave their lives for others as well as the ideals of democracy, freedom and justice that attach to particular military campaigns (Hannam and Knox 2010). Memorials and the events associated with them may serve the needs of a community in the present connected to its collective identity in order to overcome a past trauma (Johnson 1995). However, trauma itself has been critically reconceptualised as being applied to whole generations rather than just present communities (Hodgkin and Radstone 2003).

More critically, Legg (2005) has drawn attention to the ways in which such traumatic remembering is socially contested and further suggests that trauma should be understood as a collective social, political, and aesthetic condition where human agency becomes irrecoverable. Legg (2005) emphasises the embodied power relations in any form of remembering: that we remember through our bodily actions which combine moments of stillness and movement. As Hebbert (2005: 581) asserts, aspects of "memory and identity are rooted in bodily experiences of being and moving in material space." Furthermore, Edensor (2005: 829) begins his paper examining the ghosts of industrial ruins by invoking Michel De Certeau (1984: 108) who argues that places are "haunted by many different spirits, spirits one can 'invoke' or not", for "haunted places are the only ones people can live in" (1984: 108). Edensor (2005: 929) argues that "the urge to seek out the ghosts of places is bound up with the politics of remembering the past and, more specifically, with the spatialisation of memory and how memory is sought, articulated, and inscribed upon space."

Such aspects have been developed further in terms of the notion of spectral geographies by Maddern and Adey (2008) who "suggest that a careful attunement to the ghostly, spectral and the absent, can be a particularly powerful and emancipatory way of dealing with a number of problematics central to contemporary geographical thought" (Maddern and Adey 2008: 291). The problems they refer to are our increasing subjection to mediatised images of death and unexpected events that appear beyond the real. They further note a concern with "the just perceptible, the barely there, the nagging presence of an absence in a variety of spaces" (Maddern and Adey 2008: 292) that have been the mainstay of dark tourism research. However, they note that this has been under-theorised and that the concept of spectrality needs to be understood as not just a narrative, metaphorical, or allegorical device but as central to the development of a "more-than-representational" theoretical framework as discussed above.

Maddern and Adey (2008) argue that spectrality disrupts our linear sense of temporality in terms of how the ghostly confounds settled orders of past and present and linear conceptualisations of time (Wylie 2007) such that "[s]paces and times are folded, allowing distant presences, events, people and things to become rather more intimate" (Maddern and Adey 2008: 292). They explain that the "figure of the ghost is often used as a means of apprehending that which we cannot explain, do not expect, understand, or struggle to represent" (Maddern and Adey 2008: 292–293) such that "modes of experiencing uncanny agencies, unforeseen events and a morphology of almost there-ness" are then revealed. As Edensor (2005) has argued the mobilities of urban landscapes leave behind "traces of its previous form, social life, inhabitants, politics, ways of thinking and being, and modes of experience" which may subsequently translate into new material affordances for those living in these spaces haunted by past events. We can explore this further by examining the landscapes of one particular site of dark tourism, namely Chernobyl.

Mobilities and Memories at Chernobyl

The name "Chernobyl" has become a synonym for one of the worst nuclear accidents and technological disasters of all times. The nuclear accident at the Chernobyl power station occurred on 26 April 1986 as an accident during an experiment allegedly due to inexperienced staff and a weak security backup system (for a detailed review see Perez 2009). As a result, the roof of the reactor came off due to an explosion, emitting radioactive material which soon turned into a radioactive cloud spreading over Ukraine, Russia, Belarus, and most of Europe. The immediate result was significant ecological harm due to the spread of radioactive ions in the environment, 400 times more than the Hiroshima and Nagasaki nuclear bombs. Within a few days' hundreds of thousands of people were evacuated from the most contaminated areas around the Chernobyl (UNDP 2002). Most of the evacuees were residents from the nearest town to Chernobyl, Pripyat, a model Soviet town with many leisure facilities which later became known as a "ghost town." The residents were misinformed by the Soviet Government about the accident and were promised to be allowed to return within a few days and hence left all their personal belonging in their homes but were not allowed to return once the scale of the disaster was recognised. The negative health impacts (cancer, leukaemia, circulatory diseases, and other chronic diseases) have so far claimed 600,000 lives of people in the contaminated zones (International Atomic Energy Agency 2006). The most radioactively contaminated area around the Chernobyl power plant was officially designated as The Chernobyl Nuclear Power Plant Zone of Alienation, known as the "Chernobyl Exclusion Zone" or the "Zone," located in the northern territory of Ukraine. The exclusion zone extends approximately 30 km in radius from the Chernobyl nuclear reactor and covers around 2600 km^2 of the Ukrainian mainland. It includes the most visited tourist places of Chernobyl city, the town of Pripyat and roughly 180 villages that were evacuated and placed under the military control due to the disaster.

The first tourists in Chernobyl appeared in the mid-1990s, after the level of radiation had significantly fallen (Steshyn and Cots 2006). At this time, "Chernobylinterinform" was the only legal tourism organisation allowed to arrange excursions to the Zone. Initially, the "radioactive" tourist destination was especially popular among foreign tourists from the United States and Western Europe. The Chernobyl nuclear zone is now controlled by the Ukrainian Ministry of Internal Affairs and entry to the Zone is only permitted to officials and a short stay can also be arranged on a special request for tourists (Ministry of Emergencies 2011). Some areas in and around Chernobyl still have high radiation levels and all tourists must follow an official tourist guide and adhere to the health and safety requirements. According to the head of the Administration of the exclusion zone and the zone of absolute resettlement officially the visitors of the Zone can be classified into three categories; foreign scientists, Ukrainian and foreign journalists, and former residents of the territory visiting the remains of their homes and graves of relatives and friends (Golovata 2010). However, as Phillips and Ostaszewski (2012: 127) note: "[l]ax surveillance and a lack of security, along with shoddy and broken-down fencing in places around the zone's perimeter, mean that the zone of alienation has very porous borders. Wildlife and people roam in and out. In short, the area has never truly been an 'exclusion zone.'"

Nevertheless, in recent years, Chernobyl has gone through an increase in the number of visitors mainly for tourism activities but also as former residents return to the site to visit their former homes. Recent academic work has analysed photographic representations of Chernobyl in terms of the anxieties that these may suggest in terms of its symbolism for industrial decline (Dobraszczyk 2010), the postmodern sublime (Goatcher and Brunsden 2011) toxic tourism (Yankovska and Hannam 2014) and as a heterotopian space (Stone 2013). Indeed, Stone (2013: 91) asserts that, "Chernobyl is a heterotopia that allows us to gaze upon a post-apocalyptic world, in which the familiar and uncanny collide."

This sense of the uncanny is one which we wish to further explore in this chapter in terms of the mobilities and memories of Chernobyl through the reflections of some of the former residents as well as photographic evidence of the hauntedness that has been co-constructed in the landscapes of Chernobyl by visitors. The notion of the uncanny combines the familiar with the strange—where things that are hidden and secret become visible (Cixous 1976) to the tourists' gaze. Spaces that appear safe and secure but that are simultaneously "secret, obscure and inaccessible, dangerous and full of terrors" (Vidler 1999: 32 cited in Edensor 2005: 835).

Dark tourism mobilities are on the one hand practiced by former residents of the Chernobyl Exclusion Zone. One former resident reflected on his first visit back to Chernobyl as follows:

> When we came to Chernobyl first time it was easier, we took 39 people from Kolomiya, on the way we also picked up 10 people from Rivne city another 10 people from Kiev. We travelled over 1000 Km to reach our destination. All of us seemed to have good spirits, enjoyed the long journey and sang songs etc. until we got to the entry check post to Chernobyl. I felt the same tightness in my head and had flashbacks of the tragedy all over again… the whole bus was dead quiet. (Interview, November 2015)

This respondent conveys both the sense of memory in terms of flashbacks but also the way in which this affected those travelling back to visit and how this led to an embodied stillness—dead quiet.

Another former resident compared the revisit to going to a cemetery:

> The other people just look at it but when we see it we are living with it and we relive the horror each time we come back and see our land. It is like being on the cemetery where your close relatives are buried. If the same place is visited by a foreign person, he [or she] will never feel the same but if you are a native you will start remembering everything. (Interview, November 2015)

But still he demonstrates the feeling of horror which greets the former residents when they return which is also echoed by another former resident who emphasised how his heart aches and how tourists could not understand resident's experiences.

> Tourists are coming just because of their curiosity, they didn't lose anything, and they didn't go through the same pain in their life, like we did. When I go to my native city, my heart aches and I feel so hurt about what happened with my city. The tourists will never be able to understand the pain and the heartache of residents of the Zone; they can never comprehend our experience. (Interview, November 2015)

While the respondent above felt that tourists could not understand the former resident's experiences, another respondent reflected that it was a learning experience for tourists:

> The experience was tragic for us. Some young tourists travel there almost every year. A boy who was sitting with me in the bus, travelled to Chernobyl eight times already. Tourists go there because of a great curiosity. They learn the history of the place in detail. They explore the history of the accident as well. We (previous residents) only look for something that is attached in our memory, something we know already. We don't look for new things there. (Interview, November 2015)

Nevertheless, he looks for memories in his mobilities and further noted that: "I have only one physical memory left – a little liquidator pass, which was saying 'EVERYWHERE'. This pass allowed us the access to go everywhere in the Chernobyl Zone" (Interview, November 2015).

For tourists though the mobilities experienced are somewhat less embodied and more visual. Although all visitors pass through body check points to monitor radiation, most are concerned with taking photographs as visual mementos of having been there and having seen the ghostly landscapes of

Plate 13.1 Abandoned house (Photo Source: Author)

Chernobyl. Plates 13.1 and 13.2 show the empty landscapes of Chernobyl. These photographs highlight the haunted and uncanny aspects of the Chernobyl landscapes. These images are familiar in the sense we can recognise them as leisure facilities. On the other hand, they belong to ghosts— there are no living people using them and as such they are haunted by past memories from former residents which tourists attempt to understand but are unable to fully embody or comprehend.

However, these sites are not static but are subject to change as another respondent argued:

Plate 13.2 Swimming pool (Photo Source: Author)

We were following a route where the exposure to the radiation was minimum. We saw this beautiful building which looked good as new, it used to be a hospital in the old days. This was not an ordinary hospital, it was a child hospital with restaurants and pool facility. Things in the city of Pripyat change all the time as the security guards continue to steal the electrical fittings and anything that could be stripped off. They don't seem to care about the radiation and the affect it could have on people who would use the stolen things (Interview, November 2015).

Thus despite the risks, the ghosts of Chernobyl are still being recycled through both memories and material practices.

Conclusion

Contemporary tourism mobilities are as much about the fluidity of intangible memories as the tangible movement of material souvenirs. This chapter has examined haunted landscapes of Chernobyl. Former resident's memories are shaped by the trauma of the past, rewritten through attempts at pilgrimage and return in the present and contested through tourism practices which look towards the future through complex temporal interpretations of the ruins of the Chernobyl landscape (Hannam and Yankovska 2016). For tourists, the landscapes convey the ghosts of mundane leisure experiences, uncanny spaces which are difficult to comprehend but which have an affect nonetheless in disturbing the temporal and spatial ordering of tourism.

References

Adey, P. (2010). *Mobility*. London: Routledge.

Alexander, J. C. (2004). Toward a theory of cultural trauma. In J. C. Alexander, R. Eyerman, & B. Giesen (Eds.), *Cultural trauma and collective identity* (pp. 1–29). Berkeley: University of California Press.

Ashworth, G. J. (2008). The memorialization of violence and tragedy: Human trauma as heritage. In B. Graham & P. Howard (Eds.), *The Ashgate research companion to heritage and identity* (pp. 231–244). Aldershot: Ashgate.

Bartlett, F. C. (1932). *Remembering: A study in experimental and social psychology*. Cambridge: Cambridge University Press.

Birtchnell, T., & Büscher, M. (2011). Stranded: An eruption of disruption. *Mobilities, 6*(1), 1–9.

Castree, N., & Nash, C. (2006). Editorial: Post-human geographies. *Social & Cultural Geography, 7*(4), 501–504.

Coleman, S., & Crang, M. (Eds.). (2002). *Tourism: Between place and performance*. Oxford: Berghahn.

Danby, P., & Hannam, K. (2016). Entrainment: Human-equine leisure mobilities. In J. Rickly, M. Mostafanezhad, & K. Hannam (Eds.), *Tourism and leisure mobilities*. London: Routledge.

De Certeau, M. (1984). *The practice of everyday life*. Berkeley: University of California Press.

Dobraszczyk, P. (2010). Petrified ruin: Chernobyl, Pripyat and the death of the city. *City: Analysis of Urban Trends, Culture, Theory, Policy, Action, 14*(4), 370–389.

Edensor, T. (2005). The ghosts of industrial ruins: Ordering and disordering memory in excessive space. *Environment and Planning D: Society and Space, 23*, 829–849.

Eyerman, R. (2004). Cultural trauma: Slavery and the formation of African American identity. In J. C. Alexander, R. Eyerman, & B. Giesen (Eds.), *Cultural trauma and collective identity* (pp. 61–111). Berkeley: University of California Press.

Ferron, M., & Massa, P. (2014). Beyond the encyclopedia: Collective memories in Wikipedia. *Memory Studies, 7*(1), 22–45.

Goatcher, J., & Brunsden, V. (2011). Chernobyl and the sublime tourist. *Tourist Studies, 11*(2), 115–137.

Golovata, L. (2010). Chornobyl Stalkers (in Ukrainian; «Чернобильські Сталкери»). Zaxid News. Available at: http://zaxid.net/home/showSingleNews.do?chornobilski_stalkeri&objectId=1101343. Accessed 24 Apr 2013.

Hannam, K. (2006). Tourism and development III: Performance, performativities and mobilities. *Progress in Development Studies, 6*(3), 243–249.

Hannam, K., & Knox, D. (2010). *Understanding tourism*. London: Sage.

Hannam, K., & Yankovska, A. (2016). You can't go home again – Only visit: Memory, trauma and tourism at Chernobyl. In S. Marschall (Ed.), *Tourism and memories of home*. Clevedon: Channel View.

Hannam, K., Sheller, M., & Urry, J. (2006). Editorial: Mobilities, immobilities and moorings. *Mobilities, 1*(1), 1–22.

Hannam, K., Butler, G., & Paris, C. (2014). Developments and key concepts in tourism mobilities. *Annals of Tourism Research, 44*(1), 171–185.

Hebbert, M. (2005). The street as locus of collective memory. *Environment and Planning D: Society and Space, 23*, 581–596.

Heffernan, M. (1995). For ever England: The Western front and the politics of remembrance in Britain. *Ecumene, 2*, 293–323.

Hodgkin, K., & Radstone, S. (2003). Remembering suffering: Trauma and history; introduction. In S. Radstone (Ed.), *Contested pasts: The politics of memory* (pp. 97–107). London: Routledge.

Ingold, T. (2004). Culture on the ground – The world perceived through the feet. *Journal of Material Culture, 9*, 315–340.

International Atomic Energy Agency. (2006). *Chernobyl's legacy: Health, environmental and Socio-economic impacts and recommendation to the governments of Belarus, the Russian Federation and Ukraine. The Chernobyl forum 2003–2005*. Vienna: International Atomic Energy Agency. Available at: http://www.iaea.org/Publications/Booklets/Chernobyl/chernobyl.pdf. Accessed 10 May 2012.

Johnson, N. (1995). Cast in stone: Monuments, geography, and nationalism. *Environment and Planning D: Society and Space, 13*, 51–65.

Jokinen, E., & Veijola, S. (1994). The body in tourism. *Theory, Culture & Society, 11*(3), 125–151.

Kidron, C. (2013). Being there together: Dark family tourism and the emotive experience of co-presence in the holocaust past. *Annals of Tourism Research, 41*, 175–194.

Knox, D. (2006). The sacralised landscapes of Glencoe: From massacre to mass tourism, and back again. *International Journal of Tourism Research, 8*(3), 185–197.

Legg, S. (2005). Contesting and surviving memory: Space, nation, and nostalgia in Les Lieux de Memoire. *Environment and Planning D: Society and Space, 23,* 481–504.

Lorimer, J. (2009). Post-humanism/Post-humanistic Geographies. *International encyclopedia of human geographies* (pp. 344–354). Oxford: Elsevier.

Macpherson, H. (2010). Non-representational approaches to body-landscape relations. *Geography Compass, 4*(1), 1–13.

Maddern, J., & Adey, P. (2008). Editorial: Spectro-geographies. *Cultural Geographies, 15,* 291–295.

Ministry of Emergencies. (2011). Procedure of visiting of the exclusion zone. State agency of Ukraine. Available at: http://dazv.gov.ua/en/index.php?option=com_content&view=article&id=184:order-moe-of-ukraine-on-november-2-2011-1157-approving-the-visiting-of-the-exclusion-zone-and-zone-of-unconditional-mandatory-resettlement&catid=80:normativno-pravov-akti-z-pitan-scho-nalejat-do-kompetenc-dazv&Itemid=156. Accessed 12 Jun 2012.

Mostafanezhad, M., & Hannam, K. (Eds.). (2014). *Moral encounters in tourism.* Farnham: Ashgate.

Nash, C. (2000). Performativity in practice: Some recent work in cultural geography. *Progress in Human Geography, 24*(4), 653–664.

Obrador, P. (2003). Being-on-holiday: Tourist dwelling, bodies and place. *Tourist Studies, 3*(1), 47–66.

Perez, J. R. (2009). Uncomfortable heritage & dark tourism at Chernobyl. In S. Merill & L. Schmidt (Eds.), *A reader in uncomfortable heritage and dark tourism.* Cottbus: Brandenburg University of Technology.

Phillips, S., & Ostaszewski, S. (2012). An illustrated guide to the post-catastrophe future. *The Anthropology of East Europe Review, 30*(1), 127–140.

Podoshen, J. (2013). Dark tourism motivations: Simulation, emotional contagion and topographic comparison. *Tourism Management, 35,* 263–271.

Rickly, J., Mostafanezhad, M., & Hannam, K. (Eds.). (2016). *Tourism and leisure mobilities.* London: Routledge.

Sheller, M., & Urry, J. (Eds.). (2004). *Tourism mobilities: Places to play, places in play.* London: Routledge.

Steshyn, D., & Cots, E. (2006). The Komsomolska Pravda. Available from: http://www.kp.ru/daily/23696/52367/. Accessed 20 May 2012.

Stone, P. R. (2012). Dark tourism and significant other death: Towards a model of mortality mediation. *Annals of Tourism Research, 39*(3), 1565–1587.

Stone, P. R. (2013). Dark tourism, heterotopias and post-apocalyptic places: The case of Chernobyl. In L. White & E. Frew (Eds.), *Dark tourism and place identity: Managing and interpreting dark places* (pp. 79–93). London: Routledge.

UNDP, United Nations Development Program. (2002). The human consequences of the Chernobyl nuclear accident: A strategy for recovery Chernobyl Report-Final. Commissioned by UNDP and UNICEF. Available at: http://www.unicef.org/newsline/chernobylreport.pdf. Accessed 15 Jun 2012.

Yankovska, G., & Hannam, K. (2014). Dark and toxic tourism in the Chernobyl exclusion zone. *Current Issues in Tourism, 17*(10), 929–939.

Zizek, S. (2014). *Event: Philosophy in transit.* Harmondsworth: Penguin.

14

Disasters and Disaster Tourism: The Role of the Media

Richard Sharpley and Daniel Wright

Introduction

The news media love a disaster (Tarlow 2011). Even in a world of 24-hour news channels, online news sites, and social media, it is impossible to report all potentially newsworthy events and, as consequence, some types of event take precedence over or are given greater coverage than others. Thus, it is perhaps not surprising that, as Miller and Albert (2015) note, much 'past research has focused almost exclusively on identifying the most important predictors of coverage across many media types, including newsprint, network television news, Internet news sources, Twitter, and Facebook'. It is also not surprising that such research has revealed that, typically, events that involve large-scale death and suffering, such as disasters, will be given prominence over other stories; 'Disasters are unusual, dramatic, and often have great impact upon people's lives. This combination makes disasters newsworthy and creates the expectation that news outlets, which are driven by commercial imperatives, will report them' (van Belle 2000: 50). In other words, as Cockburn (2011) observes, 'the media generally assume that news of war, crime and natural disasters will always win an audience', hence the well-known adage in journalism—'if it bleeds, it leads'.

It has long been recognised that the media report disasters in a variety of ways (Houston et al. 2012; Quarantelli 1990) and that such reporting may

---

R. Sharpley (✉) • D. Wright
University of Central Lancashire, Preston, UK

© The Author(s) 2018
P. R. Stone et al. (eds.), *The Palgrave Handbook of Dark Tourism Studies*,
https://doi.org/10.1057/978-1-137-47566-4_14

have both positive and negative outcomes (Wenger 1985). That is, media reporting of disasters may on the one hand be beneficial in terms of, for example, raising public awareness of 'unknown' disasters, the Ethiopian famine in the 1980s being an oft-cited example (Franks 2013), and, in particular, supporting the work of aid agencies in raising funds for disaster relief (Kalcsics 2011). The Western media's reporting of the Indian Ocean tsunami in 2004, for example, focusing as it did on death and injury among Western tourists, arguably had a direct influence on the unusually high level of relief aid donated to such a disaster (Sharpley 2005). On the other hand, research has also frequently demonstrated that 'contrasts … exist between the realities associated with disaster responses and myths concerning disaster behaviour' (Tierney et al. 2006). In other words, it has been consistently found that, at least in the USA where the majority of such work has been undertaken, the media frequently perpetuate erroneous beliefs among the general public and others about people's behaviours following a disaster (Scanlon 1998, 2011). Moreover, many such myths are created by the media industry more generally; books and films, for example, 'have used the crucible of disaster as a setting for the espousal of tales of tragedy, chaos, suffering, love, and courage acted out by a menagerie of heroes, villains, fools, cowards, and scoundrels' (Wenger 1985: 2), such tales being the source of myths that persist both in disaster reporting and public conscientiousness. As a consequence, an unrealistic and typically negative picture is painted with regard to the outcomes of a disaster, with significant implications for both the public's understanding of disasters and, perhaps more significantly, those affected by them.

Irrespective of how they report them, however, the media play a fundamental role in informing the general public of the occurrence of disasters, thereby stimulating a specific manifestation of dark tourism, namely, disaster tourism. In other words, once a disaster has been publicised, it becomes an attraction to those who, for whatever reason, wish to travel to gaze upon it (Rojek 1997). For example, as Sharpley (2009) relates, in September 1934, when the S.S. Morro Castle, a luxury liner that sailed regularly between New York and Cuba, caught fire and subsequently drifted to the shore at Asbury, New Jersey, many thousands of people travelled to witness the smouldering wreck with the remains of many who had died still on board. Indeed, more than a quarter of a million people—'spurred on by newspaper and radio reports' (Sharpley 2009: 4)—took advantage of special excursion train fares to visit the site (Hegeman 2000). Similarly, reports of the Lockerbie disaster in December 1988, when Pan Am 103 was blown up over the Scottish town, resulted in the police having to close roads to prevent sight-seers gaining access to the crash site (http://plane-truth.com/Aoude/geocities/victim2.html).

Equally, the media may play a positive role in discouraging people to visit disaster areas or the sites of other 'dark' events. In 2002, for example, newspapers reported an appeal by the people of Soham in the UK, where two young schoolgirls had been murdered, 'for an end to the "grief tourism" that [was] bringing tens of thousands of visitors to their town' (O'Neill 2002), whilst in December 2015 and again in the UK, the media repeated the local police force's request for people not to visit the city of York to view the major floods that were affecting the city (YorkMix 2015).

Either way, the very fact that the media report on a disaster means that, as long as people have access to the site, it is likely to become a dark tourism attraction. That is, as experience has long shown, people are drawn to places of death, disaster, and tragedy, whether recent or historical, to view the site or representations/memorials of the event. Moreover, increasing academic attention has been paid over the last two decades to the phenomenon of dark tourism in general (e.g., Johnston and Mandelartz 2015; Lennon and Foley 2000; Sharpley and Stone 2009; Stone 2013), including disasters (Coats and Ferguson 2013; Gould and Lewis 2007) and motives for participating in dark tourism in particular (e.g., Isaac and Çakmak 2014; Raine 2013; Seaton 1996). However, few if any attempts have been made to explore the role of the media, specifically the news media, in dark tourism and, specifically, tourism to places of disaster. In other words, although the media inevitably report disasters, the manner in which they influence subsequent (dark) tourism to disaster sites has yet to benefit from academic scrutiny. Do tourists travel to disaster sites with particular preconceptions of what they will encounter, for example? Or will they seek out particular places or seek to confirm what they have seen or read in the media?

The purpose of this chapter is to begin to address this gap in literature. Focusing on the experience of L'Aquila, a city in Italy that in 2009 suffered a severe earthquake and which almost immediately became a dark/disaster tourism destination, it considers the extent to which media reporting of the earthquake influenced the behaviour of tourists who subsequently visited the city and the implication of this both for tourists themselves and the disaster recovery process more generally. First, however, the chapter reviews briefly what a disaster 'is', how the media report disasters, and the relationship between disasters and tourism as a framework for the case study of L'Aquila (also see Chap. 18).

Disasters, the Media, and Tourism

It has been observed that 'a disaster is perhaps easier to recognise than it is to define' (Barkun 1974: 51) and, consequently, numerous definitions are offered in both the academic and professional disaster literature. Nevertheless, the following definition captures the fundamental characteristics of a disaster:

> A serious disruption of the functioning of a community or a society involving widespread human, material, economic or environmental losses and impacts, which exceeds the ability of the affected community or society to cope using its own resources. (UNIDSR 2009: 9)

In other words, a disaster can be summarised as an extraordinary event, recovery from which demands external assistance and resources (Tierney et al. 2001). However, such a 'serious disruption' may be defined from alternative disciplinary, theoretical, or practical perspectives. Thus, von Vacano and Zaumseil (2013) cite definitions of disaster rooted in sociology, geography, anthropology, and psychology, whilst Quarantelli (1985) identifies seven conceptual perspectives on studying disasters commonly adopted in the literature. Nevertheless, a disaster is commonly perceived within the social context or in terms of its social consequences; as Fritz (1961: 655) famously puts it, a disaster is 'an event… in which a society… undergoes severe danger and incurs such losses to its members and physical appurtenances that the social structure is disrupted and the fulfilment of all or some of the essential functions of the society is prevented'.

It is the social or human cost of an 'event concentrated in time and space, in which a society or one of its subdivisions undergoes physical harm and social disruption' (Kreps 1995: 256), typically measured in a relatively significant number of deaths and injuries, that arguably renders a disaster attractive both to the media and to tourists. From the perspective of the media, and as suggested in the introduction to this chapter, disasters make good headlines. Putting it another way, the media have always inevitably been concerned with stories with human impacts and, as Ali (2013: 126) puts it, 'disasters in some sense have the most impact as they destroy a large volume of human and material elements'.

However, as widely recognised, the nature of disasters and the needs of journalists and other media personnel frequently conflict (Scanlon 1998, 2011). In other words, natural disasters and their consequences may unfold slowly; in the early stages of a disaster, little is usually known about the extent of the damage and destruction, or the number and nature of casualties. Such facts can only be established after some time. Equally, stories of individual heroism, of bravery, and of community solidarity in rescue and relief work only tend to emerge in the days and weeks after the event. Conversely, the media requires immediate 'facts'. They need to not only 'uphold their status as information provider in the eyes of the audience who thoroughly rely on the media' (Ali 2013: 127) by providing factual data on the disaster and its outcomes, but also to provide appealing stories both to satisfy their audience and to compete successfully with other news providers covering the disaster. As a consequence, reporters at disaster scenes tend to succumb to what Wenger (1985: 6) refers to as the 'who, what, when, where, why, how, how much, and how many syndrome', seeking dramatic 'facts' that cannot, at least in the early stages of a disaster when media interest is most acute, be substantiated. At the same time, they produce stories that may sell, but which may not necessarily represent reality. As Wenger (1985: 9) summarises, 'media content tends to overemphasize the chaotic, non-social, irrational, and non-traditional aspects of the event', such aspects typically including the disaster myths of looting (Tierney et al. 2006), panic, and social chaos. Indeed,

> the first popular representation of a disaster is of unchecked chaos; reporters may not have the eyes to see the local strategies that communities quickly develop to cope with their physical and emotional needs. 'Chaos' also sells better than stories about effective local disaster response. (Fernando 2010)

In short, media reporting of disasters often presents a distorted, mythical, and even inaccurate picture (Wenger 1985), but one which may appeal to media audiences, including tourists who then perhaps visit the site to verify those stories themselves. Indeed, the social disruption that is the outcome of a disaster, perhaps embellished by media stories, transforms a disaster site into a potential dark or disaster tourism destination.

In the context of this chapter, it is important to note that although disaster tourism may be considered a particular form of dark tourism, it is 'analytically distinct' (Rojek 1997: 63) from it in a number of ways. First, disaster tourism sites are typically temporary; they attract 'disaster tourists' who come to witness the consequence of the event only for as long as those consequences are in evidence. Once that evidence has been removed, a site can no longer be conceptualised as a disaster tourism destination. For example, once damaged buildings have been demolished and reconstruction has begun, the detritus resulting from flooding has been cleared, or the wreckage from an air or sea disaster has been removed (as occurred in 2014 when the wreck of the SS Costa Concordia was finally salvaged and removed from Isola del Giglio off the coast of Italy two years after it sank), a site can no longer be conceptualised as a disaster tourism destination. Nevertheless, it may evolve into a dark tourism destination should it subsequently become a place of pilgrimage or commemoration (Logan and Kier Reeves 2008), suggesting that some disaster sites may be thought of as nascent dark tourism attractions as defined in the literature.

Second, disaster sites are, in a tourism context, often unmanaged or 'raw' sites. There may be limited or no tourism services or infrastructure, although this is not always the case. For example, commercially operated Red Zone bus tours were established in Christchurch, New Zealand, following the earthquake that devastated the city in 2011 (Coats and Ferguson 2013). However, it is often the case that people will spontaneously visit and experience disaster sites as tourists without the benefit of organised tours, official guidance and interpretation, and so on. And third, not only do tourists visit dark sites for a wide variety of purposes (Raine 2013), but the assumption that tourism to dark sites is driven by a morbid fascination in death has been increasingly challenged, to the extent that it is considered not only pejorative but erroneous to refer to the 'dark tourist' (Bowman and Pezzullo 2009). In the case of tourist visits to disaster sites, however, it would be difficult to deny that such tourism is to some extent 'morbid'.

Given these characteristics of disaster tourism, it may be argued that people wishing to travel to and gaze upon disaster sites are particularly open or susceptible to the messages conveyed in the media about a disaster. That is, typically visiting the site in the early days after the event and with no formal guidance or interpretation available, tourists are not only likely to depend on the media as their primary source of information but may also, given their potentially morbid motives for visiting, respond positively to the stories in the media rather than attempting to grasp the reality of the disaster for themselves. Indeed, as the following case study of L'Aquila suggests, which is drawn from a broader empirical study by Wright (2014), what tourists came to gaze upon in the city was directly influenced by media reports of the disaster.

Case Study: L'Aquila, Italy[1]

The L'Aquila Earthquake, 2009

L'Aquila (which translates into English as 'The Eagle'), a city of some 68,000 inhabitants, is located in and is also the capital of the Abruzzo region in central Italy. It lies in a valley 720 m above sea level and it is surrounded by four

Apennine peaks of over 2000m and thus, although only about 120 km from Rome, remains relatively remote. Dating back to the thirteenth century, L'Aquila's long and varied history as a significant political and economic centre is reflected in its wealth of Baroque and Renaissance buildings. In modern times, however, it is best known as a cultural centre, home to the University of L'Aquila, and, as a tourism destination, a base for primarily domestic summer and winter mountain activities such as hiking and skiing.

The central region of Italy has a long history of earthquakes and L'Aquila in particular has suffered many. One of the first recorded occurred in December 1315, and over the following centuries, the city experienced many more, including a major tremor in 1703 which resulted in more than 300 deaths and the collapse of all the city's churches. In 1786, the city suffered its most serious earthquake in which more than 6,000 people died. Most recently, however, on 6 April 2009, L'Aquila was again struck by a significant earthquake. Measuring 5.8 on the Richter scale, it destroyed or damaged much of the city's historical centre; 309 people lost their lives, a further 1500 were injured and the majority of the population was made homeless.

Despite the city's long history of such events, the 2009 earthquake was unique in two respects. First, it was a national Italian disaster rather than a L'Aquilan disaster inasmuch as, unlike previous earthquakes, national resources and support were provided (at least, initially) to aid recovery. And second, the city immediately became a disaster tourism destination. Observers at the time noted an influx of tourists, Flamminio (2009) for example observing that whilst the ex-inhabitants of L'Aquila were living in tents, tourists were attempting to enter the old town (at that time only open to disaster response teams) in order to take pictures and to collect souvenirs. Similarly, some six months after the earthquake, an article (InAbruzzo 2009) titled *Il terremoto diventa attrattore turistico* (translated: 'The earthquake becomes a tourist attraction') suggested that the earthquake had achieved what the regional tourism authorities long failed to do. That is, during the summer months the city had, for the first time, become a popular tourist destination, although visitors came not to see L'Aquila's cultural wealth; rather they were *attrati dall'orrore della città distrutta* ('attracted to the horror of the destroyed city').

Significantly, the subsequent disaster recovery process in L'Aquila has been both slow and controversial. In the immediate aftermath of the earthquake, aid was sent to L'Aquila from around the world, construction of temporary housing was undertaken (Alexander 2010), a variety of measures were put in place to provide financial support and security for the local population (Rossi et al. 2012), and plans were put in place for the reconstruction of the city.

However, two years after the disaster, little progress had been made in rebuilding the damaged areas of the city. Reconstruction was seen to be hindered by inefficiency, excessive bureaucracy, broken promises, and corruption, and consequently, many local people felt that, having been victims of the original disaster, they were now victims of a failing recovery process (Di Nicola 2011). Four years after the earthquake, reconstruction had come to a virtual standstill; much of the historic centre remained in ruins, 22,000 residents were still living in temporary accommodation and, according to Dinmore (2013), L'Aquila had 'become a monument to Italy's economic and political paralysis'. However, as the following section reveals, not only has the Italian media painted an 'alternative' picture of the disaster recovery process in L'Aquila but also, of particular relevance to this chapter, its reporting of the earthquake was influential in how tourists visiting the city to witness the aftermath of the disaster behaved.

Media Reporting of the L'Aquila Earthquake

Prior to considering specific ways in which the media influenced tourism to the city of L'Aquila in the aftermath of the 2009 earthquake, it is important to note that media reporting of the event and, in particular, of the post-disaster recovery process was implicitly politicised. Specifically, two interrelated issues demand attention. First, it has long been accepted that the media are not neutral (Alterman 2008; Baron 2006). Newspapers in particular adopt a particular slant or bias, particularly when covering political-economic issues, that reflects their ownership (Gilens and Hertzman 2000)—in the UK, for example, many newspapers adopt recognised political positions—whilst a similar criticism is often directed at television and other media. At the time of the earthquake in L'Aquila, Silvio Berlusconi was not only the prime minister of Italy but also a media mogul and, according to Blatman (2003), the richest man in the country. His media interests included ownership, through his holding company Fininvest (in which he held an 85 per cent stake), of over 40 per cent of Mediaset, which operates three commercial television stations as well as a major advertising agency (Reuters 2013). Given that in Italy, television 'is the preferred medium of the overwhelming majority of the population and the only news source for 9 per cent' (Blatman 2003: 3), the potential conflict between Berlusconi's political activities and his commercial interests was questioned throughout his premiership. At the same time, he also owned approximately 50 per cent of Mondadori, Italy's leading publisher although, as Blatman (2003: 5) suggests, relatively diverse ownership of the country's newspapers broadly 'reflect the reality of the Italian political arena'. Nevertheless, one national paper was owned by Berlusconi's brother, whilst the country's leading news weekly, *Panorama*, was owned by the Mondadori group. Hence, the potential existed for much of the media coverage of the L'Aquila earthquake and its aftermath to reflect the government's position, particularly with respect to the recovery process.

And second, in the days immediately following the earthquake, Berlusconi promised full support from his government for that recovery process, as was reported in the British press, 'Mr. Berlusconi has put his political credibility on the line with a pledge to build a new town near L'Aquila within two years and a promise that none of the victims of the quake would be forgotten' (Squires et al. 2009). In other words, the reconstruction of L'Aquila became as much a political as a social objective. Initial scepticism regarding this pledge was well founded; as noted above, four years after the earthquake, little progress had been made. Significantly, however, and to the frustration of local residents, the media painted the opposite (and arguably politically motivated) picture:

> Then the media talks about how everything is ok, that the city is alive again. But it's all a massive lie. Today, more than three years after the earthquake, how can people report such blatant lies about the city and its people? (Research respondent cited in Wright 2014)

> It's how we are presented to the outside world, by the media and TV. I have friends in other parts of Italy and they tell me that they hear that everything in L'Aquila is now ok. And I say 'no', you come here and have a look, then tell me if you think everything is ok. (Research respondent cited in Wright 2014)

It was even noted by one resident that, when the annual cycle race, the Giro D'Italia, passed through the city in 2012:

> [the television cameras] ... seemed to ignore and hide the reality of L'Aquila... Throughout the whole section through L'Aquila, they kept the cameras tightly focused on the cyclists, which was strange. It is not the usual thing to do on the Giro D'Italia, which is to show the landscape and the terrain the cyclists are challenged by. (Research respondent cited in Wright 2014)

In short, in the years after the earthquake, the reality of L'Aquila's continuing problems was not (intentionally or otherwise) revealed by the media. Moreover, the research from which this chapter is drawn revealed that, as a consequence of this misrepresentation, local residents were increasingly happy for tourists to visit their city, to witness the lack of progress in reconstruction (Wright 2014; also Wright and Sharpley 2016):

> Even after three years, the people who come here couldn't believe the state of L'Aquila. They would say 'seriously, this is what is happening here, we didn't realise, we didn't know, that you were still living in these conditions'. Therefore, I saw the positive side of this [disaster] tourism. (Research respondent cited in Wright 2014)

In other words, the positive picture painted by the media perhaps discouraged tourists from visiting the city, although this was certainly not the case in the immediate aftermath of the earthquake. Inevitably, reports of the disaster appeared in both the national and international media, and many of these, although not succumbing to presenting many of the myths of disaster reporting discussed above, nevertheless displayed some of the challenges. For example, early reports suggested that the number of fatalities was relatively low—one report indicated that 'at least 90' (BBC 2009) had died—whilst 24 hours after the earthquake, the death toll was reported to be 235 (Hooper 2009), still significantly less than the eventual figure of 309. Some reports also resorted to typical clichés, such as local people being 'bemused' and 'dazed'.

Importantly, however, particularly in the context of this chapter, media reports of the disaster focused on one particular story that not only came to symbolise the tragedy of the earthquake but also became a focus for disaster tourists who visited L'Aquila in the days and weeks after the event. Interestingly, it subsequently also became the focus of a legal case that sought to apportion blame for the high number of casualties on four individuals who allegedly failed to ensure the safety of the building and, hence, that of the students residing in the property.[2]

As already noted, as a university city, between 8000 and 10,000 students were living in L'Aquila at the time of the earthquake (Cerqua and Di Pietro 2015). Therefore, it was inevitable that members of the student population were among the victims of the disaster, but, although precise figures are not available, it is unlikely that they comprised a significant proportion of those who lost their lives. Nevertheless, in the immediate aftermath of the earthquake, both the Italian and international media focused on attempts to rescue four students trapped in the rubble of a collapsed student house; overall, eight students died when the building collapsed.

It is unclear why the media focused on this specific outcome of the earthquake; perhaps it was because the young victims were 'outsiders' who had come to L'Aquila to study or perhaps because, as later claimed, the building they were living in was poorly constructed (Marinucci 2010). Or perhaps it was because, even though they represented only a small proportion of the total number of casualties, it was a story considered most likely to capture the public's attention (and sell newspapers). Either way, the media focus on the collapse of the student house served to establish the site both as a tourist attraction and as symbol of the earthquake. Indeed, the research revealed that most tourists visiting in the days after the disaster specifically sought out the student house, often asking local people for directions to it. As a consequence, the site also became the focus of local residents' antagonism towards these 'disaster' tourists, partly as a response to the behaviour of tourists as they wandered around and photographed the destruction of L'Aquila:

> Of course, it also annoyed me to see people who would start laughing, shouting or taking photographs in front of certain places, such as the student house, because at the end of the day people died there. (Research respondent cited in Wright 2014)

> I was extremely angry, particularly because people were coming and taking photos, capturing a tragic moment in time, a time that for us used to be our lives. Capturing it in their photos, it felt that people were preserving that time, and somehow sharing it. Yet, there were two realities, one the tourists' and the other ours, which were totally different. For us it was a death, an end. (Research respondent cited in Wright 2014)

> I cannot put up with these people, when I see them walking around the city, in front of houses which have crumbled to rubble, where friends of mine and other people I know lost their lives, taking photos… I would like to go over and break their cameras. People don't seem to care about what once used to be behind the destruction, people taking photos pretending to hold up a building which looks like it is about to collapse, this is something that hurts me. (Research respondent cited in Wright 2014)

More significantly, perhaps, the media's identification or creation of the student house as the focal point for disaster tourism impacted significantly on local residents, not least because it diverted attention from the wider tragedy that was the earthquake. As one respondent in the research lamented:

> At the student house, which is one of the most written about aspects of the earthquake around the world, eight people lost their lives. I know places in

L'Aquila where thirty, thirty-five, people died. No one went and showed their respects to these people. Why not? Because they didn't know about these places. It was what the media showed the rest of the world; they showed [collapsed] historical buildings where no one died; they showed things that they wanted to show, but not what was significant and of value to the Aquilani. (Research respondent cited in Wright 2014)

In other words, through their specific reporting of the collapse of the student house, the media initially created a situation in which tourists' attention was directed towards a specific place/event; the site became 'the place' to visit in L'Aquila. In all likelihood, this in turn prevented or dissuaded tourists from seeking out or understanding the wider impacts on the city of L'Aquila and its residents.

Within a short period of time, however, and arguably as a result of the media focus, the student house became one of the principal memorials to the victims of the earthquake. Initially this was undertaken in an informal manner; pictures of the victims were displayed on the fence surrounding the site (Plate 14.1), as was a poem written in their memory (Fig. 14.1).

Plate 14.1 Commemoration at the student house (Photo Source: Author, D. Wright)

> 'UNA GOCCIA DI RUGIADA
> PERFETTA
> SOPRA UNA FOGLIA VERDE
> PREFETTA
> SCIVOLA VIA
> LENRAMENTE
> ALLE PRIME LUCI
> DELL 'ALBA'
>
> POI
> COME SE AVESSE TIMORE
> DI COMPIERE IL SALTO
> SOSTA UN PO'
> SUL MARGINE ESTREMO.
> ALLA FINE
> DETERMINATA NELLA SCELTA
> GIA' FATTA
> AFFERRA IL CORAGGIO
> S'ABBANDONA FELICE.
> SALTA!
>
> A drop of dew, perfect on top of a green leaf, slips away slowly at the first light of dawn.
>
> Then as if it fears making the leap, it stops a moment on the extreme edge but, determined by a choice already made, takes courage and leaves happy.
>
> To all students who here have lost their lives your courage is for us, forever, for motives of pride.
>
> L'Aquila April 6, 2009, because it will not be forgotten, because it did not happen in vain.
>
> To give voice to those who are here no more.

Fig. 14.1 Poem in memory of victims (Translated by: Author, D. Wright)

As a consequence of this memorialisation of the site, along with other informal memorials at other locations around the city, not only were local people able to commemorate the victims of the earthquake but, significantly, tourists actively sought to understand its consequences both through engaging with these memorials and interacting with locals, some of whom took on the role of informal guides. As Wright (2014) states,

> Tourists who are guided around behave in different ways, because one has the ability to reinforce the reality and truth of certain places and locations. This then changes the way people act and thus, can assist in ensuring the local community is respected and therefore, the locals' attitudes will change towards the tourists.

In some cases, the messages on the memorials were more explicitly targeted towards tourists. For example, one sign stated:

> For tourists, foreigners and the curious.
> What you are visiting is not just a random place; it is NOT a tourist attraction.
> This was a part of our city, which until 16 months ago was still alive.
> It is too early to treat it like an archaeological site,
> And to stand smiling and have a photo taken.
> Have pity for whoever died under the rubble and for the people who are still crying for that loss. (Wright 2014)

In short, although the media's focus on the tragedy of the student house impacted negatively on both tourists' behaviour and the attitudes of the local community, that focus subsequently led to the transformation of the site into an unofficial memorial to victims of the earthquake, which in turn influenced positively the attitudes and behaviour of tourists.

Moreover, within two years, it had been decided that a formal public square would be created on the site of the collapsed student house to commemorate the students who died in the earthquake (Trapasso 2011), whilst a memorial to the students funded by the local fire brigade was erected on a nearby roundabout. Hence, what initially commenced as a story that the media collectively adopted as symbolic of the earthquake was eventually transformed into a place of commemoration and the principal focus for tourists who continue to visit L'Aquila.

Conclusion

As observed in the introduction to this chapter, disasters almost inevitably become headline news; when a serious disruption occurs to a society to the extent that lives are lost and external assistance is required, the media will report it. As a consequence, tourists will then visit the site to gaze on the disaster (also see Chap. 8). This was certainly the case following the earthquake in L'Aquila in 2009; the media not only reported the disaster but also the arrival of tourists, many of whom immediately sought out the most widely reported aspect of the disaster, namely, the collapsed student house. However, such a response on the part of tourists is understandable, media reports being the only initial source of information available to them, as were subsequent attitudes of local media towards both the media and tourists.

Nevertheless, over time, tourists began to proactively engage in understanding the wider implications of the disaster, particularly as more information and interpretations of the disaster were made available to them. Thus, some significant conclusions can be drawn from this research. Certainly, the media reported the disaster in a manner in which all disasters are reported. On the one hand, local media are attracted to accessible locations within a disaster zone and, particularly, towards potentially more dramatic or highly impacted areas, whilst, on the other hand, the international media (if not on location) may report through 'tainted lenses', assembling material from a variety of sources (verified or not) in the immediate aftermath. Together, this may lead to the potential reporting of 'disaster myths'. It is, then, simplistic to expect the media to adopt an alternative approach, even though in the case of L'Aquila, the emphasis on the student house resulted in antagonism towards tourists and wider disquiet among local residents. Additionally, the nature of media reporting of disasters should be anticipated, as should the arrival of tourists, and thus, one element of disaster response planning should be concerned with effective visitor management, particularly through information provision and the establishment of sites which offer the opportunity for tourists to engage with, rather than just gaze on, the disaster.

Of course, each disaster is unique and the relationship between the media and tourism in the context of L'Aquila is equally unique. Further research is, therefore, inevitably necessary, not least to explore the influence of the media in disaster destinations and how it can inadvertently impact on the organic image created in the mind of potential tourists. Research should also consider tourists themselves and explore their responses to media reporting of disasters in general, and the extent to which such reporting motivates tourists to visit specific sites in particular, thereby offering an additional dimension to understanding both disaster tourism and the phenomenon of dark tourism more generally. Nevertheless, the experience of L'Aquila reveals the inevitability of the media focusing on stories that will sell newspapers, the inevitability of disaster tourism, and the consequential need to manage tourists.

Postscript

In October 2012, six scientists were found guilty of manslaughter—for failing to predict the earthquake in L'Aquila—and were sentenced to six years in prison. Perhaps an example of trial by the media, their convictions were overturned by the Court of Appeal in November 2014 in a move that was seen as restoring the credibility of the Italian scientific community (BBC 2014).

Notes

1. This case study is drawn from a doctoral thesis that explores the responses of the local community in L'Aquila to becoming the object of the disaster tourist gaze. In particular, the quoted attitudes of local residents towards media reporting of the disaster and, specifically, the disaster recovery process provide an additional perspective on the role of the media in post-disaster tourism in L'Aquila. The thesis can be accessed at: http://clok.uclan.ac.uk/11326/
2. The student house has remained a popular topic in the Italian press (Il Centro 2015; Iilfattoquotidiano 2015), specifically with regard to recent proceedings at La Corte d'Appello (Court of Appeal, L'Aquila) in which four defendants have had their original four-year sentences confirmed. Despite little evidence to support the case, the defendants were accused of being responsible for the deaths of the students as they had allegedly failed to carry out work to ensure the safety of the building. However, the student house has remained a popular media symbol of the earthquake, and hence, these individuals may have fallen victim to the power of the media. What is certain is that the continuous media attention paid to the student house, through these court proceedings, has maintained its role as a tourist attraction.

References

Alexander, D. (2010). The L'Aquila earthquake of 6 April 2008 and Italian government policy on disaster response. *Journal of Natural Resources Policy Research, 2*(4), 325–342.

Ali, Z. (2013). Media myths and realities in natural disasters. *European Journal of Business and Social Sciences, 2*(1), 125–133.

Alterman, E. (2008). *What liberal media? The truth about bias and the news*. New York: Basic Books.

Barkun, M. (1974). *Disaster and the millennium*. New Haven: Yale University Press.

Baron, D. (2006). Persistent media bias. *Journal of Public Economics, 90*(1-2), 1–36.

BBC. (2009). Powerful Italian earthquake kills many. *BBC News*. Available at: http://news.bbc.co.uk/1/hi/world/europe/7984867.stm. Accessed 28 Jan 2016.

BBC. (2014). L'Aquila quake: Scientists see convictions overturned. *BBC News*. Available at: http://www.bbc.co.uk/news/world-europe-29996872. Accessed 12 Feb 2016.

Blatman, S. (2003). A media conflict of interest: Anomaly in Italy. Reporters sans Frontières. Available at: http://en.rsf.org/IMG/pdf/doc-2080.pdf. Accessed 2 Feb 2016.

Bowman, M., & Pezzullo, P. (2009). What's so 'dark' about 'dark tourism'? Death, tourism and performance. *Tourist Studies, 9*(3), 187–202.

Cerqua, A., & Di Pietro, G. (2015). *Natural disasters and university enrolment: Evidence from L'Aquila earthquake.* IZA Discussion Paper 9332. Available at: http://ftp.iza.org/dp9332.pdf. Accessed 4 Feb 2016.

Coats, A., & Ferguson, S. (2013). Rubbernecking or rejuvenation: Post-earthquake perceptions and the implications for business practice in a dark tourism context. *Journal of Research for Consumers, 23*(1), 32–65.

Cockburn, P. (2011). Catastrophe on camera: Why media coverage of natural disasters is flawed. Available at: http://www.independent.co.uk/news/media/tv-radio/catastrophe-on-camera-why-media-coverage-of-natural-disasters-is-flawed-2189032.html. Accessed 8 Jan 2016.

Di Nicola, P. (2011). L'Aquila: i numeri della vergogna (The numbers of shame). Available at: http://espresso.repubblica.it/dettaglio/laquila-i-numeri-della-vergogna/2148633/25. Accessed: 10 Apr 2011.

Dinmore, G. (2013). Italy: Lost in stagnation. *Financial Times.* http://www.ft.com/cms/s/0/e7f43eac-a775-11e2-bfcd-00144feabdc0.html#axzz3U5XODjh0. Accessed 11 Mar 2015.

Fernando, J. (2010). Media in disaster vs. media disasters. *Anthropology Newsletter, 51*(4), 4–4.

Flamminio, C. (2009). Tourism over the rubble of the earthquake in L'Aquila. Available at: http://www.demotix.com/photo/tourism-over-rubbles-earthquake-laquila124762. Accessed: 13 Oct 2011.

Franks, S. (2013). *Reporting disasters: Famine, aid, politics and the media.* London: C. Hurst & Co.

Fritz, C. (1961). Disasters. In R. Merton & R. Nisbet (Eds.), *Contemporary social problems* (pp. 651–694). New York: Harcourt.

Gilens, M., & Hertzman, C. (2000). Corporate ownership and news bias: Newspaper coverage of the 1996 Telecommunications Act. *The Journal of Politics, 62*(2), 369–386.

Gould, K., & Lewis, Y. (2007). Viewing the wreckage: Eco-disaster tourism in the wake of Katrina. *Societies Without Borders, 2*(2), 175–197.

Hegeman, S. (2000). Haunted by mass culture. *American Literary History, 12*(1), 298–317.

Hooper, J. (2010). *L'Aquila earthquake survivors seek answers from government.* Available at: www.theguardian.com/world/2010/apr/05/laquila-earthquake-survivors-planprotes-tmarch. Accessed 14 Nov 2012.

Houston, J. B., Pfefferbaum, B., & Rosenholtz, C. E. (2012). Disaster news: Framing and frame changing in coverage of major U.S. natural disasters, 2000–2010. *Journalism and Mass Communication Quarterly, 89*(4), 606–623.

Il Fattoquotidiano. (2015). Terremoto L'Aquila, crollo Casa dello Studente: confermate le condanne. Available at: http://www.ilfattoquotidiano.it/2015/04/28/terremoto-laquila-crollo-casa-dello-studente-confermate-le-condanne-in-appello/1634029/. Accessed 15 Feb 2016.

IlCentro. (2015). Casa dello studente, confermate in Appello 4 condanne. Available at: http://ilcentro.gelocal.it/laquila/cronaca/2015/04/28/news/casa-dello-studente-confermate-in-appello-4-condanne-1.11322516. Accessed 15 Feb 2016.

InAbruzzo. (2009). Il terremoto diventa attrattore turitico. Available at: http://www.inabruzzo.com/?p=10646. Accessed: 14 Oct 2011.

Isaac, R., & Çakmak, E. (2014). Understanding visitor's motivation at sites of death and disaster: The case of former transit camp Westerbork, The Netherlands. *Current Issues in Tourism, 17*(2), 164–179.

Johnston, T., & Mandelartz, P. (2015). *Thanatourism: Case studies in travel to the dark side*. Oxford: Goodfellow Publishers.

Kalcsics, M. (2011). A reporting disaster? The interdependence of media and aid agencies in a competitive compassion market. University of Oxford: Reuters Institute Fellowship Paper. Available at: http://reutersinstitute.politics.ox.ac.uk/sites/default/files/A%20reporting%20disaster%20The%20interdependence%20of%20media%20and%20aid%20agencies%20in%20a%20competitive%20compassion%20market%2C.pdf. Accessed 7 Dec 2015.

Kreps, G. (1995). Disasters as systemic event and social catalyst: A clarification of the subject matter. *International Journal of Mass Emergencies and Disasters, 13*(3), 255–284.

Lennon, J., & Foley, M. (2000). *Dark tourism: The attraction of death and disaster*. London: Continuum.

Logan, W., & Reeves, K. (Eds.). (2008). *Places of pain and shame: Dealing with 'difficult heritage'*. Abingdon: Routledge.

Marinucci, M. (2010). Casa dello studente, dolore e rabbia tra i familiari delle otto vittime. Available at: http://ilcentro.gelocal.it/regione/2010/01/07/news/casa-dello-studente-dolore-e-rabbia-tra-i-familiari-delle-otto-vittime-1.4556613. Accessed 22 Jan 2016.

Miller, R., & Albert, K. (2015). If it leads, it bleeds (and if it bleeds, it leads): Media coverage and fatalities in militarized interstate disputes. *Political Communication, 32*, 61–82.

O'Neill, S. (2002, August 26). Soham pleads with trippers to stay away. *Daily Telegraph*. Available at: http://www.telegraph.co.uk/news/uknews/1405391/Soham-pleads-with-trippers-to-stay-away.html. Accessed 20 Jan 2016.

Quarantelli, E. (1985). What is disaster? The need for clarification in definition and conceptualization in research. In B. Sowder (Ed.), *Disasters and mental health: Selected contemporary perspectives* (pp. 41–73). Washington, DC: US Government Printing Office.

Quarantelli, E. (1990). The mass media in disasters in the United States. Preliminary Paper 150, University of Delaware: Disaster Research Center. Available at: http://udspace.udel.edu/bitstream/handle/19716/522/PP150.pdf?sequence=3. Accessed 7 Jan 2016.

Raine, R. (2013). A dark tourist spectrum. *International Journal of Culture, Tourism and Hospitality Research, 7*(3), 242–256.

Reuters (2013). Factbox: Berlusconi's business empire. http://www.reuters.com/article/us-italy-politics-berlusconi-empire-idUSBRE97017P20130801

Rojek, C. (1997). Indexing, dragging and the social construction of tourist sites. In C. Rojek & J. Urry (Eds.), *Touring cultures: Transformations of travel and theory* (pp. 52–74). London: Routledge.

Rossi, A., Menna, C., Asprone, D., Jalayer, F., & Manfredi, G. (2012). Socio-economic resilience of the L'Aquila community in the aftermath of the 2009 earthquake. Proceedings of the 15th world conference on earthquake engineering, Lisbon. http://www.iitk.ac.in/nicee/wcee/article/WCEE2012_2225.pdf

Scanlon, J. (1998). The search for non-existent facts in the reporting of disasters. *Journalism & Mass Communication Educator, 53*(2), 45–53.

Scanlon, J. (2011). Research about the mass media and disaster: Never (well hardly ever) the twain shall meet. In J. Detrani (Ed.), *Journalism: Theory and practice* (pp. 233–269). Oakville: Apple Academic Press.

Seaton, A. (1996). Guided by the dark: From thanatopsis to thanatourism. *International Journal of Heritage Studies, 2*(4), 234–244.

Sharpley, R. (2005). Tourism and the tsunami – A comment. *Current Issues in Tourism, 8*(4), 344–349.

Sharpley, R. (2009). Shedding light on dark tourism. In R. Sharpley & P. R. Stone (Eds.), *The darker side of travel: The theory and practice of dark tourism* (pp. 3–22). Bristol: Channel View Publications.

Sharpley, R., & Stone, P. R. (2009). *The darker side of travel: The theory and practice of dark tourism*. Bristol: Channel View Publications.

Squires, N., Allen, N., & Samuel, H. (2009). Italian earthquake: Aftershocks hamper rescue effort. *The Telegraph*. Available at: http://www.telegraph.co.uk/news/worldnews/europe/italy/5122947/Italian-earthquake-aftershocks-hamper-rescue-effort.html. Accessed 2 Feb 2016.

Stone, P. R. (2013). Dark tourism scholarship: A critical review. *International Journal of Culture, Tourism and Hospitality Research, 7*(3), 307–318.

Tarlow, P. (2011). Tourism disaster management in an age of terrorism. *International Journal of Tourism Anthropology, 1*(3-4), 254–272.

Tierney, K., Lindell, M., & Perry, R. (2001). *Facing the unexpected: Disaster preparedness and response in the United States*. Washington, DC: Joseph Henry Press.

Tierney, K., Bevc, C., & Kuligowski, E. (2006). Metaphors matter: Disaster myths, media frames and their consequences in Hurricane Katrina. *The Annals of the American Academy of Political and Social Science, 604*(1), 57–81.

Trapasso, P. (2011). Una piazza della Memoria nel luogo della Casa dello Studente (translated: A memorial square at the location of the Student House). Available at: http://www.6aprile.it/author/patrizio. Accessed 2 Jan 2016.

UNISDR. (2009). *Terminology in disaster risk reduction*. Geneva: United Nations International Strategy for Disaster Reduction.

van Belle, D. (2000). New York Times and network TV news coverage of foreign disasters: The significance of insignificant variables. *Journalism and Mass Communication, 77*(1), 50–70.

von Vacano, M., & Zaumseil, M. (2013). Understanding disasters: An analysis and overview of the field of disaster research and management. In M. Zaumseil, S. Schwartz, M. von Vacano, G. Sullivan, & J. Prawitasari-Hadiyono (Eds.), *Cultural psychology of coping with disasters: The case of an earthquake in Java, Indonesia* (pp. 3–44). New York: Springer-Verlag.

Wenger, D. (1985). Mass media and disasters. Preliminary Paper 98, University of Delaware: Disaster Research Center. Available at: http://dspace.udel.edu/bitstream/handle/19716/474/PP98.pdf?sequence=3. Accessed 7 Jan 2016.

Wright, D. (2014). Residents' perceptions of dark tourism development: The case of L'Aquila, Italy. Unpublished Doctoral thesis, University of Central Lancashire, Available at http://clok.uclan.ac.uk/11326/2/Wright%20Final%20eThesis%20%28Master%20Copy%29.pdf. Accessed 30 Nov 2016.

Wright, D., & Sharpley, R. (2016). Local community perceptions of disaster tourism: The case of L'Aquila, Italy. *Current Issues in Tourism*, Online Version Available at: http://www.tandfonline.com/doi/pdf/10.1080/13683500.2016.1157141. Accessed 30 Nov 2016.

YorkMix. (2015). York floods 'unprecedented': People asked to stay out of the city and not travel. Available at: http://www.yorkmix.com/news/york-floods-unprecedented-people-asked-to-stay-out-of-the-city-and-not-travel/. Accessed 20 Jan 2016.

15

Denial of the Darkness, Identity and Nation-Building in Small Islands: A Case Study from the Channel Islands

Gilly Carr

Introduction

This chapter takes as its point of departure the opening chapter of the work of Gabriella Elgenius (2011) and, to a lesser extent, the work of Benedict Anderson (2006) who has argued that nations are but 'cultural artefacts' and 'imagined communities'. I am drawn to the idea that the nation as an entity exists first and foremost in the imagination, an artefact comprising various elements chosen to fit that imagining. For, as will be discussed in this chapter, just as nations are cultural artefacts, so too are the aspects of heritage that they choose to symbolise, imagine, define and build themselves. Elgenius argues that symbolism is an important part of the nation-building process. For her, these symbols include such things as flags, anthems and national days. She further states that 'nations are layered and their formations ongoing and visible in the adoption of national symbols' (2011, p. 1). Taking the Channel Islands as my case study, in this chapter I shall argue that the German occupation of 1940–1945 added a new layer to the islands' identity. That is, it provided a new range of symbols and events (cultural artefacts) out of which new identities were imagined and constructed. Alongside new layers of post-occupation identity that have gradually accreted since 1945, the formation of the nationhood of the Channel Islands has similarly been an ongoing process and has been subject to similar ongoing change.

G. Carr (✉)
Institute of Continuing Education, University of Cambridge, Cambridge, UK

Elgenius (2011) suggests that it is not just through symbols alone that a nation builds itself; it is also through ceremonies, museums, monuments and the land itself, which I take here to comprise national heritage sites contained within the landscape. Symbols and ceremonies, which are themselves aspects of heritage, 'mirror the pursuits of nations… the nation-ness becomes visible through these symbolic measures' (ibid, p. 2). For the purposes of this chapter, I will be focusing on heritage sites—key sites which can otherwise be termed 'national heritage' because of their importance. After all, a nation constructs itself through its heritage just as much as heritage, in turn, shapes a nation.

It will not escape the scholar of heritage or memory studies that the list of features of a nation appears to correspond closely to Pierre Nora's *lieux de mémoire*, the sites or realms of memory which Nora defines as 'any significant entity, whether material or non-material in nature, which by dint of human will or the work of time has become a symbolic element in the memorial heritage of any community' (Nora 1996, p. xvii). Nora's work demonstrates how memory binds communities together and creates social identities (Kritzman 1996, p. ix) and also, in this case, builds nations. Thus, I shall be making a direct analogy here between the cultural artefacts of Nora's sites of memory and Elgenius' symbols and sites of nationhood, for it seems to me that they can be seen as one and the same. They have both been chosen by the nation to speak for the identity of the nation.

In this chapter, it is my intention to select particular sites of memory—in this case, certain aspects of dark heritage in the Channel Islands relating to the German occupation—to observe how the islands have constructed their identities and post-war sense of nationhood over time. These will be used as a way of illustrating the difficulty that the islands have had in coming to terms with their dark past. I shall argue that the heritage chosen has been carefully selected to make a certain statement and to deny or marginalise others. Above all else, that heritage—and heritage interpretation—is partial and has involved blocking the darkness that is readily apparent to non-islanders or indeed denying that it ever existed. The Channel Islanders have had a historic inability, I shall argue, to perceive their dark past. This is perhaps unsurprising, as the islands are not large and it is surely difficult to co-exist with major dark sites in one's back yard. With every passing generation, different aspects of the German occupation have been presented to the public in heritage creation and it is only very recently that the darkness has begun to be admitted, although this has not been an even process and has been slower in some islands than others. As places which sometimes seek to be seen as nations in their own right, the islands have to consider how they are perceived by outsiders, but how has this affected their heritage?

Before we can discuss nationhood and the Channel Islands, however, we must first admit to some difficulty in accepting the islands as nations in their own right, even though they are clearly bounded. We cannot accurately refer to each of the Channel Islands as individual nations; like the Isle of Man, they are Crown Dependencies—although they certainly have many of the qualities otherwise needed to define themselves as nations on the grounds of their independence, which is an important pre-requisite. The Channel Islands have their own parliaments (the States of Deliberation in Guernsey and the States of Assembly in Jersey) which are headed by Bailiffs, the presiding officers in each island who are also presidents of the Royal Court. The Bailiffs are appointed by the Crown and are the Bailiwicks' leading citizens. The Lieutenant Governor in each of the Bailiwicks of Guernsey and Jersey acts as the monarch's personal representative but, in matters concerning the governance of the islands, the Bailiffs take precedence over the Lieutenant Governors. The Channel Islands, however, are not constitutionally independent of the UK and look to the mainland for defence, although they are not part of the UK administratively or legally. The relationship between the islands and the UK is, thus, complex because the islands are not sovereign states in their own right.

Nevertheless, while the Channel Islands may not be wholly independent of the UK, one of the proudly acknowledged characteristics of Channel Islanders is their stubbornly independent nature coupled with their strong dislike of being told what to do by outsiders. Thus, in recognition of this, as well as their independent parliamentary and legal systems, and their distinct and unique culture and history, for the purposes of this chapter, I shall treat the Bailiwicks of both Jersey and Guernsey as nations.

Channel Islands Occupation Heritage

There are many differences between the identity of the UK and the Channel Islands based on their different but linked histories over the last 800 years. The key distinctive feature of modern Channel Islands identity is the fact that while the UK was not occupied by German forces during World War II, the Channel Islands were. Moreover, that occupation plays a huge role in the self-identity of both Bailiwicks today. In this chapter, I shall examine the role of the symbols of national identity and memory that have led to the creation of heritage, arguing that this powerful triumvirate has combined to present an image of the occupation, consumed by locals and tourists alike, which effectively whitewashes the darkness out of the experience. Whether this is because Channel Islanders are in denial about the darkness and perhaps have still not come to terms with it after 70 years, or because they genuinely cannot see the darkness, is unknown. Either way, the result is the same. I argue in this chapter, therefore, that darkness is culturally constructed and is in the eye of the beholder. It is not a fixed category, unambiguous and clearly there for all to experience. Nor does it reside in a place to be emitted as an 'aura'. It clearly is not even based on knowledge of what took place at a site, for Channel Islanders are extremely interested in their local history and are generally well-informed. However, a distinction should be drawn between myth and history, because there are certain myths of the occupation (another national symbol) that are more readily consumed by and repeated among the general population. It is in the interstices—or rather, the crevasses—between history and myth where the darkness has been swept, often able to be reached and resurrected (or even detected in the first place) only by outsiders. The popularly told myths of the occupation which impact occupation heritage and concepts of identity have long since banished the darkness.

The main war narrative in the Channel Islands today is the Churchill paradigm, which gives a sanitised view of the past and is a heavy influence in the 'myth of correct relations'. Before we can discuss the Churchill paradigm and its impact, however, it is important to recognise the curious fact that, while the Channel Islands had a similar experience of war to that of other occupied countries in Western Europe (including the persecution of Jews, the deportation of people who committed acts of resistance, the importation of slave labourers, starvation and hunger, and so on), their war narrative is far removed from that of other European countries. Rather than perceiving themselves, as other Europeans do, as victims of occupation or martyrs for having been sent to their deaths in prisons or camps for acts of resistance against the Nazis, the Channel Islands have adopted the British war narrative. As Britons who were liberated by British military forces, they shared in a British victory and thus saw, and see, themselves through a Churchillian lens. According to Paul Sanders (2012, p. 25), the 'Churchillian paradigm' embraced a narrative of 'sublime and unwavering steadfastness in the face of adversity' as soon as the war came to an end. This paradigm states that 'the British were not a nation of victims, but of victors' (Sanders 2005, p. 256). It was a narrative of heroic victory which excluded any rival version of events and disregarded the multiple divergent memories of occupation. The 'myth of correct relations' plays into this, described by Sanders (2005, p. 235) as being an official narrative that began in the immediate aftermath of the occupation and held currency into the 1990s, where:

> …all or most Channel islanders had behaved as real Britishers, with an attitude and in a manner that was poised, exemplary, steadfastly consistent and scrupulously fair. Curiously, in this version the entire situation was devoid of the humiliation, desperation or compromise of principle occurring across the rest of Europe. …Even Occupation government was done 'by the book' …and the relationship with the Germans was correct, unspectacularly correct, as the islands had had the good fortune to have been run by a group of aristocratic gentlemen officers and not some red-hot Nazis.

It can be seen that the over-arching war narrative of Jersey and Guernsey dispelled the darkness from the experience of occupation from the earliest days and was responsible for an inaccurate war myth which still holds sway today among most of the population. This myth has impacted all aspects of national occupation heritage in the Channel Islands. It was an instrumental part of nation-building after the occupation and a way of helping the islands see themselves in a positive light after a humiliating and terrible experience.

Broadly, we can paint occupation heritage as existing in five areas: national days; national museums; national memorials and monuments; national symbols with continuing popular currency; and national sites in the landscape such as bunkers. Of course, as the Channel Islands are Crown Dependencies, the 'national' prefix is one that I have added myself. To all intents and purposes, however, the sites that I shall describe are principle sites of memory, acknowledged by all locally and, as such, the 'national' epithet is not misplaced.

The first and most important is probably the national day: Liberation Day, 9 May. This is a public holiday in Jersey and Guernsey, a time for commemoration and joyful festivities, and is without doubt the most important date in the islands' calendars. Shops decorate their windows with a wartime theme, articles in the local newspapers focus on the memories of the occupation generation and the islands are decorated with bunting (Plate 15.1). Significantly, the focus is on the end of the occupation (a very light heritage) and not the start of the occupation or any event of the middle (a darker heritage).

The second key aspect of occupation heritage is the occupation museums (also see Chap. 20). As discussed in detail elsewhere (Carr 2014a, p. 62), nine of these have previously existed at various times and seven remain open today (Carr 2014a, p. 62). These are not the main government-supported public

Plate 15.1 Decorations in St Peter Port in 2015 in readiness for Liberation Day (Photo Source: Author)

island museums but are, rather, privately owned by collectors of German militaria. Nonetheless, the collections that they hold are locally recognised as being of 'national' importance to the islands and their heritage.

Rather than telling the story of the occupation per se, the prime motive of the owners of the museums is to display the collections that they have built up since childhood. As such, displays are more often artistic, poetic or present a diorama which shows off a theme in a collection to its best effect. Collectors are not interested in showing items belonging to slave labourers, deported Jews or political prisoners because they argue that tourists are not interested in seeing such items (ibid, p. 75). Besides, such people were among the most dispossessed and were not known for their material possessions. While the casual visitor to a Channel Islands occupation museum might see mannequins of soldiers manning gun emplacements (although not actually pulling the trigger), they are also far more likely to see those mannequins listening to the radio, playing chess, modelling the German uniform, lying in their bunk or cooking food (Plate 15.2). The mannequins are not shown deporting, aim-

Plate 15.2 Inside the Command Bunker at Noirmont Point, Jersey (Photo Source: Author)

ing guns at, or harassing civilians. In fact, they do not interact with civilians at all. Once again, the darker side of occupation is not on show.

The third aspect of national heritage includes memorials and monuments to the occupation years. While these are to be found in great number throughout the islands, with at least 33 in St Peter Port and St Helier combined, almost a third were erected to commemorate significant anniversaries of liberation. My research has shown that, from 1985 onwards, the date at which the occupation began to be seriously memorialised, the last to be remembered have been the victims of the Nazi persecution, recognised in Jersey before Guernsey. Moreover, such memorials have been placed in marginal places and are significantly smaller than the liberation memorials (Carr 2012). It is clear once again that the darkest of narratives have been the last to be recognised and have not been allowed to challenge the national narratives of occupation.

There are two national symbols relating to the occupation that I would cite as having national currency today: The V-sign (in both Guernsey and Jersey) and the donkey (in Guernsey). Following the BBC's and Churchill's V-for-Victory campaign in 1941, which entailed encouraging the people in occupied countries to draw V-signs on walls and streets, to make the V-sound (in Morse code) and to signal to each other with V-gestures, the Channel

Islands adopted the campaign with vigour. Although the campaign was not aimed specifically at the Channel Islands, nevertheless they joined in, imagining themselves as part of a Europe-wide secret resistance army whose aim was to make the occupier feel surrounded by a hostile enemy. Subsequently, a number of islanders were caught and deported to Nazi-run prisons in France and Germany (Carr 2014b, pp. 43–63). Today, on Liberation Day, the V-sign, with its key symbolism of an Allied victory, is seen throughout the Bailiwicks and especially in garden decorations and on themed floats in the cavalcades and parades, which pass through St Peter Port and St Helier. However, it is the symbol, rather than the people imprisoned for using the symbol, which is remembered. The names of those deported are not well known.

The donkey is traditionally the mascot or 'totem animal' for Guernsey and symbolises the proudly cultivated trait of stubbornness in local people. A cartoon drawn on a birthday card towards the end of the occupation by a local newspaper cartoonist, Bert Hill, depicted a donkey standing on a map of Guernsey and kicking a rotund and clearly well-fed German out of the island. This image became iconic and is well known in the island today (Carr 2014c). It is possible now to buy cufflinks, tie pins, postcards, fridge magnets and T-shirts with the image. Again, this symbol is wholly light-hearted today and remembers a positive event (Plate 15.3).

Plate 15.3 National symbols on display in Guernsey (Photo Source: Jonathan Bartlett)

The final type of national heritage that I will discuss here, and the focus for the rest of this chapter, is the German bunker. Hundreds of these concrete fortifications are dotted around the coastlines of the Channel Islands today, and a small number have been selected to be developed into heritage sites. While some have been converted into occupation museums, others have been restored to how they would have looked when operational. While there is no single bunker that stands as a 'national monument' in either Jersey or Guernsey, there are many preserved or restored bunkers, some with a higher profile than others, which I have examined elsewhere (Carr 2014a). In 1979, Kreckler and Partridge wrote the first report which called for the preservation and scheduling of bunkers in Guernsey; subsequently five bunkers were included on the protected monuments list in 1982. More were recommended for listing in 1990 and were successfully registered soon after. In Jersey, a 1986 report recommended the protection of 15 fortifications as Sites of Special Interest (SSI) (Ginns 1986). Thus, for nearly 30 years, many bunkers have been protected as sites of national heritage. But whose stories are told inside them? How are those bunkers which have not become heritage treated? And what of the bunkers' forgotten and neglected counterpart, the labour camps, which housed the workforce who built them? Why should bunkers become an accepted part of national heritage when labour camps have not?

Bunkers and Labour Camps

Before we can explore the forgotten dark sites which are not recognised as public heritage sites, it is important to characterise them in terms of their state of existence or becoming. Only then can we understand which sites are avoided and which draw public attention and why; why darkness is acknowledged to adhere to one type of site and not the other and, indeed, why this perception may differ between tourists and locals. In order to address this, I would like to propose a schematic model, particularly suitable for the post-conflict situation, to describe the relationship between a dark event, a dark legacy, dark heritage and dark tourism (Fig. 15.1).

A dark event, such as military occupation, leaves behind it a tangible legacy or residue in the form of traces, ruins, debris, sites and objects, and an intangible legacy in the form of memories, trauma and psychological impact. All of these have the potential to be dark. If we take the example of dark sites which in this example might take the form of labour camps or military fortifications, none automatically enjoy the status of 'heritage'. Drawing on Laurajane Smith's concept of heritage, which she defines as 'the

```
              ┌──────────────┐
              │ Intervention │
              └──────────────┘
                 ↗       ↘
┌──────────┐  ┌────────────┐   ┌──────────────┐
│Dark event│  │            │   │              │
│  (e.g.   │─→│Dark legacy │   │ Dark heritage│
│Occupation)│ │            │   │              │
└──────────┘  └────────────┘   └──────────────┘
                 ↖       ↗
              ┌──────────────┐
              │   Neglect    │
              └──────────────┘
                    ↑    ↖
              ┌──────────────┐
              │ Dark tourism │
              └──────────────┘
```

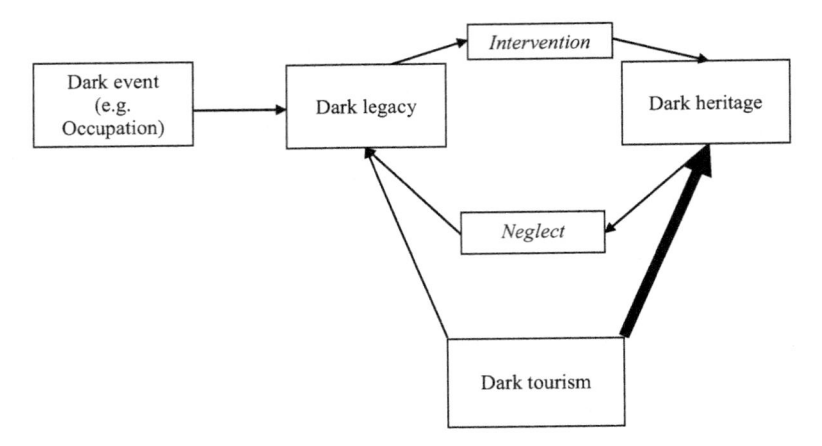

Fig. 15.1 Relationship between a dark event, a dark legacy, dark heritage and dark tourism

cultural processes of meaning and memory making and remaking rather than a thing' (2006, p. 74), I suggest that heritage has to be created or chosen through such active processes. For example, if a fortification is left untouched after a dark event, then sooner or later it will succumb to the passage of time. Plants and weeds will start to grow over it. It is still at the legacy stage with no certainty that it might ever become anything else. If not maintained, the fabric of the building will start to degrade and even collapse. This is not heritage; heritage is something (tangible or intangible) that is valued, selected and chosen to represent some aspect of identity of a group. For Channel Islanders, bunkers have been reclaimed from the weeds and from oblivion since the late 1970s. At and after this point, many have been renovated or restored. This active intervention has turned them into heritage. But heritage can just as easily be abandoned, neglected and turned back into legacy status. Thus, the passage between legacy and heritage can be cyclical and not necessarily linear. When tourists visit sites of German occupation in the Channel Islands, they are arguably more likely to visit heritage sites where there is 'something to see'; more likely (in this example) to visit bunker-museums or restored bunkers rather than abandoned bunkers hidden in the undergrowth. Because legacy sites are less known about by tourists then, predictably, more tourists visit heritage than legacy sites (represented by the different arrow thicknesses in Fig. 15.1).

This much may be true for tourists. But it is perhaps not so for non-tourists. In the Channel Islands, a popular pastime at weekends is to 'go bunkering'. This involves visiting neglected, hidden or out-of-the-way bunkers still at 'legacy' status. It is here, and not in the restored bunkers, where a non-dark narrative is provided, and where the darkness may be perceived locally. But what is the real difference between bunkers of legacy and heritage status? One might imagine that heritage-status bunkers have been more thoroughly researched and explored and, thus, the greater knowledge of the human rights abuses against slave and forced workers that took place there would lead to a heritage which proclaimed that history and acknowledged that darkness. One might also imagine that the people who have spent many years restoring and maintaining the bunkers might be those whose intimate knowledge of the sites has resulted in a familiarity with and awareness of their dark past and encourages them to embrace it. But this is not the case; these kinds of bunkers are not perceived locally to be dark places. We might conclude that perhaps long familiarity has bred contempt of the darkness, but such an assumption would be to ignore the impact of cultural identity. And it is cultural identity (and the role of the Churchillian war narrative within that) rather than historical knowledge per se that, I suggest, can dictate not only from where the darkness emanates, but who can perceive it in those places.

Rather than using bunkers as blank canvases for telling the story of an Allied victory and the post-war use of bunkers as the reclamation of Channel Island territory, the Churchillian paradigm instead dictates that bunkers are places to show off the strength and power of the enemy, an enemy that was overthrown. Thus, the display of guns and other militaria, uniforms, helmets and swastikas is to show off the spoils of war; the booty that became the property of the victor. Bunkers, therefore, did not become places to tell the story of victimhood, the narrative of the slave or forced labourer dragged across Europe to build bunkers, worked or starved to death. Bunkers, instead, became 'dark-proof', where the only admitted narrative was the defeat of the mighty Goliath told through the display of his strength, a scenario in which the Channel Islands take the role of David. Thus, it is only restored bunkers—bunkers-as-heritage—that have been converted to this use and which proclaim the dominant narrative.

The dominant Churchillian paradigm and the myth of 'correct relations' can also be seen as what Bell (2003) terms a 'governing myth' (which gains its dominance at the expense of dissident voices). Bell's 'mythscape' is the 'temporally and spatially extended discursive realm wherein the struggle for control of people's memories and the formation of nationalist myths is debated, contested and subverted incessantly' (ibid, p. 66). While the majority of restored bunkers and bunker-museums in the Channel Islands are places where the Churchillian paradigm as governing myth is writ large, there are just two which have been used for other purposes and which reveal the space within bunkers as locations of mythscapes.

In Jersey, at La Hougue Bie and at Jersey War Tunnels, there are two German fortifications where the original heritage presentation espoused the Churchillian paradigm and which now, after conversion, upgrading and reconceptualisation by heritage professionals rather than amateur enthusiasts, embrace the role of bunkers as places where people suffered. The foreign labourers who built the bunkers are given back their names and identities and their individual stories are told. This contestation and subversion of the 'governing myth' of occupation has been controversial, not least because bunkers have long been symbolic spaces where whoever owns or controls that space also controls the narrative told within it. Indeed, the darkness inherent in both of these renegotiated bunker sites has now begun to be acknowledged. I argue, therefore, that the darkness does not lie (entirely) within the 'auratic quality' which such a site might emit and to which Seaton (2009, p. 85) refers, nor in the knowledge of what it was used for, but in the dominant narrative or governing myth that prevails in a place, and which often dictates the associated heritage interpretation. I also argue that local people are more likely than tourists to be affected by or wholly cognisant of the governing myth, having grown up with it and been taught it in school and seen it enacted in the streets on both ceremonial and celebratory occasions (national days) in the local calendar, such as on Liberation Day. Visitors and tourists, conversely, will be less 'indoctrinated' into or affected by governing myths. They may be ignorant of the governing myth (and thus not inoculated against or unable to see the dark like local people) and unaware of the uninterpreted legacy sites and head only to the heritage sites. They may perceive darkness to emanate from the very sites that local people do not perceive as dark.

Labour camps in the Channel Islands are not national heritage and neither are they sites of memory. They are, instead, *lieux d'oubli* or sites of oblivion as Nancy Wood has categorised them, and it is here where the darkness really resides or has the potential to reside if uncovered or recognised as heritage. These forgotten sites are intentionally avoided by public memory 'because of the disturbing affect that their invocation is still capable of arousing' (Wood 1999, p. 10).

There were around 12 slave and forced labour camps in Jersey and around 5 each in Guernsey and Alderney, not including temporary camps or the reuse of houses and other buildings in the islands for accommodation and penal prisons of the labour force. Alderney was also the location of a concentration camp run by the SS, Lager Sylt. In these camps lived the manual labourers of the Organisation Todt (OT), a paramilitary engineering organisation with a workforce of up to 16,000 by May 1943 (Cruickshank 2004, p. 204). It comprised voluntary, conscripted and forced workers, but also slave labourers. Among these were heterogeneous groups that included Jews who had been rounded up in occupied Europe. Those sent to the Channel Islands included Poles, Czechs, Belarusians, Ukrainians, Russians, Belgians, French, North Africans, Dutch, Spanish Republicans and also German 'criminals' and political prisoners (Cohen 2000, pp. 122 and 130). Even local Channel Islanders attracted by the high rates of pay worked for the OT as cooks, interpreters, drivers and skilled labour (Ginns 2006, pp. 64–67; Bunting 1995, pp. 94–95). While various nationalities and groups of the labour force were treated better than others, and some even paid and given time off, the Russians, Ukrainians and people considered by the Nazis to be of 'Slavic origin' were categorised as *Untermenschen*, or sub-human, treated appallingly and often brutally, and given very little food. The number of deaths among these slave workers is disputed and will probably never be known with any accuracy, although it has been discussed and estimated in a variety of sources (Bunting 1995, p. 293; Cohen 2000, pp. 147–152; Cruickshank 2004, pp. 213–4; Ginns 2006, pp. 115–125; Knowles Smith 2007, pp. 9–30; Pantcheff 1981, pp. 64–74; Sanders 2005, pp. 191–230). These sources and others also record the testimony of a number of former slave workers and, consequently, the extreme suffering of these people is beyond doubt. Although a discussion of this is beyond the scope of this chapter, it will suffice to record that the unremitting hard labour involved in building bunkers, coupled with the starvation rations given to many workers, poor living and sanitary conditions, negligent working conditions, overseer violence and lack of medical attention directly contributed to or caused most of the deaths.

It can clearly be seen that labour camp sites today might be perceived as having strong residues or emanations of the darkness within them. Moreover, this darkness might be imagined to stem from their potential status as 'terrorscapes' (van der Laarse 2013). However, that same darkness is denied by local people to exist in heritage sites such as restored bunkers, even though bunkers were built by these labourers. Because darkness is something that is in the eye of the beholder, it exists in different places for different people. Different people of different cultural identities are affected by or brought up within different narratives and understandings of war.

Walter argues that one of the factors which conspires to darken sites of death is those deaths which 'challenge the collective narratives of a nation' (Walter 2009, p. 52). We have already noted that the war narrative of the Channel Islands has traditionally and specifically excluded victims, especially victims of Nazism, and therefore one of the reasons why these camps have been obliterated or ignored is because of their power to upset the heritage status quo and governing myth. Indeed, not one of these camps has become a heritage site. Each of them remains at the status of a legacy or just a memory, for most have been completely destroyed and modern buildings have been constructed on the sites. Even this is an interesting observation, for who would want to live on top of a former labour camp? It is unknown how many people are aware of the wartime history of the patch of ground in the islands upon which they live but, at the same time, it is possible that the passage of time since the war has lessened the power or perception of the darkness which might adhere to such sites.

In Alderney, for example, there are bungalows built on top of Lager Helgoland, a labour camp which was thought to house Jews (Ginns 2006, p. 85). Here, the former entrance posts to the camp are used as the entrance posts to the driveway of one of the bungalows. At Lager Norderney, now the island's camp site for tents and caravans in summer, various concrete structures are still visible in the long grass. Local people here, in such a tiny island, are surely aware of what they are living and camping on top of. The traces of Lager Borkum in Alderney today stands either side of the track that leads to the island's rubbish dump. The ruins of Lager Sylt lie abandoned, covered by the lush vegetation for which the island is famed. In 2008, this camp became the first and only one in the islands to receive a memorial plaque, but even this was placed on the entrance post of the camp by a former Polish prisoner and was not a local initiative (Plate 15.4). More so than in Jersey and Guernsey,

Plate 15.4 The entrance posts of *SS Lager* Sylt, Alderney (Photo Source: Author)

where they are less visible, the camps are sites of oblivion in Alderney. There has even been a marked reluctance to support archaeological excavation in Alderney (Sturdy Colls 2012, p. 94)—clear evidence of these camps' status as *lieux d'oubli*.

The situation is little better in Jersey and Guernsey, although fewer traces remain. Rather than being sites which people expressly avoid, more of them have been obliterated in the landscape. It seems that while traces remain, the power of the darkness of these sites is too much to tolerate. While labour camps have been categorised as merely the 'accommodation' of the men who worked on the bunkers (Ginns 2006, p. 74), a neutral word that implies nothing sinister, we know that the reports exist in Jersey of Russians being kept in cages or wire compounds within camps such as at Lager Udet in St Brelade. Moreover, some camp commandants were known for their brutality, such as at Lager Immelmann in the parish of St Peter (ibid, pp. 78–80). There are also numerous reports by local people of the torture and bad treatment of the foreign workers by their overseers. One of the better known accounts was that of Senator Edward Le Quesne in Jersey, whose diary entry for 20 February 1943 recorded that he had seen in the parish of St Ouen a Russian in the pillory with two branches of trees tied tightly around his neck with the man just able to touch the ground with his toes. As he had an armed guard standing over him, nobody was able to help him (Le Quesne 1999).

While one might have imagined the labour camps of the Channel Islands to be the prime sites of darkness today, this is apparently not the case because they are simply ignored rather than actively avoided. It is possible that these places have lost much of their darkness because they have been neutered through destruction or neglect. But, by not confronting what happened at these sites or to the people who were forced to reside there, local people are able to continue ignoring them. Nevertheless, this does not mean that these sites do not have the power to grow darker if ever they are uncovered and draw an audience. To excavate sites such as these, however, risks revealing something which people may not yet be prepared to face. It is known, for example, that Jews were among those brought to the Channel Islands to work for the OT (Cohen 2000, pp. 121–154; Sanders 2005, chapter 6), and this adds to the potential feelings of anxiety about what could yet be revealed.

While labour camps are not presented as tourist sites, it is not entirely true to say that they are not visited; local historians or researchers sometimes visit these sites, and former OT workers have also made the pilgrimage back to the sites of their suffering. Photographic evidence exists of this in Jersey, probably in 1970, when resident Spanish Republicans who stayed behind after the occupation visited the sites of camps in the island (Gary Font pers. comm.).

A similar event also took place among former prisoners when the memorial plaque was attached to the gate post of the concentration camp of Sylt in Alderney in 2008.

It is difficult to tell whether the general dissipation of the darkness of labour camps in Guernsey and Jersey happened slowly over several generations or, as is more likely, whether the real neutering of the camps took place quite early on, when they were destroyed or dismantled by the Germans and locals alike. It is not known whether the motivation for the destruction or removal of any of the camps stemmed from a desire to cover up the evidence of their crimes (in the case of the Germans) or not to be reminded of the crimes that took place on their soil (in the case of the islanders). It was probably a combination of both coupled with a need for firewood in the last harsh winter of the occupation.

While we may wonder at the lack of anxiety of islanders over the role of their islands in the Holocaust in particular, we should remember that it was not until the early 1970s, following the Eichmann trial of 1961, the 1967 Arab-Israeli war and the 1968 student protests, that the Holocaust began to assume centre stage in the consciousness of Western Europeans (Koonz 1994, p. 269). By this time, the state of preservation of most labour camp sites in the Channel Islands may not have been too different to their status today, as the photos taken around this time by Spanish Republicans in the island attest.

Should we be concerned that most of these sites have apparently lost their power to disturb? Is it sometimes a good thing for dark sites to lose their darkness? On the one hand, it means that communities can reclaim the land for the living, let go of the past and move forward, ridding themselves of the burden of war, all of which might be perceived as a thoroughly healthy and positive thing several generations after the original conflict. On the other hand, there are ethical ramifications to ignoring such sites. Even the apparently innocuous camps of many forced labourers from Western Europe (as opposed to slave labourers from Eastern Europe) housed people who were taken against their will or who had little choice but to agree to work for the OT rather than face an unknown fate in Germany (Sanders 2005, p. 205). Human rights abuses within a corrupt system were endemic inside the OT and to differentiate between camp types, or to label some as darker than others depending on who lived there and how they were treated, is to turn one's back on past suffering.

The current neglect of labour camps does not necessarily indicate their terminal position. The legacy of war does not have a pre-ordained trajectory or life cycle; something that is covered in the undergrowth or long forgotten does not have to remain in that state. Interventions by archaeologists or any other stakeholder to uncover and preserve the camps are possible, but the success of these efforts will be dictated either by the local community or by those in positions of authority who have the power to sanction or loudly welcome such interventions. However, as Geyer and Latham (1997, p. 7) wisely point out, 'no preservation, however perfect, can save these traces for the present unless they are accepted in the present'. An uncovered site imposed upon the local community as 'heritage' can return to its previously neglected state if locally rejected or disliked. The converse is also true.

But if members of the local community show no sign of wanting to change the status quo, as seems apparent in the Channel Islands, do outsiders have any right to intervene and engineer or impose a change of any kind—to force them to come face to face with the darkness? If local people are not capable of discerning the darkness at a site, or deny that the darkness exists, can and should darkness be forced upon them for educational or ethical reasons, such as raising awareness about the people who once suffered there, or to try to change the war narrative of a place through force? How possible or ethical is such an attempt? Is a desire to show respect to victims of Nazism enough to claim the moral high ground?

We must also not lose sight of why members of the local community have not turned the camps into heritage. Such a decision makes a statement about what Channel Islands identity does and does not embrace, with the associated implications that to force a change is an attempt to manipulate or misrepresent locally held concepts of identity and even collective memory. Arguably, however, the decision to ignore this legacy of occupation was taken many decades ago and the subject has never re-arisen for debate.

Since the 50th anniversary of liberation, islanders are more open to embracing and remembering victims of Nazism, especially in Jersey; progress has been slower in Guernsey, however, and is hardly detectable in Alderney. Nevertheless, if the subject of camps were discussed again today, it is possible that the outcome could be different. With this in mind, in 2014 and 2015, I began the very first excavation of a labour camp in the Channel Islands. I carried out work at Lager Wick in Jersey, a forced labour camp for French workers, Spanish Republicans and French North Africans (Carr forthcoming), and today a nature reserve for wild birds. The excavation blog was followed by people from 55 to 51 different countries in 2014 and 2015, respectively, the highest number of 'hits' coming, perhaps not surprisingly, from the UK and Jersey. While the excavation also attracted coverage by the local Channel Islands media and the associated public lecture I gave drew a large audience, I discovered that the labour camp I had excavated was either not being perceived as 'dark' by local people, or any unmistakably dark elements were either being denied permanent exposure or given a lighter spin in accordance with the Churchillian paradigm and its avoidance of a narrative of victimhood. Four examples will suffice to back up this observation.

First, the only remaining feature of Lager Wick above ground, in addition to a ruined wall of the latrine block, was its concrete entrance posts, complete with several strands of barbed wire wrapped around them (Plate 15.5). These had previously been covered in so much ivy that the posts appeared entirely indistinguishable from the surrounding trees. During the first season of excavation, I stripped back the ivy, revealing the posts once again for the first time

Plate 15.5 The entrance posts of Lager Wick, Jersey (Photo Source: Author)

in decades. Such a structure was undoubtedly, to my eyes, an almost iconic feature of a Nazi camp and my recommendation to the land owners and the local planning authorities was to leave them uncovered as part of presenting the site to the public as a heritage site. This recommendation was turned down as it was deemed more important to allow wildlife habitats to be restored to their previous state before I arrived, thus covering up once again the only recognisable dark feature of the camp. Second, I also corresponded with local historian, Michael Ginns, who lived near Lager Wick during the occupation, and showed him photographs of the barbed wire. He was most unwilling to accept that it came from the era of the labour camp and suggested instead that it was erected in 1945–1946, when the land was used for grazing cows.

Third, a few months after the first season of excavation, I was sent a PDF of an artist's impression of the camp and some text which would be placed on an information board by the side of the road by the camp. I was rather surprised to see a sanitised image of a spotlessly clean and orderly series of barrack huts with no hint of squalor or barbed wire, and the concrete entrance posts had been omitted. Representations to those who manage the site resulted in slight changes, but still no sign of barbed wire or the entrance posts graced the final image which is now in place outside the site (Plate 15.6).

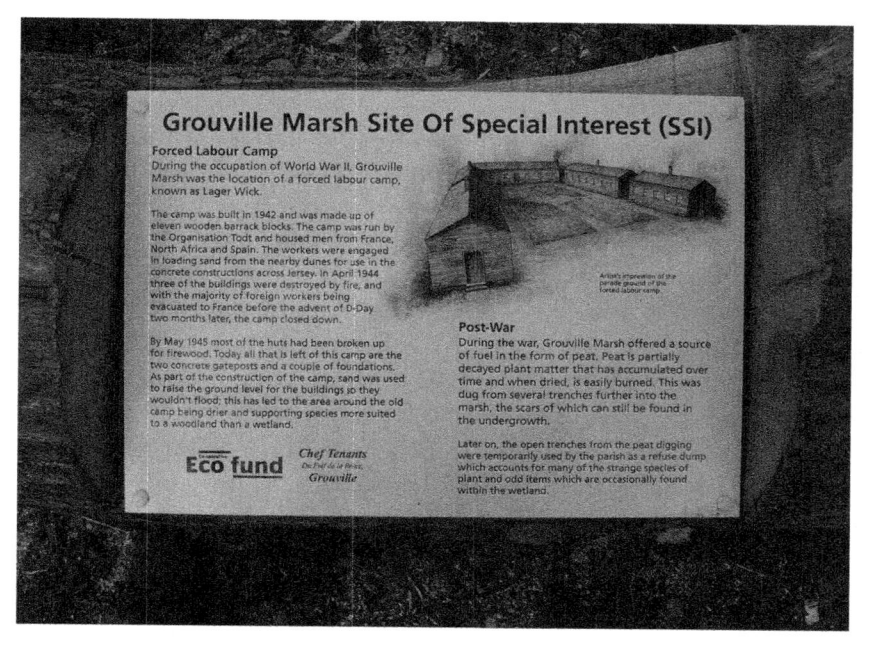

Plate 15.6 Information panel about Lager Wick, Jersey (Photo Source: Author)

Finally, during the second season of excavation, I uncovered both the ablutions block of the camp and a barrack block which, by the end of the excavation, I interpreted as belonging to the camp overseers because of the nature of the objects discovered. The excavation of the ablutions block made the lofty heights of page three of the *Jersey Evening Post*, although the article focused primarily on my call for local volunteers for the dig rather than on our discoveries. Then, on the penultimate day, I found the base of a mug which featured an eagle and swastika, the discovery of which made the front pages the following day. I imagined that this might be an opportunity to discuss the role of the overseers and their ill-treatment of the camp inmates but, after printing my quote which said that it was time to acknowledge the darker side of the island's heritage, the focus instead was on how the ablutions block would now be preserved as heritage.

Conclusion

In this chapter I have argued that the national identities of the Channel Islands changed irrevocably as a result of the German occupation. That occupation spawned a war narrative—a national myth—of 'correct relations' which, coupled with the Churchillian paradigm, deeply impacted the post-war heritage choices. In other words, these nations were re-imagined when Guernsey and Jersey chose a new range of post-war national symbols, sites, memorials and museums to rebuild and redefine their nations and identities. These, like the narratives and myths which dictated the choices, banished the victims of Nazi persecution and, with them, the darkness and the complexities of the occupation experience. It is only in recent years that they have been allowed back into the story of the occupation owing to the combined action of local politicians in Jersey and outside activism by academics.

I have argued here that the darkness in the heritage of the German occupation of the Channel Islands is in the eye of the beholder; it is primarily culturally constructed and understood, and can be denied, destroyed or marginalised by those who do not wish to (or simply cannot) see or feel it. This darkness, I have argued, comes from the ghosts of the past which haunt the ignored or buried legacies of occupation. In the Channel Islands, the Churchillian paradigm, with its avoidance of victims of Nazism and its focus on victory, and a 'governing myth' of correct relations with the Germans, has led to the avoidance and denial of the dark. Nevertheless, islanders are, on some level, haunted by these ghosts; they are aware of them but will draw instead upon less dark and less traumatic narratives of the past, even going to the extent of destroying structures which had the power to betray dark residues. While the casual tourist to the Channel Islands will see dark heritage everywhere, islanders themselves do not see their heritage in that way. Sites which have been chosen by them as heritage have been selected because they are not dark (to their eyes) and do not tell a story of darkness; rather they are made to conform to the governing myth which is part of Channel Islands' cultural identity. The dark legacies of occupation, on the other hand, are where the real darkness lies for them, and these have been destroyed, marginalised or ignored as sites of oblivion. Even when confronted with potential darkness, the eyes of these beholders paint it in lighter colours.

Acknowledgements The second half of this chapter has reproduced some of my earlier paper: Carr G. (2017) 'A culturally constructed darkness: dark legacies and dark heritage in the Channel Islands' in G. Hooper and J.J Lennon (Eds) *Dark Tourism: Practice and Interpretation*. pp. 96–107, Abingdon, Oxon: Routledge. My thanks to the publishers for allowing me to reproduce sections of that paper here.

References

Anderson, B. (2006). *Imagined communities: Reflections on the origin and spread of nationalism*. London/New York: Verso.

Bell, D. (2003). Mythscapes: Memory, mythology, and national identity. *British Journal of Sociology, 54*(1), 63–81.

Bunting, M. (1995). *The model occupation*. London: BCA.

Carr, G. (2012). Examining the memorialscape of occupation and liberation: A case study from the Channel Islands. *International Journal of Heritage Studies, 18*(2), 174–193.

Carr, G. (2014a). *Legacies of Occupation: Heritage, Memory and Archaeology in the Channel Islands*. Dordrecht: Springer International.

Carr, G. (2014b). The V-sign campaign and the fear of reprisals. In G. Carr, P. Sanders, & L. Willmot (Eds.), *Protest, defiance and resistance in the Channel Islands: German occupation 1940–1945* (pp. 43–63). London: Bloomsbury Academic.

Carr, G. (2014c). Symbolic resistance. In G. Carr, P. Sanders, & L. Willmot (Eds.), *Protest, defiance and resistance in the Channel Islands: German occupation 1940–1945* (pp. 19–41). London: Bloomsbury Academic.

Carr, G. (2016). Nazi camps on British soil: The excavation of Lager Wick forced labour camp in Jersey, Channel Islands. *Journal of Conflict Archaeology. vol 11* (2–3): 135–157.

Cohen, F. (2000). *The Jews in the Channel Islands during the German occupation*. Jersey: Jersey Heritage Trust.

Cruickshank, C. (2004 [1975]). *The German occupation of the Channel Islands.* London/Channel Islands: Oxford University Press/Guernsey Press.

Elgenius, G. (2011). *Symbols of nations and nationalism: Celebrating nationhood.* Basingstoke: Palgrave Macmillan.

Geyer, M., & Latham, M. (1997). The place of the Second World War in German memory and history. *New German Critique, 71*, 5–40.

Ginns, M. (1986). *Sites of special interest. German fortifications: Reports on sites of German defensive structures in Jersey of military and architectural importance.* Unpublished report.

Ginns, M. (2006). *The organisation Todt and the fortress engineers in the Channel Islands.* Jersey: Channel Islands Occupation Society.

Knowles Smith, H. (2007). *The changing face of the Channel Islands occupation: Record, memory and myth.* Basingstoke: Palgrave Macmillan.

Koonz, C. (1994). Between memory and oblivion: Concentration camps in German memory. In J. R. Gillis (Ed.), *Commemorations: The politics of national identity* (pp. 93–107). Princeton: Princeton University Press.

Kreckler, D., & Patridge, C. W. (1979). *Survey and classification of German military structures and sites in Guernsey, 1940–1945.* Unpublished report.

Kritzman, L. D. (1996). In remembrance of things French. In P. Nora & L. D. Kritzman (Eds.), *Realms of memory: Rethinking the French past. Volume I: Conflicts and divisions* (pp. ix–xiv). New York: Columbia University Press.

Le Quesne, E. (1999). *The occupation of Jersey day by day.* Jersey: La Haule Books Ltd.

Pantcheff, T. (1981). *Alderney: Fortress Island.* Chichester: Phillimore and Ltd.

Sanders, P. (2005). *The British Channel Islands under German occupation, 1940–1945.* Jersey: Société Jersiaise and Jersey Heritage Trust.

Sanders, P. (2012). Narratives of Britishness: UK war memory and Channel Islands occupation memory. In J. Matthews & D. Travers (Eds.), *Islands and Britishness: A global perspective* (pp. 24–39). Newcastle Upon Tyne: Cambridge Scholars Publishing.

Seaton, A. (2009). Purposeful otherness: Approaches to the management of thanotourism. In R. Sharpley & P. R. Stone (Eds.), *The darker side of travel: The theory and practice of dark tourism* (pp. 75–108). Bristol: Channel View Publications.

Smith, L. (2006). *Uses of heritage.* London/New York: Routledge.

Sturdy Colls, C. (2012). Holocaust archaeology: Archaeological approaches to landscapes of Nazi genocide and persecution. *Journal of Conflict Archaeology, 7*(2), 70–104.

Van der Laarse, R. (2013). Beyond Auschwitz? Europe's Terrorscapes in the age of postmemory. In M. Silberman & F. Vatan (Eds.), *Memory and postwar memorials: Confronting the violence of the past* (pp. 71–92). New York: Palgrave Macmillan.

Walter, T. (2009). Dark tourism: Mediating between the dead and the living. In R. Sharpley & P. R. Stone (Eds.), *The darker side of travel: The theory and practice of dark tourism* (pp. 39–55). Bristol: Channel View Publications.

Wood, N. (1999). *Vectors of memory: Legacies of trauma in postwar Europe.* Oxford/New York: Berg.

Section 4

Dark Tourism and Heritage Landscapes

Rudi Hartmann

Introduction

Over the past few decades, studies in heritage tourism have flourished and produced many results. One of the most intriguing trends has been a focus on heritage sites with a controversial history including locations of war, atrocity, and horror. These studies have fostered a debate over the nature of tourism at controversial sites. Three new concepts—dissonance in heritage (tourism), thanatourism, and dark tourism—were introduced into tourism studies during the mid-1990s and 2000s and have found widespread application (Hartmann 2014). Geographers in the USA revived a geography of memory first outlined by cultural geographer David Lowenthal. Important contributions came from Foote (1997) who examined America's landscapes of violence and tragedy, and from Owen and Alderman (2008) with a critical analysis of the management of and visitation to slavery sites as well as places associated with the civil rights movement. Remarkably, there is also a heightened interest in tourism to war and peace memorials noted early on by Smith (1998) and discussed more recently in its complexity by Butler and Suntikul (2012). A multitude of heritage landscapes elucidating the shadowed past in places with a controversial history evolved and some of these sites are now well visited by the travelling public. In the past years, tourism to places associated with 'the darker side of humanity' found increasingly the interest of researchers.

R. Hartmann (✉)
University of Colorado Denver, Denver, USA

About This Section

The chapters in this section focus on dark heritage in different contexts and on varying geographical scales of investigation. Dallen Timothy's examination in Chap. 16 of sites of suffering, tourism, and the heritage of darkness has a national focus; his chapter is based on illustrations from the USA. He argues that the path to current American civilization has been underscored by centuries of darkness. As a colonial and immigrant society, US history is full of catastrophic events and tragic moments, from the clashes and deadly conflicts the new settlers of the land had with the Native Americans to the horrific treatment of religious minorities such as the members of the Latter Day Saints (Mormon Church). Timothy not only discusses the dark heritage product regarding such human-induced catastrophes and tragedies in the USA, but also provides a list of natural disasters including volcanic eruptions (Mount St. Helens 1980) and hurricane flood sites (Hurricane Katrina 2005) which continue to receive considerable visitation.

While Timothy summarizes the growing literature on visitation to sites of slavery in the context of a broad review of examples of American heritage of suffering, Stephen Hanna, Derek Alderman, and Candice Bright's Chap. 17 is a close-up study of the past and current management practices at antebellum tourism sites in the Southeastern USA. Their contribution is aimed at examining the spatial and narrative designs of plantation tourism sites. Point of departure is a premier site, the Middleton Place Plantations and Gardens just outside Charleston, South Carolina, with a long-time focus on the 'Big House'; the architectural qualities of the structure and the surrounding gardens as well as the white owners' luxurious lifestyle. In recent years, a 'Beyond the Fields' tour was added which allows visitors to learn more about slavery and the conditions the enslaved at the plantation site faced. Hanna, Alderman, and Bright go on to discuss in great detail the ongoing changes in plantation tourism in the US South ending with a review of a remarkable example, the Whitney plantation. At this fairly new site, the emphasis of the narrative is focussed upon communicating to visitors the magnitude and severity of the traumas of slavery in general, as well as to tell several life stories of the enslaved in the specific context. The chapter's authors also contribute to the conceptual debate over dark tourism with comments on dark touristic practices they observed at the studied sites.

Tang Yong in Chap. 18 focuses on dark tourism to seismic memorial sites. Yong reviews the notion of 'disaster tourism' and discusses a variety of commemorative places in different parts of the world where natural disasters

Section 4 Dark Tourism and Heritage Landscapes   379

occurred including sites of volcanic eruptions, tsunamis, and earthquakes. In his examination of these dark touristic landscapes, Yong finds that the creation of memorial sites becomes frequently a contested phenomenon. His in-depth analysis of the commemoration practices of the 2008 Wenchuan Earthquake in Sichuan Province, China, where at least 69,000 people died is the centrepiece of the chapter. He argues that the consumption of seismic legacies holds an ethical dilemma. The chapter concludes with a discussion of the perceptions of seismic disasters and the destination images it may attach to places or regions once affected by catastrophic events.

Dominique Vanneste and Caroline Winter in Chap. 19 explore First World War battlefield tourism in Flanders, Belgium, and it is an in-depth study of the memorial sites during the centennial anniversary events of the war. After interviewing and observing visitors at the sites Vanneste and Winter argue that the Great War sites to some extent point away from the dark aspects of death and seek to enlighten and uplift. Furthermore, they suggest that researchers should go beyond the usual dark-light discourse established in the tourism literature. They notice trends to overcome the taboos of the past by openly addressing traumas. The sustained interest in the Great War battlefield sees remembrance tourism as a force for transcending past wounds and for peace among the nations once involved in the tragic conflict.

Finally, Rudi Hartmann in Chap. 20 focuses on tourism to memorial sites of the Holocaust. While he reconstructs the evolution of new commemoration practices and an expanding memorial landscape in Central and Eastern Europe now comprising a wide array of historic markers, monuments, and memorials with museums, he also discusses the changing approaches to the study of the sites associated with the victims of Nazi Germany. It was not until the late 1970s and early 1980s that researchers took notice of the new memorial sites at former concentration camps and other places of horror visited eventually by millions of people. Systematic studies and comprehensive documentations of the several thousands of memorial sites in Germany were undertaken and presented to the public in the 1990s. New approaches in the study of places with a shadowed past examined the changing commemoration practices at sites of the new heritage landscape and an observed dissonance was analysed. Researchers along a dark tourism agenda focused on the inherent curiosity visitors showed at some of the prominent memorial sites such as Auschwitz-Birkenau. Lastly, sites associated with the perpetrators such as Hitler's 'Eagles Nest' and second home in the Bavarian Alps were included in the studies with the development of new documentation and research centres.

Conclusion

All five chapters of Section 4 are contributions made by geographers. It is an indication of an increasing interest among cultural and historical geographers in tourism to places with a dark heritage. Common research foci are the spatialities and the social context framing and grounding tourism to the new heritage landscapes. Future studies are commendable to create a more comprehensive research agenda for shedding light on the nature of shadowed places in the tourism literature.

References

Butler, R., & Suntikul, W. (Eds.). (2012). *Tourism and war: A complex relationship*. London: Routledge.

Foote, K. (1997). *Shadowed ground: America's landscapes of violence and tragedy*. Austin: University of Texas Press.

Hartmann, R. (2014). Dark tourism, thanatourism, and dissonance in heritage tourism management: New directions in contemporary tourism research. *Journal of Heritage Tourism, 9*(2), 166–182.

Owen, D., & Alderman, D. (2008). *Civil rights memorials and the geography of memory*. Athens: University of Georgia Press.

Smith, V. (1998). War and tourism: An American ethnography. *Annals of Tourism Research, 25*(1), 202–227.

16

Sites of Suffering, Tourism, and the Heritage of Darkness: Illustrations from the United States

Dallen J. Timothy

Introduction

Human beings are morbidly fascinated by disastrous events, human and environmental suffering, and other morose occurrences. Such happenings can be an important part of the heritage narrative of nations or regions (Dale and Robinson 2011; Gelbman 2008; Gelbman and Timothy 2010; Jamal and Lelo 2011; Miles 2014; Stone 2011; Timothy et al. 2004) and may be key in creating destination images and touristic appeal.

Nowhere is this truer than in the United States of America. Much of the underlying character of the USA and what it means to be an American is underscored by centuries of darkness, from the earliest explorers and colonizers to the current tensions provoked by terrorism and political and economic chaos. This chapter examines one-time, localized events and sites of darkness, as well as nationwide and persistent maladies as important elements of America's heritage and how these play out in the tourism context, considering the role of scale, locale, and depth of impact in understanding the appeal of dark heritage. The chapter first examines the heritage of darkness in the United States, the importance of scale considering disasters, crises and other calamities, and the types of attractions that derive from events of darkness (also see Chap. 17).

D. J. Timothy (✉)
Arizona State University, Phoenix, AZ, USA

A Heritage of Darkness

Heritage comprises elements of the past that we inherit and utilize at present (Graham et al. 2000; Timothy 2011a). This includes both tangible and intangible ingredients that make up who we are as individuals, communities, and nations. Heritage lies at the foundation of personal and national identity and can cause entire societies either to coalesce in solidary or collapse in disunity. Heritage tells stories of people's struggles with nature and with one another. It reveals the vicissitudes of life not only among humankind's elites, but also among ordinary citizens. There is much to learn from the successes and failures of the past, and our use of yesterday and its vestiges for educational and scientific, political, artistic, cultural and touristic purposes adds value and importance to the events, places, and people that have gone before us.

Heritage usually and traditionally commemorates notable achievements and idealistic occurrences. Extraordinary architecture, remnants of ancient civilizations, renowned artworks, living cultures and folklore, cuisines and foodways, music and dance, faith and family are celebrated, packaged, and sold for consumption throughout the world. At the same time, however, heritage memorializes the darker underbelly of social and environmental interactions that generate suffering, grief, and misery. Events, places, and specific sites of darkness have always been an important part of the tourism supply, even since ancient times. However, only since the 1990s have they, and the visitor experiences and desires they elicit, been recognized systematically as a unique type of tourism (Ashworth and Hartmann 2005; Austin 2002; Dalton 2015; Foley and Lennon 1996; Hartmann 2014; Lennon and Foley 1999, 2000; Robb 2009). Packaging and promoting darkness often requires particular management approaches and specialized marketing methods, depending on the target market (e.g. children and families) or the general sensitivities of the tragedy that occurred at a given location (Austin 2002; Kelman and Dodds 2009; Kerr and Price 2016).

Based upon this understanding of heritage meaning and value, sites, and experiences associated with dark episodes are, without question, an important part of the heritage tourism product (Austin 2002; Biran et al. 2011; González-Tennant 2013; Hartmann 2009; Seaton 2002, 2009; Sharpley and Stone 2009b; Timothy 2011a; Venbrux 2010; White and Frew 2013). Some tourist destinations owe their economic well-being almost entirely to the existence of thanatouristic spaces and sites of other darkness. Locations of famous natural disasters or human-induced tragedies have long been marked, preserved, interpreted, and packaged for curious onlookers (Hartmann 2014; Lennon and Foley 2000; Timothy 2011a).

Every place has some historical element of darkness. However, settler societies have a different set of heritages to those of non-colonial states. Colonized countries have had to carve their own identities from a patrimony of native powerlessness and colonial power and the transplanted cultures of their colonizers. Much dark heritage in settler societies derives from colony-metropole relationships, many of which continue to the present day. Many colonized lands were burdened by slavery or indentured servitude, indigenous suppression, and malcontent among competing immigrant groups. Much of these countries' national heritage derives from darkness, the likes of which was not historically experienced to the same degree in the colonial motherlands. Nonetheless, even the European metropoles experienced salient events of darkness (e.g. Black Death). Like other settler societies, the United States of America experienced many of the same colonialism-imposed events that happened elsewhere.

An American Heritage of Suffering

The sheer size and cultural diversity of the United States guarantees a wide range of heritage resources that have been, or potentially could be, utilized for tourism. Much of the national heritage narrative in the United States is linked directly to darkness, and many of the country's most salient tourist attractions emerged from a patrimony of darkness (Biel 2001; Foote 1997; Newton-Matza 2014; White 1992). Likewise, dark tourism experiences in the United States are key in reinforcing national identity, patriotic pride, and sense of the American self (Tinson et al. 2015). As a colonial and immigrant society, US history is fraught with chronicles of darkness and tragedy. From this darkness, national heroes have emerged, and tragedies have coalesced national solidarity and a passionate romance with American exceptionalism.

Since America's earliest rebellions against its British rulers, which resulted in the American Revolutionary War and the Declaration of Independence, darkness has been a constant companion to the United States' nationalistic sentiment. Discontent rose quickly between the European settlers and Native Americans, often resulting in clashes and outright wars. According to the erroneous mindset of many Europeans, these 'new' American lands were *terra nullius*—lands belonging to no one that where free for the taking. This, of course, did not settle well with the natives, who already numbered in the millions by the end of the fifteenth century (Taylor 2002).

Interactions between indigenous Americans and European settlers resulted in the deaths of millions of native peoples from diseases theretofore unknown among the indigenes. The British passed legislation to destroy the Native American population wherever they posed a threat to exploration and settlement; in the eighteenth century, rewards were paid to immigrants for each Indian killed. Thousands of Native Americans were captured and sold into slavery, some even being shipped to the Caribbean to work on sugar plantations (Gallay 2002). As time passed, many tribes were expelled from their traditional hunting lands and farming settlements. In exchange for their expulsion, many tribes were forcibly resettled in less favorable areas far away from their traditional homes (Coates 2014). Eventually, white American settlers made their way from the eastern United States to the west in search of gold and land to homestead. This westward movement resulted in many skirmishes and battles between the natives and the settlers, often aided by US military intervention.

Many of these events and the places where they happened are now commemorated as sites of national interest and have become important tourist attractions (Hartmann 2009; Lemelin et al. 2013; Timothy and Boyd 2015). As scenes of human atrocity, there remains a great deal of controversy regarding these locales, how they are interpreted, conflicting historic narratives, and the various methods used to package them as tourism products (Hartmann 2009; Lemelin et al. 2013; Timothy 2011a; Willard et al. 2013).

Another blight on American history was the long period of African slavery (1640–1866) wherein Africans were captured, forcibly brought to the United States, bought and sold, and treated as personal property. Abuse, murder, rapes, forced dispersion of families, and other forms of maltreatment were part of everyday life for most slaves, who had few human rights and whose escape attempts made them worthy of execution.

Disagreements about various aspects of slavery and other states' rights issues finally led to the Civil War (1861–1865), pitting the northern non-slave states against the southern slave states. Hundreds of thousands of union (northern) and confederate (southern) soldiers and civilians died as a result of the Civil War. In the end, the conflict resulted in the abolishment of slavery in 1866. However, civil rights abuses and rampant racism against African-Americans continued far into the twentieth century. Racially motivated murders, including lynching, and discriminatory segregation were the hallmark of anti-black racism in America.

The memorialization of slaves and the condemnation of slavery is gaining momentum in the United States as a more balanced view of the country's dark patrimony unfolds. Remnants of the heritage of slavery, the Civil War and civil rights abuses in many forms (e.g. plantations, slave markets, civil rights memorials, and battlefields) are an extremely salient part of the heritage tourism supply in the eastern and southern United States (Alderman and Modlin 2016; Buzinde 2010; Chronis 2005, 2007; Dann and Seaton 2001; Miles 2015; Rice 2009; Seaton 2001). Recent changes in the interpretation and consumption of many of these locales aim to foment a sense of collective memory, truth in storytelling, and a nationwide commitment never to let such atrocities occur again (Alderman 2015; Buzinde and Santos 2008; Chronis 2008; Horton and Kardux 2004).

Persecution by the majority in the United States has not been limited to racial groups but also has occurred in relation to certain religious groups. At its founding in 1830, the Church of Jesus Christ of Latter-day Saints and its members faced a great deal of discrimination and maltreatment. Mormon history in the United States is riddled with instances of mob abuses, which resulted from the general population's unwillingness to accept some of the faith's 'peculiar' religious beliefs and unusual practices (e.g. modern-day revelation, scriptures in addition to the Bible, Mormon opposition to slavery, and the practice of polygamy among some church members from 1831 to 1890), and the perceived threat of the rapid growth of the church.

Mormon settlements were frequently raided, buildings burned, and church leaders imprisoned or murdered. In addition, several skirmishes and battles were waged between the Mormons and various state militias in the mid-1800s. One of the most malicious accounts occurred at Hauns' Mill, Missouri, only a few days after the state's governor issued the 'Extermination Order', which effectively encouraged mob warfare against the Mormons of Missouri in order to drive them out, and made killing a Mormon legal in that state. On October 30, 1838, 21 Mormon settlers were slaughtered by a mob attack at Haun's Mill. This event and several others (e.g. the assassination of Joseph Smith, the church's founder in 1844), finally led to the mass emigration of thousands of Latter-day Saints from the US east and Midwest to the Salt Lake Valley, which at the time was beyond the borders of the United States, and to other parts of the American West where they felt safe to practice their religion without persecution.

The 2092-km Mormon Trail today is a significant linear route that many tourists, both Mormons and non-Mormons, follow by car or portions by foot. Certain segments of the trail are traversed each year by groups of history enthusiasts, who dress in pioneer period attire and pull handcarts along the route (Timothy and Boyd 2015). Many of the locations where anti-Mormon atrocities took place in the eastern and Midwestern states have also been marked and preserved, monuments constructed, and historic sites and interpretive centers created. Among Latter-day Saints and some non-Mormon history buffs, these places of darkness are very popular attractions often visited as single sites or during vacation times as nodes along the linear Mormon Trail (Anderson and Anderson 1991; Hudman 1994; Hudman and Jackson 1992; Olsen 2006; Timothy and Boyd 2015). Many of these sites are owned and operated by the LDS Church or various US government agencies, including the Bureau of Land Management and the National Park Service, and function as quasi-pilgrimage destinations for history-loving Mormons, who are united not only by faith but also by the role of the persecution narrative in Mormon historical thought—solidarity through tragedy.

Economic downturns in the twentieth century and the collapse of certain resource extractive sectors, including mining and forestry, caused a rapid outmigration from traditional resource-reliant communities. Many of these small settlements became ghost towns, sitting derelict for generations. However, many of these abandoned villages and towns saw a resurgence of interest among visitors who are fascinated with abandonment, dereliction, and industrial heritage. As a result, ghost towns throughout the country have become important tourist destinations as dusty museums of former glory now frozen in time (DeLyser 1999; Prideaux and Timothy 2011).

Spaces of death and funerary rights have received considerable tourist attention on the American scene in recent years. People are morbidly fascinated by mass murders and serial killings, and the desire to visit famous crime scenes is growing (Gibson 2006), perhaps in response to the constant barrage of related information and visuals on the internet and social media. Assassinations of famous Americans, such as Abraham Lincoln and John F. Kennedy, stir much public sentiment, and the locations of these catastrophes become an indelible part of America's fascination with darkscapes, which play important commemorative propagandistic and educational roles (Foley and Lennon 1996). Public interest in the death sites, final homes, and burial locations of famous celebrities are also a growing phenomenon (Levitt 2010). Perhaps none of these is more remarkable than the grave of Elvis Presley in Memphis, Tennessee, and the thousands of secular pilgrims it draws each year (Alderman 2002).

Like all other sites of dark heritage, places of human incarceration have a role to play in the American dark heritagescape. Perhaps the most famous attraction of this sort in the United States is Alcatraz in San Francisco, California, which functioned as a prison from 1861 to 1963, housing many famous criminals and constantly being in the news for daring escape attempts (Strange and Kempa 2003). Likewise, owing largely to a sense of mistrust, from 1942 to 1946, more than 100,000 Americans of Japanese ancestry were gathered and moved to internment camps known as 'relocation centers', where they were kept until the Second World War ended. Eventually, 10 incarceration camps were erected in several western states and Arkansas. Conditions were unsavory and crowded. Many people died of diseases and lack of proper health care, and there was often a pervading sense of helplessness—US citizens being incarcerated in their own country based upon their ethnic heritage (Ng 2002). In addition to the relocation centers, there were several other kinds of facilities the US government used to gather, concentrate, and manage the Japanese-American population. In the 1980s, the US government under presidents Ronald Reagan and George H.W. Bush officially apologized for this terrible mistake and made financial restitution to survivors and their descendants (Reeves 2015). Today, many of the internment camps have been demolished, with only markers designating where they used to be, although a number of them have been renovated and serve as important dark attractions in the western part of the country (Timothy 2011b). These are especially popular among war historians and subsequent generations of those who were incarcerated.

Natural catastrophes are common in the United States. Being a very large country geographically, disasters of various sorts occur throughout the year. Several mega-disasters have happened in the past century and created increased awareness about natural processes and climate change. Many strong earthquakes have rocked California and Alaska. Volcanic eruptions have wreaked much havoc in Hawaii and Washington, and tornados are a constant threat in the Midwest during tornado season. Hurricanes are commonplace on the southeast and east coast from June to November each year. One of the worst disasters ever to happen in the United States was Hurricane Katrina in 2005. It was the costliest natural disaster in US history, destroying protective levees along the Gulf Coast, resulting in massive floods that obliterated much of the city of New Orleans and other coastal areas in Florida, Louisiana, Mississippi, and Alabama (Campbell 2008). Between 1400 and 1800 deaths occurred directly or indirectly from the storm and its aftermath. Thousands of homes, bridges, harbors, roads, and other infrastructure were destroyed and hundreds of thousands of people were displaced from their homes; the total monetary loss was estimated to be nearly $110 billion USD (Blake et al. 2011).

While there have been many hurricanes in the United States over the past few centuries, this one stands out in public memory because of its intensity, the number of lives lost, and the overwhelming economic devastation it effected. Today, much of the devastation in and around New Orleans remains in the urban and suburban landscape. Many homes and neighborhoods were never rebuilt, and large numbers of people permanently left the city. A number of entrepreneurs took advantage of the situation and its growing notoriety immediately following the disaster, offering Katrina tours to interested onlookers. These efforts to sell darkness met with much resistance with ethical concerns that tours would enable agencies to profit from the tragedies of others (Robbie 2008); that 'neighborhoods previously outside commercial tourist imaginaries were now on tourists' itineraries' (Pezzullo 2009, p. 99). In their own defense, Katrina tour providers argued that the excursions would provide opportunities for learning, civic solidarity, cultural change, redevelopment, and healing.

Modern terrorism in the United States has received widespread global attention. Relatively few times have foreign terrorists successfully struck the American homeland; as such, acts of terror are relatively rare but memorable. In February 1993, agents of the Al Qaeda network bombed the World Trade Center in New York City, killing six people and injuring many more, but the act did not destabilize the building as planned. In April 1995, spurred by anger at the federal government, Timothy McVeigh and Terry Nicholds, both Americans, bombed the Alfred P. Murrah Federal Building in Oklahoma City, killing 168 people, including 19 children. This was the most devastating case of domestic terrorism ever to have occurred in the United States (Campbell 2008).

By far the most significant act of terror in US history occurred simultaneously on September 11, 2001, in New York City; Arlington, Virginia; and in a farmer's field near Shanksville, Pennsylvania. In total, 2977 people (not including the perpetrators) died in the events of that day, while many rescue workers and others involved have fallen ill or died of 9/11-related health complications in the intervening years. This tragedy increased national solidarity and brought about a complete overhaul of the country's security apparatus with significant implications for travel and tourism. Immediately following the 9/11 events, curious gazers began flooding into New York City to catch a glimpse of the wreckage of the World Trade Center (Lisle 2004). Ground Zero, or the National September 11 Memorial and Museum, is today one of New York City's most visited attractions, and people still come from afar in a show of solidarity, to honor the victims of this tragedy, and to see the infamous site for themselves (Sather-Wagstaff 2011). While visits to the site are generally encouraged, there is some controversy surrounding how best to interpret the events of 2001 for children (Kerr and Price 2016), the 'kitchification' or commoditization of Ground Zero through souvenirs and other packaged experiences (Sharpley and Stone 2009a) and the potential of the 'teddy-bearification' of 9/11 to stifle deeper political and social discourses associated with the site and the events that created it (Potts 2012).

These examples provide only a brief snippet of the dark heritage of the United States, but they are all pivotal events in US history, many of which have helped define what it means to be American. In this way, tragic events have effectively etched a sense of identity and solidarity into the American psyche at national, local, and personal levels.

The Importance of Scale

Scale is an important geographical concept that bears upon the development of dark heritage and its consumption. From a scalar perspective, heritage may have global, national, local, or personal appeal among heritage consumers, with the possibility of overlap between these (Timothy 1997). Prominent examples of the global scale include famous and iconic heritage sites or places that exude a worldwide sense of awe and which stimulates a desire within travelers to visit. Many classic examples can be found on UNESCO's World Heritage List and on the New7Wonders of the World register, including but not limited to, the Roman Colosseum, Stonehenge, Angkor Wat, Hagia Sofia, Petra, and the Taj Mahal. Owing to their international reputations and their 'brand', these sorts of heritage places often feature prominently in national or regional marketing campaigns. These iconic heritage symbols of place tend to draw a large, universal audience and appeal to the masses.

The second scale of heritage includes sites and objects that emanate nationwide appeal. While many such locales, such as the Alamo, Taos Pueblo, St. Augustine, Historic Jamestowne, Arlington National Cemetery, and Civil War battlefields in the United States, may attract many foreign tourists, their primary audience is the US domestic consumer market. This is largely because of the nationalistic sentiments they project and their important roles in understanding and commemorating the native population, European colonization, and the country's establishment.

Third is local heritage. The local heritage product is usually comprised of monuments to community heroes or founding pioneers, historic houses, hometown museums, churches and schools, and similar historic objects that commemorate events and individuals of critical importance to regions and municipalities. From a demand perspective, such places are supported by community organizations and visited by residents, school and youth groups, and returning visitors who might have originally been from that place.

The lowest scale of heritage is what Timothy (1997) refers to as personal or familial heritage. Traveling to discover one's roots, visiting places associated with ancestral lands and properties, doing genealogy research, eating traditional foods, and attending family reunions are all important manifestations of this scale of heritage tourism. It also includes visiting sacred sites or sites of atrocity with which one has a personal or filial connection. Demand for this scale of heritage is difficult to measure and project, but it is nonetheless a salient part of tourism, particularly in source countries of historic mass emigration.

All of these scales are important in the context of dark heritage, but in the United States, the majority are of personal, local, and national prominence. Relatively few dark heritage sites in the United States can be considered global in their reach and impact. This is not to say that international tourists do not visit these sites, but these visits typically happen in conjunction with visits to other sites of more global appeal.

Understanding the Dark Heritage Product

There are two broad ways of looking at crises, catastrophes, and other manifestations of darkness in the United States. The first is one-time, mostly localized events. These occurrences become popular attractions if they are sensationalized by the media and their impact felt widely. Several of the event types and their locales noted in Table 16.1 have become and remain vital tourist attractions. These include the location in Dallas, Texas, where John F. Kennedy was assassinated; Alcatraz Prison in San Francisco; the Watergate complex in Washington, DC; the National September 11 Memorial and Museum, New York City; USS Arizona Memorial, Honolulu; Hurricane Katrina tours, New Orleans; and Mount St. Helens, Washington. Many of these one-off events contribute to the 'herofication' of individuals (e.g. Kennedy) or groups of individuals (e.g. the firefighters of 9/11) with deep nationalistic undercurrents. However, the majority of them pass quietly through history and often fall from public memory, except in the case where an event has important personal or local repercussions.

The second type of crisis is comprised of persistent, nationwide maladies that lasted a long time or continue to exist today. These have all resulted in a wide range of related dark heritage sites throughout the country. Table 16.2 illustrates some key examples of these persistent problems. Some of these overlap with the individual events in Table 16.1 and are simply manifestations of larger underlying social quandaries.

Racism/bigotry, civil unrest, and terrorism are not specific instances, although they have resulted in specific occurrences in particular locales and at particular times (e.g. plantations, slave sites, Mormon persecution sites, the Trail of Tears). Whereas the items in Table 16.1 are more connected to one-off events and related sites (except those not associated with a specific locale (e.g.

Table 16.1 Types of one-time, localized crises and catastrophes in the United States

Type of crisis/disaster	Notorious examples
Human-induced catastrophes	
Airplane crashes/air disasters	American Airlines Flight 191 (1979)
Assassinations	John F. Kennedy (1963)
Building or bridge collapses	Hyatt Regency walkway collapse (1981)
Car/highway accidents	New Orleans tour bus accident (1999)
Celebrity deaths	Elvis Presley (1977)
Crimes/thefts	Barefoot Bandit thefts (2009–2010)
Economic failures	The Great Depression (1929–1939)
Famous incarcerations	Alcatraz (1861–1963)
Financial scandals	Bernie Madoff Ponzi Scheme (1990s–2008)
Fire (buildings/cities)	MGM Grand Hotel fire (1980)
Industrial accidents	3-Mile Island (1979)
Kidnappings	Elizabeth Smart (2002–2003)
Mass hysteria	Salem Witch Trials (1692–1693)
Mass murders and serial killings	Sandy Hook Elementary shooting (2012)
Mass suicides	Heaven's Gate religious group (1997)
Migration tragedies	Donner Party tragedy (1846–1847)
Oil spills and environmental disasters	Exxon Valdez (1989)
Police raids	Waco Siege (1993)
Political scandals	Watergate (1970s)
Rebellions and riots	Los Angeles Riot (1992)
Stampedes	The Who concert disaster (1979)
Terrorism	September 11 (2001)
Train accidents	Big Bayou Canot train crash (1993)
War	Attack on Pearl Harbor (1941)
Natural calamities	
Avalanches	Loveland Pass avalanche (2013)
Blizzards/winter storms	Northeastern US Blizzard (1978)
Droughts	Dust Bowl (1931–1939)
Earthquakes	Loma Prieta Earthquake (1989)
Floods	Great Flood of 1993 (1993)
Heat waves	1980 US heat wave (1980)
Hurricanes and cyclones	Hurricane Katrina (2005)
Mudslides	Oso Mudslide (2014)
Tornados	2011 Super Outbreak (2011)
Tsunamis	Good Friday Earthquake/Tsunami (1964)
Volcanic eruptions	Mount St. Helens eruption (1980)
Mixed human-induced and natural	
Dam failures	Buffalo Creek dam burst (1972)
Epidemics and health crises	Influenza Pandemic (1918)
Explosions	West Fertilizer Company explosion (2013)
Famine/starvation	Jamestown Starving Time (1609–1610)
Fire (range/forest/wildfire)	Yarnell Hill Fire (2013)
Maritime accidents/shipwrecks	MV George Prince ferry disaster (1976)
Mining accidents	Farmington Mine Disaster (1968)

Source: Based upon Campbell's (2008) and author's compilation

Bernie Madoff scandal)), most of the sustained events in Table 16.2 provide a multi-nodal network of places that serious heritage tourists may want to visit. For example, war history buffs may desire to visit all of the former Japanese concentration camps in the United States or as many Civil War battlefields as possible.

Both types of dark situations result in similar and/or unique heritage resources that garner the attention of visitors (Fig. 16.1). As well, scale becomes an important consideration in the degree to which these attrac-

Table 16.2 Nationwide and persistent problems in the United States

Underlying cause	Famous examples and outcomes
Racism/bigotry	Slavery
	KKK/lynching's/racial segregation
	Native American maltreatment
	Religious persecution
	Japanese internment camps
Civil unrest	Civil War
	Revolutionary War
	2016 Presidential elections
Terrorism/security threats	Bombings
	Directed airplane crashes
	Mass shootings

Source: Author's compilation

Heritage Resource Types and Scales

One-time, Localized Events
- Battlefields
- Dark tours
- Ghost tours/hauntings
- Graves and cemeteries
- Historic buildings
- Historic markers
- Monuments
- No attractions at all

Scale
Personal, Local & National

Nationwide, Persistent Problems
- Battlefields
- Historic sites
- Internment camps
- Monuments
- Museums
- Prisons
- Sacred sites
- Trails and routes

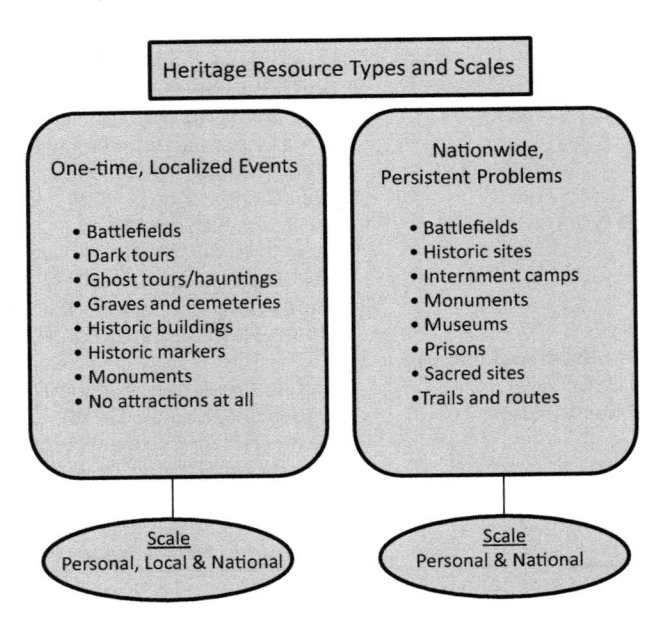

Scale
Personal & National

Fig. 16.1 Heritage resource types and scales

tions appeal to visitors. As Fig. 16.1 denotes, one-off events are often marked by battlefields, dark tour packages, ghost tours, cemeteries and graves, old buildings, historic markers, monuments, and in some cases (e.g. Bernie Madoff scandal), no attractions at all. The longer-term impact of the majority of these resources is at the personal and local scale, suggesting that natural disasters, accidents, and the like may soon be forgotten at the national level, but for the people whose family members were involved and the communities where their atrocities occurred, the severity of darkness will forever be etched in local and personal memory. Clearly there are exceptions to this scaled perspective, such as the 9/11 Memorial and the Mount St. Helens eruption, where the place-connected event lives on in personal, local and national memory.

The heritage resource type generation by nationwide, persistent problems may result in battlefields, historic sites, internment camps, monuments, museums, prisons, sacred sites, and trails and routes (Fig. 16.1). The impact scale of these happenings and site-specific attractions tend to have more personal and national heritage connections. These attractions and the experiences they inspire are especially personal for descendants of African-American slaves or Native Americans whose ancestors were forcibly dragged to unknown and inhospitable realms on the Trail of Tears. At the same time, most of the sites associated with the issues in Table 16.2 are memorialized at the national level, thereby contributing to the broader national narrative in a sustained manner for multiple generations.

Conclusion

This chapter examines the role of darkness in the heritage narrative of the United States, largely from a supply-side perspective. Without doubt, darkness underscores some of the most important historical events that molded the United States and its national ethos. The chapter identified two primary sorts of heritage that provide the attraction base for dark tourism. The first is one-time, localized events of natural and human-induced disasters and tragedies brought on by a mix of the two. The second type of darkness entails long-term, current, and nationwide problems that continue to manifest in the creation of heritage, including racism, terrorism, and civil unrest. The majority of the first type have local and personal appeal, while the second type play more into personal and national heritage narratives. Both types, however, provide a wide range of attraction types that are an important part of tourism in the United States.

Dark heritage has played a very salient role in the development of the American identity and the concept of American exceptionalism. With this frequently comes the 'herofication' of certain personalities, owing to their roles in saving lives, defeating evil, sacrificing their own lives for the cause of nationhood or community. Most sites and heroes of importance in the United States are important precisely because of their connections to disasters, crises, and other tragedies.

Such has been the chronicles of US history and the heritage that is packaged, sold, and consumed. Stone (2011) has called for a deeper analysis of dark tourism to understand its nuances. This should include examining comparative differences between the thana-experiences and other occurrences of darkness and dark visitor experiences in a wide variety of countries, both colonial states and the metropolitan countries of Europe. Only in this way can we truly begin to understand the unique experience of place and dark heritage narratives as valued and understood by difference nations and peoples.

As most heritage consumed by the cultural industries, including tourism, has focused on the grandiose, ancient, tangible, and cheery patrimony of places, many stories and experiences have been left out of national and regional storylines because they are deemed ephemeral, unnecessary, or unimportant. Unfortunately, this societal amnesia results in many dark, unsavory, or embarrassing pasts remaining untold (Timothy 2011a). Understanding dark tourism can provide a more democratized, balanced, and sustainable approach to selling heritage, since so much of the dark past involves the experiences of minorities, the imprisoned, the impoverished, and other marginalized people, whose familiarity with darkness also had a salient role to play in the world's heritage today (Timothy 2014).

References

Alderman, D. H. (2002). Writing on the Graceland wall: On the importance of authorship in pilgrimage landscapes. *Tourism Recreation Research, 27*(2), 27–33.

Alderman, D. H. (2015). The National Civil Rights Museum, Memphis, Tennessee. *Southeastern Geographer, 55*(1), 1–5.

Alderman, D. H., & Modlin, E. A. (2016). On the political utterances of plantation tourists: Vocalizing the memory of slavery on River Road. *Journal of Heritage Tourism, 11*(3), 275–289.

Anderson, W. C., & Anderson, E. (1991). *Guide to Mormon history travel*. Provo: Bushman.

Ashworth, G. J., & Hartmann, R. (2005). *Horror and human tragedy revisited: The management of sites of atrocities for tourism*. New York: Cognizant.

Austin, N. K. (2002). Managing heritage attractions: Marketing challenges at sensitive historical sites. *International Journal of Tourism Research, 4*(6), 447–457.

Biel, S. (Ed.). (2001). *American disasters*. New York: New York University Press.

Biran, A., Poria, Y., & Oren, G. (2011). Sought experiences at (dark) heritage sites. *Annals of Tourism Research, 38*(3), 820–841.

Blake, E. S., Landsea, C. W., & Gibney, E. J. (2011). *The deadliest, costliest and most intense United States tropical cyclones from 1851 to 2010 (and other frequently requested hurricane facts)*. Miami: National Weather Service.

Buzinde, C. N. (2010). Discursive constructions of the plantation past within a travel guidebook. *Journal of Heritage Tourism, 5*(3), 219–235.

Buzinde, C. N., & Santos, C. A. (2008). Representations of slavery. *Annals of Tourism Research, 35*(2), 469–488.

Campbell, B. C. (2008). *Disasters, accidents, and crises in American history: A reference guide to the nation's most catastrophic events*. New York: Facts on File.

Chronis, A. (2005). Coconstructing heritage at the Gettysburg storyscape. *Annals of Tourism Research, 32*(2), 386–406.

Chronis, A. (2007). Gettysburg co-constructed: Producing and consuming narratives in an American battlefield. *Advances in Consumer Research, 34*, 67.

Chronis, A. (2008). Co-constructing the narrative experience: Staging and consuming the American Civil War at Gettysburg. *Journal of Marketing Management, 24*(1–2), 5–27.

Coates, J. (2014). *Trail of tears*. Santa Barbara: Greenwood.

Dale, C., & Robinson, N. (2011). Dark tourism. In P. Robinson, S. Heitmann, & P. Dieke (Eds.), *Research themes for tourism* (pp. 205–217). Wallingford: CABI.

Dalton, D. (2015). *Dark tourism and crime*. London: Routledge.

Dann, G. M., & Seaton, A. V. (2001). Slavery, contested heritage and thanatourism. *International Journal of Hospitality & Tourism Administration, 2*(3–4), 1–29.

DeLyser, D. (1999). Authenticity on the ground: Engaging the past in a California ghost town. *Annals of the Association of American Geographers, 89*(4), 602–632.

Foley, M., & Lennon, J. J. (1996). JFK and dark tourism: A fascination with assassination. *International Journal of Heritage Studies, 2*(4), 198–211.

Foote, K. (1997). *Shadowed ground: America's landscapes of violence and tragedy*. Austin: University of Texas Press.

Gallay, A. (2002). *The Indian slave trade: The rise of the English empire in the American South, 1670–1671*. New Haven: Yale University Press.

Gelbman, A. (2008). Border tourism in Israel: Conflict, peace, fear and hope. *Tourism Geographies, 10*(2), 193–213.

Gelbman, A., & Timothy, D. J. (2010). From hostile boundaries to tourist attractions. *Current Issues in Tourism, 13*(3), 239–259.

Gibson, D. (2006). The relationship between serial murder and the American tourism industry. *Journal of Travel and Tourism Marketing, 20*, 45–60.

González-Tennant, E. (2013). New heritage and dark tourism: A mixed methods approach to social justice in Rosewood, Florida. *Heritage & Society, 6*(1), 62–88.

Graham, B. J., Ashworth, G. J., & Tunbridge, J. E. (2000). *A geography of heritage: Power, culture and economy*. London: Arnold.

Hartmann, R. (Ed.). (2009). *Southeast Colorado heritage tourism*. Denver: Wash Park Media.

Hartmann, R. (2014). Dark tourism, thanatourism, and dissonance in heritage tourism management: New directions in contemporary tourism research. *Journal of Heritage Tourism, 9*(2), 166–182.

Horton, J. O., & Kardux, J. C. (2004). Slavery and the contest for national heritage in the United States and The Netherlands. *American Studies International, 42*(2/3), 51–74.

Hudman, L. E. (1994). Historic sites and tourism. In S. K. Brown, D. Q. Cannon, & R. H. Jackson (Eds.), *Historical Atlas of Mormonism* (pp. 138–139). New York: Simon & Schuster.

Hudman, L. E., & Jackson, R. H. (1992). Mormon pilgrimage and tourism. *Annals of Tourism Research, 19*(1), 107–121.

Jamal, T., & Lelo, L. (2011). Exploring the conceptual and analytical framing of dark tourism: From darkness to intentionality. In R. Sharpley & P. R. Stone (Eds.), *Tourist experience: Contemporary perspectives* (pp. 29–42). London: Routledge.

Kelman, I., & Dodds, R. (2009). Developing a code of ethics for disaster tourism. *International Journal of Mass Emergencies and Disasters, 27*(3), 272–296.

Kerr, M. M., & Price, R. H. (2016). Overlooked encounters: Young tourists' experiences at dark sites. *Journal of Heritage Tourism, 11*(2), 177–185.

Lemelin, H., Powys Whyte, R., Johansen, K., Higgins-Desbiolles, F., Wilson, C., & Hemming, S. (2013). Conflicts, battlefields, indigenous peoples and tourism: Addressing dissonant heritage in warfare tourism in Australia and North America in the twenty-first century. *International Journal of Culture, Tourism and Hospitality Research, 7*(3), 257–271.

Lennon, J. J., & Foley, M. (1999). Interpretation of the unimaginable: The US Holocaust Memorial Museum, Washington, DC, and "dark tourism". *Journal of Travel Research, 38*(1), 46–50.

Lennon, J. J., & Foley, M. (2000). *Dark tourism: The attraction of death and disaster*. London: Thomson.

Levitt, L. (2010). Death on display: Reifying stardom through Hollywood's dark tourism. *The Velvet Light Trap, 65*, 62–70.

Lisle, D. (2004). Gazing at ground zero: Tourism, voyeurism and spectacle. *Journal for Cultural Research, 8*(1), 3–21.

Miles, S. (2014). Battlefield sites as dark tourism attractions: An analysis of experience. *Journal of Heritage Tourism, 9*(2), 134–147.

Miles, T. (2015). *Tales from the haunted south: Dark tourism and memories of slavery from the Civil War era*. Chapel Hill: University of North Carolina Press.

Newton-Matza, M. (Ed.). (2014). *Disasters and tragic events: An encyclopedia of catastrophes in American history, Vol. 1: 1650–1943*. Santa Barbara: ABC-CLIO.

Ng, W. (2002). *Japanese American internment during World War II: A history and reference guide*. Westport: Greenwood.

Olsen, D. H. (2006). Tourism and informal pilgrimage among the Latter-day Saints. In D. J. Timothy & D. H. Olsen (Eds.), *Tourism, religion & spiritual journeys* (pp. 254–270). London: Routledge.

Pezzullo, P. C. (2009). "This is the only tour that sells": Tourism, disaster, and national identity in New Orleans. *Journal of Tourism and Cultural Change, 7*(2), 99–114.

Potts, T. J. (2012). 'Dark tourism' and the 'kitschification' of 9/11. *Tourist Studies, 12*(3), 232–249.

Prideaux, B., & Timothy, D. J. (2011). From mining boom towns to tourist haunts: The ghost town life cycle. In M. Conlin & L. Jolliffe (Eds.), *Mining heritage and tourism: A global synthesis* (pp. 227–238). London: Routledge.

Reeves, R. (2015). *Infamy: The shocking story of the Japanese internment in World War II*. New York: Henry Holt.

Rice, A. (2009). Museums, memorials and plantation houses in the Black Atlantic: Slavery and the development of dark tourism. In R. Sharpley & P. R. Stone (Eds.), *The darker side of travel: The theory and practice of dark tourism* (pp. 224–246). Bristol: Channel View Publications.

Robb, E. M. (2009). Violence and recreation: Vacationing in the realm of dark tourism. *Anthropology and Humanism, 34*(1), 51–60.

Robbie, D. (2008). Touring Katrina: Authentic identities and disaster tourism in New Orleans. *Journal of Heritage Tourism, 3*(4), 257–266.

Sather-Wagstaff, J. (2011). *Heritage that hurts: Tourists in the Memoryscapes of September 11* (Vol. 4). Walnut Grove: Left Coast Press.

Seaton, A. V. (2001). Sources of slavery—Destinations of slavery: The silences and disclosures of slavery heritage in the UK and US. *International Journal of Hospitality & Tourism Administration, 2*(3/4), 107–129.

Seaton, A. V. (2002). Thanatourism's final frontiers? Visits to cemeteries, churchyards and funerary sites as sacred and secular pilgrimage. *Tourism Recreation Research, 27*(2), 73–82.

Seaton, A. V. (2009). Purposeful otherness: Approaches to the management of thanatourism. In R. Sharpley & P. R. Stone (Eds.), *The darker side of travel: The theory and practice of dark tourism* (pp. 75–108). Bristol: Channel View Publications.

Sharpley, R., & Stone, P. R. (2009a). (Re)presenting the macabre: Interpretation, kitschification and authenticity. In R. Sharpley & P. R. Stone (Eds.), *The darker side of travel: The theory and practice of dark tourism* (pp. 109–128). Bristol: Channel View Publications.

Sharpley, R., & Stone, P. R. (Eds.). (2009b). *The darker side of travel: The theory and practice of dark tourism*. Bristol: Channel View Publications.

Stone, P. R. (2011). Dark tourism: Towards a new post-disciplinary research agenda. *International Journal of Tourism Anthropology, 1*(3/4), 318–332.

Strange, C., & Kempa, M. (2003). Shades of dark tourism: Alcatraz and Robben Island. *Annals of Tourism Research, 30*(2), 386–405.

Taylor, A. (2002). *American colonies: Volume 1*. New York: Penguin.

Timothy, D. J. (1997). Tourism and the personal heritage experience. *Annals of Tourism Research, 34*(3), 751–754.

Timothy, D. J. (2011a). *Cultural heritage and tourism: An introduction*. Bristol: Channel View Publications.

Timothy, D. J. (2011b). Tourism and cultural heritage: Opportunities for Arizona. In B. Fahlman (Ed.), *Capitalizing on Arizona's arts and culture* (pp. 81–88). Phoenix: Arizona Town Hall.

Timothy, D. J. (2014). Contemporary cultural heritage and tourism: Development issues and emerging trends. *Public Archaeology, 13*(1–3), 30–47.

Timothy, D. J., & Boyd, S. W. (2015). *Tourism and trails: Cultural, ecological and management issues*. Bristol: Channel View Publications.

Timothy, D. J., Prideaux, B., & Kim, S. S. (2004). Tourism at borders of conflict and (de)militarized zones. In T. V. Singh (Ed.), *New horizons in tourism: Strange experiences and stranger practices* (pp. 83–94). Wallingford: CAB International.

Tinson, J. S., Saren, M. A., & Roth, B. E. (2015). Exploring the role of dark tourism in the creation of national identity of young Americans. *Journal of Marketing Management, 31*(7/8), 856–880.

Venbrux, E. (2010). Cemetery tourism: Coming to terms with death? *La Ricerca Folklorica, 61*, 41–49.

White, E. J. (1992). *Famous American disasters*. New York: Creative Television Associates.

White, L., & Frew, E. (Eds.). (2013). *Dark tourism and place identity: Managing and interpreting dark places*. London: Routledge.

Willard, P., Lade, C., & Frost, W. (2013). Darkness beyond memory: The battlefields at Culloden and Little Bighorn. In L. White & E. Frew (Eds.), *Dark tourism and place identity: Managing and interpreting dark places* (pp. 264–275). London: Routledge.

17

From Celebratory Landscapes to Dark Tourism Sites? Exploring the Design of Southern Plantation Museums

Stephen P. Hanna, Derek H. Alderman, and Candace Forbes Bright

Introduction: A Visit to Middleton

Situated just outside of Charleston, South Carolina, Middleton Place Plantations and Gardens must surely rank among the most beautiful places in the Southeastern United States. These "oldest formal gardens in North America," feature structural elements found at Versailles as well as a terraced lawn sloping down to the Ashley River. During peak season in early April, almost 1500 people come each day to gaze at the plethora of azaleas reflected in the still waters of the mill pond, or to photograph the amazing variety of wildlife that make the gardens their home.

Many visitors tour the South Flanker, the only remaining portion of the antebellum complex of majestic buildings that served as the Middleton family's home and showcase for centuries. Inside they learn that Arthur Middleton signed the Declaration of Independence while his grandson, Williams, signed the South Carolina articles of secession. Set up as a museum, the home features portraits of four generations of Middletons, as well as the family silver and other heirlooms.

S. P. Hanna (✉)
University of Mary Washington, Fredericksburg, VA, USA

D. H. Alderman
University of Tennessee, Knoxville, TN, USA

C. F. Bright
The University of Southern Mississippi, Hattiesburg, MS, USA

Yet, even visitors who limit their experiences to home and garden may catch a glimpse of the dark history underlying the beauty that brought them to this landscape. On the house tour, many guides point out the small metal tag sharing a display case with a silver tureen and Middleton family recipe book. These volunteers explain that it is an example of the tag worn by members of Middleton's enslaved community that "protected them" from bounty hunters hired to enforce fugitive slave laws. In the garden tour, interspersed among discussions of the varieties of camellias and other plants, visitors may learn that skilled enslaved laborers built the terraces and maintained the Middleton family's prized gardens.

For visitors interested in the lives of the plantation's enslaved women and men, the plantation offers the increasingly popular "Beyond the Fields" tour. On this 45-minute walk through the museum's slavery exhibit and grounds, guides explain that Middleton Place was at the center of a sprawling agrobusiness enterprise that, at any one time, comprised nearly 20 rice plantations and as many as 1000 slaves. They also share the recorded fragments of the lives of a few individuals enslaved by the Middletons to recognize their role in creating the verdant landscape that tourists enjoy today. More and more visitors, therefore, have the opportunity to learn that the grand gardens and furnishings hide what should be obvious to anyone with a rudimentary knowledge of American history; the beauty that serves as Middleton's primary attraction hides America's original sin (Plate 17.1).

Middleton Place is typical of most plantation museums in the southern United States. During the second half of the twentieth century, descendants of antebellum owners, non-profit associations, and other organizations transformed these homes into place products designed to attract tourists interested in a combination of history, architecture, and gardens. In so doing, they reproduced, and in many cases continue to reproduce, a thoroughly racialized and romanticized version of the region's social memory (Hoelscher 2006). It is a memory carefully designed to perpetuate the myth of the Lost Cause, that peculiar yet still powerful social forgetting of the enslaved, who made possible the lives of the white planter elite these sites celebrate. Usually cut off in time and space from their fields of cotton, tobacco, rice, or sugar, the remnants of plantations now serving as tourism sites are the results of selective preservation and commemorative processes that leave few traces of the dark realities of the antebellum slave-based political economy. Over time, museum administrators and curators have inscribed tour routes through the remnant landscape of the Big House and grounds that help guides explain: the significance of antique furniture; the uniqueness of architectural features; and the opulent and powerful lives of colonial or antebellum owners. Until recently, therefore,

Plate 17.1 Scenes from Middleton Place. South Flanker, reflecting pond, spring house, and chapel (Photo Source: Author—Hanna, S.P.)

the majority of plantation museum owners, docents, and visitors saw, quite literally, no place for the commemoration of the enslaved (Eichstedt and Small 2002).

Over the past decade, however, the management of tourist plantations—including Middleton—have found themselves under market and social pressure to incorporate narratives and landscape elements revealing their place and complicity in the transatlantic and domestic slave trades (Alderman et al. 2016). Thus, they increasingly employ archeologists, exhibit designers, and storytellers to find ways to respectfully commemorate the enslaved women and men who struggled in the context of bondage to create lives for themselves and their families. The end result might be a separate guided tour, such as Middleton's, that focuses on enslaved life. In a growing number of instances, plantations display the remains, restorations, reconstructions, or replicas of antebellum slave cabins. These slave quarters provide the setting where guides or signage can help visitors experience, in a very limited way, how and where the slave community lived, and the meager nature of their existence. This in no way guarantees, however, that the slave cabin will not be relegated to the physical and narrative shadows of the Big House of the planter family (Small 2013).

The Problem of Dark Tourism

As our exploration of Middleton Place makes clear, antebellum plantation museums offer a perplexing problem for tourism scholars, particularly those trying to figure out whether and exactly how these sites of southern heritage can provide meaningful dark tourism experiences. We emphasize "meaningful" to recognize that while dark tourism clearly runs the risk of commodifying and trivializing atrocity, it also carries with it a capacity for historical education and even commemorative justice for those traditionally marginalized in dominant heritage tourism narratives. Indeed, Stone (2009) calls for scholars to enhance their efforts to place dark tourism within a broader context of morality, emotion, and as we would add, historical responsibility (also see Chap. 15). The theme of historical responsibility is particularly appropriate in discussing the remembrance or forgetting of slavery within the American South. According to Griffin and Hargis (2012), the history of racialized exploitation and violence casts a long and enduring shadow across the region, and southerners as of late have explored a variety of reconciliation and restorative justice projects. At the heart of much of this transitional justice work within the South is recognizing that the cultural amnesia of difficult and painful pasts, such as been practiced at plantation museums for so many years, is not an option for racial reconciliation in America.

It is from this political and ideological perspective that we have spent the past several years studying how the spatial and narrative arrangement of tourist experiences at plantations either inhibit or facilitate the creation of moments to reflect on the nation's dark past and, in doing so, do justice to the memory of slavery and the enslaved (Alderman and Modlin 2008; Hanna

2016). Developing and transitioning to "dark" experiences has a number of loaded meanings at plantation sites, however. To darken the plantation experience, so to speak, involves a transition from a story often exclusively of white slave-owning families to one populating the plantation with previously invisible black faces and bodies. Second, a dark perspective involves transitioning from a heritage experience that represents slavery as a romanticized and benign system of servitude to recognizing the violent and dehumanizing qualities of human bondage. Third, the word dark might also encompass a recognition of the larger social geography of the plantation, moving the tourist gaze away from the day-time spaces and activities of the Big House to the night time world of slave quarters, woods, and swamps where the enslaved had perhaps their most agency and autonomy from the master's eyes and control (Ginsburg 2007; Hanna 2012).

Yet, it is no small feat to make a place for a dark, slavery-related tourism experience at sites that have historically gone to great pains to hide and deny that past. Scholars have used the framework of "surrogation" to capture the complex process of retelling the painful story of the African diaspora and how that process, by its very contentious nature, is never complete or without tension (Lambert 2007; Alderman 2010). Even in the light of current efforts to come to terms with the histories and geographies of slave life within the tours and exhibits of southern plantation museums, it is difficult if not absurd to characterize places such as Middleton Place—with their elegant mansions and lovely gardens—as dark tourism sites that prompt sober reflection on the social and emotional gravity of the slave experience and its relevance in the struggle for racial justice today. As cultural and historical geographers, we argue that for tourism plantations to realize a greater capacity to recount the darker history and legacy of antebellum slave life, there must be a direct engagement with and critique of the spatial and narrative designs of traditional plantation tourism sites. Underlying this argument is a broader recognition of the important role that landscape plays in the production, consumption, and contestation of memory—an idea of growing popularity within the literature on public commemoration (Ryan et al. 2016). And specific to our discussion here, the emplacing of stories of slavery within the plantation landscape—where and how it is grounded as well as how it is positioned in relation to broader narratives and spaces—is of critical importance to creating a surrogate to serve as a representative of the long repressed and suppressed memories of slavery. Consequently, one of the theoretical goals of this chapter is to put forward an understanding of the centrality of landscape and spatiality within dark tourism practice and analysis that has previously gone under-developed within the literature.

With this goal in mind, the purpose of our chapter is to examine the spatial and narrative designs of plantation tourism sites. Because our research has allowed us access to a number of plantation sites in the American South and we have benefited from partnerships and engagements with the tourism industry, our analysis is meant to inform and advance management as well as scholarly understandings of how the landscape can be exploited to produce critical moments of dark tourism experience. These moments can alter and destabilize the broader white myth-making that has taken place at plantations for so long (Modlin 2008). Drawing from a number of examples of prominent and successful touristic plantations, our work pays attention to how design can perpetuate the annihilation or marginalization of the enslaved before exploring how tour narratives and landscapes can be reworked to place the commemoration of enslaved women and men, as well as the broader role of slavery in American history, at the center of plantation museums. Before delving into a look at the power of specific plantation landscape designs, however, it is necessary to offer some theoretical observations meant to advance the study of dark tourism.

Surrogation and Spatial Narratives in Plantation Museum Design

Dark tourism—also called thanatourism because it often references travel associated with death, violence, and suffering—emerged as an academic field of study well over 20 years ago. Slavery heritage quickly became a topic of discussion within the dark tourism literature (Dann and Seaton 2001), and a number of studies have explored the growing popularity of travel to the slave castles of West Africa as a form of dark tourism (e.g. Mowatt and Chancellor 2011; Carter 2015). Plantation museums have tended not to be characterized in the same dark terms, a recognition that these sites have historically ignored its history of brutal enslavement and forced labor. Yet, the problem of characterizing plantations as dark sites is partly due to how we have traditionally studied dark tourism as well. Initially, scholars were most interested in identifying and categorizing destinations as dark or not. Ashworth and Isaac (2015, 316) contend that recently we have seen a shift away from classifying the degree of darkness (or lightness) of sites to analyzing the "experiences conveyed by the sites that could be dark" and the motivations and interpretations of visitors. Rudi Hartmann (2014) credits Ashworth in saying that, "there are no dark sites, only dark tourists." We would argue, more precisely, there are no dark sites or dark tourists, only dark touristic practices (also see Chap. 1).

This emphasis on practice is of particular interest to us since the narrative and spatial design of the plantation site can evoke emotions, social associations, and behavioral reactions of the traveling public that might be considered dark. Given that even individual tourists may have multiple motivations for and reactions to visiting such sites and museum management and staff play critical roles in shaping the plantation experience, a more useful approach to dark tourism analysis seeks to examine the practices and performances of different actors in creating and recreating plantation tourism sites as slavery-related heritage products. By the same token, these same practices and performances can reproduce a white-washing of this dark history for the purposes creating a plantation experience decidedly romanticized and celebratory.

Dark tourism, while seemingly a unified field of study, grew out of multiple independent strands of thought, some of which argued that developing universal taxonomies of dark sites does not capture the inherently conflicted nature of heritage, especially controversial or dark heritages (Ashworth and Isaac 2015). Often collapsed within the broad dark tourism literature is Tunbridge and Ashworth's (1996) notion of heritage dissonance, which sees disharmony rather than consensus in how heritage is produced, marketed, and consumed. Given the wide-ranging public opinions about the appropriateness and value of talking about enslavement, and the close emotional connection between slavery and the politics of racial identity in America, the dissonant heritage approach is an especially fruitful avenue for understanding the difficulty of managing dark heritage sites in general, and the specific challenges of making a place at plantation museums for dark tourism practices. Yankholmes and McKercher (2015) see the development of slavery heritage tourism as being fraught with conflict and contradictions. Rather than having a singular message presented to a homogeneous audience, slavery-related sites have contesting stakeholders "involved in the interpretation of slavery heritage, each with its own agenda, desire to remember or forget slave memories, and desire to compose different narratives" (Yankholmes and McKercher 2015, 233). This argument especially resonates with southern plantation museums, where a disharmony of views about slavery exists at the same site among tourists, tour guides, and management—all of whom have different comfort levels, personal identifications with the past, and ideological and political dispositions toward the victims and perpetrators of enslavement.

The sheer diversity of competing stakeholders is helpful to understanding the dissonant qualities of remembering slavery at tourism sites, but it does not completely capture the social and spatial dynamics at work in either marginalizing or making a place for the enslaved within plantation tourism sites.

Recent innovations in the geographical literature on race and southern memory are instructive here. Those who wish to place slavery at the center of our memories of the southern plantation struggle with the commemorative politics of both the present and the past. Alderman and Campbell (2008, 342) advance the term "symbolic excavation" recognizing that the commemoration of enslaved persons involves digging into both soil and archives to find the material necessary to reconstruct their lives and experiences. Symbolic excavation is, therefore, a form of "memory work" (Till 2012)—one made exceptionally difficult by the purposeful erasure of enslaved African-Americans from mainstream collective memories, and place representations (Alderman and Modlin 2013).

While symbolic excavation can help us understand the work curators and researchers perform to replace memories of the enslaved within plantation museums, it does not capture strategies necessary to commemorate the lives of millions of enslaved African-Americans whose existence in the historical record amounts to little more than tallies in an enslaver's inventory. Such lost lives can only be remembered through commemorative surrogation, the often dissonant process of "filling historical and emotional cavities created by the death, diasporas, and trauma of enslavement" (Alderman 2010, 94, see also Lambert 2007). The dissonant nature of surrogation is most evident when people view the surrogate—perhaps a monument, piece of public art, or a performance—as either excessive or deficient. People viewing a surrogate as deficient may argue that it does not capture slavery's brutality or recognize the institution as foundational to the American nation and economy (Baptist 2014). If viewed as excessive, a surrogate might be "responsible for opening new ruptures in the collective social memory" (Alderman 2010, 94) through overly detailed depictions of that same brutality or through glorifying a violent slave rebellion (Lambert 2007).

Commemorative surrogation is suggested here as a useful framework for understanding the political importance of design to the goal of doing justice to the memory of the enslaved within plantation tourism sites and, thereby, framing the emotional and educational experience of the dark tourist. This design process is, of course, a narrative one and involves finding the appropriate words, phrases, and discursive frameworks within which to retell and interpret the history of slavery. Yet, Waterton and Dittmer (2014) encourage us to view museums and other memorials as "assemblages" of not just narratives but also people, environments, and materials—all of which shape the experiences and the affective engagement of visitors. In particular, they consider how the designed, non-human elements of museums—including the physical layout and landscape of exhibitions and artifacts—collaborate with human elements to make a difference in the social interpretation of the past. Such a perspective does not dismiss the importance of discourse, but focuses on how the representation and performance of stories interact with and rely upon the material. Indeed, the heritage site design process also involves attaching narratives to key sites, views, and artifacts that serve to anchor stories to place thereby fixing meanings to the plantation landscape.

Eichstedt and Small (2002) spend considerable energy reviewing the many narrative and artifactual strategies used to discuss slavery or, as they found at many plantations, avoid talking about the enslaved: annihilation (no mention at all), trivialization, deflection, segregation, and limited incorporation. Our work at several plantations over the years suggests that these sites have begun to develop and adopt specific discursive and material strategies for narrating a greater presence of the enslaved. For example, Dwyer et al. (2013) note that Laura Plantation, located along Louisiana's sugar-producing River Road, began including slavery in the main tour narrative in the late 1990s, while Hanna (2016) documented the process and positioning of creating the "Slavery at Oak Alley" exhibit at a nearby plantation. Important to the design is the manner in which narratives create meaning, not simply from what they say in terms of content, but also through context and how the interpretation of surrogate narratives is shaped by what Dwyer (2004) calls an "accretion" of narratives on top or next to each other. This accretion can be the layering of allied narratives that affirm and confirm each other's interpretation of the past or a layering of antithetical narratives that contradict and work against each other's intended commemorative message.

Also important to the process of designing a surrogate for the slave experience is the role of space. Azaryahu and Foote (2008) have advanced our understanding of spatial narratives at commemorative sites by observing how the organization and configuration of interpretative signs or guide-led tours in and through landscapes affect the ways a narrative's different themes might be emphasized. Hanna (2016) notes that critical consideration of landscape design and the multi-scaled spatialities of plantation narratives are missing from many studies of plantation tourism—whether framed in the context of dark tourism or not. The locations where the histories of the enslaved are recovered and represented help frame the nature and degree to which plantation tourists engage and experience those memories. As geographers increasingly argue, the landscape is not simply incidental to public commemoration, but an active participant in the production and consumption of heritage tourism as a product and a set of values and ideas about the past (Dwyer and Alderman 2008).

An important place-making accompanies the marketing, narrating, and experiencing of the southern plantation. As our chapter suggests, understanding how allied and antagonistic memories are emplaced or spatially fixed in relation to each other determines how much and what type of room is made for the enslaved within dominant historical narratives about antebellum life and race relations. In fact, we would suggest that the process of finding a surrogate for the enslaved, as a dark heritage practice, is one that is invariably about creating an interpretative assemblage of narratives, material objects, and landscapes that has an influence on visitors that is greater than the sum of its parts. As an assemblage, the plantation museum is an open system "susceptible to new elements being introduced and old ones departing," which then open up or close down possibilities for affective engagement with the history of slavery (Waterton and Dittmer 2014).

Designing Narrative Landscapes

While the majestic white-pillared Big House with sweeping lawns and beautiful gardens was quite rare in the antebellum South (Hoelscher 2006), selective preservation and the power of late nineteenth and early twentieth century white supremacist ideology combined to turn this image into one of the South's most iconic and mythic landscapes, becoming an invented tradition for national and global audiences (Taylor 2001). Today, such plantation homes tend to be the most visited among the South's hundreds of house-museums. Oak Alley Plantation in Louisiana's sugarcane producing region, for example, attracts almost a quarter million visitors a year, and the South Carolina rice plantations, Middleton Place, Magnolia Plantation and Gardens, and Boone Hall exceed 100,000 annual visitors each. While, as heritage place-products, these museums are all different, there are some important commonalities in the spatial arrangements of the landscapes, narratives, and touristic practices that shape visitor practices.

Our observations at plantations in Louisiana, South Carolina, and Virginia suggest that, while often segregated or marginalized, guided tours and exhibits including the enslaved are more common than when Eichstedt and Small (2002) noted that most of these museums "symbolically annihilated" slavery. Thus, the potential exists for stories, artifacts, or landscape elements to serve as the commemorative surrogates necessary to open up moments for meaningful dark touristic experiences. Nevertheless, the processes of designing landscapes and narratives as surrogates for enslaved women and men involve fitting the enslaved into or alongside the traditional white-centric spatial narratives that, most commonly, continue to occupy the center of plantations as heritage tourism spaces. Therefore, it is useful to consider the spatial assemblages of plantation museums prior to the addition of slavery tours and exhibits.

The mansion or Big House remains the most prominent part of the traditional plantation landscape and is almost always the focus of the tour. As the home of the white slave-owning family, it serves as the stage upon which guides and visitors perform narratives of family history, colonial or antebellum social customs, and the most prominent family members' roles in local history and politics. Guides use portraits, furnishings, and other artifacts to authenticate these narratives. Many visitors anchor their understanding of the plantation past in these objects—this is made evident by the practice of asking questions about architectural elements, paintings, table-settings, and other curios. In this way, the practices of curators, guides, and visitors erase or trivialize the enslaved—dissonance occurs only when visitors ask about the roles of enslaved servants or recognize that the very artifacts used to illustrate the grace and charm of the white southern lifestyle also represent the wealth created from the labor of the enslaved.

Despite its prominence, the Big House is seldom the only part of the landscape that informs plantation narratives. Most sites feature footpaths leading through formal or romantic gardens to preserved outbuildings, restaurants, gift shops, and carefully contrived vistas. Even when guided tours do not follow these paths, part of the tourist experience usually involves exploring the grounds before or after the tour. At most of these heritage tourism sites, landscape elements celebrate present-day beauty instead of demonstrating the plantations' original agricultural function, thereby further obscuring the labor and lives of enslaved women and men. While the paths visitors follow through grounds and gardens are often marked with directional and interpretative signage, it is rare for these to do more than identify the antebellum kitchen or locally unique species of trees and shrubs. In other words, the sites are arranged for visitors to enjoy the beauty of the landscape rather than reflect on the struggles of the enslaved to make lives for themselves or on the central role that plantations, as slave labor camps, played in the economic and political development of the United States. At traditional plantation museums, such dissonant narratives are only present when they are brought in and vocalized by particular visitors.

As at other heritage tourism sites, a plantation's buildings and pathways are arranged not only for practical purposes, but also to preserve and represent selective memories from particular eras—to spatially configure and normalize the retelling of history (Azaryahu and Foote 2008). For those embracing their status as museums, claims of historical authenticity are highly valued by both museum management and visitors, even when exhibits, artifacts, and landscapes are by necessity staged (DeLyser 1999). Given that preservation is, at its core, a conservative practice rooted in resisting change, even as it is about narrating the past (Datel 1990), plantation museums are loath to rearrange their physical landscapes. Adding or removing structures, changing the routes of garden paths, or altering the interiors of the Big House may detract from the perceived authenticity of site. Between that and the significant financial costs involved in making major changes, the spatial arrangements of plantation museums tend to change slowly. Thus, in addition to struggling with visitors and staff who defend the honor of the southern plantation portrayed in *Gone with the Wind* and other romanticized and racialized accounts, those working to re-place the lives and experiences of enslaved women and men within these landscapes must also overcome narrow and conservative conceptualizations of what is authentic to the plantation's believed social and spatial order. For example, as one historical interpreter remarked to McDaniel (2015, 129), "I wish we could do more to interpret African American history here, but we just don't have a place to it." This comment reflects not only the disturbing assumption that the history of slavery is somehow not everywhere on the plantation, but also the reluctance of some sites to make room, literally and figuratively, for the enslaved within existing spatial narrative designs.

Nevertheless, current evidence suggests that managers, curators, and guides at many tourism plantations across the South are incorporating, or at least mentioning, the enslaved in their landscapes and narratives. When asked why they are working to add material about slavery, owners, guides, and other museum staff often state they are responding to comments from visitors or mention that a nearby, competing plantation has added a slavery tour or exhibit. Regardless of their reasons, the redesign of landscapes and narratives to accommodate the enslaved range from simply adding a few mentions in tour narratives to more fully engaging in the symbolic excavation necessary to create slavery-themed tours or exhibits.

At some plantations, efforts to replace the enslaved are rudimentary. Indeed, they appear as attempts to head off criticism more than to commemorate the enslaved in a socially responsible way. This is evident at some of the plantation museums along Virginia's James River, the region where race-based slavery became codified into colonial law in the 1660s in order to provide labor for tobacco production (Himes 1979). Shirley Plantation, for example, created an exhibit space in half of the original kitchen building. Most of the display panels explain how staff are gathering evidence about the plantation's enslaved community through archival research and archeological digs. Descriptions of the lives and experiences of the enslaved people themselves are mostly confined to four three-ring notebooks set on the room's window sills. Arranged in a frequently-asked-questions format, the binders do state that slave sales occurred at Shirley, describe how slaves were punished, and list a few local families descended from women and men formerly enslaved by the plantation's owners. Mentions of the enslaved on the tour of the mansion, however, are rare and seldom do more than passively acknowledge that slavery happened. A few miles down the road, Virginia's Berkeley Plantation takes a similar approach. This site's slavery exhibit, best described as a jumble of models, pictures, and documents describing slavery at the plantation, lines one wall of the coach house—a postbellum building containing the public restrooms. Framed copies of slave inventories hang above a model of a slave cabin next to which lies a black three-ring binder containing copies of relevant documents.

Berkeley and Shirley plantations, therefore, serve as examples of how narrative accretion and the spatial configuring of an interpretive environment can work to marginalize the enslaved. Changes in the museum's assemblage are peripheral and thus leave unchallenged the centrality of the colonial and antebellum white owners' lifestyles and contributions to local and national histories. As commemorative surrogates, both slavery exhibits can be described as deficient; they do little to encourage visitors to meaningfully reflect on the dark history of slavery more broadly or to identify with enslaved people as individuals who struggled to make lives for themselves and families. Therefore, dissonant touristic practices continue to depend on the interests visitors bring with them when visiting Shirley, Berkeley, and other plantations that marginalize the enslaved through their design practices.

Other plantation museums have done more to incorporate slavery and the enslaved into the assemblage of tour narratives, exhibits, and designed landscapes. Once again, Middleton Place serves as a useful example. At Middleton, the accretion of narrative and landscape elements commemorating the enslaved began in the early to mid-1990s—earlier than at many other tourism plantations in the United States. Eliza's House, named for the last African-American occupant of this dwelling, is a postbellum duplex that served as home to several generations of freedmen who remained at Middleton after emancipation. Displaced to make room for Middleton's restaurant, the restored building sits under a few massive live oaks across the expansive green of the sheep meadow from South Flanker where the house tour takes place (Plate 17.2). In 2005, one half of Eliza's House was transformed into an exhibit documenting "in the most personal way the lives, families, and contributions of some seven generations of African Americans at Middleton Place."[1]

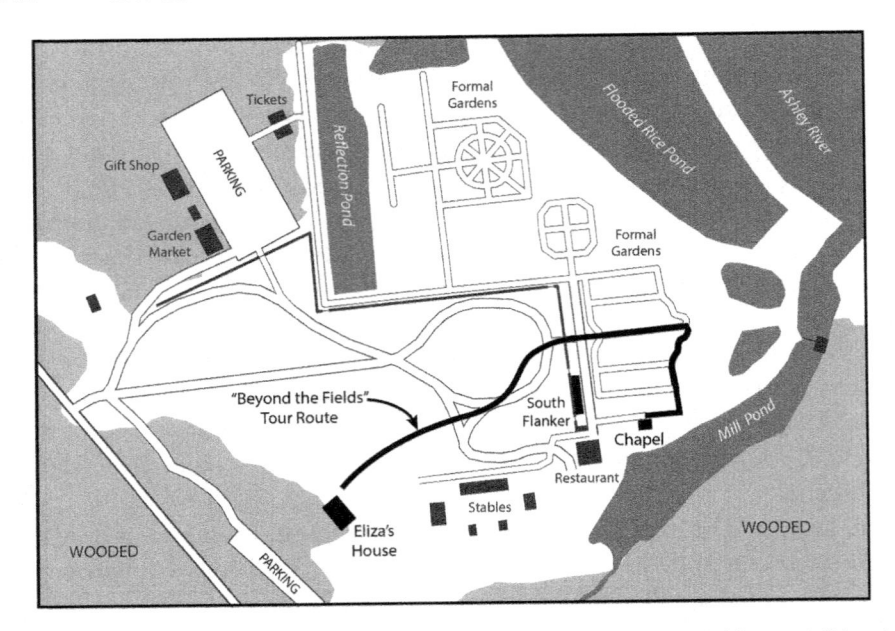

Plate 17.2 Middleton Place site plan featuring the 'Beyond the Fields Tour' (Map by Author—Hanna, S.P.)

Eliza's House also serves as the starting point for the "Beyond the Fields" tour, a guided walking tour first offered to visitors in the late 1990s. This tour combines regional histories of the roles enslaved Africans played in rice production with brief biographical facts of a few individuals enslaved by the Middleton family. Additionally, guides credit enslaved laborers for constructing the plantation's famed terraces and formal gardens. For the most part, however, the "Beyond the Fields" tour and exhibit are segregated narratively and spatially from the house tour. The inclusion of slavery and the enslaved by the volunteer guides who lead the tours of the South Flanker is highly uneven and most mentions are limited to enslaved house servants solely defined by their roles as nannies, maids, and butlers.

The additions of the "Beyond the Fields" tour and exhibit at Middleton Place are examples of heritage dissonance at a plantation museum. These additions uneasily co-exist with more traditional tours of the formal gardens that continue to emphasize the beauty of the landscape and stress that Middleton Place symbolically showcased the Middletons' place atop South Carolina's social hierarchy. Additionally, the house tour focuses almost exclusively on the significance of the family's place in the histories of South Carolina and the United States. Visitors who choose to engage with the enslaved by visiting Eliza's House or taking the "Beyond the Fields" tour may find moments and spaces where they acknowledge contributions and difficult lives of Middleton Place's enslaved population in ways that may at least complicate the narratives offered on the other tours. Thus, the design of Middleton may do more to encourage meaningful dark touristic practices than the designs of plantations such as Shirley and Berkeley.

At the same time, however, the narrative contents of the Beyond the Fields tour and exhibit as well as their spatialities ensure that the Middleton family remains at the museum's center. The tour avoids the South Flanker and this, combined with the near absence of mentions of the enslaved in the Big House tour, suggests that slavery did not exist everywhere at Middleton Place. Additionally, the "Beyond the Fields" tour ends in a small chapel built by the Middletons for the enslaved. While plainly furnished, the chapel overlooks the Mill Pond and azaleas allowing the aesthetics of the present-day gardens to intrude—visually, sensually, and politically—on a space where complex religious identities of enslaved Africans should be the focus. More problematically, guides often use the chapel to focus visitor attention on the Middleton family's concern for the spiritual well-being of their slaves—thereby creating a situation where the reputational politics of remembering the master fondly is accreted upon efforts to memorialize the enslaved. This lessens the primacy of the slave experience or, more accurately, makes it dependent upon the master narrative.

Of the traditional plantations we have visited in our studies, perhaps none has made more changes designed to incorporate the enslaved to its site and narratives than Oak Alley Plantation in Vacherie, Louisiana. Like Middleton place, Oak Alley's considerable appeal to tourists is based on its beauty. The columned antebellum mansion, the alley of 300-year-old oaks, and the elaborately costumed guides are meant to evoke nostalgia for the mythic South of moonlight and magnolias (Hanna 2016) rather than detail the slave-based sugar economy of the region. Nevertheless, due in part to visitor complaints, in 2011 the museum's manager and curators began discussing the addition of an exhibit designed to commemorate Oak Alley's enslaved. Because the original slave cabins were demolished a century ago, those involved in the discussions did not see a place within the museum where discussions of slavery could occur. Therefore, they built six replica cabins in approximately the same area where the original cabins stood and now use these structures to house or emplace the "Slavery at Oak Alley" exhibit as a dark commemorative surrogate. Completed and opened in late 2013, the exhibit is designed as a self-guided tour around and through the cabins which contain furnishings and artifacts representing the everyday lives of Oak Alley's enslaved community.

The location of this sizable slave cabin exhibit along the museum's Back Alley ensures that most visitors notice its presence and, even if they do not take the time to complete the tour, have to acknowledge the presence of the enslaved (Plate 17.3). Visitors who do spend time reading the exhibit's signage will learn about the differing experiences of house slaves and field slaves, the brutal nature of working on a sugar plantation, and, to a limited extent, the ways the enslaving family treated the women and men they enslaved. More than anything else, however, the exhibit is designed to give names to the individuals commemorated in this newly constructed space. A small sign explains that an interior cabin wall bearing the first names of 198 enslaved women and men serves as "a respectful recognition of the *people* [emphasis in original] on whose backs this plantation was built. For most of them, a name is all that remains of their story."

Here is a place designed for meaningful dark tourism experiences. Intended to be seen toward the end of the exhibit, the empty room containing this wall of names gives visitors a moment in time and space to understand that the magnificent Big House and lovely live oaks can only be enjoyed today because of slavery. Perhaps some may ponder why the majority of these 198 individuals—as well as millions of others—were robbed of the chance to be remembered as more than a single name upon a wall.

When speaking about the exhibit's design, staff talk about both the need to create a stage where the enslaved can be remembered and the need to "balance

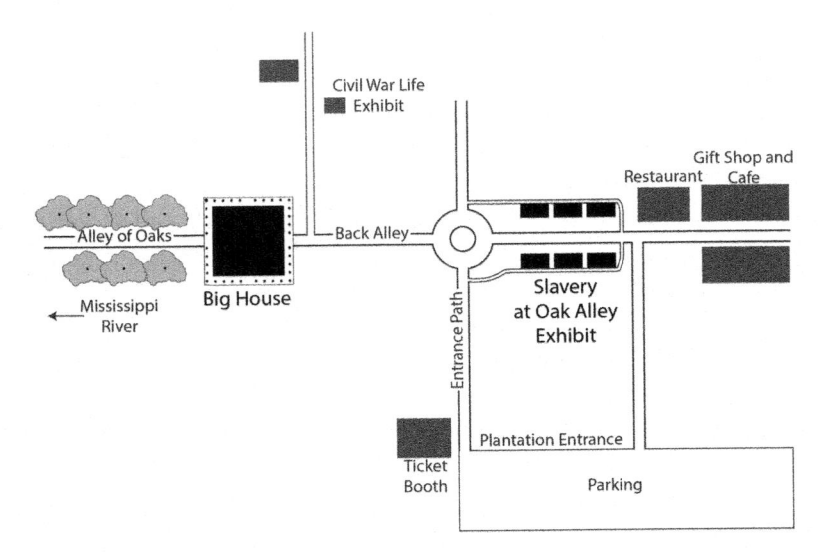

Plate 17.3 Oak Alley site plan featuring the "Slavery at Oak Alley Exhibit" (Map by Author—Hanna, S.P.)

the strong physical presence of the iconic Big House."[2] Thus, compared to the small exhibits tucked into out-buildings found at plantations such as Berkeley and Shirley, Oak Alley's slavery exhibit is expansive and centrally placed, demonstrating the difference that strategically-configured location and visibility makes in retelling and doing justice to dark heritage. The presence of the cabins is even felt in the guided tour of the Big House. As the tour reaches the second-floor gallery along the back of the mansion, guides usually advise tourists to visit the cabins after the main tour is concluded.

Yet, this massive example of narrative and commemorative accretion is less disruptive to the dominant aesthetic than one might expect. The cabins do little to challenge Oak Alley's use of beauty and landscape aesthetics to evoke nostalgia for the mythic South of the Lost Cause. The whitewashed cabins nestle seamlessly into the live oaks lining the Back Alley, and their sparsely furnished but clean interiors hardly evoke the harsh and crowded living conditions experienced by enslaved women and men in nineteenth century Louisiana. Overall, the exhibit is conservatively curated as well. The facts and stories about the enslaved are limited to those for which staff have found documentary evidence specific to Oak Alley. As a result, there are no stories about resistance and no information about the experience of being forcibly separated from family and relocated to this sugar plantation. The exhibit's designers chose not to fill these absences by drawing from contextualizing stories sourced from the surrounding area as surrogates. Thus, the exhibit cannot displace the richly detailed narratives of the master and his family guides share with audiences in the Big House.

Taken together, the examples of Shirley, Berkeley, Middleton, and Oak Alley strongly suggest that variations in the placement and design of exhibits and tours telling the stories of these plantations' enslaved community play crucial roles in their efficacy as surrogates to achieve commemorative justice through meaningful dark touristic practices. Yet, these plantations' spatial and narrative strategies for the inclusion of slavery do not displace the master's narrative from the center of the museum as assemblage. Therefore, remembering slavery and its lingering impact on racialized systems of injustice remains secondary to narratives celebrating the lives and achievements of white antebellum slave owners and landscape aesthetics reinforcing the mythical beauty of the antebellum plantation.

Reversing this hierarchy requires more radical approaches to the spatial designs of plantation museums. Whitney Plantation, opened in December 2014 within a few miles of Oak Alley, provides the best-known example of such an approach. An active sugar plantation until the 1970s, Whitney was never transformed into a traditional plantation museum. Instead, after a few decades of neglect, the plantation was purchased by lawyer John Cummings who spent 13 years and millions of dollars designing and building a museum focused on the stories and experiences of the enslaved (Amsden 2015). Thus, while Cummings and his staff began with an antebellum Big House and a few outbuildings, there were no existing white-centric tours and exhibits that had already established their primacy or etched memories of the mythic South into the landscape.

Beginning with this relatively blank slate, the Whitney staff pursued decidedly unconventional and by some accounts controversial approaches to designing the assemblage of narratives, landscapes, and experiences that now comprise the museum. Instead of simply restoring the Big House and other remaining buildings, Cummings purchased several slave cabins, a jail, and the postbellum African-American Antioch Church building and had them relocated to the site. While antithetical to more conservative historic preservation practices, this approach provided the material elements necessary to anchor the stories of the enslaved in the landscape, even if these disparate elements did not fit squarely with each other in terms of era or geographic origin. This suggests that the efficacy of finding a surrogate for retelling the dark history of slavery is sometimes about designing contextual as well as particular stand-ins for enslaved African American heritage. In addition, Whitney plantation's narrative transcends the scale of the site in ways that Oak Alley's does not. This is evident both in the massive memorials constructed on the site as well as in the use of 1930s Works Progress Administration (WPA) interviews with former slaves. The memorials contain the names of not just Whitney's enslaved population, but also of over 100,000 women, men, and children who lived, worked, and died as slaves throughout Louisiana. Selected quotes from the WPA interviews are etched into each of these memorials not because they are specific to the plantation, River Road, or even Louisiana, but because they allow for voices of the formerly enslaved—regardless of where they were enslaved—to make present their own lived experiences.

These and other design decisions permit Whitney to offer a tour that inverts the narrative and spatial arrangements found at traditional plantation tourism sites—even those that have made considerable efforts to commemorate the enslaved. The tour begins in the back of the Welcome Center, a building that contains an exhibit on the history of slavery in the Atlantic world (Plate 17.4). There, guides give a brief overview of the site's history, naming the antebellum owners as well as John Cummings, the current owner, before leading visitors to the Antioch Church where they watch a video explaining the museum's mission "as a site of memory and consciousness . . . to pay homage to all slaves on the plantation itself and to all of those who lived elsewhere in the US

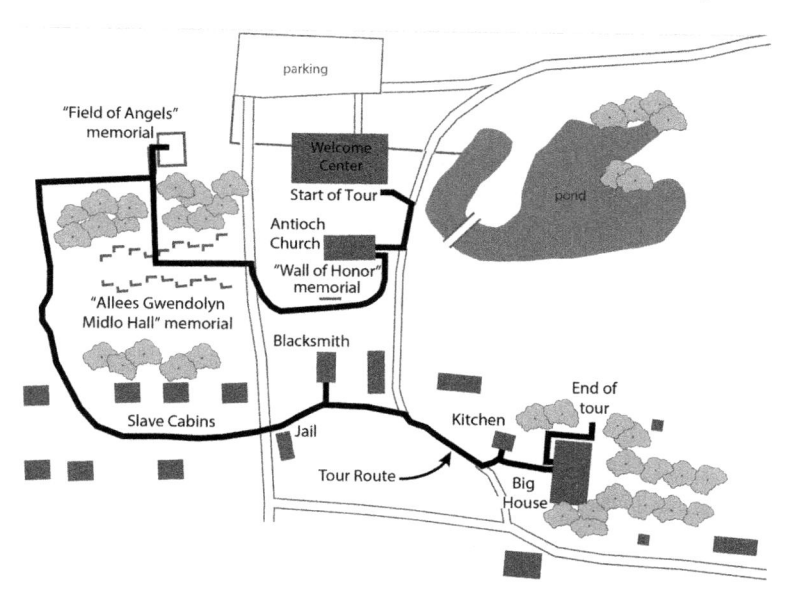

Plate 17.4 Whitney Plantation site plan featuring route of main tour (Map by Author—Hanna, S.P.)

South."[3] The tour then stops at each of the three memorials to the enslaved. There, guides tell stories about specific people enslaved at Whitney and emphasize the massive numbers of people who experienced the traumas of slavery. In addition, visitors are given time to read the names of enslaved women and men engraved on the walls of the memorials as well as the excerpts from the WPA interviews. Placing the memorials towards the beginning of the tour encourages visitors to engage in a respectful and sobering dark tourism practice—the commemoration of hundreds of thousands of women and men whose lives and deaths were shaped by their enslavement. The tour's path then leads guides and visitors to the cluster of seven slave cabins. Along this stretch, guides describe the work of planting and harvesting sugarcane as well as the grueling daily lives of enslaved field hands. After giving visitors time to look at the jail and using this artifact to talk about resistance and punishment, guides lead visitors to the restored blacksmith shop and kitchen to talk about the lives and contributions of enslaved crafts persons and cooks. The tour ends at the sparsely furnished Big House, a space used to describe the work enslaved children performed to feed, bath, and clothe their owners. In this space, the antebellum owner and his family are more present than elsewhere on the tour, but the narrative focuses on their roles as business owners and enslavers.

Whitney's design focuses the museum on the tragedy and injustice of slavery in the Southern United States and, as such, positions it to serve as a surrogate for the "historical and emotional cavities created by the death, diasporas, and trauma of enslavement" (Alderman 2010, 94). While taking place on the grounds of a plantation with many of the same landscape elements as traditional plantation museums, the tour reorganizes the assembly of these buildings and narratives to offer visitors an experience that clearly challenges the power balance of heritage interpretation from the white master to the enslaved. In addition, the museum eschews the gardens and furnishings traditional tourism plantations use to evoke nostalgia for the mythical beauty and romance of the antebellum South. Instead, the names and brief stories engraved on massive walls of dark granite recall the Vietnam Memorial in Washington, DC, while the rough and aged slave cabins and rusted jail evoke the harsh realities of the lived experiences of enslaved African-Americans. In other words, the design practices of Whitney's owners, curators, and guides create a space where dark tourism practices are encouraged—where visitors can experience sadness and anger as appropriate responses to historical injustice. This capacity to evoke strong feeling and moral reflection about slavery through narrative and landscape design is noteworthy because it inverts what Modlin et al. (2011) call the "affective inequality" historically perpetuated at plantation museums that encourages emotional investment in the lives and identities of the master at the sacrifice of knowing and identifying with the contributions and struggles of the enslaved.

Conclusion

Southern plantation museums, like other heritage tourism sites, are best understood as assemblages of narratives and landscapes accreted over time as owners, curators, guides, and tourists arrange these spaces to experience the past in order to make sense of the present as well as to entertain and hopefully educate the traveling public. Traditional ways of designing these place products leave little to no place to talk or think about slavery and, therefore, plantation museums have become sites celebrating the lives of white enslavers rather than spaces where visitors can engage in the meaningful dark tourism practices of acknowledging, empathizing with, and coming to terms with the brutal history of enslavement. Yet, heritage dissonance has always been present as the racialized and violent exploitation of millions of African-Americans haunts the plantation even as most visitors come to see beautiful gardens and reaffirm the white elite histories these museums represented and reproduced.

While more and more plantation museums are adding exhibits or tours to acknowledge this dark past, the efficacy of these additions to encourage visitors to engage intellectually with the history of slavery or emotionally with enslaved women and men as individuals varies greatly. As our exploration of plantation tourism sites in Virginia, Louisiana, and South Carolina suggests, making visible the lived experience of enslaved women and men in ways that encourage meaningful dark tourism experiences requires not only the archival and archeological excavation of stories and artifacts to serve as commemorative surrogates, but also the thoughtful spatial arrangement of landscape and narrative elements. And we would suggest, in more general ways, that dark tourism is inherently a spatial project of managing the past as heritage.

Acknowledgments The authors would like to thank Rudi Hartmann and the rest of the editors for inviting us to contribute to this volume as well as for their helpful comments and suggestions. Research for this chapter was funded by the National Science Foundation Geography and Spatial Sciences Program, grant #1359780. Finally, this chapter could not have been written without the insights and support of the other members of the plantation research team, Amy Potter, Arnold Modlin, Perry Carter, and David Butler.

Notes

1. Quote taken from the Eliza's House Brochure available for free at Middleton Place. Published by the Middleton Place Foundation.
2. From a podcast available on the Oak Alley Plantation website, http://www.oakalleyplantation.com/new-exhibit-slavery-at-oak-alley
3. Quote taken from the Whitney Plantation website: http://whitneyplantation.com/history.html

References

Alderman, D. H. (2010). Surrogation and the politics of remembering slavery in Savannah, Georgia (USA). *Journal of Historical Geography, 36*(1), 90–101.

Alderman, D. H., & Campbell, R. M. (2008). Symbolic excavation and the artifact politics of remembering slavery in the American South: Observations from Walterboro, South Carolina. *Southeastern Geographer, 48*(3), 338–355.

Alderman, D. H., & Modlin, E. A., Jr. (2008). (In)visibility of the enslaved within online plantation tourism marketing: A textual analysis of North Carolina websites. *Journal of Travel & Tourism Marketing, 25*(3–4), 265–281.

Alderman, D. H., & Modlin, E. A., Jr. (2013). Southern hospitality and the politics of African American belonging: An analysis of North Carolina tourism brochure photographs. *Journal of Cultural Geography, 30*(1), 6–31.

Alderman, D. H., Butler, D. L., & Hanna, S. P. (2016). Memory, slavery, and plantation museums: The River Road Project. *Journal of Heritage Tourism, 11*(3), 209–218.

Amsden, D. (2015, February 26). Building the first slavery museum in America. *The New York Times Magazine*. http://www.nytimes.com/2015/03/01/magazine/building-the-first-slave-museum-in-america.html?_r=0. Accessed 13 May 2016.

Ashworth, G. J., & Isaac, R. K. (2015). Have we illuminated the dark? Shifting perspectives on 'dark' tourism. *Tourism Recreation Research, 40*(3), 316–325.

Azaryahu, M., & Foote, K. E. (2008). Historical space as narrative medium: On the configuration of spatial narratives of time at historical sites. *GeoJournal, 73*(3), 179–194.

Baptist, E. (2014). *The half has never been told: Slavery and the making of American capitalism*. New York: Basic Books.

Carter, P. (2015). Placing emotional geographies via YouTube. In S. P. Hanna, A. E. Potter, E. A. Modlin Jr., P. Carter, & D. L. Butler (Eds.), *Social memory and heritage tourism methodologies* (pp. 48–67). New York: Routledge.

Dann, G. M. S., & Seaton, A. V. (2001). Slavery, contested heritage and thanatourism. *International Journal of Hospitality & Tourism Administration, 2*(3–4), 1–29.

Datel, R. E. (1990). Southern regionalism and historic preservation in Charleston, South Carolina, 1920–1940. *Journal of Historical Geography, 16*(2), 197–215.

DeLyser, D. (1999). Authenticity on the ground: Engaging the past in a California ghost town. *Annals of the Association of American Geographers, 89*(4), 602–632.

Dwyer, O. J. (2004). Symbolic accretion and commemoration. *Social & Cultural Geography, 5*(3), 419–435.

Dwyer, O. J., & Alderman, D. H. (2008). *Civil rights memorials and the geography of memory*. Chicago: University of Georgia Press.

Dwyer, O., Butler, D., & Carter, P. (2013). Commemorative surrogation and the American South's changing heritage landscape. *Tourism Geographies, 15*(3), 424–443.

Eichstedt, J., & Small, S. (2002). *Representations of slavery: Race and ideology in southern plantation museums*. Washington, DC: Smithsonian Institution Press.

Ginsburg, R. (2007). Freedom and the slave landscape. *Landscape Journal, 26*(1), 36–44.

Griffin, L. J., & Hargis, P. G. (2012). Race, memory, and historical responsibility: What do southerners do with a difficult past? *Catalyst: A Social Justice Forum, 2*(1), 2–12.

Hanna, S. P. (2012). Cartographic memories of slavery and freedom: Examining John Washington's map and mapping of Fredericksburg, Virginia. *Cartographica, 47*(1), 50–63.

Hanna, S. P. (2016). Placing the enslaved at Oak Alley Plantation: Narratives, spatial contexts, and the limits of surrogation. *Journal of Heritage Tourism, 11*(3), 219–234.

Hartmann, R. (2014). Dark tourism, thanatourism, and dissonance in heritage tourism management: New directions in contemporary tourism research. *Journal of Heritage Tourism, 9*(2), 166–182.

Himes, J. S. (1979). The emergence and crystallization of slavery in the United States. *Contemporary Sociology, 8*(5), 719–721.

Hoelscher, S. (2006). The white-pillared past: Landscapes of memory and race in the American South. In R. Schein (Ed.), *Landscape and race in the United States* (pp. 39–72). New York: Routledge.

Lambert, D. (2007). 'Part of the blood and dream': Surrogation, memory and the National Hero in the postcolonial Caribbean. *Patterns of Prejudice, 41*(3–4), 345–371.

McDaniel, G. W. (2015). Asking big questions of a small place. In M. van Balgooy (Ed.), *Interpreting African American history and culture at museums and historic sites* (pp. 129–134). New York: Rowman & Littlefield.

Modlin, E. A., Alderman, D. H., & Gentry, G. W. (2011). Tour guides as creators of empathy: The role of affective inequality in marginalizing the enslaved at plantation house museums. *Tourist Studies, 11*(1), 3–19.

Mowatt, R. A., & Chancellor, C. H. (2011). Visiting death and life: Dark tourism and slave castles. *Annals of Tourism Research, 38*(4), 1410–1434.

Ryan, M.-L., Foote, K., & Azaryahu, M. (2016). *Narrating space/spatializing narrative: Where narrative theory and geography meet*. Columbus: Ohio State Press.

Small, S. (2013). Still back of the big house: Slave cabins and slavery in southern heritage tourism. *Tourism Geographies, 15*(3), 405–423.

Stone, P. R. (2009). Dark tourism: Morality and new moral spaces. In R. Sharpley & P. R. Stone (Eds.), *The darker side of travel: The theory and practice of dark tourism* (pp. 56–72). Bristol: Channel View Publications.

Taylor, H. (2001). *Circling Dixie: Contemporary southern culture through a transatlantic lens*. New Brunswick: Rutgers University Press.

Till, K. E. (2012). Wounded cities: Memory-work and a place-based ethics of care. *Political Geography, 31*(1), 3–14.

Tunbridge, J. E., & Ashworth, G. J. (1996). *Dissonant heritage: The management of the past as a resource in conflict*. New York: Wiley.

Waterton, E., & Dittmer, J. (2014). The museum as assemblage: Bringing forth affect at the Australian War Memorial. *Museum Management and Curatorship, 29*(2), 122–139.

Yankholmes, A., & McKercher, B. (2015). Rethinking slavery heritage tourism. *Journal of Heritage Tourism, 10*(3), 233–247.

18

Dark Tourism to Seismic Memorial Sites

Yong Tang

Introduction

This chapter summarizes the major developments and ideas in the field of dark tourism to seismic memorial sites. In recent years many memorial sites regarding seismic hazards including earthquake, tsunami, and volcanic eruption have been established, and at least the epicenter of major earthquake have been marked, such as San Francisco Fire Dept. Museum in America, after the Great San Francisco Earthquake of 1906; Hokudan Earthquake Memorial Park on the west coast of Awaji Island in Japan, following the Kobe Earthquake of 1995; Wenchuan Earthquake Memorial Museum in China, following its 2008 earthquake; and Baan Nam Khem Memorial Park, Thailand, after the Sumatra-Andaman Earthquake and Tsunami of 2004. Visits to such memorials and museums represent a distinct type of contemporary tourism (Hartmann 2014). However, consumption of dark tourism attraction related to seismic memorials is highly controversial; and the continuing popularity of and fascination with such sites remains a subject of dark touristic debate within social, cultural, historical, and political contexts (Lennon and Foley 2000; Sharpley and Stone 2009; also see Chap. 14).

Y. Tang (✉)
Chengdu University of Technology, Chengdu, China

'Dark tourism' is popularized by Lennon and Foley and has been most widely used as a portmanteau expression to encompass the use of heritage sites with a controversial history and sites associated with death, disaster, and the seemingly macabre (Lennon and Foley 2000). As a recognizable field of academic study (Stone 2013; Hartmann 2014), there are many other terms applied to this form of tourism, which include 'grief tourism' (Pezzullo 2009), 'thanatourism' (Seaton 1996), and 'black spot tourism' (Rojek 1993), 'phoenix tourism' (Causevic and Lynch 2011), 'atrocity tourism' (Ashworth and Hartmann 2005), or 'dissonant heritage' (Tunbridge and Ashworth 1996) and 'morbid tourism' (Blom 2000).

As for recent literature on dark tourism, a growing body of scholarship has focused on sites either associated with man-made disaster, natural catastrophe, or something in between (Thomas 2012; Pezzullo 2009; Cioccio and Michael 2007; Xu and Grunewald 2009). Thus 'disaster tourism' is becoming an increasingly pervasive feature within the contemporary dark touristic consumption (Antick 2013; Faulkner and Vikulov 2001; Chew and Jahari 2014). Yet, less discourse has been given to the critical issue of dark sites related to seismic hazards, a subset of the totality of dark tourist attractions varying enormously, from towns of horror, through places of pilgrimages, to the battlefield, holocaust death camp, or sites of major disasters (Chronis 2012; Podoshen and Hunt 2011; Belhassen et al. 2008). However, that is by no means to say, site of earthquake has been completely overlooked; instead, earlier research into such sites has extended a broader base for understanding the phenomenon of dark tourism as a whole (Ryan and Hsu 2011; Coats and Ferguson 2013; Tang 2014a, b; Biran et al. 2014; Rittichainuwat 2008; Chew and Jahari 2014; Teigen and Glad 2011).

The purpose of this chapter is to address wide-ranging studies of dark tourism to memorial sites of seismic hazards such as earthquake, or seismic wave-induced disaster like tsunami and volcanic eruption. The chapter is structured around a series of conceptual themes and debates that have emerged from the literature. This includes an appraisal of the following aspects: creation of seismic memorial sties as a contested phenomenon; consumption of seismic legacy as an ethical dilemma; perception of travel risks mediated with destination image; multi-dimensional experiences interpreted from the visit to seismic attractions. It concludes by discussing the future research and thematic directions of dark tourism to such sites within social, cultural, historical, and political contexts.

Creation of Seismic Memorial Sites: A Contested Phenomenon

Early academic attention has largely focused on defining and categorizing dark tourism from either a supply or demand perspective. Within the matrix of dark tourism demand and supply, it is possible to locate the attraction related to site of earthquake in either 'gray' or 'black' tourism quadrant (Sharpley and Stone 2009); at the same time, it can be argued that sites of earthquake attracting visitors with dominant interests in death and suffering fall around a central to 'darker' position on the continuum of the spectrum dark tourism supply (Stone 2006).

In effect, the creation of commemorative sites is both an act of remembrance and of forgetting, and the treatment of sites of earthquake has varied substantially from case to case and place to place, as evidenced by the fact that the sites have been sanctified, designated, rectified, and in some paradoxical cases—obliterated throughout the history (Foote 2003). In the case of Haiti earthquake of 2010, where the past is too painful to carry on, the desire to forget is the initial impulse (Balaji 2011). More than 230,000 people were killed, and 250,000 residences and 30,000 commercial buildings had collapsed or were severely damaged. In contrast, people may wish to preserve a certain discourse when a natural response to the grief of community loss occurs. A striking example is the towering waves triggered by the underwater earthquake off the coast of Indonesia on December 26, 2004. This is the third largest earthquake in the world since 1900 and is the largest since the 1964 Prince William Sound, Alaska earthquake. In total, 227,898 people were killed or were missing and presumed dead, and about 1.7 million people were displaced by the earthquake and subsequent tsunami in 14 countries in South Asia and East Africa. Aceh Tsunami Museum in Banda Aceh, Indonesia, and Khao Lak-Lam Ru National Park in Thailand and Pacific Tsunami Museum in Chile were designed as symbolic reminders of the 2004 Indian Ocean earthquake and tsunami disaster, as well as an educational center and an emergency disaster shelter in case the area is ever hit by a tsunami again (Steckley and Doberstein 2011; Birkland et al. 2006; Calgaro and Lloyd 2008).

In his Shadowed Ground: America's Landscapes of Violence and Tragedy, Foote (2003) states that commemorative landscapes express not only power and heroism, but martyrdom, shame, and catharsis. As site of devastating earthquake, the memorial site should be equipped to deal with remembrance, with consigning the pain to the past and drawing lessons. However, the continuing popularity of and fascination with death and suffering gradually change the site itself or related memorial into tourist attraction. In the case of the ruins of Pompeii, the greatest thanatopic travel destination of the Romantic period has been a popular tourist destination for over 250 years (Ashworth 2002; Seaton 1996).

As touristic packaging of death has long been a theme of the 'morbid gaze' (Blom 2000), many recent seismic memorial sites are becoming increasingly pervasive features within the contemporary dark touristic landscapes, such as Tangshan Earthquake Memorial Park in Hebei, China, which is dedicated to over 240,000 victims who perished in the Tangshan Earthquake of 1976, the third deadliest earthquake of modern history. Chinese director Feng Xiaogang's 2010 film 'Aftershock' gives a dramatic account of this tragic earthquake, which leads to dark tourism in Tangshan thriving again. Tangshan Earthquake Memorial Park is one of the most visited memorial places to this deadliest natural disaster in the last century. The park is divided into four zones including earthquake ruins, lake area, rubble square area, and woods, demonstrating the theme of 'revere nature, care for human life, pursue science, and remember the past'.

Another case in China is memorials after the Wenchuan Earthquake. On Monday, May 12, 2008, an earthquake of magnitude 8.0 struck northwestern Sichuan province of China. It was the most devastating earthquake in China in more than three decades, leaving 69,197 dead, 374,176 injured, and 18,222 missing (Yang 2008; Yang et al. 2011). On May 12, 2009, China marked the first anniversary of the quake with a moment of silence as people across the nation remembered the dead. The government also opened access to the sealed ruins of the Beichuan county seat for three days, after which it was frozen in time as a state earthquake relic museum. Some 15,000 people visited this museum in Beichuan County to commemorate the fifth anniversary of the tragedy. To remind people of the terrible disaster, there were also several memorials across west Sichuan, which include Earthquake Relics Park in Donghekou Town and Epicenter Memorial Museum in Yingxiu County.

In both cases, the severe casualties and large magnitude result in sanctification whilst arousing extensive interests of tourist. The same is true to many large public memorials consecrated either at the disaster site or at a site of civic prominence, such as Memorial in Park Island Cemetery, New Zealand, after the Hawke's Bay Earthquake of 1931; Memorial Hall and Metropolitan Memorial Museum in Tokyo, after the Great Kantō Earthquake of 1923 in Japan; and Oakland Memorial Park in America, after the Loma Prieta Earthquake of 1986 (Table 18.1).

From the supply side of dark tourism, the commoditization of sites related to seismic hazards is highly contested. A good case in point is the proposed

Table 18.1 Memorial sites and attractions associated with seismic disasters

Date	Event	Country/region	Deaths/fatalities
1959 Aug 17	Hebgen Lake Earthquake	America	28
Forest Service's Earthquake Lake Visitor Center			
1964 Mar 27	Anchorage Earthquake	America	143
Anchorage Earthquake Park, Anchorage Museum			
1976 Jul 28	Tangshan Earthquake	China	242,769
Tangshan Earthquake Memorial Park and Museum; Tangshan Earthquake Memorial in Tianjin			
2009 Sept 21	Chi Chi Earthquake	China	2415
Taiwan Chi Chi Earthquake Memorial Park			
1923 Sep 1	Great Kantō Earthquake	Japan	142,800
Tokyo Memorial Hall; Tokyo Metropolitan Great Kanto Earthquake Memorial Museum			
1995 Jan 17	Kobe Earthquake (Great Hanshin-Awaji Japan Earthquake)	Japan	6434
Hokudan Earthquake Memorial Park; Port of Kobe Earthquake Memorial; Nojima Fault Preservation Museum			
1989 Oct 17	Loma Prieta Earthquake	America	63
Oakland Memorial Park			
1931 Feb 3	Hawke's Bay Earthquake	New Zealand	256
Earthquake Memorial in Park Island Cemetery			
2008 May 12	Sichuan Earthquake	China	87,587
Earthquake Relics Park in Donghekou; Earthquake Memorial Park in Beichuan; Yingxiu Epicenter Memorial Museum			
1906 Apr 18	San Francisco Earthquake	America	3000
San Francisco Fire Dept Museum			
2011 Feb 22	Christchurch Earthquake	New Zealand	181
Christ Church Cathedral			
1868 Oct 21	Hayward Earthquake	America	30
Hayward's Memorial Park			
2004 Dec 12–26	Indian Ocean Tsunami	Indonesia	230,273–310,000
Tsunami Memorial Building in Banda Aceh, North Sumatra, Indonesia; Khao Lak-Lam Ru National Park, Thailand; Baan Nam Khem Memorial Park, Thailand; Pacific Tsunami Museum in Chile			
1960 May 22	Pacific Tsunami	America	6000
Pacific Tsunami Museum in Hilo			

construction of Tsunami Memorial in the Khao Lak Lamu National Park in Thailand, following the Indian Ocean Tsunami of 2004. Not only was concern expressed over the ecological impacts of the building both during the construction and consequently as a major dark tourism attraction located with a fragile forest environment but also the scale of the project and its explicit role in attracting tourists were considered insensitive to the emotions of the friends and relatives of those who lost their lives in the tragedy. As a result of this controversy, the Tsunami Memorial has yet to be built and is replaced by three smaller, local memorials (Rittichainuwat 2008; Wegscheider et al. 2011; Mulligan et al. 2012; Birkland et al. 2006).

Beyond this controversy, recent attention has focused on drivers to dark tourism (Sharpley 2005; Lennon and Foley 2000; Gertrude 2013). It is believed that tourism plays a positive role in that it united the world in its response to the needs of the communities (Sharpley 2005). This is perhaps the reason why government acts to invigorate tourism in the aftermath of a devastated earthquake (Lennon and Foley 2000; Yang et al. 2011; Chew and Jahari 2014). As the case of Haitian tourism after the earthquake of 2013, politics is one of the central driver to smother hopes of building a tourism sector twice before (Gertrude 2013; Balaji 2011). Ironically, while dark tourism brings light to disaster zones, it can lead to numerous attempts at 'land grab' (Cohen 2011). In political geography, the implementation of 'buffer zones' for tourism development can stir feelings of discrimination, tension, and fear (Hyndman 2007).

When sending tourists a reassuring message that they can take on the trip (Causey 2007; Maximiliano and Tarlow 2013), the reconstruction may be still under way. When the city of Christchurch and the surrounding Canterbury region slowly began to rebuild in the aftermath of the 2011 Christchurch Earthquake, the nation's second deadliest natural disaster, the government of New Zealand was launching a campaign to lure Australian visitors back to the earthquake-ravaged area; ironically, New Zealanders were being urged to dive under their desks to get ready for another massive quake (Orchiston 2012, 2013; Coats and Ferguson 2013).

Similarly, just a year after the Wenchuan Earthquake of 2008, local government issued 15 million vouchers (also known as 'Panda Cards') to encourage tourists to help the recovery by sightseeing and spending. During the May Day holiday of 2009, millions of them visited the Earthquake Relics Park in Donghekou, the Yingxiu Epicenter Memorial Museum, and the nearby public cemeteries. In that case, the pain of quake survivors is being transformed into a thing for consumption, but some worried that the boom of tourism may hurt the feeling of survivors and relatives, or friends of victims perished in the tragedy (Yang et al. 2011; Yang 2008; Tang 2014a; Biran et al. 2014).

Consumption of Seismic Legacy: An Ethical Dilemma

The supply side of dark tourism does not depict a holistic picture, but it does lead to a better understanding of where to locate and explore the consumer. To follow this trend of studying the consumer side, scholars begin to look at ethical dilemma of dark touristic consumption (Sharpley and Stone 2009; Lennon and Foley 2000; Dunkley et al. 2011; Winter 2011; Hughes 2008; Podoshen and Hunt 2011; Bigley et al. 2010). Within the literature, the most attention has focused on the rights of victims in the aftermath of a disaster and contrasting motivations to visit seismic memorials (Sharpley and Stone 2009; Gertrude 2013; Coats and Ferguson 2013; Rittichainuwat 2008; Ryan and Hsu 2011; Tang 2014b).

When examining the rights of victims in 'Darker Side of Travel: The Theory and Practice of Dark Tourism', Sharpley and Stone (2009) claim that the rights of those dead are commoditized or commercialized through dark tourism and that presents an important ethical dimension deserving consideration. For instance, the humanitarian disaster after the 2010 earthquake of Haiti creates a dilemma for travelers who want to sip a rum cocktail knowing that, just down the road, malnourished children are languishing in tents (Gertrude 2013).

In other instances, Coats and Ferguson (2013) explore how residents of Christchurch, New Zealand, negotiate the balance between being the subject of unwelcome tourist gazing and commencing the path toward economic and social recovery from the devastating earthquake. The study, carried out using in-depth focus groups, said as memories of the quake faded outside Christchurch, disaster tours served to remind incoming visitors about its victims and what the city had endured. In this research, residents understood the fascination that death and disaster might exert over visitors and should not be ignored as confrontation with death allows for catharsis, acceptance, and a means of grieving (Coats and Ferguson 2013).

The ethical dilemma is not limited to the rights of victims, but extended to a wide range of studies focusing on dark touristic motivations (Ryan and Hsu 2011; Tang 2014a, b; Rittichainuwat 2008; Biran et al. 2014). We, as humans, have some sort of morbid fascination with death and suffering. For instance, sightseers wanted to visit disaster zones where more than 18,000 people were killed when a 9.0-magnitude undersea quake sent huge waves barreling into Japan in 2011 (Chew and Jahari 2014). Undoubtedly, curiosity is what draws many of us to sites like Memorial Park of Kobe Earthquake of 1995 in Japan or Park Island Cemetery for Hawke's Bay Earthquake of 1931 in New Zealand.

In addition to curiosity, dark motivations to the site of earthquake may be varied and, in most cases, mixed together. In 'Responding to Disaster: Thai and Scandinavian Tourists' Motivation to Visit Phuket, Thailand', Rittichainuwat's (2008) claim that curiosity about the outcome of the tsunami, desire to help local people, and safety are the most important travel motivations. Obviously, curiosity on thanatourism of tourists is not about death but the outcome of the disaster and that it motivated only domestic tourists rather than inbound tourists (Rittichainuwat 2008).

Addressing Rittichainuwat's (2008) call for a better understanding of tourist behavior in relation to post-disaster destinations, Biran et al. (2014) explore the motivations and intentions of potential domestic tourists (from non-hit areas) to visit Sichuan, China, in the aftermath of an earthquake in 2008. In this research, potential tourists are mainly motivated by push factors related to leisure pursuits. This suggests that in the aftermath, a destination may still be seen as suitable to fulfill such psychological needs when many of its natural and cultural resources were not affected by the earthquake, or recovered quickly (Yang et al. 2011). In terms of pull factors, safety and accessibility and tourism infrastructure are the most important attributes. Thus, the findings support the general emphasis given to communicating a safe image in reviving destinations' traditional product offers (Rittichainuwat 2011). Nevertheless, this finding also supports Tang's argument that well-educated professionals from Western counties are less attracted to visit destinations associated with earthquake, than to other traditional sites of tourism in Sichuan province, both because they tend to visit its scenery and wildlife, particularly the giant pandas native to the area (Tang 2014a).

Furthermore, we feel compassion for our fellow human beings. Visiting people suffering from a disaster, then, is more in the spirit of conveying condolences, camaraderie in suffering, and giving aid. For instance, a group of fellow Muslims, visited the victims in Pariaman of West Sumatra after the 2009 earthquake, taking donations of clothes and staple foods. This practice suggests a subtle distinction between visiting disaster sites on the basis of sense of religious duty and the more explicit, unconstructive disaster tourism emanating from the earthquake (Fraser 2013).

Ryan and Hsu (2011) examine the motives of 286 respondents relating to the 921 Earthquake Museum in Taichung, Taiwan, and conclude that the key museum roles remain the traditional ones, including knowledge seeking, information acquisition, and learning. Tang (2014b) further investigates the motivations of Chinese domestic tourists visiting seismic memorial sites after the great Wenchuan earthquake of 2008. The analysis reveals that obligation of commemoration mixed with curiosity represents a different set of travel motivation in dark tourism setting. In other words, Chinese domestic tourists are attracted in ways different from other tourist attractions both because they tend to fulfill their obligation of commemoration and are interested in destruction.

Perception of Seismic Disaster: Travel Risks and Destination Image

In recent years, there has been an increasing number of research focusing on the awareness of travel risks associated with natural disasters (Heggie 2009; Teigen and Glad 2011; Chew and Jahari 2014; Williams and Balaz 2013; Bird et al. 2010). Of course, tourists wouldn't want to put themselves in real danger, but in some extreme cases like Thailand following the Sumatra-Andaman earthquake and tsunami of 2004, tourists may die in 'paradise' (Cohen 2009).

Undoubtedly, perceived risk of no-escape natural disaster may influence placement of a destination (Huan et al. 2004; Noh and Vogt 2013). From tour operator's perspective, the perception of natural hazards can influence the adoption of appropriate mitigation and preparedness measures, and thus creating the safe images of destinations (Cavlek 2002; Rittichainuwat 2013).

Research on how individual tourists respond to risk has largely focused on risk perceptions (Fuchs and Reichel 2011; Rittichainuwat 2013; Chew and Jahari 2014). Rittichainuwat (2013) describes tourists' perceptions toward the importance of safety measures across tourists who stay at different types of accommodation. It concludes that respondents who participated in the survey six months after the March 2011 Japanese tsunami placed more importance on almost all tsunami safety measures than those who did the survey six years after the Indian Ocean tsunami.

In addition to safety measures, there are many other factors that would also influence risk perceptions. For example, potential tourists' beliefs in ghosts may deter them from traveling to disaster-hit destinations, as the case of volcanic risk in southern Iceland which challenges its tourism sector (Bird et al. 2010). As pointed out by Williams and Balaz (2013), significant differences exist between package tourists and individual 'drifter' tourists in terms of risk tolerance and competence to manage risk. In particular, age is regarded as deterrent to tourist behavior, but the evidence for risk competences was mixed. The news coverage is likely to scare away already-skittish travelers after the Tohoku Pacific earthquake and tsunami and has had significant short-term economic and travel impacts. The earthquake and tsunami hit Japan on March 11, 2011 and caused a cooling system failure at the Fukushima Daiichi Nuclear Power Plant, which is proved to be the most serious natural disaster to hit the country since the Kobe earthquake of 1995. Chew and Jahari (2014)'s discussion of the theme provides just another perspective on post-disaster places, demonstrating how perceived socio-psychological and financial risks directly affected revisit intention to post-disaster Japan.

Moreover, it is noted that cultural differences also play a role in risk perception and consequently influence travel decision (Rittichainuwat 2011, 2013). Min (2007) points out clear differences in rebound status between Japanese and American visitor arrivals that are remarkably consistent with Hofstede's conceptualization—the Japanese tended toward uncertainty avoidance more than the Americans to the case of the September 21 earthquake in 1999, the largest natural disaster of the twentieth century in Taiwan.

The previous research on perceived travel risk to site of earthquake suggests that hazards may influence travel motivations in a variety of contrasting ways (Tang 2014a). But why do they pay to walk through museums dedicated to earthquake, seismic waves, and volcanic eruption? Whether tourists are truly attracted by the death and suffering associated with earthquake or seeking fear and thrills in the seismically active region?

Visitors may be less motivated to visit because of the risk or danger sometimes attached to natural disasters while they may be motivated to visit the site of a disaster to honor the victims, learn about the disaster, see the ruins and destruction, help in the recovery, or even to experience a sense of risk, danger, or thrill associated with visiting an earthquake-prone region or other sites threatened by potential hazards (Ryan and Hsu 2011; Gertrude 2013; Tang 2014a; Rittichainuwat 2008).

Despite significant research on perceived travel risk and travel motivation to sites of earthquakes, relatively few studies have addressed the effect of perceived travel risks on the formation of destination image (Tang 2014a; Chew and Jahari 2014; Chen and Tsai 2007). From a cognitive perspective, the radiation pollution's threat in east Japan after the earthquake of 2011 did weaken the intentions of the subject students from departments of applied Japanese in Taiwan to travel to Japan; however, affective attitudes of travel safety significantly increased their hesitation in travel decisions (Chen et al. 2012). Chew and Jahari (2014) apply similar understandings of socio-psychological factors as influencing factor in a recent study, demonstrating the perceived socio-psychological factors did not have a significant influence on destination image. The same can be said for the devastating earthquake in Turkey that killed more than 30,000 people in 1999 which had a similar impact on bookings and perhaps images of Turkey's safety held by potential travelers (Sönmez 2002). In contrast, Tang (2014a) argues that the 2008 earthquake has had little effect on international tourists' travel motivations and destination images of Sichuan Province in China. In particular, the effect of negative destination images is less influential than the positive one, as most tourists avoid visiting seismic attractions. That is to say, positive image is more likely included in the process of decision-making, but negative image does not necessarily deter tourism to the extent noted in previous studies (Sönmez 2002; Chew and Jahari 2014; Chen et al. 2012).

Interpretation of Seismic Attractions: A Multi-dimensional Experience

The interpretation of dark sites and attractions has long been the focus of academic attention (Miles 2002; Biran et al. 2011; Kang et al. 2012; Hughes 2008; Frew 2012; Strange and Kempa 2003). However, limited attention has been paid to exploring seismic attractions, including how they have been interpreted and are presented to tourists and how collective memory of disasters has shaped those interpretations through media, political forces, and social change (Lennon and Foley 2000; Sharpley and Stone 2009; Teigen and Glad 2011; Balaji 2011).

Indeed, the meaning or implication of mass death and suffering is fundamental to the experience consumed at the site (Sharpley and Stone 2009). Arguably, the memorial site of earthquake gives visitors a way to properly and meaningfully engage with the tragedy. Tang (2014b) studies an essential aspect of human cognition regarding traumatic sceneries by investigating a set of travel motivations and its interplay with cognitive and affective experiences leading to the benefits gained from the visit to the memorial site of Wenchuan Earthquake of 2008. He argues that the visits lead to a successful interpretation of both cognitive and affective experiences on site. On the one hand, the cognitive experiences direct most respondents toward self-reflection, expression of sympathies to the victims, reconciliation of the imagined landscapes with topographical reality, and critically thinking of the earthquake; on other hand, tourists feel a strong sense of 'sorrow', 'scares and worries', and 'depression' due to the devastative blow effects of the disaster and the possibility of additional aftershocks. At the same time, many people express 'gratification, appreciation and satisfaction' for economic and social recovery, quick and certain recovery from the earthquake.

More importantly, a tour to a memorial site of earthquake is a multidimensional experience that can have a deep impact on one's life. For example, the 921 Earthquake Museum in Taiwan appears to satisfy many of its visitors as possessing interest, and aiding learning and knowledge acquisition, thus the museum is perceived as important as 'storage places' of history and knowledge. Therefore, it can also serve as a good place to take children (Ryan and Hsu 2011).

Dark tourism experiences can be consumed to give some phenomenological meaning to tourists' own social existence. Teigen and Glad (2011) summarize two studies of travelers exposed to the effects of natural disasters, where luck is a pivotal theme. Participants in the first study were 85 Norwegian tourists, interviewed after their return from the Tsunami disaster in Southeast Asia in December 2004. The second study reports interviews with 20 Norwegian travelers who had their travel plans disrupted by the volcanic eruption in Iceland in April 2010. Despite the differences in severity and dramatic qualities of these two disasters, downward comparisons have a self-enhancing and mood-repairing effect, reducing the impact of a threatening experience (Teigen and Glad 2011).

As a key theme in successful interpretation of dark tourism experience, authenticity is accompanied by a degree of satisfaction and enlightenment. Interestingly, the imagination offers a resilient mode and domain for place-making (Puleo 2014), as many dark touristic activities seek to reconcile comparisons between imaged landscapes and topographical reality (Podoshen 2013; Chronis 2012). In the case of 921 Earthquake Museum, Ryan's finding lends some support to the continuum of the authentic to 'pure essentialism' while arguing that the latter is a logical corollary of the concept (Ryan and Hsu 2011).

The emotional responses to the seismic hazards are gathered into what Corbin (1994) calls the 'rhetoric of pity'. In 'Who Will be My Brother's Keeper: My First Visit to Haiti', Gertrude (2013) writes, 'What we had experienced was not the Haiti Paul Farmer and Richard Frechette had written about. That part of Haiti we did not get to see at all, but what we had seen and experienced was Haiti too, albeit, one from the outer fringes'. To some extent, mediated responses to the disaster reflect the radicalization of pity and the privileging of a white view when places like Pog Suk and Phi Phi Island in Thailand were destroyed as the devastation of the 'Swedish paradise'

(Balaji 2011). Within the context of business practice and consumer research, Coats and Ferguson (2013) examine dark tourism within a framework of post-earthquake perceptions in New Zealand. They argue that inherent emotional tensions between residents of a disaster zone and subsequent visitors should always be aligned with unbiased interpretation that offers an opportunity for catharsis, acceptance, as well as grieving for a sense of loss of both people and place.

Contrary to the sympathy or emotional affection arising from the visit, visitors want to see the devastation and the monuments to those who died, and pay to witness the aftermath of others' misery. In some extreme cases, this morbid gaze is highly criticized. For instance, disheartening tales of youths turning up in their hundreds in the most devastated villages to watch, but never assist in the rescue efforts, following the west Sumatra's worst Earthquake of 2004. They used the scenes of destruction as a backdrop for 'cool' Facebook pictures, staged motorbike track races in the dislocated landscape of landslides, played 'chicken' with rescue vehicles, and racketeered by setting up parking businesses (Fraser 2013).

Conclusion

This chapter offers readers an opportunity to reassess key themes, practices, and conceptual approaches in the study of dark tourism to seismic memorial sites. In the light of recent developments, the sanctified sites of seismic disaster, marked by a monument or other types of memorials, are not only places of remembrance but also dark tourist attractions with cultural and economic power in themselves (Graham et al. 2008). In dark tourism literature, recent academic attention has largely focused on specific dark attractions like battlefields, cemetery, prisons, and Holocaust sites. Yet, less discourse has been given to the critical issue of dark tourism to seismic memorial sites. This suggests that dark tourism calls for re-ordering the empirical and conceptual focus to look at the dark touristic consumption of seismic memorial sites, because it reflects essential aspect of human cognition regarding traumatic sceneries in postmodern culture (Tang 2014b).

As discussed in this chapter, the commoditization of sites related to seismic hazards is highly contested, leading us to seek out why some events are more likely to receive treatment of commemoration, whilst arousing fascination of tourists than others, and whether it is ethical to develop, promote, or offer such sites as dark tourist attraction and how soon is too soon to have dark tourism back to the site ravaged by the disaster. These contested questions with respect to dark tourism have received considerable academic attentions but remain unclear (Lennon and Foley 2000; Ashworth 2002; Sharpley and Stone 2009; Prayag and Ryan 2012). Indeed, why do people visit the dark sites or attractions associated with seismic hazards and whether tourists are truly attracted to such sites in ways different from other dark attractions? Should the interpretation of such sites be aware of dark touristic motivations and a range of meaning that arises from the visits? Such questions are somewhat difficult to answer, because of the scarcity of information on risk perception, destination image, travel motivation, and experiences interpreted for the visit to the most recently established seismic memorial sites.

In this chapter, I only took a critical overview of current state of research in dark tourism studies related to memorial sites of seismic hazards. I argue that much of the recent research has focused on the contested phenomenon of the creation of seismic memorial sties, ethical dilemma of dark touristic consumption, and perception of travel risks mediated with destination image and the interpretation of dark touristic experiences as well as the discourse of meaning arising from the visits to these sites of disasters. To further examine the issues, the cases might be expanded to other natural disasters such as storms, tornados, wild fires, and epidemics. In addition, this suggests more conceptual and empirical contributions from a broad spectrum of disciplines to the understanding of how the commemorative landscapes of earthquake is shaped into tourist attractions when conflicts, ethnic dilemma, inequality, and social justice need to be addressed; how the shifting power between commemoration and recreation should be placed during interpretive sessions of dark touristic activities within social, cultural, historical, and political contexts.

References

Antick, P. (2013). Bhopal to Bridgehampton: Schema for a disaster tourism event. *Journal of Visual Culture, 12*(1), 165–185. https://doi.org/10.1177/1470412912470524.

Ashworth, G. J. (2002). Dark tourism: The attraction of death and disaster. *Tourism Management, 23*(2), 190–191. https://doi.org/10.1016/s0261-5177(01)00055-3.

Ashworth, G., & Hartmann, R. (2005). *Horror and human tragedy revisited: The management of sites of atrocities for tourism*. New York: Cognizant Communications Corporation.

Balaji, M. (2011). Racializing pity: The Haiti earthquake and the plight of "others". *Critical Studies in Media Communication, 28*(1). https://doi.org/10.1080/15295036.2010.545703.

Belhassen, Y., Caton, K., & Stewart, W. P. (2008). The search for authenticity in the pilgrim experience. *Annals of Tourism Research, 35*(3), 668–689. https://doi.org/10.1016/j.annals.2008.03.007.

Bigley, J. D., Lee, C. K., Chon, J., & Yoon, Y. (2010). Motivations for war-related tourism: A case of DMZ visitors in Korea. *Tourism Geographies, 12*(3), 371–394. https://doi.org/10.1080/14616688.2010.494687.

Biran, A., Poria, Y., & Oren, G. (2011). Sought experiences at (dark) heritage sites. *Annals of Tourism Research, 38*(3), 820–841. https://doi.org/10.1016/j.annals.2010.12.001.

Biran, A., Liu, W., Li, G., & Eichhorn, V. (2014). Consuming post-disaster destinations: The case of Sichuan, China. *Annals of Tourism Research, 47*, 17. https://doi.org/10.1016/j.annals.2014.03.004.

Bird, D. K., Gisladottir, G., & Dominey-Howes, D. (2010). Volcanic risk and tourism in southern Iceland: Implications for hazard, risk and emergency response education and training. *Journal of Volcanology and Geothermal Research, 189*(1-2), 33–48. https://doi.org/10.1016/j.jvolgeores.2009.09.020.

Birkland, T. A., Herabat, P., Little, R. G., & Wallace, W. A. (2006). The impact of the December 2004 Indian Ocean tsunami on tourism in Thailand. *Earthquake Spectra, 22*, S889–S900. https://doi.org/10.1193/1.2207471.

Blom, T. (2000). Morbid tourism – A postmodern market niche with an example from Althorp. *Norsk Geografisk Tidsskrift – Norwegian Journal of Geography, 54*(1), 29–36. http://dx.doi.org/10.1080/002919500423564.

Calgaro, E., & Lloyd, K. (2008). Sun, sea, sand and tsunami: Examining disaster vulnerability in the tourism community of Khao Lak, Thailand. *Singapore Journal of Tropical Geography, 29*(3), 288–306. https://doi.org/10.1111/j.1467-9493.2008.00335.x.

Causevic, S., & Lynch, P. (2011). Phoenix tourism: Post-conflict tourism role. *Annals of Tourism Research, 38*(3), 780–800. https://doi.org/10.1016/j.annals.2010.12.004.

Causey, A. (2007). 'Go back to the Batak, it's safe there': Tourism in North Sumatra during perilous times. *Indonesia and the Malay World, 35*(103), 257–271. https://doi.org/10.1080/13639810701676383.

Cavlek, N. (2002). Tour operators and destination safety. *Annals of Tourism Research, 29*(2), 478–496. https://doi.org/10.1016/S0160-7383(01)00067-6.

Chen, C. F., & Tsai, D. (2007). How destination image and evaluative factors affect behavioral intentions? *Tourism Management, 28*(4), 1115–1122. https://doi.org/10.1016/j.tourman.2006.07.007.

Chen, F.-S., Chen, M.-T., & Cheng, C.-J. (2012). A study of the students' travel Japan intentions from departments of applied Japanese in Taiwan after 311 East Japan earthquake. *Journal of Information and Optimization Sciences, 33*(2-3), 363–384. https://doi.org/10.1080/02522667.2012.10700151.

Chew, E. Y. T., & Jahari, S. A. (2014). Destination image as a mediator between perceived risks and revisit intention: A case of post-disaster Japan. *Tourism Management, 40*, 382–393. https://doi.org/10.1016/j.tourman.2013.07.008.

Chronis, A. (2012). Between place and story: Gettysburg as tourism imaginary. *Annals of Tourism Research, 39*(4), 1797–1816. https://doi.org/10.1016/j.annals.2012.05.028.

Cioccio, L., & Michael, E. J. (2007). Hazard or disaster: Tourism management for the inevitable in Northeast Victoria. *Tourism Management, 28*(1), 1–11. https://doi.org/10.1016/j.tourman.2005.07.015.

Coats, A., & Ferguson, S. (2013). Rubbernecking or rejuvenation: Post earthquake perceptions and the implications for business practice in dark tourism context. *Journal of Research for Consumers, 23*, 32–65.

Cohen, E. (2009). Death in paradise: Tourist fatalities in the tsunami disaster in Thailand. *Current Issues in Tourism, 12*(2), 183–199. https://doi.org/10.1080/13683500802531141.

Cohen, E. (2011). Tourism and land grab in the aftermath of the Indian Ocean tsunami. *Scandinavian Journal of Hospitality and Tourism, 11*(3), 224–236. https://doi.org/10.1080/15022250.2011.593359.

Corbin, A. (1994). *The lure of the sea: The discovery of the seaside in the Western world 1750–1840* (trans: Phelps, J.). London: Penguin.

Dunkley, R., Morgan, N., & Westwood, S. (2011). Visiting the trenches: Exploring meanings and motivations in battlefield tourism. *Tourism Management, 32*(4), 860–868. https://doi.org/10.1016/j.tourman.2010.07.011.

Faulkner, B., & Vikulov, S. (2001). Katherine, washed out one day, back on track the next: A post-mortem of a tourism disaster. *Tourism Management, 22*(4), 331–344. https://doi.org/10.1016/s0261-5177(00)00069-8.

Foote, K. E. (2003). *Shadowed ground: America's landscapes of violence and tragedy* (2nd ed.). Austin: University of Texas Press.

Fraser, J. (2013). The art of grieving: West Sumatra's worst earthquake in music videos. *Ethnomusicology Forum, 22*(2), 129–159. https://doi.org/10.1080/17411912.2012.707855.

Frew, E. A. (2012). Interpretation of a sensitive heritage site: The Port Arthur Memorial Garden, Tasmania. *International Journal of Heritage Studies, 18*(1), 33–48. https://doi.org/10.1080/13527258.2011.603908.

Fuchs, G., & Reichel, A. (2011). An exploratory inquiry into destination risk perceptions and risk reduction strategies of first time vs. repeat visitors to a highly volatile destination. *Tourism Management, 32*(2), 266–276. https://doi.org/10.1016/j.tourman.2010.01.012.

Gertrude, T. S. (2013). Who will be my brother's keeper – My first visit to Haiti. *Multicultural Perspectives, 15*(1), 52–57. http://dx.doi.org/10.1080/15210960.2013.754650.

Graham, B. J., Ashworth, G. J., & Tunbridge, J. E. (2008). *A geography of heritage: Power, culture and economy*. New York: Oxford University Press.

Hartmann, R. (2014). Dark tourism, thanatourism, and dissonance in heritage tourism management: New directions in contemporary tourism research. *Journal of Heritage Tourism, 9*(2), 166–182. https://doi.org/10.1080/1743873X.2013.807266.

Heggie, T. W. (2009). Geotourism and volcanoes: Health hazards facing tourists at volcanic and geothermal destinations. *Travel Medicine and Infectious Disease, 7*(5), 257–261. https://doi.org/10.1016/j.tmaid.2009.06.002.

Huan, T. C., Beaman, J., & Shelby, L. (2004). No-escape natural disaster – Mitigating impacts on tourism. *Annals of Tourism Research, 31*(2), 255–273. https://doi.org/10.1016/j.annals.2003.10.003.

Hughes, R. (2008). Dutiful tourism: Encountering the Cambodian genocide. *Asia Pacific Viewpoint, 49*(3), 318–330. https://doi.org/10.1111/j.1467-8373.2008.00380.x.

Hyndman, J. (2007). The securitization of fear in post-tsunami Sri Lanka. *Annals of the Association of American Geographers, 97*(2), 361–372. http://dx.doi.org/0.1111/j.1467-8306.2007.00542.x.

Kang, E. J., Scott, N., Lee, T. J., & Ballantyne, R. (2012). Benefits of visiting a 'dark tourism' site: The case of the Jeju April 3rd Peace Park, Korea. *Tourism Management, 33*(2), 257–265. https://doi.org/10.1016/j.tourman.2011.03.004.

Lennon, J., & Foley, M. (2000). *Dark tourism: The attraction of death and disaster.* London: Continuum.

Maximiliano, E. B., & Tarlow, P. (2013). Disasters, tourism the case of Japan earthquake. *Revista de Turismo y Patrimonio Cultural, 11*(3.Special Issue), 17–32.

Miles, W. F. S. (2002). Auschwitz: Museum interpretation and darker tourism. *Annals of Tourism Research, 29*(4), 1175–1178. https://doi.org/10.1016/s0160-7383(02)00054-3.

Min, J. C. H. (2007). Tourism behavior toward disasters: A cross-cultural comparison. *Social Behavior and Personality, 35*(8), 1031–1032.

Mulligan, M., Ahmed, I., Shaw, J., Mercer, D., & Nadarajah, Y. (2012). Lessons for long-term social recovery following the 2004 tsunami: Community, livelihoods, tourism and housing. *Environmental Hazards-Human and Policy Dimensions, 11*(1), 38–51. https://doi.org/10.1080/17477891.2011.635186.

Noh, J., & Vogt, C. (2013). Modelling information use, image, and perceived risk with intentions to travel to East Asia. *Current Issues in Tourism, 16*(5), 455–476. https://doi.org/10.1080/13683500.2012.741576.

Orchiston, C. (2012). Seismic risk scenario planning and sustainable tourism management: Christchurch and the Alpine Fault zone, South Island, New Zealand. *Journal of Sustainable Tourism, 20*(1), 59–79. https://doi.org/10.1080/09669582.2011.617827.

Orchiston, C. (2013). Tourism business preparedness, resilience and disaster planning in a region of high seismic risk: The case of the Southern Alps, New Zealand. *Current Issues in Tourism, 16*(5), 477–494. https://doi.org/10.1080/13683500.2012.741115.

Pezzullo, P. C. (2009). "This is the only tour that sells": Tourism, disaster, and national identity in New Orleans. *Journal of Tourism and Cultural Change, 7*(2), 99–114. https://doi.org/10.1080/14766820903026348.

Podoshen, J. S. (2013). Dark tourism motivations: Simulation, emotional contagion and topographic comparison. *Tourism Management, 35*, 263–271. https://doi.org/10.1016/j.tourman.2012.08.002.

Podoshen, J. S., & Hunt, J. M. (2011). Equity restoration, the Holocaust and tourism of sacred sites. *Tourism Management, 32*(6), 1332–1342. https://doi.org/10.1016/j.tourman.2011.01.007.

Prayag, G., & Ryan, C. (2012). Antecedents of tourists' loyalty to Mauritius: The role and influence of destination image, place attachment, personal involvement, and satisfaction. *Journal of Travel Research, 51*(3), 342–356. https://doi.org/10.1177/0047287511410321.

Puleo, T. (2014). Art-making as place-making following disaster. *Progress in Human Geography, 38*(4), 568–580. https://doi.org/10.1177/0309132513512543.

Rittichainuwat, N. (2008). Responding to disaster: Thai and Scandinavian Tourists' motivation to visit Phuket, Thailand. *Journal of Travel Research, 46*(4), 422–433.

Rittichainuwat, B. (2011). Ghosts: A travel barrier to tourism recovery. *Annals of Tourism Research, 38*(2), 437–459. https://doi.org/10.1016/j.annals.2010.10.001.

Rittichainuwat, B. N. (2013). Tourists' and tourism suppliers' perceptions toward crisis management on tsunami. *Tourism Management, 34*, 112–121. https://doi.org/10.1016/j.tourman.2012.03.018.

Rojek, C. (1993). *Ways of escape*. Basingstoke: Macmillan.

Ryan, C., & Hsu, S. Y. (2011). Why do visitors go to museums? The case of 921 earthquake museum, Wufong, Taichung. *Asia Pacific Journal of Tourism Research, 16*(2), 209–228. https://doi.org/10.1080/10941665.2011.556342.

Seaton, A. V. (1996). Guided by the dark: From thanatopsis to thanatourism. *International Journal of Heritage Studies, 2*(4), 234–244. http://dx.doi.org/10.1080/13527259608722178.

Sharpley, R. (2005). The tsunami and tourism: A comment. *Current Issues in Tourism, 8*(4), 344–349. https://doi.org/10.1080/13683500508668222.

Sharpley, R., & Stone, P. R. (2009). *The darker side of travel: The theory and practice of dark tourism*. Bristol: Channel View.

Sönmez, S. (2002). A distorted destination image? The case of Turkey. *Journal of Travel Research, 41*(2), 185–196.

Steckley, M., & Doberstein, B. (2011). Tsunami survivors' perspectives on vulnerability and vulnerability reduction: Evidence from Koh Phi Phi Don and Khao Lak, Thailand. *Disasters, 35*(3), 465–487. https://doi.org/10.1111/j.1467-7717.2010.01221.X.

Stone, P. R. (2006). A dark tourism spectrum: Towards a typology of death and macabre related tourist sites, attractions and exhibitions. *Tourism, 54*(2), 145–160.

Stone, P. (2013). Dark tourism scholarship: A critical review. *International Journal of Cultural, Tourism and Hospitality Reserach, 7*(3), 307–318. https://doi.org/10.1108/IJCTHR-06-2013-0039.

Strange, C., & Kempa, M. (2003). Shades of dark tourism – Alcatraz and Robben Island. *Annals of Tourism Research, 30*(2), 386–405. https://doi.org/10.1016/s0160-7383(02)00102-0.

Tang, Y. (2014a). Travel motivation, destination image and visitor satisfaction of international tourists after the 2008 Wenchuan earthquake: A structural modeling approach. *Asia Pacific Journal of Tourism Research, 19*(21), 1260–1277. https://doi.org/10.1080/10941665.2013.844181.

Tang, Y. (2014b). Dark touristic perception: Motivation, experience and benefits interpreted from the visit to seismic memorial sites in Sichuan Province. *Journal of Mountain Science, 11*(5), 1326–1341. https://doi.org/10.1007/s11629-013-2857-4.

Teigen, K. H., & Glad, K. A. (2011). "It could have been much worse": From travelers' accounts of two natural disasters. *Scandinavian Journal of Hospitality and Tourism, 11*(3), 237–249. https://doi.org/10.1080/15022250.2011.606610.

Thomas, L. L. (2012). People want to see what happened: Treme, televisual tourism, and the racial remapping of post-Katrina New Orleans. *Television & New Media, 13*(3), 213–224. https://doi.org/10.1177/1527476411433889.

Tunbridge, J. E., & Ashworth, G. J. (1996). *Dissonant heritage: The management of the past as a resource in conflict*. New York: John Wiley & Sons.

Wegscheider, S., Post, J., Zosseder, K., Muck, M., Strunz, G., Riedlinger, T., Muhari, A., & Anwar, H. Z. (2011). Generating tsunami risk knowledge at community level as a base for planning and implementation of risk reduction strategies. *Natural Hazards and Earth System Sciences, 11*(2), 249–258. https://doi.org/10.5194/nhess-11-249-2011.

Williams, A. M., & Balaz, V. (2013). Tourism, risk tolerance and competences: Travel organization and tourism hazards. *Tourism Management, 35*, 209–221. https://doi.org/10.1016/j.tourman.2012.07.006.

Winter, C. (2011). Battlefield visitor motivations: Explorations in the Great War Town of Ieper, Belgium. *International Journal of Tourism Research, 13*(2), 164–176. https://doi.org/10.1002/jtr.806.

Xu, J., & Grunewald, A. (2009). What have we learned? A critical review of tourism disaster management. *Journal of China Tourism Research, 5*(1), 102–130. https://doi.org/10.1080/19388160802711444.

Yang, W. Q. (2008). Impact of the Wenchuan earthquake on tourism in Sichuan, China. *Journal of Mountain Science, 5*(3), 194–208. https://doi.org/10.1007/s11629-008-0205-x.

Yang, W. Q., Wang, D. J., & Chen, G. J. (2011). Reconstruction strategies after the Wenchuan earthquake in Sichuan, China. *Tourism Management, 32*(4), 949–956. https://doi.org/10.1016/j.tourman.2010.07.007.

19

First World War Battlefield Tourism: Journeys Out of the Dark and into the Light

Dominique Vanneste and Caroline Winter

Introduction

Dark tourism claims within its definitions almost all tourism to places of death, and it is often assumed, therefore, that visitation to sites of war is also an example of 'dark' interest and motivation. We argue that the Great War sites, to some extent, point away from the dark aspects of death, and seek to enlighten and uplift. A century after the war, there has been a reinvigoration of interest, which does not appear to have moved towards "dark" aspects, but for many people, it has tended to emulate some of the post-war patterns of pilgrimage and its notions of quiet respect, peace and remembrance. Our argument relates to the associations between the dead, the nation, the military and families, and the reinvigoration of these aspects with the centenary in the context of the dominant and highly visual presentation of military cemeteries (also see Chap. 15).

Bowman et al. (2010: 188) argue that, at least in Western cultures, 'darkness' has negative connotations, which tends to limit tourists to those "who are likely to behave in a way some deem inappropriate". For Stone (2013) the essence of dark tourism is in fact the way it challenges

---

D. Vanneste (✉)
University of Leuven, Leuven, Belgium

C. Winter
William Angliss Institute, Melbourne, Australia

© The Author(s) 2018
P. R. Stone et al. (eds.), *The Palgrave Handbook of Dark Tourism Studies*,
https://doi.org/10.1057/978-1-137-47566-4_19

accepted norms, taboo and deviance relating to death, and that in doing so, "embodied dark leisure experiences provide for a potential construction of morality within secular society" (Stone 2013). The contribution of this chapter is not merely to present another case study about dark tourism, but it engages with the debate about a death taboo, and suggests where some of the boundaries may lie for forms of tourism which deal with the dead and sites of death. It seeks to help answer some of the questions raised by dark tourism: Who owns the dead, and at what point does taboo weaken or become susceptible to challenge? Why is it, for example, that at some sites, certain behaviours remain taboo, while at others social norms appear to have changed? We present on-site empirical research from the battlefields, in which the perceptions of visitors were analyzed. This is somewhat different to the broader study of the tourismification of war heritage (Butler and Suntikul 2013; Hartmann 2014). It is important to point out that this chapter relates to the battlefields in Belgium for the Great War of 1914–1918 and visitation to military cemeteries as well as some trench complexes and the Menin Gate at Ypres. Museums on war and peace such as the In Flanders Fields Museum or the Memorial Museum Passchendaele 1917 or the Museum at the IJzer are not included.

A Death Taboo

A taboo can be defined as "the prohibition of an action based on the belief that such behaviour is either too sacred and consecrated or too dangerous and accursed for ordinary individuals to undertake" (The Encyclopedia Brittanica 2015). Taboos exist in almost all societies, with death and sex being common concerns (The Encyclopedia Brittanica 2015). Taboos also define deviant behaviour which often attracts severe punishment. Walter (1991) suggests there are two kinds of death taboo, and we adopt his "weak taboo" that is, not talking about it rather than his stronger version (denial) which relates to the area of psychoanalysis.

There are some important reasons for which a society would seek to control and regulate the way in which people deal with death (see also Chap. 8). Not the least of these is that bereaved individuals can be emotionally difficult and dangerous to control, and the loss of social bonds through death can threaten to disrupt group identities and the social order (Reimers 1999; Walter 1999). Mary Douglas (1994: 4) argues, in relation to taboos, that "ideas about separating, purifying, demarcating and punishing transgressions have as their main function to impose system on an inherently untidy experience". As well as prohibiting certain behaviours, society also prescribes acceptable behaviours, and these are commonly expressed through rituals of mourning which are thought to help repair the disruptions caused by death (Bowman et al. 2010; Reimers 1999; Walter 1999).

There is no agreement, however, that a widespread death taboo exists in Western societies, with Walter stating that "undoubtedly, evidence exists that death is impolite in some circles, but the taboo thesis as commonly stated is grossly overdrawn and lacking in subtlety" (Walter 1991: 297). Kellehear (2007) argues that while a death taboo may exist within an elite, it is not necessarily the case for the community at large. He observes that people continue to interact with the dead "In the simple experience of reminiscence or in the act of regular talk with others, the dead live through a survivor's memories, dreams and reflections" (Kellehear 2007: 73).

Walter (2009) identified several institutions that mediate death in a society, including pilgrimage, religion, genealogy, music, sacred ancestors/heroes, photos, law, archaeology, graves, literature, family language and history, with the media and tourism being two key examples. Taboos form part of the processes of mediation. This does not mean that death is ignored by a society, but rather, that the way in which death is spoken about is carefully and strictly regulated. The task of mediating agencies then, is to specify and control the notions of socially appropriate behaviour (how to speak about death), thus avoiding the incidence of deviant behaviour and punishment.

Lebel (2011) identified three forms of bereavement, thus illustrating the social constructivist nature of mediating war death. The first of these he labelled hegemonic in which "the mobilized bereaved became an effective support base for the dominant social and political order"…with the "conversion of loss into sacrifice, and the merging of death with the rebirth of a Jewish state invested mourning with an aura of triumph" (Lebel 2011: 355). Political bereavement occurred after the Yom Kippur war of 1973, when many soldiers had been killed because of intelligence failures. The effect, he argues was that this "undercut the time-honoured heroic link between citizens and bereavement" (Lebel 2011: 359) to such an extent that protests were undertaken at remembrance sites and at funerals against politicians (Lebel 2011). In the 1990s, an era of predominantly individualistic rather than collective values, scrutiny of military decision-making with media focus on faulty planning, again saw parents being faced with the notion that their son's deaths were avoidable and now meaningless (Lebel 2011).

Mediation of the Great War Dead

The mass death of the Great War was also carefully mediated in specific ways as several authors have already outlined (Fussell 1977; Morris 1997; Vance 1997; Inglis 2005). Vance (1997: 110) comments of the Canadian experience, that "in the early 1920s, no one in their right mind wanted to wallow in the horrors of the war just ended, but neither could they go on as if the tragedy had never happened". Making sense of the war was important, in order to assure society that the mass death of their sons, brothers, husbands and friends—society's young generation, had not been in vain. Similar to Lebel's (2011) notion of hegemonic bereavement, the imagery thus created was not of darkness, but the iconography of war memorials focused on life after death, with statues of angels comforting the dead, images of salvation and resurrection after death, with the ancient red Flanders poppy playing an important role (Saunders 2013; Vance 1997; Inglis 2005). These processes created a strong and enduring form of visitation behaviour, that incorporated taboos about the war in many complex ways, and which we argue have endured to the present day.

In the Victorian era, before 1914, death was mediated through very public and highly elaborate funeral practices, but as Inglis (2005: 102) observed, "paradoxically, the war which created such unprecedented levels of bereavement may actually have tended to reduce its public expression". Audoin-Rouzeau and Becker (2012: 223) argue that a "mourning taboo" developed, such that extended public expression of grief, in the face of mass death, was not acceptable. It is not necessarily that there is a blanket denial of death but perhaps as Whitmarsh (2001: 15) suggests "one aspect of the commemorative tradition is that the reality of death is not directly mentioned". Griffin and Tobin (1997: 168) comment that "death began to move out of the centre of life and out of the family home into special, contained places created by the churches, the funeral industry and the medical profession". The issue, therefore, is not so much about the existence (or not) of a complete taboo against speaking of death, but rather that the primary control of mourning rituals has been removed from personal experience and placed with the medical and funereal institutions. As Stone comments, this has created "death sequestered societies" (Stone 2012: 1582). Stone (2012: 1583) conceptualised dark tourism as "part of wider death revivalism within popular culture, whereby dark tourism experiences help to de-sequester mortality and to mediate a range of contemporary relationships with the dead". Stone (2013) claims that "presently, therefore, a number of time-honoured taboos, such as talk of death and presenting the dead within public places, are becoming increasingly translucent and, consequently, there is a new willingness to tackle inherently ambiguous and problematic interpretations" (also see Chap. 8). In particular, Audoin-Rouzeau and Becker (2012: 3) question why the violence of the war has "remained a taboo subject".

When tourists began visiting the battlefields after the end of the war, they were positioned in opposition to the bereaved, regarded as somewhat ghoulish in their desire to tour places of death and accused of trivialising the war (Mosse 1990). That is, in terms of "dark tourism", the early tourists were perhaps seen as breaking the taboos of appropriate behaviour at sites of the war dead. Over time, however, Connelly (2009) argues that the development of visitation as pilgrimage for all visitors, helped to soften the tension between these two broad groups and provided a socially accepted way for both the bereaved and tourists to visit these sensitive places. Tour guides also played important roles in establishing and inventing these traditions, as well as associations such as the Ypres League, the Royal British Legion and the Commonwealth War Graves Commission (CWGC) or the Flemish Peace Movement.[1] Later, in the 1970s, the Holts also reinvigorated the style of pilgrimage. As previously noted, one of the early taboos was that the battlefields ought not to be treated as mere touristic entertainment, but as serious and sombre places to remember the dead.

In addition to tourism, there are, of course, some very powerful institutions which helped to establish the traditions (and taboos) for visitation to the Great War sites, especially cemeteries and other memorials, and we argue that dark tourism is inconsistent with the aims of these institutions. One of the taboos that developed was against the portrayal of the dead as other than the heroic or the innocent youth of a golden era as Vance (1997) describes. As a result, questioning of the war did not occur to any great extent until the 1960s and 1970s, after the parents of the deceased had themselves passed away (Todman 2005). Another aspect of this taboo was against speaking about the horrific effects on those involved in it. The survivors, many of whom suffered lifelong psychological and physical wounds, were living reminders of the war's damage to society's citizen-soldiers. As several studies have shown, many of these men and their families were ignored by society, and outside of the family home, their experiences were excluded from the discourse of war (Larsson 2009; Mosse 1990; Vance 1997).

Nation and Family

The two institutions of nation and the family have played instrumental roles in determining how the dead of the Great War should be treated and spoken about, and herein lies perhaps the primary reason for the establishment and strength of the Great War taboos. Our argument suggests that the taboos against inappropriate behaviour towards war death, can be seen as a form of social control with respect to protection of the nation, the social order and the integrity of families. The battlefields were quickly transformed by a number of processes which removed the evidence of war. The Commonwealth War Graves Commission on behalf of the British nations created a landscape of military cemeteries which Morris (1997: 428) argues, "reconstructed, smoothed and redeemed, enclosed and ordered – the landscape and also the bodies, and effaced mutiny, non-heroics, non-sacrificial acts of war, allied war atrocities and so on". The effect of the new burial practices was also to fuse the memory of the dead, not only with their families but as part of the public property of the nation (Heffernan 1995; Reimers 1999; Winter 1995, 2006). Of course, there was a reclamation by farmers and other forms of land use, but in most cases the position of the cemetery remained untouched and untouchable. Even as recent as 2005, the construction of the missing link between two highways (A19 and E40) was given up because it would cross the battlefield of Pilkem Ridge near Ypres, considered the resting place of many British soldiers missing in the region. Even the British government got involved in the discussion that gave rise to this decision.[2] The meaning and design of the Menin Gate Memorial at Ypres (Commonwealth) and the "Last Post" ceremony that takes place at the gate (Belgian) is also illustrative for this subtle mutual positioning (Foote and Vanneste 2011).

A taboo cautioned against glorification of the war through victorious, nationalistic displays, and most researchers agree that in the main, these sentiments were avoided in most memorials (Inglis 2005; Heffernan 1995). At the same time, Mosse (1990: 6) notes, "the aim was to make an inherently unpalatable past acceptable, important not just for the purpose of consolation but above all for the justification of the nation in whose name the war had been fought". In later years, however, the sites and memorials took on greater significance and meaning for nationalistic purposes such as pride and identity (Connelly 2009; Inglis 2005; Heffernan 1995). For the newly developing British Commonwealth nations, such as Australia, Canada and New Zealand, the war was promoted as an uplifting and noble experience (Slade 2003; Vance 1997). We argue that it is not in the interests of a nation-state that its imagined formation events are associated with the macabre, social deviance and contradictions of long-established taboos about war dead.

The traditions that were developed from 1915 for treatment of war dead remain as part of contemporary military burial practice, and as such, they retain close links with the dead of the Great War (Heffernan 1995). These associations are regularly strengthened through recovery of bodies from the battlefields and their reinternment in military cemeteries, and attended by family members, military and political figures. The application of new forensic techniques for identification are commonly applied.[3]

Other Battlefield Research

According to Lennon and Foley (1999: 47) "the emergence of simulations, replications, and virtual experiences as part of a tourism product has been a critical factor in the emergence of dark tourism" especially at Holocaust sites. While some studies have supported dark tourism theory for examination of former battlefields, others have found an absence of "dark" interest. Bowman et al. (2010) comment that there has been inadequate critique of the concept of dark tourism, perhaps with the result that to date, the association between dark tourism and battlefields appears to remain unclear.

As Seaton (2000: 72) found, "The Great War today invokes the kind of non-ironic, reverential responses which it is supposed to have destroyed. In 1998 people still left wreaths on the great Menin Gate memorial at Ypres in which the words 'honour', 'sacrifice' and 'love' may be found elegiacally copied on small cards of tribute". Miles set out to find if a thanatoptic sentiment was present in visitors' numinous and spiritual experiences at three battlefields from the Middle Ages and found that while some "darker" engagement was present, it did not form a significant feature of the visit compared with other themes and concluded there was "little evidence for a thanatoptic experience" (Miles 2014: 144). Thi Le and Pearce (2011: 461) researching the Korean War battlefields, also concluded that "Most visitors to the battlefield sites in the DMZ [demilitarized zone] do not come across as particularly 'dark'. The same goes for visitors to the Waterloo battlefield near Brussels, where Napoleon was defeated (Seaton 1999) although some small initiatives (e.g. the Belgian idea for a €2 coin in a spirit of commemoration of the fatal battle) may provoke disproportionate reactions (e.g. the veto from France[4]) which show that the darkness of battle and defeat is sometimes underestimated.

Our study then focuses on examination of visitor experiences at military cemeteries for the Great War, and whether or not there was evidence of 'dark' experiences that challenge the taboos set in place a century earlier.

The Experience from the Field

The previous paragraphs show how the concept of "taboo" can relate to war tourism, battlefield tourism, dark tourism, and even heritage or cultural tourism in a war heritage context. In the case of the Great War, we argue that one could expect that some taboos will become less influential in time, as a response to factors such as technological and attitudinal changes in Western societies. As a result, therefore, the battlefields as a focus of tourism interest renews itself which, in turn, may help to explain why (this) war tourism has endured to the present day. In testing the notion of taboo with visitors in our study area of the WWI Western Front in Belgium, we found that the present-day battlefield tourism incorporates a complex mix of taboo continuities and discontinuities.

Before going into this journey, we would like to present the study area which may not be so well known among an international audience, beyond some of the iconic sites such as Ypres (Ieper), Passchendaele (Passendale) and, of course, the poppy symbolising, among other aspects of the war, the Flemish fields that turned so sadly into one big graveyard. Even now, some visitors are impressed by the prominent presentation of the military cemeteries in the area, especially those built by the Commonwealth War Graves Commission.

> We think it is really wonderful that there are so many cemeteries. If you drive around with a car you can discover so many cemeteries. They are lovely dispersed in this region. (TC-UKAU-MC)

R1: What is it like to live in a neighbourhood like this? Which is a living cemetery really. Which it is, isn't it? So much has happened. Here. Everywhere there is a cemetery.
R2: Even in the soil…I mean everywhere…. (SW-UK-3MM)

Flanders (Belgium), and especially the far Western area called "Westhoek" (which can be translated as *corner in the west*) experienced the Great War in all of its horror and terror resulting from the trench stalemate that lasted for four years. Similarly, in the northern, flat section (the Belgian sector) the war came to a standstill with German and Belgian troops within close range of each other, trapped by the mud, the inundated land and threatened by vermin and disease as much as by force of arms. In the hillier southern section (the British sector), small differences in the topography created strategic advantages that were obstinately defended or conquered with a tremendous loss of life. An inventory of the dead has left us with approximately 200 military cemeteries for WWI of which 172 are British.[5] Some of them are well known, such as Tyne Cot, the largest Commonwealth War Graves Commission (CWGC) cemetery in the world with 11,952 soldiers buried of which 8300 are not identified and surrounded at one side by an impressive 152-meter-long wall that carries the names of another 35,000 soldiers from the UK and New Zealand who are missing or never identified. Others, however, are not so well known—who has heard of Poelcapelle British Cemetery with 7478 soldiers buried—6578 from the UK, 536 from Canada, 117 from Australia, 237 from New Zealand and 10 from South African? Or of Messines Ridge British Cemetery with 1531 graves—1003 UK soldiers, 342 Australian, 128 New Zealand, 57 South African and 1 Canadian—or the many "small" cemeteries such as Lancashire Cottage Cemetery (Komen-Waasten) with 256 Commonwealth graves and 13 German ones. The decision of the British to (re)bury their soldiers on the battlefields on which they fell and not to repatriate the bodies (contrary to decisions taken by the Belgian and French command), leave the area today with a large number of CWGC military cemeteries. German cemeteries are less dominant for a number of reasons, not the least of which is because the Belgian Service for War Graves decided to move the mortal remains of German soldiers to one of only four German cemeteries. As a consequence, the German cemeteries are few in number but very large; at Langemarck Soldatenfriedhof, for example, more than 44,000 soldiers are buried. Beyond the war cemeteries, a massive number of monuments can be found spread throughout the area, such as the Menin Gate at Ypres, the "Brooding Soldier" (Canadian monument) at Sint-Juliaan (Langemark), "The Angel" (French monument) at Mount Kemmel, the Irish Peace Park at Messines, and so on, complemented by museums, former crates (now pools and ponds), trenches, dugouts and other sites (remembrance chapels, mills, bunkers, etc.).[6] Notwithstanding that the villages and the agricultural landscape (such as fields and woods) were completely destroyed or changed beyond recognition, the civilian population is not presented in this picture, since they were deported from the area by the military for the duration of the war.

Now, 100 years later, the landscape has recovered and presents a gentle outlook on a densely populated, green and small-scale rural area with its rebuilt villages and small towns (Ypres, Veurne) dominated by a multitude of small businesses. The locals learned to live with the scars in the landscape (remnants of trenches and craters); they use the bunkers as sheds and consider the cemeteries as bright spots in the landscape like daisies in a field, as an integral part of their usual environment. Over the past century, the discovery of old ammunition has been very frequent. Nevertheless, this is seldom acknowledged unless, on occasion, a research project unearths a newsworthy find, such as the recent discovery of over 400 pieces of metal in one field with, among them, unexploded ammunition.[7] This does not mean that the local people fail to see the interest of this cultural heritage, especially since this heritage can be capitalised in terms of visitors and income, in an area which is not heavily industrialised nor stimulated by outside investments. In 2006, 310,000 overnight stays in hotels (almost 690,000 in all types of accommodation), represented 56 million euro. Even if not all of these overnight guests are motivated by WWI, a considerable number are. In 2007 one estimated the WWI motivated tourists at the Westhoek at about 370,000,[8] of which 38% stayed overnight (137,000). Of the 2.2 million day tourists in the area (2006), 9% or around 200,000 were motivated by the WWI theme in one way or another, spending 5.1 million euro.[9] In 2013, the number of WWI-motivated visitors was estimated at 415,500, based on the number of visits at 10 WWI sites[10]. Therefore, even before the centennial started, the number of visitors was already growing with 183,000 Belgian WWI visitors in 2013—up from 151,000 in 2006—and almost 155,000 British WWI visitors in 2013, compared with 133,000 in 2006. This trend resulted in nearly 790,000 visitors in 2014, of which 46% non-domestic and 500,500 in 2015, of which 54% non-domestic.[11]

This sustained interest in the Great War battlefields, together with recent large increases in visitation leads to the inevitable questions: what inspires and motivates these visitors, what are their expectations and especially, what is their interpretation of specific sites, what emotions are evoked and what image, impression and message do they take home? How easy is it to consider this mass death? This chapter relates to data collected as part of a larger study designed to help provide some answers to these questions. A series of short interviews were conducted with visitors at various Great War battlefield sites over several years, beginning in 2009, with 158 short interviews being conducted at 20 WWI-related sites,[12] In 2013, 164 interviews were conducted at Tyne Cot (central part of the Flemish Front line, British sector), Bayernwald (southern part of the Flemish Front line, German sector) and the "Trench of Death" (northern part of the Flemish Front line, Belgian sector),[13] and a further 185 interviews were held in 2014 at the same sites.[14] The data were then examined to determine whether or not there existed evidence of the operation of a death taboo, or that taboos may have been weakened. In this multitude of data, the items in Fig. 19.1 were outlined and two major groups of taboos were identified: the taboos associated with speech and taboos identified with behaviour (central trunk in the scheme). The former has to do with the subject and the discourse, while the latter is associated with (dis)respect of rules. In the analysis of our interviews, these items constitute the core nodes, while attention will be paid to sensitivities that relate to mediation on the one hand, and structure (influence) of the landscape and the landscaping, on the

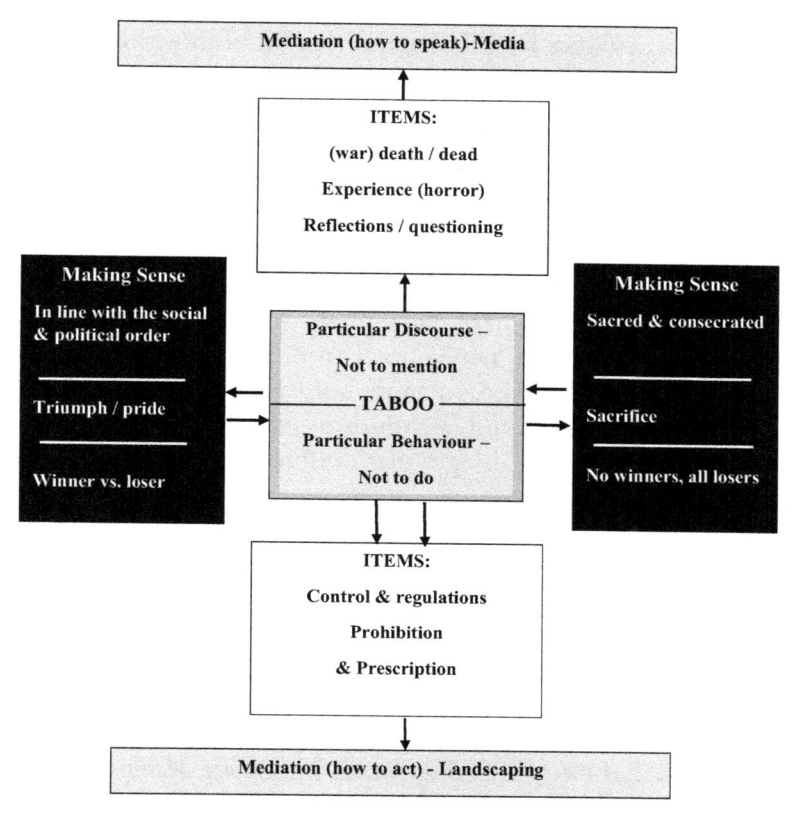

First World War Battlefield Tourism: Journeys Out of the Dark... 453

Fig. 19.1 Items from the interviews (nodes from the transcript analysis) (data from 2009, 2013 and 2014)

other hand. We also tried to gather an insight in what made behaviour and/or discourse (not) acceptable for visitors or, the other way around, what was "making sense" for visitors as well in terms of discourse as in terms of behaviour.

Before examining the visitor, we would like to highlight the position of one mediating agency which is the provincial DMO Westtoer, that has promoted and monitored battlefield tourism in the area for a very long time. Recently, they went (far) beyond that by setting up networks, by writing project proposals and organising collaboration with, among others, the North of France and the UK (refer the Interreg "2 SEAS" project *The Great War: between the lines*[15]). These organisations certainly do not consider the capitalisation of WWI heritage a taboo, but at the same time, battlefield tourism is not considered and handled as just any kind of tourism. In the case of the commemoration activities for the centennial, a lot of thought went into the ways to deal with "sensitivities" that are related to the subject "death" and the differences in interpretation according to nationalities.

An interesting sign came from the Flemish Peace Institute that was commissioned to look into the critical conditions for a peace-oriented commemoration and the way this could be justified in a normative and historical way (Van Alstein 2011). On a second level, it was mentioned that this commemoration logic had to be able to serve other objectives: the international visibility of Flanders and the stimulation of remembrance tourism. At the same time, a warning was put forward as if "remembrance tourism is an interesting medium to strengthen a peaceful recall to memory but that, at the same time, the use of a past of war as a tool to stimulate tourism, runs a risk because of its (possible) limited and commercial logic that outlines the use of the past" (Van Alstein 2011: 71).

The policy to avoid turning the centennial in a pure commercial or sensation-seeking event gave rise to a so-called Tourism+ approach with, as a subtitle "Ethical and 'many-voiced' Commemoration Tourism".[16] In the flyer, the whole message is summarised by the following sentence: "An important aspect is the use of the right tone. We have to approach the stories and the heritage from the First World War in an appropriate manner". Seven basic principles constitute a framework... *1. Respect. 2. Good hostship. 3. Accessibility. 4. 'Many-voiced'. 5. In-depth. 6. International. 7. Peace Message.* On its website,[17] the DMO Westtoer opens with "In a respectful manner..." which illustrates how sensitive the matter is considered to be. During interviews, public tourism authorities focus explicitly on this element as well (Vanneste and Foote 2013). Therefore, one could imagine that, even after a century, issues are "touchy" and taboos remain about the need to show respect through appropriate speaking and behaviour. There is also a sense that taboos have been added in relation to "international correctness" which has become an important issue. Several events are very illustrative in that respect. In 2011, Armistice Day witnessed an addition to the commemoration ceremony in Ypres of the presentation of the Olympic Flag, carried by winners of medals in Olympic Games from Belgium and abroad, and in the presence of Olympic committee officials (Plate 19.1). The relationship with war and peace focused on group spirit and unconditional devotion, especially with groups' sports where the individual effaces oneself for the team. The presence of royalty and/or the presence of representatives from different governments on all major commemoration ceremonies almost desperately try to avoid triumphalism and judgements.

[A] Ypres, Armistice Day, 2011. Winners of Olympic medals	[B] Ypres, Armistice Day 2014, Ambassadors from less evident countries (India and USA)

Plate 19.1 The international dimension of WWI commemoration events in Flanders (Photo Source [A]: Foto WO1.be, 11 Nov. 2011, Photo Source [B]: AP Photo Virginia May, 11 Nov. 2014)

Visitor Understandings of Taboos

First, it should be mentioned that we didn't use the concept of "taboo" explicitly in our interview protocol and therefore almost no one used it in his or her comments, except one middle-aged woman from the UK telling us:

> [looking away from us]…so many people died and it wasn't necessary. In some way it was because the Germans came to Belgium and somebody had to stop them…I hate war, I think if they had tried to come to an agreement with the Germans without fighting for 4 years it would have been better…[looking at us] Is this a taboo? (TC-UK-MF)[18]

In general, most visitors were forthright in giving their opinion, without considering that this may have sounded rude or offensive, they hurried to apologise or to add that they changed their minds. Some examples recorded among different nationalities (British, Australian, Dutch):

> … the British, they were more dear to us than the Germans…But [after] what we have seen yesterday and what we see now [German Cemetery Langemark], this is gone…they are all losers. (DML-NL-Fam)

> You [talks to his wife] were saying that this [German Cemetery Langemark] was quite morbid compared to the British cemeteries. But as we were driving here[…]I kind of think that the British ones[…]they glorify the sacrifice more. When you go in, they are all perfectly kept and there is architecture around them. There is a lot of thought going in them. Into this as well, but it is much

more muted, calmer, low key. And the colors are dark. The sculpture over there for example [points to the statues] I don't know...,it's quite...I don't know... (DML-UK-YC)

It's terribly annoying to say but I think that one is quickly bored by all those cemeteries. (Vl-NL-F&S)

I came to see what the biggest cemetery is like. It just gives you another feeling, to bring the reality, to discover more about the people rather than reading some numbers...it's quite surprising. (TC-Au-YM)

It is striking that visitors explicitly condemn a discourse that uses triumph or the winner-loser opposition in an attempt to give meaning to the mass death. Even more, the sacrifice and the notion to "never forget but we didn't learn any lesson" is explicitly present in many (mainstream) interpretations. Therefore, many thoughts reflect an implicit peace dimension although some fear that an explicit focus of the site on peace may erase the real message. These seem to reflect the ideas described above in the aims of the DMO Westtoer promotions.

I don't know if it is on war, I think it's on remembering what happened. Not necessarily that there was a war but remembering how many people died. And ...You know, it's not glorifying war, it's not saying "We should be at war", but it's saying "Yes it happened, and we need to remember why it happened and why it shouldn't happen anymore". (YMarket- Au-YFs)

Q: Does this site [Menin Gate] provoke a thought of war or peace? The German young women translates for her parents: "denken wir an Krieg oder Frieden wann wir hier sind" while her mother answers "Mehr an Krieg" (More about war) and her father: "Ich denke dass ist gut ist das die Leute den Krieg erinnern" (I think it's good that people remember the war) while she adds "if they focus too much on peace they maybe forget the war and the things that happened here". (YMenin Gate-G-Fam)

One could detect that a number of visitors were not affected by a taboo against speaking about the experiences during the war or asking questions about the war. As illustrated by two older women from the UK and Australia, respectively, in the past the survivors were reluctant to talk about their war experience, and while this may have been so for a range of reasons, as previously noted (Larsson 2009; Mosse 1990; Vance 1997), there was a taboo against open and public discussion about the psychological and physical effect of the war on the soldiers. Today, however, family members appear to be more willing and even desperately seeking to talk about how the war affected their relatives.

> We specifically visit the Australian ones [sites] with significance to Australians… Father…as a child I asked him what it was like and all he said was "Wet, cold and muddy."(H60-Au-OF)[I had relatives] "not who died but who were damaged by it…do not want to talk about it". (H62-UK- OF)

There was also a strong sign of the role of schools and teachers as mediating agents. For example, several teachers said they wanted the students to reflect on their impressions. Implicitly, the taboo against 'forgetting' is very strong.

> Some kids will get more angry about the way how the German cemetery is [looks like] hidden away, we got to Langemark and talked about it, how it is dark…I want them to…understand. (H62-UK-T)

> I think that this ["memorial day and stuff"] is quite a British thing actually. This total obsession with the war…what happened, you know. In a way that…well the Germans, for obvious reasons, they just want to forget about it… (DML-UK-YC)

> When you consider the enormity of what had happened, just how many people died, isn't it right to just honor them and remember them in the right way as well.[…]Should you just forget about it? Because if you forget about it, then this sort of thing can all happen again. (DML-UK-YC)

It is important to note that many of the in-depth reflections came from British visitors. It is indeed not beyond imagination that the one nationality is more "obsessed with war", as one of the respondents called this interest which represents a two-way street. On the one hand, taboos may be stronger while on the other hand, taboos may be challenged more actively. Another element is the location. Some very interesting blunt reflections could be recorded when British were confronted with the losses on the German side or vice versa. This may suggest that shock can overcome taboo. When visitors stay within their own framework, they tend to develop a less taboo challenging discourse.

> Yes this [Tyne Cot Cemetery] is a very peaceful place and also very beautiful… it is absolutely something that we cannot forget…I think because of the peacefulness and the way it is kept as well. With all the flowers and everything, it is really lovely. (TC-UK-MF)

From the research, it seems that behaviour is far more a subject of taboo. In particular, the behaviour of younger people (students) is a subject of comment in a positive as well as in a negative way as the citations below illustrate. During our interviews conducted in March and April 2014, we asked explicitly if and how visitors judged the behaviour of other visitors. Only 15 of 72 stated that the behaviour of other visitors *did not* matter, and, in general, these were families with children, claiming that children had the right to play. The large majority for whom the behaviour of others did matter, mentioned quietness and an attitude of respect as desirable or even essential, as opposed to noise (laughter, shouting). Therefore, the number of people is less important in a sense that people would like to be alone, but they accept that they can't claim the place.

Q: Is the behaviour of the other visitors important for the memory on this place? R2: "yeah".
R1: "Sort off…Yeah, just be respectful".
Q: Does it matter for you that a lot of people come to this place? Young people? R2: "You want to be alone in there, but…").
R1: "The school trips might be a problem. They see some things in a different way… They're young people and they…"
R2: "Limited time and limited patience…" (H62-UK-MCMF)

[When seeing students who placed some poppies at graves at Tyne Cot Cemetery] "I think it is really important that young people are still interested in the war, because it is something that we can never forget". (TC-UKAU-MC)

Even after 100 years, some visitors were somewhat reluctant to leave their *spatial* comfort zone, while others were happy to do so.

R: "When you think about the Germans, you think horrible things. But they were ordinary people who had to go to the war…they were forced to do the same thing just as the English people".
Q: You would also visit a German cemetery?
R: "Ah, I am not sure if I would visit a German cemetery but I don't feel they shouldn't be here" [referring to the 4 German soldiers buried at the Commonwealth Tyne Cot Cemetery] (TC-UK-MF).
Q: Do you feel different being British on a German cemetery?
R: "No[…]I think some people might. Perhaps older people might, but I don't. Really not at all". (DML-UK-YC).

This brings us to a reflection on the operation of taboo through spatial design, particularly at military cemeteries. As previously noted, the cemeteries, and the many memorials across the Western Front were designed to reflect certain values. Even so, space is given meaning only by the behaviours of those who visit (Bell 2009; May 1988). As one respondent mentioned "a great deal of thought went into their design" and therefore, they tend to mirror to some extent the old "making sense" dimension in line with the social and political order of the post-war years. The question as to whether visitors are aware of design, of the (lack of) explicit message and of (the lack of) taboo is difficult to answer from the data collected in this study. Some signs indicate that most visitors feel if the landscape tends to channel certain memories and reflections or even suspect manipulation.

> They [trenches of Hill 62] are rough and ready…In many ways this is as good if not better. (H62-UK-MCMF)

> You think that it is about 'never again', but this goes back to the earlier point where something that is respecting the dead turns into something that is glorifying the death. I don't know. But this place [German military cemetery] isn't glorifying anything. This is just sombre. (DML-UK-YC)

One of the developing elements is the change from a more introverted interest in looking at particular sites (such as those that concern familial and national sensitivities), towards an extroverted and holistic look at the broader scale of the war. While some may consider that this may weaken particular messages (such as nationalistic ones), others argue that it also opens a path for broader and more universal understanding (Levy and Sznaider 2002; Winter 2015). The weakening of certain taboos is also reflected by the fact that visitors are not ashamed to show empathy with the "other". Media might play an important role.

> I think the focus here is on what went on here between 1914 and 1918. The loss, the tremendous loss of life, the destruction of the whole county almost, you know, and the fact that they sort of picked themselves up and rebuilt this afterwards. (YMeninGate- UK- MM)

> In that book, he writes about…father who had to take part in an execution platoon and who refused. When one is at Poperinge [Dead cell], the whole story comes up again. (DM-NL-F&S)

The same ideas apply for tourism, and again, it reflects the approach taken by the DMO Westtoer to incorporate a broader perspective into commemorations.

Respondents seldom reject tourism as inappropriate, probably because they are aware that they are part of it. Further, they show awareness of the fact that, first, a balance in different types of visitors is necessary and, second, such a balance is difficult to obtain and maintain.

> It [tourism] is difficult isn't it? It's the pro's and con's... Isn't it? If you don't have enough people it isn't worth all the work that is gone to keep for the future generations but if you get too many, it could ruin it. It is very difficult. Isn't it? (SW-UK-3MM)

> We saw a lot of the British side, so now we came to have a look on the German side [Bayernwald] and it worries me still; the German people still don't take an interest and face up to what happened, I think it is very important that they should do. I think, perhaps, whoever organized German tourism, should try to encourage more to come. A lot of British people will come next year and the German people should come as well. (BW-UK-C)

> R: "You come here as a tourist, but you don't come here for tourism".
> Q: A place of remembrance? R: "Totally agree"; Q: A historical heritage place? R: "Totally agree". Q: A place for education? R: "Agree". (TC-USA-2F).

Conclusion

Taboos were developed during and in the decades following the Great War which helped to protect families and societies from the horrific experience of the war on the one hand and served the purpose of nations to justify the losses of young lives on the other hand. Ironically, they may also have protected the military and political elites who controlled the events leading up to the war, and the mass death that was its result. Some of these taboos can be identified in the literature:

- Battlefields, and cemeteries in particular must not be used or treated as places for mere touristic entertainment;
- War dead must be treated with respect, as determined by practices of quiet pilgrimage;
- War must not be glorified but sacrifice for freedom should be subject of appreciation;
- The psychological and physical effects of the war on the individuals involved in it must not be publicly discussed;

- Overt nationalistic and victorious displays must be avoided;
- There should be limited public expression of grief.

Generally, the comments made by the interview respondents tend to indicate that these taboos remain. Visitors were sometimes very blunt in the formulation of their opinion on war and quite critical of their own nationalistic approaches, thus reflecting the taboo against emphasising victorious elements, or of glorifying the war. They were, however, more willing to speak about and try to understand the experience of both "sides"—British and German, of the war.

It is important to note that noise and overly enthusiastic behaviour is the strongest taboo we could detect. Visitors expect "quietness" for themselves, and that respect for the dead must be reflected in the behaviour of others. van der Laarse (2015) states that "emptiness" (free of noise, free of objects) is a strong experience of the (difficult) past. Even when the effect of war has been lessened over time, *traumascapes lend themselves to a different form of heritization than most sites* (Baillie et al. 2010: 58). Therefore, inappropriate behaviour such as noise remains a taboo, because a visit at a war memorial involves a sense of "going back to feelings and healing". The question remains why this emptiness is so important? We argue that it is because as Audoin-Rouzeau and Becker (2012: 9) suggest, the belligerent nations have not "completely recovered from this mourning or from the distress that its lack of meaning engendered", and for many visitors, the taboo is still relevant.

The memory scape evokes a feeling of empathy with this landscape and its people, while walking through it seems to "engender deep feelings of rootedness" (Butler 2007: 370). In other words, although sites of bereavement such as cemeteries may have become less relevant to new generations, "there is something involuntary moralizing about these sites" (Pastoriza cited in Friedrich 2011: 176) and our research confirms that "respect", and the taboo about a lack of respect is primary.

Certainly, there is a challenge to the so-called pro-entertainment model which goes beyond distress and trauma for survivor communities (Baillie et al. 2010), since it brings us to the point where taboo and the notion of "darkness" can be confronted. We discovered two sides of the same coin. Behaviours regulated by boundaries of prohibition and prescription can be considered "dark" since, among others, it hinders a free experience of the site and of its heritage, while the entertainment orientation is completely absent (Sharpley 2009: 21). Breaking the taboo of "respectful" behaviour is still seen as deviant.

On the other hand, the data suggest that taboos with respect of speaking about the war are no longer as strong as they once were, in particular, those imposed by a nationalistic perspective. For sure "narratives of commemoration have 'downscaled' [from the official to the personal] or 'upscaled' [from the personal to the universal]" (Muzaini and Yeoh 2007: 1302). From that perspective, it is commonly accepted by the visitors that the sites can produce dialectically different meanings. It seems that polyvocality can take place without conflict as well as different ways of scripting. In that sense, the discourse is not dark but enlightened. This does not mean that the content of their words is "light"; the more the visitors reflect on the extent of the sacrifice and the options for a solution humankind left aside, the darker the thoughts and discourse. The "never again" *and* "they were all losers" dominate the discourse. This does not exclude a peace message; on the contrary, implicitly this implies a peace discourse which was intended by the Tourism+ approach.

In this research, the landscaping of the sites provoked interesting but also very diverse interpretations, and it supports the notion that some sites, particularly sensitive ones such as cemeteries, can influence visitors in the enactment of existing taboos. One cannot exclude then, the possibility of a multi-layered remembrance, in terms of behaviour versus discourse which can lead to "dissonance" (Tunbridge and Ashworth 1996). But places and landscapes have a high degree of "imageability" (Lynch 1960) and war-related sites have that potential, perhaps even more than other places. The whole literature on dark tourism and the attempt to explain the impact of sites in terms of darkness (Sharpley and Stone 2009) is illustrative. Re-connecting places has been proven to be a good instrument to "redraw the landscape of war memories" (refer the Japanese Network to protect War-related Sites, mentioned by Han 2012: 494, 496). It makes a balance between memories of suffering *experienced* and of suffering *caused*, as well as between remembrance related to soldiers and to civilians, and therefore, helps to change the need for the existence of taboos. The focus on the landscape as an integrated set of connected places certainly weakens the memory-nation nexus, but this integration is still not going beyond cultural boundaries (e.g. British visitors still barely visit the sites in the Belgian "sector") (Vanneste and Foote 2013).

The interviews reveal that some visitors do not have a personal connection with the memoryscape. Before visiting the landscape, no taboo makes sense to them. When experiencing the landscape, they start to understand the grief and gain empathy which makes them aware of certain behavioural taboos. Although we hope that "dark heritage sites promote dialogue and debate amongst visitors" (Baillie et al. 2010: 58), very little evidence for this was suggested by our visitors' survey. One could even presume that the attitude taboo on respectful, quiet and almost introvert behaviour implies a barrier for the meeting of and exchanging narratives with the "other".

Finally, our research found a number of important complexities that might be of use for governance and policy in war tourism. We argue that the case of taboo is highly dependent upon the circumstances of the visitor and the elements of behaviour and discourse. Since it is accepted that governance is/should be embedded in history, place, political and cultural contingencies, we recommend that governance and policy should be connected from the "as is" and not from the "as desired" perspective as suggested by Moulaert et al. (2016). In this case, this is a plea for going beyond the dark-light discourse or the breaking versus revitalising of behavioural taboos and taking into account the choices and real attitudes of the visitors. Exploring these choices might be well served by the analysis of the narratives (as we did in this chapter) for which tourism is a particularly interesting medium.

Notes

1. Vlaamse Vredesbeweging, developed from the Flemish Veterans' League.
2. http://forumeerstewereldoorlog.be/viewtopic.php?p=162793&sid=6942af2b75d10f63d6ae3e4c738f7691
3. '*Opnieuw een gesneuvelde Australiër geIdentificeerd!*' (2008) http://www.forumeerstewereldoorlog.nl/viewtopic.php?t=15261&sid=1f12207f15bca48f34a99c7252480ab9
4. '*België vermijdt Frans veto met aangepaste Waterloo-munt*', (2015) http://www.standaard.be/cnt/dmf20150608_01720478
5. http://www.wo1.be/nl/db/begraafplaatsen/britse-militaire-begraafplaatsen
6. Westtoer (2008) Toeristische valorisatie van erfgoed uit de eerste wereldoorlog in de Westhoek met het oog op 100 jaar Groote Oorlog (2014–18), pp. 22–55.
7. http://nl.metrotime.be/2015/11/09/must-read/scanner-zoekt-oorlogsmunitie/
8. Westtoer (2008) Toeristische valorisatie van erfgoed uit de eerste wereldoorlog in de Westhoek met het oog op 100 jaar Groote Oorlog (2014–18), pp. 76–77.
9. Westtoer (2008), Strategisch Beleidsplan Toerisme en Recreatie in de Westhoek 2008–2013, pp. 58–65 9per cent seems low but it is not because (i) this is before the WWI commemoration started to influencing visitors numbers, (ii) a major amusement park within that year—750,000 visitors is distorting numbers of visitors to the area, and (iii) the area is located close to a highly developed coast line that promotes visits and especially cycling in the hinterland.

10. Westtoer (2014), *Wereldoorlog I Bezoekers in the Westhoek 2013*, report, p. 9.
11. Westtoer (2015), *Herdenkingstoerisme Westhoek 2014*, Press Conference 8 April 2015; Westtoer (2016) *100 jaar Groote Oorlog in de Westhoek, Tussentijds Reflectiemoment*, 13 juni 2016, Ieper.
12. A total of 158 of which 83 with Belgians (53%), 50 with British (32%), 8 with Dutch (5%), 8 with Austrian or New-Zealand (5%) and seven with other nationalities with a low number ranging from three to one.
13. A total of 164 of which 83 with Belgians (51%) and 47 with British (29%)—37 Bayernwald, 59 Trench of Death, and 68 Tyne Cot Cemetery; period August–October 2013.
14. 185 of which 103 with Belgians (56%) and 44 with British (24%)—50 Bayernwald, 64 Trench of Death, 71 Tyne Cot Cemetery: period 6–13 November 2013 + March/April 2014.
15. http://greatwar1418.eu/en/presentation
16. Westtoer (2013), Toerisme+. Ethisch en meerstemmig Herdenkingstoerisme. 100 jaar Groote Oorlog (flyer) http://www.westtoer.be/nl/over-westtoer/nieuws/westtoer-presenteert-nieuwigheden-voor-2014
17. http://www.westtoer.be/nl/over-westtoer/nieuws/westtoer-presenteert-nieuwigheden-voor-2014'Op respectvolle wijze plaatst het provinciebedrijf Westtoer de herdenking van 100 jaar Groote Oorlog dit jaar centraal. Belangrijk zijn begrippen zoals respect, gastheerschap, meerstemmigheid en vredesboodschap'.
18. The source code includes (site-nationality-age/gender); for age: Y=young; M=middle aged; O=old; for gender: M=male; F=female; and C=couple.

References

Audoin-Rouzeau, S., & Becker, A. (2012). *Understanding the Great War 14–18*. New York: Hill and Wang.

Baillie, B., Chatzoglou, A., & Taha, S. (2010). Packaging the past. The commodification of heritage. *Heritage Management, 3*(1), 51–72.

Bell, C. (2009). *Ritual: Perspectives and dimensions*. Oxford: Oxford University Press.

Bowman, M., Pezzullo, S., & Phaedra, C. (2010). What's so 'dark' about 'dark tourism'? Death, tours, and performance. *Tourist Studies, 9*(3), 187–202.

Butler, T. (2007). Memoryscape: How audio walks can deepen our sense of place by integrating art, oral history and cultural geography. *Geography Compass, 1*(3), 360–372.

Butler, R., & Suntikul, W. (2013). *Tourism and war*. London/New York: Routledge.

Connelly, M. (2009). The Ypres League and the commemoration of the Ypres Salient, 1914–1940. *War in History, 16*(1), 51–76.

Douglas, M. (1994). *Purity and danger: An analysis of the concepts of pollution and taboo*. London: Routledge.

Foote, K. E., & Vanneste, D. (2011). The Menin Gate Memorial, Ieper. In P. Post, A. L. Molendijk, & J. E. A. Kroesen (Eds.), *Sacred places in modern Western culture* (pp. 253–257). Leuven: Peeters.

Friedrich, D. (2011). The memoryscape in Buenos Aires: Representation, memory, and pedagogy. *Journal of Curriculum Theorizing, 27*(3), 171–189.

Fussell, P. (1977). *The Great War and modern memory*. London: Oxford University Press.

Griffin, G. M., & Tobin, D. (1997). *In the midst of life… The Australian response to death* (2nd ed.). Carlton South: Melbourne University Press.

Han, J.-S. N. (2012). Conserving the heritage of shame: War remembrance and war-related sites in contemporary Japan. *Journal of Contemporary Asia, 42*(3), 493–513.

Hartmann, R. (2014). Dark tourism, thanatourism, and dissonance in heritage tourism management: New directions in contemporary tourism research. *Journal of Heritage Tourism, 9*(2), 166–182.

Heffernan, M. (1995). For ever England: The Western Front and the politics of remembrance in Britain. *Ecumene, 2*(3), 293–323.

Inglis, K. (2005). *Sacred places: War memorials in the Australian landscape*. Melbourne: Miegunyah Press at Melbourne University Press.

Kellehear, A. (2007). The end of death in late modernity: An emerging public health challenge. *Critical Public Health, 17*(1), 71–79.

Larsson, M. (2009). *Shattered ANZACs: Living with the scars of war*. Sydney: UNSW Press.

Lebel, U. (2011). Panopticon of death: Institutional design of bereavement. *Acta Sociologica, 54*(4), 351–366.

Lennon, J. J., & Foley, M. (1999). Interpretation of the unimaginable: The US Holocaust Memorial Museum, Washington, DC and "Dark Tourism". *Journal of Travel Research, 38*, 46–50.

Levy, D., & Sznaider, N. (2002). The Holocaust and the formation of cosmopolitan memory. *European Journal of Social Theory, 5*(1), 87–106.

Lynch, K. (1960). *The image of the city*. Cambridge, MA: MIT Press.

Miles, S. (2014). Battlefield sites as dark tourism attractions: An analysis of experience. *Journal of Heritage Tourism, 9*(2), 134–147.

Morris, M. S. (1997). Gardens 'forever England': Landscape, identity and the First World War British cemeteries on the Western Front. *Ecumene, 4*(4), 410–434.

Mosse, G. (1990). *Fallen soldiers: Reshaping the memory of the world wars*. New York: Oxford University Press.

Moulaert, F., Van Dyck, B., & Parra, C. (2016, January 12). Social science's say on the governance of socio-ecological development: when agents become human. Presentation at Workshop '*Ecology and social sciences*', Leuven Research Centre on Space and Society, Leuven.

Muzaini, H., & Yeoh, B. (2007). Memory-making 'from below': Rescaling remembrance at the Kranji War Memorial and Cemetery, Singapore. *Environment and Planning A, 39*, 1288–1305.

Reimers, E. (1999). Death and identity: Graves and funerals as cultural communication. *Mortality, 4*(2), 147–166.

Saunders, N. (2013). *The poppy: A history of conflict, loss, remembrance, and redemption*. London: Oneworld Publications.

Seaton, A. V. (1999). War and thanatourism: Waterloo 1815–1914. *Annals of Tourism Research, 26*(1), 130–158.

Seaton, A. V. (2000). Another weekend away looking for dead bodies… Battlefield tourism on the Somme and in Flanders. *Tourism Recreation Research, 25*(3), 63–77.

Sharpley, R. (2009). Shedding light on dark tourism: An introduction. In R. Sharpley & P. R. Stone (Eds.), *The darker side of travel. The theory and practice of dark tourism* (pp. 3–22). Bristol/Buffalo/Toronto: Channel View Publications.

Sharpley, R., & Stone, P. R. (Eds.). (2009). *The darker side of travel. The theory and practice of dark tourism*. Bristol: Channel View Publications.

Slade, P. (2003). Gallipoli thanatourism: The meaning of ANZAC. *Annals of Tourism Research, 30*(4), 779–794.

Stone, P. R. (2012). Dark tourism and significant other death: Towards a model of mortality mediation. *Annals of Tourism Research, 39*(3), 1565–1587.

Stone, P. R. (2013). A keynote address, The peace conference 2013: Post-conflict, cultural heritage and regional development. Wageningen University, The Netherlands, 9–12 October, *Deviant leisure, dark tourism and the (Re)configuration of morality in contemporary society*. http://works.bepress.com/philip_stone/43/. Accessed 8 May 2015.

The Encyclopedia Brittanica. (2015). http://www.britannica.com/topic/taboo-sociology. Accessed 30 Jul 2015.

Thi Le, D.-T., & Pearce, D. G. (2011). Segmenting visitors to battlefield sites: International visitors to the former demilitarized zone in Vietnam. *Journal of Travel and Tourism Marketing, 25*, 451–463.

Todman, D. (2005). *The Great War: Myth and memory*. London: Hambledon and London.

Tunbridge, J. E., & Ashworth, G. J. (1996). *Dissonant heritage. The management of the past as a resource in conflict*. Chichester: Wiley.

Van Alstein, M. (2011). *The Great War remembered: Commemoration and peace in Flanders Fields*. Report. Brussels: Flemish Peace Institute.

van der Laarse, R. (2015). Fatal attraction. Nazi landscapes, modernism, and Holocaust memory. In J. Kolen, J. Renes, & R. Hermans (Eds.), *Landscape biographies: Geographical, historical and archaeological perspectives on the production and transmission of landscapes* (pp. 345–375). Amsterdam: Amsterdam University Press.

Vance, J. (1997). *Death so noble: Meaning, memory and the First World War*. Vancouver: UBC Press.

Vanneste, D., & Foote, K. (2013). War, heritage, tourism, and the centenary of the Great War in Flanders and Belgium. In R. Butler & W. Suntikul (Eds.), *Tourism and war* (pp. 254–272). London/New York: Routledge.

Walter, T. (1991). Modern death: Taboo or not taboo? *Sociology, 25*(2), 293–310.

Walter, T. (1999). *On bereavement: The culture of grief.* Buckingham: Open University Press.

Walter, T. (2009). Dark tourism: Mediating between the dead and the living. In R. Sharpley & P. R. Stone (Eds.), *The darker side of travel: The theory and practice of dark tourism* (pp. 39–55). Clevedon: Channel View Publications.

Whitmarsh, A. (2001). "We will remember them" memory and commemoration in war museums. *Journal of Conservation and Museum Studies, 7,* 11–15. https://doi.org/10.5334/jcms.7013.

Winter, J. (1995). *Sites of memory, sites of mourning: The Great War in European cultural history.* Cambridge: Cambridge University Press.

Winter, J. (2006). *Remembering war: The Great War between memory and history in the twentieth century.* New Haven: Yale University Press.

Winter, C. (2015). Ritual, remembrance and war: Social memory at Tyne Cot. *Annals of Tourism Research, 54,* 16–29.

20

Tourism to Memorial Sites of the Holocaust

Rudi Hartmann

Introduction

Few historical periods in human history are so fatally associated with the destruction of human lives as Hitler's 'Third Reich'. Historic places honouring the victims of National Socialistic Germany form a wide and expanding network of heritage sites in Europe. Most of the places where the horrific events occurred during 1933–1945 have been broadly denoted as Holocaust memorial sites in the remembrance of the six million Jews who died, and the many other ethnic, religious, social, and political groups which were subjected to persecution. This chapter, therefore, reconstructs the evolution of this memorial landscape. It is important to understand that not only has the memorial landscape been substantially expanded and changed over the years but also the approaches in the study of these sites and their management practices. Ultimately, this chapter gives an overview of the various traditions of research in this field.

R. Hartmann (✉)
University of Colorado Denver, Denver, CO, USA

A Changing Memorial Landscape for the Victims of National Socialistic Germany

Beginnings: The Majdanek Memorial Site 1945/1946

During Nazi Germany's occupation of Central and Eastern Europe in 1941–1945, 20 main concentration camps, several extermination or death camps, and more than a thousand subsidiary or satellite camps were in existence (see, e.g., Gilbert's *Atlas of the Holocaust* 1982 and United States Holocaust Memorial Museum's *Historical Atlas of the Holocaust* 1996). All the main camps, death camps, as well as hundreds of satellite camps have become memorial sites for the victims of National Socialistic Germany over the past decades.

The first memorial site was established at Majdanek near Lublin, Poland, in 1945–1946. It was here that the Allied Forces (Red Army) reached the first concentration camp in July 1944. As the Soviet forces moved very quickly in the direction of Lublin, the SS had little time to destroy or conceal facilities used in the mass murder of the prisoners – as they did, for instance, in the case of the early death camps of Belzec and Sobibor which were inoperative by 1943. Thus, the physical infrastructure of the Majdanek concentration camp found at liberation was largely unchanged and still had the gas chambers and the crematorium in place, as well as the storage of collected clothes and shoes of victims. Majdanek was the proof of what had been suspected about the nature of Nazi concentration camps in the early 1940s, and (Soviet) journalists visiting the camp shortly after made it public news (reported also in *Time Magazine* 1944, p. 38).

In November 1944, the Majdanek State Museum was founded by the Polish Committee of Liberation. It declared the camp a 'memorial site of the martyrdom of the peoples of Poland and other nations' (Marcuse 2010a, p. 192/193) which became accessible to the public in 1945–1946. It is estimated that 300,000–400,000 people visited the museum and site during the first two years (Jalocha and Boyd 2014). By 1947, the Polish Parliament passed a decree that the remains of the Majdanek camp site (jointly with those at Auschwitz and other concentration camps on Polish territory) were to be preserved. In 1965, Majdanek received the status of a national museum. However, Majdanek as the second largest concentration camp in Poland would remain in the shadow of Auschwitz which became a leading symbol of the Holocaust.

The Afterlife of the Camps: Uses and Abuses of the Camps 1945–1955

The historian Harold Marcuse reconstructed in great detail what happened to the former concentration camps, the prisoners, and the SS guards in the immediate years after liberation (2010a). He lists five uses of the camps. Firstly, the Allied Forces who were confronted with horrific atrocities when reaching and liberating the camps took measures to educate the populations living in the towns nearby such as Bergen-Belsen or Dachau about the conditions they found. Secondly, there was an urgent need to bring tens of thousands of survivors back to health. A third use was directed to imprison the Germans who were held responsible for the crimes committed at the sites. Thus, former camps like Dachau became the place where SS guards and others were kept in captivity while the trials proceeded. Fourthly, efforts were made to preserve components of the camp environment which were considered important for future educational purposes. Finally, Marcuse reviews the lack of attention given to the more remote camps in the concentration camp system, such as Natzweiler and Gross-Rosen, as well as death camps such as Belzec and Sobibor in Eastern Poland. These sites as well as the majority of the satellite camps were simply abandoned and ignored before they were included in the commemoration practices much later, in the 1960s and 1970s, and some as late as in the 1980s and 1990s (Marcuse 2010a).

Camp Liberation Anniversaries as Major Events of the Commemoration Practices

In the absence of accessible and inoperative memorial sites, it was the camp liberation anniversaries in the 1950s and 1960s that had importance for the former prisoners who vividly remembered liberation which marked a turning point of their lives. The dates of liberation for the larger camps – Buchenwald on April 11 (1945), Bergen-Belsen on April 15 (1945), and Dachau on April 29 (1945) – became major annual events which brought thousands of former prisoners together. Moreover, the gatherings at the early camp liberation anniversaries served as a forum for the discussion of how to establish first memorials, markers, and exhibits on the grounds. On the tenth anniversary of the liberation of Dachau concentration camp in 1955, a prisoner organisation was formed which eventually played a crucial role in the establishment of an official memorial at the former concentration camp – the Comité International de Dachau.

While the number of surviving concentration camp prisoners has dwindled over the past decades due to natural attrition – in the case of Dachau reduced to a few hundred in 2005 and a few dozens in 2015, 50 and 60 years after the liberation of more than 30,000 prisoners – anniversary events are still held. Programmes organised for the liberation anniversaries at the memorial sites of the larger camps continue to have relevance in the public debate, with sizable coverage in the media. In 2005, the United Nations General Assembly resolution 60/7 recognised the liberation of Auschwitz on January 27 (1945) as *International Holocaust Remembrance Day*. It commemorates the genocide that resulted in the death of an estimated 6 million Jewish people, 2 million Romani people ('gypsies'), 250,000 mentally and physically disabled people, and 9000 gay men by the Nazi regime and its collaborators.

Anniversaries of the Night of Broken Glass (Kristallnacht, November 9/10, 1938)

The Night of Broken Glass ('Kristallnacht') pogroms on November 9/10, 1938 (more recently, also known as the November Pogroms) is an equally important anniversary in the commemoration of the Holocaust. A series of systematically organised vicious actions staged by the SA paramilitary forces resulted in the burning of more than 1000 synagogues and serious damage to or destruction of about 7000 shops and businesses still owned by Jews in German and Austrian cities. It marked a new stage in an openly orchestrated persecution of Jews, with the first large deportations of Jewish citizens to several concentration camps. In the years after WWII, public commemoration services have been held in many German and Austrian cities, frequently at sites of the former synagogues which were burned down. To date, civic leaders and re-founded local Jewish organisations join hands to remember the pogroms widely considered the beginning of the end of the Jewish communities in Central Europe in the late 1930s/early 1940s and of the Holocaust.

While various traditions in the commemoration practices evolved in different cities over time (see Jacobs 2008, 2010), one example should be discussed in more detail: the walk of memory ('Erinnerungsgang') in Oldenburg, a mid-size college town in northwestern Germany. It is the re-enactment of the walk through the town that Jewish citizens of Oldenburg were forced to make on November 10, 1938. The first walk of memory was in 1981. During the 1988 walk of memory, 50 years after the original event, about 1500 citizens participated. The silent, solemn walk through parts of Oldenburg each November 10th is organised by a local committee and working group ('Arbeitskreis Erinnerungsgang'). The general motive for preparing and re-enacting the walk is 'Remembering is the basis for reconciliation'. Each year a different school from Oldenburg takes on a major responsibility for the commemorative events. Thus, it has become a living body of a memory culture setting new initiatives each year.

The Slow, Complicated, and Difficult Path to Memorial Sites at Former Concentration Camps

Establishing memorials at former concentration camps and at subsidiary camps was not an easy undertaking. It took many years if not decades in some cases to reach the goal of setting up appropriate markers, memorial plaques, first exhibits, and finally official memorial sites equipped with museums and salaried staffs. A first permanent memorial at a concentration camp in Germany was established in Bergen-Belsen. A collective Jewish monument was established in September 1945. On the first anniversary of the camp liberation on April 15, 1946, a stone monument with Hebrew and English inscriptions was inaugurated by the Central Jewish Committee of the British Zone. In 1947, efforts were started to create a central memorial in the form of an obelisk and memorial wall naming 14 nations of the victims in Belsen. The memorial was formally dedicated in a commemorative ceremony in 1952 attended by West German president Theodor Heuss and the President of the Jewish World Congress Nahum Goldman. The Bergen-Belsen camp was liberated by British and Canadian troops who found horrific conditions at the site. It is estimated that more than 70,000 people died at the POW and the Concentration Camp before and during the immediate weeks following liberation. A typhus epidemic raged during the final phase of the camp, and thousands of corpses of diseased prisoners were buried in nearby mass graves. Shortly after liberation, the camp grounds had to be completely cleared for health reasons. The uncontestable, widely reported magnitude of the fatalities in Belsen, the presence of a large nearby community of displaced persons, many of them survivors of the camps, as well as the complete removal of the structures on the grounds facilitated the allocation of the memorial. This may have contributed to a relatively fast decision for a memorial and the later approval by the State of Lower Saxony in charge of the site by 1952. The memory of young author Anne Frank who died with her sister, Margot, in Belsen in March 1945 gave further momentum to the memorial site in the mid/late 1950s. The Bergen-Belsen memorial site saw more changes in the 1960s and the following years, from the addition of a small 'document house' in 1966 to the development of a new memorial site museum which opened in 2007 (Marcuse 2010a, Stiftung niedersaechsische Gedenkstaetten/Gedenkstaette Bergen-Belsen 2012).

In the case of Dachau, where at least 40,000 people died during the 12 years the camp existed, the push for a memorial site played out at a much slower pace and in more complicated ways. Early initiatives for a memorial turned out to be failures. Several proposals were turned down for a variety of reasons or were soon forgotten by the public (Marcuse 2010a). Local initiatives and plans for the closure and the demolition of the crematorium (with a first exhibit about the camp) in the early 1950s were prevented by the Paris Treaty which West Germany had signed with France in 1954. Several clauses in the treaty protected the burial sites of the concentration camp prisoners and the access to the camp. After 1955, it was most of all the re-founded *Comité International de Dachau* prisoner organisation which tenaciously stood up for the preservation of the camp site. In 1960, a first individual memorial was dedicated on the grounds by the Catholic Church. Memorials of the Jewish Community and of the Protestant Church followed in 1967. The International Memorial *Never Again* was dedicated in 1968. Eventually, a Russian Orthodox Memorial was established near the Crematorium in 1994. The official Dachau Concentration Camp Memorial with a museum and a small salaried staff funded by the State of Bavaria was opened to the public in 1965. The site was administratively integrated into the Bavarian Castle and Gardens Administration. Despite the formal establishment of the Dachau memorial site, considerable resistance among the Dachau residents persisted (Hartmann 1989; Marcuse 1990, 2001, 2005, 2010a). People living in Dachau and the County of Dachau had a hard time coming to grips with the fact that the first concentration camp of Nazi Germany was established next door to their market town. The concentration camp developed into a large military-industrial complex in 1933–1945. The predominantly Catholic community was eventually taken over by officials of the NSDAP ('Gleichschaltung') and a broadening support for the camp in the general populace developed, in particular, within the business community (Steinbacher 1993). In the years after 1965, the new memorial site on the northeastern edge of town was considered an annoying 'black spot' in the distinguished twelve hundred years past of the town. While the memorial site saw a growing number of visitors reaching close to one million per year in the mid/late 1980s, tensions between the City of Dachau and the Dachau Memorial Site continued throughout the 1980s and 1990s. These animosities re-emerged, for instance, over the City's obstruction and/or delay of approval for a new youth meeting centre ('Jugendbegegnungsstätte') in support of joint educational events with the memorial site (Stadler 1995). It was a new generation of Dachau citizens and elected politicians that sought a better and more constructive relationship in the 2000s/2010s – after the site and the entrance was restructured, many of the museum exhibits were redesigned and a new visitor centre was added (in 2003/2005/2009). In addition, more programmes in collaboration with local Dachau historians were developed (Schossig 2010).

Two other concentration camps in Germany with satellite camp systems, in Flossenbuerg in far eastern Bavaria and in Neuengamme near Hamburg, saw a complicated history in the commemoration of the sites where about 100,000 prisoners were held, with an estimated one third in Flossenbuerg and half of prisoners in Neuengamme put to death. While several memorials, monuments, and markers were placed at both sites in the late 1940s/1950s to the 1980s, appropriate memorial sites with sizable museums were developed and opened to the public only recently during the mid-2000s. For extended periods, both sites were misused Flossenbuerg for housing ethnic German refugees and low-income town residents on the camp site with new amenities and structures built on the grounds and Neuengamme for prison populations kept in an older and a new prison building. In 1989, the Hamburg Senate decided to close and relocate the prisons from the site which finally occurred in 2003/2006. Flossenbuerg, one of the largely "forgotten concentration camps" (Pelanda 1995), went through a significant transition as well, with the removal of the post-WWII structures on the camp grounds so that an expanded exhibition area on the memorial site could be opened in 2007 (Marcuse 2010a). The cases of the memorial sites at Buchenwald near Weimar, at Sachsenhausen near Berlin, and at Ravensbrueck, a camp for female prisoners North of Berlin, will be discussed in more detail later in this chapter as their development was closely tied to the agenda of the German Democratic Republic (DDR), the Communist East German state.

Memorials for the eight concentration camps in Poland, including the extermination camps of Auschwitz-Birkenau, Treblinka, Belzec, Majdanek, Sobibor, and Chelmno, underwent significant changes as well. In 1947, the remains of the camps were protected by a law passed in the Polish Parliament. The new memorials, first in Majdanek then in Auschwitz as well as at other camps, were largely set up for the purpose of designing and dedicating sites commemorating the 'martyrdom of the Polish nation (and other nations)'. The main concentration camp (Auschwitz I) saw the murder of thousands of Polish resistance fighters as well as many Polish Catholic priests and nuns including Father Maximilian Kolbe and Edith Stein now both saints within the Catholic Church. Auschwitz became the deadliest site where the 'Final Solution (of the Jewish question)' was planned and carried out by Nazi Germany during 1942–1945. It is estimated that in the three Auschwitz camps, including the death camp Auschwitz-Birkenau, at least one million Jewish lives perished. At the memorial site, an enduring and bitter conflict developed between Polish (Communist) officials as well as members of the

Polish Catholic Church and the international Jewish community. In the 1960s and 1970s, the Auschwitz memorial site was declared an 'International Monument to the Victims of Fascism' without any mention of Jewish victims in the museum exhibits. In the 1980s and 1990s, a 'War of the Crosses' raged when first a large cross was erected, then a Carmelite Convent established on the grounds which made its presence felt with close to 200 smaller wooden crosses. Pope John Paul II, a native of Krakow, Poland, eventually ordered the relocation of the nuns. Geographer Andrew Charlesworth who reconstructed and discussed the conflict between different groups over the memorialisation processes at Auschwitz argued that it was an intended and at times de facto 'De-Judaization' of the sacred site (for many) that was at the core of the long-lasting controversy (1994).

With the fall of the 'Iron Curtain' in 1989/1990, the situation at Auschwitz and other memorial sites in Poland fundamentally changed. In the following years, Auschwitz became more easily accessible to the international visitor. Subsequently, its redesigned memorial site and museum addressed the role of the Auschwitz camps in the extermination of Jews and the Holocaust. The number of tourists to Poland, in particular to Krakow with an intact old town and the nearby Auschwitz memorial site as a well-established destination, rapidly increased in the 1990s and 2000s. By the 2010s more than 1.3 million people annually visited the Auschwitz-Birkenau State Memorial and Museum. Consequently, Auschwitz had eclipsed Dachau in terms of visitation numbers while it has become 'the most widely recognized symbol of Nazi atrocities' (Marcuse 2001, p. 118).

Belzec and Sobibor, two extermination camps where an estimated 600,000 and 250,000 people respectively, almost all of them Jews, were murdered during 'Operation Reinhard' in Eastern Poland, received little recognition until the mid-1960s. Both death camps were discontinued by the SS in 1943. The sites with its structures and human remains were covered and concealed as farms. Few prisoners from neither camp survived, as all the 'Sonderkommando' prisoners were gassed as well. The last 300 Belzec inmates forced to clean up the camp were deported to Sobibor where their final fate awaited them. Seven Belzec prisoners survived WWII; and only one witness report was recorded (Reder 1946). In the late 1990s, archaeological studies were conducted at the site when, finally, an appropriate memorial site was opened in 2004. Sobibor, which saw an uprising of the prisoners in October 1943 (dramatised in the 1987 British TV film *Escape from Sobibor*), gradually gained stature as a destination as more international visitors arrived there in the 1990s/2000s, including from the Netherlands. The large majority of Dutch Jews were deported either to Auschwitz-Birkenau or to the Sobibor death camp (Schelvis 2004). In 2003, the Dutch Government made substantial contributions to the upgrades of the memorial site, with new monuments, markers, and exhibits within the grounds as well as continued research at the site.

By the 1980s/1990s, hundreds of memorial sites commemorating Nazi atrocity victims were established Europe-wide. In the German-occupied areas of Europe (1939–1945), populations had endured persecution, crime, and mass murder. Besides the above-mentioned places in Poland, many memorial sites were set up in Eastern and South Eastern Europe, France, Italy, and other countries within continental Europe. The Netherlands were occupied by Nazi Germany for five long years. Several memorial sites were developed starting in the 1970s. They included Kamp Vught (the concentration camp near 's-Hertogenbosch) and Kamp Westerbork, the former transit camp in the far Eastern Province of Drenthe which is considered the national memorial site for the Netherlands (jointly with the recently established Dutch Holocaust Memorial at the Schouwburg, the deportation center in Amsterdam). There is one Dutch site which has gained wide international recognition: the Anne Frank House. The house on 263 Prinsengracht in Amsterdam, with a Secret Annex, was the place where young Anne Frank wrote her diary 1942–1944 and which is now published in more than 60 languages and read by millions. The house was preserved and opened as a small museum in 1960. By 2007, the historic site and educational centre with the mission to disseminate Anne's oeuvre and humanistic values has received more than one million visitors annually (Hartmann 2013, 2016). Contemporary historians have compared Anne's compelling story and her short life in troubled times with an 'accessible window into the Holocaust' (Young 1999).

Former Nazi Concentration Camps Become Known as Memorial Sites of the Holocaust

The term Holocaust is a fairly new concept denoting the genocide of European Jewry (including other ethnic, religious, social, and political groups persecuted and murdered by Nazi Germany). The term became more widely used in the 1960s due to the publicity of the Eichmann Trials in 1961–1962. The highly successful NBC mini-series 'Holocaust' shown in the United States, in Germany, and other countries/TV markets in 1978/1979 was instrumental in popularising the term Holocaust and some of the historic sites such as the Theresienstadt-Terezin Ghetto and Concentration Camp and the Sobibor death camp. Holocaust movies have become a new genre, with a sizable number of film and TV productions completed and introduced to the market every year. Several Holocaust movies such as 'The Diary of Anne Frank' (1959), 'Schindler's List' (1993), and 'Son of Saul' (2015) have won Academy

Awards ('the Oscars'). These movies also remind audiences of the historic sites of the Anne Frank House in Amsterdam; of Kazimierz, the Jewish neighbourhood in Krakow; and of Auschwitz-Birkenau respectively.

By the 1980s, the term Holocaust was regularly applied to many sites where Nazi atrocities had occurred. Former concentration camps became internationally (as well as nationally in Germany) known as Holocaust memorial sites. Holocaust education formed a part of public education in many school systems worldwide (see Ehmann et al. 1995; Genger 1995 for Germany). At the same time, a parallel term emerged – 'Shoah' – a Jewish word denoting a catastrophic experience. The term found predominant use in Israel as well as in the scholarly works of European historians. While 'Holocaust' (and to a lesser degree, 'Shoah') has become the widely used term within international communication, the most common German term(s) defining the new type of memorials for the victims continued to be closely tied to the perpetrators, the NSDAP/Nazi Party: 'Gedenkstaetten fuer die Opfer des Nationalsozialismus' (memorials for the victims of National Socialism), also abbreviated as 'NS-Opfer' (NS victims), or, more specifically, the 'Opfer der Nationalsozialistischen Gewaltherrschaft' (victims of the national socialist rule of terror).

Two leading Holocaust memorial museums and of the Shoah were established outside Europe: Yad Vashem in Israel in 1953 (Krakover 2005) and the United States Holocaust Memorial Museum in Washington D.C. in 1993 (Linenthal 1995; Piper 2006). They represent a new type of carefully created places of commemoration, outside the in situ memorial sites (as discussed earlier). Besides the Holocaust museum in Washington, D.C., other Holocaust memorials and museums were formed in Los Angeles (in 1961), New York, and a few other places in the United States. In Denver, for example, a memorial to the 200,000 victims of the Babi Yar massacre in Kiev/Ukraine was established in 1982. In a public park, a walkway to a memorial and a bridge over a ravine was designed. However, a controversy evolved over the inscription originally leaving out victims of the 1941 massacre (Young 1993, pp. 294–296).

The Design of Holocaust Memorials as a New Genre

How to adorn, recognise, or characterise the places of commemoration for the victims of the Holocaust? It was a new genre in public art which evolved in the post-WWII years and decades – as convincingly shown and discussed in great detail by historians Young (1993) and Marcuse (2010b). While Young focused on about 15 sites in his seminal work 'The Texture of Memory', Marcuse preferred a close examination of exemplary memorials in a more chronological order. Young (1993, p. 13) argued that 'Holocaust memorials are neither benign nor irrelevant, but suggest themselves as the basis for political and communal action'. In his treatise Marcuse elaborates on the complexity of communal actions and political decision-making that eventually resulted in a series of new memorials, from the mid-to-late 1940s through to the late 1960s.

Majdanek, with a first memorial site at a concentration camp (as discussed earlier), was also the place where a remarkable monument was created in 1943, more than a year before liberation. The erection of a tall statue with three eagles taking flight, a proposal for 'beautification' of the camp made by Albin Boniecki and fellow prisoners, was granted by the SS camp authorities. They recognised the eagles as a Nazi symbol, whereas in the mind of the creator, the monument represented the ultimate freedom of three imprisoned groups: the men, the women, and the children at the camp (Marcuse 2010a, b, p. 56). It was a precursor of the predominantly symbolic nature of the memorials that took shape at many memorial sites. Most often, tall monuments such as obelisks were chosen for the memorials at the sites during the late 1940s and 1950s. There was an avoidance in the depiction of graphic themes for the monuments. For instance, an early memorial monument reflecting the harsh reality of the prisoner life in the camp ('Inferno') had to be redesigned by artist Fritz Koelle in Dachau. The result was a gentler, inoffensive statue of *The Unknown Concentration Camp Inmate* placed near the crematorium in 1950 (Marcuse 2010b, 72/73).

At some memorials sites, distinct and artistically impressive uses of Jewish symbols are evident. The Treblinka memorial site consists of 17,000 broken tablets 'resembling a great graggy graveyard'. In the centre of 'a landscape of fragments', an obelisk with a crack running through the monument is placed (Young 1993, 187–192). The memorial at the Babi Yar site in Kiev/Ukraine has as its prominent feature a menorah. Other examples of Jewish symbols at Holocaust memorial sites are found at Kristallnacht memorials in Germany cities. They show a desecrated Torah at the Oberstrasse synagogue in Hamburg and at the Cologne Jewish Museum:

> Without reference to the deportations and the genocide that followed the pogroms, the museum's history is framed through the imagery of a violated and tattered Torah. (Jacobs 2010, 85–2103)

Two contrasting options for the design of memorial sites were the creation of a new memorial landscape (e.g., Bergen-Belsen where the camp grounds were completely cleared) or leaving the grounds – as found at liberation – largely intact. Majdanek and Auschwitz are both examples of the latter. In the case of Auschwitz-Birkenau and the preserved rail entrance to the camp, the tracks leading to the 'gate of no return' leaves an iconic landscape for the visitors. It has become one of the most widely recognised visual marker of the Holocaust. Eventually, a memorial monument was developed within the grounds of the Birkenau site. A design competition launched in 1957/1958 led to the selection of three teams, and their winning models for the monument were built in 1967. The extensive remnants of the Auschwitz camps have remained, however, its true memorial (Young 1993, pp. 128–144; Marcuse 2010b, pp. 81–84).

In the case of the International Dachau Memorial (*Never Again* in six languages), the procedure for selecting the memorial model was decided in a design competition as well. The winning design by Nandor Glid reflected a more abstract and expressive style which became more common in the mid- and late 1950s. The chosen memorial model displayed '… a tangled mass of highly abstract emaciated bodies with angular barbed hands, supported by two fence posts with fragments of stylized barbed wire to suggest human beings entangled in the fencing that surrounded the concentration camps' (Marcuse 2010b, p. 85). The memorial was inaugurated in 1968 and continues to be a centrepiece of the Dachau memorial landscape.

A different style that became important for the design of the memorials was embedded in socialist heroic symbols. *The Monument to the Heroes of the Warsaw Ghetto* created by Nathan Rapoport was the first prominent example for this heroic, realistic design direction. Other monuments and memorials in the heroic memorialisation tradition followed in Eastern Europe including in East Germany. At the Sachsenhausen concentration camp memorial site, a central theme was the depiction of the help the inmates received from the Soviet soldiers who liberated the camp. Similarly, at the Ravensbrueck site (see, for instance, Jacobeit 1995), a concentration camp for female prisoners and their children, heroic mother and fellow inmate figures were chosen for the main monuments symbolising the support women (comrades) showed for each other in face of terror and death.

The Buchenwald Memorial Site in Former East Germany, Before and After Re-unification of Germany: Winds of Change and Lasting Implications for a New Management Style of the Memorial Sites

The memorial for the Buchenwald concentration camp, where more than 50,000 people died during 1937–1945, became a paramount project of Communist East Germany (DDR) after the establishment of the State.

Buchenwald was augmented to be a national symbol of the socialist resistance against Fascism. The 1958 Buchenwald National Site of Commemoration and Warning ('Nationale Mahn- und Gedenkstaette'), with remarkable design features, has been one of the largest and most carefully crafted memorials. The site chosen for the monumental memorial ensemble was away from the original camp hidden in the beech forests ('Buchenwald'), facing toward the City of Weimar. Thus, the new memorial site was visible from the valley floor and well suited for the representation of the Communist Party's programmes and activities at the site.

The expansive new memorial consisted of a wide sloping walkway, along 7 bas-reliefs which showed the plight and ultimately successful struggle of the prisoners against Fascism, to a large gathering place lined by an avenue of 18 featured nations with a series of massive pylons. High up from the gathering place which held up to 20,000 people was a 55-metre-tall bell tower. The main memorial monument just underneath the tower displayed a group of 11 oversized human figures heroically standing for the socialist resistance that resulted in the 'self-liberation' of the camp (according to the Communist Party's interpretation of the events during the final days at the Buchenwald camp). Prime Minister Otto Grotewohl worked closely with designer Fritz Cremer on this central sculpture project in the 1950s (Marcuse 2010a).

The new memorial was an impressive backdrop for political action. It was at the Buchenwald memorial site where soldiers and young party members took their oath, where school classes from all over the DDR came to learn about the victory of the German Communist movement and the continued successes of the East German State. The design of the memorial sites of Buchenwald, Sachsenhausen, and Ravensbrueck, as well as of Dachau, Bergen-Belsen, Flossenbuerg, and Neuengamme, reflected the Cold War situation in the 1950s and 1960s. At all the sites, most of the structures including the barracks were razed and immediately or later completely removed, for different reasons. While it was essential for the East German state to minimise the original camp environments in order to create a new memorial landscape with a distinct political mission (Young 1993; Overesch 1995; Knigge et al. 1998; Kahl 1999, pp. 892–903; Marcuse 2010a), in the West fighting a perceived Communist threat and preventing a further military expansion of the East Block became important goals for the political agenda. Dealing with the National Socialist past was no longer a high priority, while more and more former members of the Nazi Party were re-integrated in the Federal West German government. Thus, getting rid of the physical evidence of the National Socialistic past including artefacts at the sites of atrocities was allowed or even encouraged in many cases. The local populace near the camps and the new bureaucracy of the West German state generally favoured a minimisation of attention given to the 'black spots' of yesteryear. As the Cold War thawed, the East German economy stagnated and stalled and more interaction and exchanges between the citizens of the divided country were allowed during the mid- and late 1980s; the political climate changed again, and with it, the public memory of the National Socialistic era either channeled into a stale ideological version in the East or repressed and/or forgotten for many years in the West.

How did the political changes after 1989/1990, with the fall of the Berlin Wall and the re-unification of Germany, affect the Buchenwald site and its management? Free elections in the former East German states brought significant changes to the administrative body of the memorial sites. A democratisation in the decision-making processes, most of all with the inclusion of representatives from a wider societal spectrum and the various inmate and victims groups so far neglected, resulted in new guidelines and policies. The outcome was the decision for a fundamental reorientation of the memorial site to the commemoration of the victims (rather than a celebration of the successful fight against Fascism) and from the monumental memorial site back to the former concentration camp. Several memorials were added to the grounds of the former camp, among them the Jewish Memorial (1993) and a Memorial for the Sinti and Roma (1997). In 2002, a memorial for the victims at the Little Camp ('Kleine Lager') where several thousand Jewish lives perished during 1944–1945 under horrific conditions described by Buchenwald survivor Elie Wiesel and Greiser (1998) was established with support of the international Jewish community. The main museum exhibits were redesigned and a new site was added that focused on the history of the memorial site itself ('Historische Dauerausstellung: Die Geschichte der Gedenkstaette Buchenwald'). Most controversial was the establishment of a memorial and museum at the Special Camp Nr. 2 which was in existence during the Soviet occupation of the camp 1945–1950. Seven thousand persons died there, mostly members of the SS and the NSDAP who had functions at the concentration camp as well as socialists who fell out of favour in the early years of Communism in East Germany. While 'winds of change' blew across the Buchenwald memorial site in the 1990s resulting in a different political culture, all the memorials, monuments, and markers were kept in place, including a 1953 plaque for German Communist Party leader Ernst Thaelmann at the crematorium where he was shot in 1944 (Kahl 1999; Haertl and Moench 2001; Wenzel-Orf and Kirsten 2003; Azaryahu 2003; Knigge 2006).

Permanent changes in the management of the sites came with a new administrative organisation for the larger memorial sites in both the new states (in former East Germany) and in the West German states during the 1990s and

2000s. New foundations for the administrative support of the memorial sites were formed on a state level (in charge of cultural affairs). These state-supported agencies gave the memorials financial and personal stability at last. The enormous discrepancies in the staffing of the memorial sites in the East and the West from the 1980s, for example, Buchenwald with a hundred-plus staff members servicing 400,000 visitors and Dachau with less than 20 employees in charge of the administration, museum, archives, and accessibility/security of the grounds for close to one million visitors, were finally reduced. A general consensus emerged in re-unified Germany that supporting the memorial sites was a crucial public responsibility to be sufficiently and consistently taken on. New generations of school teachers and educators in the public arena joined in helping to transform the political consciousness of the country, from a mere reactive 'coming to terms with the past' approach ('Vergangenheitsbewaeltigung') to actively rediscovering the traces and remnants of the past ('Spurensuche'). Providing education at the memorial sites became more widely appreciated (see Ehmann et al. 1995; Lutz 1995; Bayerische Landeszentrale fuer Politische Bildungsarbeit 2000) and was now understood as a necessary service to the public, as 'work' ('Gedenkstaettenarbeit'). A large network of memorial sites across re-unified Germany and some of the neighbouring countries developed, and its newsletter on the internet www.gedenkstaettenforum.de formed an effective forum for the exchange of ideas and initiatives.

Memorials to Uprisings in the Ghettos and Camps: Memorial Sites to Resistance Against the National Socialistic Regime

One of the frequently asked questions younger generations have about the horrific events of the Holocaust, is whether, and if so, where and when opposition, resistance, and open revolts to the powers of Nazi Germany formed as the 'Final Solution (of the Jewish question)' took its course first in Germany and then in the German-occupied countries. Oral history and written memories of survivors support the general observation that millions of European Jews more or less obediently followed the orders to assemble for the deportations to the camps, and this without substantial resistance or a shared collective response to their fate. It also was evident that tens of millions of German citizens hardly objected to the open persecution and ultimate murder of their fellow citizens and, as Daniel Goldhagen put it, were 'Hitler's willing executioners' (1996). Were there truly acts of defiance and forms of uprising?

Memorial sites for the victims of resistance to Nazi Germany had and continue to have a considerable role in the public memory, within and beyond the international Jewish community, in and outside Germany, and in many of the German-occupied countries. The most prominent memorial in this respect is in Warsaw, now widely recognised a 'memorial icon' (Young 1989, 1993, Chap. 6). The memorial which was unveiled in 1948 at the fifth anniversary of the historic event commemorates the 13,000 resistance fighters who died during the four-week period of the Warsaw Ghetto uprising April 19–May 16, 1943. Another uprising at a Jewish Ghetto in 1943 is remembered at Bialystok. On August 16, 1948, five years after a one-week long uprising, a memorial was inaugurated in commemoration of the 71 people who died in resistance to the planned deportations from the ghetto (Grossman 1991, 102–118).

Several open revolts against the SS at the death camps, in the form of armed uprisings and prisoner escapes, have been documented for Treblinka, Sobibor, and Auschwitz-Birkenau. On August 2, 1943, 700 people launched an insurgency in Treblinka. Approximately 200 people were able to escape from the camp, and 70 are known to have survived WWII. The Sobibor uprising occurred on October 14, 1943, and precipitated the planned closure of the camp. About 300 inmates fled to nearby forests, while 58 are known to have survived. Tragically, the Auschwitz-Birkenau revolt was the least carefully planned attempt to wrestle control from the SS guards; all the escapees and 250 of the Sonderkommando inmates in the camp were eventually caught and murdered. A recent movie (Son of Saul, 2015) re-enacted the major phases of the October 7, 1943 uprising. However, about 100 Sonderkommando prisoners at one of the other Auschwitz crematoria – not directly involved in the uprising – survived with more than 5,000 prisoners who lived to see the liberation of the camp on January 27, 1945, and bore witness to the event. In all three cases, commemorative notes, plaques, and monuments as well as an oral history of the events now exist. However, at times the memory of the uprisings appear to have been lost or forgotten (see, for instance, in the case of Sobibor Blatt 2000; Roberts 2015).

In his reconstruction of the Nazi concentration camp system and the final deadliest stage, Wachsmann included a section on defiance, resistance, and uprisings entitled the 'Resistance by the Doomed' (2015, pp. 536–541). He argued that in the case of Auschwitz, prisoner attitudes were split about possible responses to the SS in the autumn of 1944. While some of the inmates working in the Sonderkommando units realised that their death was imminent because of the acquired knowledge about the mass murders in Birkenau, other prisoners simply hoped to hold on to survival until liberation – as the

Allied forces advanced. However, the last few months of Auschwitz would be also the most lethal for the inmates: 'the closer these men, women, and children came to freedom, the more likely they were to die in the concentration camps' (Wachsmann 2015, p. 541). In various recollections of Auschwitz survivors, memories of defiance in the camp were handed to the outside world. Some of the former prisoners told, for example, of the admiration they had for the courage of one camp couple, Mala Zimetbaum and Edek Galinski, doomed to die. During their public execution, they openly challenged the powers in place – Mala hitting an SS man, Edek shouting a rallying cry – and staged their final moments (Wachsmann 2015, pp. 536–537).

There were also forms of resistance at the concentration camps in Germany, most notably during the final days of Dachau and Buchenwald. However, the outcome as well as the memorialisation of the revolts differed significantly. While the Buchenwald inmates headed by the well-organised political prisoners were able to take over the camp in the final hours before the arrival of US troops, the Dachau revolt failed. The rather spontaneously initiated action by a small group of Dachau citizens and camp prisoners was 'too little, too late'. The death of six people is remembered in Dachau where a square in the Old Town was renamed Place of Resistance ('Widerstandsplatz') as were six street names for the fighters and victims (see for more information about the 'Dachauer Aufstand' Richardi et al. 1998, pp. 149–157, 210–212). In the case of Buchenwald, a 'self-liberation' myth was born and effectively disseminated by the East German state, the SED party, and the prisoner organisation throughout the 1950s to the 1980s. After the changes in the management of the memorial site in the 1990s, a different (compromise) version was told: 'the camp was freed from the inside and from the outside'. The historic facts supported the greater role the approaching US troops had in freeing all the prisoners – as the leading SS officials left the site and willingly turned over the control of the camp to the Communist elders.

The Yad Vashem memorial and museum in Jerusalem has honoured 'righteous' gentiles who in defiance of orders saved the lives of Jews. Prominent examples are Raoul Wallenberg, a Swedish diplomat and businessman who saved more than 10,000 Jews in Nazi-occupied Hungary, and Oskar Schindler, a German industrialist who courageously protected his Jewish employees in Krakow. In the latter case, it was the publication of *Schindler's Ark*, a Pulitzer Prize award-winning novel by Thomas Keneally, which subsequently served as the inspiration for Steven Spielberg's popular movie 'Schindler's List' that made Schindler's actions more widely known. In Berlin, a similar institution, The Memorial Site for Silent Heroes, honors Germans who saved or tried to save Jewish fellow citizens.

There was opposition to the Nazi Movement in Germany in particular during the early years after the Nazi seizure of power (1933/1934) and during the years of WWII (1939–1945). A multitude of forms of resistance initiated and carried out by different groups and individuals in National Socialistic Germany have been documented (see Benz and Pehle 1996). However, there was no firmly connected network of the resistant groups and the effect the various acts of defiance, protests, and challenges to the system never reached the magnitude – with few exceptions – that could have threatened the autocratic rule of Hitler and the NSDAP.

Again, differences in the commemoration of persecuted and murdered individuals and groups in the German resistance in West Germany and in East Germany were evident. Early on, the East German State paid tribute to people who were in opposition to the Nazi Regime, with focus on the resistance among Communists, Socialists, and the labour unions (Young 1993; Puvogel 1999; Endlich 1999). In particular, many memorials for anti-fascist fighters were established in and near Berlin (in the East sector of the capital city and the Soviet-controlled part of Germany). A memorial near the Berlin Dom along Karl-Liebknecht Strasse in Berlin-Mitte honoured young Socialists with Jewish backgrounds led by Herbert Baum, Marianne Cohn, Martin Kochmann, and Sala Rosenbaum ('Widerstandsgruppe um Herbert Baum'). The members of this 1938 forbidden left-wing youth group, many of them women, produced critical leaflets and were in contact with individuals in forced labour camps before they were arrested in 1942. More than 20 of the members were eventually executed (Endlich 1999, pp. 111/112).

The main official memorial to the German resistance for West Germans is in West Berlin, in the courtyard of the Bendlerblock, location of the former German Reichswehr Headquarters. It is here where Claus Schenk Graf von Stauffenberg and several other members of the military in opposition to National Socialistic Germany were shot after the unsuccessful Hitler assassination attempt on July 20, 1944. The anniversary of the attempted assassination was declared a Day of Remembrance in West Germany/Federal Republic of Germany. While the professional and personal integrity of Stauffenberg and other high military leaders involved in the coup (that could have threatened and overturned the ruling regime) has unquestionable merit and commanded respect, it did not create a sense of compassion and/or enthusiasm among younger Germans. Arguably perhaps, it was the elitist, aristocratic/high echelon background of the 'men of the 20th July 1944' that contributed to the emotional distance. 'Valkyrie' (2008), an international movie highlighting the Hitler assassination attempt (with Tom Cruise in the leading role of Claus von Stauffenberg), was a moderate success in the United States with reviewers questioning the validity of the newly introduced theme of an existing German resistance.

Two resistance events and groups have gained broad acceptance in Germany in the 1990s/2000s/2010s, with highly recognised and well-visited memorials in Berlin and in Munich: firstly, the memorial for women of Rosenstrasse who demonstrated for the release of their Jewish husbands ('die Frauen der Rosenstrasse') and, secondly, a memorial which spreads out on the grounds of the walkway to the entrance area at Munich University – depicting headlines of distributed leaflets with a call to disobedience and individual faces of members of the White Rose ('Weisse Rose') student resistance group. The Rosenstrasse memorial near Alexanderplatz has become a major stop for historic tours as well as for casual bicycle explorations in Berlin. The square where the memorial ensemble was placed in 1995 and the adjacent new Plaza Hotel offer information about this part of the old Jewish community in Berlin in general and the protest of the women in 1943 in particular. The arrest of the about 2000 Jewish men who were married to 'Aryan' women triggered a persistent unwavering push for the release of their husbands which eventually happened after several days. The events may have been embellished in the course of the first few years after WWII (with the desire and need of proof for wider protest actions against National Socialistic Germany), but nevertheless speak for themselves (Jochheim 2002; Gruner 2002). Like the 'White Rose' resistance in Munich, it was a selfless, humane form of rebellion and a courageous joint action younger generations of Germans can admire and identify with. While few of the Rosenstrasse women are known and mentioned by name during the tour stops, the six core members of the White Rose resistance group have become household names. More than a hundred high schools in Germany have been named in their honour; siblings Sophie Scholl and Hans Scholl are resistance icons in present-day German society. Moreover, Munich University has displayed a permanent exhibit since 1987, and there are close to 20 monuments and markers now in Munich, at the places where members lived, where they were arrested, held in prison, and executed, and where they are buried. Additionally, there is a memorial plaque at the Palace of Justice where the trials were held in 1943 and where a young Sophie Scholl in a most memorable way stood her ground and confronted her Nazi judge over ethics and human principles (Pfoertner 2001; Bayerische Bundeszentrale fuer politische Bildungsarbeit 2013; Kronawitter 2014, pp. 80–91).

New Perspectives, New Exhibits and Forms of Commemoration, New Sites

Over the past 20 years a multitude of new sites, new exhibits, and new commemoration practices have emerged in Germany. In the following, cases from Weimar-Buchenwald, Frankfurt, Cologne, and Berlin will be highlighted and discussed. They serve as examples and evidence that public memory of the National Socialistic era is still evolving and continues to change.

Since the early to mid-1990s, the Weimar-Buchenwald memorial site under the leadership of Volkhard Knigge has provided many stimuli in reshaping the memorial work in and outside Buchenwald. First in summer workshops, then in programmes of the new Youth Meeting Center ('Jugendbegegnungsstaette'), young people from Germany and abroad took up the laborious job of unveiling/tracing important artefacts from the 1937–1945 period, which had been 'overgrown' or deliberately removed and concealed by the 1950s/1960s authorities. Such search for lost traces ('Spurensuche') project work led to the finding and marking of the prison cell where Martin Bonhoeffer, an outspoken pastor of the 'confessing church' ('bekennende Kirche'), was held, and the uncovering of the original railway tracks and other pathways which had meaning in the arrival or the deportations of the camp prisoners (Hantsch 1994; Rook and Hofmann 1995). A unique programme was developed with the 'Zeitschneise'/timeline project inviting historically minded people to revisit sites connected to the revered German classics on the Ettersberg hill near Weimar, with a designated walk to the Buchenwald Camp (Haertl 1999). More recently, Knigge has actively participated in the discussion over a new approach and re-conceptualisation of the work at memorial sites ('Fortschreibung der Gedenkstaettenarbeit'), in particular the debate over how to address and integrate the dark heritage of the socialist state in former East Germany 1950–1989 (see Knigge 2006; Von Oehmke in Der Spiegel 21/2008).

After a long pause in the appreciation of the works of Frankfurt-born Annelies Marie 'Anne' Frank (1929), the community has taken major steps in re-integrating or taking back the worldwide known heroine and her Jewish family, with roots going back to the 1600s in the Frankfurt Jewish Ghetto. The situation changed with a 'Spurensuche' project in the Dornbusch city district, the Frankfurt neighbourhood where the Frank Family lived during 1927–1933. Two hundred people, among them many teenagers, participated. The results were markers at the house where Anne Frank was born and at another house where the family later lived, as well as the foundation of the Youth Meeting Center Anne Frank ('Jugendbegegnungsstätte Anne Frank'), with a permanent exhibit 'Anne Frank – Ein Maedchen aus Deutschland' (Anne Frank – A

Girl from Germany). The renamed Anne Frank Education Centre will be expanded, with the addition of a second floor for a larger exhibit. The Frankfurt Jewish Museum plans to have a new wing, with focus on the Frank Family in Frankfurt, a project which is in preparation for the reopening of the Museum. In 2015, the City chose as its suggested annual reading 'Frankfurt liest/ Frankfurt reads', a recently published book about the Frank Family ('Gruesse und Kuesse an alle – Die Geschichte der Familie von Anne Frank/Treasures from the Attic: Anne Frank's Family'), which was a large success (Jugendbegegnungsstaette 2004; Rahlwes and Wawra 2014; Hartmann 2016).

Cologne artist Gunter Demnig came up with a new way of commemorating Jewish citizens who became victims of National Socialism. Starting in his home town in 1992, he placed commemorative stones – stumbling blocks ('Stolpersteine') in the form of cobblestone-sized brass memorials – in front of the final home of residents who were deported and murdered during the years 1933–1945. Since 1995, more than 56,000 stumbling blocks have been installed in almost 1000 German/European cities in 22 countries. Demnig's list of cities and towns where his commemorative art project found resonance comprises major cities such as Berlin and Frankfurt as well as small towns like Dachau, with 10 stumbling blocks. However, it excludes nearby Munich where the City Council (upon recommendation of the local Jewish Community leader) rejected the project idea, though with a continued debate over individual supportive actions in town (Goebel 2010). The 'Stolpersteine' stumbling blocks, though small in size, have had quite an impact. It is a practice of commemoration that allows citizens to participate and to help to reshape the public memory in their community.

No other city in Germany has seen the establishment of so many new memorials over the past 20 years as Berlin. The city itself underwent tremendous changes after the fall of the Berlin Wall in 1989/1990 and the subsequent political, social, and economic re-integration of the West Berlin and East Berlin sectors after re-unification. Berlin used to have a large Jewish community, with distinct landmarks and neighbourhoods where once Jewish life flourished. While a revival brought back some of these qualities, a retrospective of the losses in Jewish community life during 1933–1945 has contributed to several memorials and museums. The New Synagogue on the Oranienburger Strasse restored and reopened with a museum in the mid-1990s and the Jewish Museum, a new landmark building (with a unique design by Daniel Libeskind) in Berlin opened to the public in 2001, are prominent examples for this 'museum' trend (Piper 2006). In the case of the Memorial for the Murdered Jews of Europe, the planning process and completion took many years in long drawn-out debates over how to design the memorial site. In 2005, an approximate 20,000-square-metre-large memorial site with 2700 concrete slabs and an underground information centre ('Ort der Information', with three million names of victims of the Holocaust) was finally inaugurated at the occasion of the 60th anniversary of the end of WWII. There are many other interestingly designed memorials in Berlin including a reminder of the Nazi orchestrated book burning, in form of a glass plate providing a view into a sunken room full of empty bookshelves, at the site in Berlin where it happened on May 10, 1933. Another major effort was made with the 'Topography of Terror' history museum at the former Gestapo headquarters. Commencing in 1987 it eventually resulted in indoor and outdoor exhibits with a focus on the practices and cruelties done to people held in prison there. Joint work of West and East German historians laid the basis for a new document centre which opened in 2010. Berlin also has memorials for several groups neglected for a long time in the commemoration of the victims of National Socialism. They include memorials for the persecution and murder of gay men, the prisoners with the pink triangle ('Totgeschlagen – Totgeschwiegen/put to death – put to silence' in Berlin-Schoeneberg 1989, and the formal memorial in the centre of Berlin 2008), for the Sinti and Roma (1992), and, most recently established, for mentally disabled victims (killed in the 'Euthanasia' campaign). Other ongoing projects have resulted in memorial sites at subsidiary camps/work camps for forced labour in Berlin-Schoeneweide and on Billerbecker Weg.

The Leading Memorial Sites for the Victims of National Socialistic Germany and the Holocaust

Which are the most visited and widely known destinations for this new type of 'Holocaust tourism'? Which places can be considered crucial and enduring reminders for the public memory of the fatal events? Among several thousand European and worldwide memorial sites now in existence with markers, plaques, monuments, museums, and visitor centers, about three dozen memorial sites stand out nationally and internationally.

In terms of volume of visitation to the sites, completely reliable or comparable numbers are usually not available - with the exception of sites were visitors have to pay an entrance fee. Most often, visitation of the sites is free of charge. Frequently, only estimates for the visits to, for instance, memorial sites at the former concentration camps exist. There is also a general hesitation or reluctance to fully assess and publish annual visitation trends. Most modern technological tools that would allow a precise count of the incoming visitors are not in use or are not even considered. Such methods are perceived as inappropriate surveillance of the visitors at memorial sites of the concentration camps where the prisoners once experienced tight and perpetual control by the SS guards. Websites of the major memorial sites usually offer a wealth of information (including figures about how many people died at a site) but rarely give visitation numbers to their sites which are most often buried in lengthy annual business reports.

After 70 years of expansion and adjustments to the memorial landscape for the victims of National Socialistic Germany and the Holocaust, 12 leading in situ sites evolved which receive annual visitation of 150,000 to 1.5 million and/have a wealth of programmes for incoming visitors. These are the memorials at the following concentration camps: in Dachau and Bergen-Belsen in West Germany; in Buchenwald, and Sachsenhausen in former East Germany; in Auschwitz-Birkenau, Majdanek, and Treblinka in Poland; in Mauthausen in Austria; and in Theresienstadt-Terezin in the Czech Republic. Berlin houses two top attractions: the Topography of Terror Exhibit on the grounds of the former Gestapo headquarters and the Memorial to the Murdered Jews of Europe (with an underground Holocaust Information Centre) both in the center (Stadmitte) of Berlin. Probably, the leading *in situ* site - jointly with Auschwitz-Birkenau - is the Anne Frank House in Amsterdam which receives close to 1.3 million visitors (1,295,585 in 2016). In addition, the Amsterdam historic site has developed partner organizations in Berlin (Anne Frank Zentrum), in London (Anne Frank Trust), in New York (Anne Frank Center for Mutual Respect), in Buenos Aires (Centro Ana Frank) and in Vienna (Anne Frank Verein). Two important national memorials and museums outside Europe, Yad Vashem in Jerusalem and the United States Holocaust Memorial Museum in Washington, D.C., maintain many programmes and continue to develop new ones. Visitation at each site has reached 1.5 million annually. Another highly visited and fairly recently opened Holocaust memorial and museum is found in New York ("Museum of Jewish Heritage", with extensive exhibits on the Holocaust), with annual visitation of close to 1.5 million.

Continuity and Change of the Memorial Landscape

Over the past few decades, the memorial landscape for victims of National Socialistic Germany and the Holocaust has seen consistent growth, as to the number of memorial sites, the amount and substance of information provided at visitor centres and museums, as well as the professional management of these sites. In general, there have been constructive and destructive processes which need to be addressed in the following discussion.

In many of the memorial sites, forms of improvement, modernisation, and adjustments (e.g., to the needs of new user groups) did not only include an update of the historic information given in the exhibits and in the museum technology, with the use of more interactive techniques, but also a trend to broaden the themes introduced at the sites. Starting in the 1980s, displays of art collections, literature, and poetry readings became part of the programmes – for instance, at the Dachau Memorial Site under the leadership of Barbara Distel. After the restructuring of the Buchenwald site during the 1990s, a new permanent art exhibit entitled "Tools of Survival: Testimony, Works of Art, Visual Memory" was included on the camp memorial grounds. These and other cultural offerings to expand the topics for incoming visitors and/or people living in nearby communities took aim at addressing the human condition in and outside the camps from 1933 to 1945. In some of the ghettos and camps, the performing arts and music were an essential part or a side aspect of the camp reality, for varying reasons. This applied to the early Emsland camps 1933–1936, most of all to the Boergermoor and Esterwegen camps, where the (later internationally known) 'Moorsoldaten/Peat bog soldiers' song was created by the prisoners in a show (Fackler 2000). Prisoners in many camps had to sing while marching in and out of the camps. Some of the individuals and groups at the camps felt at ease singing while on and off work, and it is known that some people broke into political songs or religious hymns when entering the gas chambers (Wachsmann 2015, p. 537). Shoshana Kalisch's (1985) collection of songs 'Yes, we sang! Songs of the Ghettos and Concentration Camps' is an indication of the role music and the arts had in even extreme situations. In Theresienstadt, groups of musicians and artists performed for camp music events and theatre performances; this may have saved the lives of some of the prisoners or delayed their deportations. Increasingly, such more general camp observations and intimate personal reflections on the situation have become part of the memory and of the commemoration practices. On a different note, by the 1990s, the Anne Frank House in Amsterdam – under the leadership of Hans Westra – broadened their educational programmes and seminars for younger visitors with the discussion of current political, social, and ethnic issues, as Anne Frank may have addressed them. All this, and a multitude of other events, have led to a greater relevance of the programmes and ultimately strengthened the mission of the memorial sites over the past years.

That said, it is sad but important to mention that there continue to be destructive forces at work. The activities of Neo-Nazis and of other hate groups have caused considerable damage to the sites. There is hardly any Jewish cemetery – often in a remote or peripheral location – that has not seen forms of vandalism. Even inner city memorial sites such as the Memorial of the Murdered Jews of Europe in Berlin have been marred by acts of vandalism, notably in 2005, 2009, and 2014. Artefacts of a highly symbolic value, such as the 'Arbeit Macht Frei' (Work Makes You Free) inscription at the gate to the Auschwitz Memorial Site and to the Dachau Memorial Site, were stolen in 2009 and in 2014 respectively. Fortunately, both gates have been retrieved and re-installed at the sites. There have been ups and downs in the numbers of occurrence which seem to follow the rise or decline in the popularity of such groups aiming at publicly denying or questioning the validity of the Holocaust and other facts about the National Socialistic era. Although they represent a fairly small segment in German/European societies, they continue to be a threat and, consequently, a challenge to the management of memorial sites (Hartmann 2017).

Changing Approaches to the Study of the Memorial Sites

Reconstructing the Holocaust 1933–1945, Reconstructing the History of the Memorials

Over the past decades, a multitude of studies have been conducted in the reconstruction of the historical events during the rule of terror of National Socialism 1933–1945. Several comprehensive studies of the Nazi concentration camps have been presented including the following: 'Der Ort des Terrors: Geschichte der nationalsozialistischen Konzentrationslager' – a series by German historians edited by Wolfgang Benz and Barbara Distel (2005–2009, with nine volumes on the history of the concentration camps published), two volumes of the Encyclopedia of Camps and Ghettos 1933–1945 edited by a United States Holocaust Memorial Museum team (Megargee 2009, 2012), and, most recently, a systematic study and detailed analysis of the history of the Nazi Concentration Camps by Nikolaus Wachsmann (2015).

While there is a tremendous wealth of information about the Holocaust, studies of the many memorial sites for the victims of National Socialistic Germany have been lagging. Systematic or selective in-depth research on the memorials and commemoration practices were not conducted until the early 1980s. Harold Marcuse, a historian with pioneering work in this field, argues that it has been a neglected topic and that there remains work to be done, particularly for the lesser known memorial sites. In the concluding section of his article on the 'afterlife of the camps', where he summarises all the efforts made in the different countries as to memorialisation of the historic events, Marcuse writes, 'the study of memorial site didactic and the effects of those memorial conceptions on the millions of visitors to former concentration camps each year is still in its infancy' (2010a, p. 204).

For the remainder of this chapter, it will be attempted to reconstruct some of the research traditions regarding an examination of the memorial sites, of their history as well as a discussion of current issues. The emphasis is particularly on visitation to the sites and their management for tourism. Furthermore, a review of the changing approaches in the heritage and tourism research field is provided, as they apply to the study of memorial sites for the victims of National Socialistic Germany.

Initial Studies About the Memorial Landscape in the 1980s/1990s

As more memorial sites were established in the 1960s and 1970s, it was noted that they received little attention and that the support for the new sites (in terms of financial resources, staff, and recognition in the bureaucracy) was negligible. Detlef Garbe (1983), an early observer – as a researcher and administrator at the sites in West Germany – talked about the forgotten legacy of the former concentrations camps in the 1970s. Though he was able to witness substantial changes by the mid/late 1980s and, in particular, after the reunification of Germany in the early 1990s, a path 'from the forgotten concentration camps to memorial sites (now) appreciated and carried by the authorities' (1992). Other authors of early studies about the memorial sites came to similar conclusions – for example, Bernd Eichmann (1985). He characterised the deplorable situation of the memorial sites at the former concentration camps with three adjectives: *Versteinert, verharmlost, vergessen* – sites which were physically and institutionally 'petrified', where the historic events were 'downplayed', with the result of the memorial sites being ultimately 'forgotten'. In a journalistic review and close-up of the leading 19 concentration camps, Konnilyn Feig (1981) critically examined a disturbing situation regarding the memorialisation of the historic events at the memorial sites as well.

Most internal studies and surveys were aimed at improving the management practices at the memorial sites for educational tourism. Dachau and other destinations were conceived as 'places of learning' ('Lernorte') for the rapidly growing incoming groups of young people after the 'Holocaust' TV series was shown and widely discussed in 1978/1979/1980. By the 1980s, memorial sites were considered an extended 'outdoor classroom' – more frequently used by committed German teachers born after 1940, with little personal baggage and involvement in the era as was often the case with representatives of the older generations. An example for this type of approach and literature in the field is Peter Steinbach's 'Modell Dachau' (1987). Here, he explains the 'Lernort' concept, its potential, and the need to educate a younger generation about the facts of a troubled past.

Another trend in the literature was the inclusion of studies that shed light on the complicated and difficult relationship several towns had with the nearby concentration camps, such as Dachau and Kaufering, with the first national socialistic concentration camp and a later series of subsidiary camps respectively – Weimar (with the Buchenwald camp) and Neuengamme near Hamburg (see Raim 1989; Hartmann 1989, Marcuse 1990, Steinbacher 1993, Schley 1996, Kaienburg 1996). Marcuse presented an in-depth study on the Dachau concentration camp (1933–2001) including the relationship the town of Dachau developed with the camp before and after 1945. He discussed and connected both periods, while the concentration camp was in existence (1933–1945) and after liberation when the site eventually became a memorial site (1965), with changes of the site up to the late 1990s (Marcuse 2001). Changes in the relationship during the 2000s between the City and the Camp were discussed by Schossig (2010).

Comprehensive Documentations of Memorial Sites to the Victims of National Socialistic Germany

By the mid/late 1980s, a need for a more comprehensive assessment of the history of the camps as well as of the history of memorial sites became evident. A new journal series, *Dachauer Hefte* for the study of the national socialistic concentration camps (Studien and Dokumente zur Geschichte der nationalsozialistischen Konzentratiosnlager), was launched in 1985. This series and related research efforts paved the way for a systematic documentation of more than 1000 memorial sites in West Germany/Federal Republic of Germany. A first version – initiated and supported by the federal agency for political education ('Bundeszentrale fuer Politische Bildung') – was published in 1987, with a revised and expanded edition presented in 1995. This volume (840 pp.) and Volume II, with focus on the memorial sites in the new states/

in former East Germany (991 pp.), have become a valuable resource and standard reference (Puvogel et al. 1995; Endlich et al. 1999). In 1998, a detailed map showing the memorial sites in re-unified Germany (as listed in the two volumes) was presented. It comprised of memorials and memorial sites in the following eight categories: larger concentration camps, subsidiary camps, memorials at synagogues, memorials at prisons/Euthanasia sites/sites associated with the German resistance, memorials at cemeteries for the victims of National Socialistic Germany, other monuments and plaques, memorials at Jewish cemeteries, and memorials for the victims at Death Marches. While this map includes close to 2000 places, the authors of the map (and of the two volumes) emphasise that it is not a complete list and that it does not include every place in the public memory of Germany.

New Approaches in Tourism Studies: Dissonance at Heritage Sites, Dark Tourism, and Thanatourism

As the memorial sites multiplied and more studies were conducted about them, new fresh approaches in the study of tourism to these sites and other sites of atrocities were introduced to the multidisciplinary field of heritage and tourism studies. Memorial sites were now understood as places with a controversial past and as a dark heritage. In the mid-1990s, three new terms appeared in the academic tourism literature denoting dissonance at contested heritage sites, including places of atrocities, and the tourist's apparent fascination with death and tragedy: *dissonant heritage, thanatourism,* and *dark tourism*. In their first overview study on the topic of dissonance, Tunbridge and Ashworth presented a book entitled *Dissonant Heritage: The Management of the Past as a Resource in Conflict* (1996). Shortly after, Lennon and Foley – they had just coined the new term of 'dark tourism' (Foley and Lennon 1996) – published a volume with a dozen case studies in *Dark Tourism: The Attraction of Death and Disaster* (2000). It received considerable attention in the media and among tourism researchers. In both texts, one of the selected case studies or chapters was Auschwitz accessible to the international tourist by 1990. For both book covers, the iconic picture of the rail tracks to the gate was chosen (Hartmann 2014).

Ashworth and Tunbridge argued that dissonance is intrinsic to all forms of heritage – whatever the scale, context, or locale. Dissonance is implicit in the commodification processes, in the creation of place products, and in the content of messages which may in some cases lead to disinheritance. Furthermore, they discuss visitor motives and management strategies for atrocity sites, elaborating on how these motives and strategies differ between three groups: the *victims*, the *perpetrators*, and the (more or less uninvolved or innocent) *bystanders*. For their discussion they chose the example of the Nazi concentration camps in Central and Eastern Europe. In separate publications, Ashworth (1996, 2002) examined the case of revived tourism in Krakow-Kazimierz, the former Jewish neighbourhood in Krakow, which was featured in the 1993 movie Schindler's List (Tunbridge and Ashworth 1996; Ashworth 1996, 2002; Ashworth and Hartmann 2005; Hartmann 2014).

The new terms of thanatourism and dark tourism are complementary concepts (or 'sister terms'). Tony Seaton (see Chap. 1) who introduced the concept of *thanatourism* (1996, 2009) recognised the deep fascination some visitors to battlefields and cemeteries have with death and dying. His analysis of the motives and lifeworld of thanatourists ('motivated by the desire for actual or symbolic encounters with death') was paralleled in studies launched by fellow researchers John Lennon (see Chap. 24) and Malcolm Foley from Glasgow Caledonian University in Scotland, who came up with a much broader, albeit more nebulous concept – *dark tourism* (1996, 2000). The 'dark tourism' agenda has been substantially expanded by Philip Stone (see book introduction and Chaps. 8, 10, and 11), founder of a dedicated university research centre (Institute for Dark Tourism Research) at the University of Central Lancashire, UK, as well having prominent online subject presence (see www.dark-tourism.org.uk). At this much visited and effective website, dark tourism was defined as 'the act of travel and visitation to sites, attractions and exhibitions which have real or recreated death, suffering or the seemingly macabre as a main theme' (Stone 2005). While Seaton focused his research largely on tourism to WWI sites, Stone included Auschwitz in his in-depth studies. Indeed, at the Institute for Dark Tourism Research, 'dark tourism' was given fresh multidisciplinary conceptual dimensions and philosophical underpinnings. Among others, Stone developed a 'Dark Tourism Spectrum' typological model, from lightest sites (such as a 'Dracula Castle' commercial venture) to darkest sites (like the Auschwitz-Birkenau State Memorial and Museum) which served for a categorisation and analysis of a multitude of sites to be included in a broadening dark tourism research agenda (Miles 2002; Sharpley 2005; Stone 2006). Stone, Sharpley (see Chap. 14), and other researchers successfully expanded their perspectives in many directions and fields (Stone and Sharpley 2008; Sharpley and Stone 2009, 2011, 2012), ultimately also including tourism to the memorial sites of the Holocaust. The notion of dark tourism – for a long time confined to scholarly research in the United Kingdom – eventually found acceptance in other countries and regions such as the United States and German-speaking countries (Quack and Steinecke 2012; Hartmann 2014).

Research About the Places Associated with the Victims, About the Places Associated with the Perpetrators

With a widely established network of memorial sites honouring the victims of the National Socialistic regime 1933–1945, a secondary type of attractions has begun to emerge in Germany and Austria: namely, sites associated with Adolf Hitler and other leaders of the Third Reich. Thus, the 'Eagle's Nest/Obersalzberg' near Berchtesgaden, Hitler's second home and alternative government centre, receives approximately 250,000–300,000 visitors annually. Subsequently, a new type of research has developed, which focuses on tourism to sites of victims *and* perpetrators ('Opfer-Orte' *und* 'Taeter-Orte'). While Petermann (2012) compared and contrasted tourism to Dachau and the Obersalzberg, John-Stucke (2012) examined visits to the Wewelsburg SS Nordic Academy and the adjacent Niederhagen Concentration Camp. The combined memorial site of the castle and the concentration camp (since 2010) has been carefully developed and recently successfully integrated in a regional heritage tourism plan (Brebeck 2008; John-Stucke 2012).

In recent years, there has been a trend of developing 'documentation centres' at sites associated with the perpetrators; for example, at the aforementioned second home of Hitler in Berchtesgaden, as well as at the Nazi Party rally grounds in Nuremberg. The new documentation centres give background information about the sites and historical events. Recently, a documentation centre has been completed in Munich ('Munich in the NS Zeit'), with a critical analysis of the role the city (then known as 'Hauptstadt der Bewegung') had during National Socialism. Another documentation centre is currently (at the time of writing) in the planning stage near Kaufering where close to 15,000 people, mostly Hungarian Jews, died in forced labour camps during the final 10 months of the National Socialistic regime. Research on the Kaufering camps conducted by a local citizen group focuses both on the victims and the perpetrators.

A four-quadrant model *Places Associated with the Victims and Perpetrators in National Socialism 1933–1945* has been introduced by Hartmann (2016; also Figs. 20.1 and 20.2). The quadrants in the schematic models illustrate:

(a) High recognition places for the victims of Nazi Germany such as Auschwitz, the Anne Frank House in Amsterdam, and the memorial site at Dachau;
(b) Little known, neglected, or forgotten places associated with the victims such as at some of the subsidiary camps;
(c) High recognition places associated with the perpetrators such as Hitler's second home in Berchtesgaden, the Gestapo headquarters in Berlin ('Topography of Terror'), and the Wannsee Villa on the outskirts of Berlin where a high-level NS Party conference on the 'Final Solution (of the Jewish Question)' was held on January 20, 1942; and
(d) Places associated with the perpetrators which are no longer accessible to the public, such as the prison cell in Landsberg where Hitler was incarcerated in 1924 and where he wrote his book *Mein Kampf*, and where, in the mid-to-late 1930s, hundreds of thousands of young Nazi Party members converged on Landsberg to see the 'Fuehrer's cell'.

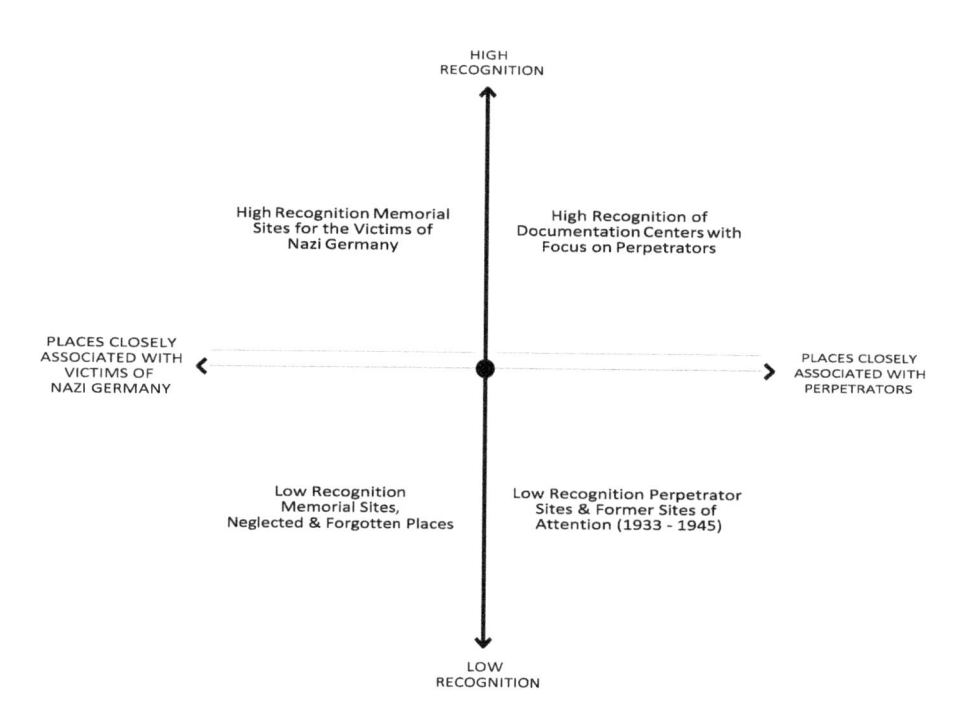

Fig. 20.1 Four-quadrant model for a categorisation of 'victims/perpetrators' places

Fig. 20.2 Diagram

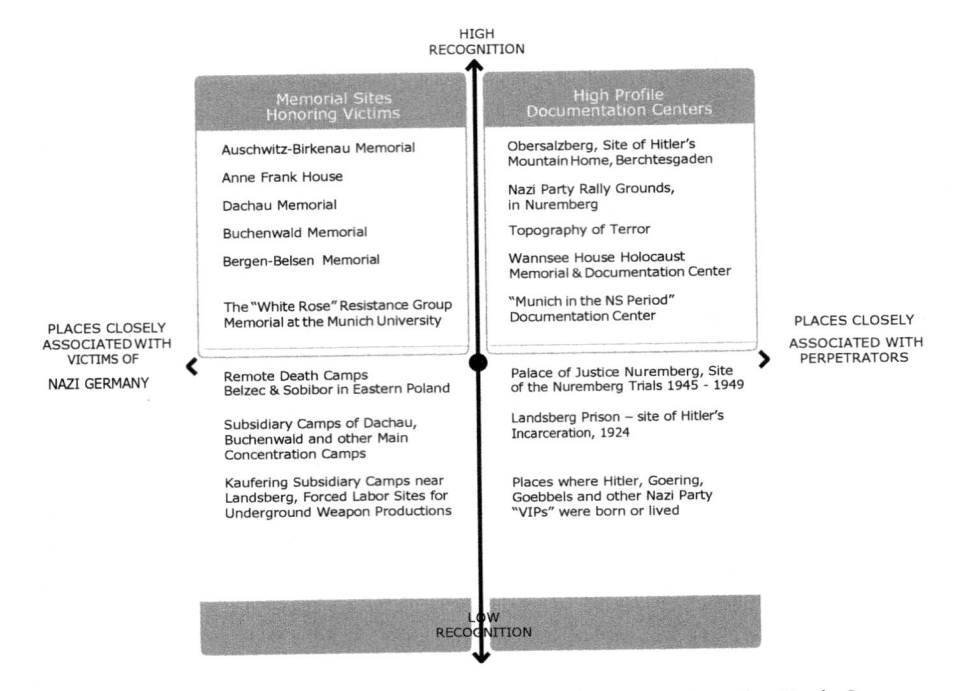

```
                           HIGH
                        RECOGNITION
                             ▲
        ┌────────────────────┼────────────────────┐
        │  Memorial Sites    │   High Profile     │
        │  Honoring Victims  │ Documentation Centers│
        │                    │                    │
        │ Auschwitz-Birkenau │ Obersalzberg, Site │
        │ Memorial           │ of Hitler's Mountain│
        │                    │ Home, Berchtesgaden│
        │ Anne Frank House   │                    │
        │                    │ Nazi Party Rally   │
        │ Dachau Memorial    │ Grounds, in Nuremberg│
        │                    │                    │
        │ Buchenwald Memorial│ Topography of Terror│
        │                    │                    │
        │ Bergen-Belsen      │ Wannsee House      │
        │ Memorial           │ Holocaust Memorial │
        │                    │ & Documentation    │
        │                    │ Center             │
        │ The "White Rose"   │                    │
        │ Resistance Group   │ "Munich in the NS  │
        │ Memorial at the    │ Period"            │
PLACES  │ Munich University  │ Documentation      │ PLACES
CLOSELY │                    │ Center             │ CLOSELY
ASSOC.  │                    │                    │ ASSOC.
WITH  ◄─┤                    │                    ├─► WITH
VICTIMS │ Remote Death Camps │ Palace of Justice  │ PERPET-
OF NAZI │ Belzec & Sobibor   │ Nuremberg, Site of │ RATORS
GERMANY │ in Eastern Poland  │ the Nuremberg      │
        │                    │ Trials 1945 - 1949 │
        │ Subsidiary Camps   │                    │
        │ of Dachau,         │ Landsberg Prison - │
        │ Buchenwald and     │ site of Hitler's   │
        │ other Main         │ Incarceration, 1924│
        │ Concentration Camps│                    │
        │                    │ Places where Hitler,│
        │ Kaufering Subsidiary│ Goering, Goebbels │
        │ Camps near         │ and other Nazi     │
        │ Landsberg, Forced  │ Party "VIPs" were  │
        │ Labor Sites for    │ born or lived      │
        │ Underground Weapon │                    │
        │ Productions        │                    │
        └────────────────────┼────────────────────┘
                             ▼
                           LOW
                        RECOGNITION
```

Fig. 20.2 Sites associated with the victims and perpetrators in Nazi Germany, 1933–1945

It should be mentioned that many of the above-mentioned victims' places, though, are also closely tied to the perpetrators. For instance, the memorial site in Auschwitz I shows the location where camp commandant Rudolf Hoess was executed by hanging in 1947. The Buchenwald memorial site offers not only several tours of the camp site with reference to the prisoners but also one tour focuses on the perpetrators. The four-quadrant model serves as a classification of the sites and is well suited for suggested further action in the commemoration of the events at various types of sites.

Conclusion

Tourism to now well-known sites closely tied to the Holocaust as well as to many of the lesser known places associated with various victim groups and the perpetrators of Nazi Germany, continues to grow with the formulation of different agendas and management concerns at the sites. This raises the question of how to best address issues and problems confronted at this new type of memorial landscape. Several approaches to the study of 'Holocaust tourism' have been developed and more studies continue to be launched. The 'dark tourism' agenda has contributed considerably to the further examination of a phenomenon which has found the attention of a wide public in and outside Germany, in many European countries and worldwide.

A need for continued research has been outlined by many researchers. Indeed, the author argues it will be more difficult to properly tell the story of victimisation as more and more Holocaust survivors pass away. What will be the task for management of the memorial sites no longer seen, revisited, and explained by the people who witnessed the fatal events (Hartmann 2005, 2014)? What are pedagogical approaches to the presentation and exploration of the sites for a younger generation which receives a lot of its information by surfing the internet, with the possibility of seeing the sites in virtual reality tours? To that end, many challenges await managers and administrators of the sites as well as academic researchers in the field.

References

Ashworth, G. (1996). Holocaust tourism and Jewish culture: The lessons of Krakow-Kazimierz. In M. Robinson, N. Evans, & P. Callaghan (Eds.), *Tourism and cultural change* (pp. 1–12). Newcastle: Centre for Travel and Tourism.

Ashworth, G. (2002). Holocaust tourism: The experience of Krakow-Kazimierz. *International Research in Geographical and Environmental Education, 11*(4), 363–367.

Ashworth, G. (2008). The memorialization of violence and tragedy: Human trauma as heritage. In B. Graham & P. Howard (Eds.), *The Ashgate companion to heritage and identity* (pp. 231–244). Aldershot: Ashgate.

Ashworth, G., & Hartmann, R. (2005). *Horror and human tragedy revisited: The management of sites of atrocities for tourism*. New York: Cognizant.

Azaryahu, M. (2003). Replacing memory: The reorientation of Buchenwald. *Cultural Geographies, 10*(1), 1–20.

Bayerische Landeszentrale fuer Politische Bildungsarbeit. (2000). *Spuren des Nationalsozialismus – Gedenkstaettenarbeit in Bayern*. Muenchen: Bayerische Landeszentrale fuer Politische Bildungsarbeit.

Bayerische Landeszentrale fuer politische Bildungsarbeit. (2013). Themenheft 1/13 Einsichten und Perspektiven, a special issue of the *Bayerische Zeitschrift fuer Politik und Geschichte* (The Bavarian Journal of History and Politics, with contributions about The White Rose Foundation at its 25th Anniversary, Change and Continuity in the Commemoration of the White Rose in Munich, A Recognition of the Impact of the White Rose Resistance Group in Munich, and the Central University Entrance Hall/Lichthof as a Place of Learning).

Benz, W., & Distel, B. (1994). Taeter und Opfer, *Dachauer Hefte*, p. 10.
Benz, W., & Pehle, W. (1996). *Encyclopedia of German resistance to the Nazi movement*. New York: Continuum International Publication Group.
Benz, W., Distel, B., & Koenigseder, A. (2005–2009). *Der Ort des Terrors: Geschichte der nationalsozialistischen Konzentrationslager*. Berlin: Metropol Verlag (with nine volumes so far published).
Blatt, T. (2000). *Sobibor – The Forgotten Revolt*. H.E.P. Google Books. ISBN 0-9649442-0-0.
Brebeck, W. E. (2008). Wewelsburg 1933–45: Ansaetze und Perspektiven zur Neukonzeption der Dauerausstellung. In W. E. Brebeck, & B. Stambolis (Eds.), *Erinnerungsarbeit kontra Verklaerung der NS-Zeit. Vom Umgang mit Tatorten, Gedenkoirten und Kulturorten* (pp. 119–141). Munich: Verlag Dr. Christian Mueller-Straten.
Charlesworth, A. (1994). Contested places of memory: The case of Auschwitz. *Environment and Planning D: Society and Space*, *12*(5), 579–593.
Ehmann, A. (1995). Ueber Sprache, Begriffe und Deutungen des nationalsozialistischen Massen- und Voelkermords. In A. Ehmann, & K. Wolf (Eds.), *Praxis der Gedenkstaettenpaedagogik*. Opladen: Leske & Budrich.
Ehmann, A., Kaiser, W., Lutz, T., Rathenow, H. F., vom Stein, C., & Weber, N. H. (1995). *Praxis der Gedenkstaettenpaedagogik*. Opladen: Leske & Budrich.
Eichmann, B. (1985). *Versteinert, verharmlost, vergessen. KZ-Gedaechtnisstaetten in der Bundesrepbulik Deutschland*. Frankfurt: Fischer.
Endlich, S. (1999). "Gedenkstaetten in Berlin", *Gedenkstaetten fuer die Opfer des Nationalsozialismus – Eine Dokumentation Band II* (pp. 27–227). Berlin: Bundeszentrale fuer politische Bildung.
Endlich, S., Goldenbogen, N., Herlemann, B., Kahl, M., & Scheer, R. (1999). *Gedenkstaetten fuer die Opfer des Nationalsozialismus – Eine Dokumentation Band II* (991 pp). Bonn: Bundeszentrale fuer politische Bildung.
Fackler, G. (2000). *Des Lagers Stimme: Musik im KZ – Alltag und Haeftlingskultur in den Konzentrationslagern 1933 bis 1936* (628 pp). Bremen: Edition Temmen.
Feig, K. (1981). *Hitler's death camps: The sanity of madness*. New York: Holmes & Meier.
Foley, M., & Lennon, J. J. (1996). JFK and dark tourism: A fascination with assassination. *International Journal of Heritage Studies*, *2*(4), 198–211.
Garbe, D. (1983). *Die vergessenen KZs? Gedenkstaetten fuer die Opfer des NS-Terrors in der Bundesrepublik*. Bornheim-Merten: Lamuv Verlag.
Garbe, D. (1992). Von den 'Vergessenen KZs; zu den 'Staatstragenden Gedenkstaetten', *Gedenkstaettenforum – Rundbrief*, Nr. 49/1992.
Genger, A. (1995). Lernen, Erinnern, Gedenken. Erfahrungen aus der Gedenkstaettenarbeit. In A. Ehmann, W. Kaiser, T. Lutz, H.-F. Rathenow, C. vom Stein, & N. H. Weber (Eds.), *Praxis der Gedenkstaettenpaedagogik* (pp. 48–54). Opladen: Leske + Budrich.
Gilbert, M. (1982). *Atlas of the Holocaust*. New York: Macmillan.

Goldhagen, D. (1996). *Hitler's willing executioners: Ordinary Germans and the Holocaust*. New York: Alfred Knopf.

Greiser, K. (1998). "Sie starben allein und ruhig, ohne zu schreien oder jemand zu rufen" Das "Kleine Lager" im Konzentrationslager Buchenwald. *Dachauer Hefte, 14*, 102–124.

Grossmann, C. (1991). Die uns verliessen und die sich erhoben: Der Aufstand im Ghetto Bialystok. *Dachauer Hefte, 7*, 102–118.

Gruner, W. (2002). Die Fabrik-Aktion und die Ereignisse in der Berliner Rosenstrasse: Fakten und Fiktionen um den 27. Februar 1943. *Jahrbuch fuer Antisemitismusforschung, 11*(2002), 137–177.

Haertl, U. (1999). *Der Ettersberg bei Weimar: Zeitschneise*. Weimar-Buchenwald: Gedenkstaette Buchenwald.

Haertl, U., & Moench, W. (2001). *Buchenwald: Relikte – Denkmale – Erinnerungen*. Weimar: Euler Verlag.

Hantsch, P. (1994, August 20). Die Spur der Steine: Jugendliche helfen bei Grabungen von Bonhoeffers Zelle in Buchenwald, *Thueringer Allgemeine*, Wochenendbeilage, p. 1.

Hartmann, R. (1989). Dachau revisited: Tourism to the memorial site and museum of the former concentration camp. *Tourism Recreation Research, 14*(1), 41–47. Reprinted in *Tourism Environment*, Tej Vir Singh, et al. (Eds.), New Delhi Inter Indian Publications, 1992, pp. 183–190.

Hartmann, R. (1997). Dealing with Dachau in geographic education. In H. Brodsky (Ed.), *Visions of land and community: Geography in Jewish studies* (pp. 357–369). College Park: University of Maryland Press.

Hartmann, R. (2003). Zielorte des Holocaust Tourismus im Wandel: die KZ-Gedenkstaette in Dachau, die Gedenkstaette in Weimar-Buchenwald und das Anne Frank Haus in Amsterdam. In C. Becker, H. Hopfinger, & A. Steinecke (Eds.), *Handbuch der Geographie der Freizeit und des Tourismus* (pp. 297–308). Munich: Oldenburg.

Hartmann, R. (2004). Das Anne-Frank-Haus in Amsterdam: Lernort, Literarische Landschaft und Gedenkstaette. In A. Brittner-Widmann, H. Quack, & H. Wachowiak (Eds.), *Festschrift C. Becker* (pp. 131–142). Trier: University of Trier Press.

Hartmann, R. (2005). Holocaust memorials without holocaust survivors: The management of museums and memorials to victims of Nazi Germany in 21st century Europe. In G. Ashworth & R. Hartmann (Eds.), *Horror and human tragedy revisited: The management of sites of atrocities for tourism* (pp. 89–107). New York: Cognizant Communication Corporation.

Hartmann, R. (2013). The Anne Frank House in Amsterdam: A museum and literary landscape goes virtual reality. *Journalism and Mass Communication, 3*(10), 625–644.

Hartmann, R. (2014). Dark tourism, thanatourism, and dissonance in heritage tourism management: New directions in contemporary tourism research. *Journal of Heritage Tourism, 9*(2), 166–182.

Hartmann, R. (2016). Special interest tourism to places closely associated with the victims of Nazi Germany: A dark heritage revisited, In: P. Williams (Ed.), *Special interest tourism*. Wallingford: CABI (forthcoming).

Hartmann, R. (2017). Places with a disconcerting past: Issues and trends in Holocaust Tourism. *EuropeNow* (10). http://www.europenowjournal.org/2017/09/05/places-with-a-disconcerting-past-issues-and-trends-in-holocaust-tourism/

Jacobs, J. (2008). Memorializing the sacred: Kristallnacht in German national memory. *Journal for the Scientific Study of Religion, 47*(3), 485–498.

Jacobs, J. (2010). Jewish memory and the emasculation of the sacred: Kristallnacht in the German landscape. In J. Jacobs (Ed.), *Memorializing the holocaust – Gender, genocide and collective memory* (pp. 83–106). New York: I.B. Taurus.

Jalocha, M., & Boyd. (2014, August 13–17). *Tourism development opportunities for the Lublin region of Poland: Emphasis beyond dark heritage*. Paper presented at tourism and transition in a time of change, Pre-Congress Meeting Krakow/Pieniny Mts, Poland.

Jocheim, G. (2002). *Frauenprotest in der Rosenstrasse 1943*. Berlin: Hentrich & Hentrich Verlag.

John-Stucke, K. (2012). Die Wewelsburg: Renaissanceschloss – "SS-Schule" – Erinnerungsort – Ausflugsziel. In: H.-D. Quack, & A. Steinecke (Eds.), *Dark Tourism – Faszination des Schreckens*, Paderborner Geographische Studien zu Tourismusforschung and Destinationsmanagement (pp. 179–191). Paderborn: Universitaet Paderborn.

Jugendbegegnunsstaette. (2004). *10 Jahre 1994–2004*. Frankfurt: Jugendbegegnungsstaette Anne Frank e.V.

Kahl, M. (1999). Gedenkstaetten in Thueringen. *Gedenkstaetten fuer die Opfer des Nationalsozialismus – Eine Dokumentation Band II* (pp. 779–913). Berlin: Bundeszentrale fuer politische Bildung.

Kaienburg, H. (1996). … sie naechtelang nicht ruhig schlafen liess – Das KZ Neuengamme und seine Nachbarn. *Dachauer Hefte*, Heft 12, 34–57.

Kaiser, W., Lutz, T., Rathenow, H. F., vom Stein, C., & Weber, N. H. (Eds.). (pp. 75–100). Opladen: Leske & Budrich.

Kalisch, S. (1985). *Yes, we sang! Songs of the ghettos and concentration camps*. New York: Harper & Row.

Knigge, V., Luettgenau, R. G., Ritscherr, B., & Stein, H. (1998). *Konzentrationslager Buchenwald 1937–1945, Spezallager Nr. 2 1945–1950 – Zwei Lager an einem Ort – Geschichte und Erinnerungskonstruktion*. Weimar-Buchenwald: Gedenkstaette Buchenwald.

Knoll, A. (1998). Totgeschlagen – totgeschwiegen: Die homosexuellen Haeftlinge im KZ Dachau. *Dachauer Hefte, 14*, 77–101.

Krakover, S. (2005). Attitudes of Israeli Visitors Towards the Holocaust Remembrance Site of Yad Vashem. In G. Ashworth & R. Hartmann (Eds.), *Horror and human tragedy revisited: The management of sites of atrocities for tourism* (pp. 108–117). New York: Cognizant Communication Corporation.

Kronawitter, H. (2014). Sophie Scholl – eine Ikone des Widerstands. *Einsichten und Perspektiven* (pp. 80–91). Muenchen: Bayerische Landeszentrale fuer politische Bildungsarbeit, 14/2.

Lennon, J. J., & Foley, M. (2000). *Dark tourism: The attraction of death and disaster.* New York: Continuum.

Linenthal, E. T. (1995). *Preserving memory: The struggle to create America's Holocaust Museum.* New York: Viking.

Lutz, T. (1995). Gedenkstaetten fuer die Opfer des NS-Regimes. Geschichte – Arbeitsweisen – gesellschaftlich Wirkungsmoeglichkeiten. In A. Ehmann, W. Kaiser, T. Lutz, H.-F. Rathenow, C. vom Stein, & N. H. Weber (Eds.), *Praxis der Gedenkstaettenpaedagogik* (pp. 37–47). Opladen: Leske + Budrich.

Marcuse, H. (1990). Das ehemalige Konzentrationslager Dachau: Der muehevolle Weg zur Gedenkstaette, 1945–1968. *Dachauer Hefte, 6,* 182–205.

Marcuse, H. (2001). *Legacies of Dachau – The uses and abuses of a concentration camp, 1933–2001.* New York: Cambridge University Press.

Marcuse, H. (2005). Reshaping Dachau for visitors: 1933–2000. In G. Ashworth & R. Hartmann (Eds.), *Horror and human tragedy revisited – The management of sites of atrocities for tourism* (pp. 118–148). New York: Cognizant Communication Corporation.

Marcuse, H. (2010a). The afterlife of the camps. In J. Kaplan & N. Wachsmann (Eds.), *Concentration camps in Nazi Germany* (pp. 186–211). New York: Routledge.

Marcuse, H. (2010b). Holocaust memorials: The emergence of a genre. *American Historical Review, 115,* 53–89.

Megargee, G. (2009). *The United States Holocaust Memorial Museum encyclopedia of camps and ghettos 1933–1945.* Bloomington: Indiana University Press. Volume I, Part A and Part B, 1659 pp.

Miles, W. (2002). Auschwitz: Museum interpretation and darker tourism. *Annals of Tourism Research, 29*(4), 1175–1178.

Nachama, A. (2012). Die fuerchterlichste Adresse Berlins – zur Konzeption eines Lernortes auf dem Gelaende der Gestapo, SS und des Reichssicherheitsdienstes. In: H.-D. Quack, & A. Steinecke (Eds.), *Dark Tourism – Faszination des Schreckens,* Paderborner Geographische Studien zu Tourismusforschung und Destinationsmanagement (pp. 153–170). Paderborn: Universitaet Paderborn.

Overesch, M. (1995). *Buchenwald und die DDR oder Die Suche nach Selbstlegitimation.* Goettingen: Vandenhoeck & Ruprecht.

Petermann, S. (2012). "You get out of it what you put into" – nationalsozialistische Opfer- und Taeterorte in Deutschland als Touristenzielorte? In H.-D. Quack, & A. Steinecke (Eds.), *Dark Tourism – Faszination des Schreckens,* Paderborner Geographische Studien zu Tourismusforschung und Destinationsmanagement (pp. 63–80). Paderborn: Universitaet Paderborn.

Pfoertner, H. (2001). *Mahnmale, Gedenkstaetten, Erinnerungsorte fuer die Opfer des Nationalsozialismus in Muenchen.* Muenchen: Herbert Utz Verlag.

Piper, K. (2006). Die Musealisierung des Holocaust: das Juedische Museum Berlin und das U.S. Holocaust Memorial Museum in Washington D.C.; ein Vergleich. *Europaeische Geschichtsdarstellungen*, Bd. 9. Koeln: Boelau.

Puvogel, U. (1999). *"Einleitung", Gedenkstaetten fuer die Opfer des Nationalsozialismus – Eine Dokumentation II: Bundeslaender Berlin, Brandenburg, Mecklenburg-Vorpommern, Sachsen-Anhalt, Sachsen, Thueringen* (pp. 11–26). Berlin: Bundeszentrale fuer Politische Bildung.

Puvogel, U., Stankowski, M., & Graf, U. (1995). *Gedenkstaetten fuer die Opfer des Nationalsozialismus – Eine Dokumentation I* (840 pp). Bonn: Bundeszentrale fuer politische Bildung.

Quack, H. D., & Steinecke, A. (2012). *Dark tourism: Faszination des Schreckens*. Paderborn: University of Paderborn Press.

Rahlwes, A., & Wawra, R. (2014). *Freiheitsrechte: Das Beispiel der Vorfahren It isund der Familie von Anne Frank*. Bildungsstaette Anne Frank and Paedagogisches Zentrum FFM Fritz Bauer Institut & Juedisches Museum Frankfurt, Materialheft: Frankfurt am Main.

Raim, E. (1989). Unternehmen Ringeltaube: Dachaus Aussenkomplex Kaufering. *Dachauer Hefte*, 5, 193–211.

Raim, E. (2000). Frauen in den Dachauer KZ-Aussenlagern Kaufering: Nationalsozialistische Vernichtungspolitik gegenueber Juedinnen. In *Spuren des Nationalsozialismus – Gedenkstaettenarbeit in Bayern* (pp. 87–110). Muenchen: Bayerische Landeszentrale fuer politische Bildung.

Reder, R. (1946). *Belzec*. Krakow: Jewish Historical Committee.

Richardi, H.-G., Philipp, E., & Luecking, M. (1998). *Dachauer Zeitgeschichtsfuehrer*. Dachau: Stadt Dachau Amt fuer Kultur, Fremdenverkehr und Zeitgeschichte.

Roberts, S. (2015, November 2). Thomas Blatt, who escaped death camp during Revolt, dies at 88. *New York Times*.

Rook, H., & Hofmann, R. (1995). *Jugendbegegnungsstaette der Gedenkstaette Buchenwald: Ein Rueckblick*. Weimar-Buchenwald: Gedenkstaette Buchenwald.

Schelvis, J. (2004). *Vernietigingskamp Sobibor*. Uitgeverij Van Soeren & Co., in translation *Sobibor: A history of a Nazi death camp*. Berg, Oxford & New Cork, 2007.

Schley, J. (1996). Weimar und Buchenwald: Beziehungen zwischen der Stadt und dem Lager. *Dachauer Hefte*, 12, 196–214.

Seaton, T. (1996). Guided by the dark: From thanatopsis to thanatourism. *International Journal of Heritage Studies*, 2(4), 234–244.

Seaton, T. (2009). Thanatourism and its discontents: An appraisal of a decade's work with some future issues and directions. In T. Jamal & M. Robinson (Eds.), *The Sage handbook of tourism studies* (pp. 521–542). London: Sage.

Sharpley, R. (2005). Travels to the edge of darkness: Towards a typology of "dark tourism". In C. Ryan, S. Page, & M. Aicken (Eds.), *Taking tourism to the limits: Issues, concepts and managerial perspectives* (pp. 187–198). Amsterdam: Elsevier.

Sharpley, R., & Stone, P. R. (Eds.). (2009). *The darker side of travel: The theory and practice of dark tourism*. London: Routledge.

Sharpley, R., & Stone, P. R. (2011). *Tourist experience: Contemporary perspectives.* London: Routledge.

Sharpley, R., & Stone, P. R. (2012). *Contemporary tourist experiences: Concepts and consequences.* London: Routledge.

Soyez, D. (2015, June 2). *Coping with uncomfortable pasts: Automotive brand worlds in Germany from a heritage (tourism) perspective.* Paper presented at the Canadian Association of Geographers Annual Meeting, Vancouver.

Stadler, S. (1995). Das Internationale Jugendbegegnungslager in Dachau. In A. Ehmann, W. Kaiser, T. Lutz, H.-F. Rathenow, C. vom Stein, & N. H. Weber (Eds.), *Praxis der Gedenkstaettenpaedagogik* (pp. 186–193). Opladen: Leske + Budrich.

Steinbach, P. (1987). *Modell Dachau: das Konzentrationslager und die Stadt in der Zeit des Nationalsozialismus und ihre Bedeutung fuer die Gegenwart.* Passau: Andreas-Haller-Verlag.

Steinbacher, S. (1993). *Dachau – Die Stadt und das Konzentrationslager in der NS-Zeit.* Muenchner Studien zur neueren und neuesten Geschichte, Band 5. Frankfurt. ISBN 978-3-631-46682-7. Frankfurt am Main: Lang.

Stiftung Gedenkstaetten Buchenwald und Mittelbau-Dora. (2003). *Ueberlebensmittel Zeugnis Kunstwerk Bildgedaechtnis – Die staendige Kunstausstellung der Gedenkstaette Buchenwald – Denkmale auf dem Lagergelaende.* Weimar: Stiftung Gedenkstaetten Buchenwald und Mittelbau-Dora.

Stone, P. R. (2005). Dark Tourism Forum, University of Central Lancashire. Retrieved from www.dark-tourism.org.uk. Accessed 31 Dec 2005.

Stone, P. R. (2006). A dark tourism spectrum: Towards a typology of death and macabre related tourist sites, attractions and exhibitions. *Tourism, 52,* 145–160.

Stone, P. R., & Sharpley, R. (2008). Consuming dark tourism: A thanatological perspective. *Annals of Tourism Research, 36*(2), 1565–1587.

Time Magazine. (1944). Vernichtungslager. *Time Magazine, 44*(8), 38.

Tunbridge, J. E., & Ashworth, G. J. (1996). *Dissonant heritage: The management of the past as a resource in conflict.* New York: Wiley.

United States Holocaust Memorial Museum. (1996). *Historical atlas of the Holocaust.* New York: Macmillan.

Wachsmann, N. (2015). *KL– A history of the Nazi concentration camps* (865 pp). New York: Farrar, Straus and Giroux.

Wenzel-Orf, H., & Kirsten, W. (2003). *Der Berg ueber der Stadt: Zwischen Goethe und Buchenwald.* Zuerich: Ammann Verlag.

Young, J. (1989). The biography of a memorial icon: Nathan Rapoport's Warsaw ghetto monument. *Representations, 26*(1), 69–106.

Young, J. (1993). *The texture of memory – Holocaust memorials and meaning.* New Haven: Yale University Press.

Young, J. (1999). The Anne Frank House: An accessible window to the Holocaust. *Anne Frank Magazine,* p. 13.

Section 5

The 'Dark Tourist' Experience

Philip R. Stone

Introduction

Dom Joly, author of *The Dark Tourist* (Joly 2010), is a comedian who used to dress up as a large penis and harangue British Members of Parliament for television viewers' amusement. He also used to masquerade for TV shows as an over-excitable squirrel and shout loudly into oversized mobile phones whilst in a cinema or in a library. Dom Joly became prominent in British popular culture for being a surreal jester—a kind of postmodern performing chump who entertained the masses by targeting the establishment or exposing deficiencies in contemporary society. Yet, by his own admission, Dom Joly thinks of himself as a 'coward' (Joly 2010: 1) and, to assuage his apparent cowardice, he decided to visit six different, *difficult destinations* in one year, including the Killing Fields of Cambodia, to see what would happen. The result is his travelogue in which Joly appears jolly on the book's front cover, photographed sitting in a deck chair against a backdrop of war carnage wearing shorts and tourist map in hand. Beside him are a suitcase and a Kalashnikov rifle. With his trademark simper, Joly proudly declares what he finally realised to be: 'I was a Dark Tourist' (Joly 2010: 5).

However, despite Dom Joly's declaration of being a 'dark tourist' (as well as the title of this section), there can be no such thing! Indeed, to categorise people who visit sites associated with pain or shame as *dark*—and somehow

P. R. Stone (✉)
University of Central Lancashire, Preston, UK

deviant—is not only misleading, it is also fruitless as a typological exercise. There can never be a so-called dark tourist as a defined taxonomy because to consume (dark) tourism is to consume experiences (Sharpley and Stone 2012; also see Chap. 1). International dark tourism has continued to expand in both scale and scope, and as tourist expectations have become more diverse and complex in response to transformations in the memoryscapes of the dead, so too have tourist experiences. The personal significance of tourism, generally, is largely defined by an individual's 'life-world', and cannot simply be detached from the socio-cultural relations in which they are embedded. Equally, the interaction of an individual tourist with a host destination, cultures, and communities is very much determined by idiosyncratic 'cultural baggage'—that is, values, experience, knowledge, attitudes, and so on. Indeed, tourism often suggests that 'you can escape from those around you but you cannot escape yourself' (Sharpley and Stone 2011: 2). The implication, therefore, is there are as many tourist experiences as they are tourists, and each is defined by the social fabric that surrounds them. Consequently, understanding the nature of (dark) tourist experiences would seem a difficult, if not impossible task.

Nevertheless, dark tourism is a social phenomenon involving the mass movement of people across global traumascapes, which cannot be fully understood without a critical examination of the meaning or significance of dark tourism to tourists themselves. Indeed, there is a need to evaluate tourist interactions with sites of death or disaster and the people they encounter, as well as the multitude of intrinsic and extrinsic factors that influence the nature and outcomes of those interactions. In short, fundamental to the study of dark tourism is the study of the tourist experience at such sites. Hence, the need exists for more focussed studies into tourist experiences within dark tourism that reflect an ever-increasing diversity and complexity, and the meanings and significance thereof. That is, the tourist experience within dark tourism can only be understood by exploring specific contexts within which it occurs, and which are conceptually located in broader meta-narrative frameworks (also see Section 2).

About This Section

The chapters in this fifth section of the Handbook offer a variety of perspectives of tourist experiences within dark tourism. The first chapter (Chap. 21) by Avital Biran and Dorina Buda examines notions of fear within dark tourism consumption. In response to calls for enhanced psychological discourse in dark tourism research, they appraise various ways in which fear of death is manifested in dark tourism engagements. In so doing, Biran and Buda draw upon Terror Management Theory (TMT) as an explanatory framework in which macro-sociological understandings of dark tourism consumption are made. The study is the first ever to comprehensively locate TMT within a dark tourism context and, in terms of mortality saliency and thanatological dark tourism experiences, expands earlier conceptual works by Stone and Sharpley (2008) and Stone (2012). Particularly, they suggest TMT may be used to empirically explore notions of ontological (in)security within the consumer experience and, specifically, examine the ways in which people negotiate existential fears in dark tourism. Importantly, whilst conceptualising dark tourism within TMT, Biran and Buda argue that dark tourism can provoke reflections of hope and health. In turn, dark tourism may provide a meaning-making mechanism in which tourist experiences are not merely about consuming narratives of death, but about contemplating life and living in the face of inevitable mortality.

The second chapter (Chap. 22) by Maximiliano Korstanje and David Baker examines dark tourism experiences through a lens of symbolic interactionism and, in particular, they explore dark tourism consumption as a way of mediating politics of the (corrupt) Other. To illustrate their discussions, they provide comparative case studies from a South American context—the Museum of ESMA (a former detention centre of the Argentinean Military Juntas where dissentients were allegedly tortured and murdered in the 1970s and early 1980s); and The Sanctuary of Cromañón (a memorial for the Buenos Aires night club accident where 194 teenagers died in 2004). Korstanje and Baker consider mediating Other death through a political (corruption) framework where an 'allegory of disaster' can be constructed and negotiated for specific visitor sites. Ultimately, they argue that dark tourism as memorial sites are potentially vulnerable or even resistant to neo-liberal market forces (within their case examples at least) and, as a result, are prone to inherent political venality.

In the third chapter (Chap. 23), Mary Margaret Kerr and Rebecca Price explore an under-researched topic within tourism generally and, dark tourism in particular. They open up a new and exciting research avenue into the experiences of children at memorial sites, where they outline multi-disciplinary child-centred research methods as a methodological blueprint for future child-related studies in dark tourism. Moreover, Kerr and Price evaluate the child's 'voice' within an exploratory case study of the Flight 93 National Memorial in Pennsylvania, USA—a site of the 9/11 atrocity. They evaluate the complexity and inimitability of children's dark tourism encounters and, specifically, evaluate four factors unique to children: (a) incomplete understanding of death, (b) lack of agency in choosing destinations, (c) youthful exploratory behaviour, and (d) emotional vulnerability. In so doing, Kerr and Price unlock a fresh and challenging yet rewarding study into children's experiences within dark tourism.

The fourth chapter (Chap. 24) by John Lennon considers the relationship between dark tourism, visualisation, and the particular role of photography (and the photographer). Lennon, who first brought to academic attention the concept of 'dark tourism' (Lennon and Foley 2000), offers a fascinating examination of the pivotal place photography occupies as both a form of dark tourism interpretation and as a pictorial record of tourist visitation and experience. Drawing upon notions of intertextuality where dark tourism images are viewed within complex relationships with texts, (hi)stories, and other images, Lennon argues that dark tourism photography, which is often distributed through mass online portals, have an infinite extension of possible meanings. The chapter specifically draws upon the work of Barthes (1981) who explored relationships between visual signifiers and mortality and how the photograph is a witness—but a witness of something that is no more. Lennon goes on to conclude that dark tourism photography as a medium provides the viewer with a testament to our painful past, our inability to move beyond it and our curious relationships with tragedy and death.

In the final chapter of this section (Chap. 25), Catherine Roberts offers a comprehensive account of educative experiences and notions of 'sensemaking' within dark tourism. In particular, Roberts explores inherent relationships between interpretation and education at specific dark tourism sites. In so doing, she critically appraises a range of factors, including attitudinal, emotional, and sensory issues, which influence capacity or propensity of visitors to engage with site interpretation. Roberts also outlines issues of learning and sensemaking from visitor behaviours and experiences, and subsequent relationships and values that might transpire. Roberts goes on to evaluate dark tourism's facility to support sensemaking within contexts of death, disaster, and atrocity. She concludes that dark tourism as a cultural mediating institution has a fundamental responsibility to support learning processes. Ultimately, Roberts suggests the rationale of dark tourism as an experiential learning experience is perhaps more relevant than simply the curation and display of distressing evidence of human suffering and misery.

As a final note, this section offers a thematic approach that is selective and not exhaustive. That said, given the dynamic and complex nature of dark tourism experiences, its global reach and the ever-increasing significance accorded to dark tourism as a focus of contemporary consumption, the 'experience economy' within dark tourism will continue to be a crucial area for scholarly exploration. It is hoped, therefore, that the chapters in this section will not only contribute to knowledge and understanding of a phenomenon that continues to grow in social and cultural significance, but will also act as a catalyst for future research within 'dark tourist' experiences.

References

Barthes, R. (1981). *Camera lucide: Reflections on photography* (trans: Howard, R.). New York: Hill and Wang.

Joly, D. (2010). *The dark tourist: Sightseeing in the world's most unlikely holiday destinations*. London: Simon & Schuster.

Lennon, J. J., & Foley, M. (2000). *Dark tourism – The attraction of death and disaster*. London: Continuum.

Sharpley, R., & Stone, P. R. (Eds.). (2011). *Tourist experience: Contemporary perspectives*. Abington: Routledge.

Sharpley, R., & Stone, P. R. (Eds.). (2012). *Contemporary tourist experience: Concepts and consequences*. Abington: Routledge.

Stone, P. R. (2012). Dark tourism and significant other death: Towards a model of mortality mediation. *Annals of Tourism Research, 39*(3), 1565–1587.

Stone, P. R., & Sharpley, R. (2008). Consuming dark tourism: A thanatological perspective. *Annals of Tourism Research, 35*(2), 574–595.

21

Unravelling Fear of Death Motives in Dark Tourism

Avital Biran and Dorina Maria Buda

Introduction

The relative simplicity of the term 'dark tourism', which has achieved a broad if not contested acceptance within academia and industry alike, is in contrast to the multifaceted nature of the phenomenon. Embedded in this complexity is the association dark tourism makes between the presentation and consumption of death in the context of tourism, as well as the complex relationships humans have with death and mortality—as individuals as well as societies. Tourism has been traditionally explored from a hedonistic perspective and, subsequently, has assumed that consumption of tourism products and destinations predominately serve the purpose of experiencing fun and pleasure (Gnoth 1997; Malone et al. 2014). Death, conflict, and atrocity sites which elicit sadness, distress, and an inherent sense of danger have been predominately considered deterring factors for tourists (Biran et al. 2014; Buda 2015a). An important aspect of dark tourism—that of human suffering—has made it difficult to apply traditional tourism motivational theories to its study (Dunkley et al. 2011). Moreover, with the seemingly pleasure-oriented consumption of tourism in places connected to death and tragedy, visits to such

A. Biran (✉)
Bournemouth University, Poole, UK

D. M. Buda
University of Groningen, Groningen, The Netherlands

sites have often been portrayed as immoral, deviant, or as a social pathology (Biran and Poria 2012; Stone and Sharpley 2013; also see Chap. 7).

As such, researchers in the rapidly emerging sub-field of dark tourism have been preoccupied with questions of tourist motivation, sought benefits, and experiences. These include but are not limited to questions such as why are tourists drawn to sites and experiences associated with death? Is it simply morbid curiosity or something else? Are dark tourism motives completely distinct from others, or are they a variety of motives for existing 'conventional' forms of tourism (such as heritage tourism, for example)? Why do tourists seemingly find gratification in visiting sites of horrible events? And, is this a 'normal' and socially accepted activity? Attempts to answer such questions have been frequently criticized as descriptive or as under-theorized and empirically fragile (Dunkley et al. 2011; Jamal and Lelo 2011; Stone 2011). Drawing upon a contemporary sociology of death, dark tourism has been conceptualized as a (post)modern-day practice for confronting death and mortality and, consequently, reducing the potential sense of dreading death (Stone and Sharpley 2008). Although this view has become widely accepted (Biran et al. 2014; Johnston 2013; Kidron 2013), there is limited investigation into the psychological mechanisms that lead people to engage with dark sites and, specifically, the role of fear of death in this.

Therefore, to address this gap in the literature, we adopt psychological theory and respond to several calls for a more critical understanding of the phenomenon of dark tourism. Particularly, Stone (2011) calls for dark tourism research to be grounded in broader (post)disciplinary frameworks that allow for a critical exploration of the phenomenon in a coherent and systematic manner. Meanwhile, Seaton (2009) appeals for enhanced psychological discourse in dark tourism research. More specifically, Buda advocates for more emotional and psychoanalytical explorations through concepts such as the death drive (Buda 2015b), desire (Buda and Shim 2014) and unconsciousness and voyeurism (Buda and McIntosh 2013). Similarly, the aim of this chapter is to adopt a psychological perspective and to discuss various ways fear of death is manifested in engagements with death in tourism. Firstly, this chapter will review the consumption of 'morbid fascination' with death in dark tourism. We then unravel the psychological interrelationships between death fears and dark tourism by drawing upon Terror Management Theory (TMT) which, in turn, provides further important explanatory power to that yielded by macro-sociological understandings of dark tourism. Ultimately, we propose death fears and anxiety shape our everyday life in various ways and, as such, these are manifested in dark tourism consumption as well as in other 'conventional' forms of tourism.

'Normalising' Dark Tourism: From 'Morbid Fascination' to Acceptable Fear of Death

Some earlier works point to dark tourism as possibly driven by 'ghoulish' interest in the macabre or, perhaps, an element of *schadenfreude* on the part of the tourist (Dann 1988; Sharpley 2009). However, more recent studies have contributed towards 'normalising' dark tourism, highlighting the role of death anxiety as a driving force which is socio-culturally accepted. Specifically, Stone and Sharpley (2008) conceptualize the phenomenon of dark tourism in terms of social congruence with how death is treated in (post)modern societies (also see Chap. 8). Their argument is that in modern society, death is sequestrated or hidden away behind medical and professional façades, with people growing detached from the process and consequences of death and dying. Traditional social institutions and rituals (for example, religion) which allowed individuals in certain 'Western' societies to give meaning to death and life and to deal with the terror that an awareness of mortality brings have gradually disappeared (also see Chap. 6).

In particular, and drawing upon Emile Durkheim's seminal work, Stone and Sharpley (2008) argue that it is this very absence of death in public discourse that makes people desire information about death. Thus, the presence of death within popular culture (as education, entertainment, or even humour) is a way of bringing death back into social consciousness and making it less threatening. Likewise, dark tourism, by offering repackaged 'Other' death as entertainment, education, memorialization, and moral instruction, allows individuals to contemplate and deal with fears of death and, subsequently, possibly restore ontological security and a sense of mortality meaning in a socially acceptable environment (Stone 2009c, 2012; Stone and Sharpley 2008). This active search (or at least consequent) of confronting death is also explored via the psychoanalytic concept of voyeurism, whereby consumption and performance of dark tourism is driven by a desire to look at something forbidden. Moving beyond a simplistic understanding of dark tourism motivations, Buda and McIntosh (2013) examine the experiential nature of dark tourism and offer a holistic and nuanced perspective of dark tourism motives and drives. Continuing in this psychoanalytic perspective, it is argued that tourists, in their quest for the unusual, whether unusual places or unusual experiences, also mobilize desire for fantasy (Buda and Shim 2014). Thus, they conjure imaginations of dark, forbidden, and possibly dangerous activities and locations. Fantasy supports desire and can be understood in connection to conscious daydreams and to unconscious psychological activities, which Sigmund Freud called 'psychical realities'.

Arguably, therefore, dark tourism is a contemporary socio-cultural, political, and spatial institution (among others) to deal with ontological anxieties, fears, and desires—particularly fear of death, of the unusual, and of the unknown. Accordingly, while earlier discussions of dark tourism consumption focused solely on motivation, these have shifted to considering drives, the actual emotional experiences, as well as consequences and benefits of dark tourism activities. Theorising dark tourism in conjunction with psychoanalysis, emotions, and the sociological condition of death in society, academic divisions evident in earlier works have started to be bridged. Particularly, Stone and Sharpley's thanatological framework, stemming from a sociology of death, has become used widely to explore dark tourism consumption (Biran and Hyde 2013). For instance, Biran et al. (2011) reinterpret previous studies of dark tourism motives in light of Stone and Sharpley's (2008) conceptualization. Their reinterpretation suggests the existence of *leisure-pursuit* motives, similar to those of visiting 'regular' sites along with *mortality-related* motives—including curiosities to understand how atrocities happened, social responsibility, identity construction, empathetic identification, and remembrance and commemoration.

Despite a common acceptance of this thanatological framework, there have been limited attempts to explore further and develop the ideas raised by this framework (Biran and Hyde 2013). As such, it still lacks empirical support, and potential advances of the theory remain incomplete. Moreover, while Stone and Sharpley (2008) emphasize the role of external socio-cultural settings and processes in shaping dark tourism engagement, there is little understanding of the internal psychological mechanisms driving this death-related touristic practice (Buda 2015b; Johnston 2013; Seaton 2009). There is also a surprising unawareness with regard to the role of fear of death and how it shapes and influences people's engagement with dark sites. To address this issue and to further an understanding of dark tourism motives and experiences, as well as their roles in confronting death and dying, we suggest the use of psychological theories, and it is this that the chapter now turns to.

The Psychology of 'Fear of Death' in Dark Tourism

The inevitability of death ensures it is present in every area of our life and human existence. Hence, social scientists have long been captivated by the seemingly 'terrifying' and 'paralysing' experience brought about by humans' awareness of their mortality, together with its cognitive and behavioural consequences (Mikulincer and Florian 2008). In psychology, the study of death was largely neglected until the mid-1920s (Feifel 1990) but has now gained scholarship. This is because of two key reasons: firstly, the growing prominence of existential psychology with an emphasis on death as a philosophical theme and, secondly, both World Wars and the Holocaust, which raised fundamental questions of meaning, purpose, and the transience of life (Feifel 1990; Kastenbaum 2000).

The relevance of a sociology of death was introduced into dark tourism research by Stone and Sharpley (2008). However, the potential contribution of psychology and, specifically, a psychology of death to this subject field have largely been overlooked thus far. An exception is Buda (2015a, b) who draws on psychoanalysis and the concept of the death drive to explore tourists' experiences of danger zones. Adopting a critical theoretical approach and employing a qualitative epistemology, Buda argues that some tourists seek to be confronted with their own death fears while engaging in danger-zone tourism. Buda also suggests that this confrontation with death fears allows individuals to reshape memories and identities as well as coming to terms with past events. Crucially, therefore, Buda stresses the need to consider the role of fear of death in shaping dark tourism experiences, as well as examining how people negotiate fear of death and dying, and giving meaning to tragic events through encounters with commoditized death. However, psychoanalysis is yet to mature within tourism studies. Indeed, some scholars critique the application of psychoanalysis within tourism research, noting it is a 'fading tradition' with loose and difficult-to-apply concepts (Pearce and Packer 2013, p. 387). Meanwhile, in human geography (Callard 2003; Kingsbury et al. 2014; Sibley 2003) and tourism geography (Buda 2015a; Kingsbury 2005; Kingsbury and Brunn 2004), psychoanalysis as a body of knowledge is employed to interpret various (tourist) experiences, especially those involving fantasy, desire, drives, and the unconscious, amongst others. However, for the purpose of this chapter, we employ the contemporary psychological theory 'Terror Management Theory' (TMT) and explore its potential role and application within dark tourism.

Terror Management Theory and Dark Tourism

Terror Management Theory is amongst the most extensively researched areas in social psychology, with over 300 experiments conducted in 15 different countries which have provided support for its hypotheses (Burke et al. 2010; Pyszczynski et al. 2006). It was developed as a formalization of the theoretical work by Ernest Becker (1971, 1973) who proposed an integrative interdisciplinary analysis of human motivation based on the works of philosophers such as Soren Kierkergaard, Otto Rank, Gergory Zilboorg, and Norman Brown. TMT's central proposition is that the juxtaposition between human cognitive ability to realize the inevitability of their mortality and the innate instinct of self-preservation results in paralysing fear (Greenberg et al. 1986; Pyszczynski et al. 2006). In the words of Becker (1973, p. xii):

> This is the terror: to have emerged from nothing, to have a name, consciousness of self, deep inner feelings, an excruciating inner yearning for life and self-expression – and with all this yet to die.

Thus, human beings are constantly battling existential fears which need to be managed so that one is not in a continuous state of terror (Goldenberg et al. 1999). The same intellectual capacities that give rise to the fear of death have also constructed the means for managing this terror through the creation of (death denying) cultural systems of belief (Goldenberg et al. 1999, 2000). TMT postulates humans cope with the feeling of terror that death induces by striving for *literal immortality* (existence after death in a form transcending the physical body, e.g., belief in the afterlife) and *symbolic immortality* (sense of being part of something greater than oneself and of infinite existence). These are achieved through two anxiety buffering processes. Firstly, the faith in a shared cultural worldview and, secondly, the preservation of one's self esteem, which is attained by living up to one's cultural worldviews (Goldenberg et al. 2000; Pyszczynski et al. 2006, 2015).

Cultural worldviews refer to the belief in the correctness and persistence of the cultural norms and values one feels belonging to. Being part of a culture and engaging with its shared values and rituals provide individuals with a sense of symbolic mortality by offering structure, continuity, and meaning to life and death (Goldenberg et al. 2000; Hofer 2013; Rieger et al. 2015). Such systems of belief ease our fear of death by answering fundamental questions such as: How did I get here? How should I live my life? What will happen when I die? Additionally, cultural worldviews provide individuals with principles for meaningful and valuable behaviour (Goldenberg et al. 2000; Goulding et al. 2013). As cultural worldviews function as an anxiety buffer against the uncertain universe, when reminded of death (i.e., our mortality becomes salient), individuals desire to behave in a manner that will reinforce and defend their cultural worldview. Indeed, this notion was supported by a range of empirical studies. It is shown that, after reminders of one's own mortality, individuals react more positively to ideas and people which share or support their worldviews and display negative reactions to those who threaten it. For example, people show greater interest in and a more positive evaluation of others sharing their religious belief or political values; conversely, people are less interested and negatively evaluate dissimilar others and those who criticize their culture (Burke et al. 2010; Pyszczynski et al. 2006, 2015).

Another way by which we negotiate our fear of death is through maintaining a high sense of self-esteem, namely one's concept of self-worth (Pyszczynski et al. 2006, 2015). Self-esteem is related to our cultural worldviews as it is derived, at least partly, from societal feedback regarding the extent to which one preforms and functions as a member of a certain cultural or social system (Goldenberg et al. 2000). People derive a sense of symbolic immortality by feeling that they meet the cultural standards of their social group and thus, are valuable members of something meaningful and long lasting. This notion of legacy includes leaving reminders of one's own existence such as children, monuments, or anything else tangible (e.g., books, music) or intangible, such as ideas and memories that will persist in perpetuity (Goldenberg et al. 2000; Pyszczynski et al. 2015; Van Marle and Maruna 2010). Moreover, notions of the afterlife that are evident in most cultures (such as Heaven, reincarnations, nirvana) reflect the promise of literal immortality if one lives up to the standards and values prescribed by her/his cultural worldviews (Goldenberg et al. 2000; Van Marle and Maruna 2010). While most studies have focused on exploring the effects of death thoughts on cultural worldview defences (Burke et al. 2010), there is evidence that people also activate their self-esteem to deal with death fears. By way of illustration, Mandel and Heine (1999) suggest that consumers exposed to death-related information favoured purchasing luxury brands (e.g., Rolex, Lexus) over non-luxury brands, as these strengthen consumers' social status in a consumer-driven culture, thus reinforcing positive self-esteem. Death-related thoughts also increase self-esteem striving in the form of risk taking, desire for fame, and preferences for self-esteem enhancing romantic partners (Burke et al. 2010; Pyszczynski et al. 2006).

The problem of death lies beneath consciousness. Hence, the contribution of TMT as a psychological tool is in the exploration of processes which are outside conscious awareness—that is, maintaining worldviews and self-esteem (Goldenberg et al. 2000; Pyszczynski et al. 2006, 2015). These two anxiety-buffer mechanisms are *distal* defences. In other words, they are unconscious, less rational, and have remote connection to the problem of death. These defences are experientially embedded through early life, namely, during childhood where we learn to associate the immersion in symbolic reality convened by parents and other cultural agents, and meeting standards of value and behaviour with a sense of meaning, love, support, safety, and security (Burke et al. 2010; Goldenberg et al. 2000; Pyszczynski et al. 2015). Yet, people also defend themselves against the fears of death by employing *proximal* defences which are more rational, conscious, and directly related to the threat of death. For example, by denying their vulnerability, pushing the problem of death to the distant future (e.g., I do not smoke that much, I am in great shape) or simply avoiding and supressing such fearful thoughts (Burke et al. 2010; Goldenberg et al. 2000; Hofer 2013; Pyszczynski et al. 2006). Proximal defences push death further from awareness yet do not negate the fear or the fact that death is inevitable—thereby ensuring such thoughts always linger (Pyszczynski et al. 2006, 2015). The core of the anxiety-buffering system according to TMT are the distal defences which prevent these implicit death-related fears from surfacing into consciousness by requiring people to view themselves as valuable parts of a meaningful world.

Nevertheless, TMT was not developed simply to explain the effects of fear of death on people's behaviour but rather why people are so invested in sustaining their belief systems and protecting their sense of value. Conversely, it illustrates the unique effect of fear of death on our lives, including behaviours which do not carry obvious and immediate relation to the problem of death. Amongst these are issues that may centre on nationalism, social judgments, interpersonal attraction and romantic love, attraction to the physical aspects of sex, charitable giving, stereotyping, health promotion behaviour, legal decision-making, and risk taking (Burke et al. 2010; Pyszczynski et al. 2006, 2015). So, the question is that if we engage with terror management in various areas of our lives, why not in tourism too? Of particular importance in this context is the application of TMT to explaining consumer behaviour which illustrates the role of consumption in dealing with death fears by enhancing one's cultural worldviews and/or sense of self-esteem. For instance, Kasser and Sheldon (2000) report that participants exposed to death reminders planned to dedicate larger sums of money to 'pleasurable spending', including travel, leisure, and entertainment. More recently, studies have considered the role of cultural goods, such as media and entertainment (e.g., music, films, literature) as buffers against fear of death (Goldenberg et al. 1999; Hofer 2013; Kneer and Rieger 2015; Rieger et al. 2015; Taylor 2013). Specifically, media psychology scholars are increasingly intrigued (perhaps similar to dark tourism scholars) with the paradoxical consumption of 'meaningful entertainment', which centres on themes of death, tragedy, violence, moral virtue and may raise mixed emotions (Klimmt 2011; Oliver et al. 2012). The few available empirical studies demonstrate the potential of such types of entertainment in addressing terror management needs (e.g., Kneer and Rieger 2015; Rieger et al. 2015). Following from these studies, we contend that dark tourism as a form of *meaningful entertainment* consumption equally functions as a psychological buffer against fears of death.

Terror Management Theory and Meaningful Entertainment Through Dark Tourism

Goldenberg et al. (1999) were the first to draw on TMT to explain the paradoxical appeal of tragedy as a form of entertainment (within the form of a tragic novel, *Farewell to Arms*). Subsequently, these authors argued that tragedies may be attractive and enjoyable since they allow people to approach their death fears and reflect on their own mortality in a safe, culturally acceptable, and relevant manner. In particular, Goldenberg et al. (1999) suggest that engaging with entertainment which is focused on death and tragedy poses no risk to the individual as it is someone else (the protagonist) who dies, and thus, the individual is not forced to reflect directly on their own mortality. Indeed, their research findings indicate that death reminders increased the appeal of tragedy, namely participants were more touched by the tragic extract and found a non-tragic book less enjoyable. Although Goldenberg's study focused on a certain form of meaningful entertainment (literature), the findings nonetheless provide some empirical support to Stone's (2011, 2012) argument that death-related tourism provides an opportunity to contemplate death of the Self through gazing upon the Significant Other Dead.

More specifically, meaningful entertainment, which arguably includes death-related tourism or 'dark tourism', often grapples with questions of life's profundities and conveys central values and worldviews (Oliver et al. 2012; Rieger et al. 2015; Stone 2009a, 2012; Stone and Sharpley 2013). Therefore, meaningful entertainment may function, for some—at least for some of the time—as a death anxiety-buffer by activating our cultural worldview defence. For example, for fans of this genre, listening to heavy metal music, which is often associated with themes of death and dying and may be considered a form of (sub)culture, can serve as a cultural buffer against existential anguish and death-related thoughts (Kneer and Rieger 2015). In short, listening to metal music can remind fans of this part of their social identity and enhance their identification with their significant cultural in-group, allowing for a sense of symbolic immortality.

Similarly, dark tourism sites may facilitate cultural worldview defences as they communicate and sustain shared values and one's sense of belonging or identification with a meaningful in-group. Following Stone (2012), it can be argued that dark tourism may activate cultural worldview defences through narratives of education, memorialization, and moral instructions. This is particularly true in relation to visiting death-related heritage sites or sites occupying the darker end of Stone's (2006) 'dark tourism spectrum' typology, which often function as political or social resources in legitimizing certain worldviews and constructing social identities (Feldman 2002; Poria et al. 2009; Stone 2006). For example, Osbaldiston and Petray (2011) note that collective rituals in Gallipoli in the form of national anthems, poems, and monuments transform the sense of horror, fear, and isolation that death can bring into feelings of patriotism and collective effervescence (and even joy). Previous studies have also noted the importance of learning about and feeling part of one's cultural heritage as a key motivation for visitors who consider these sites as part of their heritage (Biran et al. 2011; Poria et al. 2006). Similarly, we visit sites such as war memorials, battlefields, military cemeteries, and even sites of genocide which commemorate and memorialize those who have defended, fought for, or died in the name of our cultural worldview and the lasting existence of our in-group (e.g., nation, ethnic minority). As Walter (2009, p. 42) aptly notes, 'the modern state creates and recreates sacred ancestors, bestowing immortality on its heroes.'. Such sites provide meaning through literal and symbolic immortality of in-group members, the heroes or victims who will be remembered, those who have survived (for instance, genocide and other atrocities) in the face of impossible conditions, and the association of group membership with life and meaningfulness.

Moreover, 'lighter dark' sites (Stone 2006) can also bolster cultural worldviews and address terror management needs. As Stone (2012) suggests, even 'dark fun factories' such as the London Dungeon visitor attraction in the UK include educational elements and offer moral instructions which help shape, reinforce, and validate a person's worldviews and belief system. Indeed, the Dungeon experience prompts visitors to reflect on questions of justice, penal codes, as well as issues of punishment and torture by comparing past and present societal values and practices (Stone 2009a, b, 2012; Stone and Sharpley 2013). In turn, this may allow visitors to affirm the higher moral grounds of (their) modern worldviews which will not accept past (often brutal) practices (Stone 2009b, 2012). Finally, beyond dark tourism, the management of existential fears through cultural worldview anxiety-buffer is also reflected in tourism consumption in general. Consequently, religious or spiritual tourism, secular pilgrimages, visits to cultural and (not death-related) heritage sites, as well as roots/genealogy tourism that allow us to strengthen social bonds and confirm in-group systems of belief might be considered as examples.

At first glance, cultural worldview defences may be more obviously reflected in dark tourism consumption, though self-esteem striving is also manifest in dark tourism engagement. Indeed, people can derive a sense of self-worth by visiting dark sites which are of relative importance and possess symbolic meaning to their in-group and which represent the group's values and social identity (e.g., battlefields, genocide sites, or memorials). For example, visits to sites such as Gallipoli, Auschwitz, or places of genocide in Rwanda or Cambodia are encouraged, socially rewarded, and even considered obligatory, as they are seen as educational, commemorative, and central to the identity of certain social groups (Biran and Poria 2012; Biran et al. 2011; Feldman 2002; Hyde and Harman 2011; Slade 2003). Particularly, with regard to Holocaust-related sites, different agencies in Israel offer some financial support to youths whose families cannot afford to fund their participation in educative school trips to Poland (and Auschwitz-Birkenau Memorial and Museum). Hence, as visits to such sites are seen as a standard or highly valued behaviour by one's in-group, visitation affirms our adherence to the cultural worldview and values of our meaningful cultural group and, in turn, can bolster our self-esteem.

TMT studies also suggest that when faced with death fears, people tend to exhibit risky behaviour (e.g., risky driving, drug use, sun bathing, scuba diving, precarious career decision-making) as such behaviours contribute to enhancing one's positive self-esteem (Landau and Greenberg 2006; Miller et al. 2004; Pyszczynski et al. 2015; Routledge et al. 2004, 2008). Likewise, engaging with death-related tourism, which (re)presents horrific sights and atrocities and involves sensations of fear, anguish, and danger (Buda 2015a, b; Nawijn and Fricke 2015), may be seen as a (psychologically) risky behaviour. Arguably, within that context, visitors derive a sense of self-worth from the knowledge that they have faced and 'survived' these horrible events, considering themselves as emotionally strong and courageous. For example, Buda (2015b) indicates that for some tourists in danger-zones, it is all about showing and telling others that 'they were there' during a violent conflict and that it did not really scare them. This is relevant for different types of dark tourism places, even for fun factories which present gory scenes of death and violence and offer a scary and frightful experience (Bristow and Newman 2004; Stone 2009b).

Finally, addressing terror management needs through self-esteem activation takes place within the broader context of tourism and leisure consumption. For example, exploring risk-taking as a behaviour that validates and enhances self-esteem, Miller et al. (2004) found that death reminders led scuba divers with low self-esteem and self-efficacy to display greater willingness to take diving risks. Furthermore, leisure and tourism have long been considered to play a key role in individuals' self-esteem, through mastering skills and constructing positive self and social identity (e.g., Garst et al. 2001; Page and Connell 2010). Thus, it may be argued that tourism participation, as a whole, can provide opportunities for buffering existential fears through self-esteem enhancement.

Exploring the consumption of dark tourism as a form of *meaningful entertainment* through the lens of TMT suggests the appeal of dark tourism stems from its potential to buffer against death and existential fears. Compared to other sociological, thanatological, and psychoanalytic approaches adopted in dark tourism scholarship thus far, TMT offers a more nuanced understanding of *why* and *how* death-related tourism may mitigate fear of death. In other words, adopting a TMT perspective illuminates the unconscious psychological processes, cultural worldviews, and self-esteem defence mechanisms which underline the effects of fear of death on individual behaviour within the context of tourism. Additionally, the current conceptualization stresses further that fascination with death and the fear of death are embodied and socially accepted parts of the human experience and affect our behaviour in almost all areas of our lives. As such, death-related tourism may be viewed as a diverse, socio-culturally accepted and meaningful behaviour and not as a social pathology. Moreover, beyond understanding dark tourism consumption, TMT raises the need to further consider fundamental interrelationships between death fears and tourism (Buda 2015b). That is, since the ongoing and contentious need to manage the fear and terror that death can bring is manifested in other forms of tourism consumption, in which death is not necessarily the core theme of the tourism product or experience.

Conclusion

Thanatological conceptualizations of dark tourism consumption have contributed to the 'normalization' of dark tourism. Dark tourism is no longer considered only a 'deviant' behaviour of self-gratification 'sought out by necrophilic tourists' (Kidron 2013, p. 177), but can also offer meaningful experiences of contemplating death and life. We claim that dark tourism is a socially acceptable (post)modern practice for dealing with our inherent and shared fear of death. To demonstrate our claim, we draw on psychological theory and elaborate on the underlining psychological mechanisms of negotiating death fears. These fears, we argue, can shape dark tourism consumption and experiences. Within a TMT framework, it is suggested that death-related tourism allows negotiation of death fear since it may function as an anxiety-buffer mechanism by sustaining: firstly, our faith in shared cultural worldviews and, secondly, one's sense of self-esteem, which is attained by living up to one's own cultural worldview. Consequently, dark tourism facilitates a sense of symbolic and literal immortality, meaning, and continuity by satisfying one's sense of belonging to something bigger, long lasting as well as being a valuable member of a social group. Therefore, the conceptualization we have outlined in this chapter provides for a more nuanced understanding of dark tourism consumption, which considers both socio-cultural processes (as suggested by thanatological conceptualizations based on the sociology of death) and internal, individual process (as suggested here based on the psychology of death). Moreover, we suggest that other forms of tourism, which are not themed around death (e.g., religious tourism, family tourism, adventure tourism), can also be analysed and understood via a TMT conceptual application. Thus, we call for further critical explorations of various ways through which people negotiate existential fears in tourism practices.

The application of TMT, as suggested in this chapter, may advance research into the fundamental connections between death fears and (dark) tourism consumption. Specifically, central to the thanatological perspective of dark tourism consumption is the connection between ontological (in)security and patterns of behaviour (Seaton 2009; Stone and Sharpley 2008). Anxieties about the meaning of the surrounding world and our own mortality are mirrored in the consumption of (death-related) tourism, which allows for a construction of meaning in the face of death and, subsequently, a restoration of ontological security. Yet, the ontological insecurity concept has been critiqued as being too abstract and problematic to reliably operationalize (Tonry 2004; Van Marle and Maruna 2010). Thus, it may be of limited use for empirically examining the assumed role of fear of death within dark tourism experiences. Conversely, the substantial empirical evidence validating TMT (Burke et al. 2010; Pyszczynski et al. 2015) can be used to provide support and explore empirically the notion of ontological insecurity at the individual and psychological level. In this chapter, therefore, we lay the foundations and provide the tools for future research to venture into exploring 'whether dark tourism will invoke a greater or lesser extent of ontological (in)security, and whether packaged-up death provides reassurance or threatens an individuals' life-world' (Stone 2012, p. 1582).

Whilst conceptualising dark tourism within the context of TMT, we also argue that dealing with one's own fears, whether fear of death or any other type of fear, may provide (more) meaning to life. Stone (2011, 2012) similarly argues that dark tourism experiences are not merely about consuming narratives of death but about contemplating life and living in the face of inevitable mortality. Dark tourism sites provoke reflections on hope, health, and on how one should live morally and by what ethical standards. Within dark tourism experiences, the juxtaposition of death and fear alongside life and providing meaning to life is also argued by Buda (2015a, b) and Kidron (2013). Hence, this juxtaposition highlights the need to recognize the blurred boundaries between life and death and between fear and fun in dark tourism experiences.

However, despite the potential of TMT to advance an understanding of dark tourism consumption and experiences, there are several limitations worthy of note. Firstly, TMT is based on an experimental research design, which is uncommon and may be difficult to implement within tourism research. Therefore, it remains to be ascertained if and how future studies will explore the activation of terror management buffering processes in the real-world context of dark tourism. Moreover, though TMT elaborates on our reactions to psychological encounters with mortality, it is important to note that fear of death is not uni-dimensional. Indeed, there are various types of fears, including but not limited to the loss of self-fulfilment, fear of the physical decomposition of the body, as well as fear of the consequences of death to family and friends (Florian and Kravetz 1983; Mikulincer and Florian 2008). Each may shape dark tourism consumption patterns and experiences in different ways. Finally, the conceptualization in this chapter focuses on the prominent theory of TMT, but the broader field of death psychology may offer various other avenues to further explore the ways in which tourists tackle fears of death and dying.

References

Becker, E. (1971). *The birth and death of meaning*. New York: Free Press.
Becker, E. (1973). *The denial of death*. New York: Free Press Paperbacks.
Biran, A., & Hyde, K. F. (2013). New perspectives on dark tourism. *International Journal of Culture, Tourism and Hospitality Research, 7*(3), 191–198. https://doi.org/10.1108/IJCTHR-05-2013-0032.
Biran, A., & Poria, Y. (2012). Re-conceptualizing dark tourism. In R. Sharpley & P. R. Stone (Eds.), *Contemporary tourist experience: Concepts and consequences* (pp. 57–70). London: Routledge.
Biran, A., Poria, Y., & Oren, G. (2011). Sought experiences at (dark) heritage sites. *Annals of Tourism Research, 38*(3), 820–841. https://doi.org/10.1016/j.annals.2010.12.001.
Biran, A., Liu, W., Li, G., & Eichhorn, V. (2014). Consuming post-disaster destinations: The case of Sichuan, China. *Annals of Tourism Research, 47*(0), 1–17. https://doi.org/10.1016/j.annals.2014.03.004.

Bristow, R., & Newman, M. (2004). Myth vs. fact: An exploration of fright tourism. In *Proceedings of the 2004 northeastern recriation research symposium* (pp. 215–221). Westfiled: Westfiled State College.

Buda, D. M. (2015a). *Affective tourism: Dark routes in conflict*. London: Routledge.

Buda, D. M. (2015b). The death drive in tourism studies. *Annals of Tourism Research, 50*(0), 39–51. https://doi.org/10.1016/j.annals.2014.10.008.

Buda, D. M., & McIntosh, A. J. (2013). Dark tourism and voyeurism: Tourist arrested for "spying" in Iran. *International Journal of Culture, Tourism and Hospitality Research, 7*(3), 214–226. https://doi.org/10.1108/IJCTHR-07-2012-0059.

Buda, D. M., & Shim, D. (2014). Desiring the dark: 'a taste for the unusual' in north Korean tourism? *Current Issues in Tourism, 18*(1), 1–6. https://doi.org/10.1080/13683500.2014.948813.

Burke, B. L., Martens, A., & Faucher, E. H. (2010). Two decades of terror management theory: A meta-analysis of mortality salience research. *Personality and Social Psychology Review, 14*(2), 155–195. https://doi.org/10.1177/1088868309352321.

Callard, F. (2003). The taming of psychoanalysis in geography. *Social & Cultural Geography, 4*(3), 295–312. https://doi.org/10.1080/14649360309071.

Dann, G. (1988). *The dark side of tourism. Etudes et rapports, se'rie L*. Aix-en-Provence: Centre International de Recherches et d'Etudes Touristiques.

Dunkley, R. A., Morgan, N., & Westwood, S. (2011). Visiting the trenches: Exploring meanings and motivations in battlefield tourism. *Tourism Management, 32*(4), 860–868. https://doi.org/10.1016/j.tourman.2010.07.011.

Feifel, H. (1990). Psychology and death: Meaningful rediscovery. *American Psychologist, 45*(4), 537–543. https://doi.org/10.1037/0003-066X.45.4.537.

Feldman, J. (2002). Marking the boundaries of the enclave: Defining the Israeli collective rough the Poland 'experience'. *Israel Studies, 7*(2), 84.

Florian, V., & Kravetz, S. (1983). Fear of personal death: Attribution, structure, and relation to religious belief. *Journal of Personality and Social Psychology, 44*(3), 600–607. https://doi.org/10.1037/0022-3514.44.3.600.

Garst, B., Scheider, I., & Baker, D. (2001). Outdoor adventure program participation impacts on adolescent self-perception. *The Journal of Experimental Education, 24*(1), 41–49. https://doi.org/10.1177/105382590102400109.

Gnoth, J. (1997). Motivation and expectation formation. *Annals of Tourism Research, 24*(2), 283–304.

Goldenberg, J. L., Pyszczynski, T., Johnson, K. D., Greenberg, J., & Solomon, S. (1999). The appeal of tragedy: A terror management perspective. *Media Psychology, 1*(4), 313–329. https://doi.org/10.1207/s1532785xmep0104_2.

Goldenberg, J. L., Pyszczynski, T., Greenberg, J., & Solomon, S. (2000). Fleeing the body: A terror management perspective on the problem of human corporeality. *Personality and Social Psychology Review, 4*(3), 200–218. https://doi.org/10.1207/s15327957pspr0403_1.

Goulding, C., Saren, M., & Lindridge, A. (2013). Reading the body at von Hagen's 'body worlds'. *Annals of Tourism Research, 40*(0), 306–330. https://doi.org/10.1016/j.annals.2012.08.008.

Greenberg, J., Pyszczynski, T., & Solomon, S. (1986). The causes and consequences of a need for self-esteem: A terror management theory. In R. F. Baumeister (Ed.), *Public self and private self* (pp. 189–212). New York: Springer.

Hofer, M. (2013). Appreciation and enjoyment of meaningful entertainment: The role of mortality salience and search for meaning in life. *Journal of Media Psychology: Theories, Methods, and Applications, 25*(3), 109–117. https://doi.org/10.1027/1864-1105/a000089.

Hyde, K. F., & Harman, S. (2011). Motives for a secular pilgrimage to the Gallipoli battlefields. *Tourism Management, 32*(6), 1343–1351. https://doi.org/10.1016/j.tourman.2011.01.008.

Jamal, T., & Lelo, L. (2011). Exploring the conceptual and analytical framing: From darkness to intentionality. In S. Richard & P. Stone (Eds.), *Tourist experience: Contemporary perspectives*. London: Routledge.

Johnston, T. (2013). Mark twain and the innocents abroad: Illuminating the tourist gaze on death. *International Journal of Culture, Tourism and Hospitality Research, 7*(3), 199–213. https://doi.org/10.1108/IJCTHR-05-2012-0036.

Kasser, T., & Sheldon, K. M. (2000). Of wealth and death: Materialism, mortality salience, and consumption behavior. *Psychological Science, 11*(July), 348–351.

Kastenbaum, R. (2000). *The psychology of death* (3rd ed.). New York: Springer.

Kidron, C. A. (2013). Being there together: Dark family tourism and the emotive experience of co-presence in the holocaust past. *Annals of Tourism Research, 41*(0), 175–194. https://doi.org/10.1016/j.annals.2012.12.009.

Kingsbury, P. (2005). Jamaican tourism and the politics of enjoyment. *Geoforum, 36*(1), 113–132. https://doi.org/10.1016/j.geoforum.2004.03.012.

Kingsbury, P., & Brunn, S. (2004). Freud, tourism, and terror. *Journal of Travel & Tourism Marketing, 15*(2–3), 39–61. https://doi.org/10.1300/J073v15n02_03.

Kingsbury, P., Pile, S., & Blum, V. L. (2014). *Psychoanalytic geographies* (p. 2014). Burlington: Ashgate.

Klimmt, C. (2011). Media psychology and complex modes of entertainment experiences. *Journal of Media Psychology: Theories, Methods, and Applications, 23*(1), 34–38. https://doi.org/10.1027/1864-1105/a000030.

Kneer, J., & Rieger, D. (2015). The memory remains: How heavy metal fans buffer against the fear of death. *Psychology of Popular Media Culture*. https://doi.org/10.1037/ppm0000072.

Landau, M. J., & Greenberg, J. (2006). Play it safe or go for the gold? A terror management perspective on self-enhancement and self-protective motives in risky decision making. *Personality and Social Psychology Bulletin, 32*(12), 1633–1645. https://doi.org/10.1177/0146167206292017.

Malone, S., McCabe, S., & Smith, A. P. (2014). The role of hedonism in ethical tourism. *Annals of Tourism Research, 44*(0), 241–254. https://doi.org/10.1016/j.annals.2013.10.005.

Mandel, N., & Heine, S. J. (1999). Terror management and marketing: He who dies with the most toys wins. *Advances in Consumer Research, 26*(1), 527–532.

Mikulincer, M., & Florian, V. (2008). The complex and multifaced nature of the fear of personal death: The multidimensional model of victor Florian. In A. Tomer, G. T. Eliason, & P. T. P. Wong (Eds.), *Existential and spiritual issues in death attitudes* (pp. 39–64). New York: Lawrence Erlbaum Associates.

Miller, G., Taubman, O., & Ben, A. (2004). Scuba diving risk taking – A terror management theory perspective, *Journal of Sport & Exercise Psychology, 26*, 269–282.

Nawijn, J., & Fricke, M.-C. (2015). Visitor emotions and behavioral intentions: The case of concentration camp memorial Neuengamme. *International Journal of Tourism Research, 17*(3), 221–228. https://doi.org/10.1002/jtr.1977.

Oliver, M. B., Hartmann, T., & Woolley, J. K. (2012). Elevation in response to entertainment portrayals of moral virtue. *Human Communication Research, 38*(3), 360–378. https://doi.org/10.1111/j.1468-2958.2012.01427.x.

Osbaldiston, N., & Petray, T. (2011). The role of horror and dread in the sacred experience. *Tourist Studies, 11*(2), 175–190. https://doi.org/10.1177/1468797611424955.

Page, S., & Connell, J. (2010). *Leisure: An introduction*. Harlow: Prentice Hall.

Pearce, P. L., & Packer, J. (2013). Minds on the move: New links from psychology to tourism. *Annals of Tourism Research, 40*(1), 386–411. https://doi.org/10.1016/j.annals.2012.10.002.

Poria, Y., Reichel, A., & Biran, A. (2006). Heritage site management: Motivations and expectations. *Annals of Tourism Research, 33*(1), 162–178. https://doi.org/10.1016/j.annals.2005.08.001.

Poria, Y., Biran, A., & Reichel, A. (2009). Visitors' preferences for interpretation at heritage sites. *Journal of Travel Research, 48*, 92–105.

Pyszczynski, T., Greenberg, J., Solomon, S., & Maxfield, M. (2006). On the unique psychological import of the human awareness of mortality: Theme and variations. *Psychological Inquiry, 17*(4), 328–356.

Pyszczynski, T., Solomon, S., & Greenberg, J. (2015). Thirty years of terror management theory: From genesis to revelation. *Advances in Experimental Social Psychology, 52*, 1–70.

Rieger, D., Frischlich, L., Högden, F., Kauf, R., Schramm, K., & Tappe, E. (2015). Appreciation in the face of death: Meaningful films buffer against death-related anxiety. *Journal of Communication, 65*(2), 351–372. https://doi.org/10.1111/jcom.12152.

Routledge, C., Arndt, J., & Goldenberg, J. L. (2004). A time to tan: Proximal and distal effects of mortality salience on sun exposure intentions. *Personality and Social Psychology Bulletin, 30*(10), 1347–1358. https://doi.org/10.1177/0146167204264056.

Routledge, C., Arndt, J., Sedikides, C., & Wildschut, T. (2008). A blast from the past: The terror management function of nostalgia. *Journal of Experimental Social Psychology, 44*(1), 132–140. https://doi.org/10.1016/j.jesp.2006.11.001.

Seaton, A. V. (2009). Thanatourism and its discontents: An appraisal of decade's work with some future issues and directions. In T. Jamal & M. Robinson (Eds.), *The Sage handbook of tourism studies* (pp. 521–542). London: Sage.

Sharpley, R. (2009). Shedding light on dark tourism: An introduction. In R. Sharpley & P. R. Stone (Eds.), *The darker side of travel: The theory and practice of dark tourism* (pp. 3–22). Bristol: Channel View Publications.

Sibley, D. (2003). Geography and psychoanalysis: Tensions and possibilities. *Social & Cultural Geography, 4*(3), 391–399. https://doi.org/10.1080/14649360309070.

Slade, P. (2003). Gallipoli thanatourism: The meaning of ANZAC. *Annals of Tourism Research, 30*(4), 779–794. https://doi.org/10.1016/S0160-7383(03)00025-2.

Stone, P. R. (2006). Dark tourism Spectrum: Towards a typology of death and macabre related tourist sites, attractions and exhibitions. *Tourism, 54*(2), 145–160.

Stone, P. R. (2009a). Dark tourism: Morality and new moral spaces. In R. Sharpley & P. R. Stone (Eds.), *The darker side of travel: The theory and practice of dark tourism* (pp. 56–72). Bristol: Channel View Publications.

Stone, P. R. (2009b). It's a bloody guide': Fun, fear and a lighter side of dark tourism at the dungeon visitor attractions, UK. In R. Sharpley & P. R. Stone (Eds.), *The darker side of travel: The theory and practice of dark tourism* (pp. 167–185). Bristol: Channel View Publications.

Stone, P. R. (2009c). Making absent death present: Consuming dark tourism in contemporary society. In R. Sharpley & P. R. Stone (Eds.), *The darker side of travel: The theory and practice of dark tourism* (pp. 23–38). Bristol: Channel View Publications.

Stone, P. R. (2011). Dark tourism: Towards a new post-disciplinary research agenda. *International Journal of Tourism Anthropology, 1*(3/4), 318–332.

Stone, P. R. (2012). Dark tourism and significant other death: Towards a model of mortality mediation. *Annals of Tourism Research, 39*(3), 1565–1587. https://doi.org/10.1016/j.annals.2012.04.007.

Stone, P. R., & Sharpley, R. (2008). Consuming dark tourism: A thanatological perspective. *Annals of Tourism Research, 35*(2), 574–595. https://doi.org/10.1016/j.annals.2008.02.003.

Stone, P. R., & Sharpley, R. (2013). Deviance, dark tourism and 'dark leisure'. In S. Elkington & S. Gammon (Eds.), *Contemporary perspectives in leisure: Meanings, motives and lifelong learning: Meanings, motives and lifelong learning* (pp. 54–64). London: Routledge.

Taylor, L. D. (2013). Dying to watch: Thoughts of death and preferences for sexual media content. *Journal of Media Psychology: Theories, Methods, and Applications, 25*(2), 55–64. https://doi.org/10.1027/1864-1105/a000079.

Tonry, M. (2004). *Thinking about crime*. Oxford: Oxford University Press.

Van Marle, F., & Maruna, S. (2010). 'ontological insecurity' and 'terror management': Linking two free-floating anxieties. *Punishment & Society, 12*(1), 7–26. https://doi.org/10.1177/1462474509349084.

Walter, T. (2009). Dark tourism: Mediating between the dead and the living. In R. Sharpley & P. R. Stone (Eds.), *Darker side of travel: The theory and practice of dark tourism*. Clevedon: Channel View Publications.

22

Politics of Dark Tourism: The Case of Cromañón and ESMA, Buenos Aires, Argentina

Maximiliano E. Korstanje and David Baker

Introduction

Tourism has been recently catalogued as a key global industry (Shaw et al. 1990; Buckley and Witt 1990; Lee and Chang 2008). The influx of visitors not only potentially revitalises cultural resources but also generates economic resources of specific destinations. Recently, even spaces of mass-death or disasters such as Ground Zero in New York (9/11 terrorist attack), the Tsunami on Sri Lanka, or Katrina Hurricane hitting New Orleans, USA, can be 'recycled' by adopting tourism policies that take death as a main attraction (Klein 2007). Although this type of tourism has attracted criticism of post-Marxist sociologists, as the sign of sadist spectacle (Bloom 2000; Baudrillard 1996, 2006; Koch 2005), other scholars opt to explore the issue to better understand tourists' apparent fascination of 'Other' suffering. In this vein, dark tourism alludes to new forms of tourism consumption, which are different from typical tourism products of sun, sea, and sand. One of the aspects that define dark tourism is the seemingly negative (macabre) landscape that exerts fascination in Others (Stone 2012; Wilson 2008; Sharpley 2005; Korstanje 2011; Sather-Wagstaff 2011).

M. E. Korstanje (✉)
University of Palermo, Buenos Aires, Argentina

D. Baker
Tennessee State University, Nashville, TN, USA

However, this 'attraction' of death seems not to be new. For example, George H. Mead (2009), the father of symbolic interactionism, suggested that ordinary people manifested their rejection to bad news, though they exerted a strange fascination over the audience. He concluded that the Self is configured by its interaction with Others. This social dialectic alludes to the anticipation and interpretation as two pillars of the communication-process. The Self feels happiness by Other suffering because it represents a rite necessary to exercise the misfortune. Starting from the premise that the Self is morally obliged to assist the Other to reinforce its sentiment of superiority, Mead adds that this is the ethical nature of social relationships in the capitalist ethos. In a similar vein, we explore in this chapter whether voyeurism is linked to dark tourism sites. Indeed, we critically examine whether dark tourism is a platform for sadist consumption; or does dark tourism represent a way of mediating Other death (also see Chap. 8)?

To respond to these questions, we conducted fieldwork at two sites in what Philip Stone called a 'darkest subtype' in the spectrum of dark tourism consumption (Stone 2006). Visitors who are interested in these types of sites have moral interrogations about the dichotomy between life and death. In other terms, the "other" who has died offers an outstanding experience syncretised in the understanding of own death (Stone 2012). Over recent decades' numerous studies explored the motives and expectances of these 'death-seekers' but without any firm basis (Korstanje 2011). At some extent, this literature gathered interested cases of sites where tourism is adopted as main sources of profits, there are some sites that neglect all-inclusive tours. How can we study dark tourism in sites where tourism is not an alternative?

Basically, the fact that mass tourism is not adopted as a primary source of income does not mean visitors can inspect dark sites. For some local voices tourism as a commercial activity leads to moral corruption. Since eagerness and money were the key factors behind the event that took the lives of their relatives, not surprisingly tourism is viewed part of the problem and not the solution. In this chapter, we examine the ESMA Museum and Cromañón's Sanctuary, both in Argentina. These sites are not technically spaces of dark consumption, but they do provide further insights that can help expand an understanding of the politics of dark tourism. As Stone (2006) puts it, dark tourism encompasses a large spectrum of modalities and subtypes. Since not all sites become well-established tourist attractions, some sites exhibit a great mourning that impedes mass tourism. This chapter, therefore, aims to provide a study which unravels the politics of thanaptosis. Particularly, the chapter asks why some dark sites are prone to tourism, while others neglect the income this industry yields. Firstly, however a brief review of dark tourism provides a background for subsequent case study discussions.

Dark Tourism and 'Other' Death

Dark tourism has gained considerable attention and recognition over the past few years within the international study of tourism. The term 'dark tourism' was originally coined by Malcolm Foley and John Lennon in an article entitled 'JFK and Dark Tourism', published in a special issue of the International Journal of Heritage Studies (Foley and Lennon 1996). Foley and Lennon discuss the apparent touristic fascination for former US president John F Kennedy's assassination in 1963. This event marked a turning point in the political stability of the USA. Today, the media's fascination for the Kennedy's tragedy is not only educational but representative of Dallas as a tourist destination. Indeed, the city is generating considerable attraction for other audiences interested in visiting the sites where the former president was killed (Foley and Lennon 1996).

Dark tourism as a concept brought to academic attention a fascinating issue of particular sites of death, atrocity, and disaster. While a full critique of dark tourism is beyond the scope of this chapter, as an interdisciplinary subject, dark tourism has become a focus discussion not only for tourism-related scholars but also other social scientists, including but not limited to sociologists, psychologists, and anthropologists. One of the subject goals of dark tourism is to explore visitor sites and tourist experiences and to better understand experiential aspects of Other death and mortality (Stone and Sharpley 2008). Thus, this phenomenon represents a valid attempt to critically explore a contemporary representation and apparent fascination with death. Indeed, exploring why and what visitors seek at places of death is one of the key concerns of studying dark tourism in its many different guises (Foley and Lennon 1996; Seaton 1996; Miles 2002; Strange and Kempa 2003; Wight 2006; Jamal and Lelo 2011; Robb 2009; Stone and Sharpley 2008; Sharpley 2005; Korstanje 2011; Stone 2012; Kang et al. 2012). Moreover, applied-research adopts a diverse variety of methodological approaches from quantitative to more qualitative views as ethnographies. However, what is important is the subjective tourist experience which may serve to explain why people need to mediate with Other death. To understand the issue, tourists are considered as 'authoritative voices' because of the importance of their experience.

Dark tourism denotes sites where death or suffering has determined the identity of a community and where either a level of private market commoditising or public commemoration has taken place (Poria 2007; Chauhan and Khanna 2009). Its commercialisation, which was explored by Stone and Sharpley (2008), warned of the needs of defining the issue in view of the allegory of meaning. For instance, a place where a public shrine is erected confers a message which is interlinked to the practice of ordinary people within local and national communities. Though a curiosity or fascination with death might seem to be one aspect that may characterise dark tourism, it is important not to lose sight of how 'dark tourist' experiences are framed under shared values that tighten social bondage (Stone and Sharpley 2008; Stone 2012).

Furthermore, dark tourism may be defined as a (secular) pilgrimage or a 'spiritual' experience, especially considering that by sightseeing Other death, there is an inherent tendency to contemplate death of the Self through thanaptosis (Stone 2012). The concept of thanaptosis is of paramount importance in understanding the genesis of this phenomenon. Recently, Korstanje (2013) has traced the roots of 'thanaptosis' to the American Poet William Cullen Bryant (1817), who in 1817 coined the term to express the human need to anticipate death through the eyes of others. Bryant poetically suggests that Other death makes the Self feel better because we have avoided our own inevitable end, albeit temporarily. To overcome this existential obstacle, we have to listen to 'nature' as death is a vital process in the transformation of the human life cycle. To be more precise, Bryant alludes to thanaptosis as the happiness for life, which is only possible at the time of accepting our own death. However, this does not readily explain the current fascination for Other death since thanaptosis represents a pantheist concept of evolution (Korstanje 2013, 2014).

In this regard, Biran et al. (2011) argue that the specialised literature has some ingrained issues to explain the roots of thanaptosis, simply because these certain dark tourism studies have not been based on empirical evidence. Like heritage-seekers, 'dark tourists' appear to like to expand their current understanding of history (Foley and Lennon 1996; Miles 2002; Cohen 2011; Korstanje 2011; Sather-Wagstaff 2011). To explore the motivation of so-called dark tourists, one might ask to reconstruct the subject experience. However, upon closer inspection, dark tourism not only entails an apparent attachment to death as a primary reason of attraction but a quest for authentic experiences (Stone 2006; Strange and Kempa 2003; Biran et al. 2011). Of course, the diversity of tourist experiences gives rise to interpretation challenges and issues. This is especially the case when notions of authenticity and operationalisation of the concept come to the fore, as well as the pedagogical aspects of dark tourism. In sum, as Korstanje and Ivanov (2012) observe, this new trend not only gives a lesson to the community but serves as a mechanism of resilience for disasters to be prevented. Since mass-death represents a serious psychological trauma for society and survivors, which may very well affect the lines of authority, dark tourism helps revitalise the social trust in order for officialdom to keep its legitimacy. This political nature of dark tourism is combined with educational and pedagogical issues, which this chapter now turns.

The Pedagogical Nature of Dark Tourism

Adopting a pedagogical perspective, dark tourism can be used as an educational instrument to better understand why particular disasters happen (also see Chap. 25). However, the question of whether the place is authentic or not depends upon specific emotional symbolism employed to memorise tragedy. For potential dark tourists, questions of authenticity play a vital role in how space and place are configured. For example, visiting the actual place where death or disaster events occurred is one way to possess credibility of both site and experience (Cohen 2011). Miles (2002) goes on to introduce conceptual differences between places associated *with* death and spaces *of* real death or disaster. The former signals to the classification of dark tourism, whereas the latter refers to darker tourism (Stone 2006). Thus, this significant difference between dark and darker (tourism) is epitomised with the sites' authenticity and tourist experiences thereof.

Moreover, Johnston (2013) acknowledges that a particular issue with current dark tourism research is that related scholarship either adopts radical views (such as Marxist perspectives), while other views are empirically based on tourist perspectives or studies that offer conceptual frameworks and academic models in which to locate dark tourism production and consumption. Johnston (2013) also calls for a distinguishing debate of dark tourism (or thanatourism) from heritage. Indeed, Johnston associates dark tourism with the prominence of 'deathscapes', a tradition introduced by the Catholic Church in medieval Europe, whereby through the visitor's mediating gaze, death generates enough attention to motivate visitation. Johnston goes on to argue that dark tourism is stronger in those sites where social bondage is weaker. Indeed, his argument rests on the belief that so-called dark experiences may not be previously determined by the ideology of discourse but follows a kind of serendipitous logic.

Despite a number of studies that examine dark tourism pedagogically, less attention has been given to the political nature of dark tourism (also see Chap.

12). This is particularly the case at those dark sites where authorities reject tourism as an activity or view the site as an economic resource. For example, and as a case focus for this chapter, in Buenos Aires, Argentina, two sites match this criterion: firstly, the Museum of ESMA (Escuela de Mecánica de la Armada) (School of Navy) and, secondly, the Sanctuary of Cromañón. Both sites can be classified as dark tourism shrines (Stone 2006) and are discussed in more detail later in the chapter.

It is important not to lose sight that an interest for death sites as acceptable allegories of consumption depends on when the event occurred. As Frew and White (2013) note, those sites where death or disaster originally occurred are often replaced by other developments within the short-term. This suggests that any subsequent memorials which are constructed to commemorate specific deaths or disasters need to honour the memories of victims. In doing so, time and chronological distance plays a crucial role by cementing a particular discourse as well as stakeholder representations. Any factor that determines how, what, and when events are rememorised appeals to the terms of recordability and usability. Often, dark tourism shrines encompass a wider spectrum of actors such as the actual owners of sites, survivors or families of victims, and of course, the global community (Frew and White 2013).

In this vein, Stone (2006) goes on to suggest that some dark tourism sites offer darker products than others depending on the degree of suffering. Each subtype can be framed into a 'spectrum' of dark tourism suppliers. These range from a typology of 'dark fun factories' that present fictionalised death and are perceived as less authentic than, say, darker visitor attractions such as 'dark camps of genocide' like the Auschwitz-Birkenau Museum and Memorial in Poland. As tourism is embraced as a main industry at these sites, visitor experiences become increasingly diverse. However, for some shrines or sanctuaries, there is limited interest in tourism as an additional source of income. While some dark sites clearly offer a tourist spectacle, Auschwitz Memorial and Museum, for example, reluctantly accept mass visitation and plough any resultant profits into site maintenance and other Holocaust remembrance initiatives. Others dark sites may be reluctant altogether to the economy of tourism. Stone (2006) goes on to outline a typological model that can help our understanding of dark tourism, including highlighting a spectrum of dark tourism supply with varying degrees of political involvement. These suppliers include:

(a) *Dark Fun Factories* allude to those spectacles that offer an attraction to visitors and tourists, a type of entertainment that commoditises death as the primary commodity.

(b) *Dark Exhibitions* are exhibits that often merge pedagogical lessons about disasters with commercially oriented entertainment.
(c) *Dark Dungeons* signal to those spaces which correspond to a penal system or any other state sanctioned disciplinary apparatus. This subtype condenses the mix of the spectrum between darkest and lightest forms.
(d) *Dark Resting Places* focus on graves or cemeteries which can be commercialised or toured by potential visitors.
(e) *Dark Shrines* refer to temporary memorials that offer commemoration and remembrance and which remind us of a traumatic event and its immediate aftermath.
(f) *Dark Conflict Zones* encompass a set of educational, personal, and heritage activities and visitor sites associated with conflict, battlefields, or wars.
(g) *Dark Camps of Genocide* represent the darkest subtype of the spectrum and exhibit not only spaces of great suffering and pain, but also are treated with respect because of the degree of atrocity and extreme violence exerted there.

Although the term 'dark tourism' is used in many contexts to denote spaces of mourning which are visited by tourists, no less true is that the commoditisation of death seems not to be present in all sites. In this respect, Stone's conceptual insight is of importance to this chapter because of two main reasons. Firstly, it allows a conceptual classification of dark tourism sites according to the events and their impacts for society. Secondly, his explanation about why organisers of ESMA and Cromañón neglect to offer the sites to international tourists can be examined. In respect to this, Raine (2013) devoted considerable time to validate Stone's hypothesis with empirical fieldwork. She contends that the fascination for death may be operationalised in variables which range from lightest to darkest spectrum. In other words, visitors take diverse attitudes to dark tourism sites (Raine 2013). Indeed, it is important to discuss the role of dark tourism in helping society to sublimate trauma in the context of disastrous events.

Trauma and Dark Tourism

Two events caused by different reasons and in different contexts share the same platform of symbolisation. The ESMA museum reflects the same level of psychological trauma as the survivors of Cromañón's tragedy. Both are man-made disasters that suddenly shocked the community and affected the lives of many citizens. The concept of trauma and resilience are inherently enmeshed. Korstanje and Ivanov (2012) explain how dark tourism can help a community overcome loss and pain in the aftermath of disasters. By this token, survivors in post-disaster contexts need to tell their story to others, who had not experienced such a pain. Death, anthropologically speaking, undermines the lines of authorities between officialdom and members of community. In order for society not to collapse, political allegories of disaster should be orchestrated. This helps not only for survivors to start their stage of resilience but also for the event to be remembered. In view of that, politics is vital by configuring *the discourse of disaster* which varies on culture to culture and depends on many factors such as system of beliefs, types of victims, the current means of production, kinship, and others. For example, this is the difference between 9/11 which fostered social cohesion in America and Atocha that promoted the end of an administration in Spain. Arguably, a community with higher levels of resiliency has further opportunities to overcome tragedies and disasters. Therefore, the politics of dark tourism offers a fertile ground to expand the current understanding how allegories are depicted and transmitted, as well as what should be reminded and what should be ignored (Korstanje and Ivanov 2012).

Interesting outcomes obtained by Sather-Wagstaff (2011) in her autoethnography of Ground Zero in New York suggest that death produces social cohesion. Furthermore, she argues convincingly that dark tourism expands negotiation between the past and the present, so that visitors feel what victims felt. This social empathy focuses upon a discourse which is politically constructed. The influence of ideology is reversed at the time and people embrace suffering of Others. However, the discourse never shows the reason of events and, consequently, imposes a one-sided argument which is externally designed. In essence, therefore, dark tourism (as death) can wake up the society from its slumber. As Sather-Wagstaff (2011: 47) notes:

> Sites of historical and cultural importance that represent violent events are particularly prone to a social misunderstanding about their emergence; it is believed that they have come into existence only through the events that take place at particular location: war results in battlefields, genocides produce mass graves, the assassination site of a political leader delineates a national sacred place. However, historical commemorative places are not made as important sites simply because of the events that may physically mark them as distinct places through bloodshed or the destruction of building or landscapes. These places are made through ongoing human practices in time and I argue, across multiple spaces and places.

Tourists are proactive agents that produce and negotiate meanings that leave moral lessons to the rest of the community. Explaining why disaster happens is the main function of dark tourism. However, Sather-Wagstaff (2011) further argues that if heritage causes alienation on lay people's minds as post-Marxism suggested, then human suffering stimulates empathy and locates tourists in the place of victims. Therefore, dark tourism should not exist in heritage or consumption simply because the allegory is manipulated by politicians to protect their own interests. This latter point raises a profound question; that is, to what extent is dark tourism rooted in politics?

The remainder of this chapter, therefore, addresses this question and offers a critical overview of ethnographic research at the ESMA Museum and Cromañón, which are both located in Buenos Aires. Particularly, four key themes are revealed:

- *The attachment to religious discourse* which signals to the ideology of sites. Religious shrines take a different dynamic than secularised spaces.
- *The levels of internal conflicts/cohesion*. While some groups demonise external threats, others direct their resentment against other in-group members.
- *Political support or indifference*. Depending on the existent infrastructure or political resources, some groups receive more support than others. While some survivors struggle against their governments, others devote efforts in coordinating joint steps.
- *Acceptance/rejection of organised tours*. Tourism provides these sites with new income that helps maintain the monument, shrine, or sanctuary. Whereas some groups reject tourism as the precondition for corruption, others have no problems in offering a sacred sanctuary to visitors.

Case Study 1: Museo de Mecánica de la Armada (ESMA)

As the symbolic epicentre of the violation of human rights, the ESMA was an illegal detention camp where dissidents were tortured and assassinated by the last military dictatorship of Argentina. The Juntas took power in 1976 and introduced numerous liberal policies which were accompanied by violent disciplinary instruments that led towards bloodshed. People opposed to the Juntas were arrested and illegally disappeared into Argentina (Feierstein 2006). Unlike other Latin American countries, Argentina's history shows a cycle of military coups and democratically elected governments. Military forces have learned from past experiences to take action over 'glitches'—apparently caused by civilian governance—and which they considered needed to be fixed (de Imaz 1984; Haggard and Kaufman 1995). This happened in

March 1976 when military forces ended Martínez de Perón's administration. During this period, the country was subdued into a bloody climate of violence between the supporters of deceased Juan D. Peron and various left-wind terrorist cells (the so-called dirty war). To strengthen control of the political arena, the Juntas brought down the former president María Estela Martínez de Perón. At the time military forces orchestrated a plan to eradicate 'guerrilla' political dissidents. These included intellectuals, writers, and worker union leaders who were clandestinely arrested, tortured, and murdered (Feierstein 2006, 2011). This illegal repression not omitted a just trial for those persons accused of terrorism but also paved the ways for imposing policies that otherwise would have been rejected by work unions. Moreover, during this period, the Juntas government introduced a set of liberal measures which protected the interest of the elite. As a result, serious criminal acts were committed by military forces while they were in presidency (Guest 1990; Jelin 2003). Thousands of political dissidents were kidnapped or killed without trial. Similarly, in Chile and other Latin American countries, this bloody dictatorship left a great pain in the core of Argentineans (Norden 1996). Once democracy resumed in 1983, human rights violations by the armed forces received diverse judiciary treatments. The former president Raúl Alfonsin (1983–1989), who was based on the Two Demons theory, stipulated that leaders of army forces as well as those civilians who planned terrorist attacks should be brought to trial. Even so, he distinguished three types of actors in this scenario: those who had defined the plans and strategies to be followed by others of lower rank, some subordinates who took more attributes by exceeding these orders, and those who were just limited to abide by their orders. In Alfonsin's mind, at least, the first and second subtype must be brought to 'justice'. Although the trial of the military Juntas issued an exemplary message for society, this was later derogated by president Carlos Saul Menem (1989–1999). Disclaimed by their responsibility for the acts of dirty wars, the leaders of terrorist cells and Juntas were condoned. Finally, the advent of Nestor Kirchner (2003–2007) and the current president Cristina Fernandez de Kirchner, his wife, not only continued with the policies of Alfonsin, reassuming the trials to those suspected to commit human rights violations, but also incorporated into politics in a lot of organisations such as 'Abuelas de Plaza de Mayo', 'Madres de Plaza de Mayo', and so forth. Subsequently, the ESMA Navy Mechanic School (Escuela de Mecánica de la Armada), where thousands of dissidents were tortured and killed, was regenerated into a museum and is known as the 'museo de la memoria' (museum of memory).

Case Study 2: Republica de Cromañón

The Republic of Cromañón was a night club located in Buenos Aires where 194 teenagers were accidentally suffocated by carbon dioxide by a flare thrown by one of the attendants that rapidly ignited the ceiling. This tragic event occurred on 30 December 2004. This man-made disaster resonated with public opinion, who were particularly concerned with the young age of the victims. Indeed, Pope Francis—the Cardinal Primate of Argentina Jorge Bergoglio—gave a supportive message to relatives. From its inception, unlike ESMA, the Catholic Church accompanied the rise of the Republica de Cromañón's disaster. In the days after the event, a small shrine was constructed at the place where the first corpses were piled-up by police. Although those responsible for this tragedy have not faced justice, the mayor Aníbal Ibarra as well as the night club owners were subject to a trial as well as the Band Callejeros, and some inspectors who found the club showed some premises defects and organisational irregularities. Disorganised in disparate groups, relatives who had lost their sons and daughters struggled against political powers to find justice for the disaster. However, a judge did issue a national arrest order for Omar Chabán, a local businessman and former owner of the site. Former president Nestor Kirchner declared three days of national mourning, and authorities prohibited public events and concerts for a considerable period. Though police are still tracing those responsible for the disaster, the government closed many similar clubs because they did follow fire safety protocols and legal requirements. Undoubtedly, Cromañón has left a gap in the social imagination of 'porteños' who are Buenos Aires' inhabitants.

Though different in contexts, both case studies as outlined here not only represent a reminder of trauma but also suggest tourism as a valid option for remembrance. Indeed, these two case studies provide a fresh view to gain a further understanding of the issues of disaster events within the broader visitor economy. In particular, the research study of stakeholders suggests that there is a neglect of possibilities to adopt tourism as a valid economic source since profits are often associated with corruption. They suppose that 'a nuestros hijos no los mato el rock and roll sino la corrupción' (our sons have not died by the rock and roll, they were killed by financial corruption). The economic factor, therefore, means money is demonised as the reason for bribes that produced the tragedy in the first place. However, in diverse ways, the concept of evil-doers is not only present in the Sanctuary of Cromañón but also at ESMA.

Though not limited to tourists, the ethnographies conducted at both sites took the testimonies of many actors, who ranged from relatives of victims, museum curators, witnesses and officials, human rights militants, and policy makers in the Secretaria de Derechos Humanos (Secretary of Human Rights), and who have all participated in the construction of Museum. Dark sites encompass many actors, beyond visitors, who devote considerable time and effort to keep tragic memories alive. The politics of dark tourism, as argued earlier in this chapter, need something else than interviewees administered to tourists. Good ethnographies are those who tell a story, which offers a pervasive viewpoint of the issue. Therefore, we opt not to cite verbatim transcribed tape-recorded interviews which sometimes obscure more than clarify. Rather, the study offers to locate fieldwork into a coherent conceptual framework that validates Stone's 'dark tourism spectrum' model (2006).

Discussion

A direct observation of the site suggests that ESMA is based on a secular logic where religion has no place. Interviews with curators and organisers suggested that religionist organisations were in compliance with military force in arresting and torturing dissidents. Although they believe in God, they manifestly resented the course of actions followed by the Catholic Church which had supported the State. The illegal repression conducted by the 'grupo de tareas' selected and arrested people from the streets to be subject to torture sessions in clandestine buildings. In some circumstances, chaplains performed the extreme unction to dying inmates, persuading them to confess. Although the role of the Church was pervasive and respective to repression, the ESMA was founded by secular left-wing movements in sharp contrast to religiosity. Almost all rooms are decorated with pictures, allegories to dirty wars and illegal detentions perpetrated by the security forces.

In sharp contrast to Cromañón, which has not received financial support of the presidencies of Nestor Kirchner or Cristina Fernandez de Kirchner, the ESMA Museum was built by the current government as a sign of 'restoration' in view of violation of human rights perpetrated by the armed forces. Indeed, it was defined as a matter of state. Although the organisers of ESMA are loyal militants of 'Kirchnerismo', they reject tourism as a valid option to revitalise the economy of the museum. In the same argument, they believe that money engenders corruption and their cause should not be tainted by corruption. Videla's government was historically supported by the main financial powers of Argentina as well as bourgeoisie which amassed great profits with bloodshed. Ideologically, therefore, visitors to the ESMA do not feel indifference by politics (as Cromañón); they feel politics is a transformative instrument of betterment—and of course, Cristina F. de Kirchner is the leader who will lead the country to progress and development. She, anyway, should not only struggle against greater concentrated monopolies that use mass-media in their favour, but confers to 'kirchnerites'—an aura of superiority and the outstanding historical process they are facing. One of the key informants proudly stated that 'God is with us!' Evil-doers who conspire against Argentina are the economic powers as World Bank, International Monetary Fund (IMF), England, and the USA. The discourse of kirchnerites corresponds with what specialists call 'counterfeits politics', which consists in creating a gap that is filled by a conspirational plot. Since it is unchecked, conspiracy theory may feedback a social imaginary where evil-doers and international profit organisations are linked. To what extent tourism is equalled to bribes and trade, which are pejorative views for human rights organisations such as 'Abuelas de Plaza de Mayo' or 'Madres de Plaza de Mayo', seems to be one of the matters that should be investigated. In particular, are human rights organisations replicating the mistrust of military forces of trade?

A potential answer may be found in the following axiom. Historic coups against democracies in Argentina not only reflect a type of intolerance of debate or interest for populist policies by aristocracies, which resulted in the lack of punishment for militarists, but also changed substantially the commitment (militancia) of ordinary citizens respecting governmental institutions. Arguably, it is safe to say that Argentineans, in political terms at least, view democracy is only valid if their economic needs were met. However, at that time the economy did not legitimise the government, and, as a result, worker unions, civil leaders, and other actors 'allowed' the military to intervene in politics. Moreover, the social elite moved their resources to overthrow the elected government if their interests were compromised in any way. The financial factor in the social imaginary alluded to conform a distrustful conception of politics. For people who worked hard to construct the ESMA museum, bribes and greed of the great monopolies which supported in part by the Catholic Church paved the way for the (National Reorganization Process) 'proceso de Re-organización nacional' that ended Martínez de Perón's presidency.

To respond to this issue in a more accurate manner, we have to look at another case study, as outlined earlier in this chapter 'Sanctuary of Cromañón' (Santuario de Cromañón, Buenos Aires). This disaster not only put former mayor Aníbal Ibarra into question because of serious deficiencies in the protocols of Nightclub governance but also accelerated the impeachment which toppled his government. In parallel, Omar Chabán was prosecuted and condemned to prison. In the location where the first corpses were piled following the disaster, survivors and relatives constructed a makeshift 'sanctuary' which with the passing of years became a real shrine. Though from the outset, the sanctuary was visited by tourists, local residents, and others, the organisation never authorised or promoted mass visitation. Cromañón was special from many perspectives, including stakeholder dissonance as well as an unwillingness to accept the status quo. It is hard to locate leaders within this movement due to the huge number of victims. Each family allied to others forming approximately six main leading movements. Every family has been paid, but these sub-groups struggled to monopolise the subsidiaries. Not only this raises a great conflict but also helped to prevent the unification of the Cromañón movement. Indeed, their interests were based on diverse goals, and while some families looked to jail Omar Chabán, Callejeros's rock band, and Aníbal Ibarra because of their complicity with bribes, others considered the event to be simply an accident. Indeed, this movement can be sociologically framed as a cult of popular religiosity and characterised by contrasts of both economics and politics. In this case, the economy was embodied in the figure of businessman Chabán, while for politics, the former mayor Ibarra. For survivors, victims died simply because Chabán bribed the municipal inspectors who should have found managerial and maintenance irregularities of the nightclub. Their imaginary stressed that victims did not die in vain, but rather the disaster gives a reason for relatives to fight against political corruption as well, having a mission to help avoid future tragedies.

The shrine at Cromañón was constructed in January 2005 where people lay flowers, rosaries, and other objects to decorate the makeshift monument. The 194 victims were remembered as 'angels' because of their assumed purity and pristine souls. Arguably, the monument alludes to a need of justice where the sacralisation process allows victims to support a political cause. This is the reason why the process is enrooted in political remembrance. Consequently, the archetype of angels reveals two important aspects of life. Firstly, society mobilises resources to protect those groups who represent fertile ground for the next generation. That way, the group reserves its ability to survive. Whenever teenagers, pregnant women, or children are killed, the group goes into shock. The religiosity alludes to respond to a question which has no real answer or substantial contradictions of life. Secondly, all of us not only will die someday, but also we live to die. Angels are also social constructs that mediate between the gods, humans, and evil. They are not as vulnerable as men but not as powerful as gods. Any episode of sudden death confers to any victim their special and outstanding nature not only to give meaning to the death but also to guide families. It exhibits the logic of sacrifice. Following this explanation, the sacralisation operates in combination to a second element, the conflict. Aníbal Ibarra was supported not only by the former president Nestor Kirchner but also by a set of social-democratic parties. The attack to him entailed the reaction of Estela de Carlotto and other human rights militants. As Andrea Estrada (2010) puts it, Cromañón evidenced two aspects of power. One signals the struggle for fathers and mothers who had lost their sons and daughters in a man-made disaster, but secondly and more importantly, it speaks of the monopoly of memory. Estela de Carlotto, founder of the movement 'Abuelas de Plaza de Mayo', suffered the disappearance of a son by the hand of the military Juntas in Argentina. Though in the past she exerted considerable resistance to diverse governments, today she is supporting the 'frente para la Victoria' party [Front for Victory party] which led to power to Nestor Kirchner and his wife Cristina F. de Kirchner. Carlotto abruptly named Cromañón's families as 'enemies of democracy'. She was repudiated by whole families who expressed their concerns. One of the parents, Liliana Garafalo, accused Carlotto of creating an allegory of suffering where some actors are excluded. The discrepancy was given, in this token, by the monopoly of memory and under what circumstances the suffering may be manipulated in an all-encompassing discourse. The families of Cromañón represented a serious danger for democracy because they promoted the trial on Ibarra engendering political instability.

Sociologically speaking, however, the atomisation of pressure groups lacked political militancy and has resulted in a nihilist view of politics and the authorities, who were seen to be responsible for the tragedy. The higher degree of conflict against the status quo led survivors and relatives to see in money an instrument of corruption. Since tourism is a commercial activity for their social imaginary, they feel the organisation of mass tourism sites would decline the sacredness of the sanctuary. The journalist Laura Cambra (2008) acknowledges that the tragedy is mediatised by many voices. All these views are articulated by the discourse of what she calls the 'rock chabon'. This genre surfaced in the post economic crisis of 2001 where thousands of Argentines lost their trust in politicians and political parties and processes. The lack of trust revealed the daily frustrations of almost 40% of unemployment and 60% living in poverty. The rock chabon exemplified a new form of protest which was more politically radicalised. If teenagers subscribed to parties to improve the conditions of the country, rock chabon offered the opposite. Under these nihilist circumstances, supporters of rock chabon do not accept leisure or consumption as a sign of status or economic growth and view the markets and commercialisation as evils of the world.

Despite their contextual differences, both the ESMA and Cromañòn manifest a profound rejection of dark tourism because it represents an open wound that has not been cured by time. That said however, our research has revealed an additional factor: *the crisis of institutions and democracy accelerated by the*

Table 22.1 Commonalities and differences

ESMA	Cromañón
High degree of secularisation or atheism	High degree of religiosity
Homogenised discourse	Diverse discourses
Beliefs in politics and militancy	Hostility to militancy and politics
Organised performance in politics	Anarchy and dispersed interests
Struggling against liberal market	Struggling against political corruption
Identification of those responsible	Those responsible are unknown
Terrorism of state	Accident
Resentment against Catholic Church	Support of Catholic Church
Left-wing ideologies	No ideologies
Mistrust of money	Mistrust of money

military coups which affected the trust of citizenship with governments. Table 22.1 offers further description of the main features of ESMA and Cromañón. Though the return of democracy after 1983 paved the path for the end of illegal repression, the resultant social imaginary developed a negative view of economic powers. This explains, in part at least, why the ESMA museum is not prone to mass tourism. Similarly, Cromañón, a phenomenon surfaced after the disaster and alluded to the financial crisis of 2001 whereby the same hostility against money and profits were evident.

Neither ESMA nor Cromañón developed an orientation for profits. Both are involved in tragedies, where money played a vital role. The tradition of coups in daily life created a negative view of money and trade. As a result, military forces reserved the right to intervene in politics whenever they thought the nation was in danger. The same idea was replicated in other generations even though democracy had returned. The figure of civilians in army circles set the pace to politicians who are often accused of bribes, corruption, illicit enrichment, embezzlement of public money, and other public service misdemeanours. After the 2001 financial crisis where citizenship was organised under the lemma 'que se vayan todos que no quede ni uno solo' (throw all politicians out), politicians failed to achieve the commitment of the people. The political militancy of some teenagers, encouraged by 'Kirchnerismo', not only is rejected by the organisations of Cromañón but also is viewed as a sign of corruption and populism.

Conclusion

While ESMA retains legitimacy as a museum and originally institutionalised by the government, Cromañón not only struggles against the government of Cristina Fernandez de Kirchner, but also the attendant who threw the flare and caused the disaster has never been found. ESMA also centralises a clear line of power and authority, whereas Cromañón is subject to an eternal conflict in view of multiple stakeholder interests. As a makeshift shrine supported by relatives of victims and situated in the middle of an arterial street in Buenos Aires, Cromañón had faced numerous attempts of removal by the police and authorities. This not only reinforced the anti-political sentiment but also engendered a profound gap with local and national governments. The presidency of Nestor Kirchner returned a dignity to the memory of the 'disappeared persons'—a key reason why ESMA was invented and used as a dispositif of democratisation. Meanwhile, Cromañón sees in Nestor Kirchner the former president who protected Aníbal Ibarra and who was responsible for the tragedy. Apart from these substantial differences, both case study examples suggest a resistance to tourism as a commercial activity. Indeed, both movements consider corruption (and the economic forces behind such corruption) as the main factor that determined the original tragic events and/or disaster. Policy makers of Museo de la Memoria and friends of Cromañón share the same suspicions of economic powers. Upon closer inspection, the friends of Cromañón consider the corruption of Ibarra was the reason why their sons, daughters, and friends died in a tragedy which should have been prevented. In both social imaginaries, money (and consequent greed) plays a vital role as the reason and effect of their disgrace. Ultimately, therefore, this leads them to reject (dark) tourism as a main economic activity.

This chapter illustrates two important aspects of politics. On the one hand, the experience of the public was seriously determined by fear and the lack of commitment produced by military coups. On the other hand, the *political nature of dark sites*, even where tourism is rejected by the authorities, can construct, negotiate, and impose of what Korstanje (2014) dubbed 'the allegory of disaster'. However, this is a much deeper issue which warrants further scrutiny and research. What this study has revealed is that dark tourism extrapolates the political atmosphere of society. In those groups where economic factors played a negative role in society, as in Argentina and other Latin American nations, profits and profit-making have detrimental connotations. Tourism is often associated with neo-liberal market conditions and with trade and profits and, of course, corruption. This may be the real reason why those sites discussed here remain reluctant to receive organised tours.

References

Baudrillard, J. (1996). *The perfect crime*. London: Verso.
Baudrillard, J. (2006, July). Virtuality and events: The hell of power. *Baudrillard Studies, 3*(2). Availabe at http://www.ubishops.ca/BaudrillardStudies/. Bishop's University, Canada. Version translated by Chris Turner.

Biran, A., Poria, Y., & Oren, G. (2011). Sought experience at dark heritage sites. *Annals of Tourism Research, 38*(3), 820–841.

Bloom, T. (2000). Morbid-tourism – A postmodern market niche with an example from Althrop. *Norwegian Journal of Geography, 54*(1), 29–36.

Bryant, W. C. (1817). Thanatopsis. *North American Review, 5*(15), 338–341.

Buckley, P. J., & Witt, S. F. (1990). Tourism in the centrally-planned economies of Europe. *Annals of Tourism Research, 17*(1), 7–18.

Cambra, L. (2008). *Callejeros en Primera Persona.* Buenos Aires: Planeta.

Chauhan, V., & Khanna, S. (2009). Tourism: A tool for crafting peace process in Kashmir, J&K, India. *Tourismos: An International Multidisciplinary Journal of Tourism, 4*(2), 69–89.

de Imaz, J. L. (1984). *Sobre la identidad iberoamericana.* [About the Ibero-American Identity]. Buenos Aires: Editorial Sudamericana.

Estrada, A. (2010). *La Tragedia según el discruso.* Buenos Aires, Prometeo: Así se siente Cromañón.

Feierstein, D. (2006). Political violence in Argentina and its genocidal characteristics. *Journal of Genocide Research, 8*(2), 149–168.

Feierstein, D. (2014). *Genocide as social practice: Reorganizing society under the Nazis and Argentina's military juntas.* New Brunswick: Rutgers University Press.

Foley, M., & Lennon, J. J. (1996). JFK and dark tourism: A fascination with assassination. *International Journal of Heritage Studies, 2*(4), 198–211.

Frew, E., & White, L. (2013). Exploring dark tourism and place identity. In E. Frew & L. White (Eds.), *Dark tourism and place identity: Managing and interpreting dark place* (pp. 1–10). Oxford: Routledge.

Guest, I. (1990). *Behind the disappearances: Argentina's dirty war against human rights and the United Nations.* Pennsylvania: University of Pennsylvania Press.

Haggard, S., & Kaufman, R. K. (1995). *The political economy of democratic transitions.* Princeton: Princeton University Press.

Jamal, T., & Lelo, L. (2011). Exploring the conceptual and analytical framing of dark tourism: From darkness to intentionality. In *Tourist experience: Contemporary perspectives* (pp. 29–42).

Jelin, E. (2003). *State repression and the labors of memory* (Vol. 18). Minneapolis: University of Minnesota Press.

Johnston, T. (2013). Mark twain and the innocent abroad: Illuminating the tourist gaze on death. *International Journal of Culture, Tourism and Hospitality Research, 7*(3), 199–213.

Kang, E. J., Scott, N., Lee, T. J., & Ballantyne, R. (2012). Benefits of visiting a 'dark tourism' site: The case of the Jeju April 3rd peace park, Korea. *Tourism Management, 33*(2), 257–265.

Klein, N. (2007). *The shock doctrine: The rise of disaster capitalism.* New York: Macmillan.

Koch, A. (2005). Cyber citizen or cyborg citizen: Baudrillard, political agency, and the commons in virtual politics. *Journal of Mass Media Ethics, 20*(2–3), 159–175.

Korstanje, M. E. (2011). Detaching the elementary forms of dark-tourism. *Anatolia, 22*(3), 424–427.

Korstanje, M. E. (2013). Review dark tourism & place identity. *Journal of Tourism and Cultural Change, 12*(4), 369–371.

Korstanje, M. E. (2014). Chile helps Chile: Exploring the effects of earthquake Chile 2010. *International Journal of Disaster Resilience in the Built Environment, 5*(4), 1–12.

Korstanje, M. E., & Ivanov, S. (2012). Tourism as a form of new psychological resilience: The inception of dark tourism. *CULTUR-Revista de Cultura e Turismo, 6*(4), 56–71.

Lee, C. C., & Chang, C. P. (2008). Tourism development and economic growth: A closer look at panels. *Tourism Management, 29*(1), 180–192.

Mead, G. H. (2009). *Mind, self, and society: From the standpoint of a social behaviourist*. Chicago: University of Chicago Press.

Miles, W. (2002). Auschwitz: Museum interpretation and Darker Tourism. *Annals of Tourism Research, 29*(4), 1175–1178.

Norden, D. (1996). *Military rebellion in Argentina: Between coups and consolidation*. Lincoln: University of Nebraska Press.

Poria, Y. (2007). Establishing cooperation between Israel and Poland to save Auschwitz concentration camp: Globalising the responsibility for the Massacre. *International Journal of Tourism Policy, 1*(1), 45–57.

Raine, R. (2013). A dark tourism spectrum. *International Journal of Culture, Tourism and Hospitality Research, 7*(3), 242–256.

Robb, E. M. (2009). Violence and recreation: Vacationing in the realm of dark tourism. *Anthropology and Humanism, 34*(1), 51–60.

Sather-Wagstaff, J. (2011). *Heritage that hurts: Tourists in the memoryscapes of September 11* (Vol. 4). California: Left Coast Press.

Seaton, A. V. (1996). Guided by the dark: From thanatopsis to thanatourism. *International Journal of Heritage Studies, 2*(4), 234–244.

Sharpley, R. (2005). Travels to the edge of darkness: Towards a typology of dark tourism. In *Taking tourism to the limits: Issues, concepts and managerial perspectives* (pp. 215–226).

Shaw, G., Williams, A. M., & Cooper, C. (1990). Tourism, economic development and the role of entrepreneurial activity. *Progress in Tourism, Recreation and Hospitality Management, 2*, 67–81.

Stone, P. R. (2006). A dark tourism spectrum: Towards a typology of death and macabre related tourist sites, attraction and exhibitions. *Tourism, 54*(2), 145–160.

Stone, P.R. (2012). Dark tourism as mortality capital. *Annals of Tourism Research, 39*(3), 1565–1587.

Stone, P. R., & Sharpley, R. (2008). Consuming dark-tourism a Thanatological perspective. *Annals of Tourism Research, 35*(2), 574–595.

Strange, C., & Kempa, M. (2003). Shades of dark tourism: Alcatraz and Robben Island. *Annals of Tourism Research, 30*(2), 386–405.

Wight, A. C. (2006). Philosophical and methodological praxes in dark tourism: Controversy, contention and the evolving paradigm. *Journal of Vacation Marketing, 12*(2), 119–129.

Wilson, J. Z. (2008). *Prison. Cultural memory and dark tourism*. New York: Peter Lang Publishing.

23

"I Know the Plane Crashed": Children's Perspectives in Dark Tourism

Mary Margaret Kerr and Rebecca H. Price

Introduction

Researchers have noted that tourism research overlooks children altogether (Khoo-Lattimore 2015; Poria and Timothy 2014; Small 2008). Yet, a large and growing number of children tour "sites associated with death, suffering, and the seemingly macabre" (Stone 2006, p. 146). Consider these data:

- In 2013, the US Holocaust Memorial Museum received over 500,000 children and adolescents (D. Perna, personal communication, 19 November 2014).
- The Newseum in Washington, DC (with several exhibits depicting terrorism, racism, kidnapping, and war) reports that over half of its visitors are 18 years old or younger (S. Williams, personal communication, 10 November 2014).
- In 2013, the Oklahoma City Bombing Memorial admitted 18,500 children in school and other group tours (L. Barton, personal communication, 20 May 2014).
- Lastly, the Anne Frank House has received more than one million visitors since 2007, most of whom are "high-school students and young adults" (Hartmann 2014, p. 169).

M. M. Kerr (✉) • R. H. Price
University of Pittsburgh, Pittsburgh, PA, USA

Despite their numbers, young tourists receive only anecdotal mentions in the dark tourism[1] literature, because of its exclusive focus on adult experiences. This chapter seeks to introduce children's experiences into the dark tourism discourse. We first explain why children's experiences warrant investigations and then consider promising child-centered research methods from other fields. To illustrate, we offer initial exploratory studies of children's artifacts at the Flight 93 National Memorial in Pennsylvania, USA, a 9/11 site. Recommendations for future research and interpretive practice conclude the chapter.

Why Study Children at Dark Sites?

As Picard and Robinson (2012, p. 23) observed, we "need an understanding of tourists as persons and how they encounter, receive, respond, and react to the effective change in conditions which tourism ultimately entails. This is where things become complex." Indeed, if adult dark tourism research adequately addressed the complexity of children's encounters, we would need little further study. However, children's encounters differ considerably from those of adults in ways we do not yet understand. Current theories cannot account for four factors unique to children: (a) incomplete understanding of death, (b) lack of agency in choosing destinations, (c) youthful exploratory behavior, and (d) emotional vulnerability.

Incomplete Understanding of Death

Premised on a mature understanding of death, adult theories overlook children, whose incomplete understanding of the irreversibility, finality, inevitability, and causality of death renders them unable to grasp the meaning of an ostensibly dark site. This is especially true for those under age six years (Callanan 2014; Patterson 2007; Poling and Evans 2004). Biran and Poria (2012) argue that awareness is a prerequisite for perception that a site is dark (see also Miles 2014). Clearly, young tourists might lack such awareness altogether, thereby differentiating them from adults on whom current theory has focused.

Lack of Agency in Choosing Destinations

One can assume that adult travelers possess some choice and motivations to plan their itineraries. These assumptions have led to extensive debate in the dark tourism motivation literature (Ashworth and Isaac 2015; Stone 2013;

Biran and Poria 2012; Walter 2009). For an adult, a visit to a "dark site" might denote a public presentation of death, and the resulting perception and acceptance or denial of one's eventual demise (Stone 2013). An adult may journey to a dark site as a stand in for religious pilgrimage, looking toward the site and its interpretation for resolution to moral confusion—a possible life-changing experience (Collins-Kreiner 2015; Stone and Sharpley 2013; Seaton 2002). Adults may choose to visit sites for reasons of nationalism and revisiting or rewriting history (Stone 2013; Carr 2010). Or, adults may add a visit to a memorial or battlefield as an incidental side note in an itinerary (Ashworth and Isaac 2015; Walter 2009).

The current scholarly discourse and resulting theories exclude children, who do not always possess such agency (Bandura 2006). Because children have limited agency to choose their tourism destinations, the motivations often debated in the adult dark tourism literature do not necessarily apply to them (also see Chap. 21). While children influence some travel decisions, children's agency in family tourism choices is minimal (Khoo-Lattimore 2015; Carr 2006; Nanda et al. 2006; Schänzel et al. 2005). Taken further, educators typically plan school excursions and rely on factors over which children have little choice (Ritchie and Coughlan 2004). In a nationwide study of Australian schools, for example, Ritchie and Coughlan (2004) found that itinerary selection relies on many criteria, including education needs, cost-effectiveness of the visit, "destination" attractions, and the ability of attractions to cater to school groups. These decision rules may exclude children's wishes altogether.

"The general field of tourism research and the specific field of tourism motivation seem to lack a systematic interest in children's motives" (Larsen and Jenssen 2004, p. 45). Exerting little control over their travel destinations, children find themselves being taken to dark destinations like battlefields "just as children in this and other cultures find themselves being taken to church or temple" (Walter 2009, p. 53). When they arrive, they explore their surroundings in ways unique to children.

Youthful Exploratory Behavior

Children actively explore, often without regard to what the site represents to adults, as Tilden (1957) documented. While Stone (2006) suggests that dark sites may be ranked on a spectrum of least to most dark, "the same site evokes different experiences for different visitors – simply, what one visitor finds dark, another does not" (Ashworth and Isaac 2015, p. 3). This is especially true for children. Some children even play at so-called dark sites (Kerr and

Price 2016). They "play war" at battlefield sites, as noted by Bowman and Pezzullo (2010) and Carr (2010). They "play music," as noted by Knudsen (2011) at Birkenau concentration camp, or climb on war memorials, as recently depicted in social media (MetalClocker 2015). These recent posts provoked thousands of responses from adults who deemed the young visitors' behavior disrespectful and entirely inappropriate (Wagner 2015). This kind of public outcry reflects yet again differences in how adults and children experience and understand a dark destination.[2] As Sutcliffe and Kim (2014, p. 4) concluded, "research tends to examine how accompanying adults interact with children, teach children about appropriate behaviour in heritage/museum venues, or types of exhibits favoured by children. These approaches assume children to be adults in the making, and rarely approach the child's visit in the way that a child likely would, and that is from the aspect of play."

Emotional Vulnerability

While adults usually possess the maturity to manage reminders of human suffering, younger tourists may experience more distress. Some have even argued that dark sites can evoke vicarious trauma in children (Savage 2009). Such concerns derive from research in psychiatry and other fields indicating that children become distressed even when only indirectly exposed to human suffering (Burnham 2005; Pfefferbaum et al. 2000). For example, children in London exhibited signs of post-traumatic stress disorder even when their only exposure came from sitting safely in front of televisions thousands of miles away from the events of 9/11 (Holmes et al. 2007). Therefore, one can imagine that children exposed for the first time to horrifying displays such as the bones and bloodstains at Ntarama, Rwanda, the genocide memorial site (Caplan 2007), might undergo extreme distress. Researchers have yet to study children's distress at dark sites. In the words of a researcher, "a host of reactions, such as incident-related fear, should be more thoroughly explored in children less directly exposed" (Pfefferbaum et al. 2003, p. 99). Distress and PTSD seem like dire consequences of a tourist jaunt, and we simply do not yet know whether dark sites might affect children in this way.

In sum, current theories and research methods in dark tourism do not account for the differences between children and adults. To safeguard children while exploring fully what they think, feel, do, and remember at dark sites, we need additional research and different approaches. Fortunately, other disciplines have worked for decades to develop child-centered research methods, and we can adopt these to advance our efforts.

How Should We Study Children's Experiences at Dark Sites?

Research with children in any context requires special considerations (Christensen and James 2008; Woodhead and Faulkner 2008; Punch 2002), and this is equally true in tourism (Khoo-Lattimore 2015). Exploring children's experiences at memorials and other dark sites summons additional concerns, because even indirect exposure to death and suffering may evoke distress (Kerr and Price 2016; Holmes et al. 2007; Aber et al. 2004; Pfefferbaum et al. 2003; Beauchesne et al. 2002). In the next section, we discuss relevant research methods, with considerations for a unique context: children's experiences at dark sites. We discuss observing and listening, surveys, interviews, focus groups, and analysis of children's artifacts.

Observing and Listening to Children

Museum studies abound and often focus on children's learning and attention rather than their emotional experiences or motivations (also see Chap. 28). For this reason, they rely on direct observations of what and how children learn from exhibits (e.g., recording eye movements and time spent) as well as conversations that reflect their learning as they move through exhibits (Burris 2015; Eghbal-Azar and Widlok 2012). Investigators also describe how adults talk to (or teach) children, especially with those ages five to eight years, when such conversations are common during their visits (Povis and Crowley 2015; Crowley et al. 2014; Ash 2004; Allen 2002; Crowley and Jacobs 2002; Crowley et al. 2001).

Systematic observational accounts of children at dark sites are rare, anecdotal, and brief (Kerr and Price 2016; Kerr et al. 2014; Clark 2011; Knudsen 2011; Bowman and Pezzullo 2010; Carr 2010; Baldwin and Sharpley 2009). However, two museum studies offer systematic protocols useful for watching young visitors and listening to their conversations at dark sites. In their exploration of young children at a museum depicting 1840s British migrants to Southern Australia, Sutcliffe and Kim (2014) observed schoolchildren in structured and unstructured activities. The exhibits depicted death and illness, including an infant burial at sea. An ambitious observational protocol included not only children's conversations but also their behaviors, peer group associations, body language, attentiveness, and lack of engagement (e.g., fidgeting, off-task behaviors). This protocol could be used at dark sites as well.

Similarly, innovative methods appeared in Patterson's (2007) account of parent-child interactions at a museum exhibit, *Mysterious Bog People*. The researcher videoed children's conversations as they visited exhibits of mummies and artifacts found in a Northern European bog. The display included the remains of Yde, a 16-year-old girl, shown with the cord used to strangle her still around her neck; a nearby facial reconstruction depicted how she looked when alive. Though this investigation did not center on children (but on their parents' comfort level and approaches to explaining the exhibits), Patterson offered detailed analyses of the content, type, and duration of conversations captured on video as well as data from surveys, a common visitor measure.

Surveying Child Tourists

Given the safeguards needed to question minors about sensitive topics (Barker and Weller 2003b), children's surveys have yet to earn their place in the dark tourism literature. Yet, children's surveys and questionnaires appear regularly in general museum studies, particularly to assess learning and interpretive techniques. Researchers often rely on post-visit questionnaires in conjunction with observations (Hooper-Greenhill et al. 2009; Randler et al. 2007; Blud 1990). In lieu of traditional paper and pencil forms, some investigators prefer using electronic surveys to protect children's confidentiality (Lloyd and Devine 2010; Barker and Weller 2003a; De Leeuw et al. 2003). Sometimes adults read the surveys, or children hear the questions via a survey delivery system (Scott 2008). Graphics render surveys more engaging and clear for children under the age of 11 (Lloyd and Devine 2010; Scott 2008). Lastly, some adolescents simply prefer surveys (Borland et al. 2001). As one adolescent participant expressed it, "You're not going to be talked over if you've got a survey" (Hill 2006, p. 81).

Though easier than dealing with safeguards for directly querying children, inviting parents to respond on behalf of their young children may result in misinformation. Scott (2008) recommends instead that researchers trust young children's competence in responding to survey questions. She notes "...children are commonly believed to lack the communication, cognitive and social skills that are the prerequisite of good respondents. Experimental research has clearly demonstrated, however, that even preschool children are able to ... make social judgments..." (Scott 2008, p. 90).

Interviews with Children

Interviews of children have not yet appeared in the dark tourism literature. Nevertheless, we can benefit from developmental psychology and school excursion studies. Interviews offer interesting insights, even when they occur a few years after a visit. Falk and Dierking (1997), for instance, interviewed adults as well as schoolchildren and discovered that 96 percent could recall specific details of school trips from decades earlier:

> … early-elementary-school field trips are consequential experiences in children's lives. The overwhelming majority of subjects queried readily recalled their field trips – where and when they went and with whom, how they got there, and at least some details of what they did. There was no evidence that either the strength or scope of recollections significantly declined over time… These findings strongly suggest that museum field trips – regardless of type, subject matter, or nature of the lessons presented – result in highly salient and indelible memories. (Falk and Dierking 1997, pp. 215–216)

At what age can children visit a site and later recall it? Even children as young as three to six years exhibit *episodic memory*, the precise recall of events. Moreover, their recollections appear stable and highly accurate over time (Fivush 2008; Fivush and Haden 2005; Docherty and Sandelowski 1999). On the other hand, *autobiographical memory*—in which one recalls playing a role in past events—develops over time and through family and cultural influences (Fivush 2008). Western cultures, for example, promote the notion of an autonomous individual with a story to tell, whereas other cultures may not. Children in Western cultures are encouraged to rely on their autobiographical memory as early as preschool, through activities such as telling personal stories (Fivush 2008). This research implies that interviewing and inviting children to tell the story of their visit may be an appropriate research method with even very young visitors. Experts advise cueing young children (e.g., showing them photographs of a site) to help them recall their visits, and studies have shown that such techniques do not affect the content of the memory (Docherty and Sandelowski 1999).

Illustrating what we can learn from interviews even with young children, Sutcliffe and Kim (2014) conducted 15–20-minute open-ended interviews one week after children visited an immigration museum; the researchers cued with photographs of museum exhibits. Boys and girls reacted differently to exhibits and stories describing passenger illnesses and death. While both understood that death was part of the shipboard experience, the female children expressed deeper understandings and recognized with sadness that many babies and children died. Males focused on actions such as how the bodies were disposed (Sutcliffe and Kim 2014). Such gender differences warrant consideration when we conduct research with young tourists, especially when we interpret findings from interviews or when we analyze text artifacts.

Focus Group Interviews

Focus group interviews with children show promise for research at dark sites. Khoo-Lattimore (2015) invited focus groups of children ages five and six years to recount their family holidays. Based on her experiences, she outlined five principles for interviewing young tourists, summarized here:

> … phase of development, props, prompts, positionality, and pre-requisites. These five Ps require researchers to understand the development of various competences in children as well as their own skills set for interviewing children. The five Ps ask that researchers appraise their own views regarding children's role and competence and to use appropriate props and prompts that recognize children's rights. (Khoo-Lattimore 2015, p. 10)

To make children feel comfortable, researchers invite children to bring a friend to the group, interview children in familiar groups from the same classroom or neighborhood, or allow children to choose between group and individual interviews (Mayall 2008; Hill 2006).

Similar to the individual interview, the focus group seems an appropriate method for understanding children's experiences as visitors. However, researchers must remember child participants' emotional vulnerability as well as their developmental, gender, and sociocultural differences. Such considerations are essential in the interpretation of children's stories and interview responses. For example, if boys provide less detail than their female classmates do after a visit, it would be an oversimplification to assume that boys experience fewer (or weaker) emotional reactions than girls. Boys may prefer to withhold their feelings (Fivush and Buckner 2003). In preparing an interview protocol, investigators would benefit from practical guidance of experienced child researchers both within and outside the tourism field (e.g., see Angell et al. 2015; Khoo-Lattimore 2015; Christensen and James 2008; Docherty and Sandelowski 1999).

Studying Children's Artifacts

The tourism literature has embraced visitor artifacts as a rich data source (Goodson et al. 2015; Miles 2014; Stone 2012; Dockett et al. 2011; Bærenholdt et al. 2004; Haldrup and Larsen 2003). Examples include visitor comments as well as artwork, videos, and photographs that they create while touring. In addition, visitors often bring tributes or create them on site (Doss 2010; Sturken 2007). Such written artifacts and artwork can facilitate our understanding of children's feelings and thoughts (Kalvaitis and Monhardt 2012; Thomson 2008; Daiute et al. 2002; Gardner 1980). With relevance for dark tourism, White (2011, p. 2) noted that semiotic analysis of comments and drawings could offer a "useful tool for examining the sometimes multilayered images of national monuments."

Museums and other sites often encourage children to create art as part of an interpretive activity (Dockett et al. 2011; Tilden 1957). This interpretive approach yields artifacts not only familiar and enjoyable for children but also convenient for researchers. Photo elicitation activities reveal children's sense of place (Briggs et al. 2014), and children enjoy taking photographs and creating videos (Dockett et al. 2011). Moreover, many sites encourage children to write comments during a visit, suggesting another accessible source of data. Yet, it is important to be cautious here: we know little about the links between children's well-being, stress, and writing (Fivush et al. 2007). Until further research takes place, researchers must weigh the risks of including prompts that ask children to write specifically about their deepest feelings at dark sites. Open-ended prompts (e.g., "Tell us about your experience at_____") may be preferable.

Without question, a plentiful harvest awaits dark tourism researchers interested in children's experiences at particular dark sites. Some, like Uzzell and Ballantyne (2008, p. 512), might frame this inquiry as a mandate:

> Interpreters are generally willing to claim credit when visitors leave a heritage site having had a stimulating and enjoyable educational experience. Should they not also take responsibility for other effects, particularly those which are intended? How does one cater for those for whom the interpretation provides a powerful, evocative and emotional experience? What responsibility do interpreters have for the reactions of people who may have found the interpretation moving or even traumatic? Such visitors need to be catered for, as well as those for whom a place or experience is simply an intellectual encounter with the past—one which evokes little or no emotional connection.

In order for site interpreters to take responsibility for catering to—and caring for—young visitors, research must accelerate. As groundwork, Poria and Timothy (2014, p. 94) called for "small-scale exploratory qualitative studies … [that] can advance/acquire an initial understanding of children's travel experiences, including their impacts on the child."

Therefore, to begin to understand the impact of a dark site on its young visitors, we initiated small exploratory studies at the Flight 93 National Memorial in Pennsylvania, USA, where on 11 September 2001, a hijacked aircraft plowed into the earth traveling at 563 miles per hour. Cognizant of the literature on children's emotional vulnerability even when *indirectly* exposed to such an event, we cautiously began our research without interacting with young visitors. Instead, we examined artifacts they left behind in the years immediately following the crash, and it is to this work that this chapter now turns.

Children's Experiences at the Flight 93 National Memorial

On the morning of 11 September 2001, terrorists broke into the cockpit and commandeered United Flight 93, a flight from Newark, New Jersey to San Francisco, California. They diverted the plane toward Washington, DC, with the apparent intention of crashing it into the US Capitol or the White House (home and official office of the US President). Learning of the other three terrorist attacks that morning through onboard calls to loved ones, the 40 passengers and crew gathered and agreed to storm the cockpit with improvised weapons such as hot water and heavy objects. Realizing that their mission was doomed, the terrorists took the plane in a high-speed dive and crashed into a field near rural Shanksville, Pennsylvania, killing all on board. When local rescue teams arrived, they found only a smoldering crater.

The FBI immediately closed the crash site to the public. Yet, within 24 hours, mourners began to leave tributes at the "media village" 460 meters away. These tributes included banners, posters, original artwork, flowers, wreaths, and thoughts and feelings written on scraps of paper (National Park Service 2012). Beginning on 12 October 2001, all objects left at the site except for biotic materials (e.g., flowers affixed to wreaths and plants) were painstakingly gathered and stored.[3] The crash site is now part of the Flight 93 National Memorial managed by the National Park Service (NPS), a US federal agency. Today, NPS staff members collect the tributes left at the permanent memorial and minimally clean, accession, catalogue, and prepare them for storage. Under federal regulations, registered researchers may study and photograph these items,[4] with permission of the NPS curator.

In the years immediately following 9/11, hundreds of young visitors, many too young to remember the day, visited the temporary memorial site. Here we tell the story of what they left behind.

Children's Memorial Materials

Children[5] left toys, flags, stuffed animals, jewelry, and crafts, most without explanations. Many were small toys from children's fast food meals, convenient and similar to those at other US memorials (Doss 2010). Researchers have described objects like these at public memorials in the USA and elsewhere (Sather-Wagstaff 2011; Senie 2006; Sturken 2007; Simpson 2006). Some view these objects as consumerism or memorial kitsch (Sturken 2007), but Doss (2010, p. 69) defended temporary memorials: "Rather than being viewed as cultural pathologies, temporary memorials can be seen as the creative products of profound personal and public feelings. More directly, temporary memorials help to mediate the psychic crisis of sudden and inexplicable loss."

This "sudden and inexplicable loss" affected a nearby rural community of just 245 residents. Children from the area school left a toy plane at the crash site in 2002, shown in Plate 23.1.

The children drew "93" in bright colors on the tail section, and across the fuselage, "Thank you for saving our lives and for not hitting our school."

Meanwhile, Plate 23.2 shows toys and jewelry items left during the same year inside a plastic box inscribed: "To the Flight 93 people … Rock and Roll … Thank You." Media accounts at the time portrayed the phrase, "Let's roll!" as a call to action attributed to one of the passengers.[6] This upbeat message, with what might be interpreted as gifts, was likely a reference to the perceived heroes and heroines who stormed the cockpit.

One young visitor wrote on a comment card why she left a piece of handmade jewelry:

Usually im not that emotional for really anything but being here today has really made me think and I was touched I left a pink and blue lace bracelet I got from a camp called "48 hour marathon" I hope that someway these people can relize now they were heroes. God Bless!. (Original spellings)

Plate 23.1 Toy plane left in 2002 at the crash site of Flight 93 (Photo Source: Mary Anne McMullen)

Plate 23.2 Children's items left in 2002 at the crash site of Flight 93 (Photo Source: Author)

Years later, the permanent memorial was built with consideration of such tributes. Empty niches occupy space in the long granite wall that borders the crash site, and each day, visitors fill them with tributes. In 2013, we watched as 10- and 11-year-olds on a school trip—none of them alive at the time of the event—spontaneously crafted memorials with tiny scraps of paper. Many years after the crash, their creations echoed the expressions of earlier young pilgrims.

Children's Comment Cards

We examined early comment cards from the years 2001–06, because children old enough to write a card also were old enough to recall 9/11. Early visitors received blank cards for writing their comments. Starting in 2003, the NPS provided cards printed with the words, "Please share your thoughts about Flight 93 and September 11, 2001 … Your response will become part of the Tribute Collection." A display board allowed visitors to leave their comment cards for public view before they were archived.

In sifting through thousands of handwritten cards in search of those authored by children, we quickly encountered a dilemma. Many cards listed no age,[7] yet they exhibited characteristics clearly attributable to children. Ultimately, we decided to study these comments, because the cards comprise the only primary source we have from those early years. We acknowledge this limitation and outline our process for the reader.

Two researchers (with over 60 years combined experience reading children's handwriting) assessed each card by studying the signature and age (when provided), content, syntax, handwriting, symbols, spacing, and word choices. We considered age-relevant visual clues such as drawings and stickers on the cards and multiple date stamps placed as decorations around the border. In cases of disagreement, we sought a third review. We excluded any card with adult-like writing (and no doubt excluded many adolescents' comments as a result). We included cards on which adults recorded comments that children dictated; in these cases, we included only the dictated text. To illustrate the evaluation process, Plates 23.3 and 23.4 illustrate examples of rejected and accepted cards.

In all, we selected 248 cards from a collection numbering approximately 3000. Some children signed their names, gave their ages, and/or listed the states or cities in which they lived. All comments were in English—either a few words or a few lines. Some bore small drawings. None included profanity.

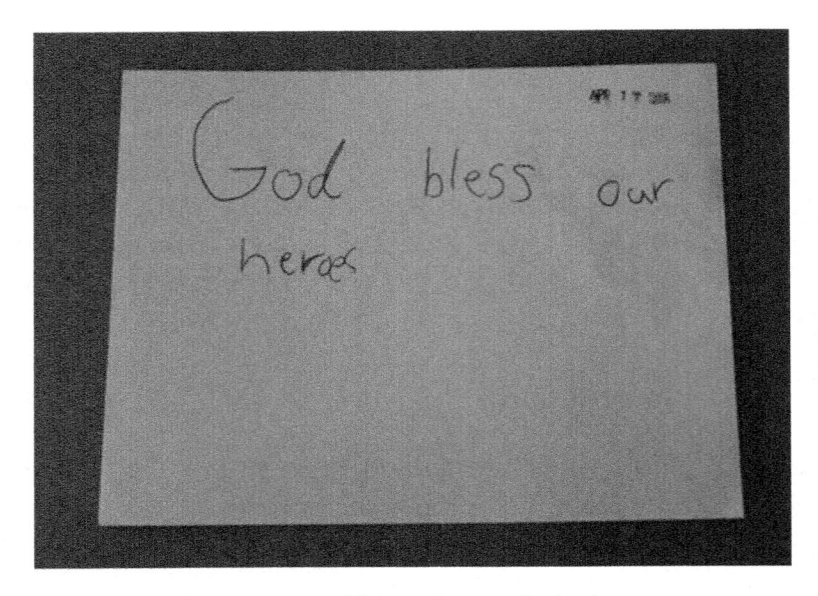

Plate 23.3 A rejected comment card (Photo Source: Author)

Plate 23.4 An accepted comment card which reads (as original): "Dear Men i Miss You i Love You i know the plane crashed. Love g p 2004 APRiL" (Photo Source: Author)

As one would expect, the comments include spelling and punctuation errors typical of young writers. Analogous to the analytic process Dockett et al. (2011) adopted, we uploaded all comments into a computer-assisted qualitative data analysis software program for line-by-line coding and the development of iterative researcher memos (Strauss 1987). Constant comparative analyses (Strauss and Corbin 1998) assessed similar patterns and themes across participants' responses. What follows is a brief synopsis of our findings.

Given the interpretive narrative associated with the Flight 93 Memorial, children wrote most frequently about the plane and heroes, offering thanks and pledging remembrance. Some wrote lengthier comments about these ideas and revealed how they were struggling to make meaning of the events. For instance, (original spellings):

- Six-year-old (gender unknown) in 2005: *I feel very sad for the good guys who died.*
- 17-year-old male in 2002: *Dear Heros, You will never be forgotten. Your sacrifice is incomprehensible. You will live on in the lives and hearts of every American, for it is because of you that we can still call ourselves American. Thank you for your completely unselfish act. I will respect you always.*
- 10-year-old female in 2004: *As I look over the feilds and try to stand all the leters, writings and so on I realise that this is life and a hard part of it. I wish I could have brought back the life's of these people. I soppurt the crew and oner them alot in what they did for this country. I support the people who take care of this place and feild. May God Bless these familys and friends as the still suffor these death's. I hope that the feel the Lord and his guidance throw this hard time. Again all my thanks to the crew for doing what they did for this country, and hope that people (if that happiness again) will stand up for what's right. God bless these family's, friends and all!*
- 14-year-old in 2005: *I have much respect for what this Memorilal stands for. I am now 14 year old and when this had happened I was 10 years old and I really did not understand what had happened so now that I have had the chance to learn more about it I understand what had happed Ive got to see this memorial and I Just wanted to thank all the people that had Joned in and helped to make this able to see and thank you to all those heros.*

As illustrated in these comments, some children drew on religion to offer comfort. For example, a seven-year-old female in 2004 wrote, "God bles all the famalys ho lost Loved ones!"

In other instances, *God* did not convey a specifically religious message. In fact, "God Bless" appeared more than any other phrase. "God Bless America" had become a popular mantra throughout the USA at the time (Domke and Coe 2007; Eberle 2007). To illustrate, a seven-year-old male in 2004 wrote "In memory of fliight 93. God. Bless America."

In their classic study of young children, Easton and Hess (1962) found that by age seven, children have learned that they are Americans, and they are firmly and emotionally attached to their nation. Also according to Easton and Hess (1962, p. 238), until "ages 9 or 10 [children] sometimes have considerable difficulty in disentangling God and country."

We find it interesting that years after the crash, older children occasionally write comment cards that recall their experiences as young children on 9/11, as shown in Plate 23.5.

Though limited in what they can reveal, the comments nevertheless provide an unprecedented glimpse into young tourists' attempts to make meaning of the crash and more broadly, the events of 9/11. "The United States is haunted by 9/11 and by what it means" (Walter 2009, p. 50). For these children, like all humans, the search for meaning played a role in managing frightening or stressful situations (Saltzman et al. 2013).

We turn now to what children shared through their art.

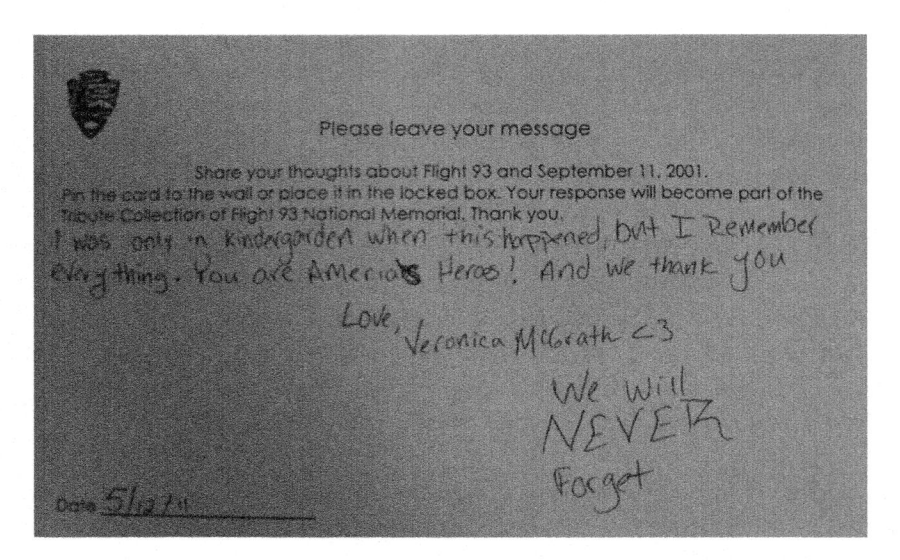

Plate 23.5 Child's message left in 2011 at the Flight 93 National Memorial (Photo Source: Author)

"I Know the Plane Crashed": Children's Perspectives in Dark Tourism 569

Children's Artwork

Young artists' drawings, paintings, and other artwork appeared at the temporary memorial during the early years. Because no art supplies were available then at the site, we believe children created these pieces elsewhere and brought them on their visit. Aided by a research team member who is both an art teacher and an art therapist, we estimated the ages of the young artists. To illustrate, we offer Plates 23.6 and 23.7, two drawings depicting the World Trade Center collapse in New York City.

Plate 23.6 Child's drawing depicting the World Trade Center crash in New York City (Of note: X-Ray technique, patriotic colors, and smiling victims) (Photo Source: Mary Anne McMullen)

Plate 23.7 Child's drawing depicting World Trade Center crash in New York City (Of note: X-ray technique and smiling victims) (Photo Source: Mary Anne McMullen)

These appear to be the work of young children, around six or seven years old. Two clues warrant this hypothesis. First, the artists used an X-ray drawing technique that allows viewers to see through buildings and planes (Di Leo 2013; Barraza 1999). Second, the smiles on the faces of people inside the buildings indicate that the artists are young children who lack experience of trauma: they depict shocking events with smiling faces. This also may reflect the young children's incomplete understanding of death, as we mentioned previously. Interestingly, children drew pictures of the World Trade Center for their visit to the Flight 93 Memorial, indicating a possible understanding of the connection between the events.

Older children and adolescents created artwork illustrative of more advanced techniques, and they often included handwritten messages such as "Sorry that your love one died," "United we stand," or "God Bless America."

"I Know the Plane Crashed": Children's Perspectives in Dark Tourism

The colors red, white, and blue (symbolic of the US flag) were ubiquitous. Even at a young age, the artists associated these colors with patriotism in America. For example, a group of children secured a display of individual painted tiles onto the temporary memorial fence. One tile seems to refer not only to the US national colors (red, white, and blue) and flag but also to the perceived heroes and heroines—the passengers and crew—who "didn't run," as illustrated in Plate 23.8.

Similar to comment cards left at the memorial, artwork often revealed children's attempts to make meaning of the events of 9/11 (Gross and Clemens 2002). One young child drew simple pictures in a multipage booklet, titling it "Surivel Stuff." She seemed to grasp the danger associated with the events and the continuing need to prepare for survival. This may reflect public service announcements from the Federal Emergency Management Agency that called on families to develop emergency plans.

Whether exposed in person or through media, children often use artwork to express their feelings and share their visions of what occurred (Gross and Clemens 2002). In this case, depictions of the World Trade Center shown above suggest that the artists had seen images of the buildings with people

Plate 23.8 Patriotic tile tied to the fence surrounding the Flight 93 crash site (Photo Source: Mary Anne McMullen)

Plate 23.9 Child's drawing depicting first responders (Photo Source: Mary Anne McMullen)

trapped inside. Similarly, other children exhibited meaning making by drawing first responders, suggesting that the children possessed some awareness that police, firefighters, and emergency medical crew played an important role in the events of 9/11. Plate 23.9 offers an example.

Content such as this could stem from adult interpretation, as some adults chose to highlight the unified response of first responders and other "heroes" as the focal point of 9/11 (Simpson 2006). In fact, many adults still choose to remember the events of 11 September 2001 as the heroic actions of Americans, rather than the actions of the hijackers (Simpson 2006).

When children visited this dark site, they left cheerful toys, simple words, and brightly colored drawings in striking contrast to somber wreaths, mourners' messages, religious medals, and photographs of the passengers and crew. Based on what we learned about children's perspectives, we subsequently redesigned the "Junior Ranger" interpretive booklet for children ages 6–12 years who may visit the Flight 93 National Memorial (Shaffer and Kerr 2015; Kerr et al. 2014; National Park Service 2014). Plate 23.10 shows a page from the booklet.

Children today find a page encouraging them to create a tribute; on another page, they see small drawings of tributes to search for while they

"I Know the Plane Crashed": Children's Perspectives in Dark Tourism 573

> **A Place of Honor**
>
> The next pages will tell you about Flight 93 National Memorial as a place of honor. This is a place where people come to show respect and to honor the brave passengers and crew. Visiting is one way to show honor. Some people leave special items on the shelves in the wall or in front of the Wall of Names. Other people may send art, poems or letters. Some people write about or tell the story of Flight 93. These are all ways to honor the brave people on Flight 93.
>
> ## Activity 6: Honoring Heroes
>
> At Flight 93 National Memorial, some visitors leave notes, flowers, flags, or badges. These items honor the passengers and crew of Flight 93. We call them **tributes**. They mean something to the person who left them, even if we do not always know why. Here are some tributes you may see today. You may not see the same item, but something like it.
>
> Circle the tributes that you saw today
>
> Flags — Religious Symbols — Flowers — Jewelry — Pins — Toys — Cards — Wreaths — Patches
>
> Junior Ranger Handbook — A Place of Honor — Page 14

Plate 23.10 Flight 93 Memorial Junior Ranger booklet page (Photo Source: Mary Anne McMullen)

roam the long walkways. One page illustrates a matching game with "helpers" such as firefighters and paramedics. Another page depicts flags of the nations represented by the passenger and crew nationalities and invites children to draw their flag. Other pages encourage quiet reflection, touch, or writing about the visit.

The artifacts also ushered in new insights for those designing the Visitor Center at the Flight 93 National Memorial. Indeed, the Visitor Center team worked hard to accommodate young children's needs while still conveying the complicated and grim narrative of the day. Disturbing artifacts, deliberately placed up high, escape young children's gaze. Large images of firefighters, medics, and police reinforce for young visitors the concept of helpers. Near the exit, a prominent glass case filled with tributes causes young visitors to stop and linger. Here, children too young to recall the events of 9/11 gaze at cheerful toys and children's vividly painted artwork and notes. Looking up at the tributes, today's young tourists experience a moment of connection with children who gazed at a charred field years ago and knew the plane crashed.

Conclusion

This chapter has sought to include children in the dark tourism discourse. In so doing, it represents only a beginning for what promises to be challenging yet rewarding research. To advance, however, scholars first must overcome difficulties that have stymied others. For example, research with children relies on approaches that must consider their interests and attempt to improve their well-being, thereby striking a delicate "balance between protection and participation" (Einarsdóttir 2007, p. 208). Researchers around the world must allocate additional time and effort to secure approvals from children, parents, sites, and institutional research review boards (IRBs) (Kerr and Price 2016). Research with children at dark sites further complicates the approval process. When there are inquiries about a child's personal experience or feelings at a potentially distressing site, an IRB may require additional levels of review, delay approval, or even prohibit research entirely (Fisher et al. 2013).

Another concern is the scholarly risk one takes when undertaking research with children. Not only might special safeguards make children difficult to access, but the researcher also must find an outlet willing to publish this new, interdisciplinary approach in the adult-dominated field of dark tourism. Moreover, the specialized knowledge required both to research with young children and to research sensitive topics may discourage some who otherwise would be interested in conducting this research (Kerr and Price 2016; Poria and Timothy 2014; Greig et al. 2012; Duffy 2007; Irwin and Johnson 2005). Even analyzing children's artifacts requires specialized skills, such as those in art theory and child development (Kerr and Price 2016).

Yet, compelling reasons may convince tentative scholars to forge ahead. First, given their insights and ability to express their feelings, capturing young tourists' perspectives can improve their experiences (and those of their families) at dark sites. Even very young children are able to make some meaning out of events and to convey that they understand (Scott 2008). At the Flight 93 National Memorial, children barely old enough to write their names were able to convey that they understood "the plane crashed" and that "heroes" "sacrificed" their lives. Research with children acknowledges children's rights to be included and to have their unique perspectives heard (Dockett et al. 2011).

Research *on* children will move us forward, but such research methods may be insufficient for fully understanding children's perspectives (Christensen and James 2008; Punch 2002). Recently, scholars have engaged children as collaborators in research design and data collection (Dockett et al. 2011). Taking collaboration another step forward, researchers have even engaged children in helping them interpret their findings from interviews (Pinter and Zandian 2015), questionnaires (Alerby and Kostenius 2011), and artifacts (Dockett et al. 2011). In every instance, the researchers applauded the benefits of engaging children and adolescents. These interactions yielded perspectives that would have been silenced or lost without children's involvement.

A second reason to undertake research with children is that their perspectives enrich interpretation, thereby benefiting children, parents, and teachers. "Although it is acknowledged that children contribute significantly as a market segment (Brochu 2003; Ward and Wilkinson 2006), they are not often considered by those undertaking research into interpretation design, practice or effectiveness" (Sutcliffe and Kim 2014, p. 3). Given the difficulty of interpreting human suffering at dark sites and the potential risks to children of grim displays, we need to understand what kinds of interpretation and exhibits facilitate meaningful visits without inducing undue distress.

Despite calls for research for the past 30 years (Graburn 1983), we still know woefully little about child tourists. We know even less about their experiences at dark sites (Kerr and Price 2016). While adult dark tourism research offers some paths to pursue, it cannot fully account for the complexities of childhood: children's incomplete understanding of death, their limited influence in choosing destinations, their youthful exploratory behavior, and their emotional vulnerability. The time has come for engaging children not only as participants but also as co-researchers. Only then will we know what young tourists think, feel, do, and remember when they visit dark sites.

Acknowledgments We acknowledge with gratitude our entire research team. Special thanks go to Mary Anne McMullen, who provided photographs and children's art consultation; Kristen Frese who assisted with artifacts analysis and writing; and, Constance DeMore Savine, who transcribed and analyzed comment cards.

Notes

1. We do not characterize young visitors as *dark tourists*, because we have no research on children's motives as tourists visiting dark sites. We do refer to *dark tourism*, for brevity, understood to mean as the "act of travel to tourist sites associated with death, suffering or the seemingly macabre" (Stone 2006, p. 146).
2. See also Frost and Laing's (2013) discussion of festivity, controversy, and generation gaps at commemorative events (pp. 163–64).
3. More recently, the National Park Service stopped archiving the small American flags seen everywhere in the United States following 9/11, because there are too many to store (See Sturken 2007, pp. 54–56).
4. Items left for public display are considered "abandoned public property." Because our research involved only such artifacts, the University's research approval board did not require parent or child consent.
5. Though we were not present, NPS staff and volunteers at the temporary memorial reported to us that children left such items.
6. Some accounts pose an alternative explanation for the words heard on a flight recording: "Let's roll" referred to rolling the heavy food service cart toward the cockpit to stop the hijackers.
7. To comply with NPS policies, site staff and volunteers refrain from asking visitors demographic information such as age or school level.

References

Aber, J. L., Gershoff, E. T., Ware, A., & Kotler, J. A. (2004). Estimating the effects of September 11th and other forms of violence on the mental health and social development of New York City's youth: A matter of context. *Applied Developmental Science, 8*(3), 111–129.

Alerby, E., & Kostenius, C. (2011). "Dammed taxi cab"–how silent communication in questionnaires can be understood and used to give voice to children's experiences. *International Journal of Research & Method in Education, 34*(2), 117–130.

Allen, S. (2002). Looking for learning in visitor talk: A methodological exploration. In G. Leinhardt, K. Crowley, & K. Knutson (Eds.), *Learning conversations in museums* (pp. 259–303). Mahwah: Lawrence Erlbaum Associates.

Angell, C., Alexander, J., & Hunt, J. A. (2015). "Draw, write and tell": A literature review and methodological development on the 'draw and write' research method. *Journal of Early Childhood Research, 3*(1), 17–28.

Ash, D. (2004). How do families use questions at dioramas? Implications for exhibit design. *Curator, 47*, 84–100.

Ashworth, G. J., & Isaac, R. K. (2015). Have we illuminated the dark? Shifting perspectives on "dark" tourism. *Tourism Recreation Research, 40*(3), 316–325.

Bærenholdt, J. O., Haldrup, M., Larsen, J., & Urry, J. (2004). *Performing tourist places*. Hants: Ashgate Publishing.

Baldwin, F., & Sharpley, R. (2009). Battlefield tourism: Bringing organised violence back to life. In R. Sharpley & P. R. Stone (Eds.), *The darker side of travel: The theory and practice of dark tourism* (pp. 186–206). Bristol: Channel View Publications.

Bandura, A. (2006). Toward a psychology of human agency. *Perspectives in Psychological Science, 1*(2), 164–180.

Barker, J., & Weller, S. (2003a). Geography of methodological issues in research with children. *Qualitative Research, 3*(2), 207–227.

Barker, J., & Weller, S. (2003b). "Is it fun?" Developing children centered research methods. *International Journal of Sociology and Social Policy, 23*(1/2), 33–58.

Barraza, L. (1999). Children's drawings about the environment. *Environmental Education Research, 5*(1), 49–66.

Beauchesne, M. A., Kelley, B. R., Patsdaughter, C. A., & Pickard, J. (2002). Attack on America: Children's reactions and parents' responses. *Journal of Pediatric Health Care, 16*(5), 213–221.

Biran, A., & Poria, Y. (2012). Reconceptualising dark tourism. *Contemporary Tourist Experience: Concepts and Consequences, 27*, 59.

Blud, L. M. (1990). Social interaction and learning among family groups visiting a museum. *Museum Management and Curatorship, 9*(1), 43–51.

Borland, M., Hill, M., Laybourn, A., & Stafford, A. (2001). *Improving consultation with children and young people in relevant aspects of policy-making and legislation in Scotland (Stationery Office)*. Edinburgh: Stationary Office.

Bowman, M. S., & Pezzullo, P. C. (2010). What's so 'dark' about 'dark tourism'? Death, tours, and performance. *Tourist Studies, 9*(3), 187–202.

Briggs, L. P., Stedman, R. C., & Krasny, M. E. (2014). Photo-elicitation methods in studies of children's sense of place. *Children, Youth, and Environments, 24*(3), 153–172.

Brochu, L. (2003). *Interpretive planning. The 5-M model for successful planning projects*. Singapore: InterpPress.

Burnham, J. J. (2005). Fears of children in the United States: An examination of the American fear survey schedule with 20 new contemporary fear items. *Measurement and Evaluation in Counseling and Development, 38*, 78–91.

Burris, A. (2015). *A Kids-eye view of the zoo*. Conference presentation, 17 July 2015, Visitor Studies Association Conference, Indianapolis.

Callanan, M. A. (2014). Diversity in children's understanding of death. *Monographs of the Society for Research in Child Development, 79*(1), 142–150.

Caplan, P. (2007). "Never again": Genocide memorials in Rwanda. *Anthropology Today, 23*(1), 20–22.

Carr, N. (2006). A comparison of adolescents' and parents' holiday motivations and desires. *Tourism and Hospitality Research, 6*(2), 129–142.

Carr, G. (2010). Shining a light on dark tourism: German bunkers in the British Channel Islands. *Public Archaeology, 9*(2), 64–84.

Christensen, P., & James, A. (2008). *Research with children: Perspectives and practices*. London: Routledge.

Clark, L. B. (2011). Never again and its discontents. *Performance Research, 16*(1), 68–79.

Collins-Kreiner, N. (2015). Dark tourism as/is pilgrimage. *Current Issues in Tourism, 19*(12), 1185–1189.

Crowley, K., & Jacobs, M. (2002). Building islands of expertise in everyday family activity. In G. Leinhardt, K. Crowley, & K. Knutson (Eds.), *Learning conversations in museums* (pp. 333–356). Mahwah: Lawrence Erlbaum Associates.

Crowley, K., Callanan, M. A., Tenenbaum, H. R., & Allen, E. (2001). Parents explain more often to boys than to girls during shared scientific thinking. *Psychological Science, 12*(3), 258–261.

Crowley, K., Pierroux, P., & Knutson, K. (2014). Informal learning in museums. In K. Sawyer (Ed.), *Cambridge handbook of the learning sciences* (pp. 461–478). Cambridge: Cambridge University Press.

Daiute, C., Buteau, E. L., Stephen J., & Smyth, J. M. (Eds.). (2012). Writing for their lives: Children's narratives as supports for physical and psychological well-being. In S. J. Lepore & J. M. Smyth (Eds.), *The writing cure: How expressive writing promotes health and emotional well-being* (pp. 53–73). Washington, DC: American Psychological Association.

De Leeuw, E., Hox, J., & Kef, S. (2003). Computer-assisted self-interviewing tailored for special populations and topics. *Field Methods, 15*(3), 223–251.

Di Leo, J. H. (2013). *Interpreting children's drawings*. London: Routledge.

Docherty, S., & Sandelowski, M. (1999). Focus on qualitative methods: Interviewing children. *Research in Nursing & Health, 22*(2), 177–185.

Dockett, S., Main, S., & Kelly, L. (2011). Consulting young children: Experiences from a museum. *Visitor Studies, 14*(1), 13–33.

Domke, D., & Coe, K. M. (2007). The God strategy: The rise of religious politics in America. *Journal of Ecumenical Studies, 42*(1), 53–75.

Doss, E. (2010). *Memorial mania: Public feeling in America*. Chicago: University of Chicago Press.

Duffy, S. (2007). Psychology. In V. Bowman (Ed.), *Scholarly resources for children and childhood studies: A research guide and annotated bibliography* (pp. 183–209). Lanham: Scarecrow Press.

Easton, D., & Hess, R. D. (1962). The child's political world. *Midwest Journal of Political Science, 6*(3), 229–246.

Eberle, G. (2007). *Dangerous words: Talking about God in an age of fundamentalism*. Boston: Trumpeter.

Eghbal-Azar, K., & Widlok, T. (2012). Potentials and limitations of mobile eye tracking in visitor studies: Evidence from field research at two museum exhibitions in Germany. *Social Science Computer Review, 31*(1), 103–118.

Einarsdóttir, J. (2007). Research with children: Methodological and ethical challenges. *Early Childhood Education Research Journal, 15*(2), 197–211.

Falk, J. H., & Dierking, L. D. (1997). School field trips: Assessing their long-term impact. *Curator: The Museum Journal, 40*(3), 211–218.

Fisher, C. B., Brunnquell, D. J., Hughes, D. L., Liben, L. S., Maholmes, V., Plattner, S., et al. (2013). Preserving and enhancing the responsible conduct of research involving children and youth: A response to proposed changes in federal regulations (Sharing Child and Youth Development Knowledge Report Vol. 27, No. 1). Retrieved from Society for Research in Child Development website. http://srcd.org/sites/default/files/spr_27-1.pdf. Accessed 10 Feb 2016.

Fivush, R. (2008). Remembering and reminiscing: How individual lives are constructed in family narratives. *Memory Studies, 1*(1), 49–58.

Fivush, R., & Buckner, J. P. (2003). Creating gender and identity through autobiographical narratives. In R. Fivush & C. A. Haden (Eds.), *Autobiographical memory and the construction of a narrative self: Developmental and cultural perspectives* (pp. 149–167). Mahwah: Lawrence Erlbaum Associates.

Fivush, R., & Haden, C. A. (2005). Parent–child reminiscing and the construction of a subjective self. In *The development of social cognition and communication*, ed. BD Homer, CS Tamis-LeMonda, pp. 315–35. Mahwah NJ: Erlbaum.

Fivush, R., Marin, K., Crawford, M., Reynolds, M., & Brewin, C. R. (2007). Children's narratives and well-being. *Cognition and Emotion, 21*(7), 1414–1434.

Frost, W., & Laing, J. (2013). *Commemorative events: Memory, identities, and conflict*. Abingdon: Routledge.

Gardner, H. (1980). *Artful scribbles: The significance of children's drawings*. New York: Basic Books.

Goodson, J. M., Soren, B. J., & Pierce, S. E. (2015). *Harnessing empathy: The path to inspiring others to take action*. Indianapolis: Visitor Studies Association.

Graburn, N. (1983). Editor's page. *Annals of Tourism Research, 10*, 1–5.

Greig, A. D., Taylor, J., & MacKay, T. (2012). *Doing research with children: A practical guide*. Thousand Oaks: Sage.

Gross, T., & Clemens, S. G. (2002). Painting a tragedy: Young children process the events of September 11. *Young Children, 57*(3), 44–51.

Haldrup, M., & Larsen, J. (2003). The family gaze. *Tourist Studies, 3*(1), 23–45.

Hartmann, R. (2014). Dark tourism, thanatourism, and dissonance in heritage tourism management: New directions in contemporary tourism research. *Journal of Heritage Tourism, 9*(2), 166–182.

Hill, M. (2006). Children's voices on ways of having a voice: Children's and young people's perspectives on methods used in research and consultation. *Childhood, 13*(1), 69–89.

Holmes, E. A., Creswell, C., & O'Connor, T. G. (2007). Post-traumatic stress symptoms in London school children following September 11, 2001: An exploratory investigation of peri-traumatic reactions and intrusive imagery. *Journal of Behavior Therapy and Experimental Psychiatry, 38*(4), 474–490.

Hooper-Greenhill, E., Phillips, M., & Woodham, A. (2009). Museums, schools and geographies of cultural value. *Cultural Trends, 18*(2), 149–183.

Irwin, L. G., & Johnson, J. (2005). Interviewing young children: Explicating our practices and dilemmas. *Qualitative Health Research, 15*(6), 821–831.

Kalvaitis, D., & Monhardt, R. M. (2012). The architecture of children's relationships with nature: A phenomenographic investigation seen through drawings and written narratives of elementary students. *Environmental Education Research, 18*(2), 209–227.

Kerr, M. M., & Price, R. H. (2016). Overlooked encounters: Young tourists' experiences at dark sites. *Journal of Heritage Tourism, 11*(2), 177–185.

Kerr, M. M., Shaffer, A., & Hartman, M. (2014, July/August). Interpreting the Flight 93 crash for children: A collaborative evaluation project. *Legacy: The Magazine of the National Association for Interpretation.*

Khoo-Lattimore, C. (2015). Kids on board: Methodological challenges, concerns and clarifications when including young children's voices in tourism research. *Current Issues in Tourism, 18*(9), 845–858.

Knudsen, B. T. (2011). Thanatourism: Witnessing difficult pasts. *Tourist Studies, 11*(1), 67–72.

Larsen, S., & Jenssen, D. (2004). The school trip: Travelling with, not to or from. *Scandinavian Journal of Hospitality and Tourism, 4*(1), 43–57.

Lloyd, K., & Devine, P. (2010). Using the internet to give children a voice: An online survey of 10-and 11-year-old children in Northern Ireland. *Field Methods, 22*(3), 270–289.

Mayall, B. (2008). Conversations with children. In P. Christensen & A. James (Eds.), *Research with children: Perspectives and practices* (pp. 109–124). London: Routledge.

MetalClocker. (2015). Parents letting their children play on the "Vietnam Women's Memorial" right in front of veterans [Reddit]. 24 March. Available from. https://www.reddit.com/r/pics/comments/304g58/parents_letting_their_children_play_on_the/. Accessed 10 Feb 2016.

Miles, S. (2014). Battlefield sites as dark tourism attractions: An analysis of experience. *Journal of Heritage Tourism, 9*(2), 134–147.

Nanda, D., Hu, C., & Bai, B. (2006). Exploring family roles in purchasing decisions during vacation planning: Review and discussions for future research. *Journal of Travel and Tourism Marketing, 20*(3–4), 107–125.

National Park Service. (2012). *Flight 93 temporary memorials and tributes: The first ten years September 11, 2001 to September 9, 2011.* Stoystown; Author.

National Park Service. (2014). *Flight 93 junior ranger program.* Stoystown: Author.

Patterson, A. R. (2007). "Dad look, she's sleeping": Parent–child conversations about human remains. *Visitor Studies, 10*(1), 55–72.

Pfefferbaum, B., Seale, T. W., McDonald, N. B., Brandt, E. N., Jr., Rainwater, S. M., Maynard, B. T., et al. (2000). Post-traumatic stress two years after the Oklahoma City bombing in youths geographically distant from the explosion. *Psychiatry, 62*(4), 358–370.

Pfefferbaum, B., Pfefferbaum, R. L., Gurwitch, R. H., Nagumalli, S., Brandt, E. N., Jr., Robertson, M. J., & Saste, V. S. (2003). Children's response to terrorism: A critical review of the literature. *Current Psychiatry Reports, 1*(2), 95–100.

Picard, D., & Robinson, M. (Eds.). (2012). *Emotion in motion: Tourism, affect and transformation*. Hants: Ashgate Publishing.

Pinter, A., & Zandian, S. (2015). "I thought it would be tiny little one phrase that we said, in a huge big pile of papers": Children's reflections on their involvement in participatory research. *Qualitative Research, 15*(2), 235–250.

Poling, D. A., & Evans, E. M. (2004). Are dinosaurs the rule or the exception? Developing concepts of death and extinction. *Cognitive Development, 19*(3), 363–383.

Poria, Y., & Timothy, D. J. (2014). Where are the children in tourism research? *Annals of Tourism Research, 47*, 93–95.

Povis, K., & Crowley, K. (2015). Observing together: Joint attention and conversation around natural history dioramas. *Visitor Studies, 18*(2), 168–182.

Punch, S. (2002). Research with children: The same or different from research with adults? *Childhood, 9*(3), 321–341.

Randler, C., Höllwarth, A., & Schaal, S. (2007). Urban park visitors and their knowledge of animal species. *Anthrozoös, 20*(1), 65–74.

Ritchie, B. W., & Coughlan, D. (2004). Understanding school excursion planning and constraints: An Australian case study. *Tourism Review International, 8*, 113–126.

Sather-Wagstaff, J. (2011). *Heritage that hurts: Tourists in the memoryscapes of September 11*. Walnut Creek: Left Coast Press.

Savage, K. (2009). *Monument wars: Washington, the National Mall, and the transformation of the memorial landscape*. Berkeley: University of California Press.

Schänzel, H. A., Smith, K. A., & Weaver, A. (2005). Family holidays: A research review and application to New Zealand. *Annals of Leisure Research, 8*(2–3), 105–123.

Scott, J. (2008). Children as respondents: The challenge for quantitative methods. In P. Christensen & A. James (Eds.), *Research with children: Perspectives and practices* (2nd ed.). Abingdon: Routledge.

Seaton, A. (2002). Thanatourism's final frontiers? Visits to cemeteries, churchyards and funerary sites as sacred and secular pilgrimage. *Tourism Recreation Research, 27*(2), 73–82.

Senie, H. F. (2006). Mourning in protest: Spontaneous memorials and the sacralization of public space. In J. Santino (Ed.), *Spontaneous shrines and the public memorialization of death* (pp. 41–56). Basingstoke: Palgrave Macmillan.

Shaffer, A., & Kerr, M. M. (2015). "Can you tell my child what happened here?" Interpreting the story of United Flight 93. *Ranger: The Journal of the Association of National Park Rangers, 31*(2), 2–3.

Simpson, D. (2006). *9/11: The culture of commemoration*. Chicago: The University of Chicago Press.

Small, J. (2008). The absence of childhood in tourism studies. *Annals of Tourism Research, 35*(3), 772–789.

Stone, P. R. (2006). A dark tourism spectrum: Towards a typology of death and macabre related tourist sites, attractions and exhibitions. *Tourism: An Interdisciplinary International Journal, 54*(2), 145–160.

Stone, P. R. (2012). Dark tourism as 'mortality capital': The case of ground zero and the significant other dead. In R. Sharpley & P. R. Stone (Eds.), *Contemporary tourist experience: Concepts and consequences* (pp. 71–94). Abington: Routledge.

Stone, P. R. (2013). Dark tourism scholarship: A critical review. *International Journal of Culture, Tourism, and Hospitality Research, 7*(3), 307–318.

Stone, P. R., & Sharpley, R. (2013). Deviance, dark tourism, and "dark leisure": Towards a (re)configuration of morality and the taboo in secular society. In S. Elkington & S. Gammon (Eds.), *Contemporary perspectives in leisure: Meanings, motives and lifelong learning* (pp. 54–64). London: Routledge.

Strauss, A. L. (1987). *Qualitative analysis for social scientists*. Cambridge: Cambridge University Press.

Strauss, A., & Corbin, J. (1998). *Basics of qualitative research: Techniques and procedures for developing grounded theory*. Thousand Oaks: Sage.

Sturken, M. (2007). *Tourists of history: Memory, kitsch, and consumerism from Oklahoma City to Ground Zero*. Durham: Duke University Press.

Sutcliffe, K., & Kim, S. (2014). Understanding children's engagement with interpretation at a cultural heritage museum. *Journal of Heritage Tourism, 9*(4), 332–348.

Thomson, P. (Ed.). (2008). *Doing visual research with children and young people*. London: Routledge.

Tilden, F. (1957). *Interpreting our heritage: Principles and practices for visitor services in parks, museums, and historic places*. Durham: University of North Carolina Press.

Uzzell, D., & Ballantyne, R. (2008). Heritage that hurts: Interpretation in a postmodern world. In G. Fairclough, R. Harrison, J. H. Jameson, & J. Schofield (Eds.), *The heritage reader* (pp. 502–513). Abington: Routledge.

Wagner, M. (2015). SEE IT: Kids play on Vietnam Women's Memorial in Washington, treat it 'like a jungle gym' – In front of veterans. *New York Daily News*. http://www.nydailynews.com/news/national/kids-play-vietnam-women-memorial-vets-glare-article-1.2162849. Date Accessed 26 Mar 2015.

Walter, T. (2009). Dark tourism: Mediating between the dead and the living. In R. Sharpley & P. R. Stone (Eds.), *The darker side of travel: The theory and practice of dark tourism* (pp. 39–55). Bristol: Channel View Publications.

Ward, C. W., & Wilkinson, E. E. (2006). *Conducting meaningful interpretation: A field guide for success*. Golden: Fulcrum.

White, L. (2011). Imagining the nation: Signifiers of national capital status in Washington, DC and Canberra. *Current Issues in Tourism, 15*(1), 121–135.

Woodhead, M., & Faulkner, D. (2008). Subjects, objects or participants? In P. Christensen & A. James (Eds.), *Research with children: Perspectives and practices* (pp. 9–35). London: Routledge.

24

Dark Tourism Visualisation: Some Reflections on the Role of Photography

John J. Lennon

In photography I can never deny the thing has been there.
Barthes (1981, p. 76)

Understanding the Connection: Dark Tourism and the Visual

This chapter considers the relationship between dark tourism, visualisation and the particular role of photography. It occupies a pivotal place within interpretation and pictorial record both as evidence of activity and visitation. The advent of smart phones and the integrated presence of high-resolution embedded cameras with significant storage has heightened the centrality of the visual record.

The fascination we have as humans with our ability to do evil, witness the evidence of horror and stare fixedly at photographic, filmic or heritage artefacts connected with death is at the heart of the phenomena known as 'dark tourism' (Lennon and Foley 1996, 2000). In a range of locations, photography is used to provide illustration, evidence and context. Tourist photography in the past was a matter of centrality, frontality, clear and centred images of objects, natural and built heritage. Now it is ubiquitous, mobile based and almost unlimited. It provides visual options, incorporating self-imagery, which is uploaded to the internet and is circulated globally on a range of social

J. J. Lennon (✉)
Glasgow Caledonian University, Glasgow, UK

media platforms (also see Chap. 30). Indeed, some 1.8 bn images are uploaded and shared each day globally (Meeker 2014). It is an exponential growth of Sontag's hypothesis that to collect photographs was to collect the world (Sontag 1977). As she presciently noted:

> Photographs really are experience captured, and the camera is the arm of consciousness in its acquisitive mood. (Sontag 1977 p. 7)

Visualisation would appear to be critical to appreciation of the divided emotions of horror and fascination. Crossing timescales and continents, the appeal of these exceptional images is central to understanding this subject and related tourist/consumer interest. Images now bear witness to visitation on a scale written records do not approach.

The nature of viewing such dark images and indeed visiting such sites is linked to the viewers/visitors often-inexpressible experience. The compulsion to visit, to stare fixedly at content and to record feelings and visual images is typical of the behavioural response of the visitor. Comparing visits to such dark sites to regular museums or heritage locations is interesting in the context of discussion of visualisation. Dark sites appear to encourage some self-reflection and photographic representation appears to work in a similar way. By looking at photographic images, the viewer ponders the motivation for both fascination and visitation.

The visualisation of dark tourism is concerned with the artefacts and manifestations of the phenomena that have been created or are lost. Imagery, like language, can never be taken at face value and the interpretation and meaning attributed to images and words have to be considered within this context. The perspectives of photographer and viewer are important here and are allied with the idea of *intertextuality* (Kristeva 1980). The images we view are inherently enmeshed in complex relationships with texts, histories and other images. For this subject area, that means that haunting and evocative images have an infinite extension of possible meanings.

Photography and the Relationship with Time and Death

The relationship between imagery and 'real' has been explored by a number of authors, notably Barthes (1972) who explored the role of such visual signifiers and their appearance as natural given truths. Barthes addressed the relationship between photography and mortality noting:

> If photography is to be discussed at a serious level, it must be described in relation to death …it's true that a photograph is a witness, but a witness of something that is no more. (Barthes 2010, p. xi)

In this context, photographic imagery can serve as a support for communication that is possibly myth dependent, and reliant upon stereotypes and clichés. The importance of these sites as physical records of atrocity, crime and tragic events merit interpretation and understanding that is unambiguous, neutral and derived from historical record. However, interpretation is further complicated by the limitations of language which when measured against visual interpretation is insuperably inadequate. As Foucault noted:

> …it is vain that we say what we see; what we see never resides in what we say. (op cit 1970, p. 18)

Words unlike numbers in say pure mathematics have no fixed value and cannot claim any single meaning. The multiplicity of meanings is a concern in any attempt at 'understanding' tragedy and dark elements of our past, which have meanings that are never fixed and remain open to interpretation. Derrida's (1977) critique of the philosophical tradition through his work on *deconstruction* is useful to this discussion. Although associated primarily with texts, it has clear applications to the visual. Decoding 'literal' images in order to understand their contexts and expose dominant ways of thinking about the tragic, pain and the nature of human evil. *Deconstruction* seeks to uncover literal and philosophical ways of thinking about text and visual imagery. The philosophical aspect aims to show that there are 'undecidables'; that is, something that cannot conform to either side of a dichotomy. In the case of the horror of something like the genocide of the Khmer Rouge or the Nazi Holocaust, it is the impossibility of reconciling the reality and unreality of such enormous evil (also see Chap. 20). This so-titled 'undecidability' is central to Derrida's reflection, when it is applied to reveal paradoxes and dichotomy in what we see and what we understand and perceive.

Photography at, and of, dark sites and atrocity locations present the visitor/viewer with a range of multiple perceptual contexts. The range is considerable: visitors may simply struggle with the horror of the site; may be (re)viewing as a retrospective witness; or may be observing others—that is, viewing those in the act of looking and considering what they see—and so forth.

This is echoed in the way we look at and perceive photographic images of the same phenomena. This degree of self-consciousness is at the heart of the ethical debate surrounding the viewing of atrocity and dark images. Do these images of suffering become aesthetically acceptable, attractively pho-

588 J. J. Lennon

Plate 24.1 Visitor at Dachau Crematoria, Dachau Concentration Camp (Photo: D. Weber)

tographed and technically composed art works? Does a collection uploaded on a social media platform anticipate that viewers will accept such images or resist them? Does such work catalyse sympathy for the victims or revulsion at the context? Does exposure to such imagery harden the viewer to atrocity and horror? Plate 24.1 captures some of these dilemmas for photographer and viewer. Previously, discussion about the ethicacy of constant utilisation of such image has caused some writers and film-makers (cf Williams 2007; Lanzman 1995) to seek alternatives to reproduction of the tragically familiar. The ubiquitousness of the 9/11 attack images or those of the Nazi Holocaust, their place in history and prevalence in a range of media may limit their ability to catalyse shock or elicit concern. According to some, they have simply become decontextualised cues for memory (Williams 2007). Their constant reproduction and multichannel distribution can make the horror strangely palpable. Of course, the alternative might be to simply ignore this element of human fascination. In essence, however, that would be to leave these dark sites without interpretation or development. To literally adopt the call for silence made by Wiesel (1960) who famously claimed that:

> Auschwitz negates any form of literature, as it defines all systems, all doctrines. (Wiesel 1960, p. 7)

In the past, the option to remain silent and not to record and interpret this content brought with it criticism that such an approach may encourage future generations to ignore or forget the incidence of these tragic events or terrible periods of human history. As Donat (1995) reminds the reader:

> … everything depends on who transmits our testament to future generations, on who writes the history of this period. History is usually written by the victor … should our murderers be victorious, should *they* write the history of this war, our destruction will be presented as one of the most beautiful pages of world history, and future generations will pay tribute to them as dauntless crusaders. Their every word will be taken for gospel. Or they may wipe out our memory altogether as if we had never existed, as if there had never been a Polish Jewry, a Ghetto in Warsaw, a Majdanek. Not even a dog will howl for us. (Donat 1995, p. 6)

Dark Tourism: Visual Record, Evidence and Place

Dark tourism has become established as a specialist focus for tourism research and has been used to discuss the wider fascination we appear to have with our own mortality and the fate of others (see, e.g. Sharpley and Stone 2009; Tunbridge and Ashworth 1998). Death, suffering, visitation and tourism have been interrelated for many centuries, but the phenomenon was first identified and categorised by Malcom Foley and John Lennon in 1996 for a special issue of the *International Journal of Heritage Studies* (Foley and Lennon 1996) and brought to further attention in their later book (Lennon and Foley 2000). Further contributions to the area in academia include issues of interpretation and selective commemoration (White and Frew 2012), cross-disciplinary studies in the field of the sociology of death/death studies (Mitchell 2007), literature and writing (Skinner 2012), problematic heritage (Sather-Wagstaff 2010) and in the area of criminology/crime sites (Botterill and Jones 2010). What the research reinforces is that for many years humans have been attracted to sites and events that are associated with death, disaster, suffering, violence and killing. From ancient Rome and gladiatorial combat to attendance at medieval public executions, death has held a steadfast and enduring appeal. What has changed, however, is the automatic pictorial recording and circulation of imagery associated with such sites on social media communication channels (also see Chap. 14).

Dark tourism as a subject field has generated much more than purely academic interest. The term has entered the mainstream and is a popular subject of media attention. It is now often used as a marketing term and the appeal of a range of global destinations associated with dark heritage shows no signs of abatement. More recently the appeal has been reinforced in New York, Paris and beyond. In Paris, the death site of Diana, Princess of Wales continues to evidence pilgrimage and visitation, and, in Africa, sites in Angola, South Africa, Sierra Leone and Rwanda have all demonstrated the appeal of dark histories and tragic events for visitors. The range varies significantly from Holocaust sites to the manufactured experience operations which recreate tableaus and 'historical' simulacra. The motivation that impels expenditure in terms of travel, payment of admission and other related costs compound the proof of appeal. Indeed, the juxtaposition of commercial services such as retail has generated some consideration in the literature (see, e.g. Macdonald 2012; Brown 2013).

Such difficult combinations of commercial operation in sites of mass killing create dreamlike images (see Plate 24.2). They present a set of tableau where the viewer (and visitor) explore the fragility of life, shared human histories and our potential to exploit our darkest past and tragic events. To gaze at such images is to confront those issues of visitation and observation. Photographs allow us to confront *temporal simultaneity*. In this respect, Bartes

Plate 24.2 Retail offer at Auschwitz-Birkenau Museum and Memorial, Poland (Photo: A. Tézenas)

(1981) locates the interest point (or punctum) of the image in relation to key time stages (temporal elements):

(a) the time the photograph/image was captured;
(b) the time of the photographer's death;
(c) the time the photograph was viewed;
(d) the time of the viewer's death.

Here then photography is considered and discussed in relation to death. The photographic image is a record or witness of something that has passed and is no more. The photograph takes the image out of its context and into another location. Whilst these images are not recreating or retrieving the past they allude to tragedy and/or places of death. We gaze at images where death or tragedy has occurred in the knowledge that these victims are already dead. They allude to the *anterior future* that Barthes (1981) identified. Cameras "… were clocks for seeing," providing certification of existence (op cit, p. xi). As viewers, we shudder over tragic events and deaths that have (of course) already occurred.

In the case of some, the compulsion to explore the limitations of this appeal is evident. By way of illustration, the photographer Ambroise Tézenas (2014) is not afraid to explore this phenomena in his work on the Sichuan Wenchuan Earthquake tour (also see Chap. 18). This site of a major earthquake in south-western China remains relatively untouched since the disaster in 2008. It was left unreconstructed on instruction of the Chinese government, so that it could become a major visitor attraction. However, it is also the death site of over 90,000 people who perished in the earthquake. The majority of bodies remain buried beneath the collapsed structures. The spectacle that such sites deliver crosses cultures and continents and the presence of the tourist (recording images of the location) reaffirms the visual commoditisation of such destinations.

The emotional attraction of such dark imagery is neither new nor culturally straightforward. This is more than reflective memory for the viewer or visitor. This type of visual record we are now faced with multiplied many fold remains critical to both historical record, memory prompt and the visitor experience/history. Photographic images of incarceration sites and execution locations contrast with the natural disaster sites, yet their visual record, uploaded and shared, appears familiar and comparable. Whatever the location, the visual nature of tragic history or suffering offers the closed circle of representation that Urry (1990) alluded to in his consideration of the Tourist Gaze. A typical example of this repetitious set of images and landscapes is provided in the website of tour operators offering excursions to the Chernobyl nuclear disaster site in Ukraine (for a useful discussion of the site, see Stone 2013; also see Chap. 13).

Pripyat, the closest but now deserted town to Chernobyl, is specifically marketed to tourists on the basis of visual and photographic appeal of the destruction, its abandonment and ecological tragedy. The post-apocalyptic appeal of Pripyat and the Chernobyl site is intensely visual (see Plate 24.3).

This dark tourism subject matter has always been intensely visual from the detritus of concentration camps to the ceaseless parade of Khmer Rouge executed prisoners in Cambodia, recorded as an essential part of an industrial scale killing operation. However, the nature of the photographic composition and its exponential rise through online circulation should not detract from an endless, repeating spectacle that crosses continents, races and cultures. Death and tragedy are the constants that reaffirm how little is learned from atrocity as its familiar repetition in Poland, Bosnia or Rwanda illustrates. The visual image which has been democratised by increasingly affordable mobile technology would appear to provide what Bordieu (1965) identified as perceptions of thought and appreciation across entire groups. What we observe in the images of tragic sites is the 'tourist gaze', visually choreographed and com-

Plate 24.3 Former residential accommodation in Pripyat, near Chernobyl (Photo: A. Tézenas)

posed (Urry 1990), framed for consumption in a discourse of tragic heritage, memory and evidence of presence. For this reason, framing darkness in Rwanda, Cambodia and Poland looks cyclically familiar.

It is logical to suppose that feelings of indignation or sadness generated by such images would seem to demand a response. Yet, one will generally, simply, emerge from such viewing back into normal life; work, eating, family and shopping, etc. This resumption of life is hopelessly inadequate in terms of a response yet, it as ubiquitous as it is irreconcilable. Consequently, it is because of the presence of historical records, artefacts and buildings with dark heritage that visual representation is extensively used. Documentary evidence in the form of photographs is employed at sites of mass killing such as the Auschwitz-Birkenau complex in Oswiecim, Poland. Historical photographs and documentation of this nature have been central in transmitting the events of World War II, ethnic cleansing and the heritage of numerous sites of tragedy or 'experience offers'. The visual heritage of these sites is indeed rich: the railway lines of Birkenau, the rows of bones and skulls in Rwanda, watchtowers at incarceration sites or barbed wire, skeletal victims and mass graves. The importance of image in informing an appreciation of the historical 'reality' is discussed elsewhere (Lennon and Foley 2000; Lennon 2007). For example, the 'Arbeit Macht Frei' gates at Auschwitz are a globally recognised image associated with the Holocaust and the Nazi regime. However, the frequency of viewing and the global circulation has served to develop a familiarity that could diminish their impact over time.

Interpretive photography within dark sites seeks to work in a subtler way. Indeed, one can see how the use of photographs can help to demonstrate the historical reality of location. In the case of Hiroshima, for example, the ruins of the Prefectural Industrial Promotion Hall are presented in the present and past. The visitor looks at the documentary photograph on the main interpretive board and can then view the identical vista (*the present*). In this way, the camera has the impact of what Barthes (2010) titles 'resurrection' (see Plate 24.4).

The photograph for Barthes (2010) is an essential witness, attesting to what has existed rather than recalling that which has been lost over time or over distance. Photography has a unique effect in recording and capturing context and reality and, as Barthes notes:

> Photography has something to do with resurrection: might we not say of it what the Byzantines said of the image of Christ which impregnated St. Veronicas napkin: that is was not made by the hand of man, *acheiropoietos*? (Barthes 2010, p. 8)

Plate 24.4 Prefectural Industrial Promotion Hall, Hiroshima, Japan (Photo: D. Mulhern)

Photographic image has the ability to transmit the reality of the death camps with immediacy and with an effect that words can rarely achieve (see Plate 24.5). In this way, the visitor can associate 'photographic time' with 'real time'. In contrast, the recurrent use of pictures of the victims, mass graves and deportation trains can blur into unreality (Lanzmann 1995). Indeed, as previously intimated, there is an inherent danger in constant recreation of the past,

Plate 24.5 Visitors at Auschwitz-Birkenau Museum and Memorial viewing historical photographic record (the past) at the current site (the present) (Photo: A. Tézenas)

particularly if there is any attempt at manipulation or stylisation which can trivialise the enormity of the issues being confronted. In this sense, the image and resurrection effect deals with what Steiner (1971) titled 'the time relation'. In this case, this relates to the contemporary nature of Auschwitz in human culture and the incomprehensible nature of its history. In discussion of the victims of Treblinka, Steiner (1967) eloquently describes this issue of simultaneous yet irreconcilable realities:

> Precisely at the same hour in which Mehring or Langer [victims of the camps] were being done to death, the overwhelming plurality of human beings, two miles away on Polish farms, five thousand miles away in New York, were sleeping or eating or going to a film or making love or worrying about the dentist. This is where my imagination balks. The two orders of simultaneous experience are so different, so irreconcilable to any common norm of human values, their co-existence is so hideous a paradox - Treblinka is both because some men have built it and almost all other men let it be.... (Steiner 1967 pp. 156–7)

Dark tourism visualisation and imagery confirm that objects and sites do not exist in isolation. They are imbued with meaning because of their relationship with other adjacent objects and locations. The meaning and interpretation of objects and sites is defined in the same way as the meaning of words. Their similarity or dissimilarity to other words allows us to create meaning and comprehension. The same comparison allows us to attempt to understand and comprehend elements of our history which may at first glance be irreconcilable with our current existence. The visual images in photography like a stone entering a pond creates ripples and rebounds with new and different connotations that move beyond their denotative level of significance.

This issue of reality and unreality and how we connect is what Wiesel (1967) referred to as 'a different planet' with our current existence and is at the core of such visual representation. The issue of *temporal* and *spatial affinity* has been dealt with in a range of ways in other visual mediums; see, for example, the valuable discussion in Wurzer (2002). However, difficulty rests with recounting something as enormous as, for example, the Holocaust or the massacres of Rwanda in narrative form. To abridge and to simplify to sentences, the enormity of such dark acts is where the limitation of language is reached. Reconstruction and replication of sites are similarly flawed in this context and can be seen as trivialising or creating destinations with clear commercial intent. Such 'visitor attractions' and 'visitor activities' developed for commercial gain remain contentious and are analogous to the use and misuse of tragic dark sites in popular visual culture such as film and television. In the case of film, the Holocaust is a subject area approached in a range of contexts by film-makers: from shamelessly exploitative and voyeuristic to use as a background for narratives, real or imagined. In contrast, the seminal approach of Lanzmann in the documentary film *Shoah* (1985) makes a useful comparison and merits consideration. Unlike many attempts to film or televise the Holocaust, *Shoah* explores the legacy of the Final Solution by drawing the viewer into the debates of the original experience. The film focuses on the death camps of: Chelmno, Belzec, Majdanek, Sobibor, Treblinka and Auschwitz in their current state to reveal and document the Nazi genocide programme. Yet, *Shoah* is not a historical documentary; rather, Lanzmann conveys the full amazement of holding in sight an item (a tower, gate and the railhead) that came from the 'different planet' with the use of extensive interviews with: victims, bystanders, perpetrators and survivors. In using contemporary 'real time' and interviews with perpetrators and linking this with long screen takes of camp sites, trains, rails and people, the connection between 'screen time' and 'real time' is established. In this way, rather than providing didactic historical commentary or Hollywood stylised narrative, the viewer is taken into the reality of the 'different planet' through this process of traumatic cultural shock. It ensures that the visitor or viewer is able to appreciate the full and dreadful aspects of this past by dealing with its symptoms and evidence in the present. Whilst Lanzmann denies the viewer the dubious privilege of being a witness, the viewer has to deal with more uncomfortable questions such as 'what does it mean to have *witnessed* it?' (Romney 1995, emphasis added). In this respect, visualisation in dark tourism offers the viewer/visitor similar dilemmas. That is, what does it mean to view these images, what does it tell us about the viewer, the inherent fascination, the repetition of themes, and what Urry (1990) referred to as the closed circle of representation. As recent history testifies, this pattern of visual evidence is a legacy that fails to offer either education or warning.

There is also parody and pastiche evident in many of the dark images of such sites which confront the sacred and the secular in ways that language would struggle to do. Photographs juxtapose the enormousness of evil and the tragedy of disaster with commercial provision of retail and related consumer services. The visitor's fascination with recorded imagery for upload, distribution and circulation echoes this juxtaposition. For instance, Facebook and Instagram visitor photographs of Auschwitz may share space with pictures of family and birthdays in a familiar pattern of display. Many images convey the collapse of any distinction between high and popular culture towards informed viewing and entertainment. As noted earlier, the earthquake site in Sichuan Wenchuan offers us as interested parties, spectacle and visual interest as it does to other visitors to the park. As Featherstone (2007) would suggest we are mixing codes; the celebration of the 'depthlessness' of popular culture and visitor appeal are ironically combined in this site. This is evidenced continually in other dark sites, from the incomprehensible graffiti found in concentration camps to the visitor tours of Chernobyl.

These distinctions between parody and reality are evident and effortlessly communicated in the visual medium of the photograph. The appropriation of the symbols of the tragic and dark past to inform the present is loaded and shared on a global scale. The issue of use of imagery within dark subject area interpretation, such as execution sites, mass graves and concentration camps, present complex issues related to evidence and experience. Orthodox museum displays condone the feeling that one can stand back from the past and be 'educated' about it. In such a context, images are used to convey a perspective of the past as separate from the present, which one travels to and visits via a combination of recreation and semi-authentic/authentic elements. In contrast, the sites themselves present a current 'reality' and elements of 'authenticity'. In such locations, it is vitally important to allow the public to differentiate between truth and falsity, replication and reality. Interpretation and how images can convey themes of dominant ideology have been explored elsewhere (Lennon and Foley 2000; Lennon and Mitchell 2007). These issues are illustrated in the interpretation of concentration camps in the former Communist states in Central and Eastern Europe or the relative non-interpretation of sites such as S-21 (the Khmer Rouge prison and execution site) in Phnom Phen, Cambodia. This type of 'political' and selective interpretation is evidenced in some imagery. History, in its visual form, is abridged and offered in episodic elements to enable the viewer to digest complex visual narratives within a busy site containing a multitude of images. In such cases, the dangers of distortion or dilution are a constant.

In some of the famous dark tourism locations such as Rwanda or Cambodia, Western viewers' perceptions of histories are often at best partial. Historical interpretation is limited and display formats are dated and abridged. Visitors are dependent upon local guides, limited narratives and historical artefacts that rarely explore the complexity that surrounds the tragic evidence being viewed. The visual record captured is similarly neither fully explained nor understood. The images are witness to the photographers and the viewer's own subjectivity. In these cases, the site itself becomes for many the visual record and data source. The problems of interpretation and understanding of the visual are akin to problems faced by interpretations of the site. They are related to the difficulties of *representation* (creating a truthful account of the

Dark Tourism Visualisation: Some Reflections on the Role... 599

reality of such places with simply an image) and *presentation* (paying tribute to and understanding the predicament of the victims and the context of the tragic history). The dilemma of avoidance of ideological distortions or deceptions is now also passed to the visitor. It becomes beholden on those visitors and viewers to consider what they are viewing and it requires them to attempt to understand what they are seeing. The alternative would appear to be to view in a passive non-inquisitive sense. Thus, whether we view a deserted fairground at Pripyat (see Plate 24.6) or an earthquake ruins tour in Sichuan, the image offers us a perspective that is multifaceted in composition, intent and meaning.

Photographs are about much more than tourism and visiting such sites. The material and subject matter should challenge the nature of our behaviour, our history and societal relationships with evil and mortality. These images are a testament to our past, our inability to move beyond it and our curious relationship with tragedy and death. Photography as with painting or writing is a medium. It mediates and is in itself an interpretation. The photographic medium comes between what is mediated and how the subject is understood. More difficult questions relate to whether anything is learned by the viewer, such as: 'what do we understand by looking at an image associated with death

Plate 24.6 Deserted fairground at Pripyat, near Chernobyl, Ukraine (Photo: A. Tézenas)

and tragedy or unusual representations of a perception of the recent past?' These images are primary visual evidence of a phenomenon. These photographs are catalysts for mental visualisation as much as they act as evidential or documentary record. Photographs of violence and execution transmitted across electronic media act as record and evidence but can also induce a heavy emotional reaction most closely related to trauma. In gazing at horror that is inexplicable and unfathomable, we are often unable to connect the location with a coherent historical or textual context. There are clear parallels here between psychological theories of how the mind copes with trauma and the impact one of these images and places can have on the viewer (Baer 2002). As the mind attempts to deal with traumatic events or images witnessed, it will endlessly replay and recall the visualisation. This is an attempt to rationalise or provide meaning for such events. Trauma, in memory, is likened to the way in which the camera arrests the forward movement of time. The horror and tragic are disconnected from the linear motion of time and it is replayed in the memory, on a website, on Facebook or Instagram. Of course, we can research or read narrative that provides information for the context; however, this is different from understanding. What is observed as an image or viewed by a visitor in the present has no place in the past. It is similarly and equally disconnected to the present, in which the precise context and history of the victims can never be truly or fully understood. This is part of our need to express our own individuality through images (Freunch 1974) which are loaded and shared on social media channels in a numbingly familiar parade of similarly framed dark places.

References

Baer, U. (2002). *Spectral evidence: The photography of trauma*. Boston: MIT Press.
Barthes, R. (1981). *Camera Lucida: Reflections on photography* (trans: Howard, R.). New York: Hill and Wang.
Berger, J. (1972). *Selected essays*. New York: Vintage.
Bordieu, P. (1965). *Photography a middle-brow art*. California: Stamford Press.
Botterill, D., & Jones, T. (2010). *Tourism and crime*. London: Goodfellow Publishers.
Brown, J. (2013). Dark tourism shops: Selling "dark" and "difficult" products. *International Journal of Culture, Tourism and Hospitality Research, 7*(3), 272–280. London: Emerald Publishing.
Derrida, J. (1997). *Of grammatology*. Baltimore: John Hopkins University Press.
Donat, A. (1965). *The new kingdom*. New York: Holt Reinhart and Winston.
Featherstone, M. (2007). *Consumer culture and postmodernism* (2nd ed.). London: Sage Publications.

Foucault, M. (1970). *The order of things: An archaeology of the human sciences.* London: Pantheon Books.
Freund, G. (1980). *Photography and society.* London/Paris: D R Godine.
Kristeva, J. (1980). *Desire in language: A semiotic approach to literature and art.* New York: Columbia University Press.
Lanzmann, C. (1995a, March 3). Why Spielberg has distorted the truth. *The Guardian Weekly*, p. 18.
Lanzmann, C. (1995b p 78) quoted in I Avisar (1988) Screening the Holocaust Bloomington and Indianapolis: Indiana University Press.
Lennon, J. J. and Mitchell, M. (2007) Dark tourism the role of sites of death in tourism pp 167–178 in Mitchell M Remember me constructing immortality – Beliefs on immortality, life and death, Routledge, London.
Lennon, J. J. (2009). Tragedy and heritage in Peril: The case of Cambodia. *Tourism Recreational Research, 3*(2), 116–123.
Lennon, J. J. (2010). Dark tourism and sites of crime. In D. Botterill & T. Jones (Eds.), *Tourism and crime* (pp. 99–121). Oxford: Goodfellow Publishers.
Lennon, J. J., & Foley, M. (2000). *Dark tourism – The attraction of death and disaster.* London/New York: Continuum.
Lennon, J. J., & Foly, M. (1996). JFK and dark tourism: A fascination with assassination. *The International Journal of Heritage Studies, 2*(1), 198–211.
Lennon, J. J., & Mitchell, M. (2007). Dark tourism the role of sites of death in tourism. In M. Mitchell (Ed.), *Remember me constructing immortality – Beliefs on immortality, life and death* (pp. 167–178). London: Routledge.
Lennon, J. J., Wei, D., & Litteljohn, D. (2012). Dark tourism: The case of the memorial to the victims of Nanjing (Nanking) Massacre, China. In L. White & E. Frew (Eds.), *Dark tourism and place identity: Marketing, managing and interpreting dark places.* Oxford: Routledge.
Levi, P. (1986). Revisiting the camps. In J. E. Young (Ed.), *The art of memory: Holocaust memorial in history.* New York: Prestel.
Levi, P. (1990). *The drowned and the saved.* London: Abacus.
Macdonald, S. (2012). Museumshop. In F. Von Bose, K. Poehis, F. Schneider, & A. Schultz (Eds.), *Museum X: Zur Neuermessung eines mehrdimensionalen Raunes* (pp. 42–55). Berlin: Panama Verlag.
Meeker, M. (2014). We now upload and share over 1.8 billion photos each day: Meeker Internet report available at: http://tech.firstpost.com/news-analysis/now-upload-share-1-8-billion-photos-everyday-meeker-report-224688.html. Accessed 2 Sep 2015.
Mitchell, M. (Ed.). (2007). *Remember me constructing immortality – Beliefs on immortality, life and death.* Oxford: Routledge.
Romney, J. (1995, January 13). Screen seen: Vital video – The Holocaust. *The Guardian Weekly*, p. T016.
Sather-Wagstaff, J. (2010). *Heritage that hurts: Tourists in the memoryscapes of September 11.* Boston: Left Coast Press.

Sharpley, R., & Stone, P. R. (2009). *The darker side of travel: The theory and practice of dark tourism*. London: Channel View Publications.
Shoah. (1985). *Documentary film directed by Claude Lanzmann*.
Skinner, J. (2012). *Writing the dark side of travel*. London: Berghahn Books.
Sontag, S. (1977). *On photography*. New York: Picador.
Steiner, G. (1967). *Language and silence: Essays in language, literature and the inhuman new*. York: Athenaeum.
Steiner, G. (1971). *In Bluebeard's castle: Some notes towards the redefinition of culture*. New Haven: Yale University Press.
Stone, P. R. (2013). Dark tourism, Heterotopias and post-apocalyptic places – The case of Chernobyl. In L. White & E. Frew (Eds.)., (2012) *Dark tourism and place identity: Managing and interpreting dark places* (pp. 81–93). Oxford: Routledge.
Tézenas, A. (2014). *I was here*. England: Dewi Lewis Publishing.
Tunbridge, J. E., & Ashworth, G. J. (1995). *Dissonant heritage: The management of the past as a resource in conflict*. Chichester: Wiley.
Urry, J. (1990). *The tourist gaze*. London: Sage Publications.
Walsh, S. (1992). *The representation of the past*. Oxford: Routledge.
White, L., & Frew, E. (2012). *Dark tourism and place identity: Managing and interpreting dark places*. Oxford: Routledge.
Wiesel, E. (1960). *Night* (trans: Rodway, S.). New York: Avon.
Wiesel, E. (1967). Jewish values in the Post Holocaust future in Judaism 16.3 (Summer).
Wiesel, E. (1968). *Legends of our fire* (trans: Donadio, S.). New York: Holt, Reinhart and Winston.
Williams, P. (2007). *Memorial museums: The global rush to commemorate atrocities*. Oxford/New York: Berg.
Wurzer, W. (Ed.). (2002). *Panorama: Philosophies of the visible*. London/New York: Continuum.

25

Educating the (Dark) Masses: Dark Tourism and Sensemaking

Catherine Roberts

Introduction

Various factors render analysis of dark tourism's interpretative and educational facility profoundly salient and significant. Its close affinities with heritage studies and practice, which privilege issues of interpretation and engagement within recognised learning frameworks and conceptualisations, suggest rich transferrable resources by which dark tourism might benchmark or reference specific learning contexts. The memorial qualities of dark tourism locations and behaviours resonate with concepts of intergenerational learning, transmission of history, and identity narratives; yet, their sensitive and provocative subject matter, allied with perceived media influence and sensationalism, evokes concerns about the commodification or trivialisation of tragedy and, consequently, moral ambiguity. Furthermore, dark tourism is located in contexts of conflict and its consequences, including heritage dissonance, contemporary conflict resolution (Braithwaite and Lee 2006), and post-conflict environments. This positioning suggests a particular real-time relevance and, indeed, a real-world responsibility, in matters of learning and interpretation and in addressing the ethical and spiritual dichotomies inherent in dark tourism themes and experiences (Wight and Lennon 2007). Hence, discussion of the problematic admixture of leisure with tragedy (Rojek 1993; Tunbridge and Ashworth 1996) and related concerns about inauthentic or inappropriate

---

C. Roberts (✉)
University of Central Lancashire, Preston, UK

© The Author(s) 2018
P. R. Stone et al. (eds.), *The Palgrave Handbook of Dark Tourism Studies*,
https://doi.org/10.1057/978-1-137-47566-4_25

qualities of dark tourism as a means of encountering human suffering and troubling events (Hewison 1987; MacCannell 1992; Walsh 1992; Urry 1995) are recurrent themes within the literature.

Hence, visitor experiences of dark tourism require further and specific research and elucidation. Furthermore, educational aspects of general tourism (i.e., excluding formal education, school, or booked specialist group visits) are currently underrepresented in the literature (but also see Chap. 23). Meanwhile, the anticipated and/or experienced educative attributes within dark tourism encounter shape touristic perceptions of Self and 'Other', and influence broader (media and academic) inferences about dark tourism, authenticity, and moral authority. However, the conceptualisation of dark touristic learning experiences and empirical testing of (informal) learning outcomes at dark tourism sites has yet to be undertaken within coherent and recognised frameworks. Academic and general discourse around dark tourism and education, and related institutional commitments to 'learning from the past' are of a speculative and, arguably, an apocryphal order. Effective investigations into how and what 'dark tourists' are learning, through encounters with sites associated with death and mortality, will represent new and rewarding avenues by which to elucidate and conceptualise perceptions and experiences of dark tourism and support responsible management of dark tourism sites.

In this chapter, therefore, I draw upon a cross-disciplinary review to outline key aspects of dark tourism discourse and its disciplinary relationships in contexts of interpretation and education, including specific considerations and conceptualisations influencing their facility at dark tourism sites. In particular, the ways in which dark tourism is perceived and expressed as a potential educative experience are reviewed, and its interpretation is explored in terms of its function as an on-site educative resource for the general tourist. Factors influencing capacity or propensity to engage with interpretation are appraised in attitudinal, emotional, and sensory contexts, informing an overview of interpretation principles as they relate to dark tourism themes. Subsequently, definitions of touristic experiences are correlated with experiential learning models. I also discuss issues of learning, sensemaking, and interpretation within specific contexts of dark tourism behaviours, destinations, and experiences and the complex network of relationships, values, and consequences that they imply. Ultimately, this chapter aims to critically appraise dark tourism's facility to support sensemaking in contexts of death, disaster, and atrocity; to suggest consequences upon perceptions, experiences, and reflections of dark tourism; to suggest relevant measures whereby understanding of dark touristic learning may be developed; and, finally, to encourage and signpost future research activity.

Dark Tourism Distinctions

Dark tourism's blended academic lineage within the disciplines of death, heritage, and tourism studies supports a rich resource portfolio. As a result, its vocabularies and thematic material are readily reflected within the critical enquiries of death studies and its modes within those of tourism studies (Roberts and Stone 2015). Their unique juxtapositioning constitutes dark tourism's thematic singularity and directs its questioning: what meanings are attached to, and carried away from, representations of death? How are they modified, and by which social means and mores? What is the significance of touristic mobility and mortality? Dark tourism research identifies significant exemplar of human behaviours in which death, memory, and travel are allied, and its intuitive resonance with contemporary cultural modes is its conceptual frameworks and interpretation of its subject are intensified. As a nexus of significant sociological theorisations and the behaviours to which they relate, 'dark tourism' is more conceptually complex and mature than the prolific recent usage of the term may suggest. Yet, inherent assumptions about tourism behaviours and their unlikely juxtaposition with the material of mortality belie the unique characteristics and essential nuances that subtly but surely differentiate dark tourism behaviours as potential meaning-making and learning experiences.

The fundamental fact of death can call into question the meaningfulness and reality of social frameworks in which an individual is implicated, potentially shattering their ontological security (Mellors 1993). Consequently, Stone (2009a) proposes that certain kinds of other death can be de-sequestered and encountered via dark tourism, which Tarlow (2005: 45) locates within active contexts at 'places where tragedies or *historically noteworthy* death has occurred and that *continue to impact on our lives*' (emphasis added). Here, complex questions arise about how death itself may be classified: what contexts and/or characteristics inform processes whereby death is rendered remarkable? This suggests the unpleasing notion of (perceived) 'value-added' death: whereby, certain factors and characteristics render death remarkable and ensure consequent (re)presentation, attention, and/or recall beyond both the private sphere and the ordinary range of public, sociocultural concern. The means and modes by which these renditions occur involve mediating agencies across varied sociocultural platforms and contexts, informing and including dark tourism praxis and participation. Thus, the way in which dark tourism themes are presented, interrogated, and contextualised at touristic sites implies potential multiple narratives and meanings, about death and mortality and about the institutional, social, and individual identities they represent. In other words, interpretation of dark tourism sites may teach us not only about certain kinds of death, but also how we manage our feelings about them through processes of differentiation. Dark tourism is in itself subject to various definitions and distinctions within academic discourse. This in part relates to its representation within particular supply/demand models (Sharpley and Stone 2009), and is perhaps more usefully understood as spatial and relational differentiations. Indeed, a brief overview of those differentiations should include a 'third way' by which site interpretation is represented as a qualifying factor in the perception of dark tourism experiences, and it is to this that the chapter now turns.

Dark Tourism: Spatial, Relational, and Mediative Dimensions

Dark tourism's sites and locations are notably diverse, ranging from the constructed attractions of the 'dartainment' industry to primary sites of atrocity and genocide; yet, they share quite specific thematic concerns of death and mortality. Ashworth and Hartmann (2005a) suggest that dark tourism is place specific and indeed much discussion of dark tourism experiences and motivation relate to place identity and destination typologies. Miles (2002: 1175) differentiates 'sites associated *with*' and 'sites *of* death, disaster, and depravity' as 'dark' and 'darker' tourism, respectively, with those shades attaching also to visit motivation and experience. This may infer a critical spatial advantage in the locational authenticity of darker sites and a consequent uniquely empowering (if not spectral) commemorative potential. This conceptualisation is echoed within alternative designations of primary sites at the location of dark events (in situ), as opposed to secondary sites constructed elsewhere (Lennon and Foley 2000; Wight 2006; Wight and Lennon 2007). It should be noted, however, that primary and secondary site designations do not confer absolute locational authenticity. Indeed, place identity may be influenced by interpretive processes that are not 'felt' to be authentic, such as re-enactments, reconstructions, and replication (Boorstin 1964; MacCannell 1973; Stone 2006). Furthermore, interpretation at primary sites may be subject to certain logistical, political, or aesthetic constraints that restrict strategic 'construction' or mediation of visitor experience and, thus, engagement (Bollag 1999; Williams 2004; Taum 2005; Wight and Lennon 2007).

Alternative conceptualisations differentiate dark tourism experiences on relational grounds. For instance, Cohen (2010) correlates tourists' levels of personal interest in the individuals and events represented by the site, and a related subjective authenticity, with levels and qualities of motivation, engagement, and experience. Taking the significance of relational aspects a stage further, Cohen (2010) posits *in populo* sites in a contravention of the in situ premises. This conceptualisation is exemplified by Yad Vashem as a population and spiritual centre of the people to whom a tragedy befell and responds to a sombre dichotomy of absence/presence with regard to the involved community: Europe's pre-Second World War Jewish communities do not exist, for the same reasons that Holocaust memorial sites do. This concept addresses a theorised 'need for the development of a person-based category in an authenticity model' (Li 2003: 250; see also Breathnach, 2003). Therefore, several studies correlate varying levels of commitment, intention, and involvement within tourist experiences with degrees of personal connection to the site (Beech 2000; Lennon and Foley 2000). Indeed, dark tourism may offer particular opportunities for 'personally meaningful' tourism (Novelli 2005; Stone and Sharpley 2008). For example, visitor sites associated with histories of slavery, conflict, and atrocity will carry particular memorial meanings for individuals depending on manifold identity and heritage factors, including but not limited to issues of ethnicity, nationality, political and moral values, and familial history (Bruner 1996; Dann and Seaton 2001; Slade 2003; Williams 2004 and Winter 1998). Clearly, then, dark tourism is most, or more than, meaningful for tourists with an intimate emotional involvement.

However, concerns about the balance between the supply and demand of dark tourism are problematised by post-modern paradigms of mobility and increasing investigation of touristic agency, creativity, and influence. It is here that the tourist is positioned within a network of stakeholders that complicates the supply-demand binary. Indeed, the encounter between tourist and site represents a third agency by which social narratives of mortality are read and written, modified, and sustained. Philip Stone's (2006) seminal 'dark tourism spectrum' typological model qualifies dark tourism within plural dimensions including perceived interpretive orientation (toward education or entertainment, history or heritage), locational (in)authenticity, and purposefulness. Thus, the 'darkness' of touristic experiences are shaded not only by spatial and relational authenticities outlined above, but by other qualifying activities including educative and interpretative constituents. Furthermore, the 'darkness' of experience is allowed by Stone's model to comprise a range of 'tonal values' across different experiential attributes of the same site or visitor experience.

Tony Walter's (2009) designation of touristic sites in terms of the activity they enable aligns, for example, shrines to care and prayer; memorials to remembrance; and museums and heritage sites to 'edutainment'. Yet, Walter also allows the likelihood that dark tourism can include any or all of the various kinds of relationships with the dead listed above, despite tendencies for certain relationships to dominate certain sites. This fluidity is useful in terms of inclusion, although it is necessarily subject to a certain neutrality of interpretation and, indeed, tolerance of other tourists and their own sought relationships. Issues of cultural contingency (Irwin-Zarecka 1994; Foote 1997) are likely at play within international tourism contexts, including cultural values that inform memorial, funerary, mourning, and other behaviours relating closely to certain dark tourism destinations. Furthermore, local populations may have different relationships—and relationality—with the in situ sites from those of tourists, and the coexistence of different behaviours may confer a certain degree of ambiguity to the touristic experience. Richard Sharpley (2005) acknowledges these and other fluidities by mapping touristic darkness across attitudinal and circumstantial axes of intention. In particular, degrees of touristic interest in site-related death intersects with the level of purpose by which that interest is matched at 'supply' level. That intersection is likely to involve some degree of interpretation, the tone of which (from educational to kitsch) influences the pale-dark shading of the experience (Sharpley 2005). This aspect and the complex ways in which dark sites are constructed (after Foote 1997) are likely open to more complex readings than Sharpley's rudimentary matrix model invites. However, that said, the matrix highlights 'third way' perspectives and presents a more nuanced notion of supply and demand binaries.

If various dark tourism experiences are obtained from perceived authenticity of place and relationality, then the role of interpretation at dark tourism sites in communicating, contextualising, and even challenging those authenticities is germane to experiential and learning processes. Indeed, dark tourism encounters constitute a means by which certain binary oppositions—fact and feeling, solemnity and sensation, the living and the dead—are (or are not) reconciled through diverse interpretive and interactive processes. Subsequently, their conceptualisation reveals the significant 'grey' areas in which those processes are located. Encounters at a site that has been 'darkened' by tragedy and atrocity may afford intuitive affects—of sadness, horror, shock, or excitement; yet those affects are dependent on cognition—that is, we can only feel for what we know. Sites of invisible and unknown violence or loss may and must exist. The absence of knowledge of memory about them and the communicated facts of the matter all constitute an absence of meaning. Conversely, awareness of dark history does not in itself constitute a meaning-making process. Moreover, an absence of experiential learning outcomes may frame dark visitation within negative contexts of voyeurism and depravity. Effective strategies of site interpretation must, then, be underpinned by a thoughtful 'philosophy of sightseeing' (Webber 1993: 286), whereby relationships between tourism, heritage, and education are established.

(Dark) Tourism and Educational Relationships

The late-twentieth century emergence of post-modern tourism (Munt 1994; Mowforth and Munt 1998) is characterised by heightened diversity and mobility and, consequently, tourism has become a pursuit of novel destinations and experiences (also see Chap. 13). In these contexts, new and descriptive typologies of 'niche' and 'special interest' tourism are generated to frame social attitudes and concerns, which are expressed as travel experiences by 'new tourists' (Poon 1993) for whom self-fulfilment and reaffirmation of identity (Craik 1997) are significant aspects of that experience. Light (2000: 153) goes on to argue that there has been an 'increasing tendency to intellectualise holidays, with an emphasis on study and learning'. As a result, tourism and especially heritage tourism, can express the avenues by which tourists may seek to increase their own cultural capital.

Theoretical convergence of tourism with heritage studies emphasise useful perspectives of (dark) tourism frameworks and transactions. As Seaton (1996: 234) notes, 'death is the one heritage that everyone shares and it has been an element of tourism longer than any other form of heritage'. This fundamental heritage commonality underpins an understanding of how and why 'dark' material attaches so readily to tourism's qualities of multitude and multiplicity. Yet its identifications within dark heritage and emergent political tourism are uneasily co-existent. For example, in their study of dark tourism development in Northern Ireland, Simone-Charteris and Boyd (2010) reveal that while perceived qualities of 'dark' and 'political' tourist attractions are relatively interchangeable, opinion on the overt interpretation—hence identification—of such sites as 'dark tourism' is divided. Therefore, on the one hand, dark tourism may be seen as a positive and transformative opportunity (Crooke 2001; Devine and Connor 2005), and conversely on the other hand, as potentially sustaining attachments to sectarianism (McDowell 2008). Indeed, auto-identification as a dark tourism site, or indeed as a 'dark tourist', is limited and liable to denote an entertainment-orientated exemplar. Furthermore, the ascription of the label 'dark tourism' rarely enjoys support from local governing bodies, official tourism associations, and local communities (Causevic and Lynch 2008). Arguably, therefore, dark tourism may represent, for many sites, a derogatory brand whereby diverse negative connotations of morbidity, moral panic, or cultural ambiguity recur within media and academic discourses (Lennon and Foley 2000; Seaton and Lennon 2004; Sharpley and Stone 2009; Bowman and Pezzullo 2010; Isaac and Ashworth 2012).

In their consideration of sites of genocide, political imprisonment, and violent conflict, William Logan and Keir Reeves (2009) introduce the terminology 'difficult heritage' in an edited volume entitled *'Places of Pain and Shame—Dealing with "Difficult Heritage"'*. Difficult heritage studies suggest a potential and relevant convergence with dark tourism research, yet only one specific reference—Young's (2009) chapter on Auschwitz-Birkenau—is made to dark tourism concepts within the text. Arguably, therefore, dark tourism has yet to be fully recognised as a mutually relevant cross-referential discipline in heritage studies and, where such references do occur in the heritage literature, they frequently relate to the 'darkest' shades of tourism. However, Frew and White (2013), in their examination of hybrid sites of 'dark heritage', suggest an emergent tendency in broader heritage research to evoke dark tourism tropes, where given sites and their associations relate to profound and historic human experience.

New perspectives of 'heritage dissonance' (Tunbridge and Ashworth 1996) and displacement are offered by dark tourism's specific analyses of iconic sites at 'darker' poles of positional spectrums. Touristic encounters at Holocaust sites (Beech 2009), places of atrocity (Ashworth and Hartmann 2005), prisons, slavery-heritage attractions, or crime sites (Dann and Seaton 2001; Wilson 2008; Rice 2009; Dalton 2013) involve significant memorial behaviours, identity markers, and narrative devices. 'Dark heritage' locations carry extraordinary semiotic weight and memorial material, and their manifestations in (dark) touristic behaviour are relevant and revealing in contexts of social memory and meaning. Importantly, dark tourism's overlap with heritage research and practice reveals further differentiation. In particular, the apprehension of shared or universal heritage (Ashworth and Hartmann 2005) at dark tourism sites represents an acquisition of relational authenticity and, consequently, offers deeper levels of engagement and openness to learning processes. The absence of this or other relationality and the low levels of engagement and empathy it implies, mark those areas of dark tourism which are liable to be transient, lacking in experiential learning opportunities, and open to criticism within moral contexts. It should be acknowledged that these areas of dark tourism are likely to attract negative perceptions about moral value and integrity, which permeate the spectrum of dark tourism experiences across a range of public, media, and academic contexts. Thus, dark tourism researchers are likely to modify overt vocabularies of dark tourism when communicating with some heritage sites and tourists, in order to avoid negative connotations. Furthermore, these 'ambiguous sites' are least likely to form the focus of serious scholarly interrogation or overlap with heritage conceptualisations. While the focus of this chapter is on site interpretation and, therefore, sets aside transient and spontaneous sites, it should be noted that their intelligent analysis is necessary to support full understanding of the dark tourism spectrum and its varying capacities to support learning experiences.

Orams (1997) and Forestell (1993) suggest that tourists are unlikely to change their post-visit behaviour if learning activities do not take place. Hence, actual encounters with educative material qualify the visit, making explicable not only the site's associated events as an incident in humanity's shared narrative, but the tourist's presence in it. Educational services represent a core element in the perception of sites of heritage dissonance or dark tourism. Indeed, the reason often provided for the existence of certain sites is purely educational and as a memorial to past events, so that 'traditional' tourism activities may not be acceptable at the site (Ashworth and Hartmann 2005a). Thus, the identity of many dark tourism sites, and by association the tourists who visit them, is qualified by perceptions and expressions of education as an orientating and motivating factor.

Yet much of the literature refutes the notion that access to educative experience represents a genuine motivating factor in visitation to dark tourism destinations. Walter (2009: 11) argues 'that most dark tourism, like much heritage tourism, is not specifically motivated'. Presented as an optional motivation, it is unlikely that 'education' will be rejected by the research subject. On the contrary, however, it is likely to be welcomed as the quality of motivation is transfused to the quality of the individual. Yet education has not been examined as either a motivation or consequence of general dark tourism. We might, therefore, more usefully discuss notions of validation as opposed to motivation: that is, validation (or *authentication*) of what tourists expect to feel and experience, and consequent validation (or *justification*) of their visit in positive contexts. Thus, educational trips or dimensions may serve as a legitimising mechanism for leisure (Schmidt 1979), or, as Cohen (2010) suggests, 'help distinguish meaningful dark tourism experiences from recreational or voyeuristic ones'. However, such a distinction is problematised by an assumption of efficacy, and that experience is necessarily made meaningful by an (unevaluated) educational dimension. Furthermore, educational dimensions might not distinguish but disguise the voyeuristic experience as meaningful. These attempts to demarcate the boundaries of educational, recreational, and voyeuristic experience may be read as moralising measures, which polarise perceptions of tourist's (static) interests and identities and contradict the potential coexistence or progression of different attitudes and experiences. However, they also reveal fundamental anxieties about the transference of darkness from site history to contemporary touristic (a)morality and (dis)respect. Arguably, connotations of shared heritage and associated educative and interpretive activity defuse perceptions that a 'search for spectacle has replaced the respect for solemnity' at sanctified sites (Rojek 1993: 141, on tombs at Pere Lachaise Cemetery in Paris). Therefore, positive identity affects are obtained through identification with educational 'solemnity' rather than mere touristic spectacle. In their study of former slavery sites, Dann and Potter (2001) argue that historicity is endowed in contemporary thought with a moral simplicity. Moreover, this is compounded by binaries of good and evil connoted by dark sites, with the nostalgic capacity of heritage speaking to a touristic 'yearning for a past they can no longer find in their own social settings' and which 'it was once possible to distinguish right from wrong' (Dann and Potter 2001: 7).

The collective nature and prevalence of touristic visitation to sites associated with death and disaster affords a ubiquity, and the various rationalisations provided by the tourism infrastructure constitute a positive cultural commentary. In turn, this is likely to support the 'sanctioning' of visitations to death-related destinations. However, that institution and its authoritative agency are not (yet) normative: both academic and media discourse call into question the ethical and moral qualities of dark tourism and its legitimacy as a mediating cultural institution. Stone and Sharpley's (2008) advocacy of dark tourism as a means by which the participant may obtain ontological security may assume too readily its sociocultural licence to do so. Additionally, negative cultural commentary relating to dysfunction, deviance, and dystopia within dark tourism contexts may problematise it. Clearly, these commentaries are tributary to dark touristic narratives, whereby both sanctioning and censure will affect perceptions of Self and place, as well as issues of learning.

(Dark) Tourism and Learning

Touristic quests to discover and engage with new places and aspects of identity meet their match in more or less formalised 'educational tourism' experiences. Arguably, it is here where opportunities for self-improvement and learning are emphasised in a post-modern take on the Grand Tour. Ritchie's (2003) market segmentation approach suggests an overarching differentiation depending on 'education first' or 'tourism first' prioritisation (the former, largely the domain of school and other formal education institutions). However, Richie (2003) acknowledges that the research scope fails to fully interrogate the 'leisure-education hybrid' (Smith and Jenner 1997). Indeed, links between travel, tourism, and education are generally under-researched (Roppolo 1996; Smith and Jenner 1997; Falk et al. 2012; Stone and Petrick 2012), whilst research into informal learning in tourism, and particularly in dark tourism, is significantly under-represented within the literature. As Mitchell (1998: 176) points out, 'little is known about touristic learning despite frequent references to educative potential within tourism marketing'. Meanwhile, Minnaert's (2012) study which offers interesting insights into social tourism and learning, emphasise that further research into touristic learning is needed, reiterating the privileging of formal education experience, whereas the unplanned learning opportunities of other forms of tourism have been left largely undiscovered. Consequently, the moral and intellectual status of dark tourism sites and visitors is dependent on educational value that is unqualified outside formal learning realms. Some authors argue that memorial sites 'should draw especially on ... the emotional appeal of a genuine historical site with authentic remains, and leave most of the intellectual learning for other, more suitable, situations' (Marcuse 2001: 391). Yet such dependence on emotional appeal without intellectual learning risks a degradation of touristic experience, literally displacing potential learning outcomes from touristic to formal educative and specialist spheres. However, Minnaert (2012) suggests that touristic learning and behavioural change can take place not only though formal learning activities, but in tourist opportunities to integrate into a community of practice.

Tourism's typological profusion reflects the diversity and fluidity of posttourism, yet contradicts its characteristic-blurred boundaries by which special and general interest merge into mixed interest (Brotherton and Himmetoglu 1997). Accordingly, twenty-first century tourists curate a portfolio of different experiences, constituting multiple typologies, within their holiday experience. Touristic hybridity is a useful concept with regard to dark tourism. Indeed, its themes and locations overlap with battlefield and other 'tourisms', and its presence in excursionary components of otherwise non-dark tourism possess qualities of historicity, issues memory, and potential dissonance, and attract different visitor groups while supporting their various objectives. Many dark tourism destinations, including First and Second World War burial grounds and battlefields (Baldwin and Sharpley 2009), are considered important destinations for 'organised trips designed to enliven learning strategies' (Lennon and Foley 2000: 163) having specific value in contexts of history, heritage, and experiential learning (Marcuse 2005). These groups affect the tilt and constitution of the visitor base and experience at museum or memorial spaces, and are generally the target groups for museology experiential learning programmes and resources.

Experiential Learning in (Dark) Tourism

Definitions of touristic experience drawn from the literature set out particular contexts for, and affinities with, experiential learning processes. The qualities expressed by these definitions may be collated to 'test' the compatibility of conceptualisations, theories, and models of informal and experiential learning that represent future dark tourism learning practices. In particular, two (interrelated) approaches to learning are identified here—Boydell's (1976) cycle of experiential learning and Kolb's[1] (1984) Experiential Learning Cycle. Whilst a full discussion is beyond the scope of this chapter, I introduce the most basic tenets here, and various developments, revisions, and challenges to the fuller expositions of these conceptualisations are well rehearsed elsewhere. Therefore, I suggest themes and offer examples that may be relevant to future discourse, particularly within the context of dark tourism. In addition to conceptual frameworks, large-scale informal and experiential learning initiatives may be interrogated in terms of their implementation and evaluation. For instance, the Inspiring Learning for All[2] framework adopted by many UK museums, galleries, and libraries refers to generic learning outcomes in planning and evaluating learning experience and include *knowledge and understanding, skills, enjoyment, inspiration and creativity, activity or progression, and attitudes and values*. These relate to further social learning outcomes and are readily associated with qualities of touristic experiences, which may be summed up as:

- The mental, spiritual, and physiological outcomes resulting from on-site recreation engagements (Schänzel and McIntosh 2000: 37);
- Aggregate and cumulative customer perceptions ... produced when humans consolidate sensory information (Carbone and Haeckel 1994: 9);
- A subjective mental state (Otto and Ritchie 1996: 166);
- The result of encountering, undergoing, or living through things (Schmitt 1999: 57);
- Sensation or knowledge acquisition resulting from participation in daily activities (Gupta and Vajic 2000: 35);
- An outcome of participation ... within a social context (Smith 2003: 233);
- Subjective personal reactions and feelings (Chen and Chen 2010: 29);
- Providing sensory, emotional, cognitive, behavioural, and relational values that replace functional values (Schmitt 1999: 57).

Of course, modifications of these qualities might be utilised in benchmarking, evaluating, and facilitating learning experiences at dark tourism sites. Moreover, this representative set reveals recurrent modes and motifs, generally comprehended by Schmitt's (1999) set. To these qualities can be added key themes arising from dark tourism production and consumption, and are discussed further in this chapter under the subheadings of *mindfulness* and *importance attitudes, emotion, empathy,* and multisensory aspects of *sense and sensibility*. The whole set can be thematically grouped as follows (some attributes may lend themselves to more than one group):

1. Mental; thought; perception; information; mental state; knowledge; reaction.
2. Spiritual; emotion; value; living through; personal reaction; feelings; empathy.
3. Physiological; recreation; activity; sensory; undergoing; sensation; participation; daily activities; reaction; feelings.
4. On-site; engagement; inter-relationship; subjective; encountering; undergoing; living through; participation; social context.
5. Aggregate; cumulative; consolidate; acquisition; outcome.

These groupings represent three experiential modes (1–3) and contextualising factors (4/5) that describe tourist experiences in significant spatial, sensory, cognitive, and affective contexts of dark tourism. In relation to Boydell's (1976) trinity of *cognition* (an increased awareness), *emotion* (changed attitudes), and *behaviour* (changed or interpersonal competence), further insights can be made. Indeed, Boydell's trinity framework may be correlated to the three experiential modes (1–3) of the tourist experience; while the contextualising factors (4/5) speak to specific qualities of place, subjectivity, social community, and encounter.

Future frameworks for the planning, provision, and evaluation of dark tourism learning might usefully identify cognitive, emotional, and behavioural modes and holistic contexts of site and the tourist community. Ambitious, if not rhetorical, educative missions to 'learn from the past' so that we may 'never again' repeat (dark) history might focus on increasing awareness, changing attitudes, and developing interpersonal competence, as represented by Boydell's conceptual trinity. Indeed, such a model represents flexible, feasible, and measurable objectives by which dark tourism learning may be developed and evaluated.

Similarly, Kolb's (1984) experiential learning model sets out the stages of learning, and which may be adapted for a range of (dark tourism) contexts and environments:

- *Concrete experience*—new experiences, or reinterpretations of experience;
- *Reflective observation*—of new experience, with a focus on consistency between experience and understanding;
- *Abstract conceptualisation*—reflection evokes new ideas, or ways to rework ideas;
- *Active experimentation*—application of new experiences and ideas in real-world contexts.

Importantly, it is not the order of these stages but their co-dependence and interrelationship which are key to Kolb's concept of effective experiential learning. Consequently, these processes reflect potential elements of dark tourism experiences (including pre- and post-visit activity), and usefully emphasise the value of a holistic attitude whereby the absence of any one stage diminishes or negates the quality of others. The stages of the learning cycle offer a checklist by which dark tourism sites and strategies can ensure that opportunities for encounters, reflection, expression, and experimentation with and of ideas and experiences are equally represented. Moreover, we might draw understanding of how to express or encounter new ideas, or to reflect upon what we have seen and done and to apply new understandings in post-visit contexts, in what are often 'difficult places' with particular protocols.

Place Protocols in Dark Tourism

, The seriousness of events memorialised at dark tourism sites tends to transfuse perceptions of the site and its representations, resulting in "sacred cow" status (Lennon and Foley 2000:119). In turn, this can problematise criticism of such sites' interpretive and logistical facilities. Thus located, to a degree, beyond criticism, such (dark) sites enhance connotations of the serious and the sacred through 'the continual reiteration of 'the educative/memorial/healing mission and purpose' of historically significant sites (Lennon and Foley 2000 95). As discussed earlier in the chapter within contexts of authenticity and validation, potential consequences to the assertion of 'educative context, often with an admonitory tone' (Lennon and Foley, ibid.: 119) and variously didactic expressions occur at dark sites and within respective communication channels. Hence, for most prospective tourists, the first (or only) point of direct communication with dark sites will be via their online representation in organisational websites and/or social media channels.

By way of illustration, some key examples offer interesting insights into educative or other 'missions' and the expressed functions and qualities prioritised within top-line messaging:

The **9/11 Memorial** website's homepage (911memorial.org, 2017) provides navigational headings relating to fundamental functions of place: *Visit, Memorial, Museum, Teach and Learn*. Further signposting to the Museum's organisational identity is offered by its Facebook categorisations (Facebook/911memorial, 2017) as *History Museum, landmark and historical place* and (again) *historical place:* implications of the profound space/time contexts in which visitation, conservation and education functions can take place.

Auschwitz Museum and Memorial expresses specific qualities of authority and authenticity through its organisational Facebook categorisations (facebook/auschwitzmemorial, 2017): *History museum; Historical Place; Government organisation* (the latter a recent, and interesting, amendment (facebook/auschwitzmemorial, 2016) to a previous designation, *Education organisation*); and through its website's homepage (Auschwitz.org, 2017) navigational headings, *Museum, History, Visiting* and *Education*,. Visiting information, prefaced by topline reference to *'the authentic memorial'* (Auschwitz.org, 2017), includes significant directives (Auschwitz.org: Visiting, 2017) that the visitor is *''required to observe the appropriate solemnity and respect' on the grounds of, and requested to read the (substantial) Rules for Visiting document before arrival at, the Museum.'* (also see Chap. 20).

Kigali Genocide Memorial Museum is defined by its website (kgm.rw, 2017) as a place for remembrance and learning, a site that honours the memory of more than one million Rwandans killed in 1994 and constitutes the final resting place for more than 250,000 victims of the Tutsi genocide. As the specificity and detail of these definitions are evocative of epitaph, and speak to memorial aspects above all others. Furthermore, place is functional, and meaningful, not only for the visitor who remembers, learns and honours; but for the dead who rest and are represented there. Navigation headings signpost standard V*isit, Memorial* and *Education* functions, but *Guestbook, Get involved* and *News* headings are suggestive of engagement, interaction and ongoing relevance that, perhaps, challenge more static notions of memorialisation. This vitality is allied with the concept of space, experience and loss shared by both visitors and the remembered dead in the site's Facebook identification (Facebook/kigaligenocidememorial, 2017) as not only a *History museum* and *Historical place,* but as a *Community.* (also see Chap. 11).

Significant variations in tone and visual identity are discernible across these online environments, reflecting very different approaches to interpretation. However, educational and memorial missions are key to the institutional identities of these in-situ dark tourism destinations and key messages from online environments represent the tip of interpretive icebergs.

As a context to an overview of interpretation strategies and modes, it is worth noting some specific considerations to their application in dark tourism realms. These speak to certain attributes of experiential learning and relate to issues of *mindfulness* and *importance attitudes, emotion, empathy*, and multisensory aspects of *sense and sensibility* as impactful on learning proclivity or problematisation.

Mindfulness and Importance Attitudes

Following Langer's (1989) representation of *mindfulness*, Moscardo (1996) and Pearce (1996) appraise the touristic experience in terms of information processing and openness to receiving new information. Distinctions between 'mindful' and 'mindless' visitors (although I regard the latter term as unfortunate, in its derogatory connotations) relate to 'mindful' interest in new subject matter and learning opportunities, and an associated greater likelihood capacity 'to enjoy, express satisfaction with, and learn more from the visit' (Moscardo 1996: 382). In contrast, the state of mindlessness suggests 'pre-existing scripts and routines are followed' (Pearce, ibid.: 13) and attention to alternative cultural values is less active. Notions of mindfulness relate closely to previous observations about relational proximity and heightened engagement. Mindful and/or highly engaged visitors are more likely to have examined interpretation activity and site information pre-visit, to recognise such opportunities on-site and to have pre-existing knowledge that enable connections and recognitions. Therefore, interpretive activity must support not only the needs and interests of mindful visitors but also, perhaps especially, enhanced learning and more meaningful engagement for the 'mindless'. In his summary of studies on audio-visual, multisensory, and dynamic interpretive techniques, Moscardo (1996) suggests that these approaches significantly enhance visitors' mindfulness attention and learning. Conversely, static interpretation recalls the 'scripts and routines of mindlessness' and, thus, risks isolating the mindful tourist.

The related psychological concept of *importance attitudes* in social perceptions and behaviour is infrequently referenced in the tourism literature (although, see Lindberg and Johnson 1997; and Um and Crompton 1990) but has clear correlation with issues of relational values and mindfulness. Studies evidence that, where personal importance is attached to an issue—that is, where an importance attitude obtains—people are far more likely to electively seek and gather information about that issue (Bizer and Krosnick 2001; Holbrook et al. 2005). Interestingly in our current contexts, these studies relate that importance attitudes generally resist change, remain stable over time and experience, and have powerful effects on thoughts and on behaviours (Boninger et al. 1995). Such qualities resonate with earlier studies on the power of tradition (Hewison 1987;

Fowler 1989; Heeley 1989; Hall and McArthur 1993) and an implied stability and continuity associated with heritage values. Touristic experience of heritage contexts may elicit purposeful information-gathering and powerful identity reinforcement, or potent dissonance and resistance, depending on the alignment of importance attitude. Significant attention is required to the management and acknowledgment of importance attitudes, more so in the contexts of especially where dark tourism representations of political, moral, and national identity concerns and the elicit heightened emotions they elicit. emotional responses.

Emotion

Moscardo and Ballantyne (2008: 247) observe of strong emotions that 'nowhere are these issues more clearly present than in interpretation of hot topics, such as war, and dark tourism places, such as sites of massacres and prisons'. The highly emotional experiences dark tourism may present to visitors (Shackley 2001) necessitate the acknowledgment in interpretive practises of emotionality and affective elements. Sharpley and Stone (2009: 115) suggest that this may enable a range of experiential processes: satisfaction of emotional needs, confrontation with or contemplation of death, making sense of tragedy or atrocity, and personal remembrance. Thus, dark site interpretation must 'authenticate the events they represent … in a manner which recognises and responds to the emotions of potential visitors' (Sharpley and Stone, ibid.: 113). Yet, this recognition and response must be finite and considered. Emotions are variable and difficult to manage, especially at sites of trauma and where attitudinal complexities exist. Balanced and responsible mediation processes preclude the prioritisation of visitor emotion over other experiential and cognitive elements. Thus, where recognising or creating opportunities to express emotion extends to strategies that, as expressed by Uzzell and Ballantyne (1998: 154) 'inject an affective component into its subject matter', interpretive integrity and experiential learning may be compromised. 'Hot' interpretation in which 'values, beliefs, relationships, interests and memories are engaged' (Sharpley and Stone, ibid.: 113), if not tempered by 'cool' approaches and reflective opportunities may 'excite a degree of emotional arousal which needs to be recognised and addressed in interpretation' in terms of risk and not success (Uzzell and Ballantyne 1998: 152). As Walter (2009) points out, there is currently no research-based insight into the potential effects of such emotional responses (although, see Best's (2007) observations on positive word-of-mouth).

Emotions are highly subjective and, therefore, difficult to articulate and analyse. Within dark tourism contexts, authenticity of feeling represents a conceptual tenet not necessarily obtained effectively via a tourist questionnaire. A high expectation of 'authentic' feelings of sadness and despair in dark tourism experience, frequently cited as a motivating factor but likely an anticipatory one, may not be matched as a result of mindlessness, failure of affective interpretation or a variety of other factors. For example, during a lecture I gave to undergraduates at the University of Central Lancashire (UK) in 2015, in discussing authenticity, a student described her disappointment during a recent trip to Auschwitz-Birkenau on being told by a guide that a portion of the site (a gallows) had been reconstructed. Yet, her disappointment was not in the reconstructive aspect per se, but in *being told*; her stated interpretive preference would have been concealment, to enable stronger feelings of sadness and shock, despite the lack of veracity that in part allowed them. Moreover, touristic feelings may include exhaustion and irritability resulting from travelling, walking, paying attention, hunger, and thirst. These are familiar, sometimes simultaneous, consequences of touristic visits to large, in situ sites where terrain and climate are physically uncomfortable, and seeking relief may be perceived as shameful or self-indulgent. These feelings may exacerbate or reduce feelings about site themes and interpretation, and may be difficult to unpick from the emotions researchers are seeking to discover. They will also, as cognitive disturbances, similarly inhibit other learning processes. In discussions of atrocity heritage, Tunbridge and Ashworth (1996) argue that the intensity of emotion evoked by dark site-specific events produces protective barriers against their understanding that block full reception of horrific realities, which would otherwise be overwhelmingly horrific. overwhelming.

Thus, perceived tourist emotions are complex and unpredictable: existing empirical research on emotional responses at sites associated with death and suffering is limited and descriptive (Preece and Price 2005; Wight 2006; Walter 2009). Most existing studies adopt qualitative methodologies and relate not to emotional intensity but to the kind of emotions expressed. Those studies which attend to touristic expressions of emotions include the following as a representative sample and with the outcomes listed:

- Austin's (2002) study of former slavery sites in Ghana, reporting feelings of anger, anguish, and sorrow;
- Krakover's (2005) study at Yad Vashem Holocaust Remembrance Site, reporting feelings of sadness and fear;
- Lisle's (2004) study at Ground Zero in New York, reporting feelings of despair, anger, frustration, sadness, hope, and love;
- Best's (2007) study of Norfolk Island's former convict settlements, reporting feelings of anger, fear, denial, grief, empathy, pride, fascination, interest, and gratitude;

- Thurnell-Read's (2009) interviews with young visitors to Auschwitz, reporting feelings of sadness and hope;
- Sharpley's (2012) study of visitor experiences at genocide sites—disgust, sadness, and hope.

It is unusual in 'darker tourism' that tourists express feelings that might be perceived as less than empathetic: even excitement, shock, horror are rarely reported, but must surely are likely to obtain. Simone-Charteris and Boyd (2010) examine visitation to in-situ sites including former prisons and sites of death, under the auspices of political as opposed todark tourism: their study reveals some of the emotions outlined above but also others including support/solidarity, commemoration, nationalism, curiosity, and enjoying the 'thrill' of political violence (also see Clarke 2000; Shackley 2001; Kliger 2005; Brin 2006; Burnhill 2007; Causevic and Lynch 2007). Arguably, therefore, attitudes to 'political' rather than 'dark' activity allow expression of feelings that may also (covertly) be obtained at dark tourism sites.

These largely negative emotions are not unexpected and must be considered in terms of the tendency of 'vexing and troublesome feelings of revulsion, grief, anger and/or shame that histories can produce' (Simon, 2011: 433) to provoke secondary effects such as anxiety, anger, and frustration, that unsettle meaning and assumed significance. It is clear that 'dark tourism will not always comfort' (Sharpley and Stone, ibid.: 54); however, its interpretation should support processing and reflection of, and degrees of relief from, strong emotion, as part of their acknowledgment.

Empathy

For Ashworth and Hartmann (2005), *empathy* relies upon the capacity of heritage consumers to identify with individual victims of the atrocity in question. Subsequently, Miles (2002: 1176) regards this enabling of empathy 'between the sightseer and the past victim over and above the evocation of historical knowledge' as essential to the success of dark tourism interpretation. Yet genuine empathy (defined[3] as 'the ability to understand and share the feelings of another') with those whose lives and deaths are represented by in-situ sites of atrocity may be impossible to achieve. Within the literature, reference to empathy as a significant factor in tourist motivation and experience is ubiquitous. However, exemplary models of interpretation are less so: this -frequently cited but ephemeral theme requires further empirical investigation to achieve a consistent understanding of what is meant by 'empathy' and how it can be evaluated. Bruner (1991) and Galani-Moutafi (2000) suggest that tourists' desire for self-transformation may be fulfilled through empathetic encounters with 'authentic' cultures. Yet this is problematised at atrocity and genocide sites that memorialise the consequences of planned obliteration of culture, or represent the ruination of cultural life. The 'authentic' cultures evoked by Auschwitz-Birkenau, for example, are both the cultures of the Nazi regime as well as the cultures (mainly largely, but not exclusively, European Jewish culture) that the regime persecuted and murdered at that site, and elsewhere. The former cannot enable empathy; the latter may evoke sympathy, but truly empathetic encounters are disabled by mortality and the absence of exchange in the encounter.

Site interpretation may support capacity for empathy by enabling fuller understanding and awareness of 'Other' life experiences. Furthermore, it can provide and promote opportunities and environments in which increased mindfulness, reflective processes, communal contexts, and meaningful exchanges with others may be experienced. Coming to know a place means coming to know its stories (Johnstone 1990), thus meaningful tourism experiences depend on the availability and communication of narratives (Arnould and Price 1993; Bruner 2005; Chronis 2005, 2012). The personal narratives encountered in interpretative material often seek to evoke empathy through individualising experience and, thus, humanising 'one of many' as 'someone'. Where storytelling is multisensory (i.e., vocal, embodied, experienced in particular physical space, and not only through visual modes of text and image) attitudes of empathy and aspects of authenticity are enhanced. Thus, encounters at in-situ dark tourism sites with 'rememberers' or storytellers are potentially self-actualising. Guided tours are effective in reinforcing a visitor's emotional experiences, particularly if the guide is a relation of a site victim/survivor or, above all, a survivor of site history themselves. These first- and second-generation storytellers (Shackley 2001; Uzzell 1989) lend relational authenticity; tourists borrow their memories and emotions in a unique 'guided' experience. Indeed, the tourist is transformed by the perceived channelling of authenticity, heightening the potential witnessing roles, and the guide takes on the qualities of ritual leader or 'spiritual advisor' (Cohen 1985). For example, Shackley's (2001) examination of tourism at Robben Island, South Africa revealed high levels of tourist satisfaction with their experience, especially with the interpretive use of recorded voices and photographs recounting former inmates' stories. Furthermore, former political prisoners, telling their own stories in new roles as tour guides, enhanced visitors' emotional experiences and generated an authentic 'spirit of place' (ibid: 356).

Dark tourism sites can and do offer access to compelling personal narratives, which may be presented so that the visitor perceives or encounters meaningful connections and commonalities. In so doing, the potential for empathy is maximised; yet, interpretation alone cannot engender empathy. A more nuanced, and feasible, understanding of empathetic experience at particular visitor sites might not be located in empathy with the victim, but with the witnessing role that acknowledgment and understanding of the victim's experiences might allow. Riches (1986) offers us a conceptualisation of the 'violence triangle' and positions the trinity of victim, perpetrator, and witness. Consequently, the imagined role of witness predominates in dark tourism interpretation, whereby touristic behaviours of gazing, recording, and documentation or recollection readily translate into onlooking, memorialisation, and 'testimonial' behaviours. Interpretive sites may seek to anchor tourists in a witness position, distant in space and time from more visceral elements (Robb 2009) yet capable of considering, processing, and reflecting upon the experience of the 'Other' in order to obtain a deeper sense of that 'Other's' Self. Knudsen (2011) discusses various witnessing tasks, including the re-establishment of first-hand witnesses' lost subjectivities (Caruth 1995) and the performance of testimonies, by which relations to past events and those who experienced them are reconfirmed or transformed (Antze and Lambek 1996; Oliver 2001; Knudsen 2003). These behaviours entail in loco performances, on behalf of but different from original witnesses, and in this sense offer a kind of shared positioning. Knudsen (2011: 58) goes on to note a third, highly nuanced, representation of witnessing through 'ethical or moral attitudes, according to which we relate to the others' with the responsibility that post-modern, globalised contexts ask of place upon us (Boltanski 1999; Chouliaraki 2006; Silverstone 2007). This represents a holistic empathetic approach to which dark tourism may rightly aspire, and by which tourists may achieve rich encounters with any historical and cultural Other.

Sense and Sensibility

Urry's (1990) seminal conceptualisation of the tourist gaze does not preclude his explicit acknowledgement that 'there will always be other senses involved' (Urry 2002: 151). However, readings of tourism as a corporeal and multisensory (Franklin and Crang 2001; Dann and Jacobsen 2002; Pan and Ryan 2009) have arguably been under-acknowledged. Indeed, critical commentary suggests that preoccupation with the tourist gaze in analyses of touristic sensemaking results in an 'absence of the body' (Veijola and Jokinen 1994: 149) and inadequate attention to 'embodied practices of sensuousness/sensuality/utility' (Crouch 2003: 28). In non-hedonic contexts, and especially at dark tourism sites, multisensory aspects are even less fully interrogated.

Yet these are significant contexts by which to understand and support embodied encounters and experiential learning through acknowledging visual, auditory, and kinaesthetic sensory learning styles (Luecke 2003) and complementary activities of seeing, hearing, and doing. Within traditional heritage interpretation, the visual sense is highly privileged: often fundamentally through the 'seeing' of iconic places and things, and further through interpretive devices of text, image, and film. However, 'post-museum' learning strategies highlight the usefulness of multisensory approaches to interpretation (although largely in consideration of children and playfulness, or visitors with sensory impairment for whom visual aspects require supplementation or replacement). The use of, for example, oral history recordings align with interpretive value attached not only to personal stories but to the human voice, and form an increasing element of heritage experiences. Thus, twenty-first century scholarship and praxis investigate taste, smell, touch, and sound in the tourist experience (Edensor 1998; Son and Pearce 2005; also see Dann and Jacobsen 2003 for a discussion of 'smellscapes'). As tourists are sightseeing, they are also *site-hearing* other languages, experiences, and sounds, through fellow-tourists, local populations, the media, and nature. Indeed, *site-feeling* changes may be found in differing temperature, the texture of physical things, site-tasting, or site-smelling of the unfamiliar and the particular. Consequently, Belk's (1990: 670) expression of nostalgia as a 'wistful mood that an object, a scene, a smell or a strain of music' evoke speaks to developing interests in multisensory experiences and interpretations of (dark) tourism.

The 'Dark Art' of Interpretation

Interpretation is defined as 'a set of information-focused communication activities, designed to facilitate a rewarding visitor experience' (Moscardo and Ballantyne 2008: 239). Interpretation is also the main communication system between a site and its visitors (Sharpley and Stone 2009; Wight and Lennon 2007) and is designed to facilitate site narrative outcomes and benefits. In sites associated with terrible events, absence of interpretation may render the site meaningless to visitors (Moscardo and Ballantyne 2008; Sharpley and Stone 2009). Furthermore, events which we may describe metaphorically as 'unspeakable' and, in turn, represent significant trauma to our identity as human beings, are problematised by our shared narrative—the story we wish to tell ourselves, about ourselves. Dark tourism requires that certain chapters in our human history are mediated, or interpreted, so that they can be confronted in the metanarrative of who we are and what we do. Meanwhile, in many cases, participants in the tragic event in question are absent: either time has elapsed, or life has been eradicated, to such a degree that we confront a void in the historical narrative. Certain voices are missing, that processes of interpretation and memorial seek to represent. This represents a grave responsibility for human society, and a specific challenge for those involved in the formal interpretation of dark tourism sites. This challenge is intensified in sites which face the 'dissonant heritage' dilemma: the dual objective of presenting heritage of death and disaster in an attractive environment (Tunbridge and Ashworth 1996; Krakover 2002). Nevertheless, broadening the appeal of these institutions does not necessarily imply that the 'integrity' of their ideological and educational agendas is compromised and/or degraded. In many cases, attracting a wider and more diversified public, when carried out in a constructive and responsible way, can fulfil the sites' objectives much more effectively than marketing solely to niche and small groups (Harrison 1993; McPherson 2006).

By way of illustration, Oren and Shani (2012) examine the Yad Vashem Holocaust Museum in Jerusalem and its seminal (Disney) concept of theming as an effective device by which artefacts, media products, and information are strategically presented. Subsequently, spatial qualities including architecture and landscape, and advanced technology, are utilised to fulfil certain outcomes or objectives. This exemplifies the liberty of secondary sites in their imaginative and strategic (but often controversial) approaches to interpretation. Conversely, Strange and Kempa (2003: 393), within contexts of in-situ former penal sites, observe that:

> *…heritage designers of dark tourism sites arrive on the scene after places of suffering have become famous. They inherit official accounts and popular stories and they constantly catch up with and cater to tourists' preconceived notions and expectations.*

This is a useful encapsulation of some of the challenges faced by contemporary interpretation practitioners at historic primary sites. Similarly, Cole's (1999) differentiation between the former Auschwitz-Birkenau Nazi concentration camp and the associated visitor destination by means of the term 'Auschwitzland' reflects that author's concerns that public consumption of the (relatively underdeveloped) site represents a risk to a sense of authenticity. Yet, this raises the paradoxical question—without its 1.75 million annual visitors, the majority of whom are tourists, who is appraising that sense? Keil (2005), in a more nuanced critique, points to the differences, in ambience and in interpretation, between Auschwitz I and Auschwitz II (Birkenau) camps. The former is the site of exhibitions, original and replica buildings and the main visitor access point for the camp complex; the latter, at some distance, is a far less structured zone of pathways, dereliction, and surprisingly limited interpretation panels. This is the area which for many guided groups is an 'independent' experience that, following from the extreme 'tour guidance' of Auschwitz I, can be somewhat disorientating. Furthermore, this area is the location of the main gas chambers, crematoria, and ash pits that materially manifest the full horror of the Final Solution; yet it is entirely feasible that the average visitor will see only a fraction of this larger portion of the large site complex. Much may be felt, yet arguably little learned, within this bleak and unmediated landscape. Regardless of the institutional concern that the site is mediated and informed by guides, the extent to which visitors can listen, or process what they are hearing and seeing, is unproven. In part, this reflects the limited opportunities for reflection and discussion within tourist groups, and in the didactic environments and navigation by which behaviours are managed. The symbolic silences at Auschwitz are met by the actual silence of tourists within the often-crowded exhibition spaces of Auschwitz I, through which they are often hastened in order to accommodate successive tour groups. Site management does not provide, nor define, reflective spaces for post-visit reflection, including evaluation or comment, and which is an essential stage in the learning process (Kolb 1984; Moutin 2003).

Examining representative and interpretive needs and processes within dark tourism, Stone & Sharpley (2009b) suggest that 'traditional forms of interpretation deny or do not allow for a relationship between the place or object and the visitor' through which meaning-making can take place. This kind of relationship is acknowledged by transformations in museum pedagogy from the colonialist acquisitions and implications of 'cabinets of curiosity' to the plural potential interpretations of the 'post-museum' (Hooper-Greenhill, 2000), and synchronous conceptualisation of 'post-tourism' Thus, contemporary interpretation involves interactive and experiential aspects, representing, as summarised by the National Park Service (2007: 6):

> ...*a bridge between the meanings of the resources and interests of the visitors... it is the role of the interpreter to ensure that those connections are built on the interests of the visitor. And it is the role of the visitor to determine which bridges will be crossed.*

Here, notions of touristic agency and creativity, current within tourism literature on experience but generally lacking in discussion of interpretive processes, are acknowledged. Further discussion of touristic engagement and participation in the creation of interpretive and learning strategies lies beyond the remit of this chapter, but is of profound significance in the contexts of mindfulness, relational value, empathy, and engagement previously discussed. It responds to the question of how to develop an interpretive approach that 'reduces the degree of dissonance, that begins to take the needs of all stakeholders into account' (Sharpley 2009b: 161), and to the challenges of making meaning, and indeed allaying anxiety, about human tragedies and ontological (in)security (Stone and Sharpley 2008).

Traditional notions of objectivity in interpretive attitudes are challenged by acknowledged and powerful emotional responses, and cultural perspectives, provoked by themes and representations of atrocity and conflict. They are further complicated by the political and cultural agendas of host destinations and managers, and by the processes of denial, dismissal, diversion, or displacement that shape interpretive material (Rayner 2012). Timothy and Boyd (2006) refer to this as a kind of 'collective amnesia' in response to traumas that resist integration into collective narratives. Hence, Wight and Lennon's (2007: 527) description of interpretation as a 'process of creating multiple constructions of the past whereby history is never an objective recall of the past, but is rather a selective interpretation'. Thus, interpretive material at dark heritage sites is highly unlikely to abstract our understanding of event landmarks from ideological hegemonies: from the simple, assumed shared values of good and bad, to the complex agendas and evolutions of political powers and nation states. Buzinde and Santos (2008) argue, in relation to former slavery plantations, that hegemonic narratives occlude alternative tellings that invoke past shame within the state identity and, thus, provoke and sustain dissonance. Meanwhile, Strange and Kempa (2003) relate the dominance of state agencies in interpretation at former prison sites. Moreover, politicisation of heritage is highlighted in touristic contexts where national identity is represented idealistically via a partial metanarrative in which expression of conflicting experience is sublimated (Pretes 2003; Palmer 2005; Goulding and Domic 2009; Patil 2011).

One outcome of selective interpretation and its political and cultural agendas is of course heritage *dissonance*. Wight and Lennon's (2007) comparative study of Lithuania's Museum of Genocide Victims and Vilna Gaon Lithuanian State Jewish Museum highlights significant difference, perhaps most explicitly in the respective absence or usage of the term 'genocide', in interpretation of shared history. They go on to examine this disparity in terms of victim/perpetrator identity and local/national experience and memory levels. Similarly, Strange and Kempa (2003) discuss Alcatraz and Robben Island as exemplifying the reconstruction of historic and dissonant sites into memorial spaces. Particular, they seek to explore the multiple ways in which dark tourism is represented, marketed, and consumed through and by complex sets of interventions, imperatives, and attitudes across networks of stakeholders, including tourists, as well as heritage and remembrance agencies at local, national, and international levels. Moreover, at Auschwitz-Birkenau, after seven decades of (physical and conceptual) reclamation, reconstruction, and reinterpretation, certain narrative dissonances are addressed by the remarkable representation of different national, and other collective Holocaust narratives within discrete exhibition spaces. Arguably, it is as if the Auschwitz-Birkenau memorial museum has allowed these disparate national identities to agree to disagree, whereby each of the former concentration camp buildings is independently curated and interpreted. The resulting variance and inconsistency of impression and experience relates not only to different narrative interpretations but also to varying resources and expertise available in different national contexts. Indeed, this can actually be experienced as an astonishing and poignant metaphor for the site's history as it represents a powerful, albeit unintentionally, evocative representation of human conflict and its fragile, reactive management.

With this in mind, Poria (2007) argues for robust interpretive strategies to create a bespoke narrative formed by interrelated expressions of a dissonant heritage event, its stakeholder network and their various feelings or involvement with the event in question. This conceptual framework is based upon axes of good/bad, active/passive, and the four permutations of 'history' that obtain. Where this framework is conceived as a continuum, flexible to evolving and diverse perceptions, and where its ownership involves stakeholders and not merely interpretation strategists, it might represent an effective benchmark for emergent dark tourism sites. Further to this continuum, Poria (2007) identifies 'bad-active' history—that is, 'owned' social identity inspiring negative emotions of shame—as least represented within heritage interpretation. Ultimately, therefore, specific and strategic approaches toward interpretation of dark tourism sites enable fluid and functional conceptualisations fundamentally associated with active and participatory meaning-making.

Conclusion

Current conceptualisation of educational tourism 'ignores many of the informal and unplanned opportunities that potentially arise for learning within tourism' (Mitchell 1998: 177). Learning, as opposed to education, is not always a structured and planned process. Indeed, Kalinowski and Weiler (1992: 17) describe learning as 'a lifelong process that is mostly incidental and natural' which, in turn, speaks to the qualities and capacities of dark tourism encounters and their positioning within lifespans. Furthermore, dark tourism's diversity of sites and participants and related needs and resources, lends itself to flexible, social, and experiential approaches to learning. Dark tourism sites represent unique opportunities for learning not only about the historical facts of atrocity and disaster, but also human experiences of and responses to them, including our own. Therefore, dark tourism's responsibility to support learning processes is intrinsic to its qualification and perception as a cultural mediating institution, to its ethical credentials, and to the relevance of its conceptualisations. Research and rationales about dark tourism as an experiential learning institution are necessary to its relevance and value as more than the curation and display of distressing evidence of human despair. Moreover, dark tourism's multidisciplinary associations and overlaps should support its identification of relevant existing theories and mechanisms, which may be usefully adapted or interrogated in order to develop coherent conceptual frameworks for experiential learning facilitation and appraisal. To that end, dark tourism scholarship is tasked with constructing coordinated approaches, if not coalitions, toward a theory and practice of dark tourism learning, its consequences and implications.

Notes

1. http://www2.le.ac.uk/departments/gradschool/training/eresources/teaching/theories/kolb
2. http://www.inspiringlearningforall.gov.uk/
3. http://www.oxforddictionaries.com/definition/english/empathy

References

Antze, P., & Lambek, M. (Eds.). (1996). *Tense past. Cultural essays in trauma and memory*. New York/London: Routledge.

Arnould, E. J., & Price, L. (1993). River magic: Extraordinary experience and the extended service encounter. *Journal of Consumer Research, 20*(1), 24–45.

Ashworth, G. J., & Hartmann, R. (Eds.). (2005a). *Horror and human tragedy revisited: The management of sites of atrocities for tourism*. New York: Cognizant Communication Corporation.

Ashworth, G. J., & Hartmann, R. (2005b). Introduction: Managing atrocity for tourism. In G. Ashworth & A. Hartmann (Eds.), *Horror and human tragedy revisited: The management of sites of atrocities for tourism* (pp. 1–14). New York: Cognizant Communication Corporation.

Ashworth, G., & Tunbridge, J. (1996). *Dissonant heritage: The resource in conflict*. New York: Wiley.

Austin, N. K. (2002). Managing heritage attractions: Marketing challenges at sensitive historical sites. *International Journal of Tourism Research, 3*(6), 447–457.

Baldwin, F., & Sharpley, R. (2009). Battlefield tourism: Bringing organised violence back to life. In R. Sharpley & P. Stone (Eds.), *The darker side of travel: The theory and practise of dark tourism* (pp. 186 - 206). Bristol: Channel View Publications.

Beech, J. (2000). The enigma of holocaust sites as tourist attractions: The case of Buchenwald. *Managing Leisure, 5*(1), 29–24.
Beech, J. (2009). Genocide tourism. In R. Sharpley & P. R. Stone (Eds.), *The darker side of travel: The theory and practice of dark tourism* (pp. 207–223). Bristol: Channel View Publications.
Belk, R. W. (1990). The role of possessions in constructing and maintaining a sense of past. In M. E. Goldberg, G. Gorn, & R. W. Pollay (Eds.), *Advances in consumer research* (Vol. 17, pp. 669–676). Provo: Association for Consumer Research.
Best, M. (2007). Norfolk Island: Thanatourism, history and visitor emotions. *Shima: The International Journal of Research into Island Cultures, 1*(2), 30–48.
Bizer, G. Y., & Krosnick, J. A. (2001). Exploring the structure of strength-related attitude features: The relation between attitude importance and attitude accessibility. *Journal of Personality and Social Psychology, 81*, 566–586.
Bollag, B. (1999). In the shadow of Auschwitz. Teaching the Holocaust in Poland. *American Educator, 23*(1), 38–49.
Boltanski, L. (1999). *Distant suffering. Morality, media and politics*. Cambridge: Cambridge University Press.
Boninger, D. S., Krosnick, J. A., Berent, M. K., & Fabrigar, L. R. (1995). The causes and consequences of attitude importance. In R. E. Petty & J. A. Krosnick (Eds.), *Attitude strength: Antecedents and consequences* (pp. 159–189). Mahwah: Lawrence Erlbaum Associates.
Boorstin, D. J. (1964). *The image: A guide to pseudo-events in America*. New York: Harper & Row.
Bowman, M. S., & Pezzullo, P. C. (2010). What's so 'dark' about 'dark tourism'? Death, tours, and performance. *Tourist Studies, 9*(3), 187–202.
Boydell, T. (1976). *Experiential learning*. Manchester: Department of Adult Education, University of Manchester.
Braithwaite, R., & Lee, Y. I. (2006). Dark tourism, hate and reconciliation: The Sandakan experience. In I. Kelly (Ed.), *Peace through tourism: A range of perspectives, Occasional Paper* (Vol. 8). Stowe: International Institute for Peace through Tourism.
Breathnach, T. (2006). Looking for the real me: Locating the self in heritage tourism. *Journal of Heritage Tourism, 1*(2), 100–120.
Brin, E. (2006). Politically oriented tourism in Jerusalem. *Tourist Studies, 6*(3), 215–243.
Brotherton, B., & Himmetoglu, B. (1997). Beyond destinations: Special interest tourism. *Anatolia: An International Journal of Tourism and Hospitality Research, 8*(3), 11–30.
Bruner, E. M. (1991). Transformation of self in tourism. *Annals of Tourism Research, 8*, 238–250.
Bruner, E. M. (1996). Tourism in Ghana: The representation of slavery and the return of the Black diaspora. *American Anthropologist, 98*(2), 290–304.
Bruner, E. M. (2005). *The role of narrative in tourism paper*. Presented at Berkeley conference 2005, On Voyage: New Directions in Tourism Theory, 7–8 October 2005.

Burnhill, E. (2007). *Weeds and wild flowers: Political tourism in West Belfast*. Retrieved from http://www.eurozine.com/articles/2007-05-08-burnhill-en.html

Buzinde, C., & Santos, C. (2008). Representations of slavery. *Annals of Tourism Research, 35*(2), 469–488.

Carbone, L. P., & Haeckel, S. H. (1994). Engineering customer experiences. *Marketing Management, 3*(3), 8–19.

Caruth, C. (Ed.). (1995). *Trauma: Explorations in memory*. Baltimore/London: The Johns Hopkins University Press.

Causevic, S., & Lynch, P. (2008). *The significance of dark tourism in the process of tourism development after a long-term political conflict: An issue of Northern Ireland*. Paper Presented at the ASA Conference 2007, Thinking Through Tourism, London Metropolitan University, London.

Chen, C. F., & Chen, F. S. (2010). Experience quality, perceived value, satisfaction and behavioral intentions for heritage tourists. *Tourism Management, 31*(1), 29–35.

Chouliaraki, L. (2006). *The spectatorship of suffering*. London: Sage Publications.

Chronis, A. (2005). Constructing heritage at the Gettysburg storyscape. *Annals of Tourism Research, 32*(2), 386–402.

Chronis, A. (2012). Tourists as story-builders: Narrative construction at a heritage museum. *Journal of Travel & Tourism Marketing, 29*(5), 444–459.

Clarke, R. (2000). Self-presentation in a contested city: Palestinian and Israeli political tourism in Hebron. *Anthropology Today, 16*(5), 12–18.

Cohen, E. (1985). The tourist guide. The origins, structure and dynamics of a role. *Annals of Tourism Research, 12*, 5–29.

Cohen, E. H. (2010). Educational dark tourism at an in populo site: The Holocaust museum. *Jerusalem Annals of Tourism Research, 38*(1), 193–209.

Cole, T. (1999). *Selling the holocaust, from Auschwitz to Schindler: How history is bought, packaged and sold*. New York: Routledge.

Craik, J. (1997). The culture of tourism. In C. Rojek & J. Urry (Eds.), *Touring cultures: Transformations of travel and theory*. London: Routledge.

Crooke, E. (2001). Confronting a troubled history: Which past in Northern Ireland's museums? *International Journal of Heritage Studies, 7*(2), 113–136.

Crouch, D. (2003). The sensuous in the tourist encounter. Introduction: The power of the body in tourist studies. *Tourist Studies, 3*(1), 5–22.

Dalton, D. (2013). *Dark tourism and crime*. Abingdon: Routledge.

Dann, G. M. S., & Jacobsen, J. K. S. (2002). Leading the tourist by the nose. In G. M. S. Dann (Ed.), *The tourist as a metaphor of the social world* (pp. 209–235). Wallingford: CABI Publishing.

Dann, G. M. S., & Jacobsen, S. (2003). Tourism smellscapes. *Tourism Geographies, 5*(1), 3–25.

Dann, G. M. S., & Potter, R. (2001). Supplanting the planters: Hawking heritage in Barbados. *International Journal of Hospitality and Tourism Administration, 2*(3/4), 51–84.

Devine, A., & Connor, R. (2005). *Cultural tourism: Promoting diversity on the aftermath of conflict*. Paper presented at conference: Tourism and Hospitality in Ireland: Exploring the Issues University of Ulster. Portrush 14/15 June 2005.

Falk, J. H., Ballantyne, R., Packer, J., & Benckendorff, P. (2012). Travel and learning: A neglected tourism research area. *Annals of Tourism Research, 39*(2), 908–927.

Foote, K. (1997). *Shadowed ground: America's landscapes of violence and tragedy*. Austin: University of Texas Press.

Forestell, P. H. (1993). If leviathan has a face, does Gaia have a soul? Incorporating environmental education in marine eco-tourisms. *Ocean and Coastal Management, 20*(3), 267–282.

Fowler, P. (1989). Heritage: A post-modernist perspective. In D. Uzzell (Ed.), *Heritage interpretation: The natural and built environment* (pp. 57–64). London: Belhaven.

Franklin, A., & Crang, M. (2001). The trouble with tourism and travel theory? *Tourist Studies, 1*(1), 5–22.

Frew, E., & White, L. (Eds.). (2013). *Dark tourism and place identity: Managing and interpreting dark places*. Oxon: Routledge.

Galani-Moutafi, V. (2000). The self and the other: Traveler, ethnographer, tourist. *Annals of Tourism Research, 27*(1), 203–224.

Gupta, S., & Vajic, M. (2000). The contextual and dialectical nature of experiences. In J. Fitzsimmons & M. Fitzsimmons (Eds.), *New service development: Creating memorable experiences* (pp. 25–43). Thousand Oaks: Sage.

Hall, C. M., & McArthur, S. (1993). Heritage management: An introductory framework. In C. M. Hall & S. McArthur (Eds.), *Heritage management in New Zealand and Australia: Visitor management, interpretation and marketing* (pp. 1–17). Auckland: Oxford University Press.

Heeley, J. (1989). Heritage and Tourism. In S. Hebenden (Ed) *Heritage, Tourism and Leisure* (pp. 3-20). Glasgow: The Planning Exchange.

Hewison, R. (1987). *The heritage industry: Britain in a climate of decline*. London: Methuen.

Hooper-Greenhill, E. (2000). *Museums and the interpretation of visual culture*. London: Routledge.

Irwin-Zarecka, I. (1994). *Frames of remembrance: The dynamics of collective memory*. New Brunswick/London: Transaction Publishers.

Isaac, R., & Ashworth, G. (2012). Moving from pilgrimage to 'dark' tourism: Leveraging tourism in Palestine. *Tourism Culture and Communication, 11*(3), 149–164.

Johnstone, B. (1990). *Stories, community, and place*. Bloomington: Indiana University Press.

Kalinowski, K. M., & Weiler, B. (1992). Educational travel. In B. Weiler & C. M. Hall (Eds.), *Special interest tourism* (pp. 5–26). London: Belhaven.

Keil, C. (2005). Sightseeing in the mansions of the dead. *Social and Cultural Geography, 6*(4), 479–494.

Kliger, R. (2005). *Solidarity boosts P.A. Tourism, but not enough*. New York: The Media Line.

Knudsen, B. T. (2003). The eyewitness and the affected viewer. September 11 in the media. *Nordicom Review, 24*(2), 117–127.

Knudsen, B. T. (2011). Thanatourism: Witnessing difficult pasts. *Tourist Studies, 11*(1), 55–72.

Kolb, D. A. (1976). *The learning style inventory: Technical manual*. Boston: McBer.

Kolb, D. A. (1984). *Experiential learning: Experience as the source of learning and development* (Vol. 1). Englewood Cliffs: Prentice-Hall.

Krakover, S. (2005). Attitudes of Israeli visitors towards the holocaust remembrance site of Yad Vashem. In G. Ashworth & R. Hartmann (Eds.), *Horror and human tragedy revisited: The Management of Sites of atrocity for tourism*. New York: Cognizant Communications Corporation.

Langer, E. J. (1989). *Mindfulness*. Reading: Addison-Wesley.

Lennon, J. J., & Foley, M. (2000). *Dark tourism: The attraction of death and disaster*. London: Continuum.

Li, Y. (2003). Heritage tourism: The contradictions between conservation and change. *Tourism and Hospitality Research, 4*(3), 247–261.

Light, D. (2000). An unwanted past: Contemporary tourism and the heritage of communism in Romania. *International Journal of Heritage Studies, 6*, 145–160.

Lindberg, K., & Johnson, R. L. (1997). Modelling resident attitudes towards tourism. *Annals of Tourism Research, 24*(2), 402–424.

Lisle, D. (2004). Gazing at ground zero: Tourism, voyeurism and spectacle. *Journal for Cultural Research, 8*(1), 3–21.

Logan, W., & Reeves, K. (Eds.). (2009). *Places of pain and shame: Dealing with 'difficult' heritage*. London: Routledge.

Luecke, R. (2003). *Business communication*. Boston: Harvard Business School Press.

MacCannell, D. (1973). Staged authenticity: Arrangements of social space in tourist settings. *American Journal of Sociology, 79*(3), 589–603.

MacCannell, D. (1992). *Empty meeting grounds: The tourist papers*. New York: Routledge.

Marcuse, H. (2001). *Legacies of Dachau: The uses and abuses of a concentration camp, 1933–2001*. Cambridge: Cambridge University Press.

Marcuse, H. (2005). Reshaping Dachau for visitors: 1933–2000. In G. Ashworth & R. Hartmann (Eds.), *Horror and human tragedies revisited: The management of sites of atrocities for tourism* (pp. 118–148). New York: Cognizant Communication Corporation.

McDowell, S. (2008). Selling conflict heritage through tourism in peacetime Northern Ireland: Transforming conflict or exacerbating difference? *International Journal of Heritage Studies, 14*(5), 405–421.

Mellor, P. (1993). Death in high modernity. In D. Clark (Ed.), *The sociology of death* (pp. 11–30). Oxford: Blackwell.

Miles, W. (2002). Auschwitz: Museum interpretation and darker tourism. *Annals of Tourism Research, 29*, 1175–1178.

Minnaert, L. (2012). Social tourism as opportunity for unplanned learning and behaviour change. *Journal of Travel Research, 51*(5), 607–616.

Mitchell, R. (1998). Learning through play and pleasure travel. *Current Issues in Tourism, 1*(2), 176–188.

Moscardo, G., & Ballantyne, R. (2008). Interpretation and attractions. In A. Fyall et al. (Eds.), *Managing visitor attractions: New directions* (pp. 237–252). Oxford: Butterworth-Heinemann.

Mouton, W. (2002). Experiential learning in travel environments as a key factor in adult learning. *Delta Kappa Gamma Bulletin, 69*(1), 36–42.

Mowforth, M., & Munt, I. (1998). *Tourism and sustainability: New tourism in the third world*. London: Routledge.

Munt, I. (1994). The "other" postmodern tourism: Culture, travel and the new middle classes. *Theory, Culture and Society, 11*, 101–123.

Novelli, M. (Ed.). (2005). *Niche tourism: Contemporary issues, trends and cases*. London: Butterworth-Heinemann.

Oliver, K. (2001). *Witnessing. Beyond recognition*. Minneapolis/London: University of Minnesota Press.

Orams, M. B. (1997). The effectiveness of environmental education: Can we turn tourists into 'greenies'? *Progress in Tourism Hospitality Research, 3*, 295–306.

Otto, J. E., & Ritchie, J. R. B. (2000). The service experience in tourism. In C. Ryan & S. Page (Eds.), *Tourism management: Towards the new millennium*. Oxford: Elsevier Science.

Pan, S., & Ryan, C. (2009). Tourism sense-making: The role of the senses and travel journalism. *Journal of Travel & Tourism Marketing, 26*(7), 625–639.

Pearce, P. L. (1996). Recent research in tourist behaviour. *Asia Pacific Journal of Tourism Research, 1*(1), 7–17.

Poon, A. (1993). *Tourism, technology and competitive strategies*. Oxford: CAB. Wallingford.

Poria, Y. (2007). Establishing cooperation between Israel and Poland to save Auschwitz concentration camp: Globalising the responsibility for the massacre. *International Journal of Tourism Policy, 1*(1), 45–57.

Preece, T., & Price, G. (2005). Motivations of participants in dark tourism: A Port Arthur example. In C. Ryan, S. Page, & M. Aicken (Eds.), *Taking tourism to the limits* (pp. 238–248). Oxford: Elsevier.

Rayner, S. (2012). Uncomfortable knowledge: The social construction of ignorance in science and environmental policy discourses. *Economy and Society, 41*(1), 107–125.

Rice, A. (2009). Revealing histories, dialoguing collections: Museums and galleries in North West England commemorating the abolition of the slave trade. *Slavery and Abolition, 30*(2), 291–309.

Riches, D. (1986). The phenomenon of violence. In D. Riches (Ed.), *The anthropology of violence* (pp. 1–27). Oxford/New York: Blackwell.

Robb, E. M. (2009). Violence and recreation: Vacationing in the realm of dark tourism. *Anthropology and Humanism, 34*, 51–60.

Roberts, C., & Stone, P. R. (2015). Dark tourism and dark heritage: Emergent themes, issues and consequences. In G. Corsane et al. (Eds.), *Displaced heritage: Responses to disaster, trauma, and loss* (pp. 10–18). Woodridge: Boydell Press.

Rojek, C. (1993). *Ways of escape: Modern transformations in leisure and travel*. London: Palgrave Macmillan.

Roppolo, C. (1996). International education: What does this mean for universities and tourism? In M. Robinson, N. Evans, & P. Callaghan (Eds.), *Tourism and cultural change*. Sunderland: Centre for Travel and Tourism and Business Editorial Press.

Schänzel, H. A., & McIntosh, A. J. (2000). An insight into the personal and emotive context of wildlife viewing at the penguin place, Otago peninsula, New Zealand. *Journal of Sustainable Tourism, 8*(1), 36–52.

Schmidt, C. (1979). The guided tour – Insulated adventure. *Urban Life, 4*, 441–467.

Schmitt, B. (1999). Experiential marketing. *Journal of Marketing Management, 15*, 53–67.

Seaton, A. V. (1996). Guided by the dark: From thanatopsis to thanatourism. *International Journal of Heritage Studies, 2*(4), 34–44.

Seaton, A. V., & Lennon, J. J. (2004). Thanatourism in the early 21st century: Moral panics, ulterior motives and Alterior desires. In T. V. Singh (Ed.), *New horizons in tourism – Strange experiences and stranger practices* (pp. 63–82). Wallingford: CABI Publishing.

Shackley, M. (2001). *Managing sacred sites*. London: Thompson.

Sharpley, R. (2005). Travels to the edge of darkness: Towards a typology of dark tourism. In C. Ryan et al. (Eds.), *Taking tourism to the limit: Issue, concepts and managerial* (pp. 215–226). London: Elsevier.

Sharpley, R. (2009a). Shedding light on dark tourism: An introduction. In R. Sharpley & P. R. Stone (Eds.), *The darker side of travel: The theory and practice of dark tourism, aspects of travel series* (pp. 3–23). Bristol: Channelview Publications.

Sharpley, R. (2009b). Dark tourism and political ideology: Towards a governance model. In R. Sharpley & P. R. Stone (Eds.), *The darker side of travel: The theory and practice of dark tourism, aspects of travel series* (pp. 145–166). Bristol: Channelview Publications.

Sharpley, R. (2012). Towards an understanding of "genocide tourism": An analysis of visitors' accounts of their experience of recent genocide sites. In *Contemporary tourist experience: Concepts and consequences*. Oxon: Routledge.

Sharpley, R., & Stone, P. R. (Eds.). (2009). *The darker side of travel: The theory and practice of dark tourism, aspects of travel series*. Bristol: Channelview Publications.

Silverstone, R. (2007). *Media and morality, on the rise of the Mediapolis*. Cambridge/Malden: Polity Press.

Simon, R. I. (2011). A shock to thought: Curatorial judgement and the public exhibition of 'difficult knowledge'. *Memory Studies, 4*(4), 432–449.

Simone-Charteris, M. T., & Boyd, S. (2010). Developing dark and political tourism in Northern Ireland: An industry perspective. In G. Gorman & Z. Mottiar (Eds.), *Contemporary issues in Irish and global tourism and hospitality*. Dublin: Dublin Institute of Technology.

Slade, P. (2003). Gallipoli thanatourism: The meaning of ANZAC. *Annals of Tourism Research, 30*(4), 779–794.

Smith, W. A. (2003). Does B&B management agree with the basic ideas behind experience management strategy? *Journal of Business and Management, 9*(3), 233–247.

Smith, C., & Jenner, P. (1997). Market segment: Educational tourism travel. *Tourism Analyst, 3*, 60–75.

Son, A., & Pearce, P. (2005). Multi-faceted image assessment: International students' views of Australia as a tourist destination. *Journal of Travel and Tourism Marketing, 18*(4), 21–35.

Stone, P. R. (2006). A dark tourism spectrum: Towards a typology of death and macabre related tourist sites, attractions and exhibitions. *Tourism, 54*(2), 145–160.

Stone, P. R. (2009a). Making absent death present: Consuming dark tourism in contemporary society. In R. Sharpley & P. R. Stone (Eds.), *The darker side of travel: The theory and practice of dark tourism, aspects of travel series* (pp. 23–38). Bristol: Channelview Publications.

Stone, M. J., & Petrick, P. F. (2013). The educational benefits of travel experiences: A literary review. *Journal of Travel Research, 52*(6), 731–744.

Stone, P. R., & Sharpley, R. (2008). Consuming dark tourism: A thanatological perspective. *Annals of Tourism Research, 35*(2), 574–595.

Strange, C., & Kempa, M. (2003). Shades of dark tourism: Alcatraz and Robben Island. *Annals of Tourism Research, 30*(2), 386–405.

Tarlow, P. E. (2005). Dark tourism: The appealing 'dark side' of tourism and more. In M. Novelli (Ed.), *Niche tourism – Contemporary issues, trends and cases* (pp. 47–58). Oxford: Butterworth-Heinemann.

Taum, Y. (2005). *Collective Cambodian memories of the Pol Pot Khmer Rouge regime*. Paper presented at the Fifth Annual Conference of the Asian Scholarship Foundation. Bangkok, 25–26 July 2005.

Thurnell-Read, T. (2009). Engaging Auschwitz: An analysis of young travellers' experiences of holocaust tourism. *Journal of Tourism Consumption and Practice, 1*(1), 26–52.

Timothy, D. J., & Boyd, S. W. (2006). Heritage tourism in the 21st century: Valued traditions and new perspectives. *Journal of Heritage Tourism, 1*(1), 1–16.

Tunbridge, J. E., & Ashworth, G. J. (1996). *Dissonant heritage: The management of the past as a resource in conflict*. New York: Wiley.

Um, S., & Crompton, J. L. (1990). Attitude determinants in tourism destination choice. *Annals of Tourism Research, 17*, 432–448.

Urry, J. (1990). *The tourist gaze: Leisure and travel in contemporary societies*. London: Sage.
Urry, J. (1995). *Consuming places*. London: Routledge.
Urry, J. (2002). *The tourist gaze* (2nd ed.). London: Sage.
Uzzell, D. L. (1989). The hot interpretation of war and conflict. In D. L. Uzzell (Ed.), *Heritage interpretation, volume I: The natural and built environment*. London: Belhaven.
Uzzell, D. L., & Ballantyne, R. (1998). Heritage that hurts: Interpretation in a postmodern world. In D. L. Uzzell & R. Ballantyne (Eds.), *Contemporary issues in heritage and environmental interpretation: Problems and prospects* (pp. 152–171). London: The Stationery Office.
Veijola, S., & Jokinen, E. (1994). The body in tourism. *Theory, Culture and Society, 11*(3), 125–151.
Walsh, J. (1992). *The representation of the past*. London: Routledge.
Walter, T. (2009). Dark tourism: Mediating between the dead and the living. In R. Sharpley & P. Stone (Eds.), *The darker side of travel: The theory and practice of dark tourism, aspects of travel series* (pp. 39–55). Bristol: Channelview Publications.
Webber, J. (1993). What does Auschwitz mean today? In T. Wiebocka (Ed.), *Auschwitz: A history in photographs* (pp. 282–291). Oswiecim: Panstowowe Muzeum Oswiecim.
Wight, C. A. (2006). Philosophical and methodological praxes in dark tourism: Controversy, contention and the evolving paradigm. *Journal of Vacation Marketing, 12*(2), 119–129.
Wight, C. A., & Lennon, J. (2007). Selective interpretation and eclectic human heritage in Lithuania. *Tourism Management, 28*(2), 519–529.
Williams, P. (2004). Witnessing genocide: Vigilance and remembrance at Tuol Sleng and Choeung Ek Holocaust. *Genocide Studies, 18*(2), 234–254.
Wilson, J. Z. (2008). *Prison: Cultural memory and dark tourism*. New York: Peter Lang.
Winter, J. (1998). *Sites of memory, sites of mourning: The great war in European cultural history*. Cambridge: Cambridge University Press.
Young, K. (2009). Auschwitz-Birkenau: The challenges of heritage management following the cold war. In W. Logan & K. Reeves (Eds.), *Places of pain and shame: Dealing with 'difficult heritage'* (pp. 50–67). Abingdon: Routledge.

Section 6

The Business of Dark Tourism

Leanne White

Introduction

Having explored the origin and history, theory and philosophy, society and culture, 'difficult heritage' landscapes, as well as 'dark tourist' experiences, this final section of the Handbook examines dark tourism from a business perspective. A key theme to emerge from chapters included in this section is that of *respect*. Indeed, a central issue identified is the extent of how the original purpose of sombre and respectful environments within 'dark tourism' are not detracted by commercial activities. Thus, for the 'dark tourism' business, the overall message from the visitor experience needs to be about empathy, respect and humility. In this section, therefore, the chapters explore how interpretation at tourist sites of dissonant heritage should be respectful, and how nonsensationalist approaches on the part of destination managers can help encourage quiet reflection and contemplation. That said, however, the destination manger ocassionally needs to remind the tourist that dark tourism sites are places which warrant a more restrained and respectful style of behaviour (Fig. 1).

As Frew and I have argued in earlier work (White and Frew 2013), the respectful development and interpretation of dark tourism sites may assist in creating places where visitors can pay their respects to those that have died, and better understand past events within the context of the site, the nation and the wider world. We have also argued that commemorative events associated with dark sites provide a focus for loved ones to deal with grief. Ultimatley,

L. White
Victoria University, Melbourne, Australia

Fig. 1 At Gallipoli in Turkey, the tourist is reminded that the cemetery is a place to be respected and is not for games and picnics (Source: Author)

the non-sensationalist aspect of staged events allow visitors to experience quiet reflectiveness and contemplation which, in turn, encourages respectfulness and can help in the healing process (Frew and White 2015).

About This Section

The final part of this Handbook incorporates five chapters that critically explore the *business of dark tourism*. As illustrated in Fig. 2, the chapters cover a range of key topics relating to dark tourism business, whereby overlapping themes include branding, retailing, exhibitions, souvenirs, and online media/marketing.

The section begins with Chap. 26 where Bird, Westcott and Thiesen examine issues surrounding the application of marketing to dark tourism. In particular, the authors examine dissonance, myth-making and the politics of heritage and how marketing plays a major role in the shaping of culture and place. The chapter also examines how marketing may be responsibly incorporated into sites of tragic memory and cultural trauma. Within the context of difficult heritage, Bird, Westcott and Thiesen argue that getting the marketing

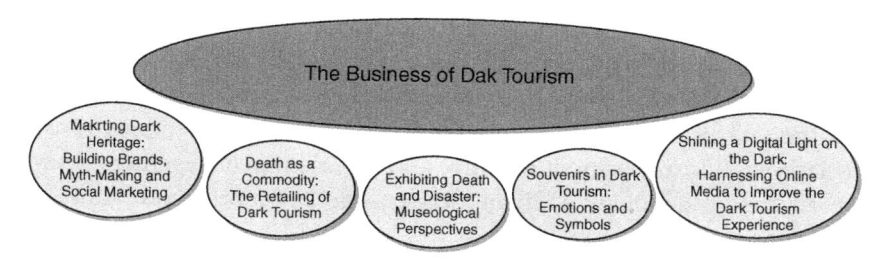

Fig. 2 This final section of the book explores the business of dark tourism focussing on the five topics of branding, retail, exhibitions, souvenirs, and online marketing

right may be a matter of ensuring dark tourism not only evokes but helps to preserve the site of memory. Consequently, the chapter highlights two dark sites—Normandy (the site of the Second World War invasion by Allied troops in 1944) and Chernobyl (the site of a nuclear disaster in 1986). The chapter argues that addressing heritage dissonance should be a key consideration in the marketing strategy of dark tourism sites. This is important to ensure relevancy and appropriateness to various target audiences. The study contends that further research is required to answer the need for theoretical and practical approaches within dark tourism marketing contexts. The chapter also puts forward a range of arguments in the hope that dark tourism site managers might be able to better understand the unique sensitivities of their site, while employing branding that supports universal concepts, including but not limited to peace and cultural understanding.

In Chap. 27, McKenzie examines the way in which the dark tourism experience is retailed. In particular, the chapter explores the impact retailing items such as souvenirs and education material can have on a range of 'light and dark' visitor sites, such as 'dark fun factories', concentration camps or 'in-between' sites which may include museums or jails. Through the use of qualitative analysis, the chapter explores the role of retailing in the supply and consumption of dark tourism from social, ethical, cultural and economic perspectives. In doing so, the chapter explores the consequences of dark tourism retailing on the increasing commodification of death within visitor economies. The chapter also raises important questions such as what type of items and products should be sold, and explores the ethical issue of whether or not the item should be sold at all. Ultimatley, the study suggests that the main purpose of retail within a dark tourism environment should be to ensure revenue-generating opportunities align with stated aims of the site.

In Chap. 28, Frew explores memorial or conflict museums and how difficult histories might be represented. The chapter finds that the challenge for museums is to delicately negotiate how contested histories are exhibited. The role of emotive interpretation is also examined in the study and, as a result, it is acknowledged that emotion occupies a special place in the debate about memorial museums. These 'new museums' occasionally employ theatrical tactics to invite emotional responses from visitors. Hence, the chapter argues that museums need to think carefully about how best to impart sensitive information to visitors using interactive and experiential engagement. Indeed, interpretation of dissonant heritage needs to be respectful. New museology takes into account the many complexities involved in representing dissonant heritage. Ultimately, this form of commemoration can combine commemorative and museological functions to assist with the interpretation of the past and try to help prevent violence in the future.

In the penultimate Chap. 29, Cave and Buda explore the role of souvenirs in dark tourism. The chapter explores the proposition that souveniring places of death, disaster, or atrocities is a more emotionally immersive experience than in other tourism contexts. The study examines existing literature on souvenirs as well as dark tourism and, subsequently, explores the role of emotion in dark tourism. The chapter suggests connections between dark tourism, souvenirs and emotions have not yet been sufficiently teased out and, as a result, calls for more attention to this particular aspect of dark tourism studies. Commercialising the dark tourism experience can help make a museum more up-to-date and connected with visitors and local people. Souvenirs also mediate tourism experiences and help (re)create emotional and multi-sensory engagement with dark places. While some dark tourism operators promote 'safe souvenirs', such as art, it may actually be the sense of risk and vicariousness which generates demand.

Finally, in Chap. 30, Bolan and Simone-Charteris examine dark tourism and online media. The chapter explores how dark tourism can take advantage of digital media to provide a more memorable experience for the tourist. In particular, the study investigates how social media platforms can be used for both marketing dark tourism destinations as well as engaging the tourist in a meaningful way. The chapter also evaluates mobile applications and how specific organisations can cater for the increasing growth of mobile technology by tourists, particularly with regard to the use of smartphones and tablets. Finally, the chapter highlights blogs and online forums, focusing on how these platforms may foster collaboration. The chapter also notes another relatively new dimension to dark tourism—the 'selfie' photograph; and contends that online media can add an extra dimension to a tourist's understanding, as well as providing new meanings for the tourist and those in dark tourism management. Recommendations for future research include the need to further investigate the experience of 'dark tourists' and how the digital can illuminate the dark.

Conclusion

The final section of this Handbook has carefully considered what happens when dark tourism and the business world meet. The five key topics of *branding, retailing, exhibitions, souvenirs* and *online media* are pivotal to the commercial operation of the dark tourism business. The chapters in this section examine dark tourism and business from both a demand and supply perspective by critically appraising existing literature, key themes and a variety of international case studies. The five chapters reinforce fundamental aspects of dark tourism and highlight the importance of understanding vital connections between dark tourism and business for both the visitor and the destination manager. In summary, this section explores the numerous ways in which aspects of dark tourism and commercial business intersect and overlap.

In terms of commercialisation, dark tourism plays a potentially vital role in our society as it provides socially acceptable environments for the individual to construct their own contemplation of mortality (Stone and Sharpley 2008). As ascertained by the variety of topics and approaches explored in this Handbook, there is little doubt that dark tourism has increasingly broad appeal. Ultimately, dark tourism affords us the opportunity to become involved in new and sometimes confronting experiences which can challenge one's sense of Self and, indeed, the wider world in which we all live.

References

Frew, E., & White, L. (2015). Commemorative events and national identity: Commemorating death and disaster in Australia. *Event Management: An International Journal, 19*(4), 509–524.

Stone, P. R., & Sharpley, R. (2008). Consuming dark tourism: A thanalogical perspective. *Annals of Tourism Research, 35*(2), 574–595.

White, L., & Frew, E. (Eds.). (2013). *Dark tourism and place identity: Managing and interpreting dark places.* Oxon: Routledge.

26

Marketing Dark Heritage: Building Brands, Myth-Making and Social Marketing

Geoffrey Bird, Morgan Westcott, and Natalie Thiesen

Introduction

This chapter examines the points of tension as well as possibilities when we fuse applications of marketing, such as branding and social marketing, with social scientific considerations of dark tourism: dissonance, myth-making, and the politics of heritage. By doing so, we are able to examine how marketing plays a major inventive role in tourism world-making (Hollinshead 2009), the shaping of culture and place. Additionally, we consider how marketing can be consciously, responsibly, and appropriately employed in politically charged sites of memory (also see Chap. 27).

Marketing is often viewed as an applied field of study, one characterised as systematic, practical, and scientific (Govers and Go 2009; McCabe 2014). Indeed, the employment of marketing is all pervasive—relevant to coffee beans and space travel, even presidential campaigns (see Kotler and Keller 2016). But in terms of dark tourism sites, there are a range of concerns raised in the literature about, for example, the Disneyfication of Auschwitz concentration camp (Cole 1999) or the repositioning of battlefields at Gallipoli/Çanakkale for contemporary political uses (Macleod 2015). The application

---

G. Bird (✉) • M. Westcott
Royal Roads University, Victoria, BC, Canada

N. Thiesen
Tourism Winnipeg, Winnipeg, MB, Canada

of marketing terms such as niche, product, positioning, segmentation, and brand, among others, can further invoke a notion that sites, cultures, histories, and experiences are increasingly viewed as the commodified or objectified products for consumption—often for profit—by the marketplace. In turn, the trajectory of this argument may conclude that marketing eviscerates any vestige of humanity, decency, authenticity, and so on and undermines commemoration, reconciliation, peace, sacredness, or other representations evoked by sites of dark heritage. Capturing the essence of this issue is the concept of *heritage dissonance* (Tunbridge and Ashworth 1996), a definition that includes the discord or conflict between the presentation of history as heritage and its interaction with the commercial and marketing elements of tourism.

Yet, despite these challenges, we argue that there are practices that site managers and scholars of dark tourism and marketing may find useful to consider. Our contribution is in advancing ways to better apply marketing within the context of dark tourism. However, our goal is not necessarily to generate more visitors, though definitely a benefit if 'forgetting' is a threat. The opportunity may be in continuing and highlighting sites and their history, perhaps to overcome the silencing or forgetting of a certain voice persecuted in the past (Allen 2016). These practices, however, may serve as a gateway for marketers to discuss further and respond to social scientific concerns, to understand audiences, and to ensure we are collectively aspiring to Morgan and Pritchard's (1998) call for more responsible forms of tourism management. Within the context of dark heritage, a working definition of 'getting it right' may be simply to ensure a dark tourism site evokes as well as preserves/conserves its aura as sites of memory. Done poorly, marketing can distort history to the point of silencing and/or forgetting.

Another key contextual question is whether dark tourism sites warrant a different approach to marketing than other forms of heritage (Biran et al. 2011). As Stone (2013b) has noted, 'dark tourism' is viewed as a research brand as opposed to something marketed for tourist consumption. Sites associated with death, atrocity, and war are typically described as something else: war heritage, remembrance tourism, even more broadly as cultural attractions. In this way, heritage marketing manuals (Misiura 2006; Chhabra 2010) have some application to dark heritage. However, on the question of the need for special consideration, as Seaton argues (2009), the unique feature of a thanatourism site is its auratic quality shaped by a universal concept—the Other of Death. This aura of death (Seaton 2009) manifests itself as a sense of hauntedness, sacredness, a spiritual element, or a distinct sense of place that is 'felt' by a tourist by visiting cemeteries, battlefields, memorials, or museums showcasing atrocity. For tourism managers, this sense of place needs to be carefully presented and conserved so as not to create a contrived, demeaning, or overly commercialised site (Seaton 2009). In this way, denoting a heritage site as *dark* may simply raise consciousness and sensitivity of marketers.

The potential scope of applications and approaches to dark tourism marketing given the spectrum of shades of dark attractions is vast (Stone 2006); we interpret this spectrum to mean that there are gradations of sensitivity and distinction in marketing that are dependent on the level of darkness. The darker end of the spectrum does indeed involve a greater degree of politics and dissonance and therefore marketing practices can be notably more questioned and contested. In this chapter, therefore, we focus our examples on the darker, more political sites, paying particular attention to two cases: Normandy, site of the Second World War invasion by Allied troops in 1944 (see Wieviorka 2008; Beevor 2009; also see Chap. 19), and Chernobyl, site of the nuclear disaster in 1986 (see Burlakova and Naydich 2012; also see Chap. 13).

Whereas marketing requires consideration of both supply and demand, our focus on the demand side will be limited and is a topic covered elsewhere in this volume. Nevertheless, it is important to consider the nature of the visitor experience to a dark heritage site. Visiting a site may involve a personal connection as a witness or by way of familial, religious, ethnic, or community ties. Other visitors with no connection with the site may come for learning (Timothy and Teye 2004) or a range of other motivations (Dunkley et al. 2011). Whereas there is an assumption that a familial tie leads to a more emotional connection with place, the learning tourist can also have a profound transformative effect in terms of social or national identities (Bird 2013). Understanding the visitor is clearly important with informing marketing and branding efforts.

Exploring marketing activities that emphasise the supply side of dark tourism, this chapter is organised into two themes: firstly, brand and myth-making, and, secondly, the interrelated concepts of Marketing 3.0 and social marketing. We begin by applying a marketing lens and related terminology to a specific dark tourism site to explore the mechanical way marketing concepts such as branding have been employed. Our first case is the landscape of war of Normandy where the D-Day and 80 days of fighting occurred in 1944, a turning point in the Second World War. The region attracts over two million visitors a year to its landing beaches, museums, and cemeteries, making it one of the most visited battlefields in the world (Atout France 2015). We then unpack dark tourism issues. We also examine myth-making, world-making, heritage force field, dissonant and political issues triggered such as silencing and forgetting, cultural memory commodification, as well as visitor meaning-making. In our second case, we explore the possibility of applying social marketing to the exclusionary zone around Chernobyl.

The challenge with this exercise is that there is a certain surreal dimension to it. Was there ever a conversation where someone asked about the brand positioning of, for example, Auschwitz-Birkenau, followed by 'who is our competition?' Some may respond to this hypothetical question by arguing that Auschwitz-Birkenau's true competition is ignorance, silencing, forgetting, and the resurrection of hatred. Clearly, our exercise in this chapter is an effort to experience and acknowledge, for some, the discomfort of employing marketing mechanisms to these sensitive sites, while at the same time getting past our initial reactions by exploring how it may be adapted for this purpose. We begin with a discussion on marketing and dark tourism concepts, followed by the two cases of Normandy and Chernobyl.

Marketing and Dark Tourism

Despite the growing amount of dark tourism literature, we are presented with a notable gap in terms of how marketing, branding, and destination marketing link with dark tourism sites. Site management, representation and interpretation of sites, moral issues, visitor motivations, and symbols of sites have been some of the main themes to date. Of course, there is the broader heritage marketing literature that adapts standard and tourism-specific marketing practices (Misiura 2006; Kotler et al. 2008). Brown et al. (2012) identify the need for the discipline and distinction of what they refer to as dark marketing. Dark marketing is defined as 'the application or adaptation of marketing principles and practices to domains of death, destruction and the ostensibly reprehensible' (Brown et al. (2013), p. 198). This conceptual research provides more questions than answers but at least identifies a need to market sites associated with death in a different manner than traditional tourism products. We refrain from using the term dark marketing because the conceptualisation is too broad; it does not readily distinguish dark tourism and heritage sites, which offer an opportunity to commemorate and teachas opposed to products such as weapons that peddle death and destruction. This distinction made, the next step in this discussion is to offer context by way of relevant marketing definitions.

The term 'marketing' is often used to denote a system of comprehensive planning that involves producing, pricing, distributing, and promoting goods and/or services in an efficient and integrated manner to the final consumer, more often than not with the objective of profitability. Inherent is the notion of satisfying the needs and wants of the consumer. Underpinning marketing is standard economic rationale: the efficient allocation of scarce resources among alternative applications to produce intended outputs (Nicholson and Synder 2007). Whether the organisation's mandate is state funded, non-profit, or for-profit, marketing elements such as brand and marketing mix work within the limitations of human and financial resources.

There are elements that distinguish marketing in tourism from the traditional practice. For example, tourist consumers often have a short yet intensive exposure to the product, service, or experience in the form of a few minutes or hours at a particular site. Another difference is that the purchase decision is open to more emotional influence, as making travel plans is not purely based on logical reasoning but rather an aspiration or hope as to the nature of the experience. The emotional appeal is also relevant as consuming the experience involves interaction with people and, therefore, the result is not entirely in the hands of the tourist or the organisation engaged in marketing and product delivery. Given the nature of the tourist experience involving a range of agencies and services, tourism marketing is characterised by complexity that depends on collaboration among various organisations such as national and regional tourism boards, transportation networks, hotels, attractions, or local visitor offices (Jetter and Chen 2012; Cox and Wray 2011; Hornby et al. 2008; Presenza and Cipollina 2010). Finally, the intangible nature of travel experience results in marketers placing a greater emphasis and importance on imagery to market a travel experience (Hsu et al. 2014). All of these characteristics come into play with dark tourism sites.

In their application to a dark tourism site, the baggage associated with marketing terms can indeed confine the marketer. Seaton (2009) argues that our 'word coinage' in the dark tourism domain is limited and that new terminology is required. This insight may be particularly evident when we consider the interaction between dark tourism and marketing. Yet, rather than viewing marketing in contest with a more humanist perspective and understanding, we can position the practice as secondary and in support of the heritage site mandate. For example, one may argue that an organisation with a goal of education and commemoration, as sites of atrocity and battlefield heritage commonly espouse in their mandates, would employ marketing practice to better articulate what it does and, with an understanding of its audience, how to do it (see for example, Chronis 2005; Worthington and Vaillancourt 2016). Interpretive planning, broader long-term strategic planning, and marketing principles are, to a large extent, interdependent.

That said, however, the devil is in the detail. Consequently, the next section provides an opportunity to examine one area of contest. We will explore branding and the collection of concepts it triggers: myth-making, world-making, cultural memory, and the heritage force field.

Considering Brand in the Context of Dark Tourism

In this section, we examine branding in terms of identity, positioning, and image. First, we present some definitions to apply to a dark tourism site—the region of Normandy where the D-Day landing beaches are located—before we analyse it from a dark tourism's conceptual perspective. We will draw upon work that explores the management of this site of war memory (Bird 2013; Bird et al. 2016).

A brand can allow the consumer to understand what is offered or at least what is promised: it does what it says on the packet. In this way, the brand can help visitors make a decision to purchase an experience or to visit a site. A consistent definition of brand, however, can be hard to pin down. The existence of a website entitled *30 Branding Definitions* (Emerge Designs 2013) suggests a number of potential definitions for 'brand' in this so-called mechanical and scientific field. However, as Ries and Ries (1998, p. 172) sum up, brand is above all 'a singular idea or concept that you own inside the mind of a prospect. It's as simple and as difficult as that'. A classic textbook definition is:

> A name, term, sign, symbol or design or a combination of these, intended to identify the goods or services of one seller or group of sellers and to differentiate them from those of competitors. (Kotler et al. 2008, p. 340)

As with a symbol, a brand evokes a certain set of attributes or ideas in the consumer. While organisations work to develop, re-enforce, and preserve *brand identity*, a *value proposition* is the product's value or benefit conveyed to the consumer. A *brand image* is defined and employed in this chapter as the actual perception held by consumers, although the term is also used with reference to visual design in the form of symbols used. For the sake of this chapter, we describe brand symbols as the language and imagery employed. Indeed, *brand position* is described by Aaker (1996, p. 71) as 'part of the brand identity and value proposition that is to be actively communicated to the target audience and that demonstrates an advantage over competing brands'. Pike (2004) and Morrison (2013) also both describe how identity, positioning, and image are interconnected. We can draw on a range of other terms such as brand equity, a measure of its total worth in terms of loyalty, awareness, quality, associations among other elements, and brand essence, the core values that form the brand identity. Certainly, a burgeoning number of books on tourism marketing take this further than this chapter allows (see for instance, Govers and Go 2009; McCabe 2014).

Myth and Tourism World-Making

Numerous scholarly debates can inform the branding of dark tourism sites. In particular, it is important to understand and consider concepts such as cultural memory, myth-making, and remembrance given the role, place, and site branding can play in world-making. Cultural memory is negotiated and dynamic, a debate between various representations of memory that results in a refashioning of the past (Sturken 1997). Tourism marketing is part of that negotiation. Inspired by Meethan (2001), Hollinshead (2009, p. 139) views tourism as a world-making agency, defined as an 'operational construct to help critically describe the creative/inventive role and function of tourism in the making of culture and place'. World-making can manifest itself in a number of different ways, through marketing, branding, managing, representing and interpreting of dark tourism sites. This concept is important because world-making shapes what is remembered, silenced, and forgotten, while drawing upon cultural memories, myths, and history.

Myth is also a central concept here because it represents taking a complex event, such as war or a nuclear disaster and, as Selwyn (1996) explains, resolving it emotionally and intellectually. In this context, Barthes' (1957, p. 142–143) perspective is often employed in marketing: '[m]yth does not deny things, on the contrary, its function is to talk about them; simply, it purifies them, it makes them innocent' and '(abolishes) the complexity of human acts, it gives them the simplicity of essences…'. Myth is therefore an important element to understand what is remembered and mediated through tourism marketing. Which myth(s) to adopt, however, and how to best position them within the tourism marketplace become more challenging matters. Given the ideological utility of heritage, particularly war remembrance and memorialisation (Mosse 1990; Brinkley 2005; Doss 2009), many question the extent to which tourism is part of an ideological reading of the landscape of war (White and Frew 2013).

Indeed, marketing and branding clearly play central roles in both making and mediating myths, but tourism does not dominate the politics of heritage. As Winter (2006, p. 6) argues, 'virtually all acts of remembrance, history and memory are braided together in the public domain, jointly informing our shifting and contested understandings of the past'. Such braiding leads to conflict in representation and interpretation at museums, such as the Smithsonian Institution's exhibit on the atomic bomb (Nobile 1995). One might go on to presume, or hope, that by understanding these concepts, destination and site marketers will be careful to avoid creating, as

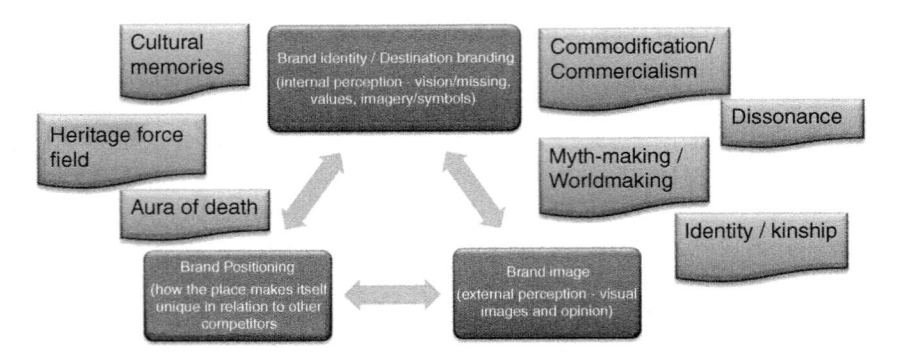

Fig. 26.1 Brand identity, positioning, and image and dark tourism-related issues and concepts (Adapted from Pike 2004; Morrison 2013)

Hollinshead (2009) describes, false or faux representations of a place and its past. However, this is not always the road taken as our Normandy case example will show.

There are many concepts related to dark tourism that we can explore but we will limit to a few in this chapter. Fig. 26.1 illustrates key elements that inform brand—identity, positioning, and image—in the traditional interconnected state. The broader context of issues and concepts, although not exhaustive, offered by dark tourism surrounds the brand, exemplifying the potential to inform, shape brand.

To consider these issues further, we now turn to our first case study—the place branding of Normandy's landscape of war.

Place Branding: Normandy's D-Day Beaches

The battlefields of D-Day and the Battle of Normandy are some of the most iconic sites of the Second World War. As Fanget and Guillemant (2016, p. 54) states, '[a] cohesive destination has a theme with a shared message between the visitors and the tourist service providers… in Normandy, that theme is remembrance'. With the passing of veterans and local witnesses of the war, Normandy as a landscape of war has been transitioning from those who come primarily to commemorate the Second World War to those interested in learning about the region's centuries of history, which includes its recent war history. To mark this shift, in 2013, public and private stakeholders (including the State Minister for Crafts, Trade, and Tourism) signed the 'Remembrance Tourism in Normandy' Destination Contract (see Bédé 2015). The mission/

vision, values, and symbols that inform brand identity, interpreted from literature and promotional documents, are outlined below:

Mission/Vision:

- to 'make Normandy the leading international destination for the remembrance of the Second World War by rallying all public and private stakeholders in the region'. (Fanget and Guillemant 2016, p. 54)

Values:

- '...[T]o improve the remembrance offering, in the interest of passing on memories to the younger generations, and also the quality of the range of services that visitors use during their stay.'
- '...a formal promotional strategy, making it possible to strengthen traditional markets and explore new ones.'

Brand symbols on promotional websites and brochures for the area employ terms such as '*devoir de la mémoire*' (the obligation to remember), education, and peace. Regional websites and brochures employ images of uninhabited landing beaches, cemeteries, Nazi bunkers, and other relics of war and younger people, as opposed to veterans, gazing upon sites.

In terms of brand image, the view held by tourists, we can gather a general sense from both quantitative and qualitative sources. The Atout France (2015) market research provides a segmented quantitative perspective. The most prominent motivation to visit Normandy was described as the '1944 sites of memory' (p. 5). Data on visitor numbers to D-Day-related museums vary from site to site, with the Normandy American Cemetery, adjacent to Omaha Beach, consistently receiving approximately on average 1.5 million visitors a year. For international visitors, the D-Day beaches remain a top-10 site in France to visit, with sites such as Omaha Beach standing as hallowed grounds for Americans, for instance. The remarks on TripAdvisor under the heading of D-Day beaches depict the area as 'moving', 'must see', 'humbling', and 'inspirational' (March to April 2016). Perhaps the best measure of brand image, however, was made evident through the international reaction to an effort to rebrand the D-Day beaches.

In 2013, local councils in the Normandy area launched a brand identity known as the 'secteur mythique' or mythic sector (Copping 2013). The decision was driven by recognition that tourist flows had historically been greater to the western sites, such as Arromanches, Omaha Beach, the Normandy American Cemetery, and Ste.-Mere-Eglise. The latter two sites gained global status in terms of the profile in films *Saving Private Ryan* (Spielberg et al. 1998) and *Band of Brothers* (Spielberg and Hanks 2001). New promotional materials demarcated the branded 'mythic' area, following the political boundaries of the participating regional councils. The battlefield itself did not align with these branded borders leaving out and, by implication, forgetting the battlefields of Juno Beach, Sword Beach, and the eastern landing area of the British and Canadian airborne at Pegasus Bridge and Merville. The participating areas represented about 70% of the D-Day beaches, in effect slicing history in two: mythic and not.

The outcry was immediate. Local and international opposition, in the form of newspaper articles and online petitions (see Larenceau n.d; Watson 2013), roundly denounced the promotional scheme, exposing dissonance between the emotional draw of these sites for people around the world and the newly created 'mythic' brand. Rationale that pointed to the fact that the 'mythic beaches' area encompassed the most popular sites associated with the 1944 landings was moot. Arguably, the furor about marketing trumping history was a factor in the decision to hold the 70th commemorative event in 2014 at a 'forgotten' beach, called Sword and adjacent to Ouistreham.

In terms of recent brand positioning (how the destination differentiates from competitors), the process for applying for World Heritage Status for the D-Day beaches began in earnest in 2012–2013. Whereas the process is not certain to result in success—it would be the only battlefield granted the coveted status—it does demonstrate the effort to position this landscape as symbolic of the Second World War. Moreover, several issues arise in the Normandy case, which this chapter now turns to.

Stakeholder Involvement and the Heritage Force Field

As mentioned earlier, Normandy and other sites associated with the Second World War are at a formative point in their evolution. As the last surviving soldiers pass away, the voice of veterans in the heritage force field is soon to be silent, leaving other stakeholders involved in managing battlefield-related sites to attempt to speak on their behalf, to educate visitors, and to perpetuate the memory (Farmer 1999). What is at stake, however, is not just remembering the past, but what and how it is remembered. To counter silencing and forgetting and to champion an inclusive perspective, developing brand identity often involves a stakeholder process.

Morrison (2013, p. 289) defines destination branding as both a process and function: 'the steps taken by a Destination Management Organisation (DMO), in collaboration with its stakeholders, to develop and communicate an identity and personality for its destination, which are difference from those of all competing destinations'. From the perspective of politics of remembrance, historian Jay Winter describes the 'multiplicity of voices' (2006, p. 152), each offering their own perspective on how war should be memorialised and remembered. Reflecting this, Seaton (2001, 2009) and Sharpley and Stone (2009) write about the *heritage force field*, acknowledging individual perspectives, often vehemently held, and the varying degrees of power and influence present in a heritage or dark tourism setting. Seaton (2009, p. 98) also argues that involving stakeholders is necessary to 'reconcile their interests and perspectives from inception, implementation and maintenance' with the concept of a force field evoking a search for equilibrium or balance. But how does this play out in terms of destination branding?

Despite the universal and legendary status of D-Day in the twentieth century, there are many voices to consider. Works such as Dolski et al. (2014) and Bird et al. (2016) provide a more comprehensive account than can occur in this chapter. Within the context of Normandy, and for that matter France in general, the sensitivities of war memory have resulted in a process of stakeholder involvement that has, in turn, evolved and shaped the *tourisme de mémoire*/remembrance tourism branding. The extent to which all participants were content when they left the process is not known nor is it clear as to whether all voices were heard. Whether we are setting brand identity with regard to a regional destination or a specific site, however, it is clear that stakeholders include the state, regional, and local governments, community groups, groups responsible for site management, and individuals represented by a particular heritage site: in this case, veterans and/or local citizens, the witnesses, and actors of the event. Of course the inherent effort to hear and even to balance all voices may result in its own form of myth-making, illustrating how the politics of memory are never concluded. Rather, they evolve, with tourism marketing in the twenty-first century now part of the mix.

But to what extent do visitors have a say as a stakeholder? It may be important to hear their voice to learn what they need, although some may argue that catering to tourists is a step towards blurring the history to be told. The media, particularly Hollywood films in the case of Normandy, have played an influential role in shaping historical perspectives of many tourists, leading to an Americanisation of the D-Day narrative. However, Lemelin and Johansen

(2014) suggest that in the face of changing motivations and generational disconnection with heritage, tourism can engage and educate these new visitors. This will require not only new interpretation but also marketing approaches. For some ideas about what these might entail, we now turn to our second case example—Chernobyl.

Chernobyl: Branding and Heterotopia

Chernobyl is the site of the 1986 nuclear accident that resulted in radioactive fallout across Europe. Some 200,000 deaths are attributed to the catastrophe, as well as 330,000 people with cancer (Greenpeace 2006). In the days that followed, the entire population in a 30-kilometre radius was evacuated, resulting in the creation of an exclusion or 'dead zone' that includes the nearby 'ghost town' of Pripyat. Over the years since the accident, tourism, first illegal and then state sanctioned, has steadily grown.

Themes associated with catastrophe and contamination are common to branding associated with this site. Thousands of visitors to Ukraine take in the day trip with official tours, an experience that evokes a range of reactions. Taking a marketing worldview first, we present some of the elements of brands and then examine key challenges and issues. We then apply the concept of social marketing—what Kotler et al. (2010) entitle Marketing 3.0—to the dark tourism site to consider how new trends may impact ways the destination is managed and marketed in the future. The intention here is to explore the extent to which social marketing may aid dark tourism destinations and sites in getting marketing right. But firstly, we offer an overview of brand identity, positioning, and image of Chernobyl and the exclusion zone, by way of reviewing key literature and observing the ways in which various destination and tour company websites position the destination, combined with visitor comments from TripAdvisor.

Visitors are frequently attracted by imagery and symbolism surrounding the town of Pripyat, referred to as 'a city frozen in time' (Isalska 2016). Pripyat was built in 1970 to house some 50,000 nuclear plant workers and today is regarded as 'most arresting "attraction" … not the ruined plant … the ghost town of Pripyat nearby' (Osborn 2011, para 32). This imagery is not lost on the local tourism industry. On their websites, tour operators employ symbols as part of their brand positioning that evoke the Soviet era during the Cold War and the resultant nuclear age: including five-point stars, gas masks, the traditional trefoil nuclear warning symbol, Geiger counters, and using colours such as red and black as well as a soviet-style font. Videos and photographs capture the ghost-town quality of the zone, reflecting lives suddenly disrupted and left behind for evermore. For example, the vacant Pripyat ferris wheel contrasts a leisure park with the fear-filled day for evacuees.

In terms of brand image held by external agencies such as the media, George Johnson's 2014 National Geographic piece, called 'Nuclear Tourism', describes his time touring Pripyat in great detail:

> What I remember most about the hours we spent in Pripyat is the sound and feel of walking on broken glass. Through the dilapidated hospital wards with the empty beds and cribs and the junk-strewn operating rooms. Through the school hallways, treading across mounds of broken-back books. Mounted over the door of an old science class was an educational poster illustrating the spectrum of electromagnetic radiation. Heat to visible light to x-rays and gamma rays—the kind that break molecular bonds and mutate DNA. How abstract that must have seemed to the schoolkids before the evacuation began.

Comments on the emptiness, destruction, and desolation are also found among TripAdvisor posts:

> I will never forget exploring Pripyat, it was the single coolest thing I've ever done. If you're into urban exploration, soviet history or even are a fan of zombie or apocalypse movies this trip is amazing. (Chris L., June 2016)

> Visiting an exclusion zone was truly a great experience. I felt [a] strange atmosphere walking on abandoned streets of the towns and villages. I tried to imagine how it looked before the evacuation, people on those streets, living in those ruined houses. Now it's all overgrown by trees, quiet and peaceful. (Matej P., May 2016)

This dark tourism site is described by Stone (2013a, p. 79) as a heterotopia: 'a ritual space that exists outside of time' (also see Chap. 10). Stone's use of Foucault's conceptualisation of 'Other places' is helpful in exploring the political and social meaning of Chernobyl and the so-called exclusion or 'dead zone' that includes the ghost town of Pripyat. The 'touristification' of the area began with the release of a 1979 film, Stalker, that depicted a tour guide's exploits in a heterotopic, post-fallout environment (Stone 2013a). While the film predates the disaster by seven years, it created a prophetic image of this type of tourism. Visitors are motivated to seek out sites from the media and popular culture such as the S.T.A.L.K.E.R video game (abandoned buildings, a car lot, and the power plant) and relish the destruction and decay of the region (Stone 2013a).

Social Marketing and Chernobyl: A Way Forward?

Social marketing, also categorised as 'Marketing 3.0' by Kotler (2010), represents a shift towards social contribution as part of establishing trust with consumers. A number of articles (Andreasen 2002; McDermott et al. 2005; and Stead et al. 2007) have identified components of social marketing including: goals to change visitor behaviour, conducting audience research and segmentation, using a social marketing mix, offering an exchange of value (incentives, rewards), and 'upstream targeting' of stakeholders including authorities and policy makers (Truong and Hall 2013). Scholars including Bright (2000) have been optimistic about the application for Marketing 3.0 in tourism, noting a synergy between the aims of tourism and the welfare-focused nature of social marketing. Social marketing has been used by hotels, for example, to reduce the environmental and economic impact of their guests through now-ubiquitous towel and linen reuse programmes (Shang et al. 2010). The emergence of social business enterprises (SBE) is held up as a more holistic example (Kotler 2010), in which businesses strive to benefit struggling populations and create positive, lasting, inter-generational impacts.

In Chernobyl, there appears to be an emerging interest amongst some local tour operators to adapt the focus of their engagement with the area. Approximately two-thirds of operators identify the region as their home; researchers found that many are emotional about the impacts of the disaster, some breaking down during interviews 'crying and upset because of their experiences' (Yankovskaa and Hannamb 2014, p. 934). An April 2016 initiative by ChernobylWEL.COMe saw the 'Chernobyl Welcome Team' and 13 volunteers work over two days to remove trash left by tourists, filling 200 trash bags (2016). The efforts were catalogued on their blog with clear links to social media, detailing their plans to counteract the impacts of 'man, who besides coming here to take photographs sometimes brought a lot of trash, and this trash covered the beautiful open air museum that is Chernobyl'. This conservation effort is touted as the first of many, with another scheduled for the autumn of 2016. Thus, as part of their marketing efforts, a regional tour operator is able to connect with internal and external stakeholders and lead a modest degree of positive change.

In addition to social initiatives like the clean-up effort, operators are beginning to incorporate imagery that reflects the changing landscape of the region.

Moving beyond the stereotypical abandoned buildings and gas masks, one operator shows a local fox eating from an outstretched tourists' hand (SoloEast n.d.). This is notable because until recently the brand symbols used to market the exclusion zone had little to do with its current, transforming state: one where animals are thriving in the absence of humans. Today once-extinct Przewalski's horses, foxes, badgers, and wolves are now reclaiming abandoned areas (Wendel 2016). The impacts of radiation on animals and plants in the zone are of interest to many in the scientific community, who have found expected negative impacts of radiation in wildlife and, at the same time, witnessed local species producing adaptive changes to the toxic environment (Fountain 2014). The excursions of two prominent scientists were documented in a 2014 New York Times online video called 'The Animals of Chernobyl'. Of course, time will tell whether the flora and fauna of Chernobyl, the science of post-radiation impacts, and the efforts of locals to conserve the area become part of the destination brand. These themes, however, may be a way to attract more diverse markets to the area and connect with potential visitors on a non-heterotopic level.

Conclusion: Possibilities for Marketing and Dark Tourism

When a marketing framework is applied to sites associated with war, disaster, atrocity, or other historic significance, there is a sense that corporate concerns or consumers ultimately dictate what forms of heritage are remembered and how. Scholars have explored some of these assumptions both within the broader context of tourism (e.g., Mosedale 2016) as well as within the context of dark tourism and destination management (e.g., White and Frew 2013). Moreover, Edwards (2009, p. 77) argues that war commemorations in Normandy can be seen as a form of commercialism, whereby he suggests '(fusing) commemoration with commerce'. This perception is also shared by Scates (2008, p. 57) in his analysis of Gallipoli when he argues '[h]istory, it seems, has been held to ransom by tourism, the memory of war popularised to the point of forgetting'. Meanwhile, Stone's work has examined the positioning of Chernobyl as a 'modern Pompeii', a heterotopia that stands as a monument to human frailty and technological and political failure (2013, p. 87).

To counter these positions, Hollinshead (2009) identified that certain assertions go unchallenged as grand clichés including those of *commodification*, *authenticity*, and *consumption*. He goes on to argue that tourism is often presumed to have a negative influence on culture by encroaching or interfering, whereas this is not automatically the case. He also identifies a tendency to perceive marketing as 'predominantly an outcome of the clever manipulation of tourists by all-powerful transnational corporations in league with local/state/national governments' (Hollinshead 2009 p. 146). To contextualise the dark tourism-marketing relationship, we may assert another grand cliché: *The marketing of dark tourism sites is a morbid and disrespectful means that aims to commodify, and profit from, the pain and anguish of the past*. We hope this chapter illustrates the need to question this oversimplification.

Some question whether it is possible to govern and manage dark tourism sites to limit heritage dissonance (Sharpley and Stone 2009). Beyond the narrative of interpretation at these sites of memory, addressing heritage dissonance needs to be a consideration in the development of any marketing strategy and promotional efforts of sites of memory. Awareness of possible dissonance in the content of promotional materials is important to ensure relevancy and appropriateness to the target audiences. Efforts to neutralise visitor reactions to war, however, and soothe tourists' apprehension about crimes against humanity and catastrophe slide into world-making/myth-making. Arguably, part of the solution involves acknowledging that visitor reactions, as part of the ever-important co-construction of meaning, evoke a deeply emotional, even angry, response to a dark heritage site. But there are a few solutions.

That said, Leopold (2007) recommends war heritage sites develop a code of conduct for site managers to address the care and sensitivity required for accurate interpretation, proper development, and ethical marketing. In the 11 guidelines in the proposed provisional code of conduct, only 1 refers to marketing, outlining the importance of developing networks to similar institutions to collaborate on marketing efforts and to create channels to disseminate promotional materials in a less commercial way (Leopold 2007). Considering the nature of marketing itself practically implies commercial activity, ethical marketing of sites of memory requires a level of sensitivity in positioning and use of the communication mix (images and text). There are no best-practice models or guidelines managers of sensitive sites can consult to lead them through the nuances and ethical considerations; many situations are unique to a particular site. Of note, however, is Austin's (2002) research that identifies challenges with targeting and selecting distribution channels for sensitive historical sites. Indeed, Austin (2002, p. 45) recommends that the focus remains on the 'historical essence of the site' rather than conflating education with entertainment, in order to attract visitors whose motivations best match the site's learning opportunities and preservation goals.

Earlier in this chapter, we suggested there may be a 'right way' for marketing dark tourism sites. Our effort to apply a social marketing lens to Chernobyl is a call to scholars to critically examine ways to apply marketing principles with a level of awareness to political and social sensitivities linked with a particular site or destination. In the case of Chernobyl, at least, there may be an ironic, and even tragic humour around caring for a natural environment that has been eviscerated by nuclear fallout. Nevertheless, the opportunity presented in such an experience may take the tourist as observer to one who is more participative, engaged, and reflective about the futility of a world radiated and destroyed. The question remains, of course, whether such an experience will ever lead to action when tourists return home?

Certainly there are ways to utilise marketing without focusing on profit: understanding the visitor (target market) in order to provide more engaging programming is an example of this. Further empirical research and international case studies—to answer the need for applied and academic approaches within the dark tourism marketing context—may help to identity useful practices appropriate for the darker spectrum of sites (after Stone 2006). Hopefully site marketers will take note of dark tourism literature—and this future research as it emerges—to better understand the unique sensitivities of these sites, while enabling branding that supports universal concepts of peace, commemoration, reconciliation, conservation, learning, remembrance, and cultural understanding.

References

Allen, M. (2016). Okinawa and the war dead. In G. R. Bird, S. Claxton, & K. Reeves (Eds.), *Managing and interpreting D-Day's sites of memory: Guardians of remembrance* (p. 255). Abingdon/Oxford: Routledge.

Andreasen, A. R. (2002). Marketing social marketing in the social change marketplace. *Journal of Public Policy and Marketing, 21*, 3–13.

Atout France. (2015). *Chiffres clés du tourisme Normand*. Comité regional de tourisme de Normandie. https://issuu.com/hebertcrtnormandie/docs/brochure_chiffres_cles_2015/1?e=25283105/36362461

Austin, N. K. (2002). Managing heritage attractions: Marketing challenges at sensitive historical sites. *International Journal of Tourism Research, 4*(6), 447–457.

Bédé, S. (2015). Les contrats de destination: nouveau souffle ou nouvelle ère de la gouvernance des destinations ? *Revue Management et Avenir, 77*, 119–136.

Beevor, A. (2009). *D-Day: The battle for Normandy*. New York: Viking.

Biran, A., Poria, Y., & Oren, G. (2011). Sought experiences at (dark) heritage sites. *Annals of Tourism Research, 38*(3), 820–841.

Bird, G. R. (2013). Place identities in the Normandy landscape of war: Touring the Canadian sites of memory. In L. White & E. Frew (Eds.), *Dark tourism and place identity: Managing and interpreting dark places* (pp. 167–186). New York: Routledge.

Bird, G. R., Claxton, S., & Reeves, K. (Eds.). (2016). *Managing and interpreting D-Day's sites of memory: Guardians of remembrance*. Oxon: Routledge.

Bright, A. D. (2000). The role of social marketing in leisure and recreation management. *Journal of Leisure Research, 32*, 12–17.

Brinkley, D. (2005). *The boys of pointe du hoc Ronald Reagan, D-Day, and the U.S. Army 2nd ranger battalion* (1st ed.). New York: W. Morrow.

Brown, S., McDonagh, P., & Shultz, C., II. (2012). Dark marketing: Ghost in the machine or skeleton in the cupboard? *European Business Review, 24*(3), 196–215.

Brown, S., McDonagh, P., & Shultz, C., II. (2013). A brand so bad it's good: The paradoxical place marketing of Belfast. *Journal of Marketing Management, 29*(11–12), 1251.

Burlakova, E. B., & Naydich, V. I. (2012). *The lessons of Chernobyl: 25 years later*. New York: Nova Science Publishers.

ChernobylWEL.COMe. (2016). We have cleaned up Chernobyl. Retrieved from http://www.chernobylwel.com/EN/blog/276/we-have-cleaned-up-chernobyl/

Chhabra, D. (2010). *Sustainable marketing of cultural and heritage tourism*. London: Routledge.

Chronis, A. (2005). Co-constructing heritage at the Gettysburg storyscape. *Annals of Tourism Research, 32*(2), 386–406.

Cole, T. (1999). *Selling the holocaust: From Auschwitz to Schindler—How history is bought, packaged, and sold*. New York: Routledge.

Copping, J. (2013, April 25). Anger as French tourism campaign 'ignores' one of the D-Day beaches. *Daily Telegraph*. http://www.telegraph.co.uk/history/britain-at-war/10015709/Anger-as-French-tourism-campaign-ignores-one-of-the-D-Day-beaches.html

Cox, C., & Wray, M. (2011). Best practice marketing for regional tourism destinations. *Journal of Travel and Tourism Marketing, 28*(5), 524–540.

Dolski, M., Edwards, S., & Buckley, J. (Eds.). (2014). *D-Day in history and memory: The Normandy landings in international remembrance and commemoration*. Denton: University of North Texas.

Doss, E. (2009). War porn: Spectacle and seduction in contemporary American war memorials. In R. Schubart (Ed.), *War isn't hell, it's entertainment: Essays on visual media and the representation of conflict*. Jefferson: McFarland.

Dunkley, R., Morgan, N., & Westwood, S. (2011). Visiting the trenches: Exploring meanings and motivations in battlefield tourism. *Tourism Management, 32*(4), 860–868.

Edwards, S. (2009). Commemoration and consumption in Normandy, 1945–1994. In M. Keren & H. H. Herwig (Eds.), *War memory and popular culture: Essays on modes of remembrance and commemoration*. London: McFarland.

Emerge Designs. (2013, August 8). *30 branding definitions*. http://emergedesigns.ca/30-branding-definitions/

Farmer, S. B. (1999). *Martyred village: Commemorating the 1944 massacre at Oradour-sur-Glane*. Berkeley: University of California Press.

Fountain, H. (2014, May 5). At Chernobyl, hints of Nature's adaptation. *The New York Times*. Retrieved from http://www.nytimes.com/2014/05/06/science/nature-adapts-to-chernobyl.html?hpw&rref=science&_r=0

Govers, R., & Go, F. (2009). *Place branding Glocal, virtual and physical identities, constructed, imagined and experienced*. Basingstoke: Palgrave Macmillan.

Greenpeace. (2006). *The Chernobyl Catastrophe: Consequences on human health*. Retrieved from http://www.greenpeace.org/international/Global/international/planet-2/report/2006/4/chernobylhealthreport.pdf

Hollinshead, K. (2009). The 'worldmaking' prodigy of tourism: The reach and power of tourism in the dynamics of change and transformation. *Tourism Analysis, 14*(1), 139–152.

Hornby, G., Brunetto, Y., & Jennings, G. (2008). The role of inter-organizational relationships in tourism operators' participation in destination marketing systems. *Journal of Hospitality and Leisure Marketing, 17*(1–2), 184–215.

Hsu, H. C., Song, C., & Song, H. (2014). A visual analysis of destinations in travel magazines. *Journal of Travel and Tourism Marketing, 31*(2), 162–177.

Isalska, A. (2016, April 26). It's hot: Chernobyl now a tourist zone. *CNN.com*. Retrieved from http://www.cnn.com/2015/04/14/travel/chernobyl-tourism/

Jetter, L., & Chen, R. J. C. (2012). An exploratory investigation of knowledge sharing and cooperative marketing in tourism alliances. *International Journal of Hospitality and Tourism Administration, 13*(2), 95–108.

Johnson, G. (2014, October). Nuclear tourism: An unforeseen legacy of the Chernobyl meltdown. *National Geographic*. Retrieved from http://ngm.nationalgeographic.com/2014/10/nuclear-tourism/johnson-text

Kotler, P., & Keller, K. (2016). *Marketing management*. Upper Saddle River: Prentice Hall.

Kotler, N., Kotler, P., & Kotler, W. (2008). *Museum marketing and strategy: Designing missions, building audiences, generating revenue and resources* (2nd ed.). San Francisco: Jossey-Bass.

Kotler, P., Kartajaya, H., & Setiawan, I. (2010). *Marketing 3.0: From products to customers to the human spirit*. Hoboken: Wiley.

Larenceau, M. (n.d.). Petitioning Bessin Seulles et Mer tourisme Secteur mythique des plages du débarquement: Suppression du secteur mythique des plages du débarquemen. https://www.change.org/p/suppression-du-secteur-mythique-des-plages-du-d%C3%A9barquement. Accessed 5 July 2016.

Lemelin, R., & Johansen, K. (2014). The Canadian National Vimy Memorial: Remembrance, dissonance and resonance. *International Journal of Culture, Tourism and Hospitality Research, 8*(2), 6–6.

Leopold, T. (2007). A proposed code of conduct for war heritage sites. In C. Ryan (Ed.), *Battlefield tourism: History, place and interpretation* (pp. 49–58). Amsterdam: Elsevier.

Macleod, J. (2015). *Gallipoli*. Oxford: Oxford University Press.

McCabe, S. (Ed.). (2014). *The Routledge handbook of tourism marketing*. Oxon: Routledge.

McDermott, L., Stead, M., & Hastings, G. (2005). What is and what is not social marketing: The challenge of reviewing the evidence. *Journal of Marketing Management, 21*, 545–553.

Misiura, S. (2006). *Heritage marketing*. London: Elsevier Butterworth-Heinemann.

Morgan, N., & Pritchard, A. (1998). *Tourism promotion and power: Creating images, creating identities*. Chichester: Wiley.

Morrison, A. (2013). *Marketing and managing tourism destinations*. Oxon: Routledge.

Mosedale, J. (2016). *Neoliberalism and the political economy of tourism*. Oxon: Routledge.

Mosse, G. L. (1990). *Fallen soldiers: Reshaping the memory of the world war*. Oxford: Oxford University Press.

Nicholson, W., & Snyder, C. (2007). *Intermediate microeconomics and its application* (10th ed.). Mason: Thomson Business and Economics.

Nobile, P. (1995). *Judgement at the Smithsonian*. New York: Marlowe.

Osborn, A. (2011, March 6). Chernobyl: The toxic tourist attraction. *The Telegraph*. Retrieved from http://www.telegraph.co.uk/news/worldnews/europe/ukraine/8363569/Chernobyl-The-toxic-tourist-attraction.html

Pike, S. (2004). *Destination marketing organisations*. New York: Elsevier.

Presenza, A., & Cipollina, M. (2010). Analysing tourism stakeholder networks. *Tourism Review, 65*(4), 17–30.

Scates, B. (2008). Memorializing Gallipoli: Manufacturing memory at Anzac. *Public History Review, 15*, 47–59.

Seaton, A. V. (2001). Sources of slavery: destinations of slavery—The silences and disclosures of slavery heritage in the UK and US. In G. Dann & A. V. Seaton (Eds.), *Slavery, contested heritage and dark tourism*. Binghamton: Haworth.

Seaton, A. V. (2009). Dark tourism and its discontents: An appraisal of a decade's work with some future issues and directions. In T. Jamal & M. Robinson (Eds.), *The SAGE handbook of tourism studies*. London: SAGE.

Shang, J., Basil, D. Z., & Wymer, W. (2010). Using social marketing to enhance hotel reuse programs. *Journal of Business Research, 63*, 166–172.

Sharpley, R., & Stone, P. R. (Eds.). (2009). *The darker side of travel: The theory and practice of dark tourism*. Bristol: Channel View.

Spielberg, S., & Hanks, T. (2001). *Band of brothers, HBO miniseries*. Hollywood: DreamWorks Pictures.

Spielberg, S., Rodat, R., Hanks, T., Burns, E., & Sizemore, T. (1998). *Saving private Ryan*. Hollywood: DreamWorks Pictures.

Stead, M., Gordon, R., Angus, K., & McDermott, L. (2007). A systematic review of social marketing effectiveness. *Health Education, 107*, 126–191.

Stone, P. R. (2013a). Dark tourism, heterotopias and post-apocalyptic places: The case of Chernobyl. In L. White & E. Frew (Eds.), *Dark tourism and place identity: Managing and interpreting dark places* (pp. 79–94). Oxon: Routledge.

Stone, P. R. (2013b). Dark tourism scholarship: A critical review. *International Journal of Culture, Tourism and Hospitality Research, 7*(3), 307–318.

Truong, V. D., & Hall, C. M. (2013). Social marketing and tourism: What is the evidence? *Social Marketing Quarterly, 19*(2), 110–135.

Tunbridge, J. E., & Ashworth, G. J. (1996). *Dissonant heritage: The management of the past as a resource in conflict*. Chichester: Wiley.

Watson, L. (2013, April 25). D-Day veterans' anger at Normandy landings tourist campaign that ignores beach where 700 British soldiers died or were wounded going ashore. *Daily Mail*. Retrieved from http://www.dailymail.co.uk/news/article-2314488/D-Day-veterans-anger-French-Normandy-landings-tourist-campaign-ignores-beach-700-British-soldiers-died-wounded-going-ashore.html#ixzz4BUpis6pa

Wendel, J. (2016, April 18). Animals rule Chernobyl 30 years after nuclear disaster. *National Geographic*. Retrieved from http://news.nationalgeographic.com/2016/04/060418-chernobyl-wildlife-thirty-year-anniversary-science/

White, L., & Frew, E. (2013). *Dark tourism and place identity: Managing and interpreting dark places*. Oxon: Routledge.

Wieviorka, O. (2008). *Normandy: The landings to the liberation of Paris*. Cambridge, MA: Belknap Press.

Winter, J. M. (2006). *Remembering war: The great war between memory and history in the twentieth century*. New Haven: Yale University Press.

Worthington, N., & Vaillancourt, M.-E. (2016). The Canadian Juno Beach Centre in Normandy, France. In G. R. Bird, S. Claxton, & K. Reeves (Eds.), *Managing and interpreting D-Day's sites of memory: Guardians of remembrance* (pp. 116–132). Oxon: Routledge.

Yankovskaa, G., & Hannamb, K. (2014). Dark and toxic tourism in the Chernobyl exclusion zone. *Current Issues in Tourism, 17*(10), 929–939.

27

'Death as a Commodity': The Retailing of Dark Tourism

Brent McKenzie

Introduction

A plush 'RMS Titanic Crew Bear' toy from the 'Titanic: The Artifact Exhibition' in Ireland, a can of 'The Last Breath of Communism' from 'Memento Park' in Budapest, and a copy of the book *Chained on the Rock: Slavery in Bermuda* from the 'Bermuda Maritime Museum'. These are all souvenirs or mementos that represent the breadth of items that can be purchased at visitor attractions related to dark tourism. Consequently, the fundamental question is whether these types of product items should be offered for sale and should you purchase them?

This chapter examines the way in which key tenets of dark tourism—death, tragedy, or the macabre—can be 'purchased' or retailed (also see Chap. 26). Thus, the focus of this study is to examine the impact retailing of such items has upon the perceived 'darkness' of a tourist site or attraction. As noted by Seaton (2009), the act of appearing to profit from Others' misfortune and tragedy has many implications. Specifically, therefore, this chapter examines the role of retailing in the supply and consumption of dark tourism from a social, ethical, cultural, and economic perspective and, by extension, the impact of retailing of dark tourism and dark tourism product has on a seemingly growing commodification of death. Arguably, there is general agreement within the literature that certain economic realities exist for 'dark' as well

---

B. McKenzie (✉)
University of Guelph, Guelph, Canada

other types of tourist attractions. However, there is greater debate as to the nature of the items, souvenirs, educational materials, memorabilia, and other similar items that should be sold at these sites.

Hence, to address this issue in this chapter, a multifaceted study was conducted, of the categories of products that are available for purchase at different dark tourism sites. In addition to examining the products that are sold at such sites, a qualitative analysis was made of visitor comments about the gift shop at dark tourism attractions. A second qualitative study was also made by way of interviews with curators of museums that focuses on issues and events related to dark tourism. The final section of this chapter presents a discussion and analysis of the role of retailing with respect to dark tourism based on the author's experiences and thoughts developed from visiting a number of dark tourism shops. To provide the greatest range of understanding of retail trade and dark tourism, attractions were selected for the study that represent the extremes of the 'dark tourism spectrum' typological model as purported by Stone (2006). Subsequently, the 'darkest' sites are exemplified by those that relate to genocide tourist attractions, and to those on the 'lightest' side—sites that are represented by what have been referred to as 'dark fun factories' (Stone 2006).

This chapter aims to contribute to the dark tourism literature by offering critical insights as to the economic and social implications, of the sale and purchase of items such as souvenirs and educational materials, at particular dark tourism sites. Of equal significance, is that this chapter helps to advance an understanding of how the concept and practice of retailing has both an impact on both the supply and demand for dark tourism attractions, museums and memorabilia, and the increased commodification of death. Furthermore, through the categorizing and analysis of the types of goods offered allows for greater understanding of the role that retail has in supporting or restricting the definition of the different shades of dark tourism.

The focus of this chapter is to examine a specific commercial aspect of dark tourism, that is, the retailing of souvenirs, mementos and other items that can be purchased at sites of dark tourism. Of course, there is debate as to what, or even if, items should be available for sale at these attractions as defined by Stone and Sharpley (2008, p. 574) as 'sites, attractions or events linked in one way or another with death, suffering, violence or disaster'. This is particularly pertinent for sites that fall within the 'darkest side' of Stone's (2006) spectrum of dark tourism. Indeed, there are a number of sites that fall within the 'darkest' side of the spectrum, as well as a number of sites that may classed on the 'lightest' side. Well-recognised examples of the former include the Auschwitz-Birkenau Memorial and Museum, and other sites that focus on genocide, atrocity, and catastrophe, while the latter include attractions and tourist sites that emphasize entertainment, derived from fictional death and macabre events, such as haunted houses (Stone 2006). Although these classifications are not universal, for example, Heuermann and Chhabra (2014) have focused on the scope of the authenticity of the dark tourism site in terms of its classification, and there are no precise categorization tools (Biran et al. 2011) of a site as 'dark' or 'light', there is certainly support that those on the far ends of the spectrum taxonomy differ from each other in numerous ways (apart from the obvious content matter).

The purpose of this chapter, therefore, is not to debate the merits of one form of classification over another, but rather to examine one variable from both extremes—that of the retail component in terms of the operations and visitor experiences. Ultimately, the selling of products at museums and other cultural heritage sites is not new (Wilkins 2011), as these shops often help provide revenues to support the continued operation of the site (Jansen-Verbeke 1998). However, what is more controversial is the existence of such shops at dark tourism sites (Toepler 2006), and it is this point that the chapter now turns to.

Dark Tourism and Retailing: A Brief Literature Review

Although the field of dark tourism is not new and continues to grow in both supply and demand (Williams 2007), the question remains as to what impact dark tourism has on the lessening of the uniqueness or individuality view of death. In other words, has the growth of dark tourism, in both visitor sites as well as scholarship, played a role in the increasing levels of insensitivity to death? As noted by Buda (2015) in her research on the psychoanalytic concept of the death drive, or the seeking out of pain or death versus pleasure and joy, there has been an increasing focus on tourists' seeking out experiences relating to fear.

Nevertheless, those who see demand increasing for tourism sites and attractions that focus on death argue that it is not an increased demand to visit and observe players with a dark history but, rather, that the number of places with such a history are now accessible to a greater number of visitors (Light 2001). An example of this growth was the fall of the Berlin Wall in 1989 and the subsequent collapse of the Soviet Union in 1991. These events now allowed tourists to visit formerly closed or highly restricted locations, many of which dealt with the oppression and often torturous regimes and deadly actions that occurred in these regions. A second significant event was the 9/11 terrorist attacks on the United Sates. These horrific events were witnessed through television or online media around the world, and the subsequent memorials, museums, and memorabilia that were created almost immediately afterwards helped to feed, or at minimum, allow a greater number of people to recall and tangentially experience these horrifying events again and again.

Of course, these types of events might help explain an apparent growth in the supply of dark tourism, but what about the demand side (Farmaki 2013)? Debates in the literature regularly focus on why people engage in dark tourism, and while there is general consensus with respect to the commodification of death, a post-modern perspective is often taken (Williams 2004). Post-modern tourism is focused on the new or unusual, and although the use of the term 'dark tourism' may have a relatively short history, the unique but universal aspect of death nonetheless drives its growth.

As discussed by Selmi et al. (2012), a major issue with dark tourism has been a question of ethics and morality, as well as the commodification of death. While the issue of (death) commodification is the focus of this chapter, it is also worth examining other issues in terms of their impact upon commodification. For instance, if visiting a growing number of 'dark sites' results in a moral dilemma for the tourist (Keil 2005)—that is, should or should they not visit—does this lessen the individual's moral concerns? Similarly, ethical questions about what should or should not be offered at a dark tourism site are raised (Stone and Sharpley 2008), and the choices and types of sites, as well as items that are offered for sale, raise fundamental issues over consumer behaviour and ethical consumption.

The work of Stone (2013) offers a compelling viewpoint that the contemporary commodification of death is evident of a broader growth of 'death sites', as well as the branding of dark tourism as a scholarly field of study. For this study, however, the question of commodification of death can be viewed as taking a direct line from changes in morality and ethics, as they relate to the supply and demand for dark tourism. One position is that by increasing tourists' exposure to sites of remembrance and tragedy, the result is a heightened understanding of personal pain and suffering and, therefore, an increased empathy for the plight of those that have experienced such events (Dale and Robinson 2011). The counter-position is that as one is exposed to more and more horrible events, one either becomes insensitive to the plight of those involved, or else an ever-increasing level of horror, gore, or realism is required to experience the earlier levels of empathy (Kerr 2015).

The linking of retailing with this commodification of death, through dark tourism, would be a specific example of the broader commodification of tourism itself (Poon 1994). As dark tourism sites continued to increase, the opportunity to build upon tourist attendance growth with commercial add-on revenues could make the difference between the success and failure of an attraction (McKenzie 2011). However, the question that remains is how can commercial activities not detract from the greater purpose of providing the dead with a sombre and respectful environment (Seaton 2009)? While research is limited in this respect, Brown (2013) offers a useful case study of how museum shops are operated at three dark sites. Brown's work is to be commended, as it provides a critical ethical review about museum shops within the context of dark tourism. Indeed, Brown further advances our understanding from two perspectives. Firstly, by examining extremes of dark tourism sites as defined by Stone (2006) and, secondly, by providing a greater linkage of similar sites within each category. Accordingly, reasons and notions of value created by souvenirs and why tourists wish to purchase them are now discussed and, subsequently, an overview of their role within dark tourism.

Souvenirs (in Dark Tourism)

Often tourists have a desire to purchase something that represents a vacation or a trip to a specific tourist attraction (also see Chap. 29). Examples of these souvenir purchases may include postcards, toys, books, or other items that are linked in some way or another to the visit. Indeed, a study by the Holiday Inn hotel chain found that 70 per cent of all people believe that purchasing a souvenir is a key part of the tourist experience, while only 20 per cent do not purchase souvenirs (www.holidayinn.com/communications). The souvenir may be purchased for oneself or as a gift for friends or family. While contemporary tourist souvenirs have been examined from a number of perspectives within the literature, original souvenirs can be found in the earliest forms of travel, including early religious pilgrimages. Indeed, badges were often provided to pilgrims that made a journey, indicating to others a 'travel status' and actual pilgrimage (Spencer 2010). Other studies have examined the significance that a souvenir provides the contemporary traveller in terms of their tangible evidence of their journey. Souvenirs can also serve as a way to remind oneself of the experiences from one's journey. Souvenir items are often novel and possess a link to a specific location, but can also be collectibles or even have functional benefits as well. For example, souvenir spoons, snow globes, cups, and tea towels are just some of the products that represent the vast majority of souvenir items sold today (Peters 2011). Research has also examined financial impacts souvenirs have for tourist attraction providers. Moreover, there are numerous travel websites that contain discussion forums related to expenditures on souvenirs, while other websites accumulate tips and recommendations on what the best souvenirs are in different cities and countries (for instance, Fodors, 2015, www.fodors.com). A leading online travel website, TripAdvisor, contains over 70,000 forum postings about souvenirs (TripAdvisor, 2015, www.tripadvisor.ca). However, while particular issues of tourist souvenirs and retailing are well rehearsed within the literature, there is limited research that focuses on retailing and gift shops at dark tourism sites. Arguably, therefore, dark tourism visitor attraction websites provide interesting insights into retail practices at particular 'dark' sites. Thus, this chapter now examines a number of these websites, from the aforementioned extremes on Stone's (2006) dark tourism spectrum taxonomy, beginning with a purposeful selection of 'darkest' visitor sites and, subsequently, 'lightest' visitor sites.

Retailing at the 'Darkest' Visitor Sites

Stone (2006) described the 'darkest' sites of dark tourism as 'Dark Camps of Genocide'. A selection and review of a number of websites related to historic examples of genocide were examined to determine the role of retailing with respect to their institution. Five sites were selected, with three sites relating to former Nazi concentration camps and the Holocaust, and two of more recent occurrences of genocide.[1]

The first relates to the Dachau Concentration Camp. A website supported by the 'Comité International de Dachau' (Comité International de Dachau, 2015, International Dachau Committee, http://www.comiteinternationaldachau.com/en/), has a 'Shop' tab on their home page where one can purchase books, DVDs, and a tour guide for visiting the Dachau concentration camp memorial. There were similar types of products sold through the Auschwitz-Birkenau Memorial and Museum website (Auschwitz-Birkenau Memorial and Museum 2015, http://auschwitz.org/en/) which contains the arguably less commercial link simply titled 'Bookstore'. Even so, this site also includes DVDs and other educational materials beyond books. The site also has a section that highlights 'new' publications, as well as a 'recommended' section (Auschwitz-Birkenau Memorial and Museum, 2015 http://auschwitz.org/en/bookstore/).

The third former Nazi concentration camp website examined was the Buchenwald and Mittelbau-Dora Memorials Foundation (Mittelbau-Dora Memorials Foundation, 2015, http://www.buchenwald.de/nc/en/896/). It had the most extensive option for searching items for purchase through its 'SHOP' link. Products were sorted by specific memorial, museum, or type of material. Again, only books, DVDs and CDs were offered for sale, but in contrast to the other two sites noted above, the ordering process was through the online retailer Amazon, versus purchasing the items directly from the home website.

The two other 'darkest' genocide websites represent atrocities committed in the early 1990s, namely, the Rwandan genocide in 1994 (see also Chap. 11) and the Srebrenica genocide that was committed in July 1995 during the Bosnian War. The first was the Kilgali Genocide Memorial. The memorial did not have its own website, but the main website at http://www.genocide-archiverwanda.org.rw (Genocide Archive of Rwanda, 2015), presents the Genocide Archive of Rwanda and provides a great deal of information about the atrocity. There were no items for purchase through the site, but one can read a number of published articles and watch a number of video documentaries about the genocide. There is additional content that can also be viewed, but only if one registers (there is no cost) with the site.

Within this review, the most recently established website is that of the Srebrenica Web Genocide Museum (Srebrenica Web Genocide Museum, 2015, http://srebrenica360.com/). As the name indicates, it relates to the genocide that occurred during the Balkan wars of the 1990s, and is aimed at educating those that would be unable to visit the Srebrenica–Potočari Memorial Centre in Bosnia and Herzegovina. There are 360-degree images from Srebrenica, but there are no items offered for purchase.

Overall, it is unsurprising that due to the level of death and terror that these dark tourism websites document, it is perhaps logical to argue that for the darkest sites, the experience of visiting the site—due to the level of intensity and experiences of pain and death—would not generally lend itself to the purchasing of something that results in an ongoing recollection of those events. This assumption is further enhanced in terms of purchasing a souvenir as a gift or keepsake.

Retailing at the 'Lightest' Visitor Sites

The 'lightest' dark tourism sites or what Stone (2006) classifies as 'Dark Fun Factories' portray death, destruction, or the macabre, but are clearly commercial-centric and have a distinct entertainment perspective (Stone 2009). One of the most researched 'Dark Fun Factories' has been the UK based Dungeon Visitor Attractions (Merlin Entertainment, 2015, http://www.merlinentertainments.biz/the-dungeons). The Dungeons are 'the ultimate live action journey through the world's murky past… [with] live action shows, exciting rides and hysterically horrible history' (The Dungeons, 2015, http://www.thedungeons.com/locations/), and offer tailored shows based upon the location of the actual attraction. Unsurprisingly, the number and types of items sold at the Dungeon sites are quite broad. Subsequently, the author visited three of the Dungeon attractions; namely the London Dungeon, (The Dungeons, 2015, http://www.thedungeons.com/london/en/); the York Dungeon, (The Dungeons, 2015, http://www.thedungeons.com/york/en/); and the Edinburgh Dungeon, (The Dungeons, 2015, http://www.thedungeons.com/edinburgh/en/). All three visitor attractions offered many of the same items, although the programme for each was specific to the attraction. The promotional 'text' used by these sites to promote their gift shops was:

- *York Dungeon*: 'The York Dungeon Shop has a fantastic range of goodies to remember your visit! Like the Dungeon it is unique experience and is accessible via Cumberland Street for gifts all year round!' (The Dungeons, 2015, http://www.thedungeons.com/york/en/plan-your-visit/facilities-and-accessibility.aspx)
- *Edinburgh Dungeon*: 'The Edinburgh Dungeon Shop of Horrors has a fantastically frightful range of goodies to take away as a souven-ear (Haha). Like the Dungeon it is a unique experience and is accessible via Market Street for gifts and trinkets all year round.' (The Dungeons, 2015, http://www.thedungeons.com/edinburgh/en/plan-your-visit/facilities-and-accessibility.aspx)
- *London Dungeon*: There is no reference to retail options for the London Dungeon on their website, but it does state that 'Before beginning your decent into The London Dungeon you will have a photograph taken together, so practice those scary faces! You will also have a photograph taken at the end of your tour during "Drop Dead" Drop Ride!' (The Dungeons, 2015, http://www.thedungeons.com/london/en/plan-your-visit/faq.aspx), which are made available for sale after the attraction.

To get a better sense of visitor experiences with the retail options at these sites, a content analysis of online postings of Dungeon visitors for the three aforementioned locations was conducted. The postings were all taken from the TripAdvisor.com website (TripAdvisor, 2015). This type of analysis has been previously shown to provide a breadth of insight on traveller perceptions and experiences (Lee et al. 2011). A selection of comments were purposefully collected by using the search terms 'London Dungeon gift shop', as well as 'Edinburgh Dungeon' and 'York Dungeon'. The purpose of the exercise was to get a sense of the role gift shops potentially play in the overall visitor experience. There were a total of 45 reviews for the Edinburgh Dungeon, 32 for the York Dungeon, and 67 for the London Dungeon. Each of these reviews was then examined by way of content analysis (Li et al. 2013). Key sentence(s) and comments directly related to the gift shop were extracted. The result was 754 words for the Edinburgh Dungeon, 492 for the York Dungeon, and 434 words for the London Dungeon. The extracted text was entered into Text Cloud software (http://tagcrowd.com/). Resultant 'word clouds' (also known as 'tag clouds') have been shown to be a useful qualitative research technique to help visualise data (Fingal 2008; McNaught and Lam 2010). Three word clouds emerged for each of the three Dungeon attractions, and a word cloud which offers an overall summary (Figs. 27.1, 27.2, 27.3, and 27.4).

The word clouds highlighted several key concepts of a gift shop in general. For the Edinburgh attraction (Fig. 27.1), key terms such as pricing and the inclusion of more terms related to death, such as the executioner, were also highlighted. For London site (Fig. 27.2), price again tended to dominate, but interestingly, there was little in the way of what might be considered 'darker aspects' of the items sold in the shop. Therefore, it may be assumed that as the London Dungeon is the original Dungeon visitor attraction within the brand, and, consequently, the site could be viewed as another 'historic' site in London, in a similar vein as the Tower of London which includes an actual historic dungeon.

The third Dungeon attraction in York (Fig. 27.3) also demonstrated financial aspects of the gift shop, though the photo souvenir also stood out. There are a number of options at the York Dungeon for purchasing a photo, which may be taken either before entering the Dungeon or during the actual Dungeon experience itself, and is clearly a personal memento of a specific visit. Interesting, the York Dungeon word cloud highlighted staff of the souvenir shop. As discussed later in the chapter, the ability for dark tourism visitor sites to market and sell additional souvenir items, has become a greater aspect of the dark tourism sector, as represented by a photograph of a specific visit.

In summary (Fig. 27.4), major terms that emerge from the word clouds do not appear to differ greatly from what one would expect to find in discussions of any gift shop at a tourist attraction (Clarke 2013). Though references to characters and items related to death such as the 'executioner' or 'coffin' focus on the dark aspects of the attractions, terms such as 'selection', 'price', and 'interesting products' perhaps apply equally to retail opportunities at other tourist attractions.

amazing bad **book** bought brilliant coffin couple end everything **buy** clock executioner expected fairly fantastic kids london momento nice expensive **priced** products quality **tour** usual ones photographs quite razors reasonably selection staff start straight things value

Fig. 27.1 Word cloud for the Edinburgh Dungeon, UK

'Death as a Commodity': The Retailing of Dark Tourism

Fig. 27.2 Word cloud for the London Dungeon, UK

Fig. 27.3 Word cloud for the York Dungeon, UK

arrived beginning bigger bit boyfriend breath **buy** change chatty chose city clear clever complaint cool course cynical **date** deadly death disappointed downer dungeons **end** enjoyed enough ensuring entrance **everyone** experience fee fire found group history hit home hour items lasts **leave lot** lovely **nice** noticed offer oh overpriced packed patient perfect performance **photo** picture **priced** pricey ps **purchase** puts quite rather recommend reduced resist room scared scariest sign small **reasonably** **souvenirs** spend **staff stock** sudden **surprise** surrounded thoroughly thought tills tiny toilets took **tour** trip unusually usual **visit** wanted whole wish **really**

Fig. 27.4 Word cloud summarising the three (UK) Dungeon attractions

Retailing at the 'In-betweens' Visitor Sites

To complete Stone's (2006) spectrum of dark tourism, those visitor sites that might fall 'in-between' the two taxonomical extremes are reviewed. This third classification of dark tourism sites, for this review at least, are referred to as 'in-betweens' as they may be consider sites 'dark' on one level, but also might be considered by some as 'light'. In order to highlight this segment, a review of the author's shopping experiences at gift shops at a number of these visitor sites is provided. The first is the Royal Air Force Museum, Cosford, UK (Royal Air Force Museum Cosford, 2015, http://www.rafmuseum.org.uk/cosford/). The gift shop is quite large by comparative standards and is markedly distinct by a large statue of the founder of the Soviet Union, V.I. Lenin. However, what makes this image interesting is that he is holding a shopping bag (Fig. 27.5). The shop offers for sale a variety of items directly and indirectly related to the museum. Moreover, the museum's web site has a tab for the online shop highlighted in yellow, suggesting the significance of retail to the museum; the museum even has a second website, solely devoted to online purchases (Royal Air Force Museum Cosford, 2015,http://www.rafmuseumshop.com/).

Fig. 27.5 Statue of Lenin holding a shopping bag (Photo Source: Author)

'Death as a Commodity': The Retailing of Dark Tourism   681

Fig. 27.6   A can of the 'last breath of communism' (Photo Source: Author)

A second example is the Memento Park in Budapest, Hungary, (Memento Park, 2015,http://www.mementopark.hu/). The online shop 'Red Star Store' offers both 'authentic' as well as 'kitschy' products connected to the Soviet Communist period, including how the period relates to Hungary (Memento Park, 2015,http://www.mementopark.hu/shop/). For example, a can of the 'last breath of Communism' (Fig. 27.6) appears to be purely for entertainment. This is in sharp contrast to the horrors and atrocities that occurred in Hungary during the period that are chronicled in the book 'In the Shadow of Stalin's Boots', and which is also available on the website as well as at the museum shop. The onsite shop is part of the museum entrance, and samples of items available for sale are displayed behind glass and have to be requested for purchase.

A third dark tourism site that might be considered as 'in-between' on Stone's dark tourism spectrum model is the Crumlin Road Gaol, Belfast, Northern Ireland (http://www.crumlinroadgaol.com/). A working prison until 1996, the transition of the site into a dark tourism attraction is relatively new. As per other gaol (or 'jail') attractions, visitors appear to be drawn to the site based on its dark history (Ross 2012). On completion of a tour of the facility, there is a fairly well-stocked gift shop. In addition to historic books for sale, Gaol branded items and other 'kitschy' souvenirs such as 'Jailhouse Rock' are also available to purchase.

Related in scope to the Crumlin Road Gaol is the Eastern State Penitentiary (ESP) in Philadelphia, Pennsylvania, USA. It is also a former working prison, but unlike the Crumlin Road Gaol it has been 'preserved' in that the majority of the sites, specifically former cells have been left to decay. Conceivably, this decay has added to the 'darkness' of the site and provides for a variety of events to be held at the ESP, including being used as a setting for theatrical films as well as being turned into a 'haunted venue and tour' during Halloween. Indeed, the product choice is quite extensive in terms of available souvenirs. For example, 'memberships' to the ESP are available, as well as specific site-related clothing, books, and DVDs. There is also a separate online store for items related to the aforementioned Halloween tours. Of particular note is an interesting 'Eastern State Penitentiary Art Kit' souvenir—a choice that might be conceived as somewhat disconnected to a penitentiary attraction. That said, however, the art kit may be viewed within the prism of a prisoner's experience in terms of keeping occupied while serving a sentence, or one may even use the kit to draw sketches of the actual penitentiary.

A final example comes from a gift shop in the city formerly known as Queenstown (now Cobh), County Cork, Ireland—a major Irish seaport. It was here that RMS Titanic made her final port call before its ill-fated maiden voyage in 1912. Items for sale include a Titanic branded plush bear (Fig. 27.7), a Titanic whistle, as well as Titanic souvenir tickets. Of course, questions as to the appropriateness of such items have been debated in the literature (Neill 2011); nonetheless, these items may help fulfil the traditional role played by other travel-related souvenirs.

Retail(ing) and the Dark Tourism Visitor Attraction

The final component of this study of the role of retailing and commerce within dark tourism offers an insight from a visitor attraction provider. Consequently, research findings reported here are based on interviews conducted by the author with curators of two museums that dealt directly with 'dark' subjects: firstly, the curator of the Museum of Occupations of Estonia (MOE), Tallinn, Estonia (Museum of Occupations of Estonia (MOE), 2015,http://www.okupatsioon.ee/en), and secondly, the Director of the Museum of the Occupation of Lativa (MOL), located in Riga, Latvia (http://okupacijasmuzejs.lv/en).

In terms of museum goals, the MOE states on its website:

Fig. 27.7 A Titanic-themed teddy bear available as a gift/souvenir (Photo Source: Author)

The Museum of Occupations provides a comprehensive overview of Estonian society during three periods of occupation: the first Soviet occupation 1940–1941, the German occupation 1941–1944, and the second Soviet occupation 1944–1991. Audio-visual displays and photos highlight the events of the era, repression and national resistance, as well as showing how people coped with the day-to-day realities of this difficult period.

Meanwhile, the MOL website states their objectives as:

- to identify, research, elucidate and commemorate the wrongdoings committed by the foreign occupation powers against the state and the people of Latvia from 1940 to 1991;
- to preserve historical memory of the Latvian people about the occupation period;
- to inform and educate the people of Latvia and other nations about the history and consequences of the occupation period in order to strengthen the Latvian state and its place amongst the free and democratic nations of the world.

The author previously visited both of these museums and, subsequently, contacted both the curator of the MOE and the Director of the MOL to conduct a research interview regarding the role of retailing within the respective museums. The interviews were conducted via SKYPE and lasted approximately 45 minutes.

Interviews with 'Dark Heritage' Professionals: A Brief Overview

The first interview at the MOE was valuable for better understanding current challenges that museums face in terms of sourcing additional revenue, but also understanding particular challenges that are faced by a museum that falls within the scope of dark tourism and difficult heritage. The MOE is a privately owned and operated museum, and thus has greater flexibility and autonomy in terms of what they sell on site. They also have a dedicated website, but at the time of writing, they did not sell any items online. With regard to the interviews, a number of specific questions were asked:

- What types of products are sold at the museum?
- Why do you believe people purchase a souvenir at your museum?
- What role does the retail shop play within the overall operations of the museum?
- How has the type of products sold at the museum changed over time?
- What role do you see retailing playing in the future success of the museum?

Overall, responses from the MOE provide some critical insights of how the museum views the role of the retail shop within its general operation. A selection of responses from the MOE to the interview questions are reported here.

'Death as a Commodity': The Retailing of Dark Tourism 685

...products sold at the museum are mostly books, as books are the biggest item in terms of money and items...we need more stories from those [Estonians] that escaped, most of the stories are about those deported to Siberia.

...some other small items as well as being able to buy a cup of coffee, a drink, ice cream...

...we have book releases at the museum...we want to do these events in the museum...

...the main reasons people purchase something because they saw the exhibits... after they walk into the museum, they think about Estonian history...

...at the moment I would like to have more museum owned products, so we are working on having more own products... we find that for younger people they want a practical product...for example a canteen for the young people as you can put it on the fire and heat it up...

...intended to or not, the concept of the museum has changed over time, the shop has become a greater part of the strategy... to buy things – things should tell a story not just to sell some artefacts, this is the main reason people are shopping...

...you can sell everything but the way to sell them must tell some kind of story... for example, even sell candy if there is a story with them... if the ice cream brand is from the Soviet time you can connect them [the visitor] with the topic of the museum.

...the Museum must see the visitor as a client... if you are a good story teller you can sell anything...

...'edu-tianment'... balance of providing education and knowledge, but make it an emotional connection to this knowledge...

The second interview with the Director of the MOL asked the same questions. Similarly to the MOE, the MOL is also privately owned, but it was founded mainly by émigré Latvians from the United States, and receives about one-third of its funding from the Latvian State (unlike the MOE, the MOL does not charge an admission fee). The MOL also has a website, where one can purchase books, DVDs, and postcards about Latvia's twentieth-century occupation periods (http://okupacijasmuzejs.lv/en/shop).

Although a number of the responses to the questions by the Director of the MOL often mirrored those of the MOE, there were some additional insights into operating such a museum. A selection of responses from the MOL to the interview questions are reported here:

...we've got a small book store, mainly books on themes on what we are doing... they are in Latvian or English, and some are in French, German or Russian...

...we have a small number of publications, with the largest percentage not by the Museum...we also have reproductions of watercolours by a well known

Latvian artist… the reason these sell so well is that we have the originals [in the museum]… the artist was a member of the French Group, who were a group that read French Literature, and because of this they were sent to the Gulag… we also have postcards of pictures that were produced in the Gulag, as well as some free give- away postcards…

…we want people to not just visit the museum but to take something back… a souvenir will give you some sort of connection with the suffering, but how do you do this in a tactical way…

…the museum works without "too much emotion"… it is an emotional experience but trying not to run out tears, in the end it is a positive experience…

…there is a fine line of what we should sell… what is tacky, what is unacceptable, what is good… the problem is this line is in different places for different people…

Although both the MOE and MOL may be exemplars of a dark tourism attraction, both museums did not appear to greatly differ from what one would expect in any typical museum shop. Most souvenir or educational items might be considered acceptable, with the caution that the museum should ensure that the official purpose or basis for offering the product for sale is at the very least understood by the museum, and, ideally, conveyed to the purchaser of the item. Interestingly, both museums believed that they had to continue to offer visitors not just new and varied exhibits, but also different types of experiences. This has proved to be quite challenging in terms of encouraging repeat visitors.

Discussion

Thus, what is the relevance of retailing with respect to the commodification of death as it relates to dark tourism? As this study has demonstrated, the degree of 'darkness' of a site may be enhanced or lessened by the type of souvenirs or other items that can be purchased. Whether the items are purchased following a visit to a dark tourism site or as a stand-alone action through an online purchase, souvenirs nevertheless represent a growing area of importance in terms of viability of a dark tourism attraction. Indeed, the ability to continually update the types of products for sale allows for greater flexibility in targeting previous visitors, in comparison to the costs involved in making changes and updates to the actual attraction.

However, a potential issue is that as the products being sold tend to become more important to the success of the dark tourism venture, the 'darkness' or original intent and purpose of the site may be lost. As evident in the interviews at both the MOE and MOL, there was a concern on how best to present the museums to younger visitors; one of the ways was to offer something unique or interesting for them to purchase. Subsequently, the inherent danger with such a strategy, in terms of a further commodification of death and a blurring or lack of understanding as to the original purpose of such a site, is that dark tourism attractions become just another place to visit to learn about history. Arguably, therefore, the level of perceived 'darkness' of a specific history may be superseded by the ability to sell enough souvenirs—either those considered authentic or kitsch (Sharpley and Stone 2009; Sturken 2007). Particularly, private enterprises without government or public support may have little choice but to cater to a wider audience, regardless of the fact that episodes of trauma and atrocity may be downplayed in order to remain financially viable. For instance, in 2016, it was announced that as of 2018, the Museum of Occupations in Tallinn will be renamed *'Vabamu'*, which in Estonian means 'Freedom'. Although the change is meant to reflect the expansion of the museum (Cavegn 2016), there was an immediate backlash as to the impact that such a change would have, specifically the belief that the change of name lessens the period of occupation in Estonia by Nazi Germany, as well as a movement towards political correctness with respect to Estonia's history (Kolga 2016).

Moreover, a related issue is that collective society now has a much greater tolerance for scenes of death and the macabre. Indeed, the popularity of films and television, and video games that depict or are based on death has added to a growing threshold of what is truly 'dark'. Consequently, the expectation is that certain dark tourism attractions will continue to depict darkest aspects of history (e.g., concentration camps), and conversely, visitors will also seek out the fun side of darkness (e.g., the dungeon-type attractions). Importantly, however, it is those sites between the extremes that appear to be the most vulnerable in terms of having to 'lighten the dark' in order to continue to operate. As evident in this study, the variety of souvenir items sold by particular dark tourism providers suggest that visitors remain interested in the historic, accurate, or even authentic items, which are still traditionally conveyed by way of books or videos. Yet, the greater impact on this commodification of death will stem from an ever-increasing exploration, if not exploitation, of what can and should be sold at particular dark tourism sites and attractions.

Conclusion

The market for dark tourism sites, experiences, and public interest in them continues to grow, though the range and type of dark tourism vary across the world. Similar to any heritage tourism site, there are ongoing dilemmas to ensure dark tourism sites are relevant and successful, in whatever way success might be measured. Indeed, commercial challenges for dark tourism sites mirror those of other heritage tourism attractions, but with the added component of the serious and solemn nature of topics being portrayed. Evidently, the focus and pursuit for revenue to continue the operation of these visitor attractions varies based on the type of site. Stone's (2006) spectrum of dark tourism provides a conceptual framework in which the retail component of these sites can be located, analysed, and critiqued. However, the challenge appears to be that unlike traditional retailing, the 'marketing' of death, destruction, and the macabre results in a more fragmented customer base.

Hence, the ability to educate, entertain, or even scare requires taking either a broad or narrow perspective in terms of what is being 'sold'. All dark tourism attractions can and generally do sell something, but determining what should be retailed versus what can be sold is fraught with difficulties. For those providers who view their attraction as, first and foremost, a way of educating visitors about a difficult and painful past (i.e., 'dark' sites such as the MOE or the MOL), there are inherent commercial and moral tensions as to how to justify selling more 'things' in order to keep the site in operation. That said, other dark tourism sites have less of a concern with such tensions as they are of a 'lighter' nature and have much greater latitude in determining what to sell.

Ultimately, therefore, the aim of this chapter was not to provide a prescriptive approach of retail components at particular dark tourism attractions. Rather, the chapter highlights a need to ensure that the focus on retail and related revenue-generating opportunities aligns with the stated aim of the visitor site in question. If the dark tourism attraction is centred on education or entertainment, retail opportunities may be created to enhance and not hinder that main focus.

Notes

1. Although there is debate on a number of events in history that may or may not have been classified as genocide, the ones selected have all been classified in this manner by the United Nations Convention on Genocide adopted in December 1948.

References

Auschwitz-Birkenau Memorial and Museum. http://auschwitz.org/en/. Accessed 4 Aug 2015.

Biran, A., Poria, Y., & Oren, G. (2011). Sought experiences at (dark) heritage sites. *Annals of Tourism Research, 38*(3), 820–841.

Brown, J. (2013). Dark tourism shops: Selling 'dark' and 'difficult' products. *International Journal of Culture, Tourism and Hospitality Research, 7*(3), 272–280.

Buda, D. (2015). The death drive in tourism studies. *Annals of Tourism Research, 50*, 39–51.

Cavegn, D. (2016). Museum of occupations to be expanded and renamed Vabamu. http://news.err.ee/v/Culture/db2ca4ab-9136-4e42-be80-df4f23d8aa5f/museum-of-occupations-to-be-expanded-and-renamed-vabamu. Accessed 20 May 2016.

Clarke, J. (2013). Experiential aspects of tourism gift consumption. *Journal of Vacation Marketing, 19*(1), 75–87.

Comité International de Dachau (International Dachau Committee). http://www.comiteinternationaldachau.com/en/. Accessed 4 Aug 2015.

Dale, C., & Robinson, N. (2011). Dark tourism. In P. Robinson, S. Heitmann, & P. Dieke (Eds.), *Research themes for tourism* (pp. 205–217). Oxfordshire: CAB International.

Farmaki, A. (2013). Dark tourism revisited: A supply/demand conceptualisation. *International Journal of Culture, Tourism and Hospitality Research, 7*(3), 281–292.

Fingal, D. (2008, November 23). Tools that create buzz: Words in a cloud. *Learning & Leading with Technology*.

Fodors. www.fodors.com. Accessed 2 Aug 2015.

Genocide Archive of Rwanda. http://www.genocidearchiverwanda.org.rw. Accessed 4 Aug 2015.

Heuermann, K., & Chhabbra, K. (2014). The darker side of dark tourism: An authenticity perspective. *Tourism Analysis, 19*, 213–225.

Jansen-Verbeke, M. (1998). The synergism between shopping and tourism. In W. Theobald (Ed.), *Global tourism* (pp. 428–446). Oxford: Butterworth-Heinemann.

Keil, C. (2005). Sightseeing in the mansions of the dead. *Social and Cultural Geography, 6*(4), 479–494.

Kerr, M. (2015). *Scream: Chilling adventures in the science of fear*. New York: Public Affairs.

Kolga, M. (2016). Welcome to the e-Occupation Museum. *Estonian Life*. http://www.eestielu.com/en/life/lifestyle/165-estonianlife-eestielu/opinion-arvamus/comment-kommentaar/5132-marcus-kolga-welcome-to-the-e-occupation-museum. Accessed 20 May 2016.

Lee, H. A., Law, R., & Murphy, J. (2011). Helpful reviewers in TripAdvisor, an online travel community. *Journal of Travel & Tourism Marketing, 28*(7), 675–688.

Li, H., Ye, Q., & Law, R. (2013). Determinants of customer satisfaction in the hotel industry: An application of online review analysis. *Asia Pacific Journal of Tourism Research, 18*(7), 784–802.

Light, D. (2001). Facing the future: Tourism and identity-building in post-socialist Romania. *Political Geography, 20*, 1053–1074.

McKenzie, B. (2011). Marketing of the dark: 'Memento Park' in Budapest. *Emerging Markets Case Studies Collection, 1*(4), 1–10.

McNaught, C., & Lam, P. (2010). Using Wordle as a supplementary research tool. *The Qualitative Report, 15*(3), 630–643.

Memento Park. http://www.mementopark.hu/. Accessed 4 Aug 2015.

Merlin Entertainment. http://www.merlinentertainments.biz/the-dungeons. Accessed 2 Aug 2015.

Mittelbau-Dora Memorials Foundation. http://www.buchenwald.de/nc/en/896/. Accessed 4 Aug 2015.

Museum of Occupations of Estonia (MOE). http://www.okupatsioon.ee/en. Accessed 4 Aug 2015.

Neill, W. (2011). The debasing of myth: The privatization of titanic memory in designing the 'post-conflict' city. *Journal of Urban Design, 16*(1), 67–86.

Peters, K. (2011). Negotiating the 'place' and 'placement' of banal tourist souvenirs in the home. *Tourism Geographies, 13*(2), 234–256.

Poon, A. (1994). The 'new tourism' revolution. *Tourism Management, 15*(2), 91–92.

Ross, J. I. (2012). Touring imprisonment: A descriptive statistical analysis of prison museums. *Tourism Management Perspectives, 4*, 113–118.

Royal Air Force Museum Cosford. http://www.rafmuseum.org.uk/cosford/. Accessed 27 Jul 2015.

Seaton, T. (2009). Purposeful otherness: Approaches to the management of Thanatourism. In R. Sharpley & P. R. Stone (Eds.), *The darker side of travel: The theory and practice of dark tourism*. Bristol: Channel View Publications.

Selmi, N., Tur, C., & Dornier, R. (2012). To what extent may sites of death be tourism destinations? The cases of Hiroshima in Japan and Struthof in France. *Asian Business & Management*, suppl. Special Issue: The Evolving Nature of Corporate Social, *11*(3), 311–328.

Sharpley, R., & Stone, P. R. (2009). (Re)presenting the macabre: Interpretation, Kitschification and authenticity. In R. Sharpley & P. R. Stone (Eds.), *The darker side of travel: The theory and practice of dark tourism*. Bristol: Channel View Publications.

Spencer, B. (2010). *Pilgrim souvenirs and secular badges*. Suffolk: Boydell Press.

Srebrenica Web Genocide Museum. http://srebrenica360.com/. Accessed 4 Aug 2015.

Stone, P. R. (2006). A dark tourism Spectrum: Towards a typology of death and macabre related tourist sites, attractions and exhibitions. *Tourism: An Interdisciplinary International Journal, 54*(2), 145–160.

Stone, P. R. (2009). 'It's a bloody guide': Fun, fear and a lighter side of dark tourism at The Dungeon visitor attractions, UK. In R. Sharpley & P. R. Stone (Eds.), *The darker side of travel: The theory and practice of dark tourism*. Bristol: Channel View Publications.

Stone, P. R. (2013). Dark tourism scholarship: A critical review. *International Journal of Culture, Tourism and Hospitality Research, 7*(3), 307–318.

Stone, P. R., & Sharpley, R. (2008). Consuming dark tourism: A Thanatological perspective. *Annals of Tourism Research, 35*(2), 574–595.

Sturken, M. (2007). *Tourists of history: Memory, kitsch, and consumerism from Oklahoma City to ground zero*. Durham/London: Duke University Press.

The Dungeons. http://www.thedungeons.com/locations/; London Dungeon, http://www.thedungeons.com/london/en/; York Dungeon, http://www.thedungeons.com/york/en/; Edinburgh Dungeon, http://www.thedungeons.com/edinburgh/en/. Accessed 2 2015.

Toepler, S. (2006). Caveat venditor? Museum merchandising, non-profit commercialisation, and the case of the metropolitan museum in New York. *Voluntas: International Journal of Voluntary and Nonprofit Organizations, 17*, 95–109.

TripAdvisor. www.tripadvisor.com. Search of visitor postings about gifts shops at the York, Edinburgh, and London, 'Dungeon' Attractions. Accessed 2 Aug 2015.

Wilkins, H. (2011). Souvenirs: What and why we buy. *Journal of Travel Research, 50*(3), 239–247.

Williams, P. (2004). Witnessing genocide: Vigilance and remembrance at Tuol Sleng and Choeung Ek. *Holocaust and Genocide Studies, 18*(2), 234–254.

Williams, P. (2007). *Memorial museums: The global rush to commemorate atrocities*. Oxford: Berg.

28

Exhibiting Death and Disaster: Museological Perspectives

Elspeth Frew

Introduction

Museums have been described as a key institution through which we understand our past and present identities. They are considered to be "trustworthy houses of authenticity" and history and, as such, they are among the most prominent institutions for education about and preservation of the past (Sodaro 2011, p. 79). Traditionally museums were places for collecting, conserving, and exhibiting artefacts of material culture with the collections and displays demonstrating the wealth and power of the collectors or the state (Carter and Orange 2012). Consequently, this tended to reflect museums' exclusivity and elitism (Ross 2004). Museums were viewed as the gatekeepers to our history and past, and spaces where our social, civic, and national identities were preserved, displayed, and shaped (Sodaro 2011).

Museology is defined as the entirety of theoretical and critical thinking within the museum field (Mairesse and Desvallées 2010). "New museology" evolved from perceived failings of original museology, and was based on the idea that the role of museums within society needed to change (McCall and Gray 2014). In other words, museums were viewed as being isolated from the modern world, elitist, obsolete, and a waste of public money (Hudson 1977). Thus, "new museology" gained prominence during the 1980s and has been described as a "current of thought principally concerned with exploring the social role of museums, along with new styles of expression and communication"

E. Frew (✉)
La Trobe University, Melbourne, Australia

(Lorente 2012, p. 241). The new museums emerging from this shift have changed their narratives with the public and define themselves as places of memory, reflecting the "postmodern shift from authoritative master discourses to the horizontal, practice-related notions of memory, place, and community" (Andermann and Arnold-de Simine 2012, p. 3). Therefore, new museology represents the changing philosophical, economic, and social approach to the way museums are conceptualized as organizations (Baddeley 2013), the way the museum functions and, the role of staff (McCall and Gray 2014). These changes also reflect the political and economic pressures which have compelled museum professionals to shift their attention from their collections towards visitors (Ross 2004).

Contemporary museums now increasingly recognize their privileged status in society as institutions for education and preservation, and they are also aware that they are not objective and neutral. Sodaro (2011) suggests that the past and the many objects representing it have always been framed by the museum's creators and caretakers, so now there are signs of a progressive opening-up of museums and a greater accessibility (Ross 2004). Indeed, Carter and Orange (2012) suggest that museums today are being recast as instigators of social activism with an increased emphasis on inclusion and diversity. Many of these new museums aim to empower community members to address social issues and human rights abuses and to have "greater social accountability for pressing contemporary issues" (Carter and Orange 2012, p. 111), such as human rights, war and genocide, the environment and climate change, immigration, and social justice.

New museology developed in response to demands that museums remain relevant to their publics, and many have now shifted to a more visitor-centred ethos. These types of museums have become more community focused and representative in their programmes and have done so in response to market forces and the economic redefinition of the public as consumers (Ross 2004; see also Chap. 27). Some new museums can be described as "issues-based" (e.g., human rights museums) and these types of museums have moved away from the centrality of the artefact and material culture and are now more focused on complex issues in contemporary society as their generating principles (Carter and Orange 2012). These issues-based museums take on historical and current problems, and are an alternative forum to recover the history of marginalized communities (Autry 2013). Such museums focus on aspects of history which were previously "sidelined or silenced in mainstream institutions" and are now encouraging "group unity without being oppositional" and, subsequently, aim to counter stereotypical thinking regarding colour and race (Autry 2013, p. 77).

The movement towards a more visitor-centred ethos by museums can be seen as entailing a corresponding shift in the identity of the museum professional, from "legislator" to "interpreter" of cultural meaning (Ross 2004). As institutions engaged in activist practices, these new types of museums and associated staff can help empower community members to address social issues and human rights abuses (Carter and Orange 2012). There has also been a move by institutions to move away from "affirming presentations of patriotism, triumph and great deeds toward an appreciation of the potential for aggression inherent in human relationships" (Simon 2011, p. 432). This has supported the proliferation of memorials built to remember and educate about past atrocity, violence, or trauma which has grown "increasingly sophisticated, technological, and apparently self-reflexive" (Sodaro 2011 p. 80). These museums examine the histories of violent conflict and traumatic loss, and the aftermath of such events (Simon 2011). This reflects that museums cannot ignore these "topics of global importance", such as war and death evident in their communities (Trofanenko 2011, p. 492). In effect, visits to these types of memorials, museums, and similar heritage places, increasingly involve deliberate "encounters with the abject – with horror, depravity or terror" (Witcomb 2013, p. 153).

Several reasons for the development of these museums are suggested including "a desire for redemption, the need to memorialise in order to grieve and the need to demarcate the present from the past while also recognising the ongoing effects of the past on the present" (Witcomb 2013, p. 153). Furthermore, Blumer (2015) notes that representation of histories of violence in cultural institutions such as museums and memorials is frequently framed in terms of conflict and hierarchies or competitions of suffering. The histories of violence can educate the public about ongoing forms of injustice and can aim to "incite social change by emphasizing the human rights lessons to be learned from human atrocity" (Blumer 2015, p. 131). Similarly, Sodaro (2011) suggests that memorial museums preserve and educate about past violence, whereby the present and future can learn from past mistakes so that "never again" will such an atrocity happen. These memorial museums vary greatly in their methodologies, displays, and approaches, but these museums seek to have some form of social and individual impact such as educating the next generation and helping to prevent future forms of atrocity by revealing the past. Even if such a museum simply increases awareness about certain human rights violations there is an enormous value in preserving sites of atrocity and the history they embody so they can never be viewed as *a-historical* or neutral venues (Hamber 2012). Instead memorial museums have become an active part of the post-conflict landscape and they reflect this context and they shape it (Hamber 2012). Memorial museums are devoted to:

> …remembering, explaining, and educating about past atrocities, conflicts, and trauma and, as such, appear to be products of a shift in the way that societies relate to the past: from the celebratory – and often forgetful – emphasis on past triumphs of the nineteenth century nation-states to a reflective effort to come to terms with the negative legacy of the past and to learn its lessons. (Sodaro 2011, p. 80)

There are many examples of memorial or conflict museums around the world such as the Anne Frank Museum in Amsterdam, the Nanjing Massacre Memorial Museum in eastern China, Robben Island in South Africa, the US Holocaust Memorial Museum in Washington, DC, the House of Terror in Budapest in Hungary, and the Kigali Genocide Memorial Centre in Rwanda (see also Chap. 11).

The Challenges of Representing National Conflict at Museums

Memorial museums cover such "difficult heritage" as slavery, apartheid, and genocide, and museum scholars and practitioners have found that legacies of trauma and violence can provide a useful basis for collective memory and learning (Failler 2015). However, (hi)stories of genocide, enslavement, and war are difficult histories because these events "of gross human injustices go against our moral understanding of what it means to be part of civilized society" (Rose 2016, p. 7). These histories about slavery, genocide, mass murder, war, disease, racism, and sexism are difficult to tell because of the pain and suffering experienced by the victims and also because the histories continue to impact our lives today (Rose 2016). Traditionally, public commemoration stresses the necessity to collectively "forget" divisive episodes particularly because in some countries, such as in the US, history has been marred by centuries of racial conflict. However, descendants of the atrocities may want to find ways to memorialize these difficult pasts and, as result, this is where memorial museums can have a role to play in consciousness-raising projects (Autry 2013). The challenge for museums, however, is to delicately negotiate the curation and exhibition of contested histories and ideas, and the inclusion of violent or traumatic subject matter in museum displays. Interpretation of these complex and sensitive topics can sometimes be difficult if curators and other museum staff are placed under pressure to package the information in a form that reflects the political and economic interests of sponsors and privileged stakeholders (Failler 2015). The difficulty of this process is recognized by Baptist (2015, p. 7) who suggested:

> To reify places that have suffered great violence; to design a site that is sure to host a reawakening of terror and grief in at least some visitors, is an aporetic puzzle and a moral burden.

Beard (2015) suggested that museum professionals who developed the National September 11 Memorial and Museum in New York faced greater challenges than most curators because of the numerous and vocal stakeholders (namely, politicians, families of the victims, developers, and the New York public), and the unique dilemmas posed of exhibiting artefacts from a massive crime scene. The museum finally opened to the public on 21 May 2014, almost 13 years after the 9/11 terrorist attacks. Sturken (2015, p. 474) goes on to note that despite the museum stating as its mission as "bearing solemn witness" to the terrorist attacks on 11 September 2001, there are other goals evident at the museum, namely:

> …to tell the story of the events of September 11, 2001, and its aftermath; to construct a political narrative of the meanings of 9/11; to commemorate those who died that day, not only in New York but at the Pentagon and in Shanksville, Pennsylvania, as well as the victims of the 1993 World Trade Center bombing; and to meaningfully provide access to key aspects of the site of Ground Zero itself.

This difficult remit is summarized by Baptist (2015) as simultaneously being a secular location and sacred place, a space for collective mourning and for individual grief. Sturken (2015, 2016) notes the mishmash and hodgepodge quality of the exhibition design at the site and suggested this reflects numerous stakeholders involved in the development of the museum and also because the 9/11 narrative jumps forward and backward, from before and after the attack. Similarly, Beard (2015, p. 151) notes the anodyne character of the exhibit scripts which "consistently eschews opinion and analysis, relying instead on eyewitness and first-person accounts to propel the narrative". Beard (2015) goes on to argue this may be appropriate given the political considerations and the deep emotional meaning for hundreds of thousands of people. Sturken (2015) suggests the museum is effective in telling the stories of survival, resilience, sacrifice, and compassion that took place in response to the attacks of 9/11, but is less effective in addressing the meaning of 9/11. Particularly, the museum's representation of Islamic faith, which is regularly attacked from Muslim leaders and constituencies (Sturken 2015). She noted that the 9/11 memorial museum represents many conflicting aspects, namely: as a memorial to those who died, a historical museum, a shrine, a sacred site, a tourist destination, and as a commercial venture (Sturken 2015).

Other examples of inherent difficulties in representing contested histories in museums are also evident. For example, "The Memorial to the Murdered Jews of Europe", also known as the "Holocaust Memorial" opened in central Berlin in 2005 after 17 years of heated debates regarding its "necessity, dedication and locale" and the challenge that the site was the "impossibility of representing the Holocaust" (Dekel 2009.p. 72). Another example is the "Changi Chapel and Museum" in Singapore which aims to "narrate, represent and perform the memory of the war as closely to how the local people (as opposed to foreigners) experienced it" (Muzaini and Yeoh 2005, p. 15). However, this proved difficult as questions were raised as to what constituted "local". Instead, Muzaini and Yeoh (2005, p. 15) suggest that perhaps the best way to commemorate the war in Singapore was to think about an "international memoryscape" where all nations involved in its "making" can also come together in its "telling".

The Role of Emotive Interpretation of Dark Historical Periods

Grief in society has been examined to determine the best means to support people who are experiencing loss (Corr and Corr 2012), and the most appropriate way to memorialize tragic events (Dauncey and Tinker 2015; Doka 2003). Local authorities have to consider the best way to allow the public to grieve and that can be a challenge for local authorities and governments to respond appropriately to perceived community needs (Kropf and Jones 2014; Nicholls 2006). Emotion has a special place in the debate about memorial museums, whether in the way emotional accounts of the past serve as vehicles for change, or the emotional nature of nostalgia in reflections on a history of political violence (Hamber 2012). These new museums "deploy strategies of applied theatrics" to invite emotional responses from visitors: to make them empathize and identify with individual sufferers and victims (Andermann and Arnold-de Simine 2012, p. 3). Therefore, victims may use atrocity heritage for a "deliberate fostering of group cohesion, place identification and ideological legitimation" (Ashworth 2002, p. 363). The overall message could be that empathy, respect, and humility are central to their purpose as human beings, where a visit can be a transformative experience and where mutual understanding and sensitive, peaceful resolve can be encouraged (Magee and Gilmore 2015).

A range of emotions can be generated by memorial museums and the associated representations of difficult histories such as fear, guilt, sympathy, empathy, disgust, and even melancholia (Rose 2016). A study of a group of Dutch people considered the intensity of emotional responses of a potential visit to a concentration camp memorial site in the Netherlands (Nawijn et al. 2015). The study revealed that individuals with a closeness to the Holocaust expected to feel most emotions more intensely. Emotions that are traditionally considered "positive" are pride, love, joy, inspiration, excitement, and affection. The respondents also expected to feel disgust, shock, compassion, and sadness. Those who looked from the viewpoint of the offenders mainly expected to feel emotions that are traditionally considered "negative", whereas those who took the point of view of victims also expected a more "positive" emotional reaction to the visit. Such findings have managerial implications regarding the way to interpret such sites (Nawijn et al. 2015). Similarly, Israeli descendants of Holocaust survivors at memorial museums who visited heritage sites and Holocaust sites of atrocity, accompanied by their survivor parents, identified a range of emotions such as "descendant empathy and identification" (Kidron 2013, p. 175). Such visits were found to help facilitate familial bonding (Kidron 2013, p. 190). In addition, Hamber (2012) found evidence of nostalgia in a study in South Africa which he named "regenerative nostalgia" due to the struggle against hardship and oppression of apartheid, followed by victory and hope for a new society and the perceived unifying peace process that ensued. Hamber goes on to note that it seems counterintuitive that nostalgia would have any place in thinking back on periods of extreme violence, but he found that nostalgia is visible in the longing for a time before the conflict and, consequently, nostalgia for the kindness shown by people during war and conflict. Indeed, recognizing nostalgia in hardship and oppression is useful for curators in that such memories are tied into sentiment and so can be used in many ways to ensure visitor experiences are poignant and memorable.

The generation of emotions via exhibits at memorial museums reflects a move away from museums having an authoritative presence and instead they have become educational and stir emotions primarily through presenting contentious issues (Trofanenko 2011; also see Chap. 25). However, Hamber (2012) notes that an overly emotional focus on the narratives of victims at such sites can limit understanding of the dynamics that cause violence.

The Role of Museums in Relation to Memory-Making, Peace-Making and Politics

In post-conflict situations, society often encourages peacebuilding via memorialization and practices of remembrance with memorials built to commemorate war, regimes of terror or violence and, moreover, reflect society's need to honour those who have died (Biran et al. 2011). Therefore, memorials are often recognized as sites for mourning, for "making politics" and for the ongoing "production of meaning" in the present (Selimovic 2013, p. 334). This reflects that commemoration can be understood as a political process, as certain memories are "spun into a coherent story" which "legitimises and delegitimises certain actions" (Selimovic 2013 p. 335). In so doing, this reflects memorials, monuments, and commemorative museums as spaces for "contentions and disjuncture" whereby victims' need and use the memorials to help them handle their loss (Selimovic 2013 p. 335). Meanwhile, Hankivsky and Dhamoon (2013) focus on one such well-publicized and controversial debate—namely, the Canadian Museum of Human Rights decision to create a separate Holocaust museum. This prompted various groups whose nations and populations have experienced genocide to make demands that the museum provides equal treatment of other national and international atrocities. Hankivsky and Dhamoon (2013, p. 900) describe this as creating a "Pandora's box of irreconcilable traumatic memory competition" which they entitled "Oppression Olympics" whereby groups compete for the mantle of the most oppressed.

Sevcenko (2010) suggests that for heritage sites to become effective resources in addressing conflict, they must continually mine their histories for perspectives on new problems. Hence, dialogues are invited on new issues as they arise and how local heritage sites can work together to build national or regional dialogue on common points of conflict. For example, the Ellis Island Immigration Station in New York as well as the Angel Island Immigration Station in San Francisco developed programmes whereby visitors "walked" in the "footsteps" of immigrants who had shaped their heritage sites and, subsequently, learnt about national debates in which those immigrants had taken part. Visitors were then encouraged to participate in a facilitated dialogue on what perspective that history provides for issues arising in their communities. These so called "Sites of Conscience" aim to develop public consciousness or acceptance of certain facts as indisputable. These sites describe particular human rights violations and then invite visitors to consider ways in which they can participate in shaping the future.

Pedagogical Challenges of Interpreting Dark Events

Regarding new museology, Trofanenko (2011, p. 492) suggests museums "cannot rest on their pedagogical laurels and continue to insist on their authoritative role". Instead they need to think about how best to impart the information to visitors using interactive and experiential engagement with the past (Sodaro 2011). Indeed, to appeal to younger generations who have grown up immersed in technology, these new experiential museums are focused more on teaching and creating an experience for the visitor than they are on more traditional museological functions of collecting and displaying. Instead of simply telling a story of the past, experiential museums seek to make the visitor experience it (Sodaro 2011). For instance, the Imperial War Museum in London "embrace the visitor's body" by using interactive audio-visual equipment to allow the visitor to become "part of the museum text" (Garton Smith 1999, p. 142). This is achieved by allowing visitors to experience sensations of the blitz (i.e., the German bombing of London during World War II) and trench warfare through the vibrations of the "bombs" and various smells. Garton Smith (1999, p. 142) believes that by using the visitor's body, the museum "unsettle the authority of the curator and the auratic object" and creates a crossover between high-culture and popular-culture.

Witcomb (2013) considered immersive experience museums that encouraged tourists to encounter the abject. Indeed, through immersive interpretation strategies, visitors explicitly take on the identity of those who were considered social outcasts or victims of atrocities and disasters. This playing, re-enactments or reconstruction help cast visitors as the role of victims and create a space for affective as well as cognitive forms of interaction (Witcomb 2013). Conversely, a study by Yair (2014) found that because of the trauma the Third Reich engendered, German memorials appear to be reluctant to advocate, direct, or lead. They provide information but shy away from manipulative educational strategies that they associate with the Third Reich. They intentionally avoided manipulating emotions or directing visitors to arrive at pre-determined moral conclusions, and refrained from using expressive props to create authentic experiences. Yair (2014) found that despite the many possibilities for introducing visitors to authentic and challenging exhibits and artefacts, German memorial sites and documentation avoided using emotive cues. Consequently, without a more challenging pedagogy, these sites are unlikely to create key educational experiences with lasting effects on visitors' identities (Yair 2014).

From an interpretative perspective, Oren and Shani (2012) suggest that theming can be effectively implemented at museums and dark tourism sites. They examined museological presentation at a memorial museum (Yad Vashem Holocaust Museum in Jerusalem), within the art of storytelling, the thematic utilization of architecture, use of up-to-date technologies and advanced museum techniques, and the promotion of a clear educational agenda. They argue theming methods enable a museum to provide multidimensional experiences that are educational and which, subsequently, draws in and impacts upon visitors through an amalgamation of storytelling, technology, and education. Theming methods enable a museum to focus the visitor more effectively on the exhibits, by combining numerous elements that involve visitors' senses throughout the visit. In the case of Yad Vashem, the theming method can also be implemented at popular dark tourism sites, by remaining committed to historical truth and by avoiding unnecessary effects that may divert visitors' attention from fundamental elements of the site (Oren and Shani 2012).

Accordingly, interpretation at a site of dissonant heritage needs to be respectful, yet often the contemporary nature of the topic makes it difficult to present in terms of standard interpretative technique and modalities of presentation. On occasion, one would prefer to "forget unpleasant pasts rather than deliberately remember an atrocity" so there should be a compelling reason to justify the "deliberate act of remembrance of past trauma" (Ashworth 2002, p. 363). The rawness of the (dark) event in the minds of the local community and society can have an impact on the way that the topic is interpreted (Frew 2012). Indeed, avoiding sensationalization and dramatization is important as is avoiding a voyeuristic approach, though emotional engagement of the visitor is critical. Thus, a balance is required to subtly engage the visitor. Such museums and memorial sites need to provide interpretation that encourages sympathy with the victims, their families, and the survivors (Frew 2012). For instance, at visitor sites associated with World War II bombings in Darwin, Australia, very few gruesome images of death are provided, which is particularly interesting given the hundreds of deaths that occurred due to the bombings. The non-sensationalist aspect of the exhibits allows the visitor to visit the sites and experience quiet reflectiveness and contemplation, which in turn encourages respectfulness (Frew 2013).

Conclusion

Dark tourism allows individuals and groups to travel to a variety of destination types, partake in different experiences and often reflect upon their own identity and the perception of the place visited. Such tourism has an increasingly broad appeal due to the opportunity to become involved in new and sometimes confronting experiences (Frew and White 2011). Indeed, there is a critical intersection between dark tourism and place identity (White and Frew 2013) and, consequently, museums have a role to play in that intersection.

Museums are changing from an "old" to a "new museology" that has shaped museum functions and roles (McCall and Gray 2014). New museology helps narrate untold stories and help repurpose museums in line with multicultural and intercultural states and communities (Shelton 2013). Many museums are beginning to "critically engage a past that is both inspiring and despairing" and have started to move away from a singular emphasis on affirming presentations of "patriotism, triumph and great deeds" towards a greater appreciation of the complexities, competing motivations, and potential for aggression inherent in human relationships (Simon 2011, p. 432). Museums maintain their mandates of collecting and exhibiting objects but are increasingly displaying difficult topics and events, which are definitive and controversial and encourage public discussion of timely and important topics (Trofanenko 2011). Therefore, the museum needs to ensure the "difficult knowledge" (Blumer 2015; Failler 2015; Segall 2014) presented by the museum creates an "unsettling – yet productive and necessary – second hand encounters... when learning about or being exposed to themes of violence, suffering and death, as well as their aftermath" (Blumer 2015, p. 127). Ultimately, Halbwachs (1992) suggest that how the past is remembered tells us more about the present than it does the past. Indeed, memorial museums tell us much more about the priorities, desires, and self-understanding of the societies that build them than they do about the terrible pasts that they remember. This "new form of commemoration" which combines commemorative and museological functions helps an interpretation of the past and may prevent violence in the future (Sodaro 2011).

References

Andermann, J., & Arnold-de Simine, S. (2012). Introduction memory, community and the new museum. *Theory, Culture and Society, 29*(1), 3–13.
Ashworth, G. J. (2002). Holocaust tourism: The experience of Krakow-Kazmierz. *International Research in Geographical and Environmental Education, 11*(4), 363–367.
Autry, R. (2013). The political economy of memory: The challenges of representing national conflict at 'identity-driven' museums. *Theory and society, 42*(1), 57–80.

Baddeley, C. (2013). *Managing the new museology: The changing role, purpose and management of Australian museums since 1980*. Unpublished dissertation, University of Canberra.

Baptist, K. W. (2015). Incompatible identities: Memory and experience at the National September 9/11 Memorial and Museum. *Emotion, Space and Society, 16*, 3–8.

Beard, R. (2015). Exhibit review: The National September 11 Memorial & Museum. *The Public Historian, 37*(1), 150–153.

Biran, A., Poria, Y., & Oren, G. (2011). Sought experiences at (dark) heritage sites. *Annals of Tourism Research, 38*(3), 820–841.

Blumer, N. (2015). Expanding museum spaces: Networks of difficult knowledge at and beyond the Canadian Museum for Human Rights. *Review of Education, Pedagogy, and Cultural Studies, 37*(2–3), 125–146.

Carter, J., & Orange, J. (2012). Contentious terrain: Defining a human rights museology. *Museum Management and Curatorship, 27*(2), 111–127.

Corr, C., & Corr, D. (2012). *Death & dying, life & living*. Belmont: Cengage Learning.

Dauncey, H., & Tinker, C. (2015). Media, memory and nostalgia in contemporary France: Between commemoration, memorialisation, reflection and restoration. *Modern & Contemporary France, 23*(2), 135–145.

Dekel, I. (2009). Ways of looking: Observation and transformation at the Holocaust Memorial, Berlin. *Memory Studies, 2*(1), 71–86.

Doka, K. J. (2003). Memorialization, ritual and public tragedy. In Lattanzi-Licht, M. & Doka, K. J. (Eds.) *Living with Grief. Coping with Public Tragedy*, Washington, DC: Hospice Foundation of America (pp. 179–189).

Failler, A. (2015). Hope without consolation: Prospects for critical learning at the Canadian Museum for Human Rights. *Review of Education, Pedagogy, and Cultural Studies, 37*(2–3), 227–250.

Frew, E. A. (2012). Interpretation of a sensitive heritage site: The Port Arthur Memorial Garden, Tasmania. *International Journal of Heritage Studies, 18*(1), 33–48.

Frew, E. A. (2013). Dark tourism in the Top End: Commemorating the bombing of Darwin. In L. White & E. A. Frew (Eds.), *Dark tourism and place identity: Managing and interpreting dark places* (pp. 248–263). Oxon: Routledge.

Frew, E. A., & White, L. K. (Eds.). (2011). *Tourism and national identities: An international perspective*. Oxon: Routledge.

Garton Smith, J. (1999). Learning from popular culture: Interpretation, visitors and critique. *International Journal of Heritage Studies, 5*(3/4), 135–148.

Halbwachs, M. (1992). *On collective memory* (trans. Coser, L. A.). Chicago: University of Chicago Press.

Hamber, B. (2012). Conflict museums, nostalgia, and dreaming of never again. *Peace and Conflict: Journal of Peace Psychology, 18*(3), 268.

Hankivsky, O., & Dhamoon, R. K. (2013). Which genocide matters the most? An intersectionality analysis of the Canadian Museum of Human Rights. *Canadian Journal of Political Science, 46*(04), 899–920.

Hudson, K. (1977). *Museums for the 1980s: A survey of world trends*. Paris/London: UNESCO/Macmillan.

Kidron, C. A. (2013). Being there together: Dark family tourism and the emotive experience of co-presence in the holocaust past. *Annals of Tourism Research, 41*, 175–194.

Kropf, N. P., & Jones, B. L. (2014). When public tragedies happen: Community practice approaches in grief, loss, and recovery. *Journal of Community Practice, 22*(3), 281–298.

Lorente, J. P. (2012). The development of museum studies in universities: From technical training to critical museology. *Museum Management and Curatorship, 27*(3), 237–252.

Magee, R., & Gilmore, A. (2015). Heritage site management: From dark tourism to transformative service experience? *The Service Industries Journal, 35*(15–16), 898–917.

Mairesse, F., & Desvallées, A. (2010). *Key concepts of museology, International Council of museums*. Paris: Armand Colin.

McCall, V., & Gray, C. (2014). Museums and the 'new museology': Theory, practice and organisational change. *Museum Management and Curatorship, 29*(1), 19–35.

Muzaini, H., & Yeoh, B. (2005). Contesting 'local' commemoration of the Second World War: The case of the Changi Chapel and Museum in Singapore. *Australian Geographer, 36*(1), 1–17.

Nawijn, J., Isaac, R-K, Gridnevskiy, K., &, van Liempt, A. (2015). Holocaust concentration camp memorial sites: An exploratory study into expected emotional response, Current Issues in Tourism, https://doi.org/10.1080/13683500.2015.1058343.

Nicholls, S. (2006). Disaster memorials as government communication [online]. *Australian Journal of Emergency Management, 21*(4), 36–43. Availability: http://search.informit.com.au/documentSummary;dn=413036481093685;res=IELHSS. ISSN: 1324-1540. Cited 04 July 15.

Oren, G., & Shani, A. (2012). The Yad Vashem Holocaust Museum: Educational dark tourism in a futuristic form. *Journal of Heritage Tourism, 7*(3), 255–270.

Rose, J. (2016). *Interpreting difficult history at museums and historic sites*. Lanham: Rowman and Littlefield.

Ross, M. (2004). Interpreting the new museology. *Museum and Society, 2*(2), 84–100.

Segall, A. (2014). Making difficult history public: The pedagogy of remembering and forgetting in two Washington DC museums. *Review of Education, Pedagogy, and Cultural Studies, 36*(1), 55–70.

Selimovic, J. M. (2013). Making peace, making memory: Peacebuilding and politics of remembrance at memorials of mass atrocities. *Peacebuilding, 1*(3), 334–348.

Sevcenko, L. (2010). Sites of conscience: New approaches to conflicted memory. *Museum International, 62*(1–2), 20–25.

Simon, R. I. (2011). A shock to thought: Curatorial judgment and the public exhibition of 'difficult knowledge'. *Memory Studies, 4*(4), 432–449.

Sodaro, A. (2011). *Exhibiting atrocity: Presentation of the past in memorial museums,* PhD, New School University, New York, USA.

Sturken, M. (2015). The 9/11 memorial museum and the remaking of ground zero. *American Quarterly, 67*(2), 471–490.

Sturken, M. (2016). The objects that lived: The 9/11 museum and material transformation. *Memory Studies, 9*(1), 13–26.

Trofanenko, B. M. (2011). On difficult history displayed: The pedagogical challenges of interminable learning. *Museum Management and Curatorship, 26*(5), 481–495.

White, L. K., & Frew, E. A. (Eds.). (2013). *Dark tourism and place identity: Managing and interpreting dark places.* Oxon: Routledge.

Witcomb, A. (2013). Understanding the role of affect in producing a critical pedagogy for history museums. *Museum Management and Curatorship, 28*(3), 255–271.

Yair, G. (2014). Neutrality, objectivity, and dissociation: Cultural trauma and educational messages in German Holocaust memorial sites and documentation centers. *Holocaust and Genocide Studies, 28*(3), 482–509.

29

Souvenirs in Dark Tourism: Emotions and Symbols

Jenny Cave and Dorina Buda

Introduction

This chapter explores the proposition that the act of 'souveniring' recent and/or ancient places of death, disaster, or atrocities is a more emotionally immersive experience—and thus less cognitively controlled—than in other tourism contexts. We introduce and explore the notion of 'dark souvenirs' (also see Chap. 27) which encompass unlikely forms, redolent of darkness, emotions, and affective experiences in the dark tourism context of places connected to death, disaster, or atrocities.

Dark tourism is often imagined as the alternate to hedonic, mass tourism. Dark tourism places are dystopic, where experiences of perceived, actual, and real risk are the norm (Isaac 2015). Yet, at heart, when narratives are co-created to define identity, they represent utopic ideals (Tinson et al. 2015). Moreover, this co-creation of tourist identity and subjectivities is performed through affects, emotions, and feelings that circulate between and amongst tourists, locals, and 'dark' places (Buda 2015a). Affective tourism, a term introduced by Buda (2015a, p. 3), refers to 'the ways in which affects, emotions, and feelings are accessed, felt, experienced and performed in encounters between touring bodies and places'.

J. Cave (✉)
University of Waikato, Hamilton, New Zealand

D. Buda
University of Groningen, Groningen, The Netherlands

Thematically, dark spaces are contradictory places of shadow versus light, postmodernity versus heritage, that are usually imbued with emotion. Attempts to construct and manage layered interpretive experiences, which include souvenirs offered for sale at sites of disaster, atrocity, death, and tragedy, might ultimately fail. Some 'dark tourists' are motivated not by entertainment or objectivity but by the affective engagements *with* and *in* those places redolent of 'darkness' (Buda 2015a), and by visceral drives to experience the site, the place, the memories, and its symbolism (Anderson and Smith 2001; Isaac 2015). The visceral drive, a Lacanian death drive of sorts, is akin to a constant force, a nuance of affect at the junction between life and death, which is not understood in a biological sense of physical demise of the body, nor in opposition to life (Buda 2015a, b). Such a psychoanalytical drive creates connections and divisions between local people, tourists, souvenirs, and dark places. This is partly because of the intensity of emotions and affects brought forth and felt in dark places, remembered, and (re)told afterwards.

Spaces and places connected to 'darkness' also parallel utopia and penalties of acts of faith, since there are similarities between constructs of mediaeval pilgrimage and dark tourism practices (Korstanje and George 2015; Collins-Kreiner 2015). Furthermore, some might argue that dark tourists 'feel' the dark space more emotionally than physically (Yan et al. 2016), encountering the essence of place without critique, and immersing themselves in echoes of danger, in the company of strangers who are there for the same 'instinctual' reasons (also see Chap. 10). Yet, divisions of the physical from the emotional can hardly be obtained, since 'instinctual reasons' are felt and performed *in* and *through* the physical body, driven by visceral intensities to push one's physical and emotional boundaries (Buda and Shim 2014; Buda 2015a).

Souvenirs belong to and represent material cultures expressive of place, subjectivity, and identity that are integral to dark tourism experiences. Most tourists collect souvenirs while visiting dark places to gather them as prized objects that mediate memories of places and experiences. Tourism generates a mobility of objects, since objects often travel in conjunction with movements of people and are rarely sets of objects fixed in place (Urry 2000). Cultures, knowledge, and attitudes also travel with and through souvenirs. Yet the majority of research regarding souvenirs engages with the mainstream context of the formal tourism industry.

The aim of this chapter, therefore, is to bring existing literature on souvenirs together with literature on dark tourism and, specifically, with theories of emotion in dark tourism. We do so to contend that souvenirs and souveniring in dark places of death, disaster, and atrocities are more imbued with emotional poignancy than in other tourism contexts and, in so doing, become tools through which (hi)stories are told and (re)negotiated.

Souvenirs and Souveniring

'Souvenirs' can be a synonym for tourism art, 'airport art', and other objects created specifically for tourists, used as a token of memory and the experiences that occur at the moment of acquisition. This action of souveniring is connected to the meaning of the word rooted in the Latin verb *subvenire* (meaning 'to remember' or 'to occur to the mind') (van den Hoven 2005).

Objects are classed as souvenirs and invested with a place-based narrative at the point of consumption (Hume 2013). However, their meaning is assigned retrospectively, upon the re-telling of travel experiences. The value to the acquirer is attributed within a hierarchy of souvenir values that span from end-of-life (when consigned to rubbish) to reincarnation status within domestic social contexts, and from sites where return of the object is possible and purposeful value remains to geographically distant sites where only the material value remains when the object is possessed (Gregson et al. 2011).

Souvenirs may be obtained during informal encounters as gifts, purchased during formal transactions in the tourism and retail industries (Cave and Buda 2013; also see Chap. 26), or acquired as detritus (Saunders 2004). Awareness of 'the Other', reciprocal gaze, and exoticism are engaged by both suppliers and purchaser/receivers (of gifts) of souvenirs in their choices to make, provide, and offer these tangible mementos to others (Morgan and Pritchard 2005; Watson and Till 2010). Souvenirs often connect to an out-of-the ordinary and/or extraordinary moment in the tourism experience.

Souveniring, as the act of acquiring an object or image that represents an experience, is central to host-guest interactions for many cultures, generating souvenir production and purchase as gift or emblem (Chan 2006), as well as less moral appropriation, pocketing, purloining, or theft. Thus, souvenirs and souveniring are inseparable from the phenomenon of travel and tourism (Cave et al. 2013a)—the act of touring, attracting tourists, and providing for their entertainment and accommodation.

The tourism industry has reached socio-cultural prominence in the global economy because of its connection to industrialisation, waged employment, and changes to labour laws to embrace weekends and holiday breaks in urban settings; yet, paradoxically, it is also connected to the anti-industrial push of travel for health. Indeed, Thomas Cook's original tours exemplify the reach of affordable recreational travel to mass markets of increasingly emancipated women and group travel for workers to escape industrial conditions. In the Western, economically developed world, the history of travellers acquiring souvenirs of place and memories occurs from Imperial Rome and Egyptian explorer-travellers, mediaeval collectors of religious relics, to pilgrims who souvenir their faiths, and to contemporary tourists and their accompanying activities. Moreover, the Grand Tour permitted social elites to 'souvenir' cultural heritage and amass private collections that demonstrated the status of 'having been' to their peers and subordinates (Jolliffe and Smith 2001).

Souvenir production can be traced back to iconographic moulds made in the fourth century for pilgrims in the Middle East (Cline 2014). Collectors sought genuine representations of sites and artistic works through acquirement of antiquities and authentic artefacts of the pre-industrial era. However, mass production of souvenirs, identified as 'cheap and inauthentic', coincided with the Industrial Revolution in the latter eighteenth century and globalised by post-World War II middle-class travel (Paraskevaidis and Andriotis 2015).

Purchased and/or collected by tourists, souvenired objects are exhibited in people's homes, private collections, and museums. Souvenirs as tangible objects epitomise memorable experiences at destinations (Hashimoto and Telfer 2007; Anderson and Littrell 1995) and are stages in the tourism experience (Lury 1997). Individuals reflexively use souvenirs as touchstones of memory that (re)create polysensual and multi-sensory tourism experiences both during and after the journey (Morgan and Pritchard 2005). The object-place relationship helps make sense of the visit during and after the experience, whereas the place-person relationship means that the souvenir symbolically embodies the qualities of a specific place and reminder of its significance, years afterwards (Swanson 2013).

Souvenirs are also trinketised miniatures of complex global forces and networks of world experience such as travel, information, and infrastructure, but which ironically are not read in the wider register (Hutnyk 2011). Souvenirs correspond with present-day mobility as some people move fluidly around the world as a result of migration, leisure and travel purposes, or displacement (Urry 2000). As such, traveller, tripper, and tourist objects give insight into role-playing, epistemological relativism, and verification of objective realities—a sense of 'one's being in the world' (Lasusa 2007) that evokes past experiences and transnational realities. Tourists are more likely to understand authenticity as implying a certain degree of participation in the life and heritage or the event. Souvenirs then are geographic artefacts, locked into the memory of the collector and the collector's experience of the site— so that the date of production, the name of the producer, and monetary value are to some extent immaterial (Hume 2013).

Geographically displaced souveniring refers to souvenirs made in a place different than the visited destination, but available in gift shops and purchased by tourists. However, the souvenir may represent a country, region, city, specific attraction, or a combination of several geographical scales (Hashimoto and Telfer 2007). Temporally speaking, souvenirs represent continua of heritage, carried from the past via the object into the current day, and are iconic constructions from the recent past or markers of specific, significant contemporary events. Many of the objects now considered as tourist souvenirs in modern society were originally produced to fulfil utilitarian needs (e.g., baskets, pottery) or religious symbols. Arguably, less knowledgeable tourists seek the object rather than seeking out high-quality craftsmanship.

From the tourist perspective, souvenirs are imbued with affective and emotional values that represent the authenticity of a tourism place or activity (Trinh, Ryan and Cave 2014). Authenticity lies at the crossroads between reality and perception, both reality and its perception being felt and performed viscerally via emotions and feelings. Reality can be considered as mediated and simulated, while authenticity is a chimaera. Conventional definitions of authenticity invoke such terms as real, genuine, true, and actual. Such terminology can be contested on grounds of the non-existence of a general truth or an autonomous reality. The form of souvenirs shifts between 'authentic' to increasingly commodified, and between local production to production in places other than their emblematic cultures. This leads to 'constructed authenticity' developed by non-cultural producers which is adopted over time by the originators as a new version of their own culture and heritage (Swanson 2013).

'Authentic' souvenirs are in fact socio-culturally and spatially constructed and imbued with emotions (Swanson 2013). In practice, however, tourists are less familiar with such debates and more likely to conform to the dichotomies of authentic/inauthentic, true/false, genuine/fake (Waitt 2000). Nonetheless, tourists can feel disappointment upon realising that the purchased items are not made of local materials or by local producers, but are mass-produced elsewhere and imported from places where labour is cheap (Staiff and Bushell 2013).

'Objective' authenticity is supported by a maker's mark, locally made attributions, and native producer's rights to legitimate cultural provenance. However, authenticity can be understood as subjectively connected by cultural bias and an individual's personal connection with the object, perceived connection with the vendor/producer or place, an uncritical view which opens a door to fakery. 'Constructive' authenticity refers to imagined souvenirs, often developed by non-native producers or corporations, that depicts archetypical and idealised views of people and place, used to market a destination or culture for tourism, but which conform to stereotypes and not contemporary realities. In some respects, the contemporary artisan constructs a translated view of culture to balance tradition with modernity. This occurs, too, in vendor transactions where historically authentic souvenirs, priced to reflect their cultural and aesthetic value, co-exist in locked display cases alongside open display racks of mass- and cheaply produced versions of the same objects at much lower prices (Swanson 2013). Souvenir vendors, therefore, have the capacity to influence the emotional tourist experience through their commercialisation practices.

Souvenirs as Commodity

Souvenirs as objects of cultures imbued with emotions and symbolic significance of heritage are embedded in the pasts they (re)present. They are global-local (g/local) representations (Ritzer 2003), valued as commodities that contribute to informal household and formal market economies. The concept of *glocalisation* is helpful in avoiding oversimplification of complex social, cultural, spatial, and economic processes involved in souveniring. The global-local relationship refers to a nexus that ties together economic factors and socio-cultural responses that mediate between globalisation and local adaptation. On the global-local continuum, souvenirs then refer to both the universality and contextuality of tourism transactions (Cave et al. 2013a).

The souveniring process plays a crucial role globally, in sustaining tourism economies, community relationships, and cultural structures. While supply can refer to production of souvenirs by locals and demand to their consumption, such a distinction is rarely clear-cut. Supply of souvenirs can happen at the place of production, in markets (Cave and Buda 2013), on the retailers' inventories, and in strategies of marketing and selling souvenirs (also see Chap. 26).

The form of souvenirs is 'agreed' communally as representations of a destination or experience and appear in 'conformity to traditional style', authorised and sustained by the community and the tourists. These may be produced in traditional and modern materials, although non-traditional techniques may also be used to produce traditional designs, or the original may be miniaturised (Hume 2013). New production 'protects the original' for objects consciously made to be shared with others, without disclosing manufacturing secrets that could result in loss of identity, traditional knowledge, or intellectual property (Cave 2009).

The role of shopping and retail activities in travel has received more attention in recent years, and souvenirs play an important role in destination economies (Ipkin and Wan 2013). Indeed, souvenirs are often offered for sale at roadside stalls, markets, producer storefronts, souvenir shops, art galleries and museums, heritage sites, events and festivals, tourist activities, retail precincts, or malls. As commodities of emotions and experiences in dark places, however, souvenirs are valued for their 'intrinsic use' value, which is recognised in the direct relation between a 'thing', emotion, and human need. The souvenir exchange value is a social process based on a logic of equivalence where an object has symbolism which commands other commodities in exchange (Watson and Kopachevsky 1994), but which varies by cultural interpretation. Commoditised objects acquire value and meaning when used within the contexts of global economic marketplaces, as well as displays in gallery and museum exhibitions, private collections, or in domestic interiors (Phillips and Steiner 1999).

Commodification of materials happens through a creative corporeal and object-oriented process of tourist encounters, wherein tourists are strolling through different spaces, sensing, bargaining, and connecting the social to the material (Regi 2014). These negotiated processes are as much socio-cultural as they are emotional, whereby the feeling of the corporeal connects the material not only to the social, but also to the emotional and affective implications of souveniring. Arguably, these implications are more intense in the context of dark tourism; for darkness, whether of places, activities, or situations, stirs deeper emotions than other tourism contexts. Souvenirs also have a 'sign value' based upon difference, usually connected to emotions, whose acquisition enhances exclusivity and a bond forged between the tourist and the 'dark' place, activity, or event as part of the dark tourism experience. Souvenirs also possess spiritual value as sacralised totems, relics, and icons (Paraskevaidis and Andriotis 2015).

The Study of Souvenirs and Souveniring

Research into the economic and socio-cultural production and consumption of souvenirs began in earnest in the 1970s as investigations into the production of handicrafts and ethnic art as transformative of traditional art (Cohen 1979, 1988) and cultural loss against a background of increased globalisation.

Particularly, Graburn's *Ethnic and Tourist Arts*, written through the lens of art history and anthropology, produced a typology of material cultures of the 'fourth world' (contemporary indigenous cultures subject to internal colonisation). Culturally plural contexts evolve as cultures encounter others, to coalesce in acculturated or hybrid forms in the modern world. Graburn's (1976) framework describes a matrix of aesthetic-formal sources/traditions that varies with intended audiences, contact with mainstream and material/technical opportunities. Hence, societal forms intended for minority fourth world consumption are categorised as minority society (functional/traditional), novel/synthetic (reintegrated), and dominant society (popular) categories, whereas forms intended for external civilisation use are respectively: minority society (commercial/fine), novel/synthetic (souvenir/novelty), and dominant society (assimilated/fine). The persistence of traditions depends upon continued internal demand, the availability of raw materials, time and work focus, skills and knowledge, peer-group reward/prestige, and a role in ritual or gift-exchange (Graburn 1976). Furthermore, over time the dominant culture appropriates the arts of the colonised to incorporate them into mainstream tourist art forms.

Stewart (1993) classified souvenirs as 'sampled' and 'representative'. Sampled souvenirs are obtained directly by the individual tourist with no intervention by the host culture and not available as consumer goods (e.g., shells or stones). Meanwhile, 'representative' souvenirs are purchasable representations of exterior sights such as miniature baskets or postcards. Gordon (1986) developed a souvenir typology that has been widely used, and, as a result, Gordon's investigation of the souvenir phenomenon offered tourism studies an initial and comprehensive typology of souvenirs. The typology offers five souvenir subcategories: pictorial images, piece of the rock souvenirs, symbolic shorthand souvenirs, marker souvenirs, and local products. Pictorial images refer to postcards and photographs, while pieces-of-the rock souvenirs represent the visited environment from which natural objects are saved. Symbolic shorthand souvenirs are manufactured rather than natural materials. Marker souvenirs act as memory-triggers and bring about images of and experiences in those places. Indigenous foods, like chillies from Mexico or olive oil from Greece, are part of the fifth subcategory of souvenirs, that of local products.

Philips and Steiner (1999) 'unpack' the complexity of how commoditised objects acquire value and meaning in the contexts of the world economic marketplace and display in gallery and museum exhibitions, private collections, and in domestic interiors. The forms of souvenirs produced are 'agreed' communally as representations of a destination and appear in 'conformity to traditional style', authorised and sustained by the community and the tourists. Nevertheless, the focus is a transcultural context, especially in former colonies, and is written from a Euro-American point of view, located in peripheral places in Africa, Asia, Oceania, and North America.

Meanwhile, Hume (2013) follows the practices of collecting and developing collections of 'Other' cultures by Western society in modern times (premodern, colonial, early modern). His work proposes a system to describe all souvenirs that use the medium, the maker's mark, relational, invitational, and iconofetish features. Fetishism aligns with souvenirs since they both substitute for phenomena that are no longer available and, thus, help to sustain the holiday after the event and recover emotionally from the emptiness left from its ending.

As noted earlier, souvenirs have also been examined as *glocalised* commodities which play a key role in sustaining culture and identity, a sense of place, and the tourism economy in tourism peripheries (Cave et al. 2013b). Recent tourist theories turn away from the dematerialised tourist landscape and see spaces (sights, places, markets, etc.) as performed consequences of human-material interactions. Thus, souvenirs are subject to materiality theory as travellers interact with the material environment and unavoidably collect and carry things home to authenticate the travel experience (Regi 2014). The production of souvenirs can also be used by cultural agents to resist, respond, and interpret global influences at local levels, but by enacting the processes of *glocalisation*, they actively preserve and sustain craft traditions, cultural structures, community relationships, and economies (Cave et al. 2013b).

Three contemporary streams of research can be identified in literature. Firstly, souvenirs are holders of meanings that embody an *object-person-place* relationship and function as props, evidence, memory, and substitute. Secondly, souvenirs are *tradable commodities* that can be researched from the perspectives of producers and distributors or retailers and consumers. Finally, souvenirs more generally as the *commodification* of material culture express the importance and value of the souvenir economy to tourism as a whole. The study of souvenirs and souveniring spans multiple disciplines, together with research into shopping, retailing, handicrafts, authenticity, material culture, gift-giving practices, and consumption, and may be examined through the lens of aesthetics, economics, or philosophy (Swanson and Timothy 2012). There is a gap, however, in understanding the production, consumption, and significance of souvenirs in general and, in particular, 'dark souvenirs' in connection to emotions, which this chapter now seeks to address.

The Study of Emotions in (Dark) Tourism and Souveniring

Emotions in tourism are crucial in that they affect the ways we travel and how we interact with others, with places, with material culture, and with 'things'. Yet, in tourism studies, limited attention has been paid to the significance of emotions and affects. Recently, however, the concept of affective tourism has been put forth to refer to 'the ways in which affects, emotions, and feelings are accessed, felt, experienced and performed in encounters between touring bodies and places' (Buda 2015a, p. 3). This responds to calls from some tourism researchers who argue that '[t]he omission of studies and narratives which locate ... 'emotion' in tourism, whether that of the tourist or the host, is a problem which has been noted and addressed by very few scholars' (Jamal and Hollinshead 2001 p. 67). Some accounts of emotions of pride and shame (Johnston 2007; Tucker 2009; Waitt et al. 2007), fear (Buda 2015b; Mura 2010), and desire (Buda and Shim 2014) in tourism have been recently published.

Specifically, Johnston (2007, p. 29) examines the 'construction and performance of lesbian tourism geographies' and argues that pride and shame are productive and lived through gendered and sexualised bodies. Meanwhile, Waitt et al. (2007) analyse emotions of shame and pride in a tourism context offered by travelling, walking, climbing, touching, and being touched by Uluru in Australia. They discuss moral gateways that shame and pride open and close as they explore joint management strategies of national parks. Probyn (2004) also analyses her everyday shame as she travels to Uluru. Similarly, Tucker (2009) recognises and discusses her own shame and discomfort in a tourist encounter in the Turkish village of Göreme. She argues 'if we are to understand tourism encounters more fully, it is necessary to examine closely their emotional and bodily dimensions' (Tucker 2009, p. 444).

Other studies in tourism view emotions as variables in quantitative approaches. Bigne and Andreu (2004, p. 682) employed 'a bi-dimensional approach to emotions – pleasure and arousal dimensions' to research consumer satisfaction in interactive museums and theme parks in Spain. Their findings offer suggestions for marketing managers to use emotion as a segmentation variable to 'maximise satisfaction and loyalty' (Bigne and Andreu 2004, p. 692). 'Consumer-related emotions' in connection to satisfaction, arousal, and pleasure are also studied by Faullant et al. (2011, p. 1423). They investigate the adventurous activity of mountaineering by analysing self-administered questionnaires completed by 240 alpinists in the Austrian Alps.

Fear and joy are considered as basic emotions influenced by 'neuroticism and extraversion, respectively, and … in conjunction with cognitive appraisals influence tourist satisfaction'. Their findings suggest that '[j]oy has direct effects on satisfaction that are not mediated by cognitions; fear's inverse effects on satisfaction are fully mediated by cognitions' (Faullant et al. 2011, p. 1423).

Research on satisfaction and loyalty concerning emotions has received some attention from tourism scholars with business and managerial approaches. For instance, Yuksel and Yuksel (2007, p. 703) examine within a specific Turkish town setting 'whether risk perceptions in shopping affect tourists emotions, their satisfaction judgment and expressed loyalty intentions'. Within tourism management, however, emotions are considered as biologically hardwired and subject to cognitive processes. Indeed, tourism management studies essentialise, universalise, and objectify emotions. Furthermore, emotions are examined as separate from affects, feelings, and senses in a body that is generally assumed white, able, and masculinist. Such studies treat emotions as items that can be measured using mathematical formulae and numerical analysis models.

Emotions, feelings, affects, and embodied senses are intensely political issues, and also highly gendered ones too. The gendered politics of knowledge production has been a key reason why embodied emotions, feelings, and senses have been marginalised in previous studies of tourism, including dark tourism (Buda 2015b). Dark tourism presents the ways anxiety, death, and atrocities are commodified as products and experiences at dark sites, focusing mainly on 'merchandising and revenue generation' (Lennon and Foley 2000 p. 12; also see Chap. 27). Encounters with emotions of fear, fascination with death, anger, and the like, felt and performed in a dark tourism place, are productive and can cause attachments and divisions between tourists, places, and the things/souvenirs collected from such a place.

Subsequently, studies by Dunkley et al. (2011) and Dunkley (2007, 2015) on battlefield tourism capture emotional aspects of the experiences of 25 tourists who participated in a tour of World War I battlefields of the Somme and Ypres. While the narrative is kept within the 'moral discourse of the 20th century frequently presented as heritage, education and history' (Seaton 1996 p. 224), Dunkley et al. recognise the importance of emotions and the potentially cathartic impacts such visits have. They even touch upon the psychoanalytic concept of voyeurism, but seem to be a bit reticent to fully engage with it: '[w]hilst there may well be elements of voyeurism in their encounters, battlefield tours emerge as complex, deeply meaningful and in some cases life-changing experiences for the individuals involved in this study' (Dunkley et al. 2011, p. 866).

Other researchers openly explore dark tourism in connection with the concept of voyeurism (Buda and McIntosh 2013), and other such psychoanalytical concepts such as desire (Buda and Shim 2014) and the death drive (Buda 2015b). In so doing, they contribute to broader emotional, affective, and sensuous engagements with places and material objects, amongst which are souvenirs too. However, connections between dark tourism, souvenirs, and emotions are not sufficiently teased out in current dark tourism studies, and in this chapter, we call for more attention to this aspect.

'Dark' and 'Emotional' Souvenirs

Souvenirs are part of multi-levelled visitor interpretation (McKinnon and Carrell 2015) and the creation of stories, symbols, and images about individuals and actions which affect those who live in the areas. They are emblematic of the events, whether current or past, and are personal or collective emotional representations of the experience, to be shared with others as well as retained as private and never shared. Irrespective of the temporal dimension of the dark event and, therefore, of the identity of a dark tourism place, emotions pervade most, if not all, experiences and transactions at such places. These dark places can be one of past or current atrocities, pain, and sorrow.

Contexts of dark tourism where dark souveniring occurs include places of on-going socio-political turmoil (Buda 2015c; Buda and Shim 2014); post-disaster sites (Korstanje and George 2015); recent and ancient heritage (Magee and Gilmore 2015; Horodnikova and Derco 2015); battlefields and submerged and land-based archaeological sites (McKinnon and Carrell 2015); post-war cemeteries (Horodnikova and Derco 2015); sites of infamous murders (Kim and Butler 2015); and sites of staged horror such as Dracula's castle and imagined movie versions.

An example of souvenir creation connected to dark tourism comes from Aotearoa in New Zealand, where souvenirs made of the iridescent paua shell set in silver in the shape of native birds were produced during World War II to supply expeditionary American forces stationed in the country with brooches to send home. The practice was continued after the war as protected employment for returned service men. Souvenirs were also made by soldiers in active theatres of war such as the sweetheart brooches fashioned from badges and shell casings (van de Wijdeven 2016). These might be considered 'dark souvenirs' since they are items souvenired by soldiers and others from theatres of war and transformed into objects of beauty and poignant remembrance, of not only the maker who may have survived but also the fallen.

Consequently, they are subliminal reminders to the wearer, maker, and observer to the 'never again' aspect of engaging in conflict and war.

The development of dark sites into places of tourism where souvenirs are sold might be explained by a 'sacralisation' model, where sites are invested with quasi-religious mystique and, thus, become a place of ritual pilgrimage for tourists who seek tangible symbols of the place, the memory, meanings, and the experience (Seaton 1999). Moreover, souvenir creation, production, and commercialisation can be concurrent with experiences of ongoing political troubles. For example, in Palestine/Israel (see also Chap. 9), current souvenirs showcase the decades-long regional conflict such as the Nativity scene surrounded by the separation wall/security fence (Isaac 2015). Dark tourism then is a complex socio-cultural and spatial phenomenon that involves atrocities, death, and disaster experienced both individually and collectively. The question remains however, should these experiences be commodified into consumptive items such as souvenirs?

In the example of Palestine/Israel, souvenirs in this area represent important tools through which (hi)stories of socio-political and economic turmoil are told and negotiated. Israeli and Palestinian manufacturers and retailers of souvenirs assert their identities, their claims in the region, and tell their stories. In the West Bank in Palestine, for example, the ongoing regional conflict has transformed the phenomenon of tourism in this region—within spatial, socio-cultural, and political contexts. 'Icons' of the ongoing Israeli-Palestinian conflict, such as the separation wall/security fence, turnstiles at checkpoints, and even refugee camps are represented in the souvenirs produced and sold to tourists. An array of emotions such as fear, fun, and excitement along with sensory engagements of the gaze at the existing separation wall/security fence, touch of the cold turnstiles at checkpoints, and the smell of olive trees, become part of souveniring experiences in these dark tourism places. Indeed, miniaturised souvenirs of olive trees, walls and the like purchased by tourists may act as emotional enhancements when the more intense in-place souveniring process ends, and tourists leave the area and (re)tell their experiences.

Similarly, in another example, the case of murder sites in the USA often means that post-touristic visits to the locations are accompanied by entertainment, eating out, photo opportunities, and the purchase of souvenirs (Gibson 2006) which bring dark tourism into the day-to-day experience of travel and tourism. Moreover, notions of kitsch or 'teddy-bearification' of the 9/11 terrorist action have been accused of trivialising and politicising the event and creating a spectacle and subjectivities that polarise opinion (Potts 2012). Shopping patterns in an area where an event of atrocity has just happened are negatively affected immediately following the event. It is not by chance that the 9/11 atrocity was immediately followed by a presidential plea to keep shopping, to keep consuming, and to keep visiting New York City, because the post-industrial American economy depends on spendthrifts (Brown et al. 2012).

Specific victim groups may possess an animosity toward touristic activity and consumption at sites where ethnic or religious persecution has taken place, and this may be reflected in avoidance of visits by those groups, thereby suggesting a potential lack of interest to visit. Indeed, it might be the reverse, that the passion and emotions associated with interest in such dark places are just too difficult to bear, or not always easy to manage and channel (Podoshen and Hunt 2011). Thus, souvenirs of the material and immaterial kinds found and experienced at these sites, if following ethical guidelines, can offer routes for tourists to negotiate, channel, and reflect on the emotions felt at the site and upon return to their homes. Arguably, such is the case with tourists in Israel/Palestine, where the emotionality of tourist places in areas of ongoing socio-political conflict are embodied in the sites, the tours, and interactions with locals by global tourists, as well as souvenirs offered for sale (Buda et.al, 2014)

Places of consumption, such as retail outlets associated with dark sites (e.g., museum gift shops), highlight a tension of economic opportunities to earn income with difficult choices about whether sales diminish the significance of the dark event by miniaturisation and symbolism. They are challenged too by issues of taste and decency, especially at places where deaths occurred (Brown 2013). Cultural standards and practices may also differ as well as familiarity with the subject matter (Biran and Hyde 2013). Museums in places of darkness, such as the Holocaust Remembrance Centre in Westerbork, the Netherlands, which commemorates victims of World War II (Isaac and Çakmak 2014), are continuously confronted not only with how history should be interpreted and presented (see also Chap. 28) but also the type of souvenirs to commercialise at such sensitive locations. Managers of museums may want to avoid the critique of commodification for profit only. In this respect, the Holocaust Remembrance Centre in Westerbork decided in 2015 to sell jewellery as souvenirs as well as works of art of a former member of the resistance during World War II (Hindriksen 2015).

Yet, commercialising such dark souvenirs makes a museum or souvenir shops more up-to-date and connected to contemporary visitors and local people. Shops can act as meaning-making vehicles by reconfirming the significance of the site or visitor attraction through its merchandise selection (Brown 2013). There are also opportunities to shape meanings to help the public make sense of dark events that can be embodied in the displays, and/

or the souvenirs available for purchase (Walby and Piché 2015). Museums in specific places of darkness, where a past atrocity occurred and is commemorated, can present their stories and souvenirs related to ideas of peace—a most cherished goal of humanity. Museums as visitor attractions may frame peace in their entire souveniring process, from views that accept war as inevitable to views strongly condemning any form of violence. Instead of creating a frame in which war or military response to violent attacks are justified, they argue for the view that any and all dark and violent attacks are crimes against humanity, requiring international co-operation and the strengthening of international law (Herborn 2014; Meijer 2016). This view corresponds with Urbain's (2013, p. 149) claim that 'when confronted with a place of trauma, there is a crucial difference between stating that "this will never happen to us again" and "this will never happen again to humanity"'. Therefore, emotions evoked by such views can generate a sense of global citizenship, which souveniring and 'collecting' commemorative places of dark events may contribute.

Conclusion

It is fair to assume that as long as people will travel, we will collect mementos and souvenirs of the place, the trip, and the activities involved. In addition, as long as disasters, death, and atrocities continue to occur, people will want to witness such events and to visit such places—whether it is during the actual occurrence or for later remembrance. Therefore, souvenirs as 'touchstones of memory' (Morgan and Pritchard 2005 p. 29) mediate tourism experiences in time and space and recreate emotional and multi-sensory engagements in and with places. These multi-sensual aspects coupled with emotional and affective experiences generated by souvenirs and souveniring processes are an important aspect of the dark tourism phenomenon.

Along with material roles of souvenirs, the symbolic significance and socio-cultural construction and production of souvenirs is also of future research interest. In a culture-bound and place-specific context, interactions between hosts, locals, tourists, and visitors can be viewed as encounters with difference. As such, they are affected by perceptions of Self versus Other as well as by perceptions of space and place. Interactions and encounters take place across a range of locales that, following 'Otherness' theory, are utopic or idealised, heterotopic or encountering difference, and dystopic - referring to places to be avoided. In a context in which most understandings of souvenirs are of Western Anglophone nature, there is an increasing need to explore souvenirs, souveniring, and 'dark experiences' from the perspectives of other cultures, such as eastern European, Indian, and Asian (see also Chap. 6).

This chapter has canvassed several issues—the act of souveniring, the nature of souvenirs and their meaning, as well as a review of the literature on their study. We conclude that the act of souveniring recent and/or ancient places of death, disaster, or atrocities is indeed more emotionally immersive—and thus less cognitively controlled—than the experience of other tourism contexts. Hence, experiences associated with souveniring are more affective, multi-layered, and less controlled than hedonistic tourism. They are charged with contradictions that are simultaneously dystopic and utopic, that both repel and attract and are more redolent of the frisson of danger and envy. Yet, conversely, such experiences are also imbued with remembrance, hope, and peace.

The issue of whether dark tourism should be commodified into consumptive items, such as souvenirs, reveals reluctance on the part of site operators to encourage trade in objects that are authentic realities. Instead, souvenir items such as art and jewellery, and so forth, are chosen to essentialise, universalise, and offer objectivity and to symbolise the realities of events that took place. They also serve to distance the consumer from the deepest emotions. As a concluding thought, event tourism that commemorate and re-enact historical battles and war scenarios can also be seen as spectacle, supported by a lively trade in militaria, and historical role play is seen as complementary to remembrance (Ryan and Cave 2007). Perhaps these are safer options, yet should tourism be safe? Is not the sense of risk and vicariousness at its heart a source of appeal that continues to generate demand? Through the generations, we may seek to relive, remember, and recoil from dark places. Indeed, a visitor who walks on the shores of ANZAC Cove at Gallipoli in Turkey, site of an infamous World War I battle, may wonder if the white pebbles underfoot should be trodden upon or viewed from a distance and, consequently, does not pick them up, but lets them lie.

References

Anderson, L., & Littrell, M. (1995). Souvenir purchase behaviour of women tourists. *Annals of Tourism Research, 22*, 328–348.

Anderson, K., & Smith, S. J. (2001). Editorial: Emotional geographies. *Transactions of the Institute of British Geographers, 26*(1), 7–10.

Bigné, J. E., & Andreu, L. (2004). Emotions in segmentation: An empirical study. *Annals of Tourism Research, 31*, 682–696.

Biran, A., & Hyde, K. F. (2013). New perspectives on dark tourism. *International Journal of Culture, Tourism and Hospitality Research, 7*, 191–198.

Brown, J. (2013). Dark tourism shops: Selling 'dark' and 'difficult' products. *International Journal of Culture, Tourism, and Hospitality Research, 7*, 272–280.

Brown, S., McDonagh, P., & Shultz, C. (2012). Dark marketing: Ghost in the machine or skeleton in the cupboard? *European Business Review, 24*, 196–215.

Buda, D. M. (2015a). *Affective tourism: Dark routes in conflict*. London: Routledge.

Buda, D. M. (2015b). The death drive in tourism studies. *Annals of Tourism Research, 50*, 39–51.

Buda, D. M. (2015c). Tourism in conflict areas complex entanglements in Jordan. *Journal of Travel Research, 55*, 835–846.

Buda, D. M., & Mcintosh, A. J. (2013). Dark tourism and voyeurism: Tourist arrested for 'spying' in Iran. *International Journal of Culture, Tourism and Hospitality Research, 7*, 214–226.

Buda, D. M., & Shim, D. (2014). Desiring the dark: 'A taste for the unusual' in North Korean tourism? *Current Issues in Tourism, 18*, 1–6.

Buda, D. M., D'Hauteserre, A.-M., & Johnston, L. (2014). Feeling and tourism studies. *Annals of Tourism Research, 46*, 102–114.

Cave, J. (2009). Embedded identity: Pacific Islanders, cultural economies and migrant tourism product. *Tourism, Culture and Communication, 9*, 65–77.

Cave, J., & Buda, D. M. (2013). Souvenirs as transactions in place and identity: Perspectives from Aotearoa New Zealand. In J. Cave, L. Jolliffe, & T. Baum (Eds.), *Tourism and souvenirs: Glocal perspectives on the margins*. Bristol: Channel View.

Cave, J., Jolliffe, L., & Baum, T. (2013a). Theorising tourism and souvenirs: Glocal perspectives. In J. Cave, L. Jolliffe, & T. Baum (Eds.), *Tourism and souvenirs: Glocal perspectives from the margins*. Bristol: Channel View Publications.

Cave, J., Jolliffe, L., & Baum, T. (Eds.). (2013b). *Tourism and souvenirs: Glocal perspectives from the margins*. Bristol: Channel View Publications.

Chan, Y. W. (2006). Coming of age of the Chinese tourists: The emergence of non-Western tourism and host–guest interactions in Vietnam's border tourism. *Tourist Studies, 6*, 187–213.

Cline, R. H. (2014). A two-sided mold and the entrepreneurial spirit of pilgrimage souvenir production in late antique Syria–Palestine. *Journal of Late Antiquity, 7*, 28–48.

Cohen, E. (1979). A phenomenology of tourist experiences. *Sociology, 13*, 179–201.

Cohen, E. (1988). Authenticity and commoditization in tourism. *Annals of Tourism Research, 15*, 371–386.

Collins-Kreiner, N. (2015). Dark tourism as/is pilgrimage. *Current Issues in Tourism, 19*(12), 1185–1189.

Dunkley, R. A. (2007). *The thanatourist: Collected tales of the thanatourism experience*. PhD, University of Wales Institute, Cardiff.

Dunkley, R. A. (2015). Beyond temporal reflections in thanatourism research. *Annals of Tourism Research, 52*, 177–179.

Dunkley, R., Morgan, N., & Westwood, S. (2011). Visiting the trenches: Exploring meanings and motivations in battlefield tourism. *Tourism Management, 32*, 860–868.

Faullant, R., Matzler, K., & Mooradian, T. A. (2011). Personality, basic emotions, and satisfaction: Primary emotions in the mountaineering experience. *Tourism Management, 32*, 1423–1430.

Gibson, D. C. (2006). The relationship between serial murder and the American tourism industry. *Journal of Travel and Tourism Marketing, 20*, 45–60.

Gordon, B. (1986). The souvenir: Messenger of the extraordinary. *Journal of Popular Culture, 20*, 135–146.

Graburn, N. (1976). *Ethnic and tourist arts: Cultural expressions from the fourth world*. Berkeley: University of California Press.

Gregson, N., Crang, M., & Watkins, H. (2011). Souvenir salvage and the death of great naval ships. *Journal of Material Culture, 16*, 301–324.

Hashimoto, A., & Telfer, D. J. (2007). Geographical representations embedded within souvenirs in Niagara: The case of geographically displaced authenticity. *Tourism Geographies, 9*, 191–217.

Hindriksen, J. (2015). *Living with Holocaust tourism: Locals' emotions in Hooghalen and Westerbork, The Netherlands*. Master of Arts, University of Groningen, Groningen.

Horodnikova, J., & Derco, J. (2015). Dark tourism, thematic routes and possibilities for innovation in the Slovak Republic. *Tourism, 63*, 241–246.

Hume, D. (2013). *Tourism art and souvenirs: The material culture of tourism*. London: Routledge.

Hutnyk, J. (2011, April 15). Tourism: Trinketization and the Manufacture of the Exotic. *Anthropologies of Tourism* [Online].http://www.anthropologiesproject.org/2011/04/tourism-trinketization-and-manufacture.html

Ipkin, A. W., & Wan, Y. K. P. (2013). A systematic approach to scale development in tourist shopping satisfaction: Linking destination attributes and shopping experience. *Journal of Travel Research, 52*, 29–41.

Isaac, R. K. (2015). Every utopia turns into dystopia. *Tourism Management, 51*, 329–330.

Isaac, R. K., & Çakmak, E. (2014). Understanding visitor's motivation at sites of death and disaster: The case of former transit camp Westerbork, the Netherlands. *Current Issues in Tourism, 17*, 164–179.

Jamal, T., & Hollinshead, K. (2001). Tourism and the forbidden zone: The underserved power of qualitative inquiry. *Tourism Management, 22*, 63–82.

Johnston, L. (2007). Mobilizing pride/shame: Lesbians, tourism and parades. *Social and Cultural Geography, 8*, 29–45.

Jolliffe, L., & Smith, R. (2001). Heritage, tourism and museums: The case of the North Atlantic islands of Skye, Scotland and Prince Edward Island. *International Journal of Heritage Studies, 7*, 149–172.

Kim, S., & Butler, G. (2015). Local community perspectives towards dark tourism development: The case of Snowtown, South Australia. *Journal of Tourism and Cultural Change, 13*, 78–89.

Korstanje, M. E., & George, B. (2015). Dark tourism: Revisiting some philosophical issues. *e-Review of Tourism Research, 12*, 127–136.

Lasusa, D. (2007). Eiffel Tower key chains and other pieces of reality: The philosophy of souvenirs. *Philosophical Forum, 38*, 271–287.

Lennon, J. J., & Foley, M. (2000). *Dark tourism*. New York: Continuum.

Lury, C. (1997). The objects of travel. In C. Rojek & J. Urry (Eds.), *Touring cultures: Transformations of travel and theory*. London: Routledge.

Magee, R., & Gilmore, A. (2015). Heritage site management: From dark tourism to transformative service experience? *Service Industries Journal, 35*, 898–917.

Mckinnon, J. F., & Carrell, T. L. (2015). *Underwater archaeology of a Pacific battlefield: The WWII battle of Saipan*. New York, NY: Springer.

Morgan, N., & Pritchard, A. (2005). On souvenirs and metonymy: Narratives of memory, metaphor and materiality. *Tourist Studies, 5*, 29–53.

Mura, P. (2010). 'Scary … but I like it!' young tourists' perceptions of fear on holiday. *Journal of Tourism and Cultural Change, 8*, 30–49.

Paraskevaidis, P., & Andriotis, K. (2015). Values of souvenirs as commodities. *Tourism Management, 48*, 1–10.

Phillips, R. B., & Steiner, C. (1999). *Unpacking culture: Art and commodity in colonial and postcolonial worlds*. Berkeley: University of California Press.

Podoshen, J., & Hunt, J. M. (2011). Equity restoration, the Holocaust and tourism of sacred sites. *Tourism Management, 32*, 1332–1342.

Potts, T. J. (2012). 'Dark tourism' and the 'kitschification' of 9/11. *Tourist Studies, 12*, 232–249.

Probyn, E. (2004). Everyday shame. *Cultural Studies, 18*, 328–349.

Regi, T. (2014). Tourism and souvenirs, glocal perspectives from the margins. *Journal of Tourism and Cultural Change, 12*, 90–92.

Ritzer, G. (2003). Rethinking globalization: Glocalization/globalization and something/nothing. *Sociological Theory, 21*, 193–209.

Ryan, C., & Cave, J. (2007). Cambridge Armistice Day celebrations: Making a carnival of war and the reality of play. In C. Ryan (Ed.), *Battlefield tourism*. Amsterdam: Elsevier.

Saunders, N. J. (Ed.). (2004). *Matters of conflict: Material culture, memory and the First World War*. London: Routledge.

Seaton, A. V. (1996). Guided by the dark: From thanatopsis to thanatourism. *International Journal of Heritage Studies, 2*, 234–244.

Seaton, A. V. (1999). War and thanatourism: Waterloo 1815–1914. *Annals of Tourism Research, 26*, 130–158.

Staiff, R., & Bushell, R. (2013). Souvenirs at the margin? Place commodities, transformations and the symbolic in Buddha sculptures from Luang Prabang, Laos. In

J. Cave, L. Jolliffe, & T. Baum (Eds.), *Tourism and souvenirs: Glocal perspectives from the margins*. Bristol: Channel View Publications.

Stewart, S. (1993). *On longing: Narratives of the miniature, the gigantic, the souvenir, the collection*. Durham: Duke University Press.

Swanson, K. (2013). Souvenirs of the American southwest: Objective or constructed authenticity. In J. Cave, L. Jolliffe, & T. Baum (Eds.), *Tourism and souvenirs: Glocal perspectives from the margins*. Bristol: Channel View Publications.

Swanson, K., & Timothy, D. J. (2012). Souvenirs: Icons of meaning, commercialization and commoditization. *Tourism Management, 33*, 489–499.

Tinson, J. S., Saren, M. A. J., & Roth, B. E. (2015). Exploring the role of dark tourism in the creation of national identity of young Americans. *Journal of Marketing Management, 31*, 856–880.

Trinh, T. T., Ryan, C., & Cave, J. (2014). Souvenirs and perceptions of authenticity—The retailers of Hoi An, Vietnam. *Tourism Management, 45*, 275–283.

Tucker, H. (2009). Recognizing emotion and its postcolonial potentialities: Discomfort and shame in a tourism encounter in Turkey. *Tourism Geographies: An International Journal of Tourism Space, Place and Environment, 11*, 444–461.

Urry, J. (2000). *Sociology beyond societies: Mobilities for the twenty-first century*. London: Routledge.

Van De Wijdeven, E. (2016). *Vintage Paua Shell Jewellery*. Auckland: Bateman Publishing.

Van Den Hoven, E. (2005). Personal souvenirs as ambient intelligent objects. sOc-EUSAI '05. 2005 joint conference on smart objects and ambient intelligence: Innovative context-aware services: Usages and technologies, 123–128.

Waitt, G. (2000). Consuming heritage: Perceived historical authenticity. *Annals of Tourism Research, 27*, 835–862.

Waitt, G., Figueroa, R., & Mcgee, L. (2007). Fissures in the rock: Rethinking pride and shame in the moral terrains of Uluru. *Transactions of the Institute of British Geographers, 32*, 248–263.

Walby, K., & Piché, J. (2015). Making meaning out of punishment: Penitentiary, prison, jail, and lock-up museums in Canada. *Canadian Journal of Criminology and Criminal Justice, 57*, 475–502.

Watson, G. L., & Kopachevsky, J. (1994). Interpretations of tourism as commodity. *Annals of Tourism Research, 21*, 643–660.

Watson, A., & Till, K. E. (2010). Ethnography and participant observation. In D. De Lyser (Ed.), *The SAGE handbook of qualitative geography*. Los Angeles: Sage.

Yan, B. J., Zhang, J., Zhang, H. L., Lu, S. J., & Guo, Y. R. (2016). Investigating the motivation-experience relationship in a dark tourism space: A case study of the Beichuan earthquake relics, China. *Tourism Management, 53*, 108–121.

Yüksel, A., & Yüksel, F. (2007). Shopping risk perceptions: Effects on tourists' emotions, satisfaction and expressed loyalty intentions. *Tourism Management, 28*, 703–713.

30

'Shining a Digital Light on the Dark': Harnessing Online Media to Improve the Dark Tourism Experience

Peter Bolan and Maria Simone-Charteris

Introduction

The tourism industry has seen some strong growth and development in recent times (Ivanov and Webster 2013). Likewise, the digital industry continues to develop and evolve at an incredible pace, infiltrating people's everyday lives and their workplaces (Chaffey 2015). All sectors and forms of tourism need to embrace the importance of digital in terms of how to market, engage with visitors and provide memorable and meaningful experiences. Every day tourists are checking out destination information, researching visitor sites and other tourist experiences, booking hotel rooms and airline flights and sharing their thoughts on social media. Tourists increasingly take their mobile devices on holiday to access and share information and enhance their overall experience (Baggio and Chiappa 2014).

This chapter, therefore, examines how dark tourism can utilise digital media to improve and provide a more immersive and memorable experience for the (dark) tourist. In addressing this crucially important aspect, a three-strand approach is taken. Firstly, the realm of social media is investigated in terms of how such platforms can be used for marketing and promotion of dark tourism destinations (see also Chap. 26) but also to engage with the dark tourist online in a meaningful and significant way, thereby establishing a relationship with such tourists and enhancing their level of experience. Secondly, the chap-

P. Bolan (✉) • M. Simone-Charteris
Ulster University Business School, Coleraine, UK

ter addresses the world of mobile applications and how to cater to the ever-growing appetites of those tourists who increasingly use their smartphones and tablets to stay connected. Indeed, harnessing such technologies as geo-location, augmented reality and gamification through mobile devices to provide new ways and new forms of interpretive information for the dark tourist that will inform, engage and immerse them in a whole new level of experience. Finally, the chapter examines the concept of blogs and related online forums, focusing on how such digital platforms can foster and develop information-sharing and research collaboration in the realm of dark tourism. Throughout all three dimensions, examples of good practice will be highlighted as well as how the technology is evolving for the future. The chapter concludes by outlining some critical insights that could help to inform new strategic directions for developing dark tourism much more effectively in the digital world.

The Dark Tourism Phenomenon

Dark tourism—the tourism of sites of tragedy—is not a new phenomenon; pilgrims as travellers have long been drawn to sites of crucifixion, sacrificial death or where death was entertainment such as the Colosseum in Roman times. During the mediaeval period, people gathered to see public executions such as at the Maumbury Rings in Dorchester, UK, (see also Chap. 2). Whilst more recently, Ground Zero in New York and the Paris tunnel where Princess Diana lost her life have become essential tourist itineraries (Stone 2006). Such is the eclecticism of macabre-related attractions from recreated death of the London Dungeon to real mass extermination sites such as the Nazi death camps in Poland and elsewhere in Europe, to the sites of famous celebrity deaths (e.g., John Lennon or Elvis Presley), or major disasters (e.g., New Orleans after Hurricane Katrina) that tourism scholars have attempted to identify different forms of dark tourism ranging from battlefield tourism, to cemetery tourism, to disaster tourism, to holocaust tourism, to political tourism, to name but a few (Simone-Charteris and Boyd 2010; Trotta 2006).

Attempts have also been made to identify different intensities of dark tourism. According to Miles (2002), for example, there is a difference between sites associated *with* death and sites *of* death. Because of this, a distinction may be made between 'dark' and 'darker' tourism with journeys to sites of death constituting a further degree of empathetic travel, namely darker tourism. Similarly, Stone (2006, p. 147) refers to 'shades of darkness'; according to the author, dark tourism products lie along a 'fluid and dynamic spectrum of intensity', whereby particular sites are conceivably 'darker' than others, depending upon various defining characteristics, perceptions and product traits. Earlier, Seaton (1996, 1999) had identified five possible categories of dark travel activity:

1. Travel to witness public enactments of death—for example, the sightseers who rush to sites of plane crashes and ship sinkings;
2. Travel to see sites of mass/individual deaths after they have occurred—for example, visits to Ground Zero in New York after 9/11;
3. Travel to internment sites of and memorials to the dead—for example, visits to monuments dedicated to the fallen soldiers of both World Wars;
4. Travel to view the material evidence, or symbolic representations of, particular deaths in locations unconnected with their occurrence—for example, visits to the Holocaust Museum in Washington DC;
5. Travel for re-enactments or simulation of death—for example, re-enactments of battles carried out by American Civil War enthusiasts in the USA.

From a demand point of view, research has endeavoured to identify motives of tourists who seek and consume dark sites and attractions, including motivations such as curiosity, nationalistic reasons, commemorative reasons, search for novelty and authenticity, educational purposes, and empathy with the victims (Ashworth 2002; Causevic and Lynch 2007; Dann 1998 as cited in Stone 2006; Seaton 1999; Stone 2006; Stone and Sharpley 2008; White and Frew 2013). However, whatever the reasons for visiting sites associated with death and suffering, the appeal of a range of destinations and individual attractions associated with dark tourism shows no sign of abatement (Ntunda 2012). Visitor interest is seemingly mirrored by the academic interest that this specialised form of tourism has generated in the last couple of decades, and which has led to the establishment of the Institute for Dark Tourism Research (iDTR) at the University of Central Lancashire (UCLan), UK, which was launched by Dr Philip Stone in 2012.

Social Media and the Dark Tourist

Although according to Stone (2006, p. 146) 'the concept of dark tourism, in its various manifestations, has generated a significant amount of research and media interest' (see also Chap. 14), there has been very little significant investigation into the digital side of dark tourism and the use of digital spaces for dark tourists to congregate and share their experiences and feelings. Furthermore, there has been little investigation into how those involved with managing and marketing such a form of tourism can harness such digital landscapes and forms of technology for tourism success. Such digital aspects include in particular social media, but also mobile or smartphone applications (or apps), and in order to harness both such aspects effectively it is vitally important to address Wi-Fi connectivity.

In terms of digital media and new technology adoption, the advent of social media has fundamentally changed the nature of business communication with the customer. In the realm of tourism this has, in turn reshaped how we communicate with the tourist. Social media can be defined as 'a type of media dispersed through online social interactions and takes a variety of forms including social networking sites, blogs, wikis, podcasts, photo and video sharing, social bookmarking and virtual environments' (Flectcher and Lee, 2012, p. 505). Whilst there are many varieties and forms of social media spaces in the realm of the digital, there are a few that dominate such a landscape. Stelzner (2015) refers to the 'big five' which are Facebook, Twitter, LinkedIn, blogging and YouTube. Additionally, we have seen some of the highest growth in recent years among the picture or image-based social platforms such as Instagram and Pinterest (Chaffey 2015). One of the areas that users of social media post about most is travel and their experiences whilst on vacation. As such, the twenty-first-century traveller now avidly utilises social media pre-trip to inform their decision-making and increasingly uses such platforms during their holiday to enhance their experience and share aspects of their experience with others (White 2009). Pace of change in this respect has been rapid. Interestingly, 'it took 38 years for the radio to attract 50 million listeners, and 13 years for television to gain the attention of 50 million viewers. The internet took only 4 years to attract 50 million participants, and Facebook reached 50 million participants in only one-and-a-half years' (Nair 2011, p. 46).

With regard to the phenomenon of dark tourism (or thanatourism as it is sometimes referred to—also see Chap. 1), this has now very much entered the realm of social media. On the more 'entertainment' side of dark tourism, the London-based 'Jack the Ripper Tour', for instance, has developed a sizeable following and growing presence on Twitter (with over 1300 followers). Jim Morrison's grave in Paris has its own Facebook page, whilst on the darker side of Stone's (2006) taxonomical 'dark tourism spectrum', the former German Nazi concentration camp at Auschwitz-Birkenau in Poland has a number of highly followed social media pages on various platforms including Facebook, Instagram and Pinterest. Some of these Auschwitz-Birkenau social pages have over 200,000 likes with some user posts receiving discussion threads of as many as 55 comments to a single post. Many have posted photographs of their visit to the concentration camp, and others have uploaded video clips. These are clear indicators that such 'dark tourists' want to mark their visit there, and to comment on what they saw and what they felt, and what they experienced. Furthermore, they want to not only share this but also to participate (at least in a virtual sense) with others who have had similar feelings and experiences. Arguably, they are searching for a sense of community with other dark tourists (elements even of a shared 'suffering') whilst also tapping into elements of history and nostalgia about such tragic events. Moreover, creation of such social media pages for these 'darkest' of visitor sites can also be viewed as a form of 'remembrance'—another way not to forget the tragedy of what happened.

It seems social media is serving to illuminate new aspects of social interaction, communication and information dissemination with regard to these dark tourism sites and locales. This is providing an avenue to not only market such destinations to tourists but to provide 'shared spaces' online for dark tourists to communicate, share experiences and discuss how such places affect and influence them. For instance, 'Dark Tourism Photography' is a public group on Facebook where subscribers are invited to share photographs that they have taken at dark tourism attractions and sites worldwide, and which currently has almost a thousand members. These social media sites may also provide a source of valuable information for industry practitioners involved in the management of dark tourism destinations, ready-made repositories of useful data to researchers of the phenomenon, as well as platforms for scholars to exchange information and engage in collaborative research projects.

With regard to the latter point, the most popular Facebook group of this kind, at present, is the 'Dark Tourism Forum' and 'Dark Tourism World'. The 'Dark Tourism Forum' was founded and is administered by Dr Philip Stone (UK) and, at the time of writing, has over 3500 'likes'. Meanwhile, 'Dark Tourism World' is administered by Jorge Coelho (Portugal); it is a bilingual group where posts are written in both English and Portuguese and, at the time of writing, has over 2500 'likes'. Both groups are dedicated to the promotion and dissemination of academic research and news related to dark tourism. Another interesting Facebook group is 'Dark Tourism Worldwide'. The group, which currently has just over 400 members, is different from the previous two in that it is not purely academic oriented but caters to a combination of academics, students and potential and seasoned 'dark tourists'. The aim of this group is 'to explore dark tourism in its furthest and newest corners: physically; morally and fundamentally' (Dark Tourism Worldwide 2016).

Harnessing social media effectively has become a necessity for any form of tourism in the modern world (Munar and Jacobsen 2014; Nusair et al. 2013), and dark tourism is no exception. People's fascination for the macabre has permeated the digital realm of the social, and this inevitably has filtered through to aspects of dark tourism. Ease of access to shared virtual content and information and the size of social media platforms (i.e., numbers of users and volume of content available) whilst impacting on people's value perceptions of online sharing (Munar and Jacobsen 2014) has captured and, indeed, enthused travellers to not only share but to actively seek out opinions and advice of other tourists through these online social media.

Virtual Dark Tourism Environments

Virtual environment displays are interactive computer displays that give users the illusion of displacement to another location. Different terms have been applied to the illusion such as artificial reality, virtual reality, cyberspace, virtual worlds and virtual environment (Ellis 2016). For tourist sites to be (re-)constructed virtually, the use of high technology is necessary as tours are not confined to two-dimensional space. In virtual tourism's 3D space, the tourist can engage not only sight and hearing but also the *equilibrioceptive* (balance, direction), *proprioceptive* (movement) and *nociceptive* (pain/wellness) senses. This is usually done in the form of Virtual Reality, Quick Time, or Flash movies that allow viewers panoramically to scan the site and zoom in and out (Kaelber 2007). Whilst some researchers raise legitimate questions concerning the efficacy of online experiences compared to those offline (Cowan 2005; Dawson 2005), others see the expansion of journeys into multimedia generated hyper-reality as the future of travel and tourism (Ritzer 2005; Kaelber 2006a, b). There are many attractions that tourists can visit virtually ranging from Canterbury Cathedral in England to the Palace of Versailles in France, to Drum Castle in Scotland. These tours are used either as internet-based experiences as tasters for future visits or as a separate visualisation by those unable to visit (Arnold 2005). With regard to dark tourism specifically, at the moment, virtual dark tourism environments are scarce.

The majority of dark tourism attractions now have websites to advertise them, but they are still primarily places that tourists have to physically visit. For example, to fully participate in the convict experience at sites of former prisons, visitors will have to feel the cold dampness of a stone prison wall, feel the claustrophobic conditions of a cramped cell, lie on an uncomfortable prison mattress and feel every lump and bump of the basic metal bed.

However, some dark tourism sites do have very sophisticated 'online doorways' through which people are led in order to entice them to visit the actual physical site. Thus, to some extent, we can journey to dark sites whilst sitting at home in front of the laptop. Perhaps one of the reasons for the shortage of virtual dark tourism environments resides in the fact that providing appropriate interpretation of the visitor attractions' topic is extremely complex. Moreover, another issue is trying to appeal to a hugely divergent set of online viewers in the short period of time that 'surfers' spend on a website, whilst at the same time maintaining sensitivity to the subject matter, is a very difficult task. Dark tourism attractions, therefore, are constrained by the divergent needs to both educate (also see Chap. 25) and entertain online viewers as they do for visitors to the physical site itself (The Digital Panopticon 2014). Nonetheless, there are a few 'places' which are nearly or wholly cyber-sites of dark tourism—among these are Alcatraz and the gas chambers of Auschwitz-Birkenau.

Indeed, the US federal prison on Alcatraz Island in California's San Francisco Bay housed some of America's most dangerous felons during its years of operation from 1934 to 1963. Among those who served time at the maximum-security facility were the notorious gangster Al 'Scarface' Capone (1899–1947) and murderer Robert 'Birdman of Alcatraz' Stroud (1890–1963). No inmate ever successfully escaped the prison despite at least a dozen attempts. Today, Alcatraz Island is a popular tourist attraction as well as a cyber-tourist destination (History 2016). There are many websites that allow people to take virtual tours of Alcatraz including www.fullscreen360.com/alcatraz, http://www.virtuar.com/alcatraz/, and http://www.digitalproperties.ca/alcatraz/. In particular, www.virtuar.com/alcatraz/ allows 'surfers' to choose between virtual tours that cover different aspects of the Island and San Francisco Bay and virtual tours that specifically focus on the prison. Prison tours available include tours of the south entrance of the building, the visitation centre where prisoners were sometimes allowed to speak with visitors, the main block which was referred to as 'Broadway', inside a cell of the main block, the shower room (which was a dangerous place where fights between inmates often occurred), the barber shop, the entrance to D block where solitary confinement cells without daylight were located, the dining hall and the inmate entrance wing on the ground floor (Virtuar 2016). The virtual tours are high definition and are so realistic that it feels as one is in the actual prison. The tours' authenticity evokes a range of emotions, which are not very different from those that the authors experienced when they visited other prisons in person—for instance, the Crumlin Road Gaol in Belfast, Northern Ireland, and the Napier Prison in Hawkes Bay, New Zealand.

For many people, Auschwitz-Birkenau stands for a moral universal *sans pareil* (unparalleled). The systematic killing of Jews by the Nazi German regime and what is now known as the Holocaust (or Shoah) has become a generalised symbol of human suffering and moral evil and provides an opportunity for humanistic learning (Alexander 2002). Visitor numbers to the Auschwitz-Birkenau Memorial and Museum in Poland have seen annual visitations grow exponentially, and in 2015 the former concentration and death camp received 1,725,700 visitors (Auschwitz-Birkenau State Museum 2015b). However, the museum faces a continuing problem of representation, for today most of it looks nothing like it did at its liberation by Soviet forces in 1945. Whilst the physical site may be difficult to reach for some and contains remnants of the past that have either disintegrated or been substantially altered, or are physically inaccessible, virtual Auschwitz tours exist that allow a different appropriation of an obliterated traumascape (Kaelber 2007). The State Museum of Auschwitz-Birkenau's (2015) website offers one of these tours. The tour, which is hosted on 'Remember.org', allows people to explore the remnants and surroundings of two large Birkenau crematoria with hotspots depicting adjacent elements in the landscape and textual explanation provided to the side. Another range of virtual tours of Auschwitz and other camps such as Dachau (near Munich, Germany), Fort Oberer Kuhberg (in Ulm, Germany), Mauthausen (in Austria) and Ravensbruck (north of Berlin, Germany) are offered by The Florida Center for Instructional Technology at the University of South Florida's website (2009). These tours of crematoria and other facilities provide more limited perspectives and at reduced resolutions than the tour offered by State Museum of Auschwitz-Birkenau.

These virtual reality tours of the Auschwitz crematoria focus on visual exploration. Unlike physical visitors who are not allowed to roam through the remnants of the crematoria, virtual visitors can get a close-up look of the facilities from the outside, the inside and above. However, hearing, touching, smelling and tasting are not engaged (Kaelber 2007) in a similar way to the virtual tours currently available of Alcatraz. Another limitation is that to be able to take these virtual tours, people must download QuickTime and Flash media players on their personal computers, which might put people off. In addition, virtual tours of dark attractions seem to have a limited lifespan as illustrated by the fact that some of the virtual tours mentioned by Kaelber (2007) such as the one provided by the Block Museum of Art as part of its online exhibit entitled 'The Last Expression', and the virtual tour provided by the British Broadcasting Corporation (*BBC*) as part of its 'Auschwitz' documentary are no longer available. It follows that until technology develops further and is able to provide 3D experiences that engage all senses, virtual dark tourism environments should be perhaps used as tasters for future visits rather than substitutes for physical visits.

Mobilising the Dark Tourism Experience

The mobile phone and the smartphone in particular have captured the public imagination. Essentially, the smartphone 'combines a cellular telephone with built-in applications and internet access. Digital voice services are combined with text messaging, email, web browsing, portable media players, digital cameras, pocket video cameras and GPS navigation' (Dickinson et al. 2014, p. 84). Smartphones are now being used like a digital 'Swiss Army Knife', replacing possessions like watches, cameras, books, diaries, laptops and even televisions. Within tourism, businesses, operators and organisations have to recognise this eagerness for mobile technology. Indeed, industry needs to fully utilise mobile technology and increasingly tap into its possibilities to improve how we market and promote products and services, as well as enhancing information provision and the overall visitor experience.

Tourists now take their smartphones and tablets on holiday, and they want to use them. Interpretive and experiential information (traditionally provided by signage, leaflets/brochures, guidebooks, maps and tour guides) can now be provided direct to the mobile device. This can include aspects such as augmented reality, broader multimedia experiences (video and audio), personalised/tailored tour functionality, gaming aspects (gamification), Global Positioning System (GPS), Location-Based Service (LBS) and Quick Response (QR) code technology.

This offers opportunities for those savvy enough to tap into this ever-increasing dependence of the mobile device and combine it with growing interests in various forms of dark tourism. One example of this is a mobile app entitled 'Killer GPS: Crime Scene, Murder Locations and Serial Killers' which provides users with over 470 locations around the globe where infamous murders were committed or bodies were dumped. Interactive maps, travel directions and profiles of famous serial killers are all provided through the app to the user's phone or tablet. According to Tussyadiah (2012, p. 783), 'increased interest in geographic technologies and their effectiveness in creating meaningful tourism experiences' suggests that a new way of approaching the needs of the tourist is necessary. The 'Killer GPS' app is one example of such an approach, attempting to meet an apparent insatiable interest in the macabre world of the serial killer with a dynamic and geographic-focused application that such 'dark tourists' can engage with on their mobile phones whilst travelling.

In 2012, an iPhone/iPad app was launched which uses the latest digital technology to tell the Jewish story of Oświęcim, the industrial town in southern Poland where the former Nazi German concentration and death camp Auschwitz-Birkenau is located. The app is called 'Oshpitzin'—the Yiddish name for the town. This example builds a new level of digital experience on the social media aspects mentioned earlier in connection with such former Nazi concentration camp sites. This type of immersive technology brings the stories and dark history surrounding such sites to life in ways that more traditional forms of interpretive information cannot. The creators of the app wanted a digital way to ensure people do not forget and saw this particular application as a modern way to help the tourist learn the 'true stories' behind the tragedies that took place (Gruber 2012).

In Northern Ireland, the 'Titanic in Belfast' app tells the story of the ill-fated ship through a GPS function. As tourists move around the 'Titanic Quarter' of the city, it geo-locates all the useful information to provide interpretation at various key points, whilst also linking the tourist to information on where to find transport or places to eat. This is another insightful example of an app focused around a dark site, but one which provides a wider range of tourist-centred information to cater to visitors' needs. Indeed, this example suggests that wider concept apps can incorporate elements of dark tourism without being explicitly concerned only with that form of tourism.

Selfies at Dark Tourism Attractions

A further dimension to the mobile side of digital tourism is the 'selfie', and this also pervades dark tourism. According to Hodalska (2015), taking selfies at horror sites, like concentration camps, Ground Zero or disaster-stricken areas, has become a growing trend on social media websites. It seems even places of tragedy and death are not exempt from the modern phenomenon of photographing oneself close-up using a smartphone. Taking photographs at dark tourist attractions is of course nothing new. Even ancient Greek and Roman visitors inscribed their names, places of origin and dates in stone at the Egyptian Valley of Kings (Quack 2016 cited by Tourism Review 2016). However, the composition and approach to taking the photographs have been changed by the 'selfie generation'.

As Hodalska (2015) notes, 'in places of death teenagers feel the urge to celebrate life in, what seems to them, the most 'creative' way'. Nevertheless, the very act of people taking apparent light-hearted selfies, not to mention ones where they are smiling, laughing and joking around, can be seen by many as highly disrespectful at places associated with suffering and death of others. As such, selfies taken at sites of great tragedy may be seen as something of ghoulish mobile souvenirs—but at what cost? Specifically, Reading (cited in Garde-Hansen 2011, p. 139) called this a kind of *memobilia* where 'mobile digital phone memories or memobilia are wearable, shareable multimedia data records of events or communications… which are deeply personal and yet instantly collective through being linked to a global memoryscape of the World Wide Web'. Indeed, selfies are usually shared on social media and receive likes, shares and tweets from online friends and followers because, arguably, a 'selfie serves as a "real time" performance of self, oriented towards an audience situated elsewhere' (Levine 2014). This view is supported by Quack (as cited by Tourism Review 2016), who states that those who take selfies are usually concerned about themselves the most—'Look, I'm in a Favela', 'Look I am at the Costa Concordia sinking site' (on the Italian Island of Giglio, where the ship Costa Concordia ran aground and capsized in 2012). According to Quack (as cited in Tourism Review 2016), 'some people visit disaster zones, such as the earthquake regions of Haiti, in order to elevate themselves… They pretend to be concerned, but are only there to tell themselves "how great that this didn't happen to me"'. Arguably, they want to witness the horrors of others as long as they are far away, and they can safely return home with their cameras' memory cards filled with gruesome photos that prove that they were there (Hodalska 2015). Of course, the question remains—is that right? Should the consequences of a nuclear catastrophe like the one that happened at the Chernobyl nuclear plant in Ukraine in 1986 serve as the background of one's own ego, like a tropical wallpaper? (Tourism Review 2016; see also Chap. 13).

The issue is that camera phones and tablets, which enable tourists to take selfies, have become socially acceptable tools for emotional detachment, which makes it possible for people to cope with the fear that lurks in the background. Furthermore, whilst taking photos is a way of certifying experience, it is also a way of refusing it (Hodalska 2015), or as Sontag (1977, p. 9) put it, 'by limiting the experience to a search for the photogenic, by converting experience into an image, a souvenir'. Essentially, through kitsch, we avert our eyes from tragedy (Harris 2002). A similar opinion is shared by Durkin (2003, p. 47) who believes that 'by rendering death into humour and entertainment we effectively neutralize it; it becomes innocuous, and thus less threatening' (also see Chap. 8). Perhaps, this is what Phoebe McWilliams was trying to accomplish in August 2012 when she took a photo of herself at Ground Zero and posted it on Twitter with a hashtag #hangover (Hodalska 2015). It follows that, whilst the smartphone and mobile devices in general bring positive aspects and advantages, particularly through social media and bespoke apps harnessing augmented reality, gamification, GPS positioning and QR code technology; they also carry a potential darker side themselves, especially when it comes to the selfie phenomenon. Whether through thoughtlessness or direct intention, there is little doubt that tourists taking jovial self-images at dark tourism locations elicit feelings of disrespect among some and even contempt in extreme cases, as advocated by authors such as Hodalska (2015).

The Dark Tourist and the Blogosphere

Blogs (a form of social media created by Tim Berners-Lee in 1992) have proliferated rapidly in recent years and are growing in popularity. According to WP Virtuoso, in 2013 there were approximately 152 million blogs on the internet, and a new blog is created somewhere in the world every half a second, which means that 172,800 blogs are added to the internet every day (WP Virtuoso 2013). Current estimates put the number of active blogs in existence as being in the order of 450 million (Bolan 2015). This trend has important implications for travel and tourism. Indeed, a key issue in tourism is the lack of direct experience with a tourism product, thus its quality and benefits cannot be evaluated before the product is consumed. The use of blogs allows potential travellers to engage in a virtual community that shares tourism experiences online (Wang et al. 2002). Traditionally, word of mouth (WOM) has been considered as a more trustworthy source of information compared to official tourist information sources, and today blogs can be considered as a new digital form of WOM. The blogosphere in tourism contains different types including consumer to consumer (C2C), business to business (B2B), business to consumer (B2C) and government to consumer (G2C) blogs, all of which have important implications for tourism and destination marketing (Schmallegger and Carson 2008).

The vast majority of travel and tourism blogs on the internet belong to the personal C2C category. Within this category, blogs are often used to publish personal travel stories and experiences online, to keep in touch with friends and relatives at home and as a way to interact socially with like-minded people, as well as to share positive and negative experiences with other travellers (Pan et al. 2007). Examples of dark tourism blogs that are used to this end include 'The Bohemian Blog', 'Travel Darkling' and 'Grief Tourism'. The Bohemian Blog is an alternative travel journal dedicated to the macabre and bizarre founded in 2011 by Darmon Richter, a British freelance writer and photographer (see also Chap. 10). Richter uses the blog as a platform to post photos that he has taken and articles that he has written about a range of dark tourism destinations and attractions such as the Tombs of Istanbul in Turkey, the Ruins of the Chisinau Ghetto in Moldova and Bulgaria's socialist-era monuments. He also uses the blog to recruit travel partners to join him on commercial travel ventures.

Similar to the Bohemian Blog, 'Travel Darkling' is a travel blog written by a freelance travel journalist and editor Anita Isalska, who has a seemingly fascination for the 'dark side'. Among her most recent posts are photos of and pieces on Soviet-era sculptures in Eastern Europe (15 December 2014), the Anatomical Theatre in Bologna, Italy, where operations and autopsies were performed for an eager-to-learn audience of Bolognese medical students across the centuries (26 April 2014), and a range of dark sites in Czech Moravia (20 February 2014). On the blog, she also posts links to articles on dark sites and attractions that she writes for *CNN Travel*, *Lonely Planet* and *TNT Magazine*. The third blog, 'Grief Tourism', is a travel blog written by Sharon Slayton and is dedicated to different types of so-called grief tourism. The most recent post dates back to 14 August 2012 and is about plantation slavery (also see Chap. 17) and prison confinement in Angola. The blogger does not post photos on her blog but provides a link to another travel blog about vacation ideas not linked to dark or grief tourism. As noted earlier, this is in line regarding mobile apps that incorporate elements of dark tourism without being explicitly concerned only with that form of tourism.

According to Schmallegger and Carson (2008), B2B blogs are used in the realm of tourism as a networking opportunity among tourism professionals, academics, businesses and tourism organisations. They are used to share opinions and information on latest industry trends, technological developments, research findings and marketing tips. On the other hand, B2C blogs and G2C blogs are used as a medium to promote tourism products/services and destinations and to build customer relationships. Both B2C and G2C blogs tend to be written by staff members to provide readers with the latest news and insider information about the company or information on different categories of interest in the destination, such as attractions, art, events, food and beverage, or entertainment. An example of a popular dark tourist attraction that uses a blog for this purpose is the National September 11 Memorial and Museum (9/11 Memorial) at the World Trade Center in New York. The blog, called 'The Memo Blog', is accessed through a link on the Memorial's website and is written by 9/11 Memorial's staff. It provides news, discussion and information about the 9/11 Memorial. Some of the most recent posts contain an entry about the availability of two new episodes of the 'Our City, Our Story' podcast series, including about Rudy Giuliani and Marilyn Goldberg who both found themselves in the midst of the unfolding disaster at the World Trade Center on 9/11 (3 June 2016). Another podcast focused on the renaming of a Brooklyn school to honour a 9/11 firefighter, Capt. Vernon A. Richard (2 June 2016).

For travel blogs to be successful and retain currency with readers, they must be updated regularly, follow-ups must be posted about previous entries, and new content must be generated often. However, this does not always happen and not only are many travel blogs not updated regularly but are also abandoned altogether. This also applies to travel blogs that focus on dark tourism. Indeed, at the time of writing, 'Travel Darkling' and 'Grief Tourism' are examples of dark tourism blogs that have not been updated for a whilst with the latest post on 'Travel Darkling' dating back to a year ago (15 December 2014) and the latest post on 'Grief Tourism' dating back to over three years ago (14 August 2012).

Another criticism of blogs and user-generated content (UGC) sites in general is the potential for 'fake' content to be posted as sites allow users to publish comments anonymously or under false identities (Cox et al. 2009; Schmallegger and Carson 2008). For instance, it is commonly known that on TripAdvisor negative comments are sometimes posted about businesses in the travel and tourism or hospitality sector from competitors or individuals instructed by competitors, as well as positive comments are sometimes posted by employees or owners themselves. Most of the time, however, fake posts are relatively easy to detect.

Wi-Fi Connectivity

Such connected experiences (through social media and mobile) can present a great opportunity for dark tourism businesses, but this will certainly impact and dictate the need for new digital strategies in the future. For this to be relevant and meaningful, it will require provision of high-quality Wi-Fi. This is something we have known for some time, and, yet, it is seldom handled well or provided properly in a high-quality way at particular event venues, in and around certain tourism attractions, or in specific hotel and accommodation establishments (certainly in the UK at least). Some operators in these sectors have made progress but many have not, at least not in a way that tourists find efficient and indeed acceptable in this second decade of the twenty-first century.

Therefore, to be truly connected in a way which tourists are already beginning to demand means we need 'smart' facilities—that is, smart hotels, smart restaurants and smart visitor attractions—where Wi-Fi is of high quality, free and always on. The benefits to free or low-cost marketing and public relations through social media on people's mobile devices will rise to new levels if this is fully addressed. Indeed, tourists at (dark) tourism sites will be able to access quality Wi-Fi freely and easily, and any specially produced bespoke apps will function more effectively if they have interactive elements tailored to the individuals and their movements. The use of beacons is increasingly filtering though in this regard. Beacons are a type of a low-cost, micro-location-based technology that use Bluetooth low energy (BLE 4.0) for communicating with beacon-enabled devices in user's smartphones or tablets. Information can then be beamed or pushed to users' mobile devices as they pass by.

Such technology is already in use in the retail sector, and we have seen it now being adopted in the field of events and event management as well. In 2015, at the US PGA Golf tournament, they used live online streaming to introduce new interactive features for mobile that included shot-by-shot laser-generated data from the course. Beacon technology is installed in the scoreboards carried by volunteers and data is then constantly updated and fed through from the beacons and also captured by remote drones and, subsequently, fed through to the tournament app which spectators have on their smartphones. Similar approaches could be used in variety of ways at dark tourism sites and locations to provide interpretive information to visitors in a dynamic and interactive way that engages the visitor and enhances their experience. 'Learning to market to the social web requires a new way to communicate with an audience in a digital environment' (Weber 2009, p. 3). Whilst for some years now authors such as Weber (2009) have advocated the importance of social and digital technology in relation to marketing in general, when it comes to tourism overall and, dark tourism in particular, then it is not only the up-front marketing aspect that deserves attention. There is an increasing need to harness what digital can do to enhance the tourist experience whilst in situ at the attraction/destination, and that requires the use of high-quality Wi-Fi and other forms of technological infrastructure such as the beacons discussed here (Bolan 2015).

Conclusion

Aspects of digital technology do not stand still. Whilst the use of tablets and smartphones is growing rapidly (including how tourists access social media), the next big thing (at the time of writing) to have an impact and a strong influence will be 'wearable tech'. Wearable tech refers to technological devices that are worn by the consumer (Chaffey 2015). Increasingly, these are technological devices that can perform many of the same functions as a smartphone or a tablet device. Early examples were in the area of health and fitness and included the concept of a fitness bracelet such as that produced by Nike—called the Fuelband. However, the latest examples likely to have a major impact are smartwatches (such as the Apple watch or the Samsung Galaxy Gear) and variations on the Google Glass concept. Such devices take what the smartphones currently do and provide it in a more immersive, portable and accessible form worn by the user. As the drive for new mobile devices grows through the advent of wearable tech, new opportunities and possibilities will open up for tourism.

With regard to dark tourism, according to Stone (2006, p. 146), 'it is crucial to the understanding of this phenomenon that an ability to extract and interrogate the motives of so-called dark tourists exists. This is particularly so within a variety of social, cultural and geographical contexts'. The authors here concur with point but further contend that this also now needs to be extended and intrinsically linked to extracting and interrogating the dark tourist in the context of the digital world. This adds an extra dimension to understanding these tourists and provides new meaning and new experiences for both the tourist and those in the arena of dark tourism management. If this is fully addressed and harnessed correctly, then we really begin to utilise digital to illuminate the realm of dark tourism and improve such experiences for all.

In summary, this chapter has taken a three-strand approach focusing on the digital realms of social media, mobile and blogging (including online forums). In conjunction with this is the crucially important aspect of Wi-Fi connectivity to help make the other aspects possible when tourists are travelling and whilst at the destination. This brings a number of important implications for the dark tourism industry. Many of the digital aspects discussed are highly beneficial if harnessed and utilised properly. Indeed, in some cases, they are becoming necessary for business success in the tourism field (Baggio and Chiappa 2014; Tussyadiah and Zach 2012). Those involved in the marketing and management of dark tourism sites and experiences need to embrace the digital expectations of today's 'dark tourist' and actively engage them through social media, through mobile devices and through bespoke apps (addressing issues such as Wi-Fi connectivity) if they are to succeed and prosper in a sustainable way for the future.

Moreover, future research may include further investigations (through qualitative and quantitative approaches) on the thoughts, views, opinions and experiences of dark tourists with regard to their use of digital in the various forms addressed in this chapter. In particular, there is a need to examine the influence of social media and the role that it plays in this form of tourism. Ultimately, future research directions should illuminate how inhabiting such digital social spaces impacts everything from decision-making to experience and shared experience within the realm of dark tourism.

References

Alexander, J. (2002). On the social construction of moral universals: The 'Holocaust' from war crime to trauma drama. *European Journal of Social Theory, 5*, 5–85.

Arnold, D. (2005). Virtual tourism: A niche in cultural heritage. In M. Novelli (Ed.), *Niche tourism: Contemporary issues, trends, and cases* (pp. 223–232). London: Elsevier.

Ashworth, G. J. (2002). Holocaust tourism: The experience of Kraków-Kazimierz. *International Research in Geographical and Environmental Education, 11*(4), 363–367.

Auschwitz-Birkenau State Museum. (2015a). *A virtual tour of Auschwitz/Birkenau by Alan and Krysia Jacobs.* Available from: http://remember.org/auschwitz/. Accessed 05 June 2016.

Auschwitz-Birkenau State Museum. (2015b). *Auschwitz report 2015*. Oswiecim: Auschwitz-Birkenau State Museum.

Baggio, R., & Chiappa, G. D. (2014). Real and virtual relationships in tourism digital ecosystems. *Information Technology and Tourism, 14*(1), 3–19.

Bolan, P. (2015). A perspective on the near future: Mobilizing events and social media. In I. Yeoman, R. Robertson, U. McMahon-Beattie, K. A. Smith, & E. Backer (Eds.), *The future of events and festivals* (pp. 200–209). London: Routledge.

Causevic, S., & Lynch, P. (2007, April 11). The significance of dark tourism in the process of tourism development after a long-term political conflict: An issue of Northern Ireland. Unpublished paper presented at: *The ASA Conference 2007: Thinking through tourism*, London Metropolitan University, London.

Chaffey, D. (2015). *Digital business and e-commerce management: Strategy, implementation and practice* (6th ed.). Harlow: Pearson.

Cowan, D. (2005). *Cyberhenge: Modern pagans on the internet*. New York: Routledge.

Cox, C., Burgess, S., Sellitto, C., & Buultjens, J. (2009). The role of user-generated content in tourists' travel planning behaviour. *Journal of Hospitality Marketing and Management, 18*, 743–764.

Dark Tourism Worldwide. (2016). *Description*. Available from: https://www.facebook.com/groups/60258462039/?ref=br_tf. Accessed 04 June 2016.

Dawson, L. (2005). The mediation of religious experience in cyberspace. In M. Højsgaard & M. Warburg (Eds.), *Religion and cyberspace* (pp. 15–37). New York: Routledge.

Dickinson, J. E., Ghali, K., Cherrett, T., Speed, C., Davies, N., & Norgate, S. (2014). Tourism and the smartphone app: Capabilities, emerging practice and scope in the travel domain. *Current Issues in Tourism, 17*(1), 84–101.

Durkin, K. F. (2003). Death, dying and the dead in popular culture. In C. D. Bryant & D. L. Peck (Eds.), *The handbook of death and dying* (pp. 43–49). New York: Sage.

Ellis, S. R. (2016). *What are virtual environments?* Available from: http://hsi.arc.nasa.gov/publications/ellis_what_ve.pdf. Accessed 04 June 2016.

Flectcher, A., & Lee, M. J. (2012). Digital heritage: Current social media uses and evaluations in American museums. *Museum Management and Curatorship, 27*(5), 505–521.

Florida Center for Instructional Technology. (2009). *Virtual reality movies*. Available from: http://fcit.usf.edu/holocaust/resource/vr.htm. Accessed 05 June 2016.

Garde-Hansen, J. (2011). *Media and memory*. Edinburgh: Edinburgh University Press.

Gruber, R. E. (2012). *iPad app tells story of Oswiecim, home of Auschwitz*. JTA – Jewish Telegraphic Agency. Available from: http://www.jta.org/2012/07/04/news-opinion/world/ipad-app-tells-story-of-oswiecim-home-of-auschwitz. Accessed 18 Dec 2015.

Harris, D. (2002). *The kitschification of Sept. 11*. Available from: http://www.salon.com/2002/01/26/kitsch_2/. Accessed 04 June 2016.

History. (2016). *Deconstructing history: Alcatraz*. Available from: http://www.history.com/topics/alcatraz. Accessed 05 June 2016.

Hodalska, J. (2015, April 23–24). Smiling Holocaust selfies: Dark tourism and digital narcissism. Unpublished paper presented at: *The international conference on the Holocaust and the contemporary world*, Krakow, Poland.

Ivanov, S. H., & Webster, C. (2013). Tourism's contribution to economic growth: A global analysis for the first decade of the millennium. *Tourism Economics, 19*(3), 477–508.

Kaelber, L. (2006a). Place and pilgrimage: Real and imagined. In W. H. Swatos (Ed.), *On the road to being there: Studies in pilgrimage and tourism* (pp. 277–295). Leiden: Brill.

Kaelber, R. (2006b). Paradigms of travel: From religious pilgrimage to postmodern tourism. In D. Timothy & D. H. Olsen (Eds.), *Tourism, religion, and spiritual journeys* (pp. 49–63). London: Routledge.

Kaelber, L. (2007). A memorial as virtual traumascape: Darkest tourism in 3D and cyber-space to the gas chambers of Auschwitz. *e-Review of Tourism Research (eRTR), 5*(2), 24–33.

Levine, A. (2014). Selfie in the age of digital recursion. *Invisible Culture: An Electronic Journal for Visual Culture, 20*. Available from: http://ivc.lib.rochester.edu/the-selfie-in-the-age-of-digital-recursion/. Accessed 04 June 2016.

Miles, W. F. S. (2002). Auschwitz: Museum interpretation and darker tourism. *Annals of Tourism Research, 29*(4), 1175–1178.

Munar, A. M., & Jacobsen, J. K. S. (2014). Motivations for sharing tourism experiences through social media. *Tourism Management, 43*, 46–54.

Nair, M. (2011, March/April). Understanding and measuring the value of social media. *The Journal of Corporate Accounting Finance, 22*(3), 45–51.

Ntunda, J. (2012, December). *Investigating the challenges of promoting dark tourism in Rwanda*. Bachelor thesis, Rwanda Tourism University College, Kigali.

Nusair, K. K., Bilgihan, A., & Okumus, F. (2013). The role of online social network travel websites in creating social interaction for gen Y travelers. *International Journal of Tourism Research, 15*, 458–472.

Pan, B., MacLaurin, T., & Crotts, J. (2007). Travel blogs and their implications for destination marketing. *Journal of Travel Research, 46*(1), 35–45.

Ritzer, G. (2005). *Enchanting a disenchanted world: Revolutionizing the means of consumption* (2nd ed.). Thousand Oaks: Sage.

Schmallegger, D., & Carson, D. (2008). Blogs in tourism: Changing approaches to information exchange. *Journal of Vacation Marketing, 14*(2), 99–110.

Seaton, A. V. (1996). From thanatopsis to thanatourism: Guided by the dark. *Journal of International Heritage Studies, 2*(2), 234–244.

Seaton, A. V. (1999). War and thanatourism: Waterloo 1815–1914. *Annals of Tourism Research, 26*(1), 130–158.

Simone-Charteris, M. T., & Boyd, S. W. (2010). Northern Ireland re-emerges from the ashes: The contribution of political tourism towards a more visited and peaceful environment. In O. Moufakkir & I. Kelly (Eds.), *Tourism, progress and peace* (pp. 179–198). Wallingford: CABI.

Sontag, S. (1977). *On photography*. London: Anchor Books Doubleday.

Stelzner, M. A. (2015). *Social media marketing industry report: How marketers are using social media to grow their businesses*, Social Media Examiner.

Stone, P. R. (2006). A dark tourism spectrum: Towards a typology of death and macabre related tourist sites, attractions and exhibitions. *Tourism, 54*(2), 145–160.

Stone, P. R., & Sharpley, R. (2008). Consuming dark tourism: A thanatological perspective. *Annals of Tourism Research, 35*(2), 574–595.

The Digital Panopticon. (2014). *Digital dark tourism: New directions in the heritage of crime and punishment?* Available from: http://www.digitalpanopticon.org/?tag=dark-tourism. Accessed 05 June 2016.

Tourism Review. (2016). *Dark tourism: Honest interest or rubbernecking?* Available from: http://www.tourism-review.com/dark-tourism-growing-in-popularity-news5007. Accessed 04 June 2016.

Trotta, J. (2006). *Grief tourism*. Available from: http://www.grief-tourism.com. Accessed 20 Dec 2015.

Tussyadiah, I. P., & Zach, F. J. (2012). The role of geo-based technology in place experiences. *Annals of Tourism Research, 39*(2), 780–800.

Virtuar. (2016). *Alcatraz*. Available from: http://www.virtuar.com/alcatraz/. Accessed 05 June 2016.

Wang, Y., Yu, Q., & Fesenmaier, D. R. (2002). Defining the virtual tourist community: Implications for tourism marketing. *Tourism Management, 23*, 407–417.

Weber, L. (2009). *Marketing to the social web: How digital customer communities build your business* (2nd ed.). London: Wiley.

White, L. (2009). Facebook, friends and photos: A snapshot into social networking for generating travel ideas. In *Tourism informatics: Visual travel recommender systems, social communities and user Interface design* (pp. 115–129). Hershey: IGI Global.

WP Virtuoso. (2013). *How many blogs are on the Internet*. Available from: http://www.wpvirtuoso.com/how-many-blogs-are-on-the-internet/. Accessed 20 Dec 2015.

Index[1]

NUMBERS AND SYMBOLS
9/11 Memorial website, 617

A
Abuses of camps 1945–1955, 471
Aceh Tsunami Museum, 425
Acocella, J., 177
Adey, P., 322, 324
Adolf Hitler, 295, 498
African slavery, 384
African-American Antioch Church building, 416
African-Americans, 384, 393, 406, 411, 418
Afterlife of camps, 471
Aftershock, 426
Agnew, J., 235
Akrotiri, 136
Al Qaeda network, 388
Alaska earthquake, 387, 425
Albert, K., 335
Alcatraz Prison, 390
Alderman, D. H., 377, 378, 406
Alderney, 366, 368–371

Alfred P. Murrah Federal Building, 388
Ali, Z., 338
Al-Nakba, 217, 220, 221
Alternative Tourism Group (ATG), 219, 220
American heritage of suffering, 383–389
American history, 384, 400, 404, 410
American Revolutionary War, 383
Anatomical museum, 90, 91
Anatomical Venus, 90
Ancestor worship, 159–164, 166, 169
Anderson, B., 355
Andreu, L., 716
Anglican doctrine, 43
The Animals of Chernobyl, 659
Anne Frank Education Centre, 489
Antebellum slave cabins, 402
Anti-black racism, 384
Anti-Catholic propaganda, 43
Anti-Catholic sympathisers, 38
Anti-Mormon atrocities, 385
Anxiety-buffer mechanisms, 521, 526
Anxiety-buffering system, 522
Aotearoa, 718

---

[1] Note: Page numbers followed by 'n' refer to notes.

© The Author(s) 2018
P. R. Stone et al. (eds.), *The Palgrave Handbook of Dark Tourism Studies*,
https://doi.org/10.1057/978-1-137-47566-4

748　Index

Apollonian, 212–215, 217, 218, 221–223
Arab-Israeli war, 370
Ariès, P., 190, 194, 195, 197–200, 202, 204, 205
Artangel exhibition, 61
Asbury, New Jersey, 336
Ashworth, G., 176, 177, 262, 266, 292, 404, 496, 606, 621
Asian thanatourism, 159, 160, 169
Asian thanatourist sites, 164
Askegaard, S., 174
Assassinations, 105, 107, 108, 110, 247, 386, 486
Athenian Glaucus, 126
Atkinson, G. C., 117, 118
Atout France market research, 653
Atrocity heritage, 262, 620, 698
Atrocity sites, 17, 497, 515
Atrocity tourism, 176, 424
Auden, W. H., 5
Audoin-Rouzeau, S., 447, 461
August Peace Memorial ceremony, 167
Auldjo, A., 128
Auschwitz-Birkenau, 245, 251, 475, 610, 620, 622, 625, 627, 648, 730, 734
Auschwitz-Birkenau Memorial and Museum, 476, 590, 595, 668, 734
　as heterotopia, 241–244
Auschwitz-Birkenau revolt, 484
Auschwitz camps, 475, 476, 480
Auschwitz Museum and Memorial's website, 493, 617
Austin, N. K., 660
Austrian, 242, 472
Authentication, 212, 213, 217, 218, 223
Authenticity value, 276–278
Authentic souvenirs, 711, 712
Azaryahu, M., 407

B
Babi Yar massacre, 478
Babi Yar site, 479
Bachelor, B., 134
Bai Guang Memorial, 163
Bailiwicks, 357, 362
Baker, D., 511
Balaz, V., 431
Ballantyne, R., 561, 619
Band of Brothers, 654
Bann, S., 105, 110
Baptist, K. W., 697
Baring-Gould, S., 5, 117–119
Barnes, J., 93
Barrett, M., 59
Barrow, J., 110
Barthes, R., 512, 586, 590, 591, 593, 651
Bartlett, F. C., 320
Battlefield, 12, 97n29, 159, 228, 393, 424, 435, 444, 447–453, 460, 461, 497, 524, 539, 540, 613, 647, 649, 654, 717, 728
Battlefield tourism, 12, 443–464, 717, 728
Battle of Bosworth, 37
Battle of Normandy, 652
Batwa ethnic group, 279
Beard, M., 126
Beard, R., 697
Becker, A., 447, 461
Becker, E., 520
Beckford, W., 10, 130
Belarusians, 367
Belgians, 93, 268, 269, 367, 449–452, 462
Belk, R. W., 624
Bell, C., 134
Belzec death camps, 470, 471, 475, 476
Benjamin, W., 92
Bergen-Belsen, 471, 473
Berkeley Plantation, 411

Berlin Wall, fall of, 26, 482, 489, 669
"Beyond the Fields" tour, 400, 412, 413
Big House, 400, 402, 403, 408–410, 413–417
Bigne, J. E., 716
Biran, A., 177, 216, 430, 511, 536
Bird, G. R., 655
Birkholz, H., 139
The Birth of Tragedy (Nietzsche), 211–213
Bizimungu, A., 271
Bizimungu, P., 271
Black Museum, 60
Black spot tourism, 424
Blatman, S., 342
Blix, G., 144
Blogosphere, 738–740
Blumer, N., 695
Bodily mutilation, 35
Bodnar, J., 165
The Bohemian Blog, 738, 739
Bond Street gallery, 60
Bonfire Night, 44
Boniecki, A., 479
Book of Common Prayer, 44
Book of Martyrs (Foxe), 43
Bordieu, P., 592
Bowie, D., 20
Bowman, M., 216, 443, 556
Boyd, S., 609, 621
Boydell, T., 614, 615
Brahmins, 160
Brand identity, 165, 650, 652, 653, 655, 656
Brand image, 650, 653, 657
Brand position, 650, 652, 654
Brand symbols, 650, 653, 659
Bright, A. D., 658
Bright, C., 378
British, 384
British travellers, 104, 111, 114, 115
Broadway, 733

Bronstein, E., 220
Brown, N., 520
Brown, S., 648
Bruner, E. M., 622
Bryant, W. C., 536
Buchenwald Memorial Site, former East Germany, 471, 480–483
Buckley-Zistel, S., 263
Buda, D., 176, 511, 516, 517, 525, 669, 707
Buddhism, 160
Buddhist monks, 160
Bulwer-Lytton, E. G., 125–128
Bunbury, S., 115
Bunhill Fields Burial Ground, 92
Bunkers, 133, 451
  labour camps and, 363–374
Burchardt, C. B., 114
Burke, E., 131
Burke, T., 67
Burton, R., 5, 117
Bush, G. W., 247, 387
Butler, R., 377
Buzinde, C., 627
Byfield, R., 38

C

Cakmak, E., 217
Calhoon, K. S., 109
California, 386, 387, 562
Cambodia, 159, 164, 525, 592, 593
Cambodian thanatourism, 164
Campbell, R. M., 406
Campbell, T., 112
Camp liberation anniversaries, 471–473
Capital punishment, 35, 36, 48, 56
Carnivalesque, 48, 54
Carr, D., 177
Carr, G., 260, 556
Carr, N., 175
Carson, D., 739

Carter, J., 694
Catastrophe, 129–133, 391
Catholic Church, 537
Cemetery
 management, 12
 visits and funereal practices, 111–114
Central Jewish Committee, 473
Ceremonies, 13, 15, 280, 283, 323, 356, 366, 454, 473
Cesarani, D., 295
Challoner, R., 44
Chamber of Horrors, 50, 60, 65, 84–86, 90, 94
Changi Chapel and Museum, 698
Channel Islanders, 356, 364
Channel Islands, 355, 357–363
Chaotic situation identity, 222
Charles XII, 104, 105
 Scandinavian memorials and history, 105–111
Charlesworth, A., 476
Chelmno, 475
Chernobyl, 319, 320, 656–658
 mobilities and memories at, 324–329
Chernobyl Exclusion Zone, 325, 326
 as heterotopia, 238–239
Chernobylinterinform, 325
Chernobyl Nuclear Power Plant Zone of Alienation, 325
Chew, E. Y. T., 432
Children distress, 556
Childrens artwork, 569–574
Childrens at dark sites
 artifacts, 561–562
 explore, 557
 factors, 554–556
 focus group, 560
 interview of, 559–560
 museum studies, 557
 survey, 558
 systematic observational accounts, 557

Children's memorial materials, 563–565
Choeung Ek Killing Fields, 164
Christchurch, New Zealand, 340
Christianity, 20
Christian Pilgrimage, 21
Churchill paradigm, 358, 365, 372
Church of Jesus Christ of Latter-day Saints, 385
Civil rights abuses, 384
Civil War, 12, 269, 384, 389, 392
Clarke, E. D., 105–109, 111, 115
Coats, A., 429, 435
Cockburn, P., 335
Cohen, E., 611
Cohen, E. H., 606
Coke, E., 43
Collins, W., 63
Cologne Jewish Museum, 479
Comité International de Dachau
 prisoner organisation, 471, 474
Commemoration, 340
 new sites, 488–490
Commemorative surrogation, 406
Comment cards, 563, 565–568, 571, 576
Commodification, 19, 91, 129, 135, 191, 251, 496, 603, 647, 667, 668, 671, 713, 715, 720
Common criminals, executions of, 44
Commonwealth War Graves Commission (CWGC), 447, 448, 450
Confessing church ('bekennende Kirche'), 488
Conflict site, 515
Connelly, M., 447
Con Son, 165, 166
Consumer culture theory (CCT), 174, 182
Consumer-led approach, 11
Contemporary folk Buddhism, 160
Contemporary museology, 265
Contemporary tourism mobilities, 330

Index

Cook, J. P., 84
Cook, T., 58
Cool authentication, 212
Cooper, M., 140
Corder, W., 56, 62, 83
Corelli, M., 117
Corporal punishment, 48
  public exhibition of, 56
Coxe, W., 105–109
Cresswell, T., 235
Crime
  drama, 63
  in eighteenth century, 48–60
  in fact and fiction in modern society, 60–69
  judicial spectacle, 34–48
  topography and transgression, 63–69
Crimewatch, 61
Criminal justice system, 35
  in England, 35
  workings of, 59
Criminal trial, public methods of, 35
Cripps, J. M., 107
Cromwell, O., 43
Cromwell, T., 38
Crone, R., 82, 83
Crouch, G. I., 175
Crown Dependencies, 357, 359
Crucifixion of Christ, 33
Crumlin Road Gaol, 681, 682, 733
Cuba, 14, 336
Cults of the dead, 196
Cultural trauma, 322
Cummings, J., 416
Cup of charity, 49
Czechs, 367

D

Dachau Concentration Camp Memorial, 471, 474, 672
Dachauer Aufstand, 485
Dachau memorial landscape, 480

Dahl, C., 127
Dallaire, R., 268
Dance of Death, 195
Danger-zone tourism, 176, 519
Dann, G., 3, 11, 294, 612
Dark camps of genocide, 538, 539, 672
Dark conflict zones, 539
Dark dungeons, 539
Darker visitor attractions, 538
Dark event, 10, 179, 337, 363, 364, 606, 701, 702, 718, 720, 721
Dark exhibitions, 539
Dark fun factories, 11, 524, 538, 668, 673
Dark heritage, 405
  context of, 390
  product, 390–393
Dark imagery, 591
Dark marketing, 648
Dark motivation, 17, 430
Darkness
  in dark tourism, 191
  of experience, 607
Dark resting places, 11, 539
Dark shrines, 539
Dark side, 212, 739
Dark sites, 10, 77, 82, 118, 158, 177, 178, 216, 228, 238, 264, 340, 356, 363, 370, 404, 405, 424, 433, 436, 516, 518, 524, 525, 534, 538, 554–562, 572, 574, 575, 586–588, 593, 596, 598, 608, 609, 616, 619, 670–672, 717, 719, 720, 729, 733, 736, 739
Dark souveniring, 718
Dark spaces, 708
Dark tourism, 9, 143–145, 157, 158, 227, 262, 496
  assumptions of, 10–11
  attractions, 732
  behaviour of, 16
  brand, 650
  categories of, 11
  colour-coded inventory of, 11

Dark tourism (*cont.*)
  conceptualisations, 606
  consumption of, 526
  criticism of, 22
  death, 173, 174, 535–537
  definition, 533, 585
  described, 515
  destinations, 613
  disasters, attraction of, 337
  dimension in, 135
  discourse of, 12
  distinctions, 605–606
  emergent perspectives of, 181–182
  emerging sub-field of, 516
  encounters of, 13, 26–28, 608
  enlightening, 191–194
  experiences, 608
  exploration of, 11
  literature on, 319
  memorial qualities of, 603
  mobilities, 326
  'morbid fascination' with death in, 516
  as motivated consumption grouping, 11
  motivational category, 9
  motivational explanation of, 11
  normalising, 517–518
  Palestinian identity through, 219
  participating in, 337
  phenomenon, 728–729
  in practice, 281–282
  as preparation, 179–181
  problem of, 402–404
  reconfiguration of, 14
  remembrance politics and, 24
  render analysis of, 603
  research, 554
  researchers, 611
  retail, 669–671
  selfies, 736–738
  as signaling, 174–178
  sites and locations, 523, 606
  stuff of, 263–268
  terror management theory and, 519–523
  thanatological conceptualizations of, 526
  traumatic memories and spectrality, 322–324
  types of, 525
  typology of, 11
Dark Tourism Forum, 731
Dark Tourism Photography, 731
Dark Tourism: The Attraction of Death and Disaster, 215, 496
Dark Tourism World, 731
Dark tourist, 246, 249, 340, 406, 536
The Dark Tourist (Joly), 248, 249
Dasent, G., 115
Davidson, P., 103
D-Day beaches, 652–654
De Amicis, E., 85
De Certeau, M., 323
de Kirchner, F., 542
Death, 13
  commodification of, 19
  fascination with, 526
  fears of, 517, 521, 522
  inevitability of, 518
  psychology of, 519
  sociological condition of, 518
  sociology of, 519
  within popular culture, 517
Death camps, 470, 471, 475–477, 484, 594, 734, 736
Death consumption, 173, 174, 178, 182
Death mentalities, 194, 195
Death of the Other, 194, 196, 197, 203, 205
Death of the Self, 194–196, 205, 523, 536
Death penalty, 59, 69
Death-related tourism, 77, 91–94, 94n1, 173, 178, 179, 192, 202, 215, 523, 525–527

Deathscapes, 189, 190, 192–194, 199, 243, 537
Death sentences, 55, 59
Death site, 10, 26, 104, 107, 121, 140, 227, 386, 515, 538, 591, 670
Debord, G., 70, 200, 229–234, 245, 248
Debordian dark tourism, 249–251
Declaration of Independence, 383, 399
Deconstruction, 90, 587
Decontextualization, 293
Demnig, G., 489
Democratisation, 482, 549
Derrida, J., 587
Des Forges, A., 268
De-sequestration of death, 199–201, 204, 205
Dhamoon, R. K., 700
Dickens, C., 3, 4, 64, 66, 78, 79, 81, 82, 86, 87, 93
Dierking, L. D., 559
Different planet, 596, 597
Digital media, 70, 727, 730
Digital voice services, 735
Dionysian catastrophe, 218
Dionysus *vs.* Apollo
  dark tourism, 215–217
  Palestinian case, 217–218
  through dark tourism, 219–222
  tragedy of modern life, 213–215
Disaster happens, 541
Disasters
  characteristics of, 338
  described, 335
  media reporting of, 336
  myths of looting, 339
  people's behaviours following, 336
  relief, 336
  unknown, 336
Disaster tourism
  characteristics of, 340
  destination of, 337
  places of, 337
  sites of, 339

Dissonant heritage, 265–268, 292, 424, 496
Dissonant Heritage: The Management of the Past as a Resource in Conflict, 496
Dittmer, J., 406
Dobraszczyk, P., 241
Dolski, M. S., 655
Donat, A., 589
Donkey symbol, 362
Doss, E., 203, 563
Douglas, M., 444
Downing, R., 54
Doyle, C., 63, 67
Dufferin, L., 5, 117, 119–121
Dungeon attraction, 60, 674, 675, 679
Dunkley, R. A., 717
Dwyer, O. J., 407

E

Earl of Kilmarnock, execution of, 51
Earthquake, 125, 129, 132, 337
  memorials, 426
  site of, 424
  See also L'Aquila Earthquake, 2009
Earthquake Relics Park, 426, 428
Earth spirit, 161
Eastern State Penitentiary (ESP), 682
Edensor, T., 139, 140, 323, 324
Edmondson, J., 3, 4
Edmondson, P., 4
Educational trips, 611
Educational value, 176, 241, 276–278, 281, 284, 613
Edward, Prince of Wales, 60
Eichmann, B., 494
Eichmann trial, 370, 477
Eichstedt, J., 407, 408
Elgenius, G., 355, 356
Elliott, C. B., 103, 109–111
Ellis, H. R., 116, 118
Elvis Presley, 15, 163, 386

Emile Durkheim's seminal work, 517
Emotional appeal, 613, 649
Emotional vulnerability, 554, 556, 560, 562, 575
Engineered and orchestrated remembrance (EOR), 15, 17, 19, 22–26, 28, 35
  commodification of death, 19
  dark tourists, 16–17
  phenomenological effect of, 27
  situational orientation of, 26
  as text and practice, 15–16
  thanatology, 19
Engineered remembrance, 13, 16, 27
  commemoration politics and, 23–24
English criminal justice, evolution of, 35
Enkelson, B., 105
Environmental change, 137
EOR, *see* Engineered and orchestrated remembrance
Equilibrioceptive, 732
Erfurt-Cooper, P., 133, 140
Escobar, P., 296, 297, 306–310, 312
Escobar, R., 299
ESMA, 541–545, 547–549
Ethiopian famine in 1980s, 336
Eurocentric attitudes, 157
European civilization, 211
European Jewry, 477
European Jews, 219, 483
European settlers, 383
Europe's pre-Second World War Jewish, 607
Executions, 48, 52, 59
  of Maria and Frederick Manning, 56
Experiential learning cycle, 614
Experiential learning model, 604, 615
Extraordinary death, 192, 201

F
Facebook, 312, 335, 435, 597, 600, 617, 730, 731
Fajardo, S., 297
Falk, J. H., 559
Famous Trials, 61
Fascination, 63, 65, 67, 69, 82, 87, 88, 90, 91, 96n13, 117, 127, 131, 144, 177, 182, 200, 202, 215, 303, 340, 386, 423, 425, 429, 435, 496, 526, 533–536, 539, 585, 586, 588, 589, 597, 620, 717, 739
Fatality, 14, 15, 20, 22, 24, 27, 28, 140, 196
Faullant, R., 716
Faux disaster, 126
Fear of death, 176, 517–522, 526–528
Featherstone, M., 598
Feig, K., 494
Ferguson, S., 429, 435
Ferguson, T., 126
Fininvest, 342
Five-point typology, 16
Flanders, J., 83
Flash media players, 734
Flaubert's Parrot (Barnes), 93
Flemish Peace Movement, 447
Fletcher, J., 140
Flight 93 Memorial Junior Ranger, 573
Flight 93 National Memorial, 554, 562–575
Florentine Venus, 90
Foley, M., 10, 17, 133, 157, 180, 204, 215, 424, 535, 589
Folk Buddhism, 160
Fonblanque, A., 88
Foote, K., 267, 292, 377, 407
Forbes, C. S., 117–119
Forbidden death, 191, 197–199, 202, 203, 205
Forestell, P. H., 611
Former Nazi concentration camps, 672, 736
  memorial sites of Holocaust, 477, 478
Forsyth, D., 143
Foucauldian dark tourism, 249–250

Foucault, M., 18, 234, 237, 241, 243, 245, 249
Fouqué, F., 136
France, 22, 60, 62, 63, 71n5, 107, 362, 453, 474, 477, 653, 655, 732
Frank, A., ix, 477, 488
Frankfurt Jewish Ghetto, 488
Frankfurt Jewish Museum, 489
French Morgue, 88
French Revolution, 60, 84, 127, 144
Freud, S., 517
Frew, E., 538, 610, 639, 641, 642
Friedrich, M., 258, 280
Friedrich, W., 134, 136
Fritz, C., 338
Fukushima Daiichi Nuclear Power Plant, 432
Functional remembrance, 18

G

Gaboriau, E., 63
Galani-Moutafi, V., 622
Gallipoli, 10, 524, 525, 645, 659, 722
Gattrel, V., 3
Genocidal tourism, 180
Genocide, 477
  places of, 525
  sites, 524
German, 367, 370, 472
  forces, 357
  occupation, 356
German Democratic Republic (DDR), 475
German refugees, 475
Germany, 362, 472
  re-unification of, 482
Gibbon, E., 34
Giddens, A., 157
Gilbert, W. S., 60
A Girl's Ride in Iceland (Tweedie), 120
Glad, K. A., 434
Global phenomenon, 157
Global tourism industry, 261

Glocalisation, 712, 715
Goffman, E., 34, 35
Goldenberg, J. L., 523
Goldhill, S., 128
Goodchild, F., 53
Gordon, B., 714
Gorer, G., 200, 202
Gourevitch, P., 268
Governing myth, 365–367, 374, 375
Graburn, N., 714
Graham, B., 264
Gram, S., 176
Grand Tour tourism, 130
Gravestone memorials, 13, 25
Gravestones, 13, 15, 18, 25
Great Kantō Earthquake of 1923 in Japan, 426
Great San Francisco Earthquake of 1906, 423
Great War battlefields, 452
Great War Dead, 446–447
Grief Tourism, 262, 337, 424, 738–740
Griffin, G. M., 446
Griffin, L. J., 402
Grim Reaper, 195, 204
Grotewohl, O., 481
Ground Zero, 127, 168, 175, 177, 179, 228, 247, 388, 533, 540, 620, 697, 728, 729, 736, 737
Guernsey, 357, 359, 361–363, 366, 368–371, 374
Gunnar's Holm, 118
Guyer, S., 267

H

Habyarimana, J., 269, 270
Haitian tourism, 428
Haiti earthquake of 2010, 425
Halden, 105, 106, 109, 111
Hallgrimsson, J., 118
Hallowed Ground, 112
Hamber, B., 699

"Hanging in chains", 41
Hankivsky, O., 700
Hanna, S., 378, 407
Hard ambiance, 230
A Hardy Norseman (Lyall), 117
Hargis, P. G., 402
Harold Marcuse, 471, 493
Harris, P., 54, 55
Harris, R., 126
Hartmann, R., 176, 177, 266, 379, 404, 499, 606, 621
Harvey, D., 235
Hass, A., 222
Hawke's Bay Earthquake of 1931, 426
Hay, D., 233
Hayward, P., 165
Head, F. B., 79, 86, 87
Hebbert, M., 323
Heidegger, M., 229
Heidelberg, W., 293, 295, 300, 304
Heine, S. J., 521
Heringman, N., 132
Heritage, 356
  of darkness, 382–383
  dissonance, 610, 646
  force field, 654
  marketing manuals, 646
  resource types and scales, 392
Heritage tourism sites, 191, 496
Heritage touristification process, 201
Herofication, 390, 394
Heterotopia
  evolving, 244–245
  principles of, 236–244
Heuss, T., 473
Heynen, H., 238
Hildebrand, B. E., 115
Hilker, M., 283
Hindu-Buddhist traditions, 159
Hiroshima Monument, 168
Hitchcock, A., 63
Hobbes, T., 195
Hodalska, J., 736

Hogarth, W., 53
Hokudan Earthquake Memorial Park, 423
Hollinshead, K., 651, 659
Holmes, S., 63, 67
Holocaust, 211, 292, 519
  death camp, 424
  national socialistic Germany and, 490, 491
Holocaust Memorial, 23, 698
  design, 478–480
  sites, 17, 469
Holocaust-related sites, 525
Home, S., 232
Homotopias, 249
Honorifics, 161
Horrific events, 108, 469, 483, 670
Hot authentication, 212, 213, 223
Howard, J., 52, 54
Hsu, S. Y., 430
Hugo, V., 92
Hume, D., 715
Hungarian National Museum, 294
Hunter, J., 90
Hunterian collection, 90
Huntington, R., 111
Hurricane Katrina, 387, 390
Hutu group, 268–270, 279, 282, 283
Hutu refugees, 271
Hutu republic, 269

Icelandic sagas, 118
Ideology, influence of, 540
Il terremoto diventa attrattore turistico, 341
Immortality, symbolic, 520, 521, 523, 524
Imperial War Museum, 701
Importance attitudes, 615, 618, 619
Incomplete understanding of death, 554, 570, 575

Indian Ocean tsunami in 2004, 336, 428, 431
Indigenous Americans, 383
Inglis, H., 110
Ingold, T., 322
"Inside", 61
Instagram, 597, 600, 730
Interahamwe group, 270
International Holocaust Remembrance Day, 472
International Jewish community, 476, 482, 484
International Memorial *Never Again*, 474
Interpretation
　definition, 624
　historical, 598
　outcome, 627
Invisible/forbidden death, 197–198
iPhone/iPad app, 736
Iqani, M., 176
Iron Curtain in 1989/1990, 26, 476
"Iron Maiden", 60
Isaac, R., 153, 217, 223, 404
Islamist terrorism attack, 179
Isola del Giglio, Italy, 339–340
Israel, 525
Israeli citizens, 180, 222
Israeli-Jewish society, 219
Israeli-Palestinian conflict, 221, 719
Ivanov, S., 536, 540

J

Jack the Ripper, 66, 89, 245
Jacobsen, M., 153, 190, 196, 199–205
Jahari, S. A., 432
Jamal, T., 216
Japanese-American population, 387
Japanese tsunami, 431
Jeffries, S., 245
Jersey, 336, 357, 359, 361, 363, 366, 368–375, 562
Jesse, J. H., 94
Jewish communities, 472, 476, 482, 484, 487, 489, 607
Jewish Ghetto, 484
Jewish Holocaust tourism, 12
Jewish organisations, 472
Jewish people, 218, 472
Jimmy Savile, 18
Johansen, K., 655
John Lennon memorial in Central Park, 10
John Paul II (Pope), 476
Johnston, L., 716
Johnston, T., 537
Joly, D., 247–249, 509
Judicial punishment, 44, 69
Justice tourism, 219, 220

K

Kaczmarek, S., 293, 310
Kagame, P., 271
Dr Kahn's Museum, 90
Kamp Vught, 477
Kamp Westerbork, 477
Kant, I., 131
Kasser, T., 522
Kaufman, V., 230
Kayibanda, G., 269
Keil, C., 625
Kellehear, A., 197, 200, 445
Kempa, M., 625, 627
Kennedy, J. F., 15, 386, 390
Kensal Green Cemetery, 92
Kerr, M. M., 511, 512
KGM, *see* Kigali Genocide Memorial
Khao Lak-Lam Ru National Park in Thailand, 425
Khmer Rouge regime in Cambodia, 164
Khoo-Lattimore, C., 560
Kierkegaard, S., 520
Kigali Genocide Memorial (KGM), 271, 276, 277, 280, 281, 284

Killer GPS app, 735
Killing Fields of Pol Pot, 164
Kim, S., 556, 557, 559
King, C., 129
King Charles I, 44, 46
King George V, 60
Kirchner, N., 542
Knigge, V., 488
Knudsen, B., 292, 556, 623
Kobe earthquake of 1995, 423, 430, 432
Kolb, D. A., 614, 615
Kolbe, M., 475
Korean Demilitarized Zone (DMZ), 264
Korean War battlefields, 449
Korstanje, M., 511, 536, 540
Korzybski, A., 251
Kotler, N., 648
Kotler, P., 656
Krakow-Kazimierz, 497
Kreckler, D., 363
Kristallnacht memorials in Germany, 479

L

Labour camp, 363–374
Lack of agency, 554–555
Ladwig, P., 160
Lager Helgoland, 368
Lager Wick, 371–373
Laing, S., 115
Langer, E. J., 618
Lanzmann, C., 597
Lao ritual cycle, 160
L'Aquila Earthquake, 2009, 340–342
  disaster recovery process in, 341
  media reporting of, 342–348
  victims, 346
L'Aquila, Italy, 337, 340–349, 350n1
The Last Days of Pompeii (Bulwer-Lytton), 125

Latter-day Saints, 385
Lee, L., 62
Legg, S., 323
Leite, N., 129
Leith, M. D., 118
Lelo, L., 216
Lemelin, R., 655
Lennon, J., 2, 10, 17, 132, 157, 180, 204, 215, 424, 512, 535, 589, 627
Leopold, T., 660
Lernort concept, 495
Levi, P., 17
Liberation Day, 359, 360, 362, 366
Light, D., 293, 294, 609
Lighter dark sites, 524
Lincoln, A., 386
Linnet, J. T., 174
Lippard, L. R., 235
Lisbon earthquake, 130, 131, 144
Literal immortality, 520, 521, 527
Little Camp, 482
Lockerbie disaster, 336
Logan, W., 610
Loma Prieta Earthquake of 1986, 426
London Dungeon, 10, 60, 216, 524, 674, 675, 677
London psychogeography, 233, 245, 246
Lorraine, P., 52
Lost traces ('Spurensuche') project, 488
Lowenthal, D., 24, 377
Luk Thung, 162
Lyall, E., 117
Lyall, J., 134

M

Macdonald, S., 292
Mackenzie, G., 121
Madame Tussauds, 10, 60, 65, 83–86, 90, 94
  waxwork exhibition, 50

Maddern, J., 324
Magna Britannia, 43
Majdanek, 470, 475, 479, 491, 589, 597
Majdanek Memorial Site 1945/1946, 470
Mamdani, M., 268
Mandel, N., 521
Manjikian, M., 127
Mann, T., 214
Manning, F., 89
Manning, M., 89
"The March of Intellect", 59
Marcuse, H., 471
Marketing
　activities, 647
　employment, 645
　framework, 659
　opportunity, 646
　social, 658
Marryat, H., 106, 113, 114
Marples, M., 2
Mass-death, 168, 169, 433, 446, 452, 456, 460, 533, 537
Mass tourism, 94, 242, 534, 547, 548, 707
May Day holiday of 2009, 428
Mayhew, H., 89
McCormick, J., 126
McIntosh, A. J., 517
McKercher, B., 16, 405
McVeigh, T., 388
Mead, G. H., 534
Meaningful entertainment, 522–526
Medellin
　bad image of, 300–301
　tourism in, 298
"Mediation" of thanatourist sites, 169
Mellor, P., 179, 199
Melvern, L., 268
Memobilia, 737
Memorial landscape, 469–473, 479–481, 491–493

Memorial landscape in 1980s/1990s, 494–495
Memorial Park of Kobe Earthquake of 1995 in Japan, 430
Memorials
　design, Holocaust, 478–480
　of Jewish Community, 474
Memorialscape, 262, 263, 268, 271, 276–285
Memorial sites
　Bergen-Belsen, 473
　earthquake, 434
　former concentration camps, 473–477
　of Holocaust, former Nazi concentration camps, 477, 478
　Majdanek, 470
　study of, 493–496
　victims of national socialistic Germany, 495–496
　victims of resistance to Nazi Germany, 484
Memory scape, 461
"Memphis Mummy", 91
Memphis, T., 386
Menem, C. S., 542
Menin Gate Memorial at Ypres, 448, 449
Metcalfe, F., 117
Middleton Place Plantations and Gardens, 399
Middleton Place site plan, 412
Middleton, A., 399
Miles, W., 537, 606, 621, 728
Military cemeteries, 443, 444, 448–451, 459, 524
Miller, R., 335
Milton, J., 20, 21
Mindfulness, 615, 618, 619, 622, 626
Minnaert, L., 613
Minoan civilisation, 136
Minoan eruption, 135
Mitchell, R., 613

Mitr Chaibancha, 161
Mobile phone, 735, 736
Modern terrorism, 388
Modlin, A., 418
Mondadori group, 343
Montserrat islands, 137–142
Moorman, E., 127
Morakabati, Y., 140
Morbid tourism, 424
More, T., 38
Moreau-Christophe, M. L., 88
Morgan, N., 646
Mormon history, 385
Mormon settlements, 385
Morris, M. S., 448
Morris, W., 5, 117
Morrison, A., 650, 655
Morten, R., 154
Moscardo, G., 618, 619
Mount St. Helens, 390
Mount Vesuvius, 125, 126, 143
Mourning taboo, 446
Mueller, F., 59
Multifaceted study, 668
Murder, cash payment for, 35
"Murder tourists", 64
"Murdrum" charge, 35
Murray, D., 175, 177
Murray, J., 78, 79, 86, 88, 91
Museo de la memoria, 542, 549
Museo de Mecánica de la Armada (ESMA), 533–549
Museology, 265, 614, 693, 694, 701, 703
Museum of Occupations of Estonia (MOE), 682, 684–688
Museum of Pathological Anatomy, 90
Museum of the Occupation of Lativa (MOL), 682–688
Museums
  description, 693
  memorial, 696
  roles, 700
  types of, 694

Myth, 64, 219, 232, 284, 336, 339, 344, 349, 358, 359, 365–367, 374, 375, 400, 404, 485, 587, 645–661
Mythic sector, 653
Mythscape, 365

N

Narconovelas, 297, 303, 312
Narrative decontextualization, 310
Narrative landscapes, designing, 408–418
Nash, C., 322
Nation and family, 447–449
National Commission for the Fight against Genocide (CNLG), 271
National heritage, 262, 356, 361, 363, 366, 383, 393
National Park Service (NPS), 386, 562, 563, 565, 572, 576n3, 576n5, 576n7, 626
National September 11 Memorial and Museum, 388, 390, 697, 739
National Socialism, 478, 489, 490, 493, 498
National Socialistic Germany, 469–473, 486, 487, 490, 491, 493–496
National socialistic Germany and holocaust, 490, 491
National Socialistic regime 1933–1945, 498
Nationhood, 355–357, 394
Nationwide and persistent problems in United States, 392
Native American population, 384
Naylor, R. A., 112
Nazi concentration camp, 373, 470, 477, 478, 484, 493, 497, 625, 672, 730, 736
Nazi Germany's occupation, 470
Nazi persecution, 361, 374

Index

Nazi regime, 241, 472, 486, 593, 622
Nazi-run prisons, 362
Nazis, 242, 292, 358, 359, 367, 371, 374
Nazism, 367, 371, 374
Nazi symbol, 479
Neiman, S., 131
Neo-Nazis, 492
New museology, 693, 694, 701, 703
New technology, 244, 730
New Zealand, 10, 128, 340, 426–430, 435, 448, 451, 464n12, 718, 733
Nicholas Hawksmoor, 245
Nicholds, T., 388
Nietzsche, F., 211–214
Night of Broken Glass ('Kristall-Nacht') pogroms on November 9/10, 1938, 472, 473
'Nobody' and 'Everybody' Research, 9
Nociceptive, 732
Non-Mormon history, 385
Non-representational theory, 321
Non-royal malefactors, executions of, 40
Non-Western emergent world regions, 157
Non-Western thanatourism, 168
Nora, P., 356
North Africans, 367, 371

O

Oak Alley Plantation, 408, 413, 419n2
Oberstrasse synagogue in Hamburg, 479
Objective authenticity, 213, 711
O'Connor, P., 89
Oklahoma City, 388, 553
Old Bailey, 48, 53, 56, 64, 85, 87
Online doorways, 733
Ontological security, 157, 517, 527, 605, 612
Orams, M. B., 611
Orange, J., 694

Orchestration, 13, 16, 24, 25, 27, 28
Orchestration of remembrance, 13, 25, 27, 28
Ordinary death, 192, 201
Oren, G., 625, 702
Organisation Todt (OT), 366, 367, 369, 370
Osbaldiston, N., 524
Oshpitzin, 736
Ostaszewski, S., 326
Otto, J. E., 294
Owen, D., 377

P

Pacific Tsunami Museum in Chile, 425
Palestine, 211–223, 719, 720
Palmer, W., 64, 84
Pan Am 103, 336
Panorama, 343
Parisian psychogeography, 233
Paris Morgue, 77, 86, 91
   corpses at, 81
   purpose of, 78
   "shuddering horror", 85
Park Island Cemetery memorial, 430
Patridge, C. W., 363
Patterson, A. R., 558
Pearce, P. L., 618
Pepys, S., 44
Performativity, 321, 322
Perreau, D., 51
Perreau, R., 51
"Personal" crimes, 40
Petford, N., 140
Petray, T., 524
Pettigrew, T., 91
Pezzullo, P. C., 216, 556
Phillips, R. B., 714
Phillips, S., 326
Phoenix tourism, 424
Photography, 71n5, 585–600

Picard, D., 554
Pike, S., 650
Pilgrimages, 10, 12, 19, 21, 44, 104, 111, 144, 166, 179, 191, 203, 219, 220, 233, 235, 295, 330, 340, 369, 386, 424, 443, 445, 447, 460, 524, 536, 555, 590, 671, 708, 719
Pillory, 35, 36, 369
Pinterest, 730
Place of Resistance ('Widerstandsplatz'), 485
Places Associated with the Victims and Perpetrators in National Socialism 1933–1945, 499
Plantation Museum, 399–419
Platenkamp, V., 153
Platz, A., 487
Plymouth, 135, 137, 139–142
Podoshen, J., 153, 174, 180, 182
Poe, E. A., 63
Poets' Corner, 94
Poland, 168, 218, 241, 242, 313n4, 470, 471, 475–477, 491, 525, 538, 590, 592, 593, 728, 730, 734, 736
Poles, 249, 367, 610
Policy maker, role of, 307–309
Polish Catholic Church, 476
Polish Committee of Liberation, 470
Polish Parliament, 470, 475
Polish prisoner, 368
Political allegories, of disaster, 540
Pompeii
　as disaster tourism trope, 133–134
　Montserrat island, 137
　Santorini, 134
Poria, Y., 216, 292, 562, 628
Porter, P., 198
Positivism, 174
Possekel, A., 137, 139
Post-9/11 world, 179
Post-Charlie Hebdo world, 173
Post-humanistic mobilities approach, 322
Post-humanistic theory, 320
Post-WWII years, 478
Potter, R., 612
Prasad, A., 182
Prasad, P., 182
Price, R., 511, 512
Pripyat
　deserted fairground at, 599
　former residential accommodation in, 592
Pritchard, A., 646
Probyn, E., 716
Pro-entertainment model, 461
Proprioceptive, 732
Proust, M., 92
Prunier, G., 268
Psychical realities, 517
Psychogeography
　bridging, 234–245
　as dark tourism, 245
　discovering, 232–234
　exploring, 229–232
Public executions, 38, 40, 43, 44, 48, 49, 51, 53, 54, 56, 59, 69, 97n19, 485, 589, 728
Public hanging, 10, 48, 50, 52, 56, 59, 69
Public spectacle, 34, 69
Pumpuang Duangjan, 162
Punishment
　in eighteenth century, 48
　in fact and fiction in modern society, 60
　judicial spectacle, 34
　topography and transgression, 63
　trial and, 33, 34

Q

Qualitative study, 562, 668
Quarantelli, E., 338
Queen Elizabeth, 38, 43

Index

Queenstown, 682
Queen Victoria, 57, 59

R

Racism, 384, 390, 393, 553, 696
Radcliffe, A., 111
Raine, R., 539
Rank, O., 520
Rapoport, N., 480
Ratcliff Highway, 64–66
Ray, G., 132
Reagan, R., 387
"The Red Barn", 56, 62, 64, 83, 97n22
Red Zone bus, 340
Reeves, K., 610
Reign of Terror, 56
Relph, E., 235
Remote and imminent death, 194
Remote camps, 471
Republic of Cromañón, 543–544
Replicas, 402, 413, 625
Resistance by the Doomed, 484
Retailing
    at in-betweens visitor sites, 680–683
    at lightest visitor sites, 673–679
Reynolds, G. W. M., 66
Rhodes, C., 18
Richardson, S., 50
Riches, D., 623
Richter, D, 739
Ritchie, J. R. B., 612
Rittichainuwat, B., 431
Rittichainuwat, N., 430
Rituals, 11, 15, 16, 34, 37, 103, 112, 116, 159–163, 165–167, 195, 196, 198, 203, 213, 237, 240, 241, 243, 246, 283, 445, 446, 517, 520, 524, 622, 657, 714, 719
Roberts, C., 512
Robinson, M., 554
Rojek, C., 143, 144
Romani people, 472
Romans, 20, 21, 33, 34, 103, 126, 127, 129, 144, 246, 389, 728, 736
Romanticism, 196, 22, 104, 196, 202
Rosenstrasse memorial, 487
Rukesha, P., 258
Rumney, R., 230
Russian Orthodox Memorial, 474
Russians, 301, 367, 369, 685
Rwanda
    memorial policymakers in, 284
    tourism developments in, 12
Rwandan commemoration process, 286
Rwandan genocide, 268–275
Rwandan Patriotic Front (RPF), 269–271
Rwandanness, 276, 277, 282
    and national identity, 282–285
Rwandan respondent, 278, 279
Rwandese Alliance for National Unity (RANU), 269

S

Sachsenhausen concentration camp memorial site, 480
Said, E., 18, 66
St Helier, 361, 362
St Peter Port, 360–362
Sanbar, E., 218
Sandberg, J., 182
Santorini, 131–142
    bronze age Pompeii, 134–138
Santos, C., 627
Satellite camp systems, 475
Sather-Wagstaff, J., 540, 541
Saving Private Ryan, 654
Sayers, M., 159, 160
Scale, 14–16, 27, 43, 66, 78, 83, 127, 132, 137, 158, 164, 167, 238, 264, 320, 321, 325, 341, 381, 389, 390, 392, 393, 416, 428, 459, 496, 586, 592, 598, 711
Scandinavia, 103–122, 430

Scandinavian graveyards, 111
Scandinavian thanatouristic sites, 105
Schaefer, S., 263
Schindler's Ark, 485
Schmallegger, D., 739
Schmitt, B., 615
Schroeder, J., 176
Scott, C. H., 112–114, 117
Scott, H., 128, 129
Scott, J., 558
Scott, Sir W., 128
Seaton, A. V., 2, 3, 106, 109, 111, 294, 516, 609, 649, 667, 729
Seaton's theory of metempsychosis, 92, 95n2
Secteur mythique, 653
SED party, 485
Segal, B., 174
Seismic disaster
  attractions, interpretation of, 433–435
  consumption of, 429–431
  memorial sites and attractions associated with, 427
  perception of, 431–433
Seismic memorial sites, 423–436
Self-esteem, 520–522, 524–527
Self, W., 232, 233
Selfies, 174–178, 736–738
Self-liberation, 481, 485
Selmi, N., 670
Selwyn, T., 221
Semmel, S., 110
September 21 earthquake in 1999, 432
Serious disruption, 338, 348
Sevcenko, L., 700
Shackley, M., 622
Shades of darkness, 158, 728
Shameful death, 197
Shani, A., 625, 702
Sharpley, R., 179, 216, 259, 336, 429, 511, 517, 518, 536, 608, 612, 619, 668

Sheldon, K. M., 522
Shilling, C., 179
Shim, D., 176
Shintoist memorial, 167, 168
Shirley plantation, 410, 411
Shoah, 478, 597, 734
Shrines, 15, 22, 28n3, 128, 161, 162, 189, 536, 538, 541, 543, 546, 549, 607, 698
Sichuan Wenchuan Earthquake tour, 591
Sierra Leone, 590
Simone-Charteris, M. T., 609, 621
Sinclair, I., 232, 233, 245
Sites of Special Interest (SSI), 363
Skinner, J., 5, 6
Slave experience, 403, 407, 413
Slavery at Oak Alley exhibit, 407, 413, 414
Slavery, in American history, 404
Slavery-related tourism experience, 403
Slavic origin, 367
Sliwinski, S., 131
Small, S., 407, 408
Smartphone, 728, 730, 735, 736, 738, 741, 742
Smith, L., 363
Smith, R. J., 166
Smith, V., 377
Sobibor, 471, 475–477, 484, 597
Sobibor death camps, 470, 476, 477
Sobibor uprising, 484
Social business enterprises (SBE), 658
Social learning outcomes, 614
Social marketing, 645–661
Social media, 140, 175–178, 335, 386, 556, 585, 586, 588, 589, 600, 616, 658, 727, 729–732, 736–738, 740–743
Social processes, 235, 292, 713
Sodaro, A., 694, 695
Sofield, T., 164

Soft ambiance, 230
Soham, UK, 337
Sontag, S., 737
South Carolina rice plantations, 408
Souveniring, 707–719, 721, 722
Souvenirs
　commodity, 712–713
　study of, 713–715
Spanish Republicans, 367, 369–371
Spatial affinity, 596
Spectacular death, 189–205
Spirits of the ancestors, 161
Sport tourism, 104
Springfield, D., 16
Spurensuche project, 488
S.S. Morro Castle, 336
Stakeholder involvement, 654–656
State Museum of Auschwitz-Birkenau, 734
Steele, S. L., 280
Stein, E., 475
Steiner, C., 714
Steiner, G., 596
Stephensen, M., 119
Stewart, S., 714
Stolpe, H., 104
Stone, O., 116, 117
Stone, P. R., 11, 152–154, 157, 158, 178–180, 215, 216, 228, 238, 240, 241, 257, 258, 264, 402, 429, 444, 446, 511, 516–518, 523, 534, 536, 538, 605, 607, 612, 619, 646, 657, 668, 670, 672, 673, 680, 728–731
Strange, C., 627
Strange, V., 625
Strasse, O., 489
Sturken, M., 697
Sullivan, A., 60
Sumatra-Andaman earthquake and tsunami of 2004, 423, 431
Suntikul, W., 377
Superstitions, 50, 114

Supply-side approach, 11
Surrogation, 403–408
Sutcliffe, K., 556, 557, 559
Swinton, A., 117
Swiss Army Knife, 735
Symbolic excavation, 406, 410
Symbolic immortality, 520, 521, 523, 524
Symbolic silences, 626
Symbolism, 27, 245, 326, 355, 362, 537, 656, 708, 713, 720

T

Taboo
　defined, 444
　glorification of war, 448
　mourning, 446
Tailing, at darkest visitor sites, 672–673
Tamed death, 194, 195, 201
Tange Kenzô, 167
Tangshan Earthquake Memorial Park, 426
Tangshan Earthquake of 1976, 426
Tang, Y., 430, 431, 433
Tarlow, P. E., 605
"Taxes on knowledge", 59
Taxonomical model, 264
Tegnér, B., 106, 115
Teigen, K. H., 434
Tercier, J., 197, 198
Terra nullius, 383
Terror Management Theory (TMT), 516, 519–528
Terrorscapes, 367
Tézenas, A., 591
Thackeray, W., 92, 131
Thaelmann, E., 482
Thanaptosis, concepts of, 536
Thanatology, 19–22
Thanatopsis, 11, 19, 117
　potential opportunity for, 158

Thanatourism, 13, 14, 19, 21, 22, 24, 27, 28, 143, 157, 158, 262, 424, 496
  ancestor worship, 160
  Asian thanatourism, 159
  definition of, 13
  memorials of war, atrocities, and disasters, 163–168
  See also Dark tourism
Thanatourist sites in Asia, 166, 168, 169
Thatcher, M., 18
Thelma (Corelli), 117
Theresienstadt-Terezin Ghetto and Concentration Camp, 477
Timbs, J., 84
Time stages, 591
Timothy, D., 378, 389
Timothy, T. J., 562
Titanic in Belfast, 736
Titanic Quarter, 736
"Titian Venus", 90
Tobacco production, 410
Tobin, D., 446
Tohoku Pacific earthquake and tsunami, 432
Topinka, R. J., 245
Topography of Terror Exhibit, 491
'Topography of Terror' history museum, 490
Tourism
  'conventional' forms of, 516
  danger-zone, 519
  dark and stormy, 125–129
  developments in Rwanda, 12
  grief, 337
  leisure and, 525
  in Medellin, 298–299
Tourismification, 444
Tourism industry, 62, 261, 282, 286, 298, 312, 404, 656, 708, 709, 727, 742
Tourism mobilities, 319–330

Tourist emotions, 620
Touristic hybridity, 613
Towner, J., 1
Tragedy, 10, 114, 117, 119, 168, 203, 211–216, 220, 240, 242, 249, 264, 278, 284, 294, 300, 301, 326, 336, 337, 344, 345, 348, 382, 383, 386, 388, 393, 394, 418, 425, 426, 428, 429, 433, 446, 496, 515, 522, 523, 535, 537, 539, 540, 543, 546–549, 587, 591–593, 597, 599, 600, 603, 605, 607, 608, 619, 626, 667, 670, 708, 728, 731, 736, 737
Tran, G. T. H., 165
Trauma, 131, 192, 201, 221, 263, 285, 322, 323, 330, 363, 406, 418, 461, 537, 539–544, 556, 570, 600, 619, 624, 687, 695, 696, 701, 702, 721
Traumatic events, 319, 323, 539, 600
Travel Darkling, 738–740
Treblinka, 475, 484, 491, 596, 597
Treblinka memorial site, 479
Trollope, A., 5, 117
Trollope, F., 78, 80, 81, 85–87, 90
Tsunami disaster in Southeast Asia in December 2004, 434
Tuan, Y., 235
Tucker, H., 716
Tunbridge, J. E., 262, 292, 496
Tussyadiah, I. P., 735
Tutsi rebel group, 269, 271
Tweedie, A., 120

U

Ukrainians, 325, 367
Unagreed society, 264
UNESCO's World Heritage List, 389
United Nations Office on Drugs and Crime (UNODC), 314n17, 302

United States (US), 130, 132, 139, 143, 165, 179, 247, 267, 296, 309, 325, 336, 381–394, 399, 400, 409, 411, 412, 416, 418, 470, 477, 478, 485, 487, 491, 493, 498, 533, 535, 545, 553, 554, 562, 563, 568, 571, 576n3, 682, 685, 696, 719, 729, 733, 741
United States Holocaust Memorial Museum in Washington D.C., 478, 491
Urry, J., 257, 591, 597, 623
USS Arizona Memorial, 390
Uzzell, D., 561, 619

V

Value proposition, 650
Vance, J., 447
Vandalism, 20, 493
Vanity Fair (Thackeray), 92
Venbrux, E., 111
Vesuvius volcano, 135
Veyriras, P., 80
Victoria and Albert Museum, 129
Victorian London, 77, 78, 82
Viebach, J., 267
Vietnam Memorial in Washington, 418
Viking sagas and sites, 114–121
The Vikings and the Victorians (Wawn), 117
Violent death, 143, 173, 200, 296
Virtual environment, 730, 732
Visitor Center team, 574
Visualisation, of dark tourism, 585–600
Visual record captured, 598
Volcanic devastation, 136
Volcanic eruptions, 104, 135, 387, 391, 423, 424, 432, 434
Volcanic risk, southern Iceland, 431
Volcanoes, 119, 125, 127, 132–137, 139–142

Volcano tourism, 133, 140, 141
Volcano tourists, 133, 135, 136
Von Hagen, G., 12
Von Vacano, M., 338
Vo Thi Sau, 166
Voyeurism, 180, 516, 517, 534, 609, 717, 718
V-sign, 361, 362
Vulnerable communities, 301–303

W

Wachsmann, N., 484
Waitt, G., 716
Walchester, K., 4, 5
Wallace, W., 37
Walled City (Hay), 233
Wallenberg, R., 485
Waller, S. E., 117
Walpole, H., 127–130, 139
Walter, T., 199, 200, 204, 205, 367, 445, 524, 607, 611
Waltham Black Act, 48
Walton, J., 2, 110
War memorials, 168, 264, 323, 446, 461, 524, 556
War of the Crosses, 476
Warbeck, P., 37
Warsaw Ghetto uprising, 484
Watergate complex, 390
Waterton, E., 406
Watson, N., 93
Wat Thap Kradan, 162, 163
Wawn, A., 117
Wenchuan earthquake, 426, 423, 591, 428, 431, 426, 433
Wenger, D., 339
West, R., 127
Western Europe, 21, 26, 194, 325, 358, 370
Western Europeans, 370
Western morality, 211
Western phenomenon, 157, 168

Western secular society, 192
Western thanatourism, 158, 159, 168
Western thanatourism, typologies of, 158
Whelan, Y., 264
Whilst monuments, 323
White Rose ('Weisse Rose') student resistance group, 487
White, L., 538, 561, 610
Whitmarsh, A., 446
Whitney Plantation, 415, 416, 419n3
Whitney Plantation site plan, 417
Wiesel, E., 588, 596
Wi-Fi connectivity, 730, 740–742
Wight, C. A., 627
William Blake, 245
William Shakespeare, 64
Williams, A. M., 431
Williams, J., 64
Williams, M. P., 233
Williams, P., 11
Willis, E., 145
Willmott, H., 179
Wilson, J. Z., 3
Winter, J. M., 651
Witcomb, A., 701
Wollstonecraft, M., 105, 106
Wolsey, C., 38
Word of mouth (WOM), 619, 738
Works Progress Administration (WPA), 416, 417
World Trade Center, 388, 569–571, 697, 739, 740
World War, 519, 729
World War I (WWI), 92, 181, 443–464, 497, 717, 722
World War II (WWII), 12, 14, 163, 166, 218, 229, 292, 357, 386, 472, 475, 476, 484, 486, 487, 490, 593, 613, 647, 652–654, 701, 702, 718, 720
Wren, C., 21
Wright, D., 259, 347
Wurzer, W., 596

Y

Yad Vashem in Israel, 478
Yad Vashem memorial and museum in Jerusalem, 485
Yair, G., 701
Yankholmes, A., 405
Yankovska, G., 259
Yoneyama, L., 166
Yong, T., 378–379
Yoshida, T., 166
Young, C., 293, 310
Young, K., 610
Youthful exploratory behavior, 554–556

Z

Zaumseil, M., 338
Zeitschneise/timeline project, 488
Zilboorg, G., 520
Zochrot, 220–222
Zola, É., 79, 87
Zulu memorials, 24